Financial Management for CA-IPC (Group-I)

With Quick Revision Book

CA (Dr) P C TULSIAN

M.Com., PhD, FCA, PGDFM

Additional Director (Former)
Board of Studies
The Institute of Chartered Accountants of India, New Delhi
Head
Department of Commerce
Ramjas College
University of Delhi
DELHI

*Recipient of an Award for **Exemplary Services Contributed to the Cause of Profession** by The Institute of Chartered Accountants of India, New Delhi*

CA BHARAT TULSIAN

Chartered Accountant
Manager, KPMG
Alumnus of Sri Ram College of Commerce (SRCC)
University of Delhi
DELHI

*Recipient of an Award for the **Best Article on Foreign Exchange** at the all-India level by The Institute of Chartered Accountants of India, New Delhi*

S Chand And Company Limited

(ISO 9001 Certified Company)

RAM NAGAR, NEW DELHI - 110 055

S Chand And Company Limited
(ISO 9001 Certified Company)
Head Office: 7361, RAM NAGAR, QUTAB ROAD, NEW DELHI - 110 055
Phone: 23672080-81-82, 66672000 Fax: 91-11-23677446
www.**schandpublishing.com**; e-mail: **info@schandpublishing.com**

Branches:

Ahmedabad : Ph: 27541965, 27542369, ahmedabad@schandpublishing.com
Bengaluru : Ph: 22268048, 22354008, bangalore@schandpublishing.com
Bhopal : Ph: 4209587, bhopal@schandpublishing.com
Chandigarh : Ph: 2625356, 2625546, 4025418, chandigarh@schandpublishing.com
Chennai : Ph: 28410027, 28410058, chennai@schandpublishing.com
Coimbatore : Ph: 2323620, 4217136, coimbatore@schandpublishing.com (Marketing Office)
Cuttack : Ph: 2332580, 2332581, cuttack@schandpublishing.com
Dehradun : Ph: 2711101, 2710861, dehradun@schandpublishing.com
Guwahati : Ph: 2738811, 2735640, guwahati@schandpublishing.com
Hyderabad : Ph: 27550194, 27550195, hyderabad@schandpublishing.com
Jaipur : Ph: 2219175, 2219176, jaipur@schandpublishing.com
Jalandhar : Ph: 2401630, jalandhar@schandpublishing.com
Kochi : Ph: 2809208, 2808207, cochin@schandpublishing.com
Kolkata : Ph: 23353914, 23357458, kolkata@schandpublishing.com
Lucknow : Ph: 4065646, lucknow@schandpublishing.com
Mumbai : Ph: 22690881, 22610885, 22610886, mumbai@schandpublishing.com
Nagpur : Ph: 2720523, 2777666, nagpur@schandpublishing.com
Patna : Ph: 2300489, 2260011, patna@schandpublishing.com
Pune : Ph: 64017298, pune@schandpublishing.com
Raipur : Ph: 2443142, raipur@schandpublishing.com (Marketing Office)
Ranchi : Ph: 2361178, ranchi@schandpublishing.com
Sahibabad : Ph: 2771235, 2771238, delhibr-sahibabad@schandpublishing.com

First Edition 2011
Subsequent Editions and Reprints 2012, 2013, 2014, 2015
Revised Edition 2016
Reprint 2017
Reprint 2018 (Twice)

ISBN: 978-93-525-3173-8 **Code**: 1007E 491

PRINTED IN INDIA

By Vikas Publishing House Pvt. Ltd., Plot 20/4, Site-IV, Industrial Area Sahibabad, Ghaziabad-201010 and Published by S Chand And Company Limited, 7361, Ram Nagar, New Delhi-110 055.

PREFACE TO THE SEVENTH EDITION

We are thankful to the readers and teachers for their response and encouragement given to the Sixth Edition. This edition is thoroughly revised and substantially expanded; all chapters have been updated and expanded.

Salient Features

The book adopts a fresh and novel approach to the study of Financial Management for the students of CA Integrated Professional Competence Course (IPC) Group-I. It has been written in a teach yourself style strictly following a student-friendly approach, and is essentially meant to serve as a tutor at home.

PEDAGOGICAL FEATURES

Simple Language	The text is presented in the simplest language "meant to serve beginners"
Heading for each Paragraph	Each paragraph has been arranged under a suitable heading for easy retention of concepts
Tabular form	Wherever possible, the text matter relating to a particular topic/ sub-topic has been presented in a tabular form
Eye-catching Screens	All important equations, formulae, figures and practical steps have been presented in screen format to catch the eye
Uniform Format of Chapter	Each chapter has been uniformly organised under suitable headings, viz., text supported by suitable illustrations, solved problems

DISTINCTIVE FEATURES

Exhibits	Over 100 exhibits to acquaint students with various accounting treatment and formats
Illustrations	Over 320 illustrations have been provided for a better understanding of the text
Solved Problems	Over 320 solved problems along with necessary working notes and alternative solution have been provided throughout the text

Tulsian's Quick Revision for Financial Management for CA-IPC (Group-I)

Section 1	**Fully Solved Scanner Chapterwise (CA Professional Examination Problems with Authentic Solutions)**
Section 2	**Revision One Day Before Examination**
Section 3	**Tulsian's Model Test Papers**
Section 4	**IPC Examination Papers**

CA (Dr) P C Tulsian
pctulsian@gmail.com

CA Bharat Tulsian
bharattulsian88@gmail.com

ACKNOWLEDGEMENTS

We wish to express our sincere thanks to several individuals who have been a source of inspiration and support, personally and professionally, including Dr. R P Tulsian, Dr. M M Goyal, Dr. S C Garg, Dr. Tanushree Jain, Ms. Madhu Aggarwal, Dr. Rajeev Goyal, Dr. S N Gupta, Dr. S S Lamba, Dr. Sarita Jain, Dr. Usha Jain, Dr. V K Aggarwal, Dr. V P Bansal, Dr. Vibha Jain, Dr. Savita Gopal, Dr. S C Gupta, Dr. S P Gupta, Dr. Naresh Gupta, Dr. Amit Singhal, Dr. J B Gupta, Dr. Madhu Gupta, Dr. Sushma Aggarwal, Dr. Renu Gupta, Dr. Manju Gupta, Dr. C P Gupta Dr. S Z H Zaidi. CA M K Aggarwal, CA S K Aggarwal, CA N D Gupta, CA Naveen Gupta, CA Anil Jindal, CA Madhu Sudan Goyal, CA Vinod Aggarwal, CA Sunil Gupta, CA Arun Jain, CA Virender Aggarwal, CA S K Gupta, CA Ishwar Khemka, CA Prem Bansal, CA Ashish Gupta, CA M K Sharda, CA Rajeev Rastogi. CA Atul Gupta, CA Kuldeep Bhardwaj, CA Neeraj Chabra, CA Kishore Paul, CA Pradeep Narang, CA S K Gupta, CA R Devarajan, CA Tapas Dutta, CA Arnav Chakrabarty, CA Seema Gupta, CA Shilpa Aggarwal, CA Vishal Pandey, Ms. Nidhi Singh, Dr. N N Sen Gupta, Prof. J P Sharma, CA Pallavi, CA Antima Jain, CA Piyush Tulsian, CA Swati Tulsian, CA Piyush and CA Prarthana Mittal.

Special word of thanks is also due to our favourite students **Piyush, Pranav, Arushi and Aman Mittal** who provided incisive comments and useful feedback.

We must conclude that this book would have never been written without the support, encouragement and prodding of our family members. Many thanks to them.

Any criticisms or suggestions for further improvement of the book will be gratefully acknowledged and appreciated.

CA (Dr) P C Tulsian
pctulsian@gmail.com

CA Bharat Tulsian
bharattulsian88@gmail.com

Tulsian's

FINANCIAL MANAGEMENT

for

CA-IPC (Group-I)

CONTENTS

Supplement to Textbook

CONTENTS

SECTION 1

FULLY-SOLVED SCANNER CHAPTERWISE

[CA PROFESSIONAL EXAMINATION PROBLEMS WITH AUTHENTIC SOLUTIONS]

SCANNER FOR CA EXAMINATION PROBLEMS

SHORT ANSWER CARRYING 4-6 MARKS &
LONG ANSWER CARRYING 8-16 MARKS

SECTION 2

REVISION ONE DAY BEFORE EXAMINATION

SECTION 3

TULSIAN'S REVISION TEST PAPERS WITH ANSWERS

SECTION 4

CA-IPC EXAMINATION PAPERS

1 INTRODUCTION TO FINANCIAL MANAGEMENT

LEARNING OBJECTIVES

After studying this chapter, you should be able to understand:

- Meaning of Business Finance
- Significance of Business Finance
- Relationship of Finance with other Disciplines
- Theories on Finance
- What is Financial Management?
- Key Elements of Financial Management
- What should be the Objective of Financial Management?
- Basic Axioms of Financial Management
- Risk-Return Trade off
- Agency Problem
- Financial Decision-Making
- Inter-Relationship Between Investment, Financing and Dividend Decisions
- Functions of a Financial Manager
- Finance Function in a Large Corporate Business Enterprise
- Various Stake Holders of the Organization
- Changing Scenario of Financial Management in India
- Inflation and Financial Management
- Impact of Taxation on Financial Management

1.0 MEANING OF BUSINESS FINANCE

Money required for any activity is known as finance. Every activity whether economic *or* non-economic, requires money to run it.

Business finance refers to money and credit employed in business. It is procured and utilized for business purposes. The following characteristics of business finance will make its meaning more clear:

1. **Includes all types of funds:** Business finance includes all types of funds used in business. (e.g., Owners' Funds, Borrowed Funds).
2. **Required in all types of organization:** Business finance is required in all types of organizations whether large *or* small, manufacturing *or* trading.
3. **Varies with Nature & Size of Business Operations:** The amount of business finance differs according to the nature and size of business operations. ***For Example***, smaller the size of business operations, smaller will be the amount of business finance required, larger the size of business operations, larger will be the amount of business finance required.

4. **Varies from time to time:** The amount of business finance varies from time to time.
5. **Required on Continuous basis:** It is required on continuous basis during the life of the business organisation unless the organisation decides to curtail its operations due to any reason(s).

2.0 SIGNIFICANCE OF BUSINESS FINANCE

Business finance is required for the establishment and existence of every business organization. Finance is required not only to start the business but also to operate it, to expand *or* modernize its operations and to secure stable growth. The importance of business finance arises basically to bridge the time gap. Manufacturers require business finance to bridge the time gap between the purchase of raw material and other supplies for production and recovery of sales. Traders require finance to bridge the time gap between the purchase of goods and recovery of sales.

The need for business finance arises for the following purposes:

1. **To acquire Fixed Assets** — Every business organization whether manufacturing *or* trading needs finance to acquire some fixed assets. Manufacturers need finance to acquire land & building, plant & machinery, furniture etc. Traders need finance to acquire shops for sale of goods, godown for storage of goods and vehicles for distribution of goods.
2. **To purchase raw-materials/goods** — Manufacturers need finance to acquire raw-materials and consumable stores for production. Traders need finance to acquire goods for distribution.
3. **To acquire services of human being** — Manufacturers need finance to pay their workers, supervisors, managers and other staff employed by them. Traders need finance to pay their staff employed by them.
4. **To meet other operating expenses** — Every organization needs finance to meet day to day other operating expenses like payment for electricity bills, water bills, telephone bills, travelling & conveyance of staff, postage & telegram expenses & so on.
5. **To adopt Modern Technology** — With fast changing technology, business organizations need finance to modernize their plans & machineries, production methods and distribution methods. An enterprise may decide to replace outdated and obsolete assets with new assets to operate more economically.
6. **To meet contingencies** — Every organization needs finance to meet the ups and downs of business and unforeseen problems.
7. **To expand existing operations** — Every organization needs finance to expand its existing operations. ***For Example***, a company manufacturing Pen Drives at a rate of 10,000 per day needs finance to increase its plant capacity to manufacture 20,000 Pen Drives per day.
8. **To diversify** — Every organization which decides to diversify, needs finance to add new products to the existing line. ***For Example***, the company manufacturing Pen Drives needs finance to add new products say Ganga Water.
9. **To avail of business opportunities** — Finance is required to avail of business opportunities. ***For Example***, where raw-materials are available at heavy cash discounts, the enterprises need finance to avail of this opportunity.

Finance is said to be life blood of business. It is required not only at the time of setting up of business but at every stage during the existence of business. It must be available at the time when it is needed. It must also be adequate for the purpose for which it is needed.

Thus, finance is required to bring a business into existence, to keep it alive and to see it growing. Men, materials, machinery and managers can be brought together and engaged in business when adequate finance is available. Many business firms are known to have failed mainly due to shortage of finance. The importance of finance has increased in modern times for two reasons viz., (i) the business activities are now undertaken on a much larger scale than in the past, and (ii) the manufacturing process has become more complex than it used to be. With the growth in size and volume of business and with the increasing complexity of production and trade, there is growing need for finance.

Without adequate finance no business can survive and without efficient financial management no business can earn profits and grow. The survival and growth of a firm is possible if it utilizes its funds in an effective manner. Collin Brooks says, ***"Bad production management and bad sales management have slain their hundreds but faulty finance has slain its thousands." If a firm ignores finance it does so at its own peril. A proper financial management provides a strong motivation to work in the right direction.***

3.0 RELATIONSHIP OF FINANCE WITH OTHER DISCIPLINES

RELATIONSHIP WITH ECONOMICS

Traditionally finance was considered as a part of economics. However, with the evolution of modern finance theory, finance evolved as an independent discipline and separated itself from economics. But even after separation both are related to each other deeply. ***For Example***, if finance manager wants to make investment decision then he shall analyze variables such as general economic environment, inflation rate, recession, boom, tax structure prevailing in the economy, etc. These variables are the products of macro economics. Similarly if finance manager wants to make financing decision then he shall be concerned with the structure of banking system, money and capital markets, fiscal and economic policies, etc. These all things come under the purview of macro economics.

RELATIONSHIP WITH ACCOUNTING

Accounting serves as an information system to finance. Information generated through accounting is used in finance for decision making. In other words, accounting is a sub part of finance. The information provided by the accounting system helps finance manager to scrutinize past performance and make future decision.

RELATIONSHIP WITH MATHEMATICS, STATISTICS AND QUANTITATIVE TECHNIQUES

In modern finance theory, some advance tools of mathematics, statistics and quantitative techniques are used in analyzing financial theories. ***For Example***, theory on valuation of options, derivatives, Capital Asset Pricing Model, risk analysis, etc. are based on advance mathematical, statistical and quantitative tools.

RELATIONSHIP WITH OTHER DISCIPLINES

Beside above the finance is also related with other disciplines such as marketing management, production management, personnel management, etc. The finance management has to operate in coordination with other parts of management to achieve its objective.

4.0 THEORIES ON FINANCE

TRADITIONAL THEORY ON FINANCE

Traditionally finance was only limited to procurements of the funds for the organization. The funds were needed to finance the expansion *or* diversification. As these activities were rare and required large amount of funds, the emphasis was on the long term resources and as a result only long term finance was considered as important. Finance function was generally concern with the issues regarding procurement of funds, administration of funds, administration of covenants imposed by supplier of funds, etc. Thus finance function was mainly an outsider looking.

MODERN THEORY ON FINANCE

Modern theory of finance considered finance as a separate discipline and have a wider perspective.

It's not only limited to procurement but increased its limit to cover efficient allocation and effective administration of fund. In modern days finance management has become an integral part of overall management.

5.0 WHAT IS FINANCIAL MANAGEMENT?

To understand the meaning of Financial Management, let us observe the following definitions:

(a) Financial Management is management of finances of an organization in order to achieve its objectives.

(b) Financial Management is that area of General Management which is concerned with the timely procurement of adequate finance from various sources and its utmost effective utilization for the attainment of organizational objectives.

(c) Financial management is an area of finance which is concerned primarily with financial decision-making within an organization.

(d) Financial management may be defined as planning, organising, directing and controlling of financial activities in an organization.

(e) Financial management is concerned with optimal procurement and effective utilization of funds in an manner that the risk, cost and control considerations are properly balanced in a given situation.

(f) Financial management is concerned with managerial decision making. Decision making is futuristic and requires information and criterion. Information is deduced from accounting. Criterion demands logic which emanates from economics.

(g) Financial management involves acquisition and management of financial resources for organization to maximize the value of stockholders' claims.

On the basis of analysis of aforesaid definitions, now financial management may be defined as follows:

Financial management is basically the application of general management principles to the areas of financial decision-making (such as Investment, Financing, Dividend & Working Capital) with a view to maximize the wealth of the Company i.e. the shareholders. Thus, Financial management answers the following basic questions:

1. Where to invest? i.e. Investment Decisions (I)
2. From where to raise funds? i.e. Financing Decision(F)
3. How much earnings to be retained and how much to be distributed?

   i.e., Dividend Decision. (D)
4. How to manage Working Capital? i.e. Working Capital Management Decision(W)

   Hence, Wealth of Company = f (I, F, D, W)

6.0 KEY ELEMENTS OF FINANCIAL MANAGEMENT

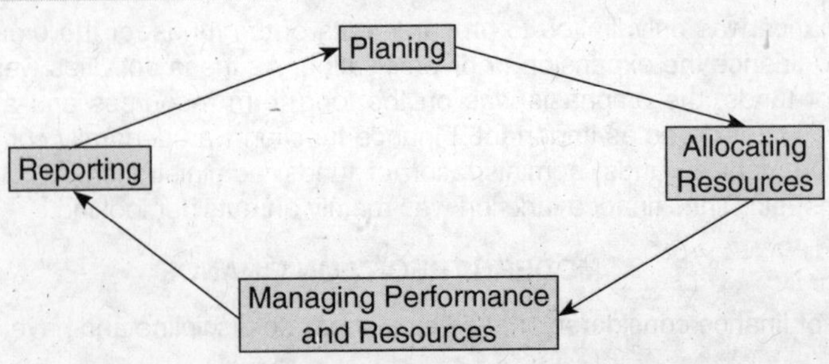

7.0 WHAT SHOULD BE THE OBJECTIVE OF FINANCIAL MANAGEMENT?

The objective of Financial Management may be:

(a) To Maximize Profit

(b) To Maximize Earning Per Share?

(c) To Minimize Costs?

(d) To Maximize Market Share?

(e) To Maximize the Current Value of the Company's Stock?

Does this mean finance manager should do anything and everything to maximize owners' wealth?

PROFIT MAXIMIZATION AS THE OBJECTIVE OF FINANCIAL MANAGEMENT

(a) Meaning of Profit Maximization

Profit Maximization implies maximizing the Rupee Income of the Firm. Profit maximization as an objective of financial management is a very vague concept. Firstly it is not clear what profits are? Whether it is absolute amount of Income *or* Earning per Share (EPS) *or* Return on Investment *or* Profit before tax *or* after tax ? On the other hand it ignores the timings of return and risk associated with it. If Profit maximization is adopted as criteria then the proposals giving returns at very later stage and with highly varying amounts may be accepted. This may be very harmful to the organization since here timings and risks are not adjusted. Beside these factors, in modern days profit maximization as an ultimate objective is considered as immoral since it ignores social responsibility and it may lead to adoption of unethical business practices. Some Arguments in favour of and Objections to Profit Maximization are given below:

(b) Arguments in favour of Profit Maximization

(i) Resources are efficiently utilized.

(ii) It is an appropriate measure of firm's performance.

(iii) It serves interest of society also.

(c) Objections to Profit Maximization

(i) It is vague

(ii) It ignores the Timing of Returns

(iii) It ignores Risk

(iv) It assumes Perfect Competition

(v) In new business environment profit maximization is regarded as

- Unrealistic
- Difficult
- Inappropriate
- Immoral

EPS MAXIMIZATION AS THE OBJECTIVE OF FINANCIAL MANAGEMENT

(a) Meaning of EPS Maximization

Maximizing EPS implies that the total earnings are retained and re-invested in the business of the firm and no portion of the earnings is distributed as dividend among the share holders so long as earnings can be re-invested at a rate of return higher than the opportunity cost of retained earnings.

(b) Objections to EPS Maximization

(i) Investors (like Senior Citizens, Low Income Group people) who prefer current dividend as against the future uncertain capital gains would not like such a policy.

(ii) EPS lacks time value of money and the risk factor.

(iii) Since market value is not a function of EPS, maximizing EPS will not result in highest price for company's shares. Hence, such a policy may not always work as Primary Goal of Financial Management

COST MINIMIZATION AS THE OBJECTIVE OF FINANCIAL MANAGEMENT

Meaning of Cost Minimization

Costs Minimization implies making the product/service available at minimum cost. Such a policy may not always result in highest sales revenue *or* highest profit. Since market value is not a function of cost, minimizing cost will not result in highest price for company's shares. Hence, such a policy may not always work as Primary Goal of Financial Management.

MARKET SHARE MAXIMIZATION AS THE OBJECTIVE OF FINANCIAL MANAGEMENT

Meaning of Market Share Maximization

Market Share Maximization implies maximizing sales revenue by serving maximum number of customers. Such a policy may not always result in highest profit. Since market value is not a function of market share, maximizing market share will not result in highest price for company's shares. Hence, such a policy may not always work as Primary Goal of Financial Management.

VALUE MAXIMIZATION AS THE OBJECTIVE OF FINANCIAL MANAGEMENT

(a) Meaning of Value Maximization

(i) Maximizing Value of the firm

(ii) Maximizing Shareholders' Value

(iii) Maximizing Share Price

The above may be considered as three equivalent goals of financial management.

The goal is to maximize Shareholders' Wealth. Wealth Maximization means maximizing the NET PRESENT VALUE (OR WEALTH) of a course of action. The wealth of owners of a company is reflected by the market value of company's shares in the Long Run.

Value is the Market Capitalization of company's common stock which is:

Number of shares × Price of shares.

(b) Arguments in favour of Wealth Maximization

(i) It maximizes the net present value of a course of action to shareholders.

(ii) It accounts for the timing and risk of the expected benefits.

(iii) Benefits are measured in terms of cash flows.

(iv) It serves the fundamental objective i. e. maximizes the market value of the firm's shares.

WEALTH MAXIMIZATION AS PRIMARY OBJECTIVE OF FINANCIAL MANAGEMENT

The primary objective of financial management is wealth maximisation. The concept of wealth in the context of wealth maximisation objective refers to the shareholders' wealth as reflected by the price of their shares in the share market. Therefore, wealth maximisation means maximisation of the market price of the equity shares of the company. However, this maximisation of the price of company's equity shares should be in the long run by making efficient decisions which are desirable for the growth of a company and are valued positively by the investors at large and not by manipulating the share prices in the short run. The long run implies a period which is long enough to reflect the normal market price of the shares irrespective of short-term fluctuations. The long run price of an equity share is a function of two basic factors:

(a) the likely rate of earnings *or* earnings per share (EPS) of the company; and

(b) the capitalisation rate reflecting the liking of the investors of a company.

The financial manager must identify those avenues of investment; modes of financing, ways of handling various components of working capital which ultimately will lead to an increase in the price of equity share. If shareholders are gaining, it implies that all other claimants are also gaining because the equity share holders are paid only after the claims of all other claimants (such as creditors, employees, lenders) have been duly paid.

OTHER OBJECTIVES

Other objectives include the following:

1. To ensure timely optimal procurement of adequate funds at reasonable cost after balancing the risk, cost and control considerations.
2. To ensure effective utilisation of funds.
3. To ensure adequate supply of funds as and when needed.
4. To ensure safety of the funds through creation of reserves, reinvestment of profits etc.

8.0 BASIC AXIOMS OF FINANCIAL MANAGEMENT

Six Basic Axioms of Financial Management are given below:

Axiom 1 Cash Flows should be preferred over Accounting Profits.

Axiom 2 Time Value of Money should be considered since today's rupee is worth more than the tomorrow's rupee.

Axiom 3 Risk-Return Trade off should be considered since additional risk is to be compensated by additional return.

Axiom 4 Incremental Cash Flows should be preferred over total cash flows since it is only the changes which matter.

Axiom 5 Taxes bias business decisions.

Axiom 6 Imperfect Capital Market bias business decisions.

RISK—RETURN TRADE OFF

Lower the risk, lower the gain and higher the risk, higher the gain. The finance manager has to strike balance between return he desires and the risk he want to take. If finance manager takes the projects with higher return involving higher risk then the expected require rate of return shall also be higher. By applying this higher rate of return to discount the higher cash flows shall result in low present value. Conversely, in case of projects with lower returns involving lower risks, the expected required rate return shall be lower and this lower rate of return shall be applied for discounting lower cash flows which shall also result in low present value. Therefore, finance manager has to find that point of return and risk which shall maximize the present value and that point is called risk return trade off.

9.0 AGENCY PROBLEM

WHAT IS AGENCY PROBLEM?

In modern organization, there is separation of ownership and management. The management acts on behalf of owners and is their agents. Consequently management should act in such a manner so as to maximize wealth of their principals i.e. owners. However this may not happen because owners and management have different interests. Due to these different interests and separation of management from ownership, management may behave in a manner which is inconsistent with the interest of owners. These behavioural problems on the part of management lead to agency problems.

WHAT IS AGENCY COST?

Agency costs are the costs that are directed to reduce the impact of agency problems. These costs may be direct *or* indirect. Example of the direct agency costs are salary, bonuses and perks paid to employees, programs such as employees stock option scheme, monitoring costs such as audit fees paid to statutory auditors *or* remuneration paid to director who is appointed in Board of Director to review their decisions, etc. There are also certain indirect agency costs, ***For Example*** management may not take certain risky projects with high returns.

WHAT ARE THE OTHER FACTORS, EXCLUDING AGENCY COSTS WHICH PREVENT AGENCY PROBLEMS?

The other factors, excluding agency costs which prevent agency problems are as follows:

- **(a) Shareholders' interference** — Sometimes big shareholders like institutional investors *or* mutual fund may intervene through their voting rights by electing their nominee in Board of Directors to represent their interest.
- **(b) Hostile takeovers** — When management is performing poorly then there is a risk that a good operating company may take over the former company. If a company is not performing well then there is possibility that its share price is quoted low in market and this may tempt other company to take over the undervalued company.
- **(c) Threat of dismissal** — If management is not performing well on a consistent basis then shareholders may force the Board of Directors to change the management.

10.0 FINANCIAL DECISION-MAKING

The finance function relates to three major decisions which the finance manager has to take: (1) Investment decision; (2) Financing decision; and (3) Dividend decision.

INVESTMENT DECISION

- **(a) Meaning** — Investment decision relates to the careful selection of assets in which funds will be invested by the firm. Investment decision can be long-term *or* short term.
- **(b) Purpose** — The purpose of investment decision is to invest financial resources for setting up new business *or* for expansion (***For Example***, to increase an existing plant capacity of 1000 tonnes to 2000 tonnes) *or* modernisation of existing business. (***For Example***, replacing an old plant by a new one).
- **(c) Decisions Taken** — The following two types of decisions are taken:
  1. **Capital Budgeting Decisions** i.e. How much to invest in a long-term asset?
  2. **Short-term Investment Decision/Working Capital Decision** (i.e. How much to invest in short-term assets such as Cash, Debtors and Inventory?)
- **(d) Factors affecting Investment Decision** — The following major factors affect the Investment decision:

In case of Capital Budgeting Decision	In case of Working Capital Decision
1. Case Flows of the Project	1. Nature of Business
2. Cost of Capital	2. Business Cycle Fluctuations
3. Investment Criteria Involved	3. Seasonal Variations
	4. Technology and Production Cycle
	5. Credit Policy
	6. Price Level Changes
	7. Market Competition

(e) Importance of Investment Decisions

The management of fixed capital *or* investment *or* capital budgeting decisions are important for the following reasons:

1. **Long term growth and effects**—These decisions affect the rate and direction of long term growth of the enterprise because a wrong decision can adversely affect the survival of the firm. ***For Example***, an unprofitable expansion of assets will result in heavy operating costs to the enterprise. These decisions have long term implication for the enterprise because the effects of investment decision extend into the future.
2. **Large amount of funds involved**—These decisions involve large investment in long term assts. Therefore these decisions are planned after careful evaluation of various projects.
3. **Risk Involved**—These decisions involve risk and uncertainty associated with the future cash flow of the project. Since the actual cash flows may not match the expected cash flows, the rate of earning may fluctuate and the firm may become more risky.
4. **Irreversible Decision**—These decisions once taken are not easily reversible without incurring heavy losses. The firm will incur heavy losses if long term assets are scrapped on reversing the investment decisions.

FINANCING DECISION

(a) Meaning — Financing decision relates to the composition of relative proportion of various sources of finance. It involves deciding the proportion of equity and debt in capital structure. Sources of financing are analysed in light of cost as well as financial risk involved. This decision determines the overall cost of capital and the financial risk of the enterprise.

(b) Purpose — The purpose of financing decision is to decide about the sources from which funds should be raised to finance the investment decisions.

(c) Decisions Taken — The following decisions are taken:

1. What should be the proportion of equity and debt in the capital structure?
2. From which sources the equity should be raised — whether by issue of equity share *or* preference shares.
3. From which sources the debt should be raised — whether by issue of debentures *or* raising long term loans.

(d) Factors affecting Financing Decision — The following major factors affect the Financing decision:

1. Risk
2. Cost
3. Control
4. Financing Leverage
5. Cash flow ability
6. Flexibility
7. Market Conditions
8. Flotation Costs
9. Legal framework

DIVIDEND DECISION

(a) Meaning — Dividend decision involves deciding whether to distribute the profits as dividend to shareholders *or* to retain profits and reinvest in the business.

(b) Objective — The main objective of dividend policy is to divide net earnings in an optimum manner so as to pay dividend to the shareholders and to retain earnings for reinvestment with the objective of maximising the wealth of shareholders.

(c) Decisions — The following decisions are taken:

1. How much earnings should be retained for reinvestment opportunities?
2. How much earnings should be distributed as dividend to shareholders?

(d) Factors affecting Dividend Decision — The following major factors affect the Dividend decision:

1. Financial Requirements of the Company
2. Stability of Dividend
3. Capital Market Considerations
4. Preferences of Shareholders
5. Legal Restrictions and Constraints on Paying Dividend
6. Bonus Shares
7. Inflation

(e) Research findings — It may be noted that the research findings suggest–

1. that by and large shareholders prefer to receive cash dividends.
2. that higher dividend normally have a salutary effect on the market price.
3. that Optimum Dividend Payout Ratio (i.e. Ratio of Dividend Per Share to Earning per Share) maximizes the Shareholders' wealth.

11.0 INTER-RELATIONSHIP BETWEEN INVESTMENT, FINANCING AND DIVIDEND DECISIONS

Investment, Financing and Dividend decisions are inter-related because the underlying, objective of all these three decisions is the same i.e. maximisation of shareholders wealth.

Let us examine how each of these decisions helps in maximizing the shareholders, wealth.

1. Investment decision is influenced by financing decisions because only that investment proposal is accepted which is expected to generate return more than the cost of financing. Acceptance of those investment proposals of which return is more than the cost of financing, will increase the return to equity shareholders and thus, maximizes their wealth.
2. Financing Decisions is influenced by investment decision because the sources from which the funds should be raised depends upon the requirements of funds for long-term and short-term purposes which are provided by investment decisions. An optimal mix of various sources increases returns to equity shareholders and thus, maximises their wealth.
3. Financing Decision is influenced by Dividend decisions because availability of retained earnings as source of funds depends on the dividend decision. An optimal mix of internal and external sources of funds increases return to equity shareholders and thus, maximises their wealth.
4. Dividend decision (i.e. how much to retain and how much to distribute as dividend) is influenced by investment decision because dividend decision also depends on the requirements of funds for future growth. An optimal dividend payout ratio maximises the shareholders' wealth.
5. Dividend decision is also influenced by financing decision because dividend decision also depends on the company's access to capital market for raising funds required for investment purposes.

Thus, it is clear that investment, financing and dividend decisions are inter-related and are to be taken jointly by keeping in view their joint impact on the shareholders' wealth.

12.0 FUNCTIONS OF A FINANCIAL MANAGER

The executive who manages the financial affairs of a business is called 'financial manager'. The financial manager essentially has to manage funds and is concerned with the optimum utilisation of funds and with their procurement in a manner that the risk, cost and control considerations are properly balanced in a given situation. All the functions of finance manager may be divided into two categories as follows:

I. Primary Functions

1. **Estimating the Capital Requirements** — Once the physical activities of the organisation have been properly forecast, the financial manager has to decide how much funds are required for long-term, mid-term and short-term purposes.
2. **Financing *or* Capital Structure Decision** — After estimating the requirements of funds, the financial manager has to decide about the sources from which funds are to be procured keeping in mind three factors viz., cost, risk and control. He should work out a proper mix of various sources in such a manner that the funds are procured at optimum cost with the least risk and the least dilution of control of the present owners. The financial manager has to decide:
   (a) What should be the proportion of equity and debt in the capital structure?
   (b) From which sources the equity should be raised — whether by issue of equity shares *or* preference shares.
   (c) From which sources the debt should be raised — whether by issue of debentures *or* raising long term loans.
3. **Utilization of Funds *or* Investment Decision** — After procuring the funds, the financial manager has to decide about the assets in which the funds are to be invested. Long-term funds should be invested only after a careful assessment of the various projects through capital budgeting techniques and uncertainty analysis. A part of long-term funds has also to be kept for financing the hard core working capital requirements. He has to participate in the formation of working capital management policies with regard to management of cash, inventories, debtors etc. The financial manager has to decide —
   (a) What should be the Fixed Assets Management Policy?
   (b) What should be the Cash Management Policy?
   (c) What should be the Inventory Management Policy?
   (d) What should be the Debtors Management Policy?
4. **Disposal of Surplus *or* Dividend Decision** — The financial manager is also concerned with the decision as to how much earnings are to be retained and how much to be distributed. Economically, this decision should depend on whether the company *or* the shareholders can make a profitable use of the funds. However, in practice, a large number of considerations like the trend of earnings, the trend of share market price, the requirements of funds for future growth, the cash flow situation, the tax brackets of shareholders are to be kept in mind with an ultimate eye on the wealth maximisation objective. The optimum dividend payout ratio maximises shareholders' wealth.
5. **Management of Cash** — The financial managers must ensure the availability of adequate cash as and when needed. To purchase raw-material, to pay wages and salaries and to meet other day to day expenses.
6. **Financial Control** — The financial manager exercises the financial control by providing planned utilisation with which actual utilisation may be compared.

II. Subsidiary Functions:

(a) Ensuring the optimum level of inventory and receivables.
(b) Supplying funds to all the parts of the organisation.
(c) Evaluating financial performance of various units of the organisation.
(d) Carrying out financial negotiations with financial institutions, banks, underwriters, inter-corporate depositors (ICD).
(e) Keeping track of stock exchange quotations and behaviour of share prices.

13.0 FINANCE FUNCTION IN A LARGE CORPORATE BUSINESS ENTERPRISE

A financial function in a large corporate business enterprise is shown below

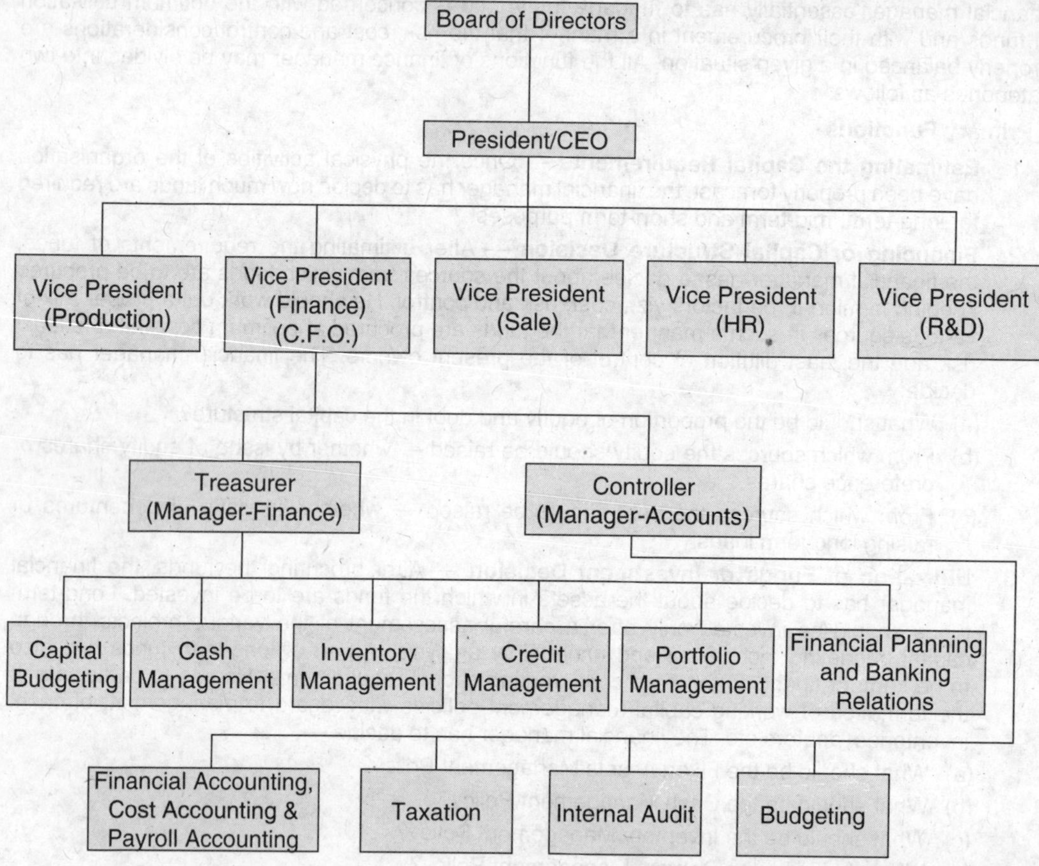

14.0 VARIOUS STAKE HOLDERS OF THE ORGANIZATION

The financial decision may have an impact on various stakeholders as follows:

INVESTORS

The providers of risk capital are concerned with the risk inherent in, and return provided by, their investments. They need information to help them determine whether they should buy, hold *or* sell. They are also interested in information which enables them to assess the ability of the enterprise to pay dividends.

EMPLOYEES

Employees and their representative groups are interested in information about the stability and profitability of their employers. They are also interested in information which enables them to assess the ability of the enterprise to provide remuneration, retirement benefits and employment opportunities.

LENDERS

Lenders are interested in information which enables them to determine whether their loans, and the interest attaching to them, will be paid when due.

SUPPLIERS AND OTHER TRADE CREDITORS

Suppliers and other creditors are interested in information which enables them to determine whether amounts owing to the will be paid when due. Trade creditors are likely to be interested in an enterprise over a shorter period than lenders unless they are dependent upon the continuance of the enterprise as a major customer.

CUSTOMERS

Customers have an interest in information about the continuance of an enterprise, especially when they have a long term involvement with, *or* are dependent on, the enterprise.

GOVERNMENTS AND THEIR AGENCIES

Governments and their agencies are interested in the allocation of resources and, therefore, the activities of enterprises. They also require information in order to regulate the activities of enterprises and determine taxation policies, and to serve as the basis for determination of national income and similar statistics.

PUBLIC

Enterprises affect members of the public in a variety of ways. ***For Example***, enterprises may make a substantial contribution to the local economy in many ways including the number of people they employ and their patronage of local suppliers. Financial statements may assist the public by providing information about the trends and recent developments in the prosperity of the enterprise and the range of its activities.

15.0 CHANGING SCENARIO OF FINANCIAL MANAGEMENT IN INDIA

Modern Financial Management has come a long way from the traditional corporate finance. As the economy is opening up and global resources are being tapped, the opportunities available to finance managers virtually have no limits. The finance manager is now responsible for shaping the fortunes of the enterprise, and is involved in the most vital decision of the allocation of capital.

Due to the changes in the global environment the finance manager needs to have a broader and far-sighted outlook, and must realize that his actions would have far-reaching consequences for the firm because they influence the size, profitability, growth, risk and survival of the firm, and as a consequence, affect the overall value of the firm.

Some of the important changes in the environment are:

1. Free pricing and book building for IPOs, seasoned equity offerings.
2. Share buybacks and Reverse Book Building.
3. Raising resources globally through ADRs/GDRs.
4. Risk Management due to introduction of Options and Futures Trading and other derivative instruments.
5. Fully Convertability of Rupee on Current Account.
6. External Commercial Borrowings.
7. Treasury Management.
8. Optimum debt-equity mix is possible. The firms have to take advantage of financial leverage to increase shareholders' wealth.
9. Interest rates have been freed from regulation.

16.0 INFLATION AND FINANCIAL MANAGEMENT

The direct consequence of inflation has been to distort the significance of operating results and utility of financial statements (based on historical cost) for various managerial accounting and financial decision making purposes. Even though it is beyond the scope of finance manager to control inflation, He is required to consider the impact of inflation on various financial management policies. Some of the prominent areas which are affected by inflation and are required to be re-oriented are as follows.

1. **Financing Decisions:** The finance manager is required to consider the impact of inflation while taking finance decisions (i.e., deciding about the sources of funds) since Interest to Suppliers of Debt, Pref. Dividend to Pref. Shareholders and Equity Dividend to Equity Shareholders are to be given out of profits and profits are affected by inflation. This involves identifying the sources from which the finance manager should raise the quantum of funds required by a company. The debentureholders and preference shareholders are interested in fixed income while equity shareholders are interested in higher profits to earn high dividend. The finance manager is required to estimate the amount of profits he is going to earn in future. While estimating the revenue and costs, he must take into consideration the inflation factor.
2. **Investment Decisions:** The finance manager is required to consider the impact of inflation on the project's profitability since the cash flows of an investment project which occur over a long period of time are affected by Inflation.
3. **Working Capital Decisions:** The finance manager is required to consider the impact of inflation while estimating the requirements of working capital since more funds may have to be tied up in inventories and receivables due to increase in input prices and manufacturing costs as a result of inflation.
4. **Dividend Decision:** The finance manager has to consider the impact of inflation while taking Dividend decision because dividend can be paid out of profits after depreciation and in a inflationary situation the depreciation provided on the basis of historical costs of assets would not provide adequate funds for replacement of fixed assets at the expiry of their useful lives.

17.0 IMPACT OF TAXATION ON FINANCIAL MANAGEMENT

Taxation affects the financial management in various ways. Some of the most significant effects are as follows:

1. Impact on Profits	Tax on profit represents cash outflow from business.
2. Impact on Dividends	Tax on Dividend distributed to shareholders represent cash outflow from business.
3. Impact on Weighted Average Cost of Capital	Weighted Average Cost of Capital is reduced if debt is used since interest on debt is tax deductible expense.
4. Impact on Cash Inflows	Cash Inflows increase since depreciation does not involve any cash outflow and at the same time it is tax deductible expense u/s 32 of The Income Tax Act, 1961.
5. Set off of Losses	Loss of loss making segment can be set off against the profits of another segment of company.
6. Unabsorbed Depreciation	Unabsorbed depreciation can be carried forwarded indefinitely and can be set off against the profits from any source in the future.
7. Carried forward & Set off of loss in case of Amalgamation	This provision helps the growth of companies and rehabilitation of sick units.
8. Tax Incentives	Tax incentives affect the decisions such as— (a) What should be the form of organisation ? (Sole Proprietorship, Partnership Firm, Company, Co-operative Society, etc.) (b) What should be the nature of industry ? (Hotel, Hospital etc.) (c) What should be the size of industry ? (whether Small, Medium *or* Large) (d) What should be the location ? (Backward Area, SEZ, etc.)

2 TIME VALUE OF MONEY

LEARNING OBJECTIVES

After studying this chapter, you should be able to understand:

- What is the Time Value of Money?
- What is Interest?
- What is the Future Value of Money?
- What are the Different Kinds of Interest?
- What is Simple Interest?
- What is Compound Interest?
- What is Effective Rate of Interest?
- What is Present Value?
- What is an Annuity?
- What is Sinking Fund?
- What is Perpetuity?
- What is Growth rate?
- How to use Compound Value and Present Value Tables
- How to find out Compound Value Factors by using Calculator
- How to find out Present Value factors by using Calculator

1.0 WHAT IS THE TIME VALUE OF MONEY?

The interest which may be earned / saved on the money held at present underlies the concept of the time value of the money. The money which is receivable at present has more value than the money receivable in the future. Hence, the relationship that exists between the value of money receivable at present and the value of money receivable at future is referred as time value of the money.

Value of money = Value of money receivable at present + Time Value of money receivable at future

From the above relationship it is clearly evident that due to the time value of the money, the money at present shall always have more value than the same amount of money at future. Due to time value of the money, a person would prefer to receive the money at present rather than in future and would like to earn interest on the money held.

2.0 WHAT IS INTEREST?

Interest is an amount that accrues on the money borrowed / lent at present for a particular period of time. The time may be one month, two months, six months, 1 year, etc. Due to the interest the time value of the money is created. The rate at which amount of interest accrues is referred as interest rate. Rate may be expressed as percentage for example 10%, 12%, etc. *or* as a fraction for example 0.10, 0.12, etc.

3.0 WHAT IS THE FUTURE VALUE OF MONEY?

Future value of money is the value of money held presently at some given future time at a given rate of interest.

Future Value of money = Value of the money at present + Interest

4.0 WHAT ARE THE DIFFERENT KINDS OF INTEREST?

There are two different kinds of interest are as follows:

(i) Simple interest

(ii) Compound interest

5.0 WHAT IS SIMPLE INTEREST?

Simple interest is the interest which accrues only on the amount originally borrowed / lent. No interest accrues on the interest accrued previously but not paid / received. A formula for calculating simple interest is given below:

Simple interest (SI) = Money borrowed/lent at present (P) × Interest Rate (R) × Time Period (t)

$$SI = P \times r \times t = Prt$$

Formulae to Calculate Future Value (FV) and Principal (P)

1. Future Value of the money (FV) (on Simple Interest basis) = P + Prt

or

$$FV = P(1 + rt)$$

2. Principal (P) = $\frac{FV}{(1 + rt)}$

ILLUSTRATION 1 [CALCULATION OF SIMPLE INTEREST AND FUTURE VALUE]

Calculate simple interest and future value of an amount of ₹ 1,00,000 borrowed at a simple interest rate of 12 % per annum for (i) 6 months, (ii) 1 year, (iii) 2 year, (iv) 1095 days. (v) 90 days

SOLUTION

STATEMENT SHOWING THE COMPUTATION OF SIMPLE INTEREST

Particulars	*for 6 moths*	*For 1 year*	*for 2 year*	*for 1095 Days*	*for 90 Days*
A. Amount borrowed (P)	1,00,000	1,00,000	1,00,000	1,00,000	1,00,000
B. Interest Rate per annum (r)	0.12	0.12	0.12	0.12	0.12
C. Time Period (in years) (t)	0.5 (i.e.6/12)	1	2	3(i.e.1095/365)	90/365
D. SI = P × r × t	6,000	12,000	24,000	36,000	2,959

STATEMENT SHOWING THE COMPUTATION OF THE FUTURE VALUE (FV)

Particulars	*for 6 moths*	*For 1 year*	*for 2 year*	*for 1095 Days*	*for 90 Days*
A. Amount borrowed (P)	1,00,000	1,00,000	1,00,000	1,00,000	1,00,000
B. SI (as calculated above)	6,000	12,000	24,000	36,000	2,959
C. FV = P + SI	1,06,000	1,12,000	1,24,000	1,36,000	1,02,959

ILLUSTRATION 2 [CALCULATION OF PRESENT VALUE (P)]

A fixed deposit receipt has a maturity value of ₹ 1,30,000. What is the amount at which fixed deposit receipt has been initially purchased if simple interest rate is 10% per year and the maturity period is 3 years.

SOLUTION

$$FV = P(1 + rt)$$
$$P = FV/(1 + rt)$$
$$P = 1{,}30{,}000 / [1 + 0.1(3)]$$
$$P = 1{,}30{,}000 / 1.30$$
$$P = 1{,}00{,}000$$

Hence, Fixed deposit receipt has been initially purchased for ₹ 1,00,000.

ILLUSTRATION 3 [CALCULATION OF SIMPLE INTEREST RATE]

A fixed deposit receipt has a maturity value of ₹ 1,30,000. It is initially purchased for ₹ 1,00,000 for 3 years. Calculate simple interest rate per year.

SOLUTION

$$FV = P(1 + rt)$$
$$1{,}30{,}000 = 1{,}00{,}000 [1 + r(3)]$$
$$1.3 = 1 + 3r$$
$$0.3 = 3r$$
$$r = 0.10$$

Hence, simple interest rate per year is 10 %

ILLUSTRATION 4 [CALCULATION OF AMOUNT OF EQUAL LOAN INSTALMENT]

X Ltd. borrows ₹ 43,60,000 from Y Ltd. at a simple interest rate of 12 % per year. It is agreed that the loan shall be payable in two equal instalments which shall be payable at the end of six months and 1 year respectively. Calculate the amount of instalment.

SOLUTION

Let the amount of instalment be 'x'

Future Value of ₹ 1 after six month $= 1 + 0.12(0.5) = 1.06$

Future Value of ₹ 1 after year $= 1 + 0.12 = 1.12$

Hence $[(x/1.06) + (x/1.12)] = 43{,}60{,}000$

$= [x\{(1/1.06) + (1/1.12)\}] = 43{,}60{,}000$

$= [x(1.12 + 1.06)/(1.12)(1.06)] = 43{,}60{,}000$

$= [2.18x / 1.1872] = 43{,}60{,}000$

$x = 43{,}60{,}000 (1.1872/2.18) = 23{,}74{,}400$

Hence the amount of instalment is ₹ 23,74,400

6.0 WHAT IS COMPOUND INTEREST?

Compound interest is the interest which accrues not only on the amount originally borrowed / lent but also on the interest accrued previously but not paid / received. A formula for calculating compound interest is given below:

Compound Interest (CI) = Future Value (FV) – Money borrowed/lent at present (P)

Whereas

Future Value (FV) = Money borrowed/lent at present (P) × [1+ Interest Rate (r)] Time Period (t)

FV = P(1 + r)^t

Note: In this formula it is assumed that interest has accrued but not paid/received

Thus, formula to calculate Money borrowed/lent at present (P) is $P = \frac{FV}{(1+r)^1}$

ILLUSTRATION 5

Calculate Future Value and Compound Interest on an amount of ₹ 1,00,000 borrowed at a compound interest rate of 12 % per annum for (i) 6 months (ii) 1 year, (iii) 2 years, (iv) 1095 days.

SOLUTION

STATEMENT SHOWING THE COMPUTATION OF COMPOUND INTEREST

Particulars	*for 6 months*	*for 1 year*	*for 2 years*	*for 1095 Days*
A. Amount borrowed (P)	1,00,000	1,00,000	1,00,000	1,00,000
B. Interest Rate (r)	0.12	0.12	0.12	0.12
C. Time Period (t)	1/2	1	2	3 (i.e. 1095/365)
D. Future Value (FV) = P (1 + r)^t	1,05,830	1,12,000	1,25,440	1,40,492.80
E. Compound Interest (CI) = FV – P	5,830	12,000	25,440	40,492.80

ILLUSTRATION 6 [CALCULATION OF PRESENT VALUE (P)]

A fixed deposit receipt has a maturity value of ₹ 1,33,100. What is the amount at which fixed deposit receipt has been initially purchased if compound interest rate is 10 % per annum and the maturity period is 3 years.

SOLUTION

$$P = \frac{FV}{(1+r)^t} = \frac{1,33,100}{(1+0.10)^3} = \frac{1,33,100}{1.331} = ₹1,00,000$$

Hence, Fixed deposit receipt has been purchased for ₹ 1,00,000.

ILLUSTRATION 7 [CALCULATION OF COMPOUND INTEREST RATE]

A fixed deposit receipt has a maturity value of ₹ 1,46,410. It is initially purchased for ₹ 1,00,000 for 4 years. Calculate the compound interest rate per annum.

SOLUTION

$$FV = P(1 + r)^t$$

$$1,46,410 = 1,00,000\,[1 + r]^4$$

$$1.46410 = (1 + r)^4$$

$$(1 + r) = \sqrt[4]{1.46410}$$

$$(1 + r) = 1.10$$

$$r = 0.10$$

Hence, compound interest rate per annum is 10 %.

ILLUSTRATION 8 [CALCULATION OF EQUAL LOAN INSTALMENT]

X Ltd. borrows ₹ 1,18,72,000 from Y Ltd. at a compound interest rate of 12 % per annum. It is agreed that the loan shall be payable in two equal instalments which shall be payable at the end of 1st year and 2nd year respectively. Calculate the amount of instalment.

SOLUTION

Let the amount of instalment be 'x'

Future Value of ₹ 1 after 1st year $= (1 + r)^1 = (1 + 0.12)^1 = 1.12$

Future Value of ₹ 1 after 2nd year $= (1 + r)^2 = (1 + 0.12)^2 = 1.2544$

Hence $[(x/1.12) + (x/1.2544)] = 1,18,72,000$

$= [\, x\,(1.12 + 1.2544)/ (1.12)(1.2544)\,] = 1,18,72,000$

$= [\, 2.3744\, x / 1.404928] = 1,18,72,000$

$x = 1,18,72,000\ (1.404928/2.3744) = 70,24,640$

Hence the amount of instalment is ₹ 70,24,640.

7.0 WHAT IS EFFECTIVE RATE OF INTEREST?

Effective rate of interest is a rate at which money held at present actually increases in a year. Sometimes it often happens that interest is compounded more than once in a year. In such circumstances effective rate of interest is different from given rate of interest.

ILLUSTRATION 9

Calculate Future value and effective rate of interest if rate of interest is r and number of compounding is n times a year.

SOLUTION

Future Value of ₹ 1 after 1 year (FV) $= [1 + (r/n)]^n$

Effective Rate of Interest $(e_r) = FV - 1$

ILLUSTRATION 10

Calculate Effective Rate of Interest if Rate of Interest is 12 % in each of the following cases:

Case (a): When interest is compounded half yearly

Case (b): When interest is compounded quarterly

Case (c): When interest is compounded monthly

Case (d): When interest is compounded twice a month

Case (e): When interest is compounded daily.

SOLUTION

STATEMENT SHOWING THE EFFECTIVE RATE OF INTEREST

Particulars	*Case (a)*	*Case (b)*	*Case (c)*	*Case (d)*	*Case (e)*
A. Interest Rate	0.12	0.12	0.12	0.12	0.12
B. No. of compounding per year (t)	2	4	12	24	365

C.	Applicable Interest Rate (r) (A / B)	0.0600	0.0300	0.0100	0.0050	0.0003
D.	Future Value (FV) = (1 + r)t	1.1236	1.1255	1.1268	1.1272	1.1275
E.	Effective Rate of Interest = (FV – 1)	0.1236	0.1255	0.1268	0.1272	0.1275

ILLUSTRATION 11

Calculate Future Value and Effective rate of interest of ₹ 1 if Rate of Interest is r and number of compounding is infinite times a year.

SOLUTION

Limit n reaches to infinity $[1 + (r / n)]^n$

By formula limit n reaches to infinity

$$[1 + (1 / n)]^n = e$$

Hence, $[1 + (r / n)]^n = [1 + \{1 / (n/r)\}]^{(n/r)}$

As n reaches infinity n / r also reaches to infinity

Hence $[1 + \{1 / (n/r)\}](n/r) = e$

Therefore $[1 + (r / n)]^n = e^r$ = Future Value (FV)

Effective Rate of Interest = FV – 1 = $e^r - 1$.

ILLUSTRATION 12

Calculate Future value if initial amount invested is P, rate of interest is r, number of compounding is n times a year and maturity period is m years.

SOLUTION

Future Value of ₹ 1 after 1 year (FV) = $[1 + (r / n)]^n$

Future Value of ₹ 1 after m years = (Future Value after 1 year)m = $[\{1 + (r / n)\}^n]^m$

$$= [1 + (r / n)]^{nm}.$$

ILLUSTRATION 13

A company offers a fixed deposit scheme whereby ₹ 10,000 matures to ₹ 12,625 after 2 years, on a half yearly compounded basis. If a company wishes to amend the scheme by compounding interest every quarter, what will be the revised maturity value?

SOLUTION

Future Value after 1 year (FV) = $[1 + (r / 2)]^2$

Future Value after 2 year = (Future value after 1 year $)^2$

$$= [\{1 + (r / 2)\}^2]^2 = [1 + r / 2]^4$$

$$10{,}000 \times [1 + r / 2]^4 = 12{,}625$$

$$[1 + r / 2]^4 = 1.2625$$

$$[1 + r / 2] = \sqrt[4]{1.2625}$$

$$1 + r / 2] = 1.06$$

$$r / 2 = 0.06$$

$$r = 0.12$$

Hence the revised future value after 1 year = $[1 +(0.12 / 4)]^4 = 1.12551$

Revised Future Value after 2 years = $(1.12551)^2 = 1.2668$

Hence, Revised Maturity Value = 10,000 × 1.2668 = ₹ 12,668.

ILLUSTRATION 14

Calculate Future Value if initial amount invested is P, Rate of Interest is r, number of compounding is infinite times a year and maturity period is m years.

SOLUTION

Future Value of ₹ 1 after 1 year (FV) as calculated in Illustration 11 = e^r

Future Value of ₹ 1 after m years = (Future value after 1 year)^m = $(e^r)m = e^{rm}$

ILLUSTRATION 15

Calculate the Future Value and Compound Interest of ₹ 1 if effective rate of interest is 12 % p.a in each of the following cases:

Case (a): When maturity period is 3 months

Case (b): When maturity period is 6 months

Case (c): When maturity period is 9 months

SOLUTION

Case (a): Let rate for 3 months be r_i

Hence, $(1 + r_i)^{(12\text{ months} / 3\text{ months})} = 1.12$

$(1 + r_i)^4 = 1.12$

$(1 + r_i) = \sqrt[4]{1.12}$

$(1 + r_i) = 1.02874$

Hence Maturity Value (Future Value) of ₹ 1 after 3 months = ₹ 1.02874

Compound Interest = Future Value – 1 = 1.02874 – 1 = 0.02874

Case (b): Let rate for 6 months be r_i

Hence, $(1 + r_i)^{(12\text{ months} / 6\text{ months})} = 1.12$

$(1 + r_i)^2 = 1.12$

$(1 + r_i) = \sqrt{1.12}$

$(1 + r_i) = 1.0583$

Hence Maturity Value (Future Value) of ₹ 1 after 6 months = ₹ 1.0583

Compound Interest = Future Value – 1

= 1.0583 – 1 = 0.0583

Case (c): Let rate for 9 months be r_i

Hence, $(1 + r_i)^{(12\text{ months} / 9\text{ months})} = 1.12$

$(1 + r_i)^{4/3} = 1.12$

$(1 + r_i) = \sqrt[4]{(1.12)^3}$

$(1 + r_i) = \sqrt[4]{1.404928}$

$(1 + r_i) = 1.0887$

Hence Maturity Value (Future Value) of ₹ 1 after 9 months = ₹ 1.0887

Compound Interest = Future Value – 1

= 1.0887 – 1 = 0.0887

8.0 WHAT IS PRESENT VALUE?

Present value of the money is today's value of tomorrow's money. In other words, it is the difference between Future Value (FV) and Interest for the period between present and future. It is Future Value of Money discounted at a given rate of interest.

Present Value of the money = Future Value of the money – Interest

Present Value (PV) = $\dfrac{\text{Money receivable / payable at future (FV)}}{[1+ \text{Interest Rate (r)}]^{\text{Time Period (t)}}}$

or **PV =** $\dfrac{FV}{(1+r)^t}$

ILLUSTRATION 16

Determine the present value of ₹ 78,67,597 receivable at the end of 4th year at an effective rate of interest of 12 % p.a?

SOLUTION

Present Value = $\dfrac{FV}{(1+r)^t} = \dfrac{₹\ 78{,}67{,}597}{(1+0.12)^4} = \dfrac{₹\ 78{,}67{,}597}{1.57353}$ = ₹ 50,00,000

ILLUSTRATION 17

Calculate the present value of ₹ 25,00,000, ₹ 30,00,000 and ₹ 40,00,000 receivable at the end of 1st year, 2nd year and 3rd year respectively at an effective rate of interest of 12% p.a.

SOLUTION

Present Value (PV) = $\dfrac{\text{Future Value (FV)}}{(1+r)^t}$

STATEMENT SHOWING THE CALCULATION OF PRESENT VALUE

Particulars	Year 1	Year 2	Year 3	Total
A. Future Value	25,00,000	30,00,000	40,00,000	95,00,000
B. Years (n)	1	2	3	
C. Rate of interest (r)	0.12	0.12	0.12	
D. P.V Factor $[1/(1+r)^n]$	0.8929	0.7972	0.7118	
E. Present Value (A × D)	22,32,250	23,91,600	28,47,200	74,71,050

ILLUSTRATION 18

Calculate the present value of ₹ 20,000, ₹ 30,000 ₹ 40,000 and ₹ 50,000 receivable at the end of 6 months, 1 year, 18 months and 2 years respectively at an effective rate of interest of 12% p.a.

SOLUTION

STATEMENT SHOWING THE CALCULATION OF PRESENT VALUE

Particulars	6 months	1 year	18 months	2 years	Total
A. Amount	20,000	30,000	40,000	50,000	1,40,000
B. Years (n)	1/2	1	3/2	2	
C. Rate of interest (r)	0.12	0.12	0.12	0.12	
D. P.V Factor $[1/(1 + r)^n]$	0.9449*	0.8929	0.8437**	0.7972	
E. Present Value (A × D)	18,898	26,787	33,748	39,860	1,19,293

*P.V Factor of 6 months = $1 / (1.12)^{1/2}$

$= 1 / 1.0583 = 0.9449$

**P.V Factor of 18 months = $1 / (1.12)^{3/2}$

$= 1 / = 1/ \sqrt{(1.12)^3} = 1/\sqrt{1.4049}$

$= 1 / 1.1853 = 0.8437$

9.0 WHAT IS AN ANNUITY?

A series of equal amount of cash flows over a certain given years is called an annuity.

ILLUSTRATION 19

Determine the present value of an annuity of amount A for n years at an effective rate of interest of r.

SOLUTION

Present Value of an annuity (P.V) $= \frac{A}{(1+r)} + \frac{A}{(1+r)^2} + \frac{A}{(1+r)^3} + ... \frac{A}{(1+r)^n}$

$= \frac{A}{(1+r)}\left[1 + \frac{A}{(1+r)} + \frac{A}{(1+r)^2} + ... \frac{A}{(1+r)^{n-1}}\right]$

These terms are in geometric progression

Therefore

$P.V = A / (1 + r) [\{1 - (1 / 1 + r)^n\} / \{1 - (1 / 1 + r)\}]$

$P.V = A / (1 + r) [\{(|1 + r|^n - 1) / (1 + r)^n\} / \{(|1 + r| - 1) / (1 + r)\}]$

$P.V = A / (1 + r) [\{ (|1 + r|^n - 1) / (1 + r)^n\} / \{r / (1 + r)\}]$

$P.V = A [(1 + r)^n - 1] / r (1 + r)^n$

$P.V = \frac{A}{r}\left[1 - \frac{1}{(1+r)^n}\right]$

ILLUSTRATION 20

Determine the present value of an annuity of ₹ 1,00,000 receivable for 5 years at an effective rate of interest of 12 % p.a.

SOLUTION

Present Value of an annuity of ₹ 1 for five years

$= \frac{A}{r}\left[1 - \frac{1}{(1+r)^n}\right] = \frac{1}{0.12}\left[1 - \frac{1}{(1+0.12)^5}\right]$

= 8.3333 [1 – 0.5674] = 8.3333 × 0.4326 = 3.605

Hence, PV of an annuity of ₹ 1,00,000

= ₹ 1,00,000 × PV of an annuity of ₹ 1 = 1,00,000 × 3.605 = ₹ 3,60,500.

ILLUSTRATION 21

Determine the present value of an annuity of ₹ 1,00,000 receivable for 5 years at an effective rate of interest of 12 % p.a. if annuity is receivable at the beginning of the year.

SOLUTION

In this case relevant number of years shall be 4 years since 5th annuity shall be payable at the beginning of 5th year which is equivalent to end of 4th year.

$$\text{Present Value of an annuity of ₹ 1} = \frac{A}{r}\left[1-\frac{1}{(1+r)^n}\right] = \frac{1}{0.12}\left[1-\frac{1}{(1+0.12)^4}\right]$$

= 8.3333 [1 – 0.6355] = 8.3333 × 0.3645 = 3.0375

This is the present value of an annuity of ₹ 1 receivable at the end of 1st year, 2nd year, 3rd year and 4th year respectively. However, in this figure ₹ 1 receivable at present is not included. Hence in this figure ₹ 1 is added to arrive at present value of an annuity of ₹ 1 for five year receivable at the beginning of the year.

Therefore, present value of an annuity of ₹ 1 for five year receivable at the beginning of the year = 3.0375 + 1 = 4.0375

Hence, PV of an annuity of ₹ 1,00,000

= ₹ 1,00,000 × PV of an Annuity of ₹ 1

= 1,00,000 × 4.0375 = ₹ 4,03,750.

ILLUSTRATION 22

Determine the present value of an annuity of ₹ 1,00,000 receivable for 5 years semi – annually at a rate of interest of 12 % p.a. compounded semi – annually.

SOLUTION

In this case r would be 0.12 / 2 = 0.06

n would be 2 × 5 years = 10 years

Present Value of an annuity of ₹ 1 for 10 years

$$= \frac{A}{r}\left[1-\frac{1}{(1+r)^n}\right] = \frac{1}{0.06}\left[1-\frac{1}{(1+0.06)^{10}}\right]$$

= 16.6666 [1 – 0.5584] = 16.6666 × 0.4416 = 7.36

Hence,

PV of an annuity of ₹ 1,00,000 = ₹ 1,00,000 × PV of an annuity of ₹ 1

= 1,00,000 × 7.36 = ₹ 7,36,000.

ILLUSTRATION 23

Determine the present value of an annuity of ₹ 1,00,000 receivable for 5 years semi – annually at a rate of interest of 12 % p.a. compounded semi – annually if annuity is payable at the beginning of semi – year.

SOLUTION

In this case relevant number of years shall be 4.5 years since 10th annuity shall be payable at the middle of 5th year which is equivalent to end of 4.5 year.

In this case r would be 0.12 / 2 = 0.06

n would be 2 × 4.5 years = 9 years

Present Value of an annuity of ₹ 1 $= \frac{A}{r}\left[1-\frac{1}{(1+r)^n}\right] = \frac{1}{0.06}\left[1-\frac{1}{(1+0.06)^9}\right]$

$= 16.6666\ [1 - 0.5919] = 16.6666 \times 0.4081 = 6.8016$

This is the present value of an annuity of ₹ 1 receivable till the end of 4.5th year. However, in this figure ₹ 1 receivable at present is not included. Hence in this figure ₹ 1 is added to arrive at present value of an annuity of ₹ 1 for 5 year receivable at the beginning of the semi – year.

Therefore, present value of an annuity of ₹ 1 for 5 years receivable at the beginning of the semi – year

= 6.8016 + 1 = 7.8016

Hence, PV of an annuity of ₹ 1,00,000

= ₹ 1,00,000 × PV of an annuity of ₹ 1

= 1,00,000 × 7.8016 = ₹ 7,80,160.

ILLUSTRATION 24

Determine the annuity payable annually to an investor if he invests ₹ 10,00,000 at present at an effective rate of interest 12 % p.a. for 10 years.

SOLUTION

Present Value of an annuity of ₹ 1 for 10 years

$= \frac{A}{r}\left[1-\frac{1}{(1+r)^n}\right] = \frac{1}{0.12}\left[1-\frac{1}{(1+0.12)^{10}}\right]$

$= 8.3333\ [1 - 0.322] = 8.3333 \times 0.678 = 5.65$

Let annuity be 'x',

Therefore, 5.65x = ₹ 10,00,000

x = 10,00,000 / 5.65 = 1,76,991

Hence, the amount of an annuity shall be ₹ 1,76,991.

ILLUSTRATION 25

Determine the annuity payable annually to an investor if he invests ₹ 10,00,000 at present at an effective rate of interest 12 % p.a. for 10 years and annuity is payable at the beginning of the year.

SOLUTION

In this case relevant number of years shall be 9 years since 10th annuity shall be payable at the beginning of 10th year which is equivalent to the end of 9th year.

Present Value of an annuity of ₹ 1 $= \frac{A}{r}\left[1-\frac{1}{(1+r)^n}\right] = \frac{1}{0.12}\left[1-\frac{1}{(1+0.12)^9}\right]$

$= 8.3333\ [1 - 0.3606] = 8.3333 \times 0.6394 = 5.3283$

This is the present value of an annuity of ₹ 1 receivable till the end of 9th year. However, in this figure ₹ 1 receivable at present is not included. Hence in this figure ₹ 1 is added to arrive at present value of an annuity of ₹ 1 for 10 year receivable at the beginning of the year.

Therefore, present value of an annuity of ₹ 1 for 10 year receivable at the beginning of the year = 5.3283 + 1 = 6.3283

Let annuity be 'x',

Therefore, 6.3283x = ₹ 10,00,000

x = 10,00,000 / 6.3283 = 1,58,020

Hence, the amount of an annuity shall be ₹ 1,58,020.

ILLUSTRATION 26

What shall be the Future Value of an annuity of ₹ 1,00,000 for 5 years at an effective rate of 12% p.a. after 5 years?

SOLUTION

Future value of an annuity of ₹ 1 (F.V) after 5 years

$$= \left(\frac{A}{r}\right)[(1+r)^n - 1] = \frac{1}{0.12}[(1+0.12)^5 - 1]$$

$$= 8.3333\ (1.7623 - 1) = 6.3525$$

Hence, FV of an annuity of ₹ 1,00,000

= ₹ 1,00,000 × FV of an annuity of ₹ 1

= 1,00,000 × 6.3525 = ₹ 6,35,250

Note: Future Value calculated above may be crossed checked with present value of an annuity of ₹ 1,00,000 determined in Illustration 22.

$$\text{Future value (F.V)} = \text{P.V}\ (1+r)^n$$

$$₹\ 6,35,250 = \text{P.V}\ (1+0.12)^5$$

$$\text{P.V} = 6,35,250/(1.12)^5 = 6,35,250 \times 0.5674 \text{ (appx.)}$$

= ₹ 3,60,441 *or* ₹ 3,60,500 (appx.)

ILLUSTRATION 27

What shall be the Future Value of an annuity of ₹ 1,00,000 (at the beginning of the year) for 5 years at an effective rate of 12 % p.a. after 5 years?

SOLUTION

In this case relevant number of years shall be 6 years since in this case 1st annuity is payable in the beginning of 1st year.

Future value of an annuity of ₹ 1 after 6 years

$$= \left(\frac{A}{r}\right)[(1+r)^n - 1] = \frac{1}{0.12}[(1+0.12)^6 - 1]$$

$$= 8.3333\ (1.9738 - 1) = 8.3333\ (0.9738) = 8.115$$

This is the Future value of an annuity of ₹ 1 after 6 years. However, in this figure ₹ 1 receivable at the end of 6 year is included. Hence in this figure ₹ 1 is deducted to arrive at Future value of an annuity of ₹ 1 for 5 year receivable at the beginning of the year.

Therefore, Future value of an annuity of ₹ 1 for 5 year receivable at the beginning of the year = 8.115 – 1 = 7.115

Hence, FV of an annuity of ₹ 1,00,000

$$= ₹\ 1,00,000 \times \text{FV of an annuity of } ₹\ 1$$

$$= 1,00,000 \times 7.115 = ₹\ 7,11,500.$$

Note: Future Value calculated above may be crossed checked with present value of an annuity of ₹ 1,00,000 determined in illustration 23.

$$\text{Future value (F.V)} = \text{P.V}\ (1 + r)^n$$

$$₹\ 7,11,500 = \text{P.V}\ (1 + 0.12)^5$$

$$\text{P.V} = 7,11,500 / (1.12)^5 = 7,11,500 \times 0.56743$$

$$= ₹\ 4,03,726 = ₹\ 4,03,740 \text{ (appx.)}.$$

10.0 WHAT IS SINKING FUND?

Sinking fund is a fund created to accumulate the specified amount of sum in a future by way of regular periodic payment for some specific purpose. Basically here the problem involves the determination of amount of Annuity for a given Future Value after a given period at a given rate of interest. Hence, formula relating to Future Value of Annuity is used for the purpose.

ILLUSTRATION 28

How much amount is required to be invested every year so as to accumulate ₹ 10,00,000 at the end of 5 years if the effective rate of interest is 12% p.a.

SOLUTION

Future value of an annuity of ₹ 1 after 5 years

$$= \left(\frac{A}{R}\right)[(1 + r)^n - 1] = \frac{1}{0.12}[1 + 0.12)^5 - 1]$$

$$= 8.3333\ (1.7623 - 1) = 8.3333\ (0.7623)$$

$$= 6.3525$$

Let the amount of an annuity be 'x'

Therefore, $6.3525x = 10,00,000$

$$x = 10,00,000/6.3525 = 1,57,418.$$

Hence, amount required to be invested every year is ₹ 1,57,418.

ILLUSTRATION 29

How much amount is required to be invested in the beginning of every year so as to accumulate ₹ 10,00,000 at the end of 5 years if the effective rate of interest is 12% p.a.

SOLUTION

In this case relevant number of years shall be 6 years since in this case 1st annuity is payable in the beginning of 1st year.

Future value of an annuity of ₹ 1 after 6 years

$$= \left(\frac{A}{R}\right)[(1 + r)^n - 1] = \frac{1}{0.12}[1 + 0.12)^6 - 1]$$

$$= 8.3333\ (1.9738 - 1) = 8.3333\ (0.9738) = 8.115$$

This is the Future value of an annuity of ₹ 1 after 6 years. However, in this figure ₹ 1 receivable at the end of 6 year is included. Hence in this figure ₹ 1 is deducted to arrive at Future value of an annuity of ₹ 1 for 5 year receivable at the beginning of the year.

Therefore, Future value of an annuity of ₹ 1 for 5 year invested at the beginning of the year

= 8.115 – 1 = 7.115

Let the amount of an annuity be 'x'

Therefore, 7.115x = 10,00,000

x = 10,00,000/7.115 = 1,40,548

Hence, amount required to be invested at the beginning of every year is ₹ 1,40,548.

11.0 WHAT IS PERPETUITY?

The stream of regular cash flows for an infinite period is called perpetuity. It may be compared to an annuity but it does not have any time limit. In perpetuity time is not finite. However, present value of perpetuity can be calculated. Example of perpetuity is preference shares which carry certain Fixed Rate of Dividend payable forever.

ILLUSTRATION 30

Determine the present value of perpetuity of amount A for infinite period at an effective rate of interest of r?

SOLUTION:

$$\text{Present Value of an annuity (P.V)} = \frac{A}{(1+r)} + \frac{A}{(1+r)^2} + \frac{A}{(1+r)^3} + \ldots \frac{A}{(1+r)^n}$$

$$= \frac{A}{(1+r)}\left[1 + \frac{1}{(1+r)} + \frac{1}{(1+r)^2} + \ldots \frac{1}{(1+r)^{n-1}}\right]$$

These terms are in geometric progression

Therefore, $P.V = A / (1 + r) [\{1 - (1 / 1 + r)^n\} / \{1 - (1 / 1 + r) \}]$

$P.V = A / (1 + r) [\{ (|1 + r|^n - 1) / (1 + r)^n\} / \{(|1 + r| - 1) / (1 + r)\}]$

$P.V = A / (1 + r) [\{ (|1 + r|^n - 1) / (1 + r)^n \} / \{r / (1 + r)\}]$

$P.V = A [(1 + r)^n - 1] / r (1 + r)^n$

$$P.V = \frac{A}{r}\left[1 + \frac{1}{(1+r)^n}\right]$$

As n tends to infinity, $[1 / (1+ r)^n]$ tends to zero therefore P.V of a perpetuity = (A / r)

ILLUSTRATION 31

Determine the present value of perpetuity ₹ 1,20,000 per year for infinite period at an effective rate of interest of 12% p.a.?

SOLUTION

P.V of perpetuity = (A / r) = ₹ 1,20,000 / 0.12 = ₹ 10,00,000

ILLUSTRATION 32

Determine the present value of perpetuity ₹ 1,20,000 per year (starting from the beginning) for infinite period at an effective rate of interest of 12% p.a.?

SOLUTION

P.V of normal perpetuity = (A / r) = ₹ 1,20,000 / 0.12 = ₹ 10,00,000

However, in this case perpetuity received in the beginning is not included therefore P.V of perpetuity starting from the beginning = P.V of normal perpetuity + Perpetuity received in the beginning = ₹ 10,00,000 + ₹ 1,20,000 = ₹ 11,20,000

ILLUSTRATION 33

Determine the present value of perpetuity of ₹ 1,00,000 per 6 months for an infinite period at an effective rate of interest of 12% p.a.

SOLUTION

In this case r would be as follows:

$$r = \left[\sqrt{(1 + \text{Effective Rate of Interest})}\right] - 1$$

$$r = \left(\sqrt{1.12}\right) - 1 = 1.0583 - 1 = 0.0583$$

$$\text{P.V of Perpetuity} = (A / r) = ₹\ 1,00,000 / 0.0583 = ₹\ 17,15,266$$

ILLUSTRATION 34

Determine the present value of perpetuity of ₹ 1,00,000 per 3 months for an infinite period at an effective rate of interest of 12% p.a.

SOLUTION

In this case r would be as follows:

$$r = \left[\sqrt[4]{(1 + \text{Effective Rate of Interest})}\right] - 1$$

$$r = \left(\sqrt[4]{1.12}\right) - 1 = 1.0287 - 1 = 0.0287$$

$$\text{P.V of Perpetuity} = (A / r) = ₹\ 1,00,000 / 0.0287 = ₹\ 34,84,321$$

ILLUSTRATION 35

Determine the perpetuity in each of the following cases if effective rate of interest is 12% p.a. and initial amount invested is ₹ 10,00,000.

Case (a): If perpetuity is payable after every year.

Case (b): If perpetuity is payable after every 6 months.

Case (c): If perpetuity is payable after every quarter.

SOLUTION

Case (a): In this case r = 0.12, P.V. of Perpetuity = A / r

$$A = (P.V)\ r = ₹\ 10,00,000 \times 0.12 = ₹\ 1,20,000$$

Hence in this case perpetuity would be ₹ 1,20,000.

Case (b): In this case r = – 1 = 0.0583, P.V. of Perpetuity = A / r

$$A = (P.V)\ r = ₹\ 10,00,000 \times 0.0583 = ₹\ 58,300$$

Hence in this case perpetuity would be ₹ 58,300.

Case (c): In this case r = – 1 = 0.0287, P.V. Perpetuity = A / r

$$A = (P.V)\ r = ₹\ 10,00,000 \times 0.0287 = ₹\ 28,700$$

Hence in this case perpetuity would be ₹ 28,700.

12.0 WHAT IS GROWTH RATE?

The rate by which future cash flows increase is called a growth rate. This growth rate may be increasing, static *or* decreasing.

ILLUSTRATION 36

Calculate the cash flows for 5 years if Cash Flow at the end of 1st year is ₹ 1,00,000 and growth rate is 5% per year in each of the following cases:

Case (a): If Growth Rate increases by 10 % per year

Case (b): If Growth Rate decreases by 10 % per year

Case (c): If Growth Rate is static

SOLUTION

Case (a):

STATEMENT SHOWING THE CASH FLOWS IF GROWTH RATE INCREASES BY 10% P.A.

Year	*Previous year's Cash Flow*	*Growth Rate*	*Year End Cash Flow (including growth)*
1	–	–	1,00,000
2	1,00,000	5 %	1,05,000
3	1,05,000	5 × 1.10 = 5.5 %	1,10,775
4	1,10,775	5.5 × 1.10 = 6.05 %	1,17,477
5	1,17,477	6.05 × 1.10 = 6.655 %	1,25,295

Case (b):

STATEMENT SHOWING THE CASH FLOWS OF GROWTH RATE DECREASES BY 10% P.A.

Year	*Previous year's Cash Flow*	*Growth Rate*	*Year End Cash Flow (including growth)*
1	–	–	1,00,000
2	1,00,000	5 %	1,05,000
3	1,05,000	5 × 0.90 = 4.5 %	1,09,725
4	1,09,725	4.5 × 0.90 = 4.05 %	1,14,169
5	1,14,169	4.05 × 0.90 = 3.645 %	1,18,330

Case (c):

STATEMENT SHOWING THE CASH FLOWS IF GROWTH RATE IS STATIC

Year	*Previous year's Cash Flow*	*Growth Rate*	*Year End Cash Flow (including growth)*
1	–	–	1,00,000
2	1,00,000	5 %	1,05,000
3	1,05,000	5 %	1,10,250
4	1,10,250	5 %	1,15,763
5	1,15,763	5 %	1,21,551

ILLUSTRATION 37

Determine the present value of an annuity of amount A if effective rate of interest is r, steady growth rate is g and the number of years is n.

SOLUTION

Present Value of an annuity (P.V) = $[A / (1 + r)] + [A (1 + g) / (1 + r)^2] + [A (1 + g)^2 / (1 + r)^3] + \ldots [A (1 + g)^{n-2} / (1 + r)^{(n-1)}] + [A (1 + g)^n - 1 / (1 + r)^n]$

$$P.V = A / (1 + r) [1 + \{(1 + g)^1 / (1 + r)^1\} + \{(1 + g)^2 / (1 + r)^2\} + \ldots\{(1 + g)^{n-2}/(1 + r)^{n-2}\} + \{(1 + g)^{(n-1)} / (1 + r)^{n-1}\}]$$

These terms are in geometric progression

Therefore

$$P.V = A / (1 + r) [\{1 - (|1 + g| / |1 + r|)^n\} / \{1 - (|1 + g| / |1 + r|)\}]$$

$$P.V = A / (1 + r) [\{(|1 + r|^n - |1 + g|^n) / (1 + r)^n\} / \{(|1 + r| - |1 + g|) / (1 + r)\}]$$

$$P.V = A / (1 + r) [\{(|1 + r|^n - |1 + g|^n) / (1 + r)^n\} / \{(r - g) / (1 + r)\}]$$

$$P.V = A [\{(1 + r)^n - (1 + g)^n\} / \{(r - g) / (1 + r)^n\}]$$

$$P.V = [\{A / (r - g)\}] [1 - \{(1 + g) / (1 + r)\}^n]$$

ILLUSTRATION 38

Calculate the present value of an annuity of ₹ 1,00,000 at an effective rate of interest of 12 % p.a. in static growth rate of 10 % per year for 5 years.

SOLUTION

Present Value of an annuity of ₹ 1 for 5 years

$$= [\{1 / (r - g)\}] [1 - \{(1 + g) / (1 + r)\}^5]$$

$$P.V = [\{1/(0.12 - 0.10)\}][1 - \{(1+ 0.10)/(1 + 0.12)\}^5]$$

$$P.V = [1 / 0.02] [1 - (1.10 / 1.12)^5]$$

$$P.V = 50 [1 - (1.61051 / 1.76234)]$$

$$P.V = 50 (1 - 0.91385)$$

$$P.V = 50 (0.08615)$$

$$P.V = 4.3075$$

PV of ₹ 1,00,000 for 5 years = ₹ 1,00,000 × PV of an annuity of ₹ 1 for 5 yrs

= ₹ 1,00,000 × 4.3075 = ₹ 4,30,750

ILLUSTRATION 39

Calculate the present value of an annuity of ₹ 1,00,000 at an effective rate of interest of 12 % p.a. in static growth rate of 10 % per year for 5 years if annuity is receivable at the beginning of the year.

SOLUTION

In this case relevant number of years shall be 4 years since 5th annuity shall be payable at the beginning of 5th year which is equivalent to end of 4th year.

Present value of an annuity of ₹ 1.10 for 4 years

$$= [\{1.10 / (r - g)\}] [1 - \{(1 + g) / (1 + r)\}^4]$$

$$P.V = [\{1.10/(0.12 - 0.10)\}][1 - \{(1 + 0.10)/(1 + 0.12)\}^4]$$

$$P.V = [1.10 / 0.02] [1 - (1.10 / 1.12)^4]$$

$$P.V = 55\ [1 - (1.4641 / 1.57352)]$$
$$P.V = 55\ (1 - 0.93046)$$
$$P.V = 55\ (0.06954)$$
$$P.V = 3.8247$$

This is the present value of an annuity of ₹ 1 receivable at the end of 1st year, 2nd year, 3rd year and 4th year respectively. However, in this figure ₹ 1 receivable at present is not included. Hence, in this figure ₹ 1 is added to arrive at present value of an annuity of ₹ 1 for five year receivable at the beginning of the year.

Therefore present value of an annuity of ₹ 1 for five year receivable at the beginning of the year

= 3.8247 + 1 = 4.8247

Hence present value of an annuity of ₹ 1,00,000 = ₹ 1,00,000 × Present value of an annuity of ₹ 1

= 1,00,000 × 4.8247 = ₹ 4,82,470.

ILLUSTRATION 40

Determine the present value of perpetuity of amount A for infinite period at an effective rate of interest of r if steady growth rate is g per year?

SOLUTION

Present value of an annuity for n years = $[\{A / (r - g)\}]\,[1 - \{(1 + g) / (1 + r)\}^n]$

As n tends to zero, $[(1 + g) / (1 + r)]^n$ tends to zero only and only if $r > g$. If $r < g$ then present value of an annuity cannot be calculated because in such circumstances present value also tends to infinity. Therefore a must condition for determining the present value of the perpetuity is $r > g$. In such a case present value shall be $[\{A / (r - g)\}]$.

ILLUSTRATION 41

Determine the present value of perpetuity of ₹ 1,00,000 for infinite period at an effective rate of interest of 12 % p.a. if steady growth rate is 10 % per year?

SOLUTION

P.V = [{ A / (r – g)}]

P.V = 1,00,000 / (0.12 – 0.10) = ₹ 1,00,000 / 0.02 = ₹ 50,00,000

ILLUSTRATION 42

Determine the present value of perpetuity of ₹ 1,00,000 for infinite period at an effective rate of interest of 12 % p.a. and steady growth rate is 10 % per year if perpetuity is payable at the beginning of the year?

SOLUTION

In such a case

P.V = A + [{ A (1 + g) / (r – g)}]

P.V = ₹ 1,00,000 + [(₹ 1,00,000 × 1.10) / (0.12 – 0.10)]

P.V = ₹ 1,00,000 + (₹ 1,10,000 / 0.02)

P.V = ₹ 1,00,000 + ₹ 55,00,000 = ₹ 56,00,000

ILLUSTRATION 43

Determine the present value of the perpetuity if ₹ 1,00,000 is payable for 5 years with growth rate of 50 % and thereafter with growth rate 8 % at an effective rate of interest of 12 % p.a.

SOLUTION

STATEMENT SHOWING THE PRESENT VALUE OF THE PERPETUITY

Year *A*	*Perpetuity* *B*	*P.V.F@12%* *C*	*Present Value* *D = B × C*
1.	1,00,000	0.893	89,300
2.	1,05,000	0.797	83,685
3.	1,10,250	0.712	78,498
4.	1,15,763	0.636	73,625
5.	34,03,426 (1,21,551 + 32,81,875)	0.567	19,29,743
		Present Value	**22,54,851**

Working Notes:

(I) CALCULATION OF AMOUNT OF PERPETUITY

Years	*Amount*	*Basis*	*Rate*	*Amount*
1		Static growth rate	5 %	1,00,000
2	1,00,000	Static growth rate	5 %	1,05,000
3	1,05,000	Static growth rate	5 %	1,10,250
4	1,10,250	Static growth rate	5 %	1,15,763
5	1,15,763	Static growth rate	5 %	1,21,551

(II) CALCULATION OF PRESENT VALUE OF PERPETUITY AFTER 5 YEARS

P.V = [{ A (1 + g) / (r – g) }]

P.V = ₹ 1,21,551 (1 + 0.08) / (0.12 – 0.08)

P.V = ₹ 1,31,275 / 0.04

P.V = ₹ 32,81,875

13.0 HOW TO USE COMPOUND VALUE AND PRESENT VALUE TABLES

Generally following four types of readymade Tables are available at the end of the book:

Type of Table	*Purpose*
CVF Table – Compound Value of Sum of ₹ 1	To find out Compound Value of a sum invested today, at the end of nth year
CVAF Table – Compound Value of Annuity ₹ 1	To find out Compound Value of an Annuity of (i.e., a series of an equal sum invested at the end of each year), for n years
PVF Table – Present Value of ₹ 1	To find out Present Value of a Future Sum to be received at the end of nth year
PVAF Table -Present Value of Annuity of ₹ 1	To Find out Present Value of an Annuity (i.e., a series of an equal Future Sum to be received at the end of each year) for n years

Notes:

(i) First Row Table Headings represent various Rates of Interest like 1%, 2% .... & so on

(ii) First Column Table Headings represent various Years 1 like 1, 2, 3, ... & so on.

(iii) To find out Table Value look under respective Rate of Interest Column and across the respective Year Row.

EXAMPLE TO ILLUSTRATE HOW TO USE CVF TABLE:

To find out the Compound Value of ₹ 1(invested now) at the end of 5th year at 10% Rate of Interest, look under 10% Rate of Interest Column and across the 5th Year Row. The Compound Value is ₹ 1.611.

TABLE CVF: COMPOUND VALUE OF ₹ 1 AT THE END OF NTH YEAR (₹ 1 INVESTED IN THE BEGINNING)

Rate of Interest	*1%*	*2%*	*3%*	*4%*	*5%*	*6%*	*7%*	*8%*	*9%*	*10%*
Year 1	1.010	1.020	1.030	1.040	1.050	1.060	1.070	1.080	1.090	1.110
2	1.020	1.040	1.061	1.082	1.103	1.124	1.145	1.166	1.188	1.210
3	1.030	1.061	1.093	1.125	1.158	1.191	1.225	1.260	1.295	1.331
4	1.041	1.082	1.126	1.170	1.216	1.262	1.311	1.360	1.412	1.464
5	1.051	1.104	1.159	1.217	1.276	1.338	1.403	1.469	1.539	1.611
6	1.062	1.126	1.194	1.265	1.340	1.419	1.501	1.587	1.677	1.772
7	1.072	1.149	1.230	1.316	1.407	1.504	1.606	1.714	1.828	1.949
8	1.083	1.172	1.267	1.369	1.477	1.594	1.718	1.851	1.993	2.144
9	1.094	1.195	1.305	1.423	1.551	1.689	1.838	1.999	2.172	2.358
10	1.105	1.219	1.344	1.480	1.629	1.791	1.967	2.159	2.367	2.594

EXAMPLES TO ILLUSTRATE HOW TO USE CVAF TABLE

Example I: To find out the Compound Value of an Annuity of ₹ 1 (to be invested at the end of each year) for 5 years at 10% Rate of Interest, look under 10% Rate of Interest Column and across the 5th Year Row. The Compound Value is ₹ 6.105.

Example II: To find out the Compound Value of an Annuity of ₹ 1 (to be invested at the beginning of each year) for 5 years at 10% Rate of Interest, look under 10% Rate of Interest Column and across the 6th year Row and deduct 1 therefrom since no deposit is made at the end of 5th year. Hence, the Compound Value is 6.616 (i.e. 7.716 – 1).

TABLE CVAF: COMPOUND VALUE OF AN ANNUITY OF ₹ 1 INVESTED AT THE END OF EACH YEAR

Rate of Interest	*1%*	*2%*	*3%*	*4%*	*5%*	*6%*	*7%*	*8%*	*9%*	*10%*
Year 1	1.000	1.000	1.000	1.000	1.000	1.000	1.000	1.000	1.000	1.000
2	2.010	2.020	2.030	2.040	2.050	2.060	2.070	2.080	2.090	2.100
3	3.030	3.060	3.091	3.122	3.153	3.184	3.215	3.246	3.278	3.310
4	4.060	4.122	4.184	4.246	4.310	4.375	4.440	4.506	4.573	4.641
5	5.101	5.204	5.309	5.416	5.526	5.637	5.751	5.867	5.985	6.105

6	6.152	6.308	6.468	6.633	6.802	6.975	7.153	7.336	7.523	7.716
7	7.214	7.434	7.662	7.898	8.142	8.394	8.654	8.923	9.200	9.487
8	8.286	8.583	8.892	9.214	9.549	9.897	10.260	10.637	11.028	11.436
9	9.369	9.755	10.159	10.583	11.027	11.491	11.978	12.488	13.021	13.579
10	10.462	10.950	11.464	12.006	12.578	13.181	13.816	14.487	15.193	15.937

EXAMPLE TO ILLUSTRATE HOW TO USE PVF TABLE:

To find out the Present Value of ₹ 1 to be received at the end of 5th year at 10% Rate of Interest, look under 10% Rate of Interest Column and across the 5th Year Row. The Present Value is ₹ 0.621.

TABLE PVF: PRESENT VALUE OF ₹ 1 RECEIVABLE AT THE END OF NTH YEAR

Rate of Interest	*1%*	*2%*	*3%*	*4%*	*5%*	*6%*	*7%*	*8%*	*9%*	*10%*
Year 1	0.990	0.980	0.971	0.962	0.952	0.943	0.935	0.926	0.917	0.909
2	0.980	0.961	0.943	0.925	0.907	0.890	0.873	0.857	0.842	0.826
3	0.971	0.942	0.915	0.889	0.864	0.840	0.816	0.794	0.772	0.751
4	0.961	0.924	0.888	0.855	0.823	0.792	0.763	0.735	0.708	0.683
5	0.951	0.906	0.863	0.822	0.784	0.747	0.713	0.681	0.650	0.621
6	0.942	0.888	0.837	0.790	0.746	0.705	0.666	0.630	0.596	0.564
7	0.933	0.871	0.813	0.760	0.711	0.665	0.623	0.583	0.547	0.513
8	0.923	0.853	0.789	0.731	0.677	0.627	0.582	0.540	0.502	0.467
9	0.914	0.837	0.766	0.703	0.645	0.592	0.544	0.500	0.460	0.424
10	0.905	0.820	0.744	0.676	0.614	0.558	0.508	0.463	0.422	0.386

EXAMPLE TO ILLUSTRATE HOW TO USE PVAF TABLE:

To Find out the Present Value of Annuity of ₹ 1 (to be received at the end of each year) for 5 years at 10% Rate of Interest, look under 10% Rate of Interest Column and across the 5th Year Row. The Present Value is ₹ 3.791

TABLE PVAF: PRESENT VALUE OF AN ANNUITY OF ₹ 1 RECEIVABLE AT THE END OF EACH YEAR

Rate of Interest	*1%*	*2%*	*3%*	*4%*	*5%*	*6%*	*7%*	*8%*	*9%*	*10%*
Year 1	0.990	0.980	0.971	0.962	0.952	0.943	0.935	0.926	0.917	0.909
2	1.970	1.942	1.913	1.886	1.859	1.833	1.808	1.783	1.759	1.736
3	2.941	2.884	2.829	2.775	2.723	2.673	2.624	2.577	2.531	2.487
4	3.902	3.808	3.717	3.630	3.546	3.465	3.387	3.312	3.240	3.170
5	4.853	4.713	4.580	4.452	4.329	4.212	4.100	3.993	3.890	3.791
6	5.795	5.601	5.417	5.242	5.076	4.917	4.767	4.623	4.486	4.355
7	6.728	6.472	6.230	6.002	5.786	5.582	5.389	5.206	5.033	4.868
8	7.652	7.325	7.020	6.733	6.463	6.210	5.971	5.747	5.535	5.335
9	8.566	8.162	7.786	7.435	7.108	6.802	6.515	6.247	5.995	5.759
10	9.471	8.983	8.530	8.111	7.722	7.360	7.024	6.710	6.418	6.145

14.0 HOW TO FIND OUT COMPOUND VALUE FACTORS BY USING CALCULATOR

Step 1: Press '1'.

Step 2: Press '.' (i.e., Decimal)

Step 3: Press '0' and then digit denoting Rate of Interest (In case Rate of Interest is a single digit number) or

Press two digits (one by one) denoting Rate of Interest (In case Rate of Interest is a double digit number)

Step 4: Press 'X' (i.e., Sign of Multiplication)

Step 5: Press '1'

Step 6: Press '=' (i.e., Sign of Equal to) to get Compound Value Factor of ₹ 1 at the end of year 1 at given Rate of Interest

Step 7: Press '=' (i.e., Sign of Equal to) again to get compound value factor of ₹ 1 at the end of year 2 at given Rate of Interest and so on.

15.0 HOW TO FIND OUT PRESENT VALUE FACTORS BY USING CALCULATOR

Step 1: Press '1'.

Step 2: Press '÷' (i.e., Sign of Division)

Step 3: Press '1'

Step 4: Press '·' (i.e., Decimal)

Step 5: Press '0' and then digit denoting Rate of Interest (in case Rate of Interest is a single digit number) or

Press two digits (one by one) denoting Rate of Interest (In case Rate of Interest is a double digit number)

Step 6: Press '=' (i.e., Sign of Equal to) to get Present Value Factor of ₹ 1 at the end of year 1 at given rate of interest

Step 7: Press '=' (i.e., Sign of Equal to) again to get Present Value Factor of ₹ 1 at the end of year 2 at given rate of interest and so on.

SOLVED PROBLEMS

PROBLEM 1

X Ltd. offers a Fixed Deposit Scheme whereby ₹ 10,000 matures to ₹ 12,544 after 2 years on yearly compounding basis. What will be the Revised Maturity Value if the company wishes to amend the scheme by compounding interest on (i) Half yearly basis (ii) Quarterly basis (iii) Monthly Basis ?

SOLUTION

Step 1: Calculation of Compound Interest Rate

$$\text{Maturity Value} = \text{Present Value } (1 + r)^t$$

$$₹\ 12{,}544 = ₹\ 10{,}000\ (1 + r)^2$$

$$1 + r = \sqrt{\frac{12{,}544}{10{,}000}} = 1.12$$

$$r = 0.12 \textit{ or } 12\%$$

Step 2: Calculation of Revised Maturity Value

$$MV = PV\ (1 + r)^t$$

on Half yearly basis	*on Quarterly basis*	*on Monthly basis*
$MV = ₹\ 10{,}000 \times \left(1+\frac{0.12}{2}\right)^4$ $= ₹\ 10{,}000 \times 1.2625$ $= ₹\ 12{,}625$	$MV = ₹\ 10{,}000 \times \left(1+\frac{0.12}{4}\right)^8$ $= ₹\ 10{,}000 \times 1.2668$ $= ₹\ 12{,}668$	$MV = ₹\ 10{,}000 \times \frac{₹\ 6{,}34{,}800}{3.174}$ $= ₹\ 10{,}000 \times 1.2697$ $= ₹\ 12{,}697$

Note: To know how to use the Compound/Present Value Factor Tables, the following problems have been solved using these tables instead of relevant formulae.

PROBLEM 2

A person deposits ₹ 1,00,000 in Deposit Account at the beginning of 1st year. Determine his account balance at the end of 4th year if Deposit interest rate is 12% p.a.

SOLUTION

Step 1: From Compound Value Factor (CVF) Table Compound sum of ₹ 1 @ 12% p.a. for 4th year = 1.574

Step 2: Account Balance after 4 years = ₹ 1,00,000 × 1.574 = ₹ 1,57,400.

PROBLEM 3

A person deposit ₹ 1,00,000 in Deposit account at the end of every year. Determine his Account balance at the end of 4th year if interest rate is 12% p.a.

SOLUTION

Step 1: From Compound Value of Annuity (CVAF) Table, The compound value of an annuity of ₹ 1 @ 12% p.a. for 4 years = 4.779

Step 2: Account Balance = ₹ 1,00,000 × 4.779 = ₹ 4,77,900

PROBLEM 4

A person deposits ₹ 1,00,000 in Deposit account at the beginning of every year. Determine his Deposit Account balance at the end of 4th year if interest rate is 12% p.a.

SOLUTION

In this problem 1st deposit is made at the beginning of 1st year and on this deposit interest shall be earned for full 4 years. Hence, in this case compound value of an annuity of ₹ 1 @ 12% p.a. for five years shall be relevant.

Step 1: From CVAF Table, the compound value of an annuity of ₹ 1 @ 12% p.a. for 5 years = 6.353

Step 2: Deduct ₹ 1 from this factor since no deposit is made at the end of 4th year

Hence, Relevant factor in this case = 6.353 – 1 = 5.353.

Step 3: Account Balance = ₹ 1,00,000 × 5.353 = ₹ 5,35,300.

PROBLEM 5

A person deposits ₹ 1,00,000, ₹ 2,00,000, ₹ 3,00,000 and ₹ 4,00,000 in his Deposit account at the beginning of 1st year, 2nd year, 3rd year and 4th year respectively. Determine his account balance at the end of 4th year if interest rate is 12% p.a.

SOLUTION

CALCULATION OF ACCOUNT BALANCE AT THE END OF 4TH YEAR

Year *A*	*Deposits* *B*	*Year*	*Compound Value Factor @ 12% p.a.* *C*	*Product* *D = B × C*
1	1,00,000	4	1.574	1,57,400
2	2,00,000	3	1.405	2,81,000
3	3,00,000	2	1.254	3,76,200
4	4,00,000	1	1.120	4,48,000
			Total Maturity Value =	**12,62,600**

PROBLEM 6

A person deposits ₹ 1,00,000, ₹ 2,00,000, ₹ 3,00,000 and ₹ 4,00,000 in his Deposit account at the end of 1st year, 2nd year, 3rd year and 4th year respectively. Determine his account balance at the end of 4th year if interest rate is 12% p.a.

SOLUTION

CALCULATION OF ACCOUNT BALANCE AT THE END OF 4TH YEAR

Year *A*	*Deposits* *B*	*Year*	*Compound Value Factor @ 12% p.a.* *C*	*Product* *D = B × C*
1	1,00,000	3	1.405	1,40,500
2	2,00,000	2	1.254	2,50,800
3	3,00,000	1	1.120	3,36,000
4	4,00,000	0	1.000	4,00,000
			Total Maturity Value =	**11,27,300**

PROBLEM 7

A person deposits ₹ 1,00,000 in his Deposit Account at the end of every quarter @ 12% p.a. compounded quarterly. Determine his account balance at the end of 4 years.

SOLUTION

Step 1: From CVAF Table, the Compound Value of an Annuity of ₹ 1 @ 3% p.a. (i.e., 12/4) for 16 years (i.e., 4 4) = 20.157

Step 2: Account Balance = ₹ 1,00,000 × 20.157 = ₹, 20,15,700

PROBLEM 8

A person deposits ₹ 1,00,000 in his Deposit Account at the beginning of every quarter @ 12% p.a. compounded quarterly. Determine his account balance at the end of 4 years.

SOLUTION

Step 1: From CVAF Table, the Compound Value of an Annuity of ₹ 1 @ 3% p.a. (i.e., 12/4) for 17 years [i.e., (4 4) + 1] = 21.761

Step 2: Relevant CVAF = 21. 761 – 1 = 20.761

Step 3: Account Balance = ₹ 1,00,000 × 20.761 = ₹ 20,76,100

PROBLEM 9

A fixed deposit receipt carrying an interest rate of 12% p.a. has a maturity value of ₹ 1,57,400 after 4 years. Determine the amount at which fixed deposit receipt was initially purchased.

SOLUTION

Step 1: From the PVF Table, the present value of 1 rupee @ 12% p.a. for 4th year = 0.636

Step 2: Initial amount = ₹ 1,57,400 × 0.636 = ₹ 1,00,106.40

PROBLEM 10

A bank granted a loan repayable in four equal annual instalment of ₹ 1,00,000 each beginning with the end of 1st year. Calculate the amount of loan granted if effective rate of interest is 12% p.a.

SOLUTION

Step 1: From the PVAF Table, the PV of an Annuity of ₹ 1 @ 12% p.a. for 4 years = 3.037

Step 2: Amount of Loan (i.e., PV of Annuity) = ₹ 1,00,000 × 3.037 = ₹ 3,03,700

PROBLEM 11

A bank granted a loan of ₹ 5,38,000 repayable in 4 equated annual instalments beginning with the end of 1st year. Determine the amount of instalment if effective rate of interest is 18 % p.a.

SOLUTION

Step 1: From PVAF Table, the PV of an Annuity of ₹ 1 @ 18% p.a. for 4 years = 2.690

Step 2: $$\text{Amount of Loan Instalment} = \frac{\text{Amount of Loan}}{\text{PV of Annuity of ₹ 1 @ 18\% p.a. for 4 years}}$$

$$= \frac{\text{₹}5,38,000}{2.690} = \text{₹ } 2,00,000$$

PROBLEM 12

A bank granted a loan of ₹ 6,34,800 repayable in 4 equated annual instalments beginning with the date of sanction of the loan. Determine the amount of instalment if effective rate of interest is 18% p.a.

SOLUTION:

In this problem 1st instalment is payable at the time of sanction of loan and last instalment shall be payable at the beginning of 4th year which is equal to the end of 3rd year. Hence, in this case the present value of an annuity of ₹ 1 @ 18% p.a. for 3 years shall be relevant.

Step 1: From PVAF Table, the PV of an annuity of ₹ 1 @ 18% p.a. for 3 years = 2.174

Step 2: In the above determined factor ₹ 1 shall be added to include the 1st instalment payable at the time of sanction of loan.

Hence, relevant factor shall be 2.174 + 1 = 3.174

Step 3: $$\text{Amount of Loan Instalment} = \frac{\text{Amount of Loan}}{(1 + \text{PV of Annuity of ₹ 1 @ 18\% p.a. for 3 years})}$$

$$= \text{₹ } 6,34,800/3.174 = \text{₹ } 2,00,000$$

PROBLEM 13

A bank granted a loan of ₹ 12,34,800 repayable in 4 annual instalments in the ratio of 1 : 2 : 3 : 4 respectively, beginning with the end of 1st year. Determine the amount of instalment if effective rate of interest is 18 % p.a.

SOLUTION:

STEP 1: DETERMINATION OF RELEVANT PRESENT VALUE FACTOR

Year *A*	*Present Value of ₹ 1 for relevant year @18% p.a.* *B*	*Ratio* *C*	*Product* *D = B × C*
1	0.847	1	0.847
2	0.718	2	1.436
3	0.609	3	1.827
4	0.516	4	2.064
		TOTAL	**6.174**

Step 2: Equivalent amount for each unit of ratio = ₹ 12,34,800 / 6.174 = ₹ 2,00,000

STEP 3: CALCULATION OF AMOUNT OF EACH INSTALMENT

Year *A*	*Equivalent Amount* *B*	*Ratio* *C*	*Amount of Instalment for each year* *D = B × C*
1	2,00,000	1	₹ 2,00,000
2	2,00,000	2	₹ 4,00,000
3	2,00,000	3	₹ 6,00,000
4	2,00,000	4	₹ 8,00,000

3 CAPITAL BUDGETING

LEARNING OBJECTIVES

After studying this chapter, you should be able to understand:

- Meaning of Management of Fixed Capital
- Meaning of Capital Budgeting
- Why are Capital Budgeting Decisions Important?
- Types of Capital Budgeting/Investment Decisions
- Capital Budgeting Process
- Techniques of Capital Budgeting
- Accounting or Average Rate of Return (ARR)
- Cash Flow Analysis
- Pay Back Period
- Discounted Payback Period
- Net Present Value (NPV) Technique
- How to Compare Mutually Exclusive Projects which are of Unequal Lives ?
- Internal Rate of Return (IRR) or Project IRR
- Why is there Conflict in Choice of Mutually Exclusive Projects by using NPV and IRR criterion?
- Which Criteria should be used when there is conflict in choice of Mutually Exclusive Projects by using NPV and IRR criterion?
- Profitability Index/Desirability Factor (PI)
- Replacement Decision
- Capital Rationing
- Modified Internal Rate of Return [MIRR]
- Equity Net Present Value [Equity NPV]
- Equity Internal Rate of Return [Equity IRR]
- How to Rank Two Mutually Exclusive Projects which are of Unequal Investment size?
- Time Adjusted Break Even point
- Social Cost Benefit Analysis
- Relation between Risk and Return

1.0 MEANING OF MANAGEMENT OF FIXED CAPITAL

Fixed capital refers to investment in long term assets. Management of fixed capital involves allocation of firm's capital to different long term assets. These decisions are called investment decisions *or* capital budgeting decisions. These decisions affect the growth, profitability and risk of the business in the long run. These long term assets yield benefits over a long period, usually more than one year.

2.0 MEANING OF CAPITAL BUDGETING

Capital Budgeting is a process of long range planning involving investment of funds in long term activities whose benefits are expected over series of years. For example, setting up of factories, installing a machinery, creating additional capacity to manufacture a part which at present is purchased from outside.

3.0 WHY ARE CAPITAL BUDGETING DECISIONS IMPORTANT?

The management of fixed capital *or* investment *or* capital budgeting decisions are important for the following reasons:

1. **Long term growth and effects-** These decisions affect the rate and direction of long term growth of the enterprise because a wrong decision can adversely affect the survival of the firm. For example, an unprofitable expansion of assets will result in heavy operating costs to the enterprise. These decisions have long term implication for the enterprise because the effects of investment decision extend into the future.
2. **Large amount of funds involved-** These decisions involve large investment in long term assts. Therefore these decisions are planned after careful evaluation of various projects.
3. **Risk Involved-** These decisions involve risk and uncertainty associated with the future cash flow of the project. Since the actual cash flows may not match the expected cash flows, the rate of earning may fluctuate and the firm may become more risky.
4. **Irreversible Decision-** These decisions once taken are not easily reversible without incurring heavy losses. The firm will incur heavy losses if long term assets are scrapped on reversing the investment decisions.

4.0 TYPES OF CAPITAL BUDGETING/INVESTMENT DECISIONS

Capital Budgeting/Investment Decisions may be classified as follows:

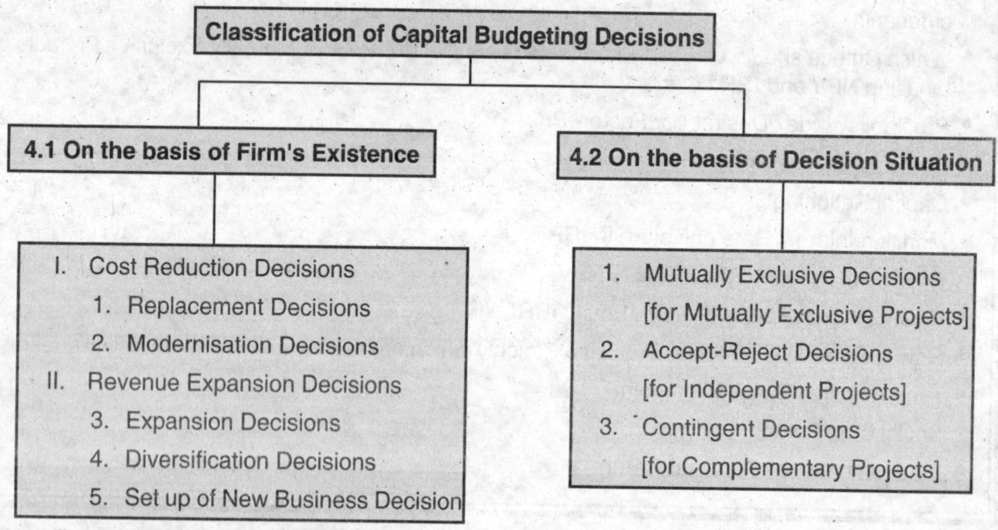

Let us discuss these decisions one by one.

1. REPLACEMENT DECISIONS

Meaning	Replacing a fixed asset due to expiry of economic life of the asset is known as Replacement Decision.

Purpose	The purpose of replacement decision is to improve operating efficiency and to reduce cost.
Example	Replacement of a Machinery on the expiry of its useful life.
Who takes	The existing firms take such decisions.

2. MODERNISATION DECISIONS

Meaning	Replacing a fixed asset due to technological obsolescence is known as Modernisation Decision.
Purpose	The purpose of modernisation decision is to improve operating efficiency and to reduce cost.
Example	Replacement of a Pentium IV computer by Intel Centrino Duo Computer
Who takes	The existing firms take such decisions.

3. EXPANSION DECISIONS

Meaning	Increasing existing production capacity is known as expansion decision.
Purpose	The purpose of expansion decision is to avoid shortage *or* delay in the delivery of products/service and to meet growth in demand of product/service and to increase revenue thereby.
Example	Increasing Oil Refining Capacity from 1000 tonnes to 2000 tonnes.
Who takes	The existing firms take such decisions.

4. DIVERSIFICATION DECISIONS

Meaning	Commencing new product/service lines is known as diversification decision.
Purpose	The purpose of diversification decision is to reduce the risk of reduction in revenues of existing product/service lines *or* to capture the new investment opportunities and to increase revenue thereby.
Example	Starting an Insurance Business by ICICI Bank.
Who takes	The existing firms take such decisions.

5. MUTUALLY EXCLUSIVE DECISIONS

Meaning	The Decisions are said to be mutually exclusive if two *or* more alternative proposals are such that the acceptance of one proposal will exclude the acceptance of the other alternative proposals. These proposals compete with each other.
Example	A firm is considering the Purchase of Machine A *or* Machine B. Firm's decision to purchase Machine A will exclude the acceptance of Machine B.

6. ACCEPT-REJECT DECISIONS/INDEPENDENT DECISIONS

Meaning	The decisions are said to be accept-reject decisions if two *or* more independent proposals are such that they do not compete with each other and any one *or* more of these proposals which meet the decision criterion adopted by the firm can be accepted subject to availability of funds.

Example	Project A, B and C are generating return of 20%, 18% and 14% respectively. If firm's minimum required rate of return is 15%. Project A and B can be accepted but project C is to be rejected.

7. CONTINGENT DECISIONS/COMPLIMENTARY DECISIONS

Meaning	The decisions are said to be Contingent decisions/Complimentary Decisions if two *or* more independent proposals are such that the acceptance of one proposal requires the acceptance of one *or* more other proposals.
Example	If a company accepts a proposal to set up a factory in remote area, it may have to invest in other infrastructure proposals e.g. building of roads, houses of employees etc.

5.0 CAPITAL BUDGETING PROCESS

The Capital Budgeting Process involves the following stages:

Stage 1: Project Planning	Project Planning involves the identification of potential investment opportunities after carrying out SWOT (i.e. Strengths, Weakness, Opportunities & Threats) Analysis. **Example:** Out of several opportunities (say A, B, C, D, E), A, C and E are expected to have potential investment opportunities
Stage 2: Project Evaluation	Project Evaluation involves (a) Determination of Cash Inflows and Cash Outflows of each proposals (b) Selection of Capital Budgeting Technique (c) Appraisal of the projects using Capital Budgeting Technique selected. **Example:** Determination of Cash Inflows & Outflows of Proposal A, C and E, Selection of Capital Budgeting Technique (say Net Present Value) and calculating NPV of Proposal A, C and E.
Stage 3: Project Selection	Project Selection involves making choice of the project so as to maximize the shareholders' wealth. **Example:** Making choice for Project E having largest NPV.
Stage 4: Project Implementation	Project Implementation involves the raising of funds, purchase of required assets and deployment of assets to carryout the project.
Stage 5: Project Control	Project Control involves monitoring the project with the help of feedback reports (say Capital Expenditure Progress Reports, Performance Reports).
Stage 6: Project Review	Project Review involves reviewing the entire project to explain its success *or* failure. It may have implication for planning and evaluation.

6.0 TECHNIQUES OF CAPITAL BUDGETING

Techniques of Capital Budgeting refer to the criteria used to evaluate the project. Some of the techniques of Capital Budgeting assuming that the proposed investment project does not involve any risk are shown below:

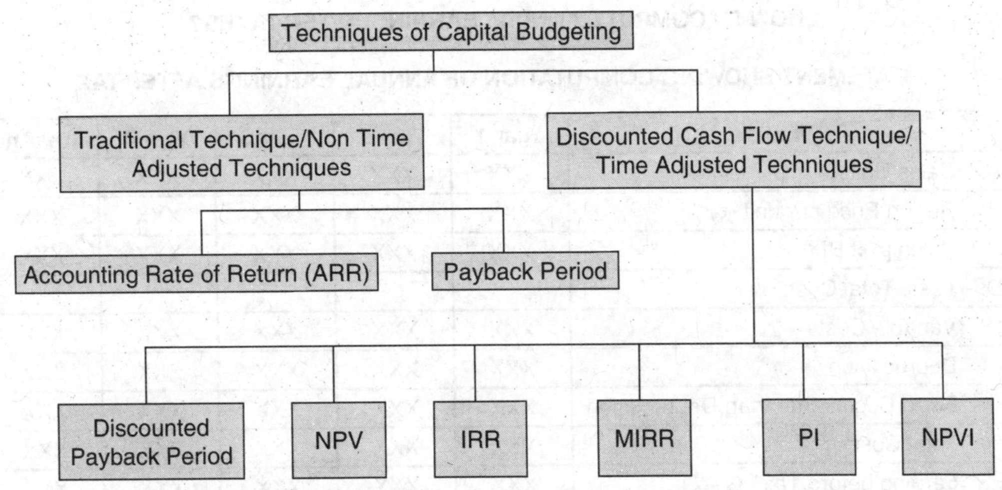

TRADITIONAL TECHNIQUES *OR* NON-TIME ADJUSTED TECHNIQUES

These techniques do not consider the Time Value of Money.

7.0 ACCOUNTING OR AVERAGE RATE OF RETURN (ARR)

WHAT IS AVERAGE RATE OF RETURN?

Accounting *or* Average Rate of Return (ARR) means the average annual yield on the project. It is found out by dividing the annual average profits after taxes by the average investments.

HOW TO COMPUTE AVERAGE RATE OF RETURN?

The calculation of Average Rate of Return involves the following practical steps:

Step 1: *Calculate Annual Average Earnings After Taxes as follows:*

$$\text{Annual Average Earnings after taxes} = \frac{\text{Total Expected Earnings after Depreciation and Taxes but before Interest on Long term Debt during Project period}}{\text{Total Period of the Project}}$$

Step 2: *Calculate Average Investment as follows:*

Average Investment(for each year) = (Opening Investment* + Closing Investment*)/2

*including Working Capital

Average Investment (during Project Period)

$$= \frac{\text{Average Investment}_1 + \text{Average Investment}_2 + \ldots\ldots \text{Average Investment}_n}{n}$$

Note: Short Cut Formula in case Straight Line Method of Depreciation is used

Average Investment = 1/2(Original Cost – Salvage Value) + Salvage Value + Working Capital

Step 3: *Calculate Accounting or Average Rate of Return (ARR) as follows:*

$$\text{Accounting or Average Rate of Return (ARR)} = \frac{\text{Annual Average Earnings after Taxes}}{\text{Average Investment}} \times 100$$

HOW TO COMPUTE ANNUAL EARNING AFTER TAXES?

STATEMENT SHOWING COMPUTATION OF ANNUAL EARNINGS AFTER TAX

Particulars	Year 1	Year 2	Year 3	Year 4	Year n
A. Sales Units	XXX	XXX	XXX	XXX	XXX
B. Selling Price per unit (₹)	XXX	XXX	XXX	XXX	XXX
C. Sales [A × B]	XXX	XXX	XXX	XXX	XXX
D. *Less:* Total Cost:					
Variable Costs	XXX	XXX	XXX	XXX	XXX
Depreciation	XXX	XXX	XXX	XXX	XXX
Fixed Costs other than Depreciation	XXX	XXX	XXX	XXX	XXX
Total Cost	XXX	XXX	XXX	XXX	XXX
E. Earning before Tax [C – D]	XXX	XXX	XXX	XXX	XXX
F. *Less:* Tax	XXX	XXX	XXX	XXX	XXX
G. Earning after Tax [E – F]	XXX	XXX	XXX	XXX	XXX

Tutorial Note: In case of Loss before Tax, Tax Savings should be calculated and deducted in order to calculate Net Loss after Tax Saving assuming that the company has taxable income from other sources against which such loss can be set off.

(a) Independent Projects	Accept the project if ARR ≥ Minimum Acceptable Rate of Return Reject the project if ARR < Minimum Acceptable Rate of Return
(b) Mutually Exclusive Projects	Projects should be ranked in the order of ARR and the project with the highestARR(but not *less* than Minimum Acceptable Rate of Return) should be selected.
(c) Complimentary Projects	If Weighted ARR of these projects is equal to *or* more than the Management's Minimum Acceptable Rate of Return, then Accept these projects otherwise Reject these projects (weights being proportion of funds used)

WHAT ARE THE MERITS AND DEMERITS OF ARR TECHNIQUE?

The merits and demerits of ARR technique are as follows:

Merits	Demerits
1. It is easy to understand and calculate.	1. It ignores the time value of money.
2. It considers the entire profits over the entire life of the projects.	2. It does not use the cash flows.
3. It uses the accounting data with which managers are familiar.	3. There is no objective way to determine the minimum acceptable rate of return.

ILLUSTRATION 1

Tulsian Ltd. provides you the following information:

1. Purchase Price of Machine	₹ 80,000
2. Installation Charges	₹ 20,000
3. Estimated Salvage Value at the end of Useful Life	₹ 40,000

4. Useful Life	4 years
5. Working Capital required	₹ 10,000
6. Annual Earnings before Depreciation and Tax	₹ 65,000
7. Tax Rate	30%

Required: Calculate the Accounting Rate of Return if the method of Depreciation is (a) Straight Line Method (SLM) (b) Written Down Value (WDV Rate 20%)

SOLUTION

(a) If Method of Depreciation is Straight Line (SLM)

Step 1: Calculation of Annual Average Earnings after tax

Particulars	Year 1	Year 2	Year 3	Year 4
A. Annual Earnings before Depreciation	65,000	65,000	65,000	65,000
B. *Less:* Depreciation*	(15,000)	(15,000)	(15,000)	(15,000)
C. Annual Earnings before tax	50,000	50,000	50,000	50,000
D. *Less:* Tax @ 30%	(15,000)	(15,000)	(15,000)	(15,000)
E. Annual Earnings after tax	35,000	35,000	35,000	35,000

* Depreciation = (₹ 80,000 + ₹ 20,000 – ₹ 40,000)/4 = ₹ 15,000

Annual Average Earnings after tax = (₹ 35,000 + ₹ 35,000 + ₹ 35,000 + ₹ 35,000)/4 = ₹ 35,000

Step 2: Calculation of Average Investment

Average Investment = 1/2 (Original Cost – Salvage Value) + Salvage Value + Working Capital

= 1/2 (₹ 80,000 + ₹ 20,000 – ₹ 40,000) + ₹ 40,000 + ₹ 10,000 = ₹ 80,000

Step 3: Accounting Rate of Return = $\frac{\text{Annual Average Earnings after tax}}{\text{Average Investment}} \times 100$

= ₹ 35,000/₹ 80,000 × 100 = 43.75%

(b) If Method of Depreciation is Written Down Value (WDV)

Step 1: Calculation of Annual Depreciation

Particulars	Year 1	Year 2	Year 3	Year 4
Opening Balance	1,00,000	80,000	64,000	51,200
Less: Depreciation @ 20%	(20,000)	(16,000)	(12,800)	(10,240)
Closing Balance	80,000	64,000	51,200	40,960

Step 2: Calculation of Annual Average Earnings after tax

Particulars	Year 1	Year 2	Year 3	Year 4
A. Annual Earnings before tax	65,000	65,000	65,000	65,000
B. *Less:* Depreciation	(20,000)	(16,000)	(12,800)	(10,240)
C. Annual Earnings before tax	45,000	49,000	52,200	54,760
D. *Less:* Tax @ 30%	(13,500)	(14,700)	(15,660)	(16,428)
E. Annual Earnings after tax	31,500	34,300	36,540	38,332

Annual Average Earnings after Tax = (₹ 31,500 + ₹ 34,300 + ₹ 36,540 + ₹ 38,332) / 4

= ₹ 35,168

Step 3: Calculation of Average Investment

Average Investment = (Opening Investment + Closing Investment) / 2

Particulars	Year 1	Year 2	Year 3	Year 4
Opening Investment (including working capital)	1,10,000	90,000	74,000	61,200
Less: Depreciation as per WDV Method (Step 1)	(20,000)	(16,000)	(12,800)	(10,240)
Closing Investment (including working capital)	90,000	74,000	61,200	50,960
Average Investment = (OI + CI) / 2	1,00,000	82,000	67,600	56,080

Average Investment = (₹ 1,00,000 + ₹ 82,000 + ₹ 67,600 + ₹ 56,080) / 4

= ₹ 76,420

Step 4: Accounting Rate of Return = $\frac{\text{Annual Average Earnings after tax}}{\text{Average Investment}} \times 100$

$= \frac{₹\ 35,168}{₹\ 76,420} \times 100 = 46.02\%$

ILLUSTRATION 2

ARR Tulsian Ltd. provides you the following information:

1.	Purchse Price of each Mchine	₹ 6,00,000
2.	Working Capital	₹ 3,00,000
3.	Useful Life of each machine	5 years
4.	Estimated Salvage Value at the end of useful life	₹ 1,00,000
5.	Method of Depreciation	Straight line
6.	Tax Rate	30%
7.	Earning before depreciation & tax:	

Machine	Year 1	Year 2	Year 3	Year 4	Year 5
Machine X	3,00,000	3,00,000	3,00,000	3,00,000	3,00,000
Machine Y	–	1,00,000	2,00,000	3,00,000	12,00,000
Machine Z	5,00,000	4,00,000	3,00,000	2,00,000	–

Required: Suggest which of the above machines should be purchased on the basis of Accounting Rate of Return Method.

SOLUTION

Machine X

STEP 1: CALCULATION OF ANNUAL AVERAGE EARNINGS AFTER TAXES

Particulars	Year 1	Year 2	Year 3	Year 4	Year 5	Total
Earning before depreciation & tax	3,00,000	3,00,000	3,00,000	3,00,000	3,00,000	
Less: Depreciation	(1,00,000)	(1,00,000)	(1,00,000)	(1,00,000)	(1,00,000)	
Earning before Tax	2,00,000	2,00,000	2,00,000	2,00,000	2,00,000	
Less: Tax @ 30 %	(60,000)	(60,000)	(60,000)	(60,000)	(60,000)	
Earning after Tax	1,40,000	1,40,000	1,40,000	1,40,000	1,40,000	7,00,000

$$\text{Annual Average Earnings after Taxes} = \frac{\text{Total Expected Earnings after Depreciation \& Taxes}}{\text{Total Period of the Project}}$$

= ₹ 7,00,000 / 5 = ₹ 1,40,000

Step 2: Average Investment = 1/2 (Original Cost – Salvage Value) + Salvage Value + Net Working Capital

= 1/2 (6,00,000 – 1,00,000) + 1,00,000 + 3,00,000 = ₹ 6,50,000

Step 3: Average Rate of Return (ARR) = $\frac{\text{Annual Average Earnings After Taxes}}{\text{Average Investment}} \times 100$

= (1,40,000 / 6,50,000) × 100 = 21.54%

Machine Y

STEP 1: CALCULATION OF ANNUAL AVERAGE EARNINGS AFTER TAXES

Particulars	Year 1	Year 2	Year 3	Year 4	Year 5	Total
Earning before depreciation & tax	–	1,00,000	2,00,000	3,00,000	12,00,000	
Less: Depreciation	(1,00,000)	(1,00,000)	(1,00,000)	(1,00,000)	(1,00,000)	
Earning before Tax	(1,00,000)	–	1,00,000	2,00,000	11,00,000	
Less: Tax @ 30 %	30,000	–	(30,000)	(60,000)	(3,30,000)	
Earning after Tax	(70,000)	–	70,000	1,40,000	7,70,000	9,10,000

Note: *Assuming that the company has taxable income from other sources against which such loss can be set off, there will be tax saving of ₹ 30,000 on negative EBT of ₹ 1,00,000.*

$$\text{Annual Average Earnings after Taxes} = \frac{\text{Total Expected Earnings after Depreciation \& Taxes}}{\text{Total Period of the Project}}$$

= ₹ 9,10,000 / 5 = ₹ 1,82,000

Step 2: Average Investment = 1/2 (Original Cost – Salvage Value) + Salvage Value + Net Working Capital

= 1/2 (6,00,000 – 1,00,000) + 1,00,000 + 3,00,000 = ₹ 6,50,000

Step 3: Average Rate of Return (ARR) = $\frac{\text{Annual Average Earnings After Taxes}}{\text{Average Investment}} \times 100$

= (1,82,000 / 6,50,000) × 100 = 28%

Machine Z

Step 1: Calculation of Annual Average Earnings after Tax

Particulars	Year 1	Year 2	Year 3	Year 4	Year 5	Total
Earning before depreciation & tax	5,00,000	4,00,000	3,00,000	2,00,000	–	
Less: Depreciation	(1,00,000)	(1,00,000)	(1,00,000)	(1,00,000)	(1,00,000)	
Earning before Tax	4,00,000	3,00,000	2,00,000	1,00,000	(1,00,000)	
Less: Tax @ 30 %	(1,20,000)	(90,000)	(60,000)	(30,000)	30,000	
Earning after Tax	2,80,000	2,10,000	1,40,000	70,000	(70,000)	6,30,000

Note: *Assuming that the company has taxable income from other sources against which such loss can be set off, there will be tax saving of ₹ 30,000 on negative EBT of ₹ 1,00,000.*

$$\text{Annual Average Earnings after Taxes} = \frac{\text{Total Expected Earnings after Depreciation \& Taxes}}{\text{Total Period of the Project}}$$

= ₹ 6,30,000 / 5 = ₹ 1,26,000

Step 2: Average Investment = 1/2 (Original Cost – Salvage Value) + Salvage Value + Net Working Capital

= 1/2 (6,00,000 – 1,00,000) + 1,00,000 + 3,00,000 = ₹ 6,50,000

Step 3: Average Rate of Return (ARR) = $\frac{\text{Annual Average Earnings After Taxes}}{\text{Average Investment}} \times 100$

= (1,26,000 / 6,50,000) × 100 = 19.38%.

Recommendation: Machine Y should be purchased since Machine Y has the highest ARR i.e. 28%.

8.0 CASH FLOW ANALYSIS

WHY SHOULD CASH FLOWS BE PREFERRED OVER ACCOUNTING PROFIT?

In Capital Budgeting, the costs and benefits of a project should be measured in terms of Cash Flows and not Accounting Profit because the accounting profit is affected by the discretionary accounting policies of the management whereas cash flows are not so affected.

WHY SHOULD CASH FLOWS BE CONSIDERED AFTER TAX?

In Capital Budgeting cash flows should be considered after tax because the tax on earnings is considered as cash outflow and the tax saving on loss/cost is considered as Cash Inflow.

HOW DOES DEPRECIATION AFFECT THE CASH FLOWS OF A PROJECT?

Depreciation affects the cash flows of a project to the extent of tax saving on depreciation since the depreciation is a deductible expense for tax purposes under Section 32 of The Income Tax Act, 1961. There are two alternative ways of considering tax saving on depreciation as follows:

Approach I	₹	Approach II	₹
A. Earnings before Depreciation & Tax	5,00,000	A. Earnings before Depreciation & Tax	5,00,000
B. *Less:* Depreciation	1,00,000	B. *Less:* Tax @ 30%	1,50,000
C. Earnings Before Tax	4,00,000	C. Earnings After Tax	3,50,000
D. *Less:* Tax @ 30%	1,20,000	D. *Add:* Tax Saving on Depreciation	30,000
E. Earnings After Tax	2,80,000	[30% of ₹ 1,00,000)	
F. *Add:* Depreciation	1,00,000	E. Cash Flows After Tax	3,80,000
G. Cash Flow After Tax	3,80,000		

Explanation as to Approach I—First Depreciation has been deducted from the Earnings to reduce the tax liability and then Depreciaton has been added back to Earnings After Tax to calculate Cash Flow After Tax since the depreciation is a non-cash operating cost.

Explanation as to Approach II—Neither Depreciation has been deducted *nor* added back later on. Only the tax saving on depreciation has been considered as Cash Inflow.

PRACTICAL STEPS IN DEVELOPING RELEVANT INFORMATION FOR CASH FLOW ANALYSIS

The following practical steps are involved in developing relevant information for Cash Flow Analysis:

Step 1: Estimation of Capital Expenditures

The following data should be procured from vendors *or* contracts *or* by making internal estimates:

(a) Cost of new equipments;

(b) Cost of removal and disposal of old equipment *less* scrap value;

(c) Cost of preparing the site and mounting of new equipment; and

(d) Cost of ancillary services required for new equipment such as new conveyors *or* new power suppliers, etc.

The impact of possible inflation on the value of capital goods must therefore be carefully assessed and estimated in working out the estimated cash flow. It is imperative that an estimate be made regarding the increase in cost of project due to delay beyond expected time. The increase will be due to many factors like inflation and increase in overhead expenditure.

Step 2: Estimation of Additional Working Capital

Every capital project involves additional working capital to finance the increase in the level of activity. The increase in working capital requirement arises due to the need for maintaining higher sundry debtors, stock-in-trade and prepaid expenses etc. At the expiry of the useful life of the project the working capital will be released and can therefore be treated as cash inflow. The impact of inflation should also be brought into the account, while working out the cash outflows on account of working capital. In an inflationary economy, the requirements of working capital may arise progressively even though there is no increase in activity of new project. This is because the value of stock etc. may rise due to inflation.

Step 3: Estimation of Production and Sales

The next step is to estimate the cash inflows for which information regarding the following items is ***Required:***

(a) Each year's production units during the life of the project.

(b) Each year's sales units during the life of the project.

(c) Selling price.

The cash inflows trend to increase considerably after the sales are break above the break even point, which is quite possible in a large capital intensive project. In the initial year of its commercial production, the company may even have cash outflows in terms of losses.

Step 4: Estimation of Cash Expenses

The next step is to estimate the amount of cash expenses that will be incurred in running the project after it goes into commercial production. To estimate the cash expenses information regarding the following items is required:

Variable Cost	Fixed Cash Cost
(i) Variable Manufacturing Expenses	(i) Fixed Cash Manufacturing Expenses
(ii) Variable Administrative Expenses	(ii) Fixed Cash Administrative Expenses
(iii) Variable Selling and Distribution Expenses	(iii) Fixed Cash Selling and Distribution Expenses

Step 5: Estimation of Cash Inflows

The last step is to estimate the Cash Inflows as follows:

STATEMENT SHOWING THE CALCULATION OF CASH INFLOW AFTER TAX (CFAT)

A. Sales Units	xxx
B. Selling Price per unit	xxx
C. Total Sales [A × B]	xxx
D. *Less:* Variable Cost	xxx
E. Contribution [C – D]	xxx

F. *Less:* Fixed Cost	
(a) Fixed Cash Cost	xxx
(b) Depreciation	xxx
G. Earning Before Tax [E – F]	xxx
H. *Less:* Tax	xxx
I. Earning After Tax [G – H]	xxx
J. *Add:* Depreciation	xxx
K. Cash Inflow After Tax (CFAT) [I + J]	xxx
L. *Add:* Release of Working Capital	xxx
M. *Add:* Net Cash Salvage Value of Asset	xxx
N. *Add:* Tax Saving on Loss on Sale of Asset	xxx
Or	
Less: Tax on Profit on Sale of Asset	xxx
O. Total CFAT for the last year	xxx

TREATMENT OF DIVIDEND AND INTEREST

Some accountants suggest that interest on long term loan funds and dividends should be deducted from gross revenue in order to calculate cash inflows. This view does not seems to be correct in view of the fact that both dividend and interest constitutes cost of capital itself. If the cost of capital itself becomes part of cash outflows, the comparison becomes vitiated.

Hence if the discounting rate (in case the discounted cash flow technique is used) is itself based on the cost of capital, there should not be any deduction for interest on long term loan funds and dividends to equity *or* preference shareholders while working out the cash inflows.

If the discounting rate is based on Cost of Equity then there should be deduction for interest on long-term loan funds and Preference Dividend while computing Cash Inflows and Repayment of long-term loan funds and Preference Share Capital should be treated as Cash Outflows.

9.0 PAY BACK PERIOD

WHAT IS PAY BACK PERIOD?

Pay back period refers to the period within which the entire cost of the project is expected to be completely recovered by way of cash inflows. Cash inflow means earnings after tax but before depreciation.

HOW TO COMPUTE PAY BACK PERIOD?

(a) In case of Equal Annual Cash Inflows

$$\text{Pay Back Period} = \frac{\text{Initial Cash Outflows}}{\text{Annual Cash Inflow}}$$

(b) In case of Unequal Annual Cash Inflows

Payback period is calculated by computing cumulative cash inflows till the Cumulative Cash Inflows become equal to Initial Cash Outflow. Thus,

$$\text{Pay Back Period} = (\text{Year upto which Cumulative CFAT is } \textit{less} \text{ than Total Cash Outflow}) + \frac{\text{Total Cash Outflow – Cumulative CFAT of the year in which Cumulative CFAT is less than Total Cash Outflow}}{\text{CFAT in next year following the year for which Cumulative CFAT has been considered in numerator}}$$

HOW TO COMPUTE CASH INFLOWS AFTER AFTER (CFAT)?

STATEMENT SHOWING THE COMPUTATION OF CASH INFLOWS AFTER TAX [CFAT]

Particulars	Year 1	Year 2	Year 3	Year 4	Year n
A. Sales Units	xxx	xxx	xxx	xxx	xxx
B. Selling Price per unit (₹)	xxx	xxx	xxx	xxx	xxx
C. Sales [A × B]	xxx	xxx	xxx	xxx	xxx
D. *Less:* Total Cost:					
Variable Costs	xxx	xxx	xxx	xxx	xxx
Depreciation	xxx	xxx	xxx	xxx	xxx
Fixed Costs other than Depreciation	xxx	xxx	xxx	xxx	xxx
Total Cost	xxx	xxx	xxx	xxx	xxx
E. Earning before Tax [C – D]	xxx	xxx	xxx	xxx	xxx
F. *Less:* Tax	(xxx)	(xxx)	(xxx)	(xxx)	(xxx)
G. Earning after Tax [E – F]	xxx	xxx	xxx	xxx	xxx
H. *Add:* Depreciation	xxx	xxx	xxx	xxx	xxx
I. Cash Flow after Taxes (CFAT) [G + H]	xxx	xxx	xxx	xxx	xxx
J. *Add:* Net Release of Working Capital					xxx
K. *Add:* Cash Salvage Value of Asset					xxx
L. *Less:* Net Tax on Profit on Sale of Asset					(xxx)
(i.e. Cash Salvage Value – Book Value)					
or					
Add: Tax Saving on Loss on Sale of Asset					xxx
(i.e. Book Value – Cash Salvage Value)					
M. Total CFAT for the last year					xxx

HOW TO COMPUTE CASH OUTFLOW?

STATEMENT SHOWING THE COMPUTATION OF CASH OUTFLOW

Particulars	Amount
1. Purchase Price of New Machinery	xxx
2. Freight, Carriage & Installation Expenses	xxx
3. Workers' Training Expenses	xxx
4. *Less:* Subsidy from Govt.	(xxx)
5. *Add:* Working Capital	xxx
6. Additional Equipment	xxx
7. Retrenchment Compensation	xxx

8. *Less:* Tax Saving on retrenchment compensation	(xxx)
Total Cash Outflow	xxx

WHAT IS ACCEPT/REJECT RULE?

(a) Independent Projects	Accept the project if Payback period < Maximum Acceptable Payback period Reject the project if Payback period > Maximum Acceptable Payback period
(b) Mutually Exclusive Projects	Projects should be ranked in the order of payback period and the project with shortest Payback period (but not exceeding Maximum Acceptable Pay Back Period) should be selected.
(c) Complimentary Projects	If combined Pay Back Period of the projects (i.e., Main Project & Complimentary Projects) is *less* than *or* equal to MAPBP then Accept these projects, otherwise Reject these projects.

WHAT ARE MERITS AND DEMERITS OF PAYBACK PERIOD?

The merit and demerits of Payback Period are as follows:

Merits	Demerits
1. It is easy to understand and calculate.	1. It ignores the time value of money.
2. It emphasises liquidity by stressing earlier cash inflows.	2. It ignores the cash flows occurring after the payback period.
3. It uses the cash flows rather than accounting data.	3. There is no objective way to determine the maximum acceptable payback period.
4. It enables the management to cope with the risk associated with the project by having a shorter payback period.	4. It is not a measure of profitability since the cash flows occurring after the payback period are ignored.
5. The reciprocal of the payback is a close approximation of the internal rate of return if the life of the project is atleast twice the payback period and the project generates equal annual cash inflows.	5. It does not necessarily maximize the wealth of the shareholders.

ILLUSTRATION 3

Calculate Payback Period for the following Projects:

Particulars	Project A	Project B	Project C
Initial Cash Outflow	₹ 4,00,000	₹ 3,50,000	₹ 2,80,000
Annual Cash Inflow After Tax	₹ 1,00,000	₹ 1,00,000	₹ 1,00,000
Life of Project	5 years	5 years	5 years

SOLUTION

$$\text{Payback Period} = \frac{\text{Initial Cash Outflow}}{\text{Annual Cash Inflow after tax}}$$

Payback Period (Project A) = ₹ 4,00,000/₹ 1,00,000 = 4 years

Payback Period (Project B) = ₹ 3,50,000/₹ 1,00,000 = 3.5 years *or* 3 years 6 months

Payback Period (Project C) = ₹ 2,80,000/₹ 1,00,000 = 2.8 years *or* 2 years 9 months & 18 days.

ILLUSTRATION 4

PB Tulsian Ltd. provides you the following information:

1.Purchase Price of Machine	₹ 1,90,000
2.Installation Expenses	₹ 10,000
3.Useful Life of Machine	5 years
4.Salvage Value at the end of Useful Life	Nil
5.Tax Rate	30%

Required: Calculate the Payback Period:

Case (a) if Earnings before depreciation and tax are ₹ 1,00,000 p.a.

Case (b) if Earnings before tax are ₹ 1,00,000 p.a.,

Case (c) if Earnings after tax are ₹ 1,00,000 p.a.

Case (d) if Annual Cash Revenues are ₹ 4,00,000 and Annual Cash Expenses are ₹ 3,00,000.

Case (e) if Operating Income before tax is ₹ 1,00,000

Case (f) if Cash Flows before tax are ₹ 1,00,000 p.a.

Case (g) if Cash Flows after tax are ₹ 1,00,000 p.a.

SOLUTION

STEP 1: CALCULATION OF CASH INFLOWS AFTER TAX (CFAT)

Particulars	Case (a)	Case (b)	Case (c)	Case (d)	Case (e)
A. Earnings before Depreciation & Tax	1,00,000	–		1,00,000	
B. *Less:* Depreciation	(40,000)	–		(40,000)	
C. Earnings before tax	60,000	1,00,000	–	60,000	1,00,000
D. *Less:* Tax @ 30%	(18,000)	(30,000)	–	(18,000)	(30,000)
E. Earnings after tax	42,000	70,000	1,00,000	42,000	70,000
F. *Add:* Depreciation	40,000	40,000	40,000	40,000	40,000
G. Cash Inflow After Tax (CFAT)	82,000	1,10,000	1,40,000	82,000	1,10,000

Step 2: Initial Cash Outflow = ₹ 1,90,000 + ₹ 10,000 = ₹ 2,00,000

Step 3: Payback Period = $\frac{\textbf{Initial Cash Outflow}}{\textbf{Annual Cash Inflow after tax}}$

Case (a) Payback Period = ₹2,00,000/₹ 82,000 = 2.439 years = 2 Years, 5 Months and 8 Days.

Case (b) Payback Period = ₹2,00,000/₹ 1,10,000 = 1.818 years = 1 Year, 9 Months and 24 Days.

Case (c) Payback Period = ₹2,00,000/₹ 1,40,000 = 1.429 years = 1 Year, 5 Months and 4 Days.

Case (d) Payback Period = ₹2,00,000/₹ 82,000 = 2.439 years = 2 Years, 5 Months and 8 Days.

Case (e) Payback Period = ₹2,00,000/₹ 1,10,000 = 1.818 years = 1 Year, 9 Months and 24 Days.

Case (f) Payback Period = ₹2,00,000/₹ 1,40,000 = 2.439 years = 2 Years, 5 Months and 8 Days.

Note: CFAT = (CFBT – T) + Tax Saving on Dep.

= (1,00,000 – 30,000) + 30% of 40,000 = ₹ 82,000.

Case (g) Payback Period = ₹2,00,000/₹ 1,00,000 = 2 years.

ILLUSTRATION 5

Tulsian Ltd. provides you the following information:

1. Purchase Price of each Machine	₹ 6,00,000
2. Working Capital	₹ 3,00,000
3. Useful Life of each machine	5 years
4. Estimated Salvage Value at the end of useful life	₹ 1,00,000
5. Cash Salvage Value at the end of useful life	₹ 1,20,000
6. Method of Depreciation	Straight line
7. Tax Rate	30%
8. Earning before depreciation & tax:	

Machine	Year 1	Year 2	Year 3	Year 4	Year 5
Machine X	3,00,000	3,00,000	3,00,000	3,00,000	3,00,000
Machine Y	–	1,00,000	2,00,000	3,00,000	12,00,000
Machine Z	5,00,000	4,00,000	3,00,000	2,00,000	–

Required: Which of the above machines should be purchased on the basis of Pay Back Period.

SOLUTION

STEP 1: COMPUTATION OF CASH INFLOW AFTER TAX (CFAT) OF MACHINE X

Particulars	Year 1	Year 2	Year 3	Year 4	Year 5
Earning before depreciation & tax	3,00,000	3,00,000	3,00,000	3,00,000	3,00,000
Less: Depreciation	(1,00,000)	(1,00,000)	(1,00,000)	(1,00,000)	(1,00,000)
Earning before Tax	2,00,000	2,00,000	2,00,000	2,00,000	2,00,000
Less: Tax @ 30 %	(60,000)	(60,000)	(60,000)	(60,000)	(60,000)
Earning after Tax	1,40,000	1,40,000	1,40,000	1,40,000	1,40,000
Add: Depreciation	1,00,000	1,00,000	1,00,000	1,00,000	1,00,000
Cash Flow after Taxes(CFAT)	2,40,000	2,40,000	2,40,000	2,40,000	2,40,000
Add: Release of Working Capital					3,00,000
Add: Actual Salvage Value of Asset					1,20,000
Less: Tax on Profit on Sale [30% of ₹ 20,000 (i.e. ₹ 1,20,000 – ₹ 1,00,000)]					(6,000)
Total CFAT for the last year					6,54,000
Cumulative CFAT	2,40,000	4,80,000	7,20,000	9,60,000	16,14,000

Step 2: Total Cash Outflow = Original Cost of the machine + Additional Working Capital

= ₹ 6,00,000 + ₹ 3,00,000 = ₹ 9,00,000

Step 3: Pay Back Period $= 3 \text{ Years} + \dfrac{\text{Total Cash Outflow} - \text{Cumulative Cash Inflow in 3rd year}}{\text{Cash Inflow in 4th year}}$

$= 3 \text{ years} + \dfrac{(₹\ 9,00,000 - ₹\ 7,20,000)}{₹\ 2,40,000} = 3.75 \text{ years}$

STEP 1: COMPUTATION OF CASH INFLOW AFTER TAX (CFAT) OF MACHINE Y

Particulars	Year 1	Year 2	Year 3	Year 4	Year 5
Earning before depreciation & tax	–	1,00,000	2,00,000	3,00,000	12,00,000
Less: Depreciation	(1,00,000)	(1,00,000)	(1,00,000)	(1,00,000)	(1,00,000)
Earning before Tax	(1,00,000)	–	1,00,000	2,00,000	11,00,000
Less: Tax @ 30 %	30,000	–	(30,000)	(60,000)	(3,30,000)
Earning after Tax	(70,000)	–	70,000	1,40,000	7,70,000
Add: Depreciation	1,00,000	1,00,000	1,00,000	1,00,000	1,00,000
Cash Flow after Taxes(CFAT)	30,000	1,00,000	1,70,000	2,40,000	8,70,000
Add: Release of Working Capital					3,00,000
Add: Cash Salvage Value of Asset.					1,20,000
Less: Tax on Profit on Sale [30% *or* ₹ 20,000 (i.e. ₹ 1, 20,000 – ₹ 1,00,000)]					(6,000)
Total CFAT for the last year					12,84,000
Cumulative Cash Inflow	30,000	1,30,000	3,00,000	5,40,000	18,24,000

Note: *Assuming that the company has taxable income from other sources against which such loss can be set off, there will be tax saving of ₹ 30,000 on negative EBT of ₹ 1,00,000.*

Step 2: Total Cash Outflow = Original Cost of the machine + Additional Working Capital

= ₹ 6,00,000 + ₹ 3,00,000 = ₹ 9,00,000

Step 3: Pay Back Period $= 4 \text{ Years} + \frac{\text{Total Cash Outflow – Cumulative Cash Inflow in 4th year}}{\text{Cash Inflow in 5th year}}$

$$= 4 \text{ years} + \frac{(₹\ 9{,}00{,}000 - ₹\ 5{,}40{,}000)}{₹\ 8{,}70{,}000} = 4.41 \text{ years}$$

Step 1: Computation of Cash Inflow After Tax (CFAT) of Machine Z

Particulars	Year 1	Year 2	Year 3	Year 4	Year 5
Earning before depreciation & tax	5,00,000	4,00,000	3,00,000	2,00,000	–
Less: Depreciation	(1,00,000)	(1,00,000)	(1,00,000)	(1,00,000)	(1,00,000)
Earning before Tax	4,00,000	3,00,000	2,00,000	1,00,000	(1,00,000)
Less: Tax @ 30 %	(1,20,000)	(90,000)	(60,000)	(30,000)	30,000
Earning after Tax	2,80,000	2,10,000	1,40,000	70,000	(70,000)
Add: Depreciation	1,00,000	1,00,000	1,00,000	1,00,000	1,00,000
Cash Flow after Taxes(CFAT)	3,80,000	3,10,000	2,40,000	1,70,000	30,000
Add: Release of Working Capital					3,00,000
Add: Cash Salvage Value of Asset.					1,20,000
Less: Tax on Ordinary Profit [30% of ₹ 20,000 (i.e. ₹ 1,20,000 – ₹ 1,00,000)]					(6,000)
Total CFAT for the last year					4,44,000
Cumulative Cash Inflow	3,80,000	6,90,000	9,30,000	11,00,000	15,44,000

Note: *Assuming that the company has taxable income from other sources against which such loss can be set off, there will be tax saving of ₹ 30,000 on negative EBT of ₹ 1,00,000.*

Step 2: Total Cash Outflow = Original Cost of the machine + Additional Working Capital

= ₹ 6,00,000 + ₹ 3,00,000 = ₹ 9,00,000

Step 3: Pay Back Period = 4 Years + $\frac{\text{Total Cash Outflow} - \text{Cumulative Cash Inflow in 4th year}}{\text{Cash Inflow in 5th year}}$

$= 2 \text{ years} + \frac{(₹\,9,00,000 - ₹\,6,90,000)}{₹\,2,40,000} = 2.875 \text{ years}$

Recommendation: Machine Z should be purchased since Machine Z has the shortest Pay Back Period i.e. 2.875 years.

DISCOUNTED CASH FLOW TECHNIQUES/TIME ADJUSTED TECHNIQUES

Discounted Cash Flow Techniques are preferred over Traditional Techniques since these techniques consider the Time Value of Money

10.0 DISCOUNTED PAYBACK PERIOD

WHAT IS DISCOUNTED PAYBACK PERIOD?

Discounted Payback Period refers to the period within which the entire cost of the project is expected to be completely recovered by way of discounted cash inflows. Cash inflow means earnings after tax but before depreciation. Discounted Cash inflow means present value of cash inflows using cost of capital as discount rate.

HOW TO COMPUTE DISCOUNTED PAYBACK PERIOD?

Discounted Payback period is calculated by computing cumulative discounted cash inflows till the cumulative discounted cash inflows become equal to the present value of Cash Outflows.

The calculation of Discounted Pay Back Period involves the following steps:

Step 1: *Calculate Cash Inflows after Tax (CFAT).*

Step 2: *Calculate Cash Outflows.*

Step 3: *Calculate Present Value of all Cash Inflows (CFAT)*

Step 4: *Calculate Present Value of all Cash Outflows*

Step 5: *Calculate Cumulative CFAT*

Step 6: *Calculate Discounted Pay Back Period as follows:*

$$\text{Discounted Pay Back Period} = \frac{(\text{Year up to which Cumulative PV of CFAT}}{\text{less than PV of Cash Outflow})}$$

$$+ \frac{\text{PV of Total Cash Outflow} - \text{Cumulative PV of CFAT of the year in which Cumulative PV of CFAT is less than PV of Cash Outflow}}{\text{PV of CFAT in next year following the year for which Cumulative PV of CFAT was considered in numerator}}$$

WHAT IS ACCEPT/REJECT RULE?

(a) Independent Projects	Accept the project if Discounted Payback period ≤ Maximum Acceptable Payback period Reject the project if Discounted Payback period > Maximum Acceptable Payback period
(b) Mutually Exclusive Projects	Projects should be ranked in the order of Discounted Payback Period and the project with shortest Discounted Payback Period(but not exceeding Maximum Acceptable Payback period) should be selected.

WHAT ARE THE MERITS AND DEMERITS OF DISCOUNTED PAYBACK PERIOD?

The merits and demerits of Discounted Payback Period are as follows:

Merits	Demerits
1. It is easy to understand and calculate. 2. It considers the time value of money. 3. It emphasises liquidity by stressing earlier cash inflows. 4. It uses the cash flows rather than accounting data. 5. It enables the management to cope with the risk associated with the project by having a shorter payback period. 6. The reciprocal of the payback is a close approximation of the internal rate of return if the life of the project is atleast twice the payback period and the project generates equal annual cash inflows.	1. It ignores the cash flows occurring after the payback period. 2. There is no objective way to determine the maximum acceptable payback period. 3. It is not a measure of profitability since the cash flows occurring after the payback period are ignored. 4. It does not necessarily maximise the wealth of the shareholders.

ILLUSTRATION 6

DPB Tulsian Ltd. provides you the following information:

1. Purchase Price of Machine	₹ 1,90,000
2. Installation Expenses	₹ 10,000
3. Useful Life of Machine	5 years
4. Salvage Value at the end of Useful Life	Nil
5. Tax Rate	30%
6. Cost of Capital	10%

Required: Calculate the Discounted Payback Period:

Case (a) if Cash Flows after tax are ₹ 1,00,000 p.a.

Case (b) if Cash Flows before tax are ₹ 1,00,000 p.a.

Note: Present Value Factors @ 10% are as follows:

Year	Year 1	Year 2	Year 3	Year 4	Year 5
Present Value Factor	0.909	0.826	0.751	0.683	0.621

SOLUTION

Case (a)

STEP 1: CALCULATION OF CUMULATIVE PRESENT VALUES OF CASH FLOWS AFTER TAX

Particulars	Year 1	Year 2	Year 3	Year 4	Year 5
A. Cash Flows After Tax	1,00,000	1,00,000	1,00,000	1,00,000	1,00,000
B. P.V. Factor @ 10%	0.909	0.826	0.751	0.683	0.621
C. PV of CFAT	90,900	82,600	75,100	68,300	62,100
D. Cumulative PV of CFAT	90,900	1,73,500	2,48,600	3,16,900	3,79,000

Step 2: Present value of Cash Outflow = (₹ 1,90,000 + ₹ 10,000) 1.000 = ₹ 2,00,000

Step 3: Calculation of Discounted Payback Period

$$\text{Discounted Payback Perid} = \frac{\text{2 years + PV of Total Cash Outflow} - \text{Cumulative PV of CFAT in 2nd year}}{\text{PV of CFAT in 3rd year}}$$

$$= \text{2 years} + \frac{₹\,2{,}00{,}000 - ₹\,1{,}73{,}500}{₹\,75{,}100}$$

= 2.353 years *or* 2 Years, 4 Months and 7 Days.

Case (b)

STEP 1: CALCULATION OF CUMULATIVE PRESENT VALUES OF CASH FLOW AFTER TAX

Particulars	Year 1	Year 2	Year 3	Year 4	Year 5
A. Cash Flows before tax	1,00,000	1,00,000	1,00,000	1,00,000	1,00,000
B. *Less:* Depreciation	(40,000)	(40,000)	(40,000)	(40,000)	(40,000)
C. Earnings before tax	60,000	60,000	60,000	60,000	60,000
D. *Less:* Tax @ 30%	(18,000)	(18,000)	(18,000)	(18,000)	(18,000)
E. Earnings after tax	42,000	42,000	42,000	42,000	42,000
F. *Add:* Depreciation	40,000	40,000	40,000	40,000	40,000
G. Cash Flows After Tax	82,000	82,000	82,000	82,000	82,000
H. P.V. Factor @ 10%	0.909	0.826	0.751	0.683	0.621
I. PV of CFAT	74,538	67,732	61,582	56,006	50,922
J. Cumulative PV of CFAT	74,538	1,42,270	2,03,852	2,59,858	3,10,780

Step 2: Present Value of Cash Outflow = (₹ 1,90,000 + ₹ 10,000) 1.000 = ₹ 2,00,000

Step 3: Calculation of Discounted Payback Period

$$\textbf{Discounted Payback Period} = \text{2 years} + \frac{\text{PV of Total Cash Outflow} - \text{Cumulative PV of CFAT in 2nd year}}{\text{PV of CFAT in 3rd year}}$$

$$= \text{2 years} + \frac{₹\,2{,}00{,}000 - ₹\,1{,}42{,}270}{₹\,61{,}582}$$

= 2.937 years *or* 2 Years, 11 Months and 7 Days.

ILLUSTRATION 7

Tulsian Ltd. provides you the following information:

1. Purchase Price of each Machine	₹ 6,00,000
2. Working Capital	₹ 3,00,000
3. Useful Life of each machine	5 years
4. Estimated Salvage Value at the end of useful life	₹ 1,00,000
5. Cash Salvage Value at the end of useful life	₹ 1,20,000
6. Method of Depreciation	Straight line
7. Tax Rate	30%
8. Cost of Capital	10%
9. Earning before depreciation & tax:	

Machine	Year 1	Year 2	Year 3	Year 4	Year 5
Machine X	3,00,000	3,00,000	3,00,000	3,00,000	3,00,000
Machine Y	–	1,00,000	2,00,000	3,00,000	12,00,000
Machine Z	5,00,000	4,00,000	3,00,000	2,00,000	–

Required: Which of the above machines should be purchased on the basis of Discounted Pay Back Period.

SOLUTION

STEP 1: CALCULATION OF CUMULATIVE PRESENT VALUE OF CFAT OF MACHINE X

Particulars	Year 1	Year 2	Year 3	Year 4	Year 5
Earning before depreciation & tax	3,00,000	3,00,000	3,00,000	3,00,000	3,00,000
Less: Depreciation	(1,00,000)	(1,00,000)	(1,00,000)	(1,00,000)	(1,00,000)
Earning before Tax	2,00,000	2,00,000	2,00,000	2,00,000	2,00,000
Less: Tax @ 30 %	(60,000)	(60,000)	(60,000)	(60,000)	(60,000)
Earning after Tax	1,40,000	1,40,000	1,40,000	1,40,000	1,40,000
Add: Depreciation	1,00,000	1,00,000	1,00,000	1,00,000	1,00,000
Cash Flow after Taxes(CFAT)	2,40,000	2,40,000	2,40,000	2,40,000	2,40,000
Add: Release of Working Capital					3,00,000
Add: Actual Salvage Value of Asset.					1,20,000
Less: Tax on Profit on Sale [30% of ₹ 20,000 (i.e. ₹ 1,20,000 – ₹ 1,00,000)]					(6,000)
Total CFAT for the last year					6,54,000
PV Factor	0.909	0.826	0.751	0.683	0.621
Present Value of CFAT	2,18,160	1,98,240	1,80,240	1,63,920	4,06,134
Cumulative PV of CFAT	2,18,160	4,16,400	5,96,640	7,60,560	11,66,694

Step 2: Total Cash Outflow = Original Cost of the machine + Additional Working Capital required

= ₹ 6,00,000 + ₹ 3,00,000 = ₹ 9,00,000

Step 3: Discounted Pay Back Period

$$= 4 \text{ Years} + \frac{\text{PV of Total Cash Outflow} - \text{Cumulative PV of CFAT in 4th year}}{\text{PV of CFAT (i.e. ₹ 2,40,000) in 5th year}}$$

$$= 4 \text{ years} + \frac{(₹\ 9,00,000 - ₹\ 7,60,560)}{₹\ 1,49,040} = 4.935 \text{ years}$$

STEP 1: CALCULATION OF CUMULATIVE PRESENT VALUE OF CFAT OF MACHINE Y

Particulars	Year 1	Year 2	Year 3	Year 4	Year 5
Earning before depreciation & tax	–	1,00,000	2,00,000	3,00,000	12,00,000
Less: Depreciation	(1,00,000)	(1,00,000)	(1,00,000)	(1,00,000)	(1,00,000)
Earning before Tax	(1,00,000)	–	1,00,000	2,00,000	11,00,000
Less: Tax @ 30 %	30,000	–	(30,000)	(60,000)	(3,30,000)
Earning after Tax	(70,000)	–	70,000	1,40,000	7,70,000
Add: Depreciation	1,00,000	1,00,000	1,00,000	1,00,000	1,00,000

Cash Flow after Taxes(CFAT)	30,000	1,00,000	1,70,000	2,40,000	8,70,000
Add: Release of Working Capital					3,00,000
Add: Cash Salvage Value of Asset					1,20,000
Less: Tax on Profit on Sale [30% of ₹ 20,000 (i.e. ₹ 1,20,000 – ₹ 1,00,000)]					(6,000)
Total CFAT for the last year					12,84,000
PV Factor	0.909	0.826	0.751	0.683	0.621
Present Value of CFAT	27,270	82,600	1,27,670	1,63,920	7,97,364
Cumulative PV of CFAT	27,270	1,09,870	2,37,540	4,01,460	11,98,824

Note: *Assuming that the company has taxable income from other sources against which such loss can be set off, there will be tax saving of ₹ 30,000 on negative EBT of ₹ 1,00,000.*

Step 2: Total Cash Outflow = Original Cost of the machine + Additional Working Capital

= ₹ 6,00,000 + ₹ 3,00,000 = ₹ 9,00,000

Step 3: Discounted Pay Back Period

$$= 4 \text{ Years} + \frac{\text{Total Cash Outflow} - \text{Cumulative PV of CFAT in 4th year}}{\text{PV of CFAT (i.e., ₹ 8,70,000) in 5th year}}$$

$$= 4 \text{ years} + \frac{(₹ 9,00,000 - ₹ 4,01,460)}{₹ 5,40,270} = 4.923 \text{ years}$$

STEP 1: CALCULATION OF CUMULATIVE PRESENT VALUE OF CFAT OF MACHINE Z

Particulars	Year 1	Year 2	Year 3	Year 4	Year 5
Earning before depreciation & tax	5,00,000	4,00,000	3,00,000	2,00,000	–
Less: Depreciation	(1,00,000)	(1,00,000)	(1,00,000)	(1,00,000)	(1,00,000)
Earning before Tax	4,00,000	3,00,000	2,00,000	1,00,000	(1,00,000)
Less: Tax @ 30 %	(1,20,000)	(90,000)	(60,000)	(30,000)	30,000
Earning after Tax	2,80,000	2,10,000	1,40,000	70,000	(70,000)
Add: Depreciation	1,00,000	1,00,000	1,00,000	1,00,000	1,00,000
Cash Flow after Taxes(CFAT)	3,80,000	3,10,000	2,40,000	1,70,000	30,000
Add: Release of Working Capital					3,00,000
Add: Cash Salvage Value of Asset					1,20,000
Less: Tax on Profit on Sale [30% of ₹ 20,000 (i.e. ₹ 1,20,000 – ₹ 1,00,000)]					(6,000)
Total CFAT for the last year					4,44,000
PV Factor	0.909	0.826	0.751	0.683	0.621
Present Value of CFAT	3,45,420	2,56,060	1,80,240	1,16,110	2,75,724
Cumulative PV of CFAT	3,45,420	6,01,480	7,81,720	8,97,830	11,73,554

Note: *Assuming that the company has taxable income from other sources against which such loss can be set off, there will be tax saving on negative EBT.*

Step 2: Total Cash Outflow = Original Cost of the machine + Additional Working Capital

= ₹ 6,00,000 + ₹ 3,00,000 = ₹ 9,00,000

Step 3: Discounted Pay Back Period

$$= 4 \text{ Years} + \frac{\text{Total Cash Outflow} - \text{Cumulative PV of CFAT in 4th year}}{\text{PV of CFAT (i.e. ₹ 30,000) in 5th year}}$$

$$= 4 \text{ years} + \frac{(₹\ 9{,}00{,}000 - ₹\ 8{,}97{,}830)}{₹\ 18{,}630} = 4.116 \text{ years}$$

Recommendation: Machine Z should be purchased since Machine Z has the shortest Discounted Pay Back Period i.e. 4.008 years.

11.0 NET PRESENT VALUE (NPV) TECHNIQUE

WHAT IS NPV TECHNIQUE?

(a) Net Present Value technique is one of the discounted cash flow techniques, which takes into account the time value of money.

(b) Net Present Value refers to the difference between the present value of all cash inflows and the present value of all cash outflows associated with the project.

(c) The present value is ascertained using the firm's overall cost of capital as the discount rate.

HOW TO COMPUTE NPV?

The calculation of NPV involves the following practical steps:

Step 1: *Calculate all the Cash Outflows associated with the project.*

Step 2: *Calculate all the Cash Inflows associated with the project.*

Step 3: *Calculate the Present Value of all Cash Outflows associated with the project.*

Step 4: *Calculate the Present Value of all Cash Inflows associated with the project.*

Step 5: *Calculate Net Present Value (NPV) as follows:*

NPV = PV of all Cash Inflows – PV of all Cash Outflows

$$= \left[\frac{CI_1}{(1+k)^1} + \frac{CI_2}{(1+k)^2} + \frac{+\,CI_3}{(1+k)^3} + \ldots + \frac{CI_n}{(1+k)^n}\right]$$

$$\text{Less } \frac{CO_1}{(1+k)^1} + \frac{CO_2}{(1+k)^2} + \frac{CO_3}{(1+k)^3} + \ldots + \frac{CO_n}{(1+k)^n}$$

$CI_1, CI_2, CI_3 \ldots$ = *Cash Inflows in different periods*

$CO_1, CO_2, CO_3 \ldots$ = *Cash Outflows in different periods*

k = *Firm's Cost of Capital used as discount rate*

n = *Expected Life of the project.*

WHAT IS ACCEPT/REJECT RULE?

(a) Independent Projects	Accept the project if NPV > 0, Reject the project if NPV < 0. Note: If NPV = 0, the management would be indifferent as to whether to accept/reject the project.
(b) Mutually Exclusive Projects	Projects should be ranked in the order of NPV and the project with the highest positive NPV should be selected.

HOW TO INTERPRET NPV?

1. NPV may be interpreted as an immediate increase in firm's wealth if the project is accepted.
2. NPV may also be interpreted as the amount, which the firm could raise at given Required Rate of Return (i.e., Cost of Capital).

WHAT ARE THE MERITS AND DEMERITS OF NPV TECHNIQUE?

The merit and demerits of NPV Technique are as follows:

Merits	Demerits
1. It considers the time value of money. 2. It considers entire cash flows over entire life of the project. 3. It is consistent with the objective of maximizing the wealth of owners since NPV may be interpreted as an immediate increase in firm's wealth if the project is accepted. 4. The ranking of projects depends upon the discount rate.	1. It requires the estimation of cash inflows and cash outflows, which is a difficult task. 2. It requires the computation of the cost of capital to be used as discount rate. 3. It may not provide satisfactory results in case of- (a) Projects involving different amounts of cash flows over entire life of the project are considered. 4. It is measure of profitability since entire cash outflows. (b) Projects having different lives. (c) Projects involving different amounts of cash outflows and having different lives. 5. It is an absolute measure. It ignores the difference in initial cash outflows, size of different projects, etc. while evaluating mutually exclusive projects.

WORTH NOTING POINTS TO BE KEPT IN MIND WHILE CALCULATING NPV

While calculating NPV, the following points should be kept in mind:

Item	How to Treat
1. Consultant' s Fees as to study the problem of choice of machine	Treat as sunk cost since it is bound to occur whether the machine is aquired *or* not.
2. Cost of New Machine.	Treat as Cash Outflow
3. Cost of Additional Equipment	Treat as Cash Outflow of the respective year
4. Expenses on Freight, Carriage & Installation of New Machine.	Treat as Cash Outflow
5. Expenses on Training of Workers for New Machine.	Treat as Cash Outflow
6. Working Capital Required	Treat as Cash Outflow of the respective year
7. Subsidy from Govt. / other agencies	Treat as Cash Inflow of the respective year
8. Release of Working Capital at the end of useful life	Treat as Cash Inflow at the end of useful life *(**Note:** Unless otherwise stated the same amount of working capital invested earlier is assumed to have been released at the end of useful life.)*

9. Cash Salvage Value of the Machine at the end of useful life	Treat as Cash Inflow at the end of useful life *(**Note:** Unless otherwise stated the same amount of savlage value estimated earlier is assumed to have been realised at the end.)*
10. Cost of Disposal of New Machine at the end of useful life	Treat as Cash Outflow at the end of useful life
11. Tax on Profit on disposal of Machine at the end of useful life Profit = [(Cash Salvage Value – Cost of Disposal) – Book Value]	Treat as Cash Outflow at the end of useful life
12. Tax Saving on Loss on disposal of Machine at the end of useful life Loss = [Book Value – (Cash Salvage Value – Cost of Disposal)]	Treat as Cash Inflow at the end of useful life
13. Annual Sales	Treat as Cash Inflow of the respective year *[**Note:** Unless otherwise stated the given sales are assumed to have been realised at the end of respective year]*
14. Variable Cost and Cash Fixed Cost	Treat as Cash Outflow of the respective year *[**Note:** Unless otherwise stated, the given variable and cash fixed cost are assumed to have been paid at the end of respective year]*
15. Tax Saving on Depreciation	Treat as Cash Inflow of the respective year *[**Note:** Calculate depreciation on net depreciable amount (i.e. Cost of New Machine + Installation Expenses + Expenses on Training of Workers – Subsidy) as per given method.]*
16. Tax on Earnings (i.e., Revenues – Cost)	Treat as Cash Outflow of the respective year
17. Tax Saving on Negative Earnings (i.e., where Cost is more than the Revenues)	Treat as Cash Inflow of the respective year. *[**Note:** Assuming that the Company has taxable income from other sources against which such loss can be set off, there will be tax saving on negative Earnings Before Tax (i.e., loss).]*

TUTORIAL NOTES

1. Ignore Depreciation and Tax while calculating Cash Flows in the following situations:
   (a) If the question is silent as to Tax Rate.
   (b) If the question states 'Ignore Taxes'.
   (c) If the question states that the Company is a zero tax company and enjoys Tax Holiday Period.
2. Unless otherwise specifically stated in the question:
   (a) The same amount of working Capital invested earlier is assumed to have been released at the end of useful life of the project
   (b) The same amount of salvage value estimated earlier is assumed to have been realised at the end of useful life of the project
   (c) The given sales are assumed to have been realised at the end of respective year.

(d) The given variable and cash fixed cost are assumed to have been paid at the end of respective year.

(e) Tax saving on negative Earning Before Tax (i.e., loss) should be calculated assuming that the company has taxable income from other sources against which such loss can be set off.

(f) Straight line Method of Depreciation is generally used to ease the computations.

(g) Block of Assets Method for depreciation should not be assumed.

(h) Subsidy from Govt./Other Agencies should be deducted from the Cost of Capital Asset while calculating depreciation.

3. If any amount is paid/received at the beginning of any year, then the Present Value Factor of the year preceding the year of payment/receipt should be used.

HOW TO CALCULATE PRESENT VALUE OF CASH OUTFLOW

STATEMENT SHOWING THE PRESENT VALUE OF CASH OUTFLOW

Particulars	Year	PV Factor	Amount	PV
1. Purchase Price of New Machinery	0	1	xxx	xxx
2. Freight, Carriage & Installation Expenses	0	1	xxx	xxx
3. Workers' Training Expenses	0	1	xxx	xxx
4. *Less:* Subsidy from Govt.	Year of receipt	PV factor of the respective yr.	(xxx)	(xxx)
5. *Add:* Initial Working Capital	0	1	xxx	xxx
6. *Add:* Additional Working Capital	Year of requirement	PV factor of the respective yr.	xxx	xxx
7. Additional Equipment	Year of acquisition	PV factor of the respective yr.	xxx	xxx
8. Retrenchment Compensation	0	1	xxx	xxx
9. *Less:* Tax Saving on Retrenchment Compensation	1	PV factor of yr. 1	(xxx)	(xxx)
Total PV of Cash Outflow				xxx

Note: *Freight etc. and Workers' training expenses are to be capitalized since these expenses have been incurred before the asset is put to use.*

ILLUSTRATION 8

From the following information calculate the Present Value of Cash Outflow:

1. Purchase Price New Machinery	₹ 10,00,000
2. Installation Expenses	₹ 1,50,000
3. Workers' Training Expenses incurred to put the asset to use	₹ 50,000
4. Subsidy from Govt.	60% of Purchase price
5. Working Capital	₹ 3,00,000
6. Cost of Capital	10%

SOLUTION

STATEMENT SHOWING THE PRESENT VALUE OF CASH OUTFLOW

Particulars	Year	PV Factor	Amount	PV
1. Purchase Price of New Machinery	0	1	10,00,000	10,00,000
2. Installation Expenses	0	1	1,50,000	1,50,000
3. Workers' Training Expenses	0	1	50,000	50,000
4. *Less:* Subsidy from Govt.	0	1	(6,00,000)	(6,00,000)
5. *Add:* Working Capital	0	1	3,00,000	3,00,000
Total PV of Cash Outflow				9,00,000

Note: *Installation Expenses and Workers' training expenses are to be capitalized since these expenses are incurred before the asset is put to use.*

ILLUSTRATION 9

From the following information, calculate the present value of cash outflow:

1.	Purchase Price of New Machinery	₹ 10,00,000
2.	Installation Expenses	₹ 1,50,000
3.	Workers' Training Expenses incurred to put the asset to use	₹ 50,000
4.	Subsidy Receivable from Govt. 50% of Purchase price now and 10% of Purchase price at the end of 1st year	
5.	Working Capital required ₹ 2,00,000 now and ₹ 1,00,000 at the beginning of 3rd year	
6.	Additional Equipment costing ₹ 3,00,000 will be needed at the beginning of 3rd year	
7.	Cost of Capital	10%

SOLUTION

STATEMENT SHOWING THE PRESENT VALUE OF CASH OUTFLOW

Particulars	Year	PV factor	Amount	PV
1. Purchase Price of New Machinery	0	1	10,00,000	10,00,000
2. Installation Expenses	0	1	1,50,000	1,50,000
3. Workers' Training Expenses	0	1	50,000	50,000
4. *Less:* Subsidy from Govt.	0	1	(5,00,000)	(5,00,000)
Less: Subsidy from Govt.	1	0.909	(1,00,000)	(90,900)
5. *Add:* Working Capital	0	1	2,00,000	2,00,000
Add: Working Capital	2	0.826	1,00,000	82,600
6. Additional Equipment	2	0.826	3,00,000	2,47,800
Total PV of Cash Outflow				11,39,500

Note: *Installation Expenses and Workers' training expenses are to be capitalized since these expenses are incurred before the asset is put to use.*

ILLUSTRATION 10

From the following information, calculate the present value of cash outflow:

1. Purchase Price of New Machinery	₹ 10,00,000
2. Installation Expenses	₹ 1,50,000
3. Workers' Training Expenses incurred to put the asset to use	₹ 50,000
4. Subsidy Receivable from Govt. 50% of Purchase price now and 10% of Purchase price at the end of 1st year	
5. Working Capital required ₹ 2,00,000 now and ₹ 1,00,000 at the beginning of 3rd year	
6. Additional Equipment costing ₹ 3,00,000 will be needed at the beginning of 3rd year	
7. Retrenchment Compensation payable to the workers due to installation of this machine ₹ 1,00,000 (fully deductible for tax purposes)	
8. Depreciation will be 100 % of the cost of machinery in year of purchase and the same will be allowed for tax purposes.	
9. Cost of Capital	10%
10. Tax Rate	30%

SOLUTION

STATEMENT SHOWING THE PRESENT VALUE OF CASH OUTFLOW

Particulars	Year	PV factor	Amount	PV
1. Purchase Price of New Machinery	0	1	10,00,000	10,00,000
2. Installation Expenses	0	1	1,50,000	1,50,000
3. Workers' Training Expenses	0	1	50,000	50,000
4. *Less:* Subsidy from Govt.	0	1	(5,00,000)	(5,00,000)
Less: Subsidy from Govt.	1	0.909	(1,00,000)	(90,900)
5. *Add:* Working Capital	0	1	2,00,000	2,00,000
Add: Working Capital	2	0.826	1,00,000	82,600
6. Additional Equipment	2	0.826	3,00,000	2,47,800
7. Retrenchment Compensation	0	1	1,00,000	1,00,000
8. *Less:* Tax Saving On retrenchment compensation	1	0.909	(30,000)	(27,270)
Total PV of Cash Outflow				12,12,230

Notes:

(i) Installation Expenses and Workers' training expenses are to be capitalized since these expenses are incurred before the asset is put to use.

(ii) Tax Saving on account of depreciation on Machinery (i.e., 30% of ₹ 6,00,000) and Additional Equipment (i.e. 30% of ₹ 3,00,000) shall be considered while calculating CFAT for the year end 1 and 3 respectively.

HOW TO CALCULATE THE PRESENT VALUE OF CASH INFLOWS AFTER TAX [CFAT]

STATEMENT SHOWING THE COMPUTATION OF PRESENT VALUE OF CASH INFLOWS AFTER TAX [CFAT]

Particulars	Year 1	Year 2	Year 3	Year 4	Year n
A. Sales Units	xxx	xxx	xxx	xxx	xxx
B. Selling Price per unit (₹)	xxx	xxx	xxx	xxx	xxx
C. Sales [A × B]	xxx	xxx	xxx	xxx	xxx
D. *Less:* Total Cost:					
Variable Costs	xxx	xxx	xxx	xxx	xxx
Depreciation	xxx	xxx	xxx	xxx	xxx
Fixed Costs other than Depreciation	xxx	xxx	xxx	xxx	xxx
Total Cost	(xxx)	(xxx)	(xxx)	(xxx)	(xxx)
E. Earning before Tax [C – D]	xxx	xxx	xxx	xxx	xxx
F. *Less:* Tax	(xxx)	(xxx)	(xxx)	(xxx)	(xxx)
G. Earning after Tax [E – F]	xxx	xxx	xxx	xxx	xxx
H. *Add:* Depreciation	xxx	xxx	xxx	xxx	xxx
I. Cash Flow after Taxes (CFAT) [G + H]	xxx	xxx	xxx	xxx	xxx
J. *Add:* Release of Working Capital					xxx
K. *Add:* Cash Salvage Value of Asset					xxx
L. *Less:* Tax on Profit on Sale (i.e. Cash Salvage Value – Book Value)					(xxx)
or					
Add: Tax on Loss on Sale (i.e Book Value – Cash Salvage Value)					xxx
M. Total CFAT for the last year					xxx
N. PV Factor @ Cost of Capital	xxx	xxx	xxx	xxx	xxx
O. PV of CFAT	xxx	xxx	xxx	xxx	xxx

ILLUSTRATION 11

Tulsian Ltd. provides you the following information:

1. Purchase Price of New Machinery	₹ 10,00,000
2. Installation Expenses	₹ 1,50,000
3. Workers' Training Expenses incurred to put the asset to use	₹ 50,000
4. Subsidy from Govt.	60% of Purchase price
5. Working Capital	₹ 3,00,000
6. Useful Life of the machine	5 years
7. Book Salvage Value	10 % of purchase price

8. Cash Salvage Value	₹ 1,20,000
9. Method of Depreciation	Straight line
10. Tax Rate	30%
11. **Sales Units:** 1st yr 1,00,000 units, 2nd yr 2,00,000 units, 3rd yr 3,00,000 units, 4th yr 4,00,000 units, 5th yr 5,00,000 units.	
12. Initial selling price per unit of ₹ 10 will continue for first 2 years and ₹ 9 thereafter. Variable cost is 40% of initial selling price. Annual fixed cost other than depreciation is ₹ 2,00,000 which will increase to ₹ 3,00,000 after 3rd year.	

Required: Calculate the Present Value of Cash Inflows after Taxes (CFAT).

SOLUTION

COMPUTATION OF PRESENT VALUE OF CASH INFLOWS AFTER TAXES (CFAT)

Particulars	Year 1	Year 2	Year 3	Year 4	Year 5
Sales Units	1,00,000	2,00,000	3,00,000	4,00,000	5,00,000
Selling Price per unit (₹)	10	10	9	9	9
Sales	10,00,000	20,00,000	27,00,000	36,00,000	45,00,000
Less: Total Cost:					
Variable Costs	4,00,000	8,00,000	12,00,000	16,00,000	20,00,000
Depreciation	1,00,000	1,00,000	1,00,000	1,00,000	1,00,000
Fixed Costs other than depreciation	2,00,000	2,00,000	2,00,000	3,00,000	3,00,000
Total Cost	(7,00,000)	(11,00,000)	(15,00,000)	(20,00,000)	(24,00,000)
Earning before Tax	3,00,000	9,00,000	12,00,000	16,00,000	21,00,000
Less: Tax @ 30%	(90,000)	(2,70,000)	(3,60,000)	(4,80,000)	(6,30,000)
Earning after Tax	2,10,000	6,30,000	8,40,000	11,20,000	14,70,000
Add: Depreciation	1,00,000	1,00,000	1,00,000	1,00,000	1,00,000
Cash Flow after Taxes(CFAT)	3,10,000	7,30,000	9,40,000	12,20,000	15,70,000
Add: Release of Working Capital					3,00,000
Add: Cash Salvage Value of Asset.					1,20,000
Less: Tax on Profit on Sale [30% of ₹ 20,000 (i.e. ₹ 1,20,000 – ₹ 1,00,000)]					(6,000)
Total CFAT for the last year					19,84,000
PV Factor @ 10%	0.909	0.826	0.751	0.683	0.621
PV of CFAT	2,81,790	6,02,980	7,05,940	8,33,260	12,32,064

HOW TO CALCULATE NET PRESENT VALUE

STATEMENT SHOWING THE COMPUTATION OF NET PRESENT VALUE

Particulars	Year	PV factor	Amount	PV
1. Purchase Price of New Machinery	0	1	(xxx)	(xxx)
2. Freight, Carriage & Installation Exp	0	1	(xxx)	(xxx)
3. Workers' Training Expenses	0	1	(xxx)	(xxx)

4. Subsidy from Govt.	year of receipt	PV factor of the respective yr.	xxx	xxx
5. Working Capital	0	1	(xxx)	(xxx)
6. Additional Working Capital	year preceding the year of requirement	PV factor of the respective yr.	(xxx)	(xxx)
7. Additional Equipment (a) Purchased at the end (b) Purchased at the beg.	year of purchase year preceding the year of purchase	PV factor of the respective yr. PV factor of the respective yr.	(xxx) (xxx)	(xxx) (xxx)
8. Retrenchment Compensation	0	1	(xxx)	(xxx)
9. Tax Saving on Retrenchment Compensation	1	PV factor of yr. 1	xxx	xxx
10. CFAT of Year 1	1	PV factor of yr. 1	xxx	xxx
11. CFAT of Year 2	2	PV factor of yr. 2	xxx	xxx
12. CFAT of Year 3	3	PV factor of yr. 3	xxx	xxx
13. CFAT of Year 4	4	PV factor of yr. 4	xxx	xxx
14. CFAT of Year 5	5	PV factor of yr. 4	xxx	xxx
15. NPV				xxx

ILLUSTRATION 12

Tulsian Ltd. provides you the following information:

1. Purchase Price of each Machine	₹ 6,00,000
2. Working Capital	₹ 3,00,000
3. Useful Life of each machine	5 years
4. Estimated Salvage Value at the end of useful life	₹ 1,00,000
5. Cash Salvage Value at the end of useful life	₹ 1,20,000
6. Method of Depreciation	Straight line
7. Tax Rate	30%
8. Cost of Capital	10%
9. Earning before depreciation & tax:	

Machine	Year 1	Year 2	Year 3	Year 4	Year 5
Machine X	3,00,000	3,00,000	3,00,000	3,00,000	3,00,000
Machine Y	–	1,00,000	2,00,000	3,00,000	12,00,000
Machine Z	5,00,000	4,00,000	3,00,000	2,00,000	–

Required: Which of the above machines should be purchased on the basis of Net Present Value.

Note: Present Value Factors @ 10% are as follows:

Year	Year 1	Year 2	Year 3	Year 4	Year 5
Present Value Factor	0.909	0.826	0.751	0.683	0.621

SOLUTION

STATEMENT SHOWING THE COMPUTATION OF CASH INFLOW AFTER TAX OF MACHINE X

Particulars	Year 1	Year 2	Year 3	Year 4	Year 5
Earning before depreciation & tax	3,00,000	3,00,000	3,00,000	3,00,000	3,00,000
Less: Depreciation	(1,00,000)	(1,00,000)	(1,00,000)	(1,00,000)	(1,00,000)
Earning before Tax	2,00,000	2,00,000	2,00,000	2,00,000	2,00,000
Less: Tax @ 30 %	(60,000)	(60,000)	(60,000)	(60,000)	(60,000)
Earning after Tax	1,40,000	1,40,000	1,40,000	1,40,000	1,40,000
Add: Depreciation	1,00,000	1,00,000	1,00,000	1,00,000	1,00,000
Cash Flow after Taxes(CFAT)	2,40,000	2,40,000	2,40,000	2,40,000	2,40,000
Add: Release of Working Capital					3,00,000
Add: Actual Salvage Value of Asset.					1,20,000
Less: Tax on Ordinary Profit on Sale [30% of ₹ 20,000 (i.e. ₹ 1,20,000 – ₹ 1,00,000)]					(6,000)
Total CFAT for the last year					6,54,000

STATEMENT SHOWING THE COMPUTATION OF CASH INFLOW AFTER TAX OF MACHINE Y

Particulars	Year 1	Year 2	Year 3	Year 4	Year 5
Earning before depreciation & tax	–	1,00,000	2,00,000	3,00,000	12,00,000
Less: Depreciation	(1,00,000)	(1,00,000)	(1,00,000)	(1,00,000)	(1,00,000)
Earning before Tax	(1,00,000)	–	1,00,000	2,00,000	11,00,000
Less: Tax @ 30 %	30,000	–	(30,000)	(60,000)	(3,30,000)
Earning after Tax	(70,000)	–	70,000	1,40,000	7,70,000
Add: Depreciation	1,00,000	1,00,000	1,00,000	1,00,000	1,00,000
Cash Flow after Taxes(CFAT)	30,000	1,00,000	1,70,000	2,40,000	8,70,000
Add: Release of Working Capital					3,00,000
Add: Cash Salvage Value of Asset.					1,20,000
Less: Tax on Profit on Sale [30% of ₹ 20,000 (i.e. ₹ 1,20,000 – ₹ 1,00,000)]					(6,000)
Total CFAT for the last year					12,84,000

Note: *Assuming that the company has taxable income from other sources against which such loss can be set off, there will be tax saving on negative EBT.*

STATEMENT SHOWING COMPUTATION OF CASH INFLOW AFTER TAX OF MACHINE Z

Particulars	Year 1	Year 2	Year 3	Year 4	Year 5
Earning before depreciation & tax	5,00,000	4,00,000	3,00,000	2,00,000	–
Less: Depreciation	(1,00,000)	(1,00,000)	(1,00,000)	(1,00,000)	(1,00,000)
Earning before Tax	4,00,000	3,00,000	2,00,000	1,00,000	(1,00,000)
Less: Tax @ 30 %	(1,20,000)	(90,000)	(60,000)	(30,000)	30,000

Earning after Tax	2,80,000	2,10,000	1,40,000	70,000	(70,000)
Add: Depreciation	1,00,000	1,00,000	1,00,000	1,00,000	1,00,000
Cash Flow after Taxes(CFAT)	3,80,000	3,10,000	2,40,000	1,70,000	30,000
Add: Release of Working Capital					3,00,000
Add: Cash Salvage Value of Asset.					1,20,000
Less: Tax on Profit on Sale [30% of ₹ 20,000 (i.e. ₹ 1,20,000 – ₹ 1,00,000)]					(6,000)
Total CFAT for the last year					4,44,000

Note: *Assuming that the company has taxable income from other sources against which such loss can be set off, there will be tax saving on negative EBT.*

STATEMENT SHOWING NET PRESENT VALUE

Particulars	Year	PV factor	Machine X		Machine X		Machine X	
			Amount	PV	Amount	PV	Amount	PV
Purchase Price of New Machinery	0	1	(6,00,000)	(6,00,000)	(6,00,000)	(6,00,000)	(6,00,000)	(6,00,000)
Working Capital	0	1	(3,00,000)	(3,00,000)	(3,00,000)	(3,00,000)	(3,00,000)	(3,00,000)
CFAT for 1st year	1	0.909	2,40,000	2,18,160	30,000	27,270	3,80,000	3,45,420
CFAT for 2nd year	2	0.826	2,40,000	1,98,240	1,00,000	82,600	3,10,000	2,56,060
CFAT for 3rd year	3	0.751	2,40,000	1,80,240	1,70,000	1,27,670	2,40,000	1,80,240
CFAT for 4th year	4	0.683	2,40,000	1,63,920	2,40,000	1,63,920	1,70,000	1,16,110
CFAT for 5th year	5	0.621	6,54,000	4,06,134	12,84,000	7,97,364	4,44,000	2,75,724
NPV				2,66,694		2,98,824		2,73,554

Recommendation: Machine Y should be purchased since Machine Y has the highest NPV of ₹ 2,98,824.

ILLUSTRATION 13

Tulsian Ltd. provides you the following information:

1. Purchase Price of New Machinery	₹ 10,00,000
2. Installation Expenses	₹ 1,50,000
3. Workers' Training Expenses incurred to put the asset to use	₹ 50,000
4. Subsidy from Govt.	60% of Purchase price
5. Working Capital	₹ 3,00,000
6. Useful Life of the machine	5 years
7. Book Salvage Value at end of useful life	10 % of purchase price
8. Cash Salvage Value at end of useful life	₹ 1,20,000
9. Method of Depreciation	Straight line
10. Tax Rate	30%
11. Cost of Capital	10%

Required: Advise the company whether the Machinery should be purchased *or* not on the basis of Net Present Value in the following cases:

Case (a) if Earnings before depreciation and tax are ₹ 5,00,000 p.a.

Case (b) if Earnings before depreciation and tax are 1st Year nil, 2nd year ₹ 5,00,000, 3rd year ₹ 5,00,000, 4th year ₹ 5,00,000, 5th year nil.

SOLUTION

Case (a) STATEMENT SHOWING THE CALCULATION OF CASH INFLOW AFTER TAX (CFAT)

Particulars	Year 1	Year 2	Year 3	Year 4	Year 5
Earning before depreciation & tax	5,00,000	5,00,000	5,00,000	5,00,000	5,00,000
Less: Depreciation	(1,00,000)	(1,00,000)	(1,00,000)	(1,00,000)	(1,00,000)
Earning before Tax	4,00,000	4,00,000	4,00,000	4,00,000	4,00,000
Less: Tax @ 30 %	(1,20,000)	(1,20,000)	(1,20,000)	(1,20,000)	(1,20,000)
Earning after Tax	2,80,000	2,80,000	2,80,000	2,80,000	2,80,000
Add: Depreciation	1,00,000	1,00,000	1,00,000	1,00,000	1,00,000
Cash Flow after Taxes(CFAT)	3,80,000	3,80,000	3,80,000	3,80,000	3,80,000
Add: Release of Working Capital					3,00,000
Add: Cash Salvage Value of Asset					1,20,000
Less: Tax on Profit on Sale [30% of ₹ 20,000 (i.e. ₹ 1,20,000 – ₹ 1,00,000)]					(6,000)
Total CFAT for the last year					7,94,000

STATEMENT SHOWING NET PRESENT VALUE

Particulars	Year	PV factor	Amount	PV
1. Purchase Price of New Machinery	0	1	(10,00,000)	(10,00,000)
2. Installation Expenses	0	1	(1,50,000)	(1,50,000)
3. Workers' Training Expenses	0	1	(50,000)	(50,000)
4. Subsidy from Govt.	0	1	6,00,000	6,00,000
5. Working Capital	0	1	(3,00,000)	(3,00,000)
6. CFAT for 1st year	1	0.909	3,80,000	3,45,420
7. CFAT for 2nd year	2	0.826	3,80,000	3,13,880
8. CFAT for 3rd year	3	0.751	3,80,000	2,85,380
9. CFAT for 4th year	4	0.683	3,80,000	2,59,540
10. CFAT for 5th year	5	0.621	7,94,000	4,93,074
NPV				7,97,294

Recommendation: The machine should be purchased since it has positive NPV.

Case (b) STATEMENT SHOWING CALCULATION OF CASH INFLOW AFTER TAX (CFAT)

Particulars	Year 1	Year 2	Year 3	Year 4	Year 5
Earning before depreciation & tax	–	5,00,000	5,00,000	5,00,000	–
Less: Depreciation	(1,00,000)	(1,00,000)	(1,00,000)	(1,00,000)	(1,00,000)
Earning before Tax	(1,00,000)	4,00,000	4,00,000	4,00,000	(1,00,000)

Less: Tax @ 30 %	30,000	(1,20,000)	(1,20,000)	(1,20,000)	30,000
Earning after Tax	(70,000)	2,80,000	2,80,000	2,80,000	(70,000)
Add: Depreciation	1,00,000	1,00,000	1,00,000	1,00,000	1,00,000
Cash Flow after Taxes (CFAT)	30,000	3,80,000	3,80,000	3,80,000	30,000
Add: Release of Working Capital					3,00,000
Add: Cash Salvage Value of Asset					1,20,000
Less: Tax on Profit on Sale [30% of ₹ 20,000 (i.e. ₹ 1,20,000 – ₹ 1,00,000)]					(6,000)
Total CFAT for the last year					4,44,000

Note: *Assuming that the company has taxable income from other sources against which such loss can be set off, there will be tax saving on negative EBT.*

STATEMENT SHOWING NET PRESENT VALUE

Particulars	Year	PV factor	Amount	PV
1. Purchase Price New of Machinery	0	1	(10,00,000)	(10,00,000)
2. Installation Expenses	0	1	(1,50,000)	(1,50,000)
3. Workers' Training Expenses	0	1	(50,000)	(50,000)
4. Subsidy from Govt.	0	1	6,00,000	6,00,000
5. Working Capital	0	1	(3,00,000)	(3,00,000)
6. CFAT for 1st year	1	0.909	30,000	27,270
7. CFAT for 2nd year	2	0.826	3,80,000	3,13,880
8. CFAT for 3rd year	3	0.751	3,80,000	2,85,380
9. CFAT for 4th year	4	0.683	3,80,000	2,59,540
10. CFAT for 5th year	5	0.621	4,44,000	2,75,724
NPV				2,61,794

Recommendation: The machine should be purchased since it has positive NPV.

ILLUSTRATION 14

Tulsian Ltd. provides you the following information:

1. Purchase Price of New Machinery	₹ 10,00,000
2. Installation Expenses	₹ 1,50,000
3. Workers' Training Expenses incurred to put the asset to use	₹ 50,000
4. Subsidy from Govt.	60% of Purchase price
5. Working Capital	₹ 3,00,000
6. Useful Life of the machine	5 years
7. Cash Salvage Value at end of useful life	₹ 1,20,000
8. Rate of Depreciation	20% on Written Down Value Basis
9. Tax Rate	30%
10. Cost of Capital	10%

11. Earnings before depreciation and tax are 1st Year nil, 2nd year ₹ 5,00,000, 3rd year ₹ 5,00,000, 4th year ₹ 5,00,000, 5th year nil.

Required: Advise the company whether the machinery should be purchased *or* not on the basis of the Net Present Value.

SOLUTION

STATEMENT SHOWING THE CALCULATION OF CASH INFLOW AFTER TAX (CFAT)

Particulars	Year 1	Year 2	Year 3	Year 4	Year 5
Earning before depreciation & tax	–	5,00,000	5,00,000	5,00,000	–
Less: Depreciation	(1,20,000)	(96,000)	(76,800)	(61,440)	(49,152)
Earning before Tax	(1,20,000)	4,04,000	4,23,200	4,38,560	(49,152)
Less: Tax @ 30 %	36,000	(1,21,200)	(1,26,960)	(1,31,568)	14,746
Earning after Tax	(84,000)	2,82,800	2,96,240	3,06,992	(34,406)
Add: Depreciation	1,20,000	96,000	76,800	61,440	49,152
Cash Flow after Taxes (CFAT)	36,000	3,78,800	3,73,040	3,68,432	14,746
Add: Release of Working Capital					3,00,000
Add: Cash Salvage Value of Asset.					1,20,000
Add: Tax Saving on Loss on Sale [30% of ₹ 76,608 (i.e. ₹ 1,96,608 – ₹ 1,20,000)]					22,982
Total CFAT for the last year					4,57,728

Note: *Assuming that the company has taxable income from other sources against which such loss can be set off, there will be tax saving on negative EBT.*

STATEMENT SHOWING NET PRESENT VALUE

Particulars	Year	PV factor	Amount	PV
1. Purchase Price New Machinery	0	1	(10,00,000)	(10,00,000)
2. Installation Expenses	0	1	(1,50,000)	(1,50,000)
3. Workers' Training Expenses	0	1	(50,000)	(50,000)
4. Subsidy from Govt.	0	1	6,00,000	6,00,000
5. Working Capital	0	1	(3,00,000)	(3,00,000)
6. CFAT for 1st year	1	0.909	36,000	32,724
7. CFAT for 2nd year	2	0.826	3,78,800	3,12,889
8. CFAT for 3rd year	3	0.751	3,73,040	2,80,153
9. CFAT for 4th year	4	0.683	3,68,432	2,51,639
10. CFAT for 5th year	5	0.621	4,57,728	2,84,249
NPV				2,61,654

Recommendation: The machine should be purchased since it has positive NPV.

Working Note: Calculation of Yearly Depreciation

Particulars	Year 1	Year 2	Year 3	Year 4	Year 5
Opening Balance [10 + 1.5 + 0.5 – 6]	6,00,000	4,80,000	3,84,000	3,07,200	2,45,760

Less: Depreciation @ 20 %	(1,20,000)	(96,000)	(76,800)	(61,440)	(49,152)
Closing Balance	4,80,000	3,84,000	3,07,200	2,45,760	1,96,608

ILLUSTRATION 15

Tulsian Ltd. provides you the following information:

1. Purchase Price of New Machinery	₹ 10,00,000
2. Installation Expenses	₹ 1,50,000
3. Workers' Training Expenses incurred to put the asset to use	₹ 50,000
4. Subsidy Receivable from Govt. at the end of 1st year 60% of Purchase price	
5. Working Capital	₹ 3,00,000
6. Useful Life of the machine	5 years
7. Book Salvage Value at end of useful life	10 % of purchase price
8. Cash Salvage Value at end of useful life	₹ 80,000
9. Method of Depreciation	Straight line
10. Tax Rate	30%
11. Cost of Capital	10%
12. Earnings before depreciation and tax are 1st Year nil, 2nd year ₹ 5,00,000, 3rd year ₹ 5,00,000, 4th year ₹ 5,00,000, 5th year nil.	

Required: Advise the company whether the machinery should be purchased *or* not on the basis of the Net Present Value.

SOLUTION

STATEMENT SHOWING THE CALCULATION OF CASH INFLOW AFTER TAX (CFAT)

Particulars	Year 1	Year 2	Year 3	Year 4	Year 5
Earning before depreciation & tax	–	5,00,000	5,00,000	5,00,000	–
Less: Depreciation	(1,00,000)	(1,00,000)	(1,00,000)	(1,00,000)	(1,00,000)
Earning before Tax	(1,00,000)	4,00,000	4,00,000	4,00,000	(1,00,000)
Less: Tax @ 30 %	30,000	(1,20,000)	(1,20,000)	(1,20,000)	30,000
Earning after Tax	(70,000)	2,80,000	2,80,000	2,80,000	(70,000)
Add: Depreciation	1,00,000	1,00,000	1,00,000	1,00,000	1,00,000
Cash Flow after Taxes (CFAT)	30,000	3,80,000	3,80,000	3,80,000	30,000
Add: Release of Working Capital					3,00,000
Add: Cash Salvage Value of Asset.					80,000
Add: Tax Saving on Loss on Sale [30% of ₹ 20,000 (i.e. ₹ 1,00,000 – ₹ 80,000)]					6,000
Total CFAT for the last year					4,16,000

Note: *Assuming that the company has taxable income from other sources.against which such loss can be set off, there will be tax saving on negative EBT.*

STATEMENT SHOWING NET PRESENT VALUE

Particulars	Year	PV factor	Amount	PV
1. Purchase Price New Machinery	0	1	(10,00,000)	(10,00,000)
2. Installation Expenses	0	1	(1,50,000)	(1,50,000)
3. Workers' Training Expenses	0	1	(50,000)	(50,000)
4. Subsidy from Govt.	1	0.909	6,00,000	5,45,400
5. Working Capital	0	1	(3,00,000)	(3,00,000)
6. CFAT for 1st year	1	0.909	30,000	27,270
7. CFAT for 2nd year	2	0.826	3,80,000	3,13,880
8. CFAT for 3rd year	3	0.751	3,80,000	2,85,380
9. CFAT for 4th year	4	0.683	3,80,000	2,59,540
10. CFAT for 5th year	5	0.621	4,16,000	2,58,336
NPV				1,89,806

Recommendation: The machine should be purchased since it has positive NPV.

ILLUSTRATION 16

Tulsian Ltd. provides you the following information:

1. Purchase Price of New Machinery	₹ 10,00,000
2. Installation Expenses	₹ 1,50,000
3. Workers' Training Expenses incurred to put the asset to use	₹ 50,000
4. Subsidy Receivable from Govt. 50% of Purchase price now and 10% of Purchase price at the end of 1st year	
5. Working Capital requirements: Beginning of 1st yr ₹ 2,00,000, beginning of 2nd yr ₹ 3,00,000, beginning of 3rd yr ₹ 2,50,000	
6. Useful Life of the machine	5 years
7. Book Salvage Value at end of useful life	10% of purchase price
8. Cash Salvage Value at end of useful life	₹ 80,000
9. Additional Equipment costing ₹ 3,00,000 will be needed at the beginning of 3rd year (useful life 3 years, Salvage Value nil)	
10. Method of Depreciation	Straight line
11. Tax Rate	30%
12. Cost of Capital	10%
13. Earnings before depreciation and tax are 1st Year nil, 2nd year ₹ 5,00,000, 3rd year ₹ 5,00,000, 4th year ₹ 5,00,000, 5th year nil.	

Required: Advise the company whether the machinery should be purchased *or* not on the basis of the Net Present Value.

SOLUTION

STATEMENT SHOWING THE CALCULATION OF CASH INFLOW AFTER TAX (CFAT)

Particulars	Year 1	Year 2	Year 3	Year 4	Year 5
Earning before depreciation and tax	–	5,00,000	5,00,000	5,00,000	–
Less: Depreciation	(1,00,000)	(1,00,000)	(1,00,000)	(1,00,000)	(1,00,000)
Less: Dep. on additional equipment	–	–	(1,00,000)	(1,00,000)	(1,00,000)
Earning before Tax	(1,00,000)	4,00,000	3,00,000	3,00,000	(2,00,000)
Less: Tax @ 30 %	30,000	(1,20,000)	(90,000)	(90,000)	60,000
Earning after Tax	(70,000)	2,80,000	2,10,000	2,10,000	(1,40,000)
Add: Depreciation	1,00,000	1,00,000	1,00,000	1,00,000	1,00,000
Add: Dep. on additional equipment	–	–	1,00,000	1,00,000	1,00,000
Cash Flow after Taxes (CFAT)	30,000	3,80,000	4,10,000	4,10,000	60,000
Add: Release of Working Capital					2,50,000
Add: Cash Salvage Value of Asset.					80,000
Add: Tax Saving on Loss on Sale [30% of ₹ 20,000 (i.e. ₹ 1,00,000 – ₹ 80,000)]					6000
Total CFAT for the last year					3,96,000

Note: *Assuming that the company has taxable income from other sources against which such loss can be set off, there will be tax saving on negative EBT.*

STATEMENT SHOWING NET PRESENT VALUE

Particulars	Year	PV factor	Amount	PV
Purchase Price of New Machinery	0	1	(10,00,000)	(10,00,000)
Installation Expenses	0	1	(1,50,000)	(1,50,000)
Workers' Training Expenses	0	1	(50,000)	(50,000)
Subsidy from Govt.	0	1	5,00,000	5,00,000
	1	0.909	1,00,000	90,900
Working Capital	0	1	(2,00,000)	(2,00,000)
	1	0.909	(1,00,000)	(90,900)
	2	0.826	50,000	41,300
Additional Equipment	2	0.826	(3,00,000)	(2,47,800)
CFAT for 1st year	1	0.909	30,000	27,270
CFAT for 2nd year	2	0.826	3,80,000	3,13,880
CFAT for 3rd year	3	0.751	4,10,000	3,07,910
CFAT for 4th year	4	0.683	4,10,000	2,80,030
CFAT for 5th year	5	0.621	3,96,000	2,45,916
NPV				68,506

Recommendation: The machine should be purchased since it has positive NPV.

ILLUSTRATION 17

Tulsian Ltd. provides you the following information:

1. Purchase Price of New Machinery	₹ 10,00,000
2. Installation Expenses	₹ 1,50,000
3. Workers' Training Expenses incurred to put the asset to use	₹ 50,000
4. Subsidy Receivable from Govt. 50% of Purchase price now and 10% of Purchase price at the end of 1st year	
5. Working Capital requirements: Beginning of 1st yr ₹ 2,00,000, beginning of 2nd yr ₹ 3,00,000, beginning of 3rd yr ₹ 2,50,000	
6. Useful Life of the machine	5 years
7. Book Salvage Value at end of useful life	10% of purchase price
8. Cash Salvage Value at end of useful life	₹ 80,000
9. Additional Equipment costing ₹ 3,00,000 will be needed at the beginning of 3rd year (useful life 3 years, Salvage Value nil)	
10. Retrenchment Compensation payable to the workers due to installation of this machine ₹ 1,00,000 (fully deductible for tax purposes)	
11. Depreciation will be 100 % of the cost of machinery (including additional equipment) in year of purchase and the same will be allowed for tax purposes.	
12. Tax Rate	30%
13. Cost of Capital	10%
14. Earnings before depreciation and tax are 1st Year nil, 2nd year ₹ 5,00,000, 3rd year ₹ 5,00,000, 4th year ₹ 5,00,000, 5th year nil.	

Required: Advise the company whether the machinery should be purchased *or* not on the basis of the Net Present Value.

SOLUTION

STATEMENT SHOWING THE CALCULATION OF CASH INFLOW AFTER TAX (CFAT)

Particulars	Year 1	Year 2	Year 3	Year 4	Year 5
Earning before depreciation and tax	–	5,00,000	5,00,000	5,00,000	–
Less: Depreciation	(6,00,000)	–	–	–	–
Less: Dep. on additional equipment	–	–	(3,00,000)	–	–
Earning before Tax	(6,00,000)	5,00,000	2,00,000	5,00,000	–
Less: Tax @ 30 %	1,80,000	(1,50,000)	(60,000)	(1,50,000)	–
Earning after Tax	(4,20,000)	3,50,000	1,40,000	3,50,000	–
Add: Depreciation	6,00,000	–	–	–	–
Add: Dep. on additional equipment	–	–	3,00,000	–	–
Cash Flow after Taxes (CFAT)	1,80,000	3,50,000	4,40,000	3,50,000	–
Add: Release of Working Capital					2,50,000
Add: Cash Salvage Value of Asset					80,000
Add: Tax on Profit on Sale [30% of ₹ 80,000]					(24,000)
Total CFAT for the last year					3,06,000

Notes:

(i) Depreciation = ₹ 10,00,000 + ₹ 1,50,000 + ₹ 50,000 – ₹ 6,00,000 = ₹ 6,00,000

(ii) Book Salvage Value has not been considered while calculating depreciation since the depreciation rate of 100% of the cost of machinery is given.

(iii) Assuming that the company has taxable income from other sources against which such loss can be set off, there will be tax saving on negative EBT.

STATEMENT SHOWING NET PRESENT VALUE

Particulars	Year	PV factor	Amount	PV
Purchase Price of New Machinery	0	1	(10,00,000)	(10,00,000)
Installation Expenses	0	1	(1,50,000)	(1,50,000)
Workers' Training Expenses	0	1	(50,000)	(50,000)
Subsidy from Govt.	0	1	5,00,000	5,00,000
	1	0.909	1,00,000	90,900
Working Capital	0	1	(2,00,000)	(2,00,000)
	1	0.909	(1,00,000)	(90,900)
	2	0.826	50,000	41,300
Additional Equipment	2	0.826	(3,00,000)	(2,47,800)
Retrenchment Compensation	0	1	(1,00,000)	(1,00,000)
Tax Saving on Retrenchment	1	0.909	30,000	27,270
Compensation				
CFAT for 1st year	1	0.909	1,80,000	1,63,620
CFAT for 2nd year	2	0.826	3,50,000	2,89,100
CFAT for 3rd year	3	0.751	4,40,000	3,30,440
CFAT for 4th year	4	0.683	3,50,000	2,39,050
CFAT for 5th year	5	0.621	3,06,000	1,90,026
NPV				33,006

Recommendation: The machine should be purchased since it has positive NPV.

ILLUSTRATION 18

Tulsian Ltd. provides you the following information:

1. Purchase Price of New Machinery	₹ 10,00,000
2. Installation Expenses	₹ 1,50,000
3. Workers' Training Expenses incurred to put the asset to use ₹ 50,000	
4. Subsidy from Govt.	60% of Purchase price
5. Working Capital	₹ 3,00,000
6. Useful Life of the machine	5 years
7. Book Salvage Value	10% of purchase price
8. Cash Salvage Value	₹ 1,20,000
9. Method of Depreciation	Straight line

10. Tax Rate	30%
11. Cost of Capital	10%
12. Sales Units: 1st yr 1,00,000 units, 2nd yr 2,00,000 units, 3rd yr 3,00,000 units, 4th yr 4,00,000 units, 5th yr 5,00,000 units.	
13. Initial selling price per unit is ₹ 10 and variable cost is 40% of initial selling price. Annual fixed cost other than depreciation is ₹ 2,00,000.	

Required: Advise the company whether the machinery should be purchased *or* not on the basis of the Net Present Value.

SOLUTION

STATEMENT SHOWING THE CALCULATION OF CASH INFLOW AFTER TAX (CFAT)

Particulars	Year 1	Year 2	Year 3	Year 4	Year 5
Sales Units	1,00,000	2,00,000	3,00,000	4,00,000	5,00,000
Selling Price per unit (₹)	10	10	10	10	10
Sales	10,00,000	20,00,000	30,00,000	40,00,000	50,00,000
Less: Total Cost					
Variable Costs	4,00,000	8,00,000	12,00,000	16,00,000	20,00,000
Depreciation	1,00,000	1,00,000	1,00,000	1,00,000	1,00,000
Fixed Costs other than Depreciation	2,00,000	2,00,000	2,00,000	2,00,000	2,00,000
Total Cost	(7,00,000)	(11,00,000)	(15,00,000)	(19,00,000)	(23,00,000)
Earning before Tax	3,00,000	9,00,000	15,00,000	21,00,000	27,00,000
Less: Tax @ 30%	(90,000)	(2,70,000)	(4,50,000)	(6,30,000)	(8,10,000)
Earning after Tax	2,10,000	6,30,000	10,50,000	14,70,000	18,90,000
Add: Depreciation	1,00,000	1,00,000	1,00,000	1,00,000	1,00,000
Cash Flow after Taxes(CFAT)	3,10,000	7,30,000	11,50,000	15,70,000	19,90,000
Add: Release of Working Capital					3,00,000
Add: Cash Salvage Value of Asset.					1,20,000
Less: Tax on Profit on sale [30% of ₹ 20,000 (i.e. ₹ 1,20,000 – ₹ 1,00,000)]					(6,000)
Total CFAT for the last year					24,04,000

STATEMENT SHOWING NET PRESENT VALUE

Particulars	Year	PV factor	Amount	PV
1. Purchase Price of New Machinery	0	1	(10,00,000)	(10,00,000)
2. Installation Expenses	0	1	(1,50,000)	(1,50,000)
3. Workers' Training Expenses	0	1	(50,000)	(50,000)
4. Subsidy from Govt.	0	1	6,00,000	6,00,000
5. Working Capital	0	1	(3,00,000)	(3,00,000)

6. CFAT for 1st year	1	0.909	3,10,000	2,81,790
7. CFAT for 2nd year	2	0.826	7,30,000	6,02,980
8. CFAT for 3rd year	3	0.751	11,50,000	8,63,650
9. CFAT for 4th year	4	0.683	15,70,000	10,72,310
10. CFAT for 5th year	5	0.621	24,04,000	14,92,884
NPV				34,13,614

Recommendation: The machine should be purchased since it has positive NPV.

ILLUSTRATION 19

Tulsian Ltd. provides you the following information:

1. Purchase Price of New Machinery	₹ 10,00,000
2. Installation Expenses	₹ 1,50,000
3. Workers' Training Expenses incurred to put the asset to use ₹ 50,000	
4. Subsidy from Govt.	60% of Purchase price
5. Working Capital	₹ 3,00,000
6. Useful Life of the machine	5 years
7. Book Salvage Value	10% of purchase price
8. Cash Salvage Value	₹ 1,20,000
9. Method of Depreciation	Straight line
10. Tax Rate	30%
11. Cost of Capital	10%
12. Sales Units: 1st yr 1,00,000 units, 2nd yr 2,00,000 units, 3rd yr 3,00,000 units, 4th yr 4,00,000 units, 5th yr 5,00,000 units.	
13. Initial selling price per unit of ₹ 10 will continue for first 2 years and ₹ 9 thereafter. Variable cost is 40% of initial selling price. Annual fixed cost other than depreciation is ₹ 2,00,000 which will increase to ₹ 3,00,000 after 3rd year.	

Required: Advise the company whether the machinery should be purchased *or* not on the basis of the Net Present Value.

SOLUTION

STATEMENT SHOWING THE CALCULATION OF CASH INFLOW AFTER TAX (CFAT)

Particulars	Year 1	Year 2	Year 3	Year 4	Year 5
Sales Units	1,00,000	2,00,000	3,00,000	4,00,000	5,00,000
Selling Price per unit (₹)	10	10	9	9	9
Sales	10,00,000	20,00,000	27,00,000	36,00,000	45,00,000
Less: Total Cost:					
Variable Costs	4,00,000	8,00,000	12,00,000	16,00,000	20,00,000
Depreciation	1,00,000	1,00,000	1,00,000	1,00,000	1,00,000
Fixed Costs Other than Depreciation	2,00,000	2,00,000	2,00,000	3,00,000	3,00,000

Total Cost	(7,00,000)	(11,00,000)	(15,00,000)	(20,00,000)	(24,00,000)
Earning before Tax	3,00,000	9,00,000	12,00,000	16,00,000	21,00,000
Less: Tax @ 30%	(90,000)	(2,70,000)	(3,60,000)	(4,80,000)	(6,30,000)
Earning after Tax	2,10,000	6,30,000	8,40,000	11,20,000	14,70,000
Add: Depreciation	1,00,000	1,00,000	1,00,000	1,00,000	1,00,000
Cash Flow after Taxes(CFAT)	3,10,000	7,30,000	9,40,000	12,20,000	15,70,000
Add: Release of Working Capital					3,00,000
Add: Cash Salvage Value of Asset.					1,20,000
Less: Tax on Profit on sale [30% of ₹ 20,000 (i.e. ₹ 1,20,000 – ₹ 1,00,000)]					(6,000)
Total CFAT for the last year					19,84,000

STATEMENT SHOWING NET PRESENT VALUE

Particulars	Year	PV factor	Amount	PV
1. Purchase Price New Machinery	0	1	(10,00,000)	(10,00,000)
2. Installation Expenses	0	1	(1,50,000)	(1,50,000)
3. Workers' Training Expenses	0	1	(50,000)	(50,000)
4. Subsidy from Govt.	0	1	6,00,000	6,00,000
5. Working Capital	0	1	(3,00,000)	(3,00,000)
6. CFAT for 1st year	1	0.909	3,10,000	2,81,790
7. CFAT for 2nd year	2	0.826	7,30,000	6,02,980
8. CFAT for 3rd year	3	0.751	9,40,000	7,05,940
9. CFAT for 4th year	4	0.683	12,20,000	8,33,260
10. CFAT for 5th year	5	0.621	19,84,000	12,32,064
NPV				27,56,034

Recommendation: The machine should be purchased since it has positive NPV.

ILLUSTRATION 20

Tulsian Ltd. provides you the following information:

1.	Purchase Price of New Machinery	₹ 10,00,000
2.	Installation Expenses	₹ 1,50,000
3.	Workers' Training Expenses incurred to put the asset to use	₹ 50,000
4.	Subsidy Receivable from Govt. 50% of Purchase price now and 10% of Purchase price at the end of 1st year	

5.	Working Capital requirements: Beginning of 1st year ₹ 2,00,000, beginning of 2nd year ₹ 3,00,000, beginning of 3rd year ₹ 2,50,000	
6.	Useful Life of the machine	5 years
7.	Book Salvage Value at end of useful life	10% of purchase price
8.	Cash Salvage Value at end of useful life	₹ 80,000
9.	Additional Equipment costing ₹ 3,00,000 will be needed at the beginning of 3rd year (useful life 3 years, Salvage Value nil)	
10.	Method of Depreciation	Straight line
11.	Tax Rate	30%
12.	Cost of Capital	10%
13.	Sales Units: 1st year 1,00,000 units, 2nd year 2,00,000 units, 3rd year 3,00,000 units, 4th year 4,00,000 units, 5th year 5,00,000 units.	
14.	Initial selling price per unit of ₹ 10 will continue for first 2 years and ₹ 9 thereafter. Variable cost is 40% of initial selling price. Annual fixed cost other than depreciation is ₹ 2,00,000 which will increase to ₹ 3,00,000 after 3rd year.	

Required: Advise the company whether the machinery should be purchased *or* not on the basis of the Net Present Value.

SOLUTION

STATEMENT SHOWING THE CALCULATION OF CASH INFLOW AFTER TAX (CFAT)

Particulars	Year 1	Year 2	Year 3	Year 4	Year 5
Sales Units	1,00,000	2,00,000	3,00,000	4,00,000	5,00,000
Selling Price per unit (₹)	10	10	9	9	9
Sales	10,00,000	20,00,000	27,00,000	36,00,000	45,00,000
Less: Total Cost:					
Variable Costs	4,00,000	8,00,000	12,00,000	16,00,000	20,00,000
Depreciation	1,00,000	1,00,000	1,00,000	1,00,000	1,00,000
Depreciation on additional Equip.	–	–	1,00,000	1,00,000	1,00,000
Fixed Costs Other than Depreciation	2,00,000	2,00,000	2,00,000	3,00,000	3,00,000
Total Cost	(7,00,000)	(11,00,000)	(16,00,000)	(21,00,000)	(25,00,000)
Earning before Tax	3,00,000	9,00,000	11,00,000	15,00,000	20,00,000
Less: Tax @ 30%	(90,000)	(2,70,000)	(3,30,000)	(4,50,000)	(6,00,000)
Earning after Tax	2,10,000	6,30,000	7,70,000	10,50,000	14,00,000
Add: Depreciation	1,00,000	1,00,000	1,00,000	1,00,000	1,00,000
Add: Dep. on additional Equipment	–	–	1,00,000	1,00,000	1,00,000
Cash Flow after Taxes(CFAT)	3,10,000	7,30,000	9,70,000	12,50,000	16,00,000
Add: Release of Working Capital					2,50,000
Add: Cash Salvage Value of Asset.					80,000

Add: Tax Saving on Loss on Sale [30% of ₹ 20,000 (i.e. ₹ 1,00,000 – ₹ 80,000)]					6,000
Total CFAT for the last year					19,36,000

STATEMENT SHOWING NET PRESENT VALUE

Particulars	Year	PV factor	Amount	PV
Purchase Price of New Machinery	0	1	(10,00,000)	(10,00,000)
Installation Expenses	0	1	(1,50,000)	(1,50,000)
Workers' Training Expenses	0	1	(50,000)	(50,000)
Subsidy from Govt.	0	1	5,00,000	5,00,000
	1	0.909	100,000	90,900
Working Capital	0	1	(2,00,000)	(2,00,000)
	1	0.909	(1,00,000)	(90,900)
	2	0.826	50,000	41,300
Additional Equipment	2	0.826	(3,00,000)	(2,47,800)
CFAT for 1st year	1	0.909	3,10,000	2,81,790
CFAT for 2nd year	2	0.826	7,30,000	6,02,980
CFAT for 3rd year	3	0.751	9,70,000	7,28,470
CFAT for 4th year	4	0.683	12,50,000	8,53,750
CFAT for 5th year	5	0.621	19,36,000	12,02,256
NPV				25,62,746

Recommendation: Machine should be purchased since it has positive NPV.

ILLUSTRATION 21

Tulsian Ltd. provides you the following information:

1. Purchase Price of New Machinery	₹ 10,00,000
2. Installation Expenses	₹ 1,50,000
3. Workers' Training Expenses incurred to put the asset to use ₹ 50,000	
4. Subsidy Receivable from Govt.: 50% of Purchase price now and 10% of Purchase price at the end of 1st year	
5. Working Capital Requirements: 50 % of Variable Cost for first 2 years and 40 % thereafter	
6. Useful Life of the machine	5 years
7. Book Salvage Value at end of useful life	10% of purchase price
8. Cash Salvage Value at end of useful life	₹ 80,000
9. Method of Depreciation	Straight line
10. Tax Rate	30%
11. Cost of Capital	10%
12. Additional Equipment costing ₹ 3,00,000 will be needed at the beginning of 3rd year (useful life 3 years, Salvage Value nil)	

13. Depreciation will be 100 % of the cost of additional equipment in year of purchase and the same will be allowed for tax purposes.
14. Retrenchment Compensation payable to the workers due to installation of this machine ₹ 1,00,000 (fully deductible for tax purposes)
15. Sales Units: 1st year 1,00,000 units, 2nd year 2,00,000 units, 3rd year 3,00,000 units, 4th year 4,00,000 units, 5th year 5,00,000 units.
16. Initial selling price per unit of ₹ 10 will continue for first 2 years and ₹ 9 thereafter. Variable cost is 40% of initial selling price. Annual fixed cost other than depreciation is ₹ 2,00,000 which will increase to ₹ 3,00,000 after 3rd year.

Required: Advise the company whether to purchase the Machinery *or* not on the basis of the Net Present Value.

SOLUTION

STATEMENT SHOWING THE CALCULATION OF CASH INFLOW AFTER TAX (CFAT)

Particulars	**Year 1**	**Year 2**	**Year 3**	**Year 4**	**Year 5**
Sales Units	1,00,000	2,00,000	3,00,000	4,00,000	5,00,000
Selling Price per unit (₹)	10	10	9	9	9
Sales	10,00,000	20,00,000	27,00,000	36,00,000	45,00,000
Less: Total Cost					
Variable Costs	4,00,000	8,00,000	12,00,000	16,00,000	20,00,000
Depreciation	1,00,000	1,00,000	1,00,000	1,00,000	1,00,000
Depreciation on additional Equip.	–	–	3,00,000	–	–
Fixed Costs Other than Depreciation	2,00,000	2,00,000	2,00,000	3,00,000	3,00,000
Total Cost	(7,00,000)	(11,00,000)	(18,00,000)	(20,00,000)	(24,00,000)
Earning before Tax	3,00,000	9,00,000	9,00,000	16,00,000	21,00,000
Less: Tax @ 30%	(90,000)	(2,70,000)	(2,70,000)	(4,80,000)	(6,30,000)
Earning after Tax	2,10,000	6,30,000	6,30,000	11,20,000	14,70,000
Add: Depreciation	1,00,000	1,00,000	1,00,000	1,00,000	1,00,000
Add: Dep on additional Equipment	–	–	3,00,000	–	–
Cash Flow after Tax (CFAT)	3,10,000	7,30,000	10,30,000	12,20,000	15,70,000
Add: Release of Working Capital					8,00,000
Add: Cash Salvage Value of Asset.					80,000
Add: Tax Saving on Loss on Sale [30% of ₹ 20,000 (i.e. ₹ 1,00,000 – ₹ 80,000)]					6000
Total CFAT for the last year					24,56,000

STATEMENT SHOWING NET PRESENT VALUE

Particulars	Year	PV factor	Amount	PV
Purchase Price of New Machinery	0	1	(10,00,000)	(10,00,000)
Installation Expenses	0	1	(1,50,000)	(1,50,000)
Workers' Training Expenses	0	1	(50,000)	(50,000)
Subsidy from Govt.	0	1	5,00,000	5,00,000
	1	0.909	1,00,000	90,900
Working Capital	0	1.000	(2,00,000)	(2,00,000)
	1	0.909	(2,00,000)	(1,81,800)
	2	0.826	(80,000)	(66,080)
	3	0.751	(1,60,000)	(1,20,160)
	4	0.683	(1,60,000)	(1,09,280)
Additional Equipment	2	0.826	(3,00,000)	(2,47,800)
Retrenchment Compensation	0	1	(1,00,000)	(1,00,000)
Tax Saving on retrenchment compensation	1	0.909	30,000	27,270
CFAT for 1st year	1	0.909	3,10,000	2,81,790
CFAT for 2nd year	2	0.826	7,30,000	6,02,980
CFAT for 3rd year	3	0.751	10,30,000	7,73,530
CFAT for 4th year	4	0.683	12,20,000	8,33,260
CFAT for 5th year	5	0.621	24,56,000	15,25,176
NPV				24,09,786

Recommendation: Machine should be purchased since it has positive NPV.

Note: *Working Capital Requirements are at the beginning of each year.*

ILLUSTRATION 22

Tulsian Ltd. provides you the following information:

1. Purchase Price of New Machinery ₹ 10,00,000
2. Installation Expenses ₹ 1,50,000
3. Workers' Training Expenses incurred to put the asset to use ₹ 50,000
4. Subsidy Receivable from Govt.: 50% of Purchase price now and 10% of Purchase price at the end of 1st year
5. Working Capital requirements: 40 % of Variable Cost for first 3 years, 30 % in 4th year and 20% in 5th year.
6. Useful Life of the machine 5 years
7. Book Salvage Value at end of useful life 10 % of purchase price.
8. Cash Salvage Value at end of useful life ₹ 80,000.
9. Method of Depreciation Straight line
10. Tax Rate 30%
11. Cost of Capital 10%
12. Additional Equipment costing ₹ 3,00,000 will be needed at the beginning of 3rd year (useful life 3 years, Salvage Value nil)

13. Depreciation will be 100 % of the cost of additional equipment in the year of purchase and the same will be allowed for tax purposes.
14. Retrenchment Compensation payable to the workers due to installation of this machine ₹ 1,00,000 (fully deductible for tax purposes)
15. The capacity of plant is 5,00,000 units p.a. but the capacity utilization during the life of plant is expected as under:

Year	1	2	3	4	5
Capacity Utilization	20%	40%	60%	80%	100%

16. Initial selling price per unit of ₹ 10 will continue for first 2 years and ₹ 9 thereafter. Variable cost is 40% of initial selling price. Annual fixed cost other than depreciation is ₹ 2,00,000 which will increase to ₹ 3,00,000 after 3rd year.
17. At the end of useful life of the project, the working capital is expected to be recovered only to the extent of 80%.

Required: Advise the company whether to purchase the machinery *or* not on the basis of Net Present Value.

SOLUTION

STATEMENT SHOWING THE CALCULATION OF CASH INFLOW AFTER TAX (CFAT)

Particulars	Year 1	Year 2	Year 3	Year 4	Year 5
Sales Units	1,00,000	2,00,000	3,00,000	4,00,000	5,00,000
Selling Price per unit (₹)	10	10	9	9	9
Sales	10,00,000	20,00,000	27,00,000	36,00,000	45,00,000
Less: Total Cost:					
Variable Costs	4,00,000	8,00,000	12,00,000	16,00,000	20,00,000
Depreciation	1,00,000	1,00,000	1,00,000	1,00,000	1,00,000
Dep on additional Equipment	–	–	3,00,000	–	–
Fixed Costs Other than Depreciation	2,00,000	2,00,000	2,00,000	3,00,000	3,00,000
Total Cost	(7,00,000)	(11,00,000)	(18,00,000)	(20,00,000)	(24,00,000)
Earning before Tax	3,00,000	9,00,000	9,00,000	16,00,000	21,00,000
Less: Tax @ 30%	(90,000)	(2,70,000)	(2,70,000)	(4,80,000)	(6,30,000)
Earning after Tax	2,10,000	6,30,000	6,30,000	11,20,000	14,70,000
Add: Depreciation	1,00,000	1,00,000	1,00,000	1,00,000	1,00,000
Add: Dep on additional Equipment	–	–	3,00,000	–	–
Cash Flow after Tax (CFAT)	3,10,000	7,30,000	10,30,000	12,20,000	15,70,000
Add: Release of Working Capital [80% of ₹ 4,00,000]					3,20,000
Add: Cash Salvage Value of Asset.					80,000
Add: Tax Saving on Loss on Sale [30% of ₹ 20,000 (i.e. ₹ 1,00,000 – ₹ 80,000)]					6,000
Total CFAT for the last year					19,76,000

STATEMENT SHOWING NET PRESENT VALUE

Particulars	Year	PV factor	Amount	PV
Purchase Price of New Machinery	0	1	(10,00,000)	(10,00,000)
Installation Expenses	0	1	(1,50,000)	(1,50,000)
Workers' Training Expenses	0	1	(50,000)	(50,000)
Subsidy from Govt.	0	1	5,00,000	5,00,000
	1	0.909	1,00,000	90,900
Working Capital	0	1.000	(1,60,000)	(1,60,000)
	1	0.909	(1,60,000)	(1,45,440)
	2	0.826	(1,60,000)	(1,32,160)
	4	0.683	80,000	54,640
Additional Equipment	2	0.826	(3,00,000)	(2,47,800)
Retrenchment Compensation	0	1	(1,00,000)	(1,00,000)
Tax Saving on retrenchment compensation	1	0.909	30,000	27,270
CFAT for 1st year	1	0.909	3,10,000	2,81,790
CFAT for 2nd year	2	0.826	7,30,000	6,02,980
CFAT for 3rd year	3	0.751	10,30,000	7,73,530
CFAT for 4th year	4	0.683	12,20,000	8,33,260
CFAT for 5th year	5	0.621	19,76,000	12,27,096
NPV				24,06,066

Recommendation: Machine should be purchased since it has positive NPV.

Note: *Working Capital requirements are in the beginning of each year.*

ILLUSTRATION 23

Tulsian Ltd. provides you the following information:

1. Purchase Price of New Machinery ₹ 10,00,000
2. Installation Expenses ₹ 1,50,000
3. Workers' Training Expenses incurred to put the asset to use ₹ 50,000
4. Subsidy Receivable from Govt.: 50% of Purchase price now and 10% of Purchase price at the end of 1st year
5. Useful Life of the machine 5 years
6. Book Salvage Value at end of useful life 10 % of purchase price.
7. Cash Salvage Value at end of useful life ₹ 80,000.
8. Method of Depreciation Straight line
9. Tax Rate 30%
10. Cost of Capital 10%
11. Additional Equipment costing ₹ 3,00,000 will be needed at the beginning of 3rd year (useful life 3 years, Salvage Value nil)
12. Depreciation will be 100 % of the cost of additional equipment in year of purchase and the same will be allowed for tax purposes.
13. Retrenchment Compensation payable to the workers due to installation of this machine ₹ 1,00,000 (fully deductible for tax purposes)

14. Sales Units: 1st yr 1,00,000 units, 2nd yr 2,00,000 units, 3rd yr 3,00,000 units, 4th yr 4,00,000 units, 5th yr 5,00,000 units.
15. Initial selling price per unit of ₹ 10 will continue for first 2 years and ₹ 9 thereafter. Variable cost is 40% of initial selling price. Annual fixed cost other than depreciation is ₹ 2,00,000 which will increase to ₹ 3,00,000 after 3rd year.
16. Debtors at the end of each year would be 20% of sales, Creditors would be 10% of variable costs (Assume that debtors are realised and creditors are paid in the following year).

Required: Advise the Company whether to purchase the Machinery *or* not on the basis of Net Present Value.

SOLUTION

STATEMENT SHOWING THE CALCULATION OF CASH INFLOW AFTER TAX (CFAT)

Particulars	Year 1	Year 2	Year 3	Year 4	Year 5	Year 6
Sales Units	1,00,000	2,00,000	3,00,000	4,00,000	5,00,000	
Selling Price per unit (₹)	10	10	9	9	9	
Sales	10,00,000	20,00,000	27,00,000	36,00,000	45,00,000	
Less: Total Cost:						
Variable Costs	4,00,000	8,00,000	12,00,000	16,00,000	20,00,000	
Depreciation	1,00,000	1,00,000	1,00,000	1,00,000	1,00,000	
Depreciation on additional Equipment	–	–	3,00,000	–	–	
Fixed Cost Other than Depreciation	2,00,000	2,00,000	2,00,000	3,00,000	3,00,000	
Total Cost	(7,00,000)	(11,00,000)	(18,00,000)	(20,00,000)	(24,00,000)	
Earning before Tax	3,00,000	9,00,000	9,00,000	16,00,000	2,100,000	
Less: Tax @ 30%	(90,000)	(2,70,000)	(2,70,000)	(4,80,000)	(6,30,000)	
Earning after Tax	2,10,000	6,30,000	6,30,000	11,20,000	14,70,000	
Add: Depreciation	1,00,000	1,00,000	1,00,000	1,00,000	1,00,000	
Add: Dep on Additional Equipment	–	–	3,00,000	–	–	
Fund Flow after taxes	3,10,000	7,30,000	10,30,000	12,20,000	15,70,000	
Less: Debtors outstanding	(2,00,000)	(4,00,000)	(5,40,000)	(7,20,000)	(9,00,000)	
Add: Receipts from debtors	–	2,00,000	4,00,000	5,40,000	7,20,000	9,00,000
Add: Creditors Outstanding	40,000	80,000	1,20,000	1,60,000	2,00,000	
Less: Payments to creditors	–	(40,000)	(80,000)	(1,20,000)	(1,60,000)	(2,00,000)
CFAT	1,50,000	5,70,000	9,30,000	10,80,000	14,30,000	7,00,000
Add: Cash Salvage Value of Asset.					80,000	
Add: Tax Saving on Loss on Sale [30% of ₹ 20,000 (i.e. ₹ 1,00,000 – ₹ 80,000)]					6,000	
CFAT for the last year					15,16,000	7,00,000

STATEMENT SHOWING NET PRESENT VALUE

Particulars	Year	PV factor	Amount	PV
Purchase Price of New Machinery	0	1	(10,00,000)	(10,00,000)
Installation Expenses	0	1	(1,50,000)	(1,50,000)
Workers' Training Expenses	0	1	(50,000)	(50,000)
Subsidy from Govt.	0	1	5,00,000	5,00,000
	1	0.909	1,00,000	90,900
Additional Equipment	2	0.826	(3,00,000)	(2,47,800)
Retrenchment Compensation	0	1	(1,00,000)	(1,00,000)
Tax Saving on retrenchment compensation	1	0.909	30,000	27,270
CFAT for 1st year	1	0.909	1,50,000	1,36,350
CFAT for 2nd year	2	0.826	5,70,000	4,70,820
CFAT for 3rd year	3	0.751	9,30,000	6,98,430
CFAT for 4th year	4	0.683	10,80,000	7,37,640
CFAT for 5th year	5	0.621	15,16,000	9,41,436
CFAT for 6th year	6	0.564	7,00,000	3,94,800
NPV				24,49,846

Recommendation: Machine should be purchased since it has positive NPV.

ILLUSTRATION 24

TULSIAN Ltd. is considering the manufacture of a new product involving a Capital Expenditure of ₹ 10 Lakh. The project consultant provides the following details:

1. Cost Price Structure at 100% Capacity (i.e. 2,00,000 Units)

Selling Price per unit	₹ 20.00
Material Cost per unit	₹ 5.00
Labour Cost per unit	₹ 3.00
Production Overheads per Unit	₹ 4.00 (50% Variable)
Administration Overheads per Unit sold	₹ 0.75 (1/3 fixed)
Commission on Sales per unit	₹ 1.00
Other Selling & Distribution Overheads per unit	₹ 1.25 (40% Variable)

Note: Fixed Production Overheads include Depreciation.

2. Expected Capacity Utilization, and Closing Stocks:

Particulars	Year 1	Year 2	Year 3	Year 4
Capacity Utilization (%)	70%	80%	90%	100%
Closing Stock of Finished Goods (Units)	40,000	30,000	20,000	Nil
Closing Stock of Materials (₹)	1,00,000	2,00,000	3,00,000	Nil

3. Cash Sales and Cash Purchases are 25% of Net Credit Sales and Net Credit Purchases respectively.
4. Trade Debtors for Goods and Trade Creditors for Materials at the end of each year would be 20% of the net credit sales and net credit purchases respectively.

5. Creditors for Wages, Commission and Overheads at the end of each year would be 10%
6. Assume that debtors are realised and creditors are paid in the following year.
7. Stock of Finished Goods is to be valued at Variable Factory Cost.
8. At the end of 4th year, it is expected that the machine will be sold for ₹ 2,50,000 and the Cost of dismantling and removal will be ₹ 50,000.
9. Method of Depreciation: Straight Line Method
10. Tax Rate : 30%
11. Cost of Capital : 10%
12. No Change in the prices of inputs *or* output are expected over the next four years.

Required: Suggest whether the manufacture of the new product is worthwhile.

SOLUTION

STATEMENT SHOWING THE COMPUTATION OF CASH FLOWS AFTER TAXES

Particulars	Year 1	Year 2	Year 3	Year 4	Year 5
Cash Sales	4,00,000	6,80,000	7,60,000	8,80,000	
Collection from Debtors	12,80,000	24,96,000	29,76,000	34,24,000	7,04,000
*Less:*Cash Purchases	(1,60,000)	(1,80,000)	(2,00,000)	(1,40,000)	
Less: Payment to Creditors	(5,12,000)	(7,04,000)	(7,84,000)	(6,08,000)	(1,12,000)
Less: Payment for other expenses	(11,70,000)	(15,16,000)	(16,66,000)	(18,24,000)	(1,84,000)
*Less:*Payment of Tax	(60,000)	(2,28,000)	(2,76,000)	(3,48,000)	–
Cash Flows after Tax (CFAT)	(2,22,000)	5,48,000	8,10,000	13,84,000	4,08,000

STATEMENT SHOWING THE COMPUTATION OF NET PRESENT VALUE

Particulars	Year	Amount	PVF @ 10%	Present Value
A	B	C	D	E = C × D
Purchase of Machine	0	(10,00,000)	1.000	(10,00,000)
CFAT for the year 1	1	(2,22,000)	0.909	(2,01,798)
CFAT for the year 2	2	5,48,000	0.826	4,52,648
CFAT for the year 3	3	8,10,000	0.751	6,08,310
CFAT for the year 4	4	13,84,000	0.683	9,45,272
CFAT for the year 5	5	4,08,000	0.621	2,53,368
Net Salvage Value(₹ 2,50,000 – ₹ 50,000)	5	2,00,000	0.621	1,24,200
NPV				11,82,000

Recommendation: The manufacture of new product is worthwile, since it generates positive NPV of ₹ 11,82,000.

Working Notes:

2. CALCULATION OF TAX PAID

Particulars	Year 1	Year 2	Year 3	Year 4
Budgeted Production (in units)	1,40,000	1,60,000	1,80,000	2,00,000

Less: Closing Stock (in units)	(40,000)	(30,000)	(20,000)	–
Add: Opening Stock (in units)	–	40,000	30,000	20,000
Sales units	1,00,000	1,70,000	1,90,000	2,20,000
Sales @ 20 per unit (Units Sold × SP)	20,00,000	34,00,000	38,00,000	44,00,000
Less: Variable Cost @ ₹ 12 per unit	(12,00,000)	(20,40,000)	(22,80,000)	(26,40,000)
Less: Fixed Cost	(6,00,000)	(6,00,000)	(6,00,000)	(6,00,000)
Profit	2,00,000	7,60,000	9,20,000	11,60,000
Tax @ 30 %	60,000	2,28,000	2,76,000	3,48,000

2. CALCULATION OF TOTAL PURCHASES, CASH PURCHASES AND PAYMENT TO CREDITORS

Particulars	Year 1	Year 2	Year 3	Year 4	Year 5
Budgeted Production (in units)	1,40,000	1,60,000	1,80,000	2,00,000	
Material Consumed @ ₹ 5 per unit	7,00,000	8,00,000	9,00,000	10,00,000	
Add: Closing Stock	1,00,000	2,00,000	3,00,000	–	
Less: Opening Stock	–	(1,00,000)	(2,00,000)	(3,00,000)	
Total Purchases	8,00,000	9,00,000	10,00,000	7,00,000	
Less: Cash Purchases (1/5 th of Total Purchases)	1,60,000	1,80,000	2,00,000	1,40,000	
Credit Purchases	6,40,000	7,20,000	8,00,000	5,60,000	
Less: Closing Balance	(1,28,000)	(1,44,000)	(1,60,000)	(1,12,000)	
Add: Opening Balance	–	1,28,000	1,44,000	1,60,000	1,12,000
Payment to Creditors	5,12,000	7,04,000	7,84,000	6,08,000	1,12,000

3. CALCULATION OF CASH SALES AND COLLECTION FROM DEBTORS

Particulars	Year 1	Year 2	Year 3	Year 4	Year 5
Sales @ 20 per unit	20,00,000	34,00,000	38,00,000	44,00,000	
Less: Cash Sales (1/5 th of Total Sales)	4,00,000	6,80,000	7,60,000	8,80,000	
Credit Sales	16,00,000	27,20,000	30,40,000	35,20,000	
Less: Closing Balance	(3,20,000)	(5,44,000)	(6,08,000)	(7,04,000)	
Add: Opening Balance		3,20,000	5,44,000	6,08,000	7,04,000
Collection from Debtors	12,80,000	24,96,000	29,76,000	34,24,000	7,04,000

4. CALCULATION OF THE PAYMENTS FOR OTHER EXPENSES

Particulars	Year 1	Year 2	Year 3	Year 4	Year 5
Labour and Variable Production overheads (Units produced × ₹ 5)	7,00,000	8,00,000	9,00,000	10,00,000	
Variable Adm., Commission & Selling & Dist. Exp (Units sold × ₹ 2 per unit)	2,00,000	3,40,000	3,80,000	4,40,000	
Fixed Overheads	6,00,000	6,00,000	6,00,000	6,00,000	

Less: Depreciation [{₹ 10 lakhs – (2.5 lakhs – 0.5 lakhs)} /4]	(2,00,000)	(2,00,000)	(2,00,000)	(2,00,000)	
Total Cash Cost other than Material Cost	13,00,000	15,40,000	16,80,000	18,40,000	
Less: O/s at the end	(1,30,000)	(1,54,000)	(1,68,000)	(1,84,000)	
Add: O/s in the beginning		1,30,000	1,54,000	1,68,000	1,84,000
Payment for other variable expenses	11,70,000	15,16,000	16,66,000	18,24,000	1,84,000

MAKING CHOICE OUT OF TWO PROJECTS ON THE BASIS OF TOTAL CASH FLOW AND DIFFERENTIAL CASH FLOW APPROACH

ILLUSTRATION 25

Tulsian Ltd. provides you the following information:

Particulars	Machine X	Machine Y
1. Purchase Price of Machine	₹ 6,00,000	₹ 9,00,000
2. Working Capital	₹ 3,00,000	₹ 5,00,000
3. Useful Life of the machine	5 years	5 years
4. Estimated Salvage Value at the end of useful life	₹ 1,00,000	₹ 2,00,000
5. Cash Salvage Value at the end of useful life	₹ 1,20,000	₹ 80,000
6. Method of Depreciation	Straight line	Straight line
7. Tax Rate	30%	30%
8. Annual Sales	₹ 10,00,000	₹ 10,00,000
9. Variable Cost	40% of Sales	30% of Sales
10. Fixed Cost (other than Depreciation) per annum	₹ 1,00,000	₹ 2,00,000
11. Annuity Factor for 5 yrs @ 10%	3.791	3.791
12. PV Factor for 5th year @ 10 %	0.621	0.621

Required: Which of the above machines should be purchased on the basis of Net Present Value.

SOLUTION

STATEMENT SHOWING THE CALCULATION OF CASH INFLOWS AFTER TAX (CFAT)

Particulars	Machine X	Machine Y	Differential Cash Flow (X–Y)
Sales	10,00,000	10,00,000	–
Less: Total Cost:			
Variable Costs	4,00,000	3,00,000	1,00,000
Depreciation	1,00,000	1,40,000	(40,000)
Fixed Costs other than Depreciation	1,00,000	2,00,000	(1,00,000)
Total Cost	(6,00,000)	(6,40,000)	(40,000)
Earning before Tax	4,00,000	3,60,000	40,000
Less: Tax @ 30%	(1,20,000)	(1,08,000)	(12,000)

Earning after Tax	2,80,000	2,52,000	28,000
Add: Depreciation	1,00,000	1,40,000	(40,000)
CFAT (for years other than last yr)	3,80,000	3,92,000	(12,000)
Add: Release of Working Capital	3,00,000	5,00,000	(2,00,000)
Add: Cash Salvage Value of Asset.	1,20,000	80,000	40,000
Less: Tax on Profit on Sale [30% of ₹ 20,000 (₹ 1,20,000 – ₹ 1,00,000)]	(6,000)	–	(6,000)
Add: Tax Saving on Loss on Sale [30% of ₹ 1,20,000 (i.e. ₹ 2,00,000 – ₹ 80,000)]	–	36,000	(36,000)
CFAT (for last yr)	7,94,000	10,08,000	(2,14,000)

STATEMENT SHOWING NET PRESENT VALUE

Particulars	Year	PV factor	Machine X		Machine Y		Differential Cash Flow	
		at 10%	Amount	PV	Amount	PV	Amount	PV
Purchase Price	0	1	(6,00,000)	(6,00,000)	(9,00,000)	(9,00,000)	(3,00,000)	(3,00,000)
Working Capital	0	1	(3,00,000)	(3,00,000)	(5,00,000)	(5,00,000)	(2,00,000)	(2,00,000)
CFAT for 1 – 4 years	1 to 4	3.17	3,80,000	12,04,600	3,92,000	12,42,640	12,000	38,040
CFAT for 5th year	5	0.621	7,94,000	4,93,074	10,08,000	6,25,968	2,14,000	1,32,894
NPV				7,97,674		4,68,608		(3,29,066)

Recommendation: Machine X should be preferred over Machine Y since net savings offered by Machine X is ₹ 3,29,066 (i.e. ₹ 7,97,674 – ₹ 4,68,608).

ILLUSTRATION 26

Tulsian Ltd. provides you the following information:

Particulars	Machine X	Machine Y
1. Purchase Price of Machine	₹ 6,00,000	₹ 9,00,000
2. Working Capital	₹ 3,00,000	₹ 5,00,000
3. Useful Life of the machine	5 years	5 years
4. Estimated Salvage Value at the end of useful life	₹ 1,00,000	₹ 2,00,000
5. Cash Salvage Value at the end of useful life	₹ 1,20,000	₹ 80,000
6. Method of Depreciation	Straight line	Straight line
7. Tax Rate	30%	30%
8. Variable Cost	₹ 4,00,000	₹ 3,00,000
9. Fixed Cost (Other than Depreciation) per annum	₹ 1,00,000	₹ 2,00,000
10. Annuity Factor for 5 yrs @ 10%	3.791	3.791
11. PV Factor for 5th year @ 10 %	0.621	0.621

Required: Which of the above machines should be purchased on the basis of Present Value.

SOLUTION

STATEMENT SHOWING THE CALCULATION OF CASH OUTFLOW AFTER TAX SAVING (COAT)

Particulars	Machine X	Machine Y	Differential Cash Flow (X–Y)
Variable Costs	4,00,000	3,00,000	1,00,000
Depreciation	1,00,000	1,40,000	(40,000)
Fixed Cost other than Depreciation	1,00,000	2,00,000	(1,00,000)
Total Cost	6,00,000	6,40,000	(40,000)
Less: Tax Saving @ 30%	(1,80,000)	(1,92,000)	(12,000)
Cost after Tax Saving	4,20,000	4,48,000	(28,000)
Less: Depreciation being non-Cash Cost	(1,00,000)	(1,40,000)	(40,000)
Cash Cost after Tax Saving (for yrs other than Last yr)	3,20,000	3,08,000	12,000
Less: Release of Working Capital	(3,00,000)	(5,00,000)	(2,00,000)
Less: Salvage Value of Asset	(1,20,000)	(80,000)	40,000
Add: Tax on Profit on Sale [30% of ₹ 20,000 (₹ 1,20,000 – ₹ 1,00,000)]	6,000	–	6,000
Less: Tax Saving on Loss on Sale [30% of ₹ 1,20,000 (i.e. ₹ 2,00,000 – ₹ 80,000)]	–	(36,000)	(36,000)
Cash Outflow after Tax Saving (COAT) for the last year	(94,000)	(3,08,000)	2,14,000

STATEMENT SHOWING TOTAL PRESENT VALUE OF CASH OUTFLOW

Particulars	Year	PV factor	Machine X		Machine Y		Differential Cash Flow	
		at 10%	Amount	PV	Amount	PV	Amount	PV
Purchase Price	0	1	6,00,000	6,00,000	9,00,000	9,00,000	(3,00,000)	(3,00,000)
Working Capital	0	1	3,00,000	3,00,000	5,00,000	5,00,000	(2,00,000)	(2,00,000)
COAT for 1 – 4 years	1 to 4	3.170	3,20,000	10,14,400	3,08,000	9,76,360	12,000	38,040
COAT for 5th year	5	0.621	(94,000)	(58,374)	(3,08,000)	1,91,268)	2,14,000	1,32,894
Total PV of Cash Outflow				18,56,026		21,85,092		(3,29,066)
NPV				7,97,674		4,68,608		(3,29,066)

Recommendation: Machine X should be preferred over Machine Y since net savings offered by Machine X is ₹ 3,29,066 (i.e. ₹ 18,56,026 – ₹ 21,85,092)

ILLUSTRATION 27

Tulsian Ltd. having no fund constraints is considering the following projects:

Project	A	B	C	D	E
Net Present Value (NPV)	(₹ 1,00,000)	0	₹ 1,00,000	₹ 2,50,000	₹ 3,00,000

Required: Suggest which projects should Tulsian Ltd. undertake:

Case (a) If all the given projects are independent projects (i.e. not mutually exclusive projects)

Case (b) If all the given projects are mutually exclusive projects

Case (c) If Project B, C, D and E are independent projects and Project A is complimentary to Project E

Case (d) If Project D and E are mutually exclusive projects and Project A is complimentary to Project E

SOLUTION

Case (a): Since the given projects are independent, all projects meeting the management's criteria should be accepted.

Project	NPV Minimum Acceptable NPV	Management's Accept/Reject	Whether to	Why to Accept/Reject
A	(₹ 1,00,000)	0	Reject	NPV is negative
B	0	0	Accept/Reject	Management is indifferent as to rejection/ acceptance.
C	₹ 1,00,000	0	Accept	NPV is positive
D	₹ 2,50,000	0	Accept	NPV is positive
E	₹ 3,00,000	0	Accept	NPV is positive

Case (b): Since the given projects are mutually exclusive, only one project having the highest rank out of projects meeting the management's criteria should be accepted.

Project	NPV Minimum Acceptable NPV	Management's Reject	Whether to	Why to Accept/Reject
A	(₹ 1,00,000)	0	Reject	NPV is negative.
B	0	0	Reject	Although it does not have negative NPV, yet it has been rejected on the ground that NPV is *less* than that of Project E.
C	₹ 1,00,000	0	Reject	Although it has positive NPV, yet it has been rejected on the ground that NPV is *less* than that of Project E.
D	₹ 2,50,000	0	Reject	Although it has positive NPV, yet it has been rejected on the ground that NPV is *less* than that of Project E.
E	₹ 3,00,000	0	Accept	It has maximum positive NPV.

Case (c): Since the Projects B, C, D and E are independent, all projects meeting the management's criteria should be accepted.

Project	NPV Minimum Acceptable NPV	Management's Accept/Reject	Whether to	Why to Accept/Reject
A	(₹ 1,00,000)	0	Accept	Although it has negative NPV, yet it has to be accepted because Project A is complementary to Project E.
B	0	0	Accept/Reject	Management is indifferent as to rejection/acceptance.
C	₹ 1,00,000	0	Accept	NPV is positive

D	₹ 2,50,000	0	Accept	NPV is positive
E	₹ 3,00,000	0	Accept	NPV is positive

Case (d): Since the Projects B and C are independent, such projects meeting the management's criteria should be accepted.

Since Projects D and E are mutually exclusive, only one project having the highest rank out of projects meeting the management's criteria should be accepted.

Project	NPV Minimum Acceptable NPV	Management's Accept/Reject	Whether to	Why to Accept/Reject
A	(₹ 1,00,000)	0	Reject	Its negative NPV, (i.e, ₹ 1,00,000)along with NPV of Project E (i.e., ₹ 3,00,000) is *less* than that of Project D.
B	0	0	Accept/Reject	Management is indifferent as to rejection/acceptance.
C	₹ 1,00,000	0	Accept	NPV is positive
D	₹ 2,50,000	0	Accept	It has maximum positive NPV.
E	₹ 3,00,000	0	Reject	Although it has positive NPV, yet it has been rejected on the ground that its NPV (i.e., ₹ 3,00,000) along with Negative NPV (i.e., ₹ 1,00,000) of Project A (which is complementary to Project E) is *less* than that of Project D.

12.0 HOW TO COMPARE MUTUALLY EXCLUSIVE PROJECTS WHICH ARE OF UNEQUAL LIVES?

The steps involved in the selection of projects having unequal lives are given below:

Step 1: *Calculate the Present Value of Cash Flows After Tax (CFAT) at the given discount rate.*

Step 2: *Calculate Annualized Equivalent Present Value as follows:*

Annualized Equivalent Present Value = Total Present Value/Present Value Factor of Annuity of ₹ 1 at given Rate of Interest at the end of the life of the project.

Or

Annualized Equivalent Present Value = Total Present Value Capital Recovery Factor at given Rate of Interest at the end of the life of the project.

Note: *Capital Recovery Factor is equal to the reciprocal of Present Value Factor of Annuity of ₹ 1 at given Rate of Interest at the end of the life of the project.*

Note: *Annualized Equivalent Present Value is the Equated Annual Instalment of present value over the useful life of the project.*

Step 3: *Select the Project as follows:*

When Net Present value of Cash Inflows is considered	Select the project having the highest Annualized Equivalent Present Value
When Present value of Cash Outflows is considered	Select the project having the lowest Annualized Equivalent Present Value

ILLUSTRATION 28

Tulsian Ltd. provides you the following information:

Particulars	Machine X	Machine Y
1. Purchase Price of Machine	₹ 5,00,000	₹ 8,00,000
2. Useful Life of the machine	5 years	8 years
3. Estimated Salvage Value at the end of useful life	Nil	Nil
4. Method of Depreciation	Straight line	Straight line
5. Tax Rate	30%	30%
6. Annual Sales	₹ 10,00,000	₹ 10,00,000
7. Variable Cost	40% of Sales	30% of Sales
8. Fixed Cost (other than Depreciation) per annum	₹ 1,00,000	₹ 2,00,000
9. Annuity Factor for 5/8 yrs @ 10%	3.791	5.335

Required: Which of the above machines should be purchased on the basis of Net Present Value.

SOLUTION

STATEMENT SHOWING THE CALCULATION OF CASH FLOW AFTER TAX (CFAT)

Particulars	Machine X	Machine Y
Sales	10,00,000	10,00,000
Less: Total Cost:		
Variable Costs	4,00,000	3,00,000
Depreciation	1,00,000	1,00,000
Fixed Cost other than Depreciation	1,00,000	2,00,000
Total Cost	(6,00,000)	(6,00,000)
Earning before Tax	4,00,000	4,00,000
Less: Tax @ 30%	(1,20,000)	(1,20,000)
Earning after Tax	2,80,000	2,80,000
Add: Depreciation	1,00,000	1,00,000
CFAT	3,80,000	3,80,000

STATEMENT SHOWING ANNUALISED NET PRESENT VALUE

Particulars	Year	PV factor at 10%	Machine X		Machine Y	
			Amount	PV	Amount	PV
Purchase Price	0	1	(5,00,000)	(5,00,000)	(8,00,000)	(8,00,000)
CFAT for 1 – 5 years	1 to 5	3.791	3,80,000	14,40,580		
CFAT for 1 – 8 years	1 to 8	5.335			3,80,000	20,27,300
NPV				9,40,580		12,27,300
Annuity Factor for 5/8 years		3.791/5.335		3.791		5.335
Annualized NPV (NPV / Annuity Factor)				2,48,109		2,30,047

Recommendation: Machine X should be purchased since Machine X has higher annualized NPV than that of Machine Y.

ILLUSTRATION 29

Tulsian Ltd. provides you the following information:

Particulars	Machine X	Machine Y
1. Purchase Price of Machine	₹ 5,00,000	₹ 8,00,000
2. Useful Life of the machine	5 years	8 years
3. Estimated Salvage Value at the end of useful life	Nil	Nil
4. Method of Depreciation	Straight line	Straight line
5. Tax Rate	30%	30%
6. Variable Cost	₹ 4,00,000	₹ 3,00,000
7. Fixed Cost (other than Depreciation) per annum	₹ 1,00,000	₹ 2,00,000
8. Annuity Factor for 5/8 yrs @ 10%	3.791	5.335

Required: Which of the above machines should be purchased on the basis of Present Value.

SOLUTION

STATEMENT SHOWING THE CALCULATION OF CASH OUTFLOW AFTER TAX SAVING (COAT)

Particulars	Machine X	Machine Y
Variable Costs	4,00,000	3,00,000
Depreciation	1,00,000	1,00,000
Fixed Costs other than Depreciation	1,00,000	2,00,000
Total Cost	6,00,000	6,00,000
Less: Tax Saving @ 30%	(1,80,000)	(1,80,000)
Cost after Tax Saving	4,20,000	4,20,000
Less: Depreciation being non-Cash Cost	(1,00,000)	(1,00,000)
Cash Cost after Tax Saving	3,20,000	3,20,000

STATEMENT SHOWING ANNUALISED PRESENT VALUE OF CASH OUTFLOW

Particulars	Year	PV factor	Machine X		Machine Y	
		at 10%	Amount	PV	Amount	PV
Purchase Price	0	1	5,00,000	5,00,000	8,00,000	8,00,000
COAT for 1 – 5 years	1 to 5	3.791	3,20,000	12,13,120		
COAT for 1 – 8 years	1 to 8	5.335			3,20,000	17,07,200
Total PV of Cash Outflow				17,13,120		25,07,200
Annuity Factor for 5/8 years		3.791/5.335		3.791		5.335
Annualized PV of Cash Outflow (PV / Annuity Factor)				4,51,891		4,69,953

Recommendation: Machine X should be purchased since Machine X has lower annualized PV of cash outflow than that of Machine Y.

ILLUSTRATION 30

Tulsian Ltd. provides you the following information:

Particulars	Machine X	Machine Y
1. Purchase Price of Machine	₹ 6,00,000	₹ 10,00,000
2. Working Capital	₹ 3,00,000	₹ 5,00,000
3. Useful Life of the machine	5 years	8 years
4. Estimated Salvage Value at the end of useful life	₹ 1,00,000	₹ 2,00,000
5. Actual Salvage Value realised at the end of useful life	₹ 1,20,000	₹ 80,000
6. Method of Depreciation	Straight line	Straight line
7. Tax Rate	30%	30%
8. Annual Sales	₹ 10,00,000	₹ 10,00,000
9. Variable Cost	40% of Sales	30% of Sales
10. Fixed Cost (other than Depreciation) per annum	₹ 1,00,000	₹ 2,00,000
11. Annuity Factor for 5/8 yrs @ 10%	3.791	5.335
12. PV Factor for 5th/8th year @ 10 %	0.621	0.467

Required: Which of the above machines should be purchased on the basis of Net Present Value.

SOLUTION

STATEMENT SHOWING THE CALCULATION OF CASH INFLOW AFTER TAX (CFAT)

Particulars	Machine X	Machine Y
Sales	10,00,000	10,00,000
Less: Total Cost:		
Depreciation	1,00,000	1,00,000
Variable Costs	4,00,000	3,00,000
Fixed Costs other than Depreciation	1,00,000	2,00,000
Total Cost	(6,00,000)	(6,00,000)
Earning before Tax	4,00,000	4,00,000
Less: Tax @ 30%	(1,20,000)	(1,20,000)
Earning after Tax	2,80,000	2,80,000
Add: Depreciation	1,00,000	1,00,000
CFAT (for years other than last yr)	3,80,000	3,80,000
Add: Release of Working Capital	3,00,000	5,00,000
Add: Cash Salvage Value of Asset	1,20,000	80,000
Less: Tax on Profit on sale [30% of ₹ 20,000 (₹ 120,000 – ₹ 1,00,000)]	(6,000)	–
Add: Tax Saving on Loss on Sale [30% of ₹ 1,20,000 (i.e. ₹ 2,00,000 – ₹ 80,000)]	–	36,000
CFAT (for last yr)	7,94,000	9,96,000

STATEMENT SHOWING ANNUALIZED NET PRESENT VALUE

Particulars	Year	PV factor	Machine X		Machine Y	
		at 10%	Amount	PV	Amount	PV
Purchase Price	0	1	(6,00,000)	(6,00,000)	(10,00,000)	(10,00,000)
Working Capital	0	1	(3,00,000)	(3,00,000)	(5,00,000)	(5,00,000)
CFAT for 1 – 4 years	1 to 4	3.17	3,80,000	12,04,600		
CFAT for 5th year	5	0.621	7,94,000	4,93,074		
CFAT for 1 – 7 years	1 to 7	4.868			3,80,000	18,49,840
CFAT for 8th year	8	0.467			9,96,000	4,65,132
NPV				7,97,674		8,14,972
Annuity Factor for 5/8 years		3.791/5.335		3.791		5.335
Annualized NPV (NPV / Annuity Factor)				2,10,413		1,52,760

Recommendation: Machine X should be purchased since Machine X has higher annualized NPV than that of Machine Y.

ILLUSTRATION 31

Tulsian Ltd. provides you the following information:

Particulars	Machine X	Machine Y
1. Purchase Price of Machine	₹ 6,00,000	₹ 10,00,000
2. Working Capital	₹ 3,00,000	₹ 5,00,000
3. Useful Life of the machine	5 years	8 years
4. Estimated Salvage Value at the end of useful life	₹ 1,00,000	₹ 2,00,000
5. Cash Salvage Value at the end of useful life	₹ 1,20,000	₹ 80,000
6. Method of Depreciation	Straight line	Straight line
7. Tax Rate	30%	30%
8. Variable Cost per annum	₹ 4,00,000	₹ 3,00,000
9. Fixed Cost (other than Depreciation) per annum	₹ 1,00,000	₹ 2,00,000
10. Annuity Factor for 5/8 yrs @ 10%	3.791	5.335
11. PV Factor for 5th/8th year @ 10 %	0.621	0.467

Required: Which of the above machines should be purchased on the basis of Present Value.

SOLUTION

STATEMENT SHOWING THE CALCULATION OF CASH OUTFLOW AFTER TAX SAVING (COAT)

Particulars	Machine X	Machine Y
Variable Costs	4,00,000	3,00,000
Depreciation	1,00,000	1,00,000
Fixed Costs other than Depreciation	1,00,000	2,00,000
Total Cost	6,00,000	6,00,000

Less: Tax Saving @ 30%	(1,80,000)	(1,80,000)
Cost after Tax Saving	4,20,000	4,20,000
Less: Depreciation being non-Cash Cost	(1,00,000)	(1,00,000)
Cash Cost after Tax Saving (for yrs other than Last yr)	3,20,000	3,20,000
Less: Release of Working Capital	(3,00,000)	(5,00,000)
Less: Salvage Value of Asset.	(1,20,000)	(80,000)
Add: Tax on Profit on Sale [30% of ₹ 20,000 (₹ 1,20,000 – ₹ 1,00,000)]	6,000	–
Less: Tax Saving on Loss on Sale [30% of ₹ 1,20,000 (i.e. ₹ 2,00,000 – ₹ 80,000)]	–	(36,000)
Cash Outflow after Tax Saving (COAT) for the last year	(94,000)	(2,96,000)

STATEMENT SHOWING ANNUALISED PRESENT VALUE OF CASH OUTFLOW

Particulars	Year	PV factor at 10%	Machine X		Machine Y	
			Amount	PV	Amount	PV
Purchase Price	0	1	6,00,000	6,00,000	10,00,000	10,00,000
Working Capital	0	1	3,00,000	3,00,000	5,00,000	5,00,000
COAT for 1 – 4 years	1 to 4	3.170	3,20,000	10,14,400		
COAT for 5th year	5	0.621	(94,000)	(58,374)		
COAT for 1 – 7 years	1 to 7	4.868			3,20,000	15,57,760
COAT for 8th year	8	0.467			(2,96,000)	(1,38,232)
Total PV of Cash Outflow				18,56,026		29,19,528
Annuity Factor for 5/8 years		3.791/5.335		3.791		5.335
Annualized PV of Cash Outflow (PV / Annuity Factor)				4,89,587		5,47,240

Recommendation: Machine X should be purchased since Machine X has lower annualized PV of cash outflow than that of Machine Y.

ILLUSTRATION 32

Tulsian Ltd. provides you the following information:

Annual Cost Saving	₹ 80,000	Cost of Project	?
Useful Life	4 years	Pay Back Period	2.855
NPV	₹ 14,560	Salvage Value	Zero
Cost of Capital	?		

Required: Ascertain the missing figures.

SOLUTION

(i) Calculation of Cost of Project

Pay Back Period = Cost of Project / Annual Cash Inflow

Cost of Project = Annual Cash Inflow × Pay Back Period

= ₹ 80,000 × 2.855 years

= ₹ 2,28,400

(ii) Calculation of PV of Cash Inflow

NPV = PV of Cash Inflow – PV of Cash Outflow

= ₹ 14,560

PV of Cash Inflow= NPV + PV of Cash Outflow

= ₹ 14,560 + ₹ 2,28,400 = ₹ 2,42,960

(iii) Calculation of Cost of Capital

PV of Cash Inflow= Annual Cash Inflow × PVF for 4 years at Cost of Capital

PVF for 4 years= ₹ 2,42,960 / ₹ 80,000 = 3.037

As per annuity table, Cumulative PVF of 3.037 corresponds to 12 %. Therefore, the Cost of Capital is 12 %.

ILLUSTRATION 33

(a) Tulsian Ltd. provides you the following information:

Cash Flow before Tax p.a.	₹ 3,64,178	Cost of Capital	15 %
Useful Life of Machine	5 years	Tax Rate	40%

Required: Calculate the Cost of Machine if the management is indifferent as to the rejection/ acceptance of machine on the basis of NPV. [Present Value of Annuity of ₹ 1 @ 15% for 5 years is ₹ 3.35]

(b) Calculate the Cost of Machine in Part (a) if Negative Net Present Value is ₹ 7,32,000

SOLUTION

CALCULATION OF PV OF CASH INFLOW AFTER TAXES

Let the Cost of Machine be x	
Cash Flow before Tax	3,64,178
Less: Tax @ 40%	(1,45,671)
Cash Flow before Tax Saving on Dep.	2,18,507
Add: Tax Saving on Depreciation [(40 % of x/5)]	0.08x
CFAT	2,18,507 + 0.08x
PV Factor @ 15 %	3.35
PV of CFAT	7,32,000 + 0.268x

(a) Calculation of the Cost of Machine

NPV = PV of CFAT – PV of Cash Outflow

= (7,32,000 + 0.268x) – x

x = 7,32,000 + 0.268x

x = ₹ 7,32,000 / 0.732 = ₹ 10,00,000

Thus, the Cost of Machine is ₹ 10,00,000

(b) Calculation of the Cost of Machine

NPV = PV of CFAT – PV of Cash Outflow

= (7,32,000 + 0.268x) – x

– ₹ 7,32,000 = ₹ 7,32,000 – 0.732 x

x = (₹ 7,32,000 + ₹ 7,32,000)/.732 = ₹ 20,00,000.

ILLUSTRATION 34

DLF Builders agreed to build a block of six flats at their own cost on the plot of land of Tulsian Ltd. and lease them out to Tulsian Ltd. for 15 years at the end of which the flats will be transferred to Tulsian Ltd. for a nominal value of ₹ 18,66,666.

DLF Builders provides you the following information:

(a)	Cost of Plot of Land	₹ 50,00,000
(b)	Cost of Construction of Building	?
(c)	Cost of Capital	10%
(d)	Tax Rate	50%
(e)	Lease Rentals to be charged:	

Years	Rentals
1 to 5	Normal
6 to 10	120% of Normal
11 to 15	150% of Normal

Normal Lease Rental per flat per annum is ₹ 1,40,000

The full cost of construction will be written off over 15 years and will be allowed for tax purposes. The present Value of Annuity of ₹ 1 @ 10% for 5 years, 10 years and 15 years are 3.79, 6.14 and 7.6 respectively. The Present Value factor @ 10% for the 15th year is 0.24.

Required: Calculate the Cost of Construction of Building.

SOLUTION

Step 1: Calculation of PV of Cash Inflow

Let the Cost of Construction of Building be x

Particulars	Years 1 – 5	Years 6 – 10	Years 11 – 15	Total
Lease Rentals	8,40,000	10,08,000	12,60,000	
Less: Tax @ 50 %	(4,20,000)	(5,04,000)	(6,30,000)	
Lease Rentals after Tax	4,20,000	5,04,000	6,30,000	
PVF @ 10%	3.79	2.35	1.46	
PV of Lease Rentals after Tax	15,91,800	11,84,400	9,19,800	36,96,000
Add: PV of Tax Saving on amount w/o [50% of (x/15)] 7.6]				0.253333x
Add: PV of Nominal Value after tax [50% of ₹ 18,66,666) 0.24]				2,24,000
PV of CFAT				39,20,000
				+ 0.253333x

Step 2: Calculation of Cost of Construction

NPV = PV of Cash Inflow – PV of Cash Outflows

= (₹ 39,20,000 + 0.253333x) – x

x = ₹ 39,20,000 / 0.746667 = ₹ 52,50,000

Thus, Cost of Construction = ₹ 52,50,000

Note: *Cost of Plot of Land has not been considered as cash outflow by builder since it has been provided by Tulsian Ltd.*

ILLUSTRATION 35

DLF Builders agreed to build a block of six flats at their own cost on the plot of land of Tulsian Ltd. and lease them out to Tulsian Ltd. for 15 years at the end of which the flats will be transferred to Tulsian Ltd. for a nominal value of ₹ 9,33,333.

DLF Builders provides you the following information:

Cost of Plot of Land	₹ 50,00,000	Cost of Capital	10%
Cost of Construction of Building	₹ 26,25,000	Tax Rate	50%

Lease Rentals to be charged:

Years	Rentals
1 to 5	Normal
6 to 10	120% of Normal
11 to 15	150% of Normal

The full cost of construction will be written off over 15 years and will be allowed for tax purposes.

The present Value of Annuity of ₹ 1 @ 10% for 5 years, 10 years and 15 years are 3.79, 6.14 and 7.6 respectively. The Present Value factor @ 10% for the 15th year is 0.24.

Required: Calculate Annual Lease rentals for each flat to be charged by builder.

SOLUTION

Step 1: Calculation of PV of Cash Inflow

Let the normal lease rentals for all 6 flats be x

Particulars	Years 1 – 5	Years 6 – 10	Years 11 – 15	Total
Lease Rentals	x	1.2x	1.5x	
Less: Tax @ 50 %	(0.5x)	(0.6x)	(0.75x)	
Lease Rentals after Tax	0.5x	0.6x	0.75x	
PVF @ 10%	3.79	2.35	1.46	
PV of Lease Rentals after Tax	1.895x	1.41x	1.095x	4.4x
Add: PV of Tax Saving on amount w/o [50% of (₹ 26,25,000/15) × 7.6]				6,65,000
Add: PV of Nominal Value after tax [50% of (₹ 9,33,333)] × 0.24				1,12,000
PV of CFAT				4.4x + 7,77,000

Step 2: Calculation of Annual Lease Rentals of Each Flat

Annual Lease Rental for 6 flats = PV of Cash Inflow equals PV of Cash Outflows

$$4.4x + 7,77,000 = 26,25,000$$

$$x = ₹\ 4,20,000$$

Thus, Normal Lease Rental per flat per annum = ₹ 4,20,000 / 6 = ₹ 70,000

for years 1-5 – ₹ 70,000
for years 6-10 – ₹ 84,000
for years 11-15 – ₹ 1,05,000

Note: *Cost of Plot of Land has not been considered as cash outflow by builder since it has been provided by Tulsian Ltd.*

13.0 INTERNAL RATE OF RETURN (IRR) OR PROJECT IRR

WHAT IS IRR TECHNIQUE?

(a) Internal Rate of Return technique is one of the discounted cash flow techniques which takes into account the time value of money.

(b) Internal Rate of Return refers to the rate, which equates the present value of all cash inflows with the present value of all cash outflows associated with the project.

(c) The Internal Rate of Return is the rate at which NPV is zero.

(d) It is called an internal rate because it depends solely upon the cash inflows and the cash outflows associated with the project and not on any rate determined outside the project.

In Algebraic Equation Form

$$\left[\frac{CI_1}{(1+r)^1}+\frac{CI_2}{(1+r)^2}+\frac{CI_3}{(1+r)^3}+\ldots\frac{CI_n}{(1+r)^n}\right]=\left[\frac{CO_1}{(1+r)^1}+\frac{CO_2}{(1+r)^2}+\frac{CO_3}{(1+r)^3}+\ldots\frac{CO_n}{(1+r)^n}\right]$$

where, $CI_1, CI_2, CI_3 \ldots$ = Cash Inflows in different periods

$CO_1, CO_2, CO_3 \ldots$ = Cash Outflows in different periods

r = Internal Rate of Return

n = Expected life of the project

WHAT IS ACCEPT/REJECT RULE?

(a) Independent Projects	Accept the project if IRR > k, Reject the project if IRR < k (i.e. Cost of Capital)
(b) Mutually Exclusive Projects	Projects should be ranked in the order of IRR and the project with **highest** IRR(but not *less* than Cost of Capital) should be selected..

HOW TO INTERPRET IRR?

1. IRR may be interpreted as the highest rate of interest, which a firm would be ready to pay on funds borrowed to finance the project without being financially worse off by repaying loan along with interest thereon out of cash inflows generated by the project.
2. IRR represents the rate of return on the unrecovered investment balance in the project.
3. IRR is the rate of return earned on the initial investment made in the project.

WHAT ARE THE MERITS AND DEMERITS OF IRR?

Merits	Demerits
1. It considers the time value of money. 2. It considers entire cash flows over entire life of the project. 3. It is consistent with the objective of maximizing the wealth of owners. 4. It is a measure of profitability since entire cash flows over entire life of the project are considered. 5. Unlike the NPV, cost of capital is not assumed to be known.	1. It requires the estimation of cash inflows and cash outflows, which is a difficult task. 2. It assumes that intermediate cash inflows are reinvested at IRR. 3. It may yield negative rates under certain circumstances. (e.g. when Cash Outflows are more than Cash Inflows). 4. It may yield multiple rates under certain circumstances (e.g. when cash flows reverse their signs during the project). 5. It is relatively difficult to compute.

	6. It ignores the absolute amount of NPV while taking decision. A project having lower IRR but higher absolute NPV may be rejected although it increases the shareholders' wealth.

COMPARISON BETWEEN NPV AND IRR

A. SIMILARITIES

1. Both consider the time value of money.
2. Both consider all cash flows over entire life of the project.
3. Both are consistent with the objective of maximizing the wealth of owners.
4. Both are equivalent as regards the acceptance/rejection of conventional investments.

B. DIFFERENCES

1. Evaluation of Non-Conventional Investments-Both are not equivalent as regards the acceptance/rejection of non-conventional investments if the projects differ in their (a) expected lives *or* (b) estimated cash outflows *or* (c) timings of cash flows.
2. Reinvestment Rate-IRR assumes that intermediate cash inflows are reinvested at IRR while NPV assumes that intermediate cash inflows are reinvested at required rate of return (i.e. firm's cost of capital).
3. Multiple/Negative Rates-IRR can yield negative rates/multiple rates under certain circumstances while there is no such possibility under NPV method.

HOW TO COMPUTE IRR?

The calculation of IRR involves the following practical steps:

I. In case of Long Life Projects (i.e. projects having life atleast twice the payback period) generating equal cash inflows:

Step 1: *Calculate the Payback Period.*

Step 2: *Calculate the reciprocal of Payback Period.*

Internal Rate of Return = Reciprocal of Payback Period = 1Payback Period

Note: *Here, the reciprocal of Pay back Period provides only a good approximation to IRR and not an exact IRR.*

II. In case of Short Life Projects (i.e. projects having life less than twice the payback period) generating equal cash inflows:

Step 1: *Calculate the Payback Period as follows:*

$$\text{Payback period} = \frac{\text{Cash Outflow}}{\text{Equal Annual Cash Inflor}}$$

Step 2: *Find out two Present Value of Annuity Factors (PVAF) within which the above Payback Period lies from the present value of annuity table.*

Step 3: *Find out the two discount rates corresponding to these above PVAF from the top row of the present value of annuity table.*

Step 4: *Calculate the IRR by interpolation as follows:*

$$IRR = \frac{\text{(PVAF at lower rate – Payback period)}}{\text{PVAF at lower rate – PVAF at higher rate}}$$

ILLUSTRATION 36

Calculate Internal Rate of Return (IRR) in the following cases:

Particulars	Project A	Project B	Project C
Cash Outflow	₹ 5,57,500	₹ 3,57,000	₹ 3,84,000
Cash Inflow After Tax p.a.	₹ 1,00,000	₹ 1,00,000	₹ 1,00,000
Life of Project	15 years	10 years	5 years

SOLUTION

Step 1: Payback Period $= \dfrac{\text{Cash Outflow}}{\text{Annual Cash Inflow after tax}}$

Project A	Project B	Project C
= ₹ 5,57,500/₹ 1,00,000	= ₹ 5,57,500/₹ 1,00,000	= ₹ 5,57,500/₹ 1,00,000
= 5.575	= 3.57	= 3.84

Step 2: *Locating the above Payback Period in the Row corresponding to the life of the project with the help of present value of Annuity Table and finding out the single discount rate at which or two discount rates within which above Payback Period lies*

Project A: 16%

Project B: 25%

Project C: 9% and 10%

$$\text{IRR} = \text{Lower Discount Rate} + \frac{\text{PVAF at lower Rate} - \text{Pay back period}}{\text{PVAF at lower rate} - \text{PVAF at higher rate}}$$

$$= 9\% + (3.89 - 3.84)/\ (3.89 - 3.791) = 9\% + 0.05/0.0099 = 9.505\%$$

III. In case of Projects generating unequal cash inflows:

Step 1: *Calculate the Fake Payback Period as follows:*

$$\text{Fake Payback Period} = \frac{\text{Cash Outflow}}{\text{Average Annual Cash Inflow}}$$

Note: *Average Annual Cash Inflow = Total Cash Inflow/Life of the project*

Step 2: *Find out two discount factors within which the above Fake Payback Period lies from the present value of annuity table.*

Step 3: *Find out the two discount rates corresponding to these above discount factors from the top row of the present value of annuity table.*

Step 4: *Calculate the NPV at both the discount rates so as to have one negative NPV and one positive NPV.*

Notes:

1. *If Both NPVs are positive, calculate again NPV at some higher discount rate so as to have negative NPV.*
2. *If Both NPVs are negative, calculate again NPV at some lower discount rate so as to have positive NPV.*
3. *Repeat this process unless you get one lower rate at which NPV is positive and one higher rate at which NPV is negative*

Step 5: *Calculate the IRR by interpolation as follows:*

$$\text{IRR} = \text{Lower Discount Rate} + \frac{\text{NPV at lower rate}}{\text{NPV at lower rate} - \text{NPV at higher rate}} \times (\text{Higher Rate} - \text{Lower Rate})$$

ILLUSTRATION 37

From the following, calculate Internal Rate of Return (IRR):

Year	0	1	2	3	4	5
Cash Flow (₹)	(3,84,000)	1,50,000	1,25,000	1,00,000	75,000	50,000

SOLUTION

Step 1: Average Annual Cash Inflow = (1,50,000 + 1,25,000 + 1,00,000 + 75,000 + 50,000)/5
= ₹ 1,00,000

Step 2: Fake Payback Period = $\frac{\text{Cash Outflow}}{\text{Average Annual Cash Inflow}} = \frac{₹\ 3,84,000}{₹1,00,000} = 3.84$

Step 3: *Discount factors corresponding to 3.84 are 9% and 10%*

Step 4: *NPV at 9% and 10%*

Year	Cash flow	PVF @ 9%	PV at 9%	PVF @ 10%	PV at 10%	PVF @ 12%	PV at 12%
0	(3,84,000)	1.000	(3,84,000)	1.000	(3,84,000)	1.000	(3,84,000)
1	1,50,000	0.917	1,37,550	0.909	1,36,350	0.893	1,33,950
2	1,25,000	0.842	1,05,250	0.826	1,03,250	0.797	99,625
3	1,00,000	0.772	77,200	0.751	75,100	0712	71,200
4	75,000	0.708	53,100	0.683	51,225	0.636	47,700
5	50,000	0.650	32,500	0.621	31,050	0.567	28,350
			21,600		12,975		(3,175)

$$\text{IRR} = \text{Lower Discount Rate} + \frac{\text{NPV at Lower Rate}}{\text{NPV at Lower Rate} - \text{NPV at Higher Rate}} \times (\text{HDR} - \text{LDR})$$

= 10% + 12,975/[12975 – (–3,175)] × (12% – 10%)

= 10% + (12,975/16,150) × 2%

= 11.607%

ILLUSTRATION 38

Tulsian Ltd. provides you the following information:

1. Purchase Price of each Machine	₹ 6,00,000
2. Working Capital	₹ 3,00,000
3. Useful Life of each machine	5 years
4. Estimated Salvage Value at the end of useful life	₹ 1,00,000
5. Cash Salvage Value at the end of useful life	₹ 1,20,000
6. Method of Depreciation	Straight line
7. Tax Rate	30%
8. Earning before depreciation & tax:	

Machine	Year 1	Year 2	Year 3	Year 4	Year 5
Machine X	3,00,000	3,00,000	3,00,000	3,00,000	3,00,000
Machine Y	–	1,00,000	2,00,000	3,00,000	12,00,000
Machine Z	5,00,000	4,00,000	3,00,000	2,00,000	–

Required: Which of the above machines should be purchased on the basis of Internal Rate of Return.

SOLUTION

STATEMENT SHOWING THE COMPUTATION OF CASH INFLOW AFTER TAXES OF MACHINE X

Particulars	Year 1	Year 2	Year 3	Year 4	Year 5
Earning before depreciation & tax	3,00,000	3,00,000	3,00,000	3,00,000	3,00,000
Less: Depreciation	(1,00,000)	(1,00,000)	(1,00,000)	(1,00,000)	(1,00,000)
Earning before Tax	2,00,000	2,00,000	2,00,000	2,00,000	2,00,000
Less: Tax @ 30 %	(60,000)	(60,000)	(60,000)	(60,000)	(60,000)
Earning after Tax	1,40,000	1,40,000	1,40,000	1,40,000	1,40,000
Add: Depreciation	1,00,000	1,00,000	1,00,000	1,00,000	1,00,000
Cash Flow after Taxes(CFAT)	2,40,000	2,40,000	2,40,000	2,40,000	2,40,000
Add: Release of Working Capital					3,00,000
Add: Actual Salvage Value of Asset.					1,20,000
Less: Tax on Profit on Sale [30% of ₹ 20,000 (i.e. ₹ 1,20,000 – ₹ 1,00,000)]					(6,000)
Total CFAT for the last year					6,54,000

Step 1: *Calculation of Fake Pay Back Period*

$$\text{Fake Pay Back Period} = \frac{\text{Cash Outflow}}{\text{Average Annual Cash Inflow}}$$

$$= 9,00,000/[(2,40,000 + 2,40,000 + 2,40,000 + 2,40,000 + 6,54,000)/5] = 2.788$$

Step 2: *Finding out two discount factors within which the above fake pay back period lies from the present value table = 2.803 and 2.745*

Step 3: *Finding out two discount rates corresponding to these above discount factors from the top row of the present value table = 23 % and 24 %*

Step 4: *Calculating the NPV at both the discount rates so as to have one negative NPV and one positive NPV.*

After applying discount rate of 23 % we get negative NPV of ₹ 80,310 now to have positive NPV we apply a lower rate of 20 % and we get negative NPV of ₹ 15,972. Again to have positive NPV we apply a lower rate of 19 % and we get positive NPV of ₹ 7,146.

STATEMENT SHOWING NET PRESENT VALUE OF MACHINE X

Particulars	Year	Amount	PV factor at 23%	PV factor at 20%	PV at factor at 19%	PV at 23%	PV at 20%	PV at 19%
Purchase Price of New Machinery	0	(6,00,000)	1	1	1	(6,00,000)	(6,00,000)	(6,00,000)
Working Capital	0	(3,00,000)	1	1	1	(3,00,000)	(3,00,000)	(3,00,000)
CFAT for 1st year	1	2,40,000	0.813	0.833	0.840	1,95,120	1,99,920	2,01,600
CFAT for 2nd year	2	2,40,000	0.661	0.694	0.706	1,58,640	1,66,560	1,69,440
CFAT for 3rd year	3	2,40,000	0.537	0.579	0.593	1,28,880	1,38,960	1,42,320
CFAT for 4th year	4	2,40,000	0.437	0.482	0.499	1,04,880	1,15,680	1,19,760
CFAT for 5th year	5	6,54,000	0.355	0.402	0.419	2,32,170	2,62,908	2,74,026
NPV						(80,310)	(15,972)	7,146

$$\text{IRR} = \text{Lower Rate} + \frac{\text{NPV at Lower Rate}}{\text{NPV at Lower Rate} - \text{NPV Higher Rate}} \times (\text{Higher Rate} - \text{Lower Rate})$$

= 19 % + [7,146/{7,146 – (–15,972)}] × (20 – 19)

= 19 + 0.309 (1)

= 19.309%

STATEMENT SHOWING THE COMPUTATION OF CASH INFLOW AFTER TAXES OF MACHINE Y

Particulars	Year 1	Year 2	Year 3	Year 4	Year 5
Earning before depreciation & tax	–	1,00,000	2,00,000	3,00,000	12,00,000
Less: Depreciation	(1,00,000)	(1,00,000)	(1,00,000)	(1,00,000)	(1,00,000)
Earning before Tax	(1,00,000)	–	1,00,000	2,00,000	11,00,000
Less: Tax @ 30 %	30,000	–	(30,000)	(60,000)	(3,30,000)
Earning after Tax	(70,000)	–	70,000	1,40,000	7,70,000
Add: Depreciation	1,00,000	1,00,000	1,00,000	1,00,000	1,00,000
Cash Flow after Taxes (CFAT)	30,000	1,00,000	1,70,000	2,40,000	8,70,000
Add: Release of Working Capital					3,00,000
Add: Cash Salvage Value of Asset.					1,20,000
Less: Tax on Ordinary Profit on Sale [30% of ₹ 20,000 (i.e. ₹ 1,20,000 – ₹ 1,00,000)]					(6,000)
Total CFAT for the last year					12,84,000

Note: *Assuming that the company has taxable income from other sources against which such loss can be set off, there will be tax saving on negative EBT.*

Step 1: *Calculation of Fake Pay Back Period*

$$\text{Fake Pay Back Period} = \frac{\text{Cash Outflow}}{\text{Average Annual Cash Inflow}}$$

= 9,00,000/[(30,000 + 1,00,000 + 1,70,000 + 2,40,000 + 12,84,000)/5]

= 2.467

Step 2: *Finding out two discount factors within which the above fake pay back period lies from the present value table = 2.483 and 2.436*

Step 3: *Finding out two discount rates corresponding to these above discount factors from the top row of the present value table = 29 % and 30 %*

Step 4: *Calculating the NPV at both the discount rates so as to have one negative NPV and one positive NPV.*

After applying discount rate of 29 % we get negative NPV of ₹ 2,91,270 now to have positive NPV we apply a lower rate of 18 % and we get negative NPV of ₹ 14,312. Again to have positive NPV we apply a lower rate of 17 % and we get positive NPV of ₹ 18,494.

STATEMENT SHOWING NET PRESENT VALUE OF MACHINE Y

Particulars	Year	Amount	PV factor at 29%	PV factor at 18%	PV at factor at 17%	PV at 29%	PV at 18%	PV at 17%
Purchase Price of New Machinery	0	(6,00,000)	1	1	1	(6,00,000)	(6,00,000)	(6,00,000)
Working Capital	0	(3,00,000)	1	1	1	(3,00,000)	(3,00,000)	(3,00,000)
CFAT for 1st year	1	30,000	0.775	0.847	0.855	23,250	25,410	25,650
CFAT for 2nd year	2	1,00,000	0.601	0.718	0.731	60,100	71,800	73,100
CFAT for 3rd year	3	1,70,000	0.466	0.609	0.624	79,220	1,03,530	1,06,080
CFAT for 4th year	4	2,40,000	0.361	0.516	0.534	86,640	1,23,840	1,28,160
CFAT for 5th year	5	12,84,000	0.28	0.437	0.456	3,59,520	5,61,108	5,85,504
NPV						(2,91,270)	(14,312)	18,494

$$IRR = \frac{\text{NPV at Lower Rate}}{\text{NPV at Lower Rate} - \text{NPV at Higher Rate}} \times \text{Lower Rate} + \times (\text{Higher Rate} - \text{Lower Rate})$$

$= 17\% + [18,494/\{18,494 - (-14,312)\}] \times (18 - 17)$

$= 17 + 0.564\ (1)$

$= 17.564\%$

STATEMENT SHOWING THE COMPUTATION OF CASH INFLOW AFTER TAXES OF MACHINE Z

Particulars	Year 1	Year 2	Year 3	Year 4	Year 5
Earning before depreciation & tax	5,00,000	4,00,000	3,00,000	200,000	–
Less: Depreciation	(1,00,000)	(1,00,000)	(1,00,000)	(1,00,000)	(1,00,000)
Earning before Tax	4,00,000	3,00,000	2,00,000	1,00,000	(1,00,000)
Less: Tax @ 30 %	(1,20,000)	(90,000)	(60,000)	(30,000)	30,000
Earning after Tax	2,80,000	2,10,000	1,40,000	70,000	(70,000)
Add: Depreciation	1,00,000	1,00,000	1,00,000	100,000	1,00,000
Cash Flow after Taxes (CFAT)	3,80,000	3,10,000	2,40,000	1,70,000	30,000
Add: Release of Working Capital					3,00,000
Add: Cash Salvage Value of Asset.					1,20,000

Less: Tax on Profit on Sale [30% of ₹ 20,000 (i.e. ₹ 1,20,000 – ₹ 1,00,000)]						(6,000)
Total CFAT for the last year						4,44,000

Note: *Assuming that the company has taxable income from other sources against which such loss can be set off, there will be tax saving on negative EBT.*

Step 1: *Calculation of Fake Pay Back Period*

$$\text{Fake Pay Back Period} = \frac{\text{Cash Outflow}}{\text{Average Annual Cash Inflow}}$$

$$= 9,00,000/[(3,80,000 + 3,10,000 + 2,40,000 + 1,70,000 + 4,44,000)/5]$$

$$= 2.915$$

Step 2: *Finding out two discount factors within which the above fake pay back period lies from the present value table = 2.926 and 2.864*

Step 3: *Finding out two discount rates corresponding to these above discount factors from the top row of the present value table = 21 % and 22 %*

Step 4: *Calculating the NPV at both the discount rates so as to have one negative NPV and one positive NPV.*

After applying discount rate of 21 % we get positive NPV of ₹ 11,744 now to have negative NPV we apply a higher rate of 22 % and we get negative NPV of ₹ 6,890.

STATEMENT SHOWING NET PRESENT VALUE OF MACHINE Z

Particulars	Year	Amount	PV factor at 29%	PV factor at 18%	PV at 18%	PV at 17%
Purchase Price New Machinery	0	(6,00,000)	1	1	(6,00,000)	(6,00,000)
Working Capital	0	(3,00,000)	1	1	(3,00,000)	(3,00,000)
CFAT for 1st year	1	3,80,000	0.826	0.820	3,13,880	3,11,600
CFAT for 2nd year	2	3,10,000	0.683	0.672	2,11,730	2,08,320
CFAT for 3rd year	3	2,40,000	0.564	0.551	1,35,360	1,32,240
CFAT for 4th year	4	1,70,000	0.467	0.451	79,390	76,670
CFAT for 5th year	5	4,44,000	0.386	0.370	1,71,384	1,64,280
NPV					11,744	(6,890)

$$\text{IRR} = \text{Lower Rate} + \frac{\text{NPV at Lower Rate}}{\text{NPV at Lower Rate} - \text{NPV at Higher Rate}} \times (\text{Higher rate} - \text{Lower rate})$$

$$= 21\% + \times (22 - 21)$$

$$= 21 + 0.630 (1)$$

$$= 21.630\%$$

Recommendation: Machine Z should be purchased since Machine Z has the highest IRR of 21.63%.

14.0 WHY IS THERE CONFLICT IN CHOICE OF MUTUALLY EXCLUSIVE PROJECTS BY USING NPV AND IRR CRITERION?

The conflict between NPV and IRR criterion in case of mutually exclusive projects situation arises due to:

(a) difference in estimated cash outflows of the projects
(b) difference in timings of cash flows of the projects
(c) difference in expected lives of the projects
(d) difference in Re-investment Rate Assumption.

NPV assumes that intermediate cash flows are reinvested at k (i.e., Cost of Capital) but IRR assumes that intermediate cash flows are reinvested at r (i.e., Internal Rate of Return). It is obvious that re-investment of funds at the cut-off rate is more possible than at the internal rate of return which at times may be very high. Moreover, net present value method also takes into account the scale of investment. Hence the net present value method using a fixed cut off rate is more reliable in ranking two *or* more projects than internal rate of return.

15.0 WHICH CRITERIA SHOULD BE USED WHEN THERE IS CONFLICT IN CHOICE OF MUTUALLY EXCLUSIVE PROJECTS BY USING NPV AND IRR CRITERION?

(a) **In case of Projects having unequal lives, 'Annualized NPV'** criterion should be used and the project having higher Annualized NPV (based on Cash Inflow) *or* lower Annualized NPV (based on Cash Outflow) should be selected.

$$\text{Annualized NPV} = \frac{\text{NPV}}{\text{Cumulative Present Value of ₹ 1 p.a. @ Cost of Capital for life of the project}}$$

(b) **In case of other projects** the project having higher NPV should be selected since NPV criterion (which selects the project giving higher return in absolute terms) is consistent with the objective of wealth maximization of shareholders.

ILLUSTRATION 39

The cash flows of two mutually exclusive Projects are as under:

Particulars	t_0	t_1	t_2	t_3	t_4	t_5	t_6
Project 'P' (₹)	(40,000)	13,000	8,000	14,000	12,000	11,000	15,000
Project 'J' (₹)	(20,000)	7,000	13,000	12,000	–	–	–

Required:

(i) Estimate the Net Present Value (NPV) of the Project 'P' and 'J' using 15% as the hurdle rate.
(ii) Estimate the Internal Rate of Return (IRR) of the Project 'P' and 'J'.
(iii) Why there is a conflict in the project choice by using NPV and IRR criterion?
(iv) Which criteria you will use in such a situation? Estimate the value at that criterion. Make a project choice.

The present value interest factor values at different rates of discount are as under:

Rate of Discount	t_0	t_1	t_2	t_3	t_4	t_5	t_6
0.15	1.00	0.8696	0.7561	0.6575	0.5718	0.4972	0.4323
0.18	1.00	0.8475	0.7182	0.6086	0.5158	0.4371	0.3704
0.20	1.00	0.8333	0.6944	0.5787	0.4823	0.4019	0.3349
0.24	1.00	0.8065	0.6504	0.5245	0.4230	0.3411	0.2751
0.26	1.00	0.7937	0.6299	0.4999	0.3968	0.3149	0.2499

SOLUTION

(I) CALCULATION OF NPV

Year	PVF @ 15%	Project P		Project J	
		Cash Flow	PV at 15%	Cash Flow	PV at 15%
0	1	(40,000)	(40,000.00)	(20,000)	(20,000.00)
1	0.8696	13,000	11,304.80	7,000	6,087.20
2	0.7561	8,000	6,048.80	13,000	9,829.30
3	0.6575	14,000	9,205.00	12,000	7,890.00
4	0.5718	12,000	6,861.60		
5	0.4972	11,000	5,469.20		
6	0.4323	15,000	6,484.50		
NPV			5,373.90		3,806.50

(ii) Calculation of IRR

Project P

Step 1: *Average Annual Cash Inflow*

= (13,000 + 8,000 + 14,000 + 12,000 + 11,000 + 15,000)/6 = ₹ 12,167

Step 2: *Fake Payback Period* $= \frac{\text{Cash Outflow}}{\text{Average Annual Cash Inflow}} = \frac{₹\,40{,}000}{₹\,12{,}167} = 3.288$

Step 3: *Discount factors corresponding to 3.288 are 20% and 21%*

Step 4: *NPV at 20% and 19%*

Year	Cash Flow	PVF @ 20%	PV at 20%	PVF @ 19%	PV at 19%
0	(40,000)	1.0000	(40,000.00)	1.0000	(40,000.00)
1	13,000	0.8333	10,832.90	0.8403	10,923.90
2	8,000	0.6944	5,555.20	0.7062	5,649.60
3	14,000	0.5787	8,101.80	0.5934	8,307.60
4	12,000	0.4823	5,787.60	0.4987	5,984.40
5	11,000	0.4019	4,420.90	0.4190	4,609.00
6	15,000	0.3349	5,023.50	0.3521	5,281.50
NPV			(278.10)		756.00

$$\text{IRR} = \text{Lower Discount Rate} + \frac{\textit{NPV at Lower Rate}}{\textit{NPV at Lower Rate} - \textit{NPV at Higher Rate}} \times (\text{HDR} - \text{LDR})$$

$$= 19\% + \frac{₹\,756}{₹\,756 - (-₹\,278.1)} \times (20\% - 19\%) = 19.73\%$$

Project 'J'

Step 1: *Average Annual Cash Inflow*

= (₹ 7,000 + ₹ 13,000 + ₹ 12,000)/3 = ₹ 10,667

Step 2: *Fake Payback Period* $= \frac{\textit{Cash Outflow}}{\textit{Average Annual Cash Inflow}} = \frac{₹\,20{,}000}{₹\,10{,}667} = 1.8749$

Step 3: *Discount factors corresponding to 1.8749 are 27% and 28%*

Step 4: *NPV at 27%, 26% and 25%*

Year	Cash Flow	PVF @ 27%	PV at 27%	PVF @ 26%	PV at 26%	PVF @ 25%	PV at 25%
0	(20,000)	1.0000	(20,000.00)	1.0000	(20,000.00)	1.000	(20,000.00)
1	7,000	0.7874	5,511.80	0.7937	5,555.90	0.800	5,600.00
2	13,000	0.6200	8,060.00	0.6299	8,188.70	0.640	8,320.00
3	12,000	0.4882	5,858.40	0.4999	5,998.80	0.512	6,144.00
NPV			(569.80)		(256.60)		64.00

$$IRR = Lower\ Discount\ Rate + \frac{NPV\ at\ Lower\ Rate}{NPV\ at\ Lower\ Rate - NPV\ at\ Higher\ Rate} \times (HDR - LDR)$$

$$= 25\% + ₹\ 64₹\ 64 - (-₹\ 256.6)\ (26\% - 25\%) = 25.20\%$$

(iii) The conflict between NPV and IRR rule in the case of mutually exclusive project situation arises due to re-investment rate assumption. NPV rule assumes that intermediate cash flows are reinvested at k and IRR assumes that they are reinvested at r. The assumption of NPV rule is more realistic.

(iv) When there is a conflict in the choice out of projects having unequal lives by using NPV and IRR criterion, one should prefer to use "Equal Annualized Criterion". According to this criterion the Annualized NPV in the case of Projects 'P' and 'J' respectively would be:

Annualized NPV = (Net Present Value/cumulative present value of ₹ 1 p.a. @15% for 6/3 years)

Project 'P' = (₹ 5,373.90/3.7845) = ₹ 1420

Project 'J' = (₹ 3,806.50/2.2832) = ₹ 1,667

Recommendation: Since the Annualized NPV in the case of Project 'J' is more than that of Project 'P', so Project J is recommended.

16.0 PROFITABILITY INDEX/DESIRABILITY FACTOR (PI)

WHAT IS PROFITABILITY INDEX?

(a) Profitability Index/Desirability Factor technique is one of the discounted cash flow techniques, which takes into account the time value of money.

(b) Profitability Index/Desirability Factor refers to the ratio of the present value of all cash inflows to the present value of all cash outflows associated with the project.

(c) The present value is ascertained using the firm's cost of capital as the discount rate.

HOW TO COMPUTE PROFITABILITY INDEX?

The calculation of Profitability Index/Desirability Factor involves the following practical steps:

Step 1: *Calculate all the Cash Outflows associated with the project.*

Step 2: *Calculate all the Cash Inflows associated with the project.*

Step 3: *Calculate the Present Value of all Cash Outflows associated with the project.*

Step 4: *Calculate the Present Value of all Cash Inflows associated with the project.*

Step 5: *Calculate Profitability Index/Desirability Factor as follows:*

$$Profitability\ Index\ (PI) = \frac{Present\ Value\ of\ all\ Cash\ Inflows}{Present\ Value\ of\ all\ Cash\ Outflows}$$

OR

$$= \frac{\left[\frac{CI_1}{(1+k)^1} + \frac{CI_2}{(1+k)^2} + \frac{+CI_3}{(1+k)^3} + ... + \frac{CI_n}{(1+k)^n}\right]}{\left[\frac{CO_1}{(1+k)^1} + \frac{CO_2}{(1+k)^2} + \frac{CO_3}{(1+k)^3} + ... + \frac{CO_n}{(1+k)^n}\right]}$$

CI_1, CI_2, CI_3 ... = *Cash Inflows in different periods*

CO_1, CO_2, CO_3 ... = *Cash Outflows in different periods*

k = *Firm's Cost of Capital used as discount rate*

n = *Expected Life of the project.*

WHAT IS ACCEPT/REJECT RULE?

(a) Independent Projects	Accept the project if PI > 1, Reject the project if PI < 1 If PI = 1, the management would be indifferent as to whether to accept/reject the project.
(b) Mutually Exclusive Projects	Mutually Exclusive Projects having same Net Present Value should be ranked in the order of PI and the project with highest PI should be selected.

HOW TO INTERPRET PROFITABILITY INDEX?

PI may be interpreted as the amount of cash inflow available per rupee of cash outflow.

USES OF PROFITABILITY INDEX

PI is useful in selection of:

(a) Mutually Exclusive Projects having the same Net Present Value.

(b) Divisible Projects [where all cash outflows are made today (i.e., at zero period)] under Capital Rationing.

CONFLICT IN PROJECT CHOICE USING PI AND NPV CRITERION

The conflict in project choice using PI and NPV criterion arises in case of mutually exclusive projects of unequal investment size having different net present values because NPV gives ranking on the basis of absolute amount whereas PI gives ranking on the basis of ratio. In such a case, mutually exclusive project having the highest NPV should be selected since it would increase the firm's wealth if the project is accepted which is consistent with the wealth maximisation objective of financial management.

WHAT ARE THE MERITS AND DEMERITS OF PROFITABILITY INDEX?

The merits and demerits of PI are as follows:

Merits	Demerits
1. It considers the time value of money.	1. It requires the estimation of cash inflows and cash outflows, which is a difficult task.
2. It considers entire cash flows over entire life of the project.	2. It requires the computation of the cost of capital to be used as discount rate.
3. It is a relative measure of profitability since the ratio of cash inflows to cash outflows is considered.	3. It may not provide satisfactory results in case of- (a) Projects involving different amounts of cash outflows. (b) Projects having different lives.

4. It guides in resolving capital rationing where projects are divisible. 5. It guides the selection of Mutually Exclusive Projects having same Net Present Value.	(c) Projects involving different amounts of cash outflows and having different lives. 4. The ranking of projects depends upon the discount rate. 5. It ignores the difference in initial cash outflows, size of different projects, etc. while evaluating mutually exclusive projects. 6. It fails to guide in resolving capital rationing where projects are indivisible. 7. It ignores the absolute amount of NPV while taking decision. A project having lower PI but higher absolute NPV may be rejected although it increases the shareholders' wealth. 8. It is not consistent with the objective of maximizing the wealth of owners since PI may not be interpreted as immediate increase in firm's wealth if the project is accepted.

ILLUSTRATION 40

From the following information, which project should be accepted on Profitability Index basis

Particulars	Project A	Project B	Project C
Present Value of Cash Inflows	1,00,000	2,00,000	3,00,000
Present value of Cash Outflow	20,000	50,000	1,00,000

SOLUTION

Particulars	Project A	Project B	Project C
Profitability Index (PI) = $\frac{\text{Present Value of all Cash Inflows}}{\text{Present Value of all Cash Outflows}}$	$\frac{1,00,000}{20,000}$	$\frac{2,00,000}{50,000}$	$\frac{3,00,000}{1,00,000}$
Profitability Index	= 5	= 4	= 3.33

Advise: Project A should be accepted because of highest PI.

ILLUSTRATION 41

Tulsian Ltd. provides you the following information:

1. Purchase Price of each Machine	₹ 6,00,000
2. Working Capital	₹ 3,00,000
3. Useful Life of each machine	5 years
4. Estimated Salvage Value at the end of useful life	₹ 1,00,000
5. Cash Salvage Value at the end of useful life	₹ 1,20,000
6. Method of Depreciation	Straight line
7. Tax Rate	30%
8. Cost of Capital	10%
9. Earning before depreciation & tax:	

Machine	Year 1	Year 2	Year 3	Year 4	Year 5
Machine X	3,00,000	3,00,000	3,00,000	3,00,000	3,00,000
Machine Y	–	1,00,000	2,00,000	3,00,000	12,00,000
Machine Z	5,00,000	4,00,000	3,00,000	2,00,000	–

Required: Which of the above machines should be purchased on the basis of Net Present Value.

Note: *Present Value Factors @ 10% are as follows:*

Year	Year 1	Year 2	Year 3	Year 4	Year 5
Present Value Factor	0.909	0.826	0.751	0.683	0.621

SOLUTION

STATEMENT SHOWING THE COMPUTATION OF CASH INFLOW AFTER TAX OF MACHINE X

Particulars	Year 1	Year 2	Year 3	Year 4	Year 5
Earning before depreciation & tax	3,00,000	3,00,000	3,00,000	3,00,000	3,00,000
Less: Depreciation	(1,00,000)	(1,00,000)	(1,00,000)	(1,00,000)	(1,00,000)
Earning before Tax	2,00,000	2,00,000	2,00,000	2,00,000	2,00,000
Less: Tax @ 30 %	(60,000)	(60,000)	(60,000)	(60,000)	(60,000)
Earning after Tax	1,40,000	1,40,000	1,40,000	1,40,000	1,40,000
Add: Depreciation	1,00,000	1,00,000	1,00,000	1,00,000	1,00,000
Cash Flow after Taxes(CFAT)	2,40,000	2,40,000	2,40,000	2,40,000	2,40,000
Add: Release of Working Capital					3,00,000
Add: Actual Salvage Value of Asset.					1,20,000
Less: Tax on Ordinary Profit on Sale [30% of ₹ 20,000 (i.e. ₹ 1,20,000 – ₹ 1,00,000)]					(6,000)
Total CFAT for the last year					6,54,000

STATEMENT SHOWING THE COMPUTATION OF CASH INFLOW AFTER TAX OF MACHINE Y

Particulars	Year 1	Year 2	Year 3	Year 4	Year 5
Earning before depreciation & tax	–	1,00,000	2,00,000	3,00,000	12,00,000
Less: Depreciation	(1,00,000)	(1,00,000)	(1,00,000)	(1,00,000)	(1,00,000)
Earning before Tax	(1,00,000)	–	1,00,000	2,00,000	11,00,000
Less: Tax @ 30 %	30,000	–	(30,000)	(60,000)	(3,30,000)
Earning after Tax	(70,000)	–	70,000	1,40,000	7,70,000
Add: Depreciation	1,00,000	1,00,000	1,00,000	1,00,000	1,00,000
Cash Flow after Taxes(CFAT)	30,000	1,00,000	1,70,000	2,40,000	8,70,000
Add: Release of Working Capital					3,00,000
Add: Cash Salvage Value of Asset.					1,20,000
Less: Tax on Profit on Sale [30% of ₹ 20,000 (i.e. ₹ 1,20,000 – ₹ 1,00,000)]					(6,000)

Total CFAT for the last year					12,84,000

Note: *Assuming that the company has taxable income from other sources against which such loss can be set off, there will be tax saving on negative EBT.*

STATEMENT SHOWING COMPUTATION OF CASH INFLOW AFTER TAX OF MACHINE Z

Particulars	Year 1	Year 2	Year 3	Year 4	Year 5
Earning before depreciation & tax	5,00,000	4,00,000	3,00,000	2,00,000	–
Less: Depreciation	(1,00,000)	(1,00,000)	(1,00,000)	(1,00,000)	(1,00,000)
Earning before Tax	4,00,000	3,00,000	2,00,000	1,00,000	(1,00,000)
Less: Tax @ 30 %	(1,20,000)	(90,000)	(60,000)	(30,000)	30,000
Earning after Tax	2,80,000	2,10,000	1,40,000	70,000	(70,000)
Add: Depreciation	1,00,000	1,00,000	1,00,000	1,00,000	1,00,000
Cash Flow after Taxes(CFAT)	3,80,000	3,10,000	2,40,000	1,70,000	30,000
Add: Release of Working Capital					3,00,000
Add: Cash Salvage Value of Asset.					1,20,000
Less: Tax on Profit on Sale [30% of ₹ 20,000 (i.e. ₹ 1,20,000 – ₹ 1,00,000)]					(6,000)
Total CFAT for the last year					4,44,000

Note: *Assuming that the company has taxable income from other sources against which such loss can be set off, there will be tax saving on negative EBT.*

STATEMENT SHOWING NET PRESENT VALUE

Particulars	Year	PV factor	Machine X		Machine Y		Machine Z	
			Amount	PV	Amount	PV	Amount	PV
Purchase Price of New Machinery	0	1	(6,00,000)	(6,00,000)	(6,00,000)	(6,00,000)	(6,00,000)	(6,00,000)
Working Capital	0	1	(3,00,000)	(3,00,000)	(3,00,000)	(3,00,000)	(3,00,000)	(3,00,000)
Total PV of Cash Outflow				9,00,000		9,00,000		9,00,000
CFAT for 1st year	1	0.909	2,40,000	2,18,160	30,000	27,270	3,80,000	3,45,420
CFAT for 2nd year	2	0.826	2,40,000	1,98,240	1,00,000	82,600	3,10,000	2,56,060
CFAT for 3rd year	3	0.751	2,40,000	1,80,240	1,70,000	1,27,670	2,40,000	1,80,240
CFAT for 4th year	4	0.683	2,40,000	1,63,920	2,40,000	1,63,920	1,70,000	1,16,110
CFAT for 5th year	5	0.621	6,54,000	4,06,134	12,84,000	7,97,364	4,44,000	2,75,724
Total PV of Cash Inflow				11,66,694		11,98,824		11,73,554

$$\text{Profitability Index (PI)} = \frac{\text{PV of all Cash Inflows}}{\text{PV of all Cash Outflows}} = \frac{11,66,694}{9,00,000} \qquad = \frac{11,98,824}{9,00,000} \qquad = \frac{11,73,554}{9,00,000}$$

$$= 1.296 \qquad = 1.332 \qquad = 1.304$$

Recommendation: Machine Y should be purchased since Machine Y has the highest PI of 1.332.

17.0 REPLACEMENT DECISION (i.e. DECISION WHETHER TO RETAIN OR REPLACE THE EXISTING MACHINE)

REPLACEMENT DECISION IN CASE THE REMAINING USEFUL LIFE OF THE EXISTING MACHINE AND THE USEFUL LIFE OF THE NEW MACHINE ARE SAME

In such a case Incremental Approach should be adopted as follows:

Step 1: *Calculate Incremental Contribution as follows:*

Particulars	Existing Machine	Machine New	Incremental (New – Old)
A. Units Produced	xxx	xxx	
B. Selling Price per unit	xxx	xxx	
C. *Less:* Direct Material Cost per unit	(xxx)	(xxx)	
D *Less:* Direct Labour Cost per unit	(xxx)	(xxx)	
E. *Less:* Variable Overheads per unit	(xxx)	(xxx)	
F. Contribution per unit [B – C – D – E]	xxx	xxx	
G. Total Contribution [A × F]	xxx	xxx	xxx

Step 2: *Calculate Incremental Depreciation (assuming Straight Line Method of Depreciation)*

Particulars	Existing Machine	Machine New	Incremental (New – Old)
A. Cost of Machine	xxx	xxx	
B. Freight, Carriage & Installation Exp.	xxx	xxx	
C. Workers' Training Expenses	xxx	xxx	
D. *Less:* Subsidy from Govt.	(xxx)	(xxx)	
E. *Less:* Estimated Salvage Value	(xxx)	(xxx)	
F. Depreciable Amount [A + B + C – D – E]	xxx	xxx	
G. Useful Life (Years)	xxx	xxx	
H. Depreciation [F/G]	xxx	xxx	xxx

Note: *In case of any other method of depreciation (say Written Down Value), depreciation should be calculated accordingly.*

Step 3: *Calculate Incremental Salvage Value and Tax Advantage*

Particulars	Existing Machine	Machine New	Incremental (New – Old)
A. Book Value at the end Useful Life	xxx	xxx	
B. *Less:* Cash Salvage Value at the end of Useful Life	(xxx)	(xxx)	xxx
C. Short Term Capital Loss (Gain) [A – B]	xxx	xxx	
D. Tax on Loss (Profit) [C × Tax Rate]	xxx	xxx	xxx

Step 4: *Calculate Incremental Cash Outflow*

Particulars	Amount
A. Purchase Price of New Machine	xxx
B. Freight, Carriage & Installation Expenses	xxx

C.	Workers' Training Expenses	xxx
D.	*Less:* Subsidy from Govt.	(xxx)
E.	Incremental Working Capital	xxx
F.	*Less:* Net Sale Proceeds of Existing Machine (Current Realizable Value – Disposal Charges)	(xxx)
G.	*Less:* Tax Saving on Loss on Sale of Existing Machine (Book Value – Net Current Realizable Value)	(xxx)
	or	
	Add: Tax on Profit on Sale of Existing Machine (Net Current Realizable Value – Book Value)	xxx
H.	Incremental Cash Outflow	xxx

REPLACEMENT DECISION IN CASE THE REMAINING USEFUL LIFE OF THE EXISTING MACHINE AND THE USEFUL LIFE OF THE NEW MACHINE ARE DIFFERENT

In such a case Annualised Present Value Approach should be adopted as per para 12.0

WORTH NOTING POINTS TO BE KEPT IN MIND WHILE TAKING REPLACEMENT DECISION

At the time of taking the decision whether to retain *or* replace the existing machine, the following points should be kept in mind:

Item	How to Treat
1. Consultant' s Fees as to study the problem of Retain *or* Replace.	Treat as sunk cost since it is bound to occur whether the existing machine is retained *or* replaced.
2. Allocation of Fixed Overheads from other Departments	Treat as irrelevant cost since it does not affect the decision to retain *or* replace
3. Undepreciated Book Value of Existing Machine.	Treat as irrelevant cost since it does not affect the decision to retain *or* replace.
4. Loss on Sale of Existing Machine.	Treat as irrelevant cost since it does not affect the decision to retain *or* replace.
5. Tax Saving on Loss on Sale of Existing Machine.	Treat as Cash Inflow
6. Market Value of Existing Machine.	Treat as Cash Inflow if its Current Market Value is more than the Exchange Value offered by supplier of New Machine.
7. Exchange Value offered by Suppliers of New Machine	Treat as Cash Inflow if Exchange Value is more than the Current Market value of the existing machine
8. Cost of Disposal and Dismantling the Existing Machine.	Treat as Cash Outflow
9. Release of Working Capital on Sale of Existing Machine.	Treat as Cash Inflow
10. Cost of New Machine.	Treat as Cash Outflow
11. Expenses on Freight, Carriage & Installation of New Machine.	Treat as Cash Outflow

12. Expenses on Training of Workers for New Machine.	Treat as Cash Outflow
13. Working Capital required if New Machine is Installed.	Treat as Cash Outflow
14. Retrenchment Compensation	Treat as Cash Outflow
15. Tax saving on Retrenchment Compensation (if it is given that Retrenchment compensation is deductible for tax)	Treat as Cash Inflow

PAY BACK PERIOD OF THE REPLACEMENT DECISION

= Year upto which CumulativeIncremental CFAT is *less* thanIncremental Cash Outflow

+

$$\frac{\text{Incremental Cash Outflow – Cumulative Incremental Cash Inflow for the year in which Cumulative Incremental Cash Inflow is less than Incremental Cash Outflow}}{\text{Incremental Cash Inflow for the next year following the year for which CumulativeIncremental Cash Inflows were considered in numerator}}$$

DISCOUNTED PAY BACK PERIOD OF THE REPLACEMENT DECISION

= Year upto which Cumulative PVof Incremental CFAT is *less* than PV of Incremental Cash Outflow

+

$$\frac{\text{PV of Incremental Cash Outflow – Cumulative PV of Incremental Cash Inflow for the year in which Cumulative PV of Incremental Cash Inflow is less than PV of Incremental Cash Outflow}}{\text{PV of Incremental Cash Inflow for the next year following the year for which Cumulative PV of Incremental Cash Inflow was considered in nummerator}}$$

NET PRESENT VALUE OF THE REPLACEMENT DECISION

= Total PV of Incremental Cash Inflow – Total PV of Incremental Cash Outflow

INTERNAL RATE OF RETURN (IRR) OF THE REPLACEMENT DECISION

IRR of the Replacement Decision is that rate at which PV of Incremental Cash Outflow becomes equal to PV of Incremental Cash Inflow. In other words, it is the rate at which NPV of Incremental Cash flows is zero. It may be calculated as under:

IRR of the Replacement Decision

$$= \text{Lower Rate} + \frac{\text{NPV at Lower Rate}}{\text{NPV at Lower Rate} - \text{NPV at Higher Rate}} \times (\text{Higher rate} - \text{Lower rate})$$

PROFITABILITY INDEX (PI) OF REPLACEMENT DECISION

PI of the Replacement Decision is the ratio of Total PV of Incremental cash Inflows to Total PV of Incremental Cash Outflows.

PI of Replacement Decision $= \dfrac{\text{Total PV of Incremental Cash Inflows}}{\text{Total PV of Incremental Cash Outflows}}$

ILLUSTRATION 42

Tulsian Ltd. is considering the replacement of its existing machine by the new one. A consultant who has charged a fee of ₹ 25,000 supplies the following information in this regard:

Particulars	Existing Machine	New Machine
1. Annual Output	8,000	10,000
2. Variable Cost per unit	₹ 60	₹ 52

3. Fixed Overheads per unit (Allocations from other Departments)	₹ 3	₹ 2.4
4. Selling Price per unit	₹ 100	₹ 120
5. Book Value of Existing Machine (Purchased 3 years ago)	₹ 2,52,000	
6. Cost of New Machine		₹ 3,80,000
7. Useful Life	8 years	5 years
8. Installation Exp.		₹ 30,000
9. Book Value at the end of useful Life.	₹ 2,000	₹ 10,000
10. Cash Salvage Value at the end of useful Life.	₹ 1,500	₹ 15,000
11. Current Realizable Value	₹ 10,600	
12. Cost of Dismantling & Removal	₹ 600	
13. Working Capital required	₹ 40,000	₹ 1,00,000

Other Information:

Method of Depreciation: Straight Line Method

Rate on Income Tax: 30 %

Company's Cost of Capital: 10 %

Exchange Value of Old Machine offered by Suppliers of New Machine: ₹ 9,000

Annuity Factor @ 10% for 5 and 8 years are ₹ 3.791 and ₹ 5.335 respectively.

PV Factor @ 10 % for 5th and 8th year are ₹ 0.621 and ₹ 0.467 respectively.

Particulars	Year 1	Year 2	Year 3	Year 4	Year 5
Present Value Factors @ 60%	0.625	0.391	0.244	0.153	0.095
Present Value Factors @ 65%	0.606	0.367	0.223	0.135	0.082

Required: Should the Company replace the existing machine?

SOLUTION

(A) CALCULATION OF INCREMENTAL CASH INFLOW AFTER TAXES (CFAT)

Particulars	₹
A. Incremental Contribution	3,60,000
B. *Less:* Incremental Depreciation	(30,000)
C. *Less:* Incremental Cash Fixed Cost	
D. Incremental Earning before Tax	3,30,000
E. *Less:* Tax @ 30%	(99,000)
F. Incremental Earning after Tax	2,31,000
G. *Add:* Incremental Depreciation	30,000
H. Incremental Cash Flow after Taxes (CFAT) (for years other than last year)	2,61,000
I. *Add:* Release of Incremental Working Capital	60,000
J. *Add:* Incremental Cash Salvage Value at the end of Useful Life	13,500
K. *Less:* Incremental Tax	(1,650)
L. Total Incremental CFAT for the last year	3,32,850

STATEMENT SHOWING THE INCREMENTAL NET PRESENT VALUE

Particulars	Year	PV factor at 10%	Amount	PV
Purchase Price of New Machine	0	1	(3,80,000)	(3,80,000)
Freight, Carriage & Installation Exp.	0	1	(30,000)	(30,000)
Incremental Working Capital	0	1	(60,000)	(60,000)
Net Sale Proceeds of Existing Machine (₹ 10,600 – ₹ 600)	0	1	10,000	10,000
Tax saving on Loss on Sale of existing machine 30% of ₹.2,42,000 (₹ 2,52,000 – ₹ 10,000)	0	1	72,600	72,600
Incremental CFAT for 1 – 4 years	1 to 4	3.170	2,61,000	8,27,370
Incremental CFAT for 5th year	5	0.621	3,32,850	2,06,700
Incremental NPV				6,46,670

Recommendation: The New Machine should be purchased since the NPV is positive.

Working Notes:

1. CALCULATION OF INCREMENTAL CONTRIBUTION

Particulars	Existing Machine	New Machine	Incremental (New – Old)
A. Units Produced	8,000	10,000	
B. Selling Price per unit	100	120	
C. *Less:* Variable Cost per unit (Qty × Rate)	(10)	(12)	
D. Contribution per unit [B – C]	40	68	
E. Total Contribution (A × D)	3,20,000	6,80,000	3,60,000

2. CALCULATION OF INCREMENTAL DEPRECIATION

Particulars	Existing Machine	New Machine	Incremental (New – Old)
A. Book Value/Cost of Machine	2,52,000	3,80,000	
B. *Add:* Installation Exp.		30,000	
C. *Less:* Estimated Salvage Value	(2,000)	(10,000)	
D. Depreciable Amount [A + B – C]	2,50,000	4,00,000	
E. Useful Life	5 yrs	5 yrs	
F. Depreciation [D/E]	50,000	80,000	30,000

3. CALCULATION OF INCREMENTAL SALVAGE VALUE AND TAX ADVANTAGE

Particulars	Existing Machine	New Machine	Incremental (New – Old)
A. Book Value at the end of useful life	2,000	10,000	
B. *Less:* Cash Salvage Value at the end of useful life	(1,500)	(15,000)	(13,500)
C. Short Term Capital Loss (Gain)	500	(5,000)	
D. Tax on Loss (Profit) @ 30 %	150	(1,500)	(1,650)

(iv) Consultant's fees has been treated as sunk cost.

(v) Since the fixed overheads are allocation from other departments, differential fixed overheads other than depreciation are irrelevant.

(vi) Exchange Value of old machine offered by Suppliers of New Machine is irrelevant since the current realizable value (i.e., ₹ 10,600) is more than the exchange value (i.e., ₹ 9,000).

ILLUSTRATION 43

CAMIJ Ltd. is considering the replacement of its existing machine by the new one. A consultant who has charged a fee of ₹ 25,000 supplies the following information in that regard:

New Machine:	
Cost Price	₹ 25 Lakh
Installation Charges	₹ 10,000
Useful Life	10 years
Book Value at the end of useful life	₹ 20,000
Disposal Value at the end of the useful life	₹ 10,000
Annual Saving in running expenses	₹ 10 Lakh
Additional Working Capital	₹ 35,000
Worker's Training Expenses	₹ 5,000
Existing Machine:	
Current Book Value	₹ 5 Lakh
Current Market Value	₹ 4.10 Lakh
Disposal Charges	₹ 10,000
Remaining Useful Life (no salvage value at the end)	10 years
Other Information:	
Income Tax Rate	30%
Cost of Capital	20%
Annuity Factor for 10 years @ 20%	4.193
Present Value Factor for 10th year @ 20%	0.162

Required: Advise the company whether to replace the existing machine *or* not.

SOLUTION

CALCULATION OF INCREMENTAL CASH INFLOW AFTER TAXES (CFAT)

Particulars	Amount
A. Total Saving in Running Expenses	10,00,000
B. *Less:* Incremental Depreciation	(1,99,500)
C. Incremental Earning before Tax	8,00,500
D. *Less:* Tax @ 30%	(2,40,150)
E. Incremental Earning after Tax	5,60,350
F. *Add:* Incremental Depreciation	1,99,500
G. Incremental Cash Flow after Taxes (CFAT) (for years other than last year)	7,59,850

H. *Add:* Release of Additional Working Capital	35,000
I. *Add:* Incremental Cash Salvage Value at the end of Useful Life	10,000
J. *Add:* Incremental Tax Advantage	3,000
K. Total Incremental CFAT for the last year	8,07,850

STATEMENT SHOWING INCREMENTAL NET PRESENT VALUE

Particulars	Year	PV factor at 20%	Amount ₹	PV at 20% ₹
Purchase Price	0	1	(25,00,000)	(25,00,000)
Installation Expenses	0	1	(10,000)	(10,000)
Workers' Training Expenses	0	1	(5,000)	(5,000)
Incremental Working Capital	0	1	(35,000)	(35,000)
Net Sale Proceeds of Existing Machine (₹ 4,10,000 – ₹ 10,000)	0	1	4,00,000	4,00,000
Tax saving on Loss on Sale of existing machine 30% of ₹.100,000 (₹ 5,00,000 – ₹ 4,00,000)	0	1	30,000	30,000
Incremental CFAT for 1 – 9 years	1 to 9	4.031	7,59,850	30,62,955
Incremental CFAT for 10th year	10	0.162	8,07,850	1,30,872
Incremental NPV				10,73,827

Recommendation: The New Machine should be purchased since the NPV is positive.

Working Notes:

1. CALCULATION OF INCREMENTAL DEPRECIATION

Particulars	Existing Machine	New Machine	Incremental (New – Old)
Cost of Machine	5,00,000	25,00,000	
Installation Expenses		10,000	
Workers' Training Expenses		5,000	
Estimated Salvage Value	–	(20,000)	
Depreciable Amount	5,00,000	24,95,000	
Useful Life	10 yrs	10 yrs	
Depreciation	50,000	2,49,500	1,99,500

2. CALCULATION OF INCREMENTAL TAX ADVANTAGE

Particulars	Existing Machine	New Machine	Incremental (New – Old)
Book Value at the end	–	20,000	
Less: Cash Salvage Value	–	(10,000)	(10,000)
Short Term Capital Loss (Gain)	–	10,000	
Tax on Loss (Profit) @ 30 %	–	3,000	3,000

(iii) Consultant's fees has been treated as sunk cost.

ILLUSTRATION 44

BS Electronics is considering a proposal to replace one of its existing machine by the new one. In this connection, the following information is available:

The Existing Machine was bought 3 years ago for ₹ 10 Lakh. It was depreciated on straight line basis. It has a remaining life of 5 years, but its maintenance cost is expected to increase by ₹ 50,000 p.a. from the 6th year of its installation. Its present realisable value is ₹ 6 Lakh.

The New Machine costs ₹ 15 Lakh and is subject to the same rate of depreciation. On sale after 5 years, it is expected to ₹ 9 Lakh. With the New Machine, Operating Cost (excluding depreciation) are expected to decrease by ₹ 1,00,000 p.a. In addition, the speed of machine would increase productivity on account of which net revenues would increase by ₹ 1.5 Lakh p.a.

Other Information: The tax rate applicable is 30% and the cost of capital 10%.

Required: Advise the company whether to replace the existing machine *or* not on the basis of Net Present Value.

Note: *Present Value Factors @ 10% are as follows:*

Particulars	Year 1	Year 2	Year 3	Year 4	Year 5
Present Value Factor	0.909	0.826	0.751	0.683	0.621

SOLUTION

CALCULATION OF INCREMENTAL CASH INFLOW AFTER TAXES

Particulars	Year 1 to 2	Year 3 to 5
A. Increase in Revenue	1,50,000	1,50,000
B. Total Saving in Running Expenses	1,00,000	1,00,000
C. Total Saving in Maintenance Expenses	—	50,000
D. *Add:* Decrease in Depreciation	5,000	5,000
E. Incremental Earning before Tax	2,55,000	3,05,000
F. *Less:* Tax @ 30%	(76,500)	(91,500)
G. Incremental Earning after Tax	1,78,500	2,13,500
H. *Less:* Incremental Depreciation	(5,000)	(5,000)
I. Incremental Cash Flow after Taxes (CFAT)	1,73,500	2,08,500
J. *Add:* Salvage Value of Asset at the end of Useful Life	–	9,00,000
K. Total Incremental CFAT for the last year	1,73,500	11,08,500

STATEMENT SHOWING INCREMENTAL NET PRESENT VALUE

Particulars	Year	PV factor 10%	Amount ₹	PV at 10% ₹
Purchase Price	0	1	(15,00,000)	(15,00,000)
Net Sale Proceeds of Existing Machine	0	1	6,00,000	6,00,000
Tax saving on Loss on Sale of existing machine 30% of ₹ 25,000 (₹ 6,25,000 – ₹ 6,00,000)	0	1	7,500	7,500
Incremental CFAT for 1 – 2 years	1 & 2	1.735	1,73,500	3,01,023
Incremental CFAT for 3 – 4 years	3 & 4	1.434	2,08,500	2,98,989

Incremental CFAT for 5th year	5	0.621	11,08,500	6,88,379
Incremental NPV				3,95,891

Recommendation: The New Machine should be purchased since the NPV is positive.

Working Notes:

(I) CALCULATION OF INCREMENTAL DEPRECIATION

Particulars	Existing Machine	New Machine	Incremental (New – Old)
Cost of Machine	10,00,000	15,00,000	
Estimated Salvage Value	–	(9,00,000)	
Depreciable Amount	10,00,000	6,00,000	
Useful Life	8 yrs	5 yrs	
Depreciation	1,25,000	1,20,000	(5,000)

(ii) The expression 'Net Revenue would increase by ₹ 1.5 lakhs p.a.' has been interpreted as net of cost.

ILLUSTRATION 45

MP Ltd. manufactures a special chemical. It is thinking of replacing its existing machine by a new one, which would cost ₹ 25 Lakh.

The company's current production is 40,000 units and is expecting to increase to 50,000 units if the new machine is bought. The Selling price of the product would remain unchanged at ₹ 160 per unit. The following is the cost of producing one unit of product using both the existing and new machine:

Particular	Existing Machine	New Machine
Variable Cost	₹ 138.4	₹ 118.4
Fixed overheads (Depreciation & Allocated corporate overheads)	₹ 8.2	₹ 12.4

The existing machine has an accounting book value of ₹ 40,000 and it is fully depreciated for tax purpose. It has a remaining economic life of 5 years.

The supplier of the new machine has offered to accept the old machine in exchange for ₹ 1,00,000. However the market price of the existing machine today is ₹ 60,000 and ₹ 15,000 after 5 years. New Machine has a life of 5 years and a salvage value of ₹ 1,00,000 at the end of its economic life.

Assume that tax rate is 30 % and cost of capital is 20%.

Required: Advise the company whether to replace the existing machine *or* not on the basis of Net Present Value.

Note: *The present value of Annuity for 5 years @ 20% is 2.991 and the present value for 5th year is 0.402.*

SOLUTION

CALCULATION OF INCREMENTAL CASH INFLOW AFTER TAXES

Particulars	₹
A. Incremental Contribution	12,16,000
B. *Less:* Incremental Depreciation	(4,80,000)

C. Incremental Earning before Tax	7,36,000
D. *Less:* Tax @ 30%	(2,20,800)
E. Incremental Earning after Tax	5,15,200
F. *Add:* Incremental Depreciation	4,80,000
G. Incremental Cash Flow after Taxes (CFAT)(for years other than last year)	9,95,200
H. *Add:* Incremental Cash Salvage Value of Asset at the end of Useful Life	85,000
I. *Add:* Incremental Tax Advantage	4,500
J. Total Incremental CFAT for the last year	10,84,700

STATEMENT SHOWING INCREMENTAL NET PRESENT VALUE

Particulars	Year	PV factor at 20%	Amount ₹	PV at 20% ₹
Purchase Price	0	1	(25,00,000)	(25,00,000)
Net Sale Proceeds of Existing Machine	0	1	1,00,000	1,00,000
Tax on Sale of existing machine @ 30% of ₹ 1,00,000	0	1	(30,000)	(30,000)
Incremental CFAT for 1 – 4 years	1 to 4	2.589	9,95,200	25,76,573
Incremental CFAT for 5th year	5	0.402	10,84,700	4,36,049
Incremental NPV				5,82,622

Recommendation: The New Machine should be purchased since the NPV is positive.

Working Notes:

(I) CALCULATION OF INCREMENTAL CONTRIBUTION

Particulars	Existing Machine	New Machine	Incremental (New – Old)
A. Unit Produced	40,000	50,000	
B. Selling Price per unit	160	160	
C. Variable Cost per unit	(138.4)	(118.4)	
D. Contribution per unit	21.6	41.6	
E. Total Contribution (A × D)	8,64,000	20,80,000	12,16,000

(II) CALCULATION OF INCREMENTAL DEPRECIATION

Particulars	Existing Machine	New Machine	Incremental (New – Old)
Cost of Machine	–	25,00,000	
Estimated Salvage Value	–	(1,00,000)	
Depreciable Amount	–	24,00,000	
Useful Life	5 yrs	5 yrs	
Depreciation	–	4,80,000	4,80,000

(III) CALCULATION OF INCREMENTAL TAX ADVANTAGE

Particulars	Existing Machine	New Machine	Incremental (New – Old)
Book Value at the end	–	1,00,000	
Less: Cash Salvage Value	(15,000)	(1,00,000)	85,000
Profit on Sale	(15,000)	–	
Tax on Profit @ 30 %	(4,500)	–	4,500

(iv) Since the fixed overheads are allocation from other departments *plus* the depreciation of plant & machinery, differential fixed overheads other than depreciation are irrelevant.

ILLUSTRATION 46

Tulsian Ltd. is considering the replacement of its existing machine by the new one. A consultant who has charged a fee of ₹ 25,000 supplies the following information in this regard:

Particulars	Existing Machine	New Machine
1. Annual Machine Hours	8,000	5,000
2. Machine Hours required per unit	1 Hour	0.5 Hour
3. Material required per unit	5 kg	4 kg
4. Material Cost per kg.	₹ 2	₹ 3
5. Labour Hours required per unit	4 Hours	3 Hours
6. Labour Cost per unit	₹ 40	₹ 30
7. Variable Overheads per unit	₹ 10	₹ 10
8. Fixed Cash Expenses per unit	₹ 10	₹ 8
9. Fixed Overheads per unit (Allocations from other Departments)	₹ 3	₹ 2.4
10. Selling Price per unit	₹ 100	₹ 120
11. Book Value of Existing Machine (Purchased 3 years ago)	₹ 2,52,000	
12. Cost of New Machine		₹ 4,30,000
13. Useful Life	8 years	5 years
14. Freight, Carriage & Installation Exp.		₹ 10,000
15. Workers' Training Expenses incurred to put the asset to use		₹ 20,000
16. Subsidy from Govt.		₹ 50,000
17. Book Value at the end of useful Life.	₹ 2,000	₹ 10,000
18. Cash Salvage Value at the end of useful Life.	₹ 1,500	₹ 15,000
19. Current Realizable Value	₹ 10,600	
20. Cost of Dismantling & Removal	₹ 600	
21. Working Capital required	₹ 40,000	₹ 1,00,000

Other Information:

Method of Depreciation: Straight Line Method

Rate on Income Tax: 30 %

Company's Cost of Capital: 10 %

Exchange Value of Old Machine offered by Suppliers of New Machine: ₹ 9,000

Annuity Factor @ 10% for 5 and 8 years are ₹ 3.791 and ₹ 5.335 respectively.

PV Factor @ 10 % for 5th and 8th year are ₹ 0.621 and ₹ 0.467 respectively.

Particulars	Year 1	Year 2	Year 3	Year 4	Year 5
Present Value Factors @ 60%	0.625	0.391	0.244	0.153	0.095
Present Value Factors @ 65%	0.606	0.367	0.223	0.135	0.082

Required:

(a) Estimate the NPV of the Replacement Decision

(b) Should the Company replace the existing machine?

(c) Estimate the Payback Period of the Replacement Decision

(d) Estimate the Discounted Payback Period of the Replacement Decision

(e) Estimate the IRR of the Replacement Decision

(f) Estimate the Profitability Index of the Replacement Decision

SOLUTION

(A) CALCULATION OF INCREMENTAL CASH INFLOW AFTER TAXES (CFAT)

Particulars	₹
A. Incremental Contribution	3,60,000
B. *Less:* Incremental Depreciation	(30,000)
C. *Less:* Incremental Cash Fixed Cost (₹ 80,000 – ₹ 80,000)	–
D. Incremental Earning before Tax	,30,000
E. *Less:* Tax @ 30%	(99,000)
F. Incremental Earning after Tax	2,31,000
G. *Add:* Incremental Depreciation	30,000
H. Incremental Cash Flow after Taxes (CFAT) (for years other than last year)	2,61,000
I. *Add:* Release of Incremental Working Capital	60,000
J. *Add:* Incremental Cash Salvage Value at the end of Useful Life	13,500
K. *Less:* Incremental Tax	(1,650)
L. Total Incremental CFAT for the last year	3,32,850

STATEMENT SHOWING THE INCREMENTAL NET PRESENT VALUE

Particulars	Year	PV factor at 10%	Amount	PV
Purchase Price of New Machine	0	1	(4,30,000)	(4,30,000)
Freight, Carriage & Installation Exp.	0	1	(10,000)	(10,000)
Workers' Training Expenses	0	1	(20,000)	(20,000)
Subsidy from Govt.	0	1	50,000	50,000
Incremental Working Capital	0	1	(60,000)	(60,000)

Net Sale Proceeds of Existing Machine (₹ 10,600 – ₹ 600)	0	1	10,000	10,000
Tax saving on Loss on Sale of existing machine 30% of ₹.2,42,000 (₹ 2,52,000 – ₹ 10,000)	0	1	72,600	72,600
Incremental CFAT for 1 – 4 years	1 to 4	3.170	2,61,000	8,27,370
Incremental CFAT for 5th year	5	0.621	3,32,850	2,06,700
Incremental NPV				6,46,670

(b) ***Recommendation:*** The New Machine should be purchased since the NPV is positive.

Working Notes:

(I) CALCULATION OF INCREMENTAL CONTRIBUTION

Particulars	Existing Machine	New Machine	Incremental (New – Old)
A. Units Produced [Annual Machine Hrs./(MH per unit]	8,000	10,000	
B. Selling Price per unit	100	120	
C. *Less:* Material Cost per unit (Qty Rate)	(10)	(12)	
D. *Less:* Labour Cost per unit (Hour Rate)	(40)	(30)	
E. *Less:* Variable Overheads per unit	(10)	(10)	
F. Contribution per unit [B – C – D – E]	40	68	
G. Total Contribution (A × D)	3,20,000	6,80,000	3,60,000

(II) CALCULATION OF INCREMENTAL DEPRECIATION

Particulars	Existing Machine	New Machine	Incremental (New – Old)
A. Book Value/Cost of Machine	2,52,000	4,30,000	
B. *Add:* Freight, Carriage & Installation Exp.		10,000	
C. *Add:* Workers' Training Expenses		20,000	
D. *Less:* Subsidy from Govt.		(50,000)	
E. *Less:* Estimated Salvage Value	(2,000)	(10,000)	
F. Depreciable Amount [A + B + C – D – E]	2,50,000	4,00,000	
G. Useful Life	5 yrs	5 yrs	
H. Depreciation [F/G]	50,000	80,000	30,000

(III) CALCULATION OF INCREMENTAL SALVAGE VALUE AND TAX ADVANTAGE

Particulars	Existing Machine	New Machine	Incremental (New – Old)
A. Book Value at the end of useful life	2,000	10,000	
B. *Less:* Cash Salvage Value at the end of useful life	(1,500)	(15,000)	(13,500)
C. Short Term Capital Loss (Gain)	500	(5,000)	
D. Tax on Loss (Profit) @ 30 %	150	(1,500)	(1,650)

(iv) Consultant's fees has been treated as sunk cost.

(v) Since the fixed overheads are allocation from other departments, differential fixed overheads other than depreciation are irrelevant.

(vi) Exchange Value of old machine offered by Suppliers of New Machine is irrelevant since the current realizable value (i.e., ₹ 10,600) is more than the exchange value (i.e., ₹ 9,000).

(C) CALCULATION OF PAY BACK PERIOD OF THE REPLACEMENT DECISION

Year	Incremental Cash Inflow	Cumulative Incremental Cash Inflow
1	2,61,000	2,61,000
2	2,61,000	5,22,000
3	2,61,000	7,83,000
4	2,61,000	10,44,000
5	3,32,850	13,76,850

Pay Back Period of the Replacement Decision:

$$= 1 \text{ Year} + \frac{\text{Total Incremental Cash outflow} - \text{Cumulative Incremental Cash Inflow in 1st year}}{\text{Incremental Cash Inflow in 2nd year}}$$

= 1 year + (₹ 3,87,400 – ₹ 2,61,000)/₹ 2,61,000 = 1.484 years

(D) CALCULATION OF DISCOUNTED PAY BACK PERIOD OF THE REPLACEMENT DECISION

Year	Incremental Cash Inflow	PVF @ 10 %	Incremental PV of Cash Inflow	Cumulative PV of Incremental Cash Inflow
1	2,61,000	0.909	2,37,249	2,37,249
2	2,61,000	0.826	2,15,586	4,52,835
3	2,61,000	0.751	1,96,011	6,48,846
4	2,61,000	0.683	1,78,263	8,27,109
5	3,32,850	0.621	2,06,700	10,33,809

Discounted Pay Back Period of the Replacement Decision: =

$$= 1 \text{ Year} + \frac{\text{Total Incremental Cash outflow} - \text{Cumulative PV of Incremental Cash Inflow in 1st year}}{\text{PV of Incremental Cash Inflow in 2nd year}}$$

= 1 year + (₹ 3,87,400 – ₹ 2,37,249)/₹ 2,15,586 = 1.696 years

(e) Calculation of IRR of the Replacement Decision

Fake Pay Back Period

= ₹ 3,87,400 / [(2,61,000 + 2,61,000 + 2,61,000 + 2,61,000 + 3,32,850) / 5] = 1.407

Year	Incremental Cash Inflow	PVF @ 60 %	Incremental PV of Cash Inflow	PVF @ 60 %	Incremental PV of Cash Inflow
0	(387,400)	1.000	(3,87,400)	1.000	(3,87,400)
1	2,61,000	0.625	1,63,125	0.606	1,58,166
2	2,61,000	0.391	1,02,051	0.367	95,787
3	2,61,000	0.244	63,684	0.223	58,203
4	2,61,000	0.153	39,933	0.135	35,235
5	3,32,850	0.095	31,621	0.082	27,294
		NPV	13,014		(12,715)

IRR of the Replacement Decision:

$$= \text{Lower Rate} + \frac{\text{NPV at Lower Rate}}{\text{NPV at Lower Rate} - \text{NPV at Higher Rate}} \times (\text{Higher rate} - \text{Lower rate})$$

= 60% + [13,014/(13,014 – 12,715)] × (65 – 60) = 60 % + 2.5291 % = 62. 5291 %

(f) PI of Replacement Decision $= \frac{\text{Total PV of Incremental Cash Inflows}}{\text{Total PV of Incremental Cash Outflows}}$

= ₹ 10,33,809/₹ 3,87,400 = 2.669

18.0 CAPITAL RATIONING

MEANING OF CAPITAL RATIONING

Capital rationing is a process where by the limited funds available are allocated amongst the financially viable projects which are not mutually exclusive under consideration so as to maximize the wealth of the shareholders. Thus, capital rationing situation is said to exist if:

(i) Limited funds are available for investment.

(ii) More than one financially viable projects which are not mutually exclusive are under consideration.

Note: *Projects are said to be not mutually exclusive if acceptance of one project does not require the rejection of other project.*

WHICH TECHNIQUE OF CAPITAL BUDGETING SHOULD BE USED UNDER THE SITUATION OF CAPITAL RATIONING

(a) Profitability Index (PI) should be used to rank the financially viable projects under the following conditions:

(i) Funds are scare today (t0) and not thereafter in subsequent years.

(ii) Projects are infinitely divisible (i.e. part of the project can be accepted).

Note: *If the question is silent projects are assumed to be indivisible (i.e. part of the project cannot be accepted).*

(iii) None of the projects can be delayed.

(iv) None of the projects can be undertaken more than once.

(v) All Cash Outflows are made today (i.e. at zero period).

How to use the Technique of PI

Step 1: *Calculate PI for each of the divisible projects.*

Step 2: *Rank the projects in descending order of PI.*

Step 3: *Select the combination of projects ranked in descending order of PI which involves funds up to a given limit.*

(b) Net Present Value Index *or* **Excess Present Value Index** (i.e. NPV/Initial Cash outflow) should be used to rank the financially viable projects under the following conditions:

(i) Funds are scare today (t0) and not thereafter in subsequent years.

(ii) Projects are infinitely divisible (i.e. part of the project can be accepted).

Note: *If the question is silent projects are assumed to be indivisible (i.e. part of the project cannot be accepted).*

(iii) None of the projects can be delayed.

(iv) None of the projects can be undertaken more than once.

(v) Cash Outflows are made not only today (i.e. at zero period) but also in future.

How to use the Technique of NPVI

Step 1: *Calculate NPVI for each of the divisible projects as follows:*

$$NPVI = \frac{NPV}{\text{Initial Cash Outflow}}$$

Step 2: *Rank the projects in descending order of NPVI.*

Step 3: *Select the combination of projects ranked in descending order of NPVI which involves funds up to a given limit.*

(c) Net Present Value should be used to rank the financially viable projects in other cases. In this case various combinations of projects should be made by applying trial and error approach and the combination which gives the maximum overall NPV should be selected.

How to use the Technique of NPV

Step 1: *Calculate NPV for each of the indivisible projects.*

Step 2: *Rank the projects in descending order of NPV.*

Step 3: *Select the combination of projects ranked in descending order of NPV involving funds up to a given limit which gives the overall maximum NPV.*

ILLUSTRATION 47

Tulsian Ltd. having limited funds of ₹ 10,10,000 and cost of capital 10 % is evaluating the desirability of following projects:

Project	A	B	C	D	E	F
Initial Cash Outflows	50,000	1,00,000	1,50,000	2,00,000	2,50,000	6,00,000
Present Value of Cash Inflows	5,00,000	9,00,000	12,00,000	14,00,000	16,25,000	38,40,000
Useful Life of Project	10 years	10 years	10 years	10 years	10 years	10 years

Required:

(a) Rank the projects according to Net Present Value and Profitability Index.

(b) Which projects should be selected assuming that the projects are divisible and there is no alternative use of money allocated for capital budgeting.

(c) Which projects should be selected assuming that the projects are indivisible and there is no alternative use of money allocated for capital budgeting.

(d) Which project should selected assuming that the risk free interest rate is 5 %.

Note: *The Compound Value of ₹ 1 @ 5% at the end of 10th year is ₹ 1.629 and the Present Value of ₹ 1 @ 10% at the end of 10th year is ₹ 0.386.*

SOLUTION

(A) RANKING OF PROJECTS ON THE BASIS OF NPV AND PI

Projects	Initial Cash Outflows	PV of Cash Inflows	NPV = PV of Cash Inflow – PV of Cash Outflow	PI = PV of Cash Inflow/ PV of Cash Outlow	Ranking as per NPV	Ranking as per PI
A	50,000	5,00,000	4,50,000	10	6	1
B	1,00,000	9,00,000	8,00,000	9	5	2
C	1,50,000	12,00,000	10,50,000	8	4	3

D	2,00,000	14,00,000	12,00,000	7	3	4
E	2,50,000	16,25,000	13,75,000	6.5	2	5
F	6,00,000	38,40,000	32,40,000	6.4	1	6

(B) SELECTION OF PROJECTS ON BASIS OF PI RANKING WHEN PROJECTS ARE DIVISIBLE

Project	Investment	PI Ranking	NPV
A	50,000	1	4,50,000
B	1,00,000	2	8,00,000
C	1,50,000	3	10,50,000
D	2,00,000	4	12,00,000
E	2,50,000	5	13,75,000
F (32,40,000 2,60,000/6,00,000)	2,60,000	6	14,04,000
	10,10,000		62,79,000

(C) SELECTION OF PROJECTS WHEN PROJECTS ARE INDIVISIBLE

Combination 1

Project	Investment	NPV Ranking	NPV
F	6,00,000	1	32,40,000
E	2,50,000	2	13,75,000
C	1,50,000	4	10,50,000
	10,00,000		56,65,000

Project D (though ranked 3 as per NPV criteria) cannot be selected because it requires initial cash outflow of ₹ 2,00,000 but we have only ₹ 1,50,000.

Combination 2

Project	Investment	NPV
A	50,000	4,50,000
B	1,00,000	8,00,000
E	2,50,000	13,75,000
F	6,00,000	32,40,000
	10,00,000	58,65,000

Combination 3

Project	Investment	NPV
A	50,000	4,50,000
C	1,50,000	10,50,000
D	2,00,000	12,00,000
F	6,00,000	32,40,000
	10,00,000	59,40,000

Conclusion: In case of indivisible projects the selection of the projects should be made on NPV criteria. In other words, the combination of projects involving funds up to a given limit, which gives the overall maximum NPV should be selected. Hence, Combination 3 (Project A, C, D, F) should be selected.

Part (d)

Note: *When the question is silent the given projects are always assumed to be indivisible. Hence, the project selection will be same as in case (c)*

Unutilised funds of ₹ 10,000 can be invested for a period of 10 years @ 5 %. The compound value of ₹ 10,000 would be ₹ 16,290 (i.e. 10,000 * 1.629) which is to be received at the end of 10th year. Now the present value of ₹ 16,290 at discount rate of 10 % (i.e. cost of capital) would be ₹ 6,288 (i.e. 16,290 * 0.386). Thus, total NPV is ₹ 59,33,712 (i.e. ₹ 59,40,000 – ₹ 6,288).

Recommendation: The company is advised to undertake project A, C, D and F since NPV of A, C, D and F is more than the NPV of any other combination and ₹ 10,000 will remain unspent.

ILLUSTRATION 48

Tulsian Ltd. having limited funds of ₹ 4,00,000 and cost of capital 10 % is evaluating the desirability of following projects:

Cash Flows at	Project A (₹)	Project B (₹)	Project C (₹)
0 year	(3,00,000)	(2,00,000)	(3,00,000)
1st year	(1,00,000)	(2,10,000)	(3,00,000)
1st year	6,00,000	4,00,000	2,00,000
2nd year	2,00,000	4,00,000	10,00,000

Required:

(a) Rank the projects according to Profitability Index (PI) and Net Present Value Index (NPVI)

(b) Which projects should be selected on basis of PI ranking assuming that the projects are divisible.

(c) Which projects should be selected on basis of NPVI ranking assuming that the projects are divisible.

Note: *The Present Value Factors @ 10% discount rate at the end of year 1 and year 2 are 0.909 and 0.826 respectively.*

SOLUTION

(A) CALCULATION OF NPV, PI AND NPVI OF THE PROJECTS

Project	Discounted Cash Flows				NPV	PI	NPVI = NPV/ Initial CF	Ranking as per PI	Ranking as per NPVI
	0	1	1	2					
A	(3,00,000)	(90,900)	5,45,400	1,65,200	3,19,700	1.82	1.07	1	3
B	(2,00,000)	(1,90,890)	3,63,600	3,30,400	3,03,110	1.78	1.52	2	1
C	(3,00,000)	(2,72,700)	1,81,800	8,26,000	4,35,100	1.76	1.45	3	2

(B) STATEMENT SHOWING THE SELECTION OF PROJECTS ON THE BASIS OF RANKING AS PER PI

Projects	Initial Cash Outflow	NPV
A	3,00,000	3,19,700
B	1,00,000	1,51,555 (i.e. 3,03,110 1,00,000/2,00,000)
Total	4,00,000	4,71,255

(C) STATEMENT SHOWING THE SELECTION OF PROJECTS ON THE BASIS OF RANKING AS PER NPVI

Projects	Initial Cash Outflow	NPV
B	2,00,000	3,03,110
C	2,00,000	2,90,067 (i.e. 4,35,100 2,00,000/3,00,000)
Total	4,00,000	5,93,177

Recommendation: Project B in full and C in part should be accepted so as to maximize the overall NPV as per NPVI ranking.

ILLUSTRATION 49

Alpha Limited is considering 5 capital projects for the years 1, 2 and 3. The company is financed by equity entirely and its cost of capital is 12%.

The expected cash flows of the projects are as detailed below:

(₹ '000)

Projects	Years and Cash flows			
	0	1	2	3
A	(70)	35	35	20
B	(40)	(30)	45	55
C	(50)	(60)	70	80
D	–	(90)	55	65
E	(60)	20	40	50

(Figures in brackets represent cash outflows.)

All projects are divisible. None of the projects can be delayed *or* undertaken more than once.

Required: Suggest which project should Alpha Ltd. undertake if the capital available for the investment is limited to ₹ 1,10,000 in year 1 and with no limitation in subsequent years.

For your analysis use the following present value of factors:

Years	0	1	2	3
Present Value Factor @ 12 %	1.00	0.89	0.80	0.71

SOLUTION

STATEMENT SHOWING THE CALCULATION OF NPV, PI AND NPVI OF THE PROJECTS

Project	Discounted Cash Flows				NPV	PI	NPVI = NPV/ Initial CF	Ranking as per PI	Ranking as per NPVI
	0	1	1	2					
A	(70)	31.15	28.00	14.20	3.35	1.05	0.05	4	4
B	(40)	(26.70)	36.00	39.05	8.35	1.13	0.21	2	2
C	(50)	(53.40)	56.00	56.80	9.40	1.09	0.19	3	3
D	–	(80.10)	44.00	46.15	10.05	–	–		
E	(60)	17.80	32.00	35.50	25.30	1.42	0.42	1	1

STATEMENT SHOWING SELECTION OF PROJECTS ON THE BASIS OF RANKING AS PER NPVI

Projects	Initial Cash Outflow	NPV
D	0	10.05
E	60,000	25.30
B	40,000	8.35
C	10,000	1.88 (i.e. 9.4 10,000/50,000)
Total	110,000	45.58

ILLUSTRATION 50

Verdi Ltd. is considering its investment programme for 2007 and 2008. The following projects are available:

Cash Flow at	Project A ₹	Project B ₹	Project C ₹	Project D ₹
1st Jan, 2007	(30,000)	(60,000)	(24,000)	(15,000)
1st Jan, 2008	(90,000)	(15,000)	(24,000)	(30,000)
1st Jan, 2009	1,20,000	90,000	40,000	90,000
1st Jan, 2010	40,000	40,000	40,000	20,000

No other projects are expected to be available for commencement on 1st Jan 2007 *or* 1st Jan 2008. None of the above projects can be delayed.

Verdi Ltd. is financed entirely by ordinary shares, and has a cost of capital of 14 %. Assume that fractions of projects may be undertaken more than once.

(a) Provide calculations showing projects Verdi Ltd. should undertake if Capital is expected to be freely available at 14 % during all future periods.

(b) Show how your answer (a) above would change if capital at 1st Jan 2007 was limited to ₹ 60,000 and expected to be freely available at 14% from 1st Jan 2008.

Note: *The Present values @ 14% at the end of year 1, 2 and 3 are 0.877, 0.769 and 0.675 respectively.*

SOLUTION

(A) STATEMENT SHOWING THE CALCULATION OF NPV, PI AND NPVI OF THE PROJECTS

Project	Discounted Cash Flows				NPV	PI	NPVI = NPV/ Initial CF	Ranking as per PI	Ranking as per NPVI
	1st Jan 2007	1st Jan 2008	1st Jan 2009	1st Jan 2010					
A	(30,000)	(78,930)	92,280	27,000	10,350	1.10	0.35	4	4
B	(60,000)	(13,155)	69,210	27,000	23,055	1.32	0.38	3	2
C	(24,000)	(21,048)	30,760	27,000	12,712	1.28	0.53	2	3
D	(15,000)	(26,310)	69,210	13,500	41,400	2.00	2.76	1	1

Recommendation: All Projects should be accepted since NPV of all projects are positive and funds are freely available at present and in future.

(B) STATEMENT SHOWING THE SELECTION OF PROJECTS ON THE BASIS OF RANKING AS PER NPVI

Projects	Initial Cash Outflow	NPV
D	15,000	41,400
C	24,000	12,712
B	21,000	8,069.25 (i.e. 23,055 21,000/60,000)
Total	60,000	62,181.25

STATEMENT SHOWING SELECTION OF PROJECTS ON THE BASIS OF RANKING AS PER PI

Projects	Initial Cash Outflow	NPV
D	15,000	41,400
B	45,000	17,291.2 (i.e., 23,055 45,000/60,000
Total	60,000	58,691

Recommendation: Project D, C in full and B in part should be accepted so as to maximize the overall NPV as per NPVI ranking.

ILLUSTRATION 51

A company has investable funds of ₹ 22 lakh in first year and there shall be no fund constraints in second year onwards. It is considering the following projects:

Project	PV Outflows	Initial Outflows	NPV	Remarks
A	3	3	12	Indivisible
B	6	5	18	Indivisible
C	10	8	20	Indivisible
D	9	6	6	Indivisible
E	4	4	5	Indivisible
F	10	8	5	Indivisible
G	10	8	(2)	Indivisible

Project C & D are mutually exclusive and Project A is complementary to G. Any uninvested amount in 1st year would result in a negative NPV of one rupee for every ten rupees of un – invested amount. Select the most desirable combination of projects.

SOLUTION

STATEMENT SHOWING THE RANKING OF THE PROJECTS AS PER NPV

Project	Initial Outflow	PV of Outflow	NPV	Ranking as per NPV
A	3	3	12	3
B	5	6	18	2
C	8	10	20	1
D	6	9	6	4
E	4	4	5	5

F	8	10	5	5
G	8	10	(2)	7

If Project C is accepted, then Project D is to be rejected. If Project D is accepted, then Project C is to be rejected.

If Project A is accepted, then Project G is also to be accepted. If Project G is accepted, then Project A is also to be accepted

Combination 1	Ranking	Initial Outflow	NPV
C	1	8	20
B	2	5	18
E	5	4	5
		17	43
Unutilised Amount		5	(0.5)
		22.00	42.50

Combination 2	Ranking	Initial Outflow	NPV
C	1	8	20
B	2	5	18
F	5	8	5
		21	43
Unutilised Amount		1	(0.1)
		22	42.90

Project A which has been recouped 3 can not be selected since its acceptance along with acceptance of project G which is complementary to Project A, requires an initial cash outflow of ₹ 11 lakh (i.e., ₹ 3 lakh + ₹ 8 lakh) but we have only ₹ 9 lakh [i.e., ₹ 22 lakh – ₹ 8 lakh (c) – ₹ 5 lakh (B)] at our disposal.

Recommendation: Combination 2 (i.e. Project B, C & F) should be taken as it has maximum NPV.

19.0 MODIFIED INTERNAL RATE OF RETURN [MIRR]

WHAT IS MIRR TECHNIQUE?

Modified Internal Rate of Return is that rate of compounding which makes the initial cash outflow in zeroth year equal to the terminal value of the cash inflows.

In algebraic equation form:

Initial Cash Outflow $(1 + r)^{n}$th = Total Terminal Value of all Cash Inflows

where, Terminal Value of Cash Inflow of Year 1 = $CI_1\,(1 + k)^{n-1}$

Terminal Value of Cash Inflow of Year 2 = $CI_2\,(1 + k)^{n-2}$

Terminal Value of Cash Inflow of Year 3 = $CI_3\,(1 + k)^{n-3}$ and so on .....

k = Reinvestment Rate (Usually the cost of capital)

r = Modified Internal Rate of Return

WHAT IS ACCEPT/REJECT RULE?

(a) Independent Projects	Accept the project if MIRR > k, Reject the project if MIRR < k (i.e. Cost of Capital)

(b) Mutually Exclusive Projects	Projects should be ranked in the order of MIRR and the project with highest MIRR(but not *less* than Cost of Capital) should be selected..

WHAT ARE THE MERITS AND DEMERITS OF MIRR?

The merits and demerits of MIRR are as follows:

Merits	Demerits
1. It considers the time value of money. 2. It considers entire cash flows over entire life of the project. 3. It is consistent with the objective of maximizing the wealth of owners. 4. It is a measure of profitability since entire cash flows over entire life of the project are considered.	1. It requires the estimation of cash inflows and cash outflows, which is a difficult task. 2. It is relatively difficult to compute. 3. It ignores the absolute amount of NPV while taking decision. A project having lower IRR but higher absolute NPV may be rejected although it increases the shareholders' wealth.

DIFFERENCE BETWEEN IRR AND MIRR

IRR differs from MIRR in the followign respects:

Basis of Distinction	IRR	MIRR
1. Reinvestment Rate	It assumes that intermediate cash inflows are reinvested at **IRR**.	It assumes that intermediate cash inflows are reinvested at **Cost of Capital**
2. Negative Rates/ Multiple Rates	It may yield negative rates/ multiple rates under certain circumstances.	It does not yield negative rates/multiple rates under any circumstances.

HOW TO COMPUTE MIRR?

The calculation of MIRR consists of the following practical steps:

Step 1: *Calculate Total Terminal Value of all Cash Inflows using Reinvestment Rate (usually Cost of Capital) as follows:*

Terminal Value of Cash Inflow of Year 1 = $CI_1\ (1+k)^{n-1}$

Terminal Value of Cash Inflow of Year 2 = $CI_2\ (1+k)^{n-2}$

Terminal Value of Cash Inflow of Year 3 = $CI_3\ (1+k)^{n-3}$ *and so on ......*

Step 2: *Calculate MIRR as follows:*

Initial Cash Outflow (1 + r)n = Total Terminal Value of all Cash Inflows

ILLUSTRATION 52

MIRR Tulsian Ltd. provides you the following information:

1. Purchase Price of Machine	₹ 1,90,000
2. Installation Expenses	₹ 10,000
3. Useful Life of Machine	4 years
4. Salvage Value at the end of Useful Life	Nil
5. Tax Rate	30%

6.	Cost of Capital	10%
7.	Cash Flow after Taxes(CFAT)	₹ 1,00,000

Required: Calculate the Modified Internal Rate of Return.

Note: *Present Value & Compound Value Factors @ 10% are as follows:*

Years	Year 1	Year 2	Year 3	Year 4
Present Value Factor	0.909	0.826	0.751	0.683
Compound Value Factor	1.1	1.21	1.331	1.464

SOLUTION

STATEMENT SHOWING TERMINAL VALUE OF CASH INFLOWS

Particulars	Year	Amount	Compounding Factor @ 10%	Terminal Value
CFAT for 1st year	1	1,00,000	1.331	1,33,100
CFAT for 2nd year	2	1,00,000	1.210	1,21,000
CFAT for 3rd year	3	1,00,000	1.100	1,10,000
CFAT for 4th year	4	1,00,000	1.000	1,00,000
Total Terminal Value of all Cash Inflows				4,64,100

Initial Cash Outflow $(1 + r)^n$ = Total Terminal Value of all Cash Inflows

(₹ 1,90,000 + ₹ 10,000) $(1 + r)^4$ = ₹ 4,64,100

$(1 + r)^4$ = ₹ 4,64,100 / ₹ 2,00,000

$(1 + r)^4$ = ₹ 2.3205

$(1 + r) = 1.2342$

$r = 1.2342 - 1 = 0.2342$

$r = 23.42\ \%$

ILLUSTRATION 53

Tulsian Ltd. provides you the following information:

1.Purchase Price of each Machine	₹ 6,00,000
2.Working Capital	₹ 3,00,000
3.Useful Life of each machine	4 years
4.Estimated Salvage Value at the end of useful life	₹ 1,00,000
5.Cash Salvage Value at the end of useful life	₹ 1,20,000
6.Method of Depreciation	Straight line
7.Tax Rate	30%
8.Cost of Capital	10%
9.Earning before depreciation & tax:	

Machine	Year 1	Year 2	Year 3	Year 4
Machine X	3,00,000	3,00,000	3,00,000	3,00,000
Machine Y	–	1,00,000	2,00,000	12,00,000
Machine Z	5,00,000	4,00,000	3,00,000	–

Required: Which of the above machines should be purchased on the basis of Modified Internal Rate of Return.

Note: *Present Value & Compound Value Factors @ 10% are as follows:*

Year	Year 1	Year 2	Year 3	Year 4	Year 5
Present Value Factor	0.909	0.826	0.751	0.683	0.621
Compound Value Factor	1.1	1.21	1.331	1.464	1.611

SOLUTION

COMPUTATION OF CASH INFLOW AFTER TAXES OF MACHINE X

Particulars	Year 1	Year 2	Year 3	Year 4
Earning before depreciation & tax	3,00,000	3,00,000	3,00,000	3,00,000
Less: Depreciation	(1,25,000)	(1,25,000)	(1,25,000)	(1,25,000)
Earning before Tax	1,75,000	1,75,000	1,75,000	1,75,000
Less: Tax @ 30 %	(52,500)	(52,500)	(52,500)	(52,500)
Earning after Tax	1,22,500	1,22,500	1,22,500	1,22,500
Add: Depreciation	1,25,000	1,25,000	1,25,000	1,25,000
Cash Flow after Taxes(CFAT)	2,47,500	2,47,500	2,47,500	2,47,500
Add: Release of Working Capital				3,00,000
Add: Actual Salvage Value of Asset.				1,20,000
Less: Tax on Profit on Sale [30% of ₹ 20,000 (i.e. ₹ 1,20,000 – ₹ 1,00,000)]				(6,000)
Total CFAT for the last year				6,61,500

TERMINAL VALUE OF CASH INFLOWS OF MACHINE X

Particulars	Year	Amount	Compounding Factor @ 10%	Terminal Value
CFAT for 1st year	1	2,47,500	1.331	3,29,423
CFAT for 2nd year	2	2,47,500	1.210	2,99,475
CFAT for 3rd year	3	2,47,500	1.100	2,72,250
CFAT for 4th year	4	6,61,500	1.000	6,61,500
Total Terminal Value of all Cash Inflows				15,62,648

Initial Cash Outflow $(1 + r)^n$ = Total Terminal Value of all Cash Inflows

(₹ 6,00,000 + ₹ 3,00,000) $(1 + r)^4$= ₹ 15,62,648

$(1 + r)^4$ = ₹ 15,62,648 / ₹ 9,00,000

$(1 + r)^4$ = ₹ 1.736

(1 + r) = (₹ 1.736)1/4

$$r = 1.1479 - 1 = 0.1479$$

$$r = 14.79\ \%$$

COMPUTATION OF CASH INFLOW AFTER TAXES OF MACHINE Y

Particulars	Year 1	Year 2	Year 3	Year 4
Earning before depreciation & tax	–	1,00,000	2,00,000	12,00,000
Less: Depreciation	(1,25,000)	(1,25,000)	(1,25,000)	(1,25,000)
Earning before Tax	(1,25,000)	(25,000)	75,000	10,75,000
Less: Tax @ 30 %	37,500	7,500	(22,500)	(3,22,500)
Earning after Tax	(87,500)	(17,500)	52,500	7,52,500
Add: Depreciation	1,25,000	1,25,000	1,25,000	1,25,000
Cash Flow after Taxes (CFAT)	37,500	1,07,500	1,77,500	8,77,500
Add: Release of Working Capital				3,00,000
Add: Cash Salvage Value of Asset				1,20,000
Less: Tax on Profit on Sale [30% of ₹ 20,000 (i.e. ₹ 1,20,000 – ₹ 1,00,000)]				(6,000)
Total CFAT for the last year				12,91,500

Note: *Assuming that the company has taxable income from other sources against which such loss can be set off, there will be tax saving on negative EBT.*

TERMINAL VALUE OF CASH INFLOWS OF MACHINE X

Particulars	Year	Amount	Compounding Factor @ 10%	Terminal Value
CFAT for 1st year	1	37,500	1.331	49,913
CFAT for 2nd year	2	1,07,500	1.210	1,30,075
CFAT for 3rd year	3	1,77,500	1.100	1,95,250
CFAT for 4th year	4	12,91,500	1.000	12,91,500
Total Terminal Value of all Cash Inflows				16,66,738

Initial Cash Outflow $(1 + r)^n$ = Total Terminal Value of all Cash Inflows

₹(6,00,000 + ₹ 3,00,000) $(1 + r)^4$ = ₹ 16,66,738

$(1 + r)^4$ = ₹ 16,66,738 / ₹ 9,00,000

$(1 + r)^4$ = ₹ 1.8519

$(1 + r)$ = (₹ 1.8519)1/4

$$r = 1.1666 - 1 = 0.1666$$

$$r = 16.66\%$$

COMPUTATION OF CASH INFLOW AFTER TAXES OF MACHINE Z

Particulars	Year 1	Year 2	Year 3	Year 4
Earning before depreciation & tax	5,00,000	4,00,000	3,00,000	–
Less: Depreciation	(1,25,000)	(1,25,000)	(1,25,000)	(1,25,000)
Earning before Tax	3,75,000	2,75,000	1,75,000	(1,25,000)

Less: Tax @ 30 %	(1,12,500)	(82,500)	(52,500)	37,500
Earning after Tax	2,62,500	1,92,500	1,22,500	(87,500)
Add: Depreciation	1,25,000	1,25,000	1,25,000	1,25,000
Cash Flow after Taxes(CFAT)	3,87,500	3,17,500	2,47,500	37,500
Add: Release of Working Capital				3,00,000
Add: Cash Salvage Value of Asset.				1,20,000
Less: Tax on Profit on Sale [30% of ₹ 20,000 (i.e. ₹ 1,20,000 – ₹ 1,00,000)]				(6,000)
Total CFAT for the last year				4,51,500

Note: *Assuming that the company has taxable income from other sources against which such loss can be set off, there will be tax saving on negative EBT.*

TERMINAL VALUE OF CASH INFLOWS OF MACHINE Z

Particulars	Year	Amount	Compounding Factor @ 10%	Terminal Value
CFAT for 1st year	1	3,87,500	1.331	5,15,763
CFAT for 2nd year	2	3,17,500	1.210	3,84,175
CFAT for 3rd year	3	2,47,500	1.100	2,72,250
CFAT for 4th year	4	4,51,500	1.000	4,51,500
Total Terminal Value of all Cash Inflows				16,23,688

Initial Cash Outflow $(1 + r)^n$= Total Terminal Value of all Cash Inflows

(₹ 6,00,000 + ₹ 3,00,000) $(1 + r)^4$= ₹ 16,23,688

$(1 + r)^4$ = ₹ 16,23,688 / ₹ 9,00,000

$(1 + r)^4$ = ₹ 1.8041

$(1 + r)$ = (₹ 1.8041)1/4

$r = 1.159 – 1 = 0.159$

$r = 15.90\%$

Recommendation: Machine Y should be purchased since Machine Y has the highest MIRR of 16.66%.

20.0 EQUITY NET PRESENT VALUE [EQUITY NPV]

MEANING OF EQUITY NPV

Equity NPV is the difference between the present value of all Cash Inflows available for Equity shareholders and the present value of Cash Outflows financed by Equity shareholders. It is ascertained using Cost of Equity as the discount rate.

EQUITY NPV IN EQUATION FORM

Equity NPV = PV of Cash Inflows available for Equity Shareholders *less* PV of Cash Outflows financed by Equity Shareholders and Repayment of Principal Amount of Loan.

where, *Cash Inflows available for Equity shareholders = Cash Inflows from the Project less Payment of Interest on Loan*

DISTINCTION BETWEEN PROJECT NPV AND EQUITY NPV

Equity NPV differs from Project NPV in the following respects:

Basis of Distinction	Project NPV	Equity NPV
1. Discount Rate	Overall Cost of Capital (k_0) is used as discount rate.	Cost of Equity (k_e) is used as discount rate.
2. Interest on Long-term Debt	It is not deducted while computing cash flows.	It is deducted while comput-ing cash flows.
3. Repayment of Long-term Debt	It is not treated as Cash Outflows.	It is treated as Cash Outflow.
4. Cash Outflow associated with Project Cost	Cash Outflow is equal to the total Project Cost (whether financed by Equity *or* Debt *or* both).	Cash Outflow is equal to only that portion of Project Cost which has been financed by Equity.

ILLUSTRATION 54

Tulsian Ltd. provides you the following information:

1. Total Cost of Plant (Life 4 years) ₹ 300 lakhs.
2. Plant is to be financed by 12% Debt and Equity so as to maintain Debt-Equity Ratio of 2: 1. Debt is to be repaid in four equal annual installments beginning from the end of the first year.
3. Annual Earning Before Interest, Depreciation and Tax: ₹ 200 lakhs.
4. Tax Rate: 50%.
5. Cost of Capital: 9%.
6. Method of Depreciation: Straight Line.

Required: Calculate the (a) Project NPV and (b) Equity NPV.

[Present Value of Annuity of ₹ 1 for 4 years at 9%, 12% and 15% are 3.24, 3.037 and 2.855 respectively]

SOLUTION

Case (a)

STEP 1: CALCULATION OF PV OF CFAT

[₹ in lakhs]

Particulars	Year 1-4
A. Earnings before Interest, Depreciation & Tax	200.00
B. *Less:* Depreciation	(75.00)
C. Earnings before tax	125.00
D. *Less:* Tax	(62.50)
E. Earnings after tax	62.50
F. *Add:* Depreciation	75.00
G. Cash Inflows After Tax (CFAT) p.a.	137.50
H. PV of Annuity Factor @ 9%	3.24
I. PV of CFAT	445.50

STEP 2: CALCULATION OF PV OF CASH OUTFLOW

Particulars	Year	PV factor	Amount	PV
Total Cost of Plant	0	1.00	300	300

Step 3: Project NPV = ₹ 445.50 – ₹ 300 = ₹ 145.50

Case (b)

STEP1: CALCULATION OF COST OF EQUITY FOR CALCULATING EQUITY NPV

Source of Finance	Amount	Proportion	After tax Cost of Source	Product
12% Debt	200	200/300	.06	.04
Equity	100	100/300	X	1/3 X
	300	1.00		.04 + 1/3 X

0.04 + X = 0.09

X = 0.09 – 0.04 =. 05

X = 0.05 3 = 0.15 *or* 15%

Hence, Cost of Equity (ke) = 15%

STEP 2: CALCULATION OF PV OF CFAT AVAILABLE FOR EQUITY SHAREHOLDERS

[₹ in lakhs]

Particulars	Year 1	Year 2	Year 3	Year 4
A. Earnings before Interest, Depreciation & Tax	200.00	200.00	200.00	200.00
B. *Less:* Interest on Long term Debt	(24.00)	(18.00)	(12.00)	(6.00)
Less: Depreciation	(75.00)	(75.00)	(75.00)	(75.00)
C. Earnings before tax [A – B]	101.00	107.00	113.00	119.00
D. *Less:* Tax @ 50%	(50.50)	(53.50)	(56.50)	(59.50)
E. Earnings after tax	50.50	53.50	56.50	59.50
F. *Add:* Depreciation	75.00	75.00	75.00	75.00
G. Cash Inflows After Tax (CFAT) p.a.	125.50	128.50	131.50	134.50
H. *Less:* Repayment of Principal	50.00	50.00	50.00	50.00
I. Cash available for Equity shareholders	75.50	78.50	81.50	84.50
J. PV of Annuity Factor @ 15%	0.87	0.756	0.658	0.572
K. PV of CFAT	65.685	59.346	53.627	48.334

Step 3: Equity NPV = PV of CFAT available for Equity shareholders – Cost of Plant financed by Equity. = ₹ 226.992 lakh – ₹ 100 lakhs = ₹ 126.992 lakhs

21.0 EQUITY INTERNAL RATE OF RETURN [EQUITY IRR]

WHAT IS EQUITY IRR?

Equity IRR is the Rate which equates the present value of cash outflows financed by equity shareholders with the present value of all cash inflows available for equity shareholders.

In Equation from:

PV of Cash Outflow financed by Equity shareholders = PV of Cash Inflow available for Equity shareholders

where, Cash Inflows available for equity shareholders = Cash Inflows from the project less Annual Payment of Interest & Principal amount of Loan.

Note: *To calculate Equity IRR, one may start discounting the cashflow with Approximate Equity IRR which is = Project IRR +* $\left[\text{Project IRR} - \text{Cost of Debt}) \times \frac{\text{Debt}}{\text{Equity}}\right]$

ILLUSTRATION 55

Calculate Project IRR and Equity IRR in Illustration 43:

Present Value of ₹ 1	29%	30%	68%	69%
for year 1	0.775	0.769	0.595	0.592
for year 2	0.601	0.592	0.354	0.350
for year 3	0.466	0.455	0.211	0.207
for year 4	0.361	0.350	0.126	0.123

SOLUTION

(a) Calculation of Project IRR

Step 1: *Payback Period* = $\frac{\text{Initial Cash Outflow}}{\text{Annual Cash Inflow after tax}} = \frac{₹\,300 \text{ lakhs}}{₹137.50 \text{ lakhs}} = 2.182$

Step 2: *Discount Factors within which Payback Period lies are 2.203 and 2.166 which correspond to discount rates of 29% and 30% respectively.*

Step 3: *Project IRR = Lower Discount Rate +* $\frac{\text{PVAF at lower Rate} - \text{Pay back period}}{\text{PVAF at lower rate} - \text{PVAF at higher rate}}$

= 29% + [(2.203 – 2.182)/(2.203 – 2.166)]

= 29% + (0.021/0.037) = 29.583%.

(b) Calculation of Equity IRR

Step 1: *Fake Payback Period*

$= \frac{\text{Initial Cash Outflows financed by Equity Shareholders}}{\text{Average Annual Cash Inflow after tax available for Equity Shareholders}}$

= ₹ *100 lakhs* ₹ *80 lakhs* = 1.25

Step 2: *Calculation of NPV at 68% and 69%*

Year	Cash Flows	PVF @ 68%	PV at 68%	PVF @ 69%	PV @ 69%
0	(100)	1.000	(100)	1.000	(100)
1	75.50	0.595	44.923	0.592	44.696
2	78.50	0.354	27.789	0.350	27.475
3	81.50	0.211	17.197	0.207	16.871
4	84.50	0.126	10.647	0.123	10.394
NPV			0.556		(0.564)

Step 3: *Equity IRR*

$= \text{Lower Discount Rate} + \frac{\text{NPV at Lower Rate}}{\text{NPV at Lower Rate} - \text{NPV at Higher Rate}} \times (\text{HDR} - \text{LDR})$

= 68% + [0.556/{0.556 – (–0.556)}] × (69% – 68%) = 68.496%

ILLUSTRATION 56 [PROJECT IRR AND EQUITY IRR]

XYZ Ltd., an infrastructure company is evaluating a proposal to build, operate and transfer a section of 35 kms. of road at a project cost of ₹ 200 crores to be financed as follows:

Equity Share Capital ₹ 50 crores, loans at the rate of interest of 15% p.a. from financial institutions ₹ 150 crores. The Project after completion will be opened to traffic and a toll will be collected for a period of 15 years from the vehicles using the road. The company is also required to maintain the road during the above 15 years and after the completion of that period, it will be handed over to the Highway authorities at zero value. It is estimated that the toll revenue will be ₹ 50 crores per annum and the annual toll collection expenses including maintenance of the roads will amount to 5% of the project cost. The company considers to write off the total cost of the project in 15 years on a straight line basis. For Corporate Income-tax purposes the company is allowed to take depreciation @ 10% on WDV basis. The financial institutions are agreeable for the repayment of the loans in 15 equal annual instalments – consisting of principal and interest.

Required: (a) Calculate Project IRR and Equity IRR. Ignore Corporate taxation.

(b) Explain the difference in Project IRR and Equity IRR

Note: *Present Values of Annuity of ₹ 1 for 15 years at 15%, 18%, 19%, 20% and 28% are ₹ 5.847, ₹ 5.092, ₹ 4.876, ₹ 4.675 and ₹ 3.483 respectively.*

SOLUTION

(a) (i) Computation of Project IRR

PV of CO = PV of CFAT

₹ 200 crore = ₹ 40 crores/$(1 + r)^{1-15}$

1. An approximation of IRR is made on the basis of cash flow data. A rough approximation may be made with reference to the pay back period. The pay back period in the given case is 5 years (i.e. ₹ 200 crores/₹ 40 crores). From the PVAF table it can be seen that Pay back Period lies between 5.092 and 4.876. This means the IRR of the project is expected to lie between 18% and 19% which correspond to 5.092 and 4.876 respectively.
2. The exact IRR by interpolating between 18% and 19% is worked out as follows:

$$\text{IRR} = \text{Lower Discount Rate} + \frac{\text{PVAF at lower Rate} - \text{Pay back period}}{\text{PVAF at lower rate} - \text{PVAF at higher rate}}$$

= 18% + (5.092 – 5.000)/(5.092 – 4.876) = 18% + (0.092/0.216) = 18.426%.

Therefore, the IRR of the project is 18.426%.

Working Notes:

(i) Toll Cash Inflow of the project

A. Toll revenue	₹ 50 crores
B. *Less:* Toll collection expenses (including maintenance of the roads) (5% of ₹ 200 crores)	₹ 10 crores
C. Net Cash inflow p.a. for 15 years [A – B]	40 crores

Note: *Since corporate taxes are not payable the impact of depreciation has not be considered.*

(a) (ii) Computation of Equity IRR

Equity IRR is computed by using the following equation:

Cash inflow from equity shareholders = PV of Cash inflow available for equity shareholders

₹ 50 crores= ₹ 14.35 crores/$(1 + r)^{1-15}$

The value of equity IRR of the project is calculated as follows:

An approximation of IRR is made on the basis of cash flow data. A rough approximation may be made with reference to the payable period. The payback period in the given case is 3.484 (i.e. ₹ 50 crores/₹ 14.35 croes). From the PVAF table at 28% the cumulative discount factor for 1 – 15 years is 3.483. Therefore, the equity IRR of project is approximately 28%.

Working Notes:

(ii) Equated Annual Instalment (i.e. principal + interest) of loan from financial institution:

$$= \frac{\text{Amount of loan from financial institution}}{\text{Cumulative discount factor for 1 – 15 years}} = \frac{₹\ 150 \text{ crores}}{5.847} = ₹\ 25.65 \text{ crores.}$$

(iii) Cash inflow available for equity shareholders

A. Net Cash Inflow of the project	₹ 40.00 crores
B. Equated yearly instalment of the project	₹ 25.65 crores
C. Cash Inflow available for equity shareholders	₹ 14.35 croes

(b) Difference in Project IRR and Equity IRR:

The project IRR is 18.426% whereas Equity IRR is 28%. This is attributed to the fact that XYZ Ltd. is earning 18.426% on the loan from financial institution but paying only 15%. The difference between the Project IRR and cost of funds from financial institution has enhanced Equity IRR. The 3.426% (i.e. 18.426% – 15%) earnings on ₹ 150 crores goes to equity shareholders who have invested ₹ 50 crore.

22.0 HOW TO RANK TWO MUTUALLY EXCLUSIVE PROJECTS WHICH ARE OF UNEQUAL INVESTMENT SIZE?

Mutually Exclusive projects which are of unequal investment size projects may *or* may not have same NPV. Such projects should be ranked as follows:

Case	How to Rank Mutually Exclusive Projects
Having different NPV	Projects should be ranked in the order of NPV and the project with highest NPV should be selected.
Having same NPV	Projects should be ranked in the order of PI and the project with highest PI should be selected.

EXAMPLE 1

Tulsian Ltd. has following two mutually exclusive projects:

Particulars	Project 'A' (in ₹)	Project 'B' (in ₹)
PV of Cash Inflow	1,00,000	18,000
PV of Cash Outflow	50,000	8,000
NPV	50,000	10,000
PI	2.00	2.25

Here, Project A should be selected since it has higher NPV than that of Project B.

EXAMPLE 2

Tulsian Ltd. has the following two mutually exclusive projects:

Particulars	Project 'A' (in ₹)	Project 'B' (in ₹)
PV of Cash Inflow	1,00,000	90,000

PV of Cash Outflow	50,000	40,000
NPV	50,000	50,000
PI	2.00	2.25

Here, Project 'B' should be selected since it has higher PI than that of Project A.

23.0 TIME ADJUSTED BREAK EVEN POINT

MEANING OF TIME ADJUSTED BREAK EVEN POINT

Time Adjusted Break Even Point refers to that level of sales at which the total present value of Cash Inflows is equal to total present value of Cash Outflows using Cost of Capital as discount rate.

HOW TO CALCULATE TIME ADJUSTED BEP

The calculation of Time Adjusted BEP involves the following practical steps:

Step 1: *Assume the Sales Units be X*

Step 2: *Calculate Cash Inflow after tax as follows:*

A. Sales Units	
B. Selling Price per unit	....
C. Total Sales [A B]	....
D. Less: Total Cost	
(a) Variable Cost	....
(b) Depreciation	....
(c) Other Fixed Cost	....
	....
E. Earnings before Tax [C – D]	....
F. Less: Tax	....
G. Earning after tax [E – F]	....
H. Add: Depreciation	....
I. Cash Flow After Tax (CFAT) [G + H]	....
J. Add: Release of Working Capital	....
K. Add: Salvage Value of Machine	....
L. Less: Tax on Profit on Sale of Machine (or Add: Tax Saving on loss)	....
M. CFAT for the last year	....

Step 3: *Calculate Total Present Value of CFAT*

Step 4: *Calculate Total Present Value of Cash Outflows*

Step 5: *Equate Total PV of CFAT with Total PV of CO & find out the value of X*

Step 6: *Time Adjusted BEP = Value of X*

ILLUSTRATION 57

From the following information, calculate the Time Adjusted Break Even Point:

1. Selling Price per unit	₹ 100

2. Variable Cost per unit	₹ 30
3. Cash Fixed Cost	₹ 30,000
4. Cost of Machine	₹ 5,10,000
5. Useful Life	5 years
6. Book Value at end of Useful Life	₹ 10,000
7. Cash Salvage Value at the end of Useful Life	₹ 15,000
8. Working Capital invested (Recovered only 16.458% at the end)	₹ 1,00,000
9. Tax Rate	30%
10. Cost of Capital	10%

Note: *The present Value of annuity for 5 years @ 10% is 3.791 and the present value for 5th year is 0.621.*

SOLUTION

Step 1: *Computation of Cash Inflows After Tax (Assume Sales units = X)*

A.	*No. of Sales Units*	X
B.	*Selling Price per unit*	100
C.	*Total Sales [A B]*	100 X
D.	*Less: Variable Cost*	(30 X)
	Cash Fixed cost	(30,000)
	Depreciation [(₹ 5,10,000 – ₹ 10,000)/5]	(1,00,000)
E.	*Earnings before Tax*	70 X – 1,30,000
F.	*Less: Tax @ 30%*	(21 X – 39,000)
G.	*Earning after tax*	49 X – 91,000
H.	*Add: Depreciation*	1,00,000
I.	*Cash Flow After Tax p.a.*	49 X + 9,000
J.	*Add: Release of Working Capital*	16,458
K.	*Add: Salvage Value*	15,000
L.	*Less: Tax on Profit on Sale (30% of ₹ 5,000)*	(1,500)
M.	*CFAT for the last year*	49 X + 38,958

Step 2: *Computation of PV of CFAT*

PV of CFAT = 3.17 (49 X + 9,000) + 0.621 (49 X + 38,958)
= 155.33 X + 28,530 + 30.429X + 24,193
= 185.759 X + ₹ 52,723

Step 3: *Time Adjusted Break Even Point*

PV of CFAT = PV of Cash Outflow

185.759 X + ₹ 52,723 = ₹ 6,10,000 (i.e., Cost of Machine + Working Capital)

X = (₹ 6,10,000 – ₹ 52,723)/185.759 = 3,000 units

Hence, Time Adjusted B.E.P = 3,000 Units

24.0 SOCIAL COST BENEFIT ANALYSIS

MEANING OF SOCIAL COST BENEFIT ANALYSIS

Social Cost Benefit Analysis is social evaluation of a project with reference to the social costs and benefits.

PURPOSE OF SOCIAL COST BENEFIT ANALYSIS

Its purpose is not to replace the existing techniques of financial analysis but to supplement and strengthen them. It is important not only for public sector but also for private sector, which has also a moral responsibility to undertake socially desirable projects. If the private sector includes social cost benefit analysis, in its project evaluation techniques, it will ensure that it is not ignoring its long term interest, since in the long run only those projects survive that are socially beneficial and acceptable to the society.

VALUATION BASIS OF SOCIAL COST BENEFIT ANALYSIS

Social cost benefit analysis is usually valued at "opportunity cost" *or* shadow prices to judge the real impact of their burden as costs to the society. Social costs and benefits need not necessarily reflect the monetary measurement of costs and benefits to the society since the market price of the goods and services are often grossly distorted due to various artificial restrictions and controls from the authorities. The social cost valuation sometimes completely change the estimates of working results of a project. A classic example of this is study of a transportation project in U.S.A. known as Victoria Line Project. From the commercial angle, its estimated costs exceed the benefits even at a discount rate of 6%. This evaluation was adjusted on account of the unrealistic fare structure, which did not reflect truly the money, value that the users placed on the services provided. An estimate was also made for the resultant saving in time and increase in comfort. All these adjustments showed that the project was socially desirable and its estimated benefits exceed the costs even at a discount rate of 8%.

NEED FOR SOCIAL COST BENEFIT ANALYSIS

The need for social cost benefit analysis arises due to the following:

(i) Market prices are used to measure costs and benefits in project analysis; they do not represent social values due to imperfections in the market.

(ii) Monetary cost benefit analysis fails to consider the external effects of the project. The external effects can be positive like development of infrastructure *or* negative like pollution and imbalance in environment.

(iii) Taxes and subsidies are transfer payments and hence ignored in social benefit cost analysis.

(iv) The SCBA is essential for measuring the redistribution effect of benefits of project, as benefits going to poorer section are more important than going to economically better off sections.

(v) Projects manufacturing tobacco products are not distinguished from those generating power *or* producing necessities of life. Thus, merit wants are important appraisal criterion for SCBA.

25.0 RELATION BETWEEN RISK AND RETURN

MEANING OF RISK

The term risk with reference to investment decision may be defined as the variability in the actual return emanating from a project in future over its working life in relation to the return estimated *or* forecasted at the time of initial capital budgeting decisions.

DIFFERENCE BETWEEN RISK & UNCERTAINTY

Risk differs from Uncertainty as follows:

Basis of Difference	Risk	Uncertainty
Meaning	Risk refers to the situation where the possibility of happening *or* non-happening of an event can be quantified and measured.	Uncertainty refers to the situation where the possibility of happening *or* non-happening of an event cannot be quantified and measured.
Assignment of Probabilities	Under risky situation, probabilities can be assigned to an event on the basis of facts and figures available regarding the decision.	Under uncertain situation, either the facts and figures are not available regarding the decision *or* probabilities cannot be assigned.

MEANING OF RETURN

The term 'return' with reference to investment decision is the motivating force and principal reward to the investment process. The return may be defined in terms of realized return and expected return.

REALISED RETURN

The realised return is the return, which was earned *or* could have been earned on investment.

EXPECTED RETURN

The expected return is the return, which the firm anticipates to earn in future over the working life of a project.

MEASUREMENT OF RETURN

The return may be measured as the total gain *or* loss to the firm over a given working life of a project and may be defined as percentage return on the initial amount invested. The formula for computing the rate of return is given below:

$$R = \frac{P_1 - P_0 + D_1}{P_0} \times 100$$

Where, P_1 = Price of Asset at the end of year

P_0 = Price of Asset at the beginning of year

D_1 = Cash Inflow for the year

The return from investment during a given period is equal to the change in value of the investment *plus* any income received from investment. It is important therefore, that any capital *or* revenue income from the investment to the investor must be included; otherwise the measure of return will be deficient.

ILLUSTRATION 58

X Ltd. requests you to calculate the rate of return on the following two assets:

Particulars	Asset A	Asset B
Price of Asset at the beginning of year	₹ 3,00,000	₹ 5,00,000
Price of Asset in the end of year	₹ 5,00,000	₹ 8,00,000
Cash Inflow for the year	₹ 20,000	₹ 40,000

SOLUTION

Return of Asset A = $\frac{P_1 - P_0 + D_1}{P_0} \times 100$ = (5,00,000 – 3,00,000 + 20,000)/3,00,000 × 100 = 73.33%

Return of Asset B = $\frac{P_1 - P_0 + D_1}{P_0} \times 100$ = (8,00,000 – 5,00,000 + 40,000)/5,00,000 × 100 = 68%

ILLUSTRATION 59

Z Ltd. is evaluating the rate of return on the project, which involves immediate cash outflow of ₹ 50,000. The cash inflow after 4 years in the project is ₹ 73,205. You are required to calculate the rate of return of Z Ltd.

SOLUTION

Initial Cash Outflow $(1 + r)^n$ = Cash Inflow after 4 year

₹ 50,000 $(1 + r)^4$ = ₹ 73,205

$(1 + r)^4$ = ₹ 73,205/₹. 50,000 = 1.4641

$1 + r = \sqrt[4]{1.4641} = 1.1$

r = 1.1 – 1.0 =. 1 *or* 10%

SOLVED PROBLEMS

ACCOUNTING RATE OF RETURN

PROBLEM 1

The MN Company Limited has decided to increase its productive capacity to meet an anticipated increase in demand for its products. The extent of this increase in capacity is still to be determined and a management meeting has been called to decide which of the following two mutually exclusive proposals-I and II-should be under taken. On the basis of the information given below you are required to evaluate the profitability (ignoring taxation) of each of the proposals on the basis of Accounting Rate of Return.

Particulars	Proposal I ₹	Proposal II ₹
Building	50,000	1,00,000
Plant	2,00,000	3,00,000
Installation	10,000	15,000
Working Capital	50,000	65,000
Net income:		
Annual pre-depreciation profits [Note (a)]	70,000	95,000
Other relevant income/expenditure:		
Sales Promotion [Note (b)]	—	15,000
Plant Scrap Value	10,000	15,000
Buildings Disposable Value [Note (c)]	30,000	60,000

Notes:

(a) The investment life is 10 years.

(b) An exceptional amount of expenditure on sales promotion of ₹ 15,000 will require to be spent in year 2 on proposal II. This has not been taken into account in calculating pre-depreciation profits.

(c) It is not the intention to dispose of the building in ten year's time, however, it is company's policy to take a notional figure into account for project evaluation purposes.

SOLUTION

EVALUATION OF THE PROFITABILITY (IGNORING TAXATION)

Particulars	Proposal I	Proposal II
A. Average Investment	₹ 2,00,000	₹ 3,10,000
B. Annual Average Earnings	₹ 48,000	₹ 59,500
C. Accounting Rate of Return	₹ 48,000/₹ 2,00,000 × 100 = 24%	₹ 59,500/₹ 3,10,000 × 100 = 19.19%

Working Notes:

(i) Average Investment= 1/2 (Original Cost – Scrap Value) + Scrap Value + Working Capital

For Proposal I = 1/2 (₹ 50,000 + ₹ 2,10,000 – ₹ 30,000 – ₹ 10,000) + ₹ 40,000 + ₹ 50,000
= ₹ 2,00,000

For Proposal II = 1/2 (₹ 1,00,000 + ₹ 3,15,000 – ₹ 60,000 – ₹ 15,000)
+ ₹ 75,000 + ₹ 65,000 = ₹ 3,10,000

(II) COMPUTATION OF DEPRECIATION (ASSUMING STRAIGHT LINE METHOD)

Particulars	Proposal I ₹	Proposal II ₹
(a) Buildings	50,000	1,00,000
Less: Disposable Value	(30,000)	(60,000
Depreciable Amount	20,000	40,000
Useful Life	10 years	10 years
Depreciation per annum (i)	₹ 2,000	₹ 4,000
(b) Plant & Installation	2,10,000	3,15,000
Less: Scrap Value	(10,000	(15,000)
Depreciable Amount	2,00,000	3,00,000
Useful Life	10 years	10 years
Depreciation per annum (ii)	₹ 20,000	₹ 30,000
Total Depreciation p.a. [(i) + (ii)]	₹ 22,000	₹ 34,000

(III) COMPUTATION OF AVERAGE EARNINGS

Earnings before depreciation & taxes	70,000	95,000
Less: Depreciation	(22,000)	(34,000
Earnings before sales promotion expenditure & taxes	48,000	61,000
Annual Average earning after promotion expenditure	= (₹ 48,000 × 10)/10 = ₹ 48,000	= (₹ 61,000 × 10) – 15,000/10 = ₹ 59,500

NET PRESENT VALUE

PROBLEM 2

A company has to make a choice between buying of two machines. Machine A would cost ₹ 1,00,000 and require cash running expenses of ₹ 32,000 p.a. Machine B would cost ₹ 1,50,000 and its cash running expenses would amount to ₹ 20,000 p.a. Both the machines have a life of 10 years with zero salvage value. The company follows straight line depreciation and is subject to 50% tax on its income. The company's required rate of return is 10%. Which machines should it buy:

Note: *Present Value of ₹ 1 per annum for 10 years at 10% discount rate is ₹ 6.1446.*

SOLUTION

CALCULATION OF CASH COST AFTER TAX SAVING

Particulars	Machine A	Machine B	Differential Cash Flow (A – B)
Cash Running Expenses	32,000	20,000	12,000
Add: Depreciation	10,000	15,000	(5,000)
Total Cost	42,000	35,000	7,000
Less: Tax Saving @ 50%	(21,000)	(17,500)	(3,500)
Cost after Tax Saving	21,000	17,500	3,500
Less: Depreciation	(10,000)	(15,000)	5,000
Cash Cost after Tax Saving	11,000	2,500	8,500

CALCULATION OF NET PRESENT VALUE

Particulars	Year	PV factor	Machine A		Machine B		Differential Cash Flow	
		at 10%	Amount	PV	Amount	PV	Amount	PV
Purchase Price	0	1	1,00,000	1,00,000	1,50,000	1,50,000	(50,000)	(50,000)
COAT for 1 – 10 years	1 to 10	6.1446	11,000	67,591	2,500	15,362	8,500	52,229
NPV				1,67,591		1,65,362		2,229

Recommendation: Machine B should be preferred over Machine A since net savings offered by Machine B is ₹ 2,229 (i.e. ₹ 1,67,591 – ₹ 1,65,362)

PROBLEM 3

The MN Company Limited has decided to increase its productive capacity to meet an anticipated increase in demand for its products. The extent of this increase in capacity is still to be determined and a management meeting has been called to decide which of the following two mutually exclusive proposals-I and II-should be undertaken. On the basis of the information given below you are required to:

(a) evaluate the profitability (ignoring taxation and investment allowance of each of the proposals) and

(b) advise management in deciding between Proposal I and Proposal II on the assumption of cost of capital of 8%:

(c) State the matters to be taken into consideration while deciding between Proposal I and Proposal II.

Particulars	Proposal I ₹	Proposal II ₹
Buildings	50,000	1,00,000
Plant	2,00,000	3,00,000
Installation	10,000	15,000
Working Capital	50,000	65,000
Net income:		
Annual pre-depreciation prcfits [Note (i)]	70,000	95,000
Other relevant Income/Expenditure including Sales promotion [Note (ii)]	—	15,000
Plant Scrap Value	10,000	15,000
Buildings Disposable Value [Note (iii)]	30,000	60,000

Notes:

(a) The investment life is 10 years.

(b) An exceptional amount of expenditure on sales promotion of ₹ 15,000 will be spent in year 2 on proposal II. This has not been taken into account in calculation pre-depreciation profits.

(c) It is not the intention to dispose of the building in ten year's time. However, it is company's policy to take a notional figure into account for project evaluation purposes.

Year	1	2	3	4	5	6	7	8	9	10	11
P.V.F. @ 8%	.926	.857	.794	.735	.681	.630	.583	.540	.500	.463	.429

SOLUTION

(A) EVALUATION OF THE PROFITABILITY OF PROPOSAL I AND II.

Year	Discount Factor at 8% ₹	PROPOSAL-I Cash Flows ₹	PROPOSAL-I Present Value of Cash Flow ₹	PROPOSAL-II Cash Flows ₹	PROPOSAL-II Present Value of Cash Flow ₹
0	1.000	(3,10,000)	(3,10,000)	(4,80,000)	(4,80,000)
1	0.926	70,000	64,820	95,000	87,970
2	0.857	70,000	59,990	80,000*	68,560
3	0.794	70,000	55,580	95,000	75,430
4	0.735	70,000	51,450	95,000	69,825
5	0.681	70,000	47,670	95,000	64,695
6	0.630	70,000	44,100	95,000	59,850
7	0.583	70,000	40,810	95,000	55,385
8	0.540	70,000	37,800	95,000	51,300
9	0.500	70,000	35,000	95,000	47,500
10	0.463	70,000	32,410	95,000	43,985
		90,000	41,670	1,40,000	64,820
Net Present Value			2,01,300		2,09,320

*Net expenditure on sales promotion.

Working Notes:

(i) Initial Cash Outflow in year 0

Particulars	PROPOSAL-I		PROPOSAL-II	
	₹	₹	₹	₹
Capital Expenditure:				
Buildings	50,000		1,00,000	
Plant	2,00,000		3,00,000	
Installations	10,000	2,60,000	15,000	4,15,000
Working Capital	50,000		65,000	
Total		3,10,000		4,80,000

(ii) Cash inflow in year 10 from scarp/disposal of plant/buildings and working capital:

Particulars	Proposal I ₹	Proposal II ₹
Scarp value of plant	10,000	15,000
Disposal value of buildings	30,000	60,000
Working capital	50,000	65,000
	90,000	1,40,000

(b) **Advice to Management:** The statement (a) above shows that on the assumption of cost of capital of 8%, the net present value of proposal II exceeds the net present value of proposal I, hence, proposal II should be accepted.

(c) **Matters to be taken into consideration when deciding between Proposals I & II.**

(i) **Degree of risk involved in the proposals:** If both the Proposals have different degree of risk, the same discounting rate should not be used. If one proposal bears a greater risk than the other its cash flows should be discounted at a higher rate to compensate for extra risk involved.

(ii) **Validity of assumptions:** In the evaluation of two proposals, various assumptions have been made. These assumptions may *or* may not prove to be a accurate in the future. Forecasts of business conditions as far as 10 years into future cannot be made with certainty. Therefore, the extent of the validity of various assumptions should be taken into consideration when deciding between Proposals I & II.

(iii) **Different initial outlay:** The initial outlay on Proposal I & Proposal II is different. Therefore, the two proposals are not strictly comparable. If additional funds are available, it is necessary to employ them gainfully, the company should accept Proposal I. If the net present value of the third project, when added to the net present value of Proposal I, exceeds the net present value of Proposal II, it will be advantageous to accept Proposal I.

(iv) **Discounting Rate:** The proposals have been evaluated on a discount rate of 8% to cover the cost of capital. It appears to be too low for the purpose of evaluation. Cash flows should be discounted at a rate which is the rate of return required by the company on a new capital project to cover the risks as well as the cost of capital. Therefore, before deciding between Proposals I & II, the adequacy of rate of 8% should be considered.

PROBLEM 4

XYZ Ltd. is planning to introduce a new product with a project life of 8 years. The projects is to be set up in Special Economic Zone (SEZ), qualifies for one time (at starting) tax free subsidy from the State Government of ₹ 25,00,000 on capital investment. Initial equipment cost will be ₹ 1.75 crores. Additional equipment costing ₹ 12,50,000 will be purchased at the end of the third year from the cash inflow of this year. At the end of 8 years, the original equipment will have no resale value, but additional equipment can be sold for ₹ 1,25,000. A working capital of ₹ 20,00,000 will be needed and it will be released at the end of eighth year. The project will be financed with sufficient amount of equity capital. The sales volumes over eight years have been estimated as follows:

Year	1	2	3	4-5	6-8
Units	72,000	1,08,000	2,60,000	2,70,000	1,80,000

A selling price of ₹ 120 per unit is expected and variable expenses will amount to 60% of sales revenue. Fixed cash operating costs will amount ₹ 18,00,000 per year. The loss of any year will be set off from the profits of subsequent two years. The company is subject to 30 per cent tax rate and considers 12 per cent to be an appropriate after tax cost of capital for this project. The company follows straight line method of depreciation.

Required: Calculate the net present value of the project and advise the management to take appropriate decision. (Figures should be rounded off in the multiple of 1,000)

Note: The Present Value Factors @ 12% discount rate are as follows:

Year	Year 1	Year 2	Year 3	Year 4	Year 5	Year 6	Year 7	Year 8
Present Value Factor	0.893	0.797	0.712	0.636	0.567	0.507	0.452	0.404

SOLUTION

COMPUTATION OF CASH INFLOWS AFTER TAX [CFAT]

(₹ in '000)

Particulars	Year 1	Year 2	Year 3	Year 4-5	Year 6-8
A. Sales Units	72	108	260	270	180
B. Selling Price per unit (₹)	120	120	120	120	120
C. Sales [A x B]	8,640	12,960	31,200	32,400	21,600
D. *Less:* Total Cost:					
Variable Costs @ 60% of Sales	5,184	7,776	18,720	19,440	12,960
Depreciation	2,188	2,188	2,188	2,413	2,413
Other Fixed Costs	1,800	1,800	1,800	1,800	1,800
Total Cost	(9,172)	(11,764)	(22,708)	(23,653)	(17,173)
E. Earning before Tax	(532)	1,196	8,492	8,747	4,427
F. *Less:* Tax @ 30%	–	(199)	(2,548)	(2,624)	(1,328)
G. Earning after Tax	(532)	997	5,944	6,123	3,099
H. *Add:* Depreciation	2,188	2,188	2,188	2,413	2,413
I. Cash Flow after Taxes (CFAT) (for years other than last year)	1,656	3,185	8,132	8,536	5,512
J. *Add:* Release of Working Capital					2,000
K. *Add:* Cash Salvage Value of Asset					125
L. Total CFAT for the last year					7,637

COMPUTATION OF NET PRESENT VALUE

(₹ in 000')

Particulars	Year	PV factor	Amount	PV
Purchase Price of New Machinery	0	1	(17,500)	(17,500)
Subsidy from Govt.	0	1	2,500	2,500
Working Capital	0	1	(2,000)	(2,000)
Additional Equipment	3	0.712	(1,250)	(890)
CFAT of Year 1	1	0.893	1,656	1,479
CFAT of Year 2	2	0.797	3,185	2,538
CFAT of Year 3	3	0.712	8,132	5,790
CFAT of Year 4	4	0.636	8,536	5,429
CFAT of Year 5	5	0.567	8,536	4,840
CFAT of Year 6	6	0.507	5,512	2,795
CFAT of Year 7	7	0.452	5,512	2,491
CFAT of Year 8	8	0.404	7,637	3,085
NPV				10,557

Recommendation: The Company should accept the project since NPV is positive.

Note: *The tax for the second year has been calculated after set off of brought forward loss of the first year. [i.e. 30% of (₹ 1,196 – ₹ 532)]*

PROBLEM 5

A doctor is planning to buy an X-Ray machine for his hospital. He has two options. He can either purchase it by making a cash payment of ₹ 5 lakhs *or* ₹ 6,15,000 are to be paid in six equal annual installments. Which option do you suggest to the doctor assuming the rate of return is 12 percent? Present value of annuity of ₹ 1 at 12 percent rate of discount for six years is 4.111.

SOLUTION

Option I: Cash Down Payment = ₹ 5,00,000

Option II: Annual Installment Basis

Annual installment = 6,15,000 × 1/6 = ₹ 1,02,500

Present Value of 1 to 6 installments @ 12% = 1,02,500 × 4.111 = ₹ 4,21,378

Advise: The doctor should buy X-Ray machine on installment basis because the present value of cash out flows is lower than cash down payment. This means Option II is better than Option I.

EVALUATION OF PROJECTS HAVING UNEQUAL LIVES

PROBLEM 6

A company is required to choose between two machines A and B. The two machines are designed differently, but have identical capacity and do exactly the same job. Machine A costs ₹ 6,00,000 and will last for 3 years. It costs ₹ 1,20,000 per year to run.

Machine B is an 'economy' model costing ₹ 4,00,000 but will last only for two years, and costs ₹ 1,80,000 per year to run. These are real cash flows. The costs are forecasted in rupees of constant purchasing power. Opportunity cost of capital is 10%. Which machine company should buy? Ignore tax.

$PVIF_{0.10,1} = 0.9091$, $PVIF_{0.10,2} = 0.8264$, $PVIF_{0.10,3} = 0.7513$.

SOLUTION

STATEMENT SHOWING EVALUATION OF TWO MACHINES

Machines	A	B
Running Cost of Machine p.a. (₹) 1,20,000	1,80,000	
Cumulative Present Value factor @ 10%.	2.4868	1.7355
Present Value of Running Cost (₹): 2,98,416	3,12,390	
Purchase Cost (₹):	6,00,000	4,00,000
Cash Outflow of Machines (₹):	8,98,416	7,12,390
Equivalent Present Value of Annual Cash Outflow (₹)	3,61,273.93	4,10,481.13

Recommendation: The Company should buy machine A since its equivalent cash outflow is *less* than that of Machine B.

PROBLEM 7

A company has to make a choice between two machines X and Y. The two machines are designed differently, but have identical capacity and do exactly the same job. Machine 'X' cost ₹ 5,50,000 and will last for three years. It costs ₹ 1,25,000 per year to run. Machine 'Y' is an economy model costing ₹ 4,00,000, but will last for two years and costs ₹ 1,50,000 per year to run. These are real cash flows. The costs re forecasted in Rupees of constant purchasing power. Opportunity cost of capital is 12%. Ignore Taxes. Which machine company should buy?

	t = 1	t = 2	t = 3
PVIF0.12	0.8929	0.7972	0.7118

PVIFA0.12,2 = 1.6901

PVIFA0.12,3 = 2.4019

SOLUTION

STATEMENT SHOWING THE CALCULATION OF ANNUALIZED NPV

Particulars	Year	PV factor	Machine X		Machine Y	
			Amount	PV	Amount	PV
Purchase Price	0	1	5,50,000	5,50,000	4,00,000	4,00,000
Cash outflow for 1 – 3 years	1 to 3	2.4019	1,25,000	3,00,238	–	–
Cash outflow for 1 – 2 years	1 to 2	1.6901	–	–	1,50,000	2,53,515
PV of Cash Outflow				8,50,238		6,53,515
Annuity Factor	3 yrs/2 yrs.	2.4019 / 1.6901		2.4019		1.6901
Annualised Present Value [PV/Annuity Factor]				3,53,985		3,86,672

Recommendation: Machine X should be purchased since its annualised present value of cash outflow is *less* than that of Machine Y.

PROBLEM 8

APZ Limited is considering to select a machine between two machines 'A' and 'B'. The two machines have identical capacity, do exactly the same job, but designed differently.

Machine 'A' costs ₹ 8,00,000, having userful life of three years. It costs ₹ 1,30,000 per year to run.

Machine 'B' is an economy model costing ₹ 6,00,000, having useful life of two years. It costs ₹ 2,50,000 per year to run.

The cash flows of machine 'A' and 'B' are real cash flows. The costs are forecasted in rupees of constant purchasing power. Ignore taxes.

The opportunity cost of capital is 10%. The present value factors at 10% are:

Year	t_1	t_2	t_3
PVIF0.10.t	0.9091	0.8264	0.7513
$PVIFA_{0.10.2}$ = 1.7355			
$PVIFA_{0.10.5}$ = 2.4868			

Which machine would you recommend the company to buy?

SOLUTION

STATEMENT SHOWING EVALUATION OF TWO MACHINES

Particulars	Machine A	Machine B
Running Cost of Machine p.a. (₹) 1,30,000	2,50,000	
Cumulative Present Value factor @ 10%.	2.4868	1.7355
Present Value of Running Cost (₹): 3,23,284	4,33,875	
Purchase Cost (₹):	8,00,000	6,00,000
Cash Outflow of Machines (₹):	11,23,284	10,33,875
Equivalent Present Value of Annual Cash Outflow (₹)	4,51,699	5,95,722

Recommendation: The Company should buy machine A since its equivalent cash outflow is *less* than that of Machine B.

Note: *Tax Saving on Depreciation has been ignored in the absence of Tax Rate.*

PROBLEM 9

A company wants to invest in a machinery that would cost ₹ 50,000 at the beginning of year 1. It is estimated that the net cash inflows from operations will be ₹ 18,000 per annum for 3 years, if the company opts to service a part of the machine at the end of the year 1 at ₹ 10,000 and the scrap value at the end of the year 3 will be ₹ 12,500. However, if the company decides not to services the part, it will have to be replaced at the end of the year 2 at ₹ 15,400. But in this case, the machine will work for the 4th year also and get operational cash inflow of ₹ 18,000 for the 4th year. It will have to be scrapped at the end of the year 4 at ₹ 9,000. Assuming cost of capital at 10% and ignoring taxes, will recommend the purchase of this machine based on the net present value of its cash flows?

If the supplier gives a discount of ₹ 5,000 for purchase, what would be your decision? (The present value factors at the end of years 0, 1, 2, 3, 4, 5 and 6 are respectively 1, 0.9091, 0.8264, 0.7513, 0.6830, 0.6209 and 0.5644).

SOLUTION

(a) If Part of Machine is Serviced

STATEMENT SHOWING NET PRESENT VALUE

Particulars	Year	PV factor at 10%	Amount ₹	PV at 10 % ₹
Purchase Price	0	1	(50,000)	(50,000)
Cost of Service	1	0.9091	(10,000)	(9,091)
CFAT for 1 – 2 years	1 to 2	1.7355	18,000	31,239
CFAT for 3rd year	3	0.7513	30,500	22,915
NPV				(4,937)
PVAF of 3 years @ 10%				2.4868
Annualized NPV (NPV/PVAF)				(1985.28)

(b) If Part of Machine is Replaced

STATEMENT SHOWING NET PRESENT VALUE

Particulars	Year	PV factor at 10%	Amount ₹	PV at 10 % ₹
Purchase Price	0	1	(50,000)	(50,000)
Cost of Replacement	2	0.8264	(15,400)	(12,727)
CFAT for 1 – 3 years	1 to 3	2.4868	18,000	44,762
CFAT for 4th year	4	0.6830	27,000	18,441
NPV				476
PVAF of 4 years @ 10%				3.1698
Annualized NPV (NPV/PVAF)				150.17

Recommendation (Without considering Supplier's Discount): The Machine should be purchased with alternative of replacing the part since this alternative has higher annualized NPV.

Recommendation (After considering Supplier's Discount): Supplier discount will not change the decision to Purchase the Machine as there is no Differntial Cash Inflow. Hence, the Machine should be purchased with alternative of replacing the part since the Annualized NPV under alternative of replacing [₹ 1,727.55 i.e. (₹ 476 + ₹ 5000)/3.1698] is more than that of Alternative of service [₹ 25.334 i.e., (₹ 5,000 – ₹ 4,937)/2.4868]

INTERNAL RATE OF RETURN (IRR)

PROBLEM 10

A company proposes to install a machine involving a Capital Cost of ₹ 3,60,000. The life of the machine is 5 years and its salvage value at the end of the life is nil. The machine will produce the net operating income after depreciation of ₹ 68,000 per annum. The company's tax rate is 45%. The Present Value factors for 5 years are as under:

Discounting Rate	14%	15%	16%	17%	18%
Cumulative factor	3.43	3.35	3.27	3.20	3.13

You are required to calculate the internal rate of return of the proposal.

SOLUTION

COMPUTATION OF CASH INFLOW

	Particulars	₹
A	Net operating income per annum	68,000
B	*Less:* Tax @ 45%	(30,600)
C	Profit after tax	37,400
D	*Add:* Depreciation (₹ 3,60,000 / 5 years)	72,000
E	Cash Inflow p.a.	1,09,400
	The IRR of the investment can be found as follows:	
	NPV = – ₹ 3,60,000 + ₹ 1,09,400 ($PVAF_5$, r)	0
	or, PVAF5 r (cumulative factor) = ₹ 3,60,000/₹ 1,09,400	3.29

COMPUTATION OF INTERNAL RATE OF RETURN

A.	Discounting rate	15%	16%
B.	Cumulative factor	3.35	3.27
C.	Total of Cash Inflow (₹)	3,66,490	3,57,738
		(₹ 1,09,400 × 3.350)	(₹ 1,09,400 × 3.27)
D.	Internal outlay (₹)	3,60,000	3,60,000
E.	NPV (₹) [C – D]	6,490	(2,262)

IRR = 15% + [6,490/(6,490 + 2,262)] = 15% + 0.74% = 15.74%.

ALTERNATIVE METHOD

$$\text{IRR} = \text{Lower Rate} + \frac{\text{PVAF at Lower Rate} - \text{Payback Period}}{\text{PVAF at Lower Rate} - \text{PVAF at Higher Rate}}$$

$$= 15\% + [(3.35 - 3.29)/(3.35 - 3.27)] = 15.75\%$$

MISCELLANEOUS

PROBLEM 11

Consider the following mutually exclusive projects:

Project	Cash Flow (₹)				
	C_0	C_1	C_2	C_3	C_4
A	–10,000	6,000	2,000	2,000	12,000
B	–10,000	2,500	2,500	5,000	7,500
C	–3,500	1,500	2,500	500	5,000
D	–3,000	0	0	3,000	6,000

Required:

(i) Calculate the payback period for each project.

(ii) If the standard payback period is 2 years, which project will you select? Will your answer differ, if standard payback period is 3 years?

(iii) If the cost of capital is 10%, compute the discounted payback period for each project. Which projects will you recommend, if standard discounted payback period is (i) 2 years; (ii) 3 years?

(iv) Compute NPV of each project. Which project will you recommend on the NPV criterion? The cost of capital is 10%. What will be the appropriate choice criteria in the case? The PV factors at 10% are:

Year	1	2	3	4
PV Factor at 10%	0.9091	0.8264	0.7513	0.6830

SOLUTION

(I) PAYBACK PERIOD

	Project A		Project B		Project C		Project D	
Year	**CI**	**Cum. CI**	**CI**	**Cum. CI**	**CI**	**Cum. CI**	**CI**	**Cum. CI**
1	6,000	6,000	2,500	2,500	1,500	1,500	0	0
2	2,000	8,000	2,500	5,000	2,500	4,000	0	0
3	2,000	10,000	5,000	10,000	500	4,500	3,000	3,000
4	12,000	22,000	7,500	17,500	5,000	9,500	6,000	9,000
Pay back	**3 years**	**3 years**	**1 year, 9 months, 18 days**			**3 years**		

(ii) If the standard payback period is 2 years, only Project C can be selected.

If the standard payback period is 3 years, all the four projects can be selected.

(III) DISCOUNTED PAYBACK PERIOD

	PVF@	Project A		Project B		Project C		Project D	
Year	**10%**	**DCI**	**Cum. DCI**	**DCI**	**Cum. DCI**	**DCI**	**Cum. DCI**	**DCI**	**Cum. DCI**
1	0.9091	5,454.6	5,454.6	2,272.75	2,272.75	1,363.65	1,363.65	0	0
2	0.8264	1,652.8	7,107.4	2,066.00	4,338.75	2,066.00	3,429.65	0	0
3	0.7513	1,502.6	8,610.0	3,756.50	8,095.25	375.65	3,805.30	2,253.90	2,253.90
4	0.6830	8,196.0	16,806.0	5,122.50	13,217.75	3,415.00	7,220.30	4,098.0	6,351.90

Discounted Payback Period (A) = 3 years + (1390/8196) = 3.17 Years *or* 3 Years, 2 Months, 1 Day.

Discounted Payback Period (B) = 3 years + (1904.75/5122.50) = 3.372 Years *or* 3 Years, 4 Months, 14 Days.

Discounted Payback Period (C) = 2 Years + (70.35/375.65) = 2.187 Years *or* 2 Years, 2 Months, 7 Days.

Discounted Payback Period (D) = 3 years + 746.10/4098 = 3.182 Years *or* 3 Years, 2 Months, 6 Days.

If Standard discounted payback period is 2 years, no project is acceptable.

If Standard discounted payback period is 3 years, Project 'C' is acceptable.

(IV) EVALUATION OF PROJECTS ON NPV CRITERION

NPV = Discounted Cash Inflow – Discounted Cash Outflow

NPV of Project A = – 10,000 + 5,454.6 + 1,652.8 + 1,502.60 + 8,196 = ₹ 6,806

NPV of Project B = – 10,000 + 2,272.75 + 2,066 + 3,756.5 + 5,122.5 = ₹ 3,217.75

NPV of Project C = – 3,500 + 1,363.65 + 2,066 + 375.65 + 3,415.00 = ₹ 3,720.3

NPV of Project D = – 3,000 + 0 + 0 + 2,253.9 + 4,098 = ₹ 3,351.9

RANKING OF MUTUALLY EXCLUSIVE PROJECTS ON NPV CRITERION

Project	NPV ₹	Ranking as per NPV
A	6,806.20	I
B	3,217.75	IV
C	3,720.30	II
D	3,351.90	III

Recommendation: Project A is acceptable under the NPV method.

PROBLEM 12

C Ltd. is considering investing in a project. The expected original investment in the project will be ₹ 2,00,000, the life of project will be 5 years with no salvage value. The expected net cash inflows after depreciation but before tax during the life of the project will be as follows:

Year	1	2	3	4	5
₹	85,000	1,00,000	80,000	80,000	40,000

The project will be depreciated at the rate of 20% on original cost. The company is subject to 30% tax rate.

Required:

(i) Calculate Pay Back Period

(ii) Average Rate of Return (ARR).

(iii) Calculate Net Present Value and Net Present Value Index, if cost of capital is 10%.

(iv) Calculate Internal Rate of Return.

Note: *The P.V. factors are:*

Year	P.V. at 10%	P.V. at 37%	P.V. at 38%	P.V. at 40%
1	0.909	0.730	0.725	0.714
2	0.826	0.533	0.525	0.510
3	0.751	0.389	0.381	0.364
4	0.683	0.284	0.276	0.260
5	0.621	0.207	0.200	0.186

SOLUTION

CALCULATION OF CASH FLOW AFTER TAX (CFAT)

Year	1 ₹	2 ₹	3 ₹	4 ₹	5 ₹
Earnings after depreciation but before tax	85,000	1,00,000	80,000	80,000	40,000
Less: Tax @ 30%	(25,500)	(30,000)	(24,000)	(24,000)	(12,000)
Earning after tax	59,500	70,000	56,000	56,000	28,000
Add: Depreciation (₹ 2,00,000 / 5)	40,000	40,000	40,000	40,000	40,000
CFAT	99,500	1,10,000	96,000	96,000	68,000
Cumulative CFAT	99,500	2,09,500	3,05,500	4,01,500	4,69,500

(i) Pay Back Period = 1 year + = 1.914 Years *or* 1 Year, 10 Months and 29 Days.

(ii) Average Rate of Return (ARR)

Step 1: *Average Earnings after Tax*

$$= \frac{₹\ 59{,}500 + ₹\ 70{,}000 + ₹\ 56{,}000 + ₹\ 56{,}000 + ₹\ 28{,}000}{5} = ₹\ 53{,}900$$

Step 2: *Average Investment = 1/2 (Original Cost – Salvage Value) + Salvage Value + Working Capital*

(Since SLM of Depreciation has been used, this shortcut formula has been applied)

= 1/2 (₹ 2,00,000 – 0) + 0 + 0 = ₹ 1,00,000

Step 3: *Average Rate of Return (ARR)*

$$= \frac{\text{Average Earnings after tax}}{\text{Average Investment}} \times 100 = \frac{₹\ 53{,}900}{₹\ 1{,}00{,}000} \times 100 = 53.9\%.$$

(III) NPV AND NPV INDEX

Particulars	Year	PV Factor	Amount	PV
Investment	0	1.000	(2,00,000)	(2,00,000)
CFAT	1	0.909	99,500	90,445.50
CFAT	2	0.826	1,10,000	90,860.00
CFAT	3	0.751	96,000	72,096.00
CFAT	4	0.683	96,000	65,568.00
CFAT	5	0.621	68,000	42,228.00
			NPV	1,61,197.50

$$\text{NPV Index} = \frac{\text{NPV}}{\text{PV of Cash Outflows}} = ₹\ 1{,}61{,}197.50/₹\ 1{,}00{,}000 = 0.81.$$

(ii) Internal Rate of Return (IRR)

Step 1: *Average Annual Cash Inflow*

$$= \frac{₹\ 99{,}500 + ₹\ 1{,}10{,}000 + ₹\ 96{,}000 + ₹\ 96{,}000 + ₹\ 68{,}000}{5} = ₹\ 93{,}900$$

Step 2: Fake Payback Period $= \frac{\text{Cash Outflow}}{\text{Average Annual Cash Inflow}} = ₹\ 2{,}00{,}000/₹\ 93{,}900 = 2.13$

Step 3: *Two Present Value of Annuity Factor within which Fake Payback Period lies are 2.143 and 2.106 which correspond to discount rates of 37% and 38% respectively.*

Step 4: *Calculation of NPV at 37% and 38%.*

Particulars	Year	Amount	PVF @ 37%	PV at 37%	PVF @ 38%	PV at 38%	PVF @ 40%	PV @ 40%
Investment	0	(2,00,000)	1.000	(2,00,000)	1.000	(2,00,000)	1.000	(2,00,000)
CFAT	1	99,500	0.730	72,635	0.725	72,138	0.714	71,043
CFAT	2	1,10,000	0.533	58,630	0.525	57,750	0.510	56,100
CFAT	3	96,000	0.389	37,344	0.381	36,576	0.364	34,944
CFAT	4	96,000	0.284	27,264	0.276	26,496	0.260	24,960
CFAT	5	68,000	0.207	14,076	0.200	13,600	0.186	12,648
NPV				9,949		6,560		(305)

$$IRR = Lower Rate + \frac{NPV at Lower Rate}{NPV at Lower Rate - NPV at Higher Rate} \times (H - L)$$

$$= 38\% + [6560/\{6560 - (-305)\}] \times (40\% - 38\%) = 39.91\%.$$

PROBLEM 13

PR Engineering Ltd. is considering the purchase of a new machine which will carry out some operations which are the present performed by manual labour. The following information related to the two alternative models – 'MX' and 'MY' are available:

Machines	Machine 'MX'	Machine 'MY'
Cost of Machine	₹ 8,00,000	₹ 10,20,000
Expected Life	6 years	6 years
Scrap Value	₹ 20,000	₹ 30,000

Estimated net income before depreciation and tax:

Year	₹	₹
1	2,50,000	2,70,000
2	2,30,000	3,60,000
3	1,80,000	3,80,000
4	2,00,000	2,80,000
5	1,80,000	2,60,000
6	1,60,000	1,85,000

Corporate tax rate for this company is 30 percent and company's required rate of return on investment proposals is 10 percent. Depreciation will be charged on straight line basis.

You are required to:

(i) Calculate the pay-back period of each proposal.

(ii) Calculate the net present value of each proposal, if the P.V. factor at 10% is – 0.909, 0.826, 0.751, 0.683, 0.621 and 0.564.

(iii) Which proposal you world recommend and why?

SOLUTION

(i) Calculation of Payback Period

CUMULATIVE CASH INFLOWS

Years	1	2	3	4	5	6
Machine 'MX'	2,14,000	4,14,000	5,79,000	7,58,000	9,23,000	10,74,000
Machine 'MY'	2,38,500	5,40,000	8,55,500	11,01,000	13,32,500	15,11,500

Pay-back Period for 'MX'

$$= 4 + \frac{(8,00,000 - 7,58,000)}{1,65,000} = 4 + \frac{42,000}{1,65,000} = 4 + 0.25$$

= 4.25 years or, 4 years and 3 months

Pay-back Period for 'MX' = 4.25 years *or* 4 years and 3 months

Pay-back Period for 'MY'

$$= 3 + \frac{(10,20,000 - 8,55,000)}{2,45,000} = 3 + \frac{1,64,500}{2,45,500} = 3 + 0.67$$

= 3.67 years or, 3 years and 8 months

Pay-back Period for 'MY' = 3.67 years *or* 3 years *or* 3 years and 8 months

(ii) Calculation of Net Present Value (NPV)

Year	PV Factor	Machine 'MX'		Machine 'MY'	
		Cash Inflows ₹	Present Value ₹	Cash Inflow ₹	Present Value ₹
0	1.000	(8,00,000)	(8,00,000)	(10,20,000)	(10,20,000)
1	0.909	2,14,000	1,94,526	2,38,500	2,16,797
2	0.826	2,00,000	1,65,200	3,01,500	2,49,039
3	0.751	1,65,000	1,23,915	3,15,500	2,36,941
4	0.683	1,79,000	1,22,257	2,45,500	1,67,677
5	0.621	1,65,000	1,02,465	2,31,500	1,43,762
6	0.564	1,51,000	85,164	1,79,000	1,00,956
Scrap Value	0.564	20,000	11,280	30,000	16,920
Net Present Value (NPV)			4,807		1,12,092

Net Present Value of Machine 'MX' = ₹ 4,807

Net Present Value of Machine 'MY' = ₹ 1,12,092

(iii) Recommendation

Particulars	Machine 'MX'	Machine 'MY'
Ranking according to Pay-back Period	II	I
Ranking according to Net Present Value (NPV)	II	I

Advise: Since machine 'MY' has higher ranking than Machine 'MX' according to both the parameters, i.e. Payback Period as well as Net Present Value, therefore, Machine 'MY' is recommended.

(i) Depreciation of Machine 'MX' = (₹ 8,00,000 – ₹ 20,000)/6 = ₹ 1,30,000

(ii) Depreciation of Machine 'MY' = (₹ 10,20,000 – ₹ 30,000)/6 = ₹ 1,65,000

(III) CASH INFLOWS OF MACHINE 'MX'

Years	1	2	3	4	5	6
Earning before Depreciation and Tax	2,50,000	2,30,000	1,80,000	2,00,000	1,80,000	1,60,000
Less: Depreciation	1,30,000	1,30,000	1,30,000	1,30,000	1,30,000	1,30,000
EBIT	1,20,000	1,00,000	50,000	70,000	50,000	30,000
Less: Tax	36,000	30,000	15,000	21,000	15,000	9,000
EBT	84,000	70,000	35,000	49,000	35,000	21,000
Add: Depreciation	1,30,000	1,30,000	1,30,000	1,30,000	1,30,000	1,30,000
CFAT	2,14,000	2,00,000	1,65,000	1,79,000	1,65,000	1,51,000

(IV) CASH INFLOWS OF MACHINE 'MY'

Years	1	2	3	4	5	6
Earning before	2,70,000	3,60,000	3,80,000	2,80,000	2,60,000	1,85,000
Depreciation and Tax						
Less: Depreciation	1,65,000	1,65,000	1,65,000	1,65,000	1,65,000	1,65,000
EBT	1,05,000	1,95,000	2,15,000	1,15,000	95,000	20,000
Less: Tax	31,500	58,500	64,500	34,500	28,500	6,000
EAT	93,500	1,36,500	1,50,500	80,500	66,500	14,000
Add: Depreciation	1,65,000	1,65,000	1,65,000	1,65,000	1,65,000	1,65,000
CFAT	2,38,500	3,01,500	3,15,500	2,45,500	2,31,500	1,79,000

PROBLEM 14

A hospital is considering to purchase a diagnostic machine costing ₹ 80,000. The projected life of the machine is 8 years and has an expected salvage value of ₹ 6,000 at the end of 8 years. The annual operating cost of the machine is ₹ 7,500. It is expected to generate revenues of ₹ 40,000 per year for eight years. Presently, the hospital is outsourcing the diagnostic work and is earning commission income of ₹ 12,000 per annum; net of taxes.

Required: Whether it would be profitable for the hospital to purchase the machine? Give your recommendation under:

(i) Net Present Value method

(ii) Profitability Index method.

PV factors at 10% are given below:

Year 1	Year 2	Year 3	Year 4	Year 5	Year 6	Year 7	Year 8
0.909	0.826	0.751	0.683	0.621	0.564	0.513	0.467

SOLUTION

CALCULATION OF CASH INFLOWS

Sales Revenue	40,000
Less: Operating Cost	7,500
Less: Depreciation [(80,000 – 6,000)/8]	9,250
Earnings before Tax	23,250
Tax @ 30%	6,975
Earnings after Tax (EAT)	16,275
Add: Depreciation	9,250
Cash inflow after tax per annum	25,525
Less: Loss of Commission Income	12,000
Net Cash inflow after tax per annum	13,525
In 8th Year:	
New Cash inflow after tax	13,525
Add: Salvage Value of Machine	6,000
Net Cash inflow in year 8	19,525

CALCULATION OF NET PRESENT VALUE (NPV)

Year	CFAT	PV Factor @ 10%	Present Value of Cash inflows
1 to 7	13,525	4.867	65,826.18
8	19,525	0.467	9,118.18
		74,944.36	
Less: Cash Outflows		80,000.00	
NPV			(5,055.64)

$$\text{Profitability Index} = \frac{\text{Sum of discounted cash inflows}}{\text{Present value of cash outflows}} = 74{,}944.36/80{,}000 = 0.937$$

Advise: Since the net present value is negative and profitability index is also *less* than 1, therefore, the hospital should not purchase the diagnostic machine.

Note: *Since the tax rate is not mentioned in the question, therefore, it is assumed to be 30 percent in the given solution.*

PROLEM 15

The management of P Limited is considering selecting a machine out of two mutually exclusive machines. The company's cost of capital is 12 percent and corporate tax rate for the company is 30 percent. Details of the machines are as follows:

Particulars	Machine – I	Machine – II
Cost of machine	₹ 10,00,000	₹ 15,00,000
Expected life	5 years	6 years
Annual income before tax and depreciation	₹ 3,45,000	₹ 4,55,000
Depreciation is to be charged on straight line basis.		

You are required to:

(i) Calculate the discounted pay-back period, net present value and internal rate of return for each machine.

(ii) Advise the management of P Limited as to which machine they should take up.

The present value factors of ₹ 1 are as follows:

Year	1	2	3	4	5	6
At 12 %	.893	.797	.712	.636	.567	.507
At 13%	.885	.783	.693	.613	.543	.480
At 14%	.877	.769	.675	.592	.519	.456
At 15%	.870	.756	.658	.572	.497	.432
At 16%	.862	.763	.641	.552	.476	.410

SOLUTION

(a)(i) Computation of Discounted Payback Period, Net Present Value (NPV) and Internal Rate of Return (IRR) for Two Machines

CALCULATION OF CASH INFLOWS

Particulars	Machine – I (₹)	Machine – II (₹)
Annual Income before Tax and Depreciation	3,45,000	4,55,000
Less: Depreciation	2,00,000	2,50,000
Income before Tax	1,45,000	2,05,000
Less: Tax @ 30%	43,500	61,500
Income after Tax	1,01,500	1,43,500
Add: Depreciation	2,00,000	2,50,000
Annual Cash Inflows	3,01,500	3,93,500

Machine – I					Machine – II		
Year	P.V. of ₹ 1 @12%	Cash flow	P.V.	Cumulative P.V	Cash flow	P.V.	Cumulative
1	0.893	3,01,500	2,69,240	2,69,240	3,93,500	3,51,396	3,51,396
2	0.797	3,01,500	2,40,296	5,09,536	3,93,500	3,13,620	6,65,016
3	0.712	3,01,500	2,14,668	7,24,204	3,93,500	2,80,172	9,45,188
4	0.636	3,01,500	1,91,754	9,15,958	3,93,500	2,50,266	11,95,454
5	0.567	3,01,500	1,70,951	10,86,909	3,93,500	2,23,115	14,18,569
6	0.507	—	—	—	3,93,500	1,99,505	16,18,074

Discounted Payback Period for:

Machine – I	Machine – II
= 4 + (10,00,000 – 9,15,958)/1,70,951	= 5 + (15,00,000 – 14,18,569)/1,99,505
= 4 + (84,042/1,70,951) = 4 + 0.4916	= 5 + (81,431/1,99,505) = 5 + 0.4082
= 4.49 years *or* 4 years and 5.9 months	**= 5.41 years *or* 5 years and 4.9 months**

Net Present Value for:

Machine – I	Machine – II
= ₹ 10,86,909 – 10,00,000 = ₹ 86,909	= ₹ 16,18,074 – 15,00,000 = ₹ 1,18,074

Internal Rate of Return (IRR) for:

Machine – I

$$\text{P.V. Factor} = \frac{\text{Initial Investment}}{\text{Annual Cash Inflow}} = 10,00,000/3,01,500 = 3.3167$$

PV factor falls between 15% and 16%

Present Value of Cash inflow at 15% and 16% will be:

Present Value at 15% = 3.353 × 3,01,500 = 10,10,930

Present Value at 16% = 3.274 × 3,01,500 = 9,87,111

IRR = 15 + [(10,10,930 – 10,00,000)/(10,10,930 – 9,87,111)] × (16 – 15)

= 15 + (10,930/23,819) × 1 = 15.4588% = 15.46%

Machine – II

P.V. Factor = 15,00,000/3,93,500 = 3.8199

Present Value of Cash inflow at 14% and 15% will be:

Present Value at 14% = 3.888 × 3,93,500 = 15,29,928

Present Value at 15% = 3.785 × 3,93,500 = 14,89,398

IRR = 14 + [(15,29,928 – 15,00,000)/(15,29,928 – 14,89,398)] × (15 – 14)

= 14 + (29,928/40,530) × 1 = 14.7384% = 14.74%

(ii) Advise to the Management

RANKING OF MACHINES IN TERMS OF THE THREE METHODS

Particulars	Machine – I	Machine – II
Discounted	I	II
Net Present Value	II	I
Internal Rate of Return	I	II

Advise: Since Machine – I has better ranking than Machine – II, therefore, Machine – I should be selected.

PROBLEM 16

A Ltd. is considering the purchase of a machine which will perform some operations which are at present performed by workers. Machines X and Y are alternative models. The following details are available:

Particulars	Machine X (₹)	Machine Y (₹)
Cost of machine	1,50,000	2,40,000
Estimated life of machine	5 years	6 years
Estimated cost of maintenance p.a.	7,000	11,000
Estimated cost of indirect material, p.c.	6,000	8,000
Estimated savings in scrap p.a.	10,000	15,000
Estimated cost of supervision p.a.	12,000	16,000
Estimated savings in wages p.a.	90,000	1,20,000

Depreciation will be charged on straight line basis. The tax rate is 30%. Evaluate the alternatives according to:

(i) Average rate of return method, and

(ii) Present value index method assuming cost of capital being 10%.

(The present value of ₹ 1.00 @ 10% p.a. for 5 years is 3.79 and for 6 years is 4.354)

SOLUTION

Evaluation of Alternatives

(i) Average Rate of Return (ARR) = $\frac{\text{Average Annual Income}}{\text{Average Investment}}$

Machine X = 31,500/75,000 × 100 = 42% Machine Y = 42,000/1,20,000 × 100 = 35%

Decision: Machine X is better.

(ii) Present Value Index Method

Present Value = Annual Cash Inflow P.V. Factor @ 10%

Machine X = 61,500 × 3.79 = ₹ 2,33,085

Machine Y = 82,000 × 4.354 = ₹ 3,57,028

P.V. Index = Present Value/Investment

Machine X = 2,33,085/1,50,000 = 1.5539 Machine Y = 3,57,028/2,40,000 = 1.4876

Decision: Machine X is better.

Working Notes:

(i) Depreciation: Machine X = 1,50,000/5 = ₹ 30,000, Machine Y = 2,40,000/6 = ₹ 40,000

(II) ANNUAL INCOME AFTER TAX AND ANNUAL CASH INFLOWS

Particulars	Machine X (₹)	Machine Y (₹)
A. Annual Savings:		
Wages	90,000	1,20,000
Scrap	10,000	15,000
Total Savings	1,00,000	1,35,000
B. Annual Estimated Cash Cost:		
Indirect Material	6,000	8,000
Supervision	12,000	16,000
Maintenance	7,000	11,000
Total Cash Cost	25,000	35,000
C. Annual Cash Savings	75,000	1,00,000
D. *Less:* Depreciation	30,000	40,000
E. Annual Savings Before Tax [C – D]	45,000	60,000
F. *Less:* Tax @ 30%	13,500	18,000
G. Annual Savings/Profit (After Tax) [E – F]	31,500	42,000
H. *Add:* Depreciation	30,000	40,000
I. Annual Cash Inflows [G + H]	61,500	82,000

PROBLEM 17

SS Limited is considering the purchase of a new automatic machine which will carry out some operations which are at present performed by manual labour. NM-A1 and NM-A2, two alternative models are available in the market. The following details are collected:

Particulars		Machine	
		NM-A1	NM -A2
Cost of Machine	(₹)	20,00,000	25,00,000
Estimated working life		5 Years	5 Years
Estimated saving in direct wages per annum	(₹)	7,00,000	9,00,000
Estimated saving in scrap per annum	(₹)	60,000	1,00,000
Estimated additional cost of indirect material per annum	(₹)	30,000	90,000
Estimated additional cost of indirect labour per annum	(₹)	40,000	50,000
Estimated additional cost of repairs and maintenance per annum	(₹)	45,000	85,000

Depreciation will be charged on a straight line method. Corporate tax rate is 30 percent and expected rate of return may be 12 percent.

You are required to evaluate the alternatives by calculating the:

(i) Pay-back Period

(ii) Accounting (Average) Rate of Return; and

(iii) Profitability Index *or* P.V. Index (P.V. factor for ₹ 1 @ 12% 0.893; 0.797; 0.712; 0.636; 0.567; 0.507)

SOLUTION

Depreciation of Machine NM-A_1 = 20,00,000/5 = 4,00,000

Depreciation on Machine NM-A_2 = 25,00,000/5 = 5,00,000

EVALUATION OF ALTERNATIVES

Particulars	Machine NMA (₹)	Machine NMA (₹)
Annual Savings:		
Direct Wages	7,00,000	9,00,000
Scraps	60,000	1,00,000
(A) Total Savings	7,60,000	10,00,000
Annual Estimated Cash Cost:		
Indirect Material	30,000	90,000
Indirect Labor	40,000	50,000
Repairs and Maintenance	45,000	85,000
(B) Total Cost	1,15,000	2,25,000
(C) Annual Cash Savings (A – B)	6,45,000	7,75,000
Less: Depreciation	4,00,000	5,00,000
Annual savings before Tax	2,45,000	2,75,000
Less: Tax @ 30%	73,500	82,5000
Annual Savings/Profits after tax	1,71,500	1,92,500
Add: Depreciation	4,00,000	5,00,000
Annual Cash Inflows	5,71,500	6,92,500

(i) Payback Period $= \frac{\text{Total Initial Capital Investment}}{\text{Annual expected after tax net cashflow}}$

Machine NM-A_1 = 20,00,000/5,71,500 = 3.50 Years

Machine NM-A_2 = 25,00,000/6,92,500 = 3.61 Years

Decision: Machine NM-A1 is better.

(ii) ARR $= \frac{\text{Average Annual Net Saving}}{\text{Average investment}} \times 100$

Machine NM-A_1 = 1,71,500/10,00,000 × 100 = 17.15%

Machine NM-A_2 = 1,92,500/12,50,000 × 100 = 15.4%

Decision: Machine NM-A1 is better.

(iii) Profitability index *or* PV Index $= \frac{\text{Present Value of Cash Inflow}}{\text{Investment}}$

Present Value Cash Inflow = Annual Cash inflow × PV factor at 12%

Machine NM-A1 = 5,71,500 × 3.605 = ₹. 20,60,258

Machine NM-A2 = 6,92,500 × 3.605 = ₹. 24,96,463

Machine NM-A_1 = 20,60,258/20,00,000 = 1.03

Machine NM-A_2 = 24,96,463/20,00,000 = 0.9

Decision: Machine NM-A1 is better.

PROBLEM 18

PQR Company Ltd. is considering to select a machine out of two mutually exclusive machines. The company's cost of capital is 12 per cent and corporate tax rate is 30 per cent. Other information relating to both machines is as follows:

Particulars	Machine – I	Machine – II
Cost of Machine	₹ 15,00,000	₹ 20,00,000
Expected Life	5 Yrs.	5 Yrs.
Annual Income (Before Tax and Depreciation)	₹ 6,25,000	₹ 8,75,000

Depreciation is to be charged on straight line basis:

Your are required to calculate: Discounted Pay Back Period; Net Present Value; Profitability Index. The present value factors of ₹ 1 @ 12% are as follows:

Year	01	02	03	04	05
PV factor @ 12%	0.893	0.797	0.712	0.636	0.567

SOLUTION

(i) Discounted Payback Period

Machine – 1

Discounted Payback Period = 3 + (15,00,000 – 12,67,056)/3,35,490

= 3 + 0.6943 = 3 years 8.28 months

Machine – II

Discounted Payback Period = 3 + (20,00,000 – 17,59,466)/4,65,870 = 3 + 0.5163

= 3 years 6.24 months

(ii) Net Present Value (NPV)

NPV of Machine – I = 19,01,639 – 15,00,000 = ₹ 4,01,639

NPV of Machine – II = 26,40,664 – 20,00,000 = ₹ 6,40,664

(iii) Profitability Index

NPV of Machine – I = 19,01,639/15,00,000 = 1.268

NPV of Machine – II = 26,40,664/20,00,000 = 1.320

RANKING OF MACHINES

Method	Machine-I	Machine-II	Rank
Discounted Payback Period	3.69 years	3.52 years	II
Net Present Value	₹ 4,01,639	₹ 6,40,664	II
Profitability Index	1.268	1.320	II

Working Notes:

1. Depreciation of Machine – I = 15,00,000/5 = ₹ 3,00,000

2. Depreciation on Machine – II = 20,00,000/5 = ₹ 4,00,000

3. CALCULATION OF CFAT

Particulars	Machine-I (₹)	Machine-II (₹)
Annual Income (before Tax and Depreciation)	6,25,000	8,75,000
Less: Depreciation	3,00,000	4,00,000
Annual Income (before Tax)	3,25,000	4,75,000
Less: Tax @ 30%	97,500	1,42,500
Annual Income (after Tax)	2,27,500	3,32,500
Add: Depreciation	3,00,000	4,00,000
CFAT	5,27,500	7,32,500

4. CALCULATION OF PV AND CUMULATIVE PV

		Machine – I			Machine – II		
Year	PV of Re 1 @ 12%	Cash flow	PV	Cumulative PV	Cash flow	PV	Cumulative PV
1	0.893	5,27,500	4,71,058	4,71,058	7,32,500	6,54,123	6,54,123
2	0.797	5,27,500	4,20,418	8,91,476	7,32,500	5,83,803	12,37,926
3	0.712	5,27500	3,75,580	12,67,056	7,32,500	5,21,540	17,59,466
4	0.636	5,27,500	3,35,490	16,02,546	7,32,500	4,65,870	22,25,336
5	0.567	5,27,500	2,99,093	19,01,639	7,32,500	4,15,328	26,40,664

PROBLEM 19

FH Hospital is considering to purchase a CT-Scan machine. Presently the hospital is outsourcing the CT -Scan Machine and is earning commission of ₹15,000 per month (net of tax). The following details are given regarding the machine:

Particulars	₹
Cost of CT -Scan machine	15,00,000
Operating cost per annum (excluding Depreciation)	2,25,000
Expected revenue per annum	7,90,000
Salvage value of the machine (after 5 years)	3,00,000
Expected life of the machine	5 years

Assuming tax rate @ 30%, whether it would be profitable for the hospital to purchase the machine?

Give your recommendation under:

(i) Net Present Value Method, and

(ii) Profitability Index Method.

PV factors at 12% are given below:

Year	1	2	3	4	5
PV factor	0.893	0.797	0.712	0.636	0.567

SOLUTION

ADVISE TO THE HOSPITAL MANAGEMENT

Determination of Cash inflows	₹
Sales Revenue	7,90,000
Less: Operating Cost	2,25,000
	5,65,000
Less: Depreciation (15,00,000 – 3,00,000)/5	2,40,000
Net Income	3,25,000
Tax @ 30%	97,500
Earnings after Tax (EAT)	2,27,500
Add: Depreciation	2,40,000
Cash inflow after tax per annum	4,67,500
Less: Loss of Commission Income	1,80,000
Net Cash inflow after tax per annum	2,87,500
In 5th Year:	
New Cash inflow after tax	2,87,500
Add: Salvage Value of Machine	3,00,000
Net Cash inflow in year 5	5,87,500

CALCULATION OF NET PRESENT VALUE (NPV)

Year	CFAT	PV Factor @10%	Present Value of Cash inflows
1 to 4	2,87,500	3.038	8,73,425.00
5	5,87,500	0.567	3,33,112.50
			12,06,537.50
Less: Cash Outflows			15,00,000.00
	NPV		(2,93,462.50)

$$\text{Profitability Index} = \frac{\text{Sum of discounted cash in flows}}{\text{Present value of cash outflows}} = \frac{12{,}06{,}537.50}{15{,}00{,}000} = 0.804$$

Advise: Since the net present value is negative and profitability index is also *less* than 1, therefore, the hospital should not purchase the CT-Scan machine.

PROBLEM 20

A company is considering the proposal of taking up a new project which requires an investment of ₹ 400 lakh on machinery and other assets. The project is expected to yield the following earnings (before depreciation and taxes) over the next five years:

Year	1	2	3	4	5
Earnings (₹ in lakhs)	160	160	180	180	150

The cost of raising the additional capital is 12% and assets have to be depreciated at 20% on 'Written Down Value' basis. The scrap value at the end of the five years' period may be taken as zero. Income-tax applicable to the company is 50%.

Required: calculate the net present value of the project and advise the management to take appropriate decision. Also calculate the Internal Rate of Return of the Project.

Note: *Present value of ₹ 1 at different rates of interest are as follows:*

Year	10%	12%	14%	16%
1	0.91	0.89	0.88	0.86
2	0.83	0.80	0.77	0.74
3	0.75	0.71	0.67	0.64
4	0.68	0.64	0.59	0.55
5	0.62	0.57	0.52	0.48

SOLUTION

STATEMENT SHOWING THE COMPUTATION OF CASH INFLOWS AFTER TAX [CFAT]

(*₹ in 000'*)

Particulars	Year 1	Year 2	Year 3	Year 4	Year 5
Earning before Depreciation & Tax	16,000	16,000	18,000	18,000	15,000
Less: Depreciation	(8,000)	(6,400)	(5,120)	(4,096)	(3,277)
Earning before Tax	8,000	9,600	12,880	13,904	11,723
Less: Tax @ 50%	(4,000)	(4,800)	(6,440)	(6,952)	(5,862)
Earning after Tax	4,000	4,800	6,440	6,952	5,861
Add: Depreciation	8,000	6,400	5,120	4,096	3,277
Cash Flow after Taxes(CFAT)	12,000	11,200	11,560	11,048	9,138
Add: Tax Saving on Loss [50% of (₹ 13,107 – 0)]	—	—	—	—	6,554
					15,692

STATEMENT SHOWING THE COMPUTATION OF NET PRESENT VALUE

(*₹ In 000'*)

Particulars	Year	Amount	PV factor at 12%	PV	PV factor at 14%	PV	PV factor at 16%	PV
Purchase Price of NewMachinery	0	(40,000)	1	(40,000)	1	(40,000)	1	(40,000)
CFAT of Year 1		12,000	0.89	10,680	0.88	10,560	0.86	10,320
CFAT of Year 2		11,200	0.80	8,960	0.77	8,624	0.74	8,288
CFAT of Year 3		11,560	0.71	8,208	0.67	7,745	0.64	7,398
CFAT of Year 4		11,048	0.64	7,071	0.59	6,518	0.55	6,076
CFAT of Year 5		15,692	0.57	8,944	0.52	8,160	0.48	7,532
NPV				3,863		1,607		(386)

Recommendation: Company should accept the project at 12 % since NPV is positive.

(ii) Calculation of Internal Rate of Return (IRR)

IRR = 14% + [1,607/(1,607 + 386) × (16% – 14%), IRR = 14 % + 1.61 % = 15.61%

PROBLEM 21

A firm can make investment in either of the following two projects. The firm anticipates its cost of capital to be 10% and the net (after tax) cash flows of the projects for five years are as follows:

(₹ '000)

Year	0	1	2	3	4	5
Project-A	(500)	85	200	240	220	70
Project-B	(500)	480	100	70	30	20

The discount factors are as under:

Year	0	1	2	3	4	5
PVF (10%)	1	0.91	0.83	0.75	0.68	0.62
PVF (20%)	1	0.83	0.69	0.58	0.48	0.41

Required:

(i) Calculate the NPV and IRR of each project.

(ii) State with reasons which project you would recommend.

(iii) Explain the inconsistency in ranking of two projects.

SOLUTION

(i) Computation of NPV and IRR

NPV FOR PROJECT A AT 10% AND 20%

Year	Cash Flows ₹ '000	PVF @ 10%	P.V. @ 10% ₹ '000	PVF @ 20%	P.V @ 20% ₹ '000
0	(500)	1.00	(500.00)	1.00	(500.00)
1	85	0.91	77.35	0.83	70.55
2	200	0.83	166.00	0.69	138.00
3	240	0.75	180.00	0.58	139.20
4	220	0.68	149.60	0.48	105.60
5	70	0.62	43.40	0.41	28.70
		NPV	+116.35		(17.95)

NPV of Project A (at 10% Cost of Capital) = ₹ 1,16,350.

$$\text{IRR} = \text{Lower Rate} + \frac{\text{NPV at Lower Rate}}{\text{NPV at Lower Rate} - \text{NPV at Higher Rate}} \times (H - L)$$

IRR = 10 + [116.35/{116.35 – (–17.95)}] × (20 – 10)% = 18.66%.

NPV FOR PROJECT B AT 10% AND 20%

Year	Cash Flows ₹ '000	PVF @ 10%	P.V. @ 10% ₹ '000	PVF @ 20%	P.V @ 20% ₹ '000
0	(500)	1.00	(500.00)	1.00	(500.00)
1	480	0.91	436.80	0.83	398.40
2	100	0.83	83.00	0.69	69.00
3	70	0.75	52.50	0.58	40.60

4	30	0.68	20.40	0.48	14.40
5	20	0.62	12.40	0.41	8.20
		NPV	+ 105.10		+30.60

NPV of Project B (at 10% Cost of Capital) = ₹ 1,05,100.

IRR = 10 + [105.10/{105.10 –30.60}] × (20 – 10)% = 24.107%.

Note: *Though in above solution discounting factors of 10% and 20% have been used. However, instead of 20%, students may assume any rate beyond 20%, say 26%, then NPV becomes negative. In such a case, the answers of IRR of Project may slightly varied from 24.10%.*

(ii) The ranking of the projects will be as under:

Particulars	Ranking as per NPV	Ranking as per IRR
Project A	1	2
Project B	2	1

Where an inconsistency is experienced, the projects yielding larger NPV is preferred because of larger cash flows which it generates. IRR criterion is rejected because of the following reasons:

(a) IRR assumes that all cash flows are re-invested at IRR.

(b) IRR is a percentage but the magnitude of cash flow is important.

(c) Multiple IRR may arise if the projects have non-conventional cash flows.

(iii) Inconsistency in ranking is due to the difference in the pattern of cash flows.

PROBLEM 22

X Ltd. provides you the following information:

Project	Cash Flow				NPV	IRR
	C_0	C_1	C_2	C_3	at 10%	
C	– ₹ 10,000	+ 2,000	+ 4,000	+ 12,000	+ ₹ 4,139	26.5%
D	– ₹ 10,000	+ 10,000	+ 3,000	+ 3,000	+ ₹ 3,823	37.6%

(i) Why there is a conflict of rankings?

(ii) Why should project C be accepted in spite of lower internal rate of return?

Particulars	Year 1	Year 2	Year 3
PVIF0.10, t	0.9090	0.8264	0.7513
PVIF0.14, t	0.8772	0.7695	0.6750
PVIF0.15, t	0.8696	0.7561	0.6575
PVIF0.30, t	0.7692	0.5917	0,4552
PVIF0.40, t	0.7143	0.5102	0.3644

SOLUTION

(I) NET PRESENT VALUE AT DIFFERENT DISCOUNTING RATES

Project	0% ₹	10% ₹	15% ₹	30% ₹	40% ₹
C	8,000	4,139	2,654	–632	–2,158

	{₹ 2,000 + ₹ 4,000 + ₹ 12,000 – ₹ 10,000}	{₹ 2,000 × 0.909 + ₹ 4,000 × 0.8264 + ₹ 12,000 × 0.7513 – ₹ 10,000}	{₹ 2,000 × 0.8696 + ₹ 4,000 × 0.7561 + ₹ 12,000 × 0.6575 – ₹ 10,000}	{₹ 2,000 × 0.7692 + ₹ 4,000 × 0.5917 + ₹ 12,000 × 0.4552 – ₹ 10,000}	{₹ 2,000 × 0.7143 + ₹ 4,000 × 0.5102 + ₹ 12,000 × 0.3644 – ₹ 10,000}
Ranking	I	I	II	II	II
D	6,000	3,823	2,967	833	–233
	{₹ 10,000 + ₹ 3,000 + ₹ 3,000 – ₹ 10,000}	{₹ 10,000 × 0.909 + ₹ 3,000 × 0.8264 + ₹ 3,000 × 0.7513 – ₹ 10,000)	{₹ 10,000 × 0.8696 + ₹ 3,000 × 0.7561 + ₹ 3,000 × 0.6675 – ₹ 10,000}	{₹ 10,000 × 0.7692 + ₹ 3,000 × 0.5917 + ₹ 3,000 × 0.4552 – ₹ 10,000}	{₹ 10,000 × 0.7143 + ₹ 3,000 × 0.5102 + ₹ 3,000 × 0.3644 – ₹ 10,000)
Ranking	II	II	I	I	I

The conflict in ranking arises because of skewness in cash flows. In the case of Project C cash flows occur more later in the life and in the case of Project D, cash flows are skewed towards the beginning. At lower discount rate, Project C's NPV will be higher than that of project D. As the discount rate increases, Project C's NPV will fall at a faster rate, due to compounding effect.

After break even discount rate, Project D has higher NPV as well as higher IRR.

(ii) If the opportunity cost of funds is 10%, project C should be accepted because the firm's wealth will increase by ₹ 316 (i.e. ₹ 4,139 – ₹ 3,823)

The following statement of incremental analysis will substantiate the above point.

Project	Cash Flow (₹)				NPV at	IRR
	C_0	C_1	C_2	C_3	10%	12.5%
₹	₹	₹	₹	₹		
C – D	0	–8,000	1,000	9,000	316	0
					{–8,000 × 0.909 + 1,000 × 0.8264 + 9,000 × 0.7513}	{–8,000 × 0.8889 + 1,000 × 0.7901 + 9,000 × 0.7023

Hence, the project C should be accepted, when opportunity cost of funds is 10%.

PROBLEM 23

A company is considering which of two mutually exclusive projects it should undertake. The Finance Director thinks that the project with the higher NPV should be chosen whereas the Managing Director thinks that the one with the higher IRR should be undertaken especially as both projects have the same initial outlay and length of life. The company anticipates cost of capital of 10% and the net after tax cash flows of the projects are as follows:

Year	0	1	2	3	4	5
(Cash flows Figs. 000)						
Project X	(200)	35	80	90	75	20
Project Y	(200)	218	10	10	4	3

Required:

(a) Calculate the NPV and IRR of each project.
(b) State, with reasons, which project you would recommend.
(c) Explain the inconsistency in the ranking of the two projects.

The discount factors are as follows:

Year	0	1	2	3	4	5
Discount Factors						
(10%)	1	0.91	0.83	0.75	0.68	0.62
(20%)	1	0.83	0.69	0.58	0.48	0.41

SOLUTION

(a) Calculation of the NPV and IRR of each project:

PROJECT X

Years	Cash Flows	Discount Factors @ 10%	Discounted Values	Discounted Factors @ 20%	Discounted Values
0	(200)	1.00	(200)	1.00	(200)
1	35	0.91	31.85	0.83	29.05
2	80	0.83	66.40	0.69	55.20
3	90	0.75	67.50	0.58	52.20
4	75	0.68	51.00	0.48	36.00
5	20	0.62	12.40	0.41	8.20
		NPV =	+ 29.15		– 19.35

IRR = 10 + [29.15/(29.15 + 19.35)] × 10 = 10 + (29.15/48.50) × 10 = 16.01%

PROJECT Y

Years	Cash Flows	Discount Factors @ 10%	Discounted Values	Discounted Factors @ 20%	Discounted Values
0	(200)	1.00	(200)	1.00	(200)
0	(200)	1.00	(200)	1.00	(200)
1	218	0.91	198.38	0.83	180.94
2	10	0.83	8.30	0.69	6.90
3	10	0.75	7.50	0.58	5,80
4	4	0.68	2.72	0.48	1.92
5	3	0.62	1.86	0.41	1.23
		NPV =	+ 18.76		–3.21

IRR = 10 + [18.76/(18.76 + 3.21)] × 10 = 10 + (18.76/21.97) × 10 = 18.54%

(b) Both the projects are acceptable because they generate the positive NPV at the company's Cost of Capital at 10%. However, the company will have to select Project X because it has a higher NPV. If the company follows IRR method, then Project Y should be selected because of higher internal rate of return (IRR). But when NPV and IRR give contradictory results, a project with high NPV is generally preferred because of higher return in absolute terms. Hence, Project X should be selected.

(c) The inconsistency in the ranking of the projects arises because of the difference in the pattern of cash flows. Projects X's major cash flows occur mainly in the middle three years, whereas Y generates the major cash flows in the first year itself.

PROBLEM 24

A company is considering the replacement of its existing machine obsolete and unable to meet the rapidly rising demand for its product. The company is faced with two alternatives: to buy Machine A which is similar to the existing machine *or* to go in for Machine B which is more expensive and has much greater capacity. The cash flows at the present level of operations under the two alternatives are as follows:

Machine	Immediate Cash outflow (in lakhs of ₹)	Cash Inflows (in lakhs of ₹) at the end of				
		Ist Year	IInd Year	III Year	IV Year	V Year
Machine A	25	—	5	20	14	14
Machine B	40	10	14	16	17	15

The company's cost of capital is 10%.

The finance manager tries to appraise the machines by calculating the following:

(a) Net Present Value; (b) Profitability Index; (c) Payback period; and (d) Discounted payback period.

At the end of his calculations, however, the finance manager is unable to make up his mind as to which machine to recommend.

You are required to make these calculations and in the light thereof to advise the finance manager about the proposed investment.

Note: *Present values of ₹ 1 at 10% discount rate are as follows:*

Year	0	1	2	3	4	5
P.V.	1.00	0.91	0.83	0.75	0.68	0.62

SOLUTION

(A) NET PRESENT VALUE

Year	Cash Flows		Present Value Factor at 10%	₹ in lakhs Present Valves	
	Machine A	Machine B		Machine A	Machine B
0 (outflows)	(25)	(40)	1.00	(25.00)	(40.00)
1 Inflows	—	10	0.91	—	9.10
2 Inflows	5	14	0.83	4.15	11.62
3 Inflows	20	16	0.75	15.00	12.00
4 Inflows	14	17	0.68	9.52	11.56
5 Inflows	14	15	0.62	8.68	9.30
			Net Present Value	12.35	13.58

(b) Profitability Index = Total Present Value of Cash Inflows/Total P.V. of Cash Outflow

PI (Machine A) = ₹ 37.35 lakhs/₹ 25.00 lakhs = 1.49

PI (Machine B) = ₹ 53.58 lakhs/₹ 40.00 lakhs = 1.34

(c) Payback Period:

Year	(₹ in lakhs) Machine A		(₹ in lakhs) Machine B	
	Cash Flows	Cumulative Cash Inflows	Cash Flows	Cumulative Cash Inflows
0	(25)	—	(40)	—
1	—	—	10	10
2	5	5	14	24
3	20	25	16	40
4	14	39	17	57
5	14	53	15	72
Payback Period		3 years		3 years

(d) Discounted Payback Period:

Year	(₹ in lakhs) Machine A		(₹ in lakhs) Machine B	
	Cash Flows	Cumulative Cash Inflows	Cash Flows	Cumulative Cash Inflows
0	(25.00)	—	(40.00)	—
1	—	—	9.10	9.10
2	4.15	4.15	11.62	20.72
3	15.00	19.15	12.00	32.72
4	9.52	28.67	11.56	44.28
5	8.68	37.35	9.30	53.58

Discounted Payback period:

For 'A' = 3 years + {(25.00 – 19.15)/9.52} = 3.6 years For 'B' = 3 years + {(40.00 – 32.72)/11.56} = 3.63 years.

Advise: The above appraisal shows that according to Net Present Value Method Machine 'B' is profitable. But Profitability Index method shows that Machine 'A' is preferable. Payback period of both the machines is the same. But discounted payback period shows that acquisition of Machine 'A' is slightly more advantageous. Thus, we find that different methods give conflicting results. In such a situation, the machine which gives the highest net present value should be accepted provided there is no problem of capital rationing. It is based on the thinking that every entrepreneur is always interested in the project which gives the maximum economic contribution in absolute terms. This condition is satisfied by Net Present Value Method. Furthers, since the demand for the company's product is rapidly rising, a machine with greater capacity would suit more. In view of this also, the company should go in for Machine B.

PROBLEM 25

Given below are the data on a capital project 'M':

Annual Cost Saving	₹ 60,000	Profitability index	1.064
Useful Life	4 years	Salvage value	0
Internal Rate of Return	15%		

You are required to calculate for this project M:

(i) Cost of Project, (ii) Payback Period, (iii) Cost of Capital, (iv) Net Present Value.

Given the following table of discount factors:

Discount factor	15%	14%	13%	12%
1 year	0.869	0.877	0.885	0.893
2 years	0.756	0.769	0.783	0.797
3 years	0.658	0.675	0.693	0.712
4 years	0.572	0.592	0.613	0.636
	2.855	2.913	2.974	3.038

SOLUTION

(i) Cost of Project 'M'

At 15% internal rate of return (IRR), the sum of total cash inflows = cost of the project i.e initial cash out lay

Hence, Total Cash inflows for 4 years for Project M = 60,000 × 2.855 = ₹ 1,71,300

Hence, Cost of the Project = ₹ 1,71,300

(ii) Payback Period

$$\text{Payback Period} = \frac{\text{Cost of the Project}}{\text{Annual Cost Savings}} = ₹\ 1{,}71{,}300/₹\ 60{,}000 = 2.855 \text{ years}$$

(iii) Cost of Capital

$$\text{Profitability index} = \frac{\text{Sum of Discounted Cash inflows}}{\text{Cost of the Project}}$$

$$1.064 = \frac{\text{Sum of Discounted Cash inflows}}{1{,}71{,}300}$$

Therefor, Sum of Discounted Cash inflows = ₹ 1,82,263.20

Since, Annual Cost Saving = ₹ 60,000

Hence, cumulative discount factor for 4 years = ₹ 1,82,263.20/₹ 60,000 = 3.038

From the discount factor table, at discount rate of 12%, the cumulative discount factor for 4 years is 3.038

Hence, Cost of Capital = 12%

(iv) Net Present Value (NPV)

NPV = Sum of Present Values of Cash inflows – Cost of the Project

= ₹ 1,82,263.20 – 1,71,300 = ₹ 10,963.20

PROBLEM 26

ANP Ltd. is providing the following information:

Annual cost of saving	₹ 96,000
Useful life	5 years
Salvage value	zero
Internal rate of return	15%
Profitability index	1.05

Table of discount factor:

Discount factor	Years					
	1	2	3	4	5	Total
15%	0.870	0.756	0.658	0.572	0.497	3.353
14%	0.877	0.769	0.675	0.592	0.519	3.432
13%	0.886	0.783	0.693	0.614	0.544	3.520

You are required to calculate:

(i) Cost of the project

(ii) Pay Back Period

(iii) Cost of Capital

(iv) Net Present Value of Cash Inflow.

SOLUTION

(i) Cost of Project 'M'

At 15% internal rate of return (IRR), the sum of total cash inflows = cost of the project i.e initial cash out lay

Hence, Total Cash inflows for 5 years for Project M = 96,000 × 3.353 = ₹ 3,21,888

Hence, Cost of the Project = ₹ 3,21,888

(ii) Payback Period

$$\text{Payback Period} = \frac{\text{Cost of the Project}}{\text{Annual Cost Savings}} = ₹\ 3{,}21{,}888/96{,}000 = 3.353 \text{ years.}$$

(iii) Cost of Capital

$$\text{Profitability index} = \frac{\text{Sum of Discounted Cash inflows}}{\text{Cost of the Project}}$$

$$1.05 = \frac{\text{Sum of Discounted Cash inflows}}{3{,}21{,}888}$$

Therefor, Sum of Discounted Cash inflows = ₹ 3,37,982.40

Since, Annual Cost Saving = ₹ 96,000

Hence, cumulative discount factor for 5 years = ₹ 3,37,982.40/96,000 = 3.52065

From the discount factor table, at discount rate of 13%, the cumulative discount factor for 5 years is 3.52065

Hence, Cost of Capital = 13%

(iv) Net Present Value (NPV)

NPV = Sum of Present Values of Cash inflows – Cost of the Project

= ₹ 3,37,982.40 – ₹ 3,21,888 = ₹ 16,094.40

4 COST OF CAPITAL

LEARNING OBJECTIVES

After studying this chapter, you should be able to understand:

- Meaning of Cost of Capital
- Components of Cost of Capital
- Relevance of Cost of Capital in Decision Making
- Is Determination of Cost of Capital an easy task ?
- Determination of Cost of Capital
- Cost of Debt
- Cost of Preference Share
- Terms Useful to Study Different Approaches as to Cost of Equity Capital
- Cost of Equity Share
- Cost of Retained Earnings or Reserves
- Cost of New Equity Share
- Cost of Depreciation Funds
- Why the Cost of Capital is most appropriately measured on an "after tax" basis ?
- Weighted Average Cost of Capital
- Marginal Cost of Capital
- How to determine New Weighted Average Cost of Capital (or Revised Weighted Average Cost of Capital)
- Effect of Financing Decision on Earning Per Share
- EPS Volatility
- How to Calculate Beta Coefficient under Capital Assets Pricing Model (CAPM)

1.0 MEANING OF COST OF CAPITAL

The cost of capital of a firm refers to the cost that a firm incurs in retaining the funds obtained from various sources (i.e. Equity Shares, Preference Shares, Debt, Retained Earnings)

2.0 COMPONENTS OF COST OF CAPITAL

The overall cost of capital of a firm consists of the costs of various segments of the total funds, which may be identified as follows:

1. Cost of Debt Capital i.e. debentures & loans from various institutions;
2. Cost of Preference Capital;

3. Cost of Equity Capital;
4. Cost of Retained Earnings.

3.0 RELEVANCE OF COST OF CAPITAL IN DECISION MAKING

1. Since the business should atleast be capable of earning so much revenue as to be able to meet its cost of capital and to finance its growth, cost of capital of a firm constitutes a crucial factor in most financial decisions.
2. It is relevant both to capital budgeting and capital structure planning, the main areas in financial management.
3. In capital budgeting decisions, cost of capital may be taken as the discounting rate. Obviously, if a particular project gives an internal rate of return higher than its cost of capital, it should be an attractive opportunity.
4. In capital structuring decisions, the cost of capital is an important consideration along with the risk factor. ***For Example*** loan may be cheaper but it entails higher risk of cash insolvency as also of variation in the earnings per share due to the financial leverage effect. It is therefore essential that the cost of each source of funds is carefully considered and compared with the risk involved in it.

4.0 IS DETERMINATION OF COST OF CAPITAL AN EASY TASK?

1. No, since both conceptually and practically a financial manager is confronted with a large number of problems in determining the cost of capital. He faces the controversy whether *or* not the cost of capital is dependent upon the method and level of financing of the company.
2. The traditional view is that cost of capital can be changed by changing the debt equity mix in the total capital while according to Modigiliani & Miller approach, the cost of capital is independent of its method *or* level of financing.

5.0 DETERMINATION OF COST OF CAPITAL

To calculate the overall cost of capital of a firm, it is necessary to find the cost of each source of finance, which has been discussed in the following paras.

6.0 COST OF DEBT

FACTORS AFFECTING THE COST OF DEBT

The considerable factors while calculating cost of debt are:

(a) Fixed Interest Rate
(b) Issue Expenses like Underwriting Commission, Brokerage
(c) Discount / Premium on Issue/Redemption
(d) Income Tax Rate

EXPLICIT AND IMPLICIT COST OF DEBT

The debt may have explicit cost as well as implicit cost.

Explicit Cost of Debt = Interest rate as per contract *plus* Cost of raising the debt (i.e. flotation cost)

For Example X Ltd. issues 1000, 9% Debentures of the face value of ₹ 100 at a discount of 5%. Underwriting, brokerage & other costs in connection with the issue ₹ 5,000.

Amount actually received by the company = ₹ 1,00,000 – ₹ 5,000 – ₹ 5,000 = ₹ 90,000.

Annual cost in form of interest = ₹ 9,000

Before tax cost = ₹ 9,000 / ₹ 90,000 100 = 10%

If income tax rate is 40%, Explicit cost after tax = 60% of 10% = 6% since interest will be allowed as a charge against revenue and to that extent tax liability of the company will be reduced.

Implicit Cost of Debt = Cost of increase in expectations of equity shareholders.

WHEN DOES IMPLICIT COST ARISE?

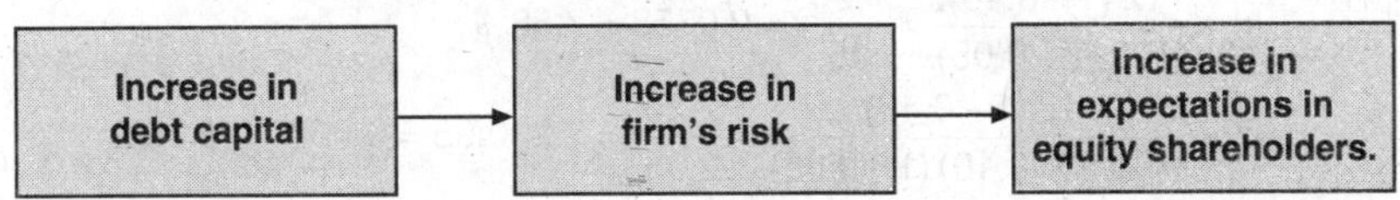

CLASSIFICATION OF DEBT ON THE BASIS OF ITS REDEEMABILITY

On the basis of Redeemability the debt may be classified as follows:

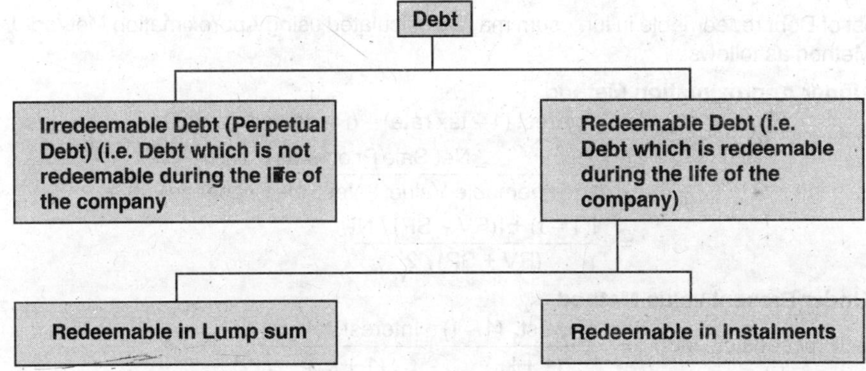

HOW TO CALCULATE THE COST OF IRREDEEMABLE DEBT (PERPETUAL DEBT)

The cost of irredeemable debt is calculated as follows:

$$\text{Cost of Debt} = \frac{\text{Interest } (1 - \text{tax rate})}{\text{Net Sale Proceeds from Issue of Debt}} = \frac{I(1-t)}{SP}$$

Where,

$$\text{Interest (I)} = \text{Face Value of a Debenture} \times \frac{\text{Rate of Interest}}{100}$$

Net Sales Proceeds from Issue of Debt (SP) = Face Value + Premium on Issue (or – Discount on Issue) – Flotation cost like underwriting commission *or* brokerage.

Tax Rate (t) = Income Tax Rate

ILLUSTRATION 1 [Cost of Perpetual/Irredeemable Debt]

Tulsian Ltd. issued ₹ 100 Lakhs 12% Debentures of ₹ 100 each. Calculate the cost of debt in each of the following cases. (Assume corporate tax rate being 40%).

Case (a) If Debentures are issued at par with no flotation cost.

Case (b) If Debentures are issued at par with 5 % flotation cost on issue price.

Case (c) If Debentures are issued at 10% premium with 5 % flotation cost on issue price.

Case (d) If Debentures are issued at 10% discount with 5 % flotation cost on issue price.

SOLUTION

Cost of Perpetual/Irredeemable Debt after tax

$$(k_d) = \frac{\text{Interest (1 – tax rate)}}{\text{Net Sale Proceeds of Debt}}$$

Case (a) $k_d = \frac{12\,(1-0.40)}{100} = \frac{7.20}{100} = 0.0720 = 7.20\%$

Case (b) $k_d = \frac{12\,(1-0.40)}{100\,(1-0.05)} = \frac{7.20}{95} = 0.0758 = 7.58\%$

Case (c) $k_d = \frac{12\,(1-0.40)}{100\,(1+0.10)\,(1-0.05)} = \frac{7.20}{0.05} = 7.200.05 = 0.0689 = 6.89\%$

Case (d) $k_d = \frac{12\,(1-0.40)}{100\,(1-0.10)\,(1-0.05)} = \frac{7.20}{85.50} = 0.0842 = 8.42\%$

HOW TO CALCULATE THE COST OF DEBT REDEEMABLE IN LUMP SUM

The Cost of Debt redeemable in lumpsum may be calculated using Approximation Method *or* Present Value Method as follows:

(a) Under Approximation Method

$$k_d = \frac{\text{Interest}\,(1-\text{tax rate}) + (\text{Redeemable Value} - \text{Net Sale Proceeds}) / N]}{(\text{Redeemable Value} + \text{Net Sale Proceeds}) / 2}$$

$$= \frac{I(1-t) + [(RV - SP) / N]}{(RV + SP) / 2}$$

(b) Under Present Value Method

$$\text{Net Proceeds of Debt} = \frac{\text{Interest}_1\,(1-t)}{(1+k_d)^1} + \frac{\text{Interest}_2\,(1-t)}{(1+k_d)^2} + \ldots$$

$$\ldots + \frac{\text{Interest}_n\,(1-t) + \text{Redeemable Value}_n}{(1+k_d)^n}$$

$$= \sum_{t=1}^{n} \frac{I_t\,(1-t)}{(1+k_d)^t} + \frac{RV_n}{(1+k_d)^n}$$

To calculate k_d the following steps may be followed:

Step 1: Calculate Total Present Value of Cash Outflow during the maturity period at two discount rates so as to have positive and negative Net Present Values (NPV).

Step 2: Find kd by interpolation technique as follows:

$$k_d = R_L + \frac{NPV_L}{NPV_L - NPV_H} \times (R_H - R_L)$$

Where, R_L = Lower Discount Rate, R_H = Higher Discount Rate

NPV_L = Positive Net Present Value at Lower Discount Rate

NPV_H = Negative Net Present Value at Higher Discount rate

NPV= Present Value of Cash outflow – Net Sale Proceeds from issue of debt.

Tutorial Note: Two Discount Rates within which kd (calculated under Approximation Method) lies may be used so as to have positive and negative Net Present Values.

ILLUSTRATION 2 [COST OF DEBT REDEEMABLE (AT PAR) IN LUMP SUM PAYMENT]

Tulsian Ltd. issued ₹ 100 Lakhs 12 % Debentures of ₹ 100 each redeemable at par after 5 years. Calculate the cost of debt according to Approximation Method in each of the following alternative cases. (Assume corporate tax rate being 40 %)

Case (a) If Debentures are issued at par with no flotation cost.

Case (b) If Debentures are issued at par with 5 % flotation cost on issue price.

Case (c) If Debentures are issued at 10% premium with 5 % flotation cost on issue price.

Case (d) If Debentures are issued at 10% discount with 5 % flotation cost on issue price.

SOLUTION

Cost of Debt Redeemable (at par) in Lump Sum Payment according to Approximation Method

$$k_d = \frac{\text{Interest } (1 - \text{tax rate}) + [(\text{Redeemable Value} - \text{Net Sale Proceeds})/N]}{(\text{Redeemable Value} + \text{Net Sale Proceeds})/2}$$

$$k_d = \frac{I(1-t) + [(RV - SP)]/N}{(RV + SP)/2}$$

Case (a) $$k_d = \frac{12\,(1 - 0.40) + [(100 - 100)/5]}{(100 + 100)/2} = 0.072 = 7.20\%$$

Case (b) $$k_d = \frac{12(1 - 0.40) + [(100 - 95)/5]}{(100 + 95)/2} = 0.0841 = 8.41\%$$

Case (c) $$k_d = \frac{12\,(1 - 0.40) + [(100 - 104.5)/5]}{(100 + 104.5)/2} = 0.0616 = 6.16\%$$

Case (d) $$k_d = \frac{12(1 - 0.40) + [(100 - 85.5)/5]}{(100 + 104.5)/2} = 0.1089 = 10.89\%$$

ILLUSTRATION 3 [COST OF DEBT REDEEMABLE (AT PAR) IN LUMP SUM PAYMENT]

Calculate the Cost of Debt in Illustration 2 according to Present Value Method.

SOLUTION

Case (a) Net Proceeds of Debt $$= \frac{\text{Interest}_1\,(1-t)}{(1+k_d)^1} + \frac{\text{Interest}_2\,(1-t)}{(1+k_d)^2} + \ldots$$

$$\ldots + \frac{\text{Interest}_n\,(1-t) + \text{Redeemable Value}_n}{(1+k_d)^n}$$

$$= \sum_{t=1}^{n} \frac{I_t\,(1-t)}{(1+k_d)^t} + \frac{RV_n}{(1+k_d)^n}$$

$$100 = \sum_{t=1}^{n} \frac{12(1-0.40)}{(1+k_d)^t} + \frac{100}{(1+k_d)^5}$$

CALCULATION OF PV AT 7% AND 8%

Year *A*	*Outflow* *B*	*PV Factor @7%* *C*	*PV Factor @8%* *D*	*PV @7%* *E = B × C*	*PV @8%* *F = B × D*
1	7.20	0.935	0.926	6.732	6.667
2	7.20	0.873	0.857	6.286	6.170
3	7.20	0.816	0.794	5.875	5.717
4	7.20	0.763	0.735	5.494	5.292
5	107.20	0.713	0.681	76.434	73.003
	(i.e. 100 + 7.2)		Total	100.821	96.849

$$k_d = R_L + \frac{NPV_L}{NPV_L - NPV_H} \times (R_H - R_L)$$

$$k_d = 7\% + \frac{0.821}{0.821 - (-3.151)} \times (8\% - 7\%) = 7.21\%$$

Case (b) Net Proceeds of Debt $= \frac{\text{Interest}_1(1-t)}{(1+k_d)^1} + \frac{\text{Interest}_2(1-t)}{(1+k_d)^2} + ... + \frac{\text{Interest}_n(1-t) + \text{Redeemable Value}_n}{(1+k_d)^n}$

$$= \sum_{t=1}^{n} \frac{I_t(1-t)}{(1+k_d)^t} + \frac{RV_n}{(1+k_d)^n}$$

$$95 = \sum_{t=1}^{5} \frac{12(1-0.40)}{(1+k_d)^t} + \frac{100}{(1+k_d)^5}$$

CALCULATION OF PV AT 8% AND 9%

Year *A*	*Outflow* *B*	*PV Factor @8%* *C*	*PV Factor @9%* *D*	*PV @8%* *E = B × C*	*PV @9%* *F = B × D*
1	7.20	0.926	0.917	6.667	6.602
2	7.20	0.857	0.842	6.170	6.062
3	7.20	0.794	0.772	5.717	5.558
4	7.20	0.735	0.708	5.292	5.098
5	107.20	0.681	0.650	73.003	69.680
	(i.e. 100 + 7.2)		Total	96.849	93.000

$$k_d = R_L + \frac{NPV_L}{NPV_L - NPV_H} \times (R_H - R_L)$$

$$k_d = 8\% + \frac{1.849}{1.849 - (-2.000)} \times (9\% - 8\%)$$

$$k_d = 8.48\%$$

Case (c) Net Proceeds of Debt $= \frac{\text{Interest}_1(1-t)}{(1+k_d)^1} + \frac{\text{Interest}_2(1-t)}{(1+k_d)^2} + ... + \frac{\text{Interest}_n(1-t) + \text{Redeemable Value}_n}{(1+k_d)^n}$

$$= \sum_{t=1}^{n} \frac{I_t(1-t)}{(1+k_d)^t} + \frac{RV_n}{(1+k_d)^n}$$

$$104.50 = \sum_{t=1}^{5} \frac{12(1-0.40)}{(1+k_d)^t} + \frac{100}{(1+k_d)^5}$$

CALCULATION OF PV AT 6% AND 7%

Year *A*	*Outflow* *B*	*PV Factor @6%* *C*	*PV Factor @7%* *D*	*PV @6%* *E = B × C*	*PV @7%* *F = B × D*
1	7.20	0.943	0.935	6.79	6.732
2	7.20	0.890	0.873	6.408	6.286
3	7.20	0.840	0.816	6.048	5.875
4	7.20	0.792	0.763	5.702	5.494
5	107.20	0.747	0.713	80.078	76.434
	(i.e. 100 + 7.2)		Total	105.026	100.821

$$k_d = R_L + \frac{NPV_L}{NPV_L - NPV_H} \times (R_H - R_L)$$

$$k_d = 6\% + \frac{0.526}{0.526 - (-3.679)} \times (7\% - 6\%)$$

$$k_d = 8.48\%$$

Case (c)Net Proceeds of Debt= $\frac{\text{Interest}_1(1-t)}{(1+k_d)^1} + \frac{\text{Interest}_2(1-t)}{(1+k_d)^2} + \ldots$

$$+ \frac{\text{Interest}_n(1-t) + \text{Redeemable Value}_n}{(1+k_d)^n}$$

$$= \sum_{t=1}^{n} \frac{I_t(1-t)}{(1+k_d)^t} + \frac{RV_n}{(1+k_d)^n}$$

$$85.50 = \frac{12(1-0.40)}{(1+k_d)^t} + \frac{100}{(1+k_d)^5}$$

CALCULATION OF PV AT 11% AND 12%

Year *A*	*Outflow* *B*	*PV Factor @11%* *C*	*PV Factor @12%* *D*	*PV @11%* *E = B × C*	*PV @12%* *F = B × D*
1	7.20	0.901	0.893	6.487	6.43
2	7.20	0.812	0.797	5.846	5.738
3	7.20	0.731	0.712	5.263	5.126
4	7.20	0.659	0.636	4.745	4.579
5	107.20	0.593	0.567	63.570	60.782
	(i.e. 100 + 7.2)		Total	85.911	82.655

$$k_d = R_L + \frac{NPV_L}{NPV_L - NPV_H} \times (R_H - R_L)$$

$$k_d = 11\% + \frac{0.411}{0.411 - (-2.845)} \times (12\% - 11\%)$$

$$k_d = 11.13\%$$

ILLUSTRATION 4 [COST OF DEBT REDEEMABLE (AT PREMIUM) IN LUMP SUM PAYMENT]

Tulsian Ltd. issued ₹ 100 Lakhs 12 % Debentures of ₹ 100 each redeemable at a premium of 5% after 5 years. Calculate the cost of debt according to Approximation Method in each of the following alternative cases: (Assume corporate tax rate being 40 %)

Case (a) If Debentures are issued at par with no flotation cost.

Case (b) If Debentures are issued at par with 5 % flotation cost on issue price.

Case (c) If Debentures are issued at 10% premium with 5 % flotation cost on issue price.

Case (d) If Debentures are issued at 10% discount of with 5 % flotation cost on issue price.

SOLUTION

Cost of Debt Redeemable in Lump Sum Payment according to Approximation Method

$$k_d = \frac{\text{Interest}(1-\text{tax rate}) + [(\text{Redeemable Value} - \text{Net Sale Proceeds})/N]}{(\text{Redeemable Value} + \text{Net Sale Proceeds})/2}$$

$$= \frac{I(I-t) + [(RV - SP)]/N}{(RV + SP)/2}$$

Case (a) $k_d = \frac{12(1-0.40) + [(105-100)/5]}{(105+100)/2} = 0.080 = 8.00\%$

Case (b) $k_d = \frac{12(1-0.40) + [(105-95)/5]}{(105+95)/2} = 0.0920 = 9.20\%$

Case (c) $k_d = \frac{12\,(1-0.40) + [(105-104.5)/5]}{(105+104.5)/2} = 0.0697 = 6.97\%$

Case (d) $k_d = \frac{12(1-0.40) + [(105-85.5)/5]}{(105+85.5)/2} = 0.1165 = 11.65\%$

ILLUSTRATION 5 [COST OF DEBT REDEEMABLE (AT PREMIUM) IN LUMP SUM PAYMENT]

Calculate the Cost of Debt in Illustration 4 according to Present Value Method.

SOLUTION

Case (a) Net Proceeds of Debt $= \frac{\text{Interest}_1\,(1-t)}{(1+k_d)^1} + \frac{\text{Interest}_2(1-t)}{(1+k_d)^2} + \ldots$

$$+ \frac{\text{Interest}_n\,(1-t) + \text{Redeemable Value}_n}{(1+k_d)^n}$$

$$= \sum_{t=1}^{n} \frac{I_t\,(1-t)}{(1+k_d)^t} + \frac{RV_n}{(1+k_d)^n}$$

$$100 = \sum_{t=1}^{5} \frac{12(1-0.40)}{(1+k_d)^t} + \frac{105}{(1+k_d)^5}$$

CALCULATION OF PV AT 8% AND 9%

Year *A*	*Outflow* *B*	*PV Factor @8%* *C*	*PV Factor @9%* *D*	*PV @8%* *E = B × C*	*PV @9%* *F = B × D*
1	7.20	0.926	0.917	6.667	6.602
2	7.20	0.857	0.842	6.170	6.062
3	7.20	0.794	0.772	5.717	5.558
4	7.20	0.735	0.708	5.292	5.098
5	112.20	0.681	0.650	76.408	72.930
	(i.e. 100 + 5 + 7.2)		Total	100.254	96.250

$$k_d = R_L + \frac{NPV_L}{NPV_L - NPV_H} \times (R_H - R_L)$$

$$k_d = 8\% + \frac{0.254}{0.254 - (-3.75)} \times (9\% - 8\%)$$

$$k_d = 8.06\%$$

Case (b) Net Proceeds of Debt $= \frac{\text{Interest}_1\,(1-t)}{(1+k_d)^1} + \frac{\text{Interest}_2(1-t)}{(1+k_d)^2} + \ldots$

$$+ \frac{\text{Interest}_n\,(1-t) + \text{Redeemable Value}_n}{(1+k_d)^n}$$

$$= \sum_{t=1}^{n} \frac{I_t\,(1-t)}{(1+k_d)^t} + \frac{RV_n}{(1+k_d)^n}$$

$$95 = \sum_{t=1}^{5} \frac{12(1-0.40)}{(1+k_d)^t} + \frac{105}{(1+k_d)^5}$$

CALCULATION OF PV AT 9% AND 10%

Year A	*Outflow* B	*PV Factor @9%* C	*PV Factor @10%* D	*PV @9%* $E = B \times C$	*PV @10%* $F = B \times D$
1	7.20	0.917	0.909	6.602	6.545
2	7.20	0.842	0.826	6.062	5.947
3	7.20	0.772	0.751	5.558	5.407
4	7.20	0.708	0.683	5.098	4.918
5	112.20	0.650	0.621	72.930	69.676
	(i.e. 100 + 5 + 7.2)		Total	96.250	92.493

$$k_d = R_L + \frac{NPV_L}{NPV_L - NPV_H} \times (R_H - R_L)$$

$$k_d = 9\% + \frac{1.25}{1.25 - (-2.507)} \times (10\% - 9\%)$$

$$k_d = 9.33\%$$

Case (c) Net Proceeds of Debt= $\frac{\text{Interest}_1(1-t)}{(1+k_d)^1} + \frac{\text{Interest}_2(1-t)}{(1+k_d)^2} + \dots$

$$+ \frac{\text{Interest}_n(1-t) + \text{Redeemable Value}_n}{(1+k_d)^n}$$

$$= \sum_{t=1}^{n} \frac{I_t(1-t)}{(1+k_d)^t} + \frac{RV_n}{(1+k_d)^n}$$

$$104.50 = \sum_{t=1}^{5} \frac{12(1-0.40)}{(1+k_d)^t} + \frac{105}{(1+k_d)^5}$$

CALCULATION OF PV AT 6% AND 7%

Year A	*Outflow* B	*PV Factor @6%* C	*PV Factor @7%* D	*PV @6%* $E = B \times C$	*PV @7%* $F = B \times D$
1	7.20	0.943	0.935	6.790	6.732
2	7.20	0.890	0.873	6.408	6.286
3	7.20	0.840	0.816	6.048	5.875
4	7.20	0.792	0.763	5.703	5.494
5	112.20	0.747	0.713	83.813	79.999
	(i.e. 100 + 5 + 7.2)		Total	108.762	104.386

$$k_d = R_L + \frac{NPV_L}{NPV_L - NPV_H} \times (R_H - R_L)$$

$$k_d = 6\% + \frac{4.262}{4.262 - (-0.114)} \times (7\% - 6\%)$$

$$k_d = 6.97\%$$

Case (c) Net Proceeds of Debt= $\frac{\text{Interest}_1(1-t)}{(1+k_d)^1} + \frac{\text{Interest}_2(1-t)}{(1+k_d)^2} + \dots$

$$+ \frac{\text{Interest}_n(1-t) + \text{Redeemable Value}_n}{(1+k_d)^n}$$

$$= \sum_{t=1}^{n} \frac{I_t(1-t)}{(1+k_d)^t} + \frac{RV_n}{(1+k_d)^n}$$

$$85.5 = \sum_{t=1}^{5} \frac{12(1-0.40)}{(1+k_d)^t} + \frac{105}{(1+k_d)^5}$$

CALCULATION OF PV AT 12% AND 11%

Year *A*	*Outflow* *B*	*PV Factor @12%* *C*	*PV Factor @11%* *D*	*PV @12%* *E = B × C*	*PV @11%* *F = B × D*
1	7.20	0.893	0.901	6.430	6.487
2	7.20	0.797	0.812	5.738	5.846
3	7.20	0.712	0.731	5.126	5.263
4	7.20	0.636	0.659	4.579	4.745
5	112.20	0.567	0.593	63.617	66.535
	(i.e. 100 + 5 + 7.2)		Total	85.49	88.876

$$k_d = R_L + \frac{NPV_L}{NPV_L - NPV_H} \times (R_H - R_L)$$

$$k_d = 11\% + \frac{3.376}{3.376-(-0.1)} \times (12\% - 11\%)$$

$$k_d = 11.997\%$$

HOW TO CALCULATE THE COST OF DEBT REDEEMABLE IN INSTALMENTS

The cost of Debt redeemable in instalments is calculated using Present Value Method as follows:

$$\text{Net Proceeds Debt} = \frac{\text{Interest}_1 (1-t) + \text{Principal}_1}{(1+k_d)^1} + \frac{\text{Interest}_2 (1-t) + \text{Principal}_2}{(1+k_d)^2} + \ldots + \frac{\text{Interest}_n (1-t) + \text{Principal}_n}{(1+k_d)^n}$$

$$= \sum_{t=1}^{n} \frac{I_t (1-t) + P_t}{(1+k_d)^t}$$

To calculate kd the following steps may be followed:

Step 1: Calculate Total Present Value of Cash Outflow during the maturity period at two discount rates so as to have positive and negative Net Present Values (NPV).

Step 2: Find kd by interpolation technique as follows:

$$k_d = RL + \frac{NPV_L}{NPV_L - NPH_H} \times (R_H - R_L)$$

ILLUSTRATION 6 [COST OF DEBT REDEEMABLE IN INSTALMENTS]

Bharat Ltd. issues ₹ 100 lakhs, 12 % Debentures of ₹ 100 each at par redeemable at par. The flotation cost being 10 % on issue price. The corporate tax rate is 40%. Calculate the cost of debt in each of the following cases:

Case (a) If 20 % Debentures are redeemable each year beginning with the end of year 1

Case (b) If Debentures are redeemable in 5 equated annual instalments beginning with the end of year 1.

Case (c) If Debentures are redeemable each year beginning with the end of year 1 in the ratio of 1 : 1 : 2 : 3 : 3.

Case (d) If 20% of Debentures are redeemable each year beginning with the end of year 2.

Case (e) If Debentures are redeemable in five equated annual instalments beginning with the end of year 2.

SOLUTION

CASE (A) CALCULATION OF CASH OUTFLOW AFTER TAX SAVING

Year A	Op. Bal. B	Interest C = B × Rate	Principal D	Instalment E = C + D	Cl. Bal. F = B + C − E	Tax Saving G = C × 40%	Cash outflow H = E − G
1	100	12.0	20	32.0	80	4.80	27.20
2	80	9.6	20	29.6	60	3.84	25.76
3	60	7.2	20	27.2	40	2.88	24.32
4	40	4.8	20	24.8	20	1.92	22.88
5	20	2.4	20	22.4	0	0.96	21.44

$$\text{Net Proceeds of Debt} = \frac{\text{Interest}_1(1-t)+\text{Principal}_1}{(1+k_d)^t} + \frac{\text{Interest}_2\,(1-t)+\text{Principal}_2}{(1+k_d)^2} + \ldots$$

$$+ \frac{\text{Interest}_n(1-t)+\text{Principal}_n}{(1+k_d)^n} = \sum_{t=1}^{n} \frac{I_t(1-t)+P_t}{(1+k_d)^t}$$

$$90 = \frac{12\,(1-.4)+20}{(1+k_d)} + \frac{9.6(1-.4)+20}{(1+k_d)^2} + \frac{7.2\,(1-.4)+20}{(1+k_d)^3} + \frac{4.8\,(1-.4)+20}{(1+k_d)^4} + \frac{2.4\,(1-.4)+20}{(1+k_d)^5}$$

CALCULATION OF PV AT 11% AND 12%

Year A	Outflow B	PV Factor @11% C	PV Factor @12% D	PV @11% E = B × C	PV @12% F = B × D
1	27.20	0.901	0.893	24.507	24.29
2	25.76	0.812	0.797	20.917	20.531
3	24.32	0.731	0.712	17.778	17.316
4	22.88	0.659	0.636	15.078	14.552
5	21.44	0.593	0.567	12.714	12.156
			Total	90.994	88.845

$$k_d = R_L + \frac{NPV_L}{NPV_L - NPV_H} \times (R_H - R_L)$$

$$k_d = 11\% + \frac{0.994}{0.994-(-1.155)} \times (12\% - 11\%)$$

$$k_d = 11.46\%$$

Case (b)

$$\text{Equated Annual Instalment} = \frac{₹\,100\text{ lakhs}}{\text{PV of Annuity of ₹ 1 for 5 years @ 12\%}} = \frac{100}{3.605} = ₹\,27.74\text{ lakh}$$

STATEMENT SHOWING THE PAYMENT OF PRINCIPAL AND INTEREST

Year A	Debentures at year beginning B	Interest C = B × Rate	Instalment D	Principal E = D − C	Debentures at at year end F = B + C − D	Tax Saving on Interest G = C × 40%	Cash Outflow H = D − G
1	100.00	12.00	27.74	15.74	84.26	4.80	22.94
2	84.26	10.11	27.74	17.63	66.63	4.04	23.70
3	66.63	8.00	27.74	19.74	46.89	3.20	24.54
4	46.89	5.63	27.74	22.11	24.78	2.25	25.49
5	24.78	*2.96	27.74	24.78	—	1.18	26.56

* Instead of Interest of ₹ 2.9736, it has been taken at 2.96 so as to bring the figure of Debentures at year end to nil. The need for this adjustment has arisen because of use of approximation in equated annual instalment.

CALCULATION OF PV AT 11% AND 12%

Year *A*	*Outflow* *B*	*PV Factor @11%* *C*	*PV Factor @12%* *D*	*PV @11%* *E = B × C*	*PV @12%* *F = B × D*
1	22.94	0.901	0.893	20.669	20.485
2	23.70	0.812	0.797	19.244	18.889
3	24.54	0.731	0.712	17.939	17.472
4	25.49	0.659	0.636	16.798	16.212
5	26.56	0.593	0.567	15.750	15.060
			Total	90.400	88.118

$$k_d = R_L + \frac{NPV_L}{NPV_L - NPV_H} \times (R_H - R_L)$$

$$k_d = 11\% + \frac{0.400}{0.400 - (-1.882)} \times (12\% - 11\%)$$

$$k_d = 11.175\%$$

CASE (C): CALCULATION OF CASH OUTFLOW AFTER TAX SAVING *(₹ lakhs)*

Year *A*	*Op. Bal.* *B*	*Interest* *C = B × Rate*	*Principal* *D*	*Instalment* *E = C + D*	*Cl. Bal.* *F = B + C − E*	*Tax Saving* *G = C × 40%*	*Cash outflow* *H = E − G*
1	100	12.0	10	22.0	90	4.80	17.20
2	90	10.8	10	20.8	80	4.32	16.48
3	80	9.6	20	29.6	60	3.84	25.76
4	60	7.2	30	37.2	30	2.88	34.32
5	30	3.6	30	33.6	0	1.44	32.16

CALCULATION OF PV AT 10% AND 11%

Year *A*	*Outflow* *B*	*PV Factor @10%* *C*	*PV Factor @11%* *D*	*PV @10%* *E = B × C*	*PV @11%* *F = B × D*
1	22.94	0.901	0.893	20.669	20.485
2	23.70	0.812	0.797	19.244	18.889
3	24.54	0.731	0.712	17.939	17.472
4	25.49	0.659	0.636	16.798	16.212
5	26.56	0.593	0.567	15.750	15.060
			Total	90.400	88.118

$$\text{Cost of Debt} = R_L + \frac{NPV_L}{NPV_L - NPV_H} \times (R_H - R_L)$$

$$k_d = 10\% + \frac{2.005}{2.005 - (-0.602)} \times (11\% - 10\%)$$

$$k_d = 10.77\%$$

Case (d)

CALCULATION OF CASH OUTFLOW AFTER TAX SAVING

Year A	Op. Bal. B	Interest C = B × Rate	Principal D	Instalment E = C + D	Cl. Bal. F = B + C – E	Tax Saving G = C × 40%	Cash outflow H = E – G
1	100	12.00	0	0	112	4.80	-4.80
2	112*	13.44	20	45.44	80	5.38	40.06
3	80	9.60	20	29.60	60	3.84	25.76
4	60	7.20	20	27.20	40	2.88	24.32
5	40	4.80	20	24.80	20	1.92	22.88
6	20	2.40	20	22.40	0	0.96	21.44

* ₹ 112 lakhs include Outstanding Interest of year 1.

CALCULATION OF PV AT 10% AND 11%

Year A	Outflow B	PV Factor @10% C	PV Factor @11% D	PV @10% E = B × C	PV @11% F = B × D
1	– 4.8	0.909	0.901	– 4.363	– 4.325
2	40.06	0.826	0.812	33.090	32.529
3	25.76	0.751	0.731	19.346	18.831
4	24.32	0.683	0.659	16.611	16.027
5	22.88	0.621	0.593	14.208	13.568
6	21.44	0.564	0.535	12.092	11.470
			Total	90.984	88.100

$$\text{Cost of Debt} = R_L + \frac{NPV_L}{NPV_L - NPV_H} \times (R_H - R_L)$$

$$k_d = 10\% + \frac{0.984}{0.984 - (-1.9)} \times (11\% - 10\%)$$

$$k_d = 10.34\%$$

Case (e)

$$\text{Equated Annual Instalment} = \frac{\text{₹ 100 lakhs}}{\text{PV of Annuity of ₹ 1 for year 2 to years @ 12\%}} = \frac{100}{3.219} = \text{₹ 31.07 lakh}$$

CALCULATION OF CASH OUTFLOW AFTER TAX SAVING

Year A	Op. Bal. B	Interest C = B × Rate	Principal D	Instalment E = C + D	Cl. Bal. F = B + C – E	Tax Saving G = C × 40%	Cash outflow H = E – G
1	100.00	12.00	0	0	112.00	4.80	–4.80
2	112.00	13.44	31.07	17.63	94.37	5.38	25.69
3	94.37	11.32	31.07	19.75	74.62	4.53	26.54
4	74.62	8.95	31.07	22.12	52.50	3.58	27.49
5	52.50	6.30	31.07	24.77	27.73	2.52	28.55
6	27.73	3.34	31.07	27.73	0	1.34	29.73

CALCULATION OF PV AT 10% AND 11%

Year *A*	*Outflow* *B*	*PV Factor @10%* *C*	*PV Factor @11%* *D*	*PV @10%* *E = B × C*	*PV @11%* *F = B × D*
1	–4.80	0.909	0.901	–4.363	–4.325
2	25.69	0.826	0.812	21.220	20.860
3	26.54	0.751	0.731	19.932	19.401
4	27.49	0.683	0.659	18.776	18.116
5	28.55	0.621	0.593	17.730	16.930
6	29.73	0.564	0.535	16.772	15.906
			Total	90.067	86.888

$$\text{Cost of Debt} = R_L + \frac{NPV_L}{NPV_L - NPV_H} \times (R_H - R_L)$$

$$k_d = 10\% + \frac{0.067}{0.067 - (-3.112)} \times (11\% - 10\%)$$

$$k_d = 10.02\%$$

ILLUSTRATION 7

Tushar Ltd. issues ₹ 100 lakhs Debentures of ₹ 100 each at par redeemable at 5% premium. The floatation cost being 10 % on issue price. The corporate tax rate is 40%. The yearly coupon rate of interest is as follows.

Year	*Coupon rate of interest*
1 - 2	10 %
3 - 4	11 %
5	12 %

Required: Calculate the cost of debt in each of the following alternative cases:

Case (a) If Debentures are redeemable after 5 years.

Case (b) If one fifth Debentures are redeemable in each year beginning with the end of year 1

SOLUTION

Case (a)

$$\text{Net Proceeds of Debt} = \frac{\text{Interest}_1(1-t)}{(1+k_d)^1} + \frac{\text{Interest}_2(1-t)}{(1+k_d)^2} + \ldots \frac{\text{Interest}_n(1-t) + \text{Redeemable value}_n}{(1+k_d)^n}$$

$$= \frac{I_t(1-t)}{(1+k_d)^t} + \frac{RV_n}{(1+k_d)^n}$$

$$90 = \frac{10\,(1-.4)}{(1+k_d)^1} + \frac{10(1-.4)}{(1+k_d)^2} + \frac{11(1-.4)}{(1+k_d)^3} + \frac{11(1-.4)}{(1+k_d)^4} + \frac{12\,(1-.4)}{(1+k_d)^5} + \frac{100}{(1+k_d)^5}$$

CALCULATION OF PV AT 9% AND 10%

Year *A*	*Outflow* *B*	*PV Factor @9%* *C*	*PV Factor @10%* *D*	*PV @9%* *E = B × C*	*PV @10%* *F = B × D*
1	6.00	0.917	0.909	5.502	5.454
2	6.00	0.842	0.826	5.052	4.956

3	6.60	0.772	0.751	5.095	4.957
4	6.60	0.708	0.683	4.673	4.508
5	112.20	0.650	0.621	72.930	69.676
	(100 + 5 + 7.2)		Total	93.252	89.551

$$k_d = R_L + \frac{NPV_L}{NPV_L - NPV_H} \times (R_H - R_L)$$

$$k_d = 9\% + \frac{3.252}{3.252 - (-0.449)} \times (10\% - 9\%)$$

$$k_d = 9.88\%$$

Case (b)

CALCULATION OF CASH OUTFLOW AFTER TAX SAVING *(₹ lakhs)*

Year A	*Op. Bal. B*	*Interest C = B × Rate D(105/5)*	*Principal (inc. Prem.)*	*Instalment E = C + D*	*Cl. Bal. F = B + D + 1*	*Tax Saving G = C × 40%*	*Cash outflow H = E – G*
1	100	10.0	21	31.0	80	4.00	27.00
2	80	8.0	21	29.0	60	3.20	25.80
3	60	6.6	21	27.6	40	2.64	24.96
4	40	4.4	21	25.4	20	1.76	23.64
5	20	2.4	21	23.4	—	0.96	22.44

$$\text{Net Proceeds of Debt} = \frac{\text{Interest}_1(1-t) + \text{Principal}_1}{(1+k_d)^t} + \frac{\text{Interest}_2\,(1-t) + \text{Principal}_2}{(1+k_d)^2} + \ldots$$

$$+ \frac{\text{Interest}_n(1-t) + \text{Principal}_n}{(1+k_d)^n} = \sum_{t=1}^{n} \frac{I_t(1-t) + P_t}{(1+k_d)^t}$$

$$90 = \frac{10\,(1-.4) + 21}{(1+k_d)^1} + \frac{8(1-.4) + 21}{(1+k_d)^2} + \frac{6.6\,(1-.4) + 21}{(1+k_d)^3} + \frac{4.4\,(1-.4) + 21}{(1+k_d)^4} + \frac{2.4\,(1-.4) + 21}{(1+k_d)^5}$$

CALCULATION OF PV AT 12% AND 13%

Year A	*Outflow B*	*PV Factor @12% C*	*PV Factor @13% D*	*PV @12% E = B × C*	*PV @13% F = B × D*
1	27.00	0.893	0.885	24.111	23.895
2	25.80	0.797	0.783	20.563	20.201
3	24.96	0.712	0.693	17.772	17.297
4	23.64	0.636	0.613	15.035	14.491
5	22.44	0.567	0.543	12.723	12.185
			Total	90.204	88.069

$$\text{Cost of Debt} = R_L + \frac{NPV_L}{NPV_L - NPV_H} \times (R_H - R_L)$$

$$k_d = 12\% + \frac{0.204}{0.204 - (-1.931)} \times (13\% - 12\%)$$

$$k_d = 12.096\%$$

ILLUSTRATION 8 [CALCULATION OF MARKET PRICE]

X Ltd.' s Debentures of the face value of ₹ 100 bear an 12% coupon rate. These debentures are redeemable after 10 years. Calculate the Market price in each of the following alternative cases:

Case (a) If Debentures of this type currently yield 16 %.

Case (b) If the maturity period is 4 years away from now and the debentures currently yield 10 %

Case (c) Would you pay ₹ 102 to purchase debentures specified in situation (b). Explain

SOLUTION

Case (a)

$$\text{Market Value of Debenture} = \frac{\text{Interest on Debenture}}{\text{Current Yield Rate}} = ₹\ 75.00$$

Case (b)

CALCULATION OF PRESENT VALUE OF A DEBENTURE

Year *A*	*Income* *B*	*PV Factor @ 10%* *C*	*PV @ 10%* *D = B × C*
1	12.00	0.909	10.908
2	12.00	0.826	9.912
3	12.00	0.751	9.012
4	112.00	0.683	76.496
		Total	106.328

Case (c)

Recommendation: As the present value of Debenture, as computed above is more than ₹ 102, hence the investor should buy the debentures at ₹ 102.

ILLUSTRATION 9 [CALCULATION OF ISSUE PRICE]

X Ltd. is planning to float a debenture issue on the following terms:

Face value : ₹ 100 per debenture

Terms of Maturity : 5 years

Premium on Redemption : 5 %

Yearly Coupon rate of Interest:

Year	*Coupon rate of interest*
1 - 2	10 %
3 - 4	11 %
5	12 %

The current market rate on similar debentures is 12 % p.a. The company proposes to price the issue so as to yield a compounded return of 13 % p.a. to the investors.

Required: Determine the issue price.

SOLUTION

CALCULATION OF PRESENT VALUE OF DEBENTURES

Year A	*Income* B	*PV Factor @ 13%* C	*PV @ 13%* D = B × C
1	10.00	0.885	8.850
2	10.00	0.783	7.830
3	11.00	0.693	7.623
4	11.00	0.613	6.743
5	117.00	0.543	63.531
			Total = 94.577

Hence, the company should issue the Debentures at ₹ 94.577.

ILLUSTRATION 10 [CALCULATION OF EFFECTIVE YIELD ON ISSUE PRICE]

X Ltd. issued ₹ 100, 12 % Debentures 5 years ago. Interest rates have been risen since then, so that debentures of the company are now selling at 15 % yield basis.

Case (a) Determine the current expected market price of the debentures. Would you buy the debentures for ₹ 75 ?

Case (b) Assuming that the debentures of the company are selling at ₹ 80 and have 5 years to run to maturity, compute the approximate effective yield an investor would earn on his investment.

SOLUTION

Case (a) Market value of Debenture $= \dfrac{\text{Interest on Debenture}}{\text{Current Yield Rate}} = \dfrac{12}{0.15} = ₹\ 80$

Recommendation: As the market value of Debenture, as computed above is more than ₹ 75, hence the investor should buy these debentures at ₹ 75.

Case (b)

Net Proceeds of Debt $= \dfrac{\text{Interest}_1}{(1+k_d)^1} + \dfrac{\text{Interest}_2}{(1+k_d)^2} + \ldots + \dfrac{\text{Interest}_1 + \text{Redeemable value}_n}{(1+k_d)^n}$

$$= \sum_{t=1}^{n} \frac{I_t(1-t)}{(1+k_d)^t} + \frac{RV_n}{(1+k_d)^n}$$

$$80.00 = \sum_{t=1}^{5} \frac{12}{(1+k_d)^t} + \frac{100}{(1+k_d)^5}$$

CALCULATION OF PRESENT VALUES AT 18% AND 19%

Year A	*Outflow* B	*PV Factor @18%* C	*PV Factor @19%* D	*PV @18%* E = B × C	*PV @19%* F = B × D
1	12.00	0.847	0.840	10.164	10.080
2	12.00	0.718	0.706	8.616	8.472
3	12.00	0.609	0.593	7.308	7.116
4	12.00	0.516	0.499	6.192	5.988
5	112.00	0.437	0.419	48.944	46.928
			Total	81.224	78.584

$$\text{Cost of Debt} = R_L + \frac{NPV_L}{NPV_L - NPV_H} \times (R_H - R_L)$$

$$k_d = 18\% + \frac{1.224}{1.224 - (-1.416)} \times (19\% - 18\%)$$

$$k_d = 18.46\%$$

7.0 COST OF PREFERENCE SHARE

FACTORS AFFECTING THE COST OF PREFERENCE SHARES

The considerable factors while calculating the cost of preference share are:

(a) Fixed Dividend Rate

(b) Issue expenses like underwriting commission, brokerage cost

(c) Discount / Premium on issue / Redemption

(d) Dividend Distribution Tax

For Example X Ltd. issues 1000 10% Preference Shares of the face value of ₹ 100 at a premium of 5%. Underwriting, brokerage & other costs in connection with the issue ₹ 5,000. Income Tax Rate 40%, Dividend Distribution Tax 20%.

Amount actually received by the company = ₹ 1,00,000 + ₹ 5,000 – ₹ 5,000 = ₹ 1,00,000.

Annual cost in form of fixed dividend = ₹ 10,000

Explicit Cost of Preference Share = Fixed Dividend + Dividend Distribution Tax

= ₹ 10,000 + 20% of ₹ 10,000 = ₹ 12,000

Explicit Cost of Preference Share = ₹ 12,000/₹ 1,00,000 × 100 = 12%

Note: There is no tax advantage since the preference dividend is not allowed as a charge against revenue. It is treated as an appropriation out of profits.

CLASSIFICATION OF PREFERENCE SHARES ON THE BASIS OF ITS REDEEMABILITY

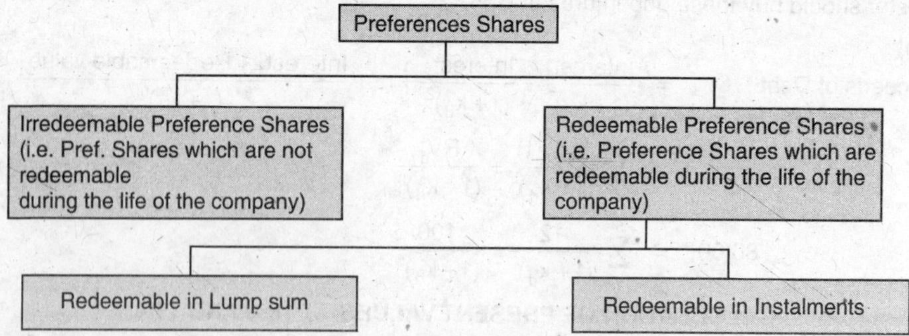

HOW TO CALCULATE THE COST OF IRREDEEMABLE PREFERENCE SHARES (PERPETUAL PREFERENCE SHARES)

The Cost of Irredeemable Preference Share is calculated as follows:

$$\text{Cost of Preference Share} = \frac{\text{Preference Dividend } (1 + \text{Dividend Tax})}{\text{Net Sale Proceeds from Issue of Preference Shares}}$$

$$k_p = \frac{D_p(1 + D_t)}{SP}$$

ILLUSTRATION 11 [CALCULATION OF COST OF IRREDEEMABLE PREFERENCE SHARES]

Tulsian Ltd. issued ₹ 100 Lakhs 12 % Preference shares of ₹ 100 each redeemable at par after 5 years. Calculate the Cost of Preference Share in each of the following cases: (Assume dividend tax rate being 20%)

Case (a) If Preference shares are issued at par with no flotation cost.

Case (b) If Preference shares are issued at par with 5 % flotation cost.

Case (c) If Preference shares are issued at 10% premium with 5 % flotation cost.

Case (d) If Preference shares are issued at 10% discount with 5 % flotation cost.

SOLUTION

Cost of An Irredeemable Preference Share

$$k_d = \frac{\text{Preference Dividend (1 + Dividend Tax)}}{\text{Net Sale Proceeds of a Preference Share}}$$

Case (a) $$k_d = \frac{12\,(1-0.20)}{100} = \frac{14.40}{100} = 0.1440 = 14.40\%$$

Case (b) $$k_d = \frac{12\,(1+0.20)}{100\,(1-0.05)} = \frac{14.40}{95} = 0.1516 = 15.16\%$$

Case (c) $$k_d = \frac{12\,(1+0.20)}{100\,(1+0.10)\,(1-0.05)} = \frac{14.40}{104.50} = 0.1378 = 13.78\%$$

Case (d) $$k_d = \frac{12\,(1+0.20)}{100\,(1-0.10)\,(1-0.05)} = \frac{14.40}{85.50} = 0.1684 = 16.84\%$$

HOW TO CALCULATE THE COST OF PREFERENCE SHARES REDEEMABLE IN LUMP SUM

The Cost of Preference Shares redeemable in lumpsum may be calculated using Approximation Method *or* Present Value Method as follows:

(a) Under Approximation Method

$$kd = \frac{\text{Preference Dividend (1 + Dividend Tax) + [(Redeemable Value – Net Sales Proceeds)/N]}}{\text{(Redeemable Value + Net Sale Proceeds)/2}}$$

$$= \frac{D_p(1+D_t) + [(RV - SP)/N]}{(RV + SP)/2}$$

(b) Under Present Value Method

$$\text{Net Proceeds of Pref. Shares} = \frac{D_1(1+D_t)}{(1+k_p)^1} + \frac{D_2(1+D_t)}{(1+k_p)^2} + \ldots + \frac{D_n(1+D_t) + \text{Redeemable Value}_n}{(1+k_p)^n}$$

$$= \sum_{t=1}^{n} \frac{D_t(1+D_t)}{(1+k_p)^t} + \frac{RV_n}{(1+k_p)^n}$$

Hence D_1, D_2 = Preference Dividend in year 1, year 2 ...

D_t = Dividend Tax Rate

To calculate kd the following steps may be followed:

Step 1: Calculate Total Present Value of Cash Outflow during the maturity period at two discount rates so as to have positive and negative Net Present Values (NPV).

Step 2: Find k_p by interpolation technique as follows:

$$k_d = R_L + \frac{NPV_L}{NPV_L - NPV_H} \times (R_H - R_L)$$

Note: NPV = Present Value of Cash Outflow – Net Sale Proceeds from issue of Preference Shares.

ILLUSTRATION 12 [Cost of Preference Shares Redeemable (at par) in Lump Sum Payment]

Tulsian Ltd. issued ₹ 100 Lakhs 12 % Preference Shares of ₹ 100 each redeemable at par after 5 years. Calculate the Cost of Preference Share According to Approximation Method in each of the following cases: (Assume dividend tax rate being 20 %)

Case (a) If Preference shares are issued at par with no flotation cost.

Case (b) If Preference shares are issued at par with 5 % flotation cost on issue price.

Case (c) If Preference shares are issued at 10% premium with 5 % flotation cost on issue price.

Case (d) If Preference shares are issued at 10% discount with 5 % flotation cost on issue price.

SOLUTION

Cost of Preference Share Redeemable in Lump Sum Payment according to Approximation Method

$$k_d = \frac{\text{Preference Dividend (1 + Dividend Tax) + [(Redeemable Value – Net Sales Proceeds)/N]}}{\text{(Redeemable Value + Net Sale Proceeds)/2}}$$

$$k_d = \frac{D_p(1+D_t)+[(RV-SP)/N]}{(RV+SP)/2}$$

Case (a) $$k_d = \frac{12\,(1+0.20)+[(100-100)/5]}{(100+100)/2} = 0.1440 = 14.40\%$$

Case (b) $$k_d = \frac{12(1+0.20)+[(100-95)/5]}{(105+95)/2} = 0.1579 = 15.79\%$$

Case (c) $$k_d = \frac{12\,(1+0.20)+[(100-104.5)/5]}{(100+104.5)/2} = 0.1320 = 13.20\%$$

Case (d) $$k_d = \frac{12(1+0.20)+[(100-85.5)/5]}{(100+85.5)/2} = 0.1865 = 18.65\%$$

ILLUSTRATION 13 [COST OF PREFERENCE SHARES REDEEMABLE IN LUMP SUM PAYMENT]

Calculate the Cost of preference shares in Illustration 12 according to Present Value Method.

SOLUTION

Case (a) Net Proceeds of a Pref. Share

$$= \frac{D_1(1+D_t)}{(1+k_p)^1} + \frac{D_2(1+D_t)}{(1+k_p)^2} + \ldots + \frac{D_n(1+D_t)+\text{Redeemable Value}_n}{(1+k_p)^n}$$

$$= \sum_{t=1}^{n} \frac{D_p\,(1+D_t)}{(1+k_p)^t} + \frac{RV_n}{(1+k_p)^n}$$

$$100 = \sum_{t=1}^{5} \frac{12\,(1+0.20)}{(1+k_p)^t} + \frac{100}{(1+k_p)^5}$$

CALCULATION OF PRESENT VALUES AT 14% AND 15%

Year *A*	*Outflow* *B*	*PV Factor @14%* *C*	*PV Factor @15%* *D*	*PV @14%* *E = B × C*	*PV @15%* *F = B × D*
1	14.40	0.877	0.870	12.629	12.528
2	14.40	0.769	0.756	11.074	10.886
3	14.40	0.675	0.658	9.720	9.475
4	14.40	0.592	0.572	8.525	8.237
5	114.40	0.519	0.497	59.374	56.857
			Total	101.322	97.983

$$k_d = R_L + \frac{NPV_L}{NPV_L - NPV_H} \times (R_H - R_L)$$

$$k_d = 14\% + \frac{1.322}{1.322 - (-2.017)} \times (15\% - 14\%)$$

$$k_d = 14.396\% \text{ or } 14.4\% \text{ (App.)}$$

Case (b)

$$\text{Net Proceeds of Pref. Shares} = \frac{D_1(1+D_t)}{(1+k_p)^1} + \frac{D_2(1+D_t)}{(1+k_p)^2} + ... + \frac{D_n(1+D_t) + \text{Redeemable Value}_n}{(1+k_p)^n}$$

$$= \sum_{t=1}^{n} \frac{D_t(1+D_t)}{(1+k_p)^t} + \frac{RV_n}{(1+k_p)^n}$$

$$95 = \sum_{t=1}^{5} \frac{12(1+0.20)}{(1+k_p)^t} + \frac{100}{(1+k_p)^5}$$

CALCULATION OF PRESENT VALUES AT 15% AND 16%

Year *A*	*Outflow* *B*	*PV Factor @15%* *C*	*PV Factor @16%* *D*	*PV @15%* *E = B × C*	*PV @16%* *F = B × D*
1	14.40	0.870	0.862	12.528	12.413
2	14.40	0.756	0.743	10.886	10.699
3	14.40	0.658	0.641	9.475	9.230
4	14.40	0.572	0.552	8.237	7.949
5	114.40	0.497	0.476	56.857	54.454
			Total	97.983	94.745

$$k_d = R_L + \frac{NPV_L}{NPV_L - NPV_H} \times (R_H - R_L)$$

$$k_d = 15\% + \frac{3.983}{2.983 - (-0.255)} \times (16\% - 15\%)$$

$$k_d = 15.92\%$$

Case (c)

$$\text{Net Proceeds of Pref. Shares} = \frac{D_1(1+D_t)}{(1+k_p)^1} + \frac{D_2(1+D_t)}{(1+k_p)^2} + ... + \frac{D_n(1+D_t) + \text{Redeemable Value}_n}{(1+k_p)^n}$$

$$= \sum_{t=1}^{n} \frac{D_t(1-D_t)}{(1+k_p)^t} + \frac{RV_n}{(1+k_p)^n}$$

$$104.50 = \sum_{t=1}^{5} \frac{12(1+0.20)}{(1+k_p)^t} + \frac{100}{(1+k_p)^5}$$

CALCULATION OF PRESENT VALUES AT 13% AND 14%

Year *A*	*Outflow* *B*	*PV Factor @13%* *C*	*PV Factor @14%* *D*	*PV @13%* *E = B × C*	*PV @14%* *F = B × D*
1	14.40	0.885	0.877	12.744	12.629
2	14.40	0.783	0.769	11.275	11.074
3	14.40	0.693	0.675	9.979	9.720
4	14.40	0.613	0.592	8.827	8.525

5	114.40	0.543	0.519	62.119	59.374
			Total	104.944	101.322

$$k_d = R_L + \frac{NPV_L}{NPV_L - NPV_H} \times (R_H - R_L)$$

$$k_d = 13\% + \frac{0.444}{0.444 - (-3.178)} \times (14\% - 13\%)$$

$$k_d = 13.12\%$$

Case (d)

$$\text{Net Proceeds of Pref. Shares} = \frac{D_1(1+D_t)}{(1+k_p)^1} + \frac{D_2(1+D_t)}{(1+k_p)^2} + \ldots + \frac{D_n(1+D_t) + \text{Redeemable Value}_n}{(1+k_p)^n}$$

$$= \sum_{t=1}^{n} \frac{D_t(1-D_t)}{(1+k_p)^t} + \frac{RV_n}{(1+k_p)^n}$$

$$85.50 = \sum_{t=1}^{5} \frac{12(1+0.20)}{(1+k_p)^t} + \frac{100}{(1+k_p)^5}$$

CALCULATION OF PRESENT VALUES AT 19% AND 20%

Year A	*Outflow* B	*PV Factor @19%* C	*PV Factor @20%* D	*PV @19%* E = B × C	*PV @20%* F = B × D
1	14.40	0.840	0.833	12.096	11.995
2	14.40	0.706	0.694	10.166	9.994
3	14.40	0.593	0.579	8.539	8.338
4	14.40	0.499	0.482	7.186	6.941
5	114.40	0.419	0.402	47.934	45.989
			Total	85.921	83.257

$$k_d = R_L + \frac{NPV_L}{NPV_L - NPV_H} \times (R_H - R_L)$$

$$k_d = 19\% + \frac{0.421}{0.421 - (-2.243)} \times (20\% - 19\%)$$

$$k_d = 19.158 \text{ or } 19.16\% \text{ (App.)}$$

ILLUSTRATION 14 [Cost of Preference Shares Redeemable (at premium) in Lump Sum Payment]

Tulsian Ltd. issued ₹ 100 Lakhs 12 % Preference Shares of ₹ 100 each redeemable at a premium of 5% after 5 years. Calculate the Cost of Preference Shares according to Approximation Method in each of the following cases. (Assume dividend tax rate 20%).

Case (a) If Preference shares are issued at par with no flotation cost.

Case (b) If Preference shares are issued at par with 5 % flotation cost on issue price.

Case (c) If Preference shares are issued at 10% premium with 5 % flotation cost on issue price.

Case (d) If Preference shares are issued at 10% discount with 5 % flotation cost on issue price.

SOLUTION

Cost of Preference Shares Redeemable in Lump Sum Payment according to Approximation Method

$$= \frac{\text{Preference Dividend } (1 + \text{Dividend Tax}) + [(\text{Redeemable Value} - \text{Net Sale Proceeds})/N]}{(\text{Redeemable Value} + \text{Net Sale Proceeds})/2}$$

$$k_d = \frac{D_p(1+D_t)+[(RV-SP)/N]}{(RV+SP)/2}$$

Case (a) $$k_p = \frac{12\,(1+0.20)+[(105-100)/5]}{(105+100)/2} = 0.1502 = 15.02\%$$

Case (b) $$k_p = \frac{12(1+0.20)+[(105-95)/5]}{(105+95)/2} = 0.1640 = 16.40\%$$

Case (c) $$k_p = \frac{12\,(1+0.20)+[(105-104.5)/5]}{(105+104.5)/2} = 0.1384 = 13.84\%$$

Case (d) $$k_p = \frac{12(1+0.20)+[(105-85.5)/5]}{(105+85.5)/2} = 0.1921 = 19.21\%$$

ILLUSTRATION 15 [COST OF PREFERENCE SHARES REDEEMABLE (AT PREMIUM) IN LUMP SUM PAYMENT]

Calculate the Cost of Preference shares in Illustration 14 according to Present Value Method.

SOLUTION

Case (a) Net Proceeds of a Pref. Share

$$= \frac{D_{p1}(1+D_t)}{(1+k_p)^1} + \frac{D_{p2}(1+D_t)}{(1+k_p)^2} + \ldots + \frac{D_{pn}(1+D_t)+\text{Redeemable Value}_n}{(1+k_p)^n}$$

$$= \sum_{t=1}^{n} \frac{D_p\,(1+D_t)}{(1+k_p)^t} + \frac{RV_n}{(1+k_p)^n}$$

$$100 = \sum_{t=1}^{5} \frac{12\,(1+0.20)}{(1+k_p)^t} + \frac{105}{(1+k_p)^5}$$

CALCULATION OF PRESENT VALUES AT 15% AND 16%

Year *A*	*Outflow* *B*	*PV Factor @15%* *C*	*PV Factor @16%* *D*	*PV @15%* *E = B × C*	*PV @16%* *F = B × D*
1	14.40	0.870	0.862	12.528	12.413
2	14.40	0.756	0.743	10.886	10.699
3	14.40	0.658	0.641	9.475	9.230
4	14.40	0.572	0.552	8.237	7.949
5	119.40	0.497	0.476	59.341	56.834
			Total	100.467	97.125

$$k_d = R_L + \frac{NPV_L}{NPV_L - NPV_H} \times (R_H - R_L)$$

$$k_d = 15\% + \frac{0.467}{0.467-(-2.875)} \times (16\% - 15\%)$$

$$k_d = 15.14\%$$

Case (b) Net Proceeds of a Pref. Share

$$= \frac{D_{p1}(1+D_t)}{(1+k_p)^1} + \frac{D_{p2}(1+D_t)}{(1+k_p)^2} + \ldots + \frac{D_{pn}(1+D_t)+\text{Redeemable Value}_n}{(1+k_p)^n}$$

$$= \sum_{t=1}^{n} \frac{D_p\,(1+D_t)}{(1+k_p)^t} + \frac{RV_n}{(1+k_p)^n}$$

$$95 = \sum_{t=1}^{5} \frac{12\,(1+0.20)}{(1+k_p)^t} + \frac{105}{(1+k_p)^5}$$

CALCULATION OF PRESENT VALUES AT 16% AND 17%

Year *A*	*Outflow* *B*	*PV Factor @16%* *C*	*PV Factor @17%* *D*	*PV @16%* *E = B × C*	*PV @17%* *F = B × D*
1	14.40	0.862	0.855	12.413	12.312
2	14.40	0.743	0.731	10.699	10.526
3	14.40	0.641	0.624	9.230	8.986
4	14.40	0.552	0.534	7.949	7.690
5	119.40	0.476	0.456	56.834	54.446
			Total	97.125	93.960

$$k_d = R_L + \frac{NPV_L}{NPV_L - NPV_H} \times (R_H - R_L)$$

$$k_d = 16\% + \frac{2.125}{2.125 - (-1.04)} \times (17\% - 16\%)$$

$$k_d = 16.67\%$$

Case (c) Net Proceeds of a Pref. Share

$$= \frac{D_{p1}(1+D_t)}{(1+k_p)^1} + \frac{D_{p2}(1+D_t)}{(1+k_p)^2} + \ldots + \frac{D_{pn}(1+D_t) + \text{Redeemable Value}_n}{(1+k_p)^n}$$

$$= \sum_{t=1}^{n} \frac{D_p\,(1+D_t)}{(1+k_p)^t} + \frac{RV_n}{(1+k_p)^n}$$

$$104.50 = \sum_{t=1}^{5} \frac{12\,(1+0.20)}{(1+k_p)^t} + \frac{105}{(1+k_p)^5}$$

CALCULATION OF PRESENT VALUES AT 13% AND 14%

Year *A*	*Outflow* *B*	*PV Factor @13%* *C*	*PV Factor @14%* *D*	*PV @13%* *E = B × C*	*PV @14%* *F = B × D*
1	14.40	0.885	0.877	12.744	12.629
2	14.40	0.783	0.769	11.275	11.074
3	14.40	0.693	0.675	9.979	9.720
4	14.40	0.613	0.592	8.827	8.525
5	119.40	0.543	0.519	64.834	61.969
			Total	107.659	103.917

$$k_d = R_L + \frac{NPV_L}{NPV_L - NPV_H} \times (R_H - R_L)$$

$$k_d = 13\% + \frac{3.159}{3.159 - (-0.583)} \times (14\% - 13\%)$$

$$k_d = 13.84\%$$

Case (d) Net Proceeds of a Pref. Share

$$= \frac{D_{p1}(1+D_t)}{(1+k_p)^1} + \frac{D_{p2}(1+D_t)}{(1+k_p)^2} + \ldots + \frac{D_{pn}(1+D_t) + \text{Redeemable Value}_n}{(1+k_p)^n}$$

$$= \sum_{t=1}^{n} \frac{D_p\,(1+D_t)}{(1+k_p)^t} + \frac{RV_n}{(1+k_p)^n}$$

$$85.5 = \sum_{t=1}^{5} \frac{12\,(1+0.20)}{(1+k_p)^t} + \frac{105}{(1+k_p)^5}$$

CALCULATION OF PRESENT VALUES AT 19% AND 20%

Year *A*	*Outflow* *B*	*PV Factor @19%* *C*	*PV Factor @20%* *D*	*PV @19%* *E = B × C*	*PV @20%* *F = B × D*
1	14.40	0.840	0.833	12.096	11.995
2	14.40	0.706	0.694	10.166	9.994
3	14.40	0.593	0.579	8.539	8.338
4	14.40	0.499	0.482	7.186	6.941
5	119.40	0.419	0.402	50.029	47.999
			Total	88.016	85.267

$$k_d = R_L + \frac{NPV_L}{NPV_L - NPV_H} \times (R_H - R_L)$$

$$k_d = 19\% + \frac{2.516}{2.516-(-0.233)} \times (20\% - 19\%)$$

$$k_d = 19.915\%$$

HOW TO CALCULATE THE COST OF PREFERENCE SHARES REDEEMABLE IN INSTALMENTS

The Cost of Preference Shares redeemable in instalments is calculated using

Present Value Method:

$$\text{Net Proceeds of Pref. Shares} = \frac{D_1\,(1+D_t) + \text{Principal}_1}{(1+k_p)^1} + \frac{D_2(1+D_t) + \text{Principal}_2}{(1+k_p)^2} + \ldots + \frac{D_n\,(1+D_t) + \text{Principal}_n}{(1+k_p)^n}$$

$$= \sum_{t=1}^{n} \frac{D_t(1+D_t)}{(1+k_p)^t} + \frac{RV_n}{(1+k_p)^n}$$

To calculate k_d the following steps may be followed:

Step 1: Calculate Total Present Value of Cash Outflow during the maturity period at two discount rates so as to have positive and negative Net Present Values (NPV).

Step 2: Find k_d by interpolation technique as follows:

$$k_d = R_L + \frac{NPV_L}{NPV_L - NPV_H} \times (R_H - R_L)$$

Note: NPV = Present Value of Cash Outflow – Net Sale Proceeds from issue of Preference Shares.

ILLUSTRATION 16

Bharat Ltd. issues ₹ 100 lakhs, 12 % Preference Shares of ₹ 100 each at par redeemable at par. The floatation cost being 10 % on issue price. The dividend tax rate is 20%. Calculate the Cost of Preference Shares in each of the following cases:

Case (a) If 20 % Preference shares are redeemable each year beginning with the end of year 1

Case (b) If Preference shares are redeemable in 5 equated annual instalment beginning with the end of year 1.

SOLUTION

Case (a)

CALCULATION OF CASH OUTFLOW (INCLUDING DIVIDEND TAX)

Year A	Op. Bal. B	Dividend C = B × Rate	Principal D	Instalment E = C + D	Cl. Bal. F = B – C	Dividend Tax G = C × 20%	Cash outflow H = E + G
1	100	12.0	20	32.0	80	2.40	34.40
2	80	9.6	20	29.6	60	1.92	31.52
3	60	7.2	20	27.2	40	1.44	28.64
4	40	4.8	20	24.8	20	0.96	25.76
5	20	2.4	20	22.4	0	0.48	22.88

Net Proceeds of Pref. Shares

$$= \frac{D_1(1+D_t)+\text{Principal}_1}{(1+k_p)^1} + \frac{D_2(1+D_t)+\text{Principal}_2}{(1+k_p)^2} + \ldots + \frac{D_n(1+D_t)+\text{Principal}_n}{(1+k_p)^n}$$

$$= \sum_{t=1}^{n} \frac{D_t(1+D_t)}{(1+k_p)^t} + \frac{RV_n}{(1+k_p)^n}$$

$$90 = \frac{12(1+.2)+20}{(1+k_p)^1} + \frac{9.6(1+.2)+20}{(1+k_p)^2} + \frac{7.2(1+.2)+20}{(1+k_p)^3} + \frac{4.8(1+.2)+20}{(1+k_p)^4} + \frac{2.4(1+.2)+20}{(1+k_p)^5}$$

CALCULATION OF PRESENT VALUES AT 19% AND 20%

Year A	Outflow B	PV Factor @19% C	PV Factor @20% D	PV @19% E = B × C	PV @20% F = B × D
1	34.40	0.840	0.833	28.896	28.655
2	31.52	0.706	0.694	22.253	21.875
3	28.64	0.593	0.579	16.984	16.583
4	25.76	0.499	0.482	12.854	12.416
5	22.88	0.419	0.402	9.587	9.198
			Total	90.574	88.727

$$k_d = R_L + \frac{NPV_L}{NPV_L - NPV_H} \times (R_H - R_L)$$

$$k_d = 19\% + \frac{0.574}{0.574-(-1.273)} \times (20\% - 19\%)$$

$$k_d = 19.31\%$$

Case (b)

$$\text{Equated Annual Instalment} = \frac{₹\ 100 \text{ lakhs}}{\text{PV of Annuity of ₹ 1 for 5 years @ 12\%}} = \frac{100}{3.605} = 27.74$$

STATEMENT SHOWING THE PAYMENT OF PRINCIPAL & INTEREST

Year A	Pref. shares at year beg. B	Preference dividend C = B × Rate	Instalment D	Principal E = D – C	Pref. shares at year end F = B – E	Dividend Tax G = C × 20%	Cash outflow H = D + G
1	100.0	12.00	27.74	15.74	84.26	2.400	30.140

2	84.26	10.11	27.74	17.63	66.63	2.022	29.762
3	66.63	8.00	27.74	19.74	46.89	1.600	29.340
4	46.89	5.63	27.74	22.11	24.78	1.126	28.866
5	24.78	2.96*	27.74	24.78	0.00	0.592	28.332

* Instead of Dividend of ₹ 2.9736, it has been taken at 2.96 so as to bring the figure of Pref. Shares at year end to nil. The need for this adjustment has arisen because of use of approximation in equated annual instalment.

CALCULATION OF PRESENT VALUES AT 19% AND 20%

Year A	*Outflow* B	*PV Factor @19%* C	*PV Factor @20%* D	*PV @19%* E = B × C	*PV @20%* F = B × D
1	30.140	0.840	0.833	25.318	25.107
2	29.762	0.706	0.694	21.012	20.655
3	29.340	0.593	0.579	17.399	16.988
4	28.866	0.499	0.482	14.404	13.913
5	28.332	0.419	0.402	11.871	11.389
			Total	90.004	88.052

$$k_d = R_L + \frac{NPV_L}{NPV_L - NPV_H} \times (R_H - R_L)$$

$$k_d = 19\% + \frac{0.004}{0.004 - (-1.948)} \times (20\% - 19\%)$$

$$k_d = 19.002\%$$

ILLUSTRATION 17

Tushar Ltd. issues ₹ 100 lakhs, Preference Shares of ₹ 100 each at par redeemable at 5% premium. The floatation cost being 10 % on issue price. The dividend tax rate is 20%. The yearly coupon rate of preference dividend is as follows:

Year	*Coupon Rate of Preference Dividend*
1 - 2	10 %
3 - 4	11 %
5	12 %

Required: Calculate the cost of preference shares in each of the following alternative cases:

Case (a) If preference shares are redeemable after 5 years.

Case (b) If one fifth preference shares are redeemable each year beginning with the end of year 1.

SOLUTION

Case (a)

$$\text{Net Proceeds of Pref. Shares} = \frac{D_1(1+D_t)}{(1+k_p)^1} + \frac{D_2(1+D_t)}{(1+k_p)^2} + \ldots + \frac{D_n(1+D_t) + \text{Redeemable Value}_n}{(1+k_p)^n}$$

$$= \sum_{t=1}^{n=5} \frac{D_t(1+D_t)}{(1+k_p)^t} + \frac{RV_n}{(1+k_p)^n}$$

$$90 = \frac{10(1+0.2)}{(1+k_p)^1} + \frac{10(1+0.2)}{(1+k_p)^2} + \frac{11(1+0.2)}{(1+k_p)^3} + \frac{11(1+0.2)}{(1+k_p)^4} + \frac{12(1+0.2)}{(1+k_p)^5} + \frac{105}{(1+k_p)^5}$$

CALCULATION OF PRESENT VALUES AT 16% AND 17%

Year *A*	*Outflow* *B*	*PV Factor @16%* *C*	*PV Factor @17%* *D*	*PV @16%* *E = B × C*	*PV @17%* *F = B × D*
1	12.00	0.862	0.855	10.344	10.26
2	12.00	0.743	0.731	8.916	8.772
3	13.20	0.641	0.624	8.461	8.237
4	13.20	0.552	0.534	7.286	7.049
5	119.40	0.476	0.456	56.834	54.446
			Total	91.841	88.764

$$k_d = R_L + \frac{NPV_L}{NPV_L - NPV_H} \times (R_H - R_L)$$

$$k_d = 16\% + \frac{1.841}{1.841 - (-1.236)} \times (17\% - 16\%)$$

$$k_d = 16.60\%$$

Case (b)

Year *A*	*Op. Bal.* *B*	*Dividend* *C = B × Rate*	*Principal (incl. Prem.)* *D = 105/5*	*Instalment* *E = C + D*	*Cl. Bal.* *F = C – D + 1*	*Dividend Tax* *G = C × 20%*	*Cash outflow* *H = E + G*
1	100	10.0	21	31.0	80	2.00	33.00
2	80	8.0	21	29.0	60	1.60	30.60
3	60	6.6	21	27.6	40	1.32	28.92
4	40	4.4	21	25.4	20	0.88	26.28
5	20	2.4	21	23.4	0	0.48	23.88

Net Proceeds of Pref. Shares

$$= \frac{D_1(1+D_t) + Principal_1}{(1+k_p)^1} + \frac{D_2(1+D_t) + Principal_2}{(1+k_p)^2} + ... + \frac{D_n(1+D_t) + Principal_n}{(1+k_p)^n}$$

$$90 = \frac{10(1+.2)+21}{(1+k_p)^1} + \frac{8(1+.2)+21}{(1+k_p)^2} + \frac{6.6(1+.2)+21}{(1+k_p)^3} + \frac{4.4(1+.2)+21}{(1+k_p)^4} + \frac{2.4(1+.2)+21}{(1+k_p)^5}$$

CALCULATION OF PRESENT VALUES AT 18% AND 19%

Year *A*	*Outflow* *B*	*PV Factor @18%* *C*	*PV Factor @19%* *D*	*PV @18%* *E = B × C*	*PV @19%* *F = B × D*
1	33.00	0.847	0.840	27.951	27.72
2	30.60	0.718	0.706	21.971	21.604
3	28.92	0.609	0.593	17.612	17.150
4	26.28	0.516	0.499	13.560	13.114
5	23.88	0.437	0.419	10.436	10.006
			Total	91.530	89.594

$$k_d = R_L + \frac{NPV_L}{NPV_L - NPV_H} \times (R_H - R_L)$$

$$k_d = 18\% + \frac{1.53}{1.53 - (-0.406)} \times (19\% - 18\%) = 18.79\%$$

ILLUSTRATION 18 [CALCULATION OF MARKET PRICE]

X Ltd.' s Preference Shares of the face value of ₹ 100 bear an 12% coupon rate. These Preference shares are redeemable after 10 years. Calculate the Market price in each of the following alternative cases:

Case (a) If Preference shares of this type currently yield 16 %.

Case (b) If the maturity period is 4 years away from now and the Preference shares currently yield 10%

Case (c) Would you pay ₹ 102 to purchase Preference shares specified in situation (b). Explain

SOLUTION

Case (a) Market value Preference Share = $\frac{\text{Dividend on Preference Share}}{\text{Current Yield Rate}} = \frac{12}{0.16} = 75.00$

Case (b)

CALCULATION OF PRESENT VALUE OF A PREFERENCE SHARE

Year *A*	*Income* *B*	*PV Factor @ 10%* *C*	*PV @ 10%* *D = B × C*
1	12.00	0.909	10.908
2	12.00	0.826	9.912
3	12.00	0.751	9.012
4	112.00	0.683	76.496
			Total = 106.328

Case (c)

Recommendation: As the present value of preference share, as computed above is more than ₹ 102, hence the investor should buy the preference share at ₹ 102.

ILLUSTRATION 19 [CALCULATION OF ISSUE PRICE]

X Ltd. is planning to float a Preference Share issue on the following terms:

Face value : ₹ 100 per Preference Share

Terms of Maturity : 5 years

Premium on Redemption : 5 %

Yearly Coupon rate of Preference Dividend:

Year	*Coupon Rate of Preference Dividend*
1 - 2	10 %
3 - 4	11 %
5	12 %

The current market rate on similar Preference shares is 12 % p.a. The company proposes to price the issue so as to yield a compounded return of 13 % p.a. to the investors.

Required: Determine the Issue Price.

SOLUTION

CALCULATION OF PRESENT VALUE OF PREFERENCE SHARE

Year A	*Income* B	*PV Factor @ 13%* C	*PV @ 13%* $D = B \times C$
1	10.00	0.885	8.850
2	10.00	0.783	7.830
3	11.00	0.693	7.623
4	11.00	0.613	6.743
5	117.00	0.543	63.531
			Total = 94.577

Hence, the company should issue the Preference shares at ₹ 94.577.

ILLUSTRATION 20 [CALCULATION OF EFFECTIVE YIELD ON ISSUE PRICE]

X Ltd. issued ₹ 100, 12 % Preference Shares 5 years ago. Dividend rates have been risen since then, so that Preference shares of the company are now selling at 15 % yield basis.

Case (a) Determine the current expected market price of the Preference Shares. Would you buy the Preference shares for ₹ 75 ?

Case (b) Assuming that the Preference shares of the company are selling at ₹ 80 and have 5 years to run to maturity, compute the approximate effective yield an investor would earn on his investment.

SOLUTION

Case (a) Market value of Preference Share $= \dfrac{\text{Dividend on Preference Share}}{\text{Current Yield Rate}} = \dfrac{12}{0.15} = 80.00$

Recommendation: As the market value of Debenture, as computed above is more than ₹ 75, hence the investor should buy these debentures at ₹ 75.

Case (b) Net Proceeds of Pref. Share

$$= \frac{D_1(1+D_t)}{(1+k_p)^1} + \frac{D_2(1+D_t)}{(1+k_p)^2} + \dots + \frac{D_n(1+D_t) + \text{Redeemable Value}_n}{(1+k_p)^n}$$

$$= \sum_{t=1}^{n} \frac{D_t\,(1+D_t)}{(1+k_p)^t} + \frac{RV_n}{(1+k_p)^n}$$

$$80.00 = \sum_{t=1}^{5} \frac{12\,(1+0.20)}{(1+k_p)^t} + \frac{100}{(1+k_p)^5}$$

CALCULATION OF PRESENT VALUES AT 18% AND 19%

Year A	*Outflow* B	*PV Factor @18%* C	*PV Factor @19%* D	*PV @18%* $E = B \times C$	*PV @19%* $F = B \times D$
1	12.00	0.847	0.840	10.164	10.080
2	12.00	0.718	0.706	8.616	8.472
3	12.00	0.609	0.593	7.308	7.116
4	12.00	0.516	0.499	6.192	5.988
5	112.00	0.437	0.419	48.944	46.928
			Total	81.224	78.584

$$k_d = R_L + \frac{NPV_L}{NPV_L - NPV_H} \times (R_H - R_L)$$

$$k_d = 18\% + \frac{1.224}{1.224 - (-1.416)} \times (19\% - 18\%)$$

$$k_d = 18.46\%$$

8.0 TERMS USEFUL TO STUDY DIFFERENT APPROACHES AS TO COST OF EQUITY CAPITAL

To study different approaches as to the Cost of Equity Share one must know:

1. What is Retention Ratio ?
2. What is Price-Earning Ratio ?
3. What is a Rate of Return on Retained Earnings ?
4. What is Growth Rate ?
5. What is Expected Dividend ?
6. What is Current Market Price ?
7. Risk of Security

Following paras answer to the aforesaid questions:

1. **Retention Ratio (b):** Retention Ratio means that proportion of earning per share (E) which is not distributed as dividend (D). It is denoted by the symbol, 'b'. The remaining proportion of earning per share which is distributed as dividend is known as 'Dividend Payout Ratio'. These are calculated as follows:

   1. $\text{Retention Ratio} = \frac{\text{Earning Per Share (E)} - \text{Dividend Per Share (D)}}{\text{Earning Per Share (E)}} \times 100$

      $b = \frac{E - D}{E} \times 100$ or, $= 1 - \text{Dividend Payout Ratio}$

      $\text{Dividend Payout Ratio} = \frac{\text{Dividend Per Share (D)}}{\text{Earning Per Share (E)}} = \frac{D}{E} \times 100$

   2. D/P Ratio = 1 – Retention Ratio (b) = 1 – b

EXAMPLE: [CALCULATION OF RETENTION RATIO (B)]

Calculate Retention Ratio (b) in each of the following alternative cases:

Case (a) Earning per share ₹ 10, Dividend per share ₹ 6

Case (b) Dividend Payout Ratio 80%.

SOLUTION

Case (a) Retention Ratio (b) $= \frac{\text{Earning Per Share} - \text{Dividend Per Share}}{\text{Earning Per Share}} \times 100$

$$= \frac{₹ 10 - ₹ 6}{₹ 10} \times 100 = 40\%$$

Case (b) Retention Ratio (b) = 100% – 80% = 20%

2. **Price Earning ratio (P/E Ratio):** Price Earning Ratio means the number of times of EPS, the share is being quoted in the market. The reciprocal of P/E Ratio indicates Earning Yield (or performance of earning in relation to market price) *or* expectations of the share holders. It is used to calculate Growth Rate (g). It is calculated as follows:

1. $\text{Price-Earning ratio} = \frac{\text{Market Price of an Equity Share (P)}}{\text{Earning Per Share (E)}} = \frac{P}{E}$
2. $\text{Price-Earning Ratio} = \frac{1}{\text{Rate of Return on Retained Earnings (t)}} = \frac{1}{r}$

EXAMPLE: [CALCULATION OF PRICE-EARNING RATIO (P/E RATIO)]

Calculate Price - Earning Ratio in each of the following alternative cases:

Case (a) Current Market Price of An Equity Share ₹ 50, Current Earning Per share ₹ 10.

Case (b) Rate of Return on Retained Earning 25%.

Case (c) Current Market Price of an Equity Share ₹ 50, Current Dividend Per Share ₹ 10, Dividend Payout Ratio 80%.

SOLUTION

Case (a) $\text{Price-Earning Ratio} = \frac{\text{Market Price per share}}{\text{Earning per share}} = \frac{P}{E} = \frac{₹\,50}{₹\,10} = 5$

Case (b) $\text{Price-Earning Ratio} = \frac{1}{\text{Rate of Return on Retained Earnings}} = \frac{1}{0.25} = 4$

Case (c) $\text{Price-Earning Ratio} = \frac{\text{Market Price per share}}{\text{Dividend per share/Dividend Payout Ratio}} = \frac{₹\,50}{₹\,10/80} = 4$

3. **Rate of Return on Retained Earnings(r):** Rate of Return on Retained Earnings(r) means the Earning yield (or performance of earning in relation to market price) *or* expectations of shareholders. It is the reciprocal of Price-Earning Ratio (P/E Ratio). It is used to calculate Growth rate (g). it is usually denoted by symbol, 'r'. It is calculated as follows:
   1. $\text{Rate of Return on Retained Earnings(r)} = \text{Earning Yield } \frac{\text{Earning Per Share}}{\text{Market Price Per Share}}$
   2. $\text{Rate of Return on Retained Earnings(r)} = \frac{1}{\text{Price Earning Ratio}} \times 100$

EXAMPLE: [CALCULATION OF RATE OF RETURN ON RETAINED EARNINGS(R)]

Calculate the Rate of Return on Retained Earnings(r) in each of the following alternative cases:

Case (a) Current Market Price of An Equity Share ₹ 50, Current Earning Per Share ₹ 10.

Case (b) Price Earning Ratio 4

Case (c) Current Market Price of earning Share ₹ 50, Current Dividend Per Share ₹ 10, Dividend Payout Ratio 80%.

SOLUTION

Case (a) $\text{Rate of Return on Retained Earnings} = \frac{\text{Earning Per Share}}{\text{Market Price Per Share}} \times 100 = \frac{₹\,10}{₹\,50} \times 100 = 20\%$

Case (b) $\text{Rate of Return on Retained Earnings} = \frac{1}{\text{Price Earning Ratio}} = \frac{1}{4} = 25\%$

Case (c) Rate of Return on Retained Earnings

$$= \frac{\text{Dividend per share/Dividend Payout Ratio}}{\text{Market Price per share}} \times 100 = \frac{₹\,10/80\%}{₹\,50} \times 100 = 25\%$$

4. **Growth Rate (g):** Growth Rate (g) means the rate at which the earnings of a company are expected to grow in future. It is denoted by the symbol, 'g '. it is calculated as follows:
   1. Growth Rate (g) = Retention Ratio (b) × Rate of Return on Retained Earnings (r) = br.
   2. Growth Rate (g) = (1 – Dividend Payout Ratio) × (1/Price – Earning Ratio)

EXAMPLE: [CALCULATION OF GROWTH RATE (G)]

Calculate Growth Rate (g) in each of the following alternative cases:

Case (a) Retention Ratio 40%, Rate of Return on Retained Earnings 20%.

Case (b) Dividend Payout Ratio 70%, Rate of Return on Retained earning 20%.

Case (c) Dividend Payout Ratio 80%, Price Earning Ratio 8.

Case (d) Dividend Payout Ratio 90%, Earning Yield 20%.

SOLUTION

Case (a) Growth Rate = Retention Ratio (b) × Ratio of Return on Retained Earnings (r)

= 0.40 0.20 = 0.08 *or* 8%

Case (b) Retention Ratio (b) = 1 – Dividend Payout Ratio = 1 – 0.70 = 0.30

Growth Rate = Retention Ratio (b) × Ratio of Return on Retained Earnings (r)

= 0.30 × 0.20 = 0.06 *or* 6%.

Case (c) Retention Ratio (b) = 1 – Dividend Payout ratio = 1 – 0.80 = 0.20

Rate of Return on Retained Earning = I/P/E Ratio = 1/8 = 0.125

Growth Rate = Retention Ratio (b) × Ratio of Return on Retained Earnings (r)

= 0.20 × 0.125 = 0.025 *or* 2.5%.

Case (d) Retention Ratio (b) = 1 – Dividend Payout Ratio = 1 – 0.90 = 0.10

Rate of Return on Retained earning (r) = Earning Yield = 0.20

Growth Rate = br = 0.10 × 0.20 = 0.02 *or* 2%

5. **Expected Dividend (D_1):** Expected Dividend (D_1) means dividend per share which is to be paid at the end of one year. It is denoted by the symbol, 'D_1'. D_1 may be calculated as follows:
   1. $D_1 = D_0 (1 + g)$
      where, D_0 = Actual Dividend Per Share paid for the last year, g = Growth Rate
   2. $D_1 = E_1 \times$ Dividend Payout Ratio
      where, E_1 = Expected Earning Per Share which means earning per share which is expected to be earned at the end of one year.

EXAMPLE: [CALCULATION OF EXPECTED DIVIDEND PER SHARE (D1)]

Calculate Expected Dividend (D1)in each of the following alternative cases:

Case (a) Present Dividend per share ₹ 10, Growth Rate 8%.

Case (b) Present Earning per share ₹ 10, Dividend Payout Ratio 60%, Growth Rate 8%.

Case (c) Expected Earning per share ₹ 10, Dividend Payout ratio 60%, Growth Rate 8%.

SOLUTION

Case (a) D_1 = D_0 (1 + g) = ₹ 10 (1 + 0.08) = ₹ 10.80

Case (b) D_0 = E_0 Dividend Payout ratio = ₹ 10 60% = ₹ 6

D_1 = D_0 (1 + g)= ₹ 6 (1 + 0.08) = ₹ 6.48

Case (c) D_1 = E_1 Dividend Payout Ratio = ₹ 10 60% = ₹ 6

6. **Current Market Price (P_0):** Current Market Price (P_0) means the price at which the share is being currently quoted in the market. It is usually denoted by the symbol, P_0. it may be calculated as follows:

1. P_0 = Current Earning Per Share × Current Price – Earning Ratio
2. $P_0 = \dfrac{\text{Current Dividend Per Share}}{\text{Current Dividend Payout Ratio}}$ × Current Price – Earning Ratio
3. $P_0 = \dfrac{\text{Expected Earning Per Share}}{(1+\text{Growth Rate})}$ × Current Price – Earning Ratio

EXAMPLE: [CALCULATION OF CURRENT MARKET PRICE (P_0)]

Calculate the Current Market Price (P_0) of an equity share in each of the following alternative cases:

Case (a) Price Earning Ratio 5, Present earning per share ₹ 10.

Case (b) Price Earning Ratio 5, Present Dividend per share ₹ 6, Dividend Payout Ratio 60%.

Case (c) Price Earning Ratio 5, Expected Earning per share ₹ 10.80, Earning Growth Rate 8%.

Case (d) Price Earning Ratio 5, Expected Dividend per share ₹ 6.48, Dividend Payout Ratio 60%, Earning Growth Rate 8%.

SOLUTION

Case (a) Current Market Price (P_0) = EPS_0 × P/E Ratio = ₹ 10 × 5 = ₹ 50

Case (b) EPS_0 = D_0/Dividend Payout Ratio = ₹ 6/60% = ₹ 10

Current Market Price (P_0) = EPS_0 × P/E Ratio = ₹ 10 × 5 = ₹ 50

Case (c) EPS_0 = EPS_1/(1 + growth rate) = ₹ 10.80/(1 + 0.08) = ₹ 10

Current Market Price (P_0) = EPS_0 × P/E Ratio = ₹ 10 × 5 = ₹ 50

Case (d) EPS_1 = D_1/Dividend Payout Ratio = ₹ 6.48/60% = ₹ 10.80

EPS_0 = EPS_1/(1 + growth rate) = ₹ 10.80/(1 + 0.08) = ₹ 10

Current Market Price (P_0) = EPS_0 × P/E Ratio = ₹ 10 × 5 = ₹ 50

7. **Risk of Security:** The total risk of security consists of the following two types of risks:

(a) Unsystematic Risk (or Diversifiable Risk):

Meaning—It represents the fluctuations in return of a specific security due to factors affecting a particular firm only. It can be eliminated through diversification (i.e. by investing in large number of well-diversified securities).

Example: The examples of unsystematic risk include:

(i) Strike by workers
(ii) Resignation by R & D Expert.
(iii) Entry of a formidable competitor.
(iv) Loosing a big contract in a bid.
(v) Inadequate Availability of Raw-Material.
(vi) Custom Duty imposed on a raw-material used by the company.

(b) Systematic Risk (or Non-diversifiable Risk *or* Market Risk)

Meaning—It represents the fluctuation in return of every security due to factors affecting the market as a whole. It arises due to tendency of every security to move together with changes in the market. It cannot be eliminated through diversification. Investors are exposed to market risk even when they hold well-diversified portfolios of securities.

Examples: The examples of systematic risk include:

(i) Change in Interest Rate Policy
(ii) Change in Corporate Tax Policy
(iii) Increase in Inflation Rate.

(iv) Govt. resorting to massive deficit financing

(v) Change in Foreign Exchange Policy.

9.0 COST OF EQUITY SHARE

MEANING OF COST OF EQUITY SHARE

It may be defined as minimum rate of return that the company must earn on that portion of its total capital employed which is financed by equity capital, so that the market price of the shares of the company remains unchanged.

FACTORS AFFECTING THE COST OF EQUITY SHARE

The computation of the Cost of an Equity Share requires an understanding of many factors basically concerning the behaviour of the investors and their expectations. The considerable factors while calculating the Cost of Equity include:

(a) Price of an Equity Share in the beginning of year.

(b) Expected Equity Dividend at the end of a year.

(c) Growth Rate.

DIFFERENT APPROACHES AS TO THE CALCULATION OF COST OF EQUITY SHARE

Since there can be different interpretations of investor's behaviour, there are many approaches regarding calculation of cost of equity shares. The six main approaches have been discussed below:

1. **Dividend Price (D/P) Ratio Approach:** Under this approach, the cost of equity share capital is calculated on the basis of the present value of the expected future streams of dividends. Here, the cost of equity capital will be the rate of expected dividend, which will maintain the market price of equity shares. This approach assumes that dividends are paid at a constant rate to perpetuity. Cost of Equity is calculated as follows:

$$k_e = \frac{D_1}{P_0}$$

Where, D_1 = Expected Dividend per share at the end of year 1.

P_0 = Current Market Price per share in the beginning of year 1.

Example: Suppose an investor subscribes to the equity shares of X Ltd. having expected dividend per share (D_1) as ₹ 6 and the current market price of the share (P_0) is ₹ 50. Cost of equity will be:

$$k_e = \frac{D_1}{P_0} = \frac{₹\ 6}{₹\ 50} = 0.12 \textit{ or } 12\%$$

Drawbacks

(i) It ignores the factor of capital appreciation *or* depreciation in the market price of shares.

(ii) A company, which declares a higher amount of dividend out of a given amount of earnings, will be placed at a premium as compared to a company, which earns the same amount of profits but utilizes a major part of same in financing its expansion programmes.

(iii) This approach cannot be used to calculate the cost of equity of companies which are not declaring dividend.

2. **Dividend Price *plus* Growth approach:** Under this approach, the cost of equity share capital is calculated on the basis of the present value of the expected future streams of dividends and the rate of growth in dividend. This growth rate in dividend (g) is equal to the compound growth rate in earnings per share. Here, the cost of capital is based upon the dividend rate and capital appreciation expected by the shareholder. Cost of equity is calculated as follows:

$$k_e = \frac{D_1}{P_0} + g$$

Where, D_1 = Expected dividend per share at the end of year 1 = D_0 (1 + g)

P_0 = Current Market Price per share at the beginning of year 1.

g = Growth rate = br

b = Retention Ratio = (1 – Dividend Payout Ratio)

$$= \frac{DPS\,(1 + D_t)}{EPS}$$

r = Internal Rate of Return on Retained Earnings

Example: Suppose an investor subscribes to the equity shares of X Ltd. having expected dividend per share (D_1) as ₹ 6 and the current market price of the share (P_0) is ₹ 50 and the earning and dividend per share are expected to grow at rate of 8% p.a., Cost of equity will be:

$$k_e = \frac{D_1}{P_0} + g = \frac{₹\,6}{₹\,50} + 0.08 = 0.20 \text{ or } 20\%$$

Drawback: It does not answer one problem—How to quantify the expectations of the investor relating to dividend and growth in dividend ?

3. **Earning Price Ratio Approach:** Under this approach, the cost of equity share capital is calculated on the basis of the present value of the expected future streams of earnings (whether distributed *or* not). Here, the cost of equity capital is based upon that rate of expected earnings, which will maintain the market price of equity shares. Cost of Equity is calculated as follows:

$$k_e = \frac{E_1}{P_0}$$

Where, E_1= Expected Earnings per share at the end of year 1.

P_0= Current market price in the beginning of year 1.

Example I: Expected Earnings per share at the end of year 1 is ₹ 10, Current Market Price is ₹ 50. here, Cost of Equity

$$(k_e) = \frac{E_1}{P_0} = \frac{₹\,10}{₹\,50} = 0.20 \text{ or } 20\%$$

Example II: If X Ltd. is expected to earn 30%; the investor who expects 20% rate of earnings will be prepared to pay ₹ 150 per share of ₹ 100 each.

Merit: In comparison to D/P approach, this approach seeks to nullify the effect of change in the dividend policy.

Drawback: Like D/P ratio approach, it also ignores the factor of capital appreciation *or* depreciation in the market price of shares.

4. **Earning Price *plus* Growth approach:** Under this approach, the cost of equity share capital is calculated on the basis of the present value of the expected future streams of earnings and the rate of growth in earnings. Here, the cost of capital is based upon the earning rate and capital appreciation expected by a shareholder. Cost of equity is calculated as follows:

$$k_e = \frac{E_1}{P_0} + g$$

Where, E_1= Expected earnings per share at the end of year 1 = E_0 (1 + g)

P_0= Current Market Price per share the beginning of year 1.

G= Growth Rate = br

b= Retention Ratio = (1 – Dividend Payout Ratio)

$$= \frac{DPS\,(1 + D_2)}{EPS}$$

r= Internal Rate of Return on Retained Earnings

Example: Expected Earnings per share (E_1) is ₹ 10 and the Current Market Price of the share (P_0) is ₹ 50 and the earning per share is expected to grow (g) at rate of 8% p.a., Cost of equity will be:

$$k_e = \frac{E_1}{P_0} + g = \frac{₹\,10}{₹\,50} + 0.08 = 0.20 + 0.08 = 28\%$$

5. **Realised Yield approach:** This approach assumes that past behaviour will be repeated in future and uses past yields instead of expected values of dividend and capital appreciation as the basis to formulate an estimate of the cost of equity capital.

6. **Capital Asset Pricing Model (CAPM)**

   1. **Who developed Capital Asset Pricing Model (CAPM)?**

      CAPM was developed by Sharp Mossin and Linter in 1960.

   2. **Main Contention of CAPM**

      The required rate of return on a security is equal to a Risk Free Rate *plus* the Risk Premium.

Now two questions arise?

(a) What is Risk Free Rate?

(b) What is Risk Premium?

3. **What is Risk Free Rate?**

   Risk Free Rate is the rate of return on risk-free security. The risk-free security is the security which has no risk of default *or* which has zero variance *or* standard deviation. ***For Example***, Government Treasury Bills *or* Bonds are usually considered risk-free securities because they normally do not have risk of default.

4. **What is Risk Premium?**

   (a) Risk Premium is the premium for systematic risk.

   (b) Systematic Risk (or Market Risk *or* Non-Diversifiable Risk) is the risk which can not be eliminated through investing in well-diversified market portfolio.

   (c) Systematic Risk is measured by beta (b)

   (d) Beta (b) is a measure of volatility of an individual security return relative to the returns of a broad based market portfolio. It indicates — how much individual security's return will change for a unit change in the market return?

   (e) the value of beta (b) can be zero *or* more than 1 *or less* than 1.

Value of Beta	*Interpretation*
1. **Beta equal to 1**	Beta equal to 1 indicates that systematic risk is equal to the aggregate market risk. It means that the security's returns fluctuate equal to market returns.
2. **Beta Greater than 1**	Beta greater than 1 indicates that systematic risk is greater than the aggregate market risk. It means that the security's returns fluctuate more than the market returns.
3. **Beta less than 1**	Beta *less* than 1 indicates that systematic risk is *less* than the aggregate market risk. it means that the security's returns fluctuate *less* than the market returns.
4. **Zero Beta**	Zero Beta indicates no volatility.

   (f) Total Risk Premium varies directly with systematic risk.

   (g) Total Risk Premium is calculated as follows:

Total Risk Premium = Beta × (Expected Rate of Market Returns – Risk Free Rate of Returns)

5. How to calculate Required Rate of Return on a security?

Required Rate of return on a security (k_e) = Risk Free Rate + Risk Premium = $R_f + \beta(R_m - R_f)$

Example: Risk Free Rate on 10 years Govt. of India Treasury Bonds is 5.5%. Rate of Return on Market Portfolio is 13.5%. Beta of the company is 1.1875. Here, the Required Rate of Return on Security will be:

$$k_e = R_f + \beta(R_m - R_f) = 5.5\% + 1.1875\ (13.5\% - 5.5\%) = 15\%$$

Note: The calculation of Beta (b) has been explained in detail in Para 19.

6. Assumptions of CAPM

The CAPM is based on the following eight assumptions:

1. **Maximization Objective:** The Investor's objective is to maximize the utility of terminal wealth;
2. **Risk Averse:** Investors are risk averse. Investors make choices on the basis of risk and return;
3. **Homogenous Expectations:** Investors have homogenous expectations of risk and return;
4. **Identical Time Horizon:** Investors have identical time horizon;
5. **Free Information:** Information is freely and simultaneously available to investors;
6. **Risk-Free Rate:** There is a risk-free asset, and investors can borrow and lend unlimited amounts at the risk-free rate;
7. **No Taxes etc.:** There are no taxes, transaction costs, restrictions on short rates, *or* other market imperfections;
8. **Marketability and Divisibility:** Total assets quantity is fixed, and all assets are marketable and divisible.

WHICH APPROACH TO USE?

Type of Company	*Approach to be used*
1. In case of companies with stable income and stable dividend policies	Dividend Price Approach
2. In case of growing companies	Dividend Price *plus* Growth Approach
3. In case of companies whose earnings accrue in cycles	E/P Ratio approach but representative figure should be taken into account to include one complete cycle.
4. In case of companies enjoying stable growth rate & stable rate of dividend.	Realized Yield Approach

ILLUSTRATION 21 [CALCULATION OF COST OF EQUITY (k_e) ACCORDING TO VARIOUS APPROACHES]

From the following information, calculate the Cost of Equity (k_e) according to (a) Dividend price Approach (b) Dividend Price *plus* Growth Approach (c) Earning Price Ratio approach (d) Earning Price *plus* Growth Approach, (e) Capital Assets Pricing Model Approach:

1. Current Market Price of an Equity Share: ₹ 100
2. Expected Earnings per Share at the end of year: ₹ 10
3. Dividend Payout Ratio: 80%.
4. Growth Rate: 6%

5. Rate of Return on Risk Free Investment: 8%
6. Rate of Return on Market Portfolio: 18%
7. Volatility of securities return relative to the return of a broad based market port folio: 1.275

SOLUTION

(a) Dividend Price Approach

$$k_e = \frac{D_1}{P_0} = \frac{80\% \text{ of } ₹\,10}{₹\,100} = 0.08 \text{ or } 8\%$$

(b) Dividend Price *plus* Growth Approach

$$k_e = \frac{D_1}{P_0} + g = \frac{80\% \text{ of } ₹\,10}{₹\,100} + 0.06 = 0.14 \text{ or } 14\%$$

(c) Earning Price Approach

$$k_e = \frac{E_1}{P_0} = \frac{₹\,10}{₹\,100} = 0.10 \text{ or } 10\%$$

(d) Earning Price *plus* Growth Approach

$$k_e = \frac{E_1}{P_0} + g = \frac{₹\,10}{₹\,100} + 0.06 = 0.16 \text{ or } 16\%$$

(e) Capital Assets Pricing Model

$k_e = R_f + (b \times \text{Average Market Risk Premium})$

or, $k_e = R_f + b\,(R_m - R_f)$

where, R_f = Rate of Return on Risk Free Investment = 8%

R_m = Rate of Return on Market Portfolio = 18%

b = Beta Coefficient i.e. measure of volatility of securities return relative to the return of a broad based market portfolio = 1.275

Thus, $k_e = 8\% + 1.275\,(18\% - 8\%) = 20.75\%$.

ILLUSTRATION 22

Calculate the Cost of Equity (ke) in each of the following alternative cases:

Case (a) An equity share of the company is currently selling for ₹ 50. The company expects to pay ₹ 6 per share at the end of current year. Dividend per share is expected to grow at the rate 8% p.a.

Case (b) An equity share of the company is currently is currently selling for ₹ 50. The company expects to earn ₹ 6 per share at the end of current year. Dividend Payout Ratio is 60%. Dividend per share is expected to grow at the rate of 8% p.a

Case (c) An equity share of the company is currently selling for ₹ 50. The company had paid dividend of ₹ 6 per share at the end of last year. Dividend per share is expected to grow at the rate of 8% p.a.

Case (d) An equity share of the company is currently selling for ₹ 50. The company had earned ₹ 6 per share at the end of last year. Dividend Payout Ratio is 60%. Dividend per share is expected to grow at the rate of 8% p.a.

Case (e) An equity share of company is currently selling for ₹ 50. The company expects to earn ₹ 6 per share at the end of current year. Dividend Payout Ratio is 60%. The company reinvests the retained earnings at a rate of 20%.

Case (f) An equity share of company is currently selling for ₹ 50. The company had earned to earn ₹ 6 per share at the end of last year. Dividend Payout ratio is 60%. The company reinvests the retained earnings at a rate of 20%.

Case (g) The price earning ratio is 5 times. The company has an earning per share of ₹ 10 per share. Dividend Payout Ratio is 60%. Dividend per share is expected to grow at the rate of 8% p.a.

Case (h) The price earning ratio is 5 times. The company has an earning per share of ₹ 10 per share. Dividend Payout ratio is 60%.

Case (i) The price earning ratio is 5 times. The company expects to earn ₹ 10.80 per share at the end of current year. Dividend Payout ratio is 60%. Dividend per share is expected to grow at the rate of 8%.

Case (j) The price earning ratio is 5 times. The company expects to earn ₹ 10.80 per share at the end of current year. Dividend Payout ratio is 60%.

Case (k) The price earning ratio is 5. The company has paid a dividend of ₹ 6 per share. Dividend payout ratio is 60%.

Case (l) The company has a policy of paying dividends at the rate of 15% of the market price of the share in the beginning. Dividend per share is expected to grow at the rate of 5%.

SOLUTION

Case (a) $$k_e = \frac{D_1}{P_0} + g$$

Where, D_1 = Expected Dividend per share at the end of year 1 = ₹ 6

P_0 = Current Market Price per share at the beginning of year 1 = ₹ 50

g = Growth Rate = 8%

k_e = ₹6/₹50 = 0.12 + 0.08 = 20%

Case (b) $$k_e = \frac{D_1}{P_0} + g$$

Where, D_1 = Expected dividend per share at the end of year 1

= EPS_1 × Dividend Payout Ratio = ₹ 6 × 60% = ₹ 3.60

P_0 = Current Market Price per share at the beginning of year 1 = ₹ 50

g = Growth rate = 8%

k_e = ₹3.60/₹50 + 0.08 = 0.072 + 0.08 = 15.2%

Case (c) $$k_e = \frac{D_1}{P_0} + g$$

Where, D_1 = Expected dividend per share at the end of year 1

= D_0 (1 + g) = ₹ 6 (1 + 0.08) = ₹ 6.48

P_0 = Current market Price per share at the beginning of year 1 = ₹ 50

g = Growth rate = 8%

k_e = ₹6.48/₹50 + 0.08 = 0.1296 + 0.08 = 20.96%

Case (d) $$k_e = \frac{D_1}{P_0} + g$$

Where, D_1 = Expected dividend per share at the end of year 1

= D_0 (1 + g) = (E_0 × Dividend Payout Ratio)(1 + g)

= (6 × 60%) (1 + 0.08) = ₹ 3.60 (1.08) = ₹ 3.888

P_0 = Current market Price per share at the beginning of year 1 = ₹ 50

g = Growth Rate = 8%

k_e = ₹3,888/₹50 = 0.0778 + 0.08 = 15.78%.

Case (e) $k_e = \frac{D_1}{P_0} + g$

Retention Ratio (b) = 1 – Dividend Payout Ratio = 1 – 0.60 = 0.40

Rate of Return on Retained Earnings (r) = 0.20

Growth Rate (g) = br = 0.40 × 0.20 = 0.08

D_1 = EPS, (1 – b) = ₹ 6 (1 – 0.4) = ₹ 3.60

P_0 = ₹ 50

k_e = (₹3.60/₹50) + 0.08 = 0.072 + 0.08 = 15.2%

Case (f) $k_e = \frac{D_1}{P_0} + g$

Retention Ratio (b) = 1 – Dividend Payout Ratio = 1 – 0.60 = 0.40

Rate of Return on Retained Earnings (r) = 0.20

Growth Rate (g) = br = 0.40 × 0.20 = 0.08

P_0 = ₹ 50

D_0 = E_0 (1 – b) = ₹ 6 (1 – 0.40) = ₹ 3.60

D_1 = D_0 (1 + g) = ₹ 3.60 (1 + 0.08) = ₹ 3.888

k_e = (₹3.888/₹50) + 0.08 = 0.0778 + .08 = 15.78%

Case (g) $k_e = \frac{D_1}{P_0} + g$

g = 8%

D_1 = D0 (1 + g) = (E_0 × Dividend Payout Ratio) (1 + g)

= (₹ 10 × 60%) (1 + 0.08) = ₹ 6.48

P_0 = EPS × P/E Ratio = ₹ 10 × 5 = ₹ 50

k_e = (₹6.48/₹50) + 0.08 = 0.1296 + 0.08 = 20.96%

Case (h) $k_e = \frac{D_1}{P_0} + g$

Retention Ratio (b) = 1 – Dividend Payout Ratio = 1 – 0.6 = 0.40

Rate of Return on Retained Earnings = 100/P/E Ratio = 100/5 = 20%

Growth Rate = br = 0.40 × 0.20 = 0.08

g = 8%

D_1 = D_0 (1 + g) = (E_0 × Dividend Payout Ratio)(1 + g)

= (₹ 10 × 60%) (1 + 0.08) = ₹ 6.48

P_0 = EPS × P/E Ratio = ₹ 10 × 5 = ₹ 50

k_e = (₹6.48/₹50) + 0.08 = 0.1296 + 0.08 = 20.96%

Case (i) Growth Rate (g) = 8%

EPS_0 = E_1/(1 + g) = ₹10.80/(1 + 0.08) = ₹ 10

D_1 = (E × Dividend Payout Ratio) = ₹ 10.80 × 60% = ₹ 6.48

P_0 = EPS0 × P/E Ratio = ₹ 10 × 5 = ₹ 50

k_e = (₹6.48/₹50) + 0.08 = 0.1296 + 0.08 = 20.96%

Case (j) Retention Ratio (b) = 1 – Dividend Payout Ratio = 1 – 0.60 = 0.40

Rate of Return of Retained earnings = 100/P/E Ratio = 100/5 = 20%

Growth Rate = br = 0.40 × 0.20 = 0.08

EPS_0 = E_1/(1 + g) = ₹10.80/(1 + 0.08) = ₹ 10

D_1 = (E_1 × Dividend Payout Ratio) = ₹ 10.80 × 60% ₹ 6.48

P_0 = E_0 × P/E Ratio = ₹ 10 × 5 = ₹ 50

k_e = (₹6.48/₹50) + 0.08 = 0.1296 + 0.08 = 20.96%

Case (k) EPS_0 = D_0/Dividend Payout Ratio = ₹ 6/60% = ₹ 10

Retention Ratio (b) = 1 – Dividend Payout ratio = 1 – 0.60 = 0.40

Rate of Return on Retained earnings (b) = 100/P/E Ratio = 100/5 = 20%

Growth Rate = br = 0.40 × 0.20 = 0.08

D_1 = D_0 (1 + g) = (E_0 × Dividend Payout Ratio)(1 + g)

= (₹ 10 × 60%) (1 + 0.08) = ₹ 6.48

P_0 = E_0 × P/E Ratio = ₹ 10 × 5 = ₹ 50

k_e = (D_1/P_0) + g = (₹6.48/₹50) + 0.08 = 0.1296 + 0.08 = 20.96%

Case (l) ke = (D_1/P_0) + g = (15% of P_0/ P_0) + 5% = 20%

ILLUSTRATION 23 [CALCULATION OF MARKET PRICE]

Mr. Investor is planning to purchase the shares of X Ltd. which has paid a dividend of ₹ 2 per share at last year. His required rate of return is 20%. What price would Mr. Investor be willing to pay for X Ltd.'s shares if he expects dividend to grow at a constant rate of (a) 10% (b) 0% (c) – 10% (d) 20% (e) 22%?

SOLUTION

(a) $P_0 = \frac{D_1}{k_e - g}$ and $D_1 = D_0 (1 + g)$

D_1 = 2 (1 + 0.10) = 2.20

P_0 = 2.20/(0.20 – 0.10) = 22.00

(b) $P_0 = \frac{D_1}{k_e - g}$ and $D_1 = D_0 (1 + g)$

D_1 = 2 (1 + 0.000) = 2.00

P_0 = 2.00/(0.20 – 0.000) = 10.00

(c) $P_0 = \frac{D_1}{k_e - g}$ and $D_1 = D_0 (1 + g)$

D_1 = 2 [1 + (– 0.10)] = 1.80

P_0 = 1.80/[0.20 – (–0.10) = 6.00

(d) $P_0 = \frac{D_1}{k_e - g}$ and $D_1 = D_0 (1 + g)$

D_1 = 2 (1 + 0.20) = 2.40

P_0 = 2.40/(0.20 – 0.20) = undefined

(e) $P_0 = \frac{D_1}{k_e - g}$ and $D_1 = D_0 (1 + g)$

D_1 = 2 (1 + 0.22) = 2.44

P_0 = 2.44/(0.20 – 0.22) = – 122.00

The result in case of (d) and (e) show that the formula gives absurd result if ke is *less* than *or* equal to the growth rate. In other words it shows that the formula has been developed on the assumption that the $k_e > g$.

ILLUSTRATION 24 [CALCULATION OF DPS PAID LAST YEAR IF DIVIDENDS ARE GROWING]

Mr. Dalal is planning to purchase the shares of X Ltd. His required rate of return is 20%. Dividends are growing at a rate of 10%. What dividend had X Ltd. paid last year if he is willing to pay ₹ 27.50 for X Ltd.'s shares?

SOLUTION

$$P_0 = \frac{D_1}{k_e - g} \text{ and } D_1 = D_0(1 + g)$$

$D_1 = D_0(1 + g)$

$P_0 = D_0(1 + 0.10)/(0.20 - 0.10) = 27.50$

$D_0(1.10) = 2.75$

$D_0 = 2.75/1.10$

$D_0 =$ ₹ 2.50

ILLUSTRATION 25 [Calculation of Required Rate of Return if Dividends are Growing]

Mr. Factor purchases an equity share of X Ltd. X Ltd. has paid dividend of ₹ 2 per share last year. Dividends are growing at a rate of 10%. What is the required rate of return of Mr. X on his equity investment if he purchases an equity share for ₹ 22 ?

SOLUTION

$$P_0 = \frac{D_1}{k_e - g} \text{ and } D_1 = D_0(1 + g)$$

$D_1 = 2(1 + 0.10) = 2.20$

$P_0 = 2.2/(k_e - 0.10) = 22.00$

$2.2 = 22(k_e - 0.10)$

$2.2 = 22k_e - 2.2$

$2.2 + 2.2 = 22k_e$

$22k_e = 4.40$

$k_e = 4.40/22$

$k_e = 0.20$ *or* 20%

ILLUSTRATION 26 [CALCULATION OF AFTER TAX COST OF EQUITY]

An Equity share of the company is currently selling for ₹ 60. The earning per share ₹ 7.50. The company reinvests the retained earning at a rate of 10%. Calculate the cost of equity share if the company's dividend payout ratio is 60%.

SOLUTION

$$K_e = \frac{D_1}{P_0} + g$$

Retention Ratio $= b = 1 -$ Dividend Payout Ratio $= 1 - 0.60 = 0.40$

$r =$ Rate of Return on Retained Earnings $= 0.10$

Growth Rate $= g = br = 0.40 \times 0.10 = 0.04$

$D_0 = EPS(1 - b) = 7.50(1 - 0.40) = 4.50$

$D_0 = 4.50 \times 1.04 = 4.68$

$k_e = 4.68/60 + 0.04$

$k_e = 0.078 + 0.04 = 0.118$ *or* 11.8%

ILLUSTRATION 27 [CALCULATION OF GROWTH RATE]

The Equity dividend per share (DPS) over the last 5 years are given below:

Year	1	2	3	4	5
DPS (₹)	2	2.4	2.88	3.46	4.15

Required: Calculate the Growth Rate:

SOLUTION

$$D\,(1+g)^4 = 4.15$$
$$2.00\,(1+g)^4 = 4.15$$
$$(1+g)^4 = 4.15/2.00$$
$$(1+g)^4 = 2.075$$
$$(1+g) = 1.20$$
$$g = 1.20 - 1.00 = 0.20$$

The compound value of ₹ 1 table suggest that ₹ 1 compounds to ₹ 2.074 after 4 years at a rate of 20%. It means the growth rate is 20%.

ILLUSTRATION 28 [CALCULATION OF GROWTH RATE]

Mr. Investor is planning to purchase the shares of X Ltd. which had paid the dividend of ₹ 2 per share last year. His required rate of return is 20%.

Required: What growth rate is he anticipating if he is willing to pay price (a) ₹ 22 (b) ₹ 10 (c) ₹ 6.

SOLUTION

(a) $P_0 = \dfrac{D_1}{k_e - g}$ and $D_1 = D_0\,(1+g)$

$$D_1 = 2\,(1+g)$$
$$P_0 = 2(1+g)/(0.20-g) = 22.00$$
$$2\,(1+g) = 4.4 - 22g$$
$$2 + 2g = 4.4 - 22g$$
$$2g + 22g = 4.4 - 2$$
$$24g = 2.4$$
$$g = 2.4/24$$
$$g = 0.10 \text{ or } 10\%$$

(b) $P_0 = \dfrac{D_1}{k_e - g}$ and $D_1 = D_0\,(1+g)$

$$D_1 = 2\,(1+g)$$
$$P_0 = 2(1+g)/(0.20-g) = 10.00$$
$$2\,(1+g) = 2 - 10g$$
$$2 + 2g = 2 - 10g$$
$$2g + 10g = 2 - 2$$
$$12g = 0$$
$$g = 0/12$$

$g = 0.00$ *or* No growth, no decline

(c) $P_0 = \dfrac{D_1}{k_e - g}$ and $D_1 = D_0\,(1+g)$

$$D_1 = 2\,(1+g)$$
$$P_0 = 2(1+g)/(0.20-g) = 6.00$$
$$2(1+g) = 1.2 - 6g$$
$$2 + 2g = 1.2 - 6g$$
$$2g + 6g = 1.2 - 2$$
$$8g = -0.8$$
$$g = -0.8/8$$

$g = -0.10$ *or* decline rate 10%

ILLUSTRATION 29 [CALCULATION OF GROWTH RATE]

The Cost of Equity is 20%. The company has a policy of paying dividend at the rate of 15% on the market price of the share in the beginning of the year. Find the Growth Rate.

SOLUTION

$$k_e = \frac{D_1}{k_e - g}$$

$$20\% = (15\% \text{ of } P_0 + g)/P_0$$

$$g = 20\% - 15\% = 5\%.$$

10.0 COST OF RETAINED EARNINGS OR RESERVES

1. Some people hold the view that retained earnings do not involve any cost on the assumption that the company has a separate identity distinct from its shareholders and it has not to pay anything for withholding the earnings in the company.
2. However, the above view does not seem to be correct due to the presence of opportunity cost of retained earnings. The cost of retained earnings may be taken as equal to the rate of return which the shareholders would have earned after investing the retained earnings passed to them in alternate investments. If earnings were distributed as dividend and simultaneously, an offer for right shares were made, the shareholders would have subscribed to the right shares on the expectations of a certain return. This return may be taken as the indicator of the cost of retained earning. Thus, the opportunity cost of retained earnings is the rate of return on dividend foregone by equity shareholders.
3. Since the shareholders generally expect dividend and capital gain from their investment, the cost of retained earnings will be equal to the shareholder's required rate of return, i.e., the Cost of Equity (k_e).
4. Since retained earnings do not involve any explicit cost (say flotation cost) the cost of retained earnings shall be *less* than the cost of new equity capital.
5. Cost of Retained Earnings may be computed as follows:

$$k_r = \frac{D_1}{P_0} + g$$

Where,
k_r = Cost of retained earnings
D_1 = Dividend per share at the end of current year
P = Current Market price of share at the beginning of the current year
g = Growth Rate

For Example — Suppose a company earns ₹ 10 per share and the current market price of share is ₹ 200. The cost of retained earning will be = = 5%

11.0 COST OF NEW EQUITY SHARE

1. Cost of new equity share is generally **higher than the cost of retained earnings due to flotation costs** involved in selling new equity shares.
2. Cost of New Equity may be ascertained by applying the following formula:

$$k_e = \frac{D_1}{P_n} + g$$

Where,
k_e= Cost of new Equity
D_1= Dividend stream to new Equity shareholders

g= Growth rate

P_n= Net Price to the firm = Issue Price – Flotation Costs

For Example — If X Ltd. issues a share at ₹ 100 and incurs 5% flotation costs, then the net price (P_n) to the firm would be ₹ 95. If the expected dividend is 20% with 10% growth rate, k_e will be

$$k_e = \frac{D_1}{P_n} + g = \frac{20}{100\,(1-0.05)} + 10\% = 31.05\%.$$

3. Explicit cost of new capital is the rate of return at which the new funds must be employed so that the existing earning per share is not affected. However it is a question whether new shares will have a cost different from that of old shares. Since the two will merge for all purposes and therefore it is possible that new shares have the same cost as old shares.

ILLUSTRATION 30 [CALCULATION OF COST OF EQUITY BEFORE ISSUE AND AFTER ISSUE]

An equity share of a company is presently selling at ₹ 125 per share. The earning per share is ₹ 20 of which 60% is paid as dividend. The shareholders expect the company to earn a constant after tax rate of 10% on its investment of retained earnings. The flotation cost of new shares is expected to be 4% of issue price. Calculate the cost of equity before and after issue.

SOLUTION

1. Retention ratio = b = 1 – Dividend Payout Patio = 1 – 0.60 = 0.40
2. Rate of Return on Retained Earnings = r = 0.10
3. Growth rate = g = br = 0.40 × 0.10 = 0.04
4. D_0 = EPS (1 – b) = 20.00 (1 – 0.40) = 12.00
5. D_1 = 12 (1.04) = 12.48
6. Cost of Equity before issue

   $$k_e = \frac{D_1}{P_0} + g = (12.48/125) + 0.04 = 0.09984 + 0.04 = 0.13984 \textit{ or } 13.984\%$$

7. Cost of Equity after issue

   $$k_e = \frac{D_1}{P_0} + g = (12.48/120) + 0.04 = 0.104 + 0.04 = 0.144 \textit{ or } 14.4\%$$

ILLUSTRATION 31 [CALCULATION OF COST OF EQUITY WHEN D_1 IS GIVEN]

Equity shares of ABC Ltd. are currently selling at ₹ 125 per share. The company expects to pay ₹ 12 per share as dividend at the end of the coming year, and the estimated growth rate in dividend is 6%. The company expects to incur 4% as flotation cost.

Required: What is the cost of existing equity capital and new equity capital ?

SOLUTION

Cost of existing equity capital: $k_e = \frac{D_1}{P_0} + g = (12/125) + 0.06 = 15.60\%$

Cost of new equity capital: $k_e = \frac{D_1}{P_0} + g = (12/120) + 0.06 = 16.00\%$

ILLUSTRATION 32 [CALCULATION OF COST OF EQUITY SHARE WHEN P/E RATIO IS GIVEN]

PCT Ltd. is planning an equity issue in the current year. It has an earning per share (EPS)of ₹ 20 and proposes to pay 60% dividend at the current year end. With a P/E ratio of 6.25, it wants to offer the issue at market price. The flotation cost is expected to be 4% of the issue price.

Required: Determine the required rate of return for equity shares (cost of equity) before issue and after the issue.

SOLUTION

1. P_0 = EPS × P/E = 20 × 6.25 = 125
2. r = Rate of Return on Retained Earnings = 100/6.25 = 16%
3. Retention ratio = b = 1 – Dividend Payout Ratio = 1 – 0.60 = 0.40
4. Growth rate = g = br = 0.40 × 0.16 = 0.064
5. $D_1 = D_0 (1 + g) = E_0 (1 - b)(1 + g)$ = ₹ 20 (1 – 0.40) (1 + 0.064) = 12.768
6. Cost of Equity before issue

   $k_e = = \frac{D_1}{P_0} + g$ = (12.768/125) + 0.064 = 0.1021 + 0.064 = 0.1661 *or* 16.61%
7. Cost of Equity after issue

   $k_e = = \frac{D_1}{P_0} + g$ = (12.768/120) + 0.064 = 0.1064 + 0.064 = 0.1704 *or* 17.04%.

ILLUSTRATION 33 [CALCULATION OF THE COST OF EQUITY WHEN P/E RATIO AND DIVIDEND TAX RATE ARE GIVEN]

Calculate the cost of equity before issue and after issue in Illustration 38 if corporate dividend tax rate is 20%.

SOLUTION

1. P_0 = EPS × P/E = 20 × 6.25 = 125
2. r = Rate of Return on Retained Earnings = 100/6.25 = 16%
3. Retention Ratio = b = 1 – Dividend Payout Ratio (1 + Dt) = 1 – 0.60 (1 + 0.2) = 0.28
4. Growth Rate = g = br = 0.28 × 0.16 = 0.0448
5. $D_1 = D_0 (1 + g) = E_0 (1 - b)(1 + g)$ = ₹ 20 (1 – 0.40) (1 + 0.0448) = 12.538
6. Cost of Equity before issue

   $$k_e = \frac{D_1(1+D_t)}{P_0} + g = \frac{12.538\,(1+0.20)}{125} + 0.0448 = 16.52\%$$
7. Cost of Equity after issue

   $$k_e = \frac{D_1\,(1+D_t)}{P_0} + g = \frac{12.538\,(1+0.20)}{120} + 0.0448 = 17.018\%$$

ILLUSTRATION 34

Bharat Ltd. is foreseeing a growth rate of 20% p.a. for next two years. The growth rate is likely to fall to 15% for the next two years. After that the growth rate is expected to continue at 10% p.a. The company paid a dividend of ₹ 2 per share last year. Investor's required rate of return is 20%. At what price would you as investor be ready to buy the shares of this company now (t = 0)?

SOLUTION

Value of Equity Share in t_0 = [PV of Dividend Payments during the years 1 – 4] + [PV of Expected Market Price at the end of the year 4]

STEP 1: CALCULATION OF PV OF DIVIDENDS PAYMENTS

Year *A*	*B*	*Dividend* *C*	*PV factor at 20%* *D*	*Total PV* *E = C × D*
1	D_1	2.40	0.833	1.999

2	D_2	2.88	0.694	1.999
3	D_3	3.31	0.579	1.916
4	D_4	3.81	0.482	1.836
				Total = 7.750

Step 2: Calculation of PV of Expected Market Price in t_4

$$P_4 = \frac{D_s}{k_e - g} = \frac{D_4(1+g)}{k_e - g} = \frac{3.81(1+0.10)}{0.20-(0.10)} = ₹\ 41.91$$

PV of $P_4 = P_4 \times$ PV factor = ₹ 41.91 × 0.482 = ₹ 20.20

Step 3: Market Price in P_0 = PV of D_{1-4} + PV of P_4 = ₹ 7.75 + ₹ 20.20 = ₹ 27.95

ILLUSTRATION 35

Tusher Ltd. is foreseeing a growth rate of 20% p.a. for next two years The growth rate is likely to fall by 25% for the next year. During fourth year the growth rate will be same as in third year. After that the growth rate is likely to fall by 33–1/3% and expected to continue thereafter. The company paid a dividend of ₹ 2 per share last year. Investor's required rate of return is 20%.

Required: At what price would you as investor be ready to buy the shares of this company now (t = 0) and at the end of the year 1 (t = 1) ?

SOLUTION

Value of Equity Share in t_0 = [PV of Dividend Payments during the years 1 – 4] + [PV of Expected Market Price at the end of the year 4]

STEP 1: CALCULATION OF PV OF DIVIDENDS PAYMENTS

Year A	B	Dividend C	PV factor at 20% D	Total PV E = C × D
1	D_1	2.40	0.833	1.999
2	D_2	2.88	0.694	1.999
3	D_3	3.31	0.579	1.916
4	D_4	3.81	0.482	1.836
			PV of D_{1-4}	Total = 7.750

Step 2: Calculation of PV of Expected Market Price in t_4

$$P_4 = \frac{D_5}{k_e - g} = \frac{D_4(1+g)}{k_e - g} = \frac{3.81(1+0.10)}{0.20-(0.10)} = ₹\ 41.91$$

PV of P_4 = $P_4 \times$ PV factor = ₹ 41.91 × 0.482 = ₹ 20.20

Step 3: Market Price in P_0 = PV of $D_{1.4}$ + PV of P_4 = ₹ 7.75 + ₹ 20.20 = ₹ 27.95

Value of Equity Share in t_1 = [PV of Dividend Payments during the years 2 – 4] + [PV of Expected Market Price at the end of the year 4]

STEP 1: CALCULATION OF PV OF DIVIDENDS PAYMENTS

Year A	B	Dividend C	PV factor at 20% D	Total PV E = C × D
2	D_2	2.88	0.833	2.399
3	D_3	3.31	0.694	2.297

4	D_4	3.81	0.579	2.206
			Total	6.902

Step 2: Calculation of PV of Expected Market Price in t_4

$$P_4 = \frac{D_5}{k_e - g} = \frac{D_4(1+g)}{k_e - g} = \frac{3.81(1+0.10)}{0.20-(0.10)} = ₹\,41.91$$

$$\text{PV of } P_4 = P_4 \times \text{PV factor} = ₹\,41.91 \times 0.579 = ₹\,24.27$$

Step 3: Market price in P_1 $= \text{PV of } D_{2,4} + \text{PV of } P_4 = ₹\,6.902 + ₹\,24.27 = ₹\,31.17$

12.0 COST OF DEPRECIATION FUNDS

Not much though has been devoted to question of cost of depreciation funds. However, these funds should not be treated as having no costs at all. Logically speaking, they should be treated on the same footing as retained earnings when it comes to their use though while calculating the cost of capital, these funds may not be considered at all.

13.0 WHY THE COST OF CAPITAL IS MOST APPROPRIATELY MEASURED ON AN "AFTER TAX" BASIS?

This is due to following two reasons:

1. Cost of capital is usually taken as cut-off rate for the evaluation of capital expenditure project and for this, the yield to shareholders is the relevant figure, which can be paid only out of after tax profits.
2. The cost of capital serves the purpose of discounting rate for discounting of cash flows, which are ascertained after deducting tax liability.

14.0 WEIGHTED AVERAGE COST OF CAPITAL

WHAT IS WEIGHTED AVERAGE COST OF CAPITAL?

It is a weighted average of costs of various sources of funds where the weights are being the proportion of each source of funds in the capital structure. It is denoted as k_0.

WHAT IS THE RELEVANCE OF WEIGHTED AVERAGE COST OF CAPITAL?

(a) Now the term cost of capital is used to refer weighted average cost of capital instead of cost of specific source of capital such as cost of debt, cost of equity etc. since there is relationship between methods of financing and their costs ***For Example***:

1. The firm's decision to use equity capital to finance its projects would enlarge its potential for borrowings in future.
2. On the other hand, the firm's decision to use debt capital to finance its projects not only adversely affects its potential for using low cost debt in future but also increases the risk of shareholders and the increased risk to shareholders will increase the cost of equity.

(b) The simple average cost of capital is not appropriate to use since firms need not necessarily use various sources of funds in equal proportion in the capital structure.

(c) It facilitates the computation of Equity Financial Break Even Point (i.e. that level of EBIT at which the firm is just able to recover the fixed interest cost of Debt, fixed Preference Dividend on Preference Shares and the Cost of Equity) as follows:

$$\text{Equity Financial B.E.P.} = \frac{\text{After-tax Weighted Average Cost of Capital}}{(1-\text{Tax Rate})} \times \text{Total Capital}$$

RATIONALE BEHIND USE OF WEIGHTED AVERAGE COST OF CAPITAL

James Van Horne in his book *'Financial Management & Policy'* expressed his view in such regard as follows:

"The rationale behind use of weighted average cost of capital is that by financing in specified proportions and accepting projects yielding more than the weighted average cost of capital, firm is able to increase the market price of its equity stock in the long run. This increase occurs because investment projects accepted are expected to yield more on their equity-financed portions than the cost of equity capital ke. Once these expectations are apparent to the market price, the market price of stock should rise, all other things remaining the same."

BOOK VALUE WEIGHTS VS. MARKET VALUE WEIGHTS

The weighted cost of capital can be computed by using book value weights *or* the market value weights.

(a) Book Value Weights represents Values as per Balance Sheet and are calculated as follows:

(BVW for Equity Shares) = Face Value of an Equity Share × No. of Equity Shares

(BVW for Preference Shares) = Face Value of a Preference Share × No. of Preference Shares

(BVW for Debentures) = Face Value of a Debenture × No. of Debentures

(BVW for Retained Earnings) = Same amount as appear in the Balance Sheet

(b) Market Value Weights represent Values as per Market Quotations and are calculated as follows:

(MVW for Equity Shares) = Current Market Price of an Equity Share × No. of Equity Shares

(MVW for Preference Shares)= Current Market Price of a Preference Share × No. of Preference Shares

(MVW for Debentures) = Current Market Price of a Debenture × No. of Debentures

Tutorial Notes:

(i) Floatation cost is not to be deducted from the Market price for computing Market Value Weights.

(ii) Retained Earnings are not shown separately since the market value of equity share represents the combined market value of equity shares and retained earnings.

(c) The same after tax cost of each source of fund is used whether the weighted average cost of capital is computed by using book value weights *or* the market value weights.

(d) The weighted cost of capital computed by using book value weights will be understated if the market value of the share is higher than the book value and vice versa.

(e) Theoretically, the market value weights should be preferred over the book value weights because the market value weights reflect the actual expectation of the investors.

(f) Why book value weights are preferred

In practice, book value weights are used because:

(i) Market value fluctuates very widely and frequently.

(ii) Generally, the firms set their capital structure targets in terms of book value.

(iii) Investors analyse Debt – Equity Ratio on book value basis to evaluate the risk of the firms.

HOW TO DETERMINE WEIGHTED AVERAGE COST OF CAPITAL?

Practical Steps involved in the Determination of Weighted Average Cost of Capital

Step 1:	Calculate the cost of each of the specific sources of funds i.e. cost of debt, cost of equity, cost of preference capital etc.) on after tax basis.
Step 2:	Calculate the weights being proportion of each source of funds in the capital structure.
Step 3:	Multiply the cost of each source by weights.
Step 4:	Add the weighted cost of all sources of funds.

FORMAT OF THE STATEMENT SHOWING THE COMPUTATION OF WEIGHTED AVERAGE COST OF CAPITAL

(A) STATEMENT SHOWING THE WEIGHTED AVERAGE COST OF CAPITAL (USING BOOK VALUE WEIGHTS)

Source of Capital *A*	*Amount of each source of capital* *B*	*Proportion of each source of capital* *C*	*After tax cost of each source of capital* *D*	*Product* *E = C × D*
Equity Share Capital	......	......	......	......
Retained Earnings	......	......	......	......
Preference Share Capital	......	......	......	......
Debentures	......	......	......	......
Total	......	1.00		......

(B) STATEMENT SHOWING THE WEIGHTED AVERAGE COST OF CAPITAL (USING MARKET VALUE WEIGHTS)

Source of Capital *A*	*Amount of each source of capital* *B*	*Proportion of each source of capital* *C*	*After tax cost of each source of capital* *D*	*Product* *E = C × D*
Equity Share Capital	......	......	......	......
Preference Share Capital	......	......	......	......
Debentures	......	......	......	......
Total	......	1.00		......

Tutorial Notes:

(i) Retained Earnings are not shown separately since the market value of equity share represents the combined market value of equity shares and retained earnings

(ii) Unless otherwise stated in the question, Book value weights should be used.

ILLUSTRATION 36

Tulsian (1) Ltd. has the following Capital Structure as per its Balance Sheet as at 31st March, 2009:

Particulars	*₹ in lakhs*
Equity Share Capital (fully paid shares of ₹ 10 each)	4
18% Preference Share Capital (fully paid shares of ₹ 100 each)	3
Retained Earnings	1
12.5% Debentures (fully paid of ₹ 100 each)	8
12% Term Loan	4

Additional Information:

(a) Currently Quoted Prices in the Stock Exchange:

Equity Shares @ ₹ 64.25, Preference Shares @ ₹ 90, Debentures @ ₹ 95.

(b) For the last year, the Company had paid equity dividend of ₹ 8 per share which is expected to grow @ 5% p.a. forever.

(c) The Corporate Tax Rate is 30%

Required: Calculate Weighted Average Cost of Capital using (a) Book Value Weights (b) Market Value Weights

SOLUTION

(A) STATEMENT SHOWING THE WEIGHTED AVERAGE COST OF CAPITAL (USING BOOK VALUE WEIGHTS)

Source of Capital *A*	*Amount of each source of capital* *B (in lakhs)*	*Proportion of each source of capital* *C*	*After tax cost of each source of capital* *D*	*Product* *E = C × D*
Equity Share Capital	4	0.20 (i.e., 4/20)	0.1807	0.0361
Retained Earnings	1	0.05 (i.e. 1/20)	0.1807	0.0090
18% Preference Share Capital	3	0.15 (i.e., 3/20)	0.2000	0.0300
12.5% Debentures	8	0.40 (i.e., 8/20)	0.0921	0.0368
12% Term Loan	4	0.20 (i.e., 4/20)	0.0840	0.0168
	20	1.00		
	Weighted Average Cost of Capital = 0.1287 *or* 12.87%			

(B) STATEMENT SHOWING THE WEIGHTED AVERAGE COST OF CAPITAL (USING MARKET VALUE WEIGHTS)

Source of Capital *A*	*Amount of each source of capital* *B (in lakhs)*	*Proportion of each source of capital* *C*	*After tax cost of each source of capital* *D*	*Product* *E = C × D*
Equity Share Capital	25.70	0.6425 (i.e., 25.7/40)	0.1807	0.1161
18% Preference Share Capital	2.70	0.0675 (i.e. 2.7/40)	0.2000	0.0135
12.5% Debentures	7.60	0.1900 (i.e. 7.6/40)	0.0921	0.0175
12% Term Loan	4.00	0.1000 (i.e. 4/40)	0.0840	0.0084
	40.00	1.0000		
	Weighted Average Cost of Capital = 0.1555 *or* 15.55%			

Working Notes:

(i) Cost of 12.5% Debentures = $\frac{\text{Interest }(1-t)}{\text{Net Sales Proceeds}} = \frac{12.5\,(1-0.3)}{₹\,9.5}$ = 0.0921 *or* 9.21%

(ii) Cost of 12% Term Loan = $\frac{\text{Interest }(1-t)}{\text{Net Sale Proceeds}} = \frac{₹\,48{,}000\,(1-0.3)}{₹\,4{,}00{,}000}$ = 0.084 *or* 8.4%

(iii) Cost of 18% Preference Share Capital = $\frac{\text{Preference Dividend}}{\text{Net Sales Proceeds}} = \frac{₹\,18}{₹\,90}$ = 0.2 *or* 20%

(iv) Cost of Equity Share Capital (k_e) $= \frac{D_1}{P_0} + g = \frac{D_0(1+g)}{P_0} + g = \frac{₹\,8(1+0.05)}{₹\,64.25} + 0.05$

$= \frac{₹\,8.4}{₹\,64.25} + 0.05 = 0.1807$ *or* 18.07%

(v) Cost of Retained Earnings = k_e = 18.07%

ILLUSTRATION 37

Tulsian (2) Ltd. has the following Capital Structure as per its Balance Sheet as at 31st March, 2009:

Particulars	*₹ in lakhs*
Equity Share Capital (fully paid shares of ₹ 10 each)	4
18% Preference Share Capital (fully paid shares of ₹ 100 each)	3
Retained Earnings	1
12.5% Debentures (fully paid of ₹ 100 each)	8
12% Term Loan	4

Additional Information:

(a) The Current market price of the company's equity share is 64.25. The dividend expected on the equity share at the end of year is at 80% which is expected to grow @ 5% p.a. forever.

(b) The Preference shares of the company which are redeemable after 10 years are currently selling at ₹ 90 per Preference Share.

(c) The Debentures of the company which are redeemable after 5 years are currently quoted at ₹ 95 per debenture.

(d) The corporate tax rate is 30%.

Required: Calculate Weighted Average Cost of Capital using (a) Book Value Weights (b) Market Value Weights

SOLUTION

(A) STATEMENT SHOWING THE WEIGHTED AVERAGE COST OF CAPITAL (USING BOOK VALUE WEIGHTS)

Source of Capital *A*	*Amount of each source of capital* *B (in lakhs)*	*Proportion of each source of capital* *C*	*After tax cost of each source of capital* *D*	*Product* *E = C × D*
Equity Share Capital	4	0.20 (i.e., 4/20)	0.1745	0.0349
Retained Earnings	1	0.05 (i.e. 1/20)	0.1745	0.0087
18% Preference Share Capital	3	0.15 (i.e., 3/20)	0.2000	0.0300
12.5% Debentures	8	0.40 (i.e., 8/20)	0.1000	0.0400
12% Term Loan	4	0.20 (i.e., 4/20)	0.0840	0.0168
Total	20	1.00		
	Weighted Average Cost of Capital = 0.1304 *or* 13.04%			

(B) STATEMENT SHOWING THE WEIGHTED AVERAGE COST OF CAPITAL (USING MARKET VALUE WEIGHT)

Source of Capital *A*	*Amount of each source of capital* *B (in lakhs)*	*Proportion of each source of capital* *C*	*After tax cost of each source of capital* *D*	*Product* *E = C × D*
Equity Share Capital	25.70	0.6425 (i.e., 25.7/40)	0.1745	0.1121
18% Preference Share Capital	2.70	0.0675 (i.e. 2.7/40)	0.2000	0.0135
12.5% Debentures	7.60	0.1900 (i.e. 7.6/40)	0.1000	0.0190
12% Term Loan	4.00	0.1000 (i.e. 4/40)	0.0840	0.0084
	40.00	1.0000		
	Weighted Average Cost of Capital = 01530 *or* 15.3%			

Working Notes:

(i) Cost of Equity Share Capital (k_e) = $\frac{D_1}{P_0} + g = \frac{₹\,8}{₹\,64.25} + 0.05 = 0.1745$ *or* 17.45%

(ii) Cost of Retained Earnings (k_r) = k_e = 17.45%

(iii) Cost of 18% Preference Share Capital (k_p)

$$= \frac{\text{Preference Dividend} + (\text{Redeemable Value} - \text{Net Sale Proceeds})/N}{(\text{Redeemable Value} + \text{Net Sale Proceeds})/2}$$

$$= \frac{₹\,18 + (₹\,100 - ₹\,90)/10}{(₹\,100 + ₹\,90)/2} = \frac{₹\,18 + ₹\,1}{₹\,95} = 0.20 \text{ or } 20\%$$

(iv) Cost of 12.5% Debentures

$$= \frac{\text{Interest}\,(1 - \text{tax rate}) + (\text{Redeemable Value} - \text{Net Sale Proceeds})/N}{(\text{Redeemable Value} + \text{Net Sale Proceeds})/2}$$

$$= \frac{₹\,12.5\,(1 - 0.3) + (₹\,100 - ₹\,95/5)}{(₹\,100 + ₹\,95)/2} = \frac{₹\,8.75 + ₹\,1}{₹\,97.5} = 0.10 \text{ or } 10\%$$

(v) Cost of 12% Term Loan = $\frac{\text{Interest}\,(1 - \text{Tax Rate})}{\text{Net Sale Proceeds}} = \frac{₹\,48{,}000\,(1 - 0.30)}{₹\,4{,}00{,}000} = 0.084$ *or* 8.4%

ILLUSTRATION 38

Tulsian (3) Ltd. has the following Capital Structure as per its Balance Sheet as at 31st March, 2009:

Particulars	*₹ in lakhs*
Equity Share Capital (fully paid share of ₹ 10 each)	4
18% Preference Share Capital (fully paid shares of ₹ 100 each)	3
Reserves & Surplus	1
12.5% Debentures (fully paid of ₹ 100 each)	8
12% Term Loan	4

Additional Information:

(a) The current market price of the company's share is ₹ 64.25. The prevailing default-risk free interest rate on 10 year GOI Treasury Bonds is 5.5%. The average market risk premium is 8%. The beta of the company is 1.1875.

(b) The Preference shares of the company which are redeemable after 10 years are currently selling at ₹ 90 per Preference Share.

(c) The Debentures of the company which are redeemable after 5 years are currently quoted at ₹ 95 per debenture.

(d) The corporate tax rate is 30%.

Required: Calculate Weighted Average Cost of Capital using (a) Book Value Weights (b) Market Value Weights

SOLUTION

(A) STATEMENT SHOWING THE WEIGHTED AVERAGE COST OF CAPITAL (USING BOOK VALUE WEIGHTS)

Source of Capital *A*	*Amount of each source of capital* *B (in lakhs)*	*Proportion of each source of capital* *C*	*After tax cost of each source of capital* *D*	*Product* *E = C × D*
Equity Share Capital	4	0.20	0.1500	0.0300
Retained Earnings	1	0.05	0.1500	0.0075
18% Preference Share Capital	3	0.15	0.2000	0.0300
12.5% Debentures	8	0.40	0.1000	0.0400
12% Term Loan	4	0.20	0.0840	0.0168
	20	1.00		
	Weighted Average Cost of Capital = 0.1243 *or* 12.43%			

(B) STATEMENT SHOWING THE WEIGHTED AVERAGE COST OF CAPITAL (USING MARKET VALUE WEIGHTS)

Source of Capital *A*	*Amount of each source of capital* *B (in lakhs)*	*Proportion of each source of capital* *C*	*After tax cost of each source of capital* *D*	*Product* *E = C × D*
Equity Share Capital	25.7	0.6425	0.1500	0.0964
18% Preference Share Capital	2.7	0.0675	0.2000	0.0135
12.5% Debentures	7.6	0.1900	0.1000	0.0190
12% Term Loan	4.0	0.1000	0.0840	0.0084
	40.0	1.0000		
	Weighted Average Cost of Capital = 0.1373 *or* 13.73%			

Working Notes:

(i) Cost of Equity (k_e) $= R_e + b(\text{Average Market Risk Premium})$

$= 5.5\% + 1.1875\ (8\%)$

$= 5.5\% + 9.5\% = 15\%$

(ii) Cost of Retained Earnings (k_r) $= k_e = 15\%$

(iii) Cost of 18% Preference Share Capital (k_p)

$$= \frac{\text{Preference Dividend} + (\text{Redeemable Value} - \text{Net Sale Proceeds})/N}{(\text{Redeemable Value} + \text{Net Sale Proceeds})/2}$$

$$= \frac{₹\,18 + (₹\,100 - ₹\,90)/10}{(₹\,100 + ₹\,90)/2} = \frac{₹\,18 + ₹\,1}{₹\,95} = 0.20 \text{ or } 20\%$$

(iv) Cost of 12.5% Debentures

$$= \frac{\text{Interest}(1-\text{tax rate}) + (\text{Redeemable Value} - \text{Net Sale Proceeds})/N}{(\text{Redeemable Value} + \text{Net Sale Proceeds})/2}$$

$$= \frac{₹\,12.5\,(1-0.3) + (₹\,100 - ₹\,95/5)}{(₹\,100 + ₹\,95)/2} = \frac{₹\,8.75 + ₹\,1}{₹\,97.5} = 0.10 \text{ or } 10\%$$

(v) Cost of 12% Term Loan $= \dfrac{\text{Interest}(1-\text{Tax Rate})}{\text{Net Sale Proceeds}} = \dfrac{₹\,48,000\,(1-0.30)}{₹\,4,00,000} = 0.084$ *or* 8.4%

15.0 MARGINAL COST OF CAPITAL

WHAT IS MARGINAL COST OF CAPITAL?

(a) Marginal Cost of Capital is nothing but weighted average cost of new *or* incremental capital using marginal weights.

(b) It may be defined as cost of raising an additional rupee of capital.

(c) The marginal weight represents the proportion of each source of new funds which the firm intends to employ.

(d) The problem of choosing between book value weights and the market value weights does not arise.

MARGINAL COST OF CAPITAL (MCC) VS. AVERAGE COST OF CAPITAL (ACC)

(a) Marginal Cost of Capital is equal to Average Cost of Capital, where the firm raises funds in proportional manner and components costs remain unchanged.

(b) Increase in ACC is faster than increase in MCC where components costs start rising.

USE OF MCC IN CAPITAL BUDGETING AND VALUATION OF FIRMS

1. MCC schedule can be used in Capital Budgeting decision ***For Example***, In NPV method, MCC can be used to determine NPV. In IRR method, MCC can be used as cut off rate.
2. MCC can be used to maximize the value of shares of the firm.
3. MCC can be used to select among several projects.

RELEVANCE OF MCC FOR DECISION-MAKING

Weighted average cost is a historical cost which has been incurred in past and should not be used in capital budgeting decisions because for decision making, it is the future cost and differential cost which is relevant and not the past cost.

HOW TO DETERMINE WEIGHTED MARGINAL COST OF CAPITAL

Weighted Marginal Cost of Capital is calculated with reference to additional new funds to be raised.

PRACTICAL STEPS INVOLVED IN THE DETERMINATION OF WEIGHTED MARGINAL COST OF CAPITAL

Step 1: Ascertain the proposed proportion of New Debt and New Equity. These are known as Marginal Weights.

Step 2: Ascertain the retained earnings which could be available (if any).

Step 3: Ascertain the External Equity to be raised as follows:

= Total Additional Funds required – Debt to be raised – Retained Earnings (if any available)

Step 4: Calculate the Cost of New Debt, New Equity and New Cost of Retained Earnings.

Step 5: Multiply the cost of each source by marginal weights.
Step 6: Add the weighted cost of all sources of funds.

FORMAT OF STATEMENT SHOWING THE COMPUTATION OF WEIGHTED MARGINAL COST OF CAPITAL

STATEMENT SHOWING WEIGHTED MARGINAL COST OF CAPITAL (USING MARGINAL WEIGHTS)

Source of Capital *A*	*Amount of each source of capital* *B*	*Proportion of each source of capital* *C*	*After tax cost of each source of capital* *D*	*Product* *E = C × D*
Equity Share Capital	......	......	......	......
Retained Earnings	......	......	......	......
New Pref. Share Capital	......	......	......	......
New Debentures	......	......	......	......
Total	......	1.00	......	......

ILLUSTRATION 39

In order to finance on expansion plan, Tulsian (4) Ltd. requires ₹ 20 lakhs and provides you the following information:

(a) Target Debt-Equity Ratio of 3 : 2.

(b) Debt will carry an Interest Rate of 12% for the first ₹ 4 lakh and 12.5% for the balance.

(c) Earning per share for the current year is ₹ 20 per share. Dividend Payout Ratio is 60%. Anticipated Dividend Growth Rate is 5%. Current Market Price per equity share is ₹ 90. Flotation Cost is ₹ 6 per share.

(d) Present Equity Share Capital ₹ 2 lakh divided into fully paid shares of ₹ 10 each.

(e) Corporate Tax Rate is 30%.

Required: Calculate Weighted Marginal Cost of Capital.

SOLUTION

STATEMENT SHOWING THE COMPUTATION WEIGHTED MARGINAL COST OF CAPITAL

Source of Capital *A*	*Amount of each source of capital* *B*	*Proportion of each source of capital* *C*	*After tax cost of each source of capital* *D*	*Product* *E = C × D*
New Equity Share Capital	6,40,000	0.32	0.2000	0.0640
Retained Earnings	1,60,000	0.08	0.1900	0.0152
12% Debt	4,00,000	0.20	0.0840	0.0168
12.5% Debt	8,00,000	0.40	0.0875	0.0350
	20,00,000	1.00		
	Weighted Average Cost of Capital = 0.1310 *or* 13.10%			

Working Notes:

(i) Retained Earnings available = (EPS × No. of Equity Shares) – (DPS × No. of Equity Shares)

= [₹ 20 × (₹ 2,00,000/₹ 10)] – [(₹ 20 × 0.60) × (₹ 2,00,000/₹ 10)]

= ₹ 4,00,000 – ₹ 2,40,000 = ₹ 1,60,000

(ii) External Debt = ₹ 20,00,000 × 3/5 = ₹ 12,00,000

12% Debt = ₹ 4,00,000, 12.5% Debt = ₹ 12,00,000 – ₹ 4,00,000 = ₹ 8,00,000

(iii) External Equity Required $= \begin{pmatrix}\text{Total Additional}\\ \text{funds required}\end{pmatrix} \times \begin{pmatrix}\text{Proportion}\\ \text{of Equity}\end{pmatrix}$ – Retained Earnings

= (₹ 20,00,000 × 2/5) – ₹ 1,60,000

= ₹ 8,00,000 – ₹ 1,60,000 = ₹ 6,40,000

(iv) Cost of New Equity (k_e) $= \frac{D_1}{P_0} + g = \frac{D_0\,(1+g)}{P_0} + g$

$= \frac{(₹\,20 \times 0.60)\,(1+0.05)}{₹\,90 - ₹\,6} + 0.05$

$= \frac{₹\,12.6}{₹\,84} + 0.05$

= 0.15 + 0.05 = 0.20 *or* 20%.

(v) Cost of New 12% Debt $= \frac{\text{Interest (1 – tax rate)}}{\text{Net Sale Proceeds}}$

$= \frac{₹\,48,000\,(1-0.30)}{₹\,4,00,000} = 0.084$ *or* 8.4%

(vi) Cost of New 12.5% Debt $= \frac{₹\,1,00,000\,(1-0.30)}{₹\,8,00,000}$

$= \frac{₹\,70,000}{₹\,8,00,000} = 0.0875$ *or* 8.75%

(vii) Cost of Retained Earnings $= \frac{D_1}{P_0} + g = \frac{D_0\,(1+g)}{P_0} + g$

$= \frac{(20 \times 0.60)\,(1+0.05)}{90} + 0.05 = 0.14 + 0.05 = 0.19$ *or* 19%

ILLUSTRATION 40

In order to finance on expansion plan, Tulsian (5) Ltd. requires ₹ 20 lakhs and provides you the following information:

(a) Target Debt-Shareholders' Funds Ratio of 3 : 2.

(b) Target Capital Gearing Ratio [(Debt + Preference) to Equity] of 3

(c) Debt will carry an Interest Rate of 12% for the first ₹ 4 lakh and 12.5% for the balance.

(d) Retained Earnings available: ₹ 1 lakh

(e) The prevailing default risk-free interest rate on 10 year GOI Treassury Bonds is 5.5%. Rate of Return on Market Portfolio is 13.5%. The beta of the Company is 1.1875.

(f) The 18% Preference Shares of ₹ 100 each redeemable after 10 years can currently be issued at ₹ 90 per Preference Share.

(g) The Corporate Tax Rate is 30%.

Required: Calculate Weighted Marginal Cost of Capital.

SOLUTION

STATEMENT SHOWING THE COMPUTATION WEIGHTED MARGINAL COST OF CAPITAL

Source of Capital *A*	*Amount of each source of capital* *B*	*Proportion of each source of capital* *C*	*After tax cost of each source of capital* *D*	*Product* *E = C × D*
New Equity Share Capital	4,00,000	0.20	0.1500	0.0300
Retained Earnings	1,00,000	0.05	0.1500	0.0075
18% Pref. Share Capital	3,00,000	0.15	0.2000	0.0300
12% Debt	4,00,000	0.20	0.0840	0.0168
12.5% Debt	8,00,000	0.40	0.0875	0.0350
Total	20,00,000	1.00		
	Weighted Marginal Cost of Capital = 0.1193 *or* 11.93%			

Working Notes:

(i) Debt = ₹ 20,00,000 × 3/5 = ₹ 12,00,000

12% Debt = ₹ 4,00,000, 12.5% Debt = ₹ 12,00,000 – ₹ 4,00,000 = ₹ 8,00,000

(ii) Shareholders' Funds = ₹ 20,00,000 × 2/5 = ₹ 8,00,000

(iii) Calculation of Preference Share Capital:

Let Preference Share Capital be 'X'

$$\text{Capital Gearing Ratio} = \frac{\text{Debt} + \text{Preference Share Capital}}{\text{Equity Shareholders' Funds}}$$

$$3 = \frac{₹\,12,00,000 + X}{₹\,8,00,000 - X}$$

$$3\,(8,00,000 - X) = (12,00,000 + X)$$

$$₹\,24,00,000 - 3X = 12,00,000 + X$$

$$4X = ₹\,12,00,000$$

18% Preference Share Capital = X = ₹ 12,00,000/4 = ₹ 3,00,000

(iv) Equity Share Capital= Shareholders' Funds – Pref. Share Capital – Retained Earnings

= ₹ 8,00,000 – ₹ 3,00,000 – ₹ 1,00,000 = ₹ 4,00,000

(v) Cost of Equity (ke) = Risk Free Rate + Average Market Risk Premium

$= R_f + \beta(R_m - R_f)$

= 5.5% + 1.1875 (13.5% – 5.5%)

= 5.5% + 9.5% = 15%

(vi) Cost of Retained Earnings (k_r) = k_e = 0.15 *or* 15%

(vii) $$\text{Cost of 12\% Debt} = \frac{\text{Interest (1 – Tax Rate)}}{\text{Net Sale Proceeds}}$$

$$= \frac{₹\,48,000\,(1 - 0.30)}{₹\,4,00,000} = 0.084 \text{ or } 8.4\%$$

(viii) $$\text{Cost of 12.5\% Debt} = \frac{\text{Interest (1 – Tax Rate)}}{\text{Net Sale Proceeds}}$$

$$= \frac{₹\,1,00,000\,(1 - 0.30)}{₹\,8,00,000} = \frac{₹\,70,000}{₹\,8,00,000} = 0.087 \text{ or } 8.75\%$$

(ix) Cost of 18% Preference Share Capital (k_p)

$$= \frac{\text{Preference Dividend} + (\text{Redeemable Value} - \text{Net Sale Proceeds})/N}{(\text{Redeemable Value} + \text{Net Sale Proceeds})/2}$$

$$= \frac{₹\,18 + (₹\,100 - ₹\,90)/10}{(₹\,100 + ₹\,90)/2}$$

$$= \frac{₹\,18 + ₹\,1}{₹\,95} = 0.20 \text{ or } 20\%$$

16.0 HOW TO DETERMINE NEW WEIGHTED AVERAGE COST OF CAPITAL (OR REVISED WEIGHTED AVERAGE COST OF CAPITAL)

PRACTICAL STEPS INVOLVED

Practical Steps involved in the determination of New Weighted Average Cost of Capital

Step 1: *Calculate the Weights being the proportion of each source (new and old) of funds in the capital structure.*

Step 2: *Calculate old and new cost of each source of funds.*

Step 3: *Multiply the cost of each source by weights as follows:*

Weight of Old Debt × Cost of Old Debt

Weight of Old Preference Shares × Cost of Old Preference Share

Weight of Old Equity × Cost of New Equity

Weight of New Equity × Cost of New Equity

Weight of New Debt × Cost of New Debt

Weight of New Preference Share × Cost of New Preference Share

Step 4: *Add the Weighted Cost of all sources of funds.*

FORMAT OF STATEMENT SHOWING THE COMPUTATION OF REVISED WEIGHTED AVERAGE COST OF CAPITAL

STATEMENT SHOWING THE REVISED WEIGHTED AVERAGE COST OF CAPITAL [USING BOOK VALUE AND MARGINAL WEIGHTS]

Source of Capital A	*Amount of each source of capital* B	*Proportion of each source of capital* C	*After tax cost of each source of capital* D	*Product* E = C × D
1. Old Equity Share Capital	......	......	New Cost	......
2. New Equity Share Capital	......	......	New Cost	......
3. Retained Earnings	......	......	New Cost (but excluding effect of flotation cost)	......
4. Old Pref. Share Capital	......	......	Old Cost	......
5. New Pref. Share Capital	......	......	New Cost	......
6. Old Debt	......	......	Old Cost	......
7. New Debt	......	......	New Cost	......
Total	......	1.00		......

17.0 EFFECT OF A FINANCING DECISION ON EARNING PER SHARE

To evaluate various methods of financing, the impact of each method of financing on earning per share should be ascertained and that method of financing should be selected under which earning per share is highest. Earning per share would be highest in case of financing which has the least cost to the company. For this purpose, EBIT-EPS chart may be prepared to show Earning per share under various alternatives of financing:

Cost of Finance	*Effect on EPS*
High Cost	EPS will be Low
Low Cost	EPS will be High

18.0 EPS VOLATILITY

EPS volatility refers to the magnitude *or* the extent of fluctuations in the earnings per share of a company in various years as compared to the average earning per share. EPS volatility shows whether a company enjoys stable earning *or* not. The main reason of EPS volatility is the fluctuations in the sales volume and the operating leverage. Higher the EPS volatility, greater the risk attached to the company. Lower the EPS volatility, lesser the risk attached to the company.

ILLUSTRATION 41 [COMPREHENSIVE]

Tulsian Ltd. provides you the following information:

(a) *Capital Structure as per Balance Sheet as at 1st April, 2008:*

Particulars	₹
15% Debentures of ₹ 100 each	10,00,000
18% Preference Shares of ₹ 100 each	2,00,000
Equity Shares of ₹ 10 each	2,00,000
Retained Earnings	4,40,000
Total	18,40,000

(b) *Currently Quoted Prices in stock exchange (as at 31st March, 2009):*

15% Debentures at ₹ 120 per Debenture

18% Preference Shares at ₹ 120 per share

Equity Shares at ₹ 78 per share

(c) *EPS and DPS*

EPS for the current year is ₹ 20 per share. Dividend Payout Ratio is 60%. Anticipated growth rate is 4%.

(d) *Corporate tax rate is 40%.*

Required:

(a) Calculate the Weighted Average Cost of Capital using (i) Book Value Weights (ii) Market Value Weights.

(b) Calculate the Cost of New Debentures, New Preference Shares, New Equity Shares and Retained Earnings if anticipated external financing opportunities are as follows:

(i) 12% Debentures of ₹ 100 each issued at par and redeemable after 5 years at 5% premium. Flotation cost is 5% of issue price.

(ii) 15% Preference Shares of ₹ 100 each issued at par and redeemable after 5 years at 5% premium. Flotation cost is 5% of the issue price.

(iii) Equity Shares of ₹ 10 each issued at ₹ 60. Flotation cost being ₹ 5 per share

(c) How much can be spent for capital investment before new equity shares must be issued?

(d) Calculate the Weighted Average Cost of Capital using Marginal Weights if the company requires ₹ 4,00,000 for future investment and intends to maintain the existing optimal capital structure.

(e) What is the required amount of capital budget if the company wants to expands its total assets by 47.50% ? There are no short term debts.

(f) How much of the capital budget must be financed by the external equity to maintain the optimal capital structure in part (e).

(g) Calculate the Weighted Average Cost of Capital using Marginal Weights in part (f) assuming that the company intends to maintain the existing optimal capital structure.

(h) Calculate the numbers of new equity shares, debentures and preference shares to be issued in part (f)

SOLUTION

CALCULATION OF RETAINED EARNINGS AS AT 31-3-2009

A.	Retained Earnings as at 1-4-2008	₹ 4,40,000
B.	Add: Current year's Retained Earnings [(20,000 × ₹ 20) × 40%]	₹ 1,60,000
C.	Retained Earnings as at 31-3-2009	₹ 6,00,000

(A) (I) STATEMENT SHOWING THE WEIGHTED AVERAGE COST OF CAPITAL (USING BOOK VALUE WEIGHTS)

Source of Capital *A*	*Amount of each source of capital* *B (in lacs)*	*Proportion of each source of capital* *C*	*After tax cost of each source of capital* *D*	*Product* *E = C × D*
Equity Share Capital	2.00	0.100	0.200	0.0200
Retained Earnings	6.00	0.300	0.200	0.0600
18% Preference Share Capital	2.00	0.100	0.150	0.0150
15% Debentures	10.00	0.500	0.075	0.0375
Total	20.00	1.000		0.1325

(A) (II) STATEMENT SHOWING THE WEIGHTED AVERAGE COST OF CAPITAL (USING MARKET VALUE WEIGHTS)

Source of Capital *A*	*Amount of each source of capital* *B (in lacs)*	*Proportion of each source of capital* *C*	*After tax cost of each source of capital* *D*	*Product* *E = C × D*
Equity Share Capital	15.60	0.520	0.200	0.104
18% Preference Share Capital	2.40	0.080	0.150	0.012
15% Debentures	12.00	0.400	0.075	0.030
Total	30.00	1.000		0.146

Cost of Equity Capital (k_e) *or* Retained Earnings (k_r)

$$= \frac{D_1}{P_0} + g = \frac{D_0(1+g)}{P_0} + g = \frac{12\,(1+0.04)}{78} + 0.04 = 0.16 + 0.04 = 0.20$$

(b) Calculation the New Cost

(i) *Cost of New Debentures (k_d)*

$$k_d = \frac{\text{Interest }(1-\text{tax rate}) + [(\text{Redeemable Value} - \text{Net Sale Proceeds})]/N}{[(\text{Redeemable Value} + \text{Net Sale Proceeds})/2]}$$

$$k_d = \frac{1(1-t) + [(RV - SP)/N]}{(RV + SP)/2} = \frac{12(1-0.4) + [(105-95)/5]}{(105+95)/2} = 0.092 \text{ or } 9.2\%$$

(ii) *Cost of New Preference Share (k_p)*

$$k_p = \frac{\text{Preference Dividend} + [(\text{Redeemable Value} - \text{Net Sale Proceeds})]/N}{[(\text{Redeemable Value} + \text{Net Sale Proceeds})/2]}$$

$$k_p = \frac{D_P + [(RV - SP)/N]}{(RV + SP)/2} = \frac{15 + [(105-95)/5]}{(105+95)/2} = 0.17 \text{ or } 17.00\%$$

(iii) *Cost of New Equity Shares (k_e)*

$$k_e = \frac{D_1}{P_0} + g = \frac{D_0(1+g)}{P_0} + g = \frac{12\,(1+0.04)}{(60-5)} + 0.04 = 0.2269 + 0.04 = 0.2669 \text{ or } 26.69\%$$

(iv) *Cost of Retained Earnings (k_r)*

$$k_r = \frac{D_1}{P_0} + g = \frac{D_0(1+g)}{P_0} + g = \frac{12\,(1+0.04)}{60} + 0.04 = 0.208 + 0.04 = 0.248 \text{ or } 24.8\%.$$

(c) Calculation of Investment before issue of equity shares

Retained earning available = Total number of shares × EPS – Dividend paid
= (20,000 × ₹ 20) – (20,000 × ₹ 12)
= ₹ 4,00,000 – ₹ 2,40,000 = ₹ 1,60,000

Total Investment = (1,60,000/0.40) = ₹ 4,00,000

Hence, the company can expand its project by ₹ 4,00,000 without issuing new equity shares.

(D) CALCULATION OF WEIGHTED AVERAGE COST BY USING MARGINAL WEIGHTS

Source of Capital A	*Amount of each source of capital* B	*Proportion of each source of capital* C	*After tax cost of each source of capital* D	*Product* E = C × D
Retained Earnings	1.60	0.400	0.248	0.0992
New 15% Pref. Share Capital	0.40	0.100	0.170	0.0170
New 12% Debentures	2.00	0.500	0.092	0.0460
Total	4.00	1.000		0.1622

(e) Required Amount of Capital Budget = 47.5% of ₹ 20 lakhs = ₹ 9.50 lakh

(f) External Equity to be raised

= Equity Portion in New Investment – Retained Earnings Available

= (40% of ₹ 9,50,000) – ₹ 1,60,000 = ₹ 2,20,000.

(G) STATEMENT SHOWING THE WEIGHTED AVERAGE COST OF CAPITAL (USING MARGINAL WEIGHTS)

Source of Capital A	*Amount of each source of capital* B	*Proportion of each source of capital* C	*After tax cost of each source of capital* D	*Product* E = C × D
New Equity Share Capital	2.20	0.232	0.267	0.0619
Retained Earnings	1.60	0.168	0.248	0.0417
New 15% Pref. Share Capital	0.95	0.100	0.170	0.0170
New 12% Debentures	4.75	0.500	0.092	0.0460
Total	9.50	1.000		0.1666

(h) Calculation of Number of New Securities

No. of New Equity Shares = ₹ 2,20,000/₹ 55 = 4,000

No. of New Pref. Shares = ₹ 95,000/₹ 95 = 1,000

No. of New Debentures = ₹ 4,75,000/₹ 95 = 5,000

ILLUSTRATION 42

A company is currently financed entirely by equity and the cost of equity is 10%. Planning to introduce a degree of debt borrowing, the company ascertains that the cost of debt will be 4 per cent. However, if the debt borrowing should exceed 20% of the company's total finance, the cost of debt will increase because of the additional risk perceived by the debenture holders, and will be given by the following expression:

$$\text{Cost of Debt} = \left(4 + \frac{X - 20\%}{30\%}\right)\%$$

where X is the market value of the debt expressed as a % of the total market value of the Co.

In addition, the cost of equity will increase if a debt is introduced into the company because shareholders will believe that there is an increased level of risk. The risk premium required (i.e. the additional return over and above the existing cost of 10%) is expected to be given by the expression:

$$\text{Risk Premium} = \frac{X}{Y} \times 4\%$$

Where X is as defined above, and Y is the market value of the equity expressed as a percentage of the total market value of the company.

Required: Calculate Ko for each of the following capital structures:

Equity	100%	80%	60%	40%	20%
Debt	NIL	20%	40%	60%	80%

SOLUTION

STATEMENT SHOWING THE CALCULATION OF WEIGHTED AVERAGE COST OF CAPITAL

Capital Structure	*Debt % (x)*	*Equity % (Y)*	$K_e = 10\% + \frac{X}{Y} \times 4\%$	$K_d = 4\% + \frac{X - 20\%}{30\%}$	$K_o = (X \times k_d) + (Y \times ke)$
I	0	1.00	$10\% + \frac{0}{100} \times 4\% = .10$	0	$K_o = (0 \times 0) + (1.00 \times .10) = .10$

II	.20	.80	$10\% + \frac{20}{80} \times 4\% = .11$	$4\% + \frac{20\% - 20\%}{30\%} = .04$	$K_0 = (.20 \times .04) + (.80 \times .11) = 0.968$
III	.40	.60	$10\% + \frac{40}{60} \times 4\% = .1267$	$4\% + \frac{40\% - 20\%}{30\%} = 0.467$	$K_0 = (.40 \times .0467) + (.60 \times .1267) = .0947$
IV	.60	.40	$10\% + \frac{60}{40} \times 4\% = .16$	$4\% + \frac{60\% - 20\%}{30\%} = 0.0533$	$K_0 = (.60 \times .0533) + (.40 \times .16) = .09598$
V	.80	.20	$10\% + \frac{80}{20} \times 4\% = .26$	$4\% + \frac{80\% - 20\%}{30\%} = 0.06$	$K_0 = (.80 \times .06) + (.20 \times .26) = 0.10$

ILLUSTRATION 43

The capital structure of the X Ltd. consists of 40% Equity, 40% Preference Capital and 20% Debt. The after tax cost of the Preference Capital and Debt are 15% and 7.20% respectively. The weighted average cost is 15.44%. Calculate after tax cost of equity.

SOLUTION

LET THE COST OF EQUITY BE X

Source of Capital A	*Amount of each each source of capital* B	*After tax cost of each source of capital* C	*Product* D = C × B
Equity Share Capital	0.400	X	0.40X
15% Preference Share Capital	0.400	0.1500	0.0600
12% Debentures	0.200	0.0720	0.0144
Total	1.000		0.0744 + 0.40X

Weighted Average Cost of Capital = 0.0744 + 0.40X

0.1544 = 0.0744 + 0.40X

0.40X = 0.1544 - 0.0744 = 0.08

X = 0.08/0.40 = 0.20

Hence, the cost of the equity = 0.20 *or* 20%

ILLUSTRATION 44

The capital structure of the Y Ltd. consists of 40% equity. The after tax cost of the Equity, Preference Shares and Debt are 20%, 15% and 7.20% respectively. Calculate the proportion of the Preference Shares and Debt in the capital structure of the company if weighted average cost of capital is 15.44%.

SOLUTION

Let the proportion of the preference share be X

Then the proportion of Debt will be (1.00 – 0.40 – X) = 0.60 – X

Source of Capital A	*Amount of each each source of capital* B	*After tax cost of each source of capital* C	*Product* D = C × B
Equity Share Capital	0.400	0.2000	0.0800

15% Preference Share Capital	X	0.1500	0.15X
12% Debentures	0.600-X	0.0720	0.0432 – 0.072X
Total	1.000		0.1232 + 0.078X

$$0.1232 + 0.078X = 0.1544 \Rightarrow 0.078X = 0.1544 - 0.1232 \Rightarrow 0.078X = 0.0312$$

$$X = 0.0312/0.078 = 0.40$$

Proportion of the Preference Share = X = 0.40 *or* 40%

Proportion of the Debt = 0.60 – X = 0.60 – 0.40 = 0.20 *or* 20%

ILLUSTRATION 45

The capital structure of the X Ltd. consists of 40% Equity, 40% Preference Capital and 20% Debt. The after tax cost of the Preference Capital and Debt are 15% and 7.20% respectively. The weighted average cost is 15.44%. X Ltd. paid currently a dividend of ₹ 4 per share. The current market price of its equity share is ₹ 44. Find the growth rate.

SOLUTION

Let the Cost of Equity = X

Source of Capital A	*Amount of each each source of capital* B	*After tax cost of each source of capital* C	*Product* D = C × B
Equity Share Capital	0.400	X	0.40X
15% Preference Share Capital	0.400	0.1500	0.0600
12% Debentures	0.200	0.0720	0.0144
Total	1.000		0.0744 + 0.40X

Weighted Average Cost of Capita = 0.0744 + 0.40X

$$0.1544 = 0.0744 + 0.40X$$

$$0.40X = 0.1544 - 0.0744 = 0.08$$

$$X = 0.08/0.40 = 0.20$$

Hence, the cost of the equity = 0.20 *or* 20%

Let the Growth Rate be Y

$$k_e = \frac{D_1}{P_0} + g = \frac{D_0(1+g)}{P_0} + g$$

$$0.20 = \frac{4\,(1+Y)}{44} + Y$$

$$0.20 = \frac{4\,(1+Y) + 44Y}{44}$$

$$0.20 \times 44 = 4 + 48Y$$

$$8.80 = 4 + 48Y$$

$$48Y = 8.80 - 4$$

$$48Y = 4.80$$

$$Y = 4.80/48$$

$$Y = 0.10$$

Hence, the Growth Rate is 0.10 *or* 10%.

19.0 HOW TO CALCULATE BETA COEFFICIENT UNDER CAPITAL ASSETS PRICING MODEL (CAPM)

MEANING OF BETA

(a) Beta (b) is a measure of volatility of an individual security return relative to the returns of a broad based market portfolio. It indicates—how much individual security's return will change for a unit change in the market return?

(b) Beta is a measure of systematic risk. Systematic Risk (or Market Risk *or* Non-Diversifiable Risk) is the risk which can not be eliminated through investing in well-diversified market portfolio.

(c) In statistical terms, Beta Co-efficient (b) is basically Regression Coefficient (bxy) of Security Return (x) on Market Return (y).

VALUE OF BETA

The value of beta (b) can be zero *or* more than 1 *or less* than 1.

Value of Beta	*Interpretation*
1. Beta equal to 1	Beta equal to 1 indicates that systematic risk is equal to the aggregate market risk. It means that the security's returns fluctuate equal to market returns.
2. Beta Greater than 1	Beta greater than 1 indicates that systematic risk is greater than the aggregate market risk. It means that the security's returns fluctuate more than the market returns.
3. Beta less than 1	Beta *less* than 1 indicates that systematic risk is *less* than the aggregate market risk. it means that the security's returns fluctuate *less* than the market returns.
4. Zero Beta	Zero Beta indicates no volatility.

HOW TO CALCULATE BETA

The calculation of the beta involves the following steps:

PRACTICAL STEPS INVOLVED IN THE CALCULATION OF BETA (B)

Step 1: *Calculate the Excess of Market Return (R_m) over Risk Free Rate (R_f) as follows and denote the same as 'M':*

$$M = R_m - R_f$$

Step 2: *Calculate M^2 and $\sum M^2$*

Step 3: *Calculate the excess of Security Return (R_s) over Risk Free Rate (R_f) as follows and denote the same as 'J':*

$$J = R_s - R_f$$

Step 4: *Calculate the product of M & J and $\sum MJ$*

Step 5: *Calculate Average R_p, Average Rm, Average M and Average J.*

Step 6: *Calculate Systematic Risk of firm or beta co-efficient (ß) as follows:*

$$\beta = \frac{\Sigma MJ - N \times \bar{M} \times \bar{J}}{\Sigma M^2 - N \cdot (\bar{M})^2} = \frac{\Sigma MJ - \dfrac{\Sigma M \cdot \Sigma J}{N}}{\Sigma M^2 - \dfrac{(\Sigma M)^2}{N}}$$

Where, M = *Excess of Market Return over Risk Free Rate* = $R_m - R_f$

J = Excess of Security Return over Risk Free Rate = $R_s - R_f$

MJ = Product of M and J

Step 7: *Calculate the Cost of the Equity (K_e) as follows:*

$K_e = R_f + \beta(R_m - R_f)$

Tutorial Note: If Correlation Coefficient of Portfolio with market (r) is given, beta coefficient (b) may be calculated as follows:

$$\text{Beta } (\beta) = \text{Correlation Coefficient (r)} \times \frac{\text{Standard Deviation of the Security}}{\text{Standard Deviation of Market Portfolio}}$$

ILLUSTRATION 46

The following figures relate to Tulsian Ltd.:

Year	*Market Return*	*Security Return*	*Risk Free Rate*
1	0.15	0.12	0.10
2	0.14	0.11	0.12
3	0.17	0.19	0.08
4	0.16	0.18	0.08
5	0.10	0.12	0.10

Required: Calculate the Beta and Cost of Equity.

SOLUTION

STATEMENT SHOWING THE CALCULATION OF THE AFTER TAX COST OF THE EQUITY

Year	*Market Return (R_m)*	*Security Return (R_s)*	*Risk Free Rate (R_f)*	*$M = R_m - R_f$*	*$J = R_s - R_f$*	*$(M)^2$*	*$M \times J$*
1	0.15	0.12	0.10	0.05	0.02	0.0025	0.0010
2	0.14	0.11	0.12	0.02	– 0.01	0.0004	– 0.0002
3	0.17	0.19	0.08	0.09	0.11	0.0081	0.0099
4	0.16	0.18	0.08	0.08	0.10	0.0064	0.0080
5	0.10	0.12	0.10	0.00	0.02	0.0000	0.0000
Total	0.72	0.72	0.48	0.24	0.24	0.0174	0.0187
Average	0.144		0.096	0.048	0.048		

$$\beta = \text{beta co-efficient} = \frac{\Sigma MJ - N \times \bar{M} \times \bar{J}}{\Sigma M^2 - N \cdot (\bar{M})^2} = \frac{0.0187 - 5 \times 0.048 \times 0.048}{0.0174 - 5 \times (.048)^2} = \frac{0.00718}{0.00588} = 1.2211$$

Alternatively,

$$\beta = \text{beta co-efficient} = \frac{\Sigma MJ - \frac{\Sigma M \cdot \Sigma J}{N}}{\Sigma M^2 - \frac{(\Sigma M)^2}{N}} = \frac{0.0187 - \frac{0.24 \times 0.24}{5}}{0.0174 - \frac{(0.24)^2}{5}} = 1.2211$$

$k_e = R_f + \beta(R_m - R_f)$

$k_e = 0.096 + 1.2211\ (0.144 - 0.096)$

$k_e = 0.154612$ *or* 15.46%

ILLUSTRATION 47

Calculate the Value of Beta (b) in the following cases:

Case (a)	Standard Deviation of Security	3
	Standard Deviation of Market Portfolio	2
	Correlation Coefficient of Portfolio with market	0.8
Case (b)	Correlation Coefficient of Portfolio with market	0.8
	Variance of Market Portfolio is 4/9th of Variance of Security	
Case (c)	Risk-Free Rate of Interest on Govt. Treasury Bonds:	5%
	Average Return on Market Portfolio:	17.5%
	Cost of Equity (k_e):	20%
Case (d)	Cost of Equity (k_e):	20%
	Average Market Risk Premium:	10%
	Risk Free Rate of Interest:	5%

SOLUTION

Case (a)

$$\text{Beta } (\beta) = \text{Correlation Coefficient of Portfolio with market} \times \frac{\text{Standard Deviation of the Security}}{\text{Standard Deviation of Market Portfolio}} = 0.8 \times \frac{3}{2} = 1.2$$

Case (b) Variance of Market Portfolio = $\frac{4}{9}$ Variance of Security

$$\frac{\text{Variance of Market Portfolio}}{\text{Variance of Security}} = \frac{4}{9}$$

$$\frac{\text{Standard Division of Market Portfolio}}{\text{Standard Deviation of Security}} = \frac{2}{3}$$

$$\text{Beta } (\beta) = \text{Correlation Coefficient of Portfolio with market} \times \frac{\text{Standard Deviation of the Security}}{\text{Standard Deviation of Market Portfolio}} = 0.8 \times \frac{3}{2} = 1.2$$

Case (c)

$$k_e = R_f + \beta(R_m - R_f)$$
$$20\% = 5\% + \beta(17.5\% - 5\%)$$
$$\beta = (20\% - 5\%)/12.5 = 1.2$$

Case (d)

$$k_e = R_f + \beta(R_m - R_f)$$
$$20\% = 5\% + \beta(10\%)$$
$$\beta = (20\% - 5\%)/10\% = 1.5$$

ILLUSTRATION 48

From the following data information, calculate the Cost of Equity (K_e):

Risk—free rate of interest	8%
Expected return of market portfolio	18%
Standard deviation of an asset	2.8%
Market standard deviation	2.3%
Correlation coefficient of portfolio with market	0.8

SOLUTION

Step 1: Beta (ß)

$$= \text{Correlation Coefficient of Portfolio with market} \times \frac{\text{Standard Deviation of the Security}}{\text{Standard Deviation of Market Portfolio}}$$

$$= 0.8 \times \frac{2.8\%}{2.3\%} = 0.974$$

Step 2: $k_e = R_f + \beta(R_m - R_f) = 8\% + 0.974\ (18\% - 8\%) = 8\% + 9.74\% = 17.74\%$

ILLUSTRATION 49

The market is giving an average return of 18%. The risk-free return is 11%.

Required:

(i) What return would be expected from an investment having a Beta factor of 0.9 ?

(ii) Beta Factor which would be necessary for an investment to yield a return of 21.6% ?

SOLUTION

(i) $k_e = R_f + \beta(R_m - R_f) = 11\% + 0.9\ (18\% - 11\%) = 17.3\%$

(ii) $k_e = R_f + \beta(R_m - R_f)$

$21.6\% = 11\% + \beta\ (18\% - 11\%)$

$\beta = (21.6\% - 11\%) / 7 = 1.5143$

ILLUSTRATION 50

Emphatic Ltd. has invested in four streams of business (A, B, C and D), the following sums: A: ₹ 10,000; B : ₹ 20,000; C : ₹ 16,000; D : ₹ 14,000.

The b values of these businesses are 0.80, 1.20, 1.40 and 1.75 respectively. If the risk free return is 4.25% and the market return is 11%,

Required:

(a) What is the b of Emphatic Ltd. & its expected return/cost of equity ?

(b) If Emphatic Ltd. encashes its Investment in business B and reinvest the funds in RBI Bonds yielding a return of 4.25%, what is the b value of the business and its expected return ?

SOLUTION

(A) (I) CALCULATION OF BETA OF THE COMPANY AS A WHOLE

Business 1	*Value* 2	*Proportion* 3	*ß of Each Business* 4	*Product* 5 = 3 × 4
A	10,000	10/60	0.80	0.1333
B	20,000	20/60	1.20	0.4000
C	16,000	16/60	1.40	0.3733
D	14,000	14/60	1.75	0.4083
	60,000	1.00		1.3149

(a) (ii) $k_e = R_f + \beta(R_m - R_f) = 4.25\% + 1.3149\ (11\% - 4.25\%) = 13.126\%$

(B) (I) CALCULATION OF BETA OF THE COMPANY AS A WHOLE (IF 'B' BUSINESS IS CLOSED & INVESTMENT IS MADE IN RISK FREE SECURITY)

Business 1	*Value* 2	*Proportion* 3	*ß of Each Business* 4	*Product* 5 = 3 × 4
A	10,000	10/60	0.80	0.1333
B	20,000	20/60	0.00	0.0000
C	16,000	16/60	1.40	0.3733
D	14,000	14/60	1.75	0.4083
	60,000	1.00		0.9149

(b) (ii) $k_e = R_f + \beta(R_m - R_f)$ = 4.25% + 0.9149 (11% – 4.25%) = 10.426%

ILLUSTRATION 51

The Beta Coefficient of Target Ltd. is 1.4. The company has been maintaining 8% rate of growth in dividend and earnings. The last dividend paid was ₹ 4 per share. Return on Government Securities is 10%. Return on market portfolio is 15%.

(i) What will be the equilibrium price per share of Target Ltd. ?

(ii) Would you advise purchasing the share if the current market price of one share of Target Ltd. is (i) ₹ 36 (ii) ₹ 50

SOLUTION

Step 1: $k_e = R_f + \beta(R_m - R_f)$ = 10% + 1.4 (15% – 10%) = 17%

Step 2: $k_e = \frac{D_1}{P_0} + g$

$$17\% = \frac{₹\,4\,(1+.08)}{P_0} + 8\%$$

$$9\% = \frac{₹\,4.32}{P_0}$$

P_0 = ₹ 4.32/9% = ₹ 48

Advice:

(i) The investor is advised to purchase the share since its current market price (i.e., ₹ 36) is *less* than the equilibrium price (i.e., ₹ 48). In otherwords, the share is under-priced.

(ii) The investor is advised not to purchase the share since its market price (i.e., ₹ 50) is more than the equilibrium price (i.e., ₹ 48). In otherwords, the share is over-priced.

ILLUSTRATION 52

An investor is holding 1,000 shares of Fatlass Company. Presently the rate of dividend being paid by the company is ₹ 2 per share and the share is being sold at ₹ 25 per share in the market. However, several factors are likely to change during the course of the year as indicated below:

Particulars	*Existing*	*Revised*
Risk Free Rate	12%	10%
Market Risk Premium	6%	4%
Beta Value	1.4	1.25
Expected Growth Rate	5%	9%

In view of the above factors whether the investor should buy, hold *or* sell the shares? and why?

SOLUTION

(i) Advice under Existing Conditions

Step 1:	Existing Rate of Return = $R_f + \beta(R_m - R_f)$ = 12% + 1.4 (6%) = 20.4%
Step 2:	Existing Price of Share = $P_0 = \frac{D_0(1+g)}{K-g} = \frac{2(1.05)}{0.204-0.05} = \frac{2.10}{0.154}$ = ₹ 13.64.
Step 3:	**Advice:** The investor is advised to sell the shares since its current market price (i.e., ₹ 25) is more than its equilibrium price (i.e., ₹ 13.63). In otherwords, the share is over-priced.
(ii) Advice under Revised Condition	
Step 1:	Revised Rate of Return = $R_f + \beta(R_m - R_f)$ = 10% + 1.25 (4%) = 15%

Step 2: Revised Price of Share = $P_0 = \frac{D_0(1+g)}{K-g} = \frac{₹\ 2(1.09)}{0.15-0.09} = \frac{2.18}{0.06}$ = ₹ 36.33

Step 3: **Advice:** the investor is advised to hold the shares since its current market price (i.e., ₹ 25) is *less* than its equilibrium price (i.e., ₹ 36.33). In other words, the share is under-priced.

ILLUSTRATION 53

From the following information, Calculate the financial leverage:

(a) Existing Capital Structure: Equity Shares ₹ 60,000, 12% Debentures ₹ 40,000

(b) Rate of Return on Risk Free Investment = 10%

(c) Rate of Return on Market Portfolio = 30%

(d) Beta Coefficient = 0.5

(e) Tax Rate = 40%

SOLUTION

STEP 1: CALCULATION OF WEIGHTED AVERAGE COST OF CAPITAL

Source of Capital A	*Amount of each source of capital* B (in lacs)	*Proportion of each source of capital* C	*After tax cost of each source of capital* D	*Product* E = C × D
Equity Share Capital	60,000	0.600	0.2000	0.1200
12% Debentures	40,000	0.400	0.0720	0.0288
Total	1,00,000	1.000		0.1488

Step 2: Expected Earnings after tax = ₹ 1,00,000 × 0.1488 = ₹ 14,880

Step 3: Expected Earnings before tax = ₹ 14,880/0.6 = ₹ 24,800

STEP 4: CALCULATION OF FINANCIAL LEVERAGE

A. EBIT	₹ 24,800
B. Less: Interest	₹ 4,800
C. EBT	₹ 20,000
D. Financial Leverage (A/C)	1.24

Working Notes:

(i) $k_e = R_f + \beta(R_m - R_f)$ = 10% + 0.5 (30% − 10%) = 20%

(ii) $k_d = 12\% (1 - 0.4) = 0.072$

SOLVED PROBLEMS

PROBLEM 1

Mr. Agent is planning to purchase the shares of X Ltd. which had paid a dividend of ₹ 2 per share at last year. Dividends are growing at a rate of 10%. What price would Mr. Agent be willing to pay for X Ltd.'s shares if he expects a rate of return of 20% ?

SOLUTION

$$P_0 = \frac{D_1}{k_e - g}; D_1 = D_0 (1 + g) = 2 (1 + 0.10) = ₹ 2.20$$

$$P_0 = ₹2.20/[0.20 - (+0.10)] = ₹ 22$$

PROBLEM 2

Mr. Factor is planning to purchase the shares of X Ltd which had paid a dividend of ₹ 2.00 per share. Dividends are declining at a rate of 10%. What price would Mr. Factor be willing to pay for X Limited's share if his required rate of return is 20%.

SOLUTION

$$P_0 = \frac{D_1}{k_e - g}; D_1 = D_0 (1 + g) = 2.00 (1 - 0.10) = ₹ 1.80$$

$$P_0 = ₹1.80/[0.20 - (-0.10)] = ₹ 6$$

PROBLEM 3

Mr. Broker is planning to purchase the shares of X Ltd. his required rate of return is 20%. Dividends are declining at a rate of 10%.

Required: What dividend had X Ltd. paid last year if he is willing to pay Rs. 9.00 for X Ltd.'s share ?

SOLUTION

$$P_0 = \frac{D_1}{k_e - g} \text{ and } D1 = D0 (1 + g)$$

$$P_0 = \frac{D_0(1 - 0.10)}{0.20 - (-0.10)} = ₹ 9.00$$

$$D_0(0.9) = ₹ 2.70$$

$$D_0 = ₹ 2.70/0.9$$

$$D_0 = ₹ 3.00$$

PROBLEM 4

Mr. Agent purchases an equity share of X Ltd. X Ltd. had paid dividend of ₹ 2 per share last year. Dividend are declining at a rate of 10%. What is the required rate of return of Mr. X on his equity investment if he purchases an equity share for ₹ 6 ?

SOLUTION

$$P_0 = \frac{D_1}{k_e - g} \text{ and } D_1(1 + g)$$

$D_1 = 2\,(1 - 0.10) = 1.80$

$P_0 = 1.8/[k_e - (-0.10)] = 6.00$

$1.8 = 6\,(k_e + 0.10)$

$1.8 = 6\,k_e + 0.6$

$1.8 - 0.6 = 6\,k_e$

$6\,k_e = 1.20$

$k_e = 1.20/6 = 0.20$

PROBLEM 5

Tulsian Ltd. is foreseeing a growth rate of 10% p.a. for next two years. The growth rate is likely to increase to 12% for the next two years. After that the growth rate is expected to continue at 8% p.a. The company paid a dividend of ₹ 5 per share last year. Investor's required rate of return is 10%.

Required: At what price would you as investor be ready to buy the shares of this company now (t = 0)?

SOLUTION

Value of Equity Share in t_0 = [PV of Dividend Payments during the years 1 – 4] + [PV of Expected Market Price at the end of the year 4]

STEP 1: CALCULATION OF PV OF DIVIDENDS PAYMENTS

Year *A*	*Dividend* *B*	*PV factor at 10%* *C*	*Total PV* *D = C × D*
1	D_1 = 5.00 (1 + 0.10) = 5.500	0.909	5.000
2	D_2 = 5.50 (1 + 0.10) = 6.050	0.826	4.997
3	D_3 = 6.05 (1 + 0.12) = 6.776	0.751	5.089
4	D_4 = 6.776 (1 + 0.12) = 7.589	0.683	5.183
		PV of D_{1-4}	20.269

Step 2: Calculation of Expected Market Price in t_4

$$P_4 = \frac{D_5}{k_e - g} = \frac{D_4(1+g)}{k_e - g} = \frac{7.589\,(1+0.08)}{0.10-(0.08)} = \frac{8.196}{0.02} = ₹\ 409.80$$

Step 3: PV of $P_4 = P_4 \times$ PV factor = ₹ 409.80 × 0.683 = ₹ 279.89

Step 4: Market price in P_0 = PV of D_4 + PV of P_4 = ₹ 20.27 + ₹ 279.89 = ₹ 300.16

PROBLEM 6

Calculate the cost of new debentures, new preference shares, new equity shares and retained earnings from the point of view of company if anticipated external financing opportunities are as follows:

(a) 13% Debentures ₹ 100 each issued at par and redeemable after 5 years at 5% premium. Floatation cost is 5% of issue price.

(b) 15% Preference Share of ₹ 100 each issued at par and redeemable after 5 years at 5% premium. Flotation cost is 5% of the issue price.

(c) Equity Shares of ₹ 10 each issued at ₹ 80. Flotation cost is ₹ 5 per share. EPS for the current year is ₹ 25 per share. Dividend Payout Ratio is 60%. Anticipated growth rate is 5%. Corporate tax rate is 40%.

SOLUTION

(a) Calculation of the Cost of New Debentures

$$\text{Approximation method} = \frac{\text{Interest }(1-\text{tax rate}) + [(\text{Redeemable value} - \text{Net Sale Proceeds})]/N}{[(\text{Redeemable value} + \text{Net Sale Proceeds})]/2}$$

$$k_d = \frac{I(1-t) + [(RV - SP)/N]}{(RV + SP)/2}$$

$$k_d = \frac{13(1-0.4) + [(105-95)/5]}{(105+95)/2} = 0.098 = 9.80\%$$

(b) Calculation of Cost of new Preference Share

$$k_d = \frac{\text{Preference Dividend} + [(\text{Redeemable Value} - \text{Net Sale Proceeds})]/N}{[(\text{Redeemable Value} + \text{Net Sale Proceeds})]/2}$$

$$k_p = \frac{D_P + [(RV - SP)/N]}{(RV + SP)/2}$$

$$k_p = \frac{15 + [(105-95)/5}{(105+95)/2} = 0.17 \text{ or } 17.00\%$$

(c) Calculation of Cost of New Equity Shares

$$\text{Cost of Equity Capital} = \frac{D_1}{P_0} + g = \frac{D_0(1+g)}{P_0} + g$$

$$k_e = \frac{15\,(1+0.05)}{(80-5)} + 0.05$$

$$k_e = 0.210 + 0.05 = 0.26 \textit{ or } 26\%.$$

(d) Calculation of New Cost of Retained Earnings

$$\text{Cost of Retained Earnings} = \frac{D_1}{P_0} + g = \frac{D_0(1+g)}{P_0} + g$$

$$k_e = \frac{15\,(1+0.05)}{80} + 0.05$$

$$k_e = 0.1969 + 0.05 = 0.2469 \textit{ or } 24.69\%$$

PROBLEM 7

Answer Problem 6 assuming dividend tax rate is 20%.

SOLUTION

(a) Calculation of Cost of New Debentures

$$\text{Approximation method} = \frac{\text{Interest }(1-\text{tax rate}) + [(\text{Redeemable Value} - \text{Net Sale Proceeds})]/N}{[(\text{Redeemable Value} + \text{Net Sale Proceeds})]/2}$$

$$k_d = \frac{I(1-t) + [(RV - SP)/N]}{(RV + SP)/2}$$

$$k_d = \frac{13(1-0.4) + [(105-95)/5]}{(105+95)/2} = 0.098 \text{ or } 9.80\%$$

(b) Calculation of Cost of New Preference Shares

$$k_p = \frac{\text{Preference Dividend }(1+\text{Dividend Tax}) + [(\text{Redeemable Value} - \text{Net Sale Proceeds})]/N}{[(\text{Redeemable Value} + \text{Net Sale Proceeds})]/2}$$

$$k_p = \frac{D_p(1+D_1) + [(RV - SP)/N]}{(RV + SP)/2}$$

$$k_p = \frac{15\,(1+0.20)+[(105-95)/5]}{(105+95)/2} = 0.20 \text{ or } 20.00\%$$

(c) Calculation of Cost of New Equity Shares

$$\text{Cost of Equity Capital} = \frac{D_1\,(1+D_t)}{P_0} + g = \frac{D_0(1+g)\,(1+D_t)}{P_0} + g$$

$$k_e = \frac{15\,(1+0.05)\,(1+0.20)}{(80-5)} + 0.05$$

$$k_e = 0.252 + 0.05 = 0.320 \text{ or } 30.2\%$$

(d) Calculation of New Cost of Retained Earnings

$$\text{Cost of Retained Earnings} = \frac{D_1(1+D_t)}{P_0} + g = \frac{D_0(1+g)\,(1+D_t)}{P_0} + g$$

$$k_e = \frac{15\,(1+.05)\,(1+0.2)}{80} + .05$$

$$k_e = 0.23625 + .05 = 0.28625 \text{ or } 28.625\%$$

LEVERAGE

LEARNING OBJECTIVES

After studying this chapter, you should be able to understand:

- Leverage Analysis
- Meaning of Risk
- Meaning of Business Risk
- Meaning of Financial Risk
- Meaning of Leverage
- Operating Leverage
- Financial Leverage
- What is Trading on Equity?
- Combined Leverage
- Indifference Point
- Uncommitted EPS Approach
- Which form of Financing should be employed?
- Financial Break Even Point (FBEP)
- Impact of Leverage on Capital Turnover Ratio and Working Turnover Ratio
- Impact of Financial Leverage on Shareholders' Wealth by Using Return-on-Investment (ROI) and Return on Equity (ROE) Analytic Framework
- How to measure Operating Risk?
- How to measure Financial Risk?

1.0 LEVERAGE ANALYSIS

Leverage Analysis is the technique, which is used to quantify risk return relationship of different alternatives of capital structure.

2.0 MEANING OF RISK

Risk exists because of lack of certainty. Risk attached to a firm can be divided into two categories—Business risk and Financial risk.

3.0 MEANING OF BUSINESS RISK

Business risk can be defined as the variability of Earnings Before Interest & Tax (EBIT). It results because of internal and external environment (***For Example,*** business cycle, technological obsolescence) in which the firm has to operate. It is an unavoidable risk so long as environment is given. It is associated with Capital Budgeting Decision (or Assets Mix Decision). It is measured by calculating Operating Leverage. Its degree does not differ with the use of different forms of financing.

4.0 MEANING OF FINANCIAL RISK

Financial risk can be defined as the variability of Earnings Before Tax (EBT). It results because of use of financial leverage (i.e. sources of funds bearing fixed financial payments like debt). It is an avoidable risk since the firm can avoid it by not using financial leverage in the capital structure. It is associated with Capital Structure Decision (or Capital Mix Decision). It is measured by calculating Financial Leverage. Its degree differs with the use of different forms of financing.

5.0 MEANING OF LEVERAGE

Leverage means use of sources of funds bearing fixed financial payments like debt in the capital structure.

6.0 OPERATING LEVERAGE

MEANING OF OPERATING LEVERAGE

Operating Leverage is a measure of Business Risk. Operating leverage is defined as the firm's ability to use fixed operating cost to magnify the effect of changes in sales on its Earnings Before Interest and Taxes [EBIT]. The percentage change in EBIT occurring due to a given percentage change in sales is known as the degree of operating leverage. The operating leverage of 1.5 means that 1% increase in sales would result in 1.5% increase in EBIT (i.e., Operating Profit).

DECISION WITH WHICH OPERATING LEVERAGE IS ASSOCIATED

It is associated with Capital Budgeting Decision (or Assets Mix Decision). Its degree does not differ with the use of different forms of financing.

WHEN DOES OPERATING LEVERAGE EXIST?

Operating Leverage exists if there are fixed costs.

HOW TO CALCULATE OPERATING LEVERAGE ?

The Degree of Operating Leverage (D.O.L) can be calculated with the help of following formulae:

1. $$\text{D.O.L.} = \frac{\text{Percentage Change in EBIT}}{\text{Percentage Change in Sales}} = \frac{\Delta\text{EBIT} / \text{EBIT}}{\Delta\text{Sales} / \text{Sales}}$$
2. $$\text{D.O.L.} = \frac{\text{Contribution}}{\text{EBIT}} = \frac{\text{Sales} - \text{Variable Costs}}{\text{Sales} - \text{Variable Costs} - \text{Fixed Costs}}$$

SIGNIFICANCE OF OPERATING LEVERAGE

Operating leverage shows the impact of change in sales on operating income (i.e. EBIT).

ILLUSTRATION 1 [CALCULATION OF OPERATING LEVERAGE]

Calculate the Degree of Operating Leverage in each of the following alternative cases:

Case (a) Contribution ₹10,000, EBIT ₹ 2,000

Case (b) Contribution ₹ 20,000, Fixed Costs ₹ 15,000.

Case (c) Sales ₹ 1,00,000, Variable Costs ₹ 40,000, Fixed Costs ₹ 30,000.

Case (d) Sales Units 10,000, Selling Price per unit ₹ 10, Variable Cost 60%, Total Operating Cost 90%.

Case (e) Installed Capacity 20,000 units, Actual Production and Sales 75% of installed capacity, Selling Price per unit ₹ 10, Fixed Cost ₹ 30,000, Total Operating Cost 80%.

Case (f) Sales ₹ 1,00,000, Cost of Goods is ₹ 20,000 *plus* 55% of Selling Price, Selling Expenses 5% of Sales, Administration Expenses ₹ 10,000.

Case (g) Increase in EBIT 200%, Increase in Sales 50%.

Case (h) Decrease in Operating Income $66\frac{2}{3}\%$, Decrease in Revenue $33\frac{1}{3}\%$

Case (i)	Sales Units	1000	1500
	Selling Price per unit	₹ 10	₹ 10
	EBIT	₹ 1,500	₹ 4,500
Case (j)	Sales Units	2000	3000
	Selling Price per unit	₹ 10	₹ 10
	Total Operating Cost	₹ 17,600	₹ 21,600

Case (k) Percentage drop in sales to make the EBIT zero : 20%.

Case (l) Percentage increase in Sales to double the EBIT : 20%.

SOLUTION

Case (a) Degree of Operating Leverage $= \frac{\text{Contribution}}{\text{EBIT}} = \frac{₹\ 10,000}{₹\ 2,000} = 5$

Case (b) Degree of Operating Leverage $= \frac{\text{Contribution}}{\text{EBIT}} = \frac{₹\ 20,000}{₹\ 20,000 - ₹\ 15,000} = 4$

Case (c) Degree of Operating Leverage $= \frac{\text{Contribution}}{\text{EBIT}} = \frac{₹\ 1,00,000 - ₹\ 40,000}{₹\ 1,00,000 - ₹\ 40,000 - ₹\ 30,000} = 2$

Case (d) Sales = 10,000 × ₹ 10 = ₹ 1,00,000

Variable Cost = 60% of ₹ 1,00,000 = ₹ 60,000

Contribution = ₹ 1,00,000 – ₹ 60,000 = ₹ 40,000

Fixed Costs = (90% of ₹ 1,00,000) – ₹ 60,000 = ₹ 30,000

EBIT = ₹ 40,000 – ₹ 30,000 = ₹ 10,000

Degree of Operating Leverage $= \frac{\text{Contribution}}{\text{EBIT}} = \frac{₹\ 40,000}{₹\ 10,000} = 4$

Case (e) Sales = (75% of 20,000 units) × ₹ 10 = ₹ 1,50,000

Variable Cost = (80% of ₹ 1,50,000) – ₹ 30,000 = ₹ 90,000

Contribution = ₹ 1,50,000 – ₹ 90,000 = ₹ 60,000

EBIT = ₹ 60,000 – ₹ 30,000 = ₹ 30,000

Degree of Operating Leverage $= \frac{\text{Contribution}}{\text{EBIT}} = \frac{₹\ 60,000}{₹\ 30,000} = 2$

Case (f)	₹
Sales	1,00,000
Less: Variable Cost (55% + 5%)	60,000
Contribution	40,000
Less: Fixed Cost (₹ 20,000 + ₹ 10,000)	30,000
EBIT	10,000

$DOL = \frac{Contribution}{EBIT} = \frac{₹\ 40,000}{₹\ 10,000} = 4$	

Case (g) Degree of Operating Leverage = $\frac{\text{Percentage Change in EBIT}}{\text{Percentage Change in Sales}} = \frac{200\%}{50\%} = 4$

Case (h) Degree of Operating Leverage = $\frac{\text{Percentage Change in EBIT}}{\text{Percentage Change in Sales}} = \frac{66\frac{2}{3}\%}{33\frac{1}{3}\%} = 2$

Case (i) Degree of Operating Leverage = $\frac{\Delta EBIT / EBIT}{\Delta Sales / Sales} = \frac{(₹4,500 - ₹1,500)/₹1,500}{(₹15,000 - ₹10,000)/₹10,000} = 4$

Case (j) EBIT (at 2000 units) = ₹ 20,000 – ₹ 17,600 = ₹ 2,400

EBIT (at 3000 units) = ₹ 30,000 – ₹ 21,600 = ₹ 8,400

$D.O.L. = \frac{\Delta EBIT / EBIT}{\Delta Sales / Sales} = \frac{(₹\ 8,400 - ₹\ 2,400)/₹\ 2,400}{(₹\ 30,000 - ₹\ 20,000)/₹\ 20,000} = 5$

Case (k) Degree of Operating Leverage = $\frac{\text{Percentage Change in EBIT}}{\text{Percentage Change in Sales}} = \frac{100\%}{20\%} = 5$

Case (l) Degree of Operating Leverage = $\frac{\text{Percentage Change in EBIT}}{\text{Percentage Change in Sales}} = \frac{100\%}{20\%} = 5$

ILLUSTRATION 2

Tulsian Ltd. a well-established firm in plastics, is considering the purchase of one of the two manufacturing companies. The financial manager of the company has developed the following information about the two companies. Both companies have total assets of ₹ 30,00,000.

Particulars	*X Ltd.* (₹)	*Y Ltd.* (₹)
Sales Revenue	60,00,000	60,00,000
Less: Cost of Goods Sold	(45,00,000)	(45,00,000)
Selling Expenses	(4,80,000)	(4,80,000)
Administrative Expenses	(1,80,000)	(3,00,000)
Depreciation	(2,40,000)	(1,80,000)
EBIT	6,00,000	5,40,000

Cost Break-ups		
Variable costs:		
Cost of goods sold	18,00,000	36,00,000
Selling expenses	3,00,000	3,00,000
Total	21,00,000	39,00,000

Required: Tulsian Ltd. wishes to buy a company which has a lower degree of business risk. Advise which company should be purchased assuming that:

(a) Sales increase by 30%

(b) Sales increase by 30% and Additional Sales generate a return of 10% on sales before interest & taxes. Variable costs bear linear function of sales.

(c) Sales increase by 30% and Return on Sales before interest & taxes improve by 5%.

SOLUTION

(A) TO (C) CALCULATION OF OPERATING LEVERAGE *(₹ IN LAKHS)*

Particulars	Case (a)		Case (b)		Case (c)	
	X Ltd. ₹	*Y Ltd.* ₹	*X Ltd.* ₹	*Y Ltd.* ₹	*X Ltd.* ₹	*Y Ltd.* ₹
A. Sales	78.00	78.00	78.00	78.00	78.00	78.00
B. *Less:* Variable cost						
(i) Cost of Goods Sold	23.40	46.80	23.40	46.80	23.40	46.80
(ii) Selling Expenses	3.90	3.90	3.90	3.90	3.90	3.90
Total Variable Expenses	27.30	50.70	27.30	50.70	27.30	50.70
C. Contribution [A – B]	50.70	27.30	50.70	27.30	50.70	27.30
D. *Less:* Fixed Cost						
(i) Cost of Goods Sold	27.00	9.00	27.00	9.00	27.00	9.00
(ii) Selling Expenses	1.80	1.80	1.80	1.80	1.80	1.80
(iii) Administrative Expenses	1.80	3.00	1.80	3.00	1.80	3.00
(iv) Depreciation	2.40	1.80	2.40	1.80	2.40	1.80
(v) Additional Fixed Cost	—	—	9.90	4.50	6.00	0.78
Total Fixed expenses	33.00	15.60	42.90	20.10	39.00	16.38
E. Earnings before Interest & Tax (EBIT) [C – D]	17.70	11.70	7.80	7.20	11.70	10.92
F. Operating Leverage (Contribution/EBIT)	2.86	2.33	6.50	3.79	4.33	2.50

Recommendation: Y Ltd. has lower degree of operating leverage in all three cases which means it has a lower degree of business risk. Therefore it is advisable for Tulsian Ltd. to purchase Y Ltd.

Working Notes:

(i) Variable Cost of Sales Ratio	X Ltd.	Y Ltd.
$= \frac{\text{Variable Cost}}{\text{Sales}} \times 100$	$\frac{₹\ 21\text{ lakhs}}{₹\ 60\text{ lakhs}} \times 100$ = 35%	$\frac{₹\ 39\text{ lakhs}}{₹\ 60\text{ lakhs}} \times 100$ = 65%
(ii) Additional Fixed Cost in case (b)		
Additional Sales	₹ 18.00 lakhs	₹ 18.00 lakhs
Less: Additional Variable Cost @ 35%/65%	₹ 6.30 lakh	₹ 11.70 lakh
Additional Contribution	₹ 11.70 lakh	₹ 6.30 lakhs
Less: Additional EBIT @ 10%	₹ 1.80 lakhs	₹ 1.80 lakhs
Additional fixed cost	₹ 9.90 lakhs	₹ 4.50 lakhs
(iii) Existing and New Rate of Return on Sales before Interest & Taxes		
$= \frac{\text{EBIT}}{\text{Sales}} \times 100$	$\frac{₹\ 6\text{ lakhs}}{₹\ 60\text{ lakhs}} \times 100$	$\frac{₹\ 5.40\text{ lakhs}}{₹\ 60\text{ lakhs}} \times 100$

	Existing Rate of Return on Sales	= 10%	= 19%
	Add: Increase in Rate	= 15%	= 15%
	New Rate of Return on Sales	= 15%	= 14%
(iv)	Additional Fixed Cost in Case (c)		
A.	Sales	₹ 78.00 lakhs	₹ 78.00 lakhs
B.	*Less:* Variable Cost @ 35% / 65%	₹ 27.30 lakhs	₹ 50.70 lakhs
C.	Contribution	₹ 50.70 lakhs	₹ 27.30 lakhs
D.	*Less:* EBIT @ 15% / 14%	₹ 11.70 lakhs	₹ 10.92 lakhs
E.	Total Fixed Cost	₹ 39.00 lakhs	₹ 16.38 lakhs
F.	*Less:* Existing Fixed Cost	₹ 33.00 lakhs	₹ 15.60 lakhs
G.	Additional Fixed Cost [Balancing Figure]	₹ 6.00 lakhs	₹ 0.78 lakhs

7.0 FINANCIAL LEVERAGE

MEANING OF FINANCIAL LEVERAGE

Financial Leverage is a measure of Financial Risk. The percentage change in Earnings Per Share [EPS] occurring due to a given percentage change in Earnings Before Interest & Tax [EBIT] is known as the degree of financial leverage. The financial leverage of 1.5 means that 1% increase in EBIT would result in 1.5% increase in EPS.

DECISION WITH WHICH FINANCIAL LEVERAGE IS ASSOCIATED

Financial Leverage is associated with Capital Structure Decision (or Capital Mix Decision). Its degree differs with the use of different forms of financing.

WHEN DOES FINANCIAL LEVERAGE EXIST?

Financial Leverage exists if there is use of funds bearing fixed financial payments like Debt.

HOW TO CALCULATE FINANCIAL LEVERAGE?

The degree of Financial Leverage can be calculated with the help of following formulae:

1. $\text{D.F.L.} = \dfrac{\text{Percentage Change in EPS}}{\text{Percentage Change in EBIT}} = \dfrac{\Delta \text{EPS}/\text{EPS}}{\Delta \text{EBIT}/\text{EBIT}}$
2. $\text{D.F.L. (if there is no preference dividend)} = \dfrac{\text{EBIT}}{\text{EBT}}$
3. $\text{D.F.L. (if there is preference dividend)} = \dfrac{\text{EBIT}}{\text{EBT} - \left(\dfrac{\text{Pref. Dividend}}{1-t}\right)}$

SIGNIFICANCE OF FINANCIAL LEVERAGE

Financial Leverage shows the impact of change in EBIT on EPS.

HOW DOES USE OF FINANCIAL LEVERAGE AFFECT THE FINANCIAL RISK?

Financial leverage affects the financial risk in two ways:

1. By increasing the variability in shareholders' earnings
2. By increasing the probability of insolvency on account of liquidity problems since the payments of financial charges are necessarily to be made irrespective of the fact whether the firm earns profits *or* not.

Effect on	*In case of High Degree of Financial Leverage*	*In case of Low Degree of Financial Leverage*
Variability in Shareholders' Earnings	Increases	Decreases
Probability of Insolvency	Increases	Decreases

EFFECT OF FINANCIAL LEVERAGE ON EPS

1. EPS will increase if ROI is more than the Cost of Debt.
2. EPS will decrease if ROI is *less* than the Cost of Debt.

ILLUSTRATION 3 [CALCULATION OF THE DEGREE OF FINANCIAL LEVERAGE]

Calculate the Degree of Financial Leverage in each of the following alternative cases:

Case (a) EBIT ₹ 2,000, EBT ₹ 500

Case (b) Contribution ₹ 20,000, Fixed Costs ₹ 15,000, 10% Debt ₹ 37,500

Case (c) Contribution ₹ 20,000, Fixed Costs ₹ 15,000, 10% Debt ₹ 37,500, 15% Preference Share Capital ₹ 3,000, Tax Rate 40%.

Case (d) Increase in EPS 300%, Increase in EBIT 200%.

Case (e) Decrease in EPS 75%, Decrease in Operating Income 6623 %

Case (f) Sales Units	2000	2800
EBIT	₹ 2,400	₹ 7,200
EPS	₹ 9.60	₹ 38.40

Case (g) Installed capacity 20000 units, Actual Production and Sales 75% of installed capacity, Selling Price per unit ₹ 10, Variable Costs 60%, Degree of Operating Leverage 2, 10% Debt ₹ 1,00,000, 15% Preference Share Capital ₹ 20,000, Tax Rate 40%.

Case (h) Percentage drop in EBIT to make EPS zero : 25%

Case (i) Percentage increase in EBIT to double the EPS : 25%.

SOLUTION

Case (a) Degree of Financial Leverage $= \frac{\text{EBIT}}{\text{EBT}} = \frac{₹\ 2{,}000}{₹\ 500} = 4$

Case (b) EBIT = ₹ 20,000 – ₹ 15,000 = ₹ 5,000

EBT = ₹ 5,000 – ₹ 3,750 = ₹ 1,250

Degree of Financial Leverage $= \frac{\text{EBIT}}{\text{EBT}} = \frac{₹\ 5{,}000}{₹\ 1{,}250} = 4$

Case (c) EBIT = ₹ 20,000 – ₹ 15,000 = ₹ 5,000

EBT = ₹ 5,000 – ₹ 3,750 = ₹ 1,250

$$\text{D.F.L.} = \frac{\text{EBIT}}{\text{EBT} - \left(\frac{\text{Preference dividend}}{1-t}\right)} = \frac{₹\ 5{,}000}{₹\ 1{,}250 - \left(\frac{15\% \text{ of } ₹\ 3{,}000}{1-0.40}\right)} = 10$$

Case (d) Degree of Financial Leverage $= \frac{\%\ \text{Change in EPS}}{\%\ \text{Change in EBIT}} = \frac{300\%}{200\%} = 1.5$

Case (e) Degree of Financial Leverage $= \frac{75\%}{66\frac{2}{3}\%} = 1.125$

Case (f) $\text{D.F.L.} = \frac{\Delta\text{EPS/EPS}}{\Delta\text{EBIT/EBIT}} = \frac{(₹\ 38.40 - ₹\ 9.60)/₹\ 9.60}{(₹\ 7200 - ₹\ 2400)/₹\ 2400} = \frac{3}{2} = 1.5$

Case (g) Sales = (75% of 20,000 units) × ₹ 10 = ₹ 1,50,000

Variable costs = 60% of ₹ 1,50,000 = ₹ 90,000

Contribution = ₹ 1,50,000 – ₹ 90,000 = ₹ 60,000

Degree of Operating Leverage = Contribution/EBIT

2 = ₹60,000/EBIT

EBIT = ₹ 60,000 / 2 = ₹ 30,000

EBTI = EBIT – Interest = ₹ 30,000 – (10% of ₹ 1,00,000) = ₹ 20,000

$$\text{Degree of Financial Leverage} = \frac{\text{EBIT}}{\text{EBT} - \left(\frac{\text{Preference Dividend}}{1-t}\right)}$$

$$= \frac{₹\ 30,000}{₹\ 20,000 - \left(\frac{15\% \text{ of } ₹\ 20,000}{1-0.40}\right)} = \frac{₹\ 30,000}{₹\ 15,000} = 2$$

Case (h) $\text{Degree of Financial Leverage} = \frac{\%\text{ Change in EPS}}{\%\text{ Change in EBIT}} = \frac{100\%}{25\%} = 4$

Case (i) $\text{Degree of Financial Leverage} = \frac{\%\text{ Change in EPS}}{\%\text{ Change in EBIT}} = \frac{100\%}{25\%} = 4$

8.0 WHAT IS TRADING ON EQUITY?

MEANING OF TRADING ON EQUITY

The use of the sources of funds with fixed cost, such as debt and preference share capital along with the owner's equity capital in the capital structure is known as 'financial leverage' *or* 'trading on equity'.

RATIONALE BEHIND THE USE OF THE TERM 'TRADING ON EQUITY'

The use of the term 'trading on equity' is derived from the fact that it is the owner's equity that is used as a basis to raise debt, which is the equity that is traded upon.

EBIT-EPS ANALYSIS

To examine the impact of leverage on the EPS (i.e., earning per share), EBIT-EPS analysis should be considered. EBIT-EPS analysis shows the impact of various alternative financial plans on EPS at various levels of EBIT.

FORMAT OF EBIT-EPS ANALYSIS STATEMENT

Particulars	*Equity Alternative*		*Debt Alternative*	
	Pessimistic EBIT	*Optimistic EBIT*	*Pessimistic EBIT*	*Optimistic EBIT*
A. EBIT	......	......	......	......
B. *Less:* Interest	......	......	......	......
C. EBT (A – B)	......	......	......	......
D. *Less:* Tax	......	......	......	......
E. Earning After Tax (C – D)	......	......	......	......
F. *Less:* Preference Dividend	......	......	......	......
G. Earning for Equity Shareholders	......	......	......	......

H. No. of Equity Shares	......	......	......	......
I. EPS (G/H)	......	......	......	......

ILLUSTRATION 4

Show the effect of financial leverage on EPS by considering the following two financial plans if EBIT is (a) ₹ 2,00,000 (b) ₹ 1,00,000.

Total Funds required	– ₹ 10,00,000
Financial Plan 'A'	– 100% Equity Shares of ₹ 10 each
Financial Plan 'B'	– 50% Equity Shares of ₹ 10 each, and 50%, 15% Debt.
Tax Rate	– 40%

SOLUTION

STATEMENT SHOWING THE EFFECT OF FINANCIAL LEVERAGE ON EPS & RETURN ON EQUITY

Particulars	*At EBIT Level of ₹ 2,00,000*		*At EBIT Level of ₹ 1,00,000*	
	Financial Plan 'B'	*Financial Plan 'B'*	*Financial Plan 'B'*	*Financial Plan 'B'*
A. Earning before interest and taxes	2,00,000	2,00,000	1,00,000	1,00,000
B. *Less:* Interest on long tern debt [15% on ₹ 5,00,000]	—	75,000	—	75,000
C. Earning before taxes [A – B]	2,00,000	1,25,000	1,00,000	25,000
D. *Less:* Taxes @ 40%	80,000	50,000	40,000	10,000
E. Earning after taxes [C – D]	1,20,000	75,000	60,000	15,000
F. *Less:* Preference dividend	—	—	—	
G. Earning after Interest, Taxes & Pref. Dividend	1,20,000	75,000	60,000	15,000
H. No. of Equity Shares	1,00,000	50,000	1,00,000	50,000
I. Earning per share [G/H]	₹ 1.20	₹ 1.50	₹ 0.60	₹ 0.30
J. Return on Equity				
$= \frac{\text{Earning after Interest, Tax and Pref. Dividend}}{\text{Equity Shareholders' Funds}}$	12%	15%	6%	3%

Analysis:

I. At EBIT level of ₹ 2,00,000, Plan B is the most attractive because EPS of ₹ 1.50 is higher than EPS of ₹ 1.20 as under plan 'A'. This is because of the following two reasons:

(a) Use of debt in financial plan 'B', and

(b) Return on Investment [i.e., 20% (i.e., ₹ 2,00,000 / ₹ 10,00,000 × 100)] is more than the Cost of debt [i.e., 15%]

II. At EBIT level of ₹ 1,00,000, Plan 'A' is the most attractive because EPS of 60 paise is higher than EPS of 30 paise as under plan 'B'. This is because of the following two reasons:

(a) Use of debt in financial plan 'B', and

(b) Return on Investment [i.e., 10% (i.e., ₹ 1,00,000 / ₹ 10,00,000 × 100)] is *less* than the Cost of Debt [i.e., 15%].

ADVANTAGE AND DISADVANTAGE OF USE OF DEBT

The financial leverage is a double-edged sword because on the one hand, it increases shareholders' return and, on the other hand, it increases their risk. It will have a favourable impact on EPS (Earning Per Share) and ROE (Return On Equity) if Return on Investment exceeds the cost of debt but it will have an unfavourable impact if Return on Investment is *less* than the cost of debt. The advantage of debt is that it saves taxes since interest is a deductible expense. The disadvantage is that it can cause financial distress. Financial distress becomes costly when the firm finds it difficult to pay interest and principal portion of debt.

ADVANTAGE AND DISADVANTAGE OF NOT USING DEBT

A firm can avoid financial risk altogether if it does not use any debt in its capital structure. But when no debt is used in the capital structure, the shareholders will be deprived of the benefit of increase in EPS arising from financial leverage (a trading on equity).

SHOULD A FIRM EMPLOY DEBT?

A firm should employ debt to the extent the financial risk perceived by the shareholders does not exceed the benefit of increased EPS. It can be shown as follows:

Case	*If ROI > Cost of Debt*		*If ROI < Cost of Debt*	
	Effect on EPS	*Effect on Financial Risk*	*Effect on EPS*	*Effect on Financial Risk*
I. Use of more debt in capital structure	Increase	Increase	Decreases & it may even lead to negative EPS.	Increases threat of insolvency
II. Use of *less* debt in capital structure	Relatively *less* increase	Relatively *less* increase	Relatively *less* decrease	Relatively *less* increase

9.0 COMBINED LEVERAGE

MEANING OF COMBINED LEVERAGE

Combined Leverage is a measure of Total Risk. The percentage change in EPS occurring due to a given percentage change in Sales is known as the degree of combined leverage. It is the product of degree of operating leverage and degree of financial leverage.

DECISION WITH WHICH COMBINED LEVERAGE IS ASSOCIATED

It is associated with Capital Budgeting Decision (or Assets Mix Decision) and Capital Structure Decision (or Capital Mix Decision). Its degree differs with the use of different forms of financing.

WHEN DOES COMBINED LEVERAGE EXIST?

Combined Leverage exists if there are *either* fixed costs *or* funds bearing fixed financial payments *or* both.

HOW TO CALCULATE COMBINED LEVERAGE?

Combined Leverage can be calculated with the help of following formulae:

1. $\text{D.C.L} = \dfrac{\text{Percentage Change in EPS}}{\text{Percentage Change in Sales}} = \dfrac{\Delta\text{EPS/EPS}}{\Delta\text{Sales/Sales}}$

2. $\text{D.C.L. (if there is no preference dividend)} = \dfrac{\text{Contribution}}{\text{EBIT}} \times \dfrac{\text{EBIT}}{\text{EBT}} = \dfrac{\text{Contribution}}{\text{EBT}}$

3. D.C.L. (if there is preference dividend) $= \dfrac{\text{Contribution}}{\text{EBIT}} \times \dfrac{\text{EBIT}}{\text{EBT} - \dfrac{\text{Preference Dividend}}{(1-t)}}$

$$= \frac{\text{Contribution}}{\text{EBT} - \dfrac{\text{Preference Dividend}}{(1-t)}}$$

4. D.C.L. = Degree of Operating Leverage Degree of Financial Leverage.

WHAT DOES COMBINED LEVERAGE INDICATE?

Combined Leverage indicates the total risk associated with the enterprise. This ratio should be as low as possible. This can be done only if one of the two leverages (i.e., Operating Leverage and Financial Leverage) is kept low. If one leverage is higher, the other should be lower. However, it is preferable to have low operating leverage and high financial leverage provided the Rate of Return on Investment is higher than the cost of funds bearing fixed financial payments. The impact of different combinations of operating leverage and financial leverage has been shown below:

Degree of Operating Leverage	*Degree of Financial Leverage*	*Nature of Situation*
High	High	Risky
High	Low	Normal
Low	High	Normal
Low	Low	Ideal

FORMAT OF STATEMENT SHOWING THE CALCULATION OF DEGREES OF VARIOUS LEVERAGES

Particulars	*Financial Plan 1*	*Financial Plan 2*
A. Sales	......	......
B. *Less:* Variable Costs	......	......
C. Contribution	......	......
D. *Less:* Fixed Costs	......	......
E. Earnings Before Interest & Tax (EBIT)	......	......
F. *Less:* Interest	......	......
G. Earnings Before Tax (EBT)	......	......
H. *Less:* Tax	......	......
I. Earnings After Tax (EAT)	......	......
J. *Less:* Preference Dividend	......	......
K. Earnings available for Equity Shareholders	......	......
L. No. of Equity Shares	......	......
M. Earnings per Share (EPS) (K/L)	......	......
N. Price Earning Ratio (P/E Ratio)	......	......
O. Market Price (EPS × P/E Ratio)	......	......
P. Operating Leverage (Contribution/EBIT)	......	......
Q. Financial Leverage	......	......

If there is no Preference Dividend = $\frac{\text{EBIT}}{\text{EBT}}$		
If there is Preference dividend = $\frac{\text{EBIT}}{\text{EBT} - \left(\frac{\text{Pref. Dividend}}{1-t}\right)}$		
R. Combined Leverage (Operating Leverage × Financial Leverage)	……	……

Tutorial Notes:

(i) In case EBT is negative, tax saving may be deducted from the loss assuming that the company has taxable income from other sources against which such loss can be set off. Alternatively, tax may be taken as Nil assuming that such loss can be carried forward to next years. Unless otherwise stated in the examination, former alternative should be used.

(ii) In case Earning After Tax (EAT) is *less* than the amount of Preference Dividend, full amount of preference dividend is to be deducted to ascertain negative EPS.

(iii) Profit Volume Ratio (or P/V Ratio) is the ratio of Contribution to Sales.

(iv) P/V Ratio may be used to calculate the sales level at which EBIT/EBT/EPS will be zero as follows:

(a) Sales Level at which EBIT will be Zero = Fixed Costs/P/V Ratio

[or, Cost Break Even Point]

(b) Sales Level at which EBT will be Zero = Fixed Costs + Interest/P/V Ratio

(c) Sales Level at which EPS will be Zero = $\frac{\text{Fixed Costs + Interest + [Pref. Dividend/(1 – t)]}}{\text{P/V Ratio}}$

ILLUSTRATION 5 [CALCULATION OF COMBINED LEVERAGE]

Calculate the Degree of Combined Leverage in each of the following alternative cases:

Case (a) Contribution ₹ 20,000, EBIT ₹ 5,000, EBT ₹ 1,250.

Case (b) Sales ₹ 1,00,000, Variable Costs 80%, Operating Costs 95%, 10% Debt ₹ 37,500.

Case (c) Operating Costs ₹ 18,000, Variable Costs ₹ 10,000, EBT ₹ 500, 10% Debt ₹ 15,000.

Case (d) Degree of Operating Leverage 5, Degree of Financial Leverage 4.

Case (e) Increase in EPS 300%, Increase in Sales 50%.

Case (f) Decrease in EPS 75%, Decrease in Sales 3313 %

Case (g) Sales Units	2000	2800
Selling Price per unit	₹ 10	₹ 10
EPS	₹ 9.60	₹ 38.40

Case (h) Installed capacity 20000 units, Actual Production and Sales 75% of installed capacity, Selling Price per unit ₹ 10, Variable Costs 60%, Degree of Operating Leverage 2, 10% Debt ₹ 1,00,000, 15% Preference Share Capital ₹ 20,000, Tax Rate 40%

Case (i) Percentage drop in Sales to make the EPS zero : 6.25%.

Case (j) Percentage increase in Sales to double the EPS : 6.25%.

SOLUTION

Case (a) D.C.L. = Degree of Operating Leverage × Degree of Financial Leverage

$$= \frac{\text{Contribution}}{\text{EBIT}} \times \frac{\text{EBIT}}{\text{EBT}} = \frac{₹\ 20{,}000}{₹\ 5{,}000} \times \frac{₹\ 5{,}000}{₹\ 1{,}250} = 16$$

Case (b) Variable Costs = 80% of ₹ 1,00,000 = ₹ 80,000

Contribution = ₹ 1,00,000 – ₹ 80,000 = ₹ 20,000

Fixed Costs = 95% of ₹ 1,00,000 – ₹ 80,000 = ₹ 15,000

EBIT = Contribution – Fixed Costs = ₹ 20,000 – ₹ 15,000 = ₹ 5,000

EBT = EBIT – Interest = ₹ 5,000 – 10% of ₹ 37,500 = ₹ 1,250.

D.C.L. = Degree of Operating Leverage × Degree of Financial Leverage

$$= \frac{\text{Contribution}}{\text{EBIT}} \times \frac{\text{EBIT}}{\text{EBT}} = \frac{₹\ 20,000}{₹\ 5,000} \times \frac{₹\ 5,000}{₹\ 1,250} = 16$$

Case (c) EBIT = EBT + Interest = ₹ 500 + 10% of ₹ 15,000 = ₹ 2,000

Contribution = EBIT + Fixed Costs = ₹ 2,000 + (₹ 18,000 – ₹ 10,000) = ₹ 10,000

D.C.L. = Degree of Operating Leverage × Degree of Financial Leverage

$$= \frac{\text{Contribution}}{\text{EBIT}} \times \frac{\text{EBIT}}{\text{EBT}} = \frac{₹\ 10,000}{₹\ 2,000} \times \frac{₹\ 2,000}{₹\ 500} = 20$$

Case (d) D.C.L. = Degree of Operating Leverage × Degree of Financial Leverage

= 5 × 4 = 20

Case (e) D.C.L. $= \frac{\text{Percentage Change in EPS}}{\text{Percentage Change in Sales}} = \frac{300\%}{50\%} = 6$

Case (f) D.C.L. $= \frac{\text{Percentage Change in EPS}}{\text{Percentage Change in Sales}} = \frac{75\%}{33\frac{1}{3}\%} = 2.25$

Case (g) D.C.L. $= \frac{\Delta\text{EPS/EPS}}{\Delta\text{Sales/Sales}} = \frac{(₹\ 38.40 - ₹\ 9.60)/₹\ 9.60}{(₹\ 28,000 - ₹\ 20,000)/₹\ 20,000} = \frac{3}{0.40} = 7.5$

Case (h) Sales = (75% of 20,000 units) × ₹ 10 = ₹ 1,50,000

Variable costs = 60% of ₹ 1,50,000 = ₹ 90,000

Contribution = ₹ 1,50,000 – ₹ 90,000 = ₹ 60,000

D.O.L. = Contribution/EBIT

2 = ₹60,000/EBIT

EBIT = ₹ 60,000/2 = ₹ 30,000

EBT = EBIT – Interest = ₹ 30,000 – (10% of ₹ 1,00,000) = ₹ 20,000

$$\text{D.F.L.} = \frac{\text{EBIT}}{\text{EBT} - \left(\frac{\text{Preference Dividend}}{1-t}\right)} = \frac{₹\ 30,000}{₹\ 20,000 - \left(\frac{15\% \text{ of } ₹\ 20,000}{1-0.40}\right)}$$

= ₹30,000/₹15,000 = 2

D.C.L. = D.O.L. × D.F.L. = 2 × 2 = 4

Alternatively, $\text{D.C.L.} = \frac{\text{Contribution}}{\text{EBT} - \frac{\text{Preference Dividend}}{(1-t)}} = \frac{₹\ 60,000}{₹\ 20,000 - \frac{15\% \text{ of } ₹\ 20,000}{(1-0.40)}} = 4$

Case (i) Degree of Combined Leverage $= \frac{\text{Percentage Change in EPS}}{\text{Percentage Change in Sales}} = \frac{100\%}{6.25\%} = 16$

Case (j) Degree of Combined Leverage $= \frac{\text{Percentage Change in EPS}}{\text{Percentage Change in Sales}} = \frac{100\%}{6.25\%} = 16$

ILLUSTRATION 6

Tulsian (6) Ltd. provides you the following information:

Operating Leverage 2, Combined Leverage 5, Profit / Volume Ratio 40%, Tax Rate 40%, Earnings After Tax ₹ 7.20 lakhs.

Required:

(a) Calculate the percentage drop is Sales to make the EBIT Zero.

(b) Calculate the percentage drop is EBIT to make the EPS Zero.

(c) Calculate the percentage drop is Sales to make the EPS Zero.

(d) At what sales level, the EBIT will be Zero ?

(e) At what sales level, the EBT will be Zero ?

(f) At what sales level, the EPS will be Zero ?

SOLUTION

(a) Percentage drop in sales to make the EBIT Zero.

$$\text{Degree of Operating Leverage} = \frac{\text{Percentage Change in EBIT}}{\text{Percentage Change in Sales}}$$

$$2 = \frac{100\%}{\text{Percentage change in Sales}}$$

Percentage change in Sales to make EBIT zero = 100%/2 = 50%.

(b) Percentage drop in EBIT to make the EPS zero.

$$\text{Degree of Operating Leverage} = \frac{\text{Percentage Change in EBIT}}{\text{Percentage Change in Sales}}$$

$$2.5 = \frac{100\%}{\text{Percentage change in Sales}}$$

Percentage change in EBIT to make EPS zero = 100%/2.5 = 40%.

(c) Percentage drop in sales to make the EPS zero.

D.C.L. = Degree of Operating Leverage × Degree of Financial Leverage = 2 × 2.5 = 5

$$\text{Degree of Operating Leverage} = \frac{\text{Percentage Change in EBIT}}{\text{Percentage Change in Sales}}$$

$$5 = \frac{100\%}{\text{Percentage change in Sales}}$$

Percentage Change in sales = 100%/5 = 20%.

Working Notes: for Part (d), (e) and (f)

EBT = EAT/(1 – Tax Rate) = ₹ 7.20 lakh/(1 – 0.40)	= ₹ 12 lakhs.
Contribution = EBT × Combined Leverage = ₹ 12 lakhs × 5	= ₹ 60 lakhs.
EBIT = Contribution / Operating Leverage = ₹ 60 lakhs / 2	= ₹ 30 lakhs.
Sales = Contribution / P/V Ratio = ₹ 60 lakhs / 0.40	= ₹ 150 lakhs.
Fixed Cost = Contribution – EBIT = ₹ 60 lakhs – ₹ 30 lakhs	= ₹ 30 lakhs.
Interest = EBIT – EBT = ₹ 30 lakhs – ₹ 12 lakhs	= ₹ 18 lakhs.

(d) **Method I**

% change in Sales to make EBIT Zero = 50% [as per part (a)]

Therefore, Sales level at which EBIT will be zero = ₹ 150 lakh – 50% of ₹ 150 lacs = ₹ 75 lacs.

Method II

Sales level at which EBIT will be zero = $\frac{\text{Fixed Cost}}{\text{P/V Ratio}} = \frac{₹ 30 \text{ lakhs}}{40\%}$ = ₹ 75 lakhs.

Method III

Assume Sales be X and Calculate EBIT in terms of X and then equate it equal to zero and find out the value of X.

(e) **Method I**

EBT zero means 100% reduction in EBT

Therefore, % drop in Sales = 100% / Combined Leverage = 100% / 5 = 20%

Sales level at which EBT will be Zero = ₹ 150 × 80% = ₹ 120 lakhs

Tutorial Note: This method is to applied only when Combined Leverage does not take Preference Dividend into consideration.

Method II

Sales level at which EBT will be zero = $\frac{\text{Fixed Cost + Interest}}{\text{P/V Ratio}} = \frac{₹ 30 \text{ lakhs} + ₹ 18 \text{ lakhs}}{40\%}$

= ₹ 120 lakhs

Method III

Assume Sales be X and calculate EBT in terms of X and then equate it equal to zero and find out the value of X.

(f) **Method I**

% change in sales to make EPS zero = 20% [as per part (c)]

Therefore, Sales level at which EPS will be zero = 80% of ₹ 150 lakhs = ₹ 120 lakhs.

Method II

Sales level at which EPS will be zero = $\frac{\text{Fixed Cost + Interest + [Pref. Dividend/(1 – t)]}}{\text{P/V Ratio}}$

= $\frac{₹ 30 \text{ lakhs} + ₹ 18 \text{ lakhs} + 0}{40\%}$ = ₹ 120 lakhs.

Method III

Assume Sales be X and Calculate EPS in terms of X and then equate it equal to zero and find out the value of X.

ILLUSTRATION 7

Tulsian Ltd. provides you the following information:

1.	Variable cost as percentage of sales	= 60%
2.	10% Debt	= ₹ 130 lakhs
3.	15% Preference Share Capital	= ₹ 20 lakhs
4.	Degree of Operating Leverage	= 2 : 1
5.	Degree of Financial Leverage	= 2.5 : 1
6.	Income Tax Rate	= 40%
7.	Equity Share Capital of ₹ 10 each	= ₹ 36 lakhs
8.	Reserves and Surplus	= ₹ 55 lakhs
9.	Miscellaneous Expenditure	= ₹ 1 lakhs

Required:

(a) Calculate the percentage drop in Sales to make the EBIT zero.

(b) Calculate the percentage drop in EBIT to make the EPS zero.

(c) Calculate the pecentage drop in Sales to make the EPS zero.

(d) At what Sales level, the EBIT will be zero?

(e) At what Sales level, the EBT will be zero?

(f) At what Sales level, the EPS will be zero?

(g) Calculate the percentage of change in EBIT, EBT and EPS if the Sales drop to ₹ 120 lakh.

(h) Determine the likely level of EBIT if EPS is ₹ 1.

SOLUTION

(a) Percentage drop in sales to make the EBIT Zero.

$$\text{Degree of Operating Leverage} = \frac{\text{Percentage Change in EBIT}}{\text{Percentage Change in Sales}}$$

$$2 = \frac{100\%}{\text{Percentage Change in Sales}}$$

Percentage change in Sales to make EBIT zero = 100%/2 = 50%.

(b) Percentage drop in EBIT to make the EPS zero.

$$\text{Degree of Financial Leverage} = \frac{\text{Percentage Change in EPS}}{\text{Percentage Change in EBIT}}$$

$$2.5 = \frac{100\%}{\text{Percentage Change in EBIT}}$$

Percentage change in EBIT to make EPS zero = 100%/2.5 = 40%.

(c) Percentage drop in sales to make the EPS zero.

D.C.L. = Degree of Operating Leverage × Degree of Financial Leverage = 2 × 2.5 = 5

$$\text{Degree of Combined Leverage} = \frac{\text{Percentage Change in EPS}}{\text{Percentage Change in Sales}}$$

$$5 = \frac{100\%}{\text{Percentage Change in Sales}}$$

Percentage Change in sales = 100%/5 = 20%.

Working Notes for Parts (d), (e) and (f):

Step 1: Calculation of Fixed Cost

$$\text{Degree of Financial Leverage} = \frac{\text{EBIT}}{\text{EBT} - \frac{\text{Pref. Dividend}}{1-t}} = \frac{\text{EBIT}}{(\text{EBIT} - \text{Interest}) - \frac{\text{Pref. Dividend}}{1-t}}$$

$$2.5 = \frac{X}{(X - ₹\,13\text{ lakh}) - \frac{₹\,3\text{ Lakh}}{(1-0.40)}} \text{ (Assuming EBIT = X)}$$

$$2.5 = \frac{X}{X - ₹\,18\text{ lakhs}}$$

$$X = ₹\,30\text{ lakhs}$$

Thus, Contribution = EBIT × D.O.L. = ₹ 30 lakh × 2 = ₹ 60 lakh.

Fixed Cost = Contribution – EBIT = ₹ 60 lakh – ₹ 30 lakh = ₹ 30 lakh.

Step 2: Calculation of EBIT, EBT and EPS assuming Sales be X

A. Sales	X
B. *Less:* Variable Cost	0.60 X
C. Contribution	0.40 X
D. *Less:* Fixed Cost	₹ 30 lakhs
E. EBIT	0.40 X – ₹ 30 lakhs
F. *Less:* Interest	₹ 13 lakh
G. EBT	0.40 X – ₹ 43 lakhs
H. *Less:* Tax	40% (.40 X – ₹ 43 lakhs)
I. EAT	0.24 X – 25.8 lakh
J. *Less:* Pref. Dividend	₹ 3 lakhs
K. Earnings available for Equity Shareholders	0.24 X – ₹ 28.8 lakhs
L. No. of Equity Shares	36 lakhs
M. EPS	$\frac{0.24\text{ X} - ₹\ 28.8\text{ lakhs}}{36\text{ lakhs}}$

(d) Sales Level at which EBIT will be zero:

0.40 X – ₹ 30 lakhs = 0

X = ₹ 30 lakhs / 0.40 = ₹ 75 lakhs

(e) Sales Level at which EBT will be zero:

0.40 X – ₹ 43 lakhs = 0

X = ₹ 43 lakhs / 0.40 = ₹ 107.50 Lakhs

(f) Sales Level at which EPS will be zero:

$$\frac{0.26\text{ X} - ₹\ 28.8\text{ lakh}}{36\text{ lakhs}} = 0$$

X = ₹ 28.8 lakhs / 0.24 = ₹ 120 Lakhs

Alternative Method for Part (d)

% Change in Sales to make EBIT zero = 50% [as per part (a)]

Therefore, Sales level at which EBIT will be zero = 150 lakh – 50% of ₹ 150 lakhs = ₹ 75 lakhs

Alternative Method for Part (f)

% change in Sales to make EPS zero = 20% [as per part (c)]

Therefore, Sales Level at which EPS will be zero = ₹ 150 lacs – 20% of ₹ 150 lacs = ₹ 120 lacs

Alternative Method based on P/V Ratio

$$\text{Profit – Volume Ratio (P/V Ratio)} = \frac{\text{Contribution}}{\text{Sales}} \times 100 = \frac{₹\ 60\text{ lakh}}{₹\ 150\text{ lakh}} \times 100 = 40\%$$

(d) Sales Level at which EBIT will be zero $= \frac{\text{Fixed Costs}}{\text{P/V Ratio}} = \frac{₹\ 30\text{ lakh}}{40\%} = ₹\ 75\text{ lakhs}$

[or Cost Break Even Point]

(e) Sales Level at which EBT will be zero $= \frac{\text{Fixed Costs + Interest}}{\text{P/V Ratio}}$

$$= \frac{₹\ 30\text{ lakh} + ₹\ 13\text{ lakh}}{40\%} = ₹\ 107.50\text{ Lakh}$$

(f) Sales Level at which EPS will be zero $= \dfrac{\text{Fixed Cost + Interest} + \dfrac{\text{Pref. Dividend}}{(1-t)}}{\text{P/V Ratio}}$

$= \dfrac{₹\,30\text{ lakh} + ₹\,13\text{ lakh} + \dfrac{₹\,3\text{ lakh}}{(1-0.40)}}{40\%} = ₹\,120\text{ Lakh}$

(g) % of fall in Sales $= \dfrac{₹\,150\text{ lakh} - ₹\,120\text{ lakh}}{₹\,150\text{ lakh}} = 20\%$

% Change in EBIT = % Change in Sales × Operating Leverage = 20% × 2 = 40%.

% Change in EPS = % Change in EBIT × Financial Leverage = 40% × 2.5 = 100%

Alternatively

% Change in EPS = % Change in Sales × Combined Leverage = 20% × 5 = 100%.

% Change in EBT $= \dfrac{\Delta EBT}{EBT} \times 100 = \dfrac{17-5}{17} \times 100 = 70.59\%$

Particulars	*Present (₹ Lakh)*	*Proposed (₹ Lakh)*	*Change (₹ Lakh)*
A. Sales	150	120	(30)
B. *Less:* Variable Cost	90	72	(18)
C. Contribution	60	48	(12)
D. *Less:* Fixed Costs	30	30	–
E. EBIT	30	18	(12)
F. *Less:* Interest	13	13	0
G. EBT	17	5	(12)

(h) % change in EBIT $= \dfrac{\text{\% change in EPS}}{\text{Degree of Financial Leverage}} = \dfrac{(₹\,2 - ₹\,1)/2}{2.5} = 20\%$

Likely Level of EBIT at EPS of ₹ 1 = EBIT (1 – 0.20) = ₹ 30 lakhs × 0.80 = ₹ 24 lakhs.

10.0 INDIFFERENCE POINT

MEANING OF INDIFFERENCE POINT

Indifference point refers to that level of EBIT (i.e. Earnings Before Interest and Tax) at which EPS (i.e., Earnings Per Share) would be same irrespective of the method of financing the new funds requirements.

RELEVANCE OF INDIFFERENCE POINT

Indifference point enables the management to know a point-

(a) before which equity alternative is favourable to raise the necessary finance.

(b) beyond which debt alternative is favourable to raise the necessary finance.

(c) at which, *either* of the alternative is favourable to raise the necessary finance.

HOW TO COMPUTE INDIFFERENCE POINT?

Indifference Point can be computed as follows:

(I) DIRECT FORMULA APPROACH

$$\frac{(EBIT - I_1)(1-t) - \text{Preference dividend}}{ES_1} = \frac{(EBIT - I_2)(1-t) - \text{Preference dividend}}{ES_2}$$

Where, I_1 represents Interest on Debt under alternative 1

ES_1 represents Number of Equity Shares under alternative 1

I_2 represents Interest on Debt under alternative 2

ES_2 represents Number of Equity Shares under alternative 2

Notes:

(i) Preference Dividends have been deducted after making adjustment of tax since Preference dividends are not deductible for tax purposes. Preference dividend is an appropriation out of profits and not charge against profits.

(ii) The total number of equity shares can be calculated as follows:

$$\text{Existing No. of Equity Shares} + \frac{\text{Desired Additional Funds}}{\text{Issue Price of an Equity Share} - \text{Flotation Costs per share}}$$

(II) STATEMENT APPROACH

Step 1: Assume that level of EBIT at which EPS would be the same under both the financial plans, equal to X.

Step 2: Calculate EPS under both the financial plans as follows:

STATEMENT SHOWING THE CALCULATION OF INDIFFERENCE POINT

Particulars	*Proposed Financial Plan 1*	*Proposed Financial Plan 2*
A. Earnings before Interest & Tax (EBIT)	X	X
B. *Less:* Interest	......	......
C. Earnings before Tax (EBT)	......	......
D. *Less:* Tax	......	......
E. Earnings after tax (EAT)	......	......
F. *Less:* Pref. Dividend	......	......
G. Earnings for Equity Shareholders	......	......
H. No. of Equity Shares	......	......
I. Earnings per Share (EPS) (Earnings for equity shareholders/No. of equity shares)	......	......

Step 3: Calculate Indifference Point by equating EPS under two Financial Plans.

WHEN SHALL THE INDIFFERENCE POINT BE INDETERMINATE?

The Indifference Point between any two financial plans shall be indeterminate if the number of equity shares under both the financial plans are equal.

SHALL THE MARKET PRICE BE SAME FOR BOTH THE FINANCIAL PLANS AT INDIFFERENCE POINT?

At indifference point, the market price per share need not necessarily be the same for all types of financial plans. The market price will be more for a share, which has higher proportion of equity in its capital structure.

GRAPHICAL REPRESENTATION

Plot two sets of EBIT-EPS coordinates for each financial plan on the graph and the point at which the two lines intersect is called Indifference Point.

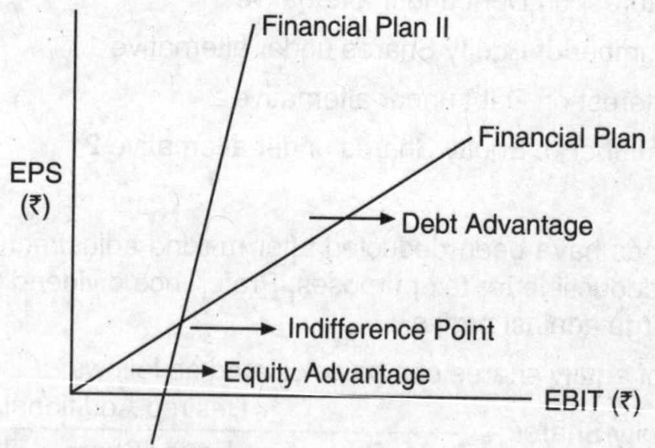

Fig. Equity Advantage, Indifference Point and Debt Advantage

ILLUSTRATION 8 [CALCULATION OF INDIFFERENCE POINT]

Tulsian (8) Ltd. provides you the following information:

1. Funds required : ₹ 10,00,000
2. Financial Plans :
   Financial Plan I : 100% Equity Shares of ₹ 10 each, Current Market Price ₹ 26, Floatation Cost Per Equity Share ₹1
   Financial Plan II : 40% Equity Shares of ₹ 10 each, Current Market Price ₹ 21, Floatation Cost Per Equity Share ₹ 1, 60%, 10% Debentures of ₹ 100 each.
   Financial Plan III : 40% Equity Shares of ₹ 10 each, Premium in Market 110%, Floatation Cost Per Equity Share ₹ 1, 40%, 10% Debentures of ₹ 100 each. 20%, 15% Preference Shares of ₹ 100 each
3. Tax Rate : 40%

Required: Calculate the Indifference Point between:

(a) Financial Plan I and II (b) Financial Plan II and III (c) Financial Plan I and III.

SOLUTION

Let the EBIT at which EPS will be same, be X

STEP 1: CALCULATION OF EPS

Particulars	*Financial Plan I*	*Financial Plan II*	*Financial Plan III*
A. EBIT	X	X	X
B. *Less:* Interest on Debt	—	60,000	40,000
C. EBT [A – B]	X	X – 60,000	X – 40,000
D. *Less:* Tax @ 40%	0.4 X	0.4 (X – 60,000)	0.4 (X – 40,000)
E. EAT [C – D]	0.6 X	0.6 X – 36,000	0.6 X – 24,000
F. *Less:* Pref. Dividend	—	—	30,000
G. Earnings for E.S.	0.6 X	0.6 X – 36,000	0.6 X – 54,000

H. No. of Equity Shares	40,000	20,000	20,000
I. EPS [G/H]	0.6X/40,000	0.6X – 36,000/20,000	0.6X – 54,000/20,000

Step 2: Calculation of Indifference Point by equating EPS under two plans:

(i) Between Financial Plan I and II

= 0.6X/40,000 = (0.6X – 36,000)/20,000

Multiplying both the sides by 40,000

0.6 X = 2 (0.6 X – 36,000)

1.2 X – 0.6 X = 72,000

X = 72,000 / 0.6 = ₹ 1,20,000

(ii) Between Financial Plan II and III

= (0.6X – 36,000)/20,000= (0.6X – 54,000)/20,000

Multiplying both the sides by 20,000

0.6 X – 36,000 = 0.6X – 54,000

0.6 X – 0.6 X = – 54,000 + 36,000

Thus, indifference point between Plans II and III is indeterminate.

(iii) Between Financial Plan I and III

= 0.6X/40,000 = (0.6X – 54,000)/20,000

Multiplying both the sides by 20,000

0.3 X = 0.6X – 54,000

X = 54,000/0.3 = ₹ 1,80,000

11.0 UNCOMMITTED EPS APPROACH

MEANING OF UNCOMMITTED EPS APPROACH

Uncommitted EPS approach is useful to the conservative decision makers who look to debt not only in the terms of interest payment, but also in terms of its repayment. Therefore, they want to get an idea of earnings, which could meet both the payments. However, this approach is of short-term significance only since after the redemption of debentures, the Debenture Redemption Reserve is to be transferred to general reserve and thus forms a part of equity shareholders' funds.

INDIFFERENCE POINT UNDER UNCOMMITTED EPS APPROACH

(a) **Meaning:** It refers to that level of EBIT at which Uncommitted Earnings Per Share (UEPS) would be same where transfers to Debenture Redemption Reserves (or Sinking Fund) are made.

$$\text{UEPS} = \frac{\text{Earnings available for Equity shareholders after transfer to Debenture Redemption Reserve}}{\text{Number of Equity Shares}}$$

(b) **How to compute Indifference Point under Uncommitted EPS Approach?**

Indifference Point can be computed as follows:

$$\frac{(\text{EBIT} - I_1)(1-t) - \text{Preference Dividend} - S_1}{ES_1} = \frac{(\text{EBIT} - I_2)(1-t) - \text{Preferece Dividend} - S_2}{ES_2}$$

Where; I_1 represents Interest on Debt under alternative 1

ES_1 represents Number of Equity Shares under alternative 1

I_2 represents Interest on Debt under alternative 2

ES_2 represents Number of Equity Shares under alternative 2

S_1 represents Sinking Fund obligations (i.e. Amount to be transferred to Debenture Redemption reserve) under alternative 1

S_2 represents Sinking Fund obligations (i.e. Amount to be transferred to Debenture Redemption reserve) under alternative 2

ILLUSTRATION 9 [CALCULATION OF INDIFFERENCE POINT UNDER UNCOMMITTED EPS APPROACH]

Tulsian (9) Ltd. provides you the following information:

1. Funds required : ₹ 10,00,000
2. Financial Plans:

   Financial Plan I : 50% Equity Shares of ₹ 10 each, Current Market Price ₹ 20, 50%, 10% Debentures of ₹ 100 each.

   Financial Plan II : 40% Equity Shares of ₹ 10 each, Premium in Market 100%, 40%, 10% Debentures of ₹ 100 each, 20%, 15% Preference Shares of ₹ 100 each.
3. Tax Rate : 40%
4. Annual Transfer to Debenture Redemption Reserve : 20% of the Face Value of Debentures.

Required: Calculate the Indifference Point under uncommitted EPS Approach.

SOLUTION

Let the EBIT at which EPS will be same, be X.

STEP 1: CALCULATION OF UNCOMMITTED EPS

Particulars	Financial Plan I	Financial Plan II
A. EBIT	X	X
B. *Less:* Interest on Debt	50,000	40,000
C. EBT [A – B]	X – 50,000	X – 40,000
D. *Less:* Tax @ 40%	0.4 (X – 50,000)	0.4 (X – 40,000)
E. EAT [C – D]	0.6 (X – 50,000)	0.6 (X – 40,000)
F. *Less:* Pref. Dividend		30,000
T/F to Debenture Redemption Reserve	1,00,000	80,000
G. Uncommitted earnings for Equity Shareholders [E – F]	0.6 X – 1,30,000	0.6 X – 1,34,000
H. No. of Equity Shares	25,000	20,000
I. Uncommitted EPS [G/H]	0.6X – 1,30,000/25,000	0.6X – 1,34,000/20,000

Step 2: Calculation of Indifference Point by equating Uncommitted EPS under two plans:

$$\frac{0.6X - 1,30,000}{25,000} = \frac{0.6X - 1,34,000}{20,000}$$

Multiplying both the sides by 20,000

$$0.8\,(0.6X - 1,30,000) = 0.6X - 1,34,000$$

$$0.48\,X - 1,04,000 = 0.6X - 1,34,000$$

$$X = ₹\ 30,000/0.12 = ₹\ 2,50,000$$

12.0 WHICH FORM OF FINANCING SHOULD BE EMPLOYED?

If the firm follows the policy of seeking to maximize the price of its shares, that form of financing should be employed under which market price of firm's share is maximum.

However, if the market price is same under both the alternatives under consideration, then firm's decision in this regard should be guided by other qualitative factors.

Examination Note: In the absence of P/E Ratio, the choice of financial plan is to be made on the basis of EPS.

ILLUSTRATION 10 [CHOICE OF FINANCIAL PLAN]

Which of the following three Financial Plans would you recommend and why?

Particulars	*Equity Plan*	*Equity Preference Share Plan*	*Equity Debt. Plan*
Earning Per Share	₹ 9.50	₹ 8	₹ 11.25
Price-Earning Ratio	20	17	16

SOLUTION

MARKET PRICE UNDER EACH FINANCIAL PLAN

Particulars	*Equity Plan*	*Equity Preference Share Plan*	*Equity Debt. Plan*
A. Earning Per Share	₹ 9.50	₹ 8	₹ 11.25
B. Price-Earning Ratio	20	17	16
C. Market Price [A × B]	₹ 190	₹ 136	₹ 180

Recommendation: The objective of financial management is to maximise the wealth of the owners, which in the context of companies means maximising the market price of the company's equity shares. The above analysis shows that the market price per share is the highest in the case of equity financing. Therefore, equity financing alternative is recommended.

ILLUSTRATION 11

Tulsian (11) Ltd. provides you the following information:

1. Funds required : ₹ 10,00,000
2. Financial Plans :

   Financial Plan I : 100% Equity Shares of ₹ 10 each, Current Market Price ₹ 25

   Financial Plan II : 40% Equity Shares of ₹ 10 each, Current Market Price ₹ 20. 60%, 10% Debentures of ₹ 100 each.

   Financial Plan III : 40% Equity Shares of ₹ 10 each, Premium in Market 100%. 40%, 10% Debentures of ₹ 100 each. 20%, 15% Preference Shares of ₹ 100 each
3. Tax Rate : 40%
4. Earnings Before Interest & Tax : 5% on Capital Employed.

Required: Which Financial Plan would you recommend and why ?

SOLUTION

STATEMENT SHOWING THE EVALUATION OF FINANCIAL PLANS

Particulars	*Financial Plan I*	*Financial Plan II*	*Financial Plan III*
A. EBIT (5% of ₹ 10,00,000)	50,000	50,000	50,000

B. *Less:* Interest	—	60,000	40,000
C. EBT	50,000	(10,000)	10,000
D. *Less:* Tax @ 40%	20,000	4,000*	(4,000)
E. EAT	30,000	(6,000)	6,000
F. *Less:* Pref. Dividend	—	—	30,000
G. Earnings for Equity shareholders (E – F)	30,000	(6,000)	(24,000)
H. No. of Equity Shares	40,000	20,000	20,000
I. EPS (G / H)	₹ 0.75	(₹ 0.30)	(₹ 1.20)

Recommendation: In the absence of P/E Ratio, the choice of Financial Plan is to be made on the basis of EPS. Hence, Financial Plan I is recommended since EPS under this Plan is the highest.

* Tax Saving has been deducted from the loss assuming that the company has taxable income from other sources against which such loss can be set off.

ILLUSTRATION 12

A Co. presents you the following figures:

Particulars		₹
EBIT		24,00,000
Less: Interest on Debentures @ 8%	2,00,000	
Less: Interest on long term loans @ 10%	2,00,000	4,00,000
EBT		20,00,000
Less: Income Tax @ 40%		8,00,000
Profit after tax : EAT		12,00,000
No. of Equity Shares (of ₹ 10 each)		4,00,000
Rulling market price		24
Undistributed Reserves & Surplus		65,00,000

The Co. need to raise ₹ 45,00,000 for repayment of Debentures and modernisation of its plants and seeks your opinion as to which of the following modes of raising the needful funds on the consideration of the probable price of the share to rule on implementation:

1. Raising the entire funds by 10% Term loans from Banks
2. Raising partly by issue of 1,00,000 equity shares @ ₹ 18 per share and the rest by 10% Term loans from Bank.

The Co. expects that the rate of return i.e., profit before tax and interest on funds employed will improve by 4% because of modernisation and that if the Debt Equity ratio (i.e. Debt/Debt *plus* Shareholders' Funds) exceeds 35%, the P.E. Ratio is to go down by 25%.

SOLUTION

STATEMENT SHOWING THE EVALUATION OF FINANCIAL PLANS

Particulars	*Debt plan* ₹	*Debt-Equity plan* ₹
A. Earnings before Interest & Tax (EBIT)	34,00,000	34,00,000
B. *Less:* Interest	6,50,000	4,70,000

C. Earnings before Tax (EBT)	27,50,000	29,30,000
D. *Less:*Tax @ 40%	11,00,000	11,72,000
E. Earning for Equity Shareholders	16,50,000	17,58,000
F. No. of Equity shares	4,00,000	5,00,000
G. Earnings per share (EPS)	4.125	3.516
H. Price Earning Ratio	6.0	8.00
I. Market Price [G × H]	24.75	28.13

Recommendation: Debt-Equity Plan is recommended since the market price of an equity share would be higher under Debt equity plan than under Debt – Plan

Working Notes:

(I) CALCULATION OF RATE OF RETURN

Funds employed	₹
Debentures [₹ 2,00,000 / 8%]	25,00,000
Long term loans [₹ 2,00,000 / 10%]	20,00,000
Equity Share Capital [4,00,000 × ₹ 10]	40,00,000
Reserves & Surplus	65,00,000
Total	150,00,000
Earnings before Interest & Tax (EBIT)	24,00,000
Rate of Return [(EBIT/Total funds employed) × 100]	16%

(II) CALCULATION OF NEW FUNDS & NEW EBIT

Particulars	₹
A. Old funds	150,00,000
B. Additonally financed	45,00,000
C. Debt Redeemption	(25,00,000)
D. New Funds [A + B – C]	170,00,000
E. New Rate of Return	20%
F. Earnings before Interest & Tax (EBIT) [D × E]	34,00,000

(III) CALCULATION OF INTEREST

Debt-Plan [(20,00,000 + 45,00,000) × 10%] = 6,50,000

Debt-Equity Plan [(20,00,000 + 27,00,000) × 10%] = 4,70,000

(IV) CALCULATION OF DEBT – EQUITY RATIO

Debt-Plan [(65,00,000/170,00,000) × 100] = 38.24%

Debt-Equity Plan [(47,00,000/170,00,000) × 100] = 27.65%

(V) CALCULATON OF NEW P/E RATIO IF D/E RATIO EXCEEDS 35%.

$$\text{Existing P/E Ratio} = \frac{\text{Market Price}}{\text{EPS}} = \frac{₹\ 24}{₹\ 12,00,000/4,00,000} = 8$$

New P/E Ratio = 75% of 8 = 6.

13.0 FINANCIAL BREAK EVEN POINT (FBEP)

MEANING OF FINANCIAL BREAK EVEN POINT (FBEP)

It refers to that level of EBIT (i.e. Earning before Interest and taxes) at which firm is just able to meet all fixed financial payments like Interest on Debt and Preference Dividend.

HOW TO CALCULATE FBEP?

FBEP can be calculated with the help of the following formula:

$$\text{FBEP} = \text{Interest} + \frac{\text{Preference Dividend}}{(1-\text{Tax})}$$

EFFECT OF FBEP ON EPS

EBIT > FBEP	EPS will have favourable effect.
EBIT < FBEP	EPS will have adverse effect.

ILLUSTRATION 13 [CALCULATION OF FINANCIAL BREAK EVEN POINT]

Calculate Financial Break Even Point for each financial plan in Illustration 11. Also indicate, if any of the plans dominate.

SOLUTION

$$\text{Financial Break Even Point (FBEP)} = \text{Interest} + \frac{\text{Preference Dividend}}{(1-\text{Tax})}$$

FBEP for Financial Plan I $= 0 + \frac{0}{(1-0.4)} = 0$

FBEP for Financial Plan II $= ₹\,60{,}000 + \frac{0}{1-0.4} = ₹\,60{,}000$

FBEP for Financial Plan III $= ₹\,40{,}000 + \frac{₹\,30{,}000}{(1-0.4)} = ₹\,90{,}000$

Domination of Plan: Plan I dominates Plan II and III as the financial BEP of Plant I is the lowest.

14.0 IMPACT OF CAPITAL TURNOVER RATIO AND CURRENT RATIO ON FINANCIAL RISK AND RETURN ON INVESTMENT

If the turnover increases without a corresponding rise in working capital, the working capital position becomes tight. If the current ratio and acid test ratio are high, the capital turnover ratio can be increased without any problem. High capital turnover ratio together with low current ratio indicates the situation of over trading, (or under capitalization) which is very risky as the risk of insolvency increases. Low Capital Turnover Ratio together with high current ratio indicates the situation of under trading, (or Over Capitalization) which represents the presence of idle funds *or* lack of profitable opportunities. The impact of Capital Turnover Ratio on Financial Risk and Return on Investment is shown below:

Situation	*Capital Turnover Rati*	*Current Ratio*	*Return on Investment*	*Financial Risk*	*Management's Action*
Over trading	High	Low	High	Exist	Raise Funds
Under trading	Low	High	Low	Does not exist	Repay funds *or* Explore new profitable opportunities

15.0 IMPACT OF FINANCIAL LEVERAGE ON SHAREHOLDERS' WEALTH BY USING RETURN-ON-INVESTMENT (ROI) AND RETURN ON EQUITY (ROE) ANALYTIC FRAMEWORK

The impact of Financial Leverage on ROE is **positive if** Return on Investment after tax (ROI after tax) is **greater** than the cost of sources of funds bearing fixed financial payments like Debt, Preference Capital and is **negative if** ROI (after tax) is **lower** than the cost of sources of funds bearing fixed financial payments like Debt, Preference Capital.

1. ROE without using ROI Rate

$$\text{ROE} = \frac{\text{Earnings after Interest, tax \& Preference Dividend}}{\text{Equity Shareholders' Funds}} \times 100$$

Note: Equity Share Holders Funds = Equity Share Capital + Reserves and Surplus − Miscellaneous Expenditure.

2. ROE using ROI Rate when there is no Preference Share Capital in the capital structure.

$$\text{ROE} = \text{ROI (after tax)} + \frac{\text{Debt}}{\text{Equity}}[\text{ROI (after tax)} - \text{Cost of Debt (after tax)}]$$

Notes: (i) $\text{ROI (After tax)} = \frac{\text{EBIT}(1-t)}{\text{Capital Employed}}$

or, = Net Operating Profit (after tax) Ratio × Capital Turnover

or, $= \frac{\text{EBIT}(1-t)}{\text{Sales}} \times \frac{\text{Sales}}{\text{Capital Employed}}$

(ii) Capital Employed = Equity Shareholders' Funds + Pref. Share Capital + Long-term Debts.

3. ROE using ROI Rate when there is also Preference Share Capital in the capital structure.

$$\text{ROE} = \text{ROI (after tax)} + \frac{\text{Debt}}{\text{Equity}}[\text{ROI (after tax)} - \text{Cost of Debt (after tax)}]$$

$$+ \frac{\text{Preference Share Capital}}{\text{Equity}}[\text{ROI (after tax)} - \text{Rate of Preference Dividend}]$$

Notes: (i) $\text{ROI (After tax)} = \frac{\text{EBIT}(1-t)}{\text{Capital Employed}}$

or, = Net Operating Profit (after tax) Ratio × Capital Turnover

or, $= \frac{\text{EBIT}(1-t)}{\text{Sales}} \times \frac{\text{Sales}}{\text{Capital Employed}}$

(ii) Capital Employed = Equity Shareholders' Funds + Pref. Share Capital + Long-term Debts.

ILLUSTRATION 14

Calculate Return on Equity Shareholders' Funds in each of the following alternative cases:

(a) EBIT ₹ 6,00,000, 15% Debt ₹ 8,00,000, Tax Rate 50% Equity Share Capital ₹ 1,00,000, Reserves and Surplus ₹ 3,00,000, Miscellaneous Expenditure ₹ 1,00,000, 18% Preference Share Capital ₹ 1,00,000.

(b) Return on Investment (before tax), 50%, Debt-Shareholders' Funds Ratio 2 : 1, Rate of Interest on Debt 15%, Tax Rate 50%.

(c) Return on Investment (before tax) 50%, Debt-Shareholders' Funds Ratio 2 : 1, Rate of Interest on Debt 15%, Tax Rate 50%, 18% Preference Share Capital to Equity Shareholders' Funds 1 : 3.

(d) Operating Profit (before tax) Ratio 40%, Capital Turnover Ratio 1.25 times, Debt-Shareholders' Funds Ratio 2 : 1, Rate of Interest on Debt 15%, Tax Rate 50%.

(e) Operating Profit (before tax) Ratio 25% Capital Turnover Ratio 2 times, Debt-Shareholders' Funds Ratio 2 : 1, Capital Gearing Ratio 3 : 1, Interest on 15% Debt ₹ 1,20,000, 18% Preference Share Capital ? Tax Rate 50%.

SOLUTION

(a) Return on Equity Shareholders' Funds $= \frac{\text{Earnings after Interest, Tax \& Pref. Dividend}}{\text{Equity Shareholders' Funds}} \times 100$

$$= \frac{₹\ 2,22,000^{*}}{₹\ 3,00,000^{**}} \times 100 = 74\%$$

Notes:

* = EBIT – Interest – Tax – Pref. Dividend

= ₹ 6,00,000 – ₹ 1,20,000 – ₹ 2,40,000 – ₹ 18,000 = ₹ 2,22,000

** = ₹ 1,00,000 + ₹ 3,00,000 – ₹ 1,00,000 = ₹ 3,00,000.

(b) Return on Equity Shareholder's Funds $= \text{ROI (after tax)} + \frac{\text{Debt}}{\text{Equity}}$ [ROI (after tax) – Cost of Debt (after tax)]

$$= 25\% + 2/1(25\% - 7.5\%) = 60\%.$$

(c) Return on Equity Shareholders' Funds

$$= \text{ROI (after tax)} + \frac{\text{Debt}}{\text{Equity Shareholders' Funds}} [\text{ROI (after tax)} - \text{Cost of Debt (after tax)}]$$

$$+ \frac{\text{Preference share Capital}}{\text{Equity Shareholders' Funds}} [\text{ROI (after tax)} - \text{Rate of Pref. Dividend}]$$

$$= 25\% + \frac{8}{3}[25\% - 7.5\%] + \frac{1}{3}[25\% - 18\%]$$

$$= 25\% + 46.67\% + 2.33\% = 74\%.$$

Note: Preference to Equity = 1 : 3

Let Preference Share Capital be 1, then Equity Shareholders' Funds = 3

$$\text{Debt – Shareholder's Funds} = \frac{\text{Long-term Debts}}{\text{Equity Shareholders' Funds + Pref. Share Capital}}$$

$$2 = \frac{\text{Long Term Debts}}{3 + 1}$$

Long Term Debt = 4 × 2 = 8

(d) Return on Investment (after tax) $= \frac{\text{OP (after tax)}}{\text{Sales}} \times \frac{\text{Sales}}{\text{Capital Employed}}$

$$= 40\% (1 - .50) \times 1.25 = 25\%.$$

Cost of Debt (after tax) = 15% (1 – .50) = 7.5%

Return on Equity Shareholders' Funds $= \text{ROI (after tax)} + \frac{\text{Debt}}{\text{Equity}}$ [ROI (after tax) – Cost of Debt (after tax)]

$$= 25\% + 2/1(25\% - 7.5\%) = 60\%$$

(e) Return on Equity Shareholders' Funds

$$= \text{ROI (after tax)} + \frac{\text{Debt}}{\text{Equity Shareholders' Funds}} [\text{ROI (after tax)} - \text{Cost of Debt (after tax)}]$$

$$+ \frac{\text{Preference share Capital}}{\text{Equity Shareholders' Funds}} [\text{ROI (after tax)} - \text{Rate of Pref. Dividend}]$$

$$= 25\% + 8/3\ [25\% - 7.5\%] + 1/3\ [25\% - 18\%]$$

$$= 25\% + 46.67\% + 2.33\% = 74\%.$$

Working Notes:

(i) ROI (after tax) = Operating Profit (after tax) Ratio × Capital Turnover Ratio

= 25% (1 – 0.5) × 2 = 25%

(ii) Cost of Debt (after tax) = 15% (1 – 0.5) = 7.5%

(iii) Cost of Pref. Share (after tax) = 18% (given)

(iv) 15% Debt = Interest / .15 = ₹ 1,20,000 / 0.15 = ₹ 8,00,000

(v) Shareholder's Funds = Long-term Debt / Debt-Shareholders' Funds Ratio = ₹ 8,00,000 / 2 = ₹ 4,00,000

(vi) Let Pref. Share Capital = X, then Equity Shareholder's Funds = ₹ 4,00,000 – X

(vii) Pref. Share Capital and Equity Shareholders Funds

$$\text{Capital Gearing Ratio} = \frac{\text{Long-term Debt + Pref. Share Capital}}{\text{Equity Shareholders' Funds}}$$

3 = (₹ 8,00,000 + X)/(₹ 4,00,000 – X)

₹ 12,00,000 – 3 X = ₹ 8,00,000 + X

X = ₹ 1,00,000

Therefore, Pref. Share capital = ₹ 1,00,000

Equity Shareholders' Funds = ₹ 4,00,000 – ₹ 1,00,000 = ₹ 3,00,000

ILLUSTRATION 15

Tulsian Ltd. provides you the following information:

1. Variable cost as percentage of sales = 60%
2. 10% Debt = ₹ 130 lakhs
3. 15% Preference Share Capital = ₹ 20 lakhs
4. Degree of Operating Leverage = 2 : 1
5. Degree of Financial Leverage = 2.5 : 1
6. Income Tax Rate = 40%
7. Equity Share Capital of ₹ 10 each = ₹ 36 lakhs
8. Reserves and Surplus = ₹ 55 lakhs
9. Miscellaneous Expenditure = ₹ 1 lakhs

Required:

(a) Calculate Return on Investment (ROI), Return on Equity Shareholders' Funds (ROE)and Price-Earning Ratio if market price of an equity share is ₹ 20. Does it have a favourable financial leverage ?

(b) Also indicate segments of ROE due to presence of Preference Share Capital and Debt.

SOLUTION

(a)Calculation of ROI and ROE

Step 1: Calculation of EBIT (Assuming EBIT = X)

$$\text{Degree of Financial Leverage} = \frac{\text{EBIT}}{\text{EBT} - \frac{\text{Pref. Dividend}}{1-t}} = \frac{\text{EBIT}}{(\text{EBIT} - \text{Interest}) - \frac{\text{Pref. Dividend}}{1-t}}$$

$$2.5 = \frac{X}{(X - ₹\,13\text{ lakh}) - \frac{₹\,3\text{ lakh}}{(1-.40)}}$$

$$2.5 = \frac{X}{X - ₹\ 18 \text{ lakhs}}$$

$$X = ₹\ 30 \text{ lakhs}$$

$$\text{Return on Investment (ROI)} = \frac{\text{EBIT}}{\text{Capital Employed}} \times 100$$

$$= \frac{₹\ 30}{(₹\ 130 + ₹\ 20 + ₹\ 36 + ₹\ 55 - ₹\ 1)} \times 100 = 12.5\%$$

$$\text{Return on Equity Shareholders' Funds (ROE)} = \frac{\text{Earnings for Equity Shareholders'}}{\text{Equity Shareholders' Funds}} \times 100$$

$$= \frac{₹\ 7.2}{(₹\ 36 + ₹\ 55 - ₹\ 1)} \times 100 = 8\%$$

EARNINGS FOR EQUITY SHAREHOLDERS

A.	EBIT	₹ 30 lakhs
B.	*Less:* Interest	₹ 13 lakhs
C.	EBT [A – B]	₹ 17 lakhs
D.	*Less:* Tax @ 40%	₹ 6.8 lakhs
E.	EAT [C – D]	₹ 10.2 lakhs
F.	*Less:* Pref. Dividend	₹ 3.0 lakhs
G.	Earnings for equity Shareholders	₹ 7.20 lakhs

H. $\text{EPS} = \frac{\text{Earnings for Equity Shareholders}}{\text{No. of Equity Shares}} = \frac{₹\ 7.20 \text{ lakh}}{3.60 \text{ lakh}} = ₹\ 2 \text{ per share}$

I. $\text{Price-Earning Ratio} = \frac{\text{Market Price}}{\text{EPS}} = \frac{₹\ 20}{₹\ 2} = 10$

The company has a favourable Financial Leverage so far as use of debt is concerned since ROI (i.e. 12.5%) is greater than the Cost of Debt. (i.e. 10%). The company has not a favourable financial leverage so far as use of preference share capital is concerned since ROI (i.e., 12.5%) is lower than the Cost of Pref. Share (i.e., 15%).

(B) SEGMENT OF ROE DUE TO PRESENCE OF PREFERENCE SHARE CAPITAL AND DEBT

Particulars	*Equity Shareholders' Funds (90)*	*Pref. Share Capital (20)*	*Debt. (130)*
A. EBIT @ 12.5%	11.25	2.5	16.25
B. *Less:* Interest	—	—	13.00
C. EBT [EBIT – Interest]	11.25	2.5	3.25
D. *Less:* Tax @ 40%	4.50	1.0	1.30
E. EAT [EBT – Tax]	6.75	1.5	1.95
F. *Less:* Pref. Dividend	—	3.0	—
G. Earnings for Equity	6.75	(1.5)	1.95

$$\text{Net \% Change due to presence of PSC and Debt} = \frac{(-1.50 + 1.95)}{₹\ 90 \text{ lakhs}} \times 100 = 0.5\%$$

Verification

ROE = Return due to use of Equity share Capital + Return due to use of Pef. Share Capital & Debt.

$$ROE = \frac{₹\ 6.75\ lakh}{₹\ 90.00\ lakhs} \times 100 + 0.5\% = 8\%$$

or, = [ROI (1 – t) + 0.5%] = 12.5% (1 – 0.40) + 0.5% = 8%.

DU-PONT CHART TO CALCULATE RETURN ON EQUITY (ROE)

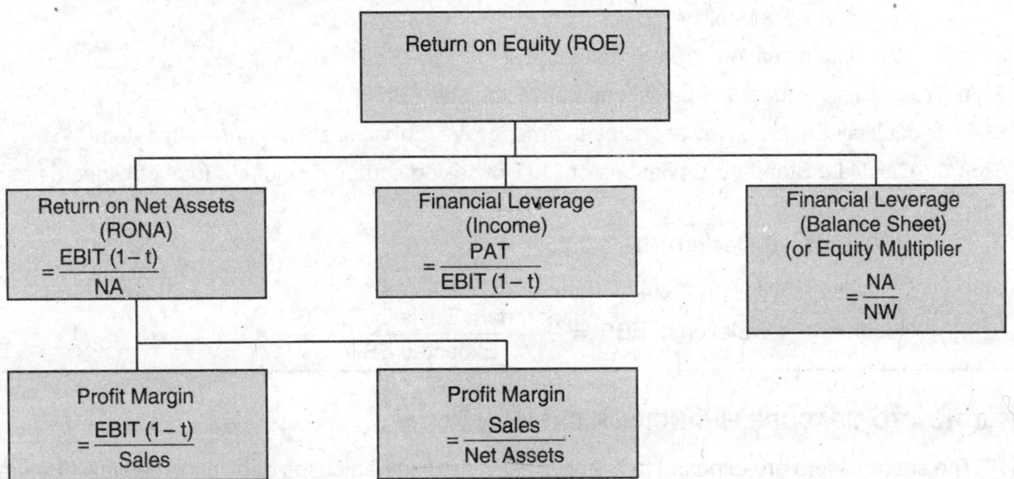

Example: EBIT ₹ 6,00,000, 15% Debt ₹ 8,00,000, Tax Rate 50%, Equity Shareholders' Funds ₹ 4,00,000, Sales ₹ 15,00,000.

SOLUTION

PAT = EBIT – Interest – Tax = ₹ 6,00,000 – ₹ 1,20,000 – ₹ 2,40,000 = ₹ 2,40,000.

1. Profit Margin = $\frac{EBIT\ (1-t)}{Sales} = \frac{₹\ 3,00,000}{₹\ 15,00,000} = 0.20$

2. Assets Turnover = $\frac{Sales}{Net\ Assets} = \frac{₹\ 15,00,000}{₹\ 12,00,000} = 1.25$

3. Return on Net Assets = $\frac{EBIT\ (1-t)}{Sales} \times \frac{Sales}{Net\ Assets} = 0.20 \times 1.25 = 0.25$

4. Financial Leverage (Income) = $\frac{PAT}{EBIT\ (1-t)} = \frac{₹\ 2,40,000}{₹\ 3,00,000} = 0.80$

5. Financial Leverage (Balance Sheet) = $\frac{NA}{NW} = \frac{₹\ 12,00,000}{₹\ 4,00,000} = 3$

6. Return on Equity (ROE) = $\frac{EBIT\ (1-t)}{NA} \times \frac{PAT}{EBIT\ (1-t)} \times \frac{NA}{NW} = 0.25 \times 0.80 \times 3 = 0.6$ *or* 60%.

16.0 HOW TO MEASURE OPERATING RISK?

1. The shareholders are always exposed to operating risk even if the company does not use debt.
2. In the absence of debt in the capital structure, the variability of EPS will be the same as the variability of EBIT.
3. Operating Risk can be measured by determining the Standard Deviation and Coefficient of Variation of Expected EBIT (i.e., Expected Earnings before Interest & Taxes).

4. **Practical Steps involved in the measurement of Operating Risk.**

   The measurement of Operating Risk involves the following steps:

Step 1: Calculate Expected EBIT as follows:

$$\text{Expected EBIT} = P_1\,(EBIT_1) + P_2\,(EBIT_2) + P_3\,(EBIT_3) + \ldots P_n\,(EBIT_n)$$

Where, P = Probability

Step 2: Calculate deviations from Expected EBIT

Step 3: Calculate squares of deviations from Expected EBIT

Step 4: Multiply Squared Deviations by the respective probabilities and obtain their total

Step 5: Calculate Standard Deviations of EBIT by taking square root of the total obtained as per Step 4, as follows:

$$\sqrt{\Sigma P\,(\text{EBIT} - \text{Expected EBIT})^2}$$

Step 6: Calculate Coefficient of Variation of EBIT as follows:

$$\text{Coefficient of Variation of EBIT} = \frac{\text{Standard Deviation of EBIT}}{\text{Expected EBIT}} \times 100$$

17.0 HOW TO MEASURE FINANCIAL RISK?

1. The shareholders are exposed to financial risk if the company uses debt in the capital structure.
2. The use of debt increases both risk and return. An increase in debt increases both the expected value of EPS and its Standard Deviation *or* Coefficient of Variation.
3. Financial Risk can measured by determining the Standard Deviation and Coefficient of Variation of Expected EPS (i.e., Expected Earning per Share).
4. **Practical Steps involved in the measurement of Financial Risk**

   The measurement of Financial Risk involves the following steps:

Step 1: Calculate Expected EPS as follows:

$$\text{Expected EPS} = P_1\,(EPS_1) + P_2\,(EPS_2) + P_3\,(EPS_3) + \ldots P_n\,(EPS_n)$$

Where, P = Probability

Step 2: Calculate deviations from Expected EPS

Step 3: Calculate squares of deviations from Expected EPS

Step 4: Multiply Squared Deviations by the respective probabilities and obtain their total

Step 5: Calculate Standard Deviations of EPS by taking square root of the total obtained as per step 4, as follows:

$$\sqrt{\Sigma P\,(\text{EPS} - \text{Expected EPS})^2}$$

Step 6: Calculate Coefficient of Variation of EPS

$$\text{Coefficient of Variation of EPS} = \frac{\text{Standard Deviation of EPS}}{\text{Expected EPS}} \times 100$$

ILLUSTRATION 16

MP Ltd. is considering expansion of its plant capacity to meet the growing demand. The company would finance the expansion *either* with 15% Debentures *or* issue of 10 lakhs equity shares at a price of ₹ 18 per share. The funds requirement is ₹ 180 lakhs. The company's profit and loss statement before expansion is as follows:

Sales	₹ 1,500 lakhs
Less: Costs	₹ 1,050 lakhs
EBIT	₹ 450 lakhs
Less: Interest	₹ 50 lakhs
EBT	₹ 400 lakhs
Less: Tax @ 40%	₹ 160 lakhs
EAT	₹ 240 lakhs
No. of Equity Shares	50 lakhs
EPS	₹ 4.8

The company's expected EBIT with associated probabilities after expansion is as follows:

EBIT ₹ (in lakh)	*Probability*
250	0.1
450	0.3
540	0.5
630	0.1

Required: Calculate the company's expected EBIT and EPS and Standard Deviation of EPS and EBIT for each plan.

SOLUTION

STEP 1: STATEMENT SHOWING THE EBIT & EPS UNDER EQUITY FINANCING PLAN

Particulars	*(₹ in lakhs)*	*(₹ in lakhs)*	*(₹ in lakhs)*	*(₹ in lakhs)*
A. Earnings before Interest & Tax (EBIT)	250	450	540	630
B. *Less:* Interest	50	50	50	50
C. Earnings before Tax (EBT)	200	400	490	580
D. *Less:* Tax @ 40%	80	160	196	232
E. Earning for Equity Shareholders	120	240	294	348
F. No. of Equity Shares	60	60	60	60
G. Earnings Per Share (EPS)	2.00	4	4.90	5.80

STEP 2: STATEMENT SHOWING THE EBIT & EPS UNDER DEBT-FINANCING PLAN

Particulars	*(₹ in lakhs)*	*(₹ in lakhs)*	*(₹ in lakhs)*	*(₹ in lakhs)*
A. Earnings before Interest & Tax (EBIT)	250	450	540	630
B. *Less:* Interest	77	77	77	77
C. Earnings before Tax (EBT)	173	373	463	553
D. *Less:* Tax @ 40%	69.20	149.20	185.20	221.20
E. Earning for Equity Shareholders	103.80	223.80	277.80	331.80
F. No. of Equity Shares	50	50	50	50
G. Earnings Per Share (EPS) (Approx.)	2.08	4.48	5.56	6.64

STEP 3: STATEMENT SHOWING THE EXPECTED EBIT UNDER BOTH THE PLANS

EBIT *A*	*Probability* *B*	*Expected EBIT* *C = A × B*
250	0.10	25
450	0.30	135
540	0.50	270
630	0.10	63
Total	1.00	493

STEP 4: STATEMENT SHOWING THE EXPECTED EPS UNDER BOTH THE PLANS

Probability Under Equity Plan *A*	*EPS Under Equity Plan* *B*	*Expected EPS Under Debt Plan* *C = A × B*	*EPS Under Debt Plan* *D*	*Expected EPS* *E = D × A*
0.10	2.00	0.20	2.08	0.208
0.30	4.00	1.20	4.48	1.344
0.50	4.90	2.45	5.56	2.780
0.10	5.80	0.58	6.64	0.664
1.00		4.43	18.76	4.996 *or* 5

STEP 5: STATEMENT SHOWING THE STANDARD DEVIATION OF EBIT UNDER BOTH THE PLANS

Probability *A*	*EBIT* *B*	*EBIT – Ex. EBIT* *C = B – 493*	*(EBIT – Ex. EBIT)²* *D = C × C*	*E = D × A*
0.10	250	– 243	59049	5904.90
0.30	450	– 43	1849	554.70
0.50	540	47	2209	1104.50
0.10	630	137	18769	1876.90
Total				9441.00

Standard Deviation of EBIT $= \sqrt{\Sigma P\ (\text{EBIT} - \text{Expected EBIT})^2} = \sqrt{9441} = 97.16$

Co-efficient of Variation of EBIT = (Standard Deviation of EBIT/Expected EBIT) × 100

= (97.16/493) × 100 = 19.71%

STEP 6: STATEMENT SHOWING STANDARD DEVIATION OF EPS UNDER BOTH THE PLANS

Probability	*Under equity Plan*				*Under Debt Plan*			
	EPS	*EPS – Ex. EPS*	*(EPS – Ex. EPS)²*	*P(EPS –Ex. EPS)²*	*EPS*	*EPS – Ex.*	*H = G²*	*G × GI = H × A*
A	*B*	*C = B – 4.43*	*D = C × C*	*E = D × A*	*F*	*G = F – 5*		
0.10	2.0	– 2.43	5.9049	0.59049	2.08	– 2.92	8.5264	0.85264
0.30	4.0	– 0.43	0.1849	0.05547	4.48	– 0.52	0.2704	0.08112
0.50	4.9	0.47	0.2209	0.11045	5.56	0.56	0.3136	0.1568
0.10	5.8	1.37	1.8769	0.18769	6.64	1.64	2.6896	0.26896
				0.9441				1.35952

Standard Deviation of EPS

Under Equity plan = $\sqrt{\Sigma P\,(\text{EPS} - \text{Expected EPS})^2} = \sqrt{0.9441} = 0.9716$

Under Debt plan = $\sqrt{1.35952} = 1.166$

Co-efficient of Variation

Under Equity Plan = (Standard Deviation of EPS/Expected EPS) × 100

= (0.9716/4.43) × 100 = 21.93%

Under Debt Plan = (Standard Deviation of EPS/Expected EPS) × 100

= (1.166/5) × 100 = 23.32%

SOLVED PROBLEMS – I

PROBLEM 1

Calculate the Operating Leverage, Financial Leverage, the Combined Leverage and Earnings after tax for the following firms:

Particulars	*A*	*B*	*C*
Output (Units)	60,000	15,000	1,00,000
Total Operating Costs	₹ 1,90,000	₹ 3,65,000	₹ 35,000
Variable Cost per unit (as % of sales)	33-1/3 %	30%	20%
10% Borrowed Capital	₹ 4,00,000	₹ 8,00,000	NIL
Selling Price per unit	₹ 6.00	₹ 50	₹ 1
Tax Rate	40%	40%	40%

SOLUTION

STATEMENT SHOWING THE CALCULATION OF DEGREE OF VARIOUS LEVERAGES

Particulars	*Firm A* ₹	*Firm B* ₹	*Firm C* ₹
A. Sales	3,60,000	7,50,000	1,00,000
B. *Less:* Variable Costs	1,20,000	2,25,000	20,000
C. Contribution	2,40,000	5,25,000	80,000
D. *Less:* Fixed Costs	70,000	1,40,000	15,000
E. Earnings before Interest & Tax (EBIT)	1,70,000	3,85,000	65,000
F. *Less:* Interest	40,000	80,000	—
G. Earnings before Tax (EBT)	1,30,000	3,05,000	65,000
H. *Less:* Tax @ 40%	52,000	1,22,000	26,000
I. Earnings after Tax (EAT)	78,000	1,83,000	39,000
J. Operating Leverage (Contribution/EBIT)	1.41	1.36	1.23
K. Financial Leverage (EBIT/EBT)	1.31	1.26	1.00
L. Combined Leverage (Operating Leverage × Financial Leverage)	1.85	1.71	1.23

PROBLEM 2

Calculate the Operating Leverage, Financial Leverage, Combined Leverage and Earning after tax under situation A, B and C and financial plans I, II and III respectively from the following information relating to the operation and capital structure of XYZ co. Also find out the combination of operating and financial leverage which give the highest value and the least value.

Installed Capacity		1200 Units
Actual Production and Sales		800 Units
Selling Price per Unit		₹ 15
Variable Cost per unit		66–2/3%
Fixed Cost:	Situation A	₹ 1,000
	Situation B	₹ 2,000
	Situation C	₹ 3,000

Tax Rate 40%	*Financial Plan*		
	I	*II*	*III*
Equity	₹ 5,000	₹ 7,500	₹ 2,500
12% Debt.	₹ 5,000	₹ 2,500	₹ 7,500

SOLUTION

CALCULATION OF DEGREE OF VARIOUS LEVERAGES (SITUATION A)

Particulars	*Plan 1* ₹	*Plan 2* ₹	*Plan 3* ₹
A. Sales	12,000	12,000	12,000
B. *Less:* Variable Costs	8,000	8,000	8,000
C. Contribution	4,000	4,000	4,000
D. *Less:* Fixed Costs	1,000	1,000	1,000
E. Earnings before Interest & Tax (EBIT)	3,000	3,000	3,000
F. *Less:* Interest	600	300	900
G. Earnings before Tax (EBT)	2,400	2,700	2,100
H. *Less:* Tax @ 40%	960	1,080	840
I. Earnings after Tax (EAT)	1,440	1,620	1,260
J. Operating Leverage (Contribution/EBIT)	1.33	1.33	1.33
K. Financial Leverage (EBIT/EBT)	1.25	1.11	1.43
L. Combined Leverage (Operating Leverage × Financial Leverage)	1.66	1.48	1.90

CALCULATION OF DEGREE OF VARIOUS LEVERAGES (SITUATION B)

Particulars	*Plan 1* ₹	*Plan 2* ₹	*Plan 3* ₹
A. Sales	12,000	12,000	12,000
B. *Less:* Variable Costs	8,000	8,000	8,000

C. Contribution	4,000	4,000	4,000
D. *Less:* Fixed Costs	2,000	2,000	2,000
E. Earnings before Interest & Tax (EBIT)	2,000	2,000	2,000
F. *Less:* Interest	600	300	900
G. Earnings before Tax (EBT)	1,400	1,700	1,100
H. *Less:* Tax @ 40%	560	680	440
I. Earnings after Tax (EAT)	840	1,020	660
J. Operating Leverage (Contribution/EBIT)	2.00	2.00	2.00
K. Financial Leverage (EBIT/EBT)	1.43	1.18	1.82
L. Combined Leverage (Operating Leverage × Financial Leverage)	2.86	2.36	3.64

CALCULATION OF DEGREE OF VARIOUS LEVERAGES (SITUATION C)

Particulars	*Plan 1* ₹	*Plan 2* ₹	*Plan 3* ₹
A. Sales	12,000	12,000	12,000
B. *Less:* Variable Costs	8,000	8,000	8,000
C. Contribution	4,000	4,000	4,000
D. *Less:* Fixed Costs	3,000	3,000	3,000
E. Earnings before Interest & Tax (EBIT)	1,000	1,000	1,000
F. *Less:* Interest	600	300	900
G. Earnings before Tax (EBT)	400	700	100
H. *Less:* Tax @ 40%	160	280	40
I. Earnings after Tax (EAT)	240	420	60
J. Operating Leverage (Contribution/EBIT)	4.00	4.00	4.00
K. Financial Leverage (EBIT/EBT)	2.50	1.43	10.00
L. Combined Leverage (Operating Leverage × Financial Leverage)	10.00	5.72	40.00

Highest value: Situation C & Financial Plan 3

Least value: Situation A & Financial Plan 2

PROBLEM 3

A firm has Sales of ₹ 10,00,000, Variable Cost of 70% Total Costs ₹ 9,00,000 and Debt of ₹ 5,00,000 at 10% Rate of Interest, Tax rate is 40%. What are the Operating, Financial, Combined Leverages and Earning after tax ? If the firm wants to double up its Earnings Before Interest and Tax (EBIT), how much of a rise in sales would be needed on a percentage basis?

SOLUTION

STATEMENT SHOWING THE CALCULATION OF DEGREE OF VARIOUS LEVERAGES

Particulars	₹
A. Sales	10,00,000

B.	*Less:* Variable Costs	7,00,000
C.	Contribution	3,00,000
D.	*Less:* Fixed Costs	2,00,000
E.	Earnings before Interest & Tax (EBIT)	1,00,000
F.	*Less:* Interest	50,000
G.	Earnings before Tax (EBT)	50,000
H.	*Less:* Tax @ 40%	20,000
I.	Earnings after Tax (EAT)	30,000
J.	Operating Leverage (Contribution/EBIT)	3.00
K.	Financial Leverage (EBIT/EBT)	2.00
L.	Combined Leverage (Operating Leverage × Financial Leverage)	6.00

Sales required to double the EBIT = [(2 × EBIT) + Fixed cost] × Sales/Contribution

= [(2 × 1,00,000) + 2,00,000] × 10/3 = 13,33,333

$$\% \text{ Income in Sales required} = \frac{₹\,13,33,333 - ₹\,10,00,000}{₹\,10,00,000} \times 100 = 33.33\%$$

$$\textbf{Alternatively, } \text{Operating Leverage} = \frac{\%\text{ change in EBIT}}{\%\text{ change in Sales}} = \frac{100\%}{\%\text{ Change in Sales}}$$

$$\%\text{ Change in Sales} = \frac{100\%}{3} = 33\frac{1}{3}\%$$

PROBLEM 4

X Ltd. has estimated that for a new product its break-even-point is 2,000 units if the items is sold for ₹ 14 per unit; the cost accounting department has currently identified variable cost of ₹ 9 per unit. Calculate the degree of operating leverage for sales volume of 2,500 units and 3,000 units. What do you infer from the degree of operating leverage at the sales volume of 2,500 and 3,000 and their difference if any?

SOLUTION

STATEMENT SHOWING THE CALCULATION OF DEGREE OF VARIOUS LEVERAGES

	Particulars	*2000 units* ₹	*2500 units* ₹	*3000 units* ₹
A.	Sales	28,000	35,000	42,000
B.	*Less:* Variable Costs	18,000	22,500	27,000
C.	Contribution	10,000	12,500	15,000
D.	*Less:* Fixed Costs	10,000	10,000	10,000
E.	Earnings before Interest & Tax (EBIT)	0.00	2,500	5,000
F.	Operating Leverage (Contribution/EBIT)	¥	5	3

At the sales volume of 3,000 units the EBIT is ₹ 5,000 which is double the EBIT of ₹ 2,500 which is at the sales volume of 2,500 units because of the fact that the operating leverage is 5 times at the sales volume of 2,500 units. Hence by increase of 20% in sales volume, the operating profit is increased by 100% i.e. 5 times of 20%. At the level of 3,000 units, the operating leverage is 3 times. Thus, as the sales volume increases from 2,000 units to 2,500 units & 3,000 units, the Operating leverage goes on decreasing from to 5 and 3 respectively.

PROBLEM 5

Two firms X and Y have the following information:

Particulars	*Sales ₹*	*Variable Costs*	*Fixed Cost ₹*
Firm X	10,00,000	25%	5,00,000
Firm Y	5,00,000	50%	1,25,000

Your are required to calculate (a) Profit to Sales ratio, (b) Break-even Point, and (c) the Degree of Operating Leverage for both firms.

Also Comment on the positions of the firms. If sales increase by 20 percent, what shall be the impact on the profitability of the two firms?

SOLUTION

STATEMENT SHOWING THE CALCULATION OF PROFIT TO SALES RATIO, BREAK-EVEN POINT & DEGREE OF OPERATING LEVERAGE

Particulars	*Firm X* ₹	*Firm Y* ₹
A. Sales	10,00,000	5,00,000
B. *Less:* Variable Costs	2,50,000	2,50,000
C. Contribution	7,50,000	2,50,000
D. *Less:* Fixed Costs	5,00,000	1,25,000
E. Earnings before Interest & Tax (EBIT)	2,50,000	1,25,000
F. Profit to Sales Ratio [E/A]	0.25	0.25
G. Break Even Sales [(D/C) × A]	6,66,667	2,50,000
H. Operating Leverage (Contribution/EBIT)	3.00	2.00

STATEMENT SHOWING THE EFFECT OF INCREASE IN SALES

Particulars	*Firm X* ₹	*Firm Y* ₹
A. Sales	12,00,000	6,00,000
B. *Less:* Variable Costs	3,00,000	3,00,000
C. Contribution	9,00,000	3,00,000
D. *Less:* Fixed Costs	5,00,000	1,25,000
E. Earnings before Interest & Tax (EBIT)	4,00,000	1,75,000
F. Operating Leverage (Contribution/EBIT)	2.25	1.71429

Comments: One can see that just by increase of 20% in sales profitability of both firms has gone up by more than 20%. This is due to the fact that operating leverage is high in both the cases.

PROBLEM 6

Consider the following information for PCT Ltd.

Particulars	₹
EBIT	10,00,000
EBT	2,00,000

Fixed cost	6,25,000

Required: Calculate percentage change in earnings per share if sales increased by 5 per cent.

SOLUTION

Step 1: Contribution = EBIT + Fixed Cost = ₹ 10,00,000 + ₹ 6,25,000 = ₹ 16,25,000

Step 2: Interest = EBIT – EBT = ₹ 10,00,000 – ₹ 2,00,000 = ₹ 8,00,000

Step 3: Percentage change in EPS

Method 1

Particulars	*Old* ₹	*New* ₹
A. Contribution	16,25,000	17,06,250
B. *Less:* Fixed Cost	6,25,000	6,25,000
C. Earnings before Interest & Tax (EBIT)	10,00,000	10,81,250
D. *Less:* Interest	8,00,000	8,00,000
E. Earnings before Tax (EBT)	2,00,000	2,81,250
F. Percentage increase in Profit *or* EPS [₹ 81,250 × 100/2,00,000]	—	40.625%

Method 2

$$\% \text{ Change in EPS} = \text{Degree of Combined Leverage} \times \% \text{ Change in Sales}$$

$$= \frac{\text{Contribution}}{\text{EBT}} \times \% \text{ Change in Sales}$$

$$= \frac{₹\ 16,25,000}{₹\ 2,00,000} \times 5\% = 40.625\%$$

Method 3

$$\% \text{ Change in EPS} = \frac{\text{Change in Contribution}}{\text{EBT}} \times 100$$

$$= \frac{5\% \text{ of } ₹\ 16,25,000}{₹\ 2,00,000} \times 100 = 40.625$$

Note: % change in contribution = % change in Sales.

PROBLEM 7

The Capital structure of X Ltd. consists of an Equity Share Capital of ₹ 10,00,000 (Shares of ₹ 100 par value) and ₹ 10,00,000, 10% Debentures, Sales increased by 20% from 1,00,000 units to 1,20,000 units, the selling price is ₹ 10 per unit, Variable costs amount to 60% and fixed expenses amount to ₹ 2,00,000. The income-tax rate is assumed to be 40%.

(a) You are required to calculate the following:
   (i) The percentage increase in earning per share;
   (ii) The degree of operating leverage, financial leverage and combined leverage at 1,00,000 units and 1,20,000 units.

(b) Comment on the behaviour of operating and financial leverage in relation to increase in production from 1,00,000 units to 1,20,000 units.

SOLUTION

STATEMENT SHOWING THE CALCULATION OF DEGREE OF VARIOUS LEVERAGES

Particulars	*1,00,000 units* ₹	*1,20,000 units* ₹
A. Sales	10,00,000	12,00,000
B. *Less:* Variable Costs	6,00,000	7,20,000
C. Contribution	4,00,000	4,80,000
D. *Less:* Fixed Costs	2,00,000	2,00,000
E. Earnings before Interest & Tax (EBIT)	2,00,000	2,80,000
F. *Less:* Interest	1,00,000	1,00,000
G. Earnings before Tax (EBT)	1,00,000	1,80,000
H. *Less:* Tax @ 40%	40,000	72,000
I. Earnings after Tax (EAT)	60,000	1,08,000
J. *Less:* Preference Dividend	—	—
K. Earnings for Equity Shareholders	60,000	1,08,000
L. No. of Equity Shares	10,000	10,000
M. Earnings per Share (EPS)	6	10.80
N. Operating Leverage (Contribution/EBIT)	2	1.71
O. Financial Leverage (EBIT/EBT)	2	1.56
P. Combined Leverage (Operating Leverage × Financial Leverage)	4	2.67

(b) In relation to increase in production and sales of 1,00,000 units to 1,20,000 units (20% increase), EPS has gone from ₹ 6 to ₹ 10.80 i.e., increase by 80%. But both the financial leverage and operating leverage have decreased consequent upon the increase in sales. Due to the reduction, both the risks i.e., business risk and financial risks of the business are reduced.

PROBLEM 8

Develop proforma income statement for the months of July, August and September for a Co. from the following information:

(a) Sales are projected at ₹ 2,25,000, ₹ 2,40,000 and ₹ 2,15,000 for July, Aug. and Sept. respectively;

(b) Cost of goods is ₹ 50,000 *plus* 30% of selling price per month;

(c) Selling Expenses are 3% of sales;

(d) Rent is 7,500 p.m., administrative expenses for July are expected to be ₹ 60,000 but are expected to rise 1% p.m. over the previous months expenses;

(e) The company has ₹ 3,00,000 of 8% loan Interest payable monthly; Corporate Tax rate is 40%.

SOLUTION

INCOME STATEMENT

Particulars	*July* ₹	*August* ₹	*September* ₹
A. Sales	2,25,000	2,40,000	2,15,000

B. *Less:* Variable Costs	67,500	72,000	64,500
C. *Less:* Fixed Costs	50,000	50,000	50,000
D. Gross Profit	1,07,500	1,18,000	1,00,500
E. *Less:* Administrative & Selling Overheads:			
(I) Rent	7,500	7,500	7,500
(ii) Administrative Expenses	60,000	60,600	61,206
(iii) Selling Expenses	6,750	7,200	6,450
Total	74,250	75,300	75,156
F. Earnings before Interest & Tax (EBIT)	33,250	42,700	25,344
G. *Less:* Interest	2,000	2,000	2,000
H. Earnings before Tax (EBT)	31,250	40,700	23,344
I. *Less:* Tax @ 40%	12,500	16,280	9,338
J. Earnings after Tax (EAT)	18,750	24,420	14,006

PROBLEM 9

The selected financial data for A, B and C companies are as follows:

Particulars	*A Ltd.*	*B Ltd.*	*C Ltd.*
Variable cost as % of sales	66-2/3	75	50
10% Debt	₹ 2000	₹ 3000	₹ 10,000
Degree of Operating Leverage	5–1	6–1	2–1
Degree of Financial Leverage	3–1	4–1	2–1
Income – Tax rate (%)	40	40	40

Required: Prepare Income Statements for A, B & C companies.

SOLUTION

INCOME STATEMENT

Particulars	*Companies*		
	A ₹	*B* ₹	*C* ₹
A. Sales	4,500	9,600	8,000
B. *Less:* Variable Costs	3,000	7,200	4,000
C. Contribution	1,500	2,400	4,000
D. *Less:* Fixed Costs	1,200	2,000	2,000
E. Earnings before Interest & Tax (EBIT)	300	400	2,000
F. *Less:* Interest	200	300	1,000
G. Earnings before Tax (EBT)	100	100	1,000
H. *Less:* Tax @ 40%	40	40	400
I. Earnings after Tax (EAT)	60	60	600

Working Notes:

(i) Calculation of Earnings before Interest (E B T) for A Ltd.

Let the E B T be x

E B T for A Ltd.:

Financial Leverage = E B I T/E B T = 3

or = (E B T + Interest)/ E B T = 3

or = (x + 200)/x = 3

or 3x = x + 200

or 2x = 200

or x = ₹ 100

E B T for B Ltd.:

Financial Leverage = (x + 300)/x = 4

4x = x + 300

x = ₹ 100

E B T for C Ltd.:

Financial Leverage = (x + 1000)/x = 2

2x = x + 1,000

x = ₹ 1,000

(II) CALCULATION OF EBIT

Particulars	*A Ltd.*	*B Ltd.*	*C Ltd.*
EBT	100	100	1,000
Add: Interest	200	300	1,000
EBIT	300	400	2,000

(iii) Calculation of Contribution.

Operating Leverage = Contribution/EBIT

Let the contribution be x

For A Ltd. = x/₹ 300 = 5

x = ₹ 300 × 5 = ₹ 1,500

For B Ltd. = x/₹ 400 = 6

x = 400 × 6 = ₹ 2,400

For C Ltd. = x/₹ 2,000 = 2

x = ₹ 2,000 × 2 = ₹ 4,000

(IV) CALCULATION OF P/V RATIO

Particulars	*A*	*B*	*C*
Variable Cost Ratio	$66\frac{2}{3}$%	75%	50%
P/V Ratio (100 – VC Ratio)	$33\frac{1}{3}$%	25%	50%

(v) Calculation of Sales

P/V Ratio = (Contribution / Sales) × 100

Let the Sales be x

For A Ltd. = ₹ 1,500/x = $33\frac{1}{3}$%

x = ₹ 1,500 × 3 = ₹ 4,500

For B Ltd. = ₹ 2,400/x = 25%

x = ₹ 2,400 × 4 = ₹ 9,600

For C Ltd. = ₹ 4,000/x = 50%

x = ₹ 4,000 × 2 = ₹ 8,000

PROBLEM 10

Prepare the Income Statement and Balance-Sheet from the following data:

Price Earning ratio	3 times
Market Price per equity share	₹ 18
No. of Equity shares of ₹ 10 each	10,000
No. of 12% Pref. Shares of ₹ 100 each	1,000
Degree of Financial Leverage	2–1
Degree of Operating Leverage	2–1
Income-Tax rate	40%
Variable Cost as % of Sales Revenue	60%
Rate of Interest on debt	10%

SOLUTION

INCOME STATEMENT

Particulars	₹
A. Sales	10,00,000
B. *Less:* Variable Costs	6,00,000
C. Contribution	4,00,000
D. *Less:* Fixed Costs	2,00,000
E. Earnings before Interest & Tax (EBIT)	2,00,000
F. *Less:* Interest	80,000
G. Earnings before Tax (EBT)	1,20,000
H. *Less:* Tax @ 40%	48,000
I. Earnings after Tax (EAT)	72,000
J. *Less:* Pref. Dividend	12,000
K. Earnings for Equity Shareholders	60,000

BALANCE SHEET

Liabilities	₹	*Assets*	₹
10,000 Equity Shares of ₹ 10 each	1,00,000	Total Assets	10,60,000
1,000, 12% Pref. Shares of ₹ 100 each	1,00,000		
Reserves & Surplus	60,000		

10% Debt	8,00,000		
	10,60,000		10,60,000

Working Notes:

(i) Earning per share = Market Price/Price Earning Ratio = ₹ 18/3 = ₹ 6

(ii) Earning for Equity shareholders = No. of Equity Shares × EPS = 10,000 × ₹ 6 = ₹ 60,000

(iii) Earning after Interest & Tax = Earnings for Equity Shareholders + Pref. Dividend
= ₹ 60,000 + ₹ 12,000 = ₹ 72,000

(iv) Earning Before Tax = Earnings after Interest & Tax + Tax = ₹ 72,000 + ₹ 48,000 = ₹ 1,20,000

(v) Earning Before Interest & Tax = $\left[\text{Earning before Tax} - \frac{\text{Pref. Dividend}}{(1-\text{tax})}\right] \times \text{Financial Leverage}$

$$= \left[₹\,1{,}20{,}000 - \frac{₹\,12{,}000}{(1-0.40)}\right] \times 2 = ₹\,2{,}00{,}000$$

(vi) Contribution = EBIT × Operating Leverage = ₹ 2,00,000 × 2 = ₹ 4,00,000

(vii) Fixed Costs = Contribution – EBIT = ₹ 4,00,000 – ₹ 2,00,000 = ₹ 2,00,000.

(viii) Contribution = Sales – Variable Cost

Let the Sales be X

$X - 0.6X = ₹\,4{,}00{,}000$

$0.4X = ₹\,4{,}00{,}000, \quad X = ₹\,4{,}00{,}000/0.4 = ₹\,10{,}00{,}000$

(ix) Interest on 10% Debt = EBIT – EBT = ₹ 2,00,000 – ₹ 1,20,000 = ₹ 80,000

(x) 10% Debt = ₹ 80,000/0.10 = ₹ 8,00,000.

(xi) It has been assumed that no equity dividend has been paid.

PROBLEM 11

The Balance Sheet of a Company is as follows:

Liabilities	₹	*Assets*	₹
Equity Shares of ₹ 10 each	60,000	Net Fixed Assets	1,50,000
10% Long Term Debt	80,000	Current Assets	50,000
Retained earnings	20,000		
Current Liabilities	40,000		
	2,00,000		2,00,000

The Company's total assets turnover ratio is 3 times. Its fixed operating costs are ₹ 1,00,000 and its variable operating cost ratio is 40%. The income-tax rate is 40%

(i) Calculate for the company the different types of leverages.

(ii) Determine the likely level of EBIT if EPS is:

(a) ₹ 1; (b) ₹ 3; (c) ₹ 0.

SOLUTION

STATEMENT SHOWING THE CALCULATION OF DEGREE OF VARIOUS LEVERAGES

Particulars	₹
A. Sales [₹ 2,00,000 × 3]	6,00,000

B. *Less:* Variable Costs	2,40,000
C. Contribution	3,60,000
D. *Less:* Fixed Costs	1,00,000
E. Earnings before Interest & Tax (EBIT)	2,60,000
F. *Less:* Interest	8,000
G. Earnings before Tax (EBT)	2,52,000
H. *Less:* Tax @ 40%	1,00,800
I. Earnings after Tax (EAT)	1,51,200
J. *Less:* Pref. Dividend	—
K. Earnings for Equity Shareholders	1,51,200
L. No. of Equity Shares	6,000
M. Earnings per Share (EPS) (Earnings for Equity Shareholders /No. of Equity Shares)	25.2
N. Operating Leverage (Contribution/EBIT)	1.385
O. Financial Leverage (EBIT/EBT)	1.032
P. Combined Leverage (Operating Leverage × Financial Leverage)	1.43

(II) CALCULATION OF THE LIKELY LEVEL OF EBIT AT DIFFERENT LEVELS OF EPS

Particulars	₹	₹	₹
A. No. of Equity Shares	6,000	6,000	6,000
B. Earnings per Share (EPS)	₹ 1	₹ 3	₹ 0
C. Earnings for Equity Shareholders (A × B)	6,000	18,000	0
D. *Add:* Pref. dividend	—	—	—
E. Earnings after Tax (EAT)(C + D)	6,000	18,000	0
F. *Add:* Tax [(E/6) × 4]	4,000	12,000	0
G. Earnings before Tax (EBT) [E + F]	10,000	30,000	0
H. *Add:* Interest	8,000	8,000	8,000
I. Earnings before Interest & Tax (EBIT) [G + H]	18,000	38,000	8,000

PROBLEM 12

MP Ltd. needs ₹ 20,00,000 for expansion. The expansion is expected to yield an annual EBIT of 16%. In choosing a financial plan, MP Ltd. has a objective of maximizing earnings per share.

It is considering the possibility of issuing equity shares and raising debt of ₹ 2,00,000, *or* ₹ 8,00,000 *or* ₹ 12,00,000. The current market price per share is ₹ 50 and is expected to drop to ₹ 40 if the funds are borrowed in excess of ₹ 10,00,000. Funds can be borrowed at the rates indicated below:

(a) Upto ₹ 2,00,000 at 8%.

(b) Over ₹ 2,00,000 and upto ₹ 10,00,000 at 12%.

(c) Over ₹ 10,00,000 at 18%. Assume tax rate of 40 per cent.

Required: Determine the EPS for the three financing alternatives.

SOLUTION

STATEMENT SHOWING ESTIMATED EPS UNDER THE VARIOUS FINANCING PLANS

Particulars	*Plan 1* ₹	*Plan 2* ₹	*Plan 3* ₹
A. Earnings before Interest & Tax (EBIT)	3,20,000	3,20,000	3,20,000
B. *Less:* Interest	16,000	88,000	1,48,000
C. Earnings before Tax (EBT)	3,04,000	2,32,000	1,72,000
D. *Less:* Tax @ 40%	1,21,600	92,800	68,800
E. Earnings after Tax (EAT)	1,82,400	1,39,200	1,03,200
F. *Less:* Pref. Dividend	0	0	0
G. Earnings for Equity Shareholders	1,82,400	1,39,200	1,03,200
H. No. of Equity Shares [Equity/Market Price]	36,000	24,000	20,000
I. Earnings Per Share (EPS)	5.07	5.80	5.16

Recommendation: Plan 2 is to be preferred since the EPS is the highest under this plan. Under this plan the borrowing is also well within the limit

Working Note:

CALCULATION OF INTEREST

On first ₹ 2,00,000 @ 8 %	16,000	16,000	16,000
On next ₹ 6,00,000 @12%	0	72,000	72,000
On next ₹ 2,00,000 @ 12%	0	0	24,000
On next ₹ 2,00,000 @ 18%	0	0	36,000
Total	16,000	88,000	1,48,000

PROBLEM 13

A company's capital structure consists of the following:

Equity shares of ₹ 100 each	₹ 20,00,000
Retained Earnings	₹ 10,00,000
9% Preference Shares	₹ 12,00,000
7% Debentures	₹ 8,00,000
Total	₹ 50,00,000

The company earns 12% on its capital. The income-tax rate is 40%. The company requires a sum of ₹ 25 lakh to finance its expansion program for which following alternatives are available to it:

(i) Issue of 20,000 Equity Shares at a premium of ₹ 25 per share.

(ii) Issue of 10% Preference Shares.

(iii) Issue of 8% Debentures.

It is estimated that the P/E ratios in the cases of Equity, Preference and Debenture financing would be 21.4,17 and 15.7 respectively.

Required: Which of the three financing alternatives would you recommend and why?

SOLUTION

STATEMENT SHOWING ESTIMATED EPS & MARKET PRICE PER EQUITY SHARE UNDER THE VARIOUS FINANCING PLANS

Particulars	*Present* ₹	*Equity Plan* ₹	*Preference Share Plan* ₹	*Debenture Plan* ₹
A. Earnings before Interest & Tax (EBIT)	6,00,000	9,00,000	9,00,000	9,00,000
B. *Less:* Interest	56,000	56,000	56,000	2,56,000
C. Earnings before Tax (EBT)	5,44,000	8,44,000	8,44,000	6,44,000
D. *Less:* Tax @ 40%	2,17,600	3,37,600	3,37,600	2,57,600
E. Earnings after Tax (EAT)	3,26,400	5,06,400	5,06,400	3,86,400
F. *Less:* Pref. Dividend	1,08,000	1,08,000	3,58,000	1,08,000
G. Earnings for Equity Shareholders	2,18,400	3,98,400	1,48,400	2,78,400
H. No. of Equity Shares	20,000	40,000	20,000	20,000
I. Earnings per Share (EPS)	10.92	9.96	7.42	13.92
J. Price Earning Ratio		21.40	17.00	15.70
K. Market Price		213.14	126.14	218.54

Recommendation: It is advised that the company should go for debt plan on account of the following reasons:

(i) Market Price Per Share is highest among the various alternative plans.

(ii) EPS is highest among the various alternatives.

(iii) Comparatively better debt equity mix.

PROBLEM 14

The operating profit (EBIT) of KP Ltd. is ₹ 3,00,000. Its capital structure consists of the following:

10% Debentures	₹ 10,00,000
12% Preference Shares	2,00,000
Equity Shares of ₹ 100 each	8,00,000

The company is in the 40% tax bracket.

Required:

(i) Determine the firm's EPS.

(ii) Determine the percentage change in EPS associated with 30 per cent increase in EBIT.

(iii) Determine the degree of Financial Leverage

(iv) Assuming present DOL is 2, determine the DCL.

SOLUTION

STATEMENT SHOWING EPS & DEGREE OF VARIOUS LEVERAGES

Particulars	*Present Situation* ₹	*Proposed 30% Increase* ₹
A. Earnings before Interest & Tax (EBIT)	3,00,000	3,90,000

B. *Less:* Interest	1,00,000	1,00,000
C. Earnings before Tax (EBT)	2,00,000	2,90,000
D. *Less:* Tax @ 40%	80,000	1,16,000
E. Earnings after Tax (EAT)	1,20,000	1,74,000
F. *Less:* Pref. Dividend	24,000	24,000
G. Earnings for Equity Shareholders	96,000	1,50,000
H. No. of Equity Shares	8,000	8,000
I. Earnings per Share (EPS)	12	18.75
J. Percentage change in EPS $\left[\frac{\Delta EPS}{EPS} \times 100\right] = \left[\frac{18.75-12}{12} \times 100\right]$	—	56.25
K. Financial leverage $\left[\frac{EBIT}{EBT - \frac{\text{Pref. Dividend}}{1-t}}\right]$	1.875	1.56
L. Operating Leverage	2.00	1.77
M. Combined Leverage (Financial Leverage × Operating Leverage)	3.75	2.7612

Working Notes: Calculation of Operating Leverage

(i) Fixed cost = EBIT × Operating Leverage – EBIT = (3,00,000 × 2) – 3,00,000 = 3,00,000

(ii) Contribution = EBIT + Fixed Cost = ₹ 3,90,000 + ₹ 3,00,000 = ₹ 6,90,000

(iii) Operating leverage = Contribution/EBIT = ₹ 6,90,000/₹ 3,90,000 = 1.77

PROBLEM 15

Tulsian Ltd's current EBIT is 10% on capital employed of ₹ 300 Lakh. One third represented by owners. Its present borrowings are:

14% Term loans	50%
Working capital borrowings from banks @16%	30%
15% Public deposits	20%

The sales of the company are growing, and to support them the company proposes to obtain an additional bank loan of ₹ 25 lakh. The increase in EBIT is expected accordingly.

Required: Calculate the change in Interest Coverage Ratio after the additional borrowing and comment.

SOLUTION

STATEMENT SHOWING INTEREST COVERAGE RATIO

Particulars	*Present Situation* ₹	*Proposed 30% Increase* ₹
A. Earnings before Interest & Tax (EBIT)	30,00,000	32,50,000
B. *Less:* Interest	29,60,000	33,60,000
C. Earnings before Tax (EBT)	40,000	(1,10,000)
D. Interest Coverage Ratio (A/B)	1.0135	0.9673

Comment: The proposal is not good since the company will not be able to pay all the fixed interest charges as the Interest Coverage Ratio has declined from 1.0135 to 0.9673

Working Note:

CALCULATION OF INTEREST

On Term Loans (200 lakhs × 50 % × 14%)	14,00,000	14,00,000
On Bank Loan (200 lakhs × 30% × 16%)	9,60,000	9,60,000
On Public deposit (200 lakhs × 20% × 15%)	6,00,000	6,00,000
On Additional borrowing (25 lakhs × 16%)		4,00,000
Total	29,60,000	33,60,000

PROBLEM 16

The Evergrowing company has to decide between debt fund and equity for its expansion programme. Its current position is as follows:

Particulars	₹
5% Debt	40,000
Equity capital (₹ 10 per share)	1,00,000
Surplus	60,000
Total Capitalization	2,00,000
Sales	6,00,000
Less: Total Cost	5,38,000
Income before interest and tax	62,000
Less: Interest	2,000
	60,000
Income tax @ 40%	24,000
Income after tax	36,000

The expansion programme is estimated to cost ₹ 1,00,000. If this is financed through debt, the rate of new debt will be 7% and the price earning ratio will be 6 times. If the expansion programme is financed through equity shares, the new shares can be sold net at ₹ 25 per share and the price to earning ratio will be 7 times. The expansion will generate additional sales of ₹ 3,00,000, with a return of 10% on sales before interest and taxes.

Required: If the company is to follow a policy of maximizing the market value of its shares, which form of financing should it choose?

SOLUTION

STATEMENT SHOWING THE EVALUATION OF FINANCIAL PLAN

Particulars	*Debt* ₹	*Equity* ₹
A. Earnings before Interest & Tax (EBIT)	92,000	92,000
B. *Less:* Interest	(9,000)	(2,000)
C. Earnings before Tax (EBT)	83,000	90,000
D. *Less:* Tax @ 40%	(33,200)	(36,000)

E. Earning for Equity Shareholders	49,800	54,000
F. No. of Equity shares	10,000	14,000
G. Earnings per share (EPS)	4.98	3.86
H. Price Earning Ratio	6.00	7.00
I. Market price [G × H]	29.88	27.02

Recommendation: The company should choose debt option for its expansion as it will maximise the market value of its shares.

PROBLEM 17

PCT Ltd. provides you the following information:

Installed Capacity	1,50,000 units
Actual Production and Sales	1,00,000 units
Selling Price per Unit	₹ 1
Variable Cost per Unit	₹ 0.50
Fixed Costs	₹ 38,000
Funds Required	₹ 1,00,000

Capital Structure	*Financial Plan*		
	A	*B*	*C*
Equity Shares of ₹ 100 each to be issued at 25% Premium	60%	40%	35%
15% Debt	40%	60%	50%
10% Pref. Shares ₹ 100 each (Assume Income tax @ 40%)	—	—	15%

Required:

(a) To calculate the Degree of Operating Leverage, Degree of Financial Leverage and Degree of Combined Leverage for each Financial Plan.

(b) To Calculate Earning Per Share and Market Price Per Share if Price Earning Ratio in A plan is 10 times and in B and C plan is 8 times.

(c) To suggest which form of financing should be employed if the firm follows the policy of seeking to maximise the price of its shares.

(d) To calculate the indifference point between A and B plan.

(e) To Calculate the Financial break even point for each plan and to suggest which plan has more financial risk.

(f) To calculate the Cost Break-Even Point.

SOLUTION

PART (A), (B) AND (C) CALCULATION OF DEGREE OF VARIOUS LEVERAGES ETC.

Particulars	*Financial Plan A* ₹	*Financial Plan B* ₹	*Financial Plan C* ₹
A. Sales	1,00,000	1,00,000	1,00,000
B. *Less:* Variable Costs	50,000	50,000	50,000

C. Contribution	50,000	50,000	50,000
D. *Less:* Fixed Costs	38,000	38,000	38,000
E. Earnings before Interest & Tax (EBIT)	12,000	12,000	12,000
F. *Less:* Interest	6,000	9,000	7,500
G. Earnings before Tax (EBT)	6,000	3,000	4,500
H. *Less:* Tax @ 40%	2400	12,00	1,800
I. Earnings after Tax (EAT)	3,600	1,800	2,700
J. *Less:* Pref. Dividend	—	—	1,500
K. Earnings for Equity Shareholders	3,600	1,800	1,200
L. No. of Equity Shares	480	320	280
M. Earnings per Share (EPS)	7.5	5.625	4.286
N. Price Earning Ratio	10	8	8
O. Market Price	75	45	34.286
P. Operating Leverage (Contribution/ EBIT)	4.167	4.167	4.167
Q. Financial Leverage (EBIT/EBT) $\left[\frac{EBIT}{EBT - \frac{\text{Pref. Dividend}}{1-t}}\right]$	2.000	4.000	6.000
R. Combined Leverage (Operating Leverage × Financial Leverage)	8.334	16.668	25.002

Recommendation: The Market price is highest under Financial Plan A, therefore Financial plan A is recommended.

(D) CALCULATION OF INDIFFERENCE POINT BETWEEN PLAN A AND PLAN B.

Particulars	*Plan A*	*Plan B*
A. EBIT	X	X
B. *Less:* Interest	6000	9000
C. EBT [A – B]	X – 6000	X – 9000
D. *Less:* Tax @ 40%	0.4X – 2400	0.4X – 3600
E. EAT [C – D]	0.6X – 3600	0.6X – 5400
F. No. of Shares	480	320
G. EPS	0.6X – 3600480	0.6X – 5400320

At indifference point, EPS under both plans will be equal.

$$\frac{0.6X - 3600}{480} = \frac{0.6X - 5400}{320}$$

$$192X - 11,52,000 = 288X - 25,92,000$$

$$96\,X = 14,40,000$$

$$X = 15,000$$

The Indifference Point between Plan A and Plan B is at the EBIT level of ₹ 15,000.

(E) STATEMENT SHOWING THE CALCULATION OF FINANCIAL BEP

Particulars	Plan A	Plan B	Plan C
A. Interest	6000	9000	7500
B. Pref. Dividend (after grossing up to tax) $\left[\frac{\text{Pref. Dividend}}{(1-t)}\right]$	—	—	2500
C. Financial BEP (A + B)	6000	9000	10,000

Comment: Since Financial BEP for Plan C is the highest, Plan C has the highest Financial Risk.

(F) STATEMENT SHOWING THE CALCULATION OF COST *OR* OPERATING BEP

(E) STATEMENT SHOWING THE CALCULATION OF FINANCIAL BEP

Particulars	Plan A	Plan B	Plan C
A. Fixed Cost	38,000	38,000	38,000
B. P/V Ratio	50%	50%	50%
C. Cost BEP (in ₹) (A/B) $\left[\frac{\text{Fixed Cost}}{\text{P/V Ratio}}\right]$	76,000	76,000	76,000
D. Cost BEP (in Units) [BEP/Selling Price per unit]	76,000	76,000	76,000

PROBLEM 18

(a) Present Data: Sales ₹ 10,00,000, Financial Leverage 1.25, Combined Leverage 1.5. Calculate the % fall in EBIT and EPS if the sales drop to ₹ 5,00,000.

(b) EBIT ₹ 1120 lakhs, EBT ₹ 320 lakhs, Fixed Cost ₹ 700 lakhs. Calculate the percentage of change in EPS if sales increased by 5%.

(c) Change in Revenue 25%, Change in Operating Income 32%, Calculate the degree of Operating leverage.

(d) Net Sales ₹ 30 crores, EBIT 12% of Net Sales, Equity ₹ 10 crores, 13% Cum-Pref. Shares ₹ 2 crores, 15% Debentures ₹ 6 crores, Income Tax Rate is 40%. Calculate ROI and Return on Equity (ROE) for the company and indicate segments of ROE due to the presence of Preference Share Capital and Borrowing (Debentures). Also, calculate Operating Leverage if Combined Leverage is 3.

SOLUTION

(a) Fall in Sales = ₹ 5,00,000 / ₹ 10,00,000 = 50%

Operating Leverage = Combined Leverage / Financial Leverage = 1.5/1.25 = 1.2

Drop in EBIT = % Fall in Sales × Operating Leverage = 50% × 1.2 = 60%

Drop in EPS = % Fall in EBIT × Financial Leverage = 60% × 1.25 = 75%

or = % Fall in Sales × Combined Leverage = 50% × 1.5 = 75%.

(b) **Step 1:** Combined Leverage = Contribution / EBT

= (₹ 1120 lakhs + ₹ 700 lakhs) / ₹ 320 lakhs = 5.6875

Step 2: % Change in EPS = % Changes in Sales × Combined Leverage

= 5% × 5.6875 = 28.4375%

(c) Degree of Operating Leverage = % Change in Operating income / % Change in Revenues

= 0.32/0.25 = 1.28

(d) ROI = EBIT/Capital employed = 12% of ₹30 crores/(₹10 crores + ₹2 crores + ₹6 crores) × 100

= 20%

ROE = Earnings for Equity Shareholders/Equity Shareholders' Funds × 100

= (EBIT – Interest – Tax – Preference Dividend)/Equity × 100

$= \frac{(₹\ 3.60 \text{ crores} - ₹\ 0.9 \text{ crores} - ₹\ 1.08 \text{ crores} - 0.26 \text{ crores})}{₹\ 10 \text{ crores}} \times 100 = 13.6\%$

SEGMENT DUE TO PRESENCE OF PREFERENCE SHARE CAPITAL AND DEBENTURES

Particulars	*Pref. Share Capital*	*Debentures*
EBIT @ 20%	0.40	1.20
Less: Interest	—	0.90
EBT	0.40	0.30
Less: Tax @ 40%	0.16	0.12
EAT	0.24	0.18
Less: Pref. Dividend	0.26	—
	(– 0.02)	0.18

Net % change due to presence of PSC and Deb. = (– 0.02 + 0.18)/10 × 100 = 1.6%

Alternative Formula of ROE indicating its segments

$$ROE = ROI(1-t) + \frac{D}{E}(ROI - k_d) + \frac{PSC}{E}(ROI - k_p)$$

$$= 20\%\ (1 - .40) + 6/10(12\% - 9\%) + 2/10(12\% - 13\%)$$

$$= 12\% + 1.8\% - 0.2\% = 13.6\%$$

$$\text{Degree of Financial Leverage} = \frac{EBIT}{EBT - \frac{\text{Preference Dividend}}{(1-t)}} = \frac{3.6}{3.6 - 0.09 - 0.43} = 1.5859$$

Degree of Combined Leverage = DFL × DOL

3 = 1.5859 × DOL

DOL = 3/1.5859 = 1.8917

SOLVED PROBLEMS–II

PROBLEM 19

ABC Corporation plans to extend assets by 50%. To finance the expansion, it is choosing between a straight 12% debt issue and Equity shares. Its Balance Sheet and Profit and Loss Account are shown below:

BALANCE SHEET AS AT 31ST MARCH, 20X9

Liabilities	*₹ (Lakhs)*	*Assets*	*₹ (Lakhs)*
11% Debentures	40.00	Total Assets	200.00
Equity shares of ₹ 10 each	100.00		
Retained Earnings	60.00		
	200.00		200.00

P & L ACCOUNT OF ABC CORPORATION FOR THE YEAR ENDED MARCH 31, 20X9

Particulars	₹ *(lakhs)*
Sales	600.00
Total Cost (Excluding int.)	540.00
Net income before taxes (EBIT)	60.00
Interest on Debentures @ 11%	4.40
Income before taxes (EBT)	55.60
Taxes @ 40%	22.24
Profit after tax (EAT)	33.36
Earning per share (₹ 33.36/10.00)	₹ 3.336
Market Price (7.5 × 3.336)	₹ 25.02

If ABC Corporation finance ₹ 1 crore expansion with debt, the rate of the incremental debt will be 12% and the price/earning ratio of the equity shares will be 5 times. If the expansion is financed by equity, the new shares can be sold at ₹ 12 per share and the price/earning ratio will remain at 7.5 times.

Required:

(a) Assuming that net income before interest and taxes (EBIT) is 10% of sales. Calculate, earnings per share at sales levels of ₹ 4 crores, ₹ 8 crores and ₹ 10 crores, when financing is with (i) Equity shares, and (ii) Debt.

(b) Using the P/E ratio, calculate the market value per share for each sales level for both the debt and the equity financing.

(c) At what level of earnings before interest and taxes (EBIT), after the new capital is acquired, would earnings per share (EPS) be the same whether new funds are raised by issuing equity shares *or* raising debt?

(d) Also determine the level of EBIT at which uncommitted earnings per shares (UEPS) would be the same if sinking fund obligations amount to ₹ 5 lakhs per year.

SOLUTION

Part (a) and (b)

STATEMENT SHOWING THE CALCULATION OF EPS AND MARKET PRICE OF SHARE UNDER DEBT PLAN

	Particulars	*Sales Level A* ₹ *(lakhs)*	*Sales Level B* ₹ *(lakhs)*	*Sales Level C* ₹ *(lakhs)*
A.	Sales	400.00	800.00	1000.00
B.	*Less:* Total Costs	360.00	720.00	900.00
C.	Earnings before Interest & Tax (EBIT)	40.00	80.00	100.00
D.	*Less:* Interest	16.40	16.40	16.40
E.	Earnings before Tax (EBT)	23.60	63.60	83.60
F.	*Less:* Tax @ 40%	9.44	25.44	33.44
G.	Earnings after Tax (EAT)	14.16	38.16	50.16
H.	*Less:* Pref. Dividend	—	—	—
I.	Earnings for Equity Shareholders	14.16	38.16	50.16

J. No. of Equity Shares	10.00	10.00	10.00
K. Earnings per Share (EPS) [I / J]	1.416	3.816	5.016
L. Price Earning Ratio	5.00	5.00	5.00
M. Market Price [K × L)	7.08	19.08	25.08

STATEMENT SHOWING CALCULATION OF EPS AND MARKET PRICE OF SHARE UNDER EQUITY PLAN

Particulars	*Sales Level A ₹ (lakhs)*	*Sales Level B ₹ (lakhs)*	*Sales Level C ₹ (lakhs)*
A. Sales	400.00	800.00	1000.00
B. *Less:* Total Costs	360.00	720.00	900.00
C. Earnings before Interest & Tax (EBIT)	40.00	80.00	100.00
D. *Less:* Interest	4.40	4.40	4.40
E. Earnings before Tax (EBT)	35.60	75.60	95.60
F. *Less:* Tax @ 40%	14.24	30.24	38.24
G. Earnings after Tax (EAT)	21.36	45.36	57.36
H. *Less:* Pref. Dividend	—	—	—
I. Earnings for Equity Shareholders	21.36	45.36	57.36
J. No. of Equity Shares	18.33	18.33	18.33
K. Earnings per Share (EPS)	1.165	2.475	3.13
L. Price Earning Ratio	7.50	7.50	7.50
M. Market Price [K × L)	₹ 8.74	₹ 18.56	₹ 23.47

(C) LEVEL OF EBIT AT WHICH EPS WILL BE SAME UNDER BOTH THE FINANCIAL PLANS (INDIFFERENCE POINT)

Particulars	*Plan A (Debt Plan)*	*Plan B (Equity Plan)*
EBIT	X	X
Less: Interest	16,40,000	4,40,000
EBT	X – 16,40,000	X – 4,40,000
Less: Tax @ 40%	0.4X – 6,56,000	0.4X – 1,76,000
EAT	0.6X – 9,84,000	0.6X – 2,64,000
Less: Pref. Dividend	—	—
Earning Available for Equity Shareholders	0.6X – 9,84,000	0.6X – 2,64,000
No. of Equity Shares	10,00,000	18,33,334
Earning Per Share (EPS)	$\frac{0.6X - 9,84,000}{10,00,000}$	$\frac{0.6X - 2,64,000}{18,33,334}$

At Indifference Point, EPS under both Plans will be equal:

$$\frac{0.6X - 9,84,000}{10,00,000} = \frac{0.6X - 2,64,000}{18,33,334}$$

$$X = ₹\ 30,80,000$$

(D) LEVEL OF EBIT AT WHICH UEPS WILL BE SAME

Particulars	*Plan A (Debt Plan)*	*Plan B (Equity Plan)*
EBIT	X	X
Less: Interest	16,40,000	4,40,000
EBT	X – 16,40,000	X – 4,40,000
Less: Tax @ 40%	0.4X – 6,56,000	0.4X – 1,76,000
EAT 0.6	X – 9,84,000	0.6X – 2,64,000
Less: Sinking Fund Obligation	5,00,000	5,00,000
Earning Available for Equity Shareholders	0.6X – 14,84,000	0.6X – 7,64,000
No. of Equity Shares	10,00,000	18,33,334
Earning Per Share (EPS)	$\frac{0.6X - 14,84,000}{10,00,000}$	$\frac{0.6X - 7,64,000}{18,33,334}$

At Indifferent level, UEPS under both Plans will be same.

$$\frac{0.6X - 14,84,000}{10,00,000} = \frac{0.6X - 7,64,000}{18,33,334}$$

$$X = ₹\ 39,13,334$$

PROBLEM 20

PCT Ltd. provides you the following information

INCOME STATEMENT

Particulars	₹
Sales (operating at 60% level of installed capacity)	6,00,000
Total costs (excluding interest but including fixed cost which is 1/6 of total cost.)	5,40,000
EBIT	60,000
Interest on Debentures @ 11%	44,000
EBT	16,000
Income tax paid @ 40%	6,400
Earning after tax	9,600
Pref. Dividend paid @ 8%	4,000
Earnings available for Equity Shareholders	5,600
Earnings per share of ₹ 100 each	₹ 11.20
Dividend paid per share	₹ 11.20

Cost of proposed expansion programme 50% of Total Assets at Present Flotation Cost associated with raising of finance ₹ 5,000

Sales expected to be increased by $33\frac{1}{3}\%$ as a result of expansion.

If PCT Ltd. finances the expansion with debt, the rate of the incremental debt will be 1% more than that at present and the price earning ratio shall be 4 times. If expansion is financed through equity shares, the new share can be sold at 70% premium and the price-earning ratio shall be 8 times.

Required:

(a) Calculate the degree of all leverages at present and proposed sales level.

(b) Calculate EPS and percentage change in EPS if financing is through (i) Debt and (ii) Equity shares

(c) Calculate the market value per equity share under both the alternatives.

(d) Which form of financing should be employed?

(e) Determine the indifference point.

(f) Determine the financial break-even point and cost break-even point at present and proposed sales levels

(g) Determine that level of EBIT at which uncommitted earnings per share (UEPS) would be same if sinking fund obligations amount to ₹ 50,000 per year.

(h) Shall the market price of share be same at the indifference point under all forms of financing?

(i) Which plan has more financial risk?

SOLUTION

Part (a), (b), (c), (d)

STATEMENT SHOWING THE CALCULATION OF DEGREE FOR VARIOUS LEVERAGES ETC.

Particulars	Present Situation ₹	Debt Plan ₹	Equity Plan ₹
A. Sales	6,00,000	8,00,000	8,00,000
B. *Less:* Variable Costs	4,50,000	6,00,000	6,00,000
C. Contribution (A – B)	1,50,000	2,00,000	2,00,000
D. *Less:* Fixed Costs	90,000	90,000	90,000
E. Earnings before Interest & Tax (EBIT) [C – D]	60,000	1,10,000	1,10,000
F. *Less:* Interest	44,000	74,600	44,000
G. Earnings before Tax (EBT) [E – F]	16,000	35,400	66,000
H. *Less:* Tax @ 40%	6400	14,160	26,400
I. Earnings after Tax (EAT) [G – H]	9,600	21,240	39,600
J. *Less:* Pref. Dividend	4,000	4,000	4,000
K. Earnings for Equity Shareholders [I – J]	5,600	17,240	35,600
L. No. of Equity Shares	500	500	2,000
M. Earnings per Share (EPS) [K/L]	11.20	34.48	17.80
N. Price Earning Ratio	—	4.00	8.00
O. Market Price [M × N]	—	137.92	142.40
P. Operating Leverage (Contribution/EBIT)	2.50	1.82	1.82
Q. Financial Leverage $\left[\frac{\text{EBIT}}{\text{EBT} - \frac{\text{Pref. Dividend}}{1-t}}\right]$	6.429	3.828	1.854
R. Combined leverage (Operating Leverage × Financial Leverage)	16.07	6.97	3.37

Recommendation: The equity financing should be employed since the market price of an equity share is higher than that under debt financing.

(E) CALCULATION OF INDIFFERENCE POINT BETWEEN THE PROPOSED PLANS

Particulars	*Debt Plan*	*Equity Plan*
EBIT	X	X
Less: Interest	74,600	X – 44,000
EBT	X – 74,600	X – 44,000
Less: Tax @ 40%	0.4X – 29,840	0.4X – 17,600
EAT	0.6X – 44,760	0.6X – 26,400
Less: Pref. Dividend	4,000	4,000
Earning Available for Equity Shareholders	0.6X – 48,760	0.6X – 30,400
No. of Equity Shares	500	2000
Earning Per Share (EPS)	$\frac{0.6X - 48,760}{500}$	$\frac{0.6X - 30,400}{2000}$

At Indifference point, EPS under both Plans will be equal:

$$\frac{0.6X - 48,760}{500} = \frac{0.6X - 30,400}{2000}$$

$$X = ₹\ 91,467$$

(F) (I) CALCULATION OF FINANCIAL BREAK EVEN POINT

Particulars	*Present Plan*	*Debt Plant*	*Equity Plan*
A. Interest on Debt	44,000	74,600	44,000
B. Pref. Dividend (after grossing up to tax) $\left[\frac{\text{Pref. Dividend}}{(1-t)}\right]$	6,667	6,667	6,667
C. Financial Break Even Point [A + B]	50,667	81,267	50,667

(II) CALCULATION OF COST BREAK EVEN POINT

Particulars	*Present Plan*	*Debt Plant*	*Equity Plan*
A. Fixed Cost	90,000	90,000	90,000
B. P/V Ratio	25%	25%	25%
C. Cost BEP (A/B) (in ₹)	3,60,000	3,60,000	3,60,000

(G) CALCULATION OF INDIFFERENCE POINT AT WHICH UEPS WILL BE SAME

Particulars	*Debt Plan*	*Equity Plan*
EBIT	X	X
Less: Interest	74,600	X – 44,000
EBT	X – 74,600	X – 44,000
Less: Tax @ 40%	0.4X – 29,840	0.4X – 17,600
EAT	0.6X – 44,760	0.6X – 26,400
Less: Sinking Fund Obligation	50,000	50,000

Less: Preference Dividend	4,000	4,000
Earning Available for Equity Shareholders	0.6X – 98,760	0.6X – 80.400
No. of Equity Shares	500	2000
Earning Per Share (EPS)	$\frac{0.6X - 98,760}{500}$	$\frac{0.6X - 80,400}{2000}$

At Indifference Level, UEPS under both Plans will be equal:

$$\frac{0.6X - 98,760}{500} = \frac{0.6X - 80,400}{2000}$$

$$X = 1,74,800$$

(h) At the Indifference Points though the EPS under both Plans will be same, but the P/E Ratio under both Plans is not same. P/E Ratio for Debt Plan is 4 and P/E Ratio for Equity Plan is 8. Therefore, market price of Shares under both Plans will be different at the Indifferent Point.

(i) Financial Risk under Debt Plan is more on account of the following reasons:

(i) Debt Plan has higher Financial Leverage.

(ii) Financial BEP is higher under Debt Plan as compared to Equity Plan.

Working Notes:

(i) *Calculation of Total Funds Required*

= (50% of Total Assets) + Flotation Cost

= [50% of (Debt + Equity + Pref. Share Capital)] + Flotation Cost

$$= \left[50\% \text{ of} \left(\frac{₹\,44,000}{11\%} + \frac{5,600}{11.20} \times 100 + \frac{4,000}{8\%}\right)\right] + ₹\,5,000$$

= [50% of (₹ 4,00,000 + ₹ 50,000 + ₹ 50,000)] + ₹ 5,000 = ₹ 2,55,000

(ii) *No. of New Equity Shares to be issued* = ₹ 2,55,000/(₹ 100 + ₹ 70) = 1,500.

PROBLEM 21

Bharat Tulsian Ltd. provides you the following information:

Capital Gearing Ratio 3, Interest Coverage Ratio 5 Times, Average Debt Collection Period 3 Months, Average Debtors. ₹ 4,00,000, Credit Sales are 2/3 rd of the Total Sales, Capital Turnover Ratio 2 Times, Fixed Cost 1/3 rd of Total Operating Cost, Equity Shares are of ₹ 10 each but 18% Preference Shares and 15% Debentures of ₹ 100 each. P/E Ratio 5, Ratio of Pref. Share to Debentures 12.5% Accumulated Reserves ₹ 2,00,000, Income Tax Rate 40%.

Required: Prepare Income Statement and Calculate the degree of Operating Leverage, Financial Leverage & Combined Leverage, Earning per Share (EPS) and Market Price.

SOLUTION

STATEMENT SHOWING THE CALCULATION OF DEGREE OF VARIOUS LEVERAGES

Particulars	₹
A. Sales	24,00,000
B. *Less:* Variable Costs	12,00,000
C. Contribution	12,00,000
D. *Less:* Fixed Costs	6,00,000
E. Earnings before Interest & Tax (EBIT)	6,00,000

F.	*Less:* Interest	1,20,000
G.	Earnings before Tax (EBT)	4,80,000
H.	*Less:* Tax @ 40%	1,92,000
I.	Earnings after Tax (EAT)	2,88,000
J.	*Less:* Pref. Dividend	18,000
K.	Earnings for Equity Shareholders	2,70,000
L.	No. of Equity Shares	10,000
M.	Earnings per Share (EPS)	27
N.	Price Earning Ratio	5
O.	Market Price [M × N]	135
P.	Operating Leverage (Contribution/EBIT)	2.00
Q.	Financial Leverage $\left[\frac{\text{EBIT}}{\text{EBT} - \frac{\text{Pref. Dividend}}{1-t}}\right]$	1.33
R.	Combined Leverage (Operating Leverage × Financial Leverage)	2.66

Working Notes:

(i) *Calculation of Total Sales*

Average Debtors = 4,00,000

Credit Sales = Average Debtors × 12 Months\Average Debt Collection Period

Credit Sales = 4,00,000 × 12 / 3 = 16,00,000

Total Sales = 16,00,000 × 3 / 2 = 24,00,000

(ii) *Calculation of Capital Employed*

Capital Employed = Total Sales /Capital Turnover Ratio

= ₹ 24,00,000/2 = ₹ 12,00,000

(iii) *Calculation of Funds bearing fixed payment & fluctuating payment*

Let Debt = X

Preference Share Capital = 0.125X

Debt + Preference Share Capital = X + 0.125X = 1.125X

Capital Gearing Ratio = Debt + Preference Share Capital /Equity Shareholder's Funds

Capital Gearing Ratio = 1.125X/(12,00,000 – 1.125X) = 3

1.125X = 3(12,00,000 – 1.125X)

1.125X = 36,00,000 – 3.375X

4.5X = 36,00,000

X = 36,00,000/4.5 = ₹ 8,00,000

Hence Debt = ₹ 8,00,000 & Preference Share Capital = ₹ 8,00,000 × 0.125 = ₹ 1,00,000

(iv) *Calculation of Interest & Preference dividend*

Interest = 8,00,000 × 0.15 = ₹ 1,20,000

Preference Dividend = 1,00,000 × 0.18 = ₹ 18,000

(v) *Calculation of Variable cost, Contribution & Fixed cost*

EBIT = Interest × Interest Coverage ratio

EBIT = 1,20,000 × 5 = 6,00,000

Total Operating Cost = Sales – EBIT

Total Operating Cost = ₹ 24,00,000 – ₹ 6,00,000 = ₹ 18,00,000

Fixed Cost = ₹ 18,00,000 / 3 = ₹ 6,00,000

Variable Cost = Total Cost – Fixed Cost

Variable Cost = ₹ 18,00,000 – ₹ 6,00,000 = ₹ 12,00,000

Contribution = Sales – Variable Cost = ₹ 24,00,000 – ₹ 12,00,000 = ₹ 12,00,000

(vi) *Calculation of Number of Shares*

Equity Shareholders' Funds = ₹ 12,00,000 – (Debt + Preference Share Capital)

Equity Shareholders' Funds = ₹ 12,00,000 – (₹ 8,00,000 + ₹ 1,00,000) = ₹ 3,00,000

Equity Share Capital = Equity Shareholders' Funds – Reserves & Surpluses

Equity Share Capital = ₹ 3,00,000 – ₹ 2,00,000 = ₹ 1,00,000

No. of Equity Shares = Equity Share Capital/₹ 10

No. of Equity Shares = ₹ 1,00,000/10 = 10,000

PROBLEM 22

Tushar Tulsian ltd. provides you the information:

Capital Gearing Ratio : 3,

Fixed Cost : 1/3rd of Total operating Cost

Dividend Yield : 6%

Operating Ratio : 75%

Ratio of 18% of Pref. Shares to 15% Debentures : 12.5%

Dividend Payment Ratio : 30%

Accumulated Reserves : ₹ 4,00,000

Capital Employed : ₹ 24,00,000

Market Price of an Equity Share of ₹ 10 : ₹ 135

Tax Rate : 40%

Required: Prepare an Income statement and Calculate the degree of operating leverage, financial leverage and combined leverage.

SOLUTION

STATEMENT SHOWING THE CALCULATION OF DEGREE OF VARIOUS LEVERAGES

Particulars	₹
A. Sales	48,00,000
B. *Less:* Variable Costs	24,00,000
C. Contribution	24,00,000
D. *Less:* Fixed Costs	12,00,000
E. Earnings before Interest & Tax (EBIT)	12,00,000
F. *Less:* Interest	2,40,000
G. Earnings before Tax (EBT)	9,60,000

H. *Less:* Tax @ 40%	3,84,000
I. Earnings after Tax (EAT)	5,76,000
J. *Less:* Pref. Dividend	36,000
K. Earnings for Equity Shareholders	5,40,000
L. No. of Equity Shares	20,000
M. Earnings per Share (EPS) [K / L]	27.00
N. Price Earning Ratio	5.00
O. Market Price [M × N]	135.00
P. Operating Leverage (Contribution/EBIT)	2.00
Q. Financial Leverage $\left[\dfrac{\text{EBIT}}{\text{EBT} - \dfrac{\text{Pref. Dividend}}{1-t}}\right]$	1.33
R. Combined Leverage (Operating leverage × Financial Leverage)	2.67

Working Notes:

(i) *Calculation of Debt, Pref. Share Capital and Equity Shareholders' Funds*

Let Debt = X

Preference Share Capital = 0.125X

Debt + Preference Share Capital = X + 0.125X = 1.125X

Capital Gearing Ratio = Debt + Preference Share Capital/Equity Shareholders' Funds

Capital Gearing Ratio = 1.125X/(24,00,000 – 1.125X) = 3

1.125X = 3(24,00,000 – 1.125X)

1.125X = 72,00,000 – 3.375X

4.5X = 72,00,000

X = 72,00,000/4.5 = 16,00,000

Hence, Debt = ₹ 16,00,000 &

Preference Share Capital = ₹ 16,00,000 × 0.125 = ₹ 2,00,000

Equity Shreholders' Funds = ₹ 24,00,000 – ₹ 16,00,000 – ₹ 2,00,000 = ₹ 6,00,000

(ii) *Interest* = ₹ 16,00,000 × 0.15 = ₹ 2,40,000

(iii) *Preference Dividend* = ₹ 2,00,000 × 0.18 = ₹ 36,000

(iv) *Calculation of EPS*

DPS = Market Price × Dividend Yield = ₹ 135 × 6% = ₹ 8.10

EPS = DPS / Dividend Payout Ratio = ₹ 8.10/0.30 = ₹ 27

(v) Calculation of number of shares

Equity Share Capital = Equity Shareholder's Funds – Reserves & Surpluses

Equity Share Capital = ₹ 6,00,000 – ₹ 4,00,000 = ₹ 2,00,000

No. of Equity Shares = Equity Share Capital/₹ 10 = ₹ 2,00,000/10 = 20,000

(VI) CALCULATION OF MISSING INFORMATION

Particulars	₹
A. Earnings per Share (EPS)	27.00
B. No. of Equity Shares	20,000

C. Earnings for Equity Shareholders [A × B]	5,40,000
D. *Add:* Pref. Dividend	36,000
E. Earnings after Tax (EAT) [C + D]	5,76,000
F. *Add:* Tax [(E/0.6) × 0.4]	3,84,000
G. Earnings before Tax (EBT) [E + F]	9,60,000
H. *Add:* Interest	2,40,000
I. Earnings before Interest & Tax (EBIT) [G + H]	12,00,000
J. Operating ratio	0.75
K. Sales [EBIT/(1 – Operating ratio)]	48,00,000
L. Total Operating Cost [J × K]	36,00,000
M. Fixed Costs [L/3]	12,00,000
N. Variable Costs [L – M]	24,00,000

PROBLEM 23

The Company's Capital structure as on 1-1-20X1 is as under:

Equity Share Capital	₹ 1,50,000
Reserves & Surplus	₹ 50,000
12% Debentures	₹ 3,00,000
	₹ 5,00,000

Expected Net Profit before Interest & Tax for the year 20X1 is ₹ 1,44,000. Current Ratio 3 : 1, Quick Ratio 2 : 1. The company has approached the bankers for the 15% loan of ₹ 2,00,000.

Required: Calculate the amount of loan which may be sanctioned by the bankers assuming that the bankers follows the policy of maintaining a Debt-Equity Ratio of not more than 2 : 1 and an Interest Coverage Ratio of not *less* than 3 times.

SOLUTION

I Maximum amount of loan as per Debt-Equity test

Let the amount of loan be X

$$\text{Debt-Equity Ratio} = \frac{₹\,3,00,000 + X}{₹\,1,50,000 + 50,000} = 2 = ₹\,3,00,000 + X = ₹\,4,00,000$$

X = ₹ 1,00,000

II Maximum amount of Loan as per Interest Coverage Test

$$\text{Interest Coverage Ratio} = \frac{\text{Net Profit before Interest}}{\text{Fixed Interest}}$$

Let the amount of the loan be X

$$\text{Interest on loan} = 0.15\,X$$

$$3 = \frac{1,44,000}{36,000 + 0.15X}$$

$$3\,(36,000 + 0.15\,X) = ₹\,1,44,000$$

$$1,08,000 + 0.45\,X = ₹\,1,44,000$$

$$0.45\,X = ₹\,36,000$$

$$X = ₹\,36,000/0.45 = ₹\,80,000$$

III Lowest of I & II is ₹ 80,000. Thus, a banker can grant a loan upto ₹ 80,000.

PROBLEM 24

A corporate business is proposed to be capitalised with an amount of ₹ 6,00,000 by any one of the following two approaches:

Securities	Approaches	
	I ₹	II ₹
Equity Shares (of ₹ 10 each)	1,00,000	5,00,000
6% Debentures (secured by assets)	3,00,000	1,00,000
7% Preference shares	2,00,000	—
	6,00,000	6,00,000

Work out the effect on the distributable profits Recommend which approach should be Preferred where:

(i) Profit before interest on debentures and tax are ₹ 1,00,000

(ii) Profit before interest on debentures and tax rise and fall by 25%

The rate of income tax is 40%.

The rate of yield on equity share is 10% for the purpose of valuation on such shares.

SOLUTION

STATEMENT SHOWING ESTIMATED EPS AND MARKET PRICE OF SHARE AT VARIOUS LEVELS OF EBIT

APPROACH I

Particulars	At Present EBIT ₹	At reduced EBIT ₹	At increased EBIT ₹
A. Earnings before Interest & Tax (EBIT)	1,00,000	75,000	1,25,000
B. *Less:* Interest	18,000	18,000	18,000
C. Earnings before Tax (EBT)	82,000	57,000	1,07,000
D. *Less:* Tax @ 40%	32,800	22,800	42,800
E. Earnings after Tax (EAT)	49,200	34,200	64,200
F. *Less:* Pref. Dividend	14,000	14,000	14,000
G. Earnings for Equity Shareholders	35,200	20,200	50,200
H. No. of Equity Shares	10,000	10,000	10,000
I. Earnings per Share (EPS)	3.52	2.02	5.02
J. Market Price per share [(EPS/Earning yield) × 100]	35.20	20.20	50.20

APPROACH II

Particulars	At Present EBIT ₹	At reduced EBIT ₹	At increased EBIT ₹
A. Earnings before Interest & Tax (EBIT)	1,00,000	75,000	1,25,000

B. *Less:* Interest	6,000	6,000	6,000
C. Earnings before Tax (EBT)	94,000	69,000	1,19,000
D. *Less:* Tax @ 40%	37,600	27,600	47,600
E. Earnings after Tax (EAT)	56,400	41,400	71,400
F. *Less:* Pref. Dividend	0	0	0
G. Earnings for Equity Shareholders	56,400	41,400	71,400
H. No. of Equity Shares	50,000	50,000	50,000
I. Earnings per Share (EPS)	1.128	0.828	1.428
J. Market Price per share [(EPS/Earning yield) × 100]	11.28	8.28	14.28

Recommendation: Approach I should be preferred since the Market value of shares are higher in approach I as compared to approach II.

PROBLEM 25

The finance advisor of JP Ltd is confronted with two alternative financing plans for raising the necessary finance to increase the total assets by 20%. One choice is 12% Debt issue. The other is to issue 8,000 equity shares at the current Market price per of ₹ 125. The modernisation and expansion programme is expected to increase the firm's existing Rate of Return on Total Assets by 25%. The firm's Balance Sheet as at March 31 of current year is given below:

Liabilities	(₹)	*Assets*	(₹)
Current liabilities	5,00,000	Current assets	16,00,000
10% Long-term loan	15,00,000	Plant and equipment (net)	34,00,000
Reserves and Surpluses	10,00,000		
Equity capital (shares of ₹100 each)	20,00,000		—
	50,00,000		50,00,000

Dividend Per Share ₹ 11.70, Tax rate 40%, Dividend Payment Ratio 60% However, the finance advisor is concerned about the effect that issuing debt might have on the firm. The average debt ratio for firms in industry is 45 per cent. He believes that if this ratio is exceeded, the P/E ratio will fall to 7 because of the potentially greater risk. If the firm increases its equity capital, he expects the P/E ratio to increase to 8.5. He also wonders as to what will happen to the dividend yield under each plan.

Required:

(a) Determine the debt ratio, under each financing plan, after the securities are issued.

(b) Determine the expected net income in the next year, expected EPS and the expected market price of the equity shares.

(c) Determine the dividend yield.

(d) Which form of financing should be employed by the company, if the company is to follow a policy of maximising market value of its shares ?

SOLUTION

(A) COMPUTATION OF DEBT RATIO

Particulars	*Debt Plan* ₹	*Equity Plan* ₹
A. Shareholders' funds	30,00,000	40,00,000

B. Long term debts	25,00,000	15,00,000
C. Other Debts	5,00,000	5,00,000
D. Total Funds employed [A + B + C]	60,00,000	60,00,000
E. Debt-Ratio (Total debts/Total Funds Employed) × 100	50.00	33.33

(B) & (C) STATEMENT SHOWING INCOME STATEMENT, EPS, MARKET PRICE OF SHARE & DIVIDEND YIELD

Particulars	*Debt Plan* ₹	*Equity Plan* ₹
A. Earnings before Interest & Tax (EBIT)	12,00,000	12,00,000
B. *Less:* Interest	2,70,000	1,50,000
C. Earnings before Tax (EBT)	9,30,000	10,50,000
D. *Less:* Tax @ 40%	3,72,000	4,20,000
E. Earnings after Tax (EAT)	5,58,000	6,30,000
F. *Less:* Pref. Dividend	—	—
G. Earnings for Equity Shareholders	5,58,000	6,30,000
H. No. of Equity Shares	20,000	28,000
I. Earnings per Share (EPS)	27.90	22.50
J. Price Earning ratio	7.00	8.50
K. Market price per share [I × J]	195.30	191.25
L. Dividend payout ratio	0.60	0.60
M. Dividend per share [I × L]	16.74	13.50
N. Dividend yield [(M/K) × 100]	8.57	7.06

(d) Recommendation: The company should use the Debt financing plan to maximize value of its shares

Working Notes:

(I) COMPUTATION OF OPERATING PROFITS / EBIT

A. Dividend per share (DPS)	11.70
B. Dividend payout ratio	0.60
C. Earnings per Share (EPS) [A/B]	19.50
D. No. of Equity Shares	20,000
E. Earnings for Equity Shareholders [C × D]	3,90,000
F. *Add:* Tax [(E/0.6) × 0.4]	2,60,000
G. Earnings before Tax (EBT) [E + F]	6,50,000
H. *Add:* Interest	1,50,000
I. Earnings before Interest & Tax (EBIT) *or* Operating profits [G + H]	8,00,000

(ii) *Computation of existing rate & new rate of return on total assets & new EBIT*

Existing Rate of Return = [(8,00,000/50,00,000) × 100] = 16%

New Rate of Return = 16% + 25% of 16% = 20 %

New EBIT = 20% of 60,00,000 = ₹ 12,00,000

PROBLEM 26

The balance sheet of CANIH Ltd. as at March 31, current year is as follows (Figures in lakhs of rupees):

Liabilities	(₹)	*Assets*	(₹)
Share capital	200	Fixed assets	500
Reserves	140	Investments	300
Long-term loans	360	Receivables	240
Short-term loans	200	Cash and bank	60
Payables	120		
Provisions	80		
	1,100		1,100

Sales for the current year were ₹ 600 lakhs. For the next year ending on March 31, they are expected to increase by 20 per cent. The net profit margin after taxes and dividend payout are expected to be 4 and 50 per cent respectively.

Required:

(a) Quantify the amount of external funds required.

(b) Determine the mode of raising the funds given the following parameters.

(i) Current Ratio should be 1.33.

(ii) Ratio of fixed assets to long-term loans should be 1.5.

(iii) Long-term debt to equity ratio should not exceed 1.06.

(iv) The funds are to be raised in the order of (1) short-term bank borrowings, (2) long-term loans and (3) equities.

SOLUTION

(A) COMPUTATION OF EXTERNAL FUNDS REQUIRED

	Particulars	₹ *(lakhs)*
A.	Earnings after tax (₹ 600 lakhs × 120% × 4%)	28.8
B.	*Less:* Dividend paid (₹ 28.8 × 50%)	14.40
C.	Retained Earnings	14.40
D.	Increase in Current Liabilities (other than short-term loans) [(120 + 80) × 20%]	40.00
E.	Total Funds Available	54.40
F.	Funds required for Incremental Assets [1,100 × 20%]	220.00
G.	External Funds required [F – E]	165.60

(b) Additional Short-term Bank Borrowings

$$1.33 = \frac{\text{Revised CA}}{\text{Revised Payable \& Provision + Short-term Borrowing}}$$

$$1.33 = \frac{₹\ 600\text{ lakh} \times 1.2}{(₹\ 120\text{ lakh} + ₹\ 80\text{ lakh}) \times 1.2 + \text{STB}}$$

$$1.33\ (₹\ 240\text{ lakh} + \text{STB}) = ₹\ 720\text{ lakhs}$$

$$\text{STB} = ₹\ 400.8/1.33 = ₹\ 301.35\text{ lakhs.}$$

$$\text{Additional STB} = ₹\ 301.35\text{ lakhs} - ₹\ 200\text{ lakhs} = ₹\ 101.35\text{ lakhs.}$$

(c) Additional Long term loans

$$\frac{\text{Revised Fixed Assets}}{\text{Long-term Loan}} = 1.5$$

$$\frac{₹\ 500 \text{ lakhs} \times 1.2}{\text{LTL}} = 1.5$$

$$\text{LTL} = ₹\ 600 \text{ lakhs}/1.5 = ₹\ 400 \text{ lakhs.}$$

$$\text{Additional LTL} = ₹\ 400 \text{ lakhs} - ₹\ 360 \text{ lakh} = ₹\ 40 \text{ lakh}$$

(d) Additional Equity = ₹ 165.60 lakh – ₹ 101.35 lakh – ₹ 40 lakh = ₹ 24.25 lakh

$$\text{LTD to Equity Ratio} = \frac{\text{Revised LTD}}{\text{Revised Equity}} = \frac{₹\ 400 \text{ lakh}}{₹\ 200 + ₹\ 140 + ₹\ 24.25 + ₹\ 14.40} = 1.056$$

Hence, New D/E Ratio does not exceed 1.06.

(e) Additional Funds to be raised as follows:

Short-term Bank Borrowings	₹ 101.35 lakhs
Long-term Loans	₹ 40.00 lakhs
Equity Share Capital	₹ 24.25 lakhs
	₹ 165.60 lakhs

PROBLEM 27

The finance manager of KP Ltd has been trying to develop a financial plan for the firm. He has, in coordination with other managers, developed the following estimates (in lakh of rupees).

Particulars	*Year*			
	1	*2*	*3*	*4*
Credit Sales	400	Increase by 20% Over Previous Year	Increase by 25% Over Previous Year	Increase by 40% Over Previous Year
Fixed Assets to **Turnover Rate**	64%	56%	48%	40%

In addition, for planning purposes, he has made the following estimates and assumptions about other results.

Operating Ratio	60%
Cash Sales	20% of Total Sales
Return on sales (after taxes)	10%
Dividend Payout Ratio	68%
Turnovers (times) based on year-end values:	
Debtors Velocity	3 Months
Stock Velocity	4 Months
Required Current Ratio	2 : 1
Required Debt Equity Ratio	1 : 2

At the beginning of year 1, the treasurer expects the firm to have capital employed of ₹ 270 lakhs and Debt-Equity Ratio of 1 : 2.

Required: Determine how much additional equity capital, if any, the firm will have to issue each year if the finance manager's estimates and assumptions are correct.

SOLUTION

STATEMENT SHOWING THE DIVIDEND PAYABLE & RETAINED EARNINGS

Particulars	Year			
	I ₹	II ₹	III ₹	IV ₹
A. Sales (Credit Sales/0.80)	500	600	750	1050
B. Operating Cost @ 60%	300	360	450	630
C. Earnings after Tax @10%	50	60	75	105
D. Dividend Payout Ratio	0.68	0.68	0.68	0.68
E. Dividend paid (C × D)	34	40.8	51	71.4
F. Retained earnings (C –E)	16	19.2	24	33.6

STATEMENT SHOWING THE REQUIREMENTS OF FUNDS

Particulars	Year			
	I ₹	II ₹	III ₹	IV ₹
A. Fixed Assets (Sales × Fixed assets to turnover ratio)	320	336	360	420
B. Current Assets:				
(i) Debtors [(Credit Sales × Debtors' Velocity)/12]	100	120	150	210
(ii) Inventory [(Operating Cost × Stock Velocity)/12]	100	120	150	210
Total Current Assets	200	240	300	420
C. Total Assets [A + B]	520	576	660	840
D. *Less:* Current Liabilities (Current assets / 2)	100	120	150	210
E. Funds Required [C – D]	420	456	510	630

BREAK–UP OF FUNDS INTO LONG–TERM DEBTS & EQUITY FUNDS

Particulars	Year			
	I ₹	II ₹	III ₹	IV ₹
A. Long term debts (Funds required /3)	140	152	170	210
B. Equity Funds [(Funds required/3) × 2]	280	304	340	420
Total	420	456	510	630

STATEMENT SHOWING THE EQUITY CAPITAL TO BE ISSUED

Particulars	Year			
	I ₹	II ₹	III ₹	IV ₹
A. Equity Funds required	280	304.00	340	420.00
B. Balance at beginning	180	280.00	304	340.00
C. *Add:* Retained earnings	16	19.20	24	33.60

D. Equity Capital at end [B + C]	196	299.20	328	373.60
E. Equity Capital to be issued [A – D]	84	4.80	12	46.40

Working Notes:

CALCULATION OF CREDIT SALES

Particulars	*(₹ in lakhs)*
I st year	400
II nd year (400 × 120/100)	480
III rd year (480 × 125/100)	600
IV th year (600 × 140/100)	840

PROBLEM 28

MJ Industries Ltd anticipates a 15 per cent increase in sales over the present level of ₹ 750 Lakhs. As it is currently operating at fully capacity, the firm is contemplating to increase its capacity by increasing its investment in assets. Its latest balance sheet as on March 31 is summarised below:

Liabilities	*₹ (Lakhs)*	*Assets*	*₹ (Lakhs)*
Equity Capital	218.35	Fixed Assets (net)	240.00
Retained Earnings	90.50	Cash and Marketable Securities	20.00
Long-term Debt	22.50	Debtors	112.50
Sundry Creditors	82.50	Inventory	127.50
Bank Loan	26.15		
Other Current Liabilities	60.00		
	500.00		500.00

(i) If M.J Industries expects to maintain its previous year's total assets turnover (based on sales) ratio, determine the expected level of total assets, and the extent of additional funds required to finance the incremental assets.

(ii) Express past year's balance sheet as a percentage of sales. Indicate which items on the balance sheet are likely to move with sales. Also, state the amount to be met by the spontaneous increase in liabilities.

(iii) If the firm maintains the current level of net profit margin on sales at 6 per cent, as also the current D/P ratio of 40 per cent, indicate the additional external financing required by the firm.

(iv) Prepare a proforma balance sheet assuming that additional financing needs, if any, can be met with an increase in bank loans.

(v) If MJ Industries had excess production capacity and did not anticipate increasing its fixed assets, what would be the requirement of additional external funds?

SOLUTION

(I) COMPUTATION OF EXPECTED LEVEL OF TOTAL ASSETS & ADDITIONAL FUNDS REQUIRED TO FINANCE THE INCREMENTAL IN ASSETS

Particulars	₹
A. Total Assets	₹ 500.00 lakhs
B. Sales	₹ 750.00 lakhs

C.	Turnover to Total Assets Ratio	1.50
D.	Estimated Sales [₹ 750 lakhs + 15% of ₹ 750 lakh]	₹ 862.50 lakhs
E.	Expected Level of Total Assets (D/C) [₹ 862.50 lakh/1.5]	₹ 575.00 lakhs
F.	Additional Funds required (E – A)	₹ 75.00 lakhs

(II) BALANCE SHEET AS PERCENTAGE OF SALES OF PREVIOUS YEAR

Liabilities	₹	*Ratio*	*Assets*	₹	*Ratio*
Equity Capital	218.35	29.11	Fixed assets	240.00	32.00
Retained earnings	90.50	12.07	Cash & Marketable Securities	20.00	2.67
Long term debts	22.50	3.00	Debtors	112.50	15.00
Sundry creditors	82.50	11.00	Inventory	127.50	17.00
Bank loan	26.15	3.49			
Other Current liabilities	60.00	8.00			
	500.00	66.67		500.00	66.67

All assets items will change with increase in sales assuming the company has no excess production capacity. Also the sundry creditors & other current liabilities will also increase.

(III) COMPUTATION OF ADDITIONAL FINANCE REQUIRED BY THE COMPANY

	Particulars	₹
A.	Earnings after Tax (862.50 × 6%)	51,75,000
B.	Dividend paid (EAT × Dividend pay out ratio)	20,70,000
C.	Retained earnings (A – B)	31,05,000
D.	Increase in Current liabilities other than Short term Loans (862.50 × 19% – 750 × 19%)	21,37,500
E.	Total funds available (C + D)	52,42,500
F.	External funds required (₹ 75,00,000 – ₹ 52,42,500)	22,57,500

(IV) PROFORMA BALANCE SHEET ASSUMING THE ADDITIONAL FINANCING IS FINANCED BY BANK

Liabilities	₹	*Assets*	₹
Equity Capital	2,18,35,000	Fixed assets	2,76,00,000
Retained earnings	1,21,55,000	Cash & Marketable Securities	23,00,000
Long term debts	22,50,000	Debtors	1,29,37,500
Sundry creditors	94,87,500	Inventory	1,46,62,500
Bank loan	48,72,500		
Other Current liabilities	69,00,000		
	5,75,00,000		5,75,00,000

(V) ADDITIONAL FINANCE IF FIXED ASSETS REMAINS SAME WITH INCREASE IN SALES

	Particulars	₹
A.	Funds required (862.50 × 34.67% – 750 × 34.67%)	39,00,000

B. Retained earnings	31,05,000
C. Increase in Current Liabilities	21,37,500
D. Total Funds Available (B + C)	52,42,500
E. Excess Funds Available (A – D)	(13,42,500)

The firm would not need any additional funds. Infact, it has excess fund.

PROBLEM 29

J.K. Limited which is considering two financing plans provides you the following information:

(a) Total funds to be raised, ₹ 4,00,000

(b) Financing Plans: A—50% Equity and Balance 8% Debt
B—50% Equity and Balance 8% Pref. Shares.

(c) Tax Rate : 35 per cent.

(d) Equity shares of the face value of ₹ 10 each will be issued at a premium of ₹ 10 per share.

(e) Expected EBIT, ₹ 1,60,000

Required: Determine for each plan:

(i) Earnings Per Share (EPS) and Financial Break-Even Point.

(ii) Indicate if any of the plans dominate, and compute the EBIT range among the plans for difference.

SOLUTION

(I) DETERMINATION OF EPS UNDER A AND B

Particulars	*Plan A*	*Plan B*
A. EBIT	₹ 1,60,000	₹ 1,60,000
B. *Less:* Interest	16,000	—
C. EBT	1,44,000	1,60,000
D. *Less:* Tax @ 35%	50,400	56,000
E. EAT	93,600	1,04,000
F. *Less:* Pref. Dividend	—	16,000
G. Earnings for Equity-holders	93,600	88,000
H. Number of Shares	10,000	10,000
I. EPS [G/H]	9.36	8.80

Financial BEP for plans, A and B

$$\text{Financial BEP} = \text{Interest} + \frac{\text{Pref. Dividend}}{(1-t)}$$

$$\text{for Plan A} = ₹\ 16{,}000 + 0 = ₹\ 16{,}000$$

$$\text{for Plan B} = ₹\ 0 + \frac{₹\ 16{,}000}{1-.35} = ₹\ 24{,}615$$

(ii) Calculation of Indifference Point among A and B:

$$\frac{(X - \text{Interest})(1-t) - \text{Pref. Dividend}}{N_1} = \frac{(X - \text{Interest})(1-t) - \text{Pref. Dividend}}{N_2}$$

$$\frac{(X - ₹\ 16{,}000)(1-.35) - 0}{10{,}000} = \frac{(X-0)(1-.35) - ₹\ 16{,}000}{10{,}000}$$

or, $0.65X - ₹ 10,400 = 0.65X - ₹ 16,000$

or, $0.65X - 0.65X = ₹ 10,400 - ₹ 16,000$

Thus, indifference point between Plans A and B is indeterminate.

Domination of Plan: Plan A dominates Plan B as the financial BEP of Plan A is lower.

PROBLEM 30

JK Ltd. has appointed you as its Finance Manager. The company wants to implement a project for which ₹ 60 lakh is required to be raised from the market as a means of financing the project. The following financing plans at options are at hand: *(Number in thousands).*

Particulars	*Plan X*	*Plan Y*	*Plan Z*
Option 1: Equity Shares	60	60	60
Option 2: Equity Shares	30	40	20
13% Preference Shares	Nil	20	20
10% Nonconvertible Debentures	30	Nil	20

Assuming corporate tax to be 35 per cent and the face value of all the shares and debentures to be ₹ 100 each, calculate the indifference points and earnings per share (EPS) for each of the financing plans. Which plan should be accepted by the company ?

SOLUTION

Determination of indifference point under plans X, Y, Z

Plan X: $\frac{X(1-t)}{N_1} = \frac{(X - \text{Interest})(1-t)}{N_2}; \frac{X(1-0.35)}{60,000} = \frac{(X - ₹ 3.0 \text{ lakh}) 0.65}{30,000}$

OR, $X - 0.35X = 2(0.65X - ₹ 1,95,000);$

$X - 0.35X = 1.3X - ₹ 3,90,000$

OR, $0.65X = ₹ 3,90,000$ *or* $X = ₹ 3,90,000/0.65 = ₹ 6,00,000$

Plan Y: $\frac{X(1-t)}{N_1} = \frac{(X - \text{Interest})(1-t) - D_P}{N_2}; \frac{X(1-0.35)}{60,000} = \frac{X(1-0.35) - ₹ 2,60,000}{40,000}$

OR, $\frac{0.65X}{60,000} = \frac{0.65X - ₹ 2,60,000}{40,000}$

$2(0.65X) = 3(0.65X - ₹ 2,60,000)$

$1.3X = 1.95X - ₹ 7,80,000$

OR, $X = ₹ 7,80,000/0.65 = ₹ 12,00,000$

Plan Z: $\frac{X(1-t)}{N_1} = \frac{(X - \text{Interest})(1-t) - D_P}{N_2}; \frac{0.65X}{60,000} = \frac{(X - ₹ 2 \text{ lakh}) 0.65 - ₹ 2,60,000}{20,000}$

OR, $\frac{0.65X}{60,000} = \frac{0.65X - ₹ 3,90,000}{20,000}$

$0.65X = 3(0.65X - ₹ 3,90,000)$

$X = ₹ 9,00,000$

DETERMINATION OF EPS UNDER PLANS X, Y AND Z FOR OPTIONS 1 AND 2

Particulars	*Plan X*		*Plan Y*		*Plan Z*	
	1	*2*	*1*	*2*	*1*	*2*
EBIT	6,00,000	6,00,000	12,00,000	12,00,000	9,00,000	9,00,000

Less: Interest	—	3,00,000	—	—	—	2,00,000
EBT	6,00,000	3,00,000	12,00,000	12,00,000	9,00,000	7,00,000
Less: Taxes @ 30%	2,10,000	1,05,000	4,20,000	4,20,000	3,15,000	2,45,000
EAT	3,90,000	1,95,000	7,80,000	7,80,000	5,85,000	4,55,000
Less: Pref. Dividend	—	—	—	2,60,000	—	2,60,000
Earning available for equity-holders	3,90,000	1,95,000	7,80,000	5,20,000	5,85,000	1,95,000
No. of Equity Shares	60,000	30,000	60,000	40,000	60,000	20,000
EPS	6.5	6.5	13	13	9.75	9.75

Conclusion: The company should adopt plan Y since the EPS is maximum under this plan.

PROBLEM 31

RTP Ltd. is in the process of raising ₹ 10,00,000 as additional capital. For this purpose two mutually exclusive alternative financial plans, have been identified. The current level of EBIT is ₹ 34,00,000 which is likely to remain unchanged. The relevant information is as follows:

Present capital structure : 6,00,000 Equity shares of ₹ 10 each, and 10% Bonds of ₹ 40,00,000

Tax rate : 50%

Current EBIT : ₹ 34,00,000

Current EPS : ₹ 2.50

Current market price : ₹ 50 per share

Financial Plan I : 40,000 equity shares @ ₹ 25 per share

Financial Plan II : 12% debentures of ₹ 10,00,000.

Required: What is the indifference level of EBIT? Identify the financial break-even levels and plot the EBIT-EPS lines on the graph paper. Which alternative financial plan is better?

SOLUTION

(A) CALCULATION OF INDIFFERENCE LEVEL

Let that level of EBIT be X *(in lakhs)*

Particulars	*Present*	*Plan I*	*Plan II*
A. EBIT	34.00	X	X
B. *Less:* Interest		4.00	5.20
C. EBT [A – B]		X – 4.00	X – 5.20
D. *Less:* Tax @ 50%		0.5 (X – 4.00)	0.5 (X – 5.20)
E. EAT [C – D]		0.5 X – 2.00	0.5 X – 2.60
F. No. of Equity Shares		6.40	6.00
G. EPS [E/F]		0.5X – 2.00/6.40	0.5X – 2.60/6.00

Equating EPS under both the plans to find Indifference Point.

$$\frac{0.5X - 2.00}{6.40} = \frac{0.5X - 2.60}{6.00}$$

$$6.00\,(0.5\,X - 2.00) = 6.40\,(0.5\,X - 2.60)$$

$$3.00\,X - 12.00 = 3.20\,X - 16.64$$

$$3.00\,X - 3.20\,X = -16.64 + 12.00$$

$$-0.20X = -4.64$$

$$X = 4.64/0.20 = 23.20$$

Thus, Indifference Level of EBIT = ₹ 23,20,000

(b) Calculation of financial BEP

Equality EPS under each plan equal to zero.

$$\text{Financial BEP under Plan I} = \frac{0.5X - 2.00}{6.40} = 0$$

$$0.5X - 2.00 = 0$$

$$X = 2.00/0.5 = 4.00$$

$$\text{Financial BEP under Plan II} = \frac{0.5X - 2.60}{6.00} = 0$$

$$0.5X - 2.60 = 0$$

$$X = 2.60/0.5 = 5.20$$

(c) Graphical Representation of EBIT-EPS, Indifference point and Financial Break Even levels.

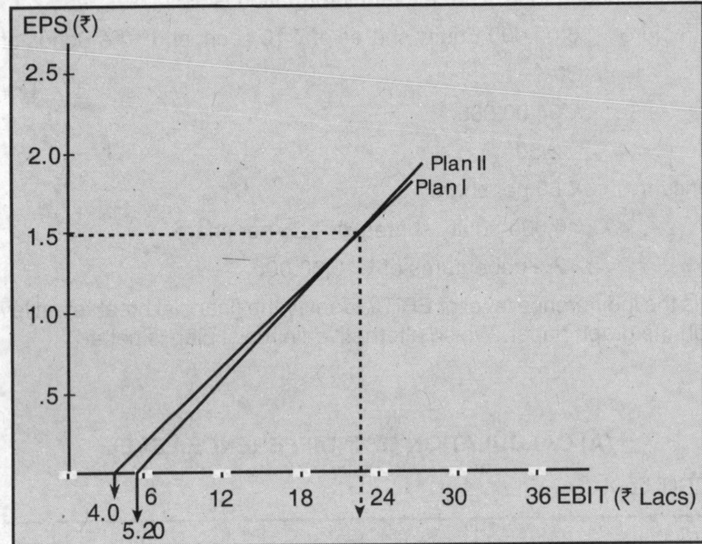

To the right of the indifference point Plan II is better, while Plan I is better for all values of EBIT below the indifference point. The horizontal intercepts identify the financial break even levels of EBIT for each plan.

(d) Choice of Financial Plan

$$\text{EPS (Plan I)} = \frac{(₹\ 34,00,000 - ₹\ 4,00,000)(1-0.5)}{6,40,000 \text{ Shares}} = ₹\ 2.34 \text{ per share}$$

$$\text{EPS (Plan II)} = \frac{(₹\ 34,00,000 - 4,00,000 - 1,20,000)(1-0.5)}{6,00,000 \text{ shares}} = ₹\ 2.40 \text{ per share}$$

In the absence of P/E Ratio, choice of financial plan is to be made on the basis of EPS. Hence, Plan II is better since EPS under Plan II is greater than that under Plan I.

PROBLEM 32

Mr. X is an enterpreneur and has recently set up manufacturing unit of Pens. He currently sells 2 million pens a year at ₹ 5 each. His variable cost to produce the pen is ₹ 3 per pen and he has ₹ 30 lakh in fixed costs. His sales to assets ratio is 5 times, and 40 per cent of his assets are financed with 10% debt, with the balance being financed by equity shares of ₹ 10 per share. The tax rate is 35 per cent.

His newly appointed finance manager Mr. Y, feels that Mr. X is doing it all wrong. By reducing his price to ₹ 4.50 per pens, he could increase his sales volume of pens by 40 per cent. Fixed costs would remain constant, and variable costs would remain ₹ 3 per unit. His sales to asset ratio would be 6.3 times. Furthermore, he could increase his debt to assets ratio to 50 per cent, with the balance in shares. It is assumed that the interest rate would go up 1% and that the price of shares would remain constant.

(a) Compute the EPS under the X and Y plans. Is Mr. Y's perception right?

(b) What is the effect on the total risk of the firm on switching from one plan to another?

SOLUTION

(A) AND (B) COMPUTATION OF EPS UNDER X AND Y PLANS

Particulars	*X Plan*	*Y Plan*
A. Sales Units	20,00,000	28,00,000
B. Selling Price per unit	₹ 5	₹ 4.50
C. Sales Revenue [A × B]	₹ 100,00,000	126,00,000
D. *Less:* Variable Cost @ ₹ 3	₹ 60,00,000	84,00,000
E. Contribution [C – D]	40,00,000	42,00,000
F. *Less:* Fixed Costs	30,00,000	30,00,000
G. EBIT [E – F]	10,00,000	12,00,000
H. *Less:* Interest (Working Note 1)	80,000	1,10,000
I. EBT [G – H]	9,20,000	10,90,000
J. *Less:* Tax @ 35%	3,22,000	3,81,500
K. EAT [I – J]	5,98,000	7,08,500
L. Number of Shares	1,20,000	1,00,000
M. EPS [K / L]	4.98	7.085
N. Degree of Operating Leverage (E/G)	4.00	3.50
O. Degree of Financial Leverage (G/I)	1.09	1.10
P. Degree of Combined Leverage (J × K)	4.36	3.85

Under Y Plan with decrease in degree of combined leverage the market price of its shares is likely to go up.

Working Note:

CALCULATION OF INTEREST ON DEBT AND NO. OF EQUITY SHARES

Particulars	*X Plan*	*Y Plan*
Assets (Sales/Assets Turnover)	₹ 20 lakh	₹ 20 lakh
Debt	40% of ₹ 20 lacs = ₹ 8 lacs	50% of ₹ 20 lacs = ₹ 10 lacs
Rate of Interest on Debt	10%	11%
Interest on Debt	₹ 80,000	₹ 1,10,000
Equity	₹ 20 lacs – ₹ 8 lacs = ₹ 12 lacs	₹ 20 lacs – ₹ 10 lacs = ₹ 10 lacs
No. of Equity Shares	1,20,000	1,00,000

PROBLEM 33

Tulsian Ltd. provides you the following information:

1. Details regarding sales etc. of existing projects and proposed projects:

Particulars	Existing	Proposed Project I	Proposed Project II
Sales	₹ 20 lakh	₹ 3 lakh	₹ 5 lakh
Variable Cost	60%	$66\frac{2}{3}\%$	64%
Fixed Costs	₹ 2 lakh	₹ 0.40 lakh	₹ 1.00 lakh
15% Debt		₹ 8 lakh	
Equity Share Capital (₹ 10 each)	₹ 4 lakh		
Investment required	—	₹ 4.00 lakh	₹ 6.00 lakh

2. Details regarding two financial plans for financing the proposed projects:
   (a) It could borrow upto ₹ 12,00,000 @ 9% for *either or* both of the projects.
   (b) It could issue 10% Preference Shares upto ₹ 6,00,000.
3. Tax Rate : 40%
4. Industry Asset Leverage : 1.2

Required:

(a) Are the existing Financial Leverage and Asset Leverage favourable to the company ?

(b) How does the acceptance of each project affect the different leverages including asset leverages ?

(c) What is the effect of financing plans on future EPS and ROI ? Also state which financial plan is better ?

SOLUTION

STATEMENT SHOWING THE CALCULATION OF DIFFERENT LEVERAGES, ROI AND EPS

(₹ in lakhs)

Particulars	Existing	Debt Plan		Debt. + Pref. Share Plan	
		Project I	*Project II*	*Project I*	*Project II*
A. Sales	20.00	3.00	5.00	3.00	5.00
B. *Less:* Variable Cost	12.00	2.00	3.20	2.00	3.20
C. Contribution	8.00	1.00	1.80	1.00	1.80
D. *Less:* Fixed Costs	2.00	0.40	1.00	0.40	1.00
E. EBIT	6.00	0.60	0.80	0.60	0.80
F. *Less:* Interest	1.20	0.36	0.54	0.36	—
G. EBT	4.80	0.24	0.26	0.24	0.80
H. *Less:* Tax @ 40%	1.92	0.096	0.104	.096	0.32
I. EAT	2.88	0.144	0.156	0.144	0.48
J. *Less:* Pref. Dividend	—	—	—	—	0.60
K. Earning after Pref. Dividend	2.88	0.144	0.156	0.144	(0.12)

L. No. of Equity Shares	0.40	0.40	0.40	0.40	0.40
M. EPS (₹ per share)	7.20	0.36	0.39	0.36	(0.30)
N. Return on investment [EBIT/Capital Employed]	50%	15%	13.33%	15%	13.33%
O. Operating Leverage [Contribution/EBIT]	1.33	1.67	2.25	1.67	2.25
P. Financing Leverage [EBIT/EBT]	1.25	2.5	3.08	2.5	1.00
Q. Combined Leverage [Contribution/EBT]	1.67	4.167	6.92	4.167	2.25
R. Asset Leverage [Sales/Total Assets]	1.67	0.75	0.83	0.75	0.83

Part (a)

(i) Yes, the company has favourable financial leverage because its ROI (i.e. 50%) is greater that the cost of debt (i.e. 12%).

(ii) Yes, the company has better asset leverage (i.e. 1.67) than the industry asset leverage (i.e. 1.2).

PART (B) EFFECT OF ACCEPTANCE OF PROJECTS ON DIFFERENT LEVERAGES

Particulars	*Existing*	*Project I*		*Project II*	
		Debt Plan	*Debt + Pref. Plan*	*Debt. Plan*	*Debt + Pref. Plan*
Operating Risk	1.33	Increases (1.67)	Increases (1.67)	Increases (2.25)	Increases (2.25)
Financial Risk	1.25	Increases (2.5)	Increases (2.5)	Increases (3.08)	Decreases (1.00)
Total Risk	1.67	Increases (4.167)	Increases (4.167)	Increases (6.92)	Increases (2.25)
Asset Leverage	1.67	Decreases (0.75)	Decreases (0.75)	Decreases (0.83)	Decreases (0.83)

PART (C) EFFECT OF FINANCING PLANS ON FUTURE EPS AND ROI

Particulars	*Existing*	*Debt Plan*	*Debt + Pref. Share Plan*
EPS	₹ 7.20	Increase by ₹ 0.75	Increases by ₹ 0.06
		(i.e. ₹ 0.36 + ₹ 0.39)	(i.e. ₹ 0.36 – ₹ 0.30)
ROI	50%	Decreases= $\frac{₹\,0.60 + ₹\,0.80}{₹\,4.00 + ₹\,6.00}$ = 14%	Decreases= $\frac{₹\,0.60 + ₹\,0.80}{₹\,4.00 + ₹\,6.00}$ = 14%

Recommendation: Debt plan is better than Debt + Pref. Share Plan because EPS under this plan will increase by ₹ 0.75.

6 CAPITAL STRUCTURE THEORIES

LEARNING OBJECTIVES

After studying this chapter, you should be able to understand:

- Meaning of Capital Structure
- Meaning of an Optimum Capital Structure
- Features of an Appropriate Capital Structure
- Factors Determining the Capital Structure
- Capital Structure Theories
- Net Income (NI) Approach
- Net Operating Income (NOI) Approach
- Traditional Approach
- Modigliani Miller (M-M) Approach
- How to Determine the Optimal Debt-Equity Mix

1.0 MEANING OF CAPITAL STRUCTURE

1. Capital structure *(also known as financial structure)* refers to the composition of long-term funds such as debentures, long-borrowings, preferences shares, equity shares (including retained earnings) in the capitalization of a company.
2. The essence of Capital Structure decision is to determine the relative proportion of equity and debt.
3. Equity here in broader sense means owner's funds which can be raised by issue of equity shares and preference shares and by retained earnings.
4. Debt can be raised by issuing debentures/bonds *or* by taking long-term borrowings.
5. The capital structure decision is a significant financial decision because it affects the shareholder's return and risk and, consequently, the market value of shares.
6. The use of the sources of funds with fixed cost, such as debt and preference share capital along with the owner's equity capital in the capital structure is described as financial leverage *or* trading on equity.
7. The use of the term 'trading on equity' is derived from the fact that it is the owner's equity which is used as a basis to raise debt, that is, the equity that is traded upon.

2.0 MEANING OF AN OPTIMUM CAPITAL STRUCTURE

THEORETICAL VIEW

(a) The financial manager should plan the 'optimum capital structure' for its company.

(b) The optimum capital structure is obtained when the market value per share is maximum in the long run. The market value will be maximised when the marginal real cost of each source of funds is the same.

(c) At optimum capital structure, the overall cost of capital is minimum and the total market value of the firm is maximum.

PRACTICAL VIEW

(a) The determination of the optimum capital structure is a difficult task because a number of factors influence the capital structure decision and it is difficult to measure a fall in the market value of an equity share on account of increase in risk due to high debt content in the capital structure.

(b) There is no one definite model which can be suggested as an ideal for all business undertaking because of the varying circumstances of various business undertaking.

(c) That's why different industries follow different capital structures and, within an industry, different companies follow different capital structures.

(d) Thus, appropriate capital structure is more realistic term than the theoretical term of optimum capital structure.

3.0 FEATURES OF AN APPROPRIATE CAPITAL STRUCTURE

1. While developing an appropriate capital structure for the company, the financial manager should aim at maximising the long-term market price of equity shares.
2. A sound *or* appropriate capital structure should have the following features:
   1. **Profitability** — The capital structure of the company should be most advantageous. Within the constraints, maximum use of the leverage at minimum cost should be made so as to obtain maximum advantage of trading on equity at minimum cost.
   2. **Solvency** — The capital structure should involve minimum risk of financial insolvency. The use of excessive debt threatens the solvency of the company.
   3. **Flexibility** — The capital structure should be flexible to meet the changing conditions. It should also be possible for the company to provide funds whenever needed to finance its profitable activities.
   4. **Conservatism** — The capital structure should be conservative in the sense that the debt capacity of the company should not be exceeded. The debt capacity of a company depends on its ability to generate cash flows. It should have enough cash to pay the fixed periodic charges (e.g., interest) and the principal sum on maturity.
   5. **Control** — The capital structure should involve minimum risk of loss of control of the company.
3. The relative importance of each of these features may differ from company to company. ***For Example***, a company may give more importance to flexibility than control while another company may be more concerned about solvency than any other requirement. Furthermore, the relative importance of these requirements may change with changing conditions.

4.0 FACTORS DETERMINING THE CAPITAL STRUCTURE

1. A variety of factors are to be considered while determining the capital structure.
2. Basically, the three basic factors i.e., Risk, Cost and Control determine the capital structure of a firm at a given point of time.
3. The finance manager should attempt to design the capital structure in such a manner that the risk and cost are the least and the control of the existing management is diluted to the least extent.
4. In addition to Risk, Cost and Control, there are also other factors like flotation costs, marketability, flexibility etc. All these factors are discussed below:
   1. **Financial Risk** — Financial risk is of two types as follows:

(a) **Risk of cash insolvency** — In case a firm uses debt in its capital structure, its risk of cash insolvency increases because of following two reasons:

(i) The firm is committed to pay fixed interest on debt irrespective of the fact that whether it has cash *or* not.

(ii) The firm is committed to pay fixed instalment of principle irrespective of the fact that whether it has cash *or* not.

(b) **Risk of Variation in Expected Earnings available to Shareholders** — In case a firm used higher debt content in its capital structure, risk of variation in expected earnings available to shareholders will be higher. Earnings available to shareholders will increase if the return on investment is higher than the cost of debt and will decrease if the return on investment is *less* than the cost of debt. In other words, the relative dispersion of expected earnings available to equity shareholders will be greater if the capital structure of a firm has higher debt content.

Thus, financial risk encompasses the volatility of earnings available to equity shareholders as well as the probability of cash insolvency.

2. **Trading on Equity (or Leverage *or* EBIT-EPS Analysis)** — The use of the sources of funds with fixed cost, such as debt and preference share capital along with the owner's equity capital in the structure is known as 'financial leverage' *or* 'trading on equity'. The use of the term 'trading on equity' is derived from the fact that it is the owner's equity that is used as basis to raise debt, that is the equity that is traded upon.

A financial manager must examine in detail how the use of proposed financing mix will affect the risk and return of the owners. The financial leverage employed by the company will depend on the amount of risk the company would like to take.

Advantages: The use of debt and preference share capital in the capital structure increases the equity shareholders' return because of following two reasons:

(a) The rate of return on investment is more than the rate of interest on debt and rate of dividend on preference capital and hence the difference is distributed to shareholders.

(b) The interest paid on debt is tax deductible and hence there is tax saving.

Disadvantages: The disadvantages of using debt in the capital structure are:

(a) There is financial risk involved as interest on debt (being a charge against profits) is to be paid even when the company is not earning sufficient profits and hence there is threat of insolvency. Debt usually has a charge on assets of the company and lenders can use for the recovery of their capital and interest.

(b) Earning per share (EPS) may decrease if the rate of return on investment is *less* than the rate of interest.

Effect of No Debt: The effect of not using debt in the capital structure are:

(a) There is no financial risk involved as no interest on debt is to be paid and hence there is no threat of insolvency.

(b) Earnings per share decreases as the same amount of earnings have to be divided among increased number of equity shares as a result of issue of additional equity shares in lieu of debt.

Thus, the company is required to achieve a trade off between return and risk while deciding upon the proportion of debt and preference share capital in its capital structure.

Examining the Impact of Leverage on EPS

To examine the impact of leverage on the EPS (i.e., earning per share), EBIT-EPS analysis should be considered. EBIT-EPS analysis shows the impact of various financing alternatives on EPS at various levels of EBIT. Let us consider the effect of financial leverage on EPS by considering two alternative plans.

EXAMPLE:

Total Funds required	—	₹ 10,00,000
Financial Plan 'A'	—	100% Equity shares of ₹ 10 each
Financial plan 'B'	—	50% Equity shares of ₹ 10 each, and 50%, 15% debt.
Tax Rate	—	40%

Level of Earnings before interest and taxes (EBIT) situation (a) ₹ 2,00,000, situation (b) ₹ 1,00,000

SOLUTION

STATEMENT SHOWING THE EFFECT OF FINANCIAL LEVERAGE ON EPS AND RETURN ON EQUITY

Particulars	*At EBIT Level of ₹ 2,00,000*		*At EBIT Level of ₹ 1,00,000*	
	Financial Plan 'A'	*Financial Plan 'B'*	*Financial Plan 'A'*	*Financial Plan 'B'*
(A) Earning before interest and taxes	2,00,000	2,00,000	1,00,000	1,00,000
(B) *Less:* Interest on long term debt (15% on ₹ 5,00,000)	—	75,000	—	75,000
(C) Earning before taxes (A – B)	2,00,000	1,25,000	1,00,000	25,000
(D) *Less:* Taxes @ 40%	80,000	50,000	40,000	10,000
(E) Earnings after taxes (C – D)	1,20,000	75,000	60,000	15,000
(F) *Less:* Preferential dividend	—	—	—	—
(G) Earning after interest, taxes and Pref. Dividend	1,20,000	75,000	60,000	15,000
(H) No. of equity shares	1,00,000	50,000	1,00,000	50,000
(I) Earnings per share (G/H)	₹ 1.20	₹ 1.50	₹ 0.60	₹ 0.30
(J) Return on Equity				
$\frac{\text{Earning after interest \& pref. dividend}}{\text{Equity shareholders' funds}}$	= 12%	= 15%	= 6%	= 3%

Analysis

I. At EBIT level of ₹ 2,00,000, Plan B is the most attractive because EPS of ₹ 1.50 is higher than EPS of ₹ 1.20 as under Plan 'A'. This is because of the following two reasons:
   (a) Use of the debt in Financial Plan 'B', and
   (b) Return on total assets [i.e. 20% (i.e. ₹ 2,00,000/₹ 10,00,000 100)] is more than the cost of debt [i.e., 15%]

II. At EBIT level of ₹ 1,00,000, Plan 'A' is the most attractive because EPS of 60 paise is higher then EPS of 30 paise as under Plan 'B'. This is because of the following two reasons:
   (a) Use of the debt in Financial Plan 'B', and
   (b) Return on total assets [i.e. 10% (i.e. ₹ 1,00,000/₹ 10,00,000 100)] is *less* than the cost of debt [i.e., 15%]

ADVANTAGE AND DISADVANTAGE OF USE OF DEBT

The financial leverage is double-edged sword because on the one hand, it increases shareholders' return and, on the other hand, it increase the risk. It will have a favourable impact on EPS(earning per share) and ROE (return on equity) if return on assets exceeds the interest cost of debt but it will have an unfavourable impact if return on assets is *less* than the cost of debt. The advantage of debt is that it saves taxes since interest is a deductible expenses. The disadvantage is that it can cause financial distress. Financial distress becomes costly when the firm finds it difficult to pay interest and capital.

ADVANTAGE AND DISADVANTAGE OF NOT USING DEBT

A firm can avoid financial risk altogether if it does not use any debt in its capital structure. But when no debt is used in the capital structure, the shareholders will be deprived of the benefit of increases in EPS arising from financial leverage (or trading on equity).

SHOULD A FIRM EMPLOY DEBT?

A firm should employ debt to the extent the financial risk perceived by the shareholders does not exceed the benefit of increased EPS. It can be shown as follows:

Case	*If ROI > Cost of Debt*		*If ROI < Cost of Debt*	
	Effect on EPS	*Effect on Financial Risk*	*Effect on EPS*	*Effect on Financial Risk*
I. Use of more debt in capital structure	Increase	Increase	Decreases & it may even lead to negative EPS.	Increases threat of insolvency
II. Use of *less* debt in capital structure	Relatively *less* increase	Relatively *less* increase	Relatively *less* decrease	Relatively *less* increase

Thus, financial leverages has two implications for companies:

(i) Use of cheaper fixed charge securities will lead to increase in return on equity as well as earnings per share.

(ii) Use of fixed charge securities increases risk of equity investors in the sense that a given change in EBIT will cause a greater change in EPS as well as return on equity.

3. **Cost of Capital** — The cost of a source of finance is the minimum return expected by its suppliers. The expected return depends on the degree of risk assumed by investors. Higher the degree of risk assumed, the higher will be the return expected by the suppliers of funds. The degree of risk assumed and return expected by suppliers of funds are shown below:

Sources of Fund	*Degree of Risk Assumed by Supplier of Fund*	*Return Expected by Supplier of Fund*
1. Debt	Lower than any other source of funds	Lower than any other source of funds
2. Preference Share Capital	Higher than debt but lower than equity share capital	Higher than debt but lower than equity share capital
3. Equity Share Capital	Higher than any other source of funds	Higher than any other source of funds

The cost of equity includes the cost of new issue of shares and the cost of retained earning. The cost of retained earnings is *less* than the cost of new issues because the company does not have to pay corporate dividend tax and also no floatation costs are incurred. Thus,

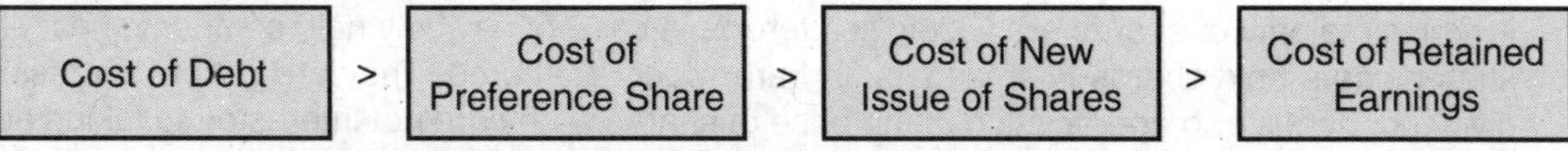

Though the cost of debt is cheaper than the cost of shares, it does not mean that a company can minimise its overall cost of capital by employing debt because, after a certain point, the debt becomes more expensive because of the increased risk of excessive debt to creditors and shareholders. Thus, the company should continue to use debt upto the point the overall cost of capital decreases but should not use debt beyond that point when the overall cost of capital starts increasing. Theoretically, the optimal debt equity mix for the company is at a point where the overall cost of capital is minimum.

Example: The cost of debt and of equity capital at various levels of debt-equity mix are estimated as follows:

Proportion of Debt (%)	*Proportion of Equity (%)*	*Cost of Debt (%)*	*Cost of Equity (%)*
0	100	10	14
20	80	10	14
40	60	11	16
50	50	12	18
60	40	13	20

Let us determine the optimal debt-equity mix.

A	*B*	*C = A × B*	*D*	*E*	*F = D × E*	*G = C + F*
Proportion of debt	*Cost of Debt %*	*Total Cost of Debt*	*Proportion of Equity*	*Cost of Equity (%)*	*Total Cost of Equity*	*Average Cost of Capital*
0.00	10	0.00	1.00	14	14.00	14.00
0.20	10	2.00	0.80	14	11.20	13.20
0.40	11	4.40	0.60	16	9.60	14.00
0.50	12	6.00	0.50	18	9.00	15.00
0.60	13	7.80	0.40	20	8.00	15.80

Conclusion: A mix of 20% debt and 80% equity will make the capital structure optimal because it has the minimum overall cost of capital.

4. **Cash Flow** — The ability of a business to discharge is fixed obligations (e.g., payment of interest on debt, payment of the principal amount of debt) depends on the availability of liquid cash. The firm may earn sufficient profits to cover the fixed charges arising out of debt but the firm may not have sufficient cash to pay, as the profits get continually invested in the form of more inventory, book debts *or* even purchase of equipment particularly if it is a growing concern. If a company is not able to generate enough cash to meet its fixed obligations, it may have to face financial insolvency. Hence, besides profitability, it is necessary to estimate the cash flows before deciding on the proportion of debt in the capital structure.

5. **Control** — The existing management group in order to retain its control over the company, may prefer to raise additional finance through the issue of preference shares *or* raising debt instead of issuing equity shares. This is because the equity shareholders have rights to elect directors and to participate in the management of the company whereas the suppliers to debt and preference shareholders do not have such rights. The risk of loss of control involved in raising finance through the issue of new equity shares can almost be avoided by distributing shares widely (e.g., by allotting shares to applications of different regions instead of allotting maximum shares to the applicants of a particular region) and in small lots (i.e., by allotting minimum number of shares (say, in lots of 100 shares) to each applicant. That's why the risk of loss of control is an important consideration in case of a closely held company (i.e., the company in which majority of the shares are held by a few members) instead of widely held company (i.e., the company in which majority of shares are widely scattered). In case of a widely held company most of the shareholders hold shares in small lots and are widely scattered. They are simply interested in dividend, bonus and appreciation in the price of shares. They are not interested to taking active part in the company's management.

   To avoid the loss of control, the company should not use the excessive debt because the restrictions imposed by the suppliers of large among of debt may curtail the freedom of the management to run the business and use of excessive debt may also cause bankruptcy which means a complete loss of control.

6. **Flexibility** — Flexibility means the firm's ability to adapt its capital structure to the needs of the changing conditions. The capital structure of a company is considered to be flexible when the company has ability to change the composition of the capital structure. The company should be in a position to raise funds whenever needed and to redeem its redeemable preference shares *or* debt whenever required.
7. **Size of the Company** — The size of a company as well as its credit standing greatly influence the availability of funds from different sources. A small company has to depend on owner's funds (i.e., capital and retained earnings) because it is often difficult for it to raise long-term loans. A large company can obtain long-term loans on easy terms and can also issue equity shares, preference shares and debentures to the public. Similarly, the company enjoying high credit standing among investors and lenders is in a better position to raise funds from various sources as compared to a company enjoying low credit standing. A company should make the best use of its size in planning the capital structure.
8. **Nature of Business** — The nature of business of a company also determines the extent to which equity *or* debt capital should be raised. If a company is engaged in business activities in which sales are subject to wide fluctuations, it is desirable to have a smaller proportion of borrowed funds because it may face financial distress during lean business due to its inability to discharge the fixed obligations. But if a company is engaged in business activities in which sales and earnings are almost stable, it may have larger proportion of borrowed funds. Similarly, the companies operating in competitive industry (e.g., readymade garments) should rely *less* on debt capital and more on equity capital.
9. **Market Conditions *or* Marketability** — Marketability here means the ability of the company to sell *or* market particular type of security in a particular period of time. It depends upon the readiness of the investors to buy the security. Due to the changing market sentiments, the company has to decide whether to raise funds through equity shares *or* through debt. During the boom period in the share market, the company should raise funds through the issue of shares instead of debenture. During the lean period, the company should raise funds through the issue of debentures instead of shares.
10. **Flotation Costs** — Flotation costs here mean the costs incurred in the issue of shares *or* debentures (***For Example***, cost of printing & distribution of prospects, underwriting commission, issue manager's commission). Flotation costs may be an important factor influencing the capital structure of a company especially in case of small companies which are interested in raising a small amount of funds through the capital market.
11. **Corporate Taxation** — Under Income Tax Act, 1961, dividend on shares is not deductible while interest paid on borrowed capital is allowed as deduction. Interest on borrowing is usually deductible in the year in which it is incurred. If it is incurred during the pre-commencement period, it is to be capitalized. Cost of issue of shares is allowed as deduction.
12. **Government Policies** — Government policies are major factor determining capital structure. ***For Example***, a change in lending policies of financial institution may mean a complete change in the financial pattern to be followed in the companies. Similarly, the Rules and Regulations framed by SEBI considerably affect the capital structure decisions. A company has to operate in the framework provided by Law. The Companies Act and the Securities and Exchange Board of India (SEBI) provide guidelines from time to time regarding the raising of funds from the public.
13. **Purpose of Financing** — The purpose of financing also to some extent affects the determination of capital structure of the company. In case funds are required for productive purposes like manufacturing etc., the company may raise funds through long term sources. On the other hand, if funds are required for non-productive sources, like welfare facilities to employees such as schools, hospitals etc., the company may rely on internal sources.
14. **Period of Finance** — The period for which finance is required also affects the determination of capital structure. In case funds are required for long term requirements say 8 to 10 years, it will be appropriate to raise borrowed funds. However, if the funds are required more *or less* permanently, it will be appropriate to raise them by issue of equity shares.

5.0 CAPITAL STRUCTURE THEORIES

Capital Structure theories explain the theoretical relationship between cost of capital and the value of the firm. The four important theories of capital structure are:

1. Net Income (NI) approach
2. Net Operating Income (NOI) approach
3. Traditional approach
4. Modigilani and Miller (MM) approach

6.0 NET INCOME (NI) APPROACH

1. Is Weighted Average Cost of Capital of a firm independent of its capital structure? According to NI approach, weighted average cost of capital of a firm is not independent of its capital structure. In other words, a firm can change its value and the cost of capital through a judicious mix of debt and equity.
2. Effect of Change in Leverage on the Weighted Average Cost of Capital and the Total Value of the firm

   The effect of change in leverage on the weighted average cost of capital and the total value of the firm has been shown below:

Effect on............	*Effect of increase in Leverage*	*Effect of decrease in Leverage*
Weighted Average Cost of Capital (k_0)	Decreases because of advantage associated with use of relatively *less* expensive debt	Increases because of disadvantage associated with use of relatively more expensive equity
Total Value of the firm (V)	Increases because of decrease in Weighted Average Cost of Capital	Decreases because of increase in Weighted Average Cost of Capital

3. **Graphical Presentation of the Effect of Change in Leverage on the Weighted Average Cost of Capital under NI APPROACH.**

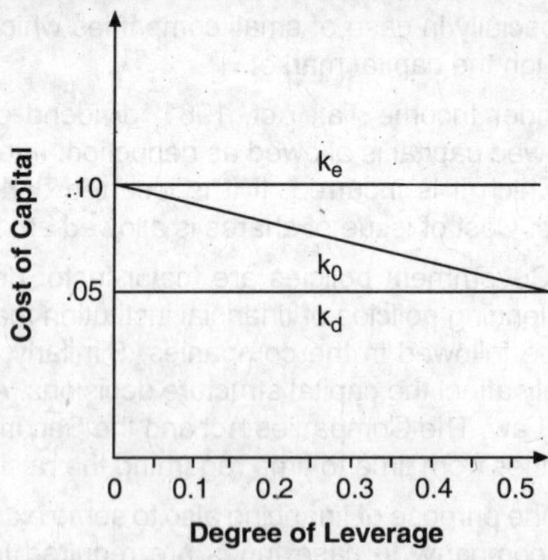

Fig. Effect of Leverage on Cost of Capital (under NI Approach)

4. **Assumptions of NI Approach**
   1. $k_d < k_e$ — The debt capitalization rate (k_d) is *less* than the equity capitalization rate (k_e).
   2. No change in risk — The use of debt content does not change the risk perception of investors. As a result, both debt capitalization rate (k_d) and equity capitalization rate (k_e) remains constant.

3. No Taxes — There are no corporate taxes.

5. **Can there be Optimum Capital Structure?**

According to NI approach, a firm can evolve an optimum capital structure at which the weighted average cost of capital would be lowest and the value of the firm would be highest through a judicious mix of debt and equity.

6. **Practical Steps involved in the calculation of Weighted Average Cost of Capital (k_0)**

Step 1: ***Calculate Market Value of Equity (S) as follows:***

$$\text{Market Value of Equity (S)} = \frac{\text{Net Income}}{k_e} = \frac{\text{NOI} - \text{Interest}}{k_e}$$

Step 2: ***Calculate Market Value of Debt (D) as follows:***

$$\text{Market Value of Debt (D)} = \frac{\text{Interest}}{\text{Rate of Interest}}$$

Step 3: ***Calculate Total Value of the Firm (V) as follows:***

Total Value of Firm (V) = Market Value of Equity (S) + Market Value of Debt (D)

Step 4: ***Calculate Weighted Average Cost of Capital (k_o)***

$$\text{Weighted Average Cost of Capital} = \frac{\text{NOI}}{\text{Total Value of the firm (V)}}$$

7. **Statement showing the Calculation of Total Value of Firm and Weighted Average Cost of Capital [Under NI Approach]**

	Particulars	*X Ltd. Levered*	*Y Ltd. Unlevered*
A	Net Operating Income (NOI)	....	....
B	*Less:* Interest on Debt (I)	....	NIL
C	Earnings for Equity Shareholders (NI)	....	....
D	Equity Capitalization Rate (k_e)	....	....
E	Market Value of Equity (S) [NI / k_e]	....	....
F	Market Value of Debt (D) [I / Rate of Interest]	....	NIL
G	Total Value of Firm (V = S + D)	....	....
H	Weighted Average Cost of Capital (ko)	....	....
	k_o = NOI/Total Value of firm (V)		
	$k_o = (k_e \times S/V) + (k_d \times D/V)$		
	Where, k_d = Rate of interest on debt		

ILLUSTRATION 1 [NET INCOME APPROACH]

The following data relate to two companies to the same risk class:

Particulars	*X Ltd.*	*Y Ltd.*
Expected Net Operating Income	₹ 2,40,000	₹ 2,40,000
10% Debt	₹ 7,20,000	
Equity Capitalization Rate	20%	15%

Required: (Use Net Income Approach)

(a) Determine the Total Value of the company and the Weighted Average Cost of Capital for each company.

(b) State the effect on the Total Value of the company and Average Cost of Capital in part (a) if the X Ltd. has decided to raise the debt by ₹ 3,80,000 and use the proceeds to buyback equity shares.

(c) State the effect on the Total Value of the company and Average Cost of Capital in part (a) if the X Ltd. has decided to issue equity shares by ₹ 3,80,000 and use the proceeds to redeem the debt.

SOLUTION

(A) CALCULATION OF TOTAL VALUE OF FIRM AND WEIGHTED AVERAGE COST OF CAPITAL

Particulars	*X Ltd.*	*Y Ltd.*
A. Net Operating Income (NOI)	₹ 2,40,000	₹ 2,40,000
B. *Less:* Interest on Debt (I)	₹ 72,000	—
C. Earnings for Equity Shareholders (NI)	₹ 1,68,000	₹ 2,40,000
D. Equity Capitalization Rate (k_e)	0.20	0.15
E. Market Value of Equity (S) [NI / k_e]	₹ 8,40,000	₹ 16,00,000
F. Market Value of Debt (D) [I / Rate of Interest]	₹ 7,20,000	—
G. Total Value of Firm (V = S + D)	₹ 15,60,000	₹ 16,00,000
H. Weighted Average Cost of Capital (k_o) $k_o = (k_e \times S / V) + (k_d \times D/V)$ *or* k_o = NOI/V	0.15385	0.15000

(B) CALCULATION OF TOTAL VALUE OF FIRM & WEIGHTED AVERAGE COST OF CAPITAL

Particulars	*X Ltd.*
A. Net Operating Income (NOI)	₹ 2,40,000
B. *Less:* Interest on Debt (I)	₹ 1,10,000
C. Earnings for Equity Shareholders (NI)	₹ 1,30,000
D. Equity Capitalization Rate (k_e)	0.20
E. Market Value of Equity (S) [NI / k_e]	₹ 6,50,000
F. Market Value of Debt (D) [I / Rate of Interest]	₹ 11,00,000
G. Total Value of Firm (V = S + D)	₹ 17,50,000
H. Weighted Average Cost of Capital (k_o) $k_o = (k_e \times S / V) + (k_d \times D/V)$ *or* k_o = NOI/V	0.13714

Effect: Increase in leverage has increased the value of the firm and decreased the weighted Average Cost of Capital.

(C) CALCULATION OF TOTAL VALUE OF FIRM & WEIGHTED AVERAGE COST OF CAPITAL

Particulars	*X Ltd.*
A. Net Operating Income (NOI)	₹ 2,40,000
B. *Less:* Interest on Debt (I)	₹ 34,000
C. Earnings for Equity Shareholders (NI)	₹ 2,06000
D. Equity Capitalization Rate (k_e)	0.20

E. Market Value of Equity (S) [NI/k_e]	₹ 10,30,000
F. Market Value of Debt (D) [I/Rate of Interest]	₹ 3,40,000
G. Total Value of Firm (V = S + D)	₹ 13,70,000
H. Weighted Average Cost of Capital (k_o) $k_o = (k_e \times S / V) + (k_d \times D/V)$ *or* k_o = NOI/V	0.17518

Effect: Decrease in Leverage has decreased the value of the firm and increased the Weighted Average Cost of Capital

7.0 NET OPERATING INCOME (NOI) APPROACH

1. Is Weighted Average Cost of Capital of a Firm Independent of its Capital Structure?

   According to NOI approach, Weighted averaged cost of capital of a firm is independent of its capital structure. In other words, a firm cannot change its value and the cost of capital through a judicious mix of debt and equity.

2. Effect of Change in Leverage on Equity Capitalization Rate, Weighted Average Cost of Capital and the Total Value of the firm

   The effect of change in leverage on the equity capitalization rate, weighted average cost of capital and the total value of the firm has been shown below:

(A) EFFECT OF INCREASE IN LEVERAGE

Effect on............	*Effect*	*Effect of Increase in Leverage*
(a) Equity Capitalization Rate (k_e)	Increase	The increase in the proportion of debt in the capital structure would lead to increase in the financial risk of equity shareholders. To compensate increased financial risk, the shareholders would expect a higher rate of return on their investments.
(b) Weighted Average Cost of Capital (k_0)	Remain Constant	The advantage associated with the use of the relatively *less* expensive debt in terms of explicit cost is exactly neutralized by the implicit cost of debt represented by the increase in the cost of equity capital.
(c) Total Value of the firm (V)	Remain Constant	Since k_o remain constant.

(B) EFFECT OF DECREASE IN LEVERAGE

Effect on............	*Effect*	*Effect of Increase in Leverage*
(a) Equity Capitalization Rate (k_e)	Increase	The decrease in the proportion of debt in the capital structure would lead to decrease in the financial risk of equity shareholders. For decreased financial risk, the shareholders would expect a lower rate of return on their investments.
(b) Weighted Average Cost of Capital (k_0)	Remain Constant	The disadvantage associated with the non-use of the relatively *less* expensive debt in terms of explicit cost is exactly neutralized by the advantage in terms of decrease in implicit cost of debt represented by the decrease in the cost of equity capital.
(c) Total Value of the firm (V)	Remain Constant	Since k_o remain constant.

3. Graphical Presentation of Effect of Change in Leverage on Equity Capitalization Rate (K_e) and Weighted Average Cost of Capital (k_o) under NOI Approach

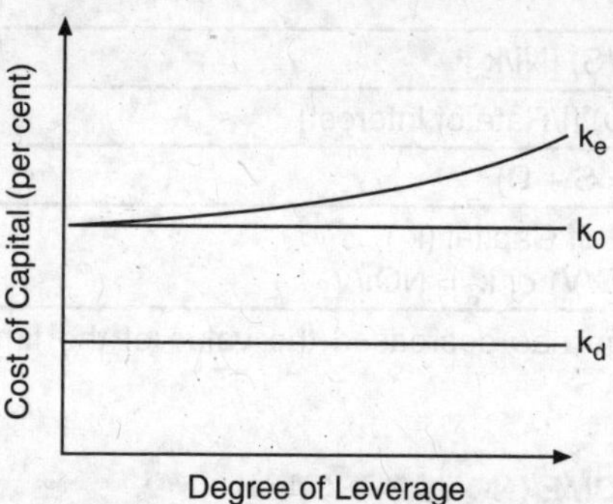

Fig.: Effect of Leverage on Cost of Capital (under NOI Approach)

4. Assumptions of NOI Approach

1. **Constant k_d** — The debt capitalization rate (k_d) is constant.
2. **Constant k_o** — The Weighted average cost of capital (k_o) is constant for all degree of debt equity mix since business risk on which (k_o) depends is assumed to remain constant.
3. **No Split** — The market capitalizes value of firm as a whole. Thus, the split between debt and equity is not important.
4. **Neutralisation** — The increase in the proportion of debt in the Capital structure would lead to increase in the financial risk of equity shareholders. The advantage associated with the use of the relatively *less* expensive debt in terms of explicit cost is exactly neutralized by the implicit cost of debt represented by the increase in the cost of equity capital.
5. **No Taxes** — There are no corporate taxes.

5. Can there be Single Optimum Capital Structure?

According to NOI approach, there is nothing like an optimum capital structure. Rather, every capital structure is an optimal one.

6. Practical Steps involved in the calculation of Equity Capitalization Rate (k_e)

Step 1: ***Calculate Total Value of the Firm (V) as follows:***

$$\text{Total Value of Firm} = \frac{\text{NOI}}{k_0}$$

Step 2: ***Calculate Market Value of Debt (D) as follows:***

$$\text{Market Value of Debt (D)} = \frac{\text{Interest}}{\text{Rate of Interest}}$$

Step 3: ***Calculate Market Value of Equity (S) as follows:***

Market Value of Equity (S) = Total Value of Firm (V) – Market Value of Debt (D)

Step 4: ***Calculate Equity Capitalization Rate (k_e)***

$$\text{Equity Capitalization Rate} = \frac{\text{Net Income}}{\text{Market Value of Equity (S)}} = \frac{\text{NOI} - \text{Interest}}{\text{Market Value of Equity (s)}}$$

7. Statement showing the calculation of Equity Capitalization Rate and Weighted Average cost of Capital [Under NOI Approach]

	Particulars	*X Ltd. Levered*	*Y Ltd. Unlevered*
A	Net Operating Income (NOI)	....	....
B	Overall Capitalization Rate (k_o)	....	....
C	Total Value of Firm [V = NOI/k_o]	....	....

D	*Less:* Market Value of Debt (D) [Interest / Rate of Interest]	....	NIL
E	Market Value of Equity (S) [C – D]	....	....
F	Earnings for Equity Shareholders (NI) [NOI – Interest]	....	....
G	Equity Capitalization Rate [k_e = NI/S]	....	....
H	Verification:		
	Weighted Average Cost of Capital (k_o)	....	....
	$k_o = (k_e \times S/V) + (k_d \times D/V)$		
	Where, k_d = Rate of interest on debt		

ILLUSTRATION 2 [NET OPERATING INCOME APPROACH]

X Ltd.'s expected annual net operating income (EBIT) is ₹ 2,40,000. The Company has 10% Debt ₹ 7,20,000. The overall capitalization rate is 15%.

Required: (use NOI Approach)

(a) Determine the Total market Value of the Company and Equity capitalization rate.

(b) Determine the Weighted Average Cost of Capital to verify the validity of the NOI Approach.

(c) State the effect on the Total Value of the company and Equity Capitalization Rate in part (a) if the X Ltd. has decided to raise the debt by ₹ 3,80,000 and use the proceeds to buy back equity shares.

(d) State the effect on the Total Value of the company and Equity Capitalization Rate in part (a) if the X Ltd. has decided to issue equity shares by ₹ 3,80,000 and use the proceeds to redeem to debt.

SOLUTION

(A) & (B) COMPUTATION OF EQUITY CAPITALIZATION RATE AND WEIGHTED AVERAGE COST OF CAPITAL

Particulars	*X Ltd.*
A. Net Operating Income (NOI)	₹ 2,40,000
B. Overall Capitalization Rate (k_o)	0.15
C. Total Value of Firm (V = NOI / k_o)	₹ 16,00,000
D. *Less:* Market Value of Debt (D) [Interest / Rate of Interest]	₹ 7,20,000
E. Market Value of Equity (S) [C – D]	₹ 8,80,000
F. Earnings for Equity Shareholders (NI) [NOI – Interest]	₹ 1,68,000
G. Equity Capitalization Rate [ke = NI/S]	0.1909
H. Verification: Weighted Average Cost of Capital (k_o) $k_o = (k_e \times S/V) + (k_d \times D/V)$	0.15

(C) COMPUTATION OF EQUITY CAPITALIZATION RATE AND WEIGHTED AVERAGE COST OF CAPITAL

Particulars	*X Ltd.*
A. Net Operating Income (NOI)	₹ 2,40,000
B. Overall Capitalization Rate (k_o)	0.15

C. Total Value of Firm ($V = NOI/k_o$)	₹ 16,00,000
D. *Less:* Market Value of Debt (D) [Interest / Rate of Interest]	₹ 11,00,000
E. Market Value of Equity (S) [C – D]	₹ 5,00,000
F. Earnings for Equity Shareholders (NI) [NOI – Interest]	₹ 1,30,000
G. Equity Capitalization Rate [ke = NI / S]	0.2600
H. Verification: Weighted Average Cost of Capital (k_o) $k_o = (k_e \times S/V) + (k_d \times D/V)$	0.15

Effect: As a result of increase in leverage, Equity Capitalization Rate has increased but the total value of the firm and Weighted Average Cost of Capital remained constant.

(D) COMPUTATION OF EQUITY CAPITALIZATION RATE AND WEIGHTED AVERAGE COST OF CAPITAL

Particulars	*X Ltd.*
A. Net Operating Income (NOI)	₹ 2,40,000
B. Overall Capitalization Rate (k_o)	0.15
C. Total Value of Firm ($V = NOI/k_o$)	₹ 16,00,000
D. *Less:* Market Value of Debt (D) [Interest / Rate of Interest]	₹ 3,40,000
E. Market Value of Equity (S) [C – D]	₹ 12,60,000
F. Earnings for Equity Shareholders (NI) [NOI - Interest]	₹ 2,06,000
G. Equity Capitalization Rate [k_e = NI / S]	0.16349
H. Verification: Weighted Average Cost of Capital (k_o) $k_o = (k_e \times S/V) + (k_d \times D/V)$	0.15

Effect: As a result of decrease in leverage, Equity Capitalization Rate has decreased but the total value of the firm and Weighted Average Cost of Capital remained constant.

8.0 TRADITIONAL APPROACH

TRADITIONAL APPROACH — AN INTERMEDIATE APPROACH

Traditional approach is also known as intermediate approach as it takes a midway between NI approach (that the value of firm is not independent of the degree of financial leverage) and the NOI approach (that the value of firm is independent irrespective of the degree of financial leverage).

CRUX OF TRADITIONAL APPROACH

The crux of traditional approach is as follows:

1. **Upto the reasonable limit of leverage,** the cost of debt *plus* the increased cost of equity (due to use of debt) will be *less* than the cost of equity (in case of equity financing only) since the advantage associated with the use of the relatively *less* expensive debt in terms of explicit cost exceeds the implicit cost of debt represented by the increase in the cost of equity capital. As a result the **overall cost of capital (k_o) decreased and the value of the firm (V) increases.** At this limit, the capital structure is optimum since the overall cost of capital is the least and the value of the firm is maximum.

2. **Beyond the reasonable limit of leverage,** the cost of debt *plus* the increased cost of equity (due to use of debt) will be more than the cost of equity (in case of equity financing only) since the financial risk of the equity shareholders and suppliers of debt also start increasing. As a result the **overall cost of capital (k_o) increases and the value of the firm (V) decreases.**

3. Graphical Presentation of Effect of Leverage on Cost of Capital under Traditional Approach

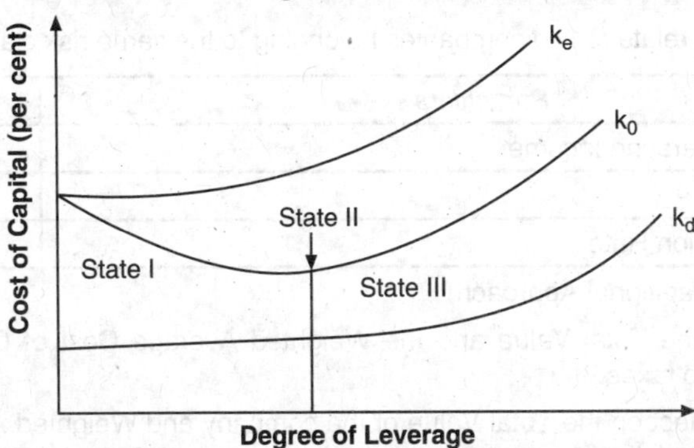

Fig. Effect of Leverage on Cost of Capital (Traditional Approach)

4. Practical Steps involved in the calculation of Weighted Average Cost of Capital

Step 1: ***Calculate Market Value of Equity (S) as follows:***

$$\text{Market Value of Equity (S)} = \frac{\text{Net Income}}{k_e} = \frac{\text{NOI} - \text{Interest}}{k_e}$$

Step 2: ***Calculate Market Value of Debt (D) as follows:***

$$\text{Market Value of Debt (D)} = \frac{\text{Interest}}{\text{Rate of Interest}}$$

Step 3: ***Calculate Total Value of the Firm (V) as follows:***

Total Value of Firm (V) = Market Value of Equity (S) + Market Value of Debt (D)

Step 4: ***Calculate Weighted Average Cost of Capital (k_o)***

Weighted Average Cost of Capital = $k_o = (k_e \times S/V) + (k_d \times D/V)$

Where, k_d = Rate of interest on Debt

5. Statement showing the calculation of Total Value of Firm and Weighted Average Cost of Capital [Under Traditional Approach]

Particulars	*X Ltd. Levered*	*Y Ltd. Unlevered*
A. Net Operating Income (NOI)	....	....
B. *Less:* Interest on Debt (I)	....	NIL
C. Earnings for Equity Shareholders (NI)	....	....
D. Equity Capitalization Rate (k_e)	....	....
E. Market Value of Equity (S) [NI/k_e]	....	....
F. Market Value of Debt (D) [Interest / Rate of Interest]	....	NIL
G. Total Value of Firm (V = S + D)	....	....
H. Weighted Average Cost of Capital (k_o)	....	....
$k_o = (k_e \times S/V) + (k_d \times D/V)$		
k_d = Rate of Interest on Debt		

6. Can there be Single Optimum Capital Structure?

According to Traditional approach, at a reasonable limit of leverage, the capital structure is optimum since the overall cost of capital is the least and the value of the firm is maximum.

ILLUSTRATION 3 [TRADITIONAL APPROACH]

The following data relate to two companies belonging to the same risk class:

Particulars	X Ltd.	Y Ltd.
Expected Net Operating Income	₹ 2,40,000	2,40,000
10% Debt	₹ 7,20,000	—
Equity Capitalization Rate	20%	15%

Required: (Use Traditional Approach)

(a) Determine the Total Value and the Weighted Average Cost of Capital for each company assuming no taxes.

(b) State the effect on the Total Value of the company and Weighted Average Cost of Capital in part (a) if X Ltd. has decided to raise the debt by ₹ 1,60,000 and use the proceeds to buyback equity shares. Due to increased financial risk kd would rise to 11% and ke to 21%.

(c) State the effect on the Total Value of the company and Weighted Average Cost of Capital in part (a) if the X Ltd. has decided to raise the debt by ₹ 1,70,000 and use the proceeds to buyback equity shares. Due to increased financial risk kd would rise to 12% and ke to 22%.

SOLUTION

(A) CALCULATION OF TOTAL VALUE OF FIRM AND WEIGHTED AVERAGE COST OF CAPITAL

Particulars	X Ltd.	Y Ltd.
A. Net Operating Income (NOI)	₹ 2,40,000	₹ 2,40,000
B. *Less:* Interest on Debt (I)	₹ 72,000	—
C. Earnings for Equity Shareholders (NI)	₹ 1,68,000	₹ 2,40,000
D. Equity Capitalization Rate (k_e)	0.20	0.15
E. Market Value of Equity (S) [NI/k_e]	₹ 8,40,000	₹ 16,00,000
F. Market Value of Debt (D) [Interest / Rate of Interest]	₹ 7,20,000	—
G. Total Value of Firm (V = S + D)	₹ 15,60,000	₹ 16,00,000
H. Weighted Average Cost of Capital (k_O) $k_O = (k_e \times S/V) + (k_D \times D/V)$ *or* $k_O = NOI/V$	0.15385	0.15000

(B) CALCULATION OF TOTAL VALUE OF FIRM AND WEIGHTED AVERAGE COST OF CAPITAL

Particulars	X Ltd.
A. Net Operating Income (NOI)	₹ 2,40,000
B. *Less:* Interest on Debt (I)	₹ 96,800
C. Earnings for Equity Shareholders (NI)	₹ 1,43,200
D. Equity Capitalization Rate (k_e)	0.21
E. Market Value of Equity (S) [NI/k_e]	₹ 6,81,904.76
F. Market Value of Debt (D) [Interest / Rate of Interest]	₹ 8,80,000
G. Total Value of Firm (V = S + D)	₹ 15,61,904.76
H. Weighted Average Cost of Capital (k_O) $k_O = (k_e \times S/V) + (k_D \times D/V)$ *or* $k_O = NOI/V$	0.15366

Effect: Increase in leverage upto ₹ 1,60,000 has increased the value of the firm and decreased the Weighted Average Cost of Capital.

(C) CALCULATION OF TOTAL VALUE OF FIRM AND WEIGHTED AVERAGE COST OF CAPITAL

Particulars	*X Ltd.*
A. Net Operating Income (NOI)	₹ 2,40,000
B. *Less:* Interest on Debt (I)	₹ 1,06,800
C. Earnings for Equity Shareholders (NI)	₹ 1,33,200
D. Equity Capitalization Rate (k_e)	0.22
E. Market Value of Equity (S) [NI/k_e]	₹ 6,05,454.55
F. Market Value of Debt (D) [Interest / Rate of Interest]	₹ 8,90,000.00
G. Total Value of Firm (V = S + D)	₹ 14,95,454.55
H. Weighted Average Cost of Capital (k_O) $k_o = (k_e \times S/V) + (k_D \times D/V)$ *or* k_o = NOI/V	0.16049

Effect: Increase in leverage beyond ₹ 1,60,000 has decreased the value of the firm and increased the Weighted Average Cost of Capital.

9.0 MODIGLIANI MILLER (M-M) APPROACH

IS WEIGHTED AVERAGE COST OF CAPITAL OF A FIRM INDEPENDENT OF ITS CAPITAL STRUCTURE?

According to M-M approach, weighted average cost of capital of a firm is Independent of its capital structure. In other words, a firm cannot change its value and the cost of capital through a judicious mix of debt and equity.

CRUX OF M-M APPROACH

The crux of M-M approach is as follows:

1. The market value of a firm and its cost of capital are independent of its capital structure. The total market value of a firm is given by capitalising the expected stream of operated earnings at a discount rate considered appropriate for its risk class.
2. The cost of capital (k_e) is equal to capitalization rate of pure equity stream *plus* a premium for financial risk. The financial risk increased with more debt content in the capital structure. As a result, ke increases in a manner to offset exactly the use of *less* expensive source of funds.
3. The cut off rate for investment purposes is completely independent of the way in which the investment is financed.
4. If the two firms, which are identical in all respects except for the degree of leverage, have different market value, arbitrage *or* switching will start and the investors will substitute personal *or* home-made leverage for corporate leverage. The switching option brings the value of the two identical firms at equilibrium point in the market.

VALUE OF A FIRM UNDER M-M APPROACH

For firms in the same risk class, the total market value of a firm is given by capitalising the Expected Net Operating Income by the overall capitalization rate appropriate to that risk class.

$$\text{Value of Firm} = \frac{\text{Expected Net Operating Income}}{\text{Expected Overall Capitalisation Rate}} = \frac{\text{NOI}}{k_o}$$

GRAPHICAL PRESENTATION OF EFFECT OF DEGREE OF LEVERAGE ON COST OF CAPITAL UNDER M-M APPROACH

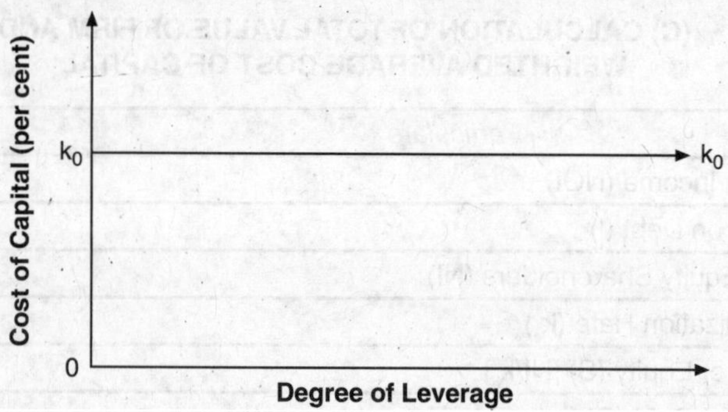

Fig. Effect of Leverage on Cost of Capital under M-M Approach

ASSUMPTIONS OF M-M APPROACH

1. **Perfect Capital Market** — This means that:
   (a) The investors are free to buy and sell securities.
   (b) They can borrow without restrictions on the same terms as the firms do.
   (c) The investors behave rationally.
   (d) There are no transaction costs.
   (e) Investors are well informed about the risk-return on all type of securities.
2. **Homogeneous Risk Class** — The firms belong to this class if their expected earning is having identical risk characteristics.
3. **No Taxes** — There are no corporate taxes.
4. **Same Expectations** — All investors have the same expectations from a firm's net operating income (EBIT) which are necessary to evaluate the value of a firm.
5. **100% Payout Ratio** — The dividend ratio is 100%. In other words, there are no retained earnings.

CRITICISMS OF M-M APPROACH

1. **No Perfect Capital Market** — The assumption of perfect capital market does not hold good in practice. Free and up-to-date information to all and at all time may not be available.
2. **Arbitrage Process may fail** — Arbitrage process may fail due to several reasons such as:
   (a) Investors may not substitute personal leverage for corporate leverage since they don't have the same risk characteristic.
   (b) The existence of transaction costs interfere with the working of arbitrage.
   (c) Institutional restrictions may not permit institutional investors to engage in home made leverage.
3. **Existence of Corporate Tax** — Since the interest on debt is tax deductible, a levered firm is in position to take the advantage of trading on equity. Hence the total market value of a levered firm is likely to exceed that of unlevered firm.

CALCULATION OF MARKET VALUE AND OVERALL CAPITALISATION RATE OF UNLEVERED FIRM

	Where No Taxes Exist	*Where Taxes Exist*
Total Market Value of Unlevered Firm (V_u)	$V_u = NOI/k_e$	$V_u = NOI\ (I - t)/k_e$
Overall Capitalisation Rate (k_o)	$k_o = k_e$ as there is no debt	$k_o = k_e$ as there is no debt

CALCULATION OF MARKET VALUE AND OVERALL CAPITALISATION RATE OF LEVERED FIRM

	Where No Taxes Exist	*Where Taxes Exist*
Total Market Value of Levered Firm (Vl)	$Vl = V_u$	$Vl = V_u + D_t$ where, t = tax rate
Equity Capitalization Rate (k_e)	$k_e = \frac{NOI - Interest}{V_l - D}$	$k_e = \frac{NOI - Interest - Tax}{V_l - D}$
Overall Capitalisation Rate (k_o)	$k_0 = \frac{NOI}{V_l}$ $k_o = (k_e \times S/V) + (k_d \times D/V)$ Note: k_d = Rate of Interest	$k_0 = \frac{(NOI - I)(1 - t) + I}{V_l}$ $k_o = (k_e \times S/V) + (k_d + D/V)$ Note: k_d = Rate of Interest

STATEMENT SHOWING THE COMPUTATION OF TOTAL MARKET VALUE AND WEIGHTED AVERAGE COST OF CAPITAL WHERE NO TAXES EXIST [UNDER M-M APPROACH]

Particulars	*X Ltd. Levered*	*Y Ltd. Unlevered*
A. Net Operating Income (NOI)	....	....
B. *Less:* Interest on Debt (I)	....	NIL
C. Earnings for Equity Shareholders (NI)	....	....
D. Overall Capitalization Rate (k_o)	....	....
E. Total Value of Firm ($V = NOI / k_o$)	....	....
F. *Less:* Market Value of Debt (D) [I / Rate of Interest]	....	NIL
G. Market Value of Equity (S)	....	....
H. Equity Capitalization Rate [ke = NI / S]	....	....
I. Weighted Average Cost of Capital (k_o)		
$k_o = (k_e \times S/V) + (k_d \times D / V)$		

STATEMENT SHOWING THE COMPUTATION OF TOTAL MARKET VALUE, EQUITY CAPITALIZATION RATE AND WEIGHTED AVERAGE COST OF CAPITAL OF LEVERED FIRM WHERE TAXES EXIST [UNDER M-M APPROACH]

Particulars	*X Ltd. Levered*
A. Value of Unlevered Firm ($NOI\ (1 - t)/ k_{e_u}$)	....
B. Present Value of Tax Savings on Interest on Debt (D_t)	....

C. Total Value of Levered Firm (V_l) [A + B]	....
D. *Less:* Market Value of Debt (D) [I / Rate of Interest]	....
E. Market Value of Equity (S)	....
F. Equity Capitalization Rate of Levered Firm [k_e = [(NOI – I) (1 – t)]/S]	....
G. Weighted Average Cost of Capital (k_o)	....
$k_o = (k_e \times S / V) + (k_d \times D / V)$ **Note:** k_d = Rate of Interest	

ILLUSTRATION 4 [M.M. APPROACH]

The following data relate to two companies belonging to the same risk class:

Particulars	*X Ltd.*	*Y Ltd.*
Expected Net Operating Income	₹ 2,40,000	2,40,000
10% Debt	₹ 7,20,000	—
Equity Capitalization Rate		15%

Required:

(a) Determine the Equilibrium Value, Equity Capitalization Rate and the Weighted Average Cost of Capital for each company assuming no taxes as per MM Approach.

(b) Determine the Equilibrium Value, Equity Capitalization Rate and the Weighted Average Cost of Capital for each company assuming 40% corporate taxes as per MM Approach.

SOLUTION

Part (a)

Unlevered Firm (u)

1. Total Value of Unlevered Firm (V_u) = [NOI/k_E] = ₹ 2,40,000 / 0.15 = ₹ 16,00,000
2. k_e of Unlevered Firm (given) = 0.15
3. k_o of Unlevered Firm (Same as above = k_E as there is no debt) = 0.15

Levered Firm (l)

(A) CALCULATION OF EQUILIBRIUM VALUE, K_e AND K_o

Particulars	*X Ltd.*	*Y Ltd.*
A. Net Operating Income (NOI)	₹ 2,40,000	₹ 2,40,000
B. *Less:* Interest on Debt (I)	₹ 72,000	—
C. Earnings for Equity Shareholders (NI)	₹ 1,68,000	₹ 2,40,000
D. Overall Capitalization Rate (k_o)	0.15	0.15
E. Total Value of Firm (V = NOI / k_o)	₹ 16,00,000	₹ 16,00,000
F. *Less:* Market Value of Debt (D) [I / Rate of Interest]	₹ 7,20,000	—
G. Market Value of Equity (S)	₹ 8,80,000	₹ 16,00,000
H. Equity Capitalization Rate [k_e = NI / S]	0.1909	0.1500
I. Weighted Average Cost of Capital (k_o) $k_o = (k_e \times S/V) + (k_o \times D/V)$	0.15	0.15

Part (b)

Unlevered Firm (u)

1. Total Value of Unlevered Firm (V_U) = [NOI (1 – t)/k_e] = ₹ 2,40,000 (1 – 0.40) / 0.15 = ₹ 9,60,000
2. k_e of Unlevered Firm (given) = 0.15
3. k_o of Unlevered Firm (Same as above = k_e as there is no debt) = 0.15

Levered Firm (l)

4. Total Value of Levered Firm (V_l) = V_U + D × t = ₹ 9,60,000 + (₹ 7,20,000 × 0.4) = ₹ 12,48,000

COMPUTATION OF EQUITY CAPITALIZATION RATE AND WEIGHTED AVERAGE COST OF CAPITAL

Particulars	*X Ltd.*
A. Net Operating Income (NOI)	₹ 2,40,000
B. *Less:* Interest on Debt (I)	₹ 72,000
C. Earnings Before Tax (EBT)	₹ 1,68,000
D. *Less:* Tax @ 40%	₹ 67,200
E. Earnings for equity shareholders (NI)	₹ 1,00,800
F. Total Value of Firm (V) as calculated above	₹ 12,48,000
G. *Less:* Market Value of Debt (D) [I / Rate of Interest]	₹ 7,20,000
H. Market Value of Equity (S)	₹ 5,28,000
I. Equity Capitalization Rate [k_e = NI / S]	0.1909
J. Weighted Average Cost of Capital (k_o) $k_o = (k_e \times S/V) + (k_o \times D/V)$	0.1385

ILLUSTRATION 5 [M.M. APPROACH]

The following data relate to two companies belonging to the same risk class:

Particulars	*X Ltd.*	*Y Ltd.*
Total Assets	₹ 12,00,000	₹ 12,00,000
Rate of Return on Total Assets	25%	25%
10% Debt	₹ 9,00,000	—
Equity Capitalization Rate		15%

Required:

(a) Determine the Equilibrium Value, and Weighted Average Cost of Capital for each company assuming no taxes as per MM Approach.

(b) Determine the Equilibrium Value, Equity Capitalization Rate and the Weighted Average Cost of Capital for each company assuming 40% corporate taxes as per MM Approach.

SOLUTION

Part (a)

Unlevered Firm (u)

1. Total Value of Unlevered Firm (V_u) = [EBIT/k_e] = ₹ 3,00,000 / 0.15 = ₹ 20,00,000
2. k_e of Unlevered Firm (given) = 0.15
3. k_o of Unlevered Firm (Same as above = k_e as there is no debt) = 0.15

Levered Firm (l)

(A) CALCULATION OF EQUILIBRIUM VALUE, K_e AND K_o

Particulars	X Ltd.	Y Ltd.
A. Net Operating Income (NOI)	₹ 3,00,000	₹ 3,00,000
B. *Less:* Interest on Debt (I)	₹ 90,000	—
C. Earnings for Equity Shareholders (NI)	₹ 2,10,000	₹ 3,00,000
D. Overall Capitalization Rate (k_o)	0.15	0.15
E. Total Value of Firm (V = NOI/k_o)	₹ 20,00,000	₹ 20,00,000
F. *Less:* Market Value of Debt (D) [I / Rate of Interest]	₹ 9,00,000	—
G. Market Value of Equity (S)	₹ 11,00,000	₹ 20,00,000
H. Equity Capitalization Rate [k_e = NI/S]	0.1909	0.15
I. Weighted Average Cost of Capital (k_o) $k_o = (k_e \times S/V) + (k_d \times D/V)$	0.15	0.15

Part (b)

Unlevered Firm (u)

1. Total Value of Unlevered Firm (V_u) = [NOI(1 – t)/k_e] = ₹ 3,00,000 × (1 – 0.40)/0.15 = ₹ 12,00,000
2. k_e of Unlevered Firm (given) = 0.15
3. k_o of Unlevered Firm (Same as above = k_e as there is no debt) = 0.15

Levered Firm (l)

4. Total Value of Levered Firm (Vl) = V_u + Dl × t = ₹ 12,00,000 + (₹ 9,00,000 × 0.4) = ₹ 15,60,000

COMPUTATION OF EQUITY CAPITALIZATION RATE AND WEIGHTED AVERAGE COST OF CAPITAL

Particulars	X Ltd.
A. Net Operating Income (NOI)	₹ 3,00,000
B. *Less:* Interest on Debt (I)	₹ 90,000
C. Earnings Before Tax (EBT)	₹ 2,10,000
D. *Less:* Tax @ 40%	₹ 84,000
E. Earnings for equity shareholders (NI)	₹ 1,26,000
F. Total Value of Firm (V) as calculated above	₹ 15,60,000
G. *Less:* Market Value of Debt (D) [I / Rate of Interest]	₹ 9,00,000
H. Market Value of Equity (S)	₹ 6,60,000
I. Equity Capitalization Rate [k_e = NI / S]	0.1909
J. Weighted Average Cost of Capital (k_o) $k_o = (k_e \times S/V) + (k_d \times D/V)$	0.1385

ILLUSTRATION 6

Compute the equilibrium values (V) and the equity capitalization rate of the two companies, X and Y on the basis of the data given below as per MM Approach. Assume that (i) there is no income tax, and (ii) the overall rate of capitalization for such companies in the market is 15%.

Particulars	X Ltd.	Y Ltd.
A. Net Operating Income (NOI)	₹ 2,40,000	₹ 2,40,000
B. *Less:* Interest on Debt (I) @ 10%	₹ 72,000	—
C. Earnings for Equity Shareholders (NI)	₹ 1,68,000	₹ 2,40,000
D. Equity Capitalization Rate (k_e)	0.20	0.15
E. Market Value of Equity (S) [NI / k_e]	₹ 8,40,000	₹ 16,00,000
F. Market Value of Debt (D) [I / Rate of Interest]	₹ 7,20,000	—
G. Total Value of Firm (V = S + D)	₹ 15,60,000	₹ 16,00,000
H. Weighted Average Cost of Capital (k_o)	0.15385	0.15000

SOLUTION

STATEMENT SHOWING THE COMPUTATION OF EQUILIBRIUM VALUES AND EQUITY CAPITALIZATION RATE

Particulars	X Ltd.	Y Ltd.
A. Net Operating Income (NOI)	₹ 2,40,000	₹ 2,40,000
B. *Less:* Interest on Debt (I)	₹ 72,000	—
C. Earnings for Equity Sharcholders (NI)	₹ 1,68,000	₹ 2,40,000
D. Overall Capitalization Rate (k_o)	0.15	0.15
E. Total Value of Firm (V = NOI/k_o)	₹ 16,00,000	₹ 16,00,000
F. *Less:* Market Value of Debt (D) [I / Rate of Interest]	₹ 7,20,000	—
G. Market Value of Equity (S)	₹ 8,80,000	₹ 16,00,000
H. Equity Capitalization Rate [k_e = NI/S]	0.1909	0.1500
I. Weighted Average Cost of Capital (k_o) $k_o = (k_e \times S / V) + (k_d \times D / V)$	0.15	0.15

ILLUSTRATION 7

From the following data, find out the value of each firm as per MM Approach and equity capitalization rate:

Particulars	Firm A ₹	Firm B ₹	Firm C ₹
A. EBIT	12,00,000	12,00,000	12,00,000
B. No. of Equity Shares	3,00,000	2,50,000	2,00,000
C. 10% Debentures		9,00,000	10,00,000

Every firm expects 12% Return on Investment.

SOLUTION

STATEMENT SHOWING THE COMPUTATION OF EQUILIBRIUM VALUES AND EQUITY CAPITALIZATION RATE

Particulars	Firm A ₹	Firm B ₹	Firm C ₹
A. Net Operating Income (EBIT)	₹ 12,00,000	₹ 12,00,000	₹ 12,00,000

B. *Less:* Interest on Debt (I)	₹ 0	₹ 90,000	₹ 1,00,000
C. Earnings for Equity Shareholders (NI)	₹ 12,00,000	₹ 11,10,000	₹ 11,00,000
D. Overall Capitalization Rate (k_o)	0.12	0.12	0.12
E. Total Value of Firm ($V = EBIT/k_o$)	₹ 1,00,00,000	₹ 1,00,00,000	₹ 1,00,00,000
F. *Less:* Market Value of Debt (D) [I / Rate of Interest]	₹ 0	₹ 9,00,000	₹ 10,00,000
G. Market Value of Equity (S)	₹ 1,00,00,000	₹ 91,00,000	₹ 90,00,000
H. Equity Capitalization Rate [$k_e = NI / S$]	0.12000	0.12198	0.12222
I. Weighted Average Cost of Capital (k_o) $k_o = (k_e \times S/V) + (k_d \times D/V)$	0.12	0.12	0.12

ILLUSTRATION 8 [CALCULATION OF EXPECTED RATE OF RETURN ON EQUITY IN CASE OF A LEVERED FIRM AT VARYING DEBT-EQUITY RATIOS ACCORDING TO M-M APPROACH]

Jalan Ltd. is an unlevered firm and its cost of equity is 15%. Tulsian Ltd. is a levered firm of the same industry using 10% Debt. Tax Rate 40%.

Required: Using M-M Approach, calculate the Cost of Equity in case of Tulsian Ltd. if the debt component in its capital structure is (a) 10% (b) 20% (c) 30% (d) 40% (e) 50% (f) 60% (g) 70% (h) 80%.

SOLUTION

$$K_{eL} = k_e \text{ for UF} + (k_e \text{ for UF} - k_d) \times \text{Debt/Equity} \times (1 - t)$$

where, K_{eL} = Cost of Equity of Levered Firm

K_{eU} = Cost of Equity of Unlevered Firm

k_d = Cost of Debt

t = Tax Rate

(a) $K_{eL} = 0.15 + (0.15 - 0.10) \times 10/90 \times (1 - 0.4) = 15.33\%$

(b) $K_{eL} = 0.15 + (0.15 - 0.10) \times 20/80 \times (1 - 0.4) = 15.75\%$

(c) $K_{eL} = 0.15 + (0.15 - 0.10) \times 30/70 \times (1 - 0.4) = 16.286\%$

(d) $K_{eL} = 0.15 + (0.15 - 0.10) \times 40/60 \times (1 - 0.4) = 17\%$

(e) $K_{eL} = 0.15 + (0.15 - 0.10) \times 50/50 \times (1 - 0.4) = 18.00\%$

(f) $K_{eL} = 0.15 + (0.15 - 0.10) \times 60/40 \times (1 - 0.4) = 19.50\%$

(g) $K_{eL} = 0.15 + (0.15 - 0.10) \times 70/30 \times (1 - 0.4) = 22\%$

(h) $K_{eL} = 0.15 + (0.15 - 0.10) \times 80/20 \times (1 - 0.4) = 27\%$

ARBITRAGE PROCESS UNDER M-M APPROACH

(a) **Meaning:** Arbitrage Process involves the selling of all securities of over valued firm and purchasing securities of under valued firm equal to the percentage of equity holdings in the over valued firm.

(b) **Activities under Arbitrage Process:**

When Levered Firm is overvalued	*When Unlevered Firm is overvalued*
(a) Investor **sells** his present equity holdings of levered firm	(a) Investor **sells** his present equity holdings of unlevered firm

(b) Investor **borrows** proportionate to his share of debt of levered firm	(b) Investor **purchases** securities of the levered firm equal to his percentage equity holdings in the unlevered firm
(c) Investor **purchases** securities of the Unlevered firm equal to his percentage equity holdings in the levered firm	

WILL THE INVESTOR GAIN BY INVESTING IN THE UNDERVALUED FIRM?

An Investor will gain by investing in undervalued firm since the same amount of present income can be earned by investing an amount, which is *less* than the present investment.

EFFECTS OF ARBITRAGE PROCESS

1. The prices of the equity shares of the overvalued firm whose shares are being sold by the investor will decrease.
2. The prices of the equity shares of the undervalued firm whose shares are being purchased by the investor will increase.
3. This process will continue till market prices of two firms become identical.

WHEN WILL THIS ARBITRAGE PROCESS COME TO AN END?

According to Modigliani and Miller, this arbitrage process will come to an end when the values of both companies become identical.

ARBITRAGE PROCESS WHEN LEVERED FIRM IS OVERVALUED

	Particulars	₹
A.	Investor's present position in overvalued firm	
	(a) Market Value of Investment	....
	(b) Dividend Income	....
B.	(a) He sells his present equity holdings for ₹	....
	(b) He borrows proportionate to his share of debt	....
	(c) Total Amount available with him [(a) + (b)]	....
C.	He purchases same % of equity holdings of undervalued firm for	....
D.	His Net Income after switching over process	
	(a) Dividend Income	....
	(b) *Less:* Interest on personal borrowings	....
	(c) Net Income [(a) – (b)]	....
E.	The amount by which Investor could reduce his outlay through the use of arbitrage process. (B – C)	....

EFFECT OF INVESTMENT OF AVAILABLE TOTAL FUNDS IN UNDERVALUED FIRM

The income of the investor shall increase by the dividend income which will be earned on additional equity holdings (over & above the present % of equity holding) of undervalued firm.

ILLUSTRATION 9 [ARBITRAGE PROCESS WHEN LEVERED FIRM IS OVER-VALUED]

The following data relate to two companies belonging to the same risk class:

Particulars	*X Ltd.*	*Y Ltd.*
Expected Net Operating Income	₹ 2,40,000	₹ 2,40,000
10% Debt	₹ 7,20,000	—
Equity Capitalization Rate	16%	15%

Required:

(a) Determine the Total Value and the Weighted Average Cost of Capital for each company assuming no taxes before the start of Arbitrage Process.

(b) Show the arbitrage process by which an investor who holds 10% equity shares in X Ltd. will be benefited by investing in Y Ltd.

(c) Will he gain by investing in the Undervalued Firm?

(d) Explain how he will be better off by investing the total funds available in undervalued firm.

(e) When will this arbitrage process come to an end?

(f) Determine the Equilibrium Value, Equity Capitalization Rate and Overall Capitalization Rate after the end of Arbitrage Process.

SOLUTION

(A) CALCULATION OF TOTAL VALUE OF FIRM AND WEIGHTED AVERAGE COST OF CAPITAL

	Particulars	*X Ltd.*	*Y Ltd.*
A.	Net Operating Income (NOI)	₹ 2,40,000	₹ 2,40,000
B.	*Less:* Interest on Debt	₹ 72,000	—
C.	Earnings for Equity Shareholders (NI)	₹ 1,68,000	₹ 2,40,000
D.	Equity Capitalization Rate (k_e)	0.16	0.15
E.	Market Value of Equity (S) [NI/k_e]	₹ 10,50,000	₹ 16,00,000
F.	Market Value of Debt (D) [I / Rate of Interest]	₹ 7,20,000	—
G.	Total Value of Firm (V = S + D)	₹ 17,70,000	₹ 16,00,000
H.	Weighted Average Cost of Capital (k_o) $k_o = (k_e \times S/V) + (k_d \times D / V)$	0.13559	0.15000

(B) ARBITRAGE PROCESS WHEN LEVERED FIRM IS OVERVALUED

	Particulars	₹
A.	Investor's present position in overvalued firm	
	(a) Market Value of Investment (10% of ₹ 10,50,000)	1,05,000
	(b) Dividend Income (10% of ₹ 1,68,000)	16,800
B.	(a) He sells his present equity holdings for ₹	1,05,000
	(b) He borrows Proportionate to his share of debt (10% of ₹ 7,20,000)	72,000
	(c) Total Amount available with him [(a) + (b)]	1,77,000
C.	He purchases 10% equity holdings of undervalued firm for (10% of ₹ 16,00,000)	1,60,000
D.	His Net Income after switching over process	
	(a) Dividend Income (15% of ₹ 1,60,000)	24,000
	(b) *Less:* Interest on personal borrowings (10% of ₹ 72,000)	7,200

(c) Net Income [(a) – (b)]	16,800
E. The amount by which Investor could reduce his outlay through the use of arbitrage process. (B – C)	17,000

(C) WILL HE GAIN BY INVESTING THE UNDERVALUED FIRM?

He will gain by investing in under valued firm since the same amount of present income can be earned by investing ₹ 1,60,000 which is *less* than the present investment of ₹ 1,77,000.

(D) CALCULATION OF THE AMOUNT BY WHICH INVESTOR COULD INCREASE HIS INCOME THROUGH THE USE OF ARBITRAGE PROCESS

Particulars	₹
A. Investor's present position in overvalued firm	
(a) Market Value of Investment (10% of ₹ 10,50,000)	1,05,000
(b) Dividend Income (10% of ₹ 1,68,000)	16,800
B. (a) He sells his present equity holdings for ₹	1,05,000
(b) He borrows Proportionate to his share of debt (10% of ₹ 7,20,000)	72,000
(c) Total Amount available with him [(a) + (b)]	1,77,000
C. He purchases equity holdings of undervalued firm for	1,77,000
D. His Net Income after switching over process	
(a) Dividend Income (15% of ₹ 1,77,000)	26,550
(b) *Less:* Interest on personal borrowings (10% of ₹ 72,000)	7,200
(c) Net Income [(a) – (b)]	19,350
E. The amount by which Investor could increase his income through the use of arbitrage process. [₹ 19,350 – ₹ 16,800]	2,550

(E) WHEN WILL THIS ARBITRAGE PROCESS COME TO AN END?

According to Modigliani and Miller, this arbitrage process will come to an end when the values of both the companies become identical.

(F) STATEMENT SHOWING THE COMPUTATION OF EQUILIBRIUM VALUES AND EQUITY CAPITALIZATION RATE

Particulars	*X Ltd.*	*Y Ltd.*
A. Net Operating Income (NOI)	₹ 2,40,000	₹ 2,40,000
B. *Less:* Interest on Debt (I)	₹ 72,000	—
C. Earnings for Equity Shareholders (NI)	₹ 1,68,000	₹ 2,40,000
D. Overall Capitalization Rate (k_o)	0.15	0.15
E. Total Value of Firm (V = NOI / k_o)	₹ 16,00,000	₹ 16,00,000
F. *Less:* Market Value of Debt (D) [I / Rate of Interest]	₹ 7,20,000	—
G. Market Value of Equity (S)	₹ 8,80,000	₹ 16,00,000
H. Equity Capitalization Rate [k_e = NI / S]	0.1909	0.1500
I. Weighted Average Cost of Capital (k_o) $k_o = (k_e \times S / V) + (k_d \times D / V)$	0.15	0.15

ILLUSTRATION 10 [ARBITRAGE PROCESS WHEN LEVERED FIRM IS OVER-VALUED]

The following data relate to two companies belonging to the same risk class:

Particulars	*X Ltd.*	*Y Ltd.*
Number of Equity Shares	10,000	17,200
Market Price per share	₹ 105	₹ 100
10% Debentures	₹ 7,20,000	—
Profit before Interest	₹ 2,40,000	₹ 2,40,000

Required: Explain how under Modigliani and Miller Approach an investor holding 10% of shares in overvalued firm will be better off in switching his holding to undervalued firm.

SOLUTION

STATEMENT SHOWING THE CALCULATION OF TOTAL VALUE OF FIRM

Particulars	*X Ltd.*	*Y Ltd.*
A. Number of Equity Shares	10,000	17,200
B. Market Price per share	₹ 105	₹ 100
C. Market Value of Equity (S) [A × B]	₹ 10,50,000	₹ 17,20,000
D. Market Value of Debt (D)	₹ 7,20,000	—
E. Total Value of Firm (V = S + D)	₹ 17,70,000	₹ 17,20,000

STATEMENT SHOWING THE CALCULATION OF EARNING FOR EQUITY SHAREHOLDERS

Particulars	*X Ltd.*	*Y Ltd.*
A. Profit before interest	₹ 2,40,000	₹ 2,40,000
B. *Less:* Interest on Debt	₹ 72,000	—
C. Earnings for Equity Shareholders	₹ 1,68,000	₹ 2,40,000

ARBITRAGE PROCESS WHEN LEVERED FIRM IS OVERVALUED

Particulars	₹
A. Investor's present position in overvalued firm	
(a) Market Value of Investment (10% of ₹ 10,50,000)	1,05,000
(b) Dividend Income (10% of ₹ 1,68,000)	16,800
B. (a) He sells his present equity holdings for ₹	1,05,000
(b) He borrows Proportionate to his share of debt (10% of ₹ 7,20,000)	72,000
(c) Total Amount available with him [(a) + (b)]	1,77,000
C. He purchases 10% equity holdings of undervalued firm for (10% of ₹ 17,20,000)	1,72,000
D. His Net Income after switching over process	
(a) Dividend Income (10% of ₹ 2,40,000)	24,000
(b) *Less:* Interest on personal borrowings (10% of ₹ 72,000)	7,200
(c) Net Income [(a) – (b)]	16,800
E. The amount by which Investor could reduce his outlay through the use of arbitrage process. (B – C)	5,000

WILL HE GAIN BY INVESTING THE UNDERVALUED FIRM?

He will gain by investing in under valued firm since the same amount of present income can be earned by investing ₹ 1,72,000 which is *less* than the present investment of ₹ 1,77,000.

WHEN WILL THIS ARBITRAGE PROCESS COME TO AN END?

According to Modigliani and Miller, this arbitrage process will come to an end when the values of both the companies become identical.

ARBITRAGE PROCESS WHEN UNLEVERED FIRM IS OVERVALUED

Particulars	₹
A. Investor's present position in overvalued firm	
(a) Market Value of Investment	....
(b) Dividend Income	....
B. He sells his present equity holding for ₹	
C. (a) He purchases equity holdings of undervalued firm for ₹	....
(b) He purchases debts of undervalued firm for ₹	....
(c) Total Amount invested [(a) + (b)]	....
D. His Net Income after switching over process	
(a) Dividend Income	....
(b) *Add:* Interest on debt	....
(c) Net Income [(a) + (b)]	....
E. The amount by which Investor could reduce his outlay through the use of arbitrage process. (B – C)	....

ILLUSTRATION 11 [ARBITRAGE PROCESS WHEN UNLEVERED FIRM IS OVERVALUED]

The following data relate to two companies belonging to the same risk class:

Particulars	*X Ltd.*	*Y Ltd.*
Expected Net Operating Income	₹ 2,40,000	2,40,000
10% Debt	₹ 7,20,000	—
Equity Capitalization Rate	20%	15%

Required:

(a) Determine the Total Value and the Weighted Average Cost of Capital for each company assuming no taxes before the start of Arbitrage Process.

(b) Show the arbitrage process by which an investor who holds 10% equity shares in Y Ltd. will be benefited by investing in X Ltd.

(c) Will be gain by investing in the Undervalued Firm?

(d) Explain how he will be better off by investing the total funds available in undervalued firm.

(e) When will this arbitrage process come to an end?

(f) Determine the Equilibrium Value, Equity Capitalization Rate and Overall Capitalization Rate after the end of Arbitrage Process.

SOLUTION

(A) CALCULATION OF TOTAL VALUE OF FIRM AND WEIGHTED AVERAGE COST OF CAPITAL

	Particulars	*X Ltd.*	*Y Ltd.*
A.	Net Operating Income (NOI)	₹ 2,40,000	₹ 2,40,000
B.	*Less:* Interest on Debt	₹ 72,000	—
C.	Earnings for equity shareholders (NI)	₹ 1,68,000	₹ 2,40,000
D.	Equity Capitalization Rate (k_e)	0.20	0.15
E.	Market Value of Equity (S) [NI/k_e]	₹ 8,40,000	₹ 16,00,000
F.	Market Value of Debt (D) [I/Rate of Interest]	₹ 7,20,000	—
G.	Total Value of Firm (V = S + D)	₹ 15,60,000	₹ 16,00,000
H.	Weighted Average Cost of Capital (k_o) $k_o = (k_e \times S / V) + (k_d \times D/V)$	0.15385	0.15000

(B) ARBITRAGE PROCESS WHEN UNLEVERED FIRM IS OVERVALUED

	Particulars	₹
A.	Investor's present position in overvalued firm	
	(a) Market Value of Investment (10% of ₹ 16,00,000)	1,60,000
	(b) Dividend Income (10% of ₹ 2,40,000)	24,000
B.	He sells his present equity holdings for ₹	1,60,000
C.	(a) He purchases equity holdings of undervalued firm for ₹ (10% of ₹ 8,40,000)	84,000
	(b) He purchases debts of undervalued firm for ₹	72,000
	(c) Total Amount invested [(a) + (b)]	1,56,000
D.	His Net Income after switching over process	
	(a) Dividend Income	16,800
	(b) *Add:* Interest on debt	7,200
	(c) Net Income [(a) + (b)]	24,000
E.	The amount by which Investor could reduce his outlay through the use of arbitrage process. (B – C)	4,000

(C) WILL HE GAIN BY INVESTING THE UNDERVALUED FIRM?

He will gain by investing in undervalued firm since the same amount of present income can be earned by investing ₹ 1,56,000 which is *less* than the present investment of ₹ 1,60,000.

(D) CALCULATION OF THE AMOUNT BY WHICH INVESTOR COULD INCREASE HIS INCOME THROUGH THE USE OF ARBITRAGE PROCESS

	Particulars	₹
A.	Investor's present position in overvalued firm	
	(a) Market Value of Investment (10% of ₹ 16,00,000)	1,60,000
	(b) Dividend Income (10% of ₹ 2,40,000)	24,000
B.	He sells his present equity holdings for ₹	1,60,000

C. (a) He purchases equity holdings of undervalued firm for [₹ 1,60,000 × ₹ 8,40,000/₹ 15,60,000]	86,154
(b) He purchases debts of undervalued firm for [₹ 1,60,000 × ₹ 7,20,000/₹ 15,60,000]	73,846
(c) Total Amount invested [(a) + (b)]	1,60,000
D. His Net Income after switching over process	
(a) Dividend Income (20% of ₹ 86,154)	17,231
(b) *Add:* Interest on debt (10% of ₹ 73,846)	7,385
(c) Net Income [(a) + (b)]	24,616
E. The amount by which Investor could increase his income through the use of arbitrage process. [D – A(b)]	616

(E) WHEN WILL THIS ARBITRAGE PROCESS COME TO AN END?

According to Modigliani and Miller, this arbitrage process will come to an end when the values of both the companies become identical.

STATEMENT SHOWING THE COMPUTATION OF EQUILIBRIUM VALUES AND EQUITY CAPITALIZATION RATE

Particulars	*X Ltd.*	*Y Ltd.*
A. Net Operating Income (NOI)	₹ 2,40,000	₹ 2,40,000
B. *Less:* Interest on Debt (I)	₹ 72,000	—
C. Earnings for Equity Shareholders (NI)	₹ 1,68,000	₹ 2,40,000
D. Overall Capitalization Rate (k_o)	0.15385	0.15385
E. Total Value of Firm (V = NOI / k_o)	₹ 15,60,000	₹ 15,60,000
F. *Less:* Market Value of Debt (D) [I / Rate of Interest]	₹ 7,20,000	—
G. Market Value of Equity (S)	₹ 8,40,000	₹ 15,60,000
H. Equity Capitalization Rate [k_e = NI / S]	0.20	0.15385
I. Weighted Average Cost of Capital (k_o) $k_o = (k_e \times S / V) + (k_d \times D / V)$	0.15385	0.15385

10.0 HOW TO DETERMINE THE OPTIMAL DEBT-EQUITY MIX

MEANING OF OPTIMAL DEBT-EQUITY MIX

Debt-Equity Mix at which the Weighted Average Cost of Capital is lowest is considered to be optimal one.

PRACTICAL STEPS INVOLVED IN DETERMINATION OF OPTIMAL DEBT-EQUITY MIX

Step 1: *Calculate the proportion of Debt (W_d) and the proportion of Equity (W_e) at various levels of Debt-Equity Mix.*

Step 2: *Calculate the Cost of Debt (k_d) and the Cost of Equity (ke) at various levels of Debt-Equity Mix.*

Step 3: *Calculate the Weighted Average Cost of Capital (k_o) at various levels of Debt-Equity Mix as follows:*

$$k_o = (k_e \times W_e) + (k_d \times W_d)$$

Step 4: *Ascertain the lowest k_o.*

Step 5: *Ascertain the Debt-Equity Mix which corresponds to lowest k_o. This Debt-Equity Mix is considered to be optimal one.*

FORMAT OF STATEMENT SHOWING THE CALCULATION OF WEIGHTED AVERAGE COST OF CAPITAL

STATEMENT SHOWING THE CALCULATION OF WEIGHTED AVERAGE COST OF CAPITAL

Case	k_e	W_e	$k_e \times W_e$	$k_d = k_i \times (1 - t)$	W_d	$k_d \times W_d$	$k_o = k_e \times W_e + k_d \times W_d$
1	0.1	0.5	0.05	0.5	0.5	0.25	0.30

ILLUSTRATION 12

In considering the most desirable capital structure of a company, the following estimates of the cost of debt and equity capital (before tax) has been made at various levels of Debt-Equity mix.

Case	*Debt Amount (₹)*	*Equity Amount (₹)*	*Cost of Debt (%)*	*Cost of Equity (%)*
1	—	5,00,000	10	12.0
2	50,000	4,50,000	10	12.0
3	1,00,000	4,00,000	10	12.5
4	1,50,000	3,50,000	11	13.0
5	2,00,000	3,00,000	12	14.0
6	2,50,000	2,50,000	13	16.0
7	3,00,000	2,00,000	14	20.0

Required: Suggest the optimal Debt-Equity Mix for the company assuming tax rate of 40%.

SOLUTION

STATEMENT SHOWING THE CALCULATION OF WEIGHTED AVERAGE COST OF CAPITAL

Case	k_e	W_e	$k_e \times W_e$	$k_d = k_i \times (1 - t)$	W_d	$k_d \times W_d$	$k_o = k_e \times W_e + k_d \times W_d$
1	0.12	1.00	0.120	0.060	0	0.000	0.1200
2	0.12	0.90	0.108	0.060	0.10	0.006	0.1140
3	0.125	0.80	0.100	0.060	0.20	0.012	0.1120
4	0.13	0.70	0.091	0.066	0.30	0.0198	0.1108
5	0.14	0.60	0.084	0.072	0.40	0.0288	0.1128
6	0.16	0.50	0.080	0.078	0.50	0.039	0.1190
7	0.20	0.40	0.080	0.084	0.60	0.0504	0.1304

Since ko is lowest in 4th case (30% Debt & 70% equity), this would be an optimal debt-equity mix for the company.

ILLUSTRATION 13

A company is currently financed entirely by equity and the cost of equity is 10%. Planning to introduce a degree of debt borrowing, the company ascertains that the cost of debt will be 4 per cent. However, if the debt borrowing should exceed 20% of the company's total finance, the cost of debt will increase because of the additional risk perceived by the debenture holders, and will be given by the following expression:

$$\text{Cost of Debt} = \left(4 + \frac{X - 20\%}{30\%}\right)\%$$

where X is the market value of the debt expressed as a % of the total market value of the Co.

In addition, the cost of equity will increase if a debt is introduced into the company because shareholders will believe that there is an increased level of risk. The risk premium required (i.e. the additional return over and above the existing cost of 10%) is expected to be given by the expression:

$$\text{Risk Premium} = \frac{X}{Y} \times 4\%$$

Where X is as defined above, and Y is the market value of the equity expressed as a percentage of the total market value of the company.

Required: Calculate K_o for each of the following capital structures and suggest the optimal debt-equity mix.

Equity	100%	80%	60%	40%	20%
Debt	NIL	20%	40%	60%	80%

SOLUTION

STATEMENT SHOWING THE CALCULATION OF WEIGHTED AVERAGE COST OF CAPITAL (K_o)

Capital Structure	Debt % (X)	Equity % (Y)	$k_e = 4 + \frac{X - 20\%}{30\%}$	$k_e = 4 + \frac{X - 20\%}{30\%}$	$K_o = (X \times k_d) + (Y \times k_e)$
I	0.00	1.00	$10\% + \frac{0}{100} \times 4\% = 0.10$	0	$K_o = (X \times k_d) + (Y \times k_e)$
II	0.20	0.80	$10\% + \frac{20}{80} \times 4\% = 0.10$	$\left(4 + \frac{20\% - 20\%}{30\%}\right) = 0.04$	$K_o = (.20 \times .04) + (.80 \times .11) = .096$
III	0.40	0.60	$10\% + \frac{40}{60} \times 4\% = 0.1267$	$\left(4 + \frac{40\% - 20\%}{30\%}\right) = 0.0467$	$K_o = (.40 \times .0467) + (.60 \times .1267) = .0947$
IV	0.60	0.40	$10\% + \frac{60}{40} \times 4\% = 0.16$	$\left(4 + \frac{60\% - 20\%}{30\%}\right) = 0.0533$	$K_o = (.60 \times .0533) + (.40 \times .16) = .09598$
V	0.80	0.20	$10\% + \frac{80}{20} \times 4\% = 0.26$	$\left(4 + \frac{80\% - 20\%}{30\%}\right) = 0.06$	$K_o = (.80 \times .06) + (.20 \times .26) = 0.10$

Since k_o is the lowest in III capital structure (i.e. 40% Debt and 60% Equity, this would be an optimal debt-equity mix.

SOLVED PROBLEMS

PROBLEM 1

The following data relate to two companies belonging to the same risk class:

Particulars	*X Ltd.*	*Y Ltd.*
Expected Net Operating Income	₹ 50,000	₹ 50,000
10% Debt	₹ 2,00,000	—

Equity Capitalization Rate	12.5%	10%

Required: (Use Net Income Approach)

(a) Determine the Total Value and the Weighted Average Cost of Capital for each of company assuming no taxed.

(b) State the effect on the Total Value and Weighted Average Cost of Capital in part (a) if X Ltd. has decided to raise the debt by ₹ 1,00,000 and use the proceeds to buyback equity shares.

(c) State the effect on the Total Value and Weighted Average Cost of Capital in part (a) if the X Ltd. has decided to issue the equity shares by ₹ 1,00,000 and use the proceeds to redeem the debt.

SOLUTION

(A) CALCULATION OF TOTAL VALUE AND WEIGHTED AVERAGE COST OF CAPITAL

Particulars	*X Ltd.*	*Y Ltd.*
A. Net Operating Income (NOI)	₹ 50,000	₹ 50,000
B. *Less:* Interest on Debt (I)	₹ 20,000	—
C. Earnings Before Tax (NI)	₹ 30,000	₹ 50,000
D. Equity Capitalization Rate (k_e)	0.125	0.10
E. Market Value of Equity (S) [NI/k_e]	₹ 2,40,000	₹ 5,00,000
F. Market Value of Debt (D) [I / Rate of Interest]	₹ 2,00,000	—
G. Total Value of Firm (V = S + D)	₹ 4,40,000	₹ 5,00,000
H. Weighted Average Cost of Capital (k_o) $k_o = (k_e \times S / V) + (k_d \times D / V)$	0.11364	0.10000

(B) CALCULATION OF TOTAL VALUE AND WEIGHTED AVERAGE COST OF CAPITAL

Particulars	*X Ltd.*
A. Net Operating Income (NOI)	₹ 50,000
B. *Less:* Interest on Debt (I)	₹ 30,000
C. Earnings Before Tax (NI)	₹ 20,000
D. Equity Capitalization Rate (k_e)	0.125
E. Market Value of Equity (S) [NI/k_e]	₹ 1,60,000
F. Market Value of Debt (D) [I / Rate of Interest]	₹ 3,00,000
G. Total Value of Firm (V = S + D)	₹ 4,60,000
H. Weighted Average Cost of Capital (k_o) $k_o = (k_e \times S/V) + (k_d \times D/V)$	0.10870

Effect: Increase in leverage has increased the value of the firm and decreased the Weighted Average Cost of Capital.

(C) CALCULATION OF TOTAL VALUE AND WEIGHTED AVERAGE COST OF CAPITAL

Particulars	*X Ltd.*
A. Net Operating Income (NOI)	₹ 50,000
B. *Less:* Interest on Debt (I)	₹ 10,000

C. Earnings Before Tax (NI)	₹ 40,000
D. Equity Capitalization Rate (k_e)	0.125
E. Market Value of Equity (S) [NI/k_e]	₹ 3,20,000
F. Market Value of Debt (D) [Interest / Rate of Interest]	₹ 1,00,000
G. Total Value of Firm (V = S + D)	₹ 4,20,000
H. Weighted Average Cost of Capital (k_o) $k_o = (k_e \times S/V) + (k_d \times D/V)$	0.11905

Effect: Decrease in leverage has decreased the Value of the Firm and increased the Weighted Average Cost of Capital.

PROBLEM 2

X Ltd.'s expected annual net operating income (EBIT) is ₹ 50,000. The Company has 10% Debt ₹ 2,00,000. The overall capitalization rate is 12.5%.

Required: (Use NOI Approach)

(a) Determine the Total market Value of the company and Equity capitalization rate.

(b) Determine the Weighted Average Cost of Capital to verify the validity of the NOI approach.

(c) State the effect on the Total Value of the company and Weighted Average Cost of Capital in part (a) if X Ltd. has decided to raise the debt by ₹ 1,00,000 and use the proceeds to buyback equity shares.

(d) State the effect on the Total Value of the company and Weighted Average Cost of Capital in part (a) if the X Ltd. has decided to issue the equity shares by ₹ 1,00,000 and use the proceeds to redeem the debt.

SOLUTION

(A) & (B) COMPUTATION OF EQUITY CAPITALIZATION RATE AND WEIGHTED AVERAGE COST OF CAPITAL

Particulars	*X Ltd.*
A. Net Operating Income (NOI)	₹ 50,000
B. Overall Capitalization Rate (k_o)	0.125
C. Total Value of Firm (V = NOI /k_o)	₹ 4,00,000
D. *Less:* Market Value of Debt (D) [I / Rate of Interest]	₹ 2,00,000
E. Market Value of Equity (S)	₹ 2,00,000
F. Earnings for equity shareholders (NI) [NOI – Interest]	₹ 30,000
G. Equity Capitalization Rate [k_e = NI / S]	0.1500
Verification:	
H. Weighted Average Cost of Capital (k_o) $k_o = (k_e \times S / V) + (k_d \times D/V)$	0.125

(C) COMPUTATION OF EQUITY CAPITALIZATION RATE AND WEIGHTED AVERAGE COST OF CAPITAL

Particulars	*X Ltd.*
A. Net Operating Income (NOI)	₹ 50,000

B. Overall Capitalization Rate (k_o)	₹ 0.125
C. Total Value of Firm (V = NOI / k_o)	₹ 4,00,000
D. *Less:* Market Value of Debt (D) [I / Rate of Interest]	₹ 3,00,000
E. Market Value of Equity (S)	₹ 1,00,000
F. Earnings for equity shareholders (NI) [NOI – Interest]	₹ 20,000
G. Equity Capitalization Rate [k_e = NI/S]	0.2000
Verification:	
H. Weighted Average Cost of Capital (k_o) $k_o = (k_e \times S/V) + (k_d \times D/V)$	0.125

Effect: As a result of increase in leverage, Equity Capitalization Rate has increased but the total value of the firm and Weighted Average Cost of Capital remained constant.

(D) COMPUTATION OF EQUITY CAPITALIZATION RATE AND WEIGHTED AVERAGE COST OF CAPITAL

Particulars	*X Ltd.*
A. Net Operating Income (NOI)	₹ 50,000
B. Overall Capitalization Rate (k_o)	₹ 0.125
C. Total Value of Firm (V = NOI / k_o)	₹ 4,00,000
D. *Less:* Market Value of Debt (D) [I / Rate of Interest]	₹ 1,00,000
E. Market Value of Equity (S)	₹ 3,00,000
F. Earnings for equity shareholders (NI) [NOI – Interest]	₹ 40,000
G. Equity Capitalization Rate [k_e = NI/S]	0.1333
Verification:	
H. Weighted Average Cost of Capital (k_o) $k_o = (k_e \times S/V) + (k_d \times D/V)$	0.125

Effect: As a result of decrease in leverage, Equity Capitalization Rate has decreased but the total value of the firm and Weighted Average Cost of Capital remained constant.

PROBLEM 3

The following data relate to two companies belonging to the same risk class: -

Particulars	*X Ltd.*	*Y Ltd.*
Expected Net Operating Income	₹ 2,40,000	₹ 2,40,000
10% Debt	₹ 7,20,000	—
Equity Capitalization Rate	16%	15%

Required: (Use Traditional Approach)

(a) Determine the Total Value and the Weighted Average Cost of Capital for each of company assuming no taxes.

(b) State the effect on the Total Value of the company and Weighted Average Cost of Capital in part (a) if X Ltd. has decided to raise the debt by ₹ 3,80,000 and use the proceeds to buyback equity shares. Due to increased financial risk kd would rise to 11% and ke to 17%.

(c) State the effect on the Total Value of the company and Weighted Average Cost of Capital in part (b) if the X Ltd. has decided to raise the debt by ₹ 1,00,000 and use the proceeds to payback equity shares. Due to increased financial risk k_d would rise to 12% and k_e to 18%.

SOLUTION

(A) CALCULATION OF TOTAL VALUE AND WEIGHTED AVERAGE COST OF CAPITAL

Particulars	*X Ltd.*	*Y Ltd.*
A. Net Operating Income (NOI)	₹ 2,40,000	₹ 2,40,000
B. *Less:* Interest on Debt (I)	₹ 72,000	—
C. Earnings for equity shareholders (NI)	₹ 1,68,000	₹ 2,40,000
D. Equity Capitalization Rate (k_e)	0.16	0.15
E. Market Value of Equity (S) [NI/k_e]	₹ 10,50,000	₹ 16,00,000
F. Market Value of Debt (D) [I / Rate of Interest]	₹ 7,20,000	—
G. Total Value of Firm (V = S + D)	₹ 17,70,000	₹ 16,00,000
H. Weighted Average Cost of Capital (k_o) $k_o = (k_e \times S/V) + (k_d \times D/V)$	0.13559	0.15000

(B) CALCULATION OF TOTAL VALUE AND WEIGHTED AVERAGE COST OF CAPITAL

Particulars	*X Ltd.*
A. Net Operating Income (NOI)	₹ 2,40,000
B. *Less:* Interest on Debt (I)	₹ 1,21,000
C. Earnings for equity shareholders (NI)	₹ 1,19,000
D. Equity Capitalization Rate (k_e)	0.17
E. Market Value of Equity (S) [NI / k_e]	₹ 7,00,000
F. Market Value of Debt (D) [I / Rate of Interest]	₹ 11,00,000
G. Total Value of Firm (V = S + D)	₹ 18,00,000
H. Weighted Average Cost of Capital (k_o) $k_o = (k_e \times S / V) + (k_d \times D / V)$	0.13333

Effect: Increase in leverage upto ₹ 3,80,000 has decreased the Weighted Average Cost of Capital and has increased the value of the firm.

(C) CALCULATION OF TOTAL VALUE AND WEIGHTED AVERAGE COST OF CAPITAL

Particulars	*X Ltd.*
A. Net Operating Income (NOI)	₹ 2,40,000
B. *Less:* Interest on Debt (I)	₹ 1,44,000
C. Earnings for equity shareholders (NI)	₹ 96,000
D. Equity Capitalization Rate (k_e)	0.18
E. Market Value of Equity (S) [NI / k_e]	₹ 5,33,333
F. Market Value of Debt (D) [I / Rate of Interest]	₹ 12,00,000
G. Total Value of Firm (V = S + D)	₹ 17,33,333
H. Weighted Average Cost of Capital (k_o) $k_o = (k_e \times S/V) + (k_d \times D / V)$	0.13846

Effect: Increase in leverage beyond ₹ 3,80,000 has increased the Weighted Average Cost of Capital and has decreased the value of the firm.

PROBLEM 4

The following data relate to two companies belonging to the same risk class:

Particulars	X Ltd.	Y Ltd.
Expected Net Operating Income	₹ 2,00,000	₹ 2,00,000
15% Debt	₹ 6,00,000	—
Equity Capitalization Rate		20%

Required:

(a) Determine the Total Market Value, Equity Capitalization Rate and Weighted Average Cost of Capital for each company assuming no taxes as per M-M Approach.

(b) Determine the Total Market Value, Equity Capitalization Rate and Weighted Average Cost of Capital for each company assuming 40% taxes as per M-M Approach.

SOLUTION

Part (a)

Unlevered Firm (u)

1. Total Value of Unlevered Firm (V_u) = [NOI/k_e] = ₹ 2,00,000 / 0.20 = ₹ 10,00,000
2. k_e of Unlevered Firm (given) = 0.20
3. k_o of Unlevered Firm (Same as above = k_e as there is no debt) = 0.20

Levered Firm (l)

CALCULATION OF TOTAL VALUE OF FIRM AND WEIGHTED AVERAGE COST OF CAPITAL

Particulars	X Ltd.	Y Ltd.
A. Net Operating Income (NOI)	₹ 2,00,000	₹ 2,00,000
B. *Less:* Interest on Debt (I)	₹ 90,000	—
C. Earnings for Equity Shareholders (NI)	₹ 1,10,000	₹ 2,00,000
D. Overall Capitalization Rate (k_o)	0.20	0.20
E. Total Value of Firm (V = NOI / k_o)	₹ 10,00,000	₹ 10,00,000
F. *Less:* Market Value of Debt (D) [I / Rate of Interest]	₹ 6,00,000	—
G. Market Value of Equity (S)	₹ 4,00,000	₹ 10,00,000
H. Equity Capitalization Rate [k_e = NI / S]	0.275	0.20
I. Weighted Average Cost of Capital (ko) $k_o = (k_e \times S/V) + (k_d \times D/V)$	0.20	0.20

Part (b)

Unlevered Firm (u)

1. Total Value of Unlevered Firm (V_u) = [NOI (1 – t)/k_e] = ₹ 2,00,000 × (1 – 0.40)/0.20 = ₹ 6,00,000
2. k_e of Unlevered Firm (given) = 0.20
3. k_o of Unlevered Firm (Same as above = k_e as there is no debt) = 0.20

Levered Firm (l)

4. Total Value of Levered Firm (V_l) = V_u + D_l × t = ₹ 6,00,000 + (₹ 6,00,000 × 0.4) = ₹ 8,40,000

COMPUTATION OF EQUITY CAPITALIZATION RATE AND WEIGHTED AVERAGE COST OF CAPITAL

Particulars	X Ltd.
A. Net Operating Income (NOI)	₹ 2,00,000
B. *Less:* Interest on Debt (I)	₹ 90,000
C. Earnings Before Tax (EBT)	₹ 1,10,000
D. *Less:* Tax @ 40%	₹ 44,000
E. Earnings for equity shareholders (NI)	₹ 66,000
F. Total Value of Firm (V) (as calculated above)	₹ 8,40,000
G. *Less:* Market Value of Debt (D) [I / Rate of Interest]	₹ 6,00,000
H. Market Value of Equity (S)	₹ 2,40,000
I. Equity Capitalization Rate [k_e = NI / S]	0.2750
J. Weighted Average Cost of Capital (k_o) $k_o = (k_e \times S/V) + (k_d \times D / V)$	0.1857

PROBLEM 5

The values of X Ltd. and Y Ltd. in accordance with the traditional approach are given below:

Particulars	X Ltd.	Y Ltd.
A. Net Operating Income (NOI)	₹ 50,000	₹ 50,000
B. Interest on Debt (I)	₹ 20,000	—
C. Earnings for Equity Shareholders (NI)	₹ 30,000	₹ 50,000
D. Equity Capitalization Rate (k_e)	0.125	0.10
E. Market Value of Equity (S) [NI/k_e]	₹ 2,40,000	₹ 5,00,000
F. Market Value of Debt (D) [I / Rate of Interest]	₹ 2,00,000	—
G. Total Value of Firm (V = S + D)	₹ 4,40,000	₹ 5,00,000
H. Weighted Average Cost of Capital (k_o)	0.11364	0.10000

Required: Compute the values of X Ltd. and Y Ltd. as per the M.M approach. Assume that (i) Corporate Income Tax do not exist and (ii) the equilibrium value of ko is 12.5%.

SOLUTION

Particulars	X Ltd.	Y Ltd.
A. Net Operating Income (NOI)	₹ 50,000	₹ 50,000
B. *Less:* Interest on Debt (I)	₹ 20,000	—
C. Earnings for Equity Shareholders (NI)	₹ 30,000	₹ 50,000
D. Overall Capitalization Rate (k_o)	0.125	0.125
E. Total Value of Firm (V = NOI/k_o)	₹ 4,00,000	₹ 4,00,000
F. *Less:* Market Value of Debt (D) [I / Rate of Interest]	₹ 2,00,000	—
G. Market Value of Equity (S)	₹ 2,00,000	₹ 4,00,000
H. Equity Capitalization Rate [k_e = NI / S]	0.1500	0.1250
I. Weighted Average Cost of Capital (k_o) $k_o = (k_e \times S/V) + (k_d \times D/V)$	0.125	0.125

PROBLEM 6

In considering the most desirable capital structure for a company, the following estimates of the cost of debt and equity capital (after tax) have been made at various levels of Debt-Equity mix:

Debt as % of Total Capital Employed	*Cost of Debt (%)*	*Cost of Equity (%)*
0	7.0	15.0
10	7.0	15.0
20	7.0	15.5
30	7.5	16.0
40	8.0	17.0
50	8.5	19.0
60	9.5	20.0

Required: Determine the optimal Debt-Equity mix for the company by calculating composite cost of capital.

SOLUTION

STATEMENT SHOWING THE CALCULATION OF WEIGHTED AVERAGE COST OF CAPITAL

Case	k_e	W_e	$k_e \times W_e$	$k_d = k_i \times (1 - t)$	W_d	$k_d \times W_d$	$k_o = k_e \times W_e + k_d \times W_d$
1	0.15	1.00	0.150	0.070	0	0.0000	0.1500
2	0.15	0.90	0.135	0.070	0.10	0.0070	0.1420
3	0.155	0.80	0.124	0.070	0.20	0.0140	0.1380
4	0.16	0.70	0.112	0.075	0.30	0.0225	0.1345
5	0.17	0.60	0.102	0.080	0.40	0.0320	0.1340
6	0.19	0.50	0.095	0.085	0.50	0.0425	0.1375
7	0.20	0.40	0.080	0.095	0.60	0.0570	0.1370

Since ko is lowest in 5th case (40% Debt & 60% equity), this would be an optimal debt-equity mix for the company.

PROBLEM 7

The following data relate to two companies belonging to the same risk class:-

Particulars	*X Ltd.*	*Y Ltd.*
Expected Net Operating Income	₹ 60,000	₹ 60,000
6% Debt	₹ 2,00,000	—
Equity Capitalization Rate	11.11%	10%

Required:

(a) Determine the Total Value and the Weighted Average Cost of Capital for each company assuming no taxes.

(b) Show the arbitrage process by which an investor who holds ₹ 2000 worth of equity shares in X Ltd. will be benefited by investing in Y Ltd.

(c) Will be gain by investing in the Undervalued Firm?

(d) When will this arbitrage process come to an end?

SOLUTION

(A) CALCULATION OF TOTAL VALUE OF FIRM AND WEIGHTED AVERAGE COST OF CAPITAL

Particulars	X Ltd.	Y Ltd.
A. Net Operating Income (NOI)	₹ 60,000	₹ 60,000
B. *Less:* Interest on Debt (I)	₹ 12,000	₹ 0
C. Earnings for equity shareholders (NI)	₹ 48,000	₹ 60,000
D. Equity Capitalization Rate (k_e)	0.1111	0.10
E. Market Value of Equity (S) [NI/k_e]	₹ 4,32,000	₹ 6,00,000
F. Market Value of Debt (D) [I / Rate of Interest]	₹ 2,00,000	₹ 0
G. Total Value of Firm (V = S + D)	₹ 6,32,000	₹ 6,00,000
H. Weighted Average Cost of Capital (k_o)	0.095	0.100

(B) ARBITRAGE PROCESS WHEN LEVERED FIRM IS OVERVALUED

Particulars	₹
A. Investor's present position in overvalued firm	
(a) Market Value of Investment	2000.00
(b) Dividend Income [(2,000/4,32,000) of ₹ 48,000]	222.22
B. (a) He sells his present equity holdings for	2000.00
(b) He borrows Proportionate to his share of debt [(2,000/4,32,000) of ₹ 2,00,000)	925.93
(c) Total Amount available with him [(a) + (b)]	2925.93
C. He purchases equity holdings of undervalued firm for [(2,000/4,32,000) of ₹ 6,00,000)	2777.78
D. His Net Income after switching over process	
(a) Dividend Income (10% of ₹ 2,777.78)	277.78
(b) *Less:* Interest on personal borrowings (6% of ₹ 925.93)	55.56
(c) Net Income [(a) – (b)]	222.22
E. The amount by which Investor could reduce his outlay through the use of arbitrage process. (B – C)	148.15

(C) WILL HE GAIN BY INVESTING THE UNDERVALUED FIRM?

He will gain by investing in undervalued firm since the same amount of present income can be earned by investing ₹ 2777.78 which is *less* than the present investment of ₹ 2,925.93.

(D) WHEN WILL THIS ARBITRAGE PROCESS COME TO AN END?

According to Modigliani and Miller, this arbitrage process will come to an end when the values of both the companies become identical.

PROBLEM 8

The following data relate to two companies belonging to the same risk class:

Particulars	X Ltd.	Y Ltd.
Expected Net Operating Income	₹ 6,60,000	₹ 6,60,000

10% Debt	₹ 30,00,000	—
Equity Capitalization Rate	20%	15%

Required:

(a) Determine the Total Value and the Weighted Average Cost of Capital for each company assuming no taxes.

(b) Show the arbitrage process by which an investor who holds 10% equity shares in X Ltd. will be benefited by investing in Y Ltd.

(c) Will be gain by investing in the Undervalued Firm?

(d) Explain how he will be better off by investing the total funds available in undervalued firm.

(e) When will this arbitrage process come to an end?

SOLUTION

(A) CALCULATION OF TOTAL VALUE & WEIGHTED AVERAGE COST OF CAPITAL

Particulars	*X Ltd.*	*Y Ltd.*
A. Net Operating Income (NOI)	₹ 6,60,000	₹ 6,60,000
B. *Less:* Interest on Debt (I)	₹ 3,00,000	—
C. Earnings for equity shareholders (NI)	₹ 3,60,000	₹ 6,60,000
D. Equity Capitalization Rate (k_e)	0.20	0.15
E. Market Value of Equity (S) [NI / k_e]	₹ 18,00,000	₹ 44,00,000
F. Market Value of Debt (D) [I / Rate of Interest]	₹ 30,00,000	—
G. Total Value of Firm (V = S + D)	₹ 48,00,000	₹ 44,00,000
H. Weighted Average Cost of Capital (k_o) $k_o = (k_e \times S / V) + (k_d \times D / V)$	0.13750	0.15000

(B) ARBITRAGE PROCESS WHEN LEVERED FIRM IS OVERVALUED

Particulars	₹
A. Investor's present position in overvalued firm	
(a) Market Value of Investment (10% of ₹ 18,00,000)	1,80,000
(b) Dividend Income (10% of ₹ 3,60,000)	36,000
B. (a) He sells his present equity holdings for ₹	1,80,000
(b) He borrows Proportionate to his share of debt (10% of ₹ 30,00,000)	3,00,000
(c) Total Amount available with him [(a) + (b)]	4,80,000
C. He purchases 10% equity holdings of undervalued firm for (10% of ₹ 44,00,000)	4,40,000
D. His Net Income after switching over process	
(a) Dividend Income (15% of ₹ 4,40,000)	66,000
(b) *Less:* Interest on personal borrowings (10% of ₹ 3,00,000)	30,000
(c) Net Income [(a) – (b)]	36,000
E. The amount by which Investor could reduce his outlay through the use of arbitrage process. (B – C)	40,000

(C) WILL HE GAIN BY INVESTING THE UNDERVALUED FIRM?

He will gain by investing in under valued firm since the same amount of present income can be earned by investing ₹ 4,40,000 which is *less* than the present investment of ₹ 4,80,000

(D) CALCULATION OF THE AMOUNT BY WHICH INVESTOR COULD INCREASE HIS INCOME THROUGH THE USE OF ARBITRAGE PROCESS

Particulars	₹
A. Investor's present position in overvalued firm	
(a) Market Value of Investment (10% of ₹ 18,00,000)	1,80,000
(b) Dividend Income (10% of ₹ 3,60,000)	36,000
B. (a) He sells his present equity holdings for ₹	1,80,000
(b) He borrows Proportionate to his share of debt (10% of ₹ 30,00,000)	3,00,000
(c) Total Amount available with him [(a) + (b)]	4,80,000
C. He purchases equity holdings of undervalued firm for (10% of ₹ 48,00,000)	4,80,000
D. His Net Income after switching over process	
(a) Dividend Income (15% of ₹ 4,80,000)	72,000
(b) *Less:* Interest on personal borrowings (10% of ₹ 3,00,000)	30,000
(c) Net Income [(a) – (b)]	42,000
E. The amount by which Investor could increase his income through the use of arbitrage process. [D – A(b)]	6,000

(E) WHEN WILL THIS ARBITRAGE PROCESS COME TO AN END?

According to Modigliani and Miller, this arbitrage process will come to an end when the values of both the companies become identical.

PROBLEM 9

The following data relate to two companies belonging to the same risk class:

Particulars	*X Ltd.*	*Y Ltd.*
Number of Equity Shares	₹ 90,000	₹ 1,50,000
Market Price per share	1.20	1.00
6% Debentures	₹ 60,000	—
Profit before Interest	₹ 18,000	₹ 18,000

All Profits after debenture interest are distributed as dividend.

Required: Explain how under Modigliani and Miller Approach an investor holding 10% of shares in overvalued firm will be better off in switching his holding to undervalued firm.

SOLUTION

STATEMENT SHOWING THE CALCULATION OF TOTAL VALUE

Particulars	*X Ltd.*	*Y Ltd.*
A. Number of Equity Shares	₹ 90,000	₹ 1,50,000
B. Market Price per share	1.20	1.00

C. Market Value of Equity (S) [A × B]	₹ 1,08,000	₹ 1,50,000
D. Market Value of Debt (D)	₹ 60,000	—
E. Total Value of Firm (V = S + D)	₹ 1,68,000	₹ 1,50,000

STATEMENT SHOWING THE CALCULATION OF EARNING FOR EQUITY SHAREHOLDERS

Particulars	*X Ltd.*	*Y Ltd.*
A. Profit before interest	₹ 18,000	₹ 18,000
B. *Less:* Interest	₹ 3,600	—
C. Earnings for Equity Shareholders	₹ 14,400	₹ 18,000

ARBITRAGE PROCESS WHEN LEVERED FIRM IS OVERVALUED

Particulars	₹
A. Investor's present position in overvalued firm	
(a) Market Value of Investment (10% of ₹ 1,08,000)	10,800
(b) Dividend Income (10% of ₹ 14,400)	1,440
B. (a) He sells his present equity holdings for ₹	10,800
(b) He borrows Proportionate to his share of debt (10% of ₹ 60,000)	6,000
(c) Total Amount available with him [(a) + (b)]	16,800
C. He purchases equity holdings of undervalued firm for (10% of ₹ 1,50,000)	15,000
D. His Net Income after switching over process	
(a) Dividend Income (10% of ₹ 18,000)	1,800
(b) *Less:* Interest on personal borrowings (6% of ₹ 6,000)	360
(c) Net Income [(a) – (b)]	1,440
E. The amount by which Investor could reduce his outlay through the use of arbitrage process. (B – C)	1,800

He will gain by investing in under valued firm since the same amount of present income can be earned by investing ₹ 16,800 which is *less* than the present investment of ₹ 15,000.

PROBLEM 10

The following data relate to two companies belonging to the same risk class:

Particulars	*X Ltd.*	*Y Ltd.*
Expected Net Operating Income	₹ 90,00,000	₹ 90,00,000
10% Debt	₹ 60,00,000	—
Equity Capitalization Rate	14%	12.5%

Required:

(a) Determine the Total Value and the Weighted Average Cost of Capital for each company assuming no taxes.

(b) Show the arbitrage process by which an investor who holds shares worth ₹ 90,000 in Y Ltd. will be benefited by investing in X Ltd.

(c) Will he gain by investing in the Undervalued Firm?

(d) When will this arbitrage process come to an end?

SOLUTION

(A) CALCULATION OF TOTAL VALUE OF FIRM AND WEIGHTED AVERAGE COST OF CAPITAL

Particulars	X Ltd.	Y Ltd.
A. Net Operating Income (NOI)	₹ 90,00,000	₹ 90,00,000
B. *Less:* Interest on Debt (I)	₹ 6,00,000	—
C. Earnings for equity shareholders (NI)	₹ 84,00,000	₹ 90,00,000
D. Equity Capitalization Rate (k_e)	0.14	0.125
E. Market Value of Equity (S) [NI / k_e]	₹ 6,00,00,000	₹ 7,20,00,000
F. Market Value of Debt (D) [I / Rate of Interest]	₹ 60,00,000	—
G. Total Value of Firm (V = S + D)	₹ 6,60,00,000	₹ 7,20,00,000
H. Weighted Average Cost of Capital (k_o) $k_o = (k_e \times S / V) + (k_d \times D / V)$	0.13636	0.12500

(B) ARBITRAGE PROCESS WHEN UNLEVERED FIRM IS OVERVALUED

Particulars	₹
A. Investor's present position in overvalued firm	
(a) Market Value of Investment	90,000
(b) Dividend Income (12.5% of ₹ 90,000)	11,250
B. He sells his present equity holdings for	90,000
C. (a) He purchases equity holdings of undervalued firm for (90,000/7,20,00,000) × (₹ 6,00,00,000)	75,000
(b) He purchases debts of undervalued firm for (90,000/7,20,00,000) × (₹ 60,00,000)	7,500
(c) Total Amount invested [(a) + (b)]	82,500
D. His Net Income after switching over process	
(a) Dividend Income (14% of ₹ 75,000)	10,500
(b) *Add:* Interest on debt (10% of ₹ 7,500)	750
(c) Net Income [(a) + (b)]	11,250
E. The amount by which Investor could reduce his outlay through the use of arbitrage process. (B – C)	7,500

(C) WILL HE GAIN BY INVESTING THE UNDERVALUED FIRM?

He will gain by investing in undervalued firm since the same amount of present income can be earned by investing ₹ 82,500 which is *less* than the present investment of ₹ 90,000.

(D) WHEN WILL THIS ARBITRATE PROCESS COME TO AN END?

According to Modigliani and Miller, this arbitrage process will come to an end when the values of both the companies become identical.

PROBLEM 11

The following data relate to two companies belonging to the same risk class:

Particulars	*X Ltd.*	*Y Ltd.*
Expected Net Operating Income	₹ 2,00,000	₹ 2,00,000
10% Debt	₹ 5,00,000	—
Equity Capitalization Rate	20%	12.5%

Required:

(a) Determine the Total Value and the Weighted Average Cost of Capital for each company assuming no taxes.

(b) Show the arbitrage process by which an investor who holds 10% equity shares in Y Ltd. will be benefited by investing in X Ltd.

(c) Will be gain by investing in the Undervalued Firm?

(d) Explain how he will be better off by investing the total funds available in undervalued firm.

(e) When will this arbitrage process come to an end?

SOLUTION

(A) CALCULATION OF TOTAL VALUE AND WEIGHTED AVERAGE COST OF CAPITAL

Particulars	*X Ltd.*	*Y Ltd.*
A. Net Operating Income (NOI)	₹ 2,00,000	₹ 2,00,000
B. *Less:* Interest on Debt (1)	₹ 50,000	—
C. Earnings for Equity Shareholders (NI)	₹ 1,50,000	₹ 2,00,000
D. Equity Capitalization Rate (k_e)	0.20	0.125
E. Market Value of Equity (S) [NI / k_e]	₹ 7,50,000	₹ 16,00,000
F. Market Value of Debt (D) [I / Rate of Interest]	₹ 5,00,000	—
G. Total Value of Firm (V = S + D)	₹ 12,50,000	₹ 16,00,000
H. Weighted Average Cost of Capital (k_o) $k_o = (k_e \times S / V) + (k_d \times D / V)$	0.160	0.125

(B) ARBITRAGE PROCESS WHEN UNLEVERED FIRM IS OVERVALUED

Statement showing the calculation of the amount by which Investor could reduce his outlay through the use of arbitrage process

Particulars	₹
A. Investor's present position in overvalued firm	
(a) Market Value of Investment (10% of ₹ 16,00,000)	1,60,000
(b) Dividend Income (12.50% of ₹ 1,60,000)	20,000
B. He sells his present equity holdings for	1,60,000
C. (a) He purchases equity holdings of undervalued firm for [10% of ₹ 7,50,000]	75,000
(b) He purchases debts of undervalued firm for [10% of ₹ 5,00,000]	50,000
(c) Total Amount invested [(a) + (b)]	1,25,000
D. His Net Income after switching over process	

(a) Dividend Income (20% of ₹ 75,000)	15,000
(b) *Add:* Interest on debt (10% of ₹ 50,000)	5,000
(c) Net Income [(a) + (b)]	20,000
E. The amount by which Investor could reduce his outlay through the use of arbitrage process. (B – C)	35,000

(C) WILL HE GAIN BY INVESTING THE UNDERVALUED FIRM?

He will gain by investing in undervalued firm since the same amount of present income can be earned by investing ₹ 1,25,000 which is *less* than the present investment of ₹ 1,60,000.

(D) STATEMENT SHOWING THE CALCULATION OF THE AMOUNT BY WHICH INVESTOR COULD INCREASE HIS INCOME THROUGH THE USE OF ARBITRAGE PROCESS

Particulars	₹
A. Investor's present position in overvalued firm	
(a) Market Value of Investment (10% of ₹ 16,00,000)	1,60,000
(b) Dividend Income (12.50% of ₹ 1,60,000)	20,000
B. He sells his present equity holdings for	1,60,000
C. (a) He purchases equity holdings of undervalued firm for [1,60,000 × 7,50,000/12,50,000]	96,000
(b) He purchases debts of undervalued firm for [1,60,000 × 5,00,000/12,50,000]	64,000
(c) Total Amount invested [(a) + (b)]	1,60,000
D. His Net Income after switching over process	
(a) Dividend Income (20% of ₹ 96,000)	19,200
(b) *Add:* Interest on debt (10% of ₹ 64,000)	6,400
(c) Net Income [(a) + (b)]	25,600
E. The amount by which Investor could reduce his outlay through the use of arbitrage process. [D – A(b)]	5,600

(E) WHEN WILL THIS ARBITRAGE PROCESS COME TO AN END?

According to Modigliani and Miller, this arbitrage process will come to an end when the values of both the companies become identical.

7 WORKING CAPITAL MANAGEMENT—ESTIMATION AND FINANCING

LEARNING OBJECTIVES

After studying this chapter, you should be able to understand:

- Meaning of Working Capital
- Purpose of Working Capital
- Need for Working Capital
- Components of Operating Cycle
- Why is Working Capital called as Circulating Capital or Revolving Capital?
- Concepts of Working Capital
- Permanent and Temporary Working Capital
- Working Capital in Case of a Stable Firm and a Growing Firm
- Meaning of Working Capital Management
- Effect of Working Capital Management Policies
- Importance of Working Capital Management
- What is an Optimum Working Capital?
- Factors Determining the Working Capital
- Estimate of Future Working Capital based on Current Assets and Current Liabilities
- Format of Statement Showing the Requirements of Working Capital
- Format of Statement Showing Profit/Loss
- Effect of Double Shift Working on Working Capital Requirements
- Sources of financing working capital
- Factoring
- Commercial Paper
- Methods of calculating the borrowing limits to finance the working capital requirements
- Recent Changes in Maximum Permissible Bank Finance
- Recommendations of Chore Committee
- Recommendations of Jilani Committee
- Recommendations of Dehejia Committee
- Treasury Management

1.0 MEANING OF WORKING CAPITAL

Working Capital refers to funds required to be invested in the business for a short period usually upto one year. It is also known as short-term capital *or* circulating capital.

2.0 PURPOSE OF WORKING CAPITAL

Working capital is required to meet day to day operating expenses and for holding stocks of raw-materials, spare parts, consumables, work in progress and finished goods and book debts (i.e. debtors balances and bills receivable). More specifically, working capital is needed:

1. to hold the stock of raw materials for such a period so as to facilitate an uninterrupted supply of raw material to production process;
2. to hold the stock of work-in-progress for process period (i.e., the time duration needed to convert the raw materials into finished products);
3. to hold the stock of finished goods for such a period so as to meet the demands of customers on continuous basis and sudden demand from some customers;
4. to grant credit to its customers for marketing and competitive reasons;
5. to hold cash balances to meet the manufacturing, office and administrative, selling and distribution expenses, taxes etc.

3.0 NEED FOR WORKING CAPITAL

1. Basically, working capital is needed because of the existence of operating cycle.
2. Operating Cycle is the duration of time between acquisition of supplies and the collection of cash from receivables.
3. Basically, working capital is required to finance operations during operating cycle for the business to run smoothly.
4. Operating cycle in a trading firm is the length of time required:
    1. to convert cash into inventory of finished goods;
    2. to convert inventory of finished goods into receivables;
    3. to convert receivables into cash;

    Operating Cycle in a Trading Firm is shown below.

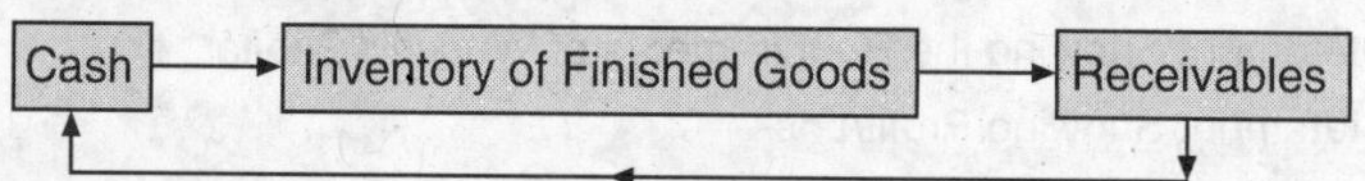

Fig. Operating Cycle in Trading Firm Selling Goods on Credit

5. Operating Cycle in a Manufacturing Firm is the length of time required:
    1. to convert cash into inventory of raw materials;
    2. to convert inventory of raw materials into work-in-progress;
    3. to convert inventory of work-in-progress into finished goods;
    4. to convert inventory of finished goods into receivables;
    5. to convert receivables into cash.

The Operating Cycle in a Manufacturing Firm is shown below:

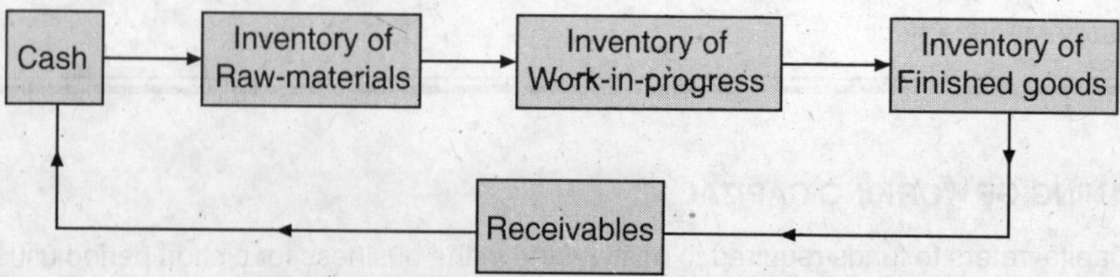

Fig. Operating Cycle in a Manufacturing Firm

6. Distinct Phases in Operating Cycle

   There are some distinct phases in the operating cycle of a manufacturing concern which are given below:

   1. Procurement of raw materials;
   2. Payment for labour, power, fuel and other manufacturing expenses;
   3. Placing the raw materials into work in progress and converting them into finished goods;
   4. Sale of finished goods for cash *or* credit. If on credit then conversion of receivables into cash.

   These phases result in cash flows going in and out of the business.

4.0 COMPONENTS OF OPERATING CYCLE

1. **Gross Operating Cycle**—Gross Operating Cycle represents the aggregate of:
   1. R = Raw Material Storage Period
   2. W = Work-in-Progress Holding Period
   3. F = Finished Goods Storage Period
   4. D = Debtors Collection Period Allowed.

   Thus, Gross Operating Cycle = R + W + F + D

2. **Net Operating Cycle** — Net operating cycle represents Gross Operating Cycle *less* Credit period allowed by supplier.

   Net Operating Cycle = Gross Operating Cycle – Credit period allowed by supplier

   Net Operating Cycle = R + W+ F + D – C

   where,
   1. R = Raw Material Storage Period
   2. W = Work-in-Progress Holding Period
   3. F = Finished Goods Storage Period
   4. D = Debtors Collection Period Allowed
   5. C = Credit Period Allowed by Supplier

3. How to Calculate Components of Operating Cycle?

   The various components of operating cycle may be calculated as shown below:

$$\text{Average Raw Material Storage Period (in days)} = \frac{\text{Average Stock of Raw Material}}{\text{Average Cost of Raw Material Consumption per day}}$$

$$\text{Average Work-in-Progress Holding Period (in days)} = \frac{\text{Average Stock of Work-in-Progress}}{\text{Average Cost of W.I.P. per day}}$$

$$\text{Average Finished Goods Storage Period (in days)} = \frac{\text{Average Stock of Finished Goods}}{\text{Average Cost of Goods Produced per day}}$$

$$\text{Average Debtors' Collection Period (in days)} = \frac{\text{Average Trade Debtors}}{\text{Average Cost of Credit Sales per day}}$$

$$\text{Average Creditors' Payment Period (in days)} = \frac{\text{Average Trade Creditors}}{\text{Average Credit Purchases per day}}$$

$$\text{Average Time Lag in Payment of Expenses (in days)} = \frac{\text{Average Creditors for Expenses}}{\text{Average Expenses per day}}$$

4. **How to Calculate Number of Operating Cycles in a year?**

   The Number of Operating Cycles in a year may be calculated as follows:

$$\text{No. of Operating Cycles in a year} = \frac{\text{No. of days in a year}}{\text{Net Operating Cycle (in days)}}$$

ILLUSTRATION 1

From the following information of Tulsian Ltd., calculate (a) Gross Operating Cycle, (b) Net Operating Cycle, and (c) No. of Operating Cycles in a year.

Particulars	₹
1. Raw Material Inventory consumed during the year	60,00,000
2. Average Stock of Raw Material	10,00,000
3. Factory Cost of Goods Produced	1,05,00,000
4. Average stock of Work-in-Progress	4,37,500
5. Office Cost of Goods Produced	1,14,00,000
6. Average stock of Finished Goods	9,50,000
7. Average Trade Debtors	11,25,000
8. Cost of Credit Sales	90,00,000
9. Average Trade Creditors	5,00,000
10. Expenses for the year	30,00,000
11. Average Creditors for Expenses	5,00,000
12. No. of working days in a year (Assume 360 days)	

SOLUTION

$$\text{Raw Material storage Period} = \frac{\text{Average Stock of Raw Material}}{\text{Average Cost of Raw Material Consumption per day}}$$

$$= \frac{₹\ 10,00,000}{₹\ 60,00,000/360} = 60 \text{ days}$$

$$\text{Work-in-progress Holding Period} = \frac{\text{Average Stock of Work-in-Progress}}{\text{Average Cost in W.I.P. per day}}$$

$$= \frac{₹\ 4,37,500}{₹\ 1,05,00,000/360} = 15 \text{ days}$$

$$\text{Finished Goods Storage Period} = \frac{\text{Average Stock of Finished Goods}}{\text{Average Cost of Goods Produced per day}}$$

$$= \frac{₹\ 9,50,000}{₹\ 1,14,00,000/360} = 30 \text{ days}$$

$$\text{Debtors Collection Period} = \frac{\text{Average Trade Debtors}}{\text{Average Cost of Credit Sales per day}}$$

$$= \frac{₹\ 11,25,000}{₹\ 90,00,000/360} = 45 \text{ days}$$

$$\text{Creditors' Payment Period} = \frac{\text{Average Trade Creditors}}{\text{Average Credit Purchases per day}}$$

$$= \frac{₹\ 5,00,000}{₹\ 60,00,000/360} = 30 \text{ days}$$

$$\text{Average Time Lag in payment of Expenses} = \frac{\text{Average Creditors for Expenses}}{\text{Average Expenses per day}}$$

$$= \frac{₹\ 5,00,000}{₹\ 30,00,000/360} = 60 \text{ days}$$

(a) Gross Operating Cycle = R + W + F + D = 60 + 15 + 30 + 45 = 150 Days

(b) Net Operating Cycle = R + W + F + D – C = 60 + 15 + 30 + 45 – 30 – 60 = 60 Days

(c) No. of Operating Cycles in a year = $\frac{\text{No. of days in a year}}{\text{Net Operating Cycle}} = \frac{360 \text{ days}}{60 \text{ days}}$

= 6 Operating Cycles in a year

5.0 WHY IS WORKING CAPITAL CALLED AS CIRCULATING CAPITAL OR REVOLVING CAPITAL?

Working capital is sometimes known as circulating capital *or* revolving capital because funds invested in current assets are continuously recovered through the realization of cash and again reinvested in current assets. Thus, the amount keeps on circulating *or* revolving from cash to current assets and back again to cash.

6.0 CONCEPTS OF WORKING CAPITAL

There are two concepts of working capital, namely, gross concept and net concept.

GROSS WORKING CAPITAL

It refers to the firm's investment in current assets. Current assets refer to the assets which are held for their conversion into cash within an operating cycle i.e., time duration between the conversion of cash into inventory items (raw-materials in case of a manufacturing firm and finished goods in case of a trading firm) and receivables and their conversion into cash.

In the form of an equation, gross working capital can be shown below:

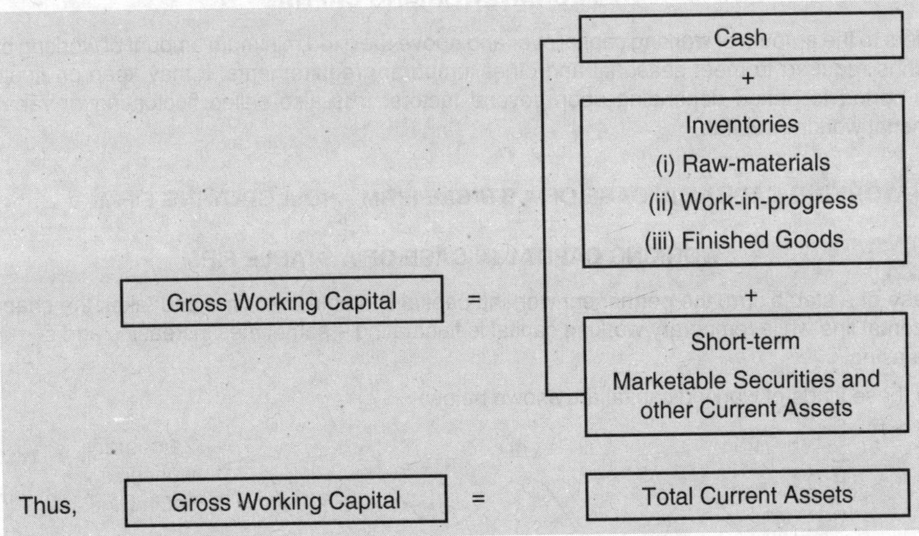

NET WORKING CAPITAL

It refers to the difference between current assets and current liabilities. Current liabilities refer to those claims of outsiders which are expected to mature for payment within an operating cycle and include creditors, bills payable, outstanding expenses, bank overdraft. It can be positive *or* negative. A positive net working capital occurs when current assets exceed current liabilities and a negative net working capital occurs when current liabilities exceed current assets.

Net working capital is a qualitative concept, which indicates:

(a) Liquidity position of the firm as it represents safety margin available to short- term creditors so as to discharge their obligations within an operating cycle.

(b) That part of the current assets which should be financed with long-term funds such as equity share capital, preference share capital, debentures, long-term borrowings.

In the form of an equation, net working capital has been shown below:

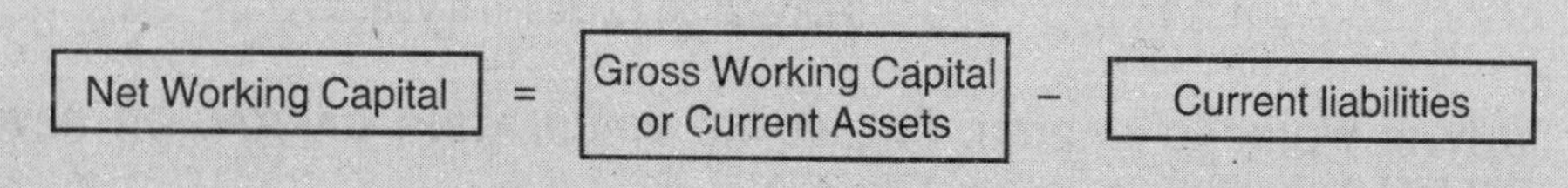

Current liabilities are source of funds in the sense that these finance current assets. For example, a company buys stocks of raw materials for cash. It implies that company is financing raw material stock from its internal sources. Suppose, the company gets a two months credit for the same purchase. It implies the stock is financed by creditors.

7.0 PERMANENT AND TEMPORARY WORKING CAPITAL

PERMANENT WORKING CAPITAL

It refers to a certain minimum level of current assets, which is essential for the firm to carry on its business irrespective of the level of operations. This is the irreducible minimum amount necessary for maintaining the circulation of the current assets. This minimum level of investment in current assets is permanently locked up in business and is, therefore, referred to as permanent *or* fixed *or* hardcore working capital. It is permanent in the same way as investment in firm's fixed assets is. This amount of working capital should be financed with long-term funds.

TEMPORARY WORKING CAPITAL

It refers to the amount of working capital over and above the fixed minimum amount of working capital, which is required to meet seasonal and other temporary requirements. It may keep on fluctuating from period to period depending upon several factors. It is also called fluctuating *or* variable *or* seasonal working capital.

8.0 WORKING CAPITAL IN CASE OF A STABLE FIRM AND A GROWING FIRM

WORKING CAPITAL IN CASE OF A STABLE FIRM

In case of a stable firm, the permanent working capital is stable over time and takes the shape of a horizontal line while temporary working capital is fluctuating – sometimes increasing and sometimes decreasing.

Both these kinds of working capital are shown below:

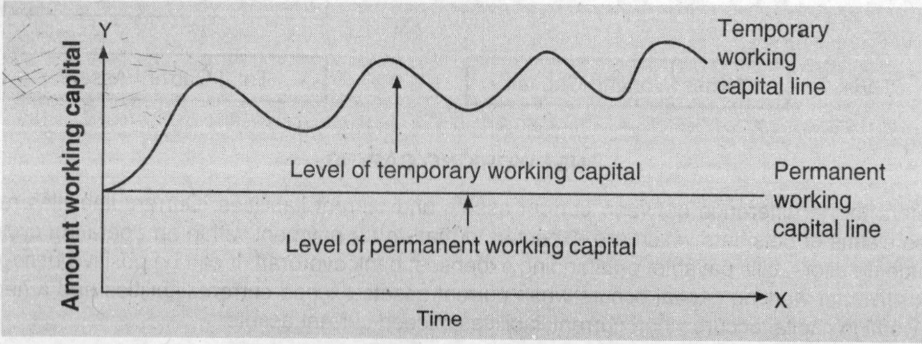

Fig. Working Capital in case of a Stable Firm

WORKING CAPITAL IN CASE OF A GROWING FIRM

In case of a growing firm, the permanent working capital may also keep on increasing over time to support a rising level of activity and hence permanent working capital line may not always be horizontal. Both these kinds of working capital are shown below:

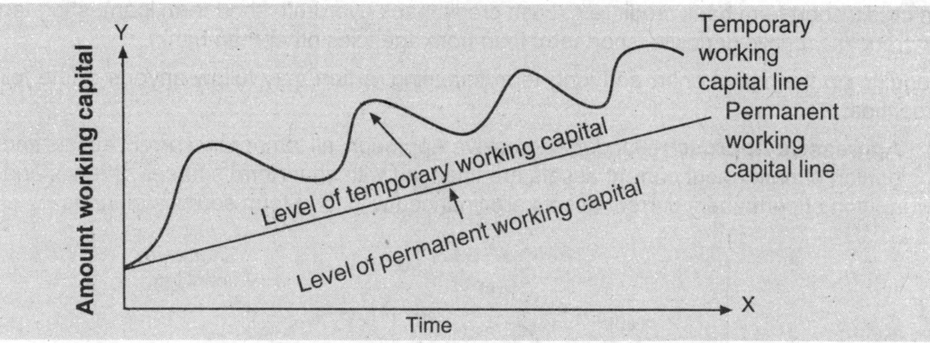

Fig. Working Capital in case of a Growing Firm

9.0 MEANING OF WORKING CAPITAL MANAGEMENT

MEANING OF WORKING CAPITAL MANAGEMENT

Working Capital Management means planning, organizing, directing and controlling of working capital. It provides an answer to following two basic questions:

(a) How much to invest in each type of Current Assets?

(b) How to finance the Current Assets?

HOW MUCH TO INVEST IN EACH TYPE OF CURRENT ASSETS?

It means what should be level of cash, receivables and inventory in the organization. How much to invest in current assets will depend on the operating cycle. Larger the operating cycle, larger the current assets. Operating cycle in a manufacturing firm is the length of time required:

(a) to convert cash into raw material and other resources such as labour, power and fuel etc;

(b) to convert raw material and other resources into work in progress;

(c) to convert work in progress into finished goods;

(d) to convert finished goods into receivables;

(e) to convert receivables into cash.

The firm's decision about the level of investment in current assets involves a trade off between risk and return *or* liquidity and profitability. The effects of excessive and inadequate investment in the current assets are shown below:

Situation	*Effect on Profitability*	*Effect on Liquidity*
1. **Excessive Investment in Current Assets**	It results in low profitability because excess investment in current assets remains idle and hence earns nothing.	It results in high liquidity and hence does not threaten solvency of the firm.
2. **Inadequate investment in current assets**	It results in high profitability since there are no idle funds.	It results in low liquidity and hence it can threaten solvency of the firm if the firm fails to meet its current obligations as and when due.

HOW TO FINANCE THE CURRENT ASSETS?

It means what portion of the working capital should be financed with long term sources of funds such as equity share capital, preference share capital, debentures, long term borrowings, retained earnings and what portion of working capital should be financed with short term sources such as trade credit, short term bank credit (e.g. cash credit, bank overdraft, short term loan), short term non bank credit (i.e. public deposits, short term loan from agencies other than bank).

Depending on the mix of short and long term financing, a firm may follow anyone of the following approaches:

(a) **Aggressive Approach**—Under Aggressive Approach, all temporary current assets and some portion of permanent current assets are financed with short-term sources of funds and some portion of permanent current assets are financed with long-term sources of funds.

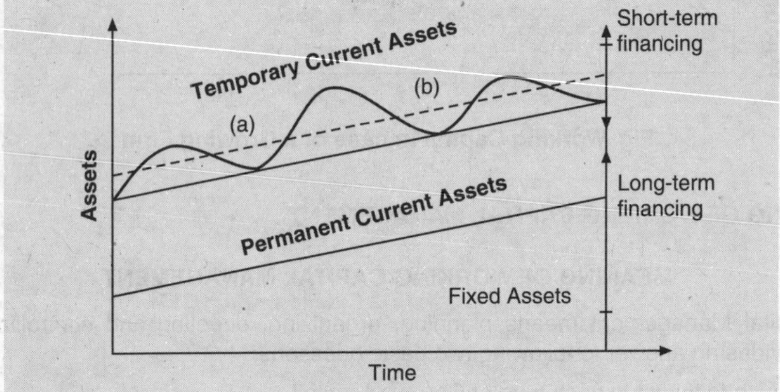

Fig. Aggressive Financing

(b) **Conservative Approach**—Under Conservative Approach, all permanent current assets and some portion of temporary current assets are financed with long term sources of funds and some portion of temporary current assets are financed with short term sources of funds.

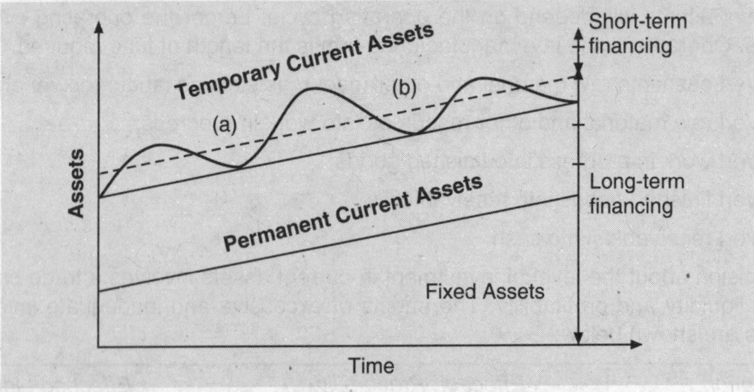

Fig. Conservative Financing

(c) **Matching Approach *or* Hedging Approach**—Under Matching Approach, all permanent current assets are financed with long term sources of fund and all the temporary current assets are financed with short-term sources of funds.

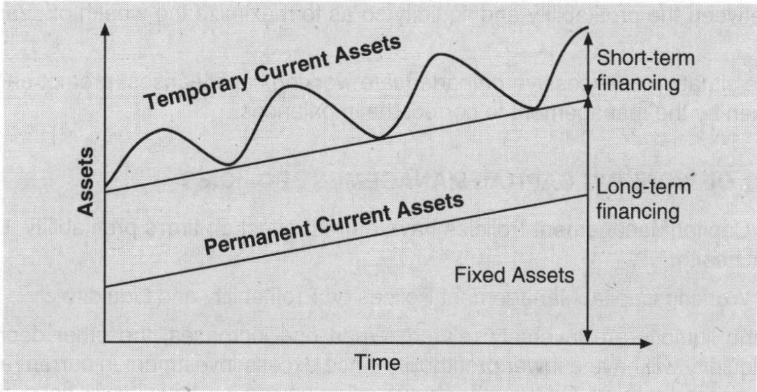

Fig. Financing under Matching Plan

COMPARATIVE STUDY OF AGGRESSIVE, CONSERVATIVE & MATCHING APPROACH

Basis of Comparision	*Aggressive Approach*	*Conservative Approach*	*Matching Approach*
I. Permanent Current Assets	o Some portion financed with Short Term sources of funds o Some portion financed with Long Term sources of funds	All permanent current assets are financed with long-term sources of funds.	All permanent current assets are financed with long-term sources of funds.
II. Temporary Current Assets	All temporary current assets are financed with Short Term sources of funds.	o Some portion financed with Long Term sources of funds. When the firm has no need for temporary current assets; the long-term finance released can be invested in marketable securities to build up the liquidity position of the firm. o Some portion financed with Short Term sources of funds.	All temporary current assets are financed with Short Term sources of funds.
III. Liquidity	Lower	Higher	Moderate
IV. Profitability	Higher	Lower	Moderate

MAJOR ISSUES IN WORKING CAPITAL MANAGEMENT

Working Capital Management refers to the administration of all aspects of current assets (i.e. cash, marketable securities, receivables and inventories) and current liabilities. It is basically concerned with:

(a) Determining the need for working capital.

(b) Determining the optimum levels of investment in various current assets.

(c) Determining the appropriate sources for financing current assets.

(d) Ensuring the payment of current liabilities as and when due.

OBJECTIVE OF WORKING CAPITAL MANAGEMENT

The objective of working capital management is to avoid the situation of excessive and inadequate working capital and to determine and maintain the optimum level of working capital after achieving a trade off between the profitability and liquidity so as to maximize the wealth of shareholders as a whole.

Whenever the situation of excessive *or* inadequate working capital arises, prompt and timely action should be taken by the management to correct the imbalances.

10.0 EFFECT OF WORKING CAPITAL MANAGEMENT POLICIES

1. Working Capital Management Policies have a great effect on firm's profitability, liquidity and its structural health.
2. Effect of Working Capital Management Polices on Profitability and Liquidity

Profitability and liquidity are inversely related. When one increases, the other decreases. A firm having high liquidity will have a lower profitability since excess investment in current assets remains idle and hence earns nothing. On the other hand, a firm having low liquidity will have high profitability since there remains no idle fund. The effects of working capital management policies on liquidity and profitability are as follows:

Policy	*Effect on Profitability*	*Effect on Liquidity*
1. **Conservative Policy i.e. Excessive Investment in Current Assets**	It results in low profitability because excess investment in current assets remains idle and hence earns nothing.	It results in high liquidity and hence does not threaten solvency of the firm.
2. **Aggressive Policy i.e. Inadequate investment in current assets**	It results in high profitability since there are no idle funds.	It results in low liquidity and hence it can threaten solvency of the firm if the firm fails to meet its current obligations as and when due. The firm would be exposed to grater risk of frequent cash shortages and stock-outs.

3. **Effect of Working Capital Management Policies on Structural Health**

   Working Capital Management also has a great impact on structural health of the organization. If different components of working capital are not properly balanced, then inspite of the fact that current ratio and quick ratios may indicate satisfactory financial position in respect of the liquidity of the firm, it may not be infact as liquid as indicated by current and quick ratio.

Effect of High investment in Inventory	It will adversely affect the liquidity of a firm if inventory mainly consists of slow moving & obsolete stock of goods.
Effect of High investment in Receivables	It will adversely affect the liquidity of a firm if receivable mainly consists of slow paying and doubtful debtors.
Effect of Higher Cash and Bank Balances	It will decrease the profitability since idle cash and bank balances do not yield any return to the firm.

4. Thus, the finance manager should chalk out such working capital management policies in respect of different components of working capital i.e. cash, receivable and inventory so as to ensure higher profitability, proper liquidity and structural health of an organization.

11.0 IMPORTANCE OF WORKING CAPITAL MANAGEMENT

THE MANAGEMENT

The management of working capital is an integral part of the overall financial management and ultimately of the overall corporate management. Neglect of management of working capital may result in technical insolvency and even liquidation of a business unit. Inefficient working capital management may cause *either* inadequate *or* excessive working capital, which is dangerous.

ADVERSE CONSEQUENCES OF EXCESSIVE WORKING CAPITAL

The adverse consequences of excessive working capital are as follows:

1. **Unnecessary Accumulation of Inventory:** It results in unnecessary accumulation of inventories. Accumulation of inventory increases the carrying cost and chances of mishandling, wastage, theft and other losses resulting in decrease in profit.
2. **Adaptation of too Liberal Credit Policy:** It results in adaptation of too liberal policy and chances of slackening of collection of receivables. As a result the chances of bad debt increases and profits decrease.
3. **Excessive Cash:** It results in excessive cash holding. Thus, profitability decreases as a result of idle cash.
4. **Encourages Speculation:** The tendency to accumulate excessive inventory is encouraged for making speculative profits so as to make dividend policy more liberal. In case the firm is unable to make speculative profits, liberal dividend policy can't be maintained.

It results in low profitability because excess investment in current assets remains idle and hence earns nothing.

ADVERSE CONSEQUENCES OF INADEQUATE WORKING CAPITAL *OR* PAUCITY OF WORKING CAPITAL

The adverse consequences of inadequate working capital are as follows:

1. **Inadequate Level of Inventory:** It results in inadequate level of inventories. Inadequate raw material and W.I.P. results in frequent production interruptions and inadequate finished goods may result in shifting of customers on regular basis.
2. **Adoption of Tight Credit Policy:** It may result in tight credit policy, which means rejection of certain types of accounts. This results in loss of sales and consequently loss of contribution.
3. **Inadequate Cash:** It may result in inadequate level of cash. As a result the firm may not:
   - meet anticipated obligations (e.g. the payment of manufacturing expenses, office and administration expenses, selling and distribution expenses, taxes, payment to creditors) as and when they become due. As a consequence, the firm may lose its reputation;
   - meet unanticipated obligations (i.e., to tackle the problem of emergency breakdown of machine, strikes of workers);
   - exploit profitable opportunities (i.e. to avail the benefits of cash discount);
   - utilize the fixed assets efficiently.

It results in low liquidity and hence it can threaten solvency of the firm if the firm fails to meet its current obligations as and when due.

Thus, The financial manager should maintain the adequate amount of working capital on a continuous basis. Financial and statistical techniques are helpful in predicting the quantum of working capital needed at different points of time.

12.0 WHAT IS AN OPTIMUM WORKING CAPITAL?

1. Optimum Working Capital can be determined only with reference to particular circumstances of a specific situation.
2. An optimum working capital is dependent upon the business situation as such and the nature and composition of various current assets.

3. A company having short conversion cycle like a Vanaspati manufacturing company may have a lower current ratio. On the other hand, a company having longer conversion cycle, like heavy equipment manufacturing company may have higher current ratio since it has to carry large inventories and debtors.
4. Traditionally, a current ratio of 2 : 1 is considered to be a satisfactory ratio. On the basis of this traditional rule, if the current ratio of 2 is more, it means the firm is adequately liquid and has the ability to meet its current obligations. The logic behind this rule is that even if the value of current assets becomes half, the firm can still meet its short-term obligations.

However, the traditional standard of 2 : 1 should not be used blindly since there may be firms having current ratio of *less* than 2 which may be working efficiently and meeting their short term obligations as and when they become due while other firms having current ratio of more than 2, may not be able to meet its obligations in time. This is so because the current ratio measures the quantity of current assets and not their quality. Current assets may consist of doubtful and slow paying debtors and slow moving and obsolete stock of goods. That is why it can be said that current ratio is no doubt a quick measurement of firm's liquidity but it is crude as well. Thus, in a company, where the inventories are easily saleable and sundry debtors are as good as liquid cash, the current ratio may be lower than 2 and yet the company may be sound.

13.0 FACTORS DETERMINING THE WORKING CAPITAL

The working capital requirements of an enterprise depend on a variety of factors. These factors affect different enterprises differently and vary from time to time. These factors are shown below:

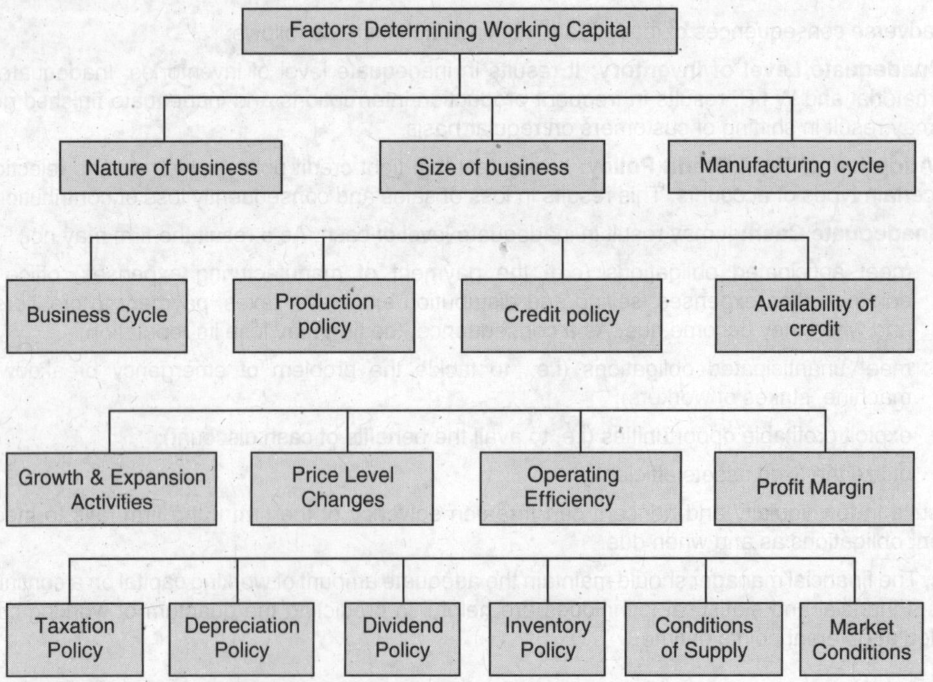

Fig. Factors Determining the Working Capital

Let us discuss these factors, which determine the working capital one by one:

NATURE OF BUSINESS

The working capital needs are basically influenced by the nature of business. The proportion of current assets to total assets measures the relative requirements of working capital of various industries.

Nature of Business	*Requirement of Working Capital*	*Reason*
1. **Small trading concern** *or* **Retail shop**	Small	Operating cycle period is small since— 1. They mostly have cash sales. 2. They carry small quantities of goods in stock. 3. They carry only small amount of debtors' balances. 4. They carry small amount of cash. 5. Goods are purchased on credit but are sold for cash.
2. **Large Trading Firms** *or* **Departmental Store dealing in large variety of goods**	Large	Operating Cycle Period is larger since— 1. They require large quantities of goods in stock. 2. They carry large debtors balances. 3. They carry large amount of cash.
3. **Manufacturing Firm**	Large	Operating Cycle period is large since— 1. They carry large quantity of raw materials. 2. They carry large quantity of work in progress. 3. They carry large quantity of finished goods. 4. They carry huge amount of debtors' balances. 5. They carry large amount of cash.

Thus, shorter the operating cycle period, smaller will be the working capital requirements. Larger the operating cycle period, larger will be the working capital requirements.

The various researches conducted in India have shown the following results:

Nature of Business	*Requirement of Working Capital*	*Reason*
1. **Public utilities** (e.g. electricity generation & supply, water supply)	Small	(a) They have cash sales. (b) They supply services and not products.
2. **Hotels, restaurants and eating houses**	Small	They mostly have cash sales and only small amount of debtors' balances.
3. **Trading firms**	Large	(a) They require large quantities of goods to be held in stock. (b) They carry large debtors' balances.
4. **Financial firms**	Large	They carry large debtors balances.
5. **Tobacco firm**	Large	They require large quantities of inventories.
6. **Construction firm**	Large	They require large quantities of raw material and work-in-progress.
7. **Manufacturing firm**		
(a) **Heavy engineering industry (e.g., BHEL)**	Large	They have larger period of operating cycle.

(b) Rice mill/cotton ®-spinning mill/ steel rolling mill	Small	They have smaller period of operating cycle.

SIZE OF BUSINESS

The size of business also affect the working capital needs. Size may be measured in terms of the scale of operations. Larger the scale of operations, larger will be the firm's working capital requirements, smaller the scale of operations, smaller will be the firm's working capital requirements.

MANUFACTURING CYCLE

Manufacturing cycle also affects the working capital needs. Manufacturing cycle refers to the time gap between the purchase of raw materials and the production of finished goods. Larger the manufacturing cycle, larger will be the firm's working capital requirements. Shorter the manufacturing cycle, smaller will be the firm's working capital requirements. For example, a distillery, which has long manufacturing cycle due to ageing process, requires heavy investment in inventory, whereas a bakery having shorter manufacturing cycle, requires low investment in inventories.

BUSINESS CYCLE

The working capital requirements depend upon the demand and sale of goods. The demand and sale of goods usually increase when the economy is going through a boom phase and decrease when the economy is going through a recessive phase. The effect of business cycle fluctuations on working capital has been shown below:

To avoid the production problems arising due to seasonal fluctuations, the firm may follow a policy of steady production in all seasons to utilize its resources to the fullest extent, which means accumulation of inventories in off-season and their quick disposal in peak season. Since seasonal fluctuations generally conform to a steady pattern, financial arrangements for seasonal working capital requirements should be made in advance.

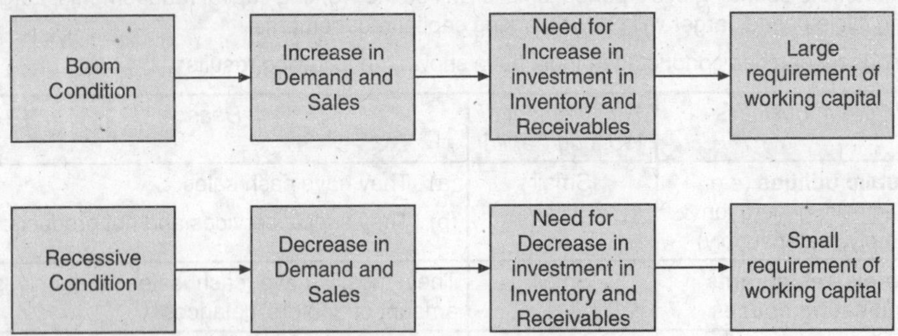

PRODUCTION POLICY

The production policy of the firm affects the working capital by influencing the level of inventories. A firm engaged in manufacture of products the demand of which is seasonal, may follow any of the following three production polices:

Production Policy	*Effect*
(1) Seasonal Production Policy (i.e., production during peak period only)	(a) Increasing production during peak period may be expensive due to increased costs of materials, labour and other expenses. (b) The firm will have to sustain its working force & physical facilities. (c) The working capital requirements will be large during peak period and small during slack period.

(2) Steady Production Policy	(a) Resources are utilized to the fullest extent. (b) Accumulation of inventories during off-season and their quick disposal during the peak season. (c) Firm will be exposed to greater inventory costs and risks. (d) The working capital requirements will follow a steady pattern.
(3) Diversified Production Policy	(a) Manufacturing of original product during the peak period. (b) Manufacturing of other product during slack period to utilize physical resources and working force. (c) The working capital requirements will vary according to the nature of the product.

CREDIT POLICY

The credit policy of the firm affects working capital by influencing the level of book debts. The credit policy of a firm depends upon industry practice, current economic conditions and the management's attitude. Its effect on working capital is shown below:

Credit Policy	*Effect*
(a) Liberal Credit Policy	Higher credit sales, higher book debts, higher working capital.
(b) Tight Credit Policy	Lower credit sales, lower book debts, lower working capital.

AVAILABILITY OF CREDIT FROM SUPPLIERS

The working capital requirements are also determined by the credit terms available to the firm from its creditors. A firm will need *less* working capital if liberal credit terms are available to it. A firm will need more working capital if no credit *or* tight credit terms are available to it.

Case	*Working Capital Requirements*
(a) If credit period received from suppliers > credit period allowed to customers.	Reduces
(b) If credit period received from suppliers < credit period allowed to customer.	Increases

GROWTH AND EXPANSION ACTIVITIES

Growing firm requires more working capital than those that are static. As a company grows, logically larger amount of working capital will be needed. It is difficult to determine precisely the relationship between growth in the volume of a company and its working capital needs. It is also important to note that the need for increased working capital funds precedes the growth in volume of business, rather than follow it. In other words, the need for working capital arises before the growth takes place. That is why an advance planning of working capital is to be made for a growing firm on continuous basis.

PRICE LEVEL CHANGES

Changes in the price level also affect the working capital requirements. However, the effects of changes in the price level may be felt differently by different prices. Generally, rising price level requires a higher investment in working capital because increased investment is required to maintain the same level of current assets. However, the firm, which can immediately revise prices of their products upwards, may not face a severe working capital problem in periods of rising price levels.

OPERATING EFFICIENCY

The operating efficiency means the optimum utilization of resources at minimum costs. The operating efficiency of management also affects the level of working capital. It is shown below:

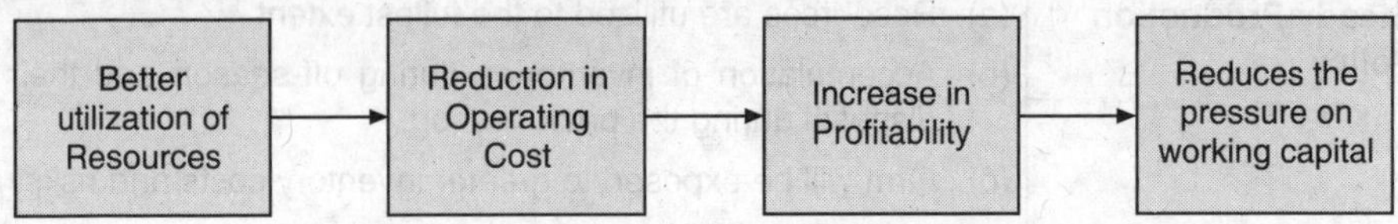

PROFIT MARGIN AND PROFIT APPROPRIATION

Profit margin also affects the level of working capital. A high net profit margin contributes towards the working capital pool. The net profit is a source of working capital to the extent it has been earned in cash. Cash from operations can be found out by adjusting non-cash items such as depreciation, losses written off etc. It can be observed from the figure shown below:

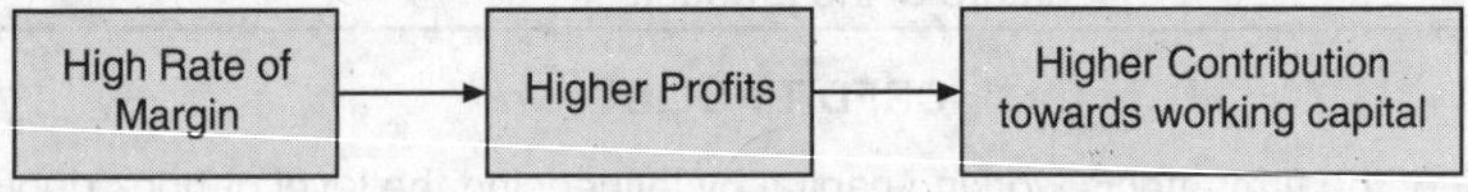

TAXATION POLICY

Taxation Policy also affects the level of working capital since taxes are to be paid in advance. The need for working capital varies with tax rates and advance tax provisions. Tax Planning also affects the level of working capital. It can be observed from the figure shown below:

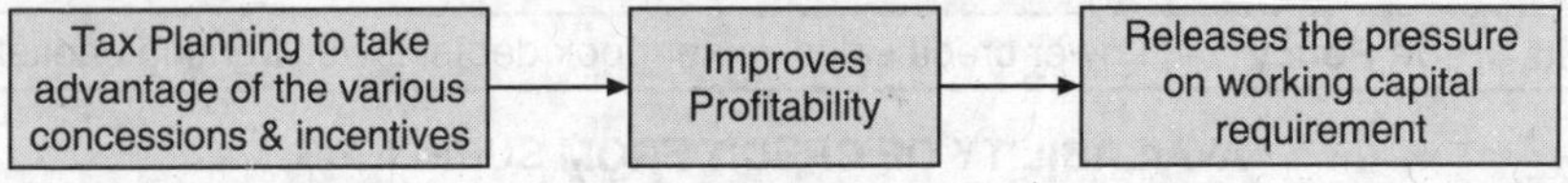

DEPRECIATION POLICY

Depreciation Policy also affects the level of working capital. It can be observed from the figure shown below:

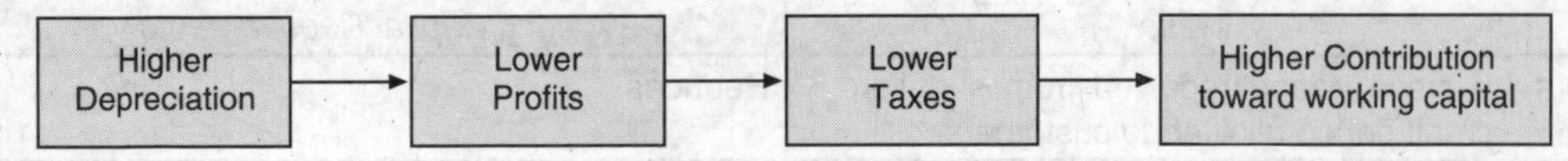

DIVIDEND POLICY

Dividend Policy also affects the level of working capital. Payment of dividend utilizes cash while retaining profits acts as a source of working capital. It can be observed from the figure shown below:

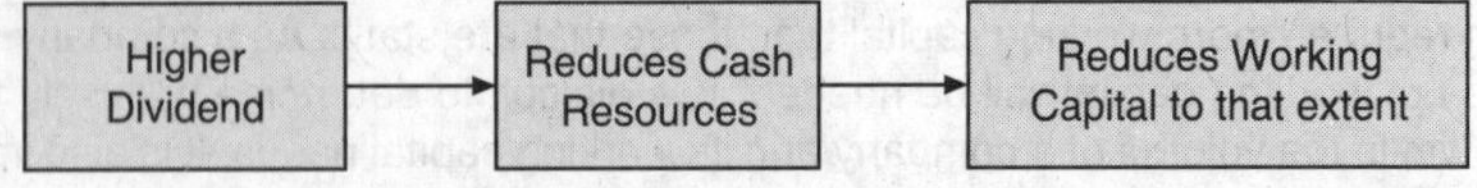

INVENTORY POLICY

Inventory Policy also affects the level of working capital since a large amount of funds is normally locked up in inventories. It can be observed from the figure shown below:

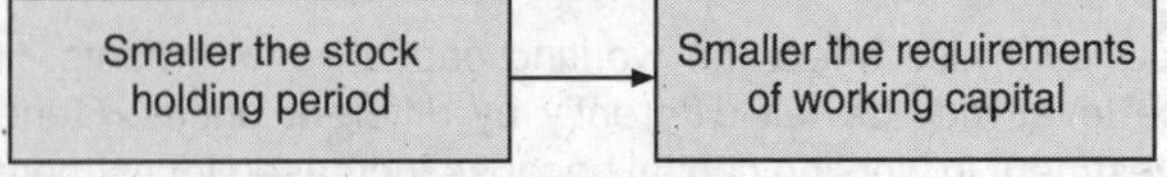

CONDITIONS OF SUPPLY

Conditions of Supply also affects the level of working capital. It can be observed from the figure shown below:

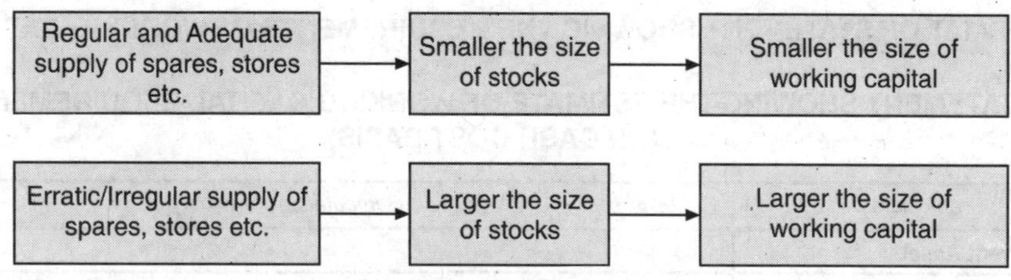

MARKET CONDITIONS

Market Conditions (like degree of competition) also affects the level of working capital. It can be observed from the figure shown below:

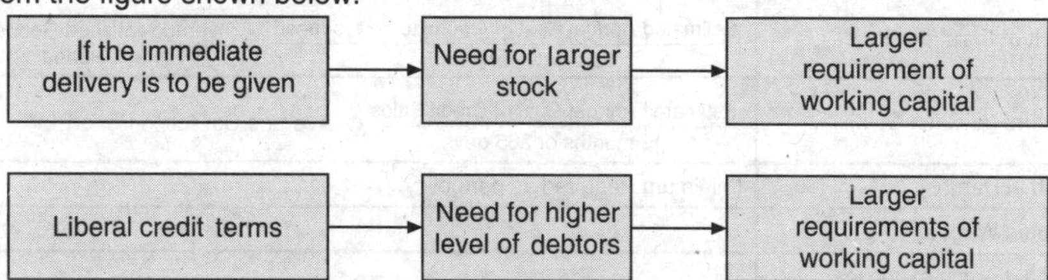

14.0 ESTIMATE OF FUTURE WORKING CAPITAL BASED ON CURRENT ASSETS AND CURRENT LIABILITIES

The holding period of various constituents of operating cycle may *either* contract *or* expand the net operating cycle period. Shorter the operating cycle, lower will be the requirement of working capital and vice versa. It may be noted that working capital requirements are to be determined on an average basis and not at any specific point of time.

The estimation of Working Capital involves the following steps.

Step 1: *Make the estimates of various Current Assets as follows:*

1. Stock of Raw material = $\frac{\text{Estimated Annual Cost of Raw Material to be Consumed}}{\text{12 months or 365 days}} \times$ Average Raw Material Holding Period

2. Stock of W.I.P. = $\frac{\text{Estimated Annual Cost of Goods to be produced}}{\text{12 months or 365 days}} \times$ Average W.I.P Holding period or Process Period

3. Stock of Finished Goods = $\frac{\text{Estimated Annual Cost of Goods to be Produced}}{\text{12 months or 365 days}} \times$ Average Finished Goods Storage Period

4. Average Trade Debtors = $\frac{\text{Estimated Annual Cost of Credit Sales}}{\text{12 months or 365 days}} \times$ Average Collection Period

5. Cash and Bank Balance = Minimum as desired by the Firm

Step 2: *Make the estimates of various Current Liabilities as follows:*

1. Average Trade Creditors = $\frac{\text{Estimated Annual Cost of Credit Purchases}}{\text{12 months or 365 days}} \times$ Average Credit Period Availed

2. Average Creditors for Expenses = $\frac{\text{Expenses for the year}}{\text{12 months or 365 days}} \times$ Average Time Lag in Payment

Step 3: *Make the Estimate of Working Capital by taking out the difference between the estimated Current Assets (as per Step 1) and the estimated Current Liabilities (as per Step 2).*

Step 4: *Add Safety Margin as % of Working Capital before adding safety margin*

or

Add Safety Margin as % of Working Capital after adding safety margin.

Step 5: *Calculate Total Working Capital after adding Safety Margin as per Step 4 to the Working Capital (excluding Safety Margin) as per Step 3.*

15.0 FORMAT OF STATEMENT SHOWING THE REQUIREMENTS OF WORKING CAPITAL

STATEMENT SHOWING THE ESTIMATE OF WORKING CAPITAL REQUIREMENTS (ON CASH COST BASIS)

Particulars	Computation	₹
A. Current Assets:		
Stock of Raw Material	$\frac{\text{Estimated Annual Cost of Raw Material to be consumed}}{\text{12 months or 365 days}}$ × Average Raw Materials Holding Period	......
Stock of Work-in-progress	As per Working Note	......
Stock of Finished Goods	$\frac{\text{Estimated Annual Cost of Goods to be produced}}{\text{12 months or 365 days}}$ × Average Finished Goods Storage Period	......
Debtors (at Cash Cost)	$\frac{\text{Estimated Annual Cost of Credit Sales}}{\text{12 months or 365 days}}$ × Average Collection Period	......
Cash in Hand	(Minimum Required as per policy)	......
Prepaid Wages		......
Prepaid Admn expenses		......
Prepaid Selling & Distri. exp.		......
Total Current Assets		......
B. Current Liabilities:		
Creditors for Raw Materials	$\frac{\text{Estimated Annual Credit Purchases}}{\text{12 months or 365 days}}$ × Avg. Credit Period Allowed by Suppliers	......
Creditors for Wages	$\frac{\text{Estimated Annual Wages for the year}}{\text{12 months or 365 days}}$ × Average Time Lag in Payment	......
Creditors for Mfg. Overheads	$\frac{\text{Estimated Annual Mfg. Overheads for the year}}{\text{12 months or 365 days}}$ × Average Time Lag in Payment	......
Cr. for Selling & Distri. Exp.	$\frac{\text{Estimated Annual Sell \& Dist. Exp. for the year}}{\text{12 months or 365 days}}$ × Average Time Lag in Payment	......
Provision for Taxation		......
Total Current Liabilities		......
C. Net Working Capital (A – B)		......
D. *Add:* Safety Margin		......
E. Total Working Capital (C + D)		......

Working Notes:

(I) CALCULATION OF STOCK OF FINISHED GOODS AND COST OF SALES

Particulars	₹
Direct Material Cost	....
Direct Labour Cost	....
Direct Expenses	....
Variable Manufacturing Expenses	....
Fixed Manufacturing Expenses (excluding Depreciation)	....
Variable Administrative Expenses	....
Fixed Administrative Expenses	....
Total Cash Cost of Goods Produced	....

Add: Opening Stock of Finished Goods	....
Total Cash Cost of Goods available	....
Less: Closing Stock of Finished Goods	....
Total Cash Cost of Goods Sold	....
Add: Variable Selling and Distribution expenses	....
Add: Fixed Selling and Distribution expenses	....
Total Cash Cost of Sales	....
Total Cash Cost of Credit Sales	....

(II) CALCULATION OF STOCK OF WORK IN PROGRESS IF PHYSICAL UNITS OF WIP ARE NOT GIVEN

Particulars	*Computation*	₹
Raw Material	$\frac{\text{Annual Cost of Raw-Materials to be consumed}}{\text{12 months}} \times \text{Process Period} \times \text{Degree of Completion}$	....
Wages	$\frac{\text{Annual Wages}}{\text{12 months}} \times \text{Process Period} \times \text{Degree of Completion}$	....
Mfg. Overheads (Variable + Fixed)	$\frac{\text{Annual Manufacturing Overheads}}{\text{12 months}} \times \text{Process Period} \times \text{Degree of Completion}$	....

Alternative Method [if Physical Units of WIP are given]

Items of Cost	*Computation*	₹
Raw-Material	WIP (units) × Degree of Completion × Raw-material Cost per unit	....
Wages	WIP (units) × Degree of Completion × Labour Cost per unit	....
Mfg. Overheads (Variable + Fixed)	WIP (units) × Degree of Completion × Mfg. Overheads per unit	....

Note: Degree of Completion

Items of Cost	*Unless otherwise stated, Degree of Completion...*
(a) In Case of Raw-Material	DOC is assumed to be 100% on the assumption that all raw materials are to be issued in the beginning of processing.
(b) In case of Wages and Manufacturing expenses	DOC is assumed to be 50% on the assumption that wages and manufacturing expenses are incurred evenly (or uniformally) throughout the process period.

Note: Cost of Packing Materials does not form part of Cost of WIP.

(III) CALCULATION OF STOCK OF FINISHED GOODS

(a) **If Stock of Finished Goods is valued at Factory Cost**

(i) ***Under FIFO Method:***

$$\frac{\text{Net Factory Cost}}{\text{No. of Units of Finished Goods Produced}} \times \text{Stock of Finished Goods (units)}$$

(ii) ***Under Weighted Average Method:***

$$\frac{\text{Net Factory Cost + Cost of Opening Stock of Finished Goods}}{\text{No. of Units of Finished Goods Produced + Opening Stock of Finished Goods}} \times \text{Stock of Finished Goods (units)}$$

(b) **If Stock of Finished Goods is valued at Cost of Goods Produced (including Administrative Expenses)**

(i) ***Under FIFO Method:***

$$\frac{\text{Cost of Goods Produced (including Adm. Exp.)}}{\text{No of Units of Finished Goods Produced}} \times \text{Stock of Finished Goods (units)}$$

(ii) ***Under Weighted Average Method:***

$$\frac{\text{Cost of Goods Produced (including Adm. Exp.)} + \text{Cost of Opening Stock of Finished Goods}}{\text{No. of Units of Finished Goods Produced} + \text{Opening Stock of Finished Goods}} \times \text{Stock of Finished Goods (units)}$$

(iv) *Unless otherwise stated, stock of finished goods is to be valued on FIFO basis at cost of goods produced (including Administrative Expenses).*

(v) *Excise Duty is calculated on the basis of Cost of Goods Produced (including Depreciation and Administrative expenses).*

(vi) *Excise Duty should form part of cost of stock of finished goods irrespective of the timings of removal of goods from the factory since it is levied on the manufacture of goods.*

(vii) *Value Added Tax (VAT) is calculated on Selling Price [i.e., Cost of Goods Produced (including Depreciation, Administrative Expenses and Excise Duty) + Selling & Distribution Expenses + Profit]*

(viii) *Debtors are valued at Cash Cost of Credit Sales plus Value Added Tax.*

(ix) *Credit Purchases of Raw-material = Raw-Materials consumed + Closing Stock of Raw-material – Opening Stock of Raw-materials.*

ILLUSTRATION 2 [CALCULATION OF STOCK OF RAW-MATERIALS]

Calculate the Stock of Raw-Material in each of the following cases:

Case (a) Budgeted Production 60,000 Units, Raw-material Cost per unit ₹ 5, Raw-material Storage Period 2 moths.

Case (b) Budgeted Production 12,000 units. Raw-material required to produce one unit 2.5 kg., Raw-Material Cost per kg ₹ 4, Raw-material Storage Period 2 months.

SOLUTION

Case (a) Stock of Raw-Material = [(60,000 units × ₹ 5)/12 months] × 2 months = ₹ 50,000

Case (b) Stock of Raw-material = [(60,000 units × 2.5 kg × ₹ 4)/12 months] × 2 months = ₹ 20,000

ILLUSTRATION 3 [CALCULATION OF STOCK OF FINISHED GOODS]

Tulsian (3) Ltd. provides you the following information:

1.	Unit Cost Structure of Product at an activity level of 60,000 units	
	Raw Material	₹ 5
	Wages	₹ 4
	Manufacturing Overheads (including Depreciation ₹ 1)	₹ 3
	Administrative Expenses	₹ 1
	Selling and Distribution expenses	₹ 2
2.	Finished Goods Storage Period – 2 months	

Required: Calculate the Cash Cost Stock of Finished Goods in each of the following alternative cases:

Case (a) If no other information is given.

Case (b) If Stock of Finished Goods is to be valued at factory cost.

SOLUTION

Case (a) Cash Cost of Goods Produced (including Adm. Exp.) per unit

= ₹ 5 + ₹ 4 + ₹ 2 + ₹ 1 = ₹ 12

Stock of Finished Goods = [(60,000 units × ₹ 12)/12 months]× 2 months = ₹ 1,20,000

Case (b) Factory Cash cost of Goods Produced = ₹ 5 + ₹ 4 + ₹ 2 = ₹ 11

Stock of Finished Goods = [(60,000 units × ₹ 11)/12 months]× 2 months = ₹ 1,10,000

ILLUSTRATION 4 [CALCULATION OF CASH COST OF DEBTORS]

Tulsian (4) Ltd. provides you the following information:

1. Cost-Price Structure of a Product an activity level of 60,000 units.	
Raw-Material	₹ 5
Wages	₹ 4
Manufacturing Overheads (including Depreciation ₹ 1)	₹ 3
Administrative expenses	₹ 1
Selling and Distribution Expenses	₹ 2
Profit	₹ 5
Selling Price	₹ 20
2. Credit Period allowed to Customers – 2 months	
3. Cash Sales – 20%	

Required: Calculate the amount of Debtors.

SOLUTION

Step 1: Cash Cost of Sales Per unit [₹ 5 + ₹ 4 + ₹ 2 + ₹ 1 + ₹ 2] = ₹ 14

Step 2: Total Cash Cost of Sales [60,000 Units × ₹ 14] = ₹ 8,40,000

Step 3: Total Cash Cost of Credit Sales [₹ 8,40,000 × 80%] = ₹ 6,72,000

Step 4: Debtors = $\frac{₹\ 6,72,000}{12 \text{ months}} \times 2$ months = ₹ 1,12,000

ILLUSTRATION 5 [CALCULATION OF STOCK OF WORK-IN-PROGRESS]

Tulsian (5) Ltd. provides you the following information:

1. Unit Cost Structure of Product at an activity level of 60,000 units.	
Raw Material	₹ 5
Wages	₹ 4
Manufacturing Overheads (including Depreciation ₹ 1)	₹ 3
Administrative Expenses	₹ 1
Selling and Distribution expenses	₹ 2
2. Production Cycle – Half Month.	

Required: Calculate the Stock of Work-in-Progress in each of the following alternative cases:

Case (a) If no other information is given.

Case (b) If expenses are incurred evenly.

Case (c) If material are issued at the start of the processing and expenses accrue evenly.

Case (d) If work-in-progress is 50% complete as to conversion cost.

Case (e) If the degree of completion is 50%.

Case (f) If the degree of completion as to material is 80% and as to conversion cost is 60%.

Case (g) If the material is required only to the extent of 50% in the beginning and the remaining is needed at a uniform rate during the process. Direct wages and other manufacturing overheads accrue similarly at a uniform rate throughout the process.

SOLUTION

$$\text{Units of WIP} = \frac{60,000 \text{ units}}{12} \times \frac{1}{2} = 2500 \text{ units}$$

CASE (A) CALCULATION OF STOCK OF WORK-IN-PROGRESS

A. Raw material [2,500 units × ₹ 5 × 100%]	₹ 12,500
B. Wages [2,500 units × ₹ 4 × 50%]	₹ 5,000
C. Manufacturing Overheads (Ex. Dep) [2,500 units × ₹ 2 × 50%]	₹ 2,500
	₹ 20,000

Notes:

(i) Administrative Expenses and Selling and Distribution Expenses do not form part of cost of stock of WIP

(ii) Stock of WIP has been calculated on Cash Cost Basis. Hence depreciation has been ignored.

Case (b) Same as in case (a)

Case (c) Same as in case (a)

Case (d) Same as in case (a)

Case (e)	
A. Raw Material [2,500 units × ₹ 5 × 50%]	₹ 6,250
B. Wages [2,500 units × ₹ 4 × 50%]	₹ 5,000
C. Manufacturing Overheads (Ex. Dep.) [2,500 units × ₹ 2 × 50%]	₹ 2,500
	₹ 13,750
Case (f)	
A. Raw Material [2,500 units × ₹ 5 × 80%]	₹ 10,000
B. Wages [2,500 units × ₹ 4 × 60%]	₹ 6,000
C. Manufacturing Overheads (Ex. Dep.) [2,500 units × ₹ 2 × 60%]	₹ 3,000
	₹ 19,000
Case (g)	
A. Raw Material [2,500 units × ₹ 2.50 × 100%]	₹ 6,250
B. Raw Material [2,500 units × ₹ 2.50 × 50%]	₹ 3,125
C. Wages [2,500 units × ₹ 4 × 50%]	₹ 5,000
D. Mfg. overheads (Ex. Dep.) [2,500 units × ₹ 2 × 50%]	₹ 2,500
	₹ 16,875

ILLUSTRATION 6 [CALCULATION OF CREDITORS FOR RAW-MATERIALS & EXPENSES]

Tulsian (6) Ltd. provides you the following information:

1. Unit Cost Structure of Product at an activity Level of 60,000 units:	
Raw Material	₹ 5
Wages	₹ 4
Manufacturing Overheads [including depreciation ₹ 1)	₹ 3
Administrative expenses	₹ 1
Selling and Distribution Expenses	₹ 2
2. Credit period allowed by supplier of materials – 2 months	
3. Cash Purchases – 20%.	
4. Time lag in payment of Wages, Manufacturing Overheads, Adm. Exp. and Selling and Distribution Expenses – 1 month.	

Required: Calculate the Creditors for Raw-Material and Expenses.

SOLUTION

1. Creditors for Raw-Material = $\dfrac{60,000 \text{ units} \times ₹\ 5 \times 80\%}{12 \text{ months}} \times 2 \text{ months} = ₹\ 40,000$

2. Creditors of Wages = $\dfrac{60,000 \text{ units} \times ₹\ 4}{12 \text{ months}} \times 1 \text{ month} = ₹\ 20,000$

3. Creditors of Manufacturing Overheads = $\dfrac{60,000 \text{ units} \times ₹\ 2}{12 \text{ months}} \times 1 \text{ month} = ₹\ 10,000$

4. Creditors for Adm. Expenses = $\dfrac{60,000 \text{ units} \times ₹\ 1}{12 \text{ months}} \times 1 \text{ month} = ₹\ 5,000$

5. Creditors for Selling & Distribution exp. = $\dfrac{60,000 \text{ units} \times ₹\ 2}{12 \text{ months}} = ₹\ 10,000$

ILLUSTRATION 7

From the following details prepare an estimate of requirements of working capital of an existing company X Ltd.:

Production	60,000 units p.a.
Selling Price	₹ 5 per unit
Raw Material	60% of selling price
Direct Wages	10% of selling price
Manufacturing Overheads (Excluding Depreciation)	20% of selling price
Materials in hand	2 months' requirements
Production time	1 month
Finished goods in store	3 month
Credit for materials	2 month
Credit allowed to customers	3 month
Average Cash Balance	₹ 20,000
Safety Margin	20%

Wages and overheads are paid in the following month. In production all the required materials are charged in the initial stage and wages and overheads accrue evenly.

SOLUTION

STATEMENT SHOWING THE REQUIREMENTS OF WORKING CAPITAL

Particulars	*Computation*	₹
A. Current Assets:		
Stock of Raw Material	₹ 1,80,000 × 2/12	30,000
Stock of Work-in-progress	As Per Working note (ii)	18,750
Stock of Finished goods	₹ 2,70,000 × 3/12	67,500
Debtors	₹ 2,70,000 × 3/12	67,500
Cash in Hand		20,000
Total Current Assets		2,03,750
B. Current Liabilities:		
Creditors for Raw materials	₹ 1,80,000 × 2/12	30,000
Creditors for Wages	₹ 30,000 × 1/12	2,500
Creditors for Manufacturing Expenses	₹ 60,000 × 1/12	5,000
Total Current Liabilities		37,500
C. Net Working Capital (A – B)		1,66,250
D. *Add:* Safety Margin	₹.1,66,250 × 20/100	33,250
E. Net Working Capital Required (C + D)		1,99,500

Working Notes:

Particulars	₹
(i) Calculation of Stock of Finished Goods and Cost of Sales	
Direct Material Cost	1,80,000
Direct Labour Cost	30,000
Manufacturing Overheads (Excluding Depreciation)	60,000
Total Cash Cost of Goods Produced	2,70,000
Add: Opening Stock of Finished Goods [₹ 2,70,000 × 3/12]	67,500
Total Cash Cost of Goods available	3,37,500
Less: Closing Stock of Finished Goods	(67,500)
Total Cash Cost of Goods Sold	2,70,000
Add: Selling and Distribution expenses	Nil
Total Cash Cost of Sales	2,70,000
(ii) Calculation of Stock of Work in progress	₹
Raw Material (₹ 1,80,000 × 1/12 × 100%)	15,000
Wages (₹ 30,000 × 1/12 × 50%)	1,250
Manufacturing Expenses (₹ 60,000 × 1/12 × 50%)	2,500
	18,750

(iii) Since it is an existing company and no specific information regarding opening stock has been given, it has been assumed that stock level is uniform throughout the year. Hence, opening stock equals closing stock.

ILLUSTRATION 8

The following annual figures relate to CAMID Ltd.

Particulars	₹
Sales (at two months' credit)	36,00,000
Materials consumed (Suppliers extend two months' Credit)	9,00,000
Wages paid (monthly in arrear)	7,20,000
Manufacturing expenses outstanding at the end of the year	
(Cash expenses are paid one month in arrear)	80,000
Total administrative expenses, paid as above	2,40,000
Total Sales promotion expenses (paid quarterly in advance)	1,20,000

The company sells its products on gross profit of 25% counting depreciation as part of the cost of production. It keeps one month's stock each of raw materials and finished goods, and a cash balance of ₹ 1,00,000. Stock of finished stocks in valued at factory cost.

Required: Assuming at 20% safety margin, work out the working capital requirements of the company on cash cost basis. Ignore work-in progress.

SOLUTION

STATEMENT SHOWING THE REQUIREMENTS OF WORKING CAPITAL

Particulars	*Computation*	₹
A. Current Assets:		
Stock of Raw Material	₹ 9,00,000 × 1/12	75,000
Stock of Finished goods	₹ 25,80,000 × 1/12	2,15,000
Debtors	₹ 29,40,000 × 2/12	4,90,000
Prepaid Sales Promotion Expenses	₹ 1,20,000 × 3/12	30,000
Cash in Hand		1,00,000
Total Current Assets		9,10,000
B. Current Liabilities:		
Creditors for Raw Materials	₹ 9,00,000 × 2/12	1,50,000
Creditors for Wages	₹ 7,20,000 × 1/12	60,000
Creditors for Manufacturing Expenses	₹ 9,60,000 × 1/12	80,000
Creditors for Office & Adm.Expenses	₹ 2,40,000 × 1/12	20,000
Total Current Liabilities		3,10,000
C. Net Working Capital (A – B)		6,00,000
D. *Add:* Safety Margin	₹ 6,00,000 × 20/100	1,20,000
E. Net Working Capital Required (C + D)		7,20,000

Working Notes:

(i) Since it is an existing company and no specific information regarding opening stock has been given, it has been assumed that stock level is uniform throughout the year. Hence, opening stock equals closing stock.

(II) CALCULATION OF STOCK OF FINISHED GOODS AND COST OF SALES

Particulars	₹
Direct Material Cost	9,00,000
Direct Labour Cost	7,20,000
Variable Manufacturing Expenses (excluding Depreciation) (₹ 80,000 × 12)	9,60,000
Total Cash Cost of Goods Produced	25,80,000
Add: Opening Stock of Finished Goods [₹ 25,80,000 × 1/12]	2,15,000
Total Cash Cost of Goods available	27,95,000
Less: Closing Stock of Finished Goods	(2,15,000)
Total Cash Cost of Goods Sold	25,80,000
Add: Office & Adm. Expenses	2,40,000
Add: Variable Selling and Distribution expenses	1,20,000
Total Cash Cost of Sales	29,40,000

ILLUSTRATION 9

CAMID Ltd. sells goods at a gross profit of 20%. It includes depreciation as part of cost of production. The following figures for the 12 months period ending 31st December, 20X7 are given to enable you to ascertain the requirements of working capital of the company on a cash cost basis.

In your working, you are required to assume that:

(i) as safety margin of 15% will be maintained;
(ii) cash is to be held to the extent of 50% of current liabilities;
(iii) there will be no work-in progress;
(iv) tax is to be ignored.
(v) the stock of finished goods is to be valued at Factory Cost.
(vi) Stocks of raw materials and finished goods are kept at one month's requirements.

Particulars	₹
Sales-at 2 months' credit	27,00,000
Materials consumed (suppliers' credit is for 2 months)	6,75,000
Wages (paid at the beginning of the next month)	5,40,000
Manufacturing expenses includes depreciation of ₹ 2,25,000	?
(cash expenses are paid one month in arrear)	
Total Administrative expenses (paid as above)	1,80,000
Sales promotion expenses-paid quarterly and advance	90,000

SOLUTION

STATEMENT SHOWING THE REQUIREMENTS OF WORKING CAPITAL

Particulars	*Computation*	₹
A. Current Assets:		
Stock of Raw Material	6,75,000 × 1/12	56,250
Stock of Finished goods	19,35,000 × 1/12	1,61,250

Debtors	22,05,000 × 2/12	3,67,500
Cash in Hand	2,32,500 × 1/2	1,16,250
Selling & Distribution Expenses	90,000 × 1/4	22,500
Total Current Assets		7,23,750
B. Current Liabilities:		
Creditors for Raw materials	6,75,000 × 2/12	1,12,500
Creditors for Wages	5,40,000 × 1/12	45,000
Creditors for Manufacturing Expenses	7,20,000 × 1/12	60,000
Creditors for Administrative Expenses	1,80,000 × 1/12	15,000
Total Current Liabilities		2,32,500
C. Net Working Capital (A – B)		4,91,250
D. *Add:* Safety Margin	4,91,250 × 15/100	73,688
E. Net Working Capital Required (C + D)		5,64,938

Working Notes:

(I) CALCULATION OF CASH MANUFACTURING EXPENSES

A.	Sales	27,00,000
B.	*Less:* Gross Profit @ 20%	(5,40,000)
C.	Cost of Goods Sold	21,60,000
D.	*Less:* Costs other than Cash Manufacturing Expenses	
	(i) Direct Material Cost	6,75,000
	(ii) Direct Labour Cost	5,40,000
	(iii) Depreciation	2,25,000
		(14,40,000)
E.	Cash Manufacturing Expenses	7,20,000

(II) CALCULATION OF STOCK OF FINISHED GOODS AND COST OF SALES

A.	Direct Material Cost	6,75,000
B.	Direct Labour Cost	5,40,000
C.	Manufacturing Expenses	7,20,000
D.	Total Cash Cost of Goods Produced	19,35,000
E.	*Add:* Opening Stock of Finished Goods	1,61,250
F.	Total Cash Cost of Goods available	20,96,250
G.	*Less:* Closing Stock of Finished Goods	(1,61,250)
H.	Total Cash Cost of Goods Sold	19,35,000
I.	Variable Administrative Expenses	1,80,000
J.	*Add:* Variable Selling and Distribution expenses	90,000
K.	Total Cash Cost of Sales	22,05,000

(iii) Since it is an existing company an no specific information regarding opening stock has been given, it has been assumed that stock level is uniform throughout the year. Hence, opening stock equals closing stock.

ILLUSTRATION 10

Determine the working capital requirements from the following particulars:

Annual budget for	*Amount (₹ in lakh)*
Raw materials	720
Supplies and components	240
Manpower Expenses	480
Factory expenses (including Depreciation ₹ 10 lakhs)	130
Administration Expenses	180
Sales	2,380

Your are given the following additional information:

(i) Stock-levels planned: Raw materials, 30 days; supplies and components, 90 days.

(ii) 50 per cent of the sales is for cash; for the remaining 20 days credit is normal.

(iii) Finished goods are held in stock for a period of 7 days before they are released for sale and are valued at factory cost.

(iv) Goods remain in process for 5 days. Materials & Components are supplied in the beginning and expenses are incurred evenly.

(v) The company enjoys 30 days credit facilities on 20 per cent of the purchases.

(vi) Cash and bank balances had been planned to be kept at the rate of half months' budgeted expenses [Assume 360 days in a year]

SOLUTION

STATEMENT SHOWING THE REQUIREMENTS OF WORKING CAPITAL

Particulars	*Computation*	₹
A. Current Assets:		
Stock of Raw Material	720 × 30/360	60.00
Stock of Supplies & Components	240 × 90/360	60.00
Stock of Work-in-progress	As per working Note	17.50
Stock of Finished goods	1560 × 7/360	30.33
Debtors	870 × 20/360	48.33
Cash in Hand	780 × 15/360	32.50
Total Current assets		248.66
B. Current Liabilities:		
Creditors for Raw materials	720 × 20% × 30/360	12.00
Creditors for Supplies & Components	240 × 20% × 30/360	4.00
Total Current Liabilities		16.00
C. Net Working Capital (A – B)		232.66

Working Notes:

(I) CALCULATION OF STOCK OF WORK-IN-PROGRESS

Particulars	*₹ (in lakhs)*
Raw Material (720 × 5/360 × 100%)	10.00

Supplies & Components (240 × 5/360 × 100%)	3.333
Wages Expenses (480 × 5/360 × 50%)	3.333
Factory Expenses (120 × 5/360 × 50%)	0.833
Total	17.50

(II) CALCULATION OF STOCK OF FINISHED GOODS AND COST OF CREDIT SALES

Particulars	*₹ (in lakhs)*
Direct Material Cost	720
Supplies & Components	240
Manpower Expenses	480
Factory Expenses (excluding depreciation) (130 – 10)	120
Cost of goods produced	1560
Add: Opening Stock of Finished Goods	30.33
Less: Closing Stock of Finished Goods	(30.33)
Add: Office & Adm. Expenses	180
Total Cash Cost of Sales	1740
Total Cash Cost of Credit Sales [₹ 1,740 lakhs × 50/100]	870

(III) CALCULATION OF BUDGETED EXPENSES

Particulars	*₹ (in lakhs)*
A. Manpower Expenses	480
B. Factory Expenses	120
C. Administrative Expenses	180
D. Total (A + B + C)	780

(iv) Since it is an existing company and no specific information regarding opening stock has been given, it has been assumed that stock level is uniform throughout the year. Hence, opening stock equals closing stock.

ILLUSTRATION 11

Suppose you are the financial director of Tulsian Ltd. The company proposes to produce 6,00,000 units of its product in the next year commencing on 1st April 20X8. The estimated cost sheet of the product is as follows:

Item	*Cost per Unit (₹)*
Raw Material	10.00
Direct Wages	2.50
Mfg. Expenses (including Depreciation 0.25)	5.25
Administrative Expenses	1.25
Selling and Distribution Expenses	1.00
Total Cost:	20.00
Profit	5.00
Selling Price	25.00

Additional Information:

(a) Company holds 2 months' raw material in stock

(b) Half a months' production remain in work in progress.

(c) On an average, finished goods remain in stock for one month.

(d) Purchases amounting to four time the cash purchase are at two months credit.

(e) Cash Sales are 75% *less* than the Credit sales and credit sales are at two and half months' credit.

(f) The company wants to maintain ₹ 25,000 as minimum cash balance and to assume 20% safety margin.

(g) All cash expenses including wages but excluding cash purchases are paid one month in arrear except sales promotion expenses totaled ₹ 1,20,000 are quarterly in advance.

(h) Closing Stocks are same as Opening Stocks.

Requirement: Forecast the working capital of the company for the next year.

SOLUTION

STATEMENT SHOWING THE REQUIREMENTS OF WORKING CAPITAL

Particulars	*Computation*	₹
A. Current Assets:		
Stock of Raw Material	₹ 60,00,000 × 2/12	10,00,000
Stock of Work-in-Progress	As per working note (ii)	3,43,750
Stock of Finished goods	₹ 1,12,50,000 × 1/12	9,37,500
Debtors	₹ 94,80,000 × 2.5/12	19,75,000
Cash in Hand		25,000
Prepaid Selling & Distribution Expenses	₹ 1,20,000 × 3/12	30,000
Total Current Assets		43,11,250
B. Current Liabilities:		
Creditors for Raw Materials	₹ 48,00,000 × 2/12	8,00,000
Creditors for Wages	₹ 15,00,000 × 1/12	1,25,000
Creditors for Manufacturing Expenses	₹ 30,00,000 × 1/12	2,50,000
Creditors for Administrative Expenses	₹ 7,50,000 × 1/12	62,500
Creditors for Selling & Distribution Expenses	₹ 4,80,000 × 1/12	40,000
Total Current Liabilities		12,77,500
C. Net Working Capital (A – B)		30,33,750
D. *Add:* Safety Margin	₹ 30,33,750 × 20/100	6,06,750
E. Net Working Capital required (C + D)		36,40,500

Working Notes:

(I) CALCULATION OF CREDIT SALES

Let credit sales be x

Cash sales = x – 3/4x

Total sales x + x – 3/4x = 150

$2x - 3/4x = 150$

$(8x - 3x)/4 = 150$

$5 \times /4 = 150$

$x = 120$

(II) CALCULATION OF STOCK OF FINISHED GOODS AND COST OF SALES

Particulars	₹
Direct Material Cost	60,00,000
Direct Labour Cost	15,00,000
Manufacturing Expenses (excluding Depreciation)	30,00,000
Administrative Expenses	7,50,000
Total Cash Cost of Goods Produced	1,12,50,000
Add: Opening Stock of Finished Goods	9,37,500
Total Cash Cost of Goods available	1,21,87,500
Less: Closing Stock of Finished Goods	(9,37,500)
Total Cash Cost of Goods Sold	1,12,50,000
Add: Selling and Distribution expenses	6,00,000
Total Cash Cost of Sales	1,18,50,000
Cash Cost of Credit Sales (1,18,50,000 × 120/150)	94,80,000

(III) CALCULATION OF STOCK OF WORK IN PROGRESS

Particulars	₹
Raw Material (₹ 60,00,000 × 0.5/12 × 100%)	2,50,000
Wages (₹ 15,00,000 × 0.5/12 × 50%)	31,250
Manufacturing Expenses (₹ 30,00,000 × 0.5/12 × 50%)	62,500
	3,43,750

(IV) CALCULATION OF CREDIT PURCHASES

Cash Purchases = x

Credit Purchases = 4x

Total Purchases = x + 4x = 60

5x = 60

x = 12

Credit Purchases = 4 × 12 = 48 lakhs

ILLUSTRATION 12 [TREATMENT OF EXCISE DUTY AND VALUE ADDED TAX]

X Ltd has an installed capacity of producing 1.25 lakh tonnes of product per annum; its present capacity utilisation is 80 per cent. The company produces product in 200 kgs bags. The estimated Cost structure per bag is as follows:

Particulars	₹
Basic Raw Materials	90

Packing material	10
Direct Labour	50
Production Overheads	25
Depreciation	15
Administrative Overheads	10
Selling overheads	30
Total Cost	230

(a) The product is subject to excise duty of 10% (levied on cost of production)

(b) Selling Price is arrived at after adding margin @ 20% on cost.

(c) Invoice Price is arrived at after adding 10% Value Added Tax..

(d) All Raw-materials are in stock for a period of 1 month.

(e) The product is in process for a period of 0.5 month (assume 50% of basic materials are required in the beginning and the balance is needed at a uniform rate during the process. Conversion costs are to be taken at 50%.)

(f) Finished goods are in stock for a period of 1 month before they are sold.

(g) Debtors are extended credit for a period 3 months. Cash Sales 20%.

(h) Average time lag in payment of excise duty, value added tax and other costs is 1.5 months.

(i) Minimum Cash Balance required ₹ 10,00,000 and Safety margin 20%.

Required: Prepare the Statement showing the requirements of Working Capital (on Cash Cost basis) in each of the following alternative cases:

Case (a) If the goods are removed from the factory immediately when the goods are finished.

Case (b) If the goods are removed from the factory only when the goods are sold.

SOLUTION

(A) STATEMENT SHOWING THE WORKING CAPITAL REQUIREMENTS (ON CASH COST BASIS)

Particulars	*Computation*	₹
A. Current Assets:		
Stock of Basic Raw-materials	5,00,000 × ₹ 90 × 1/12	37,50,000
Stock of Packing Materials	5,00,000 × ₹ 10 × 1/12	4,16,667
Stock of WIP	As per Working Note (i)	21,87,500
Stock of Finished Goods	(5,00,000 × ₹ 205 × 1/12)	85,41,667
Debtors (Credit Period 3 months)	80% × 5,00,000 × ₹ 265 × 3/12	2,65,00,000
Cash Balance		10,00,000
		4,23,95,834
B. Current Liabilities:		
Creditors for Basic Raw-materials	5,00,000 × ₹ 90 × 1.5/12	56,25,000
Creditors for Packing Materials	5,00,000 × ₹ 10 × 1.5/12	6,25,000
Creditors for Wages	5,00,000 × ₹ 50 × 1.5/12	31,25,000
Creditors for Production Overheads	5,00,000 × ₹ 25 × 1.5/12	15,62,500
Creditors for Administrative Overheads	5,00,000 × ₹ 10 × 1.5/12	6,25,000

Creditors for Selling Overheads	5,00,000 × ₹ 30 × 1.5/12	18,75,000
Creditors for Excise Duty	5,00,000 × ₹ 20 × 1.5/12	12,50,000
Creditors for Value Added Tax	5,00,000 × ₹ 30 × 1.5/12	18,75,000
		1,65,62,500
C. Working Capital [A – B]		2,58,33,334
D. *Add:* Safety Margin		51,66,666
E. Working Capital (including Safety Margin)		3,10,00,000

(b) Solution will remain same as in case (a) since excise duty is duty on manufacture, the provision for the same has to be made once the goods are manufactured irrespective of the timings of removal of finished goods.

Working Notes:

(i) No. of bags produced (80% of 1,25,000 × 1000 kg)/200 kg = 5,00,000 Bags

(II) CALCULATION OF EXCISE DUTY AND VALUE ADDED TAX

Particulars	₹
Basic Raw-materials	90
Packing Materials	10
Direct Labour	50
Production Overheads (Ex. Depreciation)	25
Depreciation	15
Administrative Overheads	10
Cost of Production	200
Excise Duty @ 10%	20
Cost of Goods Produced (including Excise Duty)	220
Selling Overheads	30
Cost of Sales	250
Profit @ 20%	50
Selling Price	300
VAT @ 10%	30
Invoice Price to Consumer	330

(III) CALCULATION OF CASH COST OF SALES

Particulars	₹
Basic Raw-material	90
Packing Material	10
Direct Labour	50
Production Overhead (Ex. Depreciation)	25
Administrative Overheads	10
Cash Cost of Goods Produced (Excluding Excise Duty)	185
Excise Duty [10% on (Cash Cost of Goods Produced + Depreciation)]	20
Cash Cost of Goods produced (including Excise Duty)	205

Selling Overheads	30
Cash Cost of Sales (Excluding VAT)	235
Value Added Tax [as per Working Note (ii)]	30
Cash Cost of Sales (Including VAT)	265

(IV) STOCK OF WIP [PROCESS PERIOD: 1/2 MONTH]

Particulars	₹
Basic Raw material (50%) [5,00,000 × ₹ 90 × 1/24 × 50%]	9,37,500
Basic Raw material (50%) [5,00,000 × ₹ 90 × 1/24 × 50% × 50%]	4,68,750
Direct Labour [5,00,000 × ₹ 50 × 1/24 × 50%]	5,20,833
Production Overheads [5,00,000 × ₹ 25 × 1/24 × 50%]	2,60,417
	21,87,500

Note: Cost of Packing Materials does not form part of Cost of WIP.

ILLUSTRATION 13 [WHEN PHYSICAL UNITS OF WIP ARE SEPARATELY GIVEN]

A newly formed company has applied to the commercial bank for the first time for financing its working capital requirements. The following information is available about the projections for the current year:

Estimated level of activity: 1,04,000 completed units of production *plus* 4,000 units of work-in-progress. Based on the above activity, estimated cost per unit is:

Raw Material	₹ 80 per unit
Direct wages	₹ 30 per unit
Overheads (inclusive of depreciation of ₹ 10 per unit)	₹ 70 per unit
Total Cost	₹ 180 per unit
Selling Price	₹ 200 per unit

Raw Materials in Stock: Average 4 weeks' consumption, work-in-progress (assume 50% completion stage in respect of conversion cost) (materials issued at the start of the processing)

Finished goods in stock	8,000 units
Credit allowed by suppliers	Average 4 weeks
Credit allowed to debtors	8 weeks
Time lag in payment of wages	Average 1½ weeks

Assume that production is carried on evenly throughout the year (52 weeks) and wages and overheads accrue similarly. All sales are on credit basis only

Required: Calculate (a) Stock of Work-in-Progress, (b) Stock of Finished Goods, (c) Debtors, (d) Stock of Raw-Materials, (e) Creditors for Raw Materials, (f) Creditors for Wages.

SOLUTION

(A) CALCULATION OF STOCK OF WORK-IN-PROGRESS

Particulars	₹
Raw Material (4,000 × ₹ 80)	3,20,000
Wages (50% of 4000 × ₹ 30)	60,000

Overhead (50% of 4000 × ₹ 60)	1,20,000
Total	5,00,000

(B) CALCULATION OF STOCK OF FINISHED GOODS AND COST OF SALES

Particulars	₹
Direct Material Cost [(1,04,000 × ₹ 80) + 3,20,000]	86,40,000
Wages [(1,04,000 × ₹ 30) + 60,000]	31,80,000
Overhead [(1,04,000 × ₹ 60) + 1,20,000]	63,60,000
Gross Factory Cost	1,81,80,000
Less: Closing WIP	(5,00,000)
Cost of goods produced	1,76,80,000
Less: Closing Stock of Finished Goods [1,76,80,000 × 8,000/1,04,000]	(13,60,000)
Total Cash Cost of Sales	1,63,20,000

(c) Debtors = ₹ 1,63,20,000 × 8/52 = ₹ 25,10,769

(d) Stock of Raw Materials = ₹ 86,40,000 × 4/52 = ₹ 6,64,615

(e) Creditors for Raw-Materials = ₹ 93,04,615 × 4/52 = ₹ 7,15,740

Note: Credit Purchases = Raw Material consumed + Closing Stock – Opening Stock
= ₹ 86,40,000 + ₹ 6,64,615 – 0 = ₹ 93,04,615

(f) Creditors for Wages = ₹ 31,80,000 × 1.5/52 = ₹ 91,731

ILLUSTRATION 14 [WHEN PHYSICAL UNITS OF WIP ARE SEPARATELY GIVEN]

CAMI Ltd. newly commencing business during 20X8 has the undermentioned Projected Profit and Loss Account:

Particulars	₹	₹
Sales		42,00,000
Cost of Goods Sold		(30,60,000)
Gross Profit		11,40,000
Administrative Expenses	2,80,000	
Selling Expenses	2,60,000	(5,40,000)
Profit before tax		6,00,000
Tax Provision		(2,00,000)
Profit after tax		4,00,000
The cost of goods sold has been arrived at as under:		
Material used		16,80,000
Wages and manufacturing expenses		12,50,000
Depreciation		4,70,000
		34,00,000
Less: Stock of finished goods (10% of goods produced not yet sold)		(3,40,000)
		30,60,000

Additional Information

(a) The figures given above relate only to finished goods and not to work in progress.

(b) Goods equal to 15% of the year's production (in terms of physical units) will be in process on the average requiring full materials but only 40% of the other expenses.

(c) The company believes in keeping material equal to two months consumption in stock.

(d) All expenses will be paid one month in arrear.

(e) Suppliers of material will extend month's credit.

(f) Sales will be 20% for cash and the rest at two months credit;

Required: Calculate (a) Stock of Work-in-Progress, (b) Stock of Finished Goods, (c) Debtors, (d) Stock of Raw-Materials, (e) Creditors for Raw Materials, (f) Creditors for Wages & Manufacturing Expenses.

SOLUTION

(A) CALCULATION OF STOCK OF WORK-IN-PROGRESS

Particulars	₹
Raw Material (₹ 16,80,000 × 15%)	2,52,000
Wages & Mfg. expenses (₹ 12,50,000 × 15% × 40%)	75,000
Total	3,27,000

(B) CALCULATION OF STOCK OF FINISHED GOODS AND COST OF SALES

Particulars	₹
Direct Material Cost [₹ 16,80,000 + ₹ 2,52,000]	19,32,000
Wages & Mfg. Exp. [₹ 12,50,000 + ₹ 75,000]	13,25,000
Gross Factory Cost	32,57,000
Less: Closing W.I.P	(3,27,000)
Cost of goods produced	29,30,000
Less: Closing Stock of Finished Goods [10% of Cost of Goods Produced]	(2,93,000)
Cost of goods sold	26,37,000
Add: Adm. Expenses.	2,80,000
Add: Selling Expenses	2,60,000
Total Cash Cost of Sales	31,77,000
Cash Cost of Credit Sales @ 80%	25,41,600

(c) Debtors = ₹ 25,41,600 × 2/12 = ₹ 4,23,600

(d) Stock of Raw-Materials = ₹ 19,32,000 × 2/12 = ₹ 3,22,000

(e) Creditors for Raw-Materials = ₹ 22,54,000 × 1.5/12 = ₹ 2,81,750

Note: Credit purchases = Raw Material consumed + Closing Stock – Opening Stock

= ₹ 19,32,000 + ₹ 3,22,000 – 0 = ₹ 22,54,000

(f) Creditors for Wages & Manufacturing expenses = ₹ 13,25,000 × 1/12 = ₹ 1,10,417

ILLUSTRATION 15 [TREATMENT OF WIP WHEN COMPLETED UNITS ARE GIVEN]

CAT Ltd. which is to commence its operations on 1st April, 20X8 proposes to produce 36,000 completed units during the coming year 20X8-20X9.

The following information is supplied:

(a) Unit Cost structure of product at production level of 36000 units	₹
Raw-material	4.00
Wages	2.00
Variable Overheads	2.00
Fixed Overheads (including ₹ 0.50 Depreciation)	1.50
Profit	3.00
Selling Price	12.50

(b) Stock of Raw-material: 1 Months' Average Consumption, Work-in-progress—1 month's completed units (materials fully supplied but 50% converted).

Stock of Finished Goods: 1 month's completed units. Stock of finished goods is valued at factory cost on FIFO basis.

(c) Credit Period allowed to customers 2 months, Credit Period allowed by Suppliers of Raw-material 3 months.

(d) Lag in Wages and Overhead payments 1 month.

(e) Cash Sales 20% and Cash Purchases 20%.

Required: Calculate (a) Stock of Work-in-progress, (b) Stock of Finished Goods, (c) Debtors, (d) Stock of Raw-materials, (e) Creditors for Raw-materials, (f) Creditors for Wages, (g) Creditors for Variable Overheads, and (h) Creditors for Fixed Overheads.

SOLUTION

CALCULATION OF EQUIVALENT PRODUCTION UNITS

Particulars	*Material (100%)*	*Labour & Oh. (50%)*
A. Actual Production	36,000	36,000
B. *Add:* Closing WIP	3,000	1,500
C. *Less:* Opening WIP	—	—
	39,000	37,500

(A) STOCK OF WORK-IN-PROGRESS [3,000 UNITS I.E. 36,000/12]

Raw-material [100% × 3,000 × ₹ 4]	₹ 12,000
Wages [50% × 3,000 × ₹ 2]	₹ 3,000
Variable Overheads [50% × 3,000 × ₹ 2]	₹ 3,000
Fixed Overheads [50% × 3,000 × ₹ 36,000/37,500]	₹ 1,440
Total	₹ 19,440

CALCULATION OF CASH COST OF GOODS PRODUCED AND CASH COST OF CREDIT SALES

Particulars	₹
A. Raw-material Consumed [(36,000 + 3,000) × ₹ 4)	1,56,000

B.	Wages [(37,500 × ₹ 2)]	75,000
C.	Variable Overheads [37,500 × ₹ 2]	75,000
D.	Fixed Overheads	36,000
E.	Gross Factory Cost [A + B + C + D]	3,42,000
F.	Adjustment for WIP	
	Add: Opening WIP	—
	Less: Closing WIP	(19,440)
G.	Cash Cost of Goods Produced	3,22,560
H.	Adjustment for Finished Stock	
	Add: Opening Stock of Finished Goods	—
	Less: Closing Stock of Finished Goods [₹ 3,22,560 × 3,000/36,000]	(26,880)
I.	Cash Cost of Goods Sold	2,95,680
J.	Cash Cost of Credit Sales (80%)	2,36,544

(b) **Stock of Finished Goods** $= \text{Cash Cost of Goods Produced} \times \frac{1 \text{ month}}{12 \text{ months}}$

$= ₹\ 3,22,560 \times 1/12 = ₹\ 26,880$

(c) **Debtors** $= \text{Cash Cost of Credit Sales} \times \frac{2 \text{ months}}{12 \text{ months}} = ₹\ 2,36,544 \times 2/12 = ₹\ 39,424$

(d) Stock of Raw-Material $= \frac{\text{Raw Material Consumed}}{12 \text{ months}} \times \text{Raw Material Storage Period}$

$= \frac{₹\ 1,56,000}{12 \text{ months}} \times 1 \text{ month} = ₹\ 13,000$

(e) **Creditors for Raw-materials**

(i) Total Purchases = Raw-material Consumed + Closing Stock – Opening Stock

= ₹ 1,56,000 + ₹ 13,000 – 0 = ₹ 1,69,000

(ii) Credit Purchases = 80% of Total Purchases = 80% of ₹ 1,69,000 = ₹ 1,35,200

(iii) Creditors for Raw-material $= \frac{₹\ 1,35,200}{12 \text{ months}} \times 3 \text{ months} = ₹\ 33,800$

(f) Creditors for Wages $= \frac{₹\ 75,000}{12 \text{ months}} \times 1 \text{ month} = ₹\ 6,250$

(g) Creditors for Variable Overheads $= \frac{₹\ 75,000}{12 \text{ months}} \times 1 \text{ month} = ₹\ 6,250$

(h) Creditors for Fixed Overheads $= \frac{₹\ 36,000}{12 \text{ months}} \times 1 \text{ month} = ₹\ 3,000$

ILLUSTRATION 16

CAMH Ltd., company newly commencing business in 2009 has the undermentioned projected Profit and Loss Accounts:

Particulars	₹	₹
Sales		2,10,000
Cost of goods sold		1,53,000
Gross Profit		57,000

Administrative Expenses	14,000	
Selling Expenses	13,000	
		27,000
Profit before tax		30,000
Provision for taxation		10,000
Profit after tax		20,000
The cost of goods sold had been arrived at as under:		
Materials used	84,000	
Wages and Manufacturing Expenses	62,500	
Depreciation	23,500	
	1,70,000	
Less: Stock of Finished goods	17,000	
(10% of goods produced not yet sold)	1,53,000	

Additional Information:

(a) The figures given above relate only to finished goods and not to work in progress.

(b) Goods equal to 15% of the year's production (in terms of physical units) will be in process on the average requiring full materials but only 40% of the other expenses.

(c) The company believes in keeping materials equal to two months' consumption in stock.

(d) All expenses will be paid one month in advance.

(e) Suppliers of materials will extend 112 months credit.

(f) Sales will be 20% for cash and the rest at two months credit.

(g) 70% of the Income tax will be paid in advance in quarterly instalments.

(h) The company wishes to keep ₹ 8,000 in cash.

Required: Prepare an estimate of (i) Total Cost of Working Capital, and (ii) Cash Cost of Working Capital.

Note: All working should form part of your answer.

SOLUTION

STATEMENT SHOWING THE REQUIREMENTS OF WORKING CAPITAL

Particulars	*On Total Cost Basis*		*On Cash Cost Basis*	
	Computation	₹	*Computation*	₹
A. Current Assets:				
Stock of Raw material	₹ 96,600 × 2/12	16,100	96,600 × 2/12	16,100
Stock of Work-in-progress	As per Working Note	17,760	As per working Note	16,350
Stock of Finished goods	₹ 1,70,000 × 10/100	17,000	1,46,500 × 10/100	14,650
Debtors	₹ 1,44,000 × 2/12	24,000	1,27,080 × 2/12	21,180
Cash in Hand	(Given)	8,000	(Given)	8,000
Prepaid Expenses:				
Wages & Mfg. expenses	₹ 66,250 × 1/12	5,521	66,250 × 1/12	5,521
Administrative expenses	₹ 14,000 × 1/12	1,167	14,000 × 1/12	1,167

Selling & Distribution Exp.	₹ 13,000 × 1/12	1,083	13,000 × 1/12	1,083
Total Current Assets		90,631		84,051
B. Current Liabilities:				
Creditors for Raw materials	1,12,700 × 1.5/12	14,088	1,12,700 × 1.5/12	14,088
Provision for Taxation	10,000 × 30/100	3,000	10,000 × 30/100	3,000
(Net of Advance Tax)				
Total Current Liabilities		17,088		17,088
C. Net Working Capital (A – B)		73,543		66,963

Working Notes:

(I) CALCULATION OF STOCK OF WORK IN PROGRESS

Particulars	*On Accounting Basis* ₹	*On Cash Cost Basis* ₹
Raw Material (84,000 × 15%)	12,600	12,600
Wages & Mfg. expenses (62,500 × 15% × 40%)	3,750	3,750
Depreciation (23,500 × 15% × 40%)	1,410	—
Total	17,760	16,350

(II) CALCULATION OF STOCK OF FINISHED GOODS AND COST OF SALES

Particulars	*On Accounting Basis* ₹	*On Cash Cost Basis* ₹
Direct Material Cost [₹ 84,000 + ₹ 12,600]	96,600	96,600
Wages & Mfg. expenses [₹ 62,500 + ₹ 3,750]	66,250	66,250
Depreciation [₹ 23,500 + ₹ 1,410]	24,910	0
Gross Factory Cost	1,87,760	1,62,850
Less: Closing W.I.P	(17,760)	(16,350)
Cost of goods produced	1,70,000	1,46,500
Less: Closing stock	(17,000)	(14,650)
Cost of goods sold	1,53,000	1,31,850
Add: Administrative Expenses	14,000	14,000
Add: Selling and Distribution expenses	13,000	13,000
Total Cash Cost of Sales	1,80,000	1,58,850
Debtors (80% of cash cost of sales)	1,44,000	1,27,080

(III) CALCULATION OF CREDIT PURCHASE

A.	Raw material consumed	96,600
B.	*Add:* Closing Stock	16,100
C.	*Less:* Opening Stock	—
D.	Purchases(A + B – C)	1,12,700

16.0 FORMAT OF STATEMENT SHOWING PROFIT/LOSS

Particulars	*Year 1*			*Year 2*		
	Units	*Per Unit* ₹	*Total* ₹	*Units*	*Per Unit* ₹	*Total* ₹
Normal Production (in units)	......			......		
Actual Production (in units)	......			......		
Sales (in units)	......			......		
A. Sales Revenue	......	......	......	......	......	......
B. *Less:* Cost of Sales						
(a) Direct Material Cost	......	......	......	......	......	......
(b) Direct Labour Cost	......	......	......	......	......	......
(c) Direct Expenses	......	......	......	......	......	......
(d) Variable Manufacturing Expenses	......	......	......	......	......	......
(e) Fixed Manufacturing Exp. (excluding Depreciation)	......	......	......	......	......	......
(f) Depreciation	......	......	......	......	......	......
(g) Variable Adm. Expenses	......	......	......	......	......	......
(h) Fixed Adm. Expenses	......	......	......	......	......	......
(i) Total Cost of Goods Produced	......	......	......	......	......	......
(j) *Add:* Opening Stock of Finished Goods	......	......	......	......	......	......
(k) Total Cost of Goods available for Sale	......	......	......	......	......	......
(l) *Less:* Closing Stock of Finished Goods	......	......	......	......	......	......
(m) Total Cost of Goods Sold	......	......	......	......	......	......
(n) *Add:* Variable Selling and Dist. expenses	......	......	......	......	......	......
(o) *Add:* Fixed Selling and Dist expenses	......	......	......	......	......	......
(p) Total Cost of Sales	......	......	......	......	......	......
C. Profit [A – B]	......	......	......	......	......	......

ILLUSTRATION 17

CAMIF Limited is launching a new project for the manufacture of a unique component. At full capacity of 24,000 units, the cost will be as follow:

Particulars	*Cost per units (₹)*
Material	80
Labour and Variable Expenses	40
Fixed Manufacturing and Administrative Expenses	20

Depreciation	10
	150

The selling price per unit is expected at ₹ 200 and the selling expenses per unit will be ₹ 10, 80% of which is variable.

In the first two years production and sales are expected to be as follows:

Year	*Production*	*Sales*
1	15,000 units	14,000 units
2	20,000 units	18,000 units

To assess working capital requirement, the following additional information is given:

(a) Stock of raw material – 3 months' average consumption, (b) Work-in-progress – Nil, (c) Debtors – 1 months average cost of sales, (d) Creditors for supply of materials – 2 months' average purchases of the year, (e) Creditors for expenses 1 month' average of all expenses during the year, (f) Cash balance – ₹ 20,000, (g) Stock of finished goods is taken at average cost.

Required: Prepare for the two years:

1. A Projected Statement of Profit/Loss.
2. A projected Statement of working capital requirements.

SOLUTION

PROJECTED STATEMENT SHOWING THE PROFIT *OR* LOSS

Particulars	*Year 1*			*Year 2*		
	Units	*Per Unit* ₹	*Total* ₹	*Units*	*Per Unit* ₹	*Total* ₹
Normal Production (in Units)	24,000			24,000		
Actual Production (in Units)	15,000			20,000		
Sales (in Units)	14,000			18,000		
A. Sales Revenue		200	28,00,000		200	36,00,000
B. *Less:* Cost of Sales						
(a) Direct Material Cost		80	12,00,000		80	16,00,000
(b) Direct Labour & Var expenses		40	6,00,000		40	8,00,000
(c) Fixed Manufacturing & Adm. Exp. (Excluding Depreciation)		32	4,80,000		24	4,80,000
(d) Depreciation		16	2,40,000		12	2,40,000
(e) Total Cost of Goods Produced	15,000	168	25,20,000	20,000	156	31,20,000
(f) *Add:* Opening Stock of Finished Goods				1,000	168	1,68,000
(g) Total Cost of Goods available	15,000	168	25,20,000	21,000		32,88,000
(h) *Less:* Closing Stock of Finished Goods	1,000	168	(1,68,000)	3,000		(4,69,714)
(i) Total Cost of Goods Sold	14,000	168	23,52,000	18,000		28,18,286
(j) *Add:* Variable Selling & Distribution Exp.		8	1,12,000		8	1,44,000
(k) *Add:* Fixed Selling & Distribution Exp.			48,000			48,000

Total Cost of Sales			25,12,000			30,10,286
C. Profit (A – B)			2,88,000			5,89,714

PROJECTED STATEMENT SHOWING THE REQUIREMENTS OF WORKING CAPITAL (ON CASH COST BASIS)

Particulars	*Year 1*		*Year 2*	
	Computation	₹	*Computation*	₹
A. Current Assets:				
Stock of Raw Material	12,00,000 × 3/12	3,00,000	16,00,000 × 3/12	4,00,000
Stock of Finished Goods		1,52,000		4,33,143
Debtors	22,88,000 × 1/12	1,90,667	27,90,857 × 1/12	2,32,571
Cash in Hand		20,000		20,000
Total Current Assets		6,62,667		10,85,714
B. Current Liabilities:				
Creditors for Raw Materials	15,00,000 × 2/12	2,50,000	17,00,000 × 2/12	2,83,333
Creditors for Wages & Variable Expenses	6,00,000 × 1/12	50,000	8,00,000 × 1/12	66,667
Creditors for Mfg. & Adm. Exp.	4,80,000 × 1/12	40,000	4,80,000 × 1/12	40,000
Creditors for Selling & Distribution Expenses	1,60,000 × 1/12	13,333	1,92,000 × 1/12	16,000
Total Current Liabilities		3,53,333		4,06,000
C. Net Working Capital (A – B)		3,09,334		6,79,714

Working Notes:

(I) CALCULATION OF CASH COST OF CLOSING STOCK AND CASH COST OF SALES

Particulars	*Year 1*			*Year 2*		
	Units	*Per Unit* ₹	*Total* ₹	*Units*	*Per Unit* ₹	*Total* ₹
Normal Production (in units)	24,000			24,000		
Actual Production (in units)	15,000			20,000		
Sales (in Units)	14,000			18,000		
A. Direct Material Cost		80	12,00,000		80	16,00,000
B. Direct Labour & Var. expenses		40	6,00,000		40	8,00,000
C. Fixed Manufacturing & Adm. Exp. (Excluding Depreciation)		32	4,80,000		24	4,80,000
D. Total Cost of Goods Produced	15,000	152	22,80,000	20,000	144	28,80,000
E. *Add:* Opening Stock Finished Goods			—	1,000	152	1,52,000
F. Cash Cost of Goods available	15,000	152	22,80,000	21,000	144.381	30,32,000
G. *Less:* Closing Stock of Finished Goods	1,000	152	(1,52,000)	3,000	144.381	(4,33,143)
H. Cash Cost of Goods Sold (G – H)	14,000	152	21,28,000	18,000	144.381	25,98,857

I.	*Add:* Variable Selling & Distribution Expenses		8	1,12,000		8	1,44,000
J.	*Add:* Fixed Selling and Distribution Expenses			48,000			48,000
K.	Cash Cost of Sales (I + J + K)			22,88,000			27,90,857

(II) CALCULATION OF CREDIT PURCHASES

	Particulars	*Year 1* ₹	*Year 2* ₹
A	Raw Material consumed	12,00,000	16,00,000
B	*Add:* Closing Stock	3,00,000	4,00,000
C	*Less:* Opening Stock	—	(3,00,000)
D	Purchases (A + B – C)	15,00,000	17,00,000

17.0 EFFECT OF DOUBLE SHIFT WORKING ON WORKING CAPITAL REQUIREMENTS

Item	Effect of Double Shift on Working Capital Requirements
1. Stock of Raw Material	Increase may not be proportionate to the rise in production since the minimum level of stocks may not be very much higher. However, the costs of raw material per unit may decrease if some trade discount is available from suppliers of raw material in view of increased purchases of raw material. However, in examination the students may increase the amount of stock of raw materials proportionately unless instructions are to the contrary.
2. Cost of Materials in Work-in-Progress	Cost of materials in Work-in-Progress will be the same as with single shift working since the work started in first shift will be completed in the second shift.
3. Cost of Labour in Work-in-progress	Cost of Labour in Work-in-Progress will be the same as with single shift working unless the second shift's workers are paid at a higher rate.
4. Fixed Expenses	Fixed Expenses will be the same as the single shift working. As a result, fixed expenses per unit in case of double shift working will reduce to half.
5. Variable Expenses	Variable Expenses will increase in proportion to increased production.
6. Semi-variable Expenses	Semi-variable Expenses will increase in proportion to variable element in them.
7. Creditors for Fixed Expenses	Creditors for fixed expenses will be the same as with single shift working.
8. Creditors for Variable Expenses	Creditors for variable expenses will increase in proportion to increased production.

ILLUSTRATION 18

M/s PCT Ltd. has been operating its manufacturing facilities till 31-03-2008 on a single shift working with the following cost structure:

Particulars	*Per Unit (₹)*
Cost of Materials	12

Wages (40% fixed)	10
Overheads (80% fixed)	10
Profit	4
Selling Price	36
Sales during 20X7 – 20X8 ₹ 8,64,000. As at 31.3.20X8, the company held:	
Stock of Raw Materials (at cost)	72,000
Work-in-Progress (valued at Prime Cost)	44,000
Finished Goods (valued at Total Cost)	1,44,000
Sundry Debtors	2,16,000

In view of increased market demand, it is proposed to double production by working an extra shift. Raw material suppliers agree to allow 10% discount in view of increase in volume of business. Credit period and selling price continue to remain same. Creditors still allow 2-month credit period. Lag in payment of wages and expenses continue to be half a month.

Required: Prepare Cost Sheet and Estimate the Working Capital Requirements for (a) single shift working and (b) double shift working.

SOLUTION

Calculation of No. of Units:

$$\text{Sales (in Units)} = \frac{\text{Sales}}{\text{Unit Selling Price}} = \frac{₹\ 8,64,000}{₹\ 36} = 24,000 \text{ units}$$

$$\text{Raw Material Inventory} = \frac{\text{Value of Stock}}{\text{Cost per unit}} = 6,000 \text{ units}$$

$$\text{W.I.P. Inventory} = \frac{\text{Value of Work-in-Progress}}{\text{Cost per unit}} = \frac{₹\ 44,000}{₹\ 22} = 2,000 \text{ units}$$

$$\text{Finished Goods Inventory} = \frac{\text{Value of Stock}}{\text{Cost per unit}} = \frac{₹\ 1,44,000}{₹\ 32} = 4,500 \text{ units}$$

$$\text{Sundry Debtors} = \frac{\text{Amount of Debtors}}{\text{Selling Price per unit}} = \frac{₹\ 2,16,000}{₹\ 36} = 6,000 \text{ units}$$

STATEMENT OF COST AT SINGLE SHIFT AND DOUBLE SHIFT WORKING

Particulars	*24,000 Units*		*48,000 Units*	
	Per unit ₹	*Total* ₹	*Per unit* ₹	*Total* ₹
Raw Materials	12.00	2,88,000	10.80	5,18,400
Wages — Variable	6.00	1,44,000	6.00	2,88,000
— Fixed	4.00	96,000	2.00	96,000
Overheads — Variable	2.00	48,000	2.00	96,000
— Fixed	8.00	1,92,000	4.00	1,92,000
Total Cost	32.00	7,68,000	24.80	11,90,400
Profit	4.00	96,000	11.20	5,37,600
Sales	36.00	8,64,000	36.00	17,28,000

STATEMENT SHOWING THE WORKING CAPITAL REQUIREMENTS (ON CASH COST BASIS)

Particulars	Single Shift Working			Double Shift Working		
	Units	Rate	₹	Units	Rate	₹
A. Current Assets:						
Stock of Materials	6,000	12	72,000	12,000	10.8	1,29,600
Stock of W.I.P.	2,000	22	44,000	2,000	18.8	37,600
Stock of Finished Goods	4,500	32	1,44,000	9,000	24.8	2,23,200
Sundry Debtors	6,000	32	1,92,000	12,000	24.8	2,97,600
	18,500		4,52,000	35,000		6,88,000
B. Current Liabilities:						
Creditors for Raw Materials	4,000	12	48,000	8,000	10.8	86,400
Creditors for Wages	1,000	10	10,000	2,000	8	16,000
Creditors for Expenses	1,000	10	10,000	2,000	6	12,000
Total Current Liabilities	6,000		68,000	12,000		1,14,400
C. Working Capital (A – B)			3,84,000			5,73,600

There is an increase in working capital required to the extent of ₹ 1,89,600 (i.e., 5,73,600 –3,84,000).

Working Notes:

(i) The quantity of material will continue to remain same due to double shift working since work started in the first shift will be completed in second shift.

(ii) Calculation of Work-in-Progress:

Particulars	Single Shift (₹)	Double Shift (₹)
Materials	12.00	10.80
Wages — Variable	6.00	6.00
Fixed	4.00	2.00
Total	22.00	18.80

18.0 SOURCES OF FINANCING WORKING CAPITAL

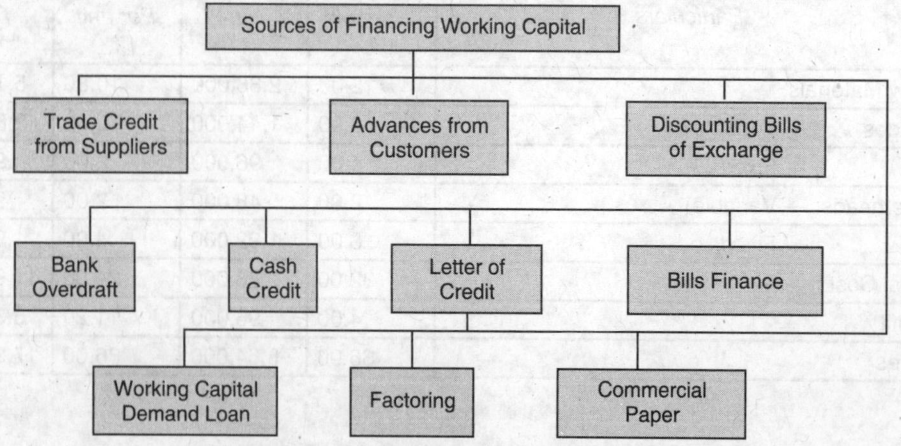

Fig. Sources of Financing Working Capital

Let us discuss the sources of financing working capital one by one:

TRADE CREDIT

Trade credit refers to an arrangement whereby the supplier of raw materials, components, stores and spare parts, finished goods, allow the customers to pay their outstanding balances within the credit period allowed by them. Generally, suppliers grant credit for a period of three to six months and thus provide short-term funds to finance current assets. The availability of trade credit depends upon various factors such as nature and size of the firm, status of the firm (i.e., credit worthiness), activity level of the firm, policy of trade credit suppliers, prevailing economic conditions etc. Trade credit may be allowed in the shape of open account of bills payable. The major advantages of trade credit include ready availability, absence of issue formalities etc. The major limitation of trade credit is that it involves loss of cash discount, which could be earned if payments were made within seven to ten days from the date of purchase. This loss is regarded as the cost of trade credit.

DOES TRADE CREDIT HAVE ANY COST?

Initially cost of trade credit may be absorbed by supplier but in the long run, he may try to pass it on to the buyer in the shape of increased prices depending upon the type of goods and elasticity of demand. In such circumstances buyer should find out alternate sources of supply to avoid costs loaded by supplier to the extent possible. It does not have any explicit cost if buyer pays the bills within normal credit period.

Merits of Trade Credit — The trade credit as a source of financing working capital has the following advantages:

1. Trade credit is readily available according to the prevailing customs.
2. Trade credit is a flexible source of finance, which can be easily adjusted to the changing needs for purchases.
3. Trade creditors generally adjust the time of payment in view of past dealings.
4. Trade credit does not involve any flotation costs.

Limitations of Trade Credit — The trade credit as a source of financing working capital has the following limitations:

1. The cost of trade credit may increase if the supplier tries to pass on it to the buyer in the shape of increased prices.
2. Payment of bill of exchange accepted *or* promissory note issued against credit is required to be made at the maturity of the bill *or* note otherwise legal action may follow to recover the payment.

Whether *or* not to Avail Cash Discount—When a supplier offers a cash discount to buyer for making a prompt payment within specified period, buyer should compare the annual opportunity cost of foregoing cash discount (or the cost of availing credit *or* implicit rate of interest) with the cost of other sources of credit to decide whether *or* not cash discount should be availed. The annual opportunity cost of foregoing cash discount can be calculated as follows:

$$\frac{\text{\% Cash Discount}}{100 - \text{\% CashDiscount}} \times \frac{\text{365 days}}{\text{Credit Period} - \text{Discount Period}}$$

Decision criteria: Avail cash discount (or do not avail credit) if the annual cost of foregoing cash discount is higher than the cost of other sources of credit, otherwise not.

ILLUSTRATION 19

X Ltd. purchases goods for ₹ 5,00,000 on credit terms of 2/10, net 40. Should X Ltd. avail cash discount if it can borrow (a) at 18% p.a. (b) at 30% p.a. ? (Assume 360 days in a year)

SOLUTION

Annual Cost of foregoing Cash Discount (or Annual Cost of availing Credit)

$$= \frac{\%\ \text{Cash Discount}}{100 - \%\ \text{Cash Discount}} \times \frac{360}{\text{Credit Period} - \text{Discount Period}}$$

$$= \frac{2}{100-2} \times \frac{360}{40-10} = 24.49\%\ \text{p.a.}$$

(a) X Ltd. should avail cash discount because the annual cost of foregoing cash discount is higher than the cost of other sources of credit (i.e. 18% p.a.)

(b) X Ltd. should not avail cash discount because the annual cost of foregoing cash discount is lower than the cost of other sources of credit (i.e. 30% p.a.)

ADVANCES FROM CUSTOMERS

Advances from customers also act as source of short-term finance. The availability of advances from customers depends upon various factors such as type of goods, elasticity of demand and creditworthiness of supplier etc.

DISCOUNTING BILLS OF EXCHANGE

When goods are sold on credit, the suppliers generally draw bills of exchange upon customers who are required to accept the same. The term of such bills of exchange may be three to six months. Instead of holding the bills till the date of maturity, companies generally prefer to get them discounted with the bank. Discounting bills of exchange refers to an act of selling of a bill to obtain payment for it before its maturity. The bank charges discount in terms of interest for the unexpired term of the bill (i.e. period from the date of discounting to the date of maturity of the bill). The bank credits the net proceeds (i.e. amount of bill *less* discount charges) to the account of the customer. On date of maturity of the bill, the bank presents the bill before the acceptor of the bill for payment and receives the full amount of the bill. If the bank does not receive the payment from the acceptor, it is known as dishonour of a bill. The bank returns the dishonoured bill to the company and debits to the account of the company. The cost of raising finance by this method is the discount charged by the bank.

BANK OVERDRAFT

Bank overdraft refers to an arrangement whereby the bank allows the customers to overdraw from its current deposit account within a specified limit. The overdraft facility is granted against the securities of assets *or* personal security as in case of cash credit. Interest is charged only on the amount actually overdrawn (i.e., debit balance) for the actual period of use (i.e., for the period the debit balance in current deposit account remains outstanding). The cost of raising finance by this method is the interest charged by the bank.

CASH CREDIT

Cash credit refers to an arrangement whereby the bank allows the borrower to draw money from time to time within a specified limit (known as cash credit limit). The cash credit facility is granted against the pledge *or* hypothecation of stock *or* pledge of marketable instruments etc. *or* personal security. During the period of credit, the borrower can draw, repay and again draw amounts within the sanctioned limit. Interest is charged only on the amount actually withdrawn for the actual period of use. The cost of raising finance by this method is the interest charged by the bank. The advantage of this source of finance is that the amount can be adjusted according to the needs of finance.

LETTER OF CREDIT

A letter of Credit is the guarantee provided by the buyer's bankers to the seller that in the case of default *or* failure of the buyer, the bank shall make the payment to the seller.

BILLS FINANCE

The banks extend assistance to the borrowers against the bills. The finance against the bills is meant to finance, the actual sale transactions. There are three forms of bill financing:

- Purchase of bills by the bank if these are payable on demand
- Discounting of bills by the bank if these are Usance bills (or time) bills.
- Advance against bills under collection from the drawees, whether sent for realisation through the bank *or* sent directly by the drawer to the drawees.

WORKING CAPITAL DEMAND LOAN

Working Capital Demand Loan is presently applicable to borrowers having working capital facilities of ₹ 10 Crore *or* more. The WCDL is granted for a fixed term on the carrying of which it has to be liquidated, renewed *or* rolled over.

19.0 FACTORING

MEANING OF FACTORING

Factoring is a financial service, which involves meaning, financing and collecting receivable. It is both a financial as well as management support to supplier of goods/services. It is a method of converting non-productive assets (receivables into productive assets (Cash). A factor makes the conversion of receivables into cash possible. Factoring may be defined as a contract between the supplier of goods/services and the factor under which the factor agrees to perform atleast two of the following functions:

(a) To finance the assigned book debts (receivables).

(b) To maintain account relating to receivables.

(c) To collect book debts.

(d) To provide protection against default in payment by debtors.

(e) To provide credit administration services to the clients to decide whether *or* not and how much credit should be extended to the customers.

Some of the major factoring firms in India are SBI Factors and Commercial Services Ltd., Canara bank Factors Ltd. (1991), Fair Growth Factors Ltd. (1992).

FACTORING COMMISSION

The commission charges by the factor for providing factoring services is known as factoring commission. It is usually expressed as a percentage of face value of receivables factored. In India, it ranges between 2.5 to 3 per cent. The commission is expect to be lower for recourse factoring since the factor does not assume the risk of bad debts. The commission is expected to be higher for non-recourse factoring since the factor assumes the risk of bad debts.

TYPES OF FACTORING

The factoring services may be classified under following categories:

1. **Non-recourse Factoring**—(Old Line Factoring)-Under Non-recourse factoring factor assumes the risk of bad debts and charges higher commission for and advances cash upto 80/90% of book debts immediately.
2. **Recourse Factoring**—Under recourse factoring, factor does not assumes the risk of bad debts and charges lower commission for and advances cash upto 70/80% of book debts.
3. **Advance Factoring**—Under advance factoring, factor advances cash against the book debts due to client immediately.

4. **Maturity Factoring**—Under maturity factoring, the factor makes the payment on maturity (i.e., in case of non-recourse factoring on collection of book debts *or* on insolvency of customers, in case of recourse factoring on collection of book debts form customers).
5. **Finance Factoring (Bulk/agency Factoring)**—Under finance factoring, the factor simply finances the book debts against bulk *either* on recourse *or* without recourse and the client continues to administer and operate sales ledger.
6. **Non-Notification Factoring**—Under non-notification factoring, the notice of assignment of receivables is not given to the debtors. But the factor performs all his functions without a disclosure to the customer that he owns the book debts.

NATURE OF OBLIGATION OF FACTOR

The nature of the obligation of the factor is of bailment contract. Factor stands in a fiduciary relationship with the client firm and the main responsibility arises out of the terms of the contract *or* agreement between the parties. Factoring firms are professionally competent with skilled persons to handle credit sales realisations for different clients in different trades for better credit management.

NEED FOR FACTOR SERVICES

Need for factor services is felt by traders to concentrate on sales and realization of credit sales be left in specialized hands to minimize the risk of bad debts arising on account of non-realisation of credit sales. If sales are realized within reasonable time, the traders need not depend much for bank finance toward scorching capital

PARTIES TO FACTORING CONTRACT

There are three parties involved generally in a factoring contract as follows:

1. Buyer of goods who has to pay for goods bought on credit terms.
2. Seller of goods who has to realize credit sales from buyer.
3. Factor who acts as agent in realizing credit sales from buyer and passes on the realized sum to seller after deducting his commission.

FACTORING OPERATING CYCLE

The factoring operating cycle comprises of the following seven steps:

Step 1: *Buyer negotiates terms of purchasing plant and machinery or other material with the seller.*

Step 2: *The factor enters into agreement with seller for rendering factor services to it.*

Step 3: *Seller delivers goods alongwith copies of invoice, delivery challan, and instructions to make payment to factor to buyer.*

Step 4: *Seller sends a deed of assignment in favour of factor alongwith copies of sales documents.*

Step 5: *On receipt of copies of sales documents as referred to above the factor makes payment to the seller of the 80% or more of the price of debt.*

Step 6: *Buyer makes payment to the factor in time or gets extension of time or in the case of default is subject to legal process at the hands of factor.*

Step 7: *The factor receives payment from the buyer on due dates and remits the money to seller after usual deduction.*

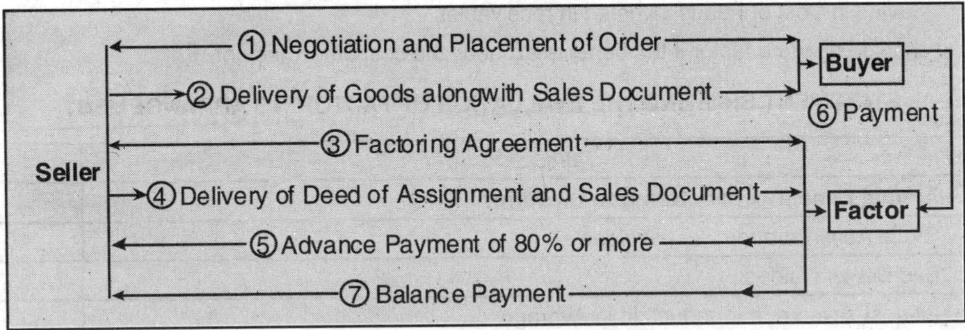

Fig. Factoring Operating Cycle

ADVANTAGES OF FACTORING

The advantages resulting from the factoring are as follow:

1. Eliminating of trade discounts.
2. Prompt payments and credits.
3. Improves scope for operating leverage.
4. Reduction of administrative cost of burden.
5. Increase in return to the client.
6. Improvement in liquidity.
7. Provides insurance against bad debts.
8. It is neither a loan *nor* a deposit but facilitates liquidity.
9. It avoids increased debts.
10. Current assets are efficiently managed thus reducing working capital requirements.
11. Better credit discipline amongst customers by regular realization of dues, effective control of sales journal, reduced credit risk, better working capital management etc.

DISADVANTAGES OF FACTORING

The disadvantages of factoring are as follows:

1. Image of the client may suffer as engaging of a Factoring Agency is not considered a good sign of efficient management.
2. Factoring may not be of much use where companies have nation-wide network branches.
3. Financial evaluation may not be accurate.
4. If the client has cheaper means of finance and credit (where goods are sold against advance payment) factoring may not be useful.

HOW TO DECIDE WHETHER *OR* NOT TO ENGAGE A FACTOR

To decide whether *or* not to engage a factor, the cost of benefits of factoring should be evaluated. The cost of factoring includes:

(a) Factoring commission;

(b) Interest on advance granted by the factor;

The benefits of factoring includes:

(a) Saving in cost of In House Credit Collection Department.

(b) Saving in Bad Debt Losses.

(c) Saving in Cost of Funds invested in receivables.

A firm should engage a factor if the benefits exceeds the cost otherwise not.

STATEMENT SHOWING THE EVALUATION OF FACTORING ARRANGEMENT

Particulars	₹
A. Annual Benefits of Factoring to the Firm:	
Credit Administration Cost avoided	....
Bad Debts avoided	....
Interest saved due to reduction in Average	....
Collection Period	
Total	....
B. Annual Cost of Factoring to the Firm:	
Factoring Commission	....
Interest charged by Factor on advance	....
Total	....
C. Net Annual Benefits/Cost of Factoring to the Firm: [A – B]	

Rate of Effective Cost of Factoring to the Firm

= (Net Annual Cost of Factoring to the Firm/Actual Advance granted) × 100

Recommendation: The company should adopt the Non-recourse Factoring alternative since the Rate of Effective Cost of Factoring to the Firm (i.e. 8% say) is *less* than the existing cost of borrowing (i.e. 15% say).

or

Recommendation: The company should adopt the Non-recourse Factoring alternative since it results in Net Annual Benefits of ₹ 5.4 lakhs (say)

or

Recommendation: The company should not adopt the Non-recourse Factoring alternative since the Rate of Effective Cost of Factoring to the Firm (i.e. 13% say) is more than the existing cost of borrowing (i.e. 12% say).

20.0 COMMERCIAL PAPER

MEANING OF COMMERCIAL PAPER

Commercial Paper is a short term issuance promissory note issued by a company in a private sector *or* public sector at such a discount/interest on face value as may be determined by the issuing company and is negotiable by endorsement and delivery. Each CP will bear a certificate from bank verifying the signatures of executants.

Though, commercial paper is said to be highly liquid because of its transferability, but in the absence of its highly developed secondary markets, its liquidity could be highly greatly affected.

FEATURES OF COMMERCIAL PAPER

The features of Commercial paper are as follows:

1. Commercial paper is a short-term money market instrument.
2. It is used by the corporate enterprises.
3. It is used for financing working capital requirements

4. It has a fixed maturity value.
5. It is a certificate evidencing an unsecured corporate debt.
6. It is issued at a discount/ interest on face value basis.
7. It contains a promise to pay some fixed amount on some future period.
8. Its issuer does not pledge any asset.
9. It can be issued directly by a company to investors *or* through banks *or* merchant bankers.

ADVANTAGES OF COMMERCIAL PAPER

The advantages of Commercial paper are as follows:

1. It can be issued with the maturities tailored to match the cash flow of the issuing company.
2. A well-rated company can diversify its sources of finance from banks to short term money markets at somewhat cheaper costs.
3. It provides investors with higher returns than they could get from the banking system.
4. It facilitates securitisation of loans resulting in creation of secondary market for the paper and efficient movement of funds providing cash surplus to cash deficit entities.
5. The companies, which are able to raise funds through commercial paper, become better known in the financial world and are thereby placed in a more favpurbale position for raising such long-term capital as they may, from time to time require. Thus, there is an in built incentive for companies to remain financially strong.

ELIGIBILITY CRITERIA FOR ISSUER OF COMMERCIAL PAPER

The issuing company shall comply with the terms and conditions stipulated from time to time, by the Reserve Bank of India relating to the issue of such CPs. The companies satisfying the following conditions are eligible to issue CPs:

1. **Minimum Tangible Net worth**—The tangible net worth of the company must be atleast ₹ 5 crore as per the latest audited balance sheet of the company. Tangible Net Worth = Paid up Capital + Free Reserves – Accumulated balance of Losses – Balance of Deferred revenue expenditure – Other fictitious Assets
2. **Fund Based Working Capital**—The fund-based working Capital must be atleast ₹ 25 crore.
3. **Minimum Current Ratio**—The minimum current asset ratio should be 1.33:1 based on the classification of current assets and current liabilities. For the purpose of computing the current ratio, the current assets and current liabilities are classified as per RBI guidelines issued from time to time.
4. **Minimum Credit Rating**—The company is required to obtain the necessary credit rating from agencies like CRISIL, ICRA, etc. The credit rating obtained from CRISIL should be not *less* than P2 while rating obtained from ICRA should not be *less* than A2.
5. **Classification of Account by Financial Bank**—The borrowers account of the company is classified as Standard Asset by financing banking company/ companies.
6. **Age of Rating**—The issuer must ensure that the credit rating at the time of applying to the RBI should not be more than 2 months old.
7. **Listed Requirement**—The companies other than public sector should be listed on one *or* more stock exchange. Closely held companies whose shares are not listed on any of the stock exchange will also be eligible to borrow under the CP scheme, provided they meet all other requirements.
8. **Issue Expenses**—All issue expenses including dealer's fees, rating agency fees and any other relevant charges connected with the issue shall be borne by the company issuing CPs.

PROCEDURE FOR ISSUE OF COMMERCIAL PAPER

1. Apply for credit rating and get certificate from Credit Rating Agency.
2. Submit application to RBI through financing bank *or* leader of consortium bank for working capital facilities together with a certificate from credit rating agency.
3. Obtain a copy of RBI's approval in writing on the amount of commercial paper to be issued.
4. Make arrangements for privately placing the issue.
5. Ensure that the proposed issue of commercial paper is complete within the period of two weeks from the date of approval of RBI.
6. Inform RBI through the bank / leader of the bank, the amount of actual issue of CP within three days of completion of issue.

GUIDELINES FOR ISSUE OF CP

Minimum Maturity Period	3 months
Maximum Maturity Period	6 months
Grace Period of Maturity	Nil
Denomination	Multiple of 10 Lakhs
Minimum Size of CP issue	₹ 50 Lakhs
Maximum Size of CP issue	upto 20% of the issue's fund based working capital limit

IMPLICATIONS OF COMMERCIAL PAPER

The implications of CP on commercial banks are as follows:

1. The banks themselves can invest in CP and show this as short-term investment.
2. The banks are likely to lose interest on working capital loan, which has been hitherto lent to the companies, which have now started borrowing through CP. Further, the larger companies might avail of the cheap funds available in the slack season worsening the banks surplus funds position, but to the banking system for borrowing during the busy season when funds are costly. This would mean the banks are loser with clear impact on profitability.

PROSPECTS OF COMMERCIAL PAPER

1. **Relaxation in credit rating**—Mandatory credit rating has been relaxed from P1 to P2 at present. If this trend continues, the credit rating will allow the investors to fix their discount rates accordingly.
2. Though CP is an unsecured promissory note, there has been no case of default as yet. There are two reasons which are as follows:
   (a) The issuing company's credit rating provides a picture for the investor about the credit-worthiness.
   (b) Companies which can issue CP are blue chip companies, these companies can not afford to take the risk of defaulting because once they do that no investor in money market will deal with them and even if someone does interest rate charged will be exorbitant.
3. **Subject to working capital limits**—CP is subject to working capital limits. To give CP a chance as visible resource option, it is suggested that CP issue should be made separate from the working capital limits of the company.
4. **Roll over Expenses**—The roll over of all issue expenses have to be incurred once again. This is a daunting factor. One solution to this can be that the maturity period of CP should increase from six months to twelve months.

5. **Competitor**—Cash credit is main competitor of CP. Currently cash credit interest rate is about twelve percent. Whereas top rating companies are able to float CPs at about nine percent.

Conclusion: CP has immense scope in India. It can be expected that within three years, CP shall takeover more than 50 percent of cash card business.

ILLUSTRATION 20

From the following information, calculate the Cost of CP Funds to Tulsian Ltd. which is planning a CP issue.

Issue Price of CP : ₹ 96,000

Face Value : ₹ 1,00,000

Maturity Period : 4 months

Issue Expenses:

Brokerage : 0.125% for 4 months

Rating Charges : 0.5% p.a.

Stamp Duty : 0.125% for 4 months

SOLUTION

$$\text{Cost of CP} = \frac{\text{Face Value} - (\text{Issue Price} - \text{Flotation Cost})}{\text{Issue Price} - \text{Flotation Cost}} \times \frac{12\text{ Months}}{\text{Maturity Period}} \times 100$$

$$= \frac{₹\,1{,}00{,}000 - (₹\,96{,}000 - ₹\,400)}{₹\,96{,}000 - ₹\,400} \times \frac{12}{4} \times 100 = 13.808\%$$

Note: Flotation Cost = ₹ 96,000 × [0.125% + (0.5/3)% + 0.125%] = ₹ 400

ILLUSTRATION 21

X Ltd. issues a 90 days CP of a face value of ₹ 1,00,000 at ₹ 97,000. The credit rating expenses are 0.5% of the size of issue, issuing & paying agent (IPA) charges 0.25% and Stamp Duty 0.5%. Calculate the Cost of CP to the company ? (assume 360 days in a year).

SOLUTION

Flotation cost of CP = (0.5% + 0.25% + 0.5%) ₹ 1,00,000 = ₹ 1,250

$$\text{Cost of CP} = \frac{\text{Face Value} - (\text{Issue Price} - \text{Flotation Cost})}{\text{Issue Price} - \text{Flotation Cost}} \times \frac{360\text{ days}}{\text{Maturity Period}} \times 100$$

$$\text{Cost of CP} = \frac{₹\,1{,}00{,}000 - (₹\,97{,}000 - ₹\,1{,}250)}{(₹\,97{,}000 - ₹\,1{,}250)} \times \frac{360}{90} \times 100 = 17.754\%$$

21.0 METHODS OF CALCULATING THE BORROWING LIMITS TO FINANCE THE WORKING CAPITAL REQUIREMENTS

Tondon committee suggested three methods of calculating the borrowing limits to finance the working capital requirements as follows:

Method	*Minimum Financing from Long Term Sources*	*Maximum Permissible Bank Finance (MPBF)*
Method 1	25% of (Current Assets – Current Liabilities other than bank borrowings)	75% of (Current Assets – Current Liabilities other than bank borrowings)
Method 2	25% of Total Current Assets	(75% of Current Assets) – Current Liabilities other than bank borrowings

Method 3	Core Current Assets + 25% of Other Current Assets	75% of (Current Assets other than Core Current Assets) – Current liabilities other than bank borrowings.

ILLUSTRATION 22

From the following information, calculate Maximum Permissible Bank Finance (MPBF) and Minimum Financing from long-term sources by different methods of Tondon Committee Norms:

Particulars	₹ *(in Lacs)*
Creditors for Purchases	100
Creditors for Expenses	40
Bills Payable	160
Bank Borrowings	100
Inventory:	
Raw Materials	100
Work – in – Progress	50
Finished Goods	140
Receivables (including	
bills discounted with bankers)	70
Cash and Bank	60

(Assume Core Current Assets as ₹ 80 lakhs)

SOLUTION

BASIC CALCULATIONS

Particulars	₹ *(in Lacs)*
A. Core Current Assets	80
B. Other Current Assets	340
C. Total Current Assets	420
D. Bank Borrowings	100
E. Current Liabilities (other than Bank Borrowings)	300

CALCULATION OF MPBF AS PER TONDON COMMITTEE NORMS

Method 1: MPBF = 75% of (C – E) = 75% of (₹ 420 – ₹ 300) = ₹ 90 lakhs

Excess bank Borrowings = ₹ 100 – ₹ 90 = ₹ 10 lakhs

Method 2: MPBF = (75% of C) – E = (75% of ₹ 420) – ₹ 300 = ₹ 315 – ₹ 300 = ₹ 15 lakhs

Excess bank Borrowings = ₹ 100 lakhs – ₹ 15 lakhs = ₹ 85 lakhs

Method 3: MPBF = (75% of B) – E = (75% of ₹ 340) – ₹ 300 = ₹ 255 – ₹ 300 = (₹ 45 lakhs)

Excess bank Borrowings = ₹ 100 lakhs + ₹ 45 lakhs = ₹ 145 lakhs

CALCULATION OF MINIMUM FINANCING FROM LONG-TERM SOURCES AS PER TONDON COMMITTEE NORMS

Method 1: 25% of (C – E) = 25% of (₹ 420 – ₹ 300) = ₹ 30 lakhs

Method 2: 25% of C = 25% of ₹ 420 = ₹ 105 lakhs

Method 3: A + 25% of B = ₹ 80 + 25% of ₹ 340 = ₹ 165 lakhs.

22.0 RECENT CHANGES IN MAXIMUM PERMISSIBLE BANK FINANCE

The important changes in credit policy affected on the beginning of 1997 are as follows:

1. RBI scrapped the concept of MPBF in order to facilitate need-based working capital without sticking to the age old policies which might have outlived their utility.
2. Indian Bank Association (IBA) proposed new system. The features of new system are as follows:

Type of Borrower	*Basis of Credit Limit*
Borrower having requirements upto ₹ 25 Lakhs	Detailed discussion with borrower.
Borrower having requirements above ₹ 25	Credit Limit upto 25% of Projected
Lakhs but upto ₹ 5 Crore	Gross sales.
Large Borrower not falling in the above categories	On the basis of cash budget system.

Notes:

1. RBI permits banks to follow Tondon/Chore Committee guidelines and retain MPBF concept with necessary modification.
2. RBI permits banks to form consortium arrangements so that the risks are spread.

23.0 RECOMMENDATIONS OF CHORE COMMITTEE

The recommendations of Chore Committee (August 1979) as accepted by RBI were as follows:

1. **Enhancement of Borrower's Contribution:** In calculating Maximum Permissible Bank Finance (MPBF), the second method of lending as recommended by Tandon Committee should be adopted. According to this method, the borrower's contribution from own funds and term finance to meet the working capital requirements should be atleast 25% of total current assets. This would give a minimum current ratio of 1.33 : 1. Excess borrowing should be treated as working capital term loan (WTCL) which could be made payable in half yearly installments within a period not exceeding 5 years.
2. **Compulsory Periodic review of Cash Credit Limits and Submission of Quarterly Statements:** All Borrowers with working capital limits of atleast ₹ 10 Lakhs. There must be compulsory periodic review of cash credit Limits atleast once a year to verify the continued viability of the borrowers and to assess the need based character of credit limits.

   All Borrowers with working capital limits of atleast ₹ 50 Lakhs. They must submit quarterly statements compulsorily prescribed under the information system designed by the Tandon Committee.
3. **No Bifurcation of cash credit into demand loan for core portion and fluctuating cash credit component:** There should be no bifurcation of cash credit into demand loan for core portion and fluctuating cash credit component and the bank should not maintain differential interest rate between these two components. For already bifurcated cash credit accounts, the necessary steps should be taken to abolish the differential interest rate with immediate effect.
4. **Separate Limits for peak and normal non- peak level periods:** The banks should fix separate limits for peak and normal non- peak level periods and indicate the duration of these periods.
5. **Drawal of funds to be regulated through quarterly statements:** The borrower should indicate before the commencement of each quarter the requirements of the funds during that quarter.
6. **Penalty for default in submission of quarterly statements:** If a borrower fails to submit these returns within prescribed time limits

(a) The bank should give notice that if default continues the account may be frozen without further notice at its discretion.

(b) The bank may charge penal interest of 1% per annum on the total outstanding for the period of default.

(c) Inspite of levy of penal interest, if default persists, bank should review the position and if it is satisfied that a stern action is necessary the operation of the account of such borrower may be frozen If the borrower has accounts with more than one bank, the decision taken by the bank to freeze the account be intimated to other concerned banks. As soon as the other financing banks receive advice, they should ensure that no operations are allowed in such accounts with them.

7. **Ad-hoc *or* temporary limits:** A request for ad-hoc *or* temporary limits to meet the unforeseen contingencies should be considered very carefully and allowed for a pre-determined period through a separate demand loan *or* non-operatable cash credit account. Banks may charge additional interest of 1% p.a. on these limits.

8. **Encouragement for Bill Finance:**

(a) **Advance against Book Debts**—Banks should replace cash credit against book debts by bill finances and should take the necessary steps for the review of existing cash credit and convert such cash credit limits into bill limits.

(b) **Drawee Bills**—The banks should earmark atleast 50% of cash credit limits against raw material to manufacturing units for drawee bills only.

(c) **Payment to small units**—Public sector undertakings and other large borrowers should give precise information in their quarterly statements about their dues to small units. On the basis of such information, banks may take such steps as to ensure timely payments to small units. One such step may be the stipulation that a portion of the credit limits for bill acceptance (drawee bills) will be utilized only for drawee bills of small-scale units.

24.0 RECOMMENDATIONS OF JILANI COMMITTEE

The recommendations of Jilani Committee (October 1993) as accepted by RBI were as follows:

1. **Bifurcation of Cash Credit Limits into Loan Component and Fluctuating Cash Credit Limits:** The cash credit limits should be bifurcated into Loan Component and Fluctuating Cash Credit Limits.
2. **Basis of Loan Component:** Loan component should be decided on the basis of current ratio.
3. **Increase in current ratio:** The bank should raise the current ratio from 1.33:1 to 1.50:1 for the existing companies with fund-based working capita limits of ₹ 10 Crore *or* more.
4. **Transfer of shortfall in working capital to Loan Account:** The shortfall in working capital should be transferred to the loan account repayable after three to five years and for which the same rate of interest is to be charged.
5. **Minimum Current Ratio 1.5:** Borrowers with limits above ₹ 50 Lakhs and above ₹ 10 Crore should be subject to Minimum current ratio of 1.5 in a phased manner after three years. Slip-backs in current ratio is to be allowed only at the discretion of banks for genuine reasons.
6. **Monitoring of Funds:** Granted needs should be monitored so as to ensure end use of funds
7. **Acceptance of Bills by Government departments:** Government departments should be advised to accept bills drawn on them.
8. **Measures to Reduce Dependence on Banks Credit:** Banks should take the necessary steps to reduce dependence on banks credit and increase reliance on long-term source.

25.0 RECOMMENDATIONS OF DEHEJIA COMMITTEE

The recommendations of Dehejia Committee (September 1969) as accepted by RBI were as follows:

1. The banks should make an appraisal of credit applications with reference to the total financial situations of the client.
2. All cash credit limit accounts with banks should be bifurcated in the following categories:
   (a) The hard core which would represent the minimum level of raw material, finished goods and stores, which any industrial concern is required to hold for maintaining certain level of production;
   (b) Fluctuating part, which would represent the short-term increase in inventories, tax, dividends and bonus payments.
3. To determine the hard core element of cash credit accounts, norms for inventory levels should be worked out by Chambers of Industry *or* by the India Bank Association.

26.0 TREASURY MANAGEMENT

MEANING OF TREASURY MANAGEMENT

The Association of Corporate Treasures defines "Treasury management as the efficient management of liquidity and financial risk in business". Treasury management is responsible for:

1. Management of cash while obtaining the optimum return from any surplus funds;
2. Management of exchange rate risks in accordance with group policy;
3. Providing both long and short term funds for the business at minimum cost;
4. Maintaining good relationships with banks and other providers of finance including shareholders;
5. Advising on aspects of corporate finance including capital structure, mergers and acquisitions.

FUNCTIONS OF TREASURY DEPARTMENT

1. **Cash Management:** The efficient collection and payment of cash both inside the group and to third parties is the function of treasury department. Treasury will normally manage surplus funds in an investment portfolio. Investment policy will consider future need for liquid funds and acceptable levels of risk as determined by company policy.
2. **Currency Management:** The treasury department manage the foreign currency risk exposure of the company in various ways such as:
   (a) By advising set-off intra-group indebtness.
   (b) By advising use of matching receipts and payments in same currency.
   (c) By advising on the currency to be used while invoicing overseas sales.
   (d) By managing any net exchange exposure in accordance with the company policy.
   (e) By entering into forward contracts to buy *or* sell currency forward to minimize the risk.
3. **Funding Management:** The treasury department provides the long term, medium and short-term funds for the business at minimum costs.
4. **Banking:** Treasury department maintains good relationship with the bankers and carry out negotiation with them.
5. **Corporate Finance:** Treasury department is involved with both acquisition and divestment activities within the group. It maintains good relationship with the investors.

SOLVED PROBLEMS

PROBLEM 1

CAMII Ltd. sells goods at a uniform rate of gross profit of 20% on sales including depreciation as per of cost of production. Its annual figures are as under:

Particulars	₹
Sales (At 2 months' credit)	24,00,000
Materials consumed (Suppliers credit 2 months)	6,00,000
Wages paid (Monthly at the beginning of the subsequent month)	4,80,000
Manufacturing expenses includes depreciation of ₹ 2,40,000 (Cash expenses are paid-one months in arrear) Administration expenses (Cash expenses are paid – one month in arrear)	1,50,000
Sales promotion expenses (Paid quarterly in advance)	75,000

The company keeps one month stock each of raw materials and finished goods. A minimum cash balance of ₹ 80,000 is always kept. The company wants to adopt a 10% safety margin in the maintenance of working capital. The company has no work in progress. The stock of finished goods is valued at factory cost.

Required: Find out the requirements of working capital of the company on cash cost basis.

SOLUTION

STATEMENT SHOWING THE REQUIREMENTS OF WORKING CAPITAL

Particulars	*Computation*	₹
A. Current Assets:		
Stock of raw material	₹ 6,00,000 × 1/12	50,000
Stock of Finished Goods	₹ 16,80,000 × 1/12	1,40,000
Debtors	₹ 19,05,000 × 2/12	3,17,500
Cash in Hand		80,000
Selling & Distribution Expenses	₹ 75,000 × 1/4	18,750
Total Current Assets		6,06,250
B. Current Liabilities:		
Creditors for Raw materials	₹ 6,00,000 × 2/12	1,00,000
Creditors for Wages	₹ 4,80,000 × 1/12	40,000
Creditors for Manufacturing Expenses	₹ 6,00,000 × 1/12	50,000
Creditors for Office & Adm. Expenses	₹ 1,50,000 × 1/12	12,500
Total Current Liabilities		2,02,500
C. Net Working Capital (A – B)		4,03,750
D. *Add:* Safety Margin	4,03,750 × 10/100	40,375
E. Net Working Capital (C + D)		4,44,125

Working Notes:

(I) CALCULATION OF CASH MANUFACTURING EXPENSES

Particulars	₹
A. Sales	24,00,000
B. *Less:* Gross Profit @ 20%	(4,80,000)
C. Cost of Goods Sold	19,20,000
D. *Less:* Costs other than Cash Manufacturing Expenses	
(i) Direct Material Cost	6,00,000
(ii) Direct Labour Cost	4,80,000
(iii) Depreciation	2,40,000
	(13,20,000)
E. Cash Manufacturing Expenses	6,00,000

(II) CALCULATION OF STOCK OF FINISHED GOODS AND COST OF SALES

Particulars	₹
Direct Material Cost	6,00,000
Direct Labour Cost	4,80,000
Cash Manufacturing Expenses	6,00,000
A. Total Cash Cost of Goods Produced	16,80,000
B. *Add:* Opening stock of Finished Goods	1,40,000
C. Total Cash cost of goods available (A + B)	18,20,000
D. *Less:* Closing Stock of Finished Goods	(1,40,000)
E. Total Cash Cost of Goods Sold (C – D)	16,80,000
F. *Add:* Cash Office & Adm. Expenses	1,50,000
G. *Add:* Variable Selling and Distribution expenses	75,000
K. Total Cash Cost of Sales (E + F + G)	19,05,000

PROBLEM 2

A proforma cost sheet of a company provides the following data:

Particulars	*Cost per unit (₹)*
Raw materials	52.00
Direct labour	19.50
Overheads (including depreciation @ ₹ 0.5)	39.50
Total cost (per unit)	111.00
Profit	19.00
Selling price	130.00

The following is the additional information available:

Average raw material in stock: one month; average materials in process: half a month; Finished Goods stock: one month; Credit allowed by suppliers: one month; credit allowed to debtors: two months. Time lag in payment of wages: one and a half weeks; overheads: one month. One-fourth of sales are on cash basis. Cash balance is expected to be ₹ 1,20,000.

Required: Prepare a statement showing the working capital needed to finance a level of activity of 70,000 units of output. You may assume that production is carried on evenly throughout the year and wages and overheads accrue similarly.

SOLUTION

STATEMENT SHOWING THE REQUIREMENTS OF WORKING CAPITAL

Particulars	*Computation*	₹
A. Current Assets:		
Stock of raw material	₹ 36,40,000 × 1/12	3,03,333
Stock of Work-in-Progress	As Per working note (ii)	2,36,980
Stock Of Finished goods	₹ 77,35,000 × 1/12	6,44,583
Debtors	₹ 58,01,250 × 2/12	9,66,875
Cash in Hand		1,20,000
Total Current Assets		22,71,771
B. Current Liabilities:		
Creditors for Raw materials	₹ 36,40,000 × 1/12	3,03,333
Creditors for Wages	₹ 13,65,000 × 1.5/52	39,375
Creditors for Manufacturing Expenses	₹ 27,30,000 × 1/12	2,27,500
Total Current Liabilities		5,70,208
C. Net Working Capital (A – B)		17,01,563

Working Notes:

(I) CALCULATION OF STOCK OF FINISHED GOODS AND COST OF SALES

Particulars	₹
Direct Material Cost [70,000 × ₹ 52]	36,40,000
Direct Labour Cost [70,000 × ₹ 19.50]	13,65,000
Manufacturing Overheads (excluding Depreciation) [70,000 × ₹ 39)	27,30,000
Total Cash Cost of Goods Produced	77,35,000
Add: Opening Stock of Finished Goods [₹ 77,35,000 × 1/12]	6,44,583
Total Cash Cost of Goods available	83,79,583
Less: Closing Stock of Finished Goods	(6,44,583)
Total Cash Cost of Goods Sold	77,35,000
Selling and Distribution expenses	Nil
Total Cash Cost of Sales	77,35,000

(II) CALCULATION OF STOCK OF WORK IN PROGRESS

Particulars	₹
Raw Material [36,40,000 × 0.5/12 × 100%]	1,51,667
Wages [13,65,000 × 0.5/12 × 50%]	28,438
Manufacturing Expenses [27,30,000 × 0.5/12 × 50%]	56,875
	2,36,980

(iii) Since it is an existing company and no specific information regarding opening stock has been given, it has been assumed that stock level is uniform throughout the year. Hence, opening stock equals closing stock.

PROBLEM 3

The management of JP & Co. Ltd. has called for a statement showing the working capital needed to finance a level of activity of 3,00,000 units of output for the year. The cost structure for the company's product, for the above mentioned activity level, is detailed below:

Particulars	*Cost per unit (₹)*
Raw materials	₹ 20
Direct Labour	5
Overheads (Including depreciation ₹ 5)	20
Total Cost	45
Profit	5
Selling price	50

Past trends indicate that the raw materials are held in stock, on an average, for two months. Work-in-process (50 per cent complete as to conversion costs) will approximate to 1/2 month's production. Finished goods remain in warehouse, on an average, for 1 month. Suppliers of materials extend 1 month's credit. Two month's credit is normally allowed to debtors. A minimum cash balance of ₹ 25,000 is expected to be maintained. The production pattern is assumed to be even during the year. Cash sales are 75% *less* than the credit sales. Safety margin 20%.

Required: prepare a Statement of working capital determination.

SOLUTION

STATEMENT SHOWING THE REQUIREMENTS OF WORKING CAPITAL

Particulars	*Computation*	₹
A. Current Assets:		
Stock of Raw Material	₹ 60,00,000 × 2/12	10,00,000
Stock of Work-in-Progress	As per Working Note (iii)	3,75,000
Stock of Finished Goods	₹ 1,20,00,000 × 1/12	10,00,000
Debtors	₹ 96,00,000 × 2/12	16,00,000
Cash in Hand		25,000
Total Current Assets		40,00,000
B. Current Liabilities:		
Creditors for Raw materials	60,00,000 × 1/12	5,00,000
Total Current Liabilities		5,00,000
C. Net Working Capital (A – B)		35,00,000
D. *Add:* Safety Margin	35,00,000 × 20/100	7,00,000
E. Net Working Capital (C + D)		42,00,000

Working Notes:

(I) CALCULATION OF CREDIT SALES

Let Credit Sales be x

Cash Sales	=	x – 3/4x
Total Sales x + x – 3/4x	=	₹ 150 lakh
2x – 3/4x	=	₹ 150 lakh
(8x – 3x)/4	=	₹ 150 lakh
5x/4	=	150, x = 150 × 4/5 ₹ 120 lakh

(II) CALCULATION OF STOCK OF FINISHED GOODS AND COST OF SALES

Particulars	₹
Direct Material Cost [3,00,000 units × ₹ 20]	60,00,000
Direct Labour Cost [3,00,000 units × ₹ 5]	15,00,000
Overheads (excluding depreciation) [3,00,000 units × ₹ 15]	45,00,000
Total Cash Cost of Goods Produced	1,20,00,000
Add: Opening stock of Finished Goods	10,00,000
Total Cash Cost of Goods available	1,30,00,000
Less: Closing Stock of Finished Goods [₹ 1,20,00,000/12]	(10,00,000)
Total Cash Cost of Goods Sold	1,20,00,000
Add: Selling and Distribution expenses	Nil
Total Cash Cost of Sales	1,20,00,000
Cash cost of credit sale (1,20,00,000 × 40/50)	96,00,000

(III) CALCULATION OF STOCK OF WORK IN PROGRESS

Particulars	₹
Raw Material [₹ 60,00,000 × 0.5/12 × 100%]	2,50,000
Wages [₹ 15,00,000 × 0.5/12 × 50%]	31,250
Manufacturing Expenses [₹ 45,00,000 × 0.5/12 × 50%]	93,750
	3,75,000

PROBLEM 4

Compute the amount of working capital for Project of BHARAT TULSIAN Ltd. from the following information:

Total Operating Cost p.a.	₹ 120.00 lakhs
Components of Cost:	
Raw Material	50%
Direct Wages	12.50%
Manufacturing Expenses (including Depreciation ₹ 6,00,000)	
Cash Office & Adm. Expenses	2.50%
Cash Selling and Distribution Expenses	5%

Raw Material Storage Period	2 Months
Conversion process period	1/2 Month
Debt. Collection period	1 Month
Finished Stock storage period	1 Month
Credit period enjoyed	1 Month
Cash in hand required	₹ 18,750
Cash Sales % *less* than credit sales	
Total Sales	₹ 200 lakhs
Safety Margin	20% of Net Working Capital (including Safety margin)
Gross Profit Ratio	44.5%
Valuation of Finished Stock	At Factory Cost.

SOLUTION

STATEMENT SHOWING THE REQUIREMENTS OF WORKING CAPITAL

Particulars	*Computation*	₹
A. Current Assets:		
Stock of Raw Material	₹ 60,00,000 × 2/12	10,00,000
Stock of Work-in-Progress	As per Working Note (iii)	3,43,750
Stock of Finished Goods	₹ 1,05,00,000 × 1/12	8,75,000
Debtors	₹ 85,50,000 × 1/12	7,12,500
Cash in Hand		18,750
Total Current Assets		29,50,000
B. Current Liabilities:		
Creditors for Raw materials	₹ 60,00,000 × 1/12	5,00,000
Creditors for Wages	₹ 15,00,000 × 1/12	1,25,000
Creditors for Manufacturing Expenses	₹ 30,00,000 × 1/12	2,50,000
Creditors for Office & Adm. Expenses	₹ 3,00,000 × 1/12	25,000
Creditors for Selling & Distribution Expenses	₹ 6,00,000 × 1/12	50,000
Total Current Liabilities		9,50,000
C. Net Working Capital (A – B)		20,00,000
D. *Add:* Safety Margin	₹ 20,00,000 × 25/100	5,00,000
E. Net Working Capital (C + D)		25,00,000

Working Notes:

(I) CALCULATION OF CASH MANUFACTURING EXPENSES

Particulars	₹ *(in lacs)*
A. Sales	200
B. *Less:* Gross Profit @ 44.5%	(89)
C. Cost of Goods Sold	111

D. *Less:* Costs other than Cash Manufacturing Expenses	
(i) Direct Material Cost	60
(ii) Direct Labour Cost	15
(iii) Depreciation	6
	(81)
E. Cash Manufacturing Expenses [C – D)	30

(II) CALCULATION OF STOCK OF FINISHED GOODS AND COST OF SALES

Particulars	₹
Direct Material Cost [50% of ₹ 120 lakh]	60,00,000
Direct Labour Cost [12.5% of ₹ 120 lakhs]	15,00,000
Cash Manufacturing Expenses	30,00,000
Total Cash Cost of Goods Produced	1,05,00,000
Add: Opening stock of Finished Goods [₹ 1,05,00,000/12]	8,75,000
Total Cash Cost of Goods available	1,13,75,000
Less: Closing Stock of Finished Goods	(8,75,000)
Total Cash Cost of Goods Sold	1,05,00,000
Cash Office & Adm. Expenses [2.5% of ₹ 120 lakh]	3,00,000
Add: Cash Selling and Distribution expenses [5% of ₹ 120 lakhs]	6,00,000
Total Cash Cost of Sales	1,14,00,000
Cash Cost of Credit Sales (₹ 1,14,00,000 × 150/200)	85,50,000

(III) CALCULATION OF CREDIT SALES

Let credit sales be x

$$\text{Cash Sales} = x - 2/3x$$
$$\text{Total Sales} = x + x - 2/3x = 200$$
$$4x/3 = 200$$
$$x = 150$$

(IV) CALCULATION OF STOCK OF WORK-IN-PROGRESS

Particulars	₹
Raw Material (60,00,000 × 0.5/12 × 100%)	2,50,000
Wages (15,00,000 × 0.5/12 × 50%)	31,250
Manufacturing Expenses (30,00,000 × 0.5/12 × 50%)	62,500
	3,43,750

PROBLEM 5

MP & Co. a firm has applied for working capital finance from a commercial bank. You are requested by the bank to prepare an estimate of the working capital requirements of the firm. You may add 10 per cent to your estimated figure to account for exigencies. The following is the firm's projected profit and loss account:

Particulars		₹
Sales		22,47,000
Cost of goods sold		16,37,100
Gross Profit		(6,09,900)
Administrative Expenses	1,49,800	
Selling Expenses	1,39,100	2,88,900
Profit before tax		3,21,000
Tax provision		(1,07,000)
Profit after tax		2,14,000

Total Cost of Goods Sold (COGS) is calculated as follows:

Particulars	₹
Materials used	8,98,800
Wages and other mfg. expenses	6,68,750
Depreciation	2,51,450
	18,19,000
Less: Stock of finished goods (10% product not yet sold)	1,81,900
Cost of goods sold	16,37,100

(a) The figures given above relate only to the goods that have been finished, and not to work in progress;

(b) Goods equal to 15 per cent of the year's production (in terms of physical units) are in progress on an average requiring full material but only 40 per cent of other expenses.

(c) The firm has a policy of keeping two months consumption of material in stock.

(d) All expenses are paid one month in arrear.

(e) Suppliers of material grant one and a half months credit;

(f) Sales are 20 per cent cash while remaining sold on two months credit.

(g) 70 per cent of the income tax has to be paid in advance in quarterly instalments.

SOLUTION

STATEMENT SHOWING THE REQUIREMENTS OF WORKING CAPITAL (ON CASH COST BASIS)

Particulars	Computation	₹
A. Current Assets:		
Stock of Raw Material	10,33,620 × 2 /12	1,72,270
Stock of Work-in-Progress	As per Working Note	1,74,945
Stock of Finished goods	15,67,550 × 10/100	1,56,755
Debtors	13,59,756 × 2/12	2,26,626
Total Current Assets		7,30,596
B. Current Liabilities:		
Creditors for Raw materials	12,05,890 × 1.5/12	1,50,736
Creditors for Wages	7,08,875 × 1/12	59,073

Creditors for Office & Adm. Expenses	1,49,800 × 1/12	12,483
Creditors for Selling & Distribution Expenses	1,39,100 × 1/12	11,592
Provision for Taxation	1,07,000 × 30/100	32,100
Total Current Liabilities		2,65,984
C. Net Working Capital (A – B)		4,64,612
D. *Add:* Safety Margin	4,64,612 × 10/100	46,461
E. Net Working Capital (C + D)		5,11,073

Working Notes:

(I) CALCULATION OF STOCK OF WORK-IN-PROGRESS

Particulars	₹
Raw Material (8,98,800 × 15%)	1,34,820
Wages & Mfg. expenses (₹ 6,68,750 × 15% × 40%)	40,125
Total	1,74,945

(II) CALCULATION OF STOCK OF FINISHED GOODS AND COST OF SALES

Particulars	₹
Direct Material Cost [₹ 8,98,800 + ₹ 1,34,820]	10,33,620
Wages & Mfg. Expenses [₹ 6,68,750 + ₹ 40,125]	7,08,875
Gross factory cost	17,42,495
Less: Closing W.I.P [As per working Note (i)]	(1,74,945)
Cost of goods produced	15,67,550
Less: Closing stock [10% of ₹ 15,67,550]	(1,56,755)
Cost of goods sold	14,10,795
Add: Office & Adm. Expenses	1,49,800
Add: Selling and Distribution expenses	1,39,100
Total Cash Cost of Sales	16,99,695
Total Cash Cost of Credit Sales (80% of ₹ 16,99,695)	13,59,756

(III) CALCULATION OF CREDIT PURCHASES

Particulars	₹
A. Raw material consumed [₹ 8,98,800 × 115%]	10,33,620
B. *Add:* Closing Stock [₹ 10,33,620 × 2/12]	1,72,270
C. *Less:* Opening Stock	Nil
D. Purchases (A + B – C)	12,05,890

PROBLEM 6

CAMII Ltd. newly commencing business 1991 has the undermentioned projected profit and Loss Account:

Particulars	₹	₹
Sales		42,00,000

Cost of Goods Sold		30,60,000
Gross Profit		11,40,000
Administrative expenses	2,80,000	
Selling expenses	2,60,000	5,40,000
Profit before tax		6,00,000
Tax Provision		2,00,000
Profit after tax		4,00,000
The cost of goods sold has been arrived at as under:		
Material used		16,80,000
Wage and manufacturing expenses		12,50,000
Depreciation		4,70,000
		34,00,000
Less: Stock of finished goods (10% of goods Produced not yet sold)		3,40,000
		30,60,000

Additional Information:

(a) The figures given above relate only to finished goods and not to work in progress.

(b) Goods equal to 15% of the years production (in terms of physical units) will be in process on the average requiring full materials but only 40% of the other expenses.

(c) The company believes in keeping material equal to two months consumption in stock.

(d) All expenses will be paid one month in arrear.

(e) Suppliers of material will extend 1? month's credit.

(f) Sales will be 20% for cash and the rest at two months credit;

(g) 90% of the income-tax will be paid in advance in quarterly instalments.

(h) The company wishes to keep ₹ 1,00,000 in cash.

Required: Prepare an estimate of the requirement of (i) working capital and (ii) cash cost of working capital.

SOLUTION

STATEMENT SHOWING THE REQUIREMENTS OF WORKING CAPITAL

Particulars	*On Accounting basis*		*On Cash Cost Basis*	
	Computation	₹	*Computation*	₹
A. Current Assets:				
Stock of raw Material	19,32,000 2/12	3,22,000	19,32,000 2/12	3,22,000
Stock of Work-in-Progress	As per working Note (i)	3,55,200	As per working Note (i)	3,27,000
Stock of Finished Goods	As per working Note (ii)	3,40,000	As per working Note (ii)	2,93,000
Debtors	28,80,000 2/12	4,80,000	25,41,600 2/12	4,23,600
Cash in Hand		1,00,000		1,00,000
Total Current Assets		15,97,200		14,65,600
B. Current Liabilities:				
Creditors for Raw Materials	22,54,000 1.5/12	2,81,750	22,54,000 1.5/12	2,81,750
Creditors for Wages	13,25,000 1/12	1,10,417	13,25,000 1/12	1,10,417

Creditors for Adm. Exp.	2,80,000 1/12	23,333	2,80,000 1/12	23,333
Creditors for Selling Exp.	2,60,000 1/12	21,667	2,60,000 1/12	21,667
Provision for Taxation	2,00,000 10/100	20,000	2,00,000 10/100	20,000
Total Current Liabilities		4,57,167		4,57,167
C. Net Working Capital (A – B)		11,40,033		10,08,433

Working Notes:

(I) CALCULATION OF STOCK OF WORK-IN-PROGRESS

Particulars	₹	₹
Raw Material (₹ 16,52,000 × 15%)	2,52,000	2,52,000
Wages & Mfg. expenses (₹ 12,50,000 × 15% × 40%)	75,000	75,000
Depreciation (₹ 4,70,000 × 15% × 40%)	28,200	—
Total	3,55,200	3,27,000

(II) CALCULATION OF STOCK OF FINISHED GOODS & CASH COST OF CREDIT SALES

Particulars	₹	₹
Direct Material Cost [₹ 16,80,000 + ₹ 2,52,000]	19,32,000	19,32,000
Wages & Mfg. Exp. [₹ 12,50,000 + ₹ 75,000]	13,25,000	13,25,000
Depreciation [₹ 4,70,000 + ₹ 28,200]	4,98,200	—
Gross Factory Cost	37,55,200	32,57,000
Less: Closing W.I.P	(3,55,200)	(3,27,000)
Cost of goods produced	34,00,000	29,30,000
Less: Closing stock [10% of Cost of Goods Produced]	(3,40,000)	(2,93,000)
Cost of goods sold	30,60,000	26,37,000
Add: Office & Adm. Expenses	2,80,000	2,80,000
Add: Selling and Distribution expenses	2,60,000	2,60,000
Total Cash Cost of Sales	36,00,000	31,77,000
Cash Cost of Credit Sales @ 80%	28,80,000	25,41,600

(III) CALCULATION OF CREDIT PURCHASES

Particulars	₹
A. Raw material consumed	19,32,000
B. *Add:* closing stock	3,22,000
C. *Less:* opening stock	Nil
D. Purchases(A + B – C)	22,54,000

PROBLEM 7

CAMIB Limited is commencing a new project for manufacture of a plastic component. The following cost information has been ascertained for annual production of 12,000 units which is the full capacity:

Particulars	*Cost per unit (₹)*
Materials	40

Direct Labour and Variable expenses	20
Fixed Manufacturing expenses	6
Depreciation	10
Fixed Administration expenses	4
	80

The selling price per unit is expected to be ₹ 96 and the selling expenses ₹ 5 per units, 80% of which is variable.

In the first two years of operations, production and sales are expected to be as follows:

Year	*Production (no. of units)*	*Sales (no. of units)*
1	6,000	5,000
2	9,000	8,500

To assess the working capital requirements, the following additional information is available:

(a)	Stock of materials	2.25 months' average consumption
(b)	Work in process	Nil
(c)	Debtors	1 month's average cost of sales
(d)	Cash balance	₹ 10,000
(e)	Creditors for supply of materials:	1 months average purchases during the year
(f)	Creditors for expenses:	1 month's average of all expenses during the year
(g)	Valuation of Finished Goods Stock	At average Cost

Required: Prepare, for the two years,

(i) A project statement of Profit/Loss (ignoring taxation); and

(ii) A projected statement of working capital requirements.

SOLUTION

PROJECTED STATEMENT OF PROFIT/LOSS

Particulars	*Year 1* Units	*Year 1* Per Unit ₹	*Year 1* Total ₹	*Year 2* Units	*Year 2* Per Unit ₹	*Year 2* Total ₹
Normal Production (in units)	12,000			12,000		
Actual Production (in units)	6,000			9,000		
Sales (in Units)	5,000			8,500		
A. Sales Revenue		96	4,80,000		96	8,16,000
B. *Less:* Cost of Sales						
(a) Direct Material Cost		40	2,40,000		40	3,60,000
(b) Direct Labour & Variable Exp.		20	1,20,000		20	1,80,000
(c) Fixed Manufacturing Exp. (excluding Depreciation)		12	72,000		8	72,000
(d) Depreciation		20	1,20,000			1,20,000
(e) Fixed Adm. Exp.		8	48,000			48,000
(f) Total Cost of Goods Produced	6,000	100	6,00,000	9,000		7,80,000

(g) *Add:* Opening Stock of Finished Goods	0		0	1,000	100	1,00,000
(h) Total Cost of Goods available	6,00,000	100	6,00,000	10,000	88	8,80,000
(i) *Less:* Closing Stock of Finished Goods	1,000	100	(1,00,000)	1,500	88	(1,32,000)
(j) Total Cost of Goods Sold	5,000	100	5,00,000	8,500	88	7,48,000
(k) *Add:* Variable Selling Exp.		4	20,000		4	34,000
(l) *Add:* Fixed Selling Exp.		2.40	12,000			12,000
Total Cost of Sales (j + k + l)			5,32,000			7,94,000
C. Profit (Loss) (A – B)			(52,000)			22,000

Note: Closing stock of finished goods has been valued Weighted Average cost.

STATEMENT SHOWING THE REQUIREMENTS OF WORKING CAPITAL (ON CASH COST BASIS)

Particulars	*Year 1*		*Year 2*	
	Computation	₹	*Computation*	₹
A. Current Assets:				
Stock of Raw Material	2,40,000 × 2.25/12	45,000	3,60,000 × 2.25/12	67,500
Stock of Finished Goods		80,000		1,11,000
Debtors	4,32,000 × 1/12	36,000	6,75,000 × 1/12	56,250
Cash In Hand		10,000		10,000
Total Current Assets		1,71,000		2,44,750
B. Current Liabilities:				
Creditors for Raw Materials	2,85,000 × 1/12	23,750	3,82,500 × 1/12	31,875
Creditors for Wages & Variable Exp.	1,20,000 × 1/12	10,000	1,80,000 × 1/12	15,000
Creditors for Mfg. Exp.	72,000 × 1/12	6,000	72,000 × 1/12	6,000
Creditors for Adm. Exp.	48,000 × 1/12	4,000	48,000 × 1/12	4,000
Creditors for Selling Exp.	32,000 × 1/12	2,667	46,000 × 1/12	3,833
Total Current Liabilities		46,417		60708
C. Net Working Capital (A – B)		1,24,583		1,84,042

Working Notes:

(I) CALCULATION OF CASH COST OF CLOSING STOCK AND CASH COST OF SALES

Particulars	*Year 1*			*Year 2*		
	Units	*Per Unit* ₹	*Total* ₹	*Units*	*Per Unit* ₹	*Total* ₹
Normal Production (in units)	12,000			12,000		
Actual Production (in units)	6,000			9,000		
Sales (in Units)	5,000			8,500		
A. Direct Material Cost		40	2,40,000		40	3,60,000
B. Direct Labour & Variable Exp. (Excluding Depreciation)		20	1,20,000		20	1,80,000

C. Fixed Manufacturing Exp.			72,000			72,000
D. Fixed Administration Exp.		8	48,000		5.33	48,000
E. Total Cost of Goods Produced (A + B + C + D)	6,000	80	4,80,000	9,000	73	6,60,000
F. *Add:* Opening Stock of Finished Goods			—	1,000	80	80,000
G. Total Cost of Goods available	6,000	80	4,80,000	10,000	74	7,40,000
H. *Less:* Closing Stock of Finished Goods	1,000	80	(80,000)	1,500	74	(1,11,000)
I. Total Cost of Goods Sold (G – H)	5,000	80	4,00,000	8,500	74	6,29,000
J. *Add:* Variable Selling & Distribution Expenses		4	20,000		4	34,000
K. *Add:* Fixed Selling & Distribution Expenses		2.40	12,000		1.41	12,000
L. Total Cost of Sales (i + j + k)			4,32,000			6,75,000

(II) CALCULATION OF CREDIT PURCHASES

Particulars	*Year 1*	*Year 2*
A. Raw material consumed	2,40,000	3,60,000
B. *Add:* Closing stock	45,000	67,500
C. *Less:* Opening stock	0	(45,000)
D. Purchases(A + B – C)	2,85,000	3,82,500

PROBLEM 8

TULSIAN Ltd. is launching a new project for the manufacture of a unique component. At full capacity of 24,000, the cost will be as follows:

Particulars	*Cost Per Unit (₹)*
Direct Material	50
Direct Labour	35
Manufacturing Expenses (50% variable)	
(40% of Fixed represent depreciation)	50
Office & Administration Expenses (1/3rd fixed)	15
Selling & Distribution Expenses (80% variable)	10
	160

In the first two year of operation, production, sales and WIP are expected to be as follows.

Year	*Production of completed Units*	*Sales*	*Closing WIP*
1	15,000 Units	14,000 Units @ ₹ 200	2,500 units Material fully supplied but 40% converted
2	20,500 Units	18,000 Units @ ₹ 220	1,250 units (Material fully supplied but 40% converted)

To assess the working Capital require works, the following additional information in given.

(a) Stock of Raw Materials-3 Months average consumption

(b) Credit allowed to Debtors-1 Month

(c) Credit allowed by suppliers of Materials-2 Months

(d) Sale Promotion Expenses ₹ 1,00,000 paid quarterly in advance

(e) Lay in payment of other expenses — 1 Month

(f) Cash Balance — 10% of current Liabilities

(g) Safety Margin — 20% of total working Capital (including safety Margin)

(h) Cash sales 75% *less* than the credit sales

(i) Credit purchases are three times the cash purchases

(j) Stock of finished goods is valued at average cost.

Required: Prepare (i) Projected Statement of Profit/Loss, (ii) Statement showing the requirements of Working Capital.

SOLUTION

PROJECTED STATEMENT OF PROFIT *OR* LOSS

Particulars	Year 1		Year 2	
	Units	*Total* ₹	*Units*	*Total* ₹
Normal Production (in units)	24,000		24,000	
Actual Production (in units)	15,000		20,500	
Sales (in units)	14,000		18,000	
A. Sales Revenue		28,00,000		39,60,000
B. *Less:* Cost of Sales				
(a) Direct Material Cost [Eq. Units × ₹ 50]		8,75,000		9,62,500
(b) Direct Labour Cost [Eq. Units × ₹ 35]		5,60,000		7,00,000
(c) Variable Mfg. Exp. [Eq. Units × ₹ 25]		4,00,000		5,00,000
(d) Fixed Manufacturing Exp. (excluding Dep.)		3,60,000		3,60,000
(e) Depreciation		2,40,000		2,40,000
(f) Gross Factory Cost (a + b + c + d + e)	17,500	24,35,000	19,250	27,62,500
(g) *Add:* Opening WIP	—		2,500	2,22,500
(h) *Less:* Closing WIP [As per working Note]	2,500	(2,22,500)	1,250	(1,07,500)
(i) Factory Cost (f + g + h)	15,000	22,12,500	20,500	28,77,500
(j) Variable Adm. Exp. [Actual Production × ₹ 10]		1,50,000		2,05,000
(k) Fixed Adm. Expenses		1,20,000		1,20,000
(l) Cost of Goods produced (i + j + k)		24,82,500	20,500	32,02,500
(m) *Add:* Opening Stock of Finished Goods		—	1,000	1,65,500
(n) Total Cost of Goods Available (l + m)	15,000	24,82,500	21,500	33,68,000
(o) *Less:* Closing Stock of Finished Goods	1,000	(1,65,500)	3,500	(5,46,768)
(p) Total Cost of Goods Sold (n – o)	14,000	23,17,000	18,000	28,21,232

(q) *Add:* Variable Selling and Distribution expenses [Sales Units × Rate]	1,12,000		1,44,000
(r) *Add:* Fixed Selling and Distribution Exp.	48,000		48,000
Total Cost of Sales (p + q + r)	24,77,000		30,13,232
C. Profit (A – B)	3,23,000		9,46,768

Note: Since Equivalent production is on FIFO basis, Stock of finished goods should also be valued on FIFO Basis.

STATEMENT SHOWING REQUIREMENTS OF WORKING CAPITAL

Particulars	*Year 1*		*Year 2*	
	Computation	₹	*Computation*	₹
A. Current Assets:				
Stock of Raw Material	8,75,000 × 3/12	2,18,750	9,62,500 × 3/12	2,40,625
Stock of Work-in-progress		2,07,500		1,01,500
Stock of Finished Goods		1,50,500		5,04,256
Debtors	18,13,600 × 1/12	1,51,133	22,33,395 × 1/12	1,86,116
Cash In Hand		27,422		28,780
Prepaid Selling Expenses	1,00,000 × 3/12	25,000	1,00,000 × 3/12	25,000
Total Current Assets		7,80,305		10,86,277
B. Current Liabilities:				
Creditors for Raw Materials	8,20,313 × 2/12	1,36,719	7,38,281 × 2/12	1,23,047
Creditors for Wages	5,60,000 × 1/12	46,667	7,00,000 × 1/12	58,333
Creditors for Mfg. Expenses	7,60,000 × 1/12	63,333	8,60,000 × 1/12	71,667
Creditors for Office & Adm. Exp. Mfg. Exp.	2,70,000 × 1/12	22,500	3,25,000 × 1/12	27,083
Creditors for Selling & Distribution expenses	60,000 × 1/12	5,000	92,000 × 1/12	7,667
Total Current Liabilities		2,74,219		2,87,797
C. Net Working capital (A – B)		5,06,086		7,98,480
D. *Add:* Safety Margin @ 25%	5,06,086 × 25/100	1,26,522	7,98,480 × 25/100	1,99,620
E. Net Working Capital (C + D)		6,32,608		9,98,100

Working Notes:

(I) CALCULATION OF EQUIVALENT UNITS IN RESPECT OF DIRECT MATERIAL, DIRECT LABOUR & MFG. EXPENSES

Particulars	*Year 1*		*Year 2*	
	Material	*Labour & Mfg. Exp.*	*Material*	*Labour & Mfg. Exp.*
A. Actual production	15,000	15,000	20,500	20,500
B. *Add:* Closing W.I.P (40% of 2500)	2,500	1,000	1,250	500
C. *Less:* Opening W.I.P.	—	—	(2,500)	(1,000)
D. Equivalent units	17,500	16,000	19,250	20,000

(II) CALCULATION OF WORK IN PROGRESS

Particulars	*Year 1* ₹	*Year 2* ₹
A. Direct material	1,25,000 (i.e. 2,500 × ₹ 50)	62,500 (i.e. 1,250 × ₹ 50)
B. Direct labour	35,000 (40% × 2,500 × ₹ 35)	17,500 (40% × 1,250 × ₹ 35)
C. Cash Mfg. Expenses		
(i) Variable	25,000 (40% × 2,500 × ₹ 25)	12,500 (40% × 1250 × ₹ 25)
(ii) Fixed (Ex. Depreciation)	22,500 (3,60,000 × 1,000/16,000)	9,000.00 (3,60,000 × 500/20,000)
Total	47,500	21,500
D. Total Cash Cost of WIP (A + B + C)	2,07,500	1,01,500
E. *Add:* Depreciation	15,000 (2,40,000 × 1000/16,000)	6,000 (2,40,000 × 500/20,000)
F. Total Cost of WIP (on accounting basis)	2,22,500	1,07,500

(III) CALCULATION OF CASH COST OF CLOSING STOCK AND CASH COST OF SALES

Particulars	*Year 1*		*Year 2*	
	Units	*Total* ₹	*Units*	*Total* ₹
Normal Production (in units)	24,000		24,000	
Actual Production (in units)	15,000		20,500	
A. Direct Material Cost		8,75,000		9,62,500
B. Direct Labour Cost		5,60,000		7,00,000
C. Variable Manufacturing Exp.		4,00,000		5,00,000
D. Fixed manufacturing Ex. (excluding Dep.)		3,60,000		3,60,000
E. Gross Factory Cost (A + B + C + D)	17,500	21,95,000	19,250	25,22,500
F. *Add:* Opening WIP			2,500	2,07,500
G. *Less:* Closing WIP	2,500	(2,07,500)	1,250	(1,01,500)
H. Cash Factory Cost (E + F – G)	15,000	19,87,500	20,500	26,28,500
I. Variable Adm. Expenses		1,50,000		2,05,000
J. Fixed Adm. Expenses		1,20,000		1,20,000
K. Cash Cost of goods produced (H + I + J)		22,57,500	20,500	29,53,500
L. *Add:* Opening Stock of Finished Goods		—	1,000	1,50,500
M. Total Cash Cost of Goods available (K + L)	15,000	22,57,500	21,500	31,04,000
N. *Less:* Closing Stock of Finished Goods	1,000	(1,50,500)	3,500	(5,04,256)
O. Total Cash Cost of Goods Sold (M – N)	14,000	21,07,000	18,000	25,99,744
P. *Add:* Variable Selling and Distribution exp.		1,12,000		1,44,000
Q. *Add:* Fixed Selling and Distribution Expenses		48,000		48,000

R. Total Cash Cost of Sales		22,67,000		27,91,744
S. Total Cash Cost of Credit Sates (80%)		18,13,600		22,33,395

(IV) CALCULATION OF CREDIT PURCHASES

Particulars	*Year 1* ₹	*Year 2* ₹
A. Raw material consumed	8,75,000	9,62,500
B. *Add:* Closing Stock	2,18,750	2,40,625
C. *Less:* Opening Stock	—	(2,18,750)
D. Purchases (A + B – C)	10,93,750	9,84,375
E. Credit Purchases (75%)	8,20,313	7,38281

(v) Computation of % Credit Sales

Let Credit Sales = 100

Cash Sales = 100 – 75 = 25

Total sales = 100 + 25 = 125

Credit Sales as a % = 100/125 × 100 = 80%

(vi) Computation of % of Credit Purchases

Let Credit Purchases = 3

Cash Purchase = 1

Total Purchase = 3 + 1 = 4

Credit purchase as % = 3/4 × 100 = 75%

PROBLEM 9

CAT (1) Ltd. which is to commence its operations on 1st April, 2009 proposes to produce 36,000 completed units during the coming year 2009–2010.

The following information is supplied:

(a) **Unit Cost Structure of product at current levels:**	₹
Raw-material	4.00
Wages	2.00
Variable Overheads	2.00
Fixed Overheads (including ₹ 1.00 Depreciation)	1.50
Profit	3.00
Selling Price	12.50

(b) **Stock of Raw-material:** 1 Month's Average Consumption, Work-in-progress-1 month's Completed units (materials fully supplied but 50% converted).

Stock of Finished Goods: 1 month's completed units. Stock of finished goods is valued at factory cost on FIFO basis.

(c) Credit Period allowed to customers 2 months, Credit Period allowed by suppliers of Raw-Material 3 months.

(d) Lag in Wages and Overhead payments 1 month.

(e) Cash Sales 20% and Cash Purchases 20%.

(f) Minimum Cash Balance required ₹ 10,556 and safely margin 25%.

Required: Prepare the Statement showing the Working Capital requirements on cash cost basis.

SOLUTION

STATEMENTS SHOWING THE WORKING CAPITAL REQUIREMENTS (ON CASH COST BASIS)

Particulars	₹
A. Current Assets:	
Stock of Raw-materials	13,000
Stock of WIP	19,440
Stock of Finished Goods	26,880
Debtors	39,424
Cash Balance	10,556
	1,09,300
B. Current Liabilities:	
Creditors for Raw-materials	33,800
Creditors for Wages	6,250
Creditors for Variable Overheads	6,250
Creditors for Fixed Overheads	3,000
	49,300
C. Working Capital [A + B]	60,000
D. *Add:* Safety Margin	15,000
E. Net Working Capital (including Safety Margin)	75,000

Working Notes:

(I) CALCULATION OF EQUIVALENT PRODUCTION UNITS

Particulars	*Material (100%)*	*Labour & Var Oh. (50%)*
A. Actual Production	36,000	36,000
B. *Add:* Closing WIP	3,000	1,500
C. *Less:* Opening WIP	—	—
	39,000	37,500

(II) STOCK OF WORK-IN-PROGRESS [3,000 UNITS I.E. 36,000/12]

Raw-material [100% × 3,000 × ₹ 4]	₹ 12,000
Wages [50% × 3,000 × 2]	₹ 3,000
Variable Overheads [50% × 3,000 × ₹ 2]	₹ 3,000
Fixed Overheads [50% × 3,000 × ₹ 0.96]	₹ 1,440
Total	₹ 19,440

(III) CALCULATION OF CASH COST OF GOODS PRODUCED AND CASH COST OF CREDIT SALES

Particulars	₹
A. Raw-material Consumed [(36,000 + 3,000) × ₹ 4)	1,56,000
B. Wages [37,500 × ₹ 2]	75,000
C. Variable Overheads [37,500 × ₹ 2]	75,000
D. Fixed Overheads	36,000
E. Gross Factory Cost [A + B + C + D]	3,42,000
F. Adjustment for WIP	
Add: Opening WIP	—
Less: Closing WIP	(19,440)
G. Cash Cost of goods Produced	3,22,560
H. Adjustment for Finished Stock	
Add: Opening Stock of Finished Goods	—
Less: Closing Stock of Finished Goods [₹ 3,22,560 x 3,000/36,000]	(26,880)
I. Cash Cost of Goods Sold	2,95,680
J. Cash Cost of Credit Sales (80%)	2,36,544

(iv) Stock of Raw-Material $= \frac{\text{Raw Material Consumed}}{\text{12 months}} \times \text{Raw Material Storage Period}$

$= \frac{₹\ 1,56,000}{\text{12 months}} \times 1\ \text{month} = ₹\ 13,000$

(v) Stock of Finished Goods = Cash Cost of Goods Produced × $\frac{\text{1 month}}{\text{12 months}}$

= ₹ 3,22,560 × 1/12 = ₹ 26,880

(vi) Debtors = Cash Cost of credit Sales × $\frac{\text{2 months}}{\text{12 months}}$ = ₹ 2,36,544 × 2/12 = ₹ 39,424

(vii) Credit Purchases of Raw-materials

Total Purchases = Raw-material Consumed + Closing Stock – Opening stock

= ₹ 1,56,000 + 13,000 – 0 = ₹ 1,69,000

Credit Purchases = 80% of Total Purchases = 80% of ₹ 1,69,000 = ₹ 1,35,200

(viii) Creditors for Raw-material $= \frac{₹\ 1,35,200}{\text{12 months}} \times 3\ \text{month} = ₹\ 33,800$

(ix) Creditors for Wages $= \frac{₹\ 75,000}{\text{12 months}} \times 1\ \text{month} = ₹\ 6,250$

(x) Creditors for Variable Overheads $= \frac{₹\ 75,000}{\text{12 months}} \times 1\ \text{month} = ₹\ 6,250$

(xi) Creditors for Fixed Overheads $= \frac{₹\ 36,000}{\text{12 months}} \times 1\ \text{month} = ₹\ 3,000$

PROBLEM 10

CAT (2) Ltd. which started its operations on 1st April 20X7 is presently producing 36,000 completed units and proposes to increase the production of completed units by 33-1/3% in the coming year 20X8-20X9.

The following information is supplied:

(a) **Unit Cost Structure of product at current level:**	₹
Raw-material	4.00
Wages	2.00
Variable Overheads	2.00
Fixed Overheads (including ₹ 0.50 Depreciation)	1.50
Profit	3.00
Selling Price	12,50

(b) **Stock of Raw-material:** 1 Month's Average Consumption, work-in-progress – 1 month's completed units (materials fully supplied but 50% converted).

Stock of Finished Goods: 1 Month's completed units. Stock of finished goods is valued at factory cost on FIFO basis.

(c) Credit Period allowed to Customers 2 months, Credit Period allowed by Suppliers of Raw-material 3 months.

(d) Lag in Wages and overheads payments 1 month.

(e) Cash Sales 20% and Cash Purchases 20%.

(f) Minimum Cash Balance required ₹ 10,556 and Safety Margin 25%.

Required: Prepare the Statement showing the Working Capital requirements (on cash cost basis) for current year and next year.

SOLUTION

STATEMENT SHOWING THE WORKING CAPITAL REQUIREMENTS (ON CASH COST BASIS)

Particulars	*Current Year* ₹	*Next Year* ₹
A. **Current Assets:**		
Stock of Raw-materials	13,000	16,333
Stock of WIP	19,440	25,480
Stock of Finished Goods	26,880	34,997
Debtors	39,424	54,912
Cash Balance	10,556	10,556
	1,09,300	1,42,278
B. **Current Liabilities:**		
Creditors for Raw-materials	33,800	39,867
Creditors for Wages	6,250	8,083
Creditors for Variable Overheads	6,250	8,083
Creditors for Fixed Overheads	3,000	3,000
	49,300	59,033
C. **Working Capital [A + B]**	60,000	83,245
D. ***Add:*** **Safety Margin**	15,000	20,811
E. **Net Working Capital (including Safety Margin) [C + D]**	75,000	1,04,056

Working Notes:

(I) CALCULATION OF EQUIVALENT PRODUCTION UNITS

Particulars	Current Year		Next Year	
	Material (100%)	*Labour & Var. Oh. (50%)*	*Material (100%)*	*Labour & Var. Oh. (50%)*
A. Actual production	36,000	36,000	48,000	48,000
B. *Add:* Closing WIP	3,000	1,500	4,000	2,000
C. *Less:* Opening WIP	—	—	(3,000)	(1,500)
	39,000	37,500	49,000	48,500

(II) STOCK OF WORK-IN-PROGRESS [3,000 UNITS I.E. 36,000/12]

Particulars	*Current Year*	*Next Year*
Raw-material	100% × 3,000 × ₹ 4 = ₹ 12,000	100% × 4,000 × ₹ 4 = ₹ 16,000
Wages	50% × 3,000 × ₹ 2 = ₹ 3,000	50% × 4,000 × ₹ 2 = ₹ 4,000
Variable Overheads	50% × 3,000 × ₹ 2 = ₹ 3,000	50% × 4,000 × ₹ 2 = ₹ 4,000
Fixed Overheads	50% × 3,000 × ₹ 0.96 = ₹ 1,440	50% × 4,000 × ₹ 0.74 = ₹ 1,480
Total	= 19,440	= ₹ 25,480

(III) CALCULATION OF CASH COST OF GOODS PRODUCED AND CASH COST OF CREDIT SALES

Particulars	*Current Year*	*Next Year*
A. Raw-material Consumed @ 4	1,56,000 [(36,000 + 3,000) × ₹ 4]	1,96,000 [49,000 × ₹ 4]
B. Wages @ ₹ 2	75,000 [(37,500 × ₹ 2)]	97,000 [48,500 × ₹ 2]
C. Variable Overheads @ ₹ 2	75,000 (37,500 × ₹ 2]	97,000 [48,500 × ₹ 2]
D. Fixed Overheads	36,000	36,000
E. Gross Factory Cost [A + B + C + D]	3,42,000	4,26,000
F. Adjustment for WIP		
Add: Opening WIP	—	19,440
Less: Closing WIP	(19,440)	(25,480)
G. Cash Cost of Goods Produced	3,22,560	4,19,960
H. Adjustment for Finished Stocks		
Add: Opening Stock of Finished Goods	—	26,880
Less: Closing Stock of Finished Goods	(26,880)	(34,997)
I. Cash Cost of Goods Sold	2,95,680	4,11,843
J. Cash Cost of Credit Sales (80%)	2,36,544	3,29,474

(iv) Stock of Raw-Material **Current Year** **Next Year**

$$= \frac{₹\,1{,}56{,}000}{12\text{ months}} \times 1\text{ month} = ₹\,13{,}000 \qquad \frac{₹\,1{,}96{,}000}{12\text{ months}} \times 1\text{ month} = ₹\,16{,}333$$

(V) STOCK OF FINISHED GOODS

Cash Cost of Goods Produced × $\frac{1 \text{ month}}{12 \text{ months}}$	₹ 3,22,560 × $\frac{1 \text{ month}}{12 \text{ months}}$ = ₹ 26,880	4,19,960 × $\frac{1 \text{ month}}{12 \text{ months}}$ = ₹ 34,997

(VI) DEBTORS

Cash Cost of Credit Sales × $\frac{2 \text{ months}}{12 \text{ months}}$	₹ 2,36,544 × $\frac{2 \text{ months}}{12 \text{ months}}$ = ₹ 39,424	₹3,29,474 × $\frac{2 \text{ months}}{12 \text{ months}}$ = ₹ 54,912

(VII) CREDIT PURCHASES OF RAW MATERIALS

Particulars	*Current Year*	*Next Year*
Raw-material Consumed	₹ 1,56,000	₹ 1,96,000
Add: Closing Stock	₹ 13,000	₹ 16,333
Less: Opening Stock	—	(₹ 13,000)
Raw-material Purchases	₹ 1,69,000	₹ 1,99,333
Credit Purchases (80%)	₹ 1,35,200	₹ 1,59,466

(viii) Creditors for Raw-material	$\frac{₹ 1,35,200}{12 \text{ months}} \times 3 \text{ months}$ = ₹ 33,800	$\frac{₹ 1,59,466}{12 \text{ months}} \times 3 \text{ months}$ = ₹ 39,867
(ix) Creditors for Wages	$\frac{₹ 75,000}{12 \text{ months}} \times 1 \text{ month}$ = ₹ 6,250	$\frac{₹ 1,59,466}{12 \text{ months}} \times 3 \text{ months}$ = ₹ 8,083
(x) Creditors of Variable Overheads	$\frac{₹ 75,000}{12 \text{ months}} \times 1 \text{ month}$ = ₹ 6,250	$\frac{₹ 97,000}{12 \text{ months}} \times 1 \text{ month}$ = ₹ 8,083
(xi) Creditors for Fixed Overheads	$\frac{₹ 36,000}{12 \text{ months}} \times 1 \text{ month}$ = ₹ 3,000	$\frac{₹ 36,000}{12 \text{ months}} \times 1 \text{ month}$ = ₹ 3,000

PROBLEM 11

Tulsian Ltd. has investigated the profitability of its assets and the cost of its funds. The results indicate:

Current Assets earn:	5%
Fixed Assets earn:	15%
Current Liabilities cost:	2%
Average Cost of Long-term Funds:	12%

The current Balance Sheet is as follows:

Liabilities	₹	*Assets*	₹
Current Liabilities	2,00,000	Current Assets	4,00,000

Long-term Funds	10,00,000	Fixed Assets	8,00,000
	12,00,000		12,00,000

Required:

(a) Calculate the net profitability of Current financial plan.

(b) The company is contemplating lowering its net working capital by (i) shifting ₹ 1,00,000 of current assets into fixed assets, *or* (ii) shifting ₹ 1,00,000 of its long-term funds into current liabilities, (iii) Shifting ₹ 1,00,000 of current assets into fixed assets and ₹ 50,000 of its long-term funds into current liabilities.

Work out the profitability of each of these alternatives. Which do you prefer ? Why ?

(c) Calculate Current Ratio and Current Assets to Fixed Assets Ratio in all plans.

SOLUTION

STATEMENT SHOWING THE PROFITABILITY OF VARIOUS FINANCIAL PLANS

Particulars	*Proposed Plans*			
	Current Plan	*Plan (i)*	*Plan (ii)*	*Plan (iii)*
A. Fixed Assets	8,00,000	9,00,000	8,00,000	9,00,000
B. Current Assets	4,00,000	3,00,000	4,00,000	3,00,000
C. Current Liabilities	2,00,000	2,00,000	3,00,000	2,50,000
D. Long-term Funds	10,00,000	10,00,000	9,00,000	9,50,000
E. Working Capital (B – C)	2,00,000	1,00,000	1,00,000	50,000
F. Profit on Fixed Assets	1,20,000	1,35,000	1,20,000	1,35,000
G. Profit on Current Assets	20,000	15,000	20,000	15,000
H. Total Profit on Assets (F + G)	1,40,000	1,50,000	1,40,000	1,50,000
I. Cost of Long-term funds	1,20,000	1,20,000	1,08,000	1,14,000
J. Cost of Short-term Funds	4,000	4,000	6,000	5,000
K. Total Cost of Financing (I + J)	1,24,000	1,24,000	1,14,000	1,19,000
L. Net Profit (H – K)	16,000	26,000	26,000	31,000
M. Current Ratio (B/C)	2	1.5	1.33	1.2
N. Current Assets to Fixed Assets (B/A)	0.5	0.33	0.5	0.33

Recommendation: Plan (iii) may be adopted because the profitability is highest under this plan but the risk has increased to the extent of decline in working capital from ₹ 2,00,000 to ₹ 50,000.

8 WORKING CAPITAL MANAGEMENT—RECEIVABLES MANAGEMENT

LEARNING OBJECTIVES

After studying this chapter, you should be able to understand:

- What is Receivable Management?
- What is the Objective of Receivable Management?
- What are Receivables?
- Why do firms grant credit?
- What is Credit Policy?
- What is the Goal of Credit Policy?
- What is Optimum Credit Policy?
- What are the major factors on which the firm's investment in Accounts receivables depend?
- Distinction between Credit Period and Average Collection Period
- Opportunity Cost of Investment in Receivables
- Practical Steps involved in Evaluation of investment in accounts receivables according to Total Approach
- Practical Steps Involved in Evaluation of investment in Accounts receivables according to Incremental Approach
- Factoring
- Methods of Monitoring Receivables
- Decision Tree analysis of credit granted

1.0 WHAT IS RECEIVABLE MANAGEMENT?

Receivable Management means planning, organising, directing and controlling of Receivables. It provides an answer to the following basic questions:

1.	**To whom credit should be allowed**	It involves an identification of customers, to whom the goods can be sold on credit after carrying out credit analysis.
2.	**How much credit period should be allowed?**	It involves the determination of Credit Period within which the customers are required to pay.
3.	**How much amount of Credit should be allowed?**	It involves the determination of amount upto which the credit can be granted to the customers.

2.0 WHAT IS THE OBJECTIVE OF RECEIVABLE MANAGEMENT?

The objective of Receivable Management is to avoid the situation of excessive and inadequate receivables and to determine and maintain optimum level of receivables after achieving a trade off between the profitability and liquidity so as to maximize the wealth of shareholders as a whole. Whenever the situation of excessive and inadequate receivables arises, prompt and timely action should be taken by management to correct imbalances. Then optimum level of receivable will lie between the two danger points of excessive and inadequate receivables. The consequences of excessive and inadequate receivables are:

Consequences of Excessive Receivables	*Consequences of Inadequate Receivables*
1. High Opportunity Cost of Investment in Receivables	1. Decrease in Sales
2. High Risk of Bad debts	2. Risk of loosing Market Share
3. High Credit Administration Cost	
4. High Risk of Liquidity	

3.0 WHAT ARE RECEIVABLES?

Receivables (also known as Book Debts) represent the amount to be collected from the customers to whom the goods *or* services have been sold on credit.

Customers from whom receivables *or* book debts have to be collected in near future are called trade debtors. Investment in Debtors represents the funds blocked for the period beginning from the date of sale and ending with the date of payment.

4.0 WHY DO FIRMS GRANT CREDIT?

The firms grant credit to retain old customers and to create new customers. In other words, the firms grant credit to maintain the existing market share and to increase their market share, which may pass on to their competitors otherwise.

5.0 WHAT IS CREDIT POLICY?

Credit Policy refers to the combination of following three decision variables:

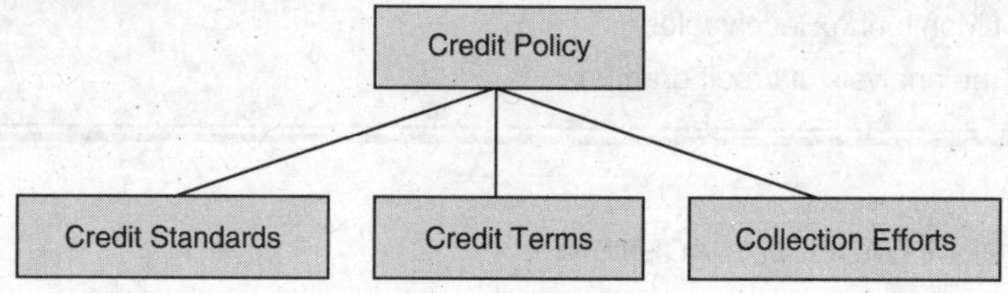

CREDIT STANDARDS

Credit standards are criteria to decide to whom credit sales can be made and to what extent. The firm may have soft standards *or* tight standards.

Type of Standard	*Effect on Sales*	*Effect on Bad Debt*	*Effect on Credit Administration Cost*
Soft Standards	Increase in Sales	Increase in bad debt	Increase in Credit administration Cost
Tight Standards	Decrease in Sales	Decrease in bad debt	Decrease in Credit administration Cost

To prepare the various categories of customers, credit analysis should be carried out. Under credit analysis, the following two factors should be considered:

(a) Average Collection Period, which means the time taken by customers to repay the credit obligation.

(b) Default Risk, which is the likelihood that a customer will not meet his obligation. Default risk is usually measured in terms of bad debt losses ratio. To determine the default risk, the credit manager should consider the following three factors:

(i) Character, which refers to the customer's willingness to pay.

(ii) Capacity, which refers to the customer's ability to pay.

(iii) Condition, which refers to economic conditions, which may affect the customer's ability to pay.

After credit analysis, the customers may be classified in various categories such as follows:

Category of Customers	*Average Collection Period*	*Default Risk*
Good	Within credit period	0
Marginal	Moderate Collection Period	Moderate
Bad	Very Large Collection Period	High

CREDIT TERMS

Credit terms refer to the stipulations under which the firm sells goods on credit to the customers. These include (a) credit period and (b) cash discount.

(a) Credit Period refers to the length of time for which credit is granted to the customer. It is usually stated in terms of net days. ***For Example***, If credit terms are "net 60", it means customers are required to pay within 60 days.

(b) A Cash Discount is a reduction in payment offered to customers to induce them to pay within a specified period of time, which will be *less* than the normal credit period. It is usually expressed as percentage of sales. Cash discount terms specify the rate of discount and the period for which it is available. If a customer wants to avail cash discount, he must make the payment in specific credit period otherwise he may make the payment within normal credit period. ***For Example***: Credit terms of "2/20 net 60" implies 2 % cash discount if payment is made within 20 days and no cash discount, if payment is made within 60 days.

CREDIT TERMS MAY BE SOFT *OR* TIGHT

Types of Terms	*Effect on Sales*	*Effect on Investment in Accounts Receivables*	*Effect on Bad Debt*	*Effect on Credit Administration Cost*
Soft Terms	Increase in Sales	Increase in Investment in Accounts receivable.	Increase in bad debt	Increase in Credit Administration Cost
Tight Terms	Decrease in Sales	Decrease in Investment in Accounts receivable.	Decrease in bad debt	Decrease in Credit Administration Cost

COLLECTION EFFORTS

Collection efforts are needed to accelerate collection from slow payers and to reduce bad debt losses. The collection policy should specify the collection procedures clearly. The following procedure is suggested when the customer has not made the payment within the credit period allowed.

(a) Send first reminder in polite wordings.

(b) If customer does not respond, send second reminder in some strong wordings.

(c) If the customer still does not respond, send third reminder in strong wordings and follow up by e-mail, fax, telephone, personal visit etc.

(d) If the customer still fails to make the payment and his financial position appears to be weak, a personal visit should be made with intention to settle the payment with compromise. On the other hand, if the financial position appears to be strong, initiate a legal action.

However individual cases should be dealt with on the merits of each individual case.

6.0 WHAT IS THE GOAL OF CREDIT POLICY?

The goal of credit policy is to maximise shareholders' wealth. It is *neither* the maximisation of sales *nor* minimisation of bad debt losses. If sales maximisation would have been the goal of firm's credit policy, the firm would follow a very lenient credit policy and would sell on credit to everyone. If minimisation of bad debt losses would have been the goal of firm's credit policy, the firm would follow tight credit policy and would not sell on credit to anyone.

7.0 WHAT IS OPTIMUM CREDIT POLICY?

Optimum Credit Policy refers to the policy, which maximises the value of the firm. The value of the firm is maximised when the incremental rate of return (also called the marginal rate of return) is equal to the incremental rate of return required by suppliers of funds (also called the marginal cost of capital) used to finance the investment. The evaluation of investment in accounts receivable may be done by following either the total approach *or* incremental approach.

8.0 WHAT ARE THE MAJOR FACTORS ON WHICH THE FIRM'S INVESTMENT IN ACCOUNTS RECEIVABLES DEPEND?

Following are the major factors on which the firm's investments in accounts receivables depend:

THE VOLUME OF CREDIT SALES

THE COLLECTION PERIOD

How to express Investment in Account Receivable. Firm's investment in Accounts receivable may be expressed in terms of sales revenue *or* cost.

Example: Average Credit Sales is ₹ 10 Lacs per day, Average collection Period is 60 days and Cost of Sales is 80%.

Thus, firm's investment in Accounts receivable *(in terms of sales revenue)*

= Daily Credit Sales × Average Collection Period (in days)

= 10 Lacs × 60 = ₹ 600 Lacs

Thus, firm's investment in Accounts receivable *(in terms of cost)*

= Cost of Daily Credit Sales × Average Collection Period (in days)

= 10 Lacs × 80% × 60 = ₹ 480 Lacs

9.0 DISTINCTION BETWEEN CREDIT PERIOD & AVERAGE COLLECTION PERIOD

CREDIT PERIOD

Credit period refers to the period for which credit is granted to the customers as per firm's credit policy. It is the period within which customers are required to make the payment. It is usually stated in terms of days. Depending upon the availability of Cash Discount, the credit period may be stated as follows:

Case	*Credit Period*
I. Where no Cash Discount is allowed	1. 'net 30' means customers are required to pay within 30 days.
II. Where Cash Discount is allowed	2. "2/10, net 30" means with 2% Cash Discount, make payment within 10 days and without Cash Discount make payment within 30 days.

AVERAGE COLLECTION PERIOD

Average Collection Period refers to the period within which the payment is actually made by the customers. It is the average credit period actually enjoyed by the customers. It may be calculated as follows:

1. Average Collection Period = $\frac{\text{12 Months/365 days}}{\text{Debtors Turnover Ratio}}$ = ... months/days

   where, Debtors Turnover Ratio = $\frac{\text{Net Credit Sales}}{\text{Average Receivables}}$

2. Average Collection Period = $\frac{\text{Average Debtors}}{\text{Average Net Credit Sales per day/month}}$ = ...month/days

3. Average Collection period

   = (Credit Period with Cash Discount × % of Customers availing Cash Discount) + (Credit period without Cash Discount × % of Customers not availing Cash Discount)

ILLUSTRATION 1 [CALCULATION OF AVERAGE COLLECTION PERIOD]

Calculate Average Collection Period in each of the following alternative cases: *(assume 360 days in year)*

Case (a) Debtors Turnover Ratio 6

Case (b) Current Level of Receivables ₹ 60 Crore, Current Annual Credit Sales ₹ 600 crores.

Case (c) Average Level of Receivables ₹ 1,00,000, Average Net Credit Sales per day ₹ 2,500.

Case (d) Credit Terms are 2/10, Net 30. 25% of the credit customers avail cash discount facility.

SOLUTION

Case (a) Average Collection Period = $\frac{\text{12 Months/360 Days}}{\text{Debtors Turnover Ratio}} = \frac{12}{6}$ = 2 Months

or = 60 Days

Case (b) Debtors Turnover Ratio = $\frac{\text{Net Credit Sales}}{\text{Average Receivables}} = \frac{\text{₹ 600 Crores}}{\text{₹ 60 Crores}}$ = 10

Average Collection Period = $\frac{\text{360 days}}{\text{Debtors Turnover Ratio}} = \frac{360}{10}$ = 36 days

Case (c) Average Collection Period = $\frac{\text{Average Receivables}}{\text{Average Net Credit Sales per day}}$

= ₹ 1,00,000/₹ 2,500 = 40 days

Case (d) Average Collection Period = (Cash Discount Period × % of Customers availing Cash Discount) + (Net Credit period × % of customers not availing Cash Discount)

= (10 days × 25%) + (30 days × 75%)

= 2.5 Days + 22.5 Days = 25 Days

10.0 OPPORTUNITY COST OF INVESTMENT IN RECEIVABLES

MEANING

Opportunity Cost of Investment in Receivables is the return foregone on funds blocked in receivables, which could have been earned if such funds would have been invested elsewhere.

USEFULNESS

It is useful in evaluating various debtors policies and in determining the optimal debtors policy.

HOW TO CALCULATE

It is calculated as follows:

$$\text{Opportunity Cost} = \text{Cost of Credit Sales} \times \frac{\text{Collection Period (days)}}{365 \text{ days}} \times \text{Required Rate of Return}$$

Note: The effect of Bad Debts and Cash Discount is to reduce the expected profit and not to increase the cost and hence Bad Debts and Cash Discount do not form part of total cost while calculating Opportunity Cost of Investment locked up in Receivables for collection period.

ILLUSTRATION 2 [CALCULATION OF OPPORTUNITY COST OF INVESTMENT IN RECEIVABLES]

Calculate the Opportunity Cost of Investment in Receivable in each of the following alternative cases (assume 360 days in a year)

Case (a) Total Sales ₹ 62,50,000, Cash Sales 20% of Total Sales, Variable Cost 85% of Sales, Fixed Cost ₹ 3,12,500, Bad Debts 5%, Average Collection Period 90 days, Required Rate of Return 12%

Case (b) Total Sales ₹ 125 lakhs, Cash Sales 25% of Credit Sales, Variable Cost 85% of Sales, Bad Debts 5%, Selling Price per unit ₹ 500, Average Cost per unit ₹ 450, Debtors Turnover Ratio 4, Required Rate of Return 12%

Case (c) Total Sales ₹ 125 lakhs, Credit Sales being four times the cash sales, Variable Cost 85% of Sales, Bad Debt 5%, Selling Price per unit ₹ 500, Average Cost per unit ₹ 450, Credit Terms are 3/24, Net 40, 25% of the credit customers avail Cash Discount facility, Required Rate of Return (after tax) 12%, Tax Rate 40%

SOLUTION

Case (a)

Step 1: Credit Sales = Total Sales – Cash Sales

= ₹ 62,50,000 – 20% of ₹ 62,50,000 = ₹ 50,00,000

Step 2: Cost of Credit Sales = 85% of ₹ 50,00,000 + 80% of ₹ 3,12,500 = ₹ 45,00,000

Step 3: Opportunity Cost of Investment in Receivables

$$= \text{Total Cost of Credit Sales} \times \frac{\text{Collection Period (days)}}{360 \text{ days}} \times \text{Required Rate of Return}$$

$$= ₹\ 45,00,000 \times \frac{90}{360} \times \frac{12}{100} = ₹\ 1,35,000$$

Case (b)

Step 1: $\text{No of units sold} = \frac{\text{Total Sales}}{\text{Selling Price per unit}} = \frac{₹\ 1,25,00,000}{₹\ 500} = 25,000 \text{ units}$

Step 2: Total Cost of Sales = Average Cost Per unit × No. of Units Sold

= ₹ 450 × 25,000 units = ₹ 1,12,50,000

Step 3: Total Cost of Credit Sales = ₹ 1,12,50,000 × 80% = ₹ 90,00,000

Step 4: Opportunity Cost of Investment in Receivables

$$= \text{Total Cost of Credit Sales} \times \frac{\text{Collection Period (days)}}{\text{360 days}} \times \text{Required Rate of Return}$$

= ₹ 90,00,000 × 90/360 × 12/100 = ₹ 2,70,000

Case (c)

Step 1: No of units sold = $\frac{\text{Total Sales}}{\text{Selling Price per unit}} = \frac{₹\ 1,25,00,000}{₹\ 500}$ = 25,000 units

Step 2: Total Cost of Sales = Average Cost Per unit No. of Units Sold

= ₹ 450 × 25,000 units = ₹ 1,12,50,000

Step 3: Total Cost of Credit Sales = ₹ 1,12,50,000 × 80% = ₹ 90,00,000

Step 4: Average Collection Period = (Cash Discount Period × % of Customers availing Cash Discount) + (Net Credit period × % Customers not availing Cash Discount)

= (24 days × 25%) + (40 days × 75%) = 36 days

Step 5: Opportunity Cost of Investment in Receivables

$$= \text{Total Cost of Credit Sales} \times \frac{\text{Collection Period (days)}}{\text{360 days}} \times \text{Required Rate of Return}$$

= ₹ 90,00,000 × 36/360 × 12/100 = ₹ 1,08,000

Note: The effect of Bad Debts and Cash Discount is to reduce the expected profit and not to increase the cost and hence Bad Debts and Cash Discount do not form part of total cost while calculating Opportunity Cost of Investment locked up in Receivables for collection period.

11.0 PRACTICAL STEPS INVOLVED IN EVALUATION OF INVESTMENT IN ACCOUNTS RECEIVABLES ACCORDING TO TOTAL APPROACH

Evaluation of Investment in Accounts Receivable according to Total Approach involves the following steps:

Step 1: Estimate Credit Sales

Step 2: Estimate Cost of Credit Sales (both Variable and Fixed)

Step 3: Estimate Bad Debt losses and Cash Discount

Step 4: Estimate **Expected Profit** (i.e. Credit Sales – Costs – Bad Debts – Cash Discount) associated with the credit policy

Step 5: Estimate Tax on Expected Profit

Step 6: Estimate **Expected Profit after Tax**

Step 7: Estimate Investment in Accounts Receivables locked up for collection period

= Cost of Annual Credit Sales × Average Collection period (in Days) / 365

Step 8: Estimate **Opportunity Cost** of Investment in Accounts Receivables

= Investment in accounts receivables in terms of cost × Required Rate of Return

Step 9: Estimate **Net Benefits** associated with the credit policy

Net Benefits = Step 6 – Step 8

Step 10: Recommendation: The credit policy having largest positive net benefits should be adopted.

Note: The effect of bad debts is to reduce the expected profit and not to increase the cost and hence bad debts do not form part of total cost while calculating Opportunity Cost of Investment locked up in Receivables for collection period.

STATEMENT SHOWING THE EVALUATION OF DEBTORS POLICIES

Particulars	Present Policy ₹	Proposed Policy I ₹	Proposed Policy II ₹	Proposed Policy III ₹
A. Expected Profit:				
(a) Credit Sales	......	......	......	......
(b) Total Cost other than Bad Debts & Cash Discount				
(i) Variable Costs	......	......	......	......
(ii) Fixed Costs	......	......	......	......
	......	......	......	......
(c) Bad Debts	......	......	......	......
(d) Cash Discount	......	......	......	......
(e) Expected Net Profit before Tax [(a) – (b) – (c) – (d)]	......	......	......	......
(f) *Less:* Tax	......	......	......	......
(g) Expected Profit after Tax	......	......	......	......
	......	......	......	......
B. Opportunity Cost of Invst. in Receivables locked up in Collection Period	......	......	......	......
C. Net Benefits (A – B)	......	......	......	......
D. Recommendation: The Policy...should be adopted since the net benefits under this policy are larger than those under other policies.				

Working Notes:

(i) Total Fixed Cost = [Average Cost per unit – Variable Cost per unit] × No. of units sold on credit under present Policy

(ii) Opportunity Cost =

$$\text{Total Cost of Credit Sales} \times \frac{\text{Collection Period (Days)}}{365} \times \frac{\text{Required Rate of Return}}{100}$$

12.0 PRACTICAL STEPS INVOLVED IN EVALUATION OF INVESTMENT IN ACCOUNTS RECEIVABLES ACCORDING TO INCREMENTAL APPROACH

Evaluation of Investment in Accounts Receivable according to Incremental Approach involves the following steps:

Step 1: Estimate Incremental Credit Sales.

Step 2: Estimate Incremental Cost of Credit Sales

Step 3: Estimate Incremental Bad Debt losses and Cash Discount

Step 4: Estimate **Incremental Expected Profit** associated with the credit policy as follows.

Incremental Expected Profit = Step 1 – Step 2 – Step 3

Step 5: Estimate Tax on Incremental Expected Profit

Step 6: Estimate **Incremental Expected Profit before Tax**

Step 7: Estimated Incremental Investment in Accounts Receivables locked up for Collection Period = Cost of Incremental Credit Sales × Average Collection Period (in Days)/365

Step 8: Estimate **Required Return on Incremental Investment** in Accounts Receivable

= Incremental Investment in Account Receivables in terms of cost × Required Rate of Return.

Step 9: Estimate **Incremental Net Benefits** associated with the credit policy

Incremental Net Benefits = Step 6 – Step 8

Step 10: Recommendation: The credit policy having largest positive net benefits should be adopted.

Note: The effect of bad debts is to reduce the expected profit and not to increase the cost and hence bad debts do not form part of total cost while calculating Opportunity Cost of Investment locked up in Receivables for collection period.

INCREMENTAL APPROACH

STATEMENT SHOWING THE EVALUATION OF DEBTORS POLICIES

Particulars	*Present Policy Days* ₹	*Proposed Policy I Days* ₹	*Proposed Policy II Days* ₹	*Proposed Policy III Days* ₹
A. Incremental Expected Profit:				
Credit Sales	....	....	....	....
(a) Incremental Credit Sales	....	....	....	....
(b) Incremental Cost of Credit Sales				
(i) Variable Costs	....	....	....	....
(ii) Fixed Costs	....	....	....	....
	....	....	....	....
(c) Incremental Bad Debt Losses	....	....	....	....
(d) Incremental Cash Discount	....	....	....	....
(e) Incremental Expected Profit (a – b – c – d)	....	....	....	....
(f) *Less:* Tax	....	....	....	....
(g) Incremental Expected Profit after Tax	....	....	....	....
B. Required Return on Incremental Investments:				
(a) Cost of Credit Sales	....	....	....	....
(b) Collection Period (in days)	....	....	....	....
(c) Investment in Receivables (a × b /365)	....	....	....	....
(d) Incremental Investment in Receivables	....	....	....	....
(e) Required Rate of Return (in %)	....	....	....	....
(f) Required Return on Incremental Investment (d × e)	....	....	....	....
C. Incremental Net Benefits (A – B)	....	....	....	....
D. Recommendation: The Policy .... should be adopted since net benefits under this policy are larger than those under other policies.				

Working Notes:

(i) Total Fixed Cost = [Average Cost per unit – Variable Cost per unit] × No. of units sold on credit under present Policy

(ii) Opportunity Cost

$$= \text{Total Cost of Credit Sales} \times \frac{\text{Collection Period (Days)}}{365} \times \frac{\text{Required Rate of Return}}{100}$$

ALTERNATIVE INCREMENTAL APPROACH

Alternative Incremental Approach involves the following practical steps:

Step 1: Estimate the Incremental Expected Profit associated with the credit policy

Step 2: Estimate the Incremental Investment in Accounts Receivables

Step 3: Estimate the Expected Rate of Return as follows:

$$\text{Expected Rate of Return} = \frac{\text{Incremental Expected Profit}}{\text{Incremental Investment in Accounts Receivables}} \times 100$$

Recommendation: The credit policy having the highest Expected Rate of Return exceeding Minimum Required Rate of Return should be adopted.

ILLUSTRATION 3

Tulsian Ltd. provides you the following information in respect of its present debtors policy and proposed debtors policies:

Particulars	*Present Policy*	*Proposed Policy I*	*Proposed Policy II*
Average Collection period	90 days	45 days	135 days
Credit Sales	₹ 25 lakh	₹ 15 lakh	₹ 75 lakh
Required Rate of Return (Pre-tax)	20%	20%	20%
Bad Debts (%)	5%	2.5%	10%
Selling Price per Unit	₹ 500	₹ 500	₹ 500
Variable Cost per unit (% of Sales)	85%	85%	85%
Average Cost per unit	₹ 450		

Required: Suggest which policy is the best ? (Assume 360 days in a year)

SOLUTION

STATEMENT SHOWING THE EVALUATION OF DEBTORS POLICIES (TOTAL APPROACH)

Particulars	*Present Policy 90 days* ₹	*Proposed Policy I 45 days* ₹	*Proposed Policy II 135 days* ₹
A. Expected Profit:			
(a) Credit Sales	25,00,000	15,00,000	75,00,000
(b) Total Costs other than Bad Debts			
(i) Variable Costs	21,25,000	12,75,000	63,75,000
(ii) Fixed Costs	1,25,000	1,25,000	1,25,000
	22,50,000	14,00,000	65,00,000
(c) Bad Debts	1,25,000	37,500	7,50,000
(d) Expected Profit [(a) – (b) – (c)]	1,25,000	62,500	2,50,000

B. Opportunity Cost of Investments in Receivables	1,12,500	35,000	4,87,500
C. Net Benefits (A – B)	12,500	27,500	(2,37,500)

Recommendation: The Proposed Policy I should be adopted since the net benefits under this policy are higher than those under other policies.

Working Notes:

(i) Fixed Cost = [Average Cost per unit – Variable Cost per Unit] × No. of Units sold

= [₹ 450 – (85% of ₹ 500)] × (₹ 25,00,000/500) = ₹ 25 × 5000 = ₹ 1,25,000

(ii) Calculation of Opportunity Cost of Average Investments locked in collection period

$$\text{Opportunity Cost} = \text{Total Cost} \times \frac{\text{Collection Period}}{360} \times \frac{\text{Required Rate of Return}}{100}$$

Present Policy = ₹ 22,50,000 × 90/360 × 20% = ₹ 1,12,500

Proposed Policy I = ₹ 14,00,000 × 45/360 × 20% = ₹ 35,000

Proposed Policy II = ₹ 65,00,000 × 135/360 × 20% = ₹ 4,87,500

STATEMENT SHOWING THE EVALUATION OF DEBTORS POLICIES (INCREMENTAL APPROACH)

Particulars	*Present Policy 90 days*	*Proposed Policy I 45 days*	*Proposed Policy II 135 days*
A. Incremental Expected Profit:			
Credit Sales	25,00,000	15,00,000	75,00,000
(a) Incremental Credit Sales		(10,00,000)	50,00,000
(b) Incremental Cost of Credit Sales			
(i) Variable Costs	21,25,000	(8,50,000)	42,50,000
(ii) Fixed Costs	1,25,000		
(c) Incremental Bad Debt Losses	1,25,000	(87,500)	6,25,000
(d) Incremental Expected Profit (a – b – c)	1,25,000	(62,500)	1,25,000
B. Required Return on Incremental Investments:			
(a) Cost of Credit Sales	22,50,000	14,00,000	65,00,000
(b) Collection Period	90	45	135
(c) Investment in Receivable (a × b/360)	5,62,500	1,75,000	24,37,500
(d) Incremental Investment in Receivables	—	(3,87,500)	18,75,000
(e) Required Rate of Return (in %)	20	20	20
(f) Required Return of Incremental Invsts (d × e)	—	(77,500)	3,75,000
C. Net Benefits (A – B)	—	15,000	(2,50,000)

Recommendation: The Proposed Policy I should be adopted since the net profits under this policy are higher than those under other policies.

Working Note: *Calculation of Fixed Cost*

Fixed Cost = [Average Cost per unit – Variable Cost per Unit] × No. of Units sold

= [₹ 450 – (85% of ₹ 500)] × (₹ 25,00,000/500) = ₹ 25 × 5000 = ₹ 1,25,000

ILLUSTRATION 4

Suggest which policy is the best in Illustration 3 if Tax Rate is 40% and the Required Rate of Return (after tax) is 12%.

SOLUTION

STATEMENT SHOWING THE EVALUATION OF DEBTORS POLICIES (TOTAL APPROACH)

Particulars	*Present Policy 90 days* ₹	*Proposed Policy I 45 days* ₹	*Proposed Policy II 135 days* ₹
A. Expected Profit:			
(a) Credit Sales	25,00,000	15,00,000	75,00,000
(b) Total Cost other than Bad Debts			
(i) Variable Costs	21,25,000	12,75,000	63,75,000
(ii) Fixed Costs	1,25,000	1,25,000	1,25,000
	22,50,000	14,00,000	65,00,000
(c) Bad Debts	1,25,000	37,500	7,50,000
(d) Expected Profit Before Tax [(a) – (b) – (c)]	1,25,000	62,500	2,50,000
(e) *Less:* Tax @ 40%	50,000	25,000	1,00,000
(f) Expected Profit after Tax	75,000	37,500	1,50,000
B. Opportunity Cost of Investments in Receivables	67,500	21,000	2,92,500
C. Net Benefits (A – B)	7,500	16,500	(1,42,500)

Recommendation: The Proposed Policy I should be adopted since the net profits under this policy are higher than those under other policies.

Working Notes:

(i) Fixed Cost = [Average Cost per unit – Variable Cost per Unit] × No. of Units sold
= [₹ 450 – (85% of ₹ 500)] × (₹ 25,00,000/500) = ₹ 25 × 5000 = ₹ 1,25,000

(ii) Calculation of Opportunity Cost of Average Investments locked in collection period

$$\text{Opportunity Cost} = \text{Total Cost} \times \frac{\text{Collection Period}}{360} \times \frac{\text{Required Rate of Return}}{100}$$

Present Policy = ₹ 22,50,000 × 90/360 × 12% = ₹ 67,500

Proposed Policy I = ₹ 14,00,000 × 45/360 × 12% = ₹ 21,000

Proposed Policy II = ₹ 65,00,000 × 135/360 × 12% = ₹ 2,92,500

STATEMENT SHOWING THE EVALUATION OF DEBTORS POLICIES (INCREMENTAL APPROACH)

Particulars	*Present Policy 90 days*	*Proposed Policy I 45 days*	*Proposed Policy II 135 days*
A. Incremental Expected Profit:			
Credit Sales	25,00,000	15,00,000	75,00,000
(a) Incremental Credit Sales		(10,00,000)	50,00,000

(b) Incremental Cost of Credit Sales			
(i) Variable Costs	21,25,000	(8,50,000)	42,50,000
(ii) Fixed Costs	1,25,000		
(c) Incremental Bad Debt Losses	1,25,000	(87,500)	6,25,000
(d) Incremental Expected Profit before tax (a – b – c)	1,25,000	(62,500)	1,25,000
(e) *Less:* Tax @ 40%	50,000	(25,000)	50,000
(f) Incremental Expected Profit after Tax	75,000	(37,500)	75,000
B. Required Return on Incremental Investments:			
(a) Cost of Credit Sales	22,50,000	14,00,000	65,00,000
(b) Collection Period	90	45	135
(c) Investment in Receivable (a × b/360)	5,62,500	1,75,000	24,37,500
(d) Incremental Investment in Receivables	—	(3,87,500)	18,75,000
(e) Required Rate of Return (in %)	12%	12%	12%
(f) Required Return on Incremental Invsts. (d × e)	—	(46,500)	2,25,000
C. Net Benefits (A – B)	—	9,000	(1,50,000)

Recommendation: The Proposed Policy I should be adopted since the net profits under this policy are higher than those under other policies.

ILLUSTRATION 5

A trader whose current sales are ₹ 6 lakhs p.a. and an average collection period of 30 days wants to pursue a more liberal policy to improve sales. A study made by a management consultant reveals the following information:

Credit Policy	*Increase In Collection Period*	*Increase In Sales*	*Present default anticipated*
A	10 days	₹ 30,000	1.50%
B	20 days	₹ 48,000	2.00%
C	30 days	₹ 75,000	3.00%
D	45 days	₹ 90,000	4.00%

The selling price per unit is ₹ 3 Average cost per unit is ₹ 2.25 & the variable cost per unit ₹ 2. The current bad debt loss is 1%. Required return on additional investment is 20%. Assume as 360 days year.

Required: Which of the above policies would you recommend for adoption?

SOLUTION

STATEMENT SHOWING THE EVALUATION OF DEBTORS POLICIES (TOTAL APPROACH)

Particulars	*Present Policy 30 days* ₹	*Proposed Policy A 40 days* ₹	*Proposed Policy B 50 days* ₹	*Proposed Policy C 60 days* ₹	*Proposed Policy D 75 days* ₹
A. Expected Profit:					
(a) Credit Sales	6,00,000	6,30,000	6,48,000	6,75,000	6,90,000

(b) Total Cost other than Bad Debts					
(i) Variable Costs [Sales ₹ 2/₹ 3]	4,00,000	4,20,000	4,32,000	4,50,000	4,60,000
(ii) Fixed Costs	50,000	50,000	50,000	50,000	50,000
	4,50,000	4,70,000	4,82,000	5,00,000	5,10,000
(c) Bad Debts	6,000	9,450	12,960	20,250	27,600
(d) Expected Profit [(a) – (b) – (c)]	1,44,000	1,50,550	1,53,040	1,54,750	1,52,400
B. Opportunity Cost of Investments in Receivables	7,500	10,444	13,389	16,667	21,250
C. Net Benefits (A – B)	1,36,500	1,40,106	1,39,651	1,38,083	1,31,150

Recommendation: The Proposed Policy A should be adopted since the net benefits under this policy are higher than those under other policies.

Working Notes:

(i) Fixed Cost = [Average Cost per unit – Variable Cost per unit] × No. of Units sold
= [₹ 2.25 – ₹ 2.00] × (₹ 6,00,000/3) = ₹ 0.25 × 2,00,000 = ₹ 50,000

(ii) Calculation of Opportunity Cost of Average Investments locked in Collection period

$$\text{Opportunity Cost} = \text{Total Cost} \times \frac{\text{Collection period}}{360} \times \frac{\text{Rate of Return}}{100}$$

A. Total Cost	4,50,000	4,70,000	4,82,000	5,00,000	5,10,000
B. Collection period	30/360	40/360	50/360	60/360	75/360
C. Required Rate of Return	20%	20%	20%	20%	20%
D. Opportunity Cost (A × B × C)	7,500	10,444	13,389	16,667	21,250

(iii) **Assumption:** Given sales are all credit sales.

EVALUATION OF DEBTORS POLICIES (INCREMENTAL APPROACH)

Particulars	*Present Policy 30 days* ₹	*Proposed Policy A 40 days* ₹	*Proposed Policy B 50 days* ₹	*Proposed Policy C 60 days* ₹	*Proposed Policy D 75 days* ₹
A. Incremental Expected Profit:					
(a) Incremental Credit Sales		30,000	48,000	75,000	90,000
(b) Incremental Costs					
(i) Variable Costs	4,00,000	20,000	32,000	50,000	60,000
(ii) Fixed Costs	50,000	—	—	—	—
(c) Incremental Bad Debt Losses	6,000	3,450	6,960	14,250	21,600
(d) Incremental Expected profit (a – b – c)		6,550	9,040	10,750	8,400
B. Required return on Incremental Investments:					
(a) Cost of Credit Sales	4,50,000	4,70,000	4,82,000	5,00,000	5,10,000

(b) Collection period	30	40	50	60	75
(c) Investment in Receivable (a x b/360)	37,500	52,222	66,944	83,333	1,06,250
(d) Incremental Investment in Receivables	—	14,722	29,444	45,833	68,750
(e) Required Rate of Return (in %)		20	20	20	20
(f) Required Return on Incremental Invsts. (d × e)	—	2,944	5,889	9,167	13,750
C. Net Benefits (A – B)	—	3,606	3,151	1,583	(5,350)

Recommendation: The Proposed Policy A should be adopted since the net benefits under this policy are higher than those under other policies.

Working Notes: Calculation of Fixed Cost

(i) Fixed Cost = [Average Cost per unit – Variable Cost per unit] × No. of Units sold
= [₹ 2.25 – ₹ 2.00] × (₹ 6,00,000/3) = ₹ 0.25 × 2,00,000 = ₹ 50,000

(ii) Calculation of Opportunity Cost of Average Investments locked in Collection period

$$\text{Opportunity Cost} = \text{Total Cost} \times \frac{\text{Collection period}}{360} \times \frac{\text{Rate of Return}}{100}$$

Alternative Approach:

$$\text{Expected Rate of Return} = \frac{\text{Incremental Expected Profit}}{\text{Incremental Investment in Receivables}} \times 100$$

$$\text{For Policy A} = \frac{₹\ 6,550}{₹\ 14,722} \times 100 = 44.49\%$$

$$\text{For Policy B} = \frac{₹\ 9,040}{₹\ 29,444} \times 100 = 30.70\%$$

$$\text{For Policy C} = \frac{₹\ 10,750}{₹\ 45,833} \times 100 = 23.45\%$$

$$\text{For Policy D} = \frac{₹\ 8,400}{₹\ 68,750} \times 100 = 12.22\%$$

Recommendation: The Proposed Policy A should be adopted since the Expected Rate of Return (i.e., 44.49%) is more than the Required Rate of Return (i.e., 20%) and is highest among the given policies.

ILLUSTRATION 6

ABC Company's present annual sales amount to ₹ 30 lakhs at ₹ 12 per unit. Variable cost are ₹ 8 per unit and fixed costs amount to ₹ 2.50 lakhs per annum. Its considering various policies. The following estimates are made for the purpose:

Particulars	*Present Policy*	*Proposed Policy I*	*Proposed Policy II*
Debtor Turnover Ratio	12	6	4
Increase in Sales (%)	—	8	30
% of Bad debt to sales	1	2	6

Fixed costs will increase by ₹ 50,000 annually after any increase in sales above 25% over the present level. The company requires a pre-tax return on investment of at least 20% for the level of risk involved.

Required: What will be the most rewarding credit policy in case of ABC Company under the above circumstances? Present your answer in a tabular form.

SOLUTION

STATEMENT SHOWING THE EVALUATION OF DEBTORS POLICIES

Particulars	*Present Policy 1 month* ₹	*Proposed Policy I 2 month* ₹	*Proposed Policy II 3 month* ₹
A. Expected Profit:			
(a) Credit Sales	30,00,000	32,40,000	39,00,000
(b) Total Cost other than Bad Debts			
(i) Variable Costs	20,00,000	21,60,000	26,00,000
(ii) Fixed Costs	2,50,000	2,50,000	3,00,000
	22,50,000	24,10,000	29,00,000
(c) Bad Debts	30,000	64,800	2,34,000
(d) Expected Profit [(a) – (b) – (c)]	7,20,000	7,65,200	7,66,000
B. Opportunity Cost of Investment in Receivables	37,500	80,333	1,45,000
C. Net Benefits (A – B)	6,82,500	6,84,867	6,21,000

Recommendation: The Proposed Policy 1 should be adopted since the net benefits under this policy are higher than those under other policies.

Working Note: Calculation of Opportunity Cost of Average Investments

$$\text{Opportunity Cost} = \frac{\text{Collection Period}}{12} \times \frac{\text{Required Rate of Return}}{100}$$

Present Policy = ₹ 22,50,000 × 1/12 × 20% = ₹ 37,500

Policy I = ₹ 24,10,000 × 2/12 × 20% = ₹ 80,333

Policy II = ₹ 29,00,000 × 3/12 × 20% = ₹ 1,45,000

ILLUSTRATION 7

STD Ltd. which sales on credit basis has ranked its customers in categories 1 to 5 in order of credit risk:

Category	*Percentage Bad Debts*	*Average Collection Period*
1	0	30 days
2	1	45 days
3	2	60 days
4	5	90 days
5	10	120 days

The company's current credit policy is to allow unlimited credit to firms in categories 1 to 3, limited credit to firm in category 4 and no additional credit to firm in category 5.

As a result, orders amounting to ₹ 25,00,000 from category 4 and ₹ 75,00,000 from category 5 customers are rejected every year. STD Ltd. makes a 10 per cent gross profit on sales and has an opportunity cost in investment in receivable of 12 per cent

Required: What would be the effect on profits of allowing full credit to all categories of customers? Should credit be extended to all categories of customers ? (Assume 360 days in a year)

SOLUTION

STATEMENT SHOWING THE EVALUATION OF DEBTORS POLICIES

Category 5

Particulars	*Category 4* ₹	*Category 5* ₹
A. Expected Profit:		
(a) Credit Sales	25,00,000	75,00,000
(b) Total Cost @ 90% of Sales	22,50,000	67,50,000
(c) Bad Debts	1,25,000	7,50,000
(d) Expected Profit [(a) – (b) – (c)]	1,25,000	0
B. Opportunity Cost of Investments in Receivables	67,500	2,70,000
C. Net Benefits (A – B)	57,500	(2,70,000)

Recommendation: The credit should not be extended to all types of customers, since it would lower the profit by ₹ 2,12,500. Credit should not be extended to category 5.

Working Note: Calculation of Opportunity Cost of Average Investments.

$$\text{Opportunity Cost} = \text{Total Cost} \times \frac{\text{Collection period}}{360} \times \frac{\text{Rate of Return}}{100}$$

Category 4 = 22,50,000 × 90/360 × 12% = 67,500

Category 5 = 67,50,000 × 120/360 × 12% = 2,70,000

ILLUSTRATION 8

The MP Company is planning to relax its credit policy to motivate customers to buy on new credit terms. It is expected that the variable costs will remain 75 per cent of sales. The incremental sales are expected to be sold on credit. For the perceived increase in risk in liberalising the credit terms, the company requires higher required return. If the following is the projected information, which credit policy should the company pursue? (Assume 360 days in a year)

Credit Policy	*Required Return*	*Collection Period*	*New Sales (₹)*
A	20%	40	3,00,000
B	25%	45	4,00,000
C	32%	55	5,00,000
D	40%	70	6,00,000

SOLUTION

STATEMENT SHOWING THE EVALUATION OF DEBTORS POLICIES

Particulars	*Proposed Policy A* ₹	*Proposed Policy B* ₹	*Proposed Policy C* ₹	*Proposed Policy D* ₹
A. Expected Profit:				
(a) Credit Sales	3,00,000	4,00,000	5,00,000	6,00,000

(b) Total Cost				
(i) Variable Costs	2,25,000	3,00,000	3,75,000	4,50,000
(c) Expected Profit [(a) – (b)]	75,000	1,00,000	1,25,000	1,50,000
B. Opportunity Cost of Invst. in Receivables	5,000	9,375	18,333	35,000
C. Net Benefits (A – B)	70,000	90,625	1,06,667	1,15,000

Recommendation: The Proposed Policy D should be adopted since the net benefits under this policy are higher than those under other policies.

Working Note: Calculation of Opportunity Cost of Average Investments

$$\text{Opportunity Cost} = \text{Total Cost} \times \frac{\text{Collection period}}{360} \times \frac{\text{Rate of Return}}{100}$$

Policy A = 2,25,000 × 40/360 × 20% = ₹ 5,000

Policy B = 3,00,000 × 45/360 × 25% = ₹ 9,375

Policy C = 3,75,000 × 55/360 × 32% = ₹ 18,333

Policy D = 4,50,000 × 70/360 × 40% = ₹ 35,000

ILLUSTRATION 9

Slow payers are regular customers of Goods Dealers Ltd., They have approached the seller for extensions of a credit facility. On an analysis of past performance, the following pattern of payment emerges in regard to Slow Payers:

Schedule	*Pattern*
At the end of 30 days	15% of the bill
At the end of 60 days	34% of the bill
At the end of 90 days	30% of the bill
At the end of 100 days	20% of the bill
Non-recovery	1% of the bill

Slow Payers want to enter into a firm commitment for purchases of goods of 15 lakhs, deliveries to be made in equal quantities on the first day of each quarter in the calendar year. The price per unit of commodity is ₹ 150 on which a profit of ₹ 5 per unit is expected to be made. It is anticipated by Goods Dealers Ltd. that taking up of this contract would mean an extra recurring expenditure of ₹ 5,000 per annum. If the opportunity cost of funds in the hands of Goods Dealers is 24% per annum, would you as the finance manager of the seller recommended the grant of credit to slow payers?

SOLUTION

STATEMENT SHOWING THE EVALUATION OF DEBTORS POLICIES

Particulars	*Proposed Policy ₹*
A. Expected Profit:	
(a) Credit Sales:	15,00,000
(b) Total Cost:	
(i) Variable Costs	14,50,000
(ii) Recurring Costs	5,000
	14,55,000
(c) Bad Debts	15,000

(d) Expected Profit [(a) – (b) – (c)]	30,000
B. Opportunity Cost of Investment in Receivables	68,787
C. Net Benefits (A – B)	(38,787)

Recommendation: The Proposed Policy should not be adopted since the net benefits under this policy are not positive

Working Note: Calculation of Opportunity Cost of Average Investments

$$\text{Opportunity Cost} = \text{Total Cost} \times \frac{\text{Collection period}}{360} \times \frac{\text{Rate of Return}}{100}$$

Particulars	*15%*	*34%*	*30%*	*20%*	*Total*
A. Total Cost	2,18,250	4,94,700	4,36,500	2,91,000	14,40,450
B. Collection period	30/365	60/365	90/365	100/365	
C. Required rate of return	24%	24%	24%	24%	
D. Opportunity Cost(A × B × C)	4,305	19,517	25,831	19,134	68,787

ILLUSTRATION 10

CANIB Limited, manufacturers of Colour TV sets, are considering the liberalisation of existing credit terms to three of their large customers A, B, and C. The credit period and likely quantity of TV sets that will be lifted by the customers are as follows:

Credit Period (Days)	*(Quantity Lifted (NO. of TV sets)*		
	A	*B*	*C*
0	1,000	1,000	—
30	1,000	1,500	—
60	1,000	2,000	1,000
90	1,000	2,500	1,500

The selling price per TV set is ₹ 9,000. The expected contribution is 20% of the selling price. The cost of carrying debtors average 20% per annum.

You are *Required:*

(a) To determine the credit period to be allowed to each customer. (Assume 360 days in a year for calculation purposes).

(b) What other problems the company might face in allowing the credit period as determined in (a) above?

SOLUTION

STATEMENT SHOWING THE EVALUATION OF POLICIES IN RESPECT OF CUSTOMER B & CUSTOMER C

(in lakhs)

Credit Period	*Customer B*				*Customer C*	
	0 days ₹	*30 days* ₹	*60 days* ₹	*90 days* ₹	*60 days* ₹	*90 days* ₹
A. Expected Profit:						
(a) Credit Sales	90.00	135.00	180.00	225.00	90.00	135.00

(b) Total Cost:						
(i) Variable Costs	72.00	108.00	144.00	180.00	72.00	108.00
(ii) Fixed Costs	0	0	0	0	0	0
	72.00	108.00	144.00	180.00	72.00	108.00
(c) Expected Profit [(a) – (b)]	18.00	27.00	36.00	45.00	18.00	27.00
B. Opportunity Cost of Investment in Receivables	0.00	1.80	4.80	9.00	2.40	5.40
C. Net Benefits(A – B)	18.00	25.20	31.20	36.00	15.60	21.60

Recommendation: Credit period of 90 days should be allowed to Customer B & C since net benefits under the policy of 90 days exceed the net benefit under other policies. No Credit period should be allowed to Customer A since allowing any credit period to Customer A will decrease the existing profit.

Working Note: Calculation of Opportunity Cost of Average Investments

$$\text{Opportunity Cost} = \text{Total Cost} \times \frac{\text{Collection period}}{360} \times \frac{\text{Rate of Return}}{100}$$

Particulars	*Customer B*				*Customer C*	
A. Total Cost	72.00	108.00	144.00	180.00	72.00	108.00
B. Collection period	0	30/360	60/360	90/360	60/360	90/360
C. Required rate of return	20%	20%	20%	20%	20%	20%
D. Opportunity cost (A × B × C)	—	1.80	4.80	9.00	2.40	5.40

(b) Other problems to be faced by the company in allowing the credit period as determined in (a) above:

When the company allows 90 days' credit to customers B and C and no credit to customer A, it might face the following problems:

(i) Customer A is lifting 1,000 TV sets without any credit facility whereas the same quantity of TV sets is lifted by customer C with 60 days credit period. A would, therefore, protest against granting 60 days credit to customer C and demand that he should also be allowed a credit period of 60 days. Alternatively he may ask for some cash discount.

(ii) At 90 days credit period, customer B would lift 2,500 TV sets whereas customer C would lift 1,500 TV sets. As such, customer B would demand either a further relaxation in credit period, say beyond 90 days, *or* some cash discount.

ILLUSTRATION 11

PM Limited is a distributors of electric equipments. Its sales in 20X1 amounted to ₹ 44 crore and profit after tax ₹ 2.20 crores.

The company has been experiencing a declining profit margin for the last three years. It is felt that this is due to the loose credit policy. On investigation, a group of slow paying customers was identified. It is recommended that the credit policy should be tightened to eliminate them. Sales to this group amounted to about 20 per cent of the company's total sales.

The following Table gives information about the company's cost structure. It is expected that if the slow-paying accounts are eliminated only variable costs would decline. It is also believed that bad debt and collection expenses are entirely attributable to these accounts. Using this information, you are required to allocate income and expenses between 'slow-paying' accounts and good accounts.

Particulars	[Per cent of Sale] Total Expenses	Fixed Expenses	Variable Expenses
Cost of goods sold	80.0		80.0
Selling Expenses	4.6	2.0	2.6
Administration Expenses	2.4	0.8	1.6
Warehousing Expenses	2.4	1.0	1.4
Bad debts Expenses	0.4	—	0.4
Collection Expenses	0.2	—	0.2

A study of credit files indicated that the collection period on 'slow-paying' accounts average to 50 days versus 35 days for all accounts. The balance of debtors for the these accounts average ₹ 120.55 lakhs during 20X1.

Required: Should the PM Limited tighten its credit policy?

SOLUTION

STATEMENT SHOWING THE ALLOCATION OF TOTAL INCOME AND EXPENSES BETWEEN GOOD CUSTOMERS AND SLOW PAYING CUSTOMERS

[₹ in Lakhs]

Particulars	Total	Good Customers (80%)	Slow-Paying Customers (20%)
A. Sales	4,400.00	3,520.00	880.00
B. *Less:* **Total Cost:**			
(a) Variable Cost:			
(i) Cost of Goods sold	3,520.00	2,816.00	704.00
(ii) Selling Expenses	114.40	91.52	22.88
(iii) Administration Expenses	70.40	56.32	14.08
(iv) Ware housing Expenses	61.60	49.28	12.32
(v) Bad Debts Expenses	17.60	—	17.60
(vi) Collection Expenses	8.80	—	8.80
Total Variable Cost	3,792.80	3,013.12	779.68
(b) Fixed Cost:			
(i) Selling Expenses	88.00	70.40	17.60
(ii) Administration Expenses	35.20	28.16	7.04
(iii) Ware housing Expenses	44.00	35.20	8.80
Total Fixed Cost	167.20	133.76	33.44
Total Cost	3960.00	3,146.88	813.12
C. Profit Before tax [A – B]	440.00	373.12	66.88
D. *Less:* **Tax @ 50% (Balancing figure)**	220.00	186.56	33.44
E. Profit After tax [C – D]	220.00	186.56	33.44

STATEMENT SHOWING THE EVALUATION OF SLOW PAYING ACCOUNT

Particulars	₹
A. Sales	880.000
B. *Less:* Variable Cost (As per Previous Statement)	779.680
C. Contribution [A – B]	100.320
D. Cost of Fund [10% of ₹ 120. 55]	12.055
E. Net Benefit [C – D]	88.265

Recommendation: It will not be advisable for the company to tighten the credit policy because this will lead to decrease in profit by ₹ 88.265 lakhs

Working Notes:

(i) After Tax rate of Return on Sales = ₹ 220 lakhs/₹ 4400 lakhs × 100 = 5%.

Before Tax Rate of Return on Sales = 5% + 5% = 10%

(ii) Cost of funds has been calculated with reference to sale value of average debtors since the rate of return has been given with reference to sales only.

(iii) Since average debtors are already given, they have not been further averaged.

ILLUSTRATION 12

CANIC Limited specialises in the manufacture of a computer component. The component is currently sold for ₹ 1,000 and its variable costs is ₹ 800. For the year ended 31st March, 20X9 the company sold on an average 400 components per month. At present the company grants one month credit to its customers. The company is thinking of extending the same to two months on account of which the following is expected:

Increase in Sales	25%
Increase in Stock	₹ 2,00,000
Increase in Creditors	₹ 1,00,000

The company expects a minimum return of 40% on the investment.

You are ***Required:*** To advise the company on whether *or* not to extend the credit terms if:

(a) all customers avail the extended credit period of two months and

(b) existing customers do not avail the new credit terms but only the new customers avail the same. Assume in this case the entire increase in sales is attributable to the new customers.

SOLUTION

STATEMENT SHOWING THE EVALUATION OF DEBTORS POLICIES

Particulars	*Present Policy* ₹	*Proposed Policy A* ₹	*Proposed Policy B* ₹
A. Expected Profit:			
(a) Credit Sales	48,00,000	60,00,000	60,00,000
(b) Total Cost:			
(i) Variable Costs	38,40,000	48,00,000	48,00,000
(c) Expected Profit (A – B)	9,60,000	12,00,000	12,00,000

B. Opportunity Cost of Investment in Receivables	1,28,000	3,60,000	2,32,000
C. Net Benefits (A – B)	8,32,000	8,40,000	9,68,000

Recommendation: The company should extend the credit terms since the net benefits are more than those under the present policy of 1 month credit period.

However the Proposed Policy B(under which only new customers avail the new credit terms) should be adopted since the net benefits under this policy are higher than those under the proposed policies

Working Notes:

(I) CALCULATION OF FUNDS ON WHICH OPPORTUNITY COST WILL BE CALCULATED

Particulars	*Present Policy* ₹	*Proposed Policy A* ₹	*Proposed Policy B* ₹
A. Total Funds	38,40,000	48,00,000	48,00,000
B. *Add:* Additional investment in stock	—	12,00,000	12,00,000
C. *Less:* Additional total creditors	—	6,00,000	6,00,000
D. Total Funds (A + B – C)	38,40,000	54,00,000	54,00,000

(II) CALCULATION OF OPPORTUNITY COST OF AVERAGE INVESTMENTS LOCKED IN COLLECTION PERIOD

$$\text{Opportunity Cost} = \text{Total Cost} \times \frac{\text{Collection Period}}{12} \times \frac{\text{Required Rate of Return}}{100}$$

Particulars	*Present Policy*	*Proposed Policy A*	*Proposed Policy B*		
A. Total Funds	38,40,000	54,00,000	38,40,000	15,60,000	Total
B. Collection Period	1/12	2/12	1/12	2/12	
C. Required Rate of Return	40%	40%	40%	40%	
D. Opportunity Cost (A × B × C)	1,28,000	3,60,000	1,28,000	1,04,000	2,32,000

ILLUSTRATION 13 [CALCULATION OF ACCEPTABLE DEGREE OF RISK OF NON-PAYMENT]

As a part of the strategy to increase sales and profits, the sales manager of a company proposes to sell goods to a group of new customers with 10% risk of non-payment. This group would require one and a half month's credit and is likely to increase sales by ₹ 1,00,000 p.a. Production and selling expenses amount to 80% of sales and the income-tax rate is 50%. The company's minimum required rate of return (after tax) is 25%.

Required: Should the sales manager's proposal accepted?

Also find the degree of risk of non-payment that the company should be willing to assume if the required rate of return (after tax) (i) 30%, (ii) 40% and (iii) 60%.

SOLUTION

STATEMENT SHOWING THE EVALUATION OF PROPOSAL

Particulars	₹
A. Expected Profit:	
(a) Net Sales	1,00,000

(b) *Less:* Production and Selling Expenses @ 80%	80,000
(c) Profit before providing for Bad Debts	20,000
(d) *Less:* Bad Debts @ 10%	10,000
(e) Profit before tax	10,000
(f) *Less:* Tax @ 50%	5,000
(g) Profit after Tax	5,000
B. Opportunity Cost of Investment in Receivables	2,500
C. Net Benefits (A – B)	2,500
D. Decision: The sales manager's proposal should be accepted.	

Working Note: Calculation of Opportunity Cost of Funds locked up

$$\text{Opportunity Cost} = \text{Total Cost of Credit Sales} \times \frac{\text{Collection Period}}{12} \times \frac{\text{Required Rate of Return}}{100}$$

= ₹ 80,000 × 1.5/12 × 25/100 = ₹ 2,500

STATEMENT SHOWING THE CALCULATION OF ACCEPTABLE DEGREE OF RISK OF NON-PAYMENT

Particulars	*Required Rate of Return*		
	30%	*40%*	*60%*
A. Sales	1,00,000	1,00,000	1,00,000
B. *Less:* Production & Sales Expenses	80,000	80,000	80,000
C. Profit before providing for Bad Debts	20,000	20,000	20,000
D. *Less:* Bad Debts (assume X)	X	X	X
E. Profit before tax	20,000 – X	20,000 – X	20,000 – X
F. *Less:* Tax @ 50%	(20,000 – X) 0.5	(20,000 – X) 0.5	(20,000 – X) 0.5
G. Profit after tax	10,000 – 0.5x	10,000 – 0.5x	10,000 – 0.5x
H. Required Return (given)	30% of 10,000* = ₹ 3,000	40% of 10,000* = ₹ 4,000	60% of 10,000* = ₹ 6,000

$$\text{* Average Debtors} = \text{Total Cost of Credit Sales} \times \frac{\text{Collection Period}}{12}$$

= ₹ 80,000 × 1.5/12 = ₹ 10,000

Now let us ascertain the value & % of X in each case

Case I 10,000 – 0.5x = 3,000

0.5x = 7,000

X = 7,000/0.5 = ₹ 14,000

Bad Debts as % of sales = ₹ 14,000/₹ 1,00,000 × 100 = 14%

Case II 10,000 – 0.5x = 4,000

0.5x = 6,000

X = 6,000/0.5 = ₹ 12,000

Bad Debts as % of sales = ₹ 12,000/₹ 1,00,000 × 100 = 12%

Case III 10,000 – 0.5x = 6,000

0.5x = 4,000

X = 4,000/0.5 = ₹ 8,000

Bad debts as % of sales = ₹ 8,000/₹ 1,00,000 × 100 = 8%

Thus, Acceptable Degree of risk of non-payment is 14%, 12% and 8% if required rate of return (after tax) is 30%, 40% and 60% respectively.

Evaluation of Debtors Policies when Cash Discount is provided

ILLUSTRATION 14

A company has a 15 per cent required rate of return. The credit sales of the company are ₹ 160 crore a year and the cost of sales is 75%. The company's collection period currently is 60 days. If company offered terms of 2/20, net 70, 60 per cent of its customers will take the discount and the collection period will be reduced to 40 days. Should the terms be changed? (Assume 360 days in a year)

SOLUTION

STATEMENT SHOWING THE EVALUATION OF DEBTORS POLICIES

Particulars	*Present Policy ₹ in crores*	*Proposed Policy ₹ in crores*
A. Expected Profit:		
(a) Credit Sales	160.00	160.00
(b) Total Cost other than Cash Discount	120.00	120.00
(c) Cash Discount	—	1.92
(d) Expected Profit [(a) – (b) – (c)]	40.00	38.08
B. Opportunity Cost of Investment in Receivables	3.00	2.00
C. Net Benefits (A – B)	37.00	36.08

Recommendation: The Present Policy should be continued since the net benefits under this policy are higher than those under the proposed policy.

Working Notes:

(i) *Calculation of Opportunity Cost of Average Investments*

$$\text{Opportunity Cost} = \text{Total Cost} \times \frac{\text{Collection period}}{360} \times \frac{\text{Rate of Return}}{100}$$

Present Policy = ₹ 120 Crore × 60/360 × 15% = 3 Crore

Proposed policy = ₹ 120 Crore × 40/360 × 15% = 2 Crore

(ii) *Calculation of Cash Discount*

Cash discount = Total Credit Sales × % of customers who takes up discount × Rate/100

= ₹ 160 Crore × 60% × 2% = ₹ 1.92 crore

ILLUSTRATION 15

MP Ltd. is considering to change its credit terms and provides you the following information.

Particulars	*Present Policy*	*Proposed Policy I*
Credit Terms	Net 30	1/10, Net 30
Sales	14,40,000	Increase in sales by ₹ 40,000

Average Collection Period	30 days	Decline in Period by 1/3rd
Bad Debts	2%	2%

It is expected that 50% of the customers will take discount and pay on 10th day. The Variable cost ratio is 70%. and the opportunity cost of investment in receivables is 10% (Pre-tax).The tax rate is 50% Should the company change its credit terms? (Assume 360 day in a year)

SOLUTION

STATEMENT SHOWING THE EVALUATION OF DEBTORS POLICIES

Particulars	*Present Policy* ₹	*Proposed Policy* ₹
A. Expected Profit:		
(a) Credit Sales	14,40,000	14,80,000
(b) Total Cost other than Bad Debts & Cash Discount	10,08,000	10,36,000
(c) Bad Debts	28,800	29,600
(d) Cash discount	—	7,400
(e) Profit Before Tax [(a) – (b) – (c) – (d)]	4,03,200	4,07,000
(f) *Less:* Tax	2,01,600	2,03,500
(g) Profit after tax	2,01,600	2,03,500
B. Opportunity Cost of Investment in Receivables	4,200	2,878
C. Net Benefits [A – B]	1,97,400	2,00,622

Recommendation: The Proposed Policy should be adopted since the net benefits under this policy are higher than those under the present policy.

Working Notes:

(i) Calculation of Opportunity Cost of Average Investments

$$\text{Opportunity Cost} = \text{Total Cost} \times \frac{\text{Collection period}}{360} \times \frac{\text{Rate of Return}}{100}$$

Present Policy = ₹ 10,08,000 × 30/360 × 5% = ₹ 4,200

Proposed policy = ₹ 10,36,000 × 20/360 × 5% = ₹ 2,878

(ii) Calculation of Cash Discount

Cash discount = Total Credit Sales × % of customers who takes up discount × Rate/100

= ₹ 14,80,000 × 50% × 1% = ₹ 7,400

ILLUSTRATION 16

The MP Company's annual credit sales are 150 crore. Cost of Sales 80%. The company's existing credit terms are 1/35, net 60. Generally 60 per cent of the customers avail the cash discount facility. The percentage default rate is 0.5 per cent. The company is thinking of two alternative changes in credit terms:

Policy	*Credit Terms*	*Expected Percentage of Customers availing Discount*	*Increase in Sales*	*Default Percentage*
A	2/10, net 60	80	5%	1.0
B	3/10, net 110	95	10%	1.5

Required: What strategy should be followed by the MP company if the required rate of return is 18 per cent ? (Take 360 days in a year)

SOLUTION

STATEMENT SHOWING THE EVALUATION OF DEBTORS POLICIES

(₹ in Crores)

Particulars	*Present Policy* ₹	*Proposed Policy A* ₹	*Proposed Policy B* ₹
A. Expected Profit:			
(a) Credit Sales	150.00	157.500	165.000
(b) Total Cost (Other than Bad Debts & Cash Discount):	120.00	126.000	132.000
(c) Bad Debts	0.75	1.575	2.475
(d) Cash Discount	0.90	2.520	4.7025
(e) Expected Profit [(a) – (B) – (c) – (d)]	28.35	27.405	25.8225
B. Opportunity Cost of Investment in Receivables	2.70	1.260	0.9900
C. Net Benefits (A – B)	25.65	26.145	24.8325

Recommendation: The Proposed Policy A should be adopted since the net benefits under this policy are higher than those under the proposed policies.

Working Notes:

(i) Present Collection Period = (35 days × 60%) + (60 days × 40%) = 45 days

(ii) Collection Period (Under Policy A) = (10 days × 80%) + (60 days × 20%) = 20 days

(iii) Collection Period (Under Policy B) = (10 days × 95%) + (110 days × 5%) = 15 days

(iv) *Calculation of Opportunity Cost of Average Investments*

$$\text{Opportunity Cost} = \text{Total Cost} \times \frac{\text{Collection Period}}{360} \times \frac{\text{Rate of Return}}{100}$$

Present Policy = 120 × 45/360 × 18% = ₹ 2.7 crore

Proposed Policy A = 126 × 20/360 × 18% = ₹ 1.26 crore

Proposed policy B = 132 × 15/360 × 18% = ₹ 0.99 crore

(v) *Calculation of Cash Discount*

Cash Discount = Total Credit Sales × % of customers who takes up discount × Rate/100

Present Policy = ₹ 150 × 60% × 1% = ₹ 0.90 crore

Policy A = ₹ 157.50 × 80% × 2% = ₹ 2.52 crore, Policy B = ₹ 165 × 95% × 3% = ₹ 4.7025 crore

ILLUSTRATION 17

X Ltd. currently makes all sales an credit and offers no cash discount. It is considering a 2% cash discount for payment within 10 days. The company's current average collection period is 60 days, sales are 4,00,000 units, selling price is ₹ 15 per unit Variable cost per unit is ₹ 10 Average Cost per unit is ₹ 12.50 at the current sales values. It is expected that the change in credit terms will result in increase in sales by 12.5% and the average collection period will fall by 25%. However, due to increased sales, increased working capital required will be ₹ 1,00,000 (it does not take into account the effect on debtors). Assuming that 50% of the credit customers will avail cash discount and 20% is the required return on investment.

Required: Should the proposed discount be offered? Also determine the effective cost of discount to X Ltd. *[Assume 360 days in a year]*

SOLUTION

STATEMENT SHOWING THE EVALUATION OF DEBTORS POLICIES

Particulars	*Present Policy [₹ in lakhs]*	*Proposed Policy [₹ in lakhs]*
A. Expected Profit:		
(a) Credit Sales	60.00	67.50
(b) Total Cost other than Cash Discount:		
(i) Variable Costs	40.00	45.00
(ii) Fixed Costs [4,00,000 units (₹ 12.50 – ₹ 10)]	10.00	10.00
	50.00	55.00
(c) Cash Discount		0.675
(d) Expected Profit [(a) – (b) – (c)]	10.00	11.825
B. Opportunity Cost of Investment in Receivables	1.667	1.575
C. Net Benefits (A – B)	8.333	10.25

Recommendation: The Proposed Policy should be adopted since the net benefits under this policy are higher than those under the present policy.

Working Notes:

(i) Calculation Opportunity Cost of Average Investments locked in Collection period

$$\text{Opportunity Cost} = \text{Total Cost} \times \frac{\text{Collection period}}{360} \times \frac{\text{Rate of Return}}{100}$$

[₹ in Lakhs]

Particulars	*Present Policy*	*Proposed Policy*		
A. Total Cost	50.00	55.00	1.00	
B. Collection Period	60/360	45/360	360/360	
C. Required Rate of Return	20%	20%	20%	
D. Opportunity Cost (A × B × C)	1.667	1.375	0.20	1.575

(ii) Calculation of Cash Discount

Cash discount = Total Credit Sales × % of Customers who takes up discount × Rate /100

= ₹ 67.50 × 50% × 2% = ₹ 0.675 lakh

ILLUSTRATION 18

The credit terms of a firm currently is net 30. It is considering to change it to Net 60. This will have the effect of increasing the firm's sales. As the firm will not relax credit standards, the bad-debt losses are expected to remain at the same percentage. i.e., 3 per cent of sales. Incremental production, selling and collection costs are 80 per cent of sales and expected to remain constant over the range of anticipated sales increases. The relevant opportunity cost for receivables is 15 per cent. Current credit sales are ₹ 600 crore and current level of receivables is ₹ 60 crore. If the credit terms are changed, the current sales are expected to change to ₹ 720 crore and the firm's receivables level will also increase. The firm's financial manager estimates that the new credit terms, will cause the firm's collection period to increase by 30 days.

Required:

(a) Determine the present collection period and the collection period after the proposed change in credit terms.

(b) What level of receivables is implied by the new collection period ?

(c) Determine the increased investment in receivables if the new credit terms are adopted.

(d) Are the new credit terms desirable ? (Assume 360 days in a year)

SOLUTION

(a) Present collection period = 360 days × Current level of Receivables/Current AnnualCredit Sales

= 360 × ₹ 60 crore/₹ 600 crore = 36 Days

New Collection Period = 36 days + 30 days = 66 days

(b) New Level of Receivables = New Sales × New Collection Period/360 days

= ₹ 720 Crores × 66 days/360 days = ₹ 132 Crores

(c) Increase in Investment in Receivables = New level of Receivables – Old level of Receivables

= 132 Crore – 60 Crore = 72 Crore

(D) STATEMENT SHOWING THE EVALUATION OF DEBTORS POLICIES

Particulars	*Present Policy [₹ in crores]*	*Proposed Policy [₹ in crores]*
A. Expected Profit:		
(a) Credit Sales	600.00	720.00
(b) Variable Cost of Credit Sales	480.00	576.00
(c) Bad Debts	18.00	21.60
(d) Expected Profit [(a) – (b) – (c)]	102.00	122.40
B. Opportunity Cost of Investment in Receivables	7.2	15.84
C. Net Benefits (A – B)	94.8	106.56

Recommendation: The Proposed Policy should be adopted since the net benefits under this policy are higher than those under the present policy.

Working Notes: Calculation of Opportunity Cost of Average Investments

$$\text{Opportunity Cost} = \text{Total Cost} \times \frac{\text{Collection period}}{360} \times \frac{\text{Rate of Return}}{100}$$

Present Policy = ₹ 480 × 36/360 × 15% = ₹ 7.2 crore

Proposed Policy = ₹ 576 × 66/360 × 15% = ₹ 15.84 crore

ILLUSTRATION 19

Tulsian Ltd. is current selling 1,00,000 units of its product @ 100 per unit. At the current level of production the cost per unit is ₹ 82. The variable cost per cent is 70% of sales. Cash sales are 75% *less* than the credit sales. The company's existing credit terms are 2/10, net 30. Generally 25% of the credit customers avail the cash discount facility. The existing default rate is 1.5% At present, the receivables are being financed by owned funds which cost 18% p.a.

The company is considering to change the credit term to 3/10, 30. As a result, following is expected:

Increase in Credit Sales: 25%

Increase in Average Stock: ₹ 2,00,000

Increase in Average Creditors: ₹ 44,444.44.

Increase in % of customers availing the cash discount: 200%

Decrease in Default Rate:

Additional funds required are to be financed by bank at a cost of 24% p.a.

Required: Should the credit terms be changed? *[Assume 360 days in a year]*

SOLUTION

Particulars	*Present Policy* ₹	*Proposed Policy* ₹
A. Expected Profit:		
(a) Credit Sales	80,00,000	1,00,00,000
(b) Total Cost other than Bad debts & Cash Discount:		
(i) Variable Costs	56,00,000	70,00,000
(ii) Fixed Costs	9,60,000	10,00,000
	65,60,000	80,00,000
(c) Bad Debts	1,20,000	1,00,000
(d) Cash discount	40,000	2,25,000
(e) Expected Profit [(a) – (b) – (c) – (d)]	12,80,000	16,75,000
B. Opportunity Cost of Investment in Receivables	82,000	90,000
C. Net Benefits [A – B]	11,98,000	15,85,000

Recommendation: The Proposed Policy should be adopted since the net benefits under this policy are higher than those under the present policy.

Working Note:

(i) Calculation of Credit Sales

Let Credit Sales be x

Then Cash Sales be x – 3/4x

$$x + x - 3/4x = 100$$
$$2x - 3/4x = 100$$
$$8x - 3x = 400$$
$$5x = 400$$
$$x = 400/5 = 80$$

Credit Sales = 80 Lakhs

Cash Sales = 100 lakhs – 80 lakhs = 20 Lakhs

Credit Sales under new policy= 80 + 80 (25/100) = 80 + 20 = 100 lakhs

(ii) Allocation of Fixed Cost to Credit Sales

Fixed Cost = Total Cost – Variable Cost = 82 × 1,00,000 units – 70% of 100 lakhs = 12 lakhs.

Fixed Cost attributable to Credit Sales = Total Fixed Cost × Credit Sales/Total Sales

For Present Policy = 12 Lakhs × 80/100 = 9.60 Lakhs

For Proposed Policy = 12 Lakhs × 100/120 = 10 Lakhs

(iii) Calculation of Average Collection Period

For Present Policy = 10 × 0.25 + 30 × 0.75 = 2.5 + 22.5 = 25 days

For Proposed Policy = 10 × 0.75 + 30 × 0.25 = 7.5 + 7.5 = 15 days

(iv) Calculation of additional funds required for Proposed Policy

A. Funds required for Present Policy = Cost of Credit Sales × 25/360

= ₹ 65,60,000 × 25/360 = ₹ 4,55,555.56

B. Funds required for Proposed Policy = ₹ 80,00,000 × 15/360 = ₹ 3,33,333.33

Add: Increase in Stock = ₹ 2,00,000.00

Less: Increased in Creditors = ₹ 44,444.44

Total Funds of Proposed Policy = ₹ 4,88,888.89

C. Additional Funds Required for Proposed Policy (A – B) = ₹ 33,333.33

(v) *Calculation of Opportunity cost of Average Investments locked up in Collection period*

$$\text{Opportunity Cost} = \text{Total Cost} \times \frac{\text{Collection period}}{360} \times \frac{\text{Rate of Return}}{100}$$

Particulars	*Present Policy*	*Proposed Policy*		
A. Cost of Average Receivables	4,55,556	4,55,556	33,333	
B. Required Rate of Return	18%	18%	24%	
C. Opportunity Cost (A × B)	82,000	82,000	8,000	90,000

(iv) *Calculation of Cash Discount*

Cash Discount = Total Credit Sales × % of Customers who avail discount × Rate/100

Present Policy = ₹ 80,00,000 × 25% × 2% = ₹ 40,000

Proposed Policy = ₹ 1,00,00,000 × 75% × 3% = ₹ 2,25,000.

13.0 FACTORING

MEANING OF FACTORING

Factoring is a financial service, which involves managing, financing and collecting receivables. It is both a financial as well as management support to supplier of goods/services. It is a method of converting non-productive assets (receivables) into productive assets (Cash). A factor makes the conversion of receivables into cash possible. Factoring may be defined as a contract between the supplier of goods/services and the factor under which the factor agrees to perform atleast two of the following functions:

(a) To finance the assigned book debts (receivables).

(b) To maintain accounts relating to receivables.

(c) To collect book debts.

(d) To provide protection against default in payment by debtors.

(e) To provide credit administration services to the clients to decide whether *or* not and how much credit should be extended to the customers.

Some of the major factoring firms in India are SBI Factors and Commercial Services Ltd., Canara Bank Factors Ltd. (1991), Fair Growth Factors Ltd. (1992)

FACTORING COMMISSION

The commission charged by the factor for providing factoring services is known as factoring commission. It is usually expressed as a percentage of face value of receivables factored. In India, it ranges between 2.5 to 3 per cent. The commission is expected to be lower for recourse factoring since the factor does not assume the risk of bad debts. The commission is expected to be higher for non-recourse factoring since the factor assumes the risk of bad debts.

TYPES OF FACTORING

The factoring services may be classified under following categories:

1. **Non-recourse Factoring** (Old Line Factoring)—Under Non-recourse factoring factor assumes the risk of bad debts and charges higher commission for and advances cash upto 80/90% of book debts immediately.
2. **Recourse Factoring**—Under recourse factoring, factor does not assume the risk of bad debts and charges lower commission for and advances cash upto 70/80% of book debts.
3. **Advance Factoring**—Under advance factoring, factor advances cash against the book debts due to client immediately.
4. **Maturity Factoring**—Under maturity factoring, the factor makes the payment on maturity (i.e., in case of non-recourse factoring on collection of book debts *or* on insolvency of customers, in case of recourse factoring on collection of book debts from customers).
5. **Financial Factoring** (Bulk/Agency Factoring)—Under finance factoring, the factor simply finances the book debts against bulk either on recourse *or* without recourse and the client continues to administer and operate sales ledger.
6. **Non-notification Factoring**—Under non-notification factoring, the notice of assignment of receivables is not given to the debtors. But the factor performs all his functions without a disclosure to the customer that he owns the book debts.

NATURE OF OBLIGATION OF FACTOR

The nature of the obligation of the factor is of bailment contract. Factor stands in a fiduciary relationship with the client firm and the main responsibility arises out of the terms of the contract *or* agreement between the parties. Factoring firms are professionally competent with skilled persons to handle credit sales realisations for different clients in different trades for better credit management.

NEED FOR FACTOR SERVICES

Need for factor services is felt by traders to concentrate on sales and realization of credit sales be left in specialized hands to minimize the risk of bad debts arising on account of non-realisation of credit sales. If sales are realized within reasonable time, the traders need not depend much for bank finance towards working capital.

PARTIES TO FACTORING CONTRACT

There are three parties involved generally in a factoring contract as follows:

1. Buyer of goods who has to pay for goods bought on credit terms.
2. Seller of goods who has to realize credit sales from buyer.
3. Factor who acts as agent in realizing credit sales from buyer and passes on the realized sum to seller after deducting his commission.

FACTORING OPERATING CYCLE

The factoring operating cycle comprises of the following seven steps:

Step 1: Buyer negotiates the terms of purchasing the asset with the seller

Step 2: The factor enters into agreement with seller for rendering factor services to it.

Step 3: Seller delivers goods along with Copies of invoice, delivery challan, and instructions to make payment to factor to buyer.

Step 4: Seller sends a deed of assignment in favour of factor alongwith copies of sales documents.

Step 5: On receipt of copies of sales documents as referred to above the factor makes payment to the seller of the 80% *or* more of the price of debt.

Step 6: Buyer makes payment to the factor in time *or* gets extension of time *or* in the case of default is subject to legal process in the hands of factor.

Step 7: The factor receives payment from the buyer on due dates and remits the money to seller after usual deduction.

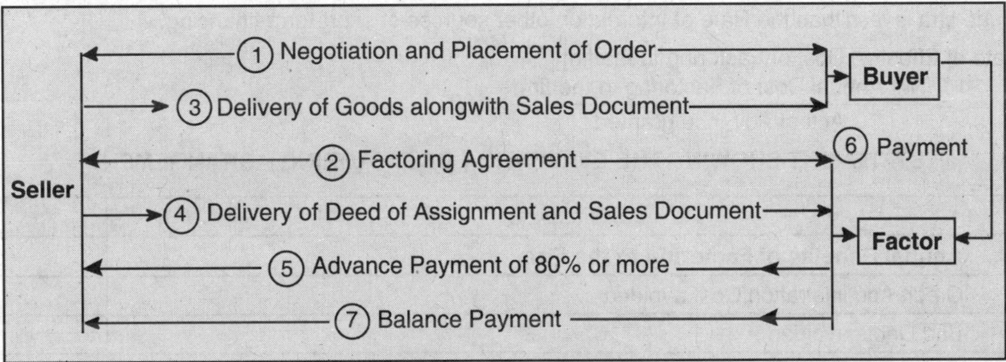

Fig. Factoring Operating Cycle

ADVANTAGES OF FACTORING

The advantages resulting from the factoring are as follows:

1. Prompt payments and credits.
2. Improves scope for operating leverage.
3. Reduction of administrative cost and burden.
4. Increase in return to the client.
5. Improvement in liquidity.
6. Provides insurance against bad debts.
7. It is *neither* a loan *nor* a deposit but facilitates liquidity.
8. Current assets are efficiently managed thus reducing working capital requirements.
9. Better credit discipline amongst customers by regular realization of dues, effective control of sales journal, reduced credit risk, better working capital management etc.

DISADVANTAGES OF FACTORING

The disadvantages of factoring are as follows:

1. Image of the client may suffer as engaging of a Factoring Agency is not considered a good sign of efficient management.
2. Factoring may not be of much use where companies have nation-side network branches.
3. Financial evaluation may not be accurate.
4. If the client has cheaper means of finance and credit (where goods are sold against advance payment) factoring may not be useful.

HOW TO DECIDE WHETHER *OR* NOT TO ENGAGE A FACTOR

To decide whether *or* not to engage a factor, the cost and benefits of factoring should be evaluated.

The cost of factoring includes:

(a) Factoring commission;

(b) Interest Charged by Factor on advance granted;

The benefits of factoring includes:

(a) Saving in costs of In House Credit Collection Department.

(b) Saving in Bad Debt losses;

(c) Saving in Cost of Funds invested in receivables due to reduction in Average Collection Period.

(d) Saving in Cash Discount allowed (if any)

A firm should engage a factor if the benefits exceed the cost *or* the Rate of Effective Cost of Factoring to the firm is *less* than the Rate of Interest on other sources of short-term financing.

Rate of Effective Cost of Factoring to the firm

$$= \frac{\text{Net Annual Cost of Factoring to the firm}}{\text{Actual Advance granted}} \times 100$$

STATEMENT SHOWING THE EVALUATION OF FACTORING ARRANGEMENT

	Particulars	₹
A.	**Annual Benefits of Factoring to the Firm:**	
	Credit Administration Cost avoided	....
	Bad Debts avoided	....
	Interest saved due to reduction in Average Collection Period	....
	[Cost of Annual Credit Sales × Rate of Interest × (Present Collection Period – New Collection Period)/365 Days]	
	Total	....
B.	**Annual Cost of Factoring to the Firm:**	
	Factoring Commission [Annual credit Sales × % of Commission]	....
	Interest Charged by Factor on advance	....
	[Annual Credit Sales – Factoring Comm. – Factoring Reserve] ×	
	$\frac{\text{Collection Period (days)}}{365}$ × Rate of Interest]	
	Total	....
C.	**Net Annual Benefits/Cost of Factoring to the Firm:**	....
	Rate of Effective Cost of Factoring to the Firm	
	$= \frac{\text{Net Annual Cost of Factoring to the Firm}}{\text{Actual Advance granted}} \times 100$	

Recommendation: The company should adopt the Non-recourse Factoring alternative since the Rate of Effective Cost of Factoring to the Firm (i.e. 12% say)is *less* than the existing cost of borrowing (i.e., 15% say).

or

Recommendation: The company should adopt the Non-recourse Factoring alternative since it results in Net Annual Benefits of ₹ 5.4 lakhs (say)

or

Recommendation: The company should not adopt the Non-recourse Factoring alternative since the Rate of Effective Cost of Factoring to the Firm (i.e., 15% say) is more than the existing cost of borrowing (i.e., 12% say).

ILLUSTRATION 20

Tulsian (1)Ltd. is considering to engage a factor and provides you the following information:

1. Total Annual Sales: ₹ 450 lakhs of which 80% on credit.
2. Existing Average Collection Period: 60 days
3. Existing Bad Debts: 2%
4. Credit Administration Cost: ₹ 9,00,000 of which one third is avoidable.
5. Factoring Commission: 2%
6. Advance Against Receivable: Factor agrees to grant an advance against receivables at an interest rate of 18% p.a. after withholding 10% as reserve.

Required: Should the company engage a factor if the company can borrow at a rate of (a)12% p.a. (b) 15% p.a. (Assume 360 days in a year).

SOLUTION

CALCULATION OF FACTORING COMMISSION, INTEREST CHARGES AND ADVANCE GRANTED BY FACTOR

	Particulars	*₹ in lakhs*
A.	Average Level of Receivables [80% of ₹ 450 × 60 days /360 days]	60.000
B.	*Less:* Factoring Commission [2% of ₹ 60 lakhs]	1.200
C.	*Less:* Factoring Reserve [10% of ₹ 60 lakhs]	6.000
D.	Eligible Amount of Advance [A – B – C]	52.800
E.	*Less:* Interest Charges [₹ 52.80 lakhs × 18% × 60/360]	1.584
F.	Actual Advance granted [D – E]	51.216

STATEMENT SHOWING THE EVALUATION OF FACTORING ARRANGEMENT

	Particulars	*₹ in lakhs*
A.	**Annual Benefits of Factoring to the Firm:**	
	Credit Administration Cost avoided [₹ 9.00 lakhs × 1/3]	3.000
	Bad Debts avoided [2% of ₹ 360 lakhs]	7.200
	Total	10.200
B.	**Annual Cost of Factoring to the Firm:**	
	Factoring Commission [2% of ₹ 360 lakhs]	7.200
	Interest Charged by Factor on advance [₹ 1.584 lakhs × 360/60]	9.504
	Total	16.704
C.	**Net Annual Cost of Factoring to the Firm:**	6.504
	Rate of Effective Cost of Factoring to the firm = ₹ 6,50,400/₹ 51,21,600 × 100	12.699%

Recommendation:

(a) The company should not adopt the Non-recourse Factoring alternative since the Rate of Effective Cost of Factoring to the Company (i.e., 12.699%) is more than the existing Cost of Borrowing (i.e., 12%).

(b) The company should adopt the Non-recourse Factoring alternative since the Rate of Effective Cost of Factoring to the the Company (i.e., 12.699%) is *less* than the existing Cost of Borrowing (i.e., 15%).

ILLUSTRATION 21

Tulsian (2) Ltd. is considering to engage a factor and provides you the following information:

1. Total Annual Sales: ₹ 450 lakhs of which 80% on credit.
2. Existing Average Collection Period: 80 days
3. Existing Bad debts: 2%
4. Credit Administration Cost: ₹ 9,00,000 of which one third is avoidable
5. Cost of sales: 80% of Sales
6. Existing Cost of Borrowing: 15% p.a.
7. Factoring Commission: 2%
8. Payment period guaranteed by factor: 60 days

Required: Should the company engage a factor ? (Assume 360 days in a year).

SOLUTION

CALCULATION OF INTEREST SAVED DUE TO REDUCTION IN AVERAGE COLLECTION PERIOD

	Particulars	*₹ in lakhs*
A.	Existing Average Level of Receivables [80% of ₹ 450 lakhs × 80 days/360 days]	80
B.	New Average Level of Receivables [80% of ₹ 450 lakhs × 60 days/360 days]	60
C.	Reduction in Debtors [A – B]	20
D.	Cost of Debtors [80% of ₹ 20 lakhs]	16
E.	Interest saved due to reduction in Average Collection period [₹ 16 lakhs × 15%]	2.4

STATEMENT SHOWING THE EVALUATION OF FACTORING ARRANGEMENT

Particulars	*₹ in lakhs*
A. Annual Benefits of Factoring to the Firm:	
Credit Administration Cost avoided [₹ 9.00 lakhs × 1/3]	3.00
Bad Debts avoided [2% of ₹ 360 lakhs]	7.20
Interest saved due to reduction in Average Collection Period [₹ 450 × 80% × 80% × 15% × (80 – 60)/360]	2.40
Total	12.60
B. Annual Cost of Factoring to the Firm:	
Factoring Commission [2% of ₹ 360 lakhs]	7.20
C. Net Annual Benefits of Factoring to the Firm:	5.40

Recommendation: The company should adopt the Non-recourse Factoring alternative since it results in Net Annual Benefits of ₹ 5.4 lakhs

ILLUSTRATION 22

Tulsian (3) Ltd. is considering to engage a factor and provides you the following information:

1. Total Annual Sales: ₹ 450 lakhs of which 80% on credit
2. Variable Cost: 80% of Sales
3. Existing Average Collection Period: 80 days
4. Existing Bad Debts: 2%
5. Credit Administration Cost: ₹ 9,00,000 of which one-third is avoidable
6. Existing Cost of Borrowing: 15% p.a.
7. Factoring Commission: 2% for non-recourse factoring
8. Advance against receivables: Factor agrees to grant advance against receivables at an interest rate of 18% p.a. after with holding 10% as reserve.
9. Payment period guaranteed by factor: 60 days

Required: Should the company engage a factor ? (Assume 360 days in a year)

SOLUTION

CALCULATION OF FACTORING COMMISSION, INTEREST CHARGES AND ADVANCE GRANTED BY FACTOR

	Particulars	*₹ in lakhs*
A.	Average Level of Receivables [80% of ₹ 450 lakhs × 60 days/360 days]	60.000
B.	*Less:* Factoring Commission [2% of ₹ 60 lakhs]	1.200
C.	*Less:* Factoring Reserve [10% of ₹ 60 lakhs]	6.000
D.	Eligible Amount of Advance [A – B – C]	52.800
E.	*Less:* Interest Charges [₹ 52.80 × 18% × 60/360]	1.584
F.	Actual Advance granted [D – E]	51.216

CALCULATION OF INTEREST SAVED DUE TO REDUCTION IN AVERAGE COLLECTION PERIOD

	Particulars	*₹ in lakhs*
A.	Existing Average Level of receivables [80% of ₹ 450 lakhs × 80 days/360 days]	80
B.	New Average Level of receivables [80% of ₹ 450 lakh × 60 days/360 days]	60
C.	Reduction in Debtors [A – B]	20
D.	Cost of Reduction in Debtors [80% of ₹ 20 lakhs]	16
E.	Interest saved due to reduction in Average Collection period [15% of ₹ 16 lakhs]	2.4

STATEMENT SHOWING THE EVALUATION OF FACTORING ARRANGEMENT

Particulars	*₹ in lakhs*
A. Annual Benefits of Factoring to the Firm:	
Credit Administration Cost avoided [₹ 9 lakhs × 1/3]	3.000
Bad Debts avoided [2% of ₹ 360 lakhs]	7.200
Interest saved due to reduction in Average Collection Period [₹ 450 × 80% × 80% × 15% × (80 – 60)/360]	2.400

	Total	12.600
B.	**Annual Cost of Factoring to the Firm:**	
	Factoring Commission [2% of ₹ 360 lakhs]	7.200
	Interest Charged by Factor on advance [₹ 1.584 × 360/60]	9.504
	Total	16.704
C.	**Net Annual cost of Factoring to the Firm:**	4.104
	Rate of Effective Cost of Factoring to the Firm = 4,10,400/₹ 51,21,600 × 100	8.013

Recommendation: The company should adopt the Non-recourse Factoring alternative since the Rate of Effective Cost of Factoring to the Company (i.e., 8.013%) is *less* than the existing cost of borrowing (i.e., 15%).

ILLUSTRATION 23

Tulsian Ltd. provides you the following information:

1. Total Annual Sales : 100 lakhs
2. Cost of Sales : 90%
3. Annual Cost of Credit Administration Dept. : ₹ 4,75,000 of which 40% is avoidable
4. Cash Sales : $33^1/_3$ % *less* than the credit sales
5. Mode of Financing Book Debts : Bank borrowings and Owned Funds in the ratio of 2 : 1
6. Cost of Funds : Bank borrowings @ 12% and Owned Funds @ 21%
7. Debtors Turnover Ratio : 4
8. Bad Debts : 1%
9. Factoring Proposal :

The following offer has been received from a factor who is prepared to realize the receivables:

Factory Commission : 2% for recourse factoring and 3% for non-recourse factoring

Discount Rate for Prepayment : 20% p.a.

Guaranteed Payment rate : 60 Days

Advance against Receivables : 80% of Receivables reduced by factoring commission

Required: Should the company continue with the In house Management of Receivable *or* accept the factoring arrangement ? (Assume 360 days in a year)

SOLUTION

CALCULATION OF FACTORING COMMISSION, INTEREST CHARGED AND ADVANCE GRANTED

Particulars	*Recourse Factoring* ₹	*Non-Recourse Factoring* ₹
Average Level of Receivables (₹ 60,00,000 × 60/360)	10,00,000	10,00,000
Less: Factoring Commission (₹ 10,00,000 × 2%), (10,00,000 × 3%)	20,000	30,000

Less: Factoring Reserve (20% of 10 lakhs)	2,00,000	2,00,000
Eligible Amount of Advance	7,80,000	7,70,000
*Less:*Interest charged (7.8 Lakhs × 20% × 60/360)		
(7.7 lakhs × 20% × 60/360)	26,000	25,667
Actual Amount of Advance granted.	7,54,000	7,44,333

STATEMENT SHOWING EVALUATION OF FACTORING ARRANGEMENT

	Particulars	*Recourse Factoring* ₹	*Non-Recourse Factoring* ₹
A.	**Annual Benefits of Factoring to the Firm:**		
	Credit Administration Cost avoided (40% of 4,75,000)	1,90,000	1,90,000
	Bad Debts (1% of ₹ 60,00,000)	—	60,000
	Interest saved due to reduction in Average Collection Period [₹ 60,00,000 × 90% × 15% × (90 – 60)/360]	67,500	67,500
	Total	2,57,500	3,17,500
B.	**Annual Cost of Factoring to the firm:**		
	Factoring commission (2% of 60 Lakhs), (3% of 60 Lakhs)	1,20,000	1,80,000
	Interest charged adv. (26,000 × 360/60); (25,667 × 360/60)	1,56,000	1,54,000
	Total	2,76,000	3,34,000
C.	**Net Annual Cost of Factoring to the firm:**	18,500	16,500
	Rate of Effective Cost of Factoring to the firm $\left(\frac{₹\,18,500}{₹\,7,54,000}\times 100\right),\left(\frac{₹\,16,500}{₹\,7,44,333}\times 100\right)$	2.45%	2.22%

Recommendation: The company should adopt the Non-recourse factoring alternative since it involves the least cost.

Working Notes:

(i) Calculation of Credit Sales

Let Credit Sales be x

$$\text{Cash Sales} = (x - 1/3x)$$
$$\text{Total Sales} = (x + x - 1/3x)$$
$$100 \text{ Lakhs} = x + x - 1/3x$$

Multiplying the equation by 3

$$300 \text{ Lakh} = 3x + 3x - 1x$$
$$5x = 300 \text{ Lakh}$$
$$x = 300 \text{ Lakh}/5 = 60 \text{ Lakhs}$$

(ii) Credit Collection Period = 360 Days/Debtors Turnover Ratio = 360/4 = 90 Days

(iii) Weighted Average Cost of Funds = (12% × 2/3) + (21% × 1/3) = 15%

14.0 METHODS OF MONITORING RECEIVABLES

There are four methods of monitoring receivables:

AVERAGE AGE OF RECEIVABLE (AVERAGE COLLECTION PERIOD)

Average Collection period means the time taken by customers to repay the credit obligation. It measures the quantity of receivables, since it indicates the speed of their collectability. To judge collection efficiency, average collection period should be compared with the credit period allowed as per credit policy of the firm.

Case	*Effect on Liquidity*	*Effect on Risk of Bad Debt*	*Effect on Profitability*	*Quality of Collection Efforts*
Average Collection Period is more than Credit Period allowed	Decrease in liquidity	Increase in risk of Bad Debt	Decrease in profitability	It indicates poor quality of collection efforts
Average Collection Period is *less* than Credit Period allowed	Increase in liquidity	Decrease in risk of Bad Debt	Decrease in profitability if rate of cash discount offered is *less* than cost of funds.	It indicates good quality of collection efforts

However, there are two major limitations of average collection period as a tool to monitor receivables as follows:

(a) It does not provide the specific information about the age of outstanding receivable since it is based on aggregate debtors and aggregate sales.

(b) The period of receivables does not necessarily coincide with the period of sales.

AGEING SCHEDULE

Ageing schedule classifies the receivables according to their age (the period for which they have been outstanding). An ageing schedule may contain the following contents:

(a) Age classes (in days) (say 1 to 30 days, 31 to 60 days and so on).
(b) Month of sale.
(c) Outstanding balance of receivables.
(d) Percentage of agewise outstanding to total outstanding.

An ageing schedule may be prepared as under:

Age Classes (days)	*As on 31st December 2008*			*As on 31st March 2009*		
	Month of Sale	*Balance of receivables*	*% to total*	*Month of Sale*	*Balance of receivables*	*% to total*
1-30	December	2,50,000	50	March	3,20,000	40
31-60	November	1,25,000	25	February	2,40,000	30
61-90	October	62,500	12.5	January	1,20,000	15
91-120	Earlier	12,500	2.5	Earlier	40,000	5
120 and above	Earlier	12,500	2.5	Earlier	40,000	5
		5,00,000			8,00,000	

To ascertain the condition of receivables for control purposes, one should compare:

(a) Current liquidity of receivables with the past liquidity of receivables.
(b) Current liquidity of receivables of one firm with that of other firms.

Thus, the ageing schedule:

(a) Indicates a tendency for old accounts to accumulate.
(b) Helps the firm in designing its collection policy.
(c) Enables the firm to have a close control over the quality of other accounts.

COLLECTION PROGRAMME

(a) Monitoring the state of receivables.
(b) Information to customers when due date approaches.
(c) Telegraphic and telephonic advice to customers on the due date.
(d) Threat of legal action on Overdue Accounts.
(e) Legal action on Overdue Accounts.

COLLECTION EXPERIENCE MATRIX

Collection Experience Matrix relates outstanding receivables of a period with credit sales of same period. The practical steps involved in preparing Collection Experience Matrix are given on next page.

Step 1: Show credit sales over a period of time horizontally.

Step 2: Show associated outstanding receivables of the same period vertically in the column of credit sales of same period.

Step 3: Show the outstanding receivables in each column as percentage of credit sales of that column.

Step 4: Study the percentages diagonally and ascertain the trend whether increasing *or* decreasing.

For Example: The top diagonal show the manner in which current months sales are collected, the next diagonal shows the manner in which one month older outstanding receivables are collected and so on.

Step 5: Interpret the trend as follows:

If the percentages are increasing as moving down any diagonal	The firm is unable to collect its receivables speedily
If the percentages are decreasing as moving down any diagonal	The firm is able to collect its receivables speedily.

ILLUSTRATION 24 FROM THE FOLLOWING, PREPARE COLLECTION EXPERIENCE MATRIX

Month	*April*	*May*	*June*	*July*	*Aug.*	*Sep.*
Credit Sales	250	300	320	350	400	300
Outstanding Receivables						
April		200				
May		150	240			
June		100	210	288		
July		0	90	280	315	
August		0	0	80	280	300
September	0	0	0	70	280	270

SOLUTION

COLLECTION EXPERIENCE MATRIX

Month	*April*	*May*	*June*	*July*	*Aug.*	*Sep.*
Credit Sales	250	300	320	350	400	300

Outstanding Receivables as % of Credit Sales						
April		80				
May		60	80			
June		40	70	90		
July		0	30	87.5	90	
August		0	0	25	80	75
September	0	0	0	20	70	90

Interpretation:

1. About 20% of the sales in a given month are collected in the same month.
2. During the second month, the collection varied from 2.5% to 20%.
3. During the third month, the remaining receivables were collected so that the balance of book debts became nil at the end of third month and the collection varied from 40% to 67.5%.

15.0 DECISION TREE ANALYSIS OF CREDIT GRANTED

The decision whether to grant credit *or* not is a decision involving costs and benefits. When a customer pays, the seller makes profit (i.e., sales-cost of sales), but when he fails to pay, the seller incurs loss equal to the cost of sales. If the relative chances of recovering the dues from the customer can be estimated, the decision whether to grant credit *or* not may be taken on the basis of expected net benefits. It can be observed from the following table:

Nature of Expected Net Benefits	*Decision whether to grant credit or not*
(a) If Expected Net Benefits are positive	Credit may be granted
(b) If Expected Net Benefits are Negative	Credit may be not granted.
(c) If Expected Net Benefits are zero	Credit management would be indifferent as to the decision whether to grant credit *or* not.

ILLUSTRATION 25

PCT Ltd. received an order for supply of a product from X Ltd. for ₹ 10 lakh. Cost of Sales is 80% of sales. It has been estimated that the probability of non-recovery in case X Ltd. is bankrupt is (a) 25%, (b) 15%, (c) 20%.

On the basis of above information, determine whether PCT Ltd. should accept the order ?

SOLUTION

Sales	₹ 10,00,000
Cost of Sales	₹ 8,00,000

Case (a)

Probable Profit on Recovery [₹ 2,00,000 × 75/100]	₹ 1,50,000
Less: Probable Loss in case of Non-Recovery [₹ 8,00,000 × 25/100]	₹ 2,00,000
Net Expected Loss	₹ 50,000

Recommendation: The order should not be accepted since there is net expected loss to the extent of ₹ 50,000.

Case (b)

Probable Profit on Recovery [₹ 2,00,000 × 85/100]	₹ 1,70,000
Less: Probable Loss in case of Non-Recovery [₹ 8,00,000 × 15/100]	₹ 1,20,000
Net Expected Benefit	50,000

Recommendation: The order should be accepted since the net expected benefits are positive.

Case (c)

Probable Profit on Recovery [₹ 2,00,000 × 80/100]	₹ 1,60,000
Less: Probable Loss in case of Non-Recovery [₹ 8,00,000 × 20/100]	₹ 1,60,000
Net Expected Benefit	Nil

Recommendation: The management would be indifferent as to the decision whether order should be accepted *or* not since the net expected benefits are zero.

SOLVED PROBLEMS

PROBLEM 1

MNQ Ltd. wants to relax its credit on sales from the current level of 1 month to 2 months. Due to this, sales would increase to ₹ 72 lakhs from the present level of ₹ 60 lakhs per annum but the percentage of bad debt losses is likely to go up by 2% of sales which is now at 3% of sales. The company's variable cost is 75% of sales and fixed expenses are ₹ 12 lakhs per annum.

Required: Advice the company on the implications of revising the credit policy. The firm's required rate of return is 10%.

SOLUTION

STATEMENT SHOWING THE EVALUATION OF DEBTORS POLICIES

Particulars	*Present Policy 1 month* ₹	*Proposed Policy 2 months* ₹
A. Expected Profit:		
(a) Credit Sales	60,00,000	72,00,000
(b) Total Cost other than Bad Debts:		
(i) Variable Costs	45,00,000	54,00,000
(ii) Fixed Costs	12,00,000	12,00,000
	57,00,000	66,00,000
(c) Bad Debts	1,80,000	3,60,000
(d) Expected Profit [(a) – (b) – (c)]	1,20,000	2,40,000
B. Opportunity Cost of Investment Receivables	47,500	1,10,000
C. Net Benefits [A – B]	72,500	1,30,000

Recommendation: The Proposed Policy should be adopted since the net benefits under this policy are higher than those under the present policy.

Working Note:

$$\text{Opportunity Cost} = \text{Total Cost} \times \frac{\text{Collection Period}}{12} \times \frac{\text{Rate of Return}}{100}$$

Present Policy = ₹ 57,00,000 × 1/12 × 10% = ₹ 47,500

Proposed Policy = ₹ 66,00,000 × 2/12 × 10% = ₹ 1,10,000

PROBLEM 2

A firm sells 40,000 units of its product per annum @ ₹ 35 per unit. This average cost per unit is ₹ 31 and the variable cost per unit is ₹ 28. The Debtor Turnover Ratio 6 times. Bad debt losses are 4% of sales and the collection charges amount to ₹ 15,000. The firm is considering proposal to follow a strict collection policy which would reduce bad debt losses to 3% of sales and the Debtor Turnover Ratio to 8 times. It would, however, reduce sale volumes by 1000 units. The firm's required rate of return is 20%.

Required: Would you recommended the adoption of the new collection policy ? (Assume 360 days in a year)

SOLUTION

STATEMENT SHOWING THE EVALUATION OF DEBTORS POLICIES

Particulars	*Present Policy 60 days* ₹	*Proposed Policy 45 days* ₹
A. Expected Profit:		
(a) Credit Sales	14,00,000	13,65,000
(b) Total Cost other than Bad Debts:		
(i) Variable Costs	11,20,000	10,92,000
(ii) Fixed Costs	1,20,000	1,20,000
	12,40,000	12,12,000
(c) Bad Debts	56,000	40,950
(d) Expected Profit [(a) – (b) – (c)]	1,04,000	1,12,050
B. Opportunity Cost of Investment in Receivables	41,333	30,300
C. Net Benefits [A – B]	62,667	81,750

Recommendation: The Proposed Policy should be adopted since the net benefits under this policy are higher than those under the present policy.

Working Note:

$$\text{Opportunity Cost} = \text{Total Cost} \times \frac{\text{Collection Period}}{12} \times \frac{\text{Rate of Return}}{100}$$

Present Policy = ₹ 12,40,000 × 60/360 × 20% = ₹ 41,333

Proposed Policy = ₹ 12,12,000 × 45/360 × 20% = ₹ 30,300

Assumption: Fixed Cost include Collection Charges.

PROBLEM 3

(a) A Company sells a product at ₹ 30 per unit with a variable cost of ₹ 20 per unit. The Fixed Costs amount to ₹ 6,25,000 per annum and the total annual sales to ₹ 75 lakhs. It is estimated that if the present credit facility of one month were doubled, sales could be increased by ₹ 6,00,000 per annum. The Company expects a return on investment of at least 20% prior to taxation. ***Required:*** Justify by calculation that this course can be adopted.

(b) There is the possibility of an additional overseas order being procured which would not affect the home market. 10,000 extra units could be sold, but additional costs on the order would amount to ₹ 300 while the risk of a bad debt is estimated at 25%. Also credit would have to be extended to the customer to 90 days.

Required: Should the order be accepted?

SOLUTION

PART (A) STATEMENT SHOWING THE EVALUATION OF DEBTORS POLICIES

Particulars	*Present Policy 1 month* ₹	*Proposed Policy 2 months* ₹
A. Expected Profit:		
(a) Credit Sales:	75,00,000	81,00,000
(b) Total Cost:		
(i) Variable Costs	50,00,000	54,00,000
(ii) Fixed Costs	6,25,000	6,25,000
	56,25,000	60,25,000
(c) Expected Profit [(a) – (b)]	18,75,000	20,75,000
B. Opportunity Cost of Investment in Receivables	93,750	2,00,833
C. Net Benefits [A – B]	17,81,250	18,74,167

Recommendation: The Proposed Policy should be adopted since the net benefits under this policy are higher than those under the present policy.

Working Note: *Calculation of Opportunity Cost of Average Investments*

$$\text{Opportunity Cost} = \text{Total Cost} \times \frac{\text{Collection Period}}{12} \times \frac{\text{Rate of Return}}{100}$$

Present Policy = ₹ 56,25,000 × 1/12 × 20% = ₹ 93,750

Proposed Policy = ₹ 60,25,000 × 2/12 × 20% = ₹ 2,00,833

Part (b)

Particulars	₹
A. Expected Profit:	
(a) Additional Sales (10,000 units @ ₹ 30)	3,00,000
(b) *Less:* Variable Cost (10,000 units @ ₹ 20)	2,00,000
(c) *Less:* Additional Costs	300
(d) Bad Debts (₹ 3,00,000 × 25/100)	75,000
(e) Expected Profit [(a) – (b) – (c) – (d)]	24,700
B. Opportunity Cost (₹ 2,00,000 × 90/365 × 20/100)	9,863
C. Net Benefits (A – B)	14,837

Recommendation: The Overseas Order should be accepted.

PROBLEM 4

CAS Corporation is considering relaxing its present credit policy and is in the process of evaluating two proposed policies. The firm is required to give a return of 25% on the investment in new accounts receivable. The Company's variable costs are 70% of the selling price. Given the following information, which is the better option?

Particulars	*Present Policy*	*Proposed Policy I*	*Proposed Policy II*
Annual Credit sales	₹ 50 lakhs	₹ 60 lakhs	₹ 67.5 lakhs
Account Receivable Turnover Ratio	4 times	3 times	2.4 times
Bad debt losses	3%	5%	6.66666%

SOLUTION

STATEMENT SHOWING THE EVALUATION OF DEBTORS POLICIES

Particulars	*Present Policy* ₹	*Proposed Policy I* ₹	*Proposed Policy II* ₹
A. Expected Profit:			
(a) Credit Sales	50,00,000	60,00,000	67,50,000
(b) Total Cost other than Bad Debts:			
(i) Variable costs	35,00,000	42,00,000	47,25,000
(c) Bad debts	1,50,000	3,00,000	4,50,000
(d) Expected Profit [(a) – (b) – (c)]	13,50,000	15,00,000	15,75,000
B. Opportunity Cost of Investment in Receivables	2,18,750	3,50,000	4,92,188
C. Net Benefits [A – B]	11,31,250	11,50,000	10,82,812

Recommendation: The Proposed Policy 1 should be adopted since the net benefits under this policy are higher than those under other policies.

Working Note: *Calculation of Opportunity Cost of Average Investments*

$$\text{Opportunity Cost} = \text{Total Cost} \times \frac{\text{Collection Period}}{12} \times \frac{\text{Rate of Return}}{100}$$

Present Policy = ₹ 35,00,000 × 3/12 × 25% = ₹ 2,18,750

Proposed Policy I = ₹ 42,00,000 × 4/12 × 25% = ₹ 3,50,000

Proposed Policy II = ₹ 47,25,000 × 5/12 × 25% = ₹ 4,92,188

PROBLEM 5

The credit management of ABC Company had to decide on a proposal for liberal extension of credit which will result in a slowing process of the average collection period from one to two months. The companies product was sold for ₹ 20 per unit of which ₹ 15 represented variable cost (including credit department cost). The current actual sales amounted to ₹ 24 lakhs, represented entirely by credit sales. The average total cost per unit was ₹ 18. The relaxation in credit policy was expected to result in a 25% increase in sales, i.e., ₹ 30 lakhs annually. The corporate management aimed at a return of 25% on additional investment.

Required: You are required to make relevant calculations to help the credit manager in examining the financial implications of liberalising the credit policy. (Assume 360 days in a year).

SOLUTION

STATEMENT SHOWING THE EVALUATION OF DEBTORS POLICIES

Particulars	*Present Policy* ₹	*Proposed Policy* ₹
A. Expected Profit:		
(a) Credit Sales	24,00,000	30,00,000
(b) Total Cost:		
(i) Variable Costs	18,00,000	22,50,000
(ii) Fixed Costs	3,60,000	3,60,000
	21,60,000	26,10,000
(c) Expected Profit [(a) – (b)]	2,40,000	3,90,000
B. Opportunity Cost of Investment in Receivables	45,000	1,08,750
C. Net Benefits [A – B]	1,95,000	2,81,250

Recommendation: The Proposed Policy 1 should be adopted since the net benefits under this policy are higher than those under other policies.

Working Note:

(i) Calculation of Fixed cost

A. No. of units sold = $\frac{\text{Total Sales}}{\text{Selling Price}} = \frac{₹\ 24,00,000}{₹\ 20} = 1,20,000$

B. Total Costs = Average Cost × No. of units sold = ₹ 18 × 1,20,000 = ₹ 21,60,000

C. Total Variable cost = 1,20,000 × ₹ 15 = ₹ 18,00,000

D. Fixed Cost = ₹ 21,60,000 – ₹ 18,00,000 = ₹ 3,60,000

(ii) Calculation of Opportunity Cost of Average Investments locked up in collection period

$$\text{Opportunity Cost} = \text{Total Cost} \times \frac{\text{Collection Period}}{12} \times \frac{\text{Rate of Return}}{100}$$

Present Policy = ₹ 21,60,000 × 1/12 × 25% = ₹ 45,000

Proposed Policy = ₹ 26,10,000 × 2/12 × 25% = ₹ 1,08,750

PROBLEM 6

A company currently has annual sales of ₹ 2,50,000 and an average collection period of 30 days. It is considering a more liberal credit policy. If the credit period is extended, the company expects sales and bad-debt losses to increase in the following manner.

Credit Policy	*Increase in Credit Period*	*Increase in Sales ₹*	*Bad-debt %*
A	$33^1/_3$%	5%	1.2
B	50%	7%	1.5
C	100%	8%	1.8
D	140%	10%	2.2

The selling price per unit is ₹ 4. Average cost per unit at the current level of operation is ₹ 3.00 and variable cost per unit is ₹ 2.40. If the current bad-debt loss is 1 per cent of sales and the required rate of return investment is 20 per cent, which credit policy should be undertaken ? Ignore taxes, and assume 360 days in a year.

SOLUTION

STATEMENT SHOWING THE EVALUATION OF DEBTORS POLICIES

Particulars	*Present Policy* ₹	*Proposed Policy A* ₹	*Proposed Policy B* ₹	*Proposed Policy C* ₹	*Proposed Policy D* ₹
A. Expected Profit:					
(a) Credit Sales	2,50,000	2,62,500	2,67,500	2,70,000	2,75,000
(b) Total Cost other than Bad Debts:					
(i) Variable costs	1,50,000	1,57,500	1,60,500	1,62,000	1,65,000
(ii) Fixed Cost	37,500	37,500	37,500	37,500	37,500
	1,87,500	1,95,000	1,98,000	1,99,500	2,02,500
(c) Bad Debts	2,500	3,150	4,013	4,860	6,050
(d) Expected Profit [(a) – (b) – (c)]	60,000	64,350	65,487	65,640	66,450
B. Opportunity Cost of Investment in Receivables	3,125	4,333	4,950	6,650	8,100
C. Net Benefits (A – B)	56,875	60,017	60,537	58,990	58,350

Recommendation: The Proposed Policy B should be adopted since the net benefits under this policy are higher than those under other policies.

Working Note: Calculation of Opportunity Cost of Average Investments locked up in collection period

$$\text{Opportunity Cost} = \text{Total Cost} \times \frac{\text{Collection Period}}{360} \times \frac{\text{Rate of Return}}{100}$$

A. Total cost	1,87,500	1,95,000	1,98,000	1,99,500	2,02,500
B. Collection period	30/360	40/360	45/360	60/360	72/360
C. Required Rate of Return	20%	20%	20%	20%	20%
D. Opportunity cost (A × B × C)	3,125	4,333	4,950	6,650	8,100

PROBLEM 7

A group of customers want to enter into a contract with you to buy goods worth ₹ 20 lakhs during 20X1 the deliveries to be made in four equal instalments quarterly. The price of the commodity is ₹ 20 per unit on which you expect a profit of ₹ 10. The acceptance of this proposal would mean an additional recurring expenditure of ₹ 10,000 p.a. on your part.

The aging schedule of accounts receivables in respect of this group of customers in the past was as follows:

Period	*Percentage of bills for which payment received*
At the end of 30 days	15%
At the end of 60 days	25%
At the end of 90 days	40%
At the end of 120 days	20%

Assuming an opportunity cost of 20% of the funds locked up in accounts receivables, will it be desirable to accept this proposal? [Assume 360 days in a year]

SOLUTION

STATEMENT SHOWING THE EVALUATION OF DEBTORS POLICIES

Particulars	*Proposed Policy (₹)*
A. Expected Profit:	
(a) Credit Sales	20,00,000
(b) Total Cost:	
(i) Variable Costs	10,00,000
(ii) Fixed Costs	10,000
	10,10,000
(c) Expected Profit [(a) – (b)]	9,90,000
B. Opportunity Cost of Investment in Receivables	44,609
C. Net Benefits [A – B]	9,45,391

Recommendation: The Proposed Policy should be adopted since the net benefits under this policy are positive.

Working Note: Calculation of Opportunity Cost of Average Investments locked up in collection period

$$\text{Opportunity Cost} = \text{Total Cost} \times \frac{\text{Collection Period}}{360} \times \frac{\text{Rate of Return}}{100}$$

Particulars	*15%*	*25%*	*40%*	*20%*	*Total*
A. Total Cost	1,51,500	2,52,500	4,04,000	2,02,000	10,10,000
B. Collection Period	30/360	60/360	90/360	120/360	
C. Required Rate of Return	20%	20%	20%	20%	
D. Opportunity Cost (A × B × C)	2,525	8,417	20,200	13,467	44,609

PROBLEM 8

PM Ltd. is considering of introducing a cash discount and provides you the following information:

Particulars	*Present Policy*	*Proposed Policy*
Credit Firms	Net 40	1/10, Net 50
Sales	120 lakhs	120 lakhs
Average Collection Period	60 Days	30 Days

It is expected that 50% of the customers will take advantage of the changed credit terms. The Cost of Sales Ratio is 80% The required rate of return (pre-tax) in 15% and tax rate is 50%.

Required: Should the company change its credit terms ? (Assume 360 days)

SOLUTION

STATEMENT SHOWING THE EVALUATION OF DEBTORS POLICIES

Particulars	*Present Policy (₹ in lakhs)*	*Proposed Policy (₹ in lakhs)*
A. Expected Profit:		
(a) Credit Sales	120	120

(b) Variable Costs of Sales	96	96
(c) Cash discount	—	0.6
(d) Expected Profit before tax [(a) – (b) – (c)]	24	23.4
(e) *Less:* Tax @ 50%	12.00	11.7
(f) Expected Profit after tax	12.00	11.7
B. Opportunity Cost of Investment in Receivables	1.2	0.60
C. Net Benefits [A – B]	10.8	11.1

Recommendation: The Proposed Policy should be adopted since the benefits under this policy are higher than those under the present policy.

Working Note:

(i) Calculation of Opportunity Cost of Average Investments locked in collection period

Opportunity Cost $= \text{Total Cost} \times \frac{\text{Collection Period}}{360} \times \frac{\text{Rate of Return}}{100}$

Present Policy = ₹ 96 lakhs × 60/360 × 7.5% = ₹ 1.2 lakhs

Proposed Policy = ₹ 96 lakhs × 30/360 × 7.5% = ₹ 0.6 lakhs

(ii) Calculation of Cash Discount

Cash Discount = Total Credit Sales × % of customers who takes up discount × Rate/100

= ₹ 120 lakhs × 50% × 1% = ₹ 0.6. Lakhs

PROBLEM 9

X Ltd. has credit sales of ₹ 360 lakhs and its average collection period is 30 days. The financial controller estimates that bad debt losses are around 2% of credit sales. The firm spends ₹ 1,40,000 annually on debtors administraion. This cost comprises of telephonic and fax bills along with salaries of staff members. These are the avodable costs. A Factoring firm has offered to buy the firm's receiveables. The factor will charge 1% commission and will pay an advance against receivables on an interest @ 15% p.a. after withholding 10% as reserve.

Required: Should the company engage factor ? (Assume 360 days in a year).

SOLUTION

CALCULATION OF FACTORING COMMISSION, INTEREST CHARGES AND ADVANCE GRANTED BY FACTOR

Particulars	₹
A. Average Level of Receivables [₹ 360 lakhs × 30 days/360 days]	30,00,000
B. *Less:* Factoring Commission [1% of ₹ 30 lakhs]	30,000
C. *Less:* Factoring Reserve [10% of ₹ 30 lakhs]	3,00,000
D. Eligible Amount of Advance [A – B – C]	26,70,000
E. *Less:* Interest Charges [₹ 26.7 lakhs × 15% × 30 days/360 days]	33,375
F. Actual Advance granted [D – E]	26,36,625

STATEMENT SHOWING THE EVALUATION OF FACTORING ARRANGEMENT

Particulars	₹
A. Annual Benefits of Factoring to the Firm:	
Credit Administration Cost avoided	1,40,000

Bad Debts avoided [2% of 360 lakhs]	7,20,000
Total	8,60,000
B. Annual Cost of Factoring to the Firm:	
Factoring Commission [1% ₹ 360 lakhs]	3,60,000
Interest Charged by Factor on advance [₹ 33,375 × 360 days/30 days]	4,00,500
Total	7,60,500
C. Net Annual Benefits of Factoring to the Firm:	99,500

Recommendation: The company should adopt the Non-recourse Factoring alternative since it results in Net Annual Benefits of ₹ 99,500.

PROBLEM 10

CAMIC Limited is manufacturer of various electronic gadgets. The annual turnover for the year 20X2 was ₹ 730 lakhs. The company has a wide network of sales outlets all over the country.

The turnover is spread evenly for each of the 50 weeks of the working year. All sales are for credit and sales within the week are also spread evenly over each of the five working days.

All invoicing of credit sales is carried out at the Head office in Bombay. Sales documentation sent by post daily from each location to the Head office for the past two years. Delays in preparing and despatching invoices were noticed. As a result, only some of the invoices were despatched in the same week and the remainder in the following week.

An analysis of the delay in invoicing [being the interval between the date of sale and the date of despatch of the invoice] indicated the following pattern:

No. of days of delay in invoicing	3	4	5	6
% of Weeks sales	20	10	40	30

A further analysis indicated that the debtors take on an average 36 days of credit before paying. This period is measured from the day of despatch of the invoice rather than the date of sale.

It is proposed to hire an agency for undertaking the invoicing work at various locations. The agency has assured that the maximum delay would be reduced to three days under the following pattern:

No. of days of delay in invoicing	0	1	3
% of weeks sales	40	40	20

The agency has also offered additionally to monitor the collections which will reduce the credit period to 30 days. CAMIC Limited expects to save ₹ 4,000 per month in postage costs. All working funds are borrowed from a local bank at simple interest rate of 20% p.a.

The agency has quoted a fee of ₹ 2,00,000 p.a. for the invoicing work and ₹ 2,50,000 p.a. for monitoring collections and is willing to offer a discount of ₹ 50,000 provided both the works are given. You are required to advise CAMIC Limited about the acceptance of agency's proposal.

SOLUTION

STATEMENT SHOWING THE EVALUATION OF PROPOSAL

Particulars	*Present Policy*	*Proposed Policy*		
		Invoicing Work	*Monitoring Work*	*Both Work*
A. Opportunity Cost				
(a) Due to delay Invoicing	1,92,000	40,000	1,92,000	40,000

(b) Due to delay payment	14,40,000	14,40,000	12,00,000	12,00,000
Total (a) + (b)	16,32,000	14,80,000	13,92,000	12,40,000
B. Fixed Cost	48,000	2,00,000	2,98,000	4,00,000
			[i.e. 2.50 + .48]	[i.e. 2 + 2.50 – .50]
C. Total (A + B)	16,80,000	16,80,000	16,90,000	16,40,000

Recommendation: Proposed policy III is recommended since the cost of proposed policy (III) is *less* than that of other policies.

Working Notes:

(i) Calculation of Opportunity Cost of funds locked up in debtors.

(a) Due to delay Invoicing = Sales subject to delay × $\frac{\text{Rate}}{100} \times \frac{\text{Period of Delay}}{365}$

For Present Policy and Policy II = ₹ 730 lakhs × 20% × 20/100 × 3/365 = ₹ 24,000

= ₹ 730 lakhs × 10% × 20/100 × 4/365 = ₹ 16,000

= ₹ 730 lakhs × 40% × 20/100 × 5/365 = ₹ 80,000

= ₹ 730 lakhs × 30% × 20/100 × 6/365 = ₹ 72,000

₹ 1,92,000

For Proposed Policy I = ₹ 730 lakhs × 40% × 20/100 × 0/365 = 0

and Proposed Policy III = ₹ 730 lakhs × 40% × 20/100 × 1/365 = ₹ 16,000

= ₹ 730 lakhs × 20% × 20/100 × 3/365 = ₹ 24,000

₹ 40,000

(b) Due to delay payment = Sales × $\frac{\text{Rate}}{100} \times \frac{\text{Collection Period}}{365}$

For Present & proposed policy I = ₹ 730 lakhs × 20/100 × 36/365 = ₹ 14,40,000

For Proposed Policy II and III = ₹ 730 lakhs × 20/100 × 30/365 = ₹ 12,00,000

PROBLEM 11

MP Limited has annual sales of ₹ 400 crore. It sells 80 per cent of its products on a 60-day credit. Its average collection period is 80 days. The company's bad debts, based on the past experience, could be estimated as 0.9 per cent of credit sales. The company's annual cost of administering credit sales is 0.46875%. It is possible to avoid 40,00,000 of these costs if credit administration is transferred by the company to a factor. The factor will charge 1.75 per cent non-recourse commission for his services. He can also extend advance against receivables to the company at an interest rate of 16.5 per cent after withholding 10 per cent as reserve.

Required: Should the company hire services of the factors ? (Assume Required Rate of return 15% and 360 days in a year)

SOLUTION

CALCULATION OF FACTORING COMMISSION, INTEREST CHARGED AND ADVANCE GRANTED

Particulars	*(₹ in Crores)*
Average Level of Receivable (320 crores × 80/360)	71.11
Less: Factoring Commission (1.75% × 71.11)	1.24

Less: Factoring Reserve (10% of 71.11)	7.11
Eligible Amount of Advance	62.76
Less: Interest charged on advance (62.76 × 16.5% × 80/360)	2.30
Actual amount of advance granted	60.46

STATEMENT SHOWING THE EVALUATION OF FACTORING ARRANGEMENT

Particulars	*(₹ in Crores)*
A. Annual Benefits of Factoring to the firm:	
Credit Administration cost avoided	0.40
Bad Debts avoided (0.9% of 320 crores)	2.88
Total	3.28
B. Annual Cost of Factoring to the firm:	
Factoring Commission (1.75% of 320 crores)	5.60
Interest Charged on advance granted (2.3012 × 360/80)	10.36
Total	15.96
C. Net Annual Cost of Factoring to the firm:	12.68
Rate of Effective Cost = Net Annual Cost/Actual advance granted = 12.68/60.46 × 100	20.97%

Recommendation: The company should continue with its in house credit management since its Rate of Effective Cost is *less* than the cost of other sources of financing (i.e., 15%)

Working Notes:

(i) Credit Sales = 400 crore × 80% = 320 crores

(ii) Assumption: The factor will make the payment within 60 days.

(iii) Interest saved due to reduction in debtors for 20 days (i.e., 80 days – 60 days) has not been calculated in the absence of cost of owned funds used to finance book debts.

PROBLEM 12

The PJ Ltd. has current annual sales (turnover) amount to ₹ 2160 lakhs The cash Sales were *less* than the credit sales. The credit terms of PJ Ltd. are 2/10, net 30. On the current level of sales, the bad debts are 1 per cent. The past experience shows that 50 per cent of the customers avail of the cash discount; the remaining customers pay on an average 70 days after the date of sale.

The book debts (receivables) of PJ Ltd are at present being financed on 2 : 1 basis by a mix of bank borrowings and owned funds which cost per annum 25 per cent and 28 per cent respectively.

As an alternative to the in-house management of receivable, PS Ltd. is contemplating the use of advance non-recourse factoring deal with the Goods Factors Ltd. The main elements of such a deal structure by the factor are (i) factor reserve, 15 per cent; (ii) guaranteed payment date, 24 days after the date of purchase; (iii) discount charge, 22 per cent and (iv) commission for other services, 4 per cent of the value of receivables.

The finance management PJ Ltd seeks your advice, as a consultant, on the cost-benefit of the factoring arrangement. What advise would your give? your can make your own assumptions, where necessary. *(Assume 360 days in a year)*

SOLUTION

(I) CALCULATION OF FACTORING COMMISSION, INTEREST CHARGED AND ADVANCE GRANTED

Particulars	*(₹ in lakhs)*
Average Level of Receivables (₹ 1620 Lakhs × ₹, 24/360)	108.00
Less: Factoring Commission (4% of ₹ 108 Lakhs)	4.32
Less: Factoring Reserve (15% of ₹ 108 Lakhs)	16.20
Eligible Amount of Advance	87.48
Less: Interest Charged on advance (22% of ₹ 87.48 Lakhs × 24/360)	1.28
Actual amount of advance granted	86.20

(II) STATEMENT SHOWING EVALUATION OF FACTORING ARRANGEMENT

Particulars	*(₹ in lakhs)*
A. Annual Benefits of Factoring to the Firm:	
Cash Discount (1,620 lakhs × 50% × 2%)	16.20
Credit Administration cost avoided	—
Bad Debts avoided (1% of 1620 Lakhs)	16.20
Interest saved due to reduction in Average Collection Period [₹ 1620 lakh × 26% × (40 – 24)/360]	18.72
Total	51.12
B. Annual Cost of Factoring to the firm:	
Factoring Commission (4% of 1620 Lakhs)	64.800
Interest Charged on advance granted. (22% of ₹ 87.48 lakhs)	19.245
Total	84.045
C. Net Annual Cost of Factoring to the firm	32.925
Rate of Effective Cost = Net Annual Cost/Actual advance granted = 32.925/86.20 × 100	38.19%

Recommendation: The company should continue with its in house management alternative since its Rate of Effective Cost is *less* than the Cost of other resources of financing (i.e., 26%)

Working Notes:

(i) Calculation of credit Sales

Let Credit Sales be x

Cash Sales = x – 2/3x

Total Sales = x + x – 2/3x

2160 Lakhs = x + x – 2/3x

Multiplying the equation by 3

6480 Lakh = 3x + 3x – 2x

4x = 6480 Lakh

x = 6480 Lakh/4 = 1620 Lakhs

(ii) Existing Average Collection Period = 0.5 (10 days) + 0.5 (70 days) = 5 + 35 = 40 days

(iii) Cash Discount = Credit Sales × Cash discount × Customers availing cash discount
= ₹ 1620 Lakhs × 50% × 2% = ₹ 16.2 Lakhs

(iv) Average Cost of Funds = (0.25 × 2/3) + (0.28 × 1/3) = 0.26 *or* 26%

(v) Calculation of Interest Saved Due to Reduction in Average Collection Period

Particulars	*(₹ in lakhs)*
A. Existing Level of Receivables (₹ 1620 Lakhs × 40/360)	180
B. New Level of Receivables (₹ 1620 Lakhs × 24/360)	108
C. Reduction in Debtors	72
D. Interest saved on reduction in Debtors (26% of ₹ 72 lakhs)	18.72

Note: In the absence of Cost of Credit Sales, interest saved has been calculated on sales and not on cost of sales.

PROBLEM 13

The following factors relate to the K.P Ltd:

Annual Turnover in the current financial year ₹ 3,000 lakhs

Annual Cash Turnover 75% *less* than the credit turnover

Average collection period, 75 days;

Cost of Funds 21% annum;

Annual credit and collection expenditure: ₹ 40 lakh of which three-fourths is avoidable;

Bad debts: 1 per cent of sales

The Factors Ltd. offers a factoring deal to the KP. It proposes to charge a commission as percentage of the value of the book debts of 2 per cent for recourse factoring and 3.5 per cent for non-recourse factoring. In addition, it would charge 22 per cent per annum as discount/interest for pre-payment (advance against uncollected and not due receivables) to the extent of 80 per cent of the value of the receivables. The guaranteed payment/collection date is 60 days.

Required: Making your own assumption where necessary, what advice would you give to KP, to continue with the in-house management of receivables *or* accept the factoring arrangement? *[Assume 360 days in a year]*

SOLUTION

CALCULATION OF FACTORING COMMISSION, INTEREST CHARGED AND ADVANCE GRANTED

Particulars	*Recourse Factoring [₹ in lakhs]*	*Non-Recourse Factoring [₹ in lakhs]*
Average Level of Receivables: (₹ 2400 Lakhs × 60/360)	400	400
Less: Factoring Commission (₹ 400 Lakhs × 2%), (3.5% of 400 Lakhs)	8	14
Less: Factoring Reserve (20% of ₹ 400 lakhs)	80	80
Eligible Amount of Advance	312	306
Less: Interest charged on advance (₹ 312 Lakhs × 22% × 60/360), (₹ 306 lakhs × 22% × 60/360)	11.44	11.22
Actual Amount of Advance granted	300.56	294.78

CALCULATION OF INTEREST SAVED ON REDUCTION OF AVERAGE COLLECTION PERIOD

Particulars	(₹ in lakhs)
Existing Average level of Receivables (₹ 2400 lakhs × 75/360)	500
New Average level of Receivables (₹ 2400 Lakhs × 60/360)	400
Reduction in Debtors	100
Cost of Debtors	100
Interest saved due to reduction of Averagecollection period (21% of 100 Lakhs)	21

STATEMENT SHOWING EVALUATION OF FACTORING THE FIRM

Particulars	Recourse Factoring [₹ in lakhs]	Non-Recourse Factoring [₹ in lakhs]
A. Annual Benefits of Factoring to the firm:		
Credit Administration Cost avoided (₹ 40 Lakhs × 3/4)	30,00,000	30,00,000
Bad Debts avoided (1% of ₹ 2400 Lakhs)		24,00,000
Interest saved due to reduction of Average Collection Period [₹ 2,400 lakh × 21% × (75 – 60)/360]	21,00,000	21,00,000
Total	51,00,000	75,00,000
B. Annual Cost of factoring to the firm:		
Factoring Commission (2% of ₹ 2400 lakhs), (3.5% of ₹ 2400 lakhs)	48,00,000	84,00,000
Interest Charged on advance granted (₹ 11.44 Lakhs × 360/60), (₹ 11.22 Lakhs × 360/60)	68,64,000	67,32,000
Total	1,16,64,000	1,51,32,000
C. Net Annual Cost of Factoring to the firm:	65,64,000	76,32,000
Rate of Effective Cost of factoring: $\left(\frac{₹\ 65.64 \text{ lakhs}}{₹\ 300.56 \text{ lakhs}} \times 100\right), \left(\frac{₹\ 76.32 \text{ lakhs}}{₹\ 294.78 \text{ lakhs}} \times 100\right)$	21.84%	25.89%

Recommendation: The company should continue in-house credit management since its effective cost involved is least.

Working Note: Calculation of credit Sales

Let Credit Sales be x

$$\text{Cash Sales} = x - 3/4x$$

$$\text{Total Sales} = x + x - 3/4x$$

$$3{,}000 \text{ Lakhs} = x + x - 3/4x$$

Multiplying the equation by 4

$$12{,}000 \text{ Lakh} = 4x + 4x - 3x$$

$$5x = 12{,}000 \text{ Lakh}$$

$$x = 12{,}000 \text{ Lakh}/5 = 2{,}400 \text{ Lakhs}$$

9 WORKING CAPITAL MANAGEMENT—INVENTORY MANAGEMENT

LEARNING OBJECTIVES

After studying this chapter, you should be able to understand:

- What is Inventory Management?
- What is the Objective of Inventory Management?
- Need for Holding Inventory
- Re-order Quantity or Economic Order Quantity (EOQ)
- Re-order Level/Re-order Point
- Other Stock Levels
- ABC Analysis
- Inventory Turnover Ratio
- Analysis of Investment in Inventory

1.0 WHAT IS INVENTORY MANAGEMENT?

Inventory Management means planning, organising, directing and controlling of inventory. It provides an answer to the following two basic questions:

HOW MUCH TO ORDER?

It means what should be the size of an order. How much to order will depend upon the annual consumption, carrying cost per unit per annum, ordering cost per order and stock out cost. It involves the determination of E.O.Q.

WHEN TO PLACE AN ORDER?

It means when the fresh order should be placed with supplier to procure additional inventory. It involves the determination of Re-order level/point.

2.0 WHAT IS THE OBJECTIVE OF INVENTORY MANAGEMENT?

The objective of Inventory Management is to avoid the situation of excessive and inadequate inventory and to determine and maintain optimum level of inventory after achieving a trade off between the profitability and liquidity so as to maximize the wealth of shareholders as a whole. Whenever the situation of excessive and inadequate inventory arises, prompt and timely action should be taken by management to correct imbalances.

Then optimum level of inventory will lie between the two danger points of excessive and inadequate inventory. The consequences of excessive and inadequate inventory are:

Consequences of Excessive Receivables	*Consequences of Inadequate Receivables*
1. Opportunity Costs of funds tied up in inventory 2. Excessive Carrying Costs such as storage costs, handling cost, insurance etc. 3. Risk of Liquidity	1. Interruption in Production 2. Excessive stock out costs

Thus, an effective management should ensure the procurement of inventory

- of right quality,
- in the right quantity,
- at right time,
- at right place,
- from right source.

3.0 NEED FOR HOLDING INVENTORY

Following are the three principle motives for holding inventory:

TRANSACTION MOTIVE

It is the need to hold inventories to facilitate smooth production and sales.

1. Stock of raw material is to be held to facilitate continous supply of material to production department for uninterrupted production.
2. Stock of W.I.P. is to be held because of production cycle, which is the time span between introduction of raw material into production and emergence of finished product.
3. Stock of finished goods is to be held to facilitate continous supply of product to customers.

PRECAUTIONARY MOTIVE

It is the need to hold inventory to meet contingencies in future.

SPECULATIVE MOTIVE

It is the need to hold inventory in order to take advantage of profitable opportunities as and when they arise.

4.0 RE-ORDER QUANTITY OR ECONOMIC ORDER QUANTITY (EOQ)

MEANING OF ECONOMIC ORDER QUANTITY (EOQ)

Re-order quantity is the quantity for which order is placed when the stock reaches re-order level. It is known as economic order quantity when it is the quantity which is most economical to order.

EOQ refers to the quantity of inventory, at which total of ordering costs and the carrying costs is minimum. At EOQ the ordering costs are equal to carrying costs.

OBJECTIVE OF ECONOMIC ORDER QUANTITY (EOQ)

The objective of EOQ is to determine that order size which is most economical to order.

FACTORS TO BE CONSIDERED

EOQ is determined after considering the following factors:

(a) Ordering Costs	**(b) Carrying Costs**
The term 'Ordering Costs' refer to the costs incurred for acquiring inputs. These costs include - (i) Cost of placing an order, (ii) Cost of transportation, (iii) Cost of receiving goods,	The term 'Carrying Costs' refer to the costs incurred in maintaining a given level of inventory. These costs include- (i) Cost of storage space, (ii) Cost of handling materials, (iii) Cost of Insurance,

(iv) Cost of inspecting goods.		(iv) Cost of deterioration *or* obsolescence, (v) Cost of store staff.	
There is an inverse relationship between order size and ordering cost.		There is positive relationship between order size and carrying cost.	
Larger the order size **Smaller the order size**	Lower the ordering costs because of fewer orders Higher the ordering costs because of more orders	**Larger the order size** **Smaller the order size**	Higher the carrying costs because of high average inventory. Lower the carrying costs because of low average inventory.
(c) Annual Consumption (Usage) of inventory.			

IMPORTANCE OF EOQ

The EOQ technique solves one of the major problems of the inventory management i.e. the order quantity problem by answering to the question: 'How much inventory should be ordered at a particular point of time ?'

ASSUMPTIONS OF EOQ TECHNIQUE

Following are the assumptions of EOQ:

1. Annual Usage (consumption) of inventory is known.
2. Rate of usage is known and constant.
3. Ordering Costs are known and constant.
4. Carrying Costs are known and constant.
5. Zero lead-time/delivery period. (i.e., Inputs are supplied as and when ordered)

HOW TO DETERMINE EOQ?

EOQ may be determined by any of the following three methods:

(a) Graphical Method (b) Tabular Method (c) Formula Method

(a) Graphical Method: The optimum quantity of inventory which should be ordered at a point of time is determined after achieving a trade off between ordering cost and carrying costs.

Practical Steps involved in the determination of EOQ according to Graphical Method

Step 1: Take order sizes on X-axis and costs on Y-axis.

Step 2: Draw carrying cost line going upward indicating carrying cost increases as order size increases.

Step 3: Draw ordering cost line sloping downward indicating ordering cost decreases as order size increases.

Step 4: Draw total cost line which first slopes downward and then goes upward after a certain minimum point.

Step 5: Locate the point a which both the carrying cost line and ordering cost line cut each other and draw a perpendicular from this point on X-axis.

Step 6: Locate the point at which the perpendicular touches X-axis. This point gives us the Economic Order Quantity.

Step 7: Locate the point at which the perpendicular (when extended upward)cuts the total cost line. This point gives us the minimum total cost at economic order quantity.

TUTORIAL NOTES

(i) Annual total cost of ordering and carrying is minimum at EOQ order size.

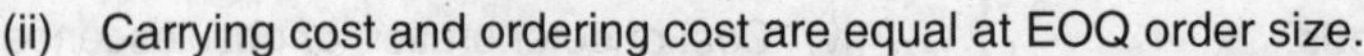

(ii) Carrying cost and ordering cost are equal at EOQ order size.

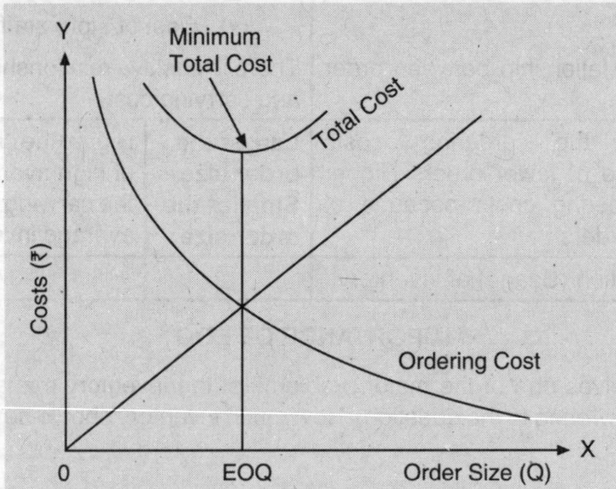

(b) Tabular *or* Trial and Error Method: The ordering and carrying costs for different order sizes are computed and the order size with lowest total cost (ordering and carrying) of inventory is the EOQ as follows:

Particulars	*Order size I*	*Order size II*	*Order size III*
A. Annual Consumption (Units)	....	....	....
B. Order Size (Units)	....	....	....
C. No. of Orders (A/B)	....	....	....
D. Cost per order (₹)	....	....	....
E. Total Ordering Cost (C × D)	....	....	....
F. Average Inventory (Units) (Order Size/2)	....	....	....
G. Carrying Cost per unit	....	....	....
H. Total Carrying cost (F × G)	....	....	....
I. Total Cost (E + H)			

Alternatively, total annual ordering and carrying cost at different order sizes may be computed as follows:

Total Annual Ordering and Carrying Cost at any order size

= [(No. of Orders × Ordering Cost per order) + (Avg. Inventory × Carrying Cost per unit p.a)]

or, $$= \left[\left(\frac{\text{Annual Consumption}}{\text{Order size}} \times \text{Ordering cost per order}\right) + \left(\frac{\text{Order Size}}{2} \times \text{Carrying Cost per unit p.a.}\right)\right]$$

TUTORIAL NOTE

Where quantity discounts are offered by the supplier of inputs, the most economical purchase level is that order size at which the total cost (i.e., Total annual Ordering & Carrying Costs + Total Purchase price of annual consumption of inputs) is minimum.

(c) Formula Method: EOQ may be calculated with the help of following formula:

1. **EOQ** $= \sqrt{\frac{2\,AO}{C}}$

where, A = Annual Consumption of Input (in units)

O = Ordering Costs Per order

C = Carrying Costs per unit p.a.

2. **No. of Orders per year** = Total Annual Consumption (in Units)/Order Size
3. **Frequency of Orders** = 365 days/No. of orders per year
4. **Total Annual Ordering and Carrying Cost at EOQ** = $\sqrt{2\ AOC}$

LIMITATIONS OF EOQ TECHNIQUE

1. Expected annual usage may not be same as the actual due to unusual and unexpected demand for inventory.
2. Rate of usage may not be constant due to unusual and unexpected demand for inventory.
3. Ordering and carrying costs may not be constant due to fluctuations in the costs of various components comprising costs.
4. Lead-time may not be constant due to reason beyond supplier's control.

ILLUSTRATION 1

From the following information, calculate (a) Economic order quantity, (b) for EOQ, the number of orders per year, (c) for EOQ how frequently should orders be placed, (d) for EOQ, Total Ordering Cost, (e) for EOQ, Total Carrying Cost and (f) Total Annual Carrying and Ordering Cost at that quantity.

Annual Consumption of input	48,000 units	Purchase Price of input unit	₹ 25
Annual Carrying Cost	12%	Ordering Cost per order	₹ 180

SOLUTION

(a) $\text{EOQ} = \sqrt{\frac{2\ AO}{C}} = \sqrt{\frac{2 \times 48000 \times ₹\ 180}{₹\ 3}} = 2400 \text{ units}$

where, A = Annual consumption of Input (in units) = 48,000 units

O = Ordering Costs Per order = ₹ 180

C = Carrying costs per unit p.a. = ₹ 25 × 12% = ₹ 3.

(b) No. of orders per year $= \frac{\text{Total Annual Consumption}}{\text{Order Size}} = \frac{48{,}000 \text{ Units}}{2{,}400 \text{ Units}} = 20 \text{ Orders}$

(c) Frequency of Orders $= \frac{365 \text{ days}}{\text{No. of Order}} = \frac{365 \text{ days}}{20 \text{ Orders}} = 18.25 \text{ Days.}$

(d) Total Ordering Cost $= \frac{\text{Annual Consumption}}{\text{Order Size}} \times \text{Ordering Cost per order}$

$= \frac{48{,}000}{2{,}400} \times ₹\ 180 = ₹\ 3{,}600$

(e) Total Carrying Cost $= \frac{\text{Order Size}}{2} \times \text{Carrying Cost per unit p.a.} = 2{,}400/2 \times ₹\ 3 = ₹\ 3{,}600$

(f) Total Annual Carrying & Ordering Cost

$= \left[\left(\frac{\text{Annual Consumption}}{\text{Order size}} \times \text{Ordering cost per order}\right) + \left(\frac{\text{Order Size}}{2} \times \text{Carrying Cost per unit p.a.}\right)\right]$

$= \left(\frac{48{,}000}{2{,}400} \times ₹\ 180\right) + \left(\frac{2{,}400}{2} \times ₹\ 3\right)$

= ₹ 3,600 + ₹ 3,600 = ₹ 7,200

Alternatively,

Total Annual Carrying Ordering cost at EOQ = $\sqrt{2\ AOC} = \sqrt{2 \times 48000 \times ₹\ 180 \times ₹\ 3} = ₹\ 7{,}200$

ILLUSTRATION 2

X Ltd. manufactures a special product 'ZED' and provides the following information:

Demand of ZED varies from 500 units to 1500 units per month.

Semi-Annual carrying cost 6%	Raw-material required per unit of finished product	2 kg
Ordering cost per order ₹ 90	Purchase price of input unit	₹ 25 per kg

Required: Calculate (a) Economic order quantity and Total Cost at that quantity, (b) Advise the company if it proposes to place orders on monthly basis, (c) Would your advise in part (b) differ if the company has been offered a discount of 4% on monthly orders?

SOLUTION

(a) $\text{EOQ} = \sqrt{\frac{2\text{ AO}}{\text{C}}} = \sqrt{\frac{2 \times 24000 \times ₹\ 90}{₹\ 3}} = 1200 \text{ units}$

where, A = Annual Consumption of Input units = (500 + 1500)/2 × 12 × 2 = 24000 units

O = Ordering Costs Per order = ₹ 90

C = Carrying Costs per unit p.a. = ₹ 25 × 6% × 2 = ₹ 3.

STATEMENT SHOWING THE CALCULATION OF TOTAL COST FOR PART (A), (B) & (C)

A.	Annual usage	24,000	24,000	24,000
B.	Order Size	1,200	2,000	2,000
C.	No. of orders	20	12	12
D.	Ordering cost per order	₹ 90	₹ 90	₹ 90
E.	Total ordering cost (C × D)	₹ 1,800	₹ 1,080	₹ 1,080
F.	Average inventory (B/2)	600	1,000	1,000
G.	Carrying cost per unit	₹ 3	₹ 3	₹ 2.88
H.	Total carrying cost (F × G)	₹ 1,800	₹ 3,000	₹ 2,880
I.	Total ordering & carrying cost (E + H)	₹ 3,600	₹ 4,080	₹ 3,960
J.	Purchase price offered	₹ 25	₹ 25	₹ 24
K.	Total purchase price (A × J)	₹ 6,00,000	₹ 6,00,000	₹ 5,76,000
L.	Total cost (I + K)	₹ 6,03,600	₹ 6,04,080	₹ 5,79,960

(b) Advice to Management: The company should not place orders on monthly basis as it results in an additional expenditure of ₹ 480 (i.e., ₹ 6,04,080 – ₹ 6,03,600).

(c) Advice to Management: The company should accept the 4% discount offer as it results in saving of ₹ 23,640 (i.e., ₹ 6.03,600 – ₹ 5,79,960).

ILLUSTRATION 3

Monthly demand of product X – 1500 units

Requirement of component to produce 1 unit of product X : 5 units

Ordering, receiving and handling cost: ₹ 10 per order

Trucking Costs: ₹ 5 per order

Deterioration and obsolescence Cost: ₹ 10 per unit p.a.

Interest Rate: 15% p.a.

Storage Cost: ₹ 4,50,000 for 90,000 units

Purchase Price of a component: ₹ 100

Required: Calculate Economic Order Quantity.

SOLUTION

A = Annual consumption of Input units = (1,500 units × 5) × 12 = 90,000 units

O = Ordering Costs Per order = ₹ 10 + ₹ 5 = ₹ 15 per order

C = Carrying costs per unit p.a. = ₹ 10 + 15% of ₹ 100 + (₹ 4,50,000 / 90,000) = ₹ 30

$$EOQ = \sqrt{\frac{2\ AO}{C}} = \sqrt{\frac{2 \times 90,000}{30}} = 300 \text{ units}.$$

ILLUSTRATION 4

X Limited, manufactures of a special product, follows the policy of EOQ (Economic Order Quantity) for one of its components. The component's details are as follows:

Purchase Price per component	₹ 200
Cost of an order	₹ 100
Annual cost of carrying one unit in inventory	10% of purchase price
Total cost of carrying inventory and ordering per annum	₹ 4,000

The company has been offered a discount of 2% on the price of the component provided the lot size is 2,000 components at a time.

Required: (a) Compute the EOQ (b) Advise whether the quantity discount offer can be accepted. (Assume that the inventory carrying cost does not vary according to discount policy.) (c) Would your advise differ if the company is offered 5% discount on a single order ?

SOLUTION

(a) Let Annual usage be 'A'

Ordering cost per order (O) = ₹ 100

Carrying cost per unit (C) = 10% of ₹ 200 = ₹ 20

Total cost of carrying Inventory and ordering p.a. = $\sqrt{2AOC}$ = ₹ 4,000

$$\sqrt{2A \times 100 \times 20} = ₹\ 4,000$$

$$\sqrt{2A \times 2000} = ₹\ 4,000$$

$$2A \times 2000 = 4,000 \times 4,000$$

$$A = (4,000 \times 4,000)/4,000 = 4,000$$

$$EOQ = \sqrt{\frac{2\ AO}{C}} = \sqrt{\frac{2 \times 4000 \times 100}{20}} = 200 \text{ units.}$$

For (b) and (c)

STATEMENT SHOWING TOTAL COST AT PURCHASE PRICE OF ₹ 200, ₹ 196 AND ₹ 190

A. Annual usage	4,000	4,000	4,000
B. Order Size	200	2000	4000
C. No. of orders	20	2	1
D. Ordering cost per order	100	100	100
E. Total ordering cost (C D)	2,000	200	100

F. Average inventory (B/2)	100	1000	2000
G. Carrying cost / unit	20	20	20
H. Total carrying cost (F G)	2,000	20,000	40,000
I. Total ordering & carrying cost (E + H)	4,000	20,200	40,100
J. Purchase price offered	200	196	190
K. Total purchase price (A J)	8,00,000	7,84,000	7,60,000
L. Total cost (I + K)	8,04,000	8,04,200	8,00,100

(b) **Advice to Management:** The 2% quantity discount offer should not be accepted as it results in an additional expenditure of ₹ 200 (i.e., ₹ 8,04,200 – ₹ 8,04,000).

(c) **Advice to Management:** The 5% quantity discount offer should be accepted as it results in saving of ₹ 3,900 (i.e., ₹ 8,04,000 – ₹ 8,00,100).

ILLUSTRATION 5

EXE Limited has received an offer of quantity discounts on its order of materials as under:

Price per tonne (₹)	*Tonnes (Nos.)*
1,200	Less than 500
1,180	500 and *less* than 1,000
1,160	1,000 and *less* than 2,000
1,140	2,000 and *less* than 3,000
1,120	3,000 and above

The annual requirement for the materials is 5,000 tonnes. The ordering cost per order is ₹ 1,200 and the stock holding cost is estimated at 20% of material cost per annum.

Required:

(a) Compute the most economical purchase level.

(b) What will be your answer to the question which precedes this if there are no discounts offered and the price per tonne is ₹ 1,500 ?

SOLUTION

(A) STATEMENT SHOWING THE TOTAL COST AT VARIOUS ORDER SIZES

Total Annual Requirements A	*Order Size (Tonnes)* B	*No. of Orders* C = A/B ₹	*Price per tonne* D ₹	*Total Purchase Price of* E = A × D ₹	*Ordering Cost* F = C × ₹1200 ₹	*Carrying Cost p.u. 1/2 × B × 20% of Price* G ₹	*Total Cost* H = E + F + G ₹
5,000	250	20	1,200	60,00,000	24,000	30,000 (125 × ₹ 240)	60,54,000
5,000	500	10	1,180	59,00,000	12,000	59,000 (250 × ₹ 236)	59,71,000
5,000	1,000	5	1,160	58,00,000	6,000	1,16,000 (500 × ₹ 232)	59,22,000
5,000	2,000	2.5	1,140	57,00,000	3,000	2,28,000 (1000 × ₹ 228)	59,31,000
5,000	3,000	1.666	1,120	56,00,000	2,000	3,36,000 (1500 × ₹ 224)	59,38,000

The most economical purchase level is 1000 tonnes because total cost is minimum (₹ 59,22,000) at this order size.

(b) $EOQ = \sqrt{\frac{2\ AO}{C}}$

where, A = Annual Usage,

O = Ordering Cost per order

C = Carrying Cost per unit per annum.

$$= \sqrt{\frac{2 \times 5000 \times ₹\,1200}{20\% \times ₹\,1500}} = 200 \text{ tonnes.}$$

ILLUSTRATION 6

SHRI RANI SATI & CO. which manufactures a product 'Ever Young', provides you the following information:

Monthly demand of 'Ever Young'	= 900 units
Cost of Placing an order	= ₹ 75
Carrying Cost per unit p.m.	= 2%
Cost of Input to be purchased	= ₹ 50 per kg.
Output per kg. of Input	= 1.5 units

Required:

(i) What percentage of discount in the price of input should be negotiated if the company proposes to rationalize placements of orders on monthly basis ?

(ii) Suppose the company followed the policy of economic order quantity and at the end of the year, it was found that the cost of placing an order was ₹ 108 instead of ₹ 75 and all other estimates were correct. What is the difference in cost on account of this error ?

SOLUTION

(i) Carrying Cost per unit p.a. (C) = 2% × 12 × ₹ 50 = ₹ 12

Annual Usage (A) = (900 × 12)/1.5 = 7200 kg.

$$EOQ = \sqrt{\frac{2\ AO}{C}} = \sqrt{\frac{2 \times 7200 \times 75}{12}} = 300 \text{ kg.}$$

Total cost when order quantity is 300 kg.

= Ordering Cost + Carrying Cost + Purchase Cost

$$= \left(\frac{7200}{300} \times ₹\,75\right) + \left(\frac{1}{2} \times 300 \times ₹\,12\right) + (7200 \times ₹\,50)$$

= ₹ 1,800 + ₹ 1,800 + ₹ 3,60,000 = ₹ 3,63,600

Suppose new negotiated purchase price is X, carrying cost will be 24X.

Now, Total Cost when order quantity is 600 kg. will be—

$$= \left(\frac{7200}{600} \times ₹\,75\right) + \left(\frac{1}{2} \times 600 \times 0.24X\right) + (7200\ X)$$

= 900 + 72X + 7200X = ₹ 900 + 7272 X

In order to rationalise the placements of orders on monthly basis, the above cost should be equal to total cost when order size is of economic order quantity.

Thus, ₹ 900 + 7272 X = ₹ 3,63,600

7272 X = ₹ 3,63,600 – ₹ 900

X = ₹ 3,62,700/7272 = ₹ 49.88 App.

Discount Desired = ₹ 50 – ₹ 49.88 = ₹ 0.12

% of Discount to be negotiated = ₹ 0.12/50 × 100 = 0.24%

(ii) Revised EOQ = $\sqrt{\dfrac{2 \times 7200 \times 108}{12}}$ = 360 units

(a) Revised Total Ordering and Carrying Cost

$= \left(\dfrac{7200}{360} \times ₹\,108\right) + \left(\dfrac{1}{2} \times 360 \times ₹\,12\right) = ₹\,2{,}160 + ₹\,2{,}160 = ₹\,4{,}320$

(b) Total Ordering and Carrying Cost at actual economic order size of 300 and correct ordering cost of ₹ 108

$= \left(\dfrac{7200}{300} \times ₹\,108\right) + \left(\dfrac{1}{2} \times 300 \times ₹\,12\right) = ₹\,2{,}592 + ₹\,1{,}800 = ₹\,4{,}392$

(c) Difference in the relevant Cost on account of wrong estimation of ordering cost [B – A]

= ₹ 4,392 – ₹ 4,320 = ₹ 72.

5.0 RE-ORDER LEVEL/RE-ORDER POINT [R.O.L.]

MEANING OF RE-ORDER LEVEL/RE-ORDER POINT [R.O.L.]

Re-order level is that level of stock at which fresh order should be placed for replenishment of stock. It is fixed somewhere between maximum and minimum levels in such a way that fresh supplies are received in such a way that fresh supplies are received just before the minimum level is reached. It is the level at which purchase requisition should be made out for fresh supplies.

OBJECTIVE OF R.O.L.

The objective of fixing Re-order Level is to determine when the fresh order should be placed for replenishment of stock.

IMPORTANCE OF R.O.L.

The Re-order Level technique solves one of the major problems of the inventory management i.e., order point problem by answering to the question-when the fresh order should be placed to procure additional inventory ?

HOW TO DETERMINE R.O.L.?

(a) Under Certainty—By certainty, we mean that usage and lead time are constant. Under assumption of certainty, the re-order level is calculated as follows:

Re-order Level = Normal Consumption during Normal Lead Time

= Normal daily/weekly/monthly usage (in units) × Normal Lead Time (in days/weeks/months)

ILLUSTRATION 7

Annual Usage of a firm is 3,60,000 units and 2 to 4 days as taken in receiving delivery of inventory after placing an order. Calculate Re-order Level under assumption of certainty. (Assume 360 days in a year).

SOLUTION

Normal daily usage = 3,60,000/360 = 1,000 units,

Normal lead time = (2 + 4)/2 = 3 days

Re-order level = Normal daily usage (in units) × Normal Lead time (in days)

= 1,000 units × 3 days = 3,000 Units.

ILLUSTRATION 8

The consumption of materials varies from 30 units to 70 units, Normal usage being 60 units. The re-order period varies from 3 to 7 weeks, normal re-order period being 6 weeks. Calculate Re-order level under assumption of certainty.

SOLUTION

ROL = Normal usage × Normal Re-order Period

= 60 units × 6 weeks = 360 units.

(b) Under Uncertainty—By uncertainty, we mean that usage and lead time are not constant. Since the usage & /or lead-time may increase, the firm may face a problem of stock out. To guard against stock out, the firm may maintain safety stock. Safety stock is buffer inventory as cushion against expected increase in usage & /or lead time. Under assumption of uncertainty, the re-order level is calculated as follows:

Re-order Level = ROL under certainty + Safety Stock.

Re-order Level = Normal Consumption during normal lead time + Safety Stock

= Normal daily/ weekly/ monthly usage (in units) × Normal Lead time (in days/ weeks/ months) + Safety Stock.

Safety Stock = (Expected Rate of Consumption × Expected increase in delivery time) + (Expected increase in Rate of Consumption × Normal Re-order period)

Alternative Formula:

Re-order Level under Uncertainty = Maximum Usage × Maximum Re-order Period

ILLUSTRATION 9

Annual Usage of a firm is 3,60,000 units and 2 to 4 days are taken in receiving delivery of inventory after placing an order. Calculate Re-order Level in each of the following alternative cases:

Case (a) If expected delay in delivery time is 1 day

Case (b) If the reasonable expected stock out is 100 units per day

Case (c) If the reasonable expected stock out is 100 units per day and expected delay in delivery time is 1 day. [Assume 360 days in a year]

SOLUTION

Normal daily usage = 3,60,000/360 = 1,000 units, Normal lead time = (2 + 4)/2 = 3 days

Safety Stock = (Expected Rate of Consumption × Expected increase in delivery time) + (Expected increase in Rate of Consumption × Normal Re-order period)

Case (a)

Safety Stock = 1,000 units × 1 day = 1,000 units

Re-order level = Normal daily usage (in units) × Normal Lead time (in days) + Safety Stock

= (1,000 units × 3) + 1,000 units = 4000 Units

Case (b)

Safety Stock = 100 units × 3 days = 300 units

Re-order level = Normal daily usage (in units) × Normal Lead Time (in days) + Safety Stock

= (1,000 units × 3) + 300 units = 3,300 Units

Case (c)

Safety Stock = (1,100 units × 1 day) + (100 units × 3 days) = 1,400 units

Re-order level = Normal daily usage (in units) × Normal Lead time (in days) + Safety Stock

= (1,000 units × 3) + 1,400 units = 4,400 Units

ILLUSTRATION 10

The consumption of materials varies from 30 units to 70 units, Normal usage being 60 units. The re-order period varies from 3 to 7 weeks, normal re-order period being 6 weeks. Calculate Re-order level under assumption of uncertainty.

SOLUTION

ROL = Maximum Usage × Maximum Re-order Period = 70 units × 7 weeks = 490 units.

ASSUMPTIONS OF ROL

Following are the assumptions of Re-order level:

1. The rate of daily usage of inventory is known and constant.
2. Constant Lead-time (i.e., the time normally taken in receiving the delivery of inventory after placing an order with the supplier is fixed).

In other words, certainty is assumed by re-order level model.

6.0 OTHER STOCK LEVELS

Setting of various stock levels is one of the techniques of inventory control. The main purpose of setting various stock levels is to avoid the situation of under stocking and over stocking. These levels are not permanent but need revision according to the changes in the factors which determine these levels.

MAXIMUM STOCK LEVEL

1. Meaning	Maximum Stock Level is that level of stock above which the stock in hand should not normally be allowed to exceed. It is the largest quantity of a particular material which may be held in the store at any time.
2. Objective	The objective of fixing the maximum stock level is to avoid the costs of over-stocking such as—Cost of storage, Cost of investment in stock, Cost of insurance, risk of obsolescence etc.
3. Factors	This Level is fixed after considering the following factors: (a) Re-order Level (b) Re-order Quantity (c) Minimum Rate of Consumption (d) Minimum Re-order Period

	(e) Availability of Working Capital (f) Availability of Storage space (g) Extra Cost of Storage (h) Extra Cost of Insurance (i) Risk of obsolescence and deterioration (j) Supply of Imported Materials (k) Price Fluctuations
4. Formula	Maximum Stock Level is computed with the help of following formula: Maximum Level = Re-order Level + Re-order Quantity – (Minimum Consumption × Minimum Re-order Period)

MINIMUM STOCK LEVEL

1. Meaning	Minimum Stock Level is that level of stock below which the stock in hand should not normally be allowed to fall. It is the lowest quantity of a particular material which must be held in the store at all times.
2. Objective	The objective of fixing the minimum stock level is to avoid the costs of under-stocking such as-Cost of stoppage of production due to shortage of materials like cost of idle labour, cost of idle plant & machinery etc.
3. Factors	This level is fixed after considering the following factors: (a) Re-order Level (b) Normal Rate of Consumption (c) Normal Re-order period
4. Formula	Minimum Stock Level is computed with the help of following formula: Minimum Level = Re-order Level – (Normal Consumption × Normal Re-order Period)

AVERAGE STOCK LEVEL

1. Meaning	Average Stock Level indicates the average stock held by the organisation.
2. Formula	This level of stock may be computed by using any one of the following formula: Average Inventory Level = Minimum Level + 1/2 Re-order quantity $OR = \frac{\text{Maximum Level + Minimum Level}}{2}$ **Note:** The Results under both these formulae need not be the same.

DANGER LEVEL

1. Meaning	Danger level is the level at which normal issues of the raw material inventory are stopped and emergency issues are only made on special requisition approved by the competent authority. When stock reaches this level an urgent action is required for the fresh supplies of materials. It is generally below the minimum level. However, some enterprises treat minimum level as danger level whereas some others fix the danger level above the minimum level but below the re-order level. Fixing danger level below the minimum level is meant for taking urgent corrective action whereas fixing it above the minimum level is for preventive action.

2. Objective	The objective of fixing danger level (below minimum level) is to determine when an urgent action is required for fresh supplies of materials.
3. Factors	This level is fixed after considering the following factors: (a) Average Consumption (b) Maximum Re-order Period for emergency purchases
4. Formula	Danger Level is computed with the help of following formula: Danger Level = Average Consumption × Maximum Re-order Period for emergency purchases

ILLUSTRATION 11

Shriram Enterprises manufactures a special product 'ZED'. The following particulars were collected for the year 20X1:

Monthly demand of ZED : 1,000 units.	Minimum Usage : 25 units per week.
Cost of placing an order : ₹ 100.	Maximum Usage : 75 units per week.
Annual carrying cost per unit : 6.5%.	Re-order Period : 4 to 6 weeks.
Purchase Price of input unit : ₹ 200.	For emergency purchase 3 weeks.

Required: *Compute from the above—*

(a) Re-order quantity, (b) Re-order level, (c) Minimum level, (d) Maximum level, (e) Average Stock Level, (f) Danger level, (g) Total cost p.a. if order size is of (i) EOQ (ii) 130 units (iii) 260 units, (h) When should the next order be placed assuming that the present inventory level is 100 units ?

SOLUTION

(a) Re-order quantity = $\sqrt{\frac{2\text{ AO}}{\text{C}}} = \sqrt{\frac{2 \times 2600 \times ₹\,100}{₹\,13}}$ = 200 units

where, A = Annual demand of Input units = 52 weeks × (75 + 25)/2 = 2600 units

O = Ordering Costs Per order = ₹ 100

C = Annual Carrying cost per unit = of ₹ 200 = ₹ 13.

(b) Re-order Level (ROL) = Maximum Rate of Consumption × Maximum Re-order Period

= 75 units × 6 Weeks = 450 units

(c) Minimum Level = Re-order level – (Normal Rate of Consumption × Normal Re-order period)

= 450 units – (50 units × 5 weeks)

= 450 units – 250 units = 200 units

(d) Maximum Level = Re-order level + Re-order quantity – (Minimum Rate of Consumption × Minimum Re-order Period)

= 450 units + 200 units – (25 units × 4 weeks) = 550 units

(e) Average Stock Level = 1/2 (Minimum Stock Level + Maximum Stock Level)

= 1/2 (200 units + 550 units) = 375 units.

Alternatively, = Minimum Level + 1/2 Re-order Quantity

= 200 units + 200 × 1/2 = 300 units

(f) Danger Level = Normal Rate of Consumption × Lead time for emergency purchases

= 50 units per week × 3 = 150 units

(G) STATEMENT SHOWING TOTAL COST AT DIFFERENT ORDER SIZES

A. Annual usage	2,600	2,600	2,600
B. Order Size	200	130	260
C. No. of orders (A/B)	13	20	10
D. Ordering cost per order	100	100	100
E. Total ordering cost (C × D)	1,300	2,000	1,000
F. Average inventory (Order size/2)	100	65	130
G. Carrying cost per unit (6.5% of ₹ 200)	13	13	13
H. Total Carrying Cost (F × G)	1,300	845	1,690
I. Total ordering & carrying cost (E + H)	2,600	2,845	2,690
J. Purchase price (2600 × ₹ 200)	5,20,000	5,20,000	5,20,000
K. Total cost (I + J)	5,22,600	5,22,845	5,22,690

(h) Per Week Normal Requirement = (25 + 75) / 2 = 50 units

Weeks Requirement served by present level = 100 / 50 = 2 weeks

Since Re-order Period (i.e., 3 weeks to 6 weeks) exceeds 2 weeks, the next order for the replenishment of supplies should be placed immediately.

7.0 ABC ANALYSIS

1. Meaning	ABC analysis is a system of inventory control. It exercises discriminating control over different items of stores classified on the basis of the investment involved. It is based on the principle of management by exception i.e. concentrate more on critical areas than others.
2. Working	Usually all items of stores are classified into 3 categories according to their importance (i.e. their value and frequency of replenishment during a period) as follows:

Category	Composition	Control
A	It consists of those items which require large investments *(say about 70% of total value of stores)* but constitute a small percentage *(say about 10%)* of total items of stores.	High degree of control is exercised by use of various techniques such as Fixing Stock Levels like Max level, Min. Level, Reorder level, Determining EOQ.
B	It consists of those items which require relatively moderate investment *(say about 20% of total value of stores)* but constitute relatively moderate percentage *(say about 20%)* of total items of stores.	Moderate degree of control is exercised. Orders are placed on a periodic review basis.

C	It consists of those items which require small investment *(say 10% of total value of stores)* but constitute a large percentage *(say about 70%)* of total items of stores.	Lower degree of control is exercised. Orders of large size are placed *either* after 6 months *or* once in a year to minimise ordering costs and to take advantages of bulk purchase.

3. Illustration

Following illustration will make clear this concept:

Category	*No. of items*	*% of total no. of items*	*Value*	*% of total value*
A	100	10	70,000	70
B	200	20	20,000	20
C	700	70	10,000	10
	1000	100	1,00,000	100

4. Graphical Representation

5. Advantages

The advantages of ABC analysis are the following:

(i) It ensures effective control on costly items (i.e. A category items) which require large investment.

(ii) It saves time and cost by exercising economic systems of control over low value items (i.e. C category items).

(iii) It ensures optimum investment in inventory considering the operational requirements and financial resources with the use of economic order quantities.

(iv) It ensures minimum total cost (i.e. ordering costs and carrying costs) of inventory.

(v) It helps in the maintenance of high inventory turnover rate.

6. Steps involved in ABC Classification

PRACTICAL STEPS INVOLVED IN ABC CLASSIFICATION

Step 1: Calculate the consumption value of each item by multiplying the annual consumption of each item (in units) by their respective unit prices.

Step 2: Calculate the total consumption value of all items.

Step 3: Calculate the percentage of consumption value of each item in relation to total consumption value of all items.

Step 4: Assign the ranking to aforesaid percentages i.e. rank 1 to highest %, rank 2 to second highest % & so on.

Step 5: Classify the items having nearly 70% value under A category, having nearly 20% value under B category and having nearly 10% value under C category.

Step 6: Calculate the percentage of each item in relation to total number of all items.

Step 7: Classify the items having nearly 10% of total no. of items under A category, having nearly 20% of total no. of items under B category and having nearly 70% of total no. of items under C category.

ILLUSTRATION 12

The following information is known about a group items. Classify the material in ABC classification.

Model Number	*Annual Consumption in Pieces*	*Unit price in paise*
501	30,000	10
502	2,80,000	15
503	3,000	10
504	1,10,000	5
505	4,000	5
506	2,20,000	10
507	15,000	5
508	80,000	5
509	60,000	15
510	8,000	10

SOLUTION

STATEMENT SHOWING ABC CLASSIFICATION

Category	*Model No.*	*% of Total Items*	*Consumption value*	*% of Total value*	*Ranking*
A Category	502	10%	42,000	48%	1
	506	10%	22,000	25%	2
	Total	20%	64,000	73%	
B Category	504	10%	9,000	10%	3
	509	10%	5,500	6%	4
	508	10%	4,000	5%	5
	Total	30%	18,500	21%	
C Category	501	10%	3,000	3-1/2%	6
	510	10%	800	1%	7
	507	10%	750	1%	8
	503	10%	300	1/4%	9
	505	10%	200	1/4%	10
	Total	50%	5,050	6%	
	G. Total	100%	87,550	100%	

Working Note:

STATEMENT SHOWING RANKING OF ITEMS

Model No. *A*	*Annual Consumption in Pieces* *B*	*Unit Price* *₹* *C*	*Annual Consumption Value* *D = B × C*	*Rank (According to value)*
501	30,000	0.10	3,000	6
502	2,80,000	0.15	42,000	1
503	3,000	0.10	300	9
504	1,10,000	0.05	5,500	4
505	4,000	0.05	200	10
506	2,20,000	0.10	22,000	2
507	15,000	0.05	750	8
508	80,000	0.05	4,000	5
509	60,000	0.15	9,000	3
510	8,000	0.10	800	7

8.0 INVENTORY TURNOVER RATIO

1. Meaning	Inventory Turnover Ratio is one of the techniques of inventory control. It expresses the relationship between the cost of material consumed and the average stock held.
2. Objective	The objective of computing the Inventory Turnover Ratio is to determine the efficiency with which inventories are maintained. In other words, the objective is to find out – (a) Fast Moving Stock i.e. stock in great demand (b) Slow Moving Stock i.e. stock in low demand (c) Dormant Stock i.e. stock having no demand at present (d) Obsolete Stock i.e. stock no longer in demand
3. Formula	Inventory Turnover Ratio is computed with the help of following formula: Inventory Turnover Ratio $= \frac{\text{Cost of Materials consumed during the period}}{\text{Cost of Average Stock held during the period}}$ = ... times *where,* (i) Cost Materials Consumed = Opening Stock + Purchases – Closing Stock (ii) Average Stock = 1/2 (Opening Stock + Closing Stock) **Note:** This ratio is usually expressed as 'X' number of times. Avg. No. of days for which an avg. inventory is held = $\frac{\text{365 days}}{\text{Inventory Turnover}}$
4. Interpretation	It indicates the speed with which the inventory is consumed. In general, a high ratio indicates fast moving stock and a low ratio indicates slow moving stock. However, too high ratio and too low ratio call for further investigation. A too high ratio may be the result of a very low inventory levels which may

	result in frequent stock-outs and thus the firm may incur high stock-outs. On the other hand, a too low ratio may be the result of excessive inventory levels, slow-moving *or* dormant *or* obsolete inventory and thus, the firm may incur high carrying costs. Thus, a firm should have *neither* a very high *nor* a very low stock turnover ratio, it should have a satisfactory level. To judge whether the ratio is satisfactory *or* not, it should be compared with its own past ratios *or* with the ratio of similar firms in the same industry *or* with industry average.
5. Usefulness	On the basis of Inventory Turnover Ratio, the management may take the necessary corrective action such as – (a) Decision as to how to prevent the under-stocking of fast moving stock items. (b) Decision as to how to prevent the over-stocking of slow moving stock items. (c) Decision as to whether to retain *or* scrap the dormant stock items. (d) Decision as to scrapping *or* discard of obsolete stock items.

ILLUSTRATION 13

From the following data calculate the Inventory Turnover Ratio of the two items, and put forward your comments on them.

Particulars	*Material A* ₹	*Material B* ₹
Opening Stock	10,000	9,000
Purchases during the year	52,000	27,000
Closing Stock	6,000	11,000

SOLUTION

Particulars	*Material A* ₹	*Material B* ₹
A. Opening Stock	10,000	9,000
B. *Add:* Purchases during the year	52,000	27,000
C. *Less:* Closing Stock	6,000	11,000
D. Consumption of Material during the year	56,000	25,000
E. Average Inventory:		
(Opening Stock + Closing Stock)/2	(10,000 + 6,000)/2 = 8,000	(9,000 + 11,000)/2 = 10,000
F. Inventory Turnover Ratio:		
$= \frac{\text{Consumption of materials during the period}}{\text{Average inventory during the period}}$	56,000/8,000 = 7 times,	25,000/10,000 = 2.5 times
Alternatively (in number of days):		
$= \frac{\text{No. of days in a year}}{\text{Inventory turnover ratio}}$	365/7 = 52 days	365/2.5 = 146 days

Comments: The turnover of material A is substantially higher than that of material B. Hence, material A is fast moving as compared to Material B.

9.0 ANALYSIS OF INVESTMENT IN INVENTORY

The objective of inventory policy is to maximise the value of firm. The value of the firm will be maximised when the marginal rate of return of investment in inventory is equal to marginal cost of funds used to finance the investment in inventory. The marginal rate of return is calculated by dividing the incremental operating profit by the incremental investment in inventories. The cost of funds is the required rate of the suppliers of funds. A change in inventory policy should be made if the incremental rate of return exceeds the required rate of return. The evaluation of inventory policy involves the following steps:

PRACTICAL STEPS INVOLVED IN THE EVALUATION OF INVENTORY POLICY

Step 1: *Estimate the Incremental Operating Profit as follows:*

Incremental Operating Profit = Incremental Contribution – Incremental Costs

Step 2: *Estimate the Incremental Investment as follows:*

Incremental Investment = Increase in inventory + Increase in other net working capital.

Note: Average Inventory = Cost of Goods Sold / Inventory Turnover.

Step 3: *Estimate the Incremental Rate of Return as follows:*

$$\text{Incremental Rate of Return} = \frac{\text{Incremental Operating Profit}}{\text{Incremental Investment}}$$

Step 4: *Compare the incremental rate of return with the required rate of return.*

Step 5: *Adopt that inventory policy at which incremental rate of return is equal to the required rate of return since the value of the firm is maximised at this point. However, a conservative firm may adopt that inventory policy at which incremental rate of return exceeds the required rate of return since there can be an error of estimation in incremental rate of return & the required rate of return.*

ILLUSTRATION 14

A Ltd. uses inventory turnover as one performance measure to evaluate its production manager. Currently, its inventory turnover (based on Cost of Goods Sold/Average Inventory) is 10 times per annum, as compared with industry average of 4. Average sales are ₹ 4,50,000 p.a. variable costs of inventory have consistently remained at 70% of sales with fixed costs of ₹ 10,000. Carrying costs of inventory (excluding financing costs) are 5% per annum. Sales force complained that low inventory levels are resulting in lost-sales due to stock outs. Sales manager has made an estimate based on stock out reports as under:

Inventory Policy	*Inventory Turnover*	*Sales (in ₹)*
Current	10	4,50,000
A	8	5,00,000
B	6	5,40,000
C	4	5,65,000

On the basis of above estimates, assuming a 40% tax rate and an after tax required return of 20% on investment in inventory, which policy would you recommend ?

SOLUTION

STEP 1: CALCULATION OF COST OF GOODS SOLD

Policy A	*Variable Cost* (₹) B	*Fixed Cost* (₹) C	*Total Cost* (₹) $D = B + C$	*Inventory Turnover* E	*Average Investment* $F = D / E$
Current	4,50,000 × 0.7 = 3,15,000	10,000	3,25,000	10	32,500
A	5,00,000 × 0.7 = 3,50,000	10,000	3,60,000	8	45,000
B	5,40,000 × 0.7 = 3,78,000	10,000	3,88,000	6	64,667
C	5,65,000 × 0.7 = 3,95,500	10,000	4,05,500	4	1,01,375

STEP 2: STATEMENT SHOWING THE EVALUATION OF INVENTORY POLICIES

Particulars	*Current (₹)*	*A (₹)*	*B (₹)*	*C (₹)*
A. Sales	4,50,000	5,00,000	5,40,000	5,65,000
B. *Less:* Cost of Goods Sold	3,25,000	3,60,000	3,88,000	4,05,500
C. Contribution	1,25,000	1,40,000	1,52,000	1,59,500
D. *Less:* Carrying Cost @ 5%	1,625	2,250	3,233	5,069
E. Profit before tax	1,23,375	1,37,750	1,48,767	1,54,431
F. *Less:* Tax @ 40%	49,350	55,100	59,507	61,772
G. Profit after tax	74,025	82,650	89,260	92,659
H. Incremental Profit (After Tax)		8,625	15,235	18,634
I. Incremental Investment		12,500	32,167	68,875
J. Increment Rate of Return (H/I × 100)		69%	47.36%	27.05%

Conclusion: Since the incremental rate of return is highest with inventory policy A, therefore, policy A should be followed.

SOLVED PROBLEMS

PROBLEM 1

A customer has been ordering 90,000 special design metal columns at the rate of 18,000 per order during the past years. The production cost comprises ₹ 120 for material, ₹ 60 for labour and ₹ 20 for fixed overheads. It costs ₹ 1500 to set up for one run of 18,000 column and inventory carrying cost is 15%. Since this customer may buy at least 5000 columns this year, the company would like to avoid making five different production runs. Find the most economic production in.

SOLUTION

$$\text{Economic Production Run} = \sqrt{\frac{2 \times \text{Annual Output} \times \text{Set up cost per production run}}{\text{Inventory Carrying Cost per unit p.a.}}}$$

$$= \sqrt{\frac{2 \times 90{,}000 \times ₹\ 1500}{₹\ 30}} = 3000 \text{ units.}$$

PROBLEM 2

X Ltd. is committed to supply 24,000 bearings per annum to Y Ltd. on a steady basis. It is estimated that it costs 10 paise as inventory holding cost per bearing per month and that the set-up cost per run of bearing manufacture is ₹ 324.

(a) What would be the optimum run size for bearing manufacture?

(b). What is the minimum inventory holding cost at optimum run size?

(c) Assuming that the company has a policy of manufacturing 6,000 bearings per run, how much extra costs would the company be incurring as compared to the optimum run suggested in (a)?

SOLUTION

(a) Optimum production run size (Q) = $\sqrt{\frac{2\ AO}{C}}$

where, A = No. of units to be produced within one year.

O = Set-up cost per production run

C = Carrying cost per unit per annum.

$= \sqrt{\frac{2 \times 24{,}000 \times ₹\ 324}{0.10 \times 12}} = 3{,}600$ bearings

(b) Minimum inventory holding cost, if run size is 3600 bearings

= Average inventory × carrying cost per unit

= (3600/2) × (0.10 × 12) = ₹ 2,160.

(C) STATEMENT SHOWING TOTAL COST AT PRODUCTION RUN SIZES OF 3,600 AND 6,000 BEARINGS

A. Annual requirements	24,000	24,000
B. Run Size	3,600	6,000
C. No. of runs (A/B)	6.667	4
D. Set up cost per run	₹ 324	₹ 324
E. Total set up cost (C × D)	₹ 2,160	₹ 1,296
F. Average inventory (B/2)	1,800	3,000
G. Carrying cost p.a.	1.20	1.20
H. Total carrying cost (F × G)	2,160	3,600
I. Total cost (E + H)	4,320	4,896

Extra cost incurred, if run size is of 6,000 = ₹ 4,896 – ₹ 4,320 = ₹ 576.

PROBLEM 3

(a) The annual demand for an item of raw material is 4,000 units and the purchase price is expected to be ₹ 90 per unit. The cost of processing an order is ₹ 135 and the cost of storage is estimated to be ₹ 12 per unit. What is the optimal order quantity and total relevant cost of this order quantity?

(b) Suppose that ₹ 135 as estimated to be the incremental cost of processing an order is incorrect and should have been ₹ 80. All other estimates are correct. What is the difference in cost on account of this error ?

(c) Assume at the commencement of the period that a supplier offers 4,000 units at a price of ₹ 86. The materials will be delivered immediately and placed in the stores. Assume that the incremental cost of placing the order is zero and original estimate of ₹ 135 for placing an order for the economic batch is correct. Should the order be accepted ?

SOLUTION

(a) Optimal order quantity = $\sqrt{\frac{2\ AO}{C}}$

where, A = Annual requirements of raw material in units = 4000 units

O = Ordering cost per order = ₹ 135

C = Carrying cost per unit per annum. = ₹ 12

$$= \sqrt{\frac{2 \times 4,000 \times ₹\ 135}{₹\ 12}} = 300 \text{ units}$$

Total relevant cost when order quantity is 300 units = Ordering cost + Carrying cost

= (No. of orders × Ordering cost per order) + (Avg. inventory Carrying cost p.a.)

$$= \left(\frac{4,000}{300 \text{ units}} \times ₹\ 135\right) + [(1/2 \times 300 \text{ units} \times ₹\ 12]$$

= ₹ 1,800 + ₹ 1,800 = 3,600

(b) Difference in the Relevant cost on account of wrong estimation

Revised optimum order quantity = $\sqrt{\frac{2 \times 4,000 \times ₹\ 80}{₹\ 12}}$ = 231 units

Revised relevant cost when order quantity is 231 units

$$= \left(\frac{4,000 \text{ units}}{231 \text{ units}} \times ₹\ 80\right) + [(1/2 \times 231 \text{ units}) \times ₹\ 12]$$

= ₹ 1,385.28 + ₹ 1,386

= ₹ 2,771.28 (or, ₹ 2,771) ...(A)

Since, the estimate of ordering cost was detected as wrong at the end of the year and all other estimates were found to be correct, therefore, the relevant cost under such a situation would be as follows:

$$= \left(\frac{4,000 \text{ units}}{300 \text{ units}} \times ₹\ 80\right) + [(1/2 \times 300 \text{ units}) \times ₹\ 12]$$

= ₹ 1,066.67 + ₹ 1,800

= ₹ 2,866.67 (or, ₹ 2,867 say) ...(B)

Difference in the relevant cost (B – A) on account of wrong estimation of ordering cost

= ₹ 2,867 – ₹ 2,771 = ₹ 96

(c) Evaluation of purchases at a price of ₹ 86.

STATEMENT OF COST AT SPECIAL OFFER AND AT THE ORIGINAL ESTIMATE

Total units purchases	*Price* ₹	*Order Size (in units)*	*Total Cost of Purchase* ₹	*Ordering Cost* ₹	*Carrying Cost* ₹	*Total cost* ₹
4,000	86	4,000	3,44,000 (4,000 × ₹ 86)	Nil	24,000	3,68,000
4,000	90	300	3,60,000 (4,000 × ₹ 90)	1,800	1,800	3,63,600
						4,400

Recommendation: Since the special offer of ₹ 86 per unit on the initial purchase of 4,000 units imposes an additional cost of ₹ 4,400, therefore such a purchase is not recommended.

10 WORKING CAPITAL MANAGEMENT—CASH MANAGEMENT

LEARNING OBJECTIVES

After studying this chapter, you should be able to understand:

- Meaning of Cash Management
- Objective of Cash Management
- Need for Cash
- Nature of Cash Management
- Cash Planning
- Cash Budget
- Methods of Cash Forecasting
- Cash Management Control
- How to Determine Optimum Cash Balance
- Baumol's Model
- The Miller–Orr Model
- Management of Marketable Securities

1.0 MEANING OF CASH MANAGEMENT

Cash Management means planning, organising, directing and controlling of cash. It provides an answer to the following basic questions:

(a) **How much to maintain cash balance?**

It means what should be level of cash in the organisation. How much to maintain cash balance will depend upon the cash operating cycle. Larger the operating cycle, larger the cash balance required.

(b) **How to finance deficit** (i.e., excess of estimated cash outflows over estimated cash inflows)?

(c) **How to invest surplus** (i.e., excess of estimated cash inflows over estimated cash outflows)?

2.0 OBJECTIVE OF CASH MANAGEMENT

The objective of cash management is to avoid the situation of excessive and inadequate cash and to determine and maintain the optimum level of cash after achieving a trade off between the profitability and liquidity so as to maximize the wealth of shareholders as a whole.

Whenever the situation of surplus *or* deficit cash arises, prompt and timely action should be taken by the management to correct the imbalances.

3.0 NEED FOR CASH

The following are the three principal motives for holding cash:

TRANSACTION MOTIVE

The transaction motive is the need to hold cash to make routine payments while conducting business in the ordinary course. Example: To make payments for purchases, manufacturing expenses, office and selling expenses, taxes etc.

SPECULATIVE MOTIVE

The speculative motive is the need to hold cash in order to take advantage of profitable opportunities as and when they arise. Example: To make purchases for future requirements if it is expected that material prices will increase.

PRECAUTIONARY MOTIVE

The precautionary motive is the need to hold cash to meet contingencies in the future. The precautionary balance may be kept in cash *or* marketable securities. Safety as is typified by the saying that a man has only three friends-an old wife, an old dog and money.

4.0 NATURE OF CASH MANAGEMENT

Organisational Structure of an enterprise helps in determining the exact nature of cash management. In a highly centralised organization, the central *or* head office controls the inflows and outflows of cash on routine and daily basis. In a decentralised organisation, the decentralised offices control the inflows and outflows of cash on routine and daily basis.

5.0 CASH PLANNING

Cash planning is the first step in the cash management. Cash planning is the technique to plan and control the use of cash. Cash planning may be done on daily, weekly *or* monthly basis. Cash planning involves:

(a) Estimating the timings and amount of expected cash inflows.

(b) Estimating the timings and amount of expected cash outflows.

(c) Estimating the timings and amount of cash deficit.

(d) Estimating the timings and amount of surplus cash.

For this purpose, Cash Flow Statements and Cash Budgets are required to be prepared.

6.0 CASH BUDGET

MEANING OF CASH BUDGET

Cash budget is a statement showing the estimated cash inflows, cash outflows and the resultant cash balances over a given budget period.

PURPOSE OF CASH BUDGET

Cash Budget serves as a device for planning and controlling the inflows and outflows of cash to ensure the availability of cash when it is needed.

UTILITY OF CASH BUDGET

The utilities of preparing Cash Budget are summarised as follows:

(i) It enables the management to determine the timings when there is likely to be surplus/shortage of cash.

(ii) It enables the management to determine the quantum of surplus/shortage of cash.

(iii) It enables the management to determine the period for which the situation of surplus/shortage is likely to be continued.

(iv) It enables the management to prepare the borrowing schedule.

(v) It enables the management to prepare the repayment schedule well in advance.

(vi) It enables the management to plan for dividend payment well in advance.

(vii) It enables the management to plan for financing the expansion/modernization of the existing plant.

(viii) It enables the management to plan for financing a new project.

(ix) It enables the management to take the advantage of cash discount.

However, it should be understood that the cash budget is only as much useful as the accuracy of the forecasts that are used in its preparation.

7.0 METHODS OF CASH FORECASTING

RECEIPTS AND PAYMENTS METHOD

The steps involved in preparation of cash budget as per Receipts and Payments Method are as follows:

PRACTICAL STEPS INVOLVED IN THE PREPARATION OF CASH BUDGET

Step 1: Ascertain the Opening Balance

Step 2: Identify, Analyse and Estimate the Cash inflows such as:

(a) Operating Cash inflows (i.e., Cash inflows relating to operating activities such as cash sales, collection from debtors and trading commission).

(b) Investing Cash inflows (i.e., Cash inflows relating to relating to investing activities such as sale of investments, sale of fixed assets, interest and dividend on investments).

(c) Financing Cash inflows (i.e., Cash inflows relating to financing activities such as proceeds from issue of shares, debentures).

Step 3: Identify, Analyse and Estimate the Cash Outflows such as:

(a) Operating Cash outflows (i.e., Cash outflows relating to operating activities such as cash purchases, payment to creditors, payment of operating expenses).

(b) Investing Cash outflows (i.e., Cash outflows relating to investing activities such as purchases of investments, purchase of fixed assets).

(c) Financing Cash outflows (i.e., Cash outflows relating to financing activities such as redemption of shares and debentures, payment of interest, tax and dividend).

Step 4: Estimate the Deficit *or* Surplus & make the necessary arrangement:

In case of deficit, the necessary arrangement (say by borrowing *or* by selling Marketable Securities) should be made to finance the deficit. In case of surplus, the necessary arrangement (say by Repayment of borrowing *or* by purchasing Marketable Securities) should be made to invest the surplus.

SPECIMEN OF CASH BUDGET
CASH BUDGET
for the Budget period ending ......

Particulars	*Period*			
	April (₹)	*May* (₹)	*June* (₹)	*July* (₹)
A. Total Cash Available:				
1. Opening Cash Balance	....	....	....	....
2. Cash Sales	....	....	....	....
3. Collections from Debtors	....	....	....	....
4. Proceeds from Issue of Shares/Debentures	....	....	....	....
5. Proceeds from sale of Fixed Assets	....	....	....	....
6. Misc. Non-operating Income received	....	....	....	....
Total (1 + 2 + 3 + 4 + 5 + 6)	....	....	....	....
B. Total Cash Payments:				
7. Cash Purchases of Material	....	....	....	....
8. Payments to Suppliers of Materials	....	....	....	....
9. Payments of Direct Labour Wages	....	....	....	....
10. Payment of Factory Overheads	....	....	....	....
(Excluding Non-Cash Costs like Dep.)				
11. Payment of Administration Expenses				
(Excluding Non-Cash Costs like Dep.)				
12. Payment of Selling and Distribution Exp.	....	....	....	....
(Excluding Non-Cash Costs like Dep.)				
13. Redemption of Redeemable	....	....	....	....
Pref. shares/Debentures/Buy Back of Shares				
14. Payment for Purchase of Fixed Asset	....	....	....	....
15. Payment for Misc. Non-operating expenses	....	....	....	....
16. Advance Payment of Income-tax	....	....	....	....
17. Payment of Dividend	....	....	....	....
Total (7 + ... + 17)	....	....	....	....
18. Surplus (Shortage) (A – B)	....	....	....	....
19. Effects of Short-term Financing & Investing:				
Proceeds of Short-term Borrowings	....	....	....	....
Proceeds of Marketable Securities	....	....	....	....
Less: Repayment of loan principal	(......)	(......)	(......)	(......)
Less: Repayment of Interest on loan	(......)	(......)	(......)	(......)
Less: Investment in Marketable Securities	(......)	(......)	(......)	(......)
20. Closing Cash Balance (18 + 19)	....	....	....	....

Working Note:

Calculation of Cash Sales, Collection from Debtors, Cash Purchases and Payments to Suppliers.

Particulars	*Jan.*	*Feb.*	*Mar.*	*Apr.*	*May*	*Jun.*	*July*
A. No. of Units Sold	....	....	....	....	....	....	....
B. Selling Price per unit	....	....	....	....	....	....	....
C. Total Sales (A × B)	....	....	....	....	....	....	....
D. *Less:* Cash Sales	....	....	....	....	....	....	....
E. Credit Sales (C – D)	....	....	....	....	....	....	....
F. *Less:* Bad Debts	....	....	....	....	....	....	....
G. Good Debtors (E – F)	....	....	....	....	....	....	....
H. Collection from Debtors:							
In month following month of Sales	....	....	....	....	....	....	....
In Second month	....	....	....	....	....	....	....
In Third month	....	....	....	....	....	....	....
I. Gross Profit on Sales (C × GP%)	....	....	....	....	....	....	....
J. Total Purchases (C – I)	....	....	....	....	....	....	....
K. *Less:* Cash Purchases	....	....	....	....	....	....	....
L. Credit Purchases (J – K)	....	....	....	....	....	....	....
M. Payment to Suppliers	....	....	....	....	....	....	....

Working Notes: When Opening and Closing Stock, Trade Debtors, Trade Creditors and Creditors for Expenses are given:

(I) CALCULATION OF CASH SALES AND COLLECTION FROM DEBTORS

Particulars	*Jan.*	*Feb.*	*Mar.*	*Apr.*	*May*	*Jun.*
A. Sales (Units)	....	....	....	....	....	....
B. Selling Price per unit	....	....	....	....	....	....
C. Total Sales	....	....	....	....	....	....
D. *Less:* Cash Sales	....	....	....	....	....	....
E. Credit Sales	....	....	....	....	....	....
F. *Add:* Opening Trade Debtors	....	....	....	....	....	....
G. *Less:* Closing Trade Debtors	....	....	....	....	....	....
H. Collection from Debtors	....	....	....	....	....	....

(II) CALCULATION OF CASH PURCHASES AND PAYMENT TO CREDITORS

Particulars	*Jan.* ₹	*Feb.* ₹	*Mar.* ₹	*Apr.* ₹	*May* ₹	*Jun.* ₹
A. Total Sales	....	....	....	....	....	....
B. *Less:* Gross Profit	....	....	....	....	....	....
C. Cost of Goods Sold	....	....	....	....	....	....

D. *Add:* Closing Stock	....	....	....	....	....	....
E. *Less:* Opening Stock	....	....	....	....	....	....
F. *Less:* Wages	....	....	....	....	....	....
G. Total Purchases	....	....	....	....	....	....
H. *Less:* Cash Purchases	....	....	....	....	....	....
I. Credit Purchases	....	....	....	....	....	....
J. *Add:* Opening Trade Creditors	....	....	....	....	....	....
K. *Less:* Closing Trade Creditors	....	....	....	....	....	....
L. Payment to Creditors	....	....	....	....	....	....

(III) PAYMENT OF EXPENSES (EXCLUDING DEPRECIATION)

Particulars	*April (₹)*	*May (₹)*	*June (₹)*
A. Expenses (Excluding Depreciation)	....	....	....
B. *Add:* Opening Creditors for Expenses	....	....	....
C. *Less:* Closing Creditors for Expenses	....	....	....
D. Total Payment	....	....	....

ILLUSTRATION 1 [CALCULATION OF THE AMOUNT OF CASH SALES AND COLLECTION FROM THE DEBTORS]

Tulsian (1) Ltd. provides you the following information:

(a) Sales (in units):

January	*February*	*March*	*April*	*May*	*June*
1,000	2,000	3,000	4,000	5,000	6,000

(b) 20% of the Sales are on cash basis and the balance on credit basis.

(c) Uniform Selling Price—₹ 20 per unit.

Required: Calculate the amount of Cash Sales and Collection from Debtors for the months, April to June in each of the following alternative cases:

Case (a) If credit period allowed to customers is 1 month

Case (b) If credit period allowed to customers is 2 months.

Case (c) If credit period allowed to customers is 3 months.

Case (d) If 50% of credit sales are collected in the month of sales and the balance in the month following.

Case (e) If 50% of credit sales are collected within one month and the balance in two months.

Case (f) If 2% of credit sales constitute bad debt losses. 50% of the good accounts receivables are collected in the month of the sales and the rest in the next month.

Case (g) If realisation from debtors are 30% in the month of sales, 60% in the month following that and the balance in the month after that.

Case (h) If 50% of credit sales are collected in the month following the sales, 50% of the remaining in the second month and the balance in the third month.

SOLUTION

CALCULATION OF CASH AND CREDIT SALES

Particulars	*Jan.*	*Feb.*	*Mar.*	*Apr.*	*May*	*Jun.*
A. Sales (Units)	1,000	2,000	3,000	4,000	5,000	6,000
B. Selling Price per unit	20	20	20	20	20	20
C. Total Sales (A × B)	20,000	40,000	60,000	80,000	1,00,000	1,20,000
D. *Less:* Cash Sales @20%	4,000	8,000	12,000	16,000	20,000	24,000
E. Credit Sales @ 80%	16,000	32,000	48,000	64,000	80,000	96,000

Particulars	*April* ₹	*May* ₹	*June* ₹
Case (a)			
Cash Sales	16,000	20,000	24,000
Collection from Debtors	48,000	64,000	80,000
Case (b)			
Cash Sales	16,000	20,000	24,000
Collection from Debtors	32,000	48,000	64,000
Case (c)			
Cash Sales	16,000	20,000	24,000
Collection from Debtors	16,000	32,000	48,000
Case (d)			
Cash Sales	16,000	20,000	24,000
Collection from Debtors:			
50% of the Current Month's Sales	32,000	40,000	48,000
50% of Previous Month's Sales	24,000	32,000	40,000
	56,000	72,000	88,000
Case (e)			
Cash Sales	16,000	20,000	24,000
Collection from Debtors:			
50% of Previous Month's Sales	24,000	32,000	40,000
50% of Previous to Previous Month's Sales	16,000	24,000	32,000
	40,000	56,000	72,000
Case (f)			
Cash Sales	16,000	20,000	48,000
Collection from Debtors			
50% of Current Month's Good Receivables	31,360	39,200	47,040
50% of Previous Month's Good Receivables	23,520	31,360	39,200
	54,880	70,560	86,240

Working Note:

CALCULATION OF GOOD ACCOUNT RECEIVABLE

Particulars	*Jan.* ₹	*Feb.* ₹	*Mar.* ₹	*Apr.* ₹	*May* ₹	*Jun.* ₹
Credit Sales	16,000	32,000	48,000	64,000	80,000	96,000
Less: 2% Bad Debts	320	640	960	1,280	1,600	1,920
Good Account Receivables	15,680	31,360	47,040	62,720	78,400	94,080

Particulars	*April* ₹	*May* ₹	*June* ₹
Case (g)			
Cash Sales	16,000	20,000	24,000
Collection from Debtors			
30% of Current Month's Sales	19,200	24,000	28,800
60% of Previous Month's Sales	28,800	38,400	48,000
10% of Previous to Previous Month's Sales	3,200	4,800	6,400
	51,200	67,200	83,200
Case (h)			
Cash Sales	16,000	20,000	24,000
Collection from Debtors			
50% of Previous Month's Sales	24,000	32,000	40,000
25% of Previous to Previous Month's Sales	8,000	12,000	16,000
25% of Third Previous Month's Sales	4,000	8,000	12,000
	36,000	52,000	68,000

ILLUSTRATION 2 [CALCULATION OF THE AMOUNT OF CASH SALES AND COLLECTION FROM THE DEBTORS]

Tulsian (2) Ltd. provides you the following information:

(a) Sales (in units) and Closing Trade Debtors:

Particulars	*January*	*February*	*March*	*April*	*May*	*June*
Sales (units)	1,000	2,000	3,000	4,000	5,000	6,000
Closing Trade Debtors (₹)	16,000	40,000	64,000	88,000	1,12,000	1,36,000

(b) 20% of the Sales are on Cash basis and the balance on credit basis.

(c) Uniform Selling Price-₹ 20 per unit.

Required: Calculate the amount of Cash Sales and Collection from Debtors for the months Jan. to June.

SOLUTION

CALCULATION OF CASH SALES AND COLLECTION FROM TRADE DEBTORS

Particulars	January	February	March	April	May	June
A. Sales (Units)	1,000	2,000	3,000	4,000	5,000	6,000
B. Selling Price per unit (₹)	20	20	20	20	20	20
C. Total Sales (A × B)	20,000	40,000	60,000	80,000	1,00,000	1,20,000
D. *Less:* Cash Sales@20%	(4,000)	(8,000)	(12,000)	(16,000)	(20,000)	(24,000)
E. Credit Sales	16,000	32,000	48,000	64,000	80,000	96,000
F. *Add:* Opening Debtors	—	16,000	40,000	64,000	88,000	1,12,000
G. *Less:* Closing Debtors	(16,000)	(40,000)	(64,000)	(88,000)	(1,12,000)	(1,36,000)
H. Collection from Debtors [E + F – G]	—	8,000	24,000	40,000	56,000	72,000

ILLUSTRATION 3 [CALCULATION OF THE AMOUNT OF CASH PURCHASES AND PAYMENT TO CREDITORS]

Tulsian (3) Ltd. provides you the following information:

(a) Sales (in units):

January	February	March	April	May	June	July
1,000	2,000	3,000	4,000	5,000	6,000	7,000

(b) 25% of the Purchases are on cash basis and the balance on credit basis.

(c) Uniform Selling Price—₹ 20 per unit. This price was fixed after adding 25% to cost.

(d) No stock remains at the end of a month.

Required: Calculate the amount of Cash Purchases and Payment to Creditors for the months, April to June in each of the following alternative cases:

Case (a) If credit period allowed by suppliers is 1 month

Case (b) If credit period allowed by suppliers is 2 months.

Case (c) If credit period allowed by suppliers is 3 months.

Case (d) If 50% of Credit purchases are paid in the month of purchases and the balance in the month following.

Case (e) If 50% of Credit purchases are paid within one month and the balance in two months.

Case (f) If purchases are made one month in advance and credit purchases are paid after one month.

SOLUTION

CALCULATION OF CASH PURCHASES AND CREDIT PURCHASES

Particulars	Jan.	Feb.	Mar.	Apr.	May	Jun.	July
A. Sales (Units)	1,000	2,000	3,000	4,000	5,000	6,000	7,000
B. Selling Price per unit (₹)	20	20	20	20	20	20	20
C. Total Sales (A B)	20,000	40,000	60,000	80,000	1,00,000	1,20,000	1,40,000
D. *Less:* Gross Profit @ 20%	(4,000)	(8,000)	(12,000)	(16,000)	(20,000)	(24,000)	(28,000)

E. Total Purchases (C – D)	16,000	32,000	48,000	64,000	80,000	96,000	1,12,000
F. *Less:* Cash Purchases@25%	(4,000)	(8,000)	(12,000)	(16,000)	(20,000)	(24,000)	(28,000)
G. Credit Purchases (E – F)	12,000	24,000	36,000	48,000	60,000	72,000	84,000

Particulars	*April* ₹	*May* ₹	*June* ₹
Case (a)			
Cash Purchases (25% of Current Month's Purchases)	16,000	20,000	24,000
Payment of Creditors (preceding Month's Credit Purchases)	36,000	48,000	60,000
Case (b)			
Cash Purchases (25% of Current Month's Purchases)	16,000	20,000	24,000
Payment to Creditors (Second Preceding Month's Credit Purchases)	24,000	36,000	48,000
Case (c)			
Cash Purchases (25% of Current Month's Purchases)	16,000	20,000	24,000
Payment to Creditors (3rd Preceding Month's Credit Purchases)	12,000	24,000	36,000
Case (d)			
Cash Purchases	16,000	20,000	24,000
Payment to Creditors:			
50% of Current Month's Credit Purchases	24,000	30,000	36,000
50% of Preceding Month's Credit Purchases	18,000	24,000	30,000
	42,000	54,000	66,000
Case (e)			
Cash Purchases	16,000	20,000	24,000
Payment to Creditors:			
50% of Preceding Month's Credit Purchases	18,000	24,000	30,000
50% of Second Preceding Month's Credit Purchases	12,000	18,000	24,000
	30,000	42,000	54,000
Case (f)			
Cash Purchases (25% of Next Month's Purchases)	20,000	24,000	28,000
Payment to Creditors (75% of Current Month's Purchases)	48,000	60,000	72,000
	68,000	84,000	1,00,000

ILLUSTRATION 4 [CALCULATION OF THE AMOUNT OF CASH PURCHASES AND PAYMENTS TO CREDITORS]

Tulsian (4) Ltd. provides you the following information:

(a) Sales (in units) and Closing Stock (in units) and Closing Trade Creditors:

Particulars	*January*	*February*	*March*	*April*	*May*	*June*	*July*
Sales (units)	1,000	2,000	3,000	4,000	5,000	6,000	7,000
Closing Stock (Units)	100	200	300	400	500	600	700

Closing Trade Creditors (₹)	11,400	28,650	45,975	62,850	79,500	96,150	1,12,800
Wages	2,400	3,000	3,600	4,800	6,000	7,200	8,400

(b) 25% of the Purchases are on Cash basis and the balance on credit basis.

(c) Uniform Selling Price-₹ 20 per unit. This price was fixed after adding 25% to cost.

Required: Calculate the amount of Cash Purchases and Payment to Creditors for the months Jan. to July.

SOLUTION

CALCULATION OF CASH PURCHASES AND PAYMENT TO TRADE CREDITORS

	Particulars	*Jan.*	*Feb.*	*Mar.*	*Apr.*	*May*	*Jun.*	*July*
A.	Sales (Units)	1,000	2,000	3,000	4,000	5,000	6,000	7,000
B.	Selling Price per unit (₹)	20	20	20	20	20	20	20
C.	Total Sales (A × B) (₹)	20,000	40,000	60,000	80,000	1,00,000	1,20,000	1,40,000
D.	*Less:* Gross Profit@20%	(4,000)	(8,000)	(12,000)	(16,000)	(20,000)	(24,000)	(28,000)
E.	Cost of Goods Sold (C – D)	16,000	32,000	48,000	64,000	80,000	96,000	1,12,000
F.	*Add:* Closing Stock	1,600	3,200	4,800	6,400	8,000	9,600	11,200
G.	*Less:* Opening Stock	—	(1,600)	(3,200)	(4,800)	(6,400)	(8,000)	(9,600)
H.	*Less:* Wages	(2,400)	(3,000)	(3,600)	(4,800)	(6,000)	(7,200)	(8,400)
I.	Total Purchases	15,200	30,600	46,000	60,800	75,600	90,400	1,05,200
J.	*Less:* Cash Purchases @ 25%	(3,800)	(7,650)	(11,500)	(15,200)	(18,900)	(22,600)	(26,300)
K.	Credit Purchases (I – J)	11,400	22,950	34,500	45,600	56,700	67,800	78,900
L.	*Add:* Opening Creditors	—	11,400	28,650	45,975	62,850	79,500	96,150
M.	*Less:* Closing Creditors	(11,400)	(28,650)	(45,975)	(62,850)	(79,500)	(96,150)	(1,12,800)
N.	Payment to Creditors [K + L – M]	—	5,700	17,175	28,725	40,050	51,150	62,250

ILLUSTRATION 5 [CALCULATION OF THE AMOUNT OF EXPENSES PAID]

Tulsian (5) Ltd. provides you the following information:

Particulars	*March (₹)*	*April (₹)*	*May (₹)*	*June (₹)*
Budgeted Expenses	30,000	50,000	70,000	90,000

Budgeted expenses for each month include depreciation amounting to ₹ 10,000.

Required: Calculate the amount of expenses paid during the months April to June in each of the following alternative cases:

Case (a) If no time lag is given

Case (b) If time lag is 1 month

Case (c) If time lag is 1/2 month

Case (d) If time lag is 1/4 month

Case (e) If time lag is 1/8 month

Case (f) If time lag is 1/3 month.

SOLUTION

Particulars	*April (₹)*	*May (₹)*	*June (₹)*
Case (a)			
Payment of Expenses [Current Month's Expenses]	40,000	60,000	80,000
Case (b)			
Payment of Expenses	20,000	40,000	60,000
Case (c)			
Payment of Expenses:			
1/2 of Current Month's Expenses	20,000	30,000	40,000
1/2 of Previous Month's Expenses	10,000	20,000	30,000
	30,000	50,000	70,000
Case (d)			
Payment of Expenses:			
3/4 of Current Month's Expenses	30,000	45,000	60,000
1/4 of Previous Month's Expenses	5,000	10,000	15,000
	35,000	55,000	75,000
Case (e)			
Payment of Expenses:			
7/8 of Current Month's Expenses	35,000	52,500	70,000
1/8 of Previous Month's Expenses	2,500	5,000	7,500
	37,500	57,500	77,500
Case (f)			
Payment of Expenses:			
2/3 of Current Month's Expenses	26,666.67	40,000	53,333
1/3 of Previous Month's Expenses	6,666.67	13,333	20,000
	33,333.34	53,333	73,333

ILLUSTRATION 6 [CALCULATION OF THE AMOUNT OF EXPENSES PAID]

Tulsian (6) Ltd. provides you the following information:

Particulars	*March (₹)*	*April (₹)*	*May (₹)*	*June (₹)*
Budgeted Expenses	40,000	70,000	1,30,000	1,00,000
Closing Creditors for Expenses	10,000	20,000	40,000	30,000

Budgeted Expenses for each month include depreciation amounting to ₹ 10.000.

Required: Calculate the amount of expenses paid during the months April to June.

SOLUTION

CALCULATION OF EXPENSES PAID

Particulars	*April (₹)*	*May (₹)*	*June (₹)*
A. Budgeted Expenses	70,000	1,30,000	1,00,000

B. *Less:* Depreciation	(10,000)	(10,000)	(10,000)
C. Cash Expenses	60,000	1,20,000	90,000
D. *Add:* Opening Creditors	10,000	20,000	40,000
E. *Less:* Closing Creditors	(20,000)	(40,000)	(30,000)
F. Expenses Paid	50,000	1,00,000	1,00,000

ILLUSTRATION 7

Prepare Cash Budget of Tulsian (7) Ltd. for April to June from the following information:

1. Estimated Sales, Purchases and Expenses are as follows:

Particulars	*Jan.* ₹	*Feb.* ₹	*March* ₹	*April* ₹	*May* ₹	*June* ₹
Sales	2,00,000	4,00,000	6,00,000	8,00,000	10,00,000	12,00,000
Purchases	1,52,000	3,06,000	4,60,000	6,08,000	7,56,000	9,04,000
Wages	24,000	30,000	36,000	48,000	60,000	72,000
Adm. Expenses	30,000	40,000	50,000	60,000	70,000	80,000
Selling & Dist. Exp.	30,000	50,000	70,000	90,000	1,10,000	1,00,000

2. Cash Sales are 20% of total sales.
3. 50% of Credit Sales are paid within one month and the balance in two months.
4. Cash Purchases are 25% of Total Purchases.
5. 50% of Credit Purchases are paid within one month and the balance in two months.
6. No Stock remains at the end of a month.
7. Commission on Sales—10%.
8. The time lag in the payment of Wages is one third of the month and that of Adm. Expenses one month.
9. Adm. Expenses for each month include depreciation amounting to ₹ 10,000.
10. 12% ₹ 2,00,000 Debentures of ₹ 100 each were issued on 1st Jan. (Half yearly interest payable on 30th June and 31st Dec.)
11. 36,000 Equity Shares of ₹ 10 each were issued on 1st May at 5% premium.
12. Cash balance at the end of March ₹ 4,00,000.

SOLUTION

CASH BUDGET FOR APRIL TO JUNE

Particulars	*April (₹)*	*May (₹)*	*June (₹)*
A. Total Cash Available:			
Cash in hand	4,00,000	2,66,750	4,99,250
Cash Sales	1,60,000	2,00,000	2,40,000
Collection from Debtors	4,00,000	5,60,000	7,20,000
Issue of Equity Shares	—	3,78,000	—
	9,60,000	14,04,750	14,59,250

B. Total Cash Payments:			
Cash Purchases	1,52,000	1,89,000	2,26,000
Payment to Creditors for Purchases	2,87,250	4,00,500	5,11,500
Wages	44,000	56,000	68,000
Administrative Expenses	40,000	50,000	60,000
Selling and Distribution Expenses	90,000	1,10,000	1,00,000
Commission on Sales	80,000	1,00,000	1,20,000
Interest on Debentures		—	12,000
	6,93,250	9,05,500	10,97,500
C. Closing Balance [A – B]	2,66,750	4,99,250	3,61,750

Working Notes:

(I) CALCULATION OF CASH SALES AND COLLECTION FROM DEBTORS

Particulars	*Jan.*	*Feb.*	*March*	*April*	*May*	*June*
A. Total Sales	2,00,000	4,00,000	6,00,000	8,00,000	10,00,000	12,00,000
B. *Less:* Cash Sales @ 20%	(40,000)	(80,000)	(1,20,000)	(1,60,000)	(2,00,000)	(2,40,000)
C. Credit Sales	1,60,000	3,20,000	4,80,000	6,40,000	8,00,000	9,60,000
D. Collection from Debtors:						
50% of Previous months		80,000	1,60,000	2,40,000	3,20,000	4,00,000
50% of Previous to Prev. Month			80,000	1,60,000	2,40,000	3,20,000
Total Collection from Debtors		80,000	2,40,000	4,00,000	5,60,000	7,20,000

(II) CALCULATION OF CASH PURCHASES AND PAYMENT TO CREDITORS

Particulars	*Jan.* ₹	*Feb.* ₹	*March* ₹	*April* ₹	*May* ₹	*June* ₹
A. Total Purchases	1,52,000	3,06,000	4,60,000	6,08,000	7,56,000	9,04,000
B. *Less:* Cash Pur. @ 25%	(38,000)	(76,500)	(1,15,000)	(1,52,000)	(1,89,000)	(2,26,000)
C. Credit Purchases	1,14,000	2,29,500	3,45,000	4,56,000	5,67,000	6,78,000
D. Payment to Creditors						
50% of Previous Month		57,000	1,14,750	1,72,500	2,28,000	2,83,500
50% of Previous to Prev. Month			57,000	1,14,750	1,72,500	2,28,000
Total Payment to Creditors		57,000	1,71,750	2,87,250	4,00,500	5,11,500

(III) PAYMENT OF WAGES

Particulars	*April (₹)*	*May (₹)*	*June (₹)*
2/3rd of Current Month's	32,000	40,000	48,000
1/3rd of Previous Month's	12,000	16,000	20,000
	44,000	56,000	68,000

(iv) In the absence of any time lag Selling and Distribution Expenses and Commission on Sales are assumed to have been paid in the same month of incurrence.

ILLUSTRATION 8

Prepare Cash Budget of Tulsian (8) Ltd. for April to June from the following information:

1. Sales Jan. 1,000 units. Sales are expected to be increased by 1,000 units per month.
2. Uniform Selling Price of ₹ 100 per unit was fixed after adding 25% to cost.
3. Cash sales are 25% of Net Credit Sales.
4. 2% of Accounts receivable constitute bad debt losses. 50% of the good accounts receivable are collected in the month following the sales, 50% of the remaining in the second month and the balance in the third month.
5. Cash Purchases are 33-1/3% of Net Credit Purchases.
6. 50% of Credit Purchases are paid within one month and the balance in two months.
7. No Stock remains at the end of a month.
8. The estimated expenses are as follows:

Particulars	*Jan. (₹)*	*Feb. (₹)*	*March (₹)*	*April (₹)*	*May (₹)*	*June (₹)*
Wages	12,000	15,000	18,000	24,000	30,000	36,000
Adm. Expenses	15,000	20,000	25,000	30,000	35,000	40,000
Selling & Dist. Expenses	15,000	25,000	35,000	45,000	55,000	50,000

9. Commission on Sales—10%
10. The time lag in the payment of Wages is one third of the month and that of Adm. Expenses one month.
11. Adm. Expenses for each month include depreciation amounting to ₹ 5,000.
12. 12% ₹ 1,00,000 Debentures of ₹ 100 each were issued on 1st Jan. (Half yearly interest payable on 30th June and 31st Dec.)
13. 18,000 Equity Shares of ₹ 10 each were issued on 1st May at 5% premium.
14. Estimated Advance Tax for the Assessment Year 2009–2010 is ₹ 1,00,000. First installment of Advance Tax is 15%.
15. Cash balance at the end of March ₹ 2,00,000.

SOLUTION

CASH BUDGET FOR APRIL TO JUNE

Particulars	*April (₹)*	*May (₹)*	*June (₹)*
A. Total Cash Available:			
Cash in hand	2,00,000	1,17,775	2,16,825
Cash Sales	80,000	1,00,000	1,20,000
Collection from Debtors	1,76,400	2,54,800	3,33,200
Issue of Equity Shares	—	1,89,000	—
	4,56,400	6,61,575	6,70,025
B. Total Cash Payments:			
Cash Purchases	74,000	92,500	1,11,000
Payment to Creditors for Purchases	1,37,625	1,94,250	2,49,750
Wages	22,000	28,000	34,000
Administrative Expenses	20,000	25,000	30,000

Selling and Distribution Expenses	45,000	55,000	50,000
Commission on Sales	40,000	50,000	60,000
Interest on Debentures	—	—	6,000
Advance Tax		—	15,000
	3,38,625	4,44,750	5,55,750
C. Closing Balance [A – B]	1,17,775	2,16,825	1,14,275

Working Notes:

(I) CALCULATION OF CASH SALES AND COLLECTION FROM DEBTORS

Particulars	*Jan.*	*Feb.*	*March*	*April*	*May*	*June*
A. Sales (Units)	1,000	2,000	3,000	4,000	5,000	6,000
B. Selling Price per Unit	100	100	100	100	100	100
C. Total Sales	1,00,000	2,00,000	3,00,000	4,00,000	5,00,000	6,00,000
D. *Less:* Cash Sales @ 20%	(20,000)	(40,000)	(60,000)	(80,000)	(1,00,000)	(1,20,000)
E. Credit Sales @ 80%	80,000	1,60,000	2,40,000	3,20,000	4,00,000	4,80,000
F. *Less:* 2% Bad Debts	(1,600)	(3,200)	(4,800)	(6,400)	(8,000)	(9,600)
G. Good A/c Receivable	78,400	1,56,800	2,35,200	3,13,600	3,92,000	4,70,400
50% of Previous Month				1,17,600	1,56,800	1,96,000
25% of Previous to Previous				39,200	58,800	78,400
25% of Third Previous Month				19,600	39,200	58,800
				1,76,400	2,54,800	3,33,200

(II) CALCULATION OF CASH PURCHASES AND PAYMENT TO CREDITORS

Particulars	*Jan.* ₹	*Feb.* ₹	*March* ₹	*April* ₹	*May* ₹	*June* ₹
A. Total Sales	1,00,000	2,00,000	3,00,000	4,00,000	5,00,000	6,00,000
B. *Less:* Gross Profit @ 20%	(20,000)	(40,000)	(60,000)	(80,000)	(1,00,000)	(1,20,000)
C. Cost of Goods Sold	80,000	1,60,000	2,40,000	3,20,000	4,00,000	4,80,000
D. *Less:* Wages	(12,000)	(15,000)	(18,000)	(24,000)	(30,000)	(36,000)
E. Total Purchases	68,000	1,45,000	2,22,000	2,96,000	3,70,000	4,44,000
F. *Less:* Cash Purchases @ 25%	(17,000)	(36,250)	(55,500)	(74,000)	(92,500)	(1,11,000)
G. Credit Purchases	51,000	1,08,750	1,66,500	2,22,000	2,77,500	3,33,000
H. Payment to Creditors						
50% of Previous Month				83,250	1,11,000	1,38,750
50% of Previous to Previous				54,375	83,250	1,11,000
				1,37,625	1,94,250	2,49,750

(III) PAYMENT OF WAGES

Particulars	*April (₹)*	*May (₹)*	*June (₹)*
2/3rd of Current Month's	16,000	20,000	24,000
1/3rd of Previous Month's	6,000	8,000	10,000
	22,000	28,000	34,000

(iv) In the absence of any time lag Selling and Distribution Expenses and Commission on Sales, the payment has been paid in the same month.

(v) Depreciation being non-cash expenses will not appear in the Cash Budget.

(vi) The first instalments of Advance Tax in case of a company assessee is payable on/before 15th June.

ILLUSTRATION 9

Prepare Cash Budget of Tulsian (9) Ltd. for April to June from the following information:

1. Sales Jan. 1,000 units. Sales are expected to be increased by 1,000 units per month.
2. Uniform Selling Price of ₹ 100 per unit was fixed after adding 25% to cost.
3. Cash Sales are 25% of Net Credit Sales.
4. Cash Purchases are 33—1/3% of Net Credit Purchases.
5. The Estimated Expenses, Closing Stock, Closing Trade Debtors and Closing Creditors are as follows:

Particulars	*Jan.* ₹	*Feb.* ₹	*March* ₹	*April* ₹	*May* ₹	*June* ₹
Wages	12,000	15,000	18,000	24,000	30,000	36,000
Adm. Expenses	15,000	20,000	25,000	30,000	35,000	40,000
Selling & Dist. Exp.	15,000	25,000	35,000	45,000	55,000	50,000
Closing Stock (Units)	100	200	300	400	500	600
Closing Trade Debtors (₹)	80,000	2,00,000	3,20,000	4,40,000	5,60,000	6,80,000
Closing Trade Creditors (₹)	57,000	1,43,250	2,29,875	3,14,250	3,97,500	4,80,750
Closing Creditors for Selling & Dist. Exp. (₹)	5,000	10,000	20,000	15,000	30,000	25,000

6. Commission on Sales—10%
7. The time lag in the payment of Wages is one third of the month and that of Adm. Expenses one month.
8. Adm. Expenses for each month include depreciation amounting to ₹ 5,000.
9. 12% ₹ 1,00,000 Debentures of ₹ 100 each were issued on 1st Jan. (Half yearly interest payable on 30th June and 31st Dec.)
10. 18,000 Equity Shares of ₹ 10 each were issued on 1st May at 5% premium.
11. Estimated Advance Tax for the Assessment Year 2009-2010 is ₹ 1,00,000. First instalment of Advance Tax is 15%.
12. Cash balance at the end of March ₹ 2,00,000.

SOLUTION

CASH BUDGET FOR APRIL TO JUNE

Particulars	*April (₹)*	*May (₹)*	*June (₹)*
A. Total Cash Available:			
Cash in hand	2,00,000	1,28,375	2,59,625
Cash Sales	80,000	1,00,000	1,20,000
Collection from Debtors	2,00,000	2,80,000	3,60,000

	Issue of Equity Shares	—	1,89,000	—
	Total Cash Available	4,80,000	6,97,375	7,39,625
B.	**Total Cash Payments:**			
	Cash Purchases	76,000	94,500	1,13,000
	Payment to Creditors for Purchases	1,43,625	2,00,250	2,55,750
	Wages	22,000	28,000	34,000
	Administrative Expenses	20,000	25,000	30,000
	Selling and Distribution Expenses	50,000	40,000	55,000
	Commission on Sales	40,000	50,000	60,000
	Interest on Debentures	—	—	6,000
	Advance Tax	—	—	15,000
		3,51,625	4,37,750	5,68,750
C.	**Surplus [A – B]**	1,28,375	2,59,625	1,70,875

Working Notes:

(I) CALCULATION OF CASH SALES AND COLLECTION FROM DEBTORS

	Particulars	*Jan.*	*Feb.*	*March*	*April*	*May*	*June*
A.	Sales (Units)	1,000	2,000	3,000	4,000	5,000	6,000
B.	Selling Price per Unit	100	100	100	100	100	100
C.	Total Sales	1,00,000	2,00,000	3,00,000	4,00,000	5,00,000	6,00,000
D.	*Less:* Cash Sales @ 20%	(20,000)	(40,000)	(60,000)	(80,000)	(1,00,000)	(1,20,000)
E.	Credit Sales	80,000	1,60,000	2,40,000	3,20,000	4,00,000	4,80,000
F.	*Add:* Opening Trade Debtors	—	80,000	2,00,000	3,20,000	4,40,000	5,60,000
G.	*Less:* Closing Trade Debtors	(80,000)	(2,00,000)	(3,20,000)	(4,40,000)	(5,60,000)	(6,80,000)
H.	Collection from Debtors	0	40,000	1,20,000	2,00,000	2,80,000	3,60,000

(II) CALCULATION OF CASH PURCHASES AND PAYMENT TO CREDITORS

	Particulars	*Jan.* ₹	*Feb.* ₹	*March* ₹	*April* ₹	*May* ₹	*June* ₹
A.	Total Sales	1,00,000	2,00,000	3,00,000	4,00,000	5,00,000	6,00,000
B.	*Less:* Gross Profit @ 20%	(20,000)	(40,000)	(60,000)	(80,000)	(1,00,000)	(1,20,000)
C.	Cost of Goods Sold	80,000	1,60,000	2,40,000	3,20,000	4,00,000	4,80,000
D.	*Add:* Closing Stock	8,000	16,000	24,000	32,000	40,000	48,000
E.	*Less:* Opening Stock	—	(8,000)	(16,000)	(24,000)	(32,000)	(40,000)
F.	*Less:* Wages	(12,000)	(15,000)	(18,000)	(24,000)	(30,000)	(36,000)
G.	Total Purchases	76,000	1,53,000	2,30,000	3,04,000	3,78,000	4,52,000
H.	*Less:* Cash Purchases @ 25%	(19,000)	(38,250)	(57,500)	(76,000)	(94,500)	(1,13,000)
I.	Credit Purchases	57,000	1,14,750	1,72,500	2,28,000	2,83,500	3,39,000
J.	*Add:* Opening Trade Creditors	—	57,000	1,43,250	2,29,875	3,14,250	3,97,500
K.	*Less:* Closing Trade Creditors	(57,000)	(1,43,250)	(2,29,875)	(3,14,250)	(3,97,500)	(4,80,750)
L.	Payment to Creditors	0	28,500	85,875	1,43,625	2,00,250	2,55,750

(III) PAYMENT OF WAGES

Particulars	*April (₹)*	*May (₹)*	*June (₹)*
2/3rd of Current Month's	16,000	20,000	24,000
1/3rd of Previous Month's	6,000	8,000	10,000
	22,000	28,000	34,000

(IV) PAYMENT OF SELLING AND DISTRIBUTION EXPENSES

Particulars	*April (₹)*	*May (₹)*	*June (₹)*
Selling and Distribution Expenses	45,000	55,000	50,000
Add: Opening Creditors for Expenses	20,000	15,000	30,000
Less: Closing Creditors for Expenses	(15,000)	(30,000)	(25,000)
	50,000	40,000	55,000

(v) Depreciation being non-cash expenses will not appear in the Cash Budget.

(vi) The first instalments of Advance Tax in case of a company assessee is payable on/before 15th June.

ILLUSTRATION 10

TULSIAN (10) Ltd. is considering the manufacture of a new product involving a Capital Expenditure of ₹ 8 lacs for machine. The project consultant provides the following details:

1. Cost Price Structure at 100% Capacity (i.e. 2,00,000 Units)

Selling Price per unit	₹ 20.00
Material Cost per unit	₹ 5.00
Labour Cost per unit	₹ 3.00
Production Overheads per Unit	₹ 4.00 (50% Variable)
Administration Overheads per Unit sold	₹ 0.75 (1/3 fixed)
Commission on Sales per unit	₹ 1.00
Other Selling & Distribution Overheads per unit	₹ 1.25 (40% Variable)

Note: Fixed Production Overheads include Depreciation on Straight Line basis. The useful life of the machine is 4 months.

2. 12% Loan of ₹ 8 lacs (to be taken on 1st April to purchase the machine) is repayable in four equal monthly instalments. Interest on outstanding Balance is payable at the end of each month.

3. Expected Capacity Utilization and Closing Stocks:

Month	*April*	*May*	*June*	*July*
Capacity Utilization (%)	70%	80%	90%	100%
Closing Stock of Finished Goods (Units)	40,000	30,000	20,000	Nil
Closing Stock of Materials (₹)	1,00,000	2,00,000	3,00,000	Nil

4. Cash Sales and Cash Purchases are 25% of Net Credit Sales and Net Credit Purchases respectively.

5. Trade Debtors for Goods and Trade Creditors for Materials at the end of each month would be 20% of the net credit sales and net credit purchases respectively.

6. Creditors for Wages, Commission and Overheads at the end of each month would be 10%.
7. Assume that debtors are realised and creditors are paid in the following month.
8. No change in the prices of inputs *or* output are expected over the next four months.
9. Minimum balance required to be maintained is ₹ 1,00,000. Interest @ 12% p.a. is payable on outstanding balance at the end of each month. Money can be borrowed/repaid in the multiple of ₹ 10,000.

Required: Prepare Cash budget for April to August.

SOLUTION

CASH BUDGET FOR 5 MONTHS

	Particulars	*April*	*May*	*June*	*July*	*Aug*
A.	**Total Cash Available:**					
	Cash in hand	3,00,000	1,00,000	4,98,300	13,80,300	29,10,300
	Cash Sales	4,00,000	6,80,000	7,60,000	8,80,000	—
	Collection from Debtors	12,80,000	24,96,000	29,76,000	34,24,000	7,04,000
	12% Loan	8,00,000	—	—	—	—
	Total	27,80,000	32,76,000	42,34,300	56,84,300	36,14,300
B.	**Total Cash Payments**					
	Purchase of Machine	8,00,000	—	—	—	—
	Cash Purchases	1,60,000	1,80,000	2,00,000	1,40,000	—
	Payment to Creditors for Purchases	5,12,000	7,04,000	7,84,000	6,08,000	1,12,000
	Payment of Wages	3,78,000	4,74,000	5,34,000	5,94,000	60,000
	Payment for Production Overheads	4,32,000	5,16,000	5,56,000	5,96,000	60,000
	Payment for Administrative Overheads	90,000	1,31,500	1,44,000	1,58,500	16,000
	Payment for Selling and Distribution Overheads	1,80,000	2,31,500	2,44,000	2,58,500	26,000
	Commission on Sales	90,000	1,63,000	1,88,000	2,17,000	22,000
	Total	26,42,000	24,00,000	26,50,000	25,72,000	2,96,000
C.	**Surplus(Deficit)**	1,38,000	8,76,000	15,84,300	31,12,300	33,18,300
D.	*Add:* Bank Borrowings	1,70,000				
E.	*Less:* Repayment of 12% Loan	(2,00,000)	(2,00,000)	(2,00,000)	(2,00,000)	
F.	*Less:* Interest on 12% Loan	(8,000)	(6,000)	(4,000)	(2,000)	
G.	*Less:* Repayment of Borrowings		(1,70,000)			
H.	*Less:* Interest on Borrowings		(1,700)			
I.	Closing Balance	1,00,000	4,98,300	13,80,300	29,10,300	33,18,300

Working Notes:

(I) CALCULATION OF UNITS SOLD

Particulars	*April*	*May*	*June*	*July*	*Aug*
Units produced	1,40,000	1,60,000	1,80,000	2,00,000	
Add: Opening stock		40,000	30,000	20,000	

Less: Closing stock	(40,000)	(30,000)	(20,000)		
Units sold		1,00,000	1,70,000	1,90,000	2,20,000

(II) CALCULATION OF CASH PURCHASES AND PAYMENT TO CREDITORS

Particulars	*April*	*May*	*June*	*July*	*Aug*
A. Production (in units)	1,40,000	1,60,000	1,80,000	2,00,000	
B. Material Consumed @₹ 5	7,00,000	8,00,000	9,00,000	10,00,000	
C. *Add:* Closing Stock	1,00,000	2,00,000	3,00,000		
D. *Less:* Opening Stock		(1,00,000)	(2,00,000)	(3,00,000)	
E. Total Purchases	8,00,000	9,00,000	10,00,000	7,00,000	
F. *Less:* Cash Purchases	(1,60,000)	(1,80,000)	(2,00,000)	(1,40,000)	
G. Credit Purchases	6,40,000	7,20,000	8,00,000	5,60,000	
H. *Add:* Opening Trade Creditors		1,28,000	1,44,000	1,60,000	1,12,000
I. *Less:* Closing Trade Creditors	(1,28,000)	(1,44,000)	(1,60,000)	(1,12,000)	
J. Payment to Creditors	5,12,000	7,04,000	7,84,000	6,08,000	1,12,000

(III) CALCULATION OF CASH SALES AND COLLECTION FROM DEBTORS

Particulars	*April*	*May*	*June*	*July*	*Aug*
A. Total Sales	20,00,000	34,00,000	38,00,000	44,00,000	
B. *Less:* Cash Sales @20%	(4,00,000)	(6,80,000)	(7,60,000)	(8,80,000)	
C. Credit Sales	16,00,000	27,20,000	30,40,000	35,20,000	
D. *Add:* Opening Trade Debtors		3,20,000	5,44,000	6,08,000	7,04,000
E. *Less:* Closing Trade Debtors	(3,20,000)	(5,44,000)	(6,08,000)	(7,04,000)	
F. Collection from debtors	12,80,000	24,96,000	29,76,000	34,24,000	7,04,000

(IV) CALCULATION OF PAYMENT FOR WAGES

Particulars	*April*	*May*	*June*	*July*	*Aug*
A. Wages	4,20,000	4,80,000	5,40,000	6,00,000	
B. *Add:* Outstanding Wages at the beg.		42,000	48,000	54,000	60,000
C. *Less:* Outstanding Wages at the end	(42,000)	(48,000)	(54,000)	(60,000)	
D. Payment for Wages	3,78,000	4,74,000	5,34,000	5,94,000	60,000

(V) CALCULATION OF PAYMENT FOR PRODUCTION OVERHEADS

Particulars	*April*	*May*	*June*	*July*	*Aug*
A. Production Overheads — Variable	2,80,000	3,20,000	3,60,000	4,00,000	
— Fixed	2,00,000	2,00,000	2,00,000	2,00,000	
B. *Add:* Outstanding Overheads at the beg.		48,000	52,000	56,000	60,000
C. *Less:* Outstanding Overheads at the end	(48,000)	(52,000)	(56,000)	(60,000)	
D. Payment for Production Overheads	4,32,000	5,16,000	5,56,000	5,96,000	60,000

(VI) CALCULATION OF PAYMENT FOR ADMINISTRATION OVERHEADS

Particulars	April	May	June	July	Aug
A. Adm. Overheads — Variable	50,000	85,000	95,000	1,10,000	
— Fixed	50,000	50,000	50,000	50,000	
B. *Add:* Outstanding Overheads at the beg.		10,000	13,500	14,500	16,000
C. *Less:* Outstanding Overheads at the end	(10,000)	(13,500)	(14,500)	(16,000)	
D. Payment for Adm. Overheads	90,000	1,31,500	1,44,000	1,58,500	16,000

(VII) CALCULATION OF PAYMENT FOR SELLING AND DISTRIBUTION OVERHEADS

Particulars	April	May	June	July	Aug
A. Selling and Distribution Overheads					
— Variable	50,000	85,000	95,000	1,10,000	
— Fixed	1,50,000	1,50,000	1,50,000	1,50,000	
B. *Add:* Outstanding Overheads at the beg.		20,000	23,500	24,500	26,000
C. *Less:* Outstanding Overheads at the end	(20,000)	(23,500)	(24,500)	(26,000)	
D. Payment for Selling & Distribution Overheads	1,80,000	2,31,500	2,44,000	2,58,500	26,000

(VIII) CALCULATION OF PAYMENT FOR COMMISSION ON SALES

Particulars	April	May	June	July	Aug
A. Commission on Sales	1,00,000	1,70,000	1,90,000	2,20,000	
B. *Add:* Outstanding Commission at the beg.		10,000	17,000	19,000	22,000
C. *Less:* Outstanding Commission at the end	(10,000)	(17,000)	(19,000)	(22,000)	
D. Payment for Commission	90,000	1,63,000	188,000	2,17,000	22,000

ILLUSTRATION 11 [CALCULATION OF BORROWINGS/SALES OF SECURITIES TO MAINTAIN MINIMUM CASH BALANCE]

Tulsian (11) Ltd. provides you the following information:

(a) Sales, Purchases etc.

Particulars	April ₹	May ₹	June ₹	July ₹	August ₹	September ₹
Cash Sales	8,000	12,000	16,000	20,000	24,000	28,000
Collected from Debtors	16,000	32,000	48,000	64,000	80,000	96,000
Cash Purchases	8,000	12,000	16,000	20,000	24,000	28,000
Payment to Creditors	12,000	24,000	36,000	48,000	60,000	72,000
Payment of Expenses	12,000	5,000	7,800	2,950	27,000	20,000

(b) The opening cash balance of ₹ 10,000 is the minimum cash balance to be maintained.

(c) Any short fall in the minimum cash balance is to be met by Bank borrowings in the multiple of ₹ 5,000 @ 12% p.a. *or* by sale of marketable securities in the multiple of ₹ 10,000. Bank interest is payable for a minimum period of a month.

(d) Any surplus cash is to be used to repay the borrowings in the multiple of ₹ 5,000 *or* to purchase the marketable securities in the multiple of ₹ 10,000. [Ignore Interest on securities received and paid].

Required: Prepare the Cash Budget for April to September.

SOLUTION

CASH BUDGET FOR APRIL TO SEPTEMBER

Particulars	*April* ₹	*May* ₹	*June* ₹	*July* ₹	*August* ₹	*September* ₹
A. Total Cash Available:						
Opening Cash Balance	10,000	12,000	14,900	14,000	12,000	15,000
Cash Sales	8,000	12,000	16,000	20,000	24,000	28,000
Collection from Debtors	16,000	32,000	48,000	64,000	80,000	96,000
	34,000	56,000	78,900	98,000	1,16,000	1,39,000
B. Total Cash Payments:						
Cash Purchases	8,000	12,000	16,000	20,000	24,000	28,000
Payment to Creditors	12,000	24,000	36,000	48,000	60,000	72,000
Payment of Expenses	12,000	5,000	7,800	2,950	27,000	20,000
	32,000	41,000	59,800	70,950	1,11,000	1,20,000
C. Surplus (Deficit) [A – B]	2,000	15,000	19,100	27,050	5,000	19,000
Financing and Investment:						
D. Borrowings	10,000	—	—	—	—	—
E. Sales of Securities	—	—	—	—	10,000	—
F. *Less:* Repayment of Borrowings	—	—	(5,000)	(5,000)	—	—
G. *Less:* Interest on Borrowings	—	(100)	100)	(50)	—	—
H. *Less:* Purchase of Securities	—	—	—	(10,000)	—	—
I. Closing Cash Balance [C + D + E – F – G – H]	12,000	14,900	14,000	12,000	15,000	19,000

ILLUSTRATION 12

Prepare the Cash Budget for April to June if the following information is also provided in Illustration 8: "The company maintains a minimum cash balance of ₹ 2,00,000. Any short fall in the minimum cash balance may be met by borrowing from bank *or* the sale of securities. The bank interest @ 12% p.a. is payable for the whole month on monthly basis. Bank borrowings can be made *or* repaid in the multiple of ₹ 5,000. Cash in excess of ₹ 1,10,000 is to be invested in Govt. Securities in the multiple of ₹ 10,000. Ignore interest on securities."

SOLUTION

CASH BUDGET FOR APRIL TO JUNE

Particulars	*April (₹)*	*May (₹)*	*June (₹)*
A. Total Cash Available:			
Cash in hand	2,00,000	2,02,775	2,05,975

Cash Sales	80,000	1,00,000	1,20,000
Collection from Debtors	1,76,400	2,54,800	3,33,200
Issue of Equity Shares	—	1,89,000	—
	4,56,400	7,46,575	6,59,175
B. Total Cash Payments:			
Cash Purchases	74,000	92,500	1,11,000
Payment to Creditors for Purchases	1,37,625	1,94,250	2,49,750
Wages	22,000	28,000	34,000
Administrative Expenses	20,000	25,000	30,000
Selling and Distribution Expenses	45,000	55,000	50,000
Commission on Sales	40,000	50,000	60,000
Interest on Debentures	—	—	6,000
Advance Tax	—	—	15,000
	3,38,625	4,44,750	5,55,750
C. Surplus (Deficit)	1,17,775	3,01,825	1,03,425
D. *Add:* Bank Borrowings	85,000	—	90,000
E. *Add:* Sale of Securities	—	—	10,000
F. *Less:* Interest on Borrowings	—	(850)	—
G. *Less:* Repayment of Borrowings	—	(85,000)	—
H. *Less:* Purchase of Securities	—	(10,000)	—
I. Closing Balance	2,02,775	2,05,975	2,03,425

Working Notes: Same as in Illustration 8.

ILLUSTRATION 13

Prepare the Cash Budget for April to October at 20X8 from the information supplied by Shah Agency Trading concern.

(A) BALANCE SHEET AS AT 31ST MARCH 20X9

Particulars		₹
Proprietor's Capital		1,00,000
Outstanding liabilities		17,000
Cash		20,500
Stock in trade		50,500
Sundry debtors		26,000
Furniture	25,000	
Less: Depreciation	5,000	20,000

(B) ESTIMATED SALES AND EXPENDITURE ON SALARIES

Months	*Sales*	*Salaries*
April	30,000	3,000

May	52,000	3,500
June	50,000	35,000
July	75,000	4,000
August	90,000	4,000
September	35,000	3,000
October	25,000	3,000
November	25,000	3,000

(c) The other monthly expenses are: Rent ₹ 1,000, Depreciation ₹ 1,000, Misc. Expenses ₹ 500 and Commission 1% of Sales.

(d) Of the sales, 80% is on credit and 20% for cash.

(e) 70% of the credit sales are collected in one month and the balance in two months. There are no bad debt losses.

(f) Gross margin on sales on an average is 30%.

(g) Purchases equal to next month's sales are made every month and they are paid during the month in which they are made.

(h) The film maintains a minimum cash balance of ₹ 10,000.

(i) Cash deficiencies are made up by bank loans which are repaid at the earliest available opportunity and cash in excess of ₹ 15,000 is invested in securities (interest on bank loans and securities is to be ignored).

(j) Outstanding liabilities remain unchanged.

(k) Credit Sales in February and March were equal.

SOLUTION

CASH BUDGET FOR APRIL-OCTOBER 20X9

	Particulars	*April* ₹	*May* ₹	*June* ₹	*July* ₹	*Aug.* ₹	*Sep.* ₹	*Oct.* ₹
A.	**Total Cash Available:**							
	Opening Balance	20,500	10,000	10,000	10,000	10,000	10,000	15,000
	Cash Sales	6,000	10,400	10,000	15,000	18,000	7,000	5,000
	Collection from Debtors	20,000	22,800	36,320	40,480	54,000	68,400	41,200
	Total	46,500	43,200	56,320	65,480	82,000	85,400	61,200
B.	**Total Cash Payments:**							
	Creditors	36,400	35,000	52,500	63,000	24,500	17,500	17,500
	Salaries	3,000	3,500	35,000	4,000	4,000	3,000	3,000
	Rent	1,000	1,000	1,000	1,000	1,000	1,000	1,000
	Commission on Sales (1% of Sales)	300	520	500	750	900	350	250
	Misc. Expenses	500	500	500	500	500	500	500
	Total	41,200	40,520	89,500	69,250	30,900	22,350	22,250
C.	**Surplus (Deficit)**	5,300	2,680	(33,180)	(3,770)	51,100	63,050	38,950
	Financing & Investment							

D.	Borrowing to maintain minimum cash balance of ₹ 10,000	4,700	7,320	43,180	13,770		
E.	Repayment after Maintaining minimum Cash Balance of ₹ 10,000		—	—	—	(41,100)	(27,870)	
F.	Investment in Security after maintaining minimum Balance ₹ 15,000		—	—	—	—	(20,180)	(23,950)
G.	Closing cash balance (C + D – E – F)	10,000	10,000	10,000	10,000	10,000	15,000	15,000

Working Notes:

(I) SCHEDULE OF COLLECTION FROM DEBTORS

Particulars	*April*	*May*	*June*	*July*	*Aug.*	*Sep.*	*Oct.*
Total Sales	30,000	52,000	50,000	75,000	90,000	35,000	25,000
Cash Sales	6,000	10,400	10,000	15,000	18,000	7,000	5,000
Credit (80%)	24,000	41,600	40,000	60,000	72,000	28,000	20,000
Collection from Debtors:							
70% in one month	14,000	16,800	29,120	28,000	42,000	50,400	19,600
30% in two months	6,000	6,000	7,200	12,480	12,000	18,000	21,600
Total Collection	20,000	22,800	36,320	40,480	54,000	68,400	41,200

(II) SCHEDULE OF PAYMENTS TO TRADE CREDITORS

Particulars	*April*	*May*	*June*	*July*	*Aug.*	*Sep.*	*Oct.*	*Nov.*
Sales	30,000	52,000	50,000	75,000	90,000	35,000	25,000	25,000
Purchases 70% of sales of next month	36,400	35,000	52,500	63,000	24,500	17,500	17,500	

(iii) Assumptions:

(a) It has been assumed that collection of 70% and 30% of credit sales is effected in one month and 2 months respectively from the month of sale.

(b) Sundry Debtors of ₹ 26,000 outstanding on 31st March represent 30% of credit sales for February and 100% of credit sales for March i.e., ₹ 6,000 and ₹ 20,000 respectively. Accordingly, ₹ 6,000 February's outstanding credit sales is collected in April and ₹ 20,000 credit sales for March is collected in the ratio of 70% (₹ 14,000) and 30% (₹ 6,000) in April and May respectively.

ADJUSTED NET INCOME METHOD

Under this method, cash inflows and outflows are estimated usually for a year. This method is useful when the management is interested in long range planning. The cash budget prepared on the basis of this method is also called 'Cash Flow Statement'.

8.0 CASH MANAGEMENT CONTROL

1. To ensure that projected cash flows do not significantly differ from actual cash flows, there must be proper control of cash collection and disbursement. The objective in managing the cash flow should be:

A. To accelerate cash collection as much as possible.

B. To decelerate *or* delay disbursements as much as possible within allowed limits.

HOW TO ACCELERATE CASH COLLECTION?

Cash collection can be accelerated:

(a) By reducing processing time in raising the invoice to the customer.

(b) By reducing the time gap between the time a customer sends the cheque and the time the cheque is received by the firm.

(c) By reducing the processing time between the time the cheque is received by the firm and the time the cheque is deposited into bank.

(d) By reducing the collection time between the time the cheque is deposited in bank and the time the cheque is credited to firm's bank account.

The amount of cheques sent by customers, which are not yet collected is called collection *or* deposit float.

METHODS OF ACCELERATING CASH COLLECTION

A firm can use Concentration Banking and Lock Box system to speed up cash collections.

1. Concentration Banking

Meaning—Concentration banking is a system of operating through a number of collection centers in different regions instead of a single collection center centralised at the head office.

Purpose—The purpose of concentration banking is to minimise the gap between the mailing time from customers to the firm and the time when the funds become available for use.

Functions—The collection centers perform the following functions:

(a) They collect cheques from customers.

(b) They deposit the collected cheques in their local bank accounts.

(c) They transfer surplus funds to the concentration bank each day.

Concentration Bank—The concentration bank is the one with which the company has its major bank account and is usually located at the head office.

Decision—Whether a concentration bank system should be used *or* not should be decided on the basis of its costs and benefits. If its benefits exceed its costs, the system should be introduced, otherwise not.

How to decide whether *or* not to establish Concentration Banking/Lock Box System

PRACTICAL STEPS INVOLVED IN DECIDING WHETHER OR NOT TO ESTABLISH CONCENTRATION BANKING/LOCK BOX SYSTEM

Step 1: *Calculate **Average Collection per day** as follows:*

= Annual Credit Sales/365

Step 2: *Calculate **Reduction in Mailing and Processing Time** as follows:*

= Existing Mailing and Processing Time – Mailing and Processing time after introducing system

Step 3: *Calculate **Annual Interest saved** as follows:*

= (Average Collection per day × Reduction in Mailing and Processing Time) × Rate of Interest p.a.

Step 4: *Calculate the **Annual Cost** of Concentration Banking/Lock Box System.*

Step 5: *Introduce the Proposed System if Annual Interest saved (as per Step 3) exceeds Annual Cost (as per Step 4), otherwise not.*

ILLUSTRATION 14

Annual Credit Sales	₹ 1825 lakhs
Mailing and Processing Time	5 days
Rate of Borrowing	18% p.a.
Cost of maintaining Concentration Banking System	₹ 0.8 Lakh

If concentration banking system is introduced, mailing and processing time is reduced to 3 days. Should the system be introduced ?

SOLUTION

Step 1: Average Collection per day = ₹ 1825 lakhs/365 = ₹ 5 Lakhs.

Step 2: Reduction in mailing and processing time = 5 – 3 days = 2 days.

Step 3: Annual Interest Saved = ₹ 5 lakh × 2 days × 18% = ₹ 1.8 Lakhs.

Step 4: Cost of maintaining Concentration Banking System = ₹ 0.8 Lakh.

Recommendation: The system should be introduced since the anticipated savings exceed the cost of maintaining the system.

2. Lock Box System

Purpose — The purpose of lock box system is to eliminate the time gap between the receipt of cheque and its deposit into the bank.

Working — The working of lock box system is as follows:

(a) The firm establishes a number of collection centers considering customer's location and volume of remittances.

(b) The firm hires a local post office box at each center.

(c) The firm instructs its customers to mail their remittances to the lock boxes.

(d) The firm authorises its local bank at each center to pick up their remittance from local box.

(e) The bank fixes up the mail several times a day and deposits the cheques in firm's bank account.

Decision — Whether a lock box system should be used *or* not should be decided on the basis of its costs and benefits. If its benefits exceed its costs, the system should be introduced, otherwise not.

Playing the Float — The difference between the total amount of cheques drawn and the bank balance as per bank books is called float. The period during which cheques issued are expected to be presented for encashment is called float period. The finance manager can accurately estimate the time when the cheques issued will be presented for encashment, he can utilize float period to the advantage by issuing more cheques but having only so much bank balance as will be sufficient to honour those cheques which are actually expected to be presented on a particular date.

EXAMPLE:

Bank balance as per Company's books	₹ 10 lakh
Bank balance as per Bank's books	₹ 10 lakh
Issue of an outstation cheque for ₹ 1 lakh (expected to be presented on 8th day)	
Reduction in Bank balance as per	
Company's books on issue of cheque—	₹ 1 lakh

Thus, company has a payment float of ₹ 1 Lakh available for 7 days.

Kind of Float — Different kinds of float with reference to management of cash are as follows:

1. **Billing Float** — Billing float refers to the time between the sale and mailing the invoice to the customer.
2. **Mail Float** — Mail float refers to the gap between the time a customer sends the cheque and the time the cheque is received by the firm.
3. **Cheque Processing Float** — Cheque Processing float refers to the gap between the time the cheques is received by the firm and the time the cheque is deposited into the bank.
4. **Banking Processing Float** — Banking Processing float refers to the gap between the time the cheque is deposited into the bank and the time the cheque is credited to firm's bank account.

DECELERATE *or* DELAY DISBURSEMENTS

Delaying disbursement results in maximum availability of funds. The firm should make maximum use of trade credit as an interest free source of funds. A centralized system may be followed for disbursements. A payment from single central account will increase the credit period by the time. The firm should delay the payment as much as possible but within allowed limits and not at the cost of credit standing.

ILLUSTRATION 15

MP Ltd. is currently following a centralised collection system. Most of its customers are located in the cities of Northern India. The remittances mailed by customers to the central location take four days to reach. Before depositing the remittances in the bank, the firm loses two days in processing them. The daily average collection of the firm is ₹ 2,00,000.

The company is thinking of establishing a lock-box system. It is expected that such system will reduce mailing time by one day and processing time by one day.

(i) Find out the reduction in cash balances expected to result from the adoption of the lock-box system.

(ii) Determine the opportunity cost of the present centralised collection system if the interest rate is assumed to be 15%.

(iii) Should the lock-box system be introduced if its annual cost is ₹ 50,000 ?

SOLUTION

(i) Reduction in Cash Balances = Average Daily Collection × Time saved

= ₹ 2,00,000 × 2 days = ₹ 4,00,000

(ii) Opportunity Cost = 15% of ₹ 4,00,000 = ₹ 60,000

(ii) The lock-box system should be introduced since the cost of the lock box system (i.e., ₹ 50,000) is *less* than the opportunity cost of existing system (i.e., ₹ 60,000)

ILLUSTRATION 16

PM Ltd. undertakes large turnkey projects. It is situated in Delhi and receives large payments on contracts as and when work progresses. The cheques received from customers are deposited in a local branch of a nationalised bank and the money becomes available after 10 days. The cheques are mostly drawn on a bank in Chennai. The company is thinking of collecting the funds sooner by sending an accounts executive to Chennai. A visit to Chennai may cost ₹ 15,000. If Company's opportunity cost of capital is 15%, what minimum amount of cheque will justify sending a person to Chennai. *[Assume 360 days in a year]*

SOLUTION

Let us Simple Interest formula to find out Principal

Rate = 15%, Time = 10 days, Interest = 15,000. Principal?

Principal × Rate × Time = ₹ 15,000

Principal × 15/100 × 10/360 = ₹ 15,000

Principal = ₹ 15,000 × 100/15 × 360/10 = ₹ 36,00,000.

ILLUSTRATION 17

IP Limited is considering whether *or* not to go for a lock-box system. The cost of the system is expected to be ₹ 2.50 per cheque. The average cheque size will be ₹ 9,000. The firm can invest the funds received earlier by using the lock-box system in the money market instruments earning a return of 10% per annum. How much should be the reduction in the cheque collection time for IP Limited to be able to the accept the decision about the lock-box ? *[Assume 360 days in a year]*

SOLUTION

Let us use Simple Interest formula to find out Time:

Rate = 10%, Time = ?, Interest = ₹ 2.50, Principal = 9,000

Interest = Principal × Rate × Time

$$₹\ 2.50 = ₹\ 9{,}000 \times \frac{10}{100} \times \frac{\text{Time (days)}}{360}$$

$$\text{Time} = \frac{₹\ 2.50 \times 100 \times 360}{₹\ 9{,}000 \times 10} = 1 \text{ day.}$$

ILLUSTRATION 18

MI Ltd. has annual sales of ₹ 365 lakh. The company has investment opportunities in the money market to earn a return of 15% per annum. If the company could reduce its float by 3 days, what would be the increase in company's total return ?

SOLUTION

1. Average sales per day = $\frac{₹\ 365 \text{ lakhs}}{365 \text{ days}}$ = ₹ 1 lakh.
2. Increase in Total Returns = ₹ 1 lakh × 3 days × 15% = ₹ 45,000.

ILLUSTRATION 19

KP Ltd. uses a continuous billing system that results in an average daily receipt of ₹ 50 lakhs. It is contemplating the institution of concentration banking, instead of the current system of centralised billing and collection. It is estimated that such a system would reduce the collection period of accounts receivable by 2 days.

Concentration on banking would cost ₹ 2,00,000 annually and 10% can be earned by the firm on its investments. It is also found that a lock-box system could reduce the overall collection time by 4 days and would cost annually ₹ 4,00,000.

(i) How much would cash be released with the concentration banking system?

(ii) How much money can be saved due to reduction in the collection period by 2 days? Should the firm institute the concentration banking system?

(iii) How much could cash be freed by lock-box system?

(iv) How much can be saved with lock-box?

(v) Between concentration banking and lock-box system, which is better?

SOLUTION

(i) Cash released = Average Daily Receipts × Time Saved
= ₹ 50 lakhs × 2 days = ₹ 100 lakhs

(ii) Saving due to Concentration Banking = (Cash released × Rate of Interest) – Cost
= (₹ 100 lakh × 10%) – ₹ 2 lakh = ₹ 8 lakh

Recommendation: Yes since it results in saving of ₹ 8 lakh

(iii) Cash released by lock box system = ₹ 50 lakh × 4 days = ₹ 200 lakh

(iv) Saving due to lock box = (₹ 200 lakhs × 10%) – ₹ 4 lakh = ₹ 16 lakh

(v) Lock box system is better than Concentration Banking because its savings exceed those of Concentration Banking.

ILLUSTRATION 20

The following information is available about a firm:

(a) On an average, accounts receivable are collected after 80 days; inventories have an average of 110 days and accounts payables are paid approximately 70 days after they arise.

(b) The firm spends a total of ₹ 300 lakh annually at a constant rate.

(c) It can earn 12% on investments.

Required: *Calculate:* (i) The firm's cash cycle; (ii) Cash turnover assuming a 360-days year; (iii) Minimum amount of cash to be maintained to meet payments as they become due; (iv) Savings by reducing the average age of inventories to 70 days.

SOLUTION

(i) Cash cycle = 80 days + 110 days – 70 days = 120 days.

(ii) Cash Turnover = $\frac{\text{360 days}}{\text{Cash cycle}} = \frac{\text{360 days}}{\text{120 days}}$ = 3 times.

(iii) Minimum Cash Balance = $\frac{\text{Total Operating Cash Outflow}}{\text{Cash Turnover}} = \frac{₹\ 300\text{ lakh}}{3}$ = ₹ 100 lakh.

(iv) Savings = Annual Operating Cash Outflow × Time saved × Rate
= ₹ 300 lakhs × 40/360 × 12/100 = ₹ 4 lakhs.

9.0 HOW TO DETERMINE OPTIMUM CASH BALANCE

1. Various cash management models have been developed to determine the optimum cash balance to be maintained by the organization.
2. The purpose of all these models is to avoid the situation of excessive and inadequate cash and to determine and maintain the optimum level of cash after achieving a trade off between the profitability and liquidity so as to maximise the wealth of shareholders as a whole.
3. Whenever the situation of excessive *or* inadequate cash arises, prompt and timely action should be taken by the management to correct the imbalances.
4. The popular cash management models are Baumol's Model and Miller-Orr Model

10.0 BAUMOL'S MODEL

APPLICATION

The Baumol's Model helps in determining the optimum cash balance when the demand for cash is certain.

OPTIMUM CASH BALANCE

According to Baumol's model, optimum cash balance is that level of cash where the total of carrying costs (or holding costs) and transactions costs is the minimum.

MEANING OF ECONOMIC LOT SIZE

The Economic Lot Size refers to the size of lot, at which total of transaction costs and the holding costs is minimum. At Economic Lot Size, total transaction costs are equal to total holding costs.

FACTORS TO BE CONSIDERED

Economic Lot Size is determined after considering the following factors:

(a) Transaction Costs: The transaction costs refer to the costs involved in converting the marketable securities into cash. This happen when the firm falls short of cash and has to sell the securities resulting in clerical, brokerage, registration and other costs. The transaction cost per transaction is assumed to be constant. Total transaction cost is calculated as follows:

Total Transaction Cost = Total No. of Transactions × Per Transaction Cost

$$= \frac{\text{Annual Cash Requirements (A)}}{\text{Economic Lot Size (C)}} \times \text{Per Transaction Cost (T)} = \frac{A}{C} \times T$$

There is an Inverse relationship between lot size and transaction cost.

Larger the lot size Lower the transaction costs because of fewer lots

Smaller the lot size Higher the transaction costs because of more lots

(b) Holding Costs: The holding cost *or* opportunity cost refers to the return foregone on marketable securities *or* the cost incurred in maintaining an Average Cash Balance. It varies with the Average Cash Balance.

There is positive relationship between lot size and holding cost.

Larger the lot size Higher the holding costs because of high average cash balance.

Smaller the lot size Lower the holding costs because of low average cash balance

The total holding cost is calculated as follows:

Total Holding Cost = Average Cash Balance Holding Cost p.a.

$$= \frac{\text{Economic Lot Size (C)}}{2} \times \text{Holding Cost p.a. (H)} = \frac{C}{2} \times H$$

(c) Annual Requirements of Cash.

IMPORTANCE OF ECONOMIC LOT SIZE

The Economic Lot Size technique solves one of the major problems of the cash management i.e., the lot size problem by answering to the question: 'How much marketable securities should be sold at a particular point of time?'

ASSUMPTIONS OF ECONOMIC LOT SIZE TECHNIQUE

Following are the assumptions of Economic Lot Size:

1. Constant Annual Requirements of Cash
2. Constant Rate of Demand for Cash

3. Constant Transaction Costs
4. Constant Holding Costs, and
5. Zero Conversion Period

HOW TO DETERMINE ECONOMIC LOT SIZE?

Economic Lot Size may be determined by any of the following three methods:

(a) Graphical Method (b) Tabular Method (c) Formula Method

(a) Graphical Method: The optimum lot size of marketable securities which should be sold at a point of time is determined after achieving a trade off between transaction cost and holding cost.

PRACTICAL STEPS INVOLVED IN THE DETERMINATION OF ECONOMIC LOT SIZE ACCORDING TO GRAPHICAL METHOD

Step 1: *Take lot sizes on X-axis and costs on Y-axis.*

Step 2: *Draw Holding cost line going upward indicating holding cost increases as lot size increases.*

Step 3: *Draw transaction cost line sloping downward indicating transaction cost decreases as lot size increases.*

Step 4: *Draw total cost line which first slops downward and then goes upward after a certain minimum point.*

Step 5: *Locate the point at which both the holding cost line and transaction cost line cut each other and draw a perpendicular from this point on X-axis.*

Step 6: *Locate the point at which the perpendicular touches X-axis. This point gives us the Economic Lot Size.*

Step 7: *Locate the point at which the perpendicular (when extended upward) cuts the total cost line. This point gives us the minimum total cost at Economic Lot Size.*

TUTORIAL NOTES:

(i) Annual total cost of transaction and holding is minimum at Economic Lot Size.

(ii) Holding cost and transaction cost are equal at Economic Lot Size.

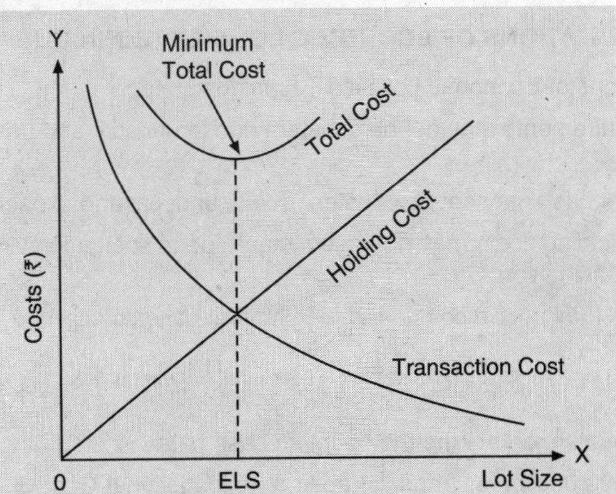

(b) Tabular *or* Trial and Error Method: The transaction and holding costs for different lot sizes are computed and the lot size with lowest total cost (transaction and holding) of marketable securities is the Economic Lot Size as follows:

Particulars	*Different Lot Sizes*		
	Lot size I	*Lot size II*	*Lot size III*
A. Annual Requirements of Cash	....	....	....
B. Lot Size	....	....	....
C. No. of Lots (A/B)	....	....	....
D. Cost per Lot (₹)	....	....	....
E. Total Transaction Cost (C × D)	....	....	....
F. Average Balance (Lot Size/2)	....	....	....
G. Holding Cost	....	....	....
H. Total Holding cost (F × G)	....	....	....
I. Total Cost (E + H)	....	....	....

Alternatively, total annual transaction and holding cost at different lot sizes may be computed as follows:

Total annual transaction and holding cost at any lot size

= [(No. of lots × Transaction cost per lot) + (Average Balance × Holding cost p.a.)

$$\text{or,} = \left[\left(\frac{\text{Annual Requirements}}{\text{Lot size}} \times \text{Transaction cost per lot}\right) + \left(\frac{\text{Lot size}}{2} \times \text{Holding cost p.a.}\right)\right]$$

(c) Formula Method: Economic Lot Size may be calculated with the help of following formula:

1. Economic Lot Size (C) = $\sqrt{\frac{2\,AT}{H}}$

   Where, A = Annual Cash Requirements

   T = Transaction costs per lot

   H = Holding costs p.a.

2. No. of Lots per year= Total Annual Cash Requirements/Economic Lot Size
3. Economic Lot Frequency = 365 days/No. of lots per year
4. Total annual transaction and holding cost at Economic Lot Size = $\sqrt{2ATH}$

LIMITATIONS OF ECONOMIC LOT SIZE TECHNIQUE

Following are the limitations of Economic Lot Size Technique:

1. Annual Cash Requirements may not be constant due to unusual and unexpected demand for cash.
2. Rate of demand for cash may not be constant due to unusual and expected demand for cash.
3. Transaction and holding costs may not be constant due to fluctuations in the costs of various components comprising costs.
4. Conversion period may not be constant due to market conditions.

ILLUSTRATION 21

From the following information, determine the optimum cash balance according to Baumol's Model.

Total Disbursement ₹ 1,20,000 p.m., Administrative & Transactional Cost of Transferring cash to disbursement account ₹ 37.50 per transfer, Marketable Securities earn 1% p.m.

SOLUTION

A = Annual Cash requirement = 1,20,000 × 12 = ₹ 14,40,000

T = Transaction Cost per transaction = ₹ 37.50

H = Holding Cost = 1% p.m. *or* 0.12 p.a.

C = Optimum Cash Balance, $\sqrt{\frac{2AT}{H}} = \sqrt{\left(\frac{2 \times 14,40,000 \times 37.50}{0.12}\right)}$ = ₹ 30,000

ILLUSTRATION 22

CAS limited estimates its total cash requirement of ₹ 8 lakh next year. The company's opportunity cost of funds is 15% per annum. The company will have to incure ₹ 600 per transaction when it converts its short term securities into cash. Determine the optimum cash balance according to Baumol's model.

SOLUTION

A = Annual Cash requirement = ₹ 8,00,000 (given)

T = Transaction Cost per transaction = ₹ 600 (given)

H = Holding Cost of one rupee p.a. = 15% (given)

Optimum Cash Balance (C) = $\sqrt{\frac{2\ AT}{H}} = \sqrt{\frac{2 \times ₹\ 8\ \text{lakhs} \times 600}{0.15}}$ = ₹ 80,000

11.0 THE MILLER-ORR MODEL

APPLICATION

The Miller-Orr's Model helps in determining the optimum cash balance **when the demand for cash is uncertain.**

CONTROL LIMITS

In the Miller-Orr's model, control limits are set for cash balances. These limits consist of upper limit (h), the return point (z) & the lower limit (o).

1. Upper Limit (h) It is that level of cash balance at which the marketable securities are purchased to bring down the cash balance back to the normal level.

2. Lower Limit (o) It is that level of cash balance at which the marketable securities are sold to bring up cash balance back to the normal level.

3. Return Point (z) It is normal level of cash balance which lies between the upper limit and lower limit and which is to be attained after purchase/sale of marketable securities.

These limits satisfy the demands for cash at the lowest possible total costs (i.e., Transaction Cost + Cash Holding Cost).

THE WORKING OF THIS MODEL IS SUMMARIZED AS FOLLOWS

(i) When the cash balance touches the **upper limit,** the marketable securities are **purchased** for cash equal to (h – z) in order to bring the cash balance back to the normal level (return point).

(ii) When the cash balance touches the lower limit, the marketable securities are sold for cash equal to (z – o) in order to bring the cash balance back to the normal level (return point)

(iii) When the cash balance stays **between (h, z) & (z,o), no transaction** between cash & marketable security account is made.

(iv) The high & low limit of cash balance are set on the basis of following three factors:

T = Transaction Cost per transaction.

H = Holding Cost *or* Opportunity Cost foregone on marketable securities

= Degree of likely fluctuations in cash balances *or* the standard deviation of net cash flows.

HOW TO DETERMINE THE DISTANCE BETWEEN UPPER & LOWER LIMITS?

The distance between upper limit & lower limit is based on value of Z which is determined as follows:

1. $$Z = \left(\frac{\frac{3}{4} \times \text{Transaction Cost} \times \text{Daily Cash Flow Variance}}{\text{Holding Cost (i.e., Daily Interest Rate)}}\right)^{1/3} = \left(\frac{\frac{3}{4}T\sigma^2}{H}\right)^{1/3} = \sqrt[3]{\frac{\frac{3}{4}T\sigma^2}{H}}$$

   Z is inversely related to interest rate.

2. Upper limit is three times above the lower limit and the return point lies between the upper limit and the lower limit. Thus,

   Upper limit = Lower Limit + 3Z, Return Point (z) = Lower limit + Z

3. The net effect is that the firms hold the average cash balance equal to:

   Average Cash Balance = Lower limit + 4/3 Z.

GRAPHICAL PRESENTATION

The following diagram illustrates the Miller-Orr model:

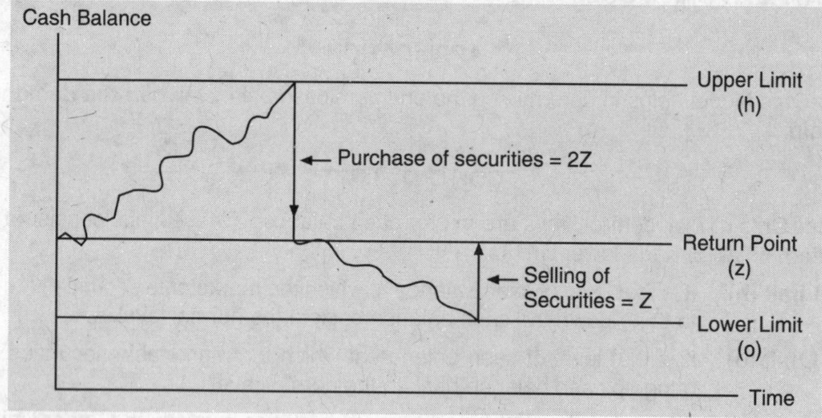

Fig. Miller-Orr Model

ILLUSTRATION 23

M/s PCT Ltd. provides following information:

The company maintains a minimum cash balance of ₹ 10,00,000. The standard deviation of the company's daily cash flow is ₹ 3,60,000. The annual interest rate is 12%. The transaction cost of buying & selling securities is ₹ 180 per transaction. (Assume 360 days in a year).

Required: Calculate upper limit, return point, and Average Cash Balance as per the Miller-Orr model.

SOLUTION

1. Z = [3/4 × 180 × (3,60,000)2/(0.12 / 360)]1/3 = ₹ 17,57,500

2. Upper limit = Lower limit + 3Z = 10,00,000 + (3 × 17,57,500) = ₹ 62,72,500
3. Return Point = Lower limit + Z = 10,00,000 + 17,57,500 = ₹ 27,57,500
4. Average Cash Balance = Lower Limit + 4/3 Z = 10,00,000 + (4/3 × 17,57,500) = ₹ 33,43,333.

If the cash balance touches the lower limit of ₹ 10,00,000, it will sell marketable securities worth (Z) ₹ 17,57,500 & restore point to ₹ 27,57,500 cash balance level. On the other hand, if PCT Ltd's cash balance touches upper limit of ₹ 62,72,500, it will buy marketable securities worth (2Z), i.e., ₹ 62,72,500 – ₹ 35,15,000 = ₹ 27,57,500.

12.0 MANAGEMENT OF MARKETABLE SECURITIES

1. The excess cash held to meet variable cash requirements and future contingencies should be temporarily invested in marketable securities.
2. The selection of securities should be guided by three principles—Safety, Maturity and Marketability.
3. **Safety**

   Returns and risks are directly related to each other. Higher the default risk, higher the return from securities and lower the default risk, lower the return from securities. The default risk means the possibility of default in the payment of interest or/and principal on time. To minimize the default risk, the excess cash should be invested in safe securities.
4. **Maturity**

   Maturity refers to the time period over which interest and principal are to be paid. Matching of maturity and forecasting cash need is essential. Prices of long term securities fluctuate more with changes in interest rate and are therefore, more risky. To avoid the fluctuations in the prices of securities, the excess cash should be invested in Short-term securities.
5. **Marketability**

   It refers to the convenience, speed and cost at which a securities can be converted into cash. If the securities can be sold quickly without loss of time and price, it is highly liquid *or* marketable, for example—Government treasury bills. To avoid the loss of time in realizing the securities, the excess cash should be invested in highly liquid marketable securities.
6. **Types of Marketable Securities**

   To invest surplus cash, the following marketable securities are available in India:

	Issued by	*Safety*	*Maturity*	*Marketability*
Treasury Bills	Government	No Default risk	Short Term	Highly marketable
Commercial Papers (CPs)	Credit worthy Large Companies	Low default risk	Short Term	Highly marketable
Certificate of Deposits (CDs)	Banks	Low default risk	Short Term	Highly marketable
Bank Deposits	Banks	No default risk in case nationalized banks. Low default risk in case of other banks	Short Term	Highly marketable
Inter-Corporate Deposits (ICD)	Companies	High default risk	Short Term	Less marketable
Money Market Mutual Funds (MMMFs)	Mutual Funds	Low default risk	Short Term	Highly marketable

SOLVED PROBLEMS-I

PROBLEM 1

X Ltd. is to start production on 1st January. The prime cost of a unit is expected to ₹ 40 out of which ₹ 16 is for materials and ₹ 24 for labour. In addition variable expenses per unit are expected to be ₹ 8 and fixed expenses per month ₹ 30,000. Payment for materials is to be made in the month following the purchases. One third of sale will be for cash and the rest on credit for settlement in the following month. Expenses are payable in the month in which they are incurred. The selling price is fixed at ₹ 80 per unit. The number of units manufacture and sold are expected to be as under:

January	900	April	2,100
February	1,200	May	2,100
March	1,800	June	2,400

Required: Draw up a statement showing requirements of cash from month to month, ignoring the question of stock.

SOLUTION

STATEMENT SHOWING REQUIREMENTS OF CASH FOR 6 MONTHS FROM JANUARY TO JUNE

Particulars	*January* ₹	*February* ₹	*March* ₹	*April* ₹	*May* ₹	*June* ₹
A. Total Cash Available:						
Cash Sales	24,000	32,000	48,000	56,000	56,000	64,000
Collection from Debtors	—	48,000	64,000	96,000	1,12,000	1,12,000
	24,000	80,000	1,12,000	1,52,000	1,68,000	1,76,000
B. Total Cash Payments:						
Payment to Creditors	—	14,400	19,200	28,800	33,600	33,600
Labour	21,600	28,800	43,200	50,400	50,400	57,600
Variable Expenses	7,200	9,600	14,400	16,800	16,800	19,200
Fixed Expenditure	30,000	30,000	30,000	30,000	30,000	30,000
	58,800	82,800	1,06,800	1,26,000	1,30,800	1,40,400
C. Surplus (Deficit) [A – B]	(34,800)	(2,800)	5,200	26,000	37,200	35,600
D. Cum. Surplus (Deficit)	(34,800)	(37,600)	(32,400)	(6,400)	30,800	66,400

PROBLEM 2

X & Co. has furnished the following information. Based on this, prepare a cash budget for three months i.e., June, July and August:

Month	*Sales* ₹	*Materials Purchases* ₹	*Wages* ₹	*Production Overheads* ₹	*Office & Selling expenses* ₹
June	72,000	25,000	10,000	6,000	5,500
July	97,000	31,000	12,100	6,300	6,700
Aug.	86,000	25,500	10,600	6,000	7,500

(a) Cash balance in hand as on 1st June: ₹ 72,500.
(b) 50% of sales are Cash sales.
(c) A fixed assets has to be purchased for ₹ 8,000 in July 2008.
(d) Debtors are allowed one month's credit.
(e) Creditors for materials grant one month's credit.
(f) Sales commission at 3% on sales is paid to the salesman each month.

SOLUTION

CASH BUDGET FOR THREE MONTHS FOR JUNE TO AUG.

Particulars	*June* ₹	*July* ₹	*August* ₹
A. Total Cash Available:			
Opening Balance	72,500	84,840	1,08,330
Cash Sales	36,000	48,500	43,000
Collection from Debtors	—	36,000	48,500
	1,08,500	1,69,340	1,99,830
B. Total Cash Payments:			
Creditors	—	25,000	31,000
Sales Commission 3%	2,160	2,910	2,580
Wages	10,000	12,100	10,600
Production Overheads	6,000	6,300	6,000
Office & Selling Expenses	5,500	6,700	7,500
Fixed Assets	—	8,000	—
	23,660	61,010	57,680
C. Closing Balance [A – B]	84,840	108,330	1,42,150

Note: It has been assumed that the Wages, Production Overheads and Office & Selling expenses will be paid in the same month in which these are incurred.

PROBLEM 3

Make out Cash Budget from the following details for October to December

(a) Cash and Bank Balance on 1st Oct.: ₹ 40,000.

(B) SALES (ACTUAL AND ESTIMATED)

	Actual (₹)		*Estimated (₹)*
July	1,00,000	October	1,00,000
August	1,10,000	November	1,20,000
September	90,000	December	90,000

(C) PURCHASES (ACTUAL AND ESTIMATED):

	Actual (₹)		*Estimated (₹)*
July	50,000	October	50,000

August	60,000	November	70,000
September	50,000	December	50,000

(D) WAGES AND EXPENSES (ACTUAL AND ESTIMATED):

	Actual			*Estimated*	
	Wages	*Expenses*		*Wages*	*Expenses*
July	8,000	16,000	October	15,000	9,000
August	16,000	8,000	November	18,000	10,000
September	12,000	9,000	December	12,000	10,000

(e) Machine to be purchased in Oct. ₹ 35,000.

(f) Income-tax to be paid in Nov. ₹ 30,000.

(g) ₹ 500 rent payable every month in addition to Expenses.

(h) Cash sales are 75% *less* than the credit sales and credit purchases are four times the cash purchases.

(i) Time-lag: Credit Sales 2 months. Credit purchases 1 month. Wages 1/2 month. Expenses 1/4 month.

SOLUTION

CASH BUDGET FOR 3 MONTHS FROM OCT. TO 31ST DEC.

Particulars	*Oct. (₹)*	*Nov. (₹)*	*Dec. (₹)*
A. Total Cash Available:			
Opening Balance	40,000	40,000	25,250
Cash Sales	20,000	24,000	18,000
Collection from Debtors	88,000	72,000	80,000
Total	1,48,000	1,36,000	1,23,250
B. Total Cash Payments:			
Cash Purchases	10,000	14,000	10,000
Payments to creditors for goods	40,000	40,000	56,000
Wages	13,500	16,500	15,000
Expenses	9,000	9,750	10,000
Rent	500	500	500
Advance Income Tax	—	30,000	—
Machinery	35,000	—	—
	1,08,000	1,10,750	91,500
C. Closing Balance [A – B]	40,000	25,250	31,750

Working Notes:

(I) CALCULATION OF WAGES

Month	*50% of Previous Month*	*50% of Current Month*	*Total*
Oct.	₹ 6,000	₹ 7,500	₹ 13,500
Nov.	7,500	9,000	16,500
Dec.	9,000	6,000	15,000

(II) CALCULATION OF EXPENSES

Month	*25% of Previous*	*75% of Current*	*Total*
Oct.	₹ 2,250	₹ 6,750	₹ 9,000
Nov.	2,250	7,500	9,750
Dec.	2,500	7,500	10,000

(III) CALCULATION OF COLLECTION ON ACCOUNT SALES

Month	*July*	*Aug.*	*Sept.*	*Oct.*	*Nov.*	*Dec.*
Sales	1.00	1.10	.90	1.00	1.20	.90
Cash Sales @ 20%	.20	.22	.18	.20	.24	.18
Credit Sales @ 80%	.80	.88	.72	.80	.96	.72
Collection from Debtors			.80	.88	.72	.80

PROBLEM 4

From the following prepare Cash Budget for the period from 1st March to 31st August when the opening cash balance was ₹ 12,000.

Month	*Sales*	*Selling Exp.*	*Purchases*	*Wages*	*Factory and Adm. Overheads*
Jan.	17,000	700	8,000	1,500	1,500
Feb.	16,000	750	8,400	1,600	1,650
March	18,200	650	8,300	1,680	1,250
April	15,500	680	8,300	1,200	1,525
May	16,500	740	7,600	1,800	1,740
June	20,000	700	6,800	1,600	1,530
July	18,000	600	7,000	1,700	1,300
August	22,000	550	5,800	1,650	1,510

(a) Period for credit allowed by suppliers and to customers: 1 month.

(b) Lag in payment of:

(a) Wages 1/8 month, (b) Factory and Admn. Exp. 1 month, (c) Selling Exp. 1 month.

(c) Machinery purchased for ₹ 5,000 in March payable on delivery.

(d) Building purchased in April for ₹ 15,000 payable in two equal instalment in May and July.

(e) Commission of 3% on sales payable two month after sales.

SOLUTION

CASH BUDGET FOR SIX MONTHS FROM 1ST MARCH TO 31ST AUG.

Particulars	*March* ₹	*April* ₹	*May* ₹	*June* ₹	*July* ₹	*August* ₹
A. Total Cash Available:						
Opening Balance	12,000	10,020	16,280	11,504	15,834	17,121
Collection from Debtors	16,000	18,200	15,500	16,500	20,000	18,000
	28,000	28,220	31,780	28,004	35,834	35,121

B. Total Cash Payments:						
Payments to creditors for goods	8,400	8,300	8,300	7,600	6,800	7,000
Wages	1,670	1,260	1,725	1,625	1,688	1,656
Factory & Adm. Expenses	1,650	1,250	1,525	1,740	1,530	1,300
Selling Exp.	750	650	680	740	700	600
Selling Comm.	510	480	546	465	495	600
Vendor of building	—	—	7,500	—	7,500	—
Purchase of Machinery	5,000	—	—	—	—	—
	17,980	11,940	20,276	12,170	18,713	11,156
C. Closing Balance [A – B]	10,020	16,280	11,504	15,834	17,121	23,965

Working Notes:

(I) CALCULATION OF WAGES

Particulars	*March* ₹	*April* ₹	*May* ₹	*June* ₹	*July* ₹	*August* ₹
A. 1/8 of previous month	200	210	150	225	200	212
B. 7/8 of current month	1,470	1,050	1,575	1,400	1,488	1,444
	1,670	1,260	1,725	1,625	1,688	1,656

(II) CALCULATION OF COMMISSION ON SALES

Particulars	*Jan.* ₹	*Feb.* ₹	*March* ₹	*April* ₹	*May* ₹	*June* ₹	*July* ₹	*Aug.* ₹
Sales	510	480	546	465	495	600	540	660
Commission payment On Account			510	480	546	465	495	600

PROBLEM 5

You are required to prepare Cash Budget three months ended 31st Dec. based on the following information:

(a) Cash at Bank on 1st Oct. ₹ 60,000.

(b) Salaries and wages estimated monthly ₹ 20,000.

(c) Interest payable – Aug., Nov. ₹ 10,000.

(D) SALES, PURCHASES AND EXPENSES

Particulars	*September*	*October*	*November*	*December*
Cash Sales		2,80,000	3,04,000	2,42,000
Credit Sales	2,00,000	1,60,000	2,80,000	2,40,000
Purchases	3,20,000	3,40,000	4,80,000	3,60,000
Other Expenses		40,000	44,000	42,000

(e) Credit Sales are collected 50% in the month sales are made and 50% in the month following.

(f) Collection from credit sales are subject to 5% discount of payment if received during the month of sales and 212 % if payment is received in the month following.

(g) Creditors are paid *either* on a prompt *or* 30 days basis, 10% of the creditors are estimated to be in the prompt category.

SOLUTION

CASH BUDGET FOR THREE MONTHS FROM 1ST OCT. TO 31ST DEC.

Particulars	*October* ₹	*November* ₹	*December* ₹
A. Total Cash Available:			
Opening Balance	60,000	1,31,500	2,18,500
Cash Sales	2,80,000	3,04,000	2,42,000
Collection from Debtors	1,73,500	2,11,000	2,50,500
	5,13,500	6,46,500	7,11,000
B. Total Cash Payments:			
Cash Purchases	34,000	48,000	36,000
Payments to creditors	2,88,000	3,06,000	4,32,000
Salaries & Wages	20,000	20,000	20,000
Interest	—	10,000	—
Other Expenses	40,000	44,000	42,000
	3,82,000	4,28,000	5,30,000
C. Closing Balance [A – B]	1,31,500	2,18,500	1,81,000

Working Notes:

CALCULATION OF COLLECTION FROM DEBTORS

(₹ *in lakhs*)

Particulars	*Sep.*	*Oct.*	*Nov.*	*Dec.*
A. Sales	2.00	1.60	2.80	2.40
B. 50% of sales	1.00	0.80	1.40	1.20
C. Collection in the month of sales @ 95% of B	0.95	0.76	1.33	1.14
D. Remaining 50% of sales (A – B)	1.00	0.80	1.40	1.20
E. Collection in the month following sales @ 97.5%	—	0.975	0.78	1.365
F. Total Collection (C + E)	0.95	1.735	2.11	2.505

PROBLEM 6

Prepare Cash Budget (on the basis of Receipts and Payments Method) for the period from the January to 30th June 2009 from the following information:

Months	*Credit Sales* ₹	*Credit Purchases* ₹	*Wages* ₹	*Production Overheads* ₹	*Adm. Overheads* ₹	*Selling Exp.* ₹	*Distribution* ₹	*R & D Exp.* ₹
Oct. '08	20,000	10,000	2,500	1,600	850	1,250	750	250
Nov.	15,000	7,500	2,250	2,000	825	1,125	625	250
Dec.	10,000	5,000	2,000	1,875	875	750	500	250
Jan. '09	12,500	10,000	2,250	2,000	925	1,100	600	300

Feb.	15,000	12,500	2,500	2,125	975	1,200	650	300
Mar.	20,000	15,000	2,750	2,250	900	1,300	725	300
Apr.	17,500	12,500	2,250	2,000	875	1,250	650	375
May	15,000	7,500	2,000	1,875	925	1,200	625	375
Jun.	12,500	10,000	2,250	2,000	975	1,125	600	375

(a) Period for credit allowed by suppliers is 2 months.

(b) Period of credit allowed to customers is 3 months.

(c) Lag in payments of overheads to be 1 month and that of wages 1/8 month.

(d) The cash balance on 1st January is expected to be ₹ 25,000.

(e) Plant and machinery to be installed in April at cost of ₹ 30,000 which will be paid in monthly instalments of ₹ 5,000 each commencing from 1st May.

(f) A sales commission of 10% on sales is to be paid within the month following actual sales.

(g) Cash sales of ₹ 1,250 per month are expected (No commission is payable on them).

(h) The company has a hire-purchases agreement under which ₹ 1,250 a month is being paid for plant purchased before the budget period. The last payment will be in the month of March.

(i) Preference Share dividend of 8% on capital of ₹ 5 lakhs to be paid on 1st April.

(j) Tax of ₹ 25,000 is due on 1st April.

(k) Dividends from investments amounting to ₹ 17,500 are expected on 1st May.

(l) Calls of 25% on Equity Share Capital of ₹ 50,000 are due on 1st January, 1st March and 1st June.

(m) A minimum balance of ₹ 10,000 is to be maintained. The Company enjoys overdraft facility to the extent of ₹ 50,000.

SOLUTION

CASH FORECAST FOR THE PERIOD FROM 1ST JAN. TO 30TH JUNE 2009

Particulars	*Jan.* ₹	*Feb.* ₹	*Mar.* ₹	*Apr.* ₹	*May* ₹	*June* ₹
A. Total Cash Available:						
Opening Balance	25,000	42,531	43,887	46,918	10,000	10,000
Debtors	20,000	15,000	10,000	12,500	15,000	20,000
Cash sales	1,250	1,250	1,250	1,250	1,250	1,250
Dividends	—	—	—	—	17,500	—
Capital	12,500	—	12,500	—	—	12,500
Total	58,750	58,781	67,637	60,668	43,750	43,750
B. Total Cash Payments:						
Purchases	7,500	5,000	10,000	12,500	15,000	12,500
Wages	2,219	2,469	2,719	2,312	2,031	2,219
Production Overheads	1,875	2,000	2,125	2,250	2,000	1,875
Admn. Overheads	875	925	975	900	875	925
Selling Expenses	750	1,100	1,200	1,300	1,250	1,200
Distribution Expenses	500	600	650	725	650	625

R & D Expenses	250	300	300	300	375	375
Commission	1,000	1,250	1,500	2,000	1,750	1,500
Income Tax	—	—	—	25,000	—	—
Dividends	—	—	—	40,000	—	—
Capital Expenses	1,250	1,250	1,250	—	5,000	5,000
Total	16,219	14,894	20,719	87,287	28,931	26,219
C. Surplus (Deficit) [A – B]	42,531	43,887	46,918	(26,619)	14,819	17,531
D. Borrowings (Repayment)	—	—	—	36,619	(4,819)	(7,531)
E. Closing Balance (C ± D)	42,531	43,887	46,918	10,000	10,000	10,000

PROBLEM 7

From the information and the assumption that the cash balance in hand on 1 January is ₹ 1,72,500, prepare a Cash Budget.

Month	*Sales* ₹	*Materials Purchases* ₹	*Salaries & Wages* ₹	*Production Overheads* ₹	*Office and Selling Overheads* ₹
January	72,000	25,000	10,000	6,000	5,500
February	97,000	31,000	12,100	6,300	6,700
March	86,000	25,500	10,600	6,000	7,500
April	88,600	30,600	25,000	6,500	8,900
May	1,02,500	37,000	22,000	8,000	11,000
June	1,08,700	38,800	23,000	8,200	11,500

Assume that 50 per cent of total sales are cash sales. Assets are to be acquired in the months of February and April. Therefore, provisions should be made for the payment of ₹ 8,000 and ₹ 25,000 for the same. An application has been made to the bank for the grant of a loan of ₹ 30,000 and it is hoped that the loan amount will be received in the month of May. It is anticipated that a dividend of ₹ 35,000 will be paid in June. Debtors are allowed one month's credit. Creditors for materials purchased and overheads grant one month's credit. Sales commission at 3 per cent on sales is paid to the salesman each month.

SOLUTION

CASH BUDGET FROM JAN. TO JUNE

Particulars	*Jan.* ₹	*Feb.* ₹	*Mar.* ₹	*Apr.* ₹	*May* ₹	*June* ₹
A. Total Cash Available:						
Opening Balance	1,72,500	1,96,340	2,21,330	2,55,650	2,51,292	3,05,767
Cash sales	36,000	48,500	43,000	44,300	51,250	54,350
Collection from Debtors	—	36,000	48,500	43,000	44,300	51,250
Bank loan	—	—	—	—	30,000	—
Total	2,08,500	2,80,840	3,12,830	3,42,950	3,76,842	4,11,367
B. Total Cash Payments:						
Materials	—	25,000	31,000	25,500	30,600	37,000

Salaries and wages	10,000	12,100	10,600	25,000	22,000	23,000
Production Overheads	—	6,000	6,300	6,000	6,500	8,000
Office and selling Overheads	—	5,500	6,700	7,500	8,900	11,000
Sales commission	2,160	2,910	2,580	2,658	3,075	3,261
Capital expenditure		8,000	—	25,000		—
Dividend	—	—	—	—	—	35,000
Total	12,160	59,510	57,180	91,658	71,075	1,17,261
C. **Closing Balance (A – B)**	1,96,340	2,21,330	2,55,650	2,51,292	3,05,767	2,94,106

PROBLEM 8

X Ltd. is to be performed to take over a running business. It has been decided to raise ₹ 55 lakhs by issuing equity shares, and the balance of capital required in the first six months is to be financed by a financial institution against a issue of ₹ 5 lakhs 8% debentures (interest payable in its favour).

Initially outlay consist of	₹
Freehold premises	25,00,000
Plant & Machinery	10,00,000
Stock	6,00,000
Vehical & other items	5,00,000

(Payment on above items are to be made in the month of incorporation) sales during the six month ending on June 30, are estimated as under:

January	₹ 14 lakhs	April	₹ 25 lakhs
February	₹ 15 lakhs	May	₹ 26.50 lakhs
March	₹ 18.50 lakhs	June	₹ 28 lakhs

Lag in payment Debtors 2 months; Creditors 1 month.

Other Information:

(a) Preliminary Expenses: ₹ 50,000 (Payable in February)

(b) General Expenses: ₹ 50,000 per month, at the end of each month.

(c) Monthly Wages & Salaries (payable ion the first day of the next month). ₹ 80,000 for the first three months and ₹ 95,000 thereafter.

(d) Gross Profit rate is expected to be 20% on sales.

(e) The Shares and Debentures are to be issued on 1st January.

(f) The Stock level throughout is to be the same as the outlay. Prepare a Cash Budget for the six months ended June 30.

SOLUTION

X LTD.
CASH BUDGET FOR THE SIX MONTHS ENDING JUNE 30, 20.. *(₹ in Lakhs)*

Particulars	*Jan.*	*Feb.*	*Mar.*	*Apr.*	*May.*	*June*	*Total*
A. Total Cash Available:							
(a) Opening Balance	—	13.50	1.30	2.80	2.50	0.50	—
(b) Issue of Shares	55.00						55.00

(c) Issue of 8% Debentures	5.00						5.00
(d) Sales			14.00	15.00	18.50	25.00	72.50
	60.00	13.50	15.30	17.80	21.00	25.50	132.50
B. Total Cash Payments:							
(a) Fixed Assets:							
Freehold Premises	25.00						25.00
Plant & Machinery	10.00						10.00
Vehicals	5.00						5.00
(b) Preliminary Expenses		0.50					0.50
(c) Wages and Salaries		0.80	0.80	0.80	0.95	0.95	4.30
(d) Gen. expenses	0.50	0.50	0.50	0.50	0.50	0.50	3.00
(e) Purchases	6.00	10.40	11.20	14.00	19.05	20.25	80.90
	46.50	12.20	12.50	15.30	20.50	21.70	128.70
C. Closing Balance (A – B)	13.50	1.30	2.80	2.50	0.50	3.80	3.80

Working Notes:

SCHEDULE OF PAYMENTS TO CREDITORS

Particulars	*Jan.*	*Feb.*	*Mar.*	*Apr.*	*May*	*June*
A. Sales	14.00	15.00	18.50	25.00	26.50	28.00
B. Cost of Goods Sold @ 80%	11.20	12.00	14.80	20.00	21.20	22.40
C. *Less:* Wages & Salaries	(0.80)	(0.80)	(0.80)	(0.95)	(0.95)	(0.95)
D. Purchases	10.40	11.20	14.00	19.05	20.25	21.45
E. Payments	6.00	10.40	11.20	14.00	19.05	20.25

PROBLEM 9

In May 2009, Shri Anath got ₹ 10,000 in Delhi lottery and started a business to manufacture a certain components for BHEL during the same month, he purchased machinery for ₹ 5,00,000 out of gift of ₹ 1,00,000 from his father-in-law and a loan ₹ 4,00,000 from bank. Interest at 9% per annum, payable quarterly in arrears from the month borrowing. The principal is repayable at ₹ 20,000 every half year. He commenced manufacture on 2009 and his production and delivery schedule as under:

Particulars	*30th June*	*31st July*	*31st Aug.*	*30th Sept.*	*31st Oct.*
Production & delivery	1000	1500	2000	2500	3000

and thereafter 3,000 units every month.

He gets ₹ 10 per unit from BHEL. His variable cost is ₹ 6 per unit. He has fixed expenses to the extent of ₹ 1,000 per month. He also want to draw ₹ 1,000 per month for his maintenance. His bills are settled after 30 days from the date of supply. His variable cost is to be met by actual payment in the every month. The fixed cost and his drawings are met on the first day of the next month. He desires always to carry a minimum cash balance of ₹ 2,000 and a maximum one of ₹ 10,000.

Required: Prepare a Cash Budget for each of the 9 months from May 2009 to Jan. 2010 Assume a Temporary overdraft from the bank, whenever required with in the above-maintained minimum & maximum cash balance requirements. Ignore interest on the overdraft.

SOLUTION

CASH BUDGET FOR THE PERIOD MAY 2009 TO JAN. 2010 (₹ in '000)

Particulars	May ₹	June ₹	July ₹	Aug. ₹	Sept. ₹	Oct. ₹	Nov. ₹	Dec. ₹	Jan. ₹
A. Total Cash Available:									
(a) Opening Balance	—	10	4	3	2	5	10	2	2
(b) Lottery receipts	10	—	—	—	—	—	—	—	—
(c) Gift from Father-in-law	100	—	—	—	—	—	—	—	—
(d) Loan from Bank	400	—	—	—	—	—	—	—	—
(e) Supply Bills Collected	—	—	10	15	20	25	30	30	30
	510	10	14	18	22	30	40	32	32
B. Total Cash Payments:									
(a) Machineries	500	—	—	—	—	—	—	—	—
(b) Interest on Loan	—	—	—	9	—	—	9	—	—
(c) Loan repayments (Investment)	—	—	—	—	—	—	20	—	—
(d) Variable cost	—	6	9	12	15	18	18	18	18
(e) Drawing and fixed costs	—	—	2	2	2	2	2	2	2
	500	6	11	23	17	20	49	20	20
C. Surplus (Deficit)	10	4	3	(5)	5	10	(9)	12	12
D. *Add:* Overdraft from Bank to Maintain a min. balance of ₹ 2,000	—	—	—	7	—	—	11	—	—
E. *Less:* Repayment of overdraft After keeping min. balance of ₹ 2,000	—	—	—	—	—	—	—	(10)	(8)
F. Closing Balance (C + D – E)	10	4	3	2	5	10	2	2	4

SOLVED PROBLEMS-II

PROBLEM 10

Prepare Cash Budget for July-December from the following information:

(A) THE ESTIMATED SALES, EXPENSES ETC. ARE AS FOLLOWS (₹ in Lakhs)

Particulars	June	July	Aug.	Sept.	Oct.	Nov.	Dec.
Sales	35	40	40	50	50	60	65
Purchases	14	16	17	20	20	25	28
Wages and Salaries	12	14	14	18	18	20	22
Misc. Expenses	5	6	6	6	7	7	7
Interest Received	2	—	—	2	—	—	2
Sale of Shares	—	—	20	—	—	—	—

(b) 20% of the sales are on cash and the balance on credit.

(c) 1% of the credit sales are returned by the customers. 2% of the Gross accounts receivable constitute bad debt losses. 50% of the good accounts receivables are collected in the month of the sales, and the rest in the next month.

(d) The time lag in the payment of misc. expenses and purchases is one month. Wages and salaries are paid fortnightly with a time lag of 15 days.

(e) The company keeps a minimum cash balance of ₹ 5 lakhs. Cash in excess of ₹ 7 lakhs is invested in Govt. securities in the multiple of ₹ 1 lakh. Shortfalls in the minimum cash balance are made good by borrowing from banks. Ignore interest received and paid.

SOLUTION

CASH BUDGET FOR JULY-DECEMBER *(₹ in Lakhs)*

Particulars	*Jul.* ₹	*Aug.* ₹	*Sept.* ₹	*Oct.* ₹	*Nov.* ₹	*Dec.* ₹
A. Total Cash Available:						
Opening Cash in hand	5.00	7.10	7.14	7.06	7.86	7.54
Cash sales	8.00	8.00	10.00	10.00	12.00	13.00
Collection from Debtors	29.10	31.04	34.92	38.80	42.68	48.50
Interest Received	—	—	2.00	—	—	2.00
Sale of Shares	—	20.00	—	—	—	—
	42.10	66.14	54.06	55.86	62.54	71.04
B. Total Cash Payments:						
Creditors for suppliers	14.00	16.00	17.00	20.00	20.00	25.00
Wages & Salaries	13.00	14.00	16.00	18.00	19.00	21.00
Misc. expenses	5.00	6.00	6.00	6.00	7.00	7.00
Total Payments	32.00	36.00	39.00	44.00	46.00	53.00
C. Surplus (Deficit) [A – B]	10.10	30.14	15.06	11.86	16.54	18.04
Financing & Investment:						
D. Borrowing/Sales of Govt. Securities to maintain minimum cash balance	—	—	—	—	—	—
E. Investment in Govt. securities (in excess of ₹ 7 lakhs in the multiple of ₹ 1 lakhs)	(3.00)	(23.00)	(8.00)	(4.00)	(9.00)	(11.00)
F. Closing Cash Balance (C + D – E)	7.10	7.14	7.06	7.86	7.54	7.04

Working Notes:

(I) COLLECTION FROM DEBTORS *(₹ in lakhs)*

Particulars	*Jun.*	*Jul.*	*Aug.*	*Sept.*	*Oct.*	*Nov.*	*Dec.*
A. Sales	35.00	40.00	40.00	50.00	50.00	60.00	65.00
B. Cash Sales @ 20%	7.00	8.00	8.00	10.00	10.00	12.00	13.00
C. Credit Sales @ 80% [A – B]	28.00	32.00	32.00	40.00	40.00	48.00	52.00
D. *Less:* Returns (1%)	0.28	0.32	0.32	0.40	0.40	0.48	0.52
E. *Less:* Bad Debts (2%)	0.56	0.64	0.64	0.80	0.80	0.96	1.04
F. Good accounts receivable	27.16	31.04	31.04	38.80	38.80	46.56	50.44
G. Collection 50% in the month of Sales	13.58	15.52	15.52	19.40	19.40	23.28	25.22
H. Balance 50% in the next month	—	13.58	15.52	15.52	19.40	19.40	23.28
I. Total Collection in a month (G + H)	13.58	29.10	31.04	34.92	38.80	42.68	48.50

* The wordings used in the question may also be interpreted to mean that bad debts at 2% is to be worked out from net credit sales figures after returns

(II) PAYMENT OF WAGES & SALARIES (FORTNIGHTLY WITH A LAG OF 15 DAYS) *(₹ in Lakhs)*

Particulars	*July*	*August*	*Sept.*	*Oct.*	*Nov.*	*Dec.*
1/2 to be paid in the same month	7.00	7.00	9.00	9.00	10.00	11.00
1/2 to be paid in the next month	6.00	7.00	7.00	9.00	9.00	10.00
Total Wages & Salaries paid	13.00	14.00	16.00	18.00	19.00	21.00

PROBLEM 11

Prepare Cash Budget for Jan.-June from the following information:

(a) The estimated sales and expenses are as follows:

Particulars	*Nov.*	*Dec.*	*Jan.*	*Feb.*	*Mar.*	*Apr.*	*May*	*June*
Sales	2,00,000	2,20,000	1,20,000	1,00,000	1,50,000	2,40,000	2,00,000	2,00,000
Salaries	30,000	30,000	24,000	24,000	24,000	30,000	27,000	27,000
Misc. Expenses	27,000	27,000	21,000	30,000	24,000	27,000	27,000	27,000

(b) Cash Sales are 75% *less* than the credit sales.

(c) The firm has a gross margin of 25% on sales.

(d) 50% of the credit sales are collected in the month following the sales, 60% of the remaining in the second month and balance in the third month.

(e) Material for the sale of each month is purchased one month advance on a credit for two months.

(f) The time lag in the payment of salaries is one third of month and miscellaneous expenses one month.

(g) 12% Debentures ₹ 40,000 were issued on 1st January. (Half yearly interest due on 30th June & 31st Dec.)

(h) The firm maintains a minimum cash balance of ₹ 40,000. Funds can be borrowed @ 12% p.a. in the multiple of ₹ 1,000 the interest being payable on monthly basis.

(i) Cash balance at the end of December is ₹ 60,000.

SOLUTION

CASH BUDGET FOR JAN.-JUNE

Particulars	*Jan.* ₹	*Feb.* ₹	*Mar.* ₹	*Apr.* ₹	*May* ₹	*June* ₹
A. Total Cash Available:						
Cash in hand	60,000	42,000	59,800	64,800	51,500	40,500
Cash sales	24,000	20,000	30,000	48,000	40,000	40,000
Collection from Debtors	1,36,000	1,32,800	1,04,000	1,03,200	1,48,000	1,61,600
Issue of Debentures	40,000	—	—	—	—	—
	2,60,000	1,94,800	1,93,800	2,16,000	2,39,500	2,42,100
B. Total Cash Payments:						
Creditors for suppliers	1,65,000	90,000	75,000	1,12,500	1,80,000	1,50,000

	Salaries	26,000	24,000	24,000	28,000	28,000	27,000
	Misc. Expenses	27,000	21,000	30,000	24,000	27,000	27,000
	Interest on debentures	—	—	—	—	—	2,400
		2,18,000	1,35,000	1,29,000	1,64,500	2,35,000	2,06,400
C.	**Surplus (Deficit) [A – B]**	42,000	59,800	64,800	51,500	4,500	35,700
	Financing:						
D.	Borrowing to maintain ₹ 40,000	—	—	—	—	36,000	5,000
E.	Payment of Interest @ 12% p.a.	—				—	(360)*
F.	**Closing Cash Balance (C + D – E)**	42,000	59,800	64,800	51,500	40,500	40,340

Working Notes:

(I) COLLECTION FROM DEBTORS

(₹ *in '000*)

Particulars	*Nov.*	*Dec.*	*Jan.*	*Feb.*	*Mar.*	*Apr.*	*May*	*June*
Sales	200	220	120	100	150	240	200	200
Cash Sales (20%)	40	44	24	20	30	48	40	40
Credit sales (80%)	160	176	96	80	120	192	160	160
Collection from Debtors:								
50% in next month		80	88	48.0	40.0	60.0	96	80.0
30% in 2nd month			48	52.8	28.8	24.0	36	57.6
20% in 3rd month		—	—	32.0	35.2	19.2	16	24.0
		80	136	132.8	104.0	103.2	148	161.6

(II) PAYMENT TO CREDITORS

(₹ *in '000*)

Particulars	*Nov.*	*Dec.*	*Jan.*	*Feb.*	*Mar.*	*Apr.*	*May*	*June*
75% of Sales	150	165	90	75	112.50	180	150	150
Purchase one month in advance	165	90	75	112.5	180	150	150	150*
Payment to Suppliers on 2 month credit			165	90	75	112.5	180	150

(III) PAYMENT OF SALARIES

(₹ *in '000*)

Particulars	*Nov.*	*Dec.*	*Jan.*	*Feb.*	*Mar.*	*Apr.*	*May*	*June*
Due for the month	30	30	24	24	24	30	27	27
1/3 of last month	—	10	10	8	8	8	10	9
2/3 of current month	20	20	16	16	16	20	18	18
Total Payment	20	30	26	24	24	28	28	27

(iv) Assumptions

(a) Purchases for the month of June is assumed as in may in the absence of sales figure for July.

(b) In the absence of information about sales of Oct. nil collection for that month is assumed.

PROBLEM 12

From the information given below, prepare a Cash Budget of M/s. Ram Ltd. for the first half year of 2009, assuming that cost would remain unchanged:

(a) Sales are both on credit and for cash the latter being one-third of the former;

(b) Realisations from debtors are 25% in the month of sale, 60% in month following that and the balance in the month after that;

(c) The company adopts uniform pricing policy of the selling price being 25% over cost;

(d) Budgeted sales of each month are purchased and paid for in the preceding month;

(e) The company has outstanding debentures of ₹ 2 lakhs on 1st Jan. which carry interest at 15% per annum payable on the last date of each quarter on calendar years basis. 20% of the debentures are due for redemption on 30th June 2009;

(f) The company has to pay the last instalment of advance tax, for assessment year 2008-2009, amounting to ₹ 54,000;

(g) Anticipated office costs for the six month period are; Jan. ₹ 25,000 Feb. ₹ 20,000 Mar. ₹ 40,000 Apr. ₹ 35,000 May ₹ 30,000 and June ₹ 45,000;

(h) The operating cash balance of ₹ 10,000 is the minimum cash balance to be maintained Deficits have to be met by borrowals in multiples of ₹ 10,000 on which interest on monthly basis has to be paid on the first date of the subsequent month at 12% p.a. Interest is payable for a minimum period of a month.

(i) Rent payable is ₹ 2,000 per month.

(g) Sales forecast for the different months are:

Oct. 2008 ₹ 1,60,000, Nov. ₹ 1,80,000, Dec. ₹ 2,00,000, Jan. 2009 ₹ 2,20,000, Feb. ₹ 1,40,000 Mar. ₹ 1,60,000, Apr. 1,50,000, May ₹ 2,00,000, June ₹ 1,80,000 and July ₹ 1,20,000.

SOLUTION

M/S. RAM LTD.
CASH BUDGET JAN. TO JUNE 2009

	Particulars	*Jan.* ₹	*Feb.* ₹	*Mar.* ₹	*Apr.* ₹	*May* ₹	*June* ₹
A.	**Total Cash Available:**						
	Opening balance	10,000	77,500	1,10,250	44,500	10,875	17,775
	Cash sales (1/4 of total sales)	55,000	35,000	40,000	37,500	50,000	45,000
	Collection from Debtors	1,51,500	1,47,750	1,17,750	1,15,875	1,23,000	1,40,625
		2,16,500	2,60,250	2,68,000	1,97,875	1,83,875	2,03,400
B.	**Total Cash Payments:**						
	Purchases	1,12,000	1,28,000	1,20,000	1,60,000	1,44,000	96,000
	Office Expenses	25,000	20,000	40,000	35,000	30,000	45,000
	Rent	2,000	2,000	2,000	2,000	2,000	2,000
	Debenture Interest	—	—	7,500	—	—	7,500
	Advance Tax	—	—	54,000	—	—	—
	Redemption of Debentures	—	—	—	—	—	40,000
		1,39,000	1,50,000	2,23,500	1,97,000	1,76,000	1,90,500
C.	**Surplus (Deficit) [A – B]**	77,500	1,10,250	44,500	875	7,875	12,900

D.	*Add:* **Borrowing to maintain Minimum Cash Balance**	—	—	—	10,000	10,000	—
E.	*Less:* **Interest on Borrowings**	—	—	—	—	(100)	(200)
F.	**Closing Balance**	77,500	1,10,250	44,500	10,875	17,775	12,700

Working Notes:

(I) CALCULATION OF CREDIT SALES

Particulars	*2008*		*009*					
	Nov. ₹	*Dec.* ₹	*Jan.* ₹	*Feb.* ₹	*Mar.* ₹	*Apr.* ₹	*May* ₹	*June* ₹
Credit Sales @ 75%	135	150	165	105	120	112.50	150	135

(II) CASH COLLECTION FROM DEBTORS *(₹ in '000)*

Particulars	*Jan.*	*Feb.*	*Mar.*	*Apr.*	*May*	*June*
(a) 25% in the same month	41.25	26.25	30.00	28.125	37.50	33.75
(b) 60% in the next month	90.00	99.00	63.00	72.000	67.50	90.00
(c) 15% in the third month	20.25	22.50	24.75	15.750	18.00	16.875
Collection from Debtors	151.50	147.75	117.75	115.875	123.00	140.625

PROBLEM 13

From the following information relating to a departmental store for the three months period ending 31st January, 2009, you are required to prepare the Monthly cash budget on receipts and payments basis.

(a) It is anticipated that the working capital items as on 1st November, 20X8 will be as follows:

Particulars	*₹ 000's*
Cash in hand and at bank	545
Short-term investments	300
Debtors	2,570
Stock	1,300
Trade Creditors	2,110
Creditors for Expenses	200
Dividends Due	485
Tax Due	320

(B) BUDGETED PROFIT STATEMENT *₹ 000's*

Sales	2,100	1,800	1,700
Cost of goods sold	(1,635)	(1,405)	(1,330)
Gross Profit	465	395	370
Administrative, selling and Distribution expenses and interest	(315)	(270)	(255)
Net Profit prior to tax	150	125	115

(C) BUDGETED BALANCES AT THE END OF EACH MONTH ₹ 000's

Particulars	30th Nov.	31st Dec.	31st Jan.
Short-term investments	700	—	200
Debtors	2,600	2,500	2,350
Stock	1,200	1,100	1,000
Trade Creditors	2,000	1,950	1,900
Creditors for Expenses	200	200	200
Dividends Due	485	—	—
Tax Due	320	320	320

(d) Depreciation amounting to ₹ 60,000 is included in the budgeted expenditure for each month.

(e) Capital expenditure amounting to ₹ 8,00,000 is expected to be incurred during December 2008.

(f) Process from the sale of plant equipment of ₹ 50,000 are expected in January, 2009.

SOLUTION

CASH BUDGET FOR THREE MONTHS ENDING 31ST JAN. 2009

Particulars	Nov. 2008 (₹ '000)	Dec. 2008 (₹ '000)	Jan. 2009 (₹ '000)
A. Total Cash Available:			
Opening Cash balance	545	315	65
Receipts from Debtors	2,070	1,900	1,850
Sale of Investments	—	700	—
Sale of Plant	—	—	50
	2,615	2,915	1,965
B. Total Cash Payments:			
Trade Creditors	1,645	1,355	1,280
Creditors for expenses	255	210	195
Capital expenditure	—	800	—
Payment of dividend	—	485	—
Purchase of Investments	400	—	200
	2,300	2,850	1,675
C. Surplus (Deficit) [A – B]	315	65	290

Working Notes:

(I) CALCULATION OF PAYMENTS TO TRADE CREDITORS (₹ in '000)

Particulars	Nov.	Dec.	Jan.
(a) Cost of goods sold	1,635	1,405	1,330
(b) *Add:* Closing Stock	1,200	1,100	1,000
	2,835	2,505	2,330
(c) *Less:* Opening Stock	(1,300)	(1,200)	(1,100)

(d) Purchases	1,535	1,305	1,230
(e) *Add:* Opening Trade Creditors	2,110	2,000	1,950
	3,645	3,305	3,180
(f) *Less:* Closing Trade Creditors	(2,000)	(1,950)	(1,900)
(g) Payments made to Trade Creditors	1,645	1,355	1,280

(II) CALCULATION OF RECEIPTS FROM DEBTORS *(₹ in '000)*

Particulars	*Nov.*	*Dec.*	*Jan.*
(a) Opening Debtors	2,570	2,600	2,500
(b) *Add:* Sales	2,100	1,800	1,700
	4,670	4,400	4,200
(c) *Less:* Closing Debtors	(2,600)	(2,500)	(2,350)
(d) Receipts from Debtors	2,070	1,900	1,850

(III) CALCULATION OF PAYMENTS TO CREDITORS FOR EXPENSES *(₹ in '000)*

Particulars	*Nov.*	*Dec.*	*Jan.*
(a) Adm. Selling & distribution expenses & interest	315	270	255
(b) *Less:* Depreciation	(60)	(60)	(60)
(c) Cash expenses	255	210	195
(d) *Add:* Opening creditors for expenses	200	200	200
(e) *Less:* Closing creditors for expenses	(200)	(200)	(200)
	255	210	195

PROBLEM 14

Prepare monthly Cash Budget for 6 months beginning from April 2009, on the basis of following information:

(a) Estimated monthly sales are as follows:

Particulars	₹	*Particulars*	₹
Jan.	1,00,000	June	80,000
Feb.	1,20,000	July	1,00,000
March	1,40,000	Aug.	80,000
April	80,000	Sept.	60,000
May	60,000	Oct.	1,00,000

(b) Wages and Salaries are estimated to be payable as follows:

Particulars	₹	*Particulars*	₹
April	9,000	July	10,000
May	8,000	Aug.	9,000
June	10,000	Sept.	9,000

(c) Cash sales are 75% *less* than the credit sales. 75% of credit sales are collected within one month and the balance in two months. There are no bad debt losses.

(d) Purchases amount to 80% of sales and are made and paid for in the month preceding the sale.

(e) The firm has 10% Debentures of ₹ 1,20,000. Interest on these has to be paid quarterly in Jan., Apr. and so on.

(f) The firm is to be make an advance payment of tax of ₹ 5,000 in July, 2009.

(g) The firm had a cash balance of ₹ 20,000 on April 1, 2009, which is the minimum desired level of cash balance. Any cash surplus/deficit above/below this level is made up by temporary investment/liquidation of temporary investments *or* Temporary borrowings at the end of each month (interest on these to be ignored).

SOLUTION

MONTHLY CASH BUDGET FOR THE SIX MONTHS FROM APR. TO SEPT., 2009 *(₹ '000)*

Particulars	*April* ₹	*May* ₹	*June* ₹	*July* ₹	*Aug.* ₹	*Sept.* ₹
A. Total Cash Available:						
Opening Cash balance	20	20	20	20	20	20
Cash sales	16	12	16	20	16	12
Collection from debtors	108	76	52	60	76	68
	144	108	88	100	112	100
B. Total Cash Payments:						
Purchases	48	64	80	64	48	80
Wages & salaries	9	8	10	10	9	9
Interest on Debn.	3	—	—	3	—	—
Tax Payment	—	—	—	5	—	—
	60	72	90	82	57	89
C. Surplus (Deficit) [A – B]	84	36	(2)	18	55	11
D. Investment/Financing:						
Temp. investments After keeping min.						
Cash balance of ₹ 20,000	(64)	(16)	—	—	(35)	—
E. Realisation of temporary Investments to maintain Cash balance of ₹ 20,000	—	—	22	2	—	9
F. Closing Cash Balance (C + D + E)	20	20	20	20	20	20

Working Notes:

(I) SCHEDULE OF COLLECTIONS FROM DEBTORS *(₹ in '000)*

Particulars	*Feb.*	*Mar.*	*Apr.*	*May.*	*June*	*July*	*Aug.*	*Sept.*
Total Sales	120	140	80	60	80	100	80	60
Credit Sales (80% of total sales)	96	112	64	48	64	80	64	48
Collection:								
One month (75%)		72	84	48	36	48	60	48
Two month (25%)			24	28	16	12	16	20
Total Collections			108	76	52	60	76	68

(II) SCHEDULE OF PAYMENTS TO TRADE CREDITORS

(₹ in '000)

Particulars	*Apr.*	*May*	*June*	*July*	*Aug.*	*Sept.*	*Oct.*
A. Total Sales	80	60	80	100	80	60	100
B. Purchasing being 80% of sales of next month	48	64	80	64	48	80	

PROBLEM 15

Sri Ramesh has given the sales forecast for January to July 2009 and actual sales for November, December 2008 were as under. With the other particulars given, prepare Cash Budget for five months January/May 2009:

1. SALES

Particulars	₹
November 2008	80,000
December	70,000
January 2009	80,000
February	1,00,000
March	80,000
April	1,00,000
May	90,000
June	1,20,000
July	1,00,000

2. Sales 20% cash 80% credit payable in the third month (January sales in March)
3. Variable expenses 5% on turnover time lag half month.
4. Commission 5% on credit sales payable in the third month.
5. Purchases 60% of the sales of the third month.
6. Payment 3rd month of purchases.
7. Rent and other expenses ₹ 3,000 paid every month.
8. Other payments: Fixed Assets Purchase March ₹ 50,000, Taxes April ₹ 20,000
9. Opening Cash Balance ₹ 25,000

SOLUTION

CASH BUDGET FROM JANUARY TO MARCH 2009

Particulars	*Jan.* ₹	*Feb.* ₹	*March* ₹	*April* ₹	*May* ₹	*Total* ₹
A. Total Cash Available:						
Opening Balance	25,000	47,050	52,750	24,050	32,550	25,000*
Cash Sales	16,000	20,000	16,000	20,000	18,000	90,000
Collection from Debtors	64,000	56,000	64,000	80,000	64,000	3,28,000
Total Cash Inflow	1,05,000	1,23,050	1,32,750	1,24,050	1,14,550	4,43,000

B. Total Cash Payments:						
Payment to S. Creditors	48,000	60,000	48,000	60,000	54,000	2,70,000
Expenses—						
Variable Expenses	3,750	4,500	4,500	4,500	4,750	22,000
Commission	3,200	2,800	3,200	4,000	3,200	16,400
Rent	3,000	3,000	3,000	3,000	3,000	15,000
Other Payments:						
Fixed Assets	—	—	50,000	—	—	50,000
Taxes	—	—	—	20,000	—	20,000
Total Cash Outflow	57,950	70,300	1,08,700	91,500	64,950	3,93,400
C. Closing Balance [A – B]	47,050	52,750	24,050	32,550	49,600	49,600

*Opening Balance

Working Notes:

(I) CASH SALES AND REALISATION FROM DEBTORS

Particulars	*Nov. '08* ₹	*Dec.* ₹	*Jan. '09* ₹	*Feb.* ₹	*March* ₹	*April* ₹	*May* ₹
Total Sales	80,000	70,000	80,000	1,00,000	80,000	1,00,000	90,000
Cash Sales 20%	(16,000)	(14,000)	(16,000)	(20,000)	(16,000)	(20,000)	(18,000)
Credit Sales 80%	64,000	56,000	64,000	80,000	64,000	80,000	72,000
Realisation from Debtors			64,000	56,000	64,000	80,000	64,000

(ii) Payment for Purchases: Purchases made for the third month requirements i.e., Nov. purchases will be for Jan. Sales: Further payment is made in third month from the purchase i.e., Nov. purchases will be paid in January. In effect it means payment for purchases will be 60% of sales of each month's sale, goods having been purchased two months earlier.

Particulars	*Jan.* ₹	*Feb.* ₹	*March* ₹	*April* ₹	*May* ₹
Payment for purchases:					
Equal to 60% of sales of current month	48,000	60,000	48,000	60,000	54,000

(III) COMMISSION @ 5% ON CREDIT SALE PAID IN THE THIRD MONTH I.E., FOR NOV. 2008 SALES PAID IN JAN. 2009.

Particulars	*Nov.* ₹	*Dec.* ₹	*Jan.* ₹	*Feb.* ₹	*March* ₹	*April* ₹	*May* ₹
Credit Sales	64,000	56,000	64,000	80,000	64,000	80,000	72,000
Commission @ 5%	3,200	2,800	3,200	4,000	3,200	4,000	3,600
(iv) Variable Expenses 5% of Total Sales	4,000	3,500	4,000	5,000	4,000	5,000	4,500
1/2 of previous month			1,750	2,000	2,500	2,000	2,500
& 1/2 of Current month			2,000	2,500	2,000	2,500	2,250
			3,750	4,500	4,500	4,500	4,750

11 SOURCES OF FINANCE

LEARNING OBJECTIVES

After studying this chapter, you should be able to understand:

- Financial Needs
- Sources of Raising Finance
- Long Term Sources of Finance
- Equity Shares
- Preference Shares
- Distinction Between an Equity Share and Preference Share
- Retained Profits
- Debentures
- Distinction Between a Share and a Debenture
- Long Term Loans from Financial Institutions
- Loans from Commercial Banks
- Venture Capital Financing
- Lease Financing
- Asset Securitisation
- International Financing
- Short-Term Sources of Finance
- Trade Credit
- Advances from Customers
- Discounting Bills of Exchange
- Bank Overdraft
- Clean Overdraft
- Cash Credit
- Factoring
- Advances Against Goods
- Advances Against Documents of Title to Goods
- Advances Against Supply of Bills
- Financing of Export Trade by Banks
- Inter Corporate Deposits (ICD)
- Certificate of Deposit (CD)
- Public Deposits
- Other Sources of Financing
- New Instruments

1.0 FINANCIAL NEEDS

A company needs funds to meet its different types of financial needs. A basic principle is that short-term financial needs should be met from short-term sources, medium-term financial needs from medium-term sources and long-term financial needs from long-term sources. Accordingly, the method of raising the funds is to be decided with reference to the period for which funds are required.

The purpose, period and sources of various finances available in India are summarised as under:

Types of Needs	*Meaning*	*Period*	*Sources*
Long Term Needs	Such needs refer to the requirement of funds to finance permanent *or* hardcore working capital like building, plant, and furniture.	Exceeding 5 years	1. Equity Shares 2. Preference Shares 3. Retained Profits 4. Debentures 5. Loans from Financial Institutions 6. Loans from Commercial Banks 7. Venture Capital Funding 8. Lease Financing 9. Asset Securitisation 10. International Financing
Medium Term Needs	Such needs refer to the requirement of funds to finance deferred revenue expenditure like advertisement expenses	Exceeding 1 year but not exceeding 5 years	1. Commercial Banks 2. Public Deposits 3. State Financial Corporation 4. Redeemable Debentures 5. Redeemable Preference Shares 6. Loans from Financial Institutions 7. Euro-shares 8. Foreign Currency Bonds 9. Lease Financing/ Hire Purchase Financing
Short Term Needs	Such needs refer to the requirement of funds to finance temporary working capital	Normally not exceeding 1 year	1. Trade Credit from Suppliers 2. Advances from Customers 3. Bill Discounting facility 4. Overdraft 5. Cash Credit 6. Factoring 7. Public Deposits

2.0 SOURCES OF RAISING FINANCE

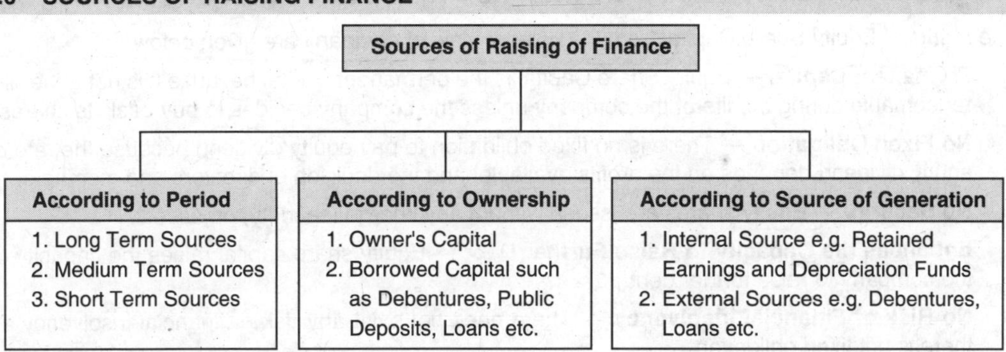

However, for the sake of convenience, the different sources of funds can also be classified into the following categories:

(i) Security Financing — Financing through Shares and Debentures

(ii) Internal Financing — Financing through Retained Earnings, Depreciation.

(iii) Loan Financing — Financing through both short term and long-term loans.

(iv) International Financing.

(v) Other Sources.

3.0 LONG TERM SOURCES OF FINANCE

The different sources of Long-term sources of finance are as follows :

1. Equity Shares
2. Preference Shares
3. Retained Profits
4. Debentures
5. Loans from Financial Institutions
6. Loans from Commercial Banks
7. Venture Capital Funding
8. Lease Financing
9. Asset Securitisation
10. International Financing

4.0 EQUITY SHARES

MEANING OF EQUITY SHARE

An equity share is a share, which is not a preference share. In other words, it is a share, which does not carry two preferential rights (viz., right to receive dividend and right to receive repayment of capital) attached to a preference share. The capital raised through equity shares is called Equity Share Capital and the persons who contribute money through equity shares are called Equity Shareholders. Since dividend to Equity Shareholders can be paid only when there are distributable profits, these shares have least risk involved. But the cost of capital of this source is highest because the shareholders usually expect a higher rate of return on their investments. A company having substantial Equity Share Capital may find it easier to raise further funds since equity shares provide a security to other sources of finance. A public limited company may raise funds from promoters *or* from the public by way of issue of equity shares.

MERITS OF EQUITY SHARE CAPITAL FROM THE POINT OF VIEW OF COMPANY

The merits of Equity Share Capital from the point of view of company are given below:

1. **Permanent Capital** — Equity Share Capital is the permanent capital because it is not generally redeemable during the life of the company unless the company decides to buy back its shares.
2. **No Fixed Obligation** — There is no fixed obligation to pay equity dividend because the rate of equity dividend depends on the profits available, and the decision of directors and members.
3. **No Security** — Equity shares are issued without any charge (security) on assets.
4. **Enhances the Capacity to Raise Further Debt** — Equity share capital raises the capacity of the company to raise further debt.
5. **No Risk of Financial Insolvency** — There does not exist any risk of financial insolvency as there is not fixed obligation.
6. **Right issue** — The company can make further issue of share capital by making a right issue.

LIMITATIONS OF EQUITY SHARE CAPITAL FROM THE POINT OF VIEW OF COMPANY

1. High Cost
2. Control gets diluted
3. Risk of Hostile takeover
4. Increased Agency Cost

MERITS OF EQUITY SHARE CAPITAL FROM THE POINT OF VIEW OF SHAREHOLDERS

The merits of Equity Share Capital from the point of view of shareholders are given below:

1. **Voting Rights** — They enjoy voting rights. They have rights to elect directors and to participate in the management of the company.
2. **High Dividend** — They may get high rates of dividend in profitable years.
3. **Bonus Shares** — They may get bonus shares in profitable years.
4. **Capital Appreciation** — They may get capital appreciation in the value of their shares.
5. **High Liquidity** — They may sell shares in the share market to get liquid funds.

LIMITATIONS OF EQUITY SHARE CAPITAL FROM THE POINT OF VIEW OF SHAREHOLDERS

The limitations of Equity Share Capital from the point of view of shareholders are discussed below:

1. **Uncertainty of Earnings** — They bear high degree of risk associated with uncertainty of earnings of the company. They may not get any dividend in the years of losses *or* lesser profits.
2. **High Risks** — They bear high degree of risk associated with the fluctuation in the market prices of their shares.
3. **Inability to participate in the Management** — In case of widely held company, they are practically not in a position to participate in the management of the company as they are usually scattered and hold shares in small lots.
4. **No Security** — They may get less *or* nothing at the time of liquidation because they are repaid at the last only and that their shares are not secured against any asset.
5. **No Control over Increase in Rate of Dividend** — They cannot increase the rates of equity dividend as proposed by the board of directors.

5.0 PREFERENCE SHARES

MEANING OF PREFERENCE SHARE

According to Section 85 of the Companies Act, 1956, a preference share is one, which carries the following two rights:

1. A right to receive dividend at a stipulated rate *or* of a fixed amount before any dividend is paid on equity shares; and
2. A right to receive repayment of capital on winding up of the company, before the capital of equity shareholders is returned.

Preference share is a hybrid form of financing which partakes some characteristics of equity because preference dividend like equity dividend is not a tax-deductible payment. It resembles debt payment because the rate of preference dividend is fixed. Typically, when preference dividend is skipped, it is payable in future because of cumulative feature associated with most of preference shares.

KINDS OF PREFERENCE SHARES

In addition to the aforesaid two preferential rights, a preference share may carry some other rights. On the basis of additional rights, preference shares can be classified into seven types as under:

1. Cumulative Preference Share is the share on which arrears of dividend accumulate. Unless stated otherwise, a preference share is always deemed to be a cumulative share.
2. Non-cumulative Preference Share is the share on which, arrears of dividend do not accumulate as per the express provision in the articles of association.
3. Participating Preference Share is that share, which, in addition to two basic preferential rights, also carries one *or* more of the following rights as per the articles of association:
   (i) a right to participate in the surplus profits left after paying dividend to equity shareholders; and
   (ii) a right to participate in the surplus assets left after the repayment of capital to equity shareholders on the winding up of the company.
4. Non-participating Preference Share is the share, which is not a participating share. Unless stated otherwise, a preference share is always deemed to be a non-participating preference share.
5. Convertible Preference Share is the share, which confers on its holder a right of conversion into equity share.
6. Non-Convertible Preference Share is the share, which does not confer on its holder a right of conversion into equity share. Unless stated otherwise, a preference share is always deemed to be a non-convertible share.
7. Redeemable Preference Share is the share, which is redeemable in accordance with the provisions of Sections 80 and 80A of the Companies Act, 1956. After the commencement of the Companies (Amendment) Act, 1988, no company limited by shares can issue any preference share, which is irredeemable.

MERITS OF PREFERENCE SHARE CAPITAL FROM THE POINT OF VIEW OF COMPANY

The merits of preference share capital from the point of view of company are discussed below:

1. **Dividend Not Charge** — Preference dividend is payable at a fixed rate and is payable as an appropriation and not as a charge. In other words, it is payable only if there are profits.
2. **No Risk of Loss of Control** — There does not exist any risk of loss of control as the preference shareholders do not have any voting rights (except at their class meetings) and they cannot participate in the management of the company.
3. **No Security** — Preference shares are issued without any charge (security) on assets.

4. **No Risk of Financing Insolvency** — There does not exist any risk of financial insolvency in relation to payment of preference dividend because preference dividend is an appropriation out of profits and not a charge against the profits.
5. **Low Cost** — The cost of preference share is lower than the cost of equity shares.
6. **Advantage of Trading on Equity** — The Company has an advantage of trading on equity if the rate of return on investment exceeds the rate of preference dividend. In this case, equity shareholders get higher rate of return on their investment.

LIMITATIONS OF PREFERENCE SHARE CAPITAL FROM THE POINT OF VIEW OF COMPANY

The limitations of preference share capital from the point of view of company are discussed below:

1. **Cost higher than that of Debt** — The cost of preference share is higher than the cost of debt because of the following four reasons:
   (i) Preference shareholders expect high rates of return in comparison to suppliers of debt.
   (ii) Dividends are not tax deductible as dividend is treated as an appropriation out of profits and not as a charge against the profits.
   (iii) Flotation cost of new issue of preference share is higher than that of issue of debentures.
2. **Not Permanent Capital** — Preference share capital is not a permanent capital because it is to be redeemed within a period which can never exceed 20 years.
3. **Not Attracts many investors** — Issue of Preference shares does not attract many investors because of risk of no dividend in case of losses *or* inadequate profits.

MERITS OF PREFERENCE SHARE CAPITAL FROM THE POINT OF VIEW OF SHAREHOLDERS

The merits of preference share capital from the point of view of shareholders are discussed below:

1. **Preferential right as to the payment of dividend** — They enjoy preferential right as to the payment of dividend as the payment of preference dividend is made before the payment of equity dividend.
2. **Preferential right as to the repayment of capital** — They enjoy preferential right as to the repayment of preference share capital as the repayment of preference share capital is made before the repayment of equity share capital.
3. **No Reduction in Dividend** — The rate of preference dividend cannot be reduced as it is already fixed.
4. **Accumulation of Dividend** — In case of cumulative preference shares, the arrears of dividend also accumulate.
5. **Redeemable** — The shares are redeemable during the life time of the company.

LIMITATIONS OF PREFERENCE SHARE CAPITAL FROM THE POINT OF VIEW OF SHAREHOLDERS

The limitations of preference share capital from the point of view of shareholders are discussed below:

1. **No Voting Rights** — Shareholders do not have any voting rights except at their class meetings. They do not have right to appoint directors and to participate in the management of the company.
2. **No Capital Appreciation** — Shareholders do not get any capital appreciation in the value of their shares as in the case with equity shares.
3. **No Increase in Dividend** — Shareholders do not get increased rates of dividend in the years of high profits as the rate of preference dividend is fixed.

6.0 DISTINCTION BETWEEN AN EQUITY SHARE AND PREFERENCE SHARE

An equity share and a preference share can be distinguished as follows:

Basis of Distinction	*An Equity Share*	*A Preference Share*
1. Preferential right as to the payment of dividend	Payment of equity dividend is made after the payment of preference dividend.	Payment of preference dividend is made before the payment of equity dividend.
2. Preferential right as to the repayment of capital	Repayment of Equity Share Capital is made after the repayment of preference share capital.	Repayment of Preference Share Capital is made before the repayment of equity share capital.
3. Rate of dividend - Fixed *or* Fluctuating	The rate of equity dividend may fluctuate from year to year depending upon the decision of directors and members.	The rate of preference dividend is fixed.
4. Arrears of dividend	In case of an equity share, arrears of dividend cannot accumulate in any case.	In case of preference shares, arrears of dividend may accumulate.
5. Convertibility	It cannot be convertible.	It may be convertible.
6. Redeemability	It is not redeemable during the lifetime of the company unless the company decides to buy-back its shares.	It is redeemable during the lifetime of the company.
7. Right to receive premium on redemption	It cannot carry a right to receive premium on redemption.	It may carry a right to receive premium on redemption.
8. Voting rights	Equity shareholders generally enjoy voting rights.	Preference share holders do not have any voting rights except at their class meetings.
9. Fluctuation in Market Value	Its market value fluctuates.	Its market value usually does not fluctuate.

7.0 RETAINED PROFITS

MEANING OF RETAINED PROFITS

That portion of the profits which is not distributed but is retained and reinvested in the business is known as retained profits. The retained profit is an internal source of finance. This method of financing is also known as reinvestment of profits *or* ploughing back of profits *or* self-financing *or* internal financing.

Such funds belong to the ordinary shareholders and increase the net worth of the company. A public limited company must plough back a reasonable amount of profit every year keeping in view the legal requirements in this regard and its own expansion plans.

Creation — Under this method of financing, a certain proportion of profits is transferred to reserves, which are shown under the head 'Reserves and Surplus'.

Part of Shareholders' funds — Since retained profits actually belong to the shareholders of the company, these are treated as part of shareholders' funds.

Use — The retained profits may be used to meet long-term, medium-term and short-term financial needs.

ADVANTAGES OF USING RETAINED PROFITS

The main advantages of using retained profits as a source of financing are as follows:

1. **No Explicit Cost** — It does not involve any explicit cost in term of flotation costs (e.g. expenses on printing, advertisement and distribution of prospectus, brokerage, underwriting commission). Hence, it is cheaper than issue of shares.
2. **More Dependable** — It is more dependable than external sources since it is not required to depend upon external investors who may *or* may not subscribe the issue.
3. **No Fixed Obligation** — It does not involve any fixed obligation to pay any dividend on profits reinvested.
4. **Not Affect Control** — Its use does not affect the control over the management of the company since there is no addition to the number of shareholders.
5. **No Security** — It does not require the security of assets to be offered.
6. **Increases Capacity to Raise Debt** — It increases the capacity of the company to raise further debt.
7. **Increases Financial Strength** — Accumulation of reserves increases financial strength to the company.
8. **Source for Bonus Shares** — It acts as a source of issuing Bonus Shares.

LIMITATIONS OF USING RETAINED PROFITS

The main limitations of using retained profits as a source of financing are as follows:

1. **Available only to Profitable companies** — This source of financing is available only to profitable companies.
2. **Concentration of Economic Power** — Growth of companies through accumulation of reserves leads to concentration of economic power.
3. **Involves Opportunity Cost** — It involves opportunity cost (i.e. the return which the shareholders could have earned if the profits were distributed). The management sometimes does not consider this cost while declaring dividend to equity share holders.
4. **Danger of Over-capitalisation** — There is always a danger of over-capitalization if the company retains profits on continuous basis year after year without requirements of funds for profitable investments.

8.0 DEBENTURES

MEANING OF DEBENTURES

A debenture is a written instrument acknowledging a debt and containing provisions as regards the repayment of principal and the payment of interest at a fixed rate. According to Sec. 2 (12) of The Companies Act, 1956, debenture includes debentures, stock, bonds and any other securities of a company whether constituting a charge on the assets of the company *or* not. Debenture represents a debt. The persons who contribute money through debentures are called debentureholders. The main features of the debentures are discussed below:

1. **Fixed Interest** — The rate of interest payable on debentures is fixed and is payable on the face value of the debentures.
2. **No Voting Rights** — The debentureholders do not enjoy voting rights except at their class meetings. They do not have rights to elect directors and to participate in the management.
3. **Redeemable** — The debentures are redeemable during the life of the company.

KINDS OF DEBENTURES

Depending upon the terms and conditions of the issue and redemption, the debentures may be of the various types as given below:

1. **Naked Debentures *or* Unsecured Debentures** are those, which are not secured on any asset. The holders of these debentures are treated as ordinary creditors.
2. **Secured Debentures** are those, which are secured *either* on a particular asset *or* on all the assets of the company in general. According to SEBI Guidelines, non-convertible debentures for a term exceeding 18 months must be secured.
3. **First Mortgage Debentures** are those, which have a first claim on the assets charged.
4. **Second Mortgage Debentures** are those, which have a second claim on the assets charged.
5. **Redeemable Debentures** are those, which are repayable after a specified period in lumpsum *or* by installments during the lifetime of the company
6. **Irredeemable Debentures (or Perpetual Debentures)** are those, which are not redeemable during the lifetime of the company.
7. **Registered Debentures** are those, which are payable to the persons whose names appear in the Register of Debenture-holders. These can be transferred only by executing a transfer deed. Interest is paid to the registered holder.
8. **Bearer Debentures** are those, which are payable to bearer thereof. These can be transferred merely by delivery. Interest is paid to the person who produces the interest coupon attached to such debentures.
9. **Convertible Debentures** are those, the holders of which have a right to convert them into shares.

   A convertible debenture is one, which entitles its holder a right of conversion into share. The portion of debenture, which is fully convertible into shares, is termed as FCD (i.e. Fully Convertible Debenture) portion and the remaining portion, which is not convertible into shares, is termed as NCD (i.e. Non-convertible Debenture) portion.

   The issue of Convertible Debenture has distinct advantages from the point of view of issuing company:

   (i) The issue enables the management to raise equity capital indirectly without diluting the equity holding, until the capital raised has started earning an added return to support to the additional issue.

   (ii) Such securities can be issued even when the equity market is not very good.

   (iii) The convertible bonds are normally unsecured and therefore, their issuance may ordinarily not impair the borrowing capacity.

   The worth noting points in this regard are as follows:

   (i) Conversion takes place as per the terms of issue.

   (ii) Conversion can take place —

   — at a specified date (e.g. at 31st Dec. 2009)

   — after a specified period (e.g. on the expiry of 6 months from the date of allotment)

   — Within a specified period (e.g. after the expiry of 1 year but within 3 years from the date of allotment).

   (iii) Conversion can take place even before the expiry of the specified period after passing the necessary resolution at the meeting of debenture-holders e.g., Convertible Debenture (Part III) of Reliance Petrochemicals Ltd. were converted before the expiry of specified period of 5 years. However, in such a case conversion is optional.

10. **Non-convertible (NCD)** are those, the holders of which do not have a right to convert them into shares. Unless otherwise stated, the debentures are deemed to be non-convertible debentures.

MERITS OF DEBENTURES FROM THE POINT OF VIEW OF THE COMPANY

The merits of debentures from the point of view of the company are discussed below:

1. **Low Cost** — The cost of debt is lower than the cost of share because of the following reasons:
   (i) Debenture holders expect low rates of interest as they assume low degree of risk.
   (ii) Interest is tax deductible expense. In other words, interest is allowed as deduction while computing total income on which tax liability is calculated. As a result, tax liability is reduced.
2. **No Risk of Loss of Control** — There does not exist any risk of loss of control as the debenture holders do not have any voting rights (except at their class meeting) and cannot participate in the management of the company.
3. **Advantage of Trading on Equity** — The company has an advantage of trading on equity if the rate of return on investment exceeds the rate of interest payable on debentures. In this case, equity shareholders get higher rate of return on their investment.

LIMITATIONS OF DEBENTURES FROM THE POINT OF VIEW OF THE COMPANY

The limitations of debentures from the point of view of the company are discussed below:

1. **Risk of Financial Insolvency** — There exists the risk of financial insolvency because of the following two reasons:
   (i) Interest on debentures is a charge against the profits and is to be paid even if the company suffers losses.
   (ii) Debentures are to be redeemed at the scheduled time of redemption during the life time of the company.

   The use of debt can cause financial distress when the firm finds it difficult to pay interest and principal.
2. **Security** — Non-convertible debentures (NCD) for a term exceeding 18 months are to be secured against assets.
3. **Increases Risk of Shareholders** — The use of debt increases the risk of shareholders because it will have unfavourable impact if return on assets is *less* than the cost of debt.

9.0 DISTINCTION BETWEEN A SHARE AND A DEBENTURE

A share and debenture can be distinguished as follows:

Basis of Distinction	*A Share*	*A Debenture*
1. Capital vs Loan	Share is a part of owned capital.	Debenture constitutes a loan.
2. Reward for investment	Reward is the payment of dividend.	Reward is the payment of interest.
3. Rate of interest and dividend - Fluctuating *or* Fixed	The rate of dividend may fluctuate from year to year depending upon the profit, decisions of directors and members.	The rate of interest is fixed.
4. Charge vs Appropriation	Payment of dividend is an appropriation out of profit and this cannot be made if there is no profit.	Payment of interest is a charge against profits and is to be made even if there is no profit.

5. Priority as to payment of interest/ dividend	Payment of dividend gets no priority over the payment of interest.	Payment of interest gets priority over the payment of dividend.
6. Priority as to repayment of principal during winding up	Payment of share capital is made after the repayment of debentures.	Payment of debentures is made before the payment of share capital.
7. Secured by charge	Shares are not secured by any charge.	Non-convertible debentures for a term exceeding 18 months are always secured by a charge.
8. Restriction on issue at discount	Sec. 79 of the Companies Act, 1956, imposes certain restrictions on issue of shares at discount.	No restriction is imposed on the issue of debentures at discount.
9. Voting rights	Shareholders generally enjoy voting rights.	Debentureholders do not have any voting rights (except at their class meetings).
10. Convertibility	Equity shares can never be convertible.	Debentures can be convertible.
11. Trust Deed	Share Trust Deed is not required to be executed.	Debentures trust deed is required to be executed.

10.0 LONG TERM LOANS FROM FINANCIAL INSTITUTIONS

MEANING OF TERM LOANS

Term Loans represent secured borrowings for a period normally exceeding 5 years and at present it is most important source of finance for new projects. They generally carry a rate of interest inclusive of interest tax, depending on the credit rating of the borrower, the perceived risk of lending and the cost of funds. These loans are generally repayable over a period of 6 to 10 years in annual, semi-annual *or* quarterly installments. Long-term loans are raised by the companies from financial institutions like the Industrial Development Bank of India (IDBI), Industrial Credit and Investment Corporation of India (ICICI) etc.

Before a term loan is sanctioned, a company has to satisfy the concerned financial institution regarding the technical, commercial, economical, financial and managerial viability of a project for which a loan is required. Such loans are available at different rates of interest under different schemes of financial institutions and are to be repaid according to the stipulated repayment schedule. The loans in many cases stipulate a number of conditions regarding the management and certain other financial policies of the company.

The merits and limitations of long-term loans from the point of view of the company are discussed below:

MERITS OF LONG-TERM LOANS

The merits of long-term loans from the point of view of the company are given below:

1. **Low Cost** — The cost of term loans is lower than the cost of equity *or* preference share capital because interest is a tax deductible expense and the rate of interest is lower than the rate of dividend.
2. **Advantage of Trading on Equity** — The company has an advantage of trading on equity if the Rate of Return on Investment (ROI) exceeds the rate of interest payable on term loan.

LIMITATIONS OF LONG-TERM LOANS

The limitations of long-term loans from the point of view of the company are given below:

1. **Risk of Financial Insolvency** — There exists the risk of financial insolvency because of the following two reasons:
   (i) Interest on term loan is a charge against the profits and is to be paid even if the company is suffering losses.
   (ii) Term loans are to be repaid at the scheduled time during the life time of the company.
2. **Security** — The term loans are to be secured by securities by way of mortgage, hypothecation etc.
3. **Increases the Risk of Shareholders** — The use of term loan increases the risk of shareholders because it will have unfavourable impact if return on assets is *less* than the cost of debt.
4. **Interference with Management** — Usually the financial institutions nominate one *or* two directors to have some degree of control over the functioning of the company. These nominee directors may interfere the management of the affairs of the company.
5. **Restrictive Clauses** — The loan agreement may also provide for conversion of loans into equity capital after a stated period if the lending institution so desires. The loan agreement may impose restriction on dividend payments to shareholders *or* may prevent the company from taking additional loans.
6. **Long Processing Time** — The lending institutions usually take a long time in sanctioning loans.

11.0 LOANS FROM COMMERCIAL BANKS

Loans are raised by companies from commercial banks against the security of assets. The banks do not interfere with the management of the company. Such loans can be repaid in parts and interest can be saved to that extent. Banks extend credit term after a proper appraisal of term loans. The term financing by bank disciplines both the banker and the borrower as long term planning is required to ensure that cash flows would be adequate to meet the instruments of repayments and allow an active turnover of bank loans. The adoption of the formal term loan lending by commercial banks will not in any way hamper the criteria of liquidity and as a matter of fact, it will introduce flexibility in the operations of banking system.

Bridge Finance: Bridge finance refers to the loan taken by a company normally from commercial banks for a short period pending disbursement of loans sanctioned by financial institutions. The bridge loans are repaid out of the term loans as and when disbursed by the concerned institutions. Bridge loans are normally secured by hypothecating movable assets, personal guarantees and demand promissory notes. The rate of interest on bridge loans is higher as compared to term loans.

12.0 VENTURE CAPITAL FINANCING

MEANING OF VENTURE CAPITAL FINANCING

The venture capital financing refers to the financing of new high risky venture promoted by qualified entrepreneurs who lack experience and funds to give shape to their ideas. In a broad sense, under venture capital financing, venture capitalist make investment to purchase equity *or* debt securities from inexperienced entrepreneurs who undertake highly risky venture with potential of success.

METHODS OF VENTURE CAPITAL FINANCING

Some common methods of venture capital financing are as follows:

(a) **Equity Financing:** The venture capital undertakings generally require funds for a longer period but may not be able to provide returns to the investors during the initial stages. Therefore, the venture capital finance is generally provided by way of equity share capital. The equity contribution of venture capital firm does not exceed 49% of total capital of venture capital undertakings so that the effective control and ownership remains with the entrepreneur.

(b) **Conditional Loan:** A conditional loan is repayable in the form of a royalty after the venture is able to generate sales. No interest is paid on such loans. In India, venture capital financers charge royalty ranging between 2 and 15%; actual rate depends on other factors of the venture such as gestation period, cash flow patterns, riskiness and other factors of the enterprises. Some venture capital financers give a choice to the enterprise of the paying a high rate of interest (which could be well above 20%) instead of royalty on sales once it becomes commercially sound.

(c) **Income Note:** It is a hybrid security which combines the feature of both conventional loan and conditional loan. The entrepreneur has to pay both interest and royalty on sales but at substantially low rates. IDBI's VCF provides funding equal to 80% - 87.5% of the projects cost for commercial application of indigenous technology.

(d) **Participating Debentures:** Such security carries charges in three phases - in the start up phase, no interest is charged, next phase a low rate of interest is charged upon a particular level of operation, after that, a high level of interest is required to be paid.

13.0 LEASE FINANCING

Leasing is an alternative to the purchase of an asset out of owned *or* borrowed funds. Under leasing, the asset is purchased initially by the lessor (leasing company) and thereafter leased to the user (lessee company) which pays specified rent (Lease rent) at specified intervals. Lessor gets the advantage of depreciation allowance being tax deductible and lessee has advantage of lease rent being tax deductible.

WHAT IS MEANT BY THE TERM 'LEASE'?

A lease is an agreement whereby the owner of an asset grants to the user the right to use an asset for payment of periodic rentals over agreed period of time.

WHO IS A 'LESSOR' IN THE LEASE AGREEMENT?

A Lessor is a person *or* entity who owns the asset and who grants the right to use the asset for payment of periodic rentals over agreed period of time.

WHO IS A 'LESSEE' IN THE LEASE AGREEMENT?

A lessee is a person *or* entity who acquires the right to use the asset from the owner of the asset for a payment of periodic rentals over agreed period of time.

WHAT ARE 'LEASE RENTALS'?

A series of periodic payments over agreed period of time by the user of the asset to the owner of the asset for acquiring the right to use the asset, are called 'Lease Rentals'.

WHAT IS 'LEASE TERM'?

It is the non-cancellable period for which the lessee has agreed to take on lease the asset together with any further period for which the lessee has the option to continue the lease of asset, with *or* without further payment, and at the inception of the lease it is reasonably certain that this option will be exercised by the lessee.

CLASSIFICATION OF LEASE

(a) What is the basic principle regarding classification of leases?

The classification of lease is based on the extent to which risks and rewards incident to ownership of a leased assets lie with the lessor *or* lessee. Risks include the possibilities of losses from idle capacity *or* technological obsolescence and of variations in return due to changing economic conditions. Rewards may be represented by the expectation of profitable operation over the economic life of the asset and of gain from appreciation in value *or* realization of residual value.

(b) When is the lease classified as a Finance Lease?

A lease is classified as a finance lease if it transfers substantially all the risks and rewards incident to ownership of an asset.

In other words, financial leases are long-term non-cancellable leases where all risks as to the asset are borne by the lessee and all returns of the asset are enjoyed by the lessee.

(c) When is the lease classified as Operating Lease?

An operating lease is a lease other than a finance lease. In other words, operating leases are short term, cancellable leases where the risk of obsolescence is borne by the lessor and annual maintenance cost is also borne by the lessor unless contract provides otherwise.

(d) Distinction between Finance Lease and Operating Lease

A Finance Lease differs from an Operating Lease in the following respects:

Basis of Difference	*Finance Lease*	*Operating Lease*
(i) Lease Term	Lease term is for the major part of the economic life of the assets.	Lease term is significantly *less* than the economic life of the assets.
(ii) Are Risk and Rewards transferred?	Under finance lease, the Lessor transfers substantially all the risks and rewards incident to ownership of an asset to the Lessee.	Under operating lease, the Lessor does not transfer substantially all the risks and rewards incident to ownership of an asset to the Lessee.
(iii) Who bears Risk of obsolescence?	The risk of obsolescence falls on the Lessee.	The risk of obsolescence falls on the Lessor.
(iv) Is Continuation of Lease certain?	Continuation of lease is reasonably certain.	Continuation of lease is not reasonably certain.
(v) Is the lease cancellable?	Finance Leases are generally non-cancellable unless contract provides otherwise.	Operating leases are generally cancellable unless contract provides otherwise.
(vi) Who bears Annual Maintenance Cost?	Annual maintenance cost is generally borne by the lessee unless contract provides otherwise.	Annual maintenance cost is borne by the lessor unless contract provides otherwise.

OPEN ENDED AND CLOSE ENDED LEASE

A Lease is said to be an open ended lease when the lessee has the option of purchasing the leased asset at the end of lease period. A lease is said to be a close ended lease when the lessee has no option of purchasing the leased asset at the end of lease period and the asset gets transferred to the lessor at the end of lease period. The risk of obsolescence, residual values etc. remain with the lessor being the legal owner of the asset.

14.0 ASSET SECURITISATION

MEANING OF ASSET SECURITISATION

Asset securitisation is defined as a process whereby loans and other receivables are packaged, underwritten and sold in the form of asset-backed securities. The assets which can be securitised include receivables from government, trade receivables, credit card receivables etc.

ASSETS WHICH CAN BE SECURITISED

For an asset to be securitised, it must fulfill certain conditions. These conditions are:

(i) The cash flows of the assets should be dependable and periodically in accordance with a determinable and demonstrated historical payment pattern.

(ii) The asset should be of good quality and readily marketable, *either* on its own merit *or* with some other form of credit enhancement so that the risk of default is sustainably reduced.

(iii) The pool of assets must have similar interest payment dates and maturities.

(iv) The total amount of assets to be securitised must be large enough to make the transaction a worthwhile proposition keeping in view the high transaction costs involved at the moment in India.

DEBT SECURITISATION PROCESS

Under Debt securitisation, a financial institution-

1. pools and packages individual loans and receivables,
2. creates securities against them,
3. gets them rated and
4. sells them to the investors at large through public offering *or* private placements (Trustee).

The asset cash flow (inflow from the original borrower) are remitted to the trustee who in turn pays scheduled interest and principal payments to the investors.

Thus "Securitisation is a synthetic technique of converting asset into securities, security into liquidity, liquidity into assets and asset into securities on an ongoing basis" thereby providing flexibility in yield, pricing pattern, risks and marketability of instruments used to the advantage of both borrowers and lenders/investors.

Debt securitisation process can be classified in the following three functions;

(i) **The Originating Function:** A borrower seeks a loan from a finance company, bank, housing company *or* a lease from a leasing company. The creditworthiness of borrower is evaluated and a contract is entered into with repayment schedule structured over the life of the loan.

(ii) **The Pooling Function:** Similar loans *or* receivables are clubbed together to create an underlying pool of assets. The pool is transferred in favour of a SPV (Special Purpose Vehicle) which acts as a trustee for the investor. Once the assets are transferred, they are held in originators portfolio.

(iii) **The Securitisation Function:** It is the SPV's job now to structure and issue the securities on the basis of asset pool. The securities carry a coupon and an expected maturity which can be asset based *or* mortgaged based. These are generally sold to investors through merchant bankers. The investors interested in this type of securities are generally institutional investors like mutual funds, insurance companies etc. The originator usually keeps the spread available (i.e. difference) between yield from secured assets and interest paid to investors.

ADVANTAGES OF DEBT SECURITISATION TO THE ORIGINATOR

(i) The assets are shifted off the balance sheet, thus giving the originator recourse to off balance sheet funding.

(ii) It converts illiquid assets to liquid portfolio.

(iii) It helps in enhancing credit rating of originator.

(iv) It facilitates better balance sheet management as assets are transferred off balance sheet facilitating satisfaction of capital adequacy norms.

For an investor, securitisation opens up new investment avenues. Though the investor bears credit risk, the securities are tied up to definite assets. Securitisation is a long term source of finance as compared to factoring, bill discounting and cash credit etc. In Indian context, Debt securitisation has began to take off. The ideal candidates for this are hire purchase and leasing companies, asset finance and real estate companies. ICICI, HDFC, Citibank, Bank of America etc have *or* are planning to raise funds by securitisation.

15.0 INTERNATIONAL FINANCING

The essence of financial management is to raise and utilise the funds effectively. This also holds goods for the procurement of funds in the international capital markets, for a multi-national organisation in any currency. There are various avenues for a multi-national organisation to raise funds *either* through internal *or* external sources. Internal funds comprise share capital, loans from parent company and retained earnings. Now a days external fund can be raised from a number of sources, as follows:-

COMMERCIAL BANKS

Like domestic loans, commercial banks all over the world extend foreign currency loans also for international operations. These banks also provide facility to overdraw, over and above the loan amount. Interest is also changed on overdrawn amount.

DEVELOPMENT BANKS AND FINANCIAL INSTITUTIONS

In almost all the countries development banks offer long and medium term loans including foreign currency component. Many agencies at the national level offer a number of concessions to foreign companies to invest within their country and to finance exports from their countries. Examples in this respect may be quoted of EXIM Bank of United States of America, which offers loans to buyers outside USA for purchasing US manufactured goods. Similarly the EXIM Bank of India also performs a similar role by providing a number of facilities to Indian businessmen and foreign importers.

DISCOUNTING OF TRADE BILLS

Discounting of trade bills is used as short term financing method. This method is widely used in Europe and Asian countries to finance both domestic and international business. Under this arrangement, companies holding bills of exchange, get the bills discounted by commercial banks before their maturity.

INTERNATIONAL AGENCIES

A number of international agencies have emerged during the recent years to finance international trade and business. The International Finance Corporation (IFC), the International Bank for Reconstruction and Development (IBRD), the Asian Development Bank (ADB), the International Monetary Fund (IMF), the Aid India Club etc. are some of the agencies, which may be quoted in this respect. These agencies finance projects both in public and private sectors.

INTERNATIONAL CAPITAL MARKET

It is well known today that modern organisations including multinationals largely depend upon sizable borrowings in rupees as well as in foreign currencies to finance their projects involving huge outlays. The taxation benefits available on borrowings as against the capital often influence this course as interest payment on borrowed funds is an allowable expenditure for tax purpose.

In order to cater to the financial needs of such organisations, international capital markets of financial centres have sprung up wherever international trade centres have developed. Lending and borrowing in foreign currencies to finance the international trade and industry has led to the development of international capital market.

In domestic capital markets of various countries, international capital transactions also take place. For instance, USA, Japan, UK, Switzerland, West Germany have active domestic capital markets. Foreign borrowers raise money in these capital markets through issue of 'Foreign Bonds'.

In international market, international bond is known as a "Euro-bond". The issue of Euro-bond is managed by a syndicate of international banks and placed with investors and lenders worldwide. The issue may be denominated in any of the currencies for which liquid market exist. In international capital market, the availability of foreign currency is assured under the four main systems viz.

1. Euro-currency market;
2. Export Credit Facilities;
3. Bonds issues, and
4. Financial Institutions.

Euro-Currency markets were originated with dollar dominated bank deposits and provide loans in Europe particularly, in London. Euro-dollar deposits form the main ingredient of Euro-currency market. Euro-dollar deposits are dollar denominated time deposits available at foreign branches of US banks and at some foreign banks. These deposits are acquired by these banks from Foreign

Governments and various firms and individuals who want to hold dollars outside USA. Banks based in Europe accept dollar denominated deposits and make dollar denominated loans to the customers. This forms the basis of Euro-currency market spread over various parts of the world. In Euro-currency market, funds are made available as loans through syndicated Euro-credit *or* instruments known as Floating Rate Notes PRNs/FRCDs (Certificates of deposits). London has remained as the main centre for Euro-currency credit.

The creditors however insist on bank guarantees. Several multinational banks of Japanese, American, British, German and French origin, operate all over the world, extending financial assistance for trade and projects. Several multinational banks like Citi Bank, ANZ Grindlays bank, Standard Chartered bank, American Express, Bank of America, etc. are aggressive players in India and they issue specific bank guarantees to facilitate business transactions between various parties, including government agencies. Commercial borrowings as well as Exim Bank finance however, constitute major part.

FINANCIAL INSTRUMENTS IN INTERNATIONAL MARKET

The liberalised measures have boosted the confidence of foreign investors and also provided an opportunity to Indian companies to explore the possibility of tapping the European market for their financial requirements, where the resources are raised through the mechanism of Euro-issues i.e. Global Depository Receipts (GDRs) and Euro-bonds.

Euro Bonds	Euro bonds are debt instruments denominated in a currency issued outside the country of that currency. Example A Dollar note floated in India.
Foreign Bonds	Foreign Bonds are debts instruments denominated in a currency which is foreign to the borrower and is sold in the country of that currency. An Indian firm placing Dollar denominated bonds in USA. In these bonds, the risk of currency fluctuation exists.
Fully Hedged Bonds	Fully Hedged Bonds are the foreign bonds in which the risk of currency fluctuation does not exists. These bonds eliminate the risk of currency fluctuation by selling in the forward markets the entire stream of principal and interest payments.
Floating Rate Notes	Floating Rate Notes are the instruments issued upto seven-year period with floating rate of interest depending upon prevailing exchange rates.
Euro Commercial Papers (ECP)	ECPs are short-term market instruments with maturity of *less* than 1 year and are usually designated in US dollar.
Foreign Currency Options	Foreign Currency Option is the right to buy *or* sell, spot, future *or* forward, a specified foreign currency. It provides a hedge against financial and economic risk.
Foreign Currency Futures	Foreign Currency Futures are the obligations to buy *or* sell a specified currency in the present for settlement at a future date.

EURO-ISSUES

The term Euro-issue, in the Indian context, denotes that the issue is listed on a European Stock Exchange. However, subscription can come from any part of the world except India. Finance can be raised by Global Depository Receipts (GDRs), Foreign Currency Convertible Bond(FCCBs) and pure debt bonds. However, GDRs and FCCBs are more popular instruments.

GLOBAL DEPOSITORY RECEIPTS (GDRS)

(a) Meaning of Global Depository Receipts (GDRs)

"Global Depository Receipts" means any instrument in the form of a depository receipt *or* certificate [by whatever name it is called] created by the Overseas Depository Bank outside India and issued to non-resident investors against the issue of Ordinary Shares *or* Foreign Currency Convertible Bonds of issuing company;

Notes:

(i) **"Issuing Company"** means an Indian company permitted to issue Foreign Currency Convertible Bonds *or* ordinary shares of that company against Global Depository Receipts;

(ii) **"Overseas Depository Bank"** means a bank authorised by the issuing company to issue global depository receipts against issue of Foreign Currency Convertible bonds *or* ordinary shares of the issuing company;

(b) Characteristics of GDRs

1. Denomination-GDRs are denominated in US dollars.
2. No Voting Rights-Holders of GDRs do not have voting rights.
3. Who can issue Bonds/Shares for Foreign market-An Indian company is permitted to issue foreign currency convertible Bonds *or* ordinary shares against GDRs.
4. Who can issue GDRs- An Overseas Depository Bank outside India is authorised to issue GDRs.
5. To When GDRs issued-GDRs are issued to non-resident investors.
6. Where listed-GDRs are listed on the Luxemberg stock exchange.
7. Cancellation-An investor may get the GDR cancelled any time after a cooling off period of 45 days.

(c) Mechanism of GDRs

The mechanism of a GDRs issue may be described with the help of following diagram.

An Indian Company issues

↓

Its Ordinary Shares or FCCB

↓

Keeps with Overseas Depository Banks

↓

Against which GDRs (denominated in US Dollars) are issued

↓

To Foreign investors

AMERICAN DEPOSITORY RECEIPTS (ADRS)

(a) Meaning of American Depository Receipts (ADRs) — Depository receipts issued by a company in the United State of America (USA) is known as American Depository Receipts (ADRs). Such receipts have to be issued in accordance with the provisions of the Securities and Exchange Commission of USA (SEC) which are very stringent.

(b) Characteristics of ADRs

1. An ADR is generally created by deposit of the securities of a Non-United States company with a custodian bank in the country of incorporation of the issuing company. The Custodian bank informs the depository in the United States that the ADRs can be issued.
2. ADRs are United States dollar denominated and are traded in the same way as are the securities of United State companies.
3. The ADR holder is entitled to the same rights and advantages as owners of underlying securities in the home country.

Several variations of ADRs have developed over time to meet more specialized demands in different markets. One such variations is the GDRs which are identical in structure to an ADR, the only difference being that they can be traded in more than one currency and within as well as outside the United States.

(c) Advantages of ADRs

1. The major advantage of ADRs of the investor is that dividends are paid promptly and in United States dollars.
2. The facilities are registered in the United States so that some assurance is provided to the investor with respect to the protection of ownership rights.
3. These instruments also obviate the need to transport physically securities between markets.
4. In general, ADRs increase access to United States capital markets by lowering the costs of investing in the securities of Non-United States companies and by providing the benefits of a convenient, familiar and well-regulated trading environment.
5. Issues of ADRs can increase the liquidity of an emerging market issuer's shares, and can potentially lower the future cost of raising equity capital by raising the company's visibility and international familiarity with the company's name, and by increasing the size of the potential investor base.

(d) Disadvantages of ADRs

1. High costs of meeting the partial *or* full reporting requirements of the Securities and Exchange Commission, As per the estimates, the cost of preparing and filing US GAAP account only ranges from $5,00,000 to $ 10,00,000 with the ongoing cost of $ 1,50,000 to $ 2,00,000 per annum. Because of the additional work involved, legal fees are considerably higher for a US listing, which ranges between $ 2,50,000 to $ 3,50,000 for the underwriters, to be reimbursed by the issuer.
2. The initial Securities Exchange Commission registration fees which are based on a percentage of the issue size as well as 'blue sky' registration costs (permitting the securities to be offered in all States of the US) are required to be met.
3. It has further been observed that while implied legal responsibility lies on a company's directors for the information contained in the offering document as required by any stock exchange, the US is widely recognised as the 'most litigious market in the world'. Accordingly, the broader the target investor base in the US (such as retail investors), the higher the potential legal liability.

DIFFERENCE BETWEEN GDRS AND ADRS

Though GDRs and ADRs are similar in many respects but they also have their points of differences. ADRs carry more clout with investors as they are listed on one of the major stock exchanges in the US. Since stock exchange regulations are extremely stringent in the US, ADRs are subject to much stricter disclosure requirements than GDRs. Also the annual legal and accounting costs of maintaining an ADR are much higher.

OTHER TYPES OF INTERNATIONAL ISSUES

Foreign Euro Bonds *or* Foreign Currency Bonds	In domestic capital markets of various countries, the Bonds issues referred to above are known by different names such as Yankee bonds in US, Swiss Frances in Switzerland, Samurai Bonds in Tokyo and Bulldogs in UK.
Euro Convertible Bonds *or* Foreign Currency Convertible Bonds	A convertible bond is a debt instrument, which gives the holders of a bond an option to convert the bonds into a pre-determined number of equity shares of the company. Usually, the price of equity shares at the time of conversion will have a premium element. These bonds will carry a fixed rate of interest and if the issuer company so desires may also include a Call option *or* a Put option.
Euro Bonds	Plain Euro Bonds are debt instruments but they are not very attractive for an investor interested in valuable addition to his investments.
Euro Convertible Zero Bonds	These bonds are structured as a convertible bond carrying no interest. At the time of maturity, conversion takes place at a determined price. These bonds have a five-year maturity period.
Euro Bonds with Equity Warrants	These bonds are attached with a warrant which carries a coupon rate. The persons interested in fixed interest income invest in these bonds.

FOREIGN DIRECT INVESTMENTS (FDI)

International Investment is one of the most important vehicle, of global operations. Economic growth and development of countries depend to a large extent on adequate capital and technological inputs. Most often, these inputs are not sufficiently available in a number of countries. So importation of these inputs is made to supplement domestic resources that enhance investment as well as productivity. Foreign capital can come to countries seeking it in various forms. It can be a loan capital, direct investment and also portfolio investment, etc. The growing international production and trade require increased amount of international investment. As a result, the flow of international investment has been increasing. The country requires international investment for enhancing the production, trade and distribution, capabilities. The need for international investment is more pronounced in the developing countries where the capital is in scarce.

16.0 SHORT-TERM SOURCES OF FINANCE

To finance temporary working capital, short-term capital is required for a short period (normally not exceeding one year).

The principal sources of raising short-term capital in case of a company are shown below:

1. Trade Credit from Suppliers
2. Advances from Customers
3. Discounting Bills of Exchange
4. Bank Overdraft
5. Cash Credit
6. Factoring
7. Public Deposits

17.0 TRADE CREDIT

MEANING OF TRADE CREDIT

Trade credit refers to an arrangement whereby the suppliers of raw materials, components, stores and spare parts, finished goods, allow the customers to pay their outstanding balances within the credit period allowed by them. Generally, suppliers grant credit for a period of three to six months and thus provide short-term funds to finance current assets. The availability of trade credit depends upon various factors such as nature and size of the firm, status of the firm (i.e., credit worthiness), activity level of the firm, policy of trade credit suppliers, prevailing economic conditions etc. Trade credit may be allowed in the shape of open account of bills payable. The major advantages of trade credit include ready availability, absence of issue formalities etc. The major limitation of trade credit is that it involves loss of cash discount which could be earned if payments were made within seven to ten days from the date of purchase. This loss is regarded as the cost of trade credit.

DOES TRADE CREDIT HAVE ANY COST?

Initially cost of trade credit may be absorbed by supplier but in the long run, he may try to pass it on to the buyer in the shape of increased prices depending upon the type of goods and elasticity of demand. In such circumstances buyer should find out alternate sources of supply to avoid costs loaded by supplier to the extent possible. It does not have any explicit cost if buyer pays the bills within normal credit period.

MERITS OF TRADE CREDIT

The trade credit as a source of short-term finance has the following advantages:

1. Trade credit is readily available according to the prevailing customs.
2. Trade credit is a flexible source of finance which can be easily adjusted to the changing needs for purchases.
3. Trade creditors generally adjust the time of payment in view of past dealings.
4. Trade credit does not involve any flotation costs.

LIMITATIONS OF TRADE CREDIT

The trade credit as a source of short term finance has the following limitations:

1. The cost of trade credit may increase if the supplier tries to pass on it to the buyer in the shape of increased prices.
2. Payment of bill of exchange accepted *or* promissory note issued against credit is required to be made at the maturity of the bill *or* note otherwise legal action may follow to recover the payment.

18.0 ADVANCES FROM CUSTOMERS

Advances from customers also act as source of short-term finance. The availability of advances from customers depends upon various factors such as type of goods, elasticity of demand and creditworthiness of supplier etc.

19.0 DISCOUNTING BILLS OF EXCHANGE

When goods are sold on credit, the suppliers generally draw bills of exchange upon customers who are required to accept the same. The term of such bills of exchange may be three to six months. Instead of holding the bills till the date of maturity, companies generally prefer to get them discounted with the bank. Discounting bills of exchange refers to an act of selling of a bill to obtain payment for it before its maturity. The bank charges discount in terms of interest for the unexpired term of the bill (i.e., period from the date of discounting to the date of maturity of the bill). The bank credits the net proceeds (i.e., amount of bill *less* discount charges) to the account of the customer. On date of maturity of the bill, the bank presents the bill before the acceptor of the bill for payment and receives the full amount of the bill. If the bank does not receive the payment from the acceptor, it is known as dishonour of a bill. The bank returns the dishonoured bill to the company and debits to the account of the company. The cost of raising finance by this method is the discount charged by the bank.

20.0 BANK OVERDRAFT

Bank overdraft refers to an arrangement whereby the bank allows the customers to overdraw from its current deposit account within a specified limit. The overdraft facility is granted against the securities of assets *or* personal security as in case of cash credit. Interest is charged only on the amount actually overdrawn (i.e., debit balance) for the actual period of use (i.e., for the period the debit balance in current deposit account remains outstanding). The cost of raising finance by this method is the interest charged by the bank.

21.0 CLEAN OVERDRAFT

Banks may entertain clean advances form those customers, which are financially, sound and reputed for their integrity. The banks in this case rely upon the personal security of borrower. Banks are responsible for ensuring customer's credit worthiness before providing them with clean overdraft as there is no asset securing the amount of advance. The banks normally take guarantee from the persons whom they believe to be credit worthy.

22.0 CASH CREDIT

Cash credit refers to an arrangement whereby the bank allows the borrower to draw money from time to time within a specified limit (known as cash credit limit). The cash credit facility is granted against the pledge *or* hypothecation of stock *or* pledge of marketable instruments etc. *or* personal security. During the period of credit, the borrower can draw, repay and again draw amounts within the sanctioned limit. Interest is charged only on the amount actually withdrawn for the actual period of use. The cost of raising finance by this method is the interest charged by the bank. The advantage of this source of finance is that the amount can be adjusted according to the needs of finance. Hypothecation is an equitable charge on movable property for an amount of debt where *neither* possession *nor* ownership is passed to the creditor. Under pledge, the borrower delivers the possession of movable property to the lender as security for repayment of debt.

23.0 LETTER OF CREDIT

A letter of Credit is the guarantee provided by the buyer's bankers to the seller that in the case of default *or* failure of the buyer, the bank shall make the payment to the seller.

24.0 BILLS FINANCE

The banks extend assistance to the borrowers against the bills. The finance against the bills is meant to finance, the actual sale transactions. There are three forms of bill financing:

- Purchase of bills by the bank if these are payable on demand
- Discounting of bills by the bank if these are Usance bills (or time) bills.
- Advance against bills under collection from the drawees, whether sent for realisation through the bank *or* sent directly by the drawer to the drawees.

25.0 WORKING CAPITAL DEMAND LOAN

Working Capital Demand Loan is presently applicable to borrowers having working capital facilities of Rs. 10 Crore *or* more. The WCDL is granted for a fixed term on the carrying of which it has to be liquidated, renewed *or* rolled over.

26.0 FACTORING

MEANING OF FACTORING

Factoring is a financial service, which involves meaning, financing and collecting receivable. It is both a financial as well as management support to supplier of goods/services. It is a method of converting non-productive assets (receivables into productive assets (Cash). A factor makes the conversion *or* receivables into cash possible. Factoring may be defined as a contract between the supplier of goods/services and the factor under which the factor agrees to perform atleast two of the following functions :

(a) To finance the assigned book debts (receivables).

(b) To maintain account relating to receivables.

(c) To collect book debts.

(d) To provide protection against default in payment by debtors.

(e) To provide credit administration services to the clients to decide whether *or* not and how much credit should be extended to the customers.

Some of the major factoring firms in India are SBI Factors and Commercial Services Ltd., Canara bank Factors Ltd. (1991), Fair Growth Factors Ltd. (1992).

FACTORING COMMISSION

The commission charges by the factor for providing factoring services is known as factoring commission. It is usually expressed as a percentage of face value of receivables factored. In India, it ranges between 2.5 to 3 per cent. The commission is expect to be lower for recourse factoring since the factor does not assume the risk of bad debts. The commission is expected to be higher for non-recourse factoring since the factor assumes the risk of bad debts.

TYPES OF FACTORING

The factoring services may be classified under following categories:

1. **Non-recourse Factoring-(Old Line Factoring)**—Under Non-recourse factoring factor assumes the risk of bad debts and charges higher commission for and advances cash upto 80/90% of book debts immediately.

2. **Recourse Factoring**—Under recourse factoring, factor does not assumes the risk of bad debts and charges lower commission for and advances cash upto 70/80% of book debts.

3. **Advance Factoring**—Under advance factoring, factor advances cash against the book debts due to cleint immediately.

4. **Maturity Factoring**—Under maturity factoring, the factor makes the payment on maturity (i.e., in case of non-recourse factoring on collection of book debts *or* on insolvency of customers, in case of recourse factoring on collection of book debts form customers).

5. **Finance Factoring (Bulk/agency Factoring)**—Under finance factoring, the factor simply finances the book debts against bulk *either* on recourse *or* without recourse and the client continues to administer and operate sales ledger.

6. **Non-Notification Factoring**—Under non-notification factoring, the notice of assignment of receivables is not given to the debtors. But the factor performs all his functions without a disclosure to the customer that he owns the book debts.

NATURE OF OBLIGATION OF FACTOR

The nature of the obligation of the factor is of bailment contract. Factor stands in a fiduciary relationship with the client firm and the main responsibility arises out of the terms of the contract *or* agreement between the parties. Factoring firms are professionally competent with skilled persons to handle credit sales realisations for different clients in different trades for better credit management.

NEED FOR FACTOR SERVICES

Need for factor services is felt by traders to concentrate on sales and realization of credit sales be left in specialized hands to minimize the risk of bad debts arising on account of non-realisation of credit sales. It sales are realized within reasonable time, the traders need not depend much for bank finance toward scorching capital

PARTIES TO FACTORING CONTRACT

There are three parties involved generally in a factoring contract as follows:

1. Buyer of goods who has to pay for goods bought on credit terms.
2. Seller of goods who has to realize credit sales from buyer.
3. Factor who acts as agent in realizing credit sales from buyer and passes on the realized sum to seller after deducting his commission.

FACTORING OPERATING CYCLE

The factoring operating cycle comprises of the following seven steps :

Step 1: Buyer negotiates terms of purchasing plant and machinery *or* other material with the seller.

Step 2: The factor enters into agreement with seller for rendering factor services to it.

Step 3: Seller delivers goods alongwith copies of invoice, delivery challan, and instructions to make payment to factor to buyer.

Step 4: Seller sends a deed of assignment in favour of factor alongwith copies of sales documents.

Step 5: On receipt of copies of sales documents as referred to above the factor makes payment to the seller of the 80% *or* more of the price of debt.

Step 6: Buyer makes payment to the factor in time *or* gets extension of time *or* in the case of default is subject to legal process at the hands of factor.

Step 7: The factor receives payment from the buyer on due dates and remits the money to seller after usual deduction.

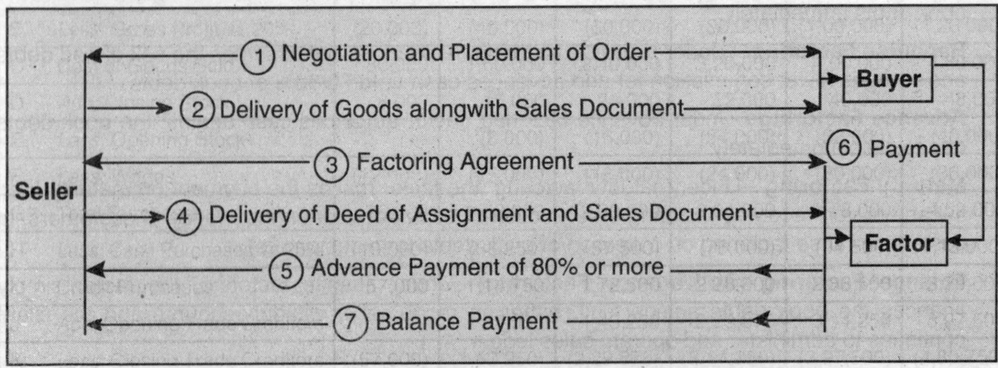

Fig. Factoring Operating Cycle

ADVANTAGES OF FACTORING

The advantages resulting from the factoring are as follow:

1. Eliminating of trade discounts.
2. Prompt payments and credits.
3. Improves scope for operating leverage.
4. Reduction of administrative cost of burden.
5. Increase in return to the client.
6. Improvement in liquidity.
7. Provides insurance against bad debts.
8. It is *neither* a loan *nor* a deposit but facilitates liquidity.
9. It avoids increased debts.
10. Current assets are efficiently managed thus reducing working capital requirements.
11. Better credit discipline amongst customers by regular realization of dues, effective control of sales journal, reduced credit risk, better working capital management etc.

DISADVANTAGES OF FACTORING

The disadvantages of factoring are as follows :

1. Image of the client may suffer as engaging of a Factoring Agency is not considered a good sign of efficient management.
2. Factoring may not be of much use where companies have nation-wide network branches.
3. Financial evaluation may not be accurate.
4. If the client has cheaper means of finance and credit (where goods are sold against advance payment) factoring may not be useful.

HOW TO DECIDE WHETHER *or* NOT TO ENGAGE A FACTOR

To decide whether *or* not to engage a factor, the cost of benefits of factoring should be evaluated. The cost of factoring includes:

(a) Factoring commission;

(b) Interest on advance granted by the factor;

The benefits of factoring includes:

(a) Saving in cost of In House Credit Collection Department.

(b) Saving in Bad Debt Losses.

(c) Saving in Cost of Funds invested in receivables.

A firm should engage a factor if the benefits exceeds the cost otherwise not.

27.0 COMMERCIAL PAPER

MEANING OF COMMERCIAL PAPER

Commercial Paper is a short term issuance promissory note issued by a company in a private sector *or* public sector at such a discount/interest on face value as may be determined by the issuing company and is negotiable by endorsement and delivery. Each CP will bear a certificate from bank verifying the signatures of executants.

Though, commercial paper is said to be highly liquid because of its transferability, but in the absence of its highly developed secondary markets, its liquidity could be highly greatly affected.

FEATURES OF COMMERCIAL PAPER

The features of Commercial paper are as follows:

1. Commercial paper is a short-term money market instrument.
2. It is used by the corporate enterprises.
3. It is used for financing working capital requirements
4. It has a fixed maturity value.
5. It is a certificate evidencing an unsecured corporate debt.
6. It is issued at a discount/ interest on face value basis.
7. It contains a promise to pay some fixed amount on some future period.
8. Its issuer does not pledge any asset.
9. It can be issued directly by a company to investors *or* through banks *or* merchant bankers.

ADVANTAGES OF COMMERCIAL PAPER

The advantages of Commercial paper are as follows:

1. It can be issued with the maturities tailored to match the cash flow of the issuing company.
2. A well-rated company can diversify its sources of finance from banks to short term money markets at somewhat cheaper costs.
3. It provides investors with higher returns than they could get from the banking system.
4. It facilitates securitisation of loans resulting in creation of secondary market for the paper and efficient movement of funds providing cash surplus to cash deficit entities.
5. The companies, which are able to raise funds through commercial paper, become better known in the financial world and are thereby placed in a more favourbale position for raising such long-term capital as they may, from time to time require. Thus, there is an in built incentive for companies to remain financially strong.

ELIGIBILITY CRITERIA FOR ISSUER OF COMMERCIAL PAPER

The issuing company shall comply with the terms and conditions stipulated from time to time, by the Reserve Bank of India relating to the issue of such CPs. The companies satisfying the following conditions are eligible to issue CPs:

1. **Minimum Tangible Net worth** — The tangible net worth of the company must be atleast Rs. 5 crore as per the latest audited balance sheet of the company. Tangible Net Worth = Paid up Capital + Free Reserves – Accumulated balance of Losses-Balance of Deferred revenue expenditure – Other fictitious Assets
2. **Fund Based Working Capital** — The fund-based working Capital must be atleast Rs. 25 crore.
3. **Minimum Current Ratio** — The minimum current asset ratio should be 1.33:1 based on the classification of current assets and current liabilities. For the purpose of computing the current ratio, the current assets and current liabilities are classified as per RBI guidelines issued from time to time.
4. **Minimum Credit Rating** — The company is required to obtain the necessary credit rating from agencies like CRISIL, ICRA, etc. The credit rating obtained from CRISIL should be not *less* than P2 while rating obtained from ICRA should not be *less* than A2.
5. **Classification of Account by Financial Bank** — The borrowers account of the company is classified as Standard Asset by financing banking company/ companies.
6. **Age of Rating** — The issuer must ensure that the credit rating at the time of applying to the RBI should not be more than 2 months old.

7. **Listed Requirement** — The companies other than public sector should be listed on one *or* more stock exchange. Closely held companies whose shares are not listed on any of the stock exchange will also be eligible to borrow under the CP scheme, provided they meet all other requirements.
8. **Issue Expenses** — All issue expenses including dealer's fees, rating agency fees and any other relevant charges connected with the issue shall be borne by the company issuing CPs.

PROCEDURE FOR ISSUE OF COMMERCIAL PAPER

1. Apply for credit rating and get certificate from Credit Rating Agency.
2. Submit application to RBI through financing bank *or* leader of consortium bank for working capital facilities together with a certificate from credit rating agency.
3. Obtain a copy of RBI's approval in writing on the amount of commercial paper to be issued.
4. Make arrangements for privately placing the issue.
5. Ensure that the proposed issue of commercial paper is complete within the period of two weeks from the date of approval of RBI.
6. Inform RBI through the bank / leader of the bank, the amount of actual issue of CP within three days of completion of issue.

GUIDELINES FOR ISSUE OF CP

Minimum Maturity Period	3 months
Maximum Maturity Period	6 months
Grace Period of Maturity	Nil
Denomination	Multiple of 10 Lakhs
Minimum Size of CP issue	Rs. 50 Lakhs
Maximum Size of CP issue	upto 20% of the issue's fund based working capital limit

IMPLICATIONS OF COMMERCIAL PAPER

The implications of CP on commercial banks are as follows:

1. The banks themselves can invest in CP and show this as short-term investment.
2. The banks are likely to lose interest on working capital loan, which has been hitherto lent to the companies, which have now started borrowing through CP. Further, the larger companies might avail of the cheap funds available in the slack season worsening the banks surplus funds position, but to the banking system for borrowing during the busy season when funds are costly. This would mean the banks are loser with clear impact on profitability.

PROSPECTS OF COMMERCIAL PAPER

1. **Relaxation in Credit Rating** — Mandatory credit rating has been relaxed from P1 to P2 at present. If this trend continues, the credit rating will allow the investors to fix their discount rates accordingly.
2. Though CP is an unsecured promissory note, there has been no case of default as yet. There are two reasons which are as follows:
   (a) The issuing company's credit rating **provides** a picture for the investor about the credit-worthiness.
   (b) Companies which can issue CP are blue chip companies, these companies can not afford to take the risk of defaulting because once they do that no investor in money market will deal with them and even if someone does interest rate charged will be exorbitant.

3. **Subject to Working Capital Limits** — CP is subject to working capital limits. To give CP a chance as visible resource option, it is suggested that CP issue should be made separate from the working capital limits of the company.
4. **Roll over Expenses** — The roll over of all issue expenses have to be incurred once again. This is a daunting factor. One solution to this can be that the maturity period of CP should increase from six months to twelve months.
5. **Competitor** — Cash credit is main competitor of CP. Currently cash credit interest rate is about twelve percent. Whereas top rating companies are able to float CPs at about nine percent.

Conclusion: CP has immense scope in India. It can be expected that within three years, CP shall takeover more than 50 percent of cash card business.

28.0 ADVANCES AGAINST GOODS

Another important tool for obtaining bank credit facility is advance against goods. 'Goods' has the same meaning as in Sale of Goods Act. In order to avail bank credit, a customer *either* hypothecates *or* pledges the goods, which the banker accepts as security. Following are some of the benefits of securing goods as a mode of advance:

(i) the assets is highly liquid;

(ii) the turnover rate is usually high;

(iii) source of payment is reliable;

As the value of goods keep on changing, the banker must continuously assess the value of hypothecated/ pledged goods.

29.0 ADVANCES AGAINST DOCUMENTS OF TITLE TO GOODS

Documents of title to Goods refer to those documents of which possession is recognised by law *or* business custom as possession of goods. ***For Example***: Bill of lading, railway receipt, lorry receipt, dock warehouse keeper certificate etc. Such documents can be endorsed *or* delivered to any person to take delivery of goods in his right. An advance against the pledge of document is equivalent to advance against pledge goods itself.

30.0 ADVANCES AGAINST SUPPLY OF BILLS

Under this category, advances against bills for supply of goods to government *or* government agencies against firm order after acceptance of tender fall. These bills are clean bills without being accompanied by any documents of title of goods. These bills evidence supply of goods to government agencies. Sometimes, these bills may be accompanied inspection notes from representatives of government agencies for having inspected the goods before they are dispatched. If bills are without inspection report, banks like to examine them with the accepted tender *or* contract for verifying that the goods supplied under the bills strictly confirm to the terms and conditions in the acceptance tender. These supply bills represent debt which is assigned to the bank by endorsement of supply bills and executing irrevocable power of attorney in favour of banks for receiving the bills from government *or* government agencies. The banks also take separate letters from the suppliers instructing the government body to pay the bills directly to the bank. It may be noted that the supply bills are not negotiable instruments.

31.0 FINANCING OF EXPORT TRADE BY BANKS

The advances by commercial banks for export financing are in the form of:

1. Pre-shipment Finance i.e. before the shipment of goods
2. Post-shipment Finance i.e. after the shipment of goods

PRE-SHIPMENT FINANCE

This finance is generally in the form of packing credit. Packing credit is an advance granted by a bank to the exporter for the purpose of buying, manufacturing, processing, packing, shipping to the overseas buyers. Generally, banks require to loose the irrevocable letters of credit opened in favour of customers by the overseas buyer and a firm sale contract. These two documents not only serve as evidence of a definite arrangement for realisation of export sales proceed but also indicate the amount of finance required by the exporter. Such advance is required to be liquidated within 180 days of its date of commitment by negotiation of export bills *or* receipt of export proceeds.

Types of Packing Credit	*Details*
Clean Packing Credit	This is an advance made available to an exporter only on production of a firm export order *or* a letter of credit without exercising any charge *or* control over raw material *or* finished goods. It is a clean type of export advance. Each proposal is weighed according to particular requirements of the trade and credit worthiness of the exporter. A suitable margin has to be maintained. Also, Export Credit Guarantee Corporation (ECGC) cover should be obtained by the bank.
Packing Credit against Hypothecation of Goods	Export finance is also made available on certain terms and conditions where the exporter has pledged interest and the goods are hypothecated to the bank as security with the stipulated margin. At the time of utilizing the advance, the exporter is required to submit, alongwith the firm export order *or* letter of credit relative stock statements and thereafter continue submitting them every fortnight and / *or* whenever there is any movement of stock.
Packing Credit against Pledge of Goods	Export finance is made available on certain terms and condition where the exportable finished goods are pledged to the bank with approved clearing agents who will ship the same from time to time as required by the exporter. The possession of the goods so pledged lies with the bank under lock and key.
E.C.G.C. guarantee	Any loan given to an exporter for the manufacture, purchasing, processing *or* packing of goods meant for export against a firm order qualifies for the packing. Credit guarantee is issued by Export Credit Guarantee Corporation (ECGC)
Forward Exchange Contract	Another requirement of packing credit facility is that if the export bill is to be drawn in a foreign currency, the exporter should enter into a forward exchange contract with the banks thereby avoiding risk involved in the possible change in the rate of exchange.

DOCUMENTS REQUIRED FOR OBTAINING PRE-SHIPMENT FINANCE

In Case of a Partnership Firm	*In Case of a Company*
1. Joint and several demands promote signed on behalf of the firm as well as by the partners individually.	1. Demand pro-note
2. Letter of Continuity (signed on behalf of the firm as well as by the partners individually)	2. Letter of Continuity.
3. Letter of pledge to secure demand cash credit against goods (in case of pledge) Or Agreement of Hypothecation to secure demand cash credit (in case of hypothecation)	3. Letter of pledge Or Agreement of Hypothecation signed on behalf of the company.

4. Letter of authority to open the account.	4. General Guarantee of directors of the company in their joint and personal capacities.
5. Declaration of Partnership.	5. Certified copy of Board of Directors' Resolution
6. Agreement to utilise the money drawn in terms of contract.	6. Letter of Hypothecation (for bills).
7. Letter of Hypothecation (for bills).	7. Agreement to utilise the money drawn in terms of contract should bear the seal of the company.

POST-SHIPMENT FINANCE

This finance is generally in the form of:

(i) **Purchase / Discounting of Documentary export bills:** Post shipment is given to an exporter by a bank by purchasing export bills drawn payable at sight *or* by discounting usance export bills against a confirm sales order and backed by documents of title of goods such as bill of lading *or* air consignment notes.

Since such type of finance also qualifies for post - shipment export credit guarantee, the exporter should obtain contract shipment risk policy of Export Credit Guarantee Corporation (ECGC). The corporation while granting the policy fixes credit limit for individual exporter. The corporation's liability is limited to the extent of the limits so fixed.

(ii) **Advance against Export bills sent for collection:** Post-shipment Finance is also provided to exporters by banks by way of advance against export bills forwarded through them for collection after considering the nature of goods exported and the creditworthiness of the drawer and the drawee. While granting such advance following documents are usually obtained:

(a) Demand promissory notes.

(b) Letter of continuity.

(c) Letter of hypothecation

(d) General guarantee of directors *or* partners of the firm (as the case may be).

(iii) **Advance against duty drawbacks, cash subsidiary:** Post-shipment Finance is also provided to exporters by way of duty drawbacks, cash subsidiary etc. against export performance. Such advance is required to be liquidated within 180 days from the days of shipment. While granting such advance following documents are usually obtained:

(a) Demand promissory notes.

(b) Letter of continuity.

(c) Undertaking from the borrowers that they will deposit the cheque/payments received from the appropriate authorities immediately with the bank and will not utilise such amount in any other way.

(d) General guarantee of directors *or* partners of the firm (as the case may be).

Other facilities extended to exporters:

(a) Issue letter of credit.

(b) Guarantee of waiver of excise duty etc. due to performance of contracts, bond in lieu of cash security deposit, guarantee for advance payments etc.

(c) Providing finance to approved clients undertaking export on deferred payment terms.

(d) Securing status report of buyer and their trade information on various commodities through correspondents.

(e) Providing economic intelligence on various countries.

32.0 INTER CORPORATE DEPOSITS (ICD)

The companies can borrow funds even for a single day from other companies having surplus liquidity. The rate of interest on ICDs vary depending upon the time period and the amount involved.

33.0 CERTIFICATE OF DEPOSIT (CD)

Certificate of Deposit is a document of title similar to a time deposit receipt issued by a bank except that:

(i) There is no prescribed rate of interest.
(ii) Banker is not required to encash the deposits before maturity period.

However, the investor can sell the CD in the market.

34.0 PUBLIC DEPOSITS

MEANING OF PUBLIC DEPOSITS

Public deposits are raised by companies by inviting their shareholders, employees and the general public to deposit their savings with the companies. It may be noted that a private company cannot invite general public to deposit their savings with the company. Such deposits can be accepted for a period not *less* than six months but not exceeding three years at a time. Thus, public deposits can be raised by companies to meet their short-term and medium-term financial needs.

MERITS OF PUBLIC DEPOSITS FROM THE POINT OF VIEW OF COMPANY

The merits of public deposits are discussed below:

1. **No Security** — The deposits are not required to be covered by securities by way of mortgage, hypothecation etc.
2. **Easy Invitation** — The deposits can be easily invited by offering a rate of interest higher than the interest on bank deposits.

35.0 OTHER SOURCES OF FINANCING

SEED CAPITAL ASSISTANCE

The Seed Capital Assistance is for professionally *or* technically qualified entrepreneurs.

For projects with Project Cost	*Suppliers of Seed Capital*
1. Upto ₹ 5 lakhs	National Equity Fund of SIDBI
2. Upto ₹ 2 Crore	IDBI
3. Exceeding ₹ 2 Crore	Risk Capital and Technology Corporation Ltd. (RCTC)

The Seed Capital Assistance from IDBI —

Maximum assistance – 50% of the required contribution *or* ₹ 15 lakhs.

Interest – Interest Free.

Service Charges – 1% per annum for the first 5 years and at increasing rate thereafter.

Repayment schedule – It is fixed depending upon the repaying capacity of the unit with an initial moratorium upto 5 years.

INTERNAL CASH ACCRUAL

In case of existing profit making companies, which undertake an expansion *or* diversification program, the surplus generated from operation after meeting all the contractual, statutory working requirement of funds is available for financing capital expenditure.

UNSECURED LOANS

Who provides: Promoters to meet their contribution Loan

Rate of Interest: Rate of Interest chargeable on these loan should be *less* than *or* equal to Rate of Interest on institutional loans

Payment of Interest — Interest on these loans can be payable only after the payment of institutional dues.

Repayment of Loan — Such loans cannot be repaid without approval of institution.

Part of Equity — These loans are treated as part of Equity for the purpose of calculating Debt Equity Ratio.

DEFERRED PAYMENT FACILITY

Who provides: Supplier of machinery provide this facility under which payment for purchase of machinery can be made over a period of time.

Bank Guarantee: Generally the supplier of machinery requires the buyer to furnish bank guarantee.

CAPITAL INCENTIVES

(a) What consist of: These incentives consist of lumpsum subsidy and exemption from/or deferment of sales tax and octroi duty.

(b) Quantum: Its quantum is sanctioned by the implementing agency as a % of its fixed capital investment subject to an overall selling.

(c) Requirements: Special capital incentives are sanctioned and released to the units only after they have complied with the requirements of the relevant scheme. The requirements may be classified into the initial effective steps and final effective steps.

Initial Effective Steps	*Final Effective Steps*
1. Formation of firm/ company	1. Obtaining clearance under FEMA.
2. Acquisition of Land in backward area and registration.	2. Capital Goods clearance/import licence
3. Registration for manufacture of the License	3. Conversion of Letter of Intent to Industrial products.
	4. Tie up of the means of Finance
	5. All clearance required for setting up of the unit
	6. Aggregate Expense incurred for the project should exceed 25% of the project cost and at least 10% of the fixed assets should have been created/ acquired site

The release of special capital incentives by the concerned State Government generally takes one *or* two years. The promoters therefore find it convenient to avail bridge finance against the capital incentives.

ACCRUAL ACCOUNT/ PROVISIONS

The outstanding expenses are self generating and hence spontaneous source of finance.

36.0 NEW INSTRUMENTS

Following are some of new instruments and their features:

Types of Instruments	*Rate of Interest*	*Feature*
Deep Discount Bonds	Zero Interest	There is no interest payout during lock in period. Sold at discounted value. Interest is represented by difference in Value of maturity and issue price.
Secured Premium Notes		These are issued along with detachable warrant. Detachable warrants are convertible into equity shares within a specified period. It has a maturity period of 4 to 7 years
Zero Interest Fully Convertible Debentures	Zero Interest	Fully convertible debentures which are compulsorily and automatically converted after a specified period into equity shares of the company at predetermined price.
Zero Coupon Bonds	Zero Interest	Sold at discounted value. Interest is represented by difference in Value of maturity and issue price
Double option Bonds	15% p.a. compounding half yearly.	Each bond has 2 parts, principal part and other for interest. Investor may sell *either* one *or* both parts at any time.
Option Bonds	Payable on maturity *or* periodically.	Cumulative and Non - Cumulative bonds; may be redeemable at premium. Recently issued by IDBI, ICICI.
Inflation Bonds	Adjusted for Inflation (Normal Interest rate + Inflation rate)	Protect the investor from Inflation.
Floating rate Bonds	Not Fixed, depends upon market conditions.	There is volatility in the Interest rates. Issued by financial institutions like IDBI, ICICI.

12 RATIO ANALYSIS

LEARNING OBJECTIVES

After studying this chapter, you should be able to understand:

- Meaning of Ratio Analysis
- Meaning of a Ratio
- Expression of Ratio
- Objectives of Ratio Analysis
- Advantages and Uses of Ratio Analysis
- Limitations of Ratio Analysis
- Benchmarks
- Classification of Ratios on the Basis of Financial Statements
- Classification of Ratios from User's Point of New
- Liquidity Ratios
- Solvency Ratios
- Activity Ratios
- Profitability Ratios

1.0 MEANING OF RATIO ANALYSIS

(a) Ratio Analysis is one of the most important tools of Financial Statement Analysis.

(b) Ratio Analysis is the process of establishing and interpreting the quantitative relationship between two related items of Financial Statements to make a qualitative judgement about the:

1. Liquidity (Short-term Solvency)
2. Long-term Solvency
3. Operating Efficiency and
4. Profitability of the enterprise.

2.0 MEANING OF A RATIO

(a)	Since we are using the term 'Ratio' in relation to financial statement analysis, it may properly mean 'An Accounting Ratio' *or* 'Financial Ratio'.
(b)	An Accounting Ratio is a mathematical expression of a quantitative relationship between two related items (having mutual cause & effect relationship) of Financial Statements which the analyst may use to make a qualitative judgement about the: 1. Liquidity (Short-term Solvency) 2. Long-term Solvency 3. Operating Efficiency and 4. Profitability of the enterprise.

Example I *The figure of Gross Profit can be said to be significantly related to the figure of Revenue from Operations.*

Example II *The figure of Gross Profit cannot be said to be related to the figure of Securities Premium.*

3.0 EXPRESSION OF RATIO

Ratios can be expressed as:

1. **Percentage say,** Gross Profit Ratio is 20% of Revenue from Operations [calculated by dividing Gross Profit (₹ 20,000) by Revenue from Operations (₹ 1,00,000) and multiplying by 100];
2. **Proportion say,** Current Ratio is 2 : 1 [calculated by dividing current assets (₹ 1,00,000) by Current Liabilities (₹ 50,000)];
3. **Fraction say,** Proprietors'Funds are one-tenth of Total Assets [calculated by dividing Proprietors'Funds(₹ 10,000) by Total Assets (₹ 1,00,000)];
4. **Times say,** Debtors Turnover Ratio is 5 times [calculated by dividing Credit Revenue from Operations (₹ 1,00,000) by Average Trade Receivables (₹ 20,000)].

4.0 OBJECTIVES OF RATIO ANALYSIS

The main Objectives of Ratio Analysis are:

1. **To determine Liquidity (Short-term Solvency)** (i.e., ability of the enterprise to meet its short-term obligations as and when they become due).
2. **To determine Long-term Solvency** (i.e., ability of the enterprise to pay the interest regularly and to repay the principal on maturity *or* in pre-determined instalments at due dates).
3. **To determine Operating Efficiency** with which Resources are utilised in generating Revenue
4. **To determine Profitability with respect to Revenue from Operations and Investment**
5. **To compare Intra Firm Position** (i.e., Evaluating the Financial Position and Performance of the same enterprise over a period of time) and to identify the strong and week areas (if any) and to take the necessary corrective action.
6. **To compare Inter Firm Position** (i.e., Evaluating the Relative Financial Position and Performance of the enterprise in the industry) and to identify the strong and week areas (if any) and to take the necessary corrective action.

5.0 ADVANTAGES AND USES OF RATIO ANALYSIS

The various Advantages and Uses of Ratio Analysis are as follows:

1. **Useful in determining Liquidity (Short-term Solvency):** The short-term creditors like bankers and suppliers of material can determine the ability of the enterprise to meet its short-term obligations as and when they become due with the help of Liquidity Ratios such as Current Ratio and Quick Ratio.
2. **Useful in determining Long-term Solvency:** The long-term creditors like debenture-holders and financial institutions can determine the ability of the enterprise to pay the interest regularly and to repay the principal on maturity *or* in pre-determined instalments at due dates with the help of Solvency Ratios such as Debt Equity Ratio.
3. **Useful in determining Operating Efficiency:** The management can determine the Operating Efficiency with which Resources are utilized in generating Revenue with the help of Activity Ratios such as Working Capital Turnover Ratio, Inventory Turnover Ratio, Debtors Turnover Ratio etc.

4. **Useful in determining Profitability:** The management and the investors can determine the Profitability with respect to Revenue from Operations and Investment with the help of Profitability Ratios such as Gross Profit Ratio, Operating Profit Ratio, Net Profit Ratio, Return on Investment etc. After analysing the relevant ratios, the present investors can decide whether to hold, sell *or* purchase the shares and the prospective investor can decide whether *or* not to buy the shares.
5. **Useful in Intra Firm Comparison:** Ratio Analysis is useful (a) in evaluating the Financial Position and Performance of the same enterprise over a period of time by comparing the ratios of one period with those of another period, (b) in identifying the strong and week areas (if any) and (c) in taking the necessary corrective action.
6. **Useful in Inter Firm Comparison:** Ratio Analysis is useful (a) in evaluating the relative Financial Position and Performance of the enterprise in comparision to a standard enterprise belonging to the same industry by comparing the actual ratios of the enterprise with the ratios of a standard enterprise belonging to the same industry, (b) in identifying the strong and weak areas (if any) and (c) in taking the necessary corrective action.
7. **Useful in Pattern/Industry Comparison:** Ratio Analysis is useful in evaluating the relative Financial Position and Performance of the enterprise in the industry by comparing the actual ratios of the enterprise with the ratios of industry to which the firm belongs, (a) in identifying the strong and weak areas (if any) and (b) in taking the necessary corrective action.

6.0 LIMITATIONS OF RATIO ANALYSIS

The major limitations of Ratio Analysis are as follows:

1. **Ratio Analysis ignores Qualitative Factors:** The ratio analysis is only quantitative analysis and not qualitative analysis. ***For Example***, while conducting the credit analysis of a customer seeking credit, he may deserve a credit to be granted on the basis of financial statements submitted by him but in reality his character (i.e., intention to repay) and credit worthiness may be doubtful.
2. **Ratio Analysis ignores Price-level changes:** A ratio can be accurately interpreted only if the effect of change in prices which may have taken place, is adjusted in the figures used in the ratio. ***For Example***, Fixed Asset Turnover Ratio would not give a brighter picture than that justified by the circumstances unless the fixed assets are revalued at their current replacement cost.
3. **Ratio Analysis is not free from Personal Bias:** In many situations, the accountant has to make choice out of various alternatives available, e.g., choice in the method of depreciation (e.g., Straight line *or* Written Down), choice in the method of inventory valuation (e.g., FIFO, LIFO etc.). Since the subjectivity is inherent in personal judgement, the financial statements, are therefore not free from personal bias. As a result, the ratio analysis also cannot be said to be free from personal bias.
4. **Ratio Analysis is a Historical analysis:** Ratio analysis is basically historical in nature because the financial statements on the basis of which the ratios are established, are historical in nature unless the ratio analysis is based on the projected financial statements prepared to plan for the future.
5. **Ratio Analysis provides Only symptoms and not cure:** Ratios are at best only symptoms and like the symptoms displayed by a human body may have their origin at a place different from where the symptom appears. Like doctor, it becomes the duty of the management to unearth underlying causes.
6. **Ratio Analysis does not consider the reality behind the Financial Statements:** The relationship between the two figures can be well interpreted only after studying the reality behind the statements on the basis of which the ratio has been established. ***For Example***, the Quick Ratio of a dry fruit merchant, calculated just 10-15 days before Deepawali (i.e., an

Indian festival) may be lower because of heavy accumulation of inventories. An analyst may conclude that the short-term financial position of this concern is not a satisfactory one unless he takes into account the fact that the accumulation of inventories is in anticipation of demand in near future.

7. **The quality of the Ratio Analysis depends upon the Accuracy of the accounts:** The quality of the ratios very much depends upon the quality of the accounts on the basis of which these are established. ***For Example***, if the closing Inventory is over-valued, not only the profitability will be overstated but also the financial position will appear to be better. Thus, the ratios are as accurate as the accounts.

7.0 BENCHMARKS

Benchmark is a yardstick against which actual ratio is to be compared in order to make a qualitative judgement about the various aspects of the financial position and performance of an enterprise. Benchmark may be:

<table>
<tr><td>A Past Ratio of the same enterprise</td><td>A ratio could be compared with the past ratio of the same enterprise. This type of comparisons is known as Intra-firm comparision as is done under Time Series Analysis.</td></tr>
<tr><td>Same Industry Ratio of Similar</td><td>A ratio could be compared with the ratio of similar firms belonging to the same industry at the same point of time. This type of comparison is known as inter-firm comparison as is done under Cross Sectional Analysis.</td></tr>
<tr><td>Industry Average</td><td>A ratio could be compared with the industry average at the same point of time. This type of comparison is known as pattern comparison as in done under Cross Sectional Analysis.</td></tr>
<tr><td>Rule of Thumb</td><td>Rule of Thumb have evolved over a period of time. A ratio could be compared with rule of thumb. However these rules of thumb should be used cautiously.
<table>
<tr><th>Ratio</th><th>Rule of Thumb</th><th>Meaning</th></tr>
<tr><td>1. Current Ratio</td><td>2:1</td><td>Current Assets should be twice the Current Liabilities.</td></tr>
<tr><td>2. Quick Ratio</td><td>1:1</td><td>Quick Assets should be equal to Current Liabilities.</td></tr>
<tr><td>3. Debt-Equity Ratio</td><td>2:1</td><td>Debt could be twice the Shareholders' Funds.</td></tr>
</table>
</td></tr>
</table>

8.0 CLASSIFICATION OF RATIOS ON THE BASIS OF FINANCIAL STATEMENTS

1. Income Statement Ratios	These ratios are calculated on the basis of Income Statement Items. **Example:** Gross Profit Ratio, Operating Profit Ratio, Net Profit Ratio
2. Position Statement Ratios	These ratios are calculated on the basis of Position Statement (i.e. Balance Sheet) Items. **Example:** Current Ratio, Quick Ratio, Debt-Equity Ratio,
3. Composite Ratios	These ratios are calculated on the basis of Items of both the Income Statement and Position Statement. **Example:** Inventory Turnover Ratio, Debtors Turnover Ratio, Creditors Turnover Ratio, Return on Investment

9.0 CLASSIFICATION OF RATIOS FROM USER'S POINT OF NEW

In view of the requirements of various users (e.g., Short-term Creditors, Long-term Creditors, Management, Investors) of the ratios, one may classify the ratios into the following four groups:

CLASSIFICATION OF RATIOS

1. Liquidity Ratios
2. Solvency Ratios
3. Activity Ratios
4. Profitability Ratios

10.0 LIQUIDITY RATIOS

Meaning	Liquidity Ratios measure the Short-term solvency which means the ability of the enterprise to meet its short-term obligations as and when they become due.
Liquidity Ratios	Usually the following liquidity ratios are calculated to judge the short term solvency of the enterprise: 1. Current Ratio, 2. Quick Ratio

11.0 CURRENT RATIO

MEANING OF CURRENT RATIO

Current ratio establishes a relationship between Current Assets and Current Liabilities.

OBJECTIVE OF CURRENT RATIO

The objective of computing Current Ratio is to measure the ability of the firm to meet its short-term obligations as and when due. In other words, the objective is to measure the safety margin available for short-term creditors.

COMPONENTS OF CURRENT RATIO

There are two components of Current Ratio as follows:

1. **Current Assets:** Current Assets refer to those assets which either are in the form of Cash *or* Cash Equivalent *or* are held for their conversion into Cash within Operating Cycle *or* 12 months from the date of Balance Sheet. An asset is classified either as a Current Asset *or* Non-current Asset on the basis of the purpose for which an asset is held in the hands of user.

EXAMPLES OF CURRENT ASSETS

1. Current Investments	*[e.g. Investments having maturity of more than 3 months but not more than 1 year from the date of acquisition]*
2. Inventories	*[e.g. Raw Materials, Work-in-Progress, Finished Goods, Stores & Spares, Loose Tools]*
3. Trade Receivables	*[e.g. Trade Trade Receivables, Bills Receivables to be realized within 12 months]*
4. Cash and Cash Equivalents	*[e.g. Bank Balance, Cheques/Drafts on hand, Cash Balance, Investments having maturity of 3 months or less]*
5. Short-term Loans & Advances	*[e.g. Loans & Advances receivable within 12 months, Advance tax]*
6. Other Current Assets	*[e.g.Prepaid Expenses, Incomes accrued but not received, Advance Tax]*

TUTORIAL NOTES

1. *The 'Provision for doubtful Trade Receivables' is deducted from the total amount of Trade Receivables in order to ascertain the realisable value of Trade Receivables.*
2. *Non-realizable portion of Current Investments is also deducted from the total value of Current Investments in order to ascertain the realizable value of Current Investments.*
3. *Unless otherwise stated, it is assumed that Trade Receivables and Current Investments are realizable at their given book values.*

CALCULATION OF CURRENT ASSETS

1. Current Assets = Current Investments + Inventories + Trade Receivables + Cash and Cash Equivalents + Short-term Loans and Advances + Other Current Assets
2. Current Assets = Current Liabilities + Working Capital

   [**Note:** Working Capital = Current Assets – Current Liabilities]
3. Current Assets = Total Assets – Non-Current Assets

2. **Current Liabilities:** Current Liabilities refer to those liabilities which are expected to be settled within Operating Cycle *or* 12 months from the date of Balance Sheet.

EXAMPLES OF CURRENT LIABILITIES

1. Short-Term Borrowings	*[e.g. Loans repayable on demand or within 12 months, Deposits/Advances repayable within 12 months]*
2. Trade Payables	*[e.g. Trade Receivables, Bills Payables to be settled within 12 months]*
3. Other Current Liabilities	*[e.g. Bank Overdraft,Unpaid Dividend, Unpaid matured Deposits, Unpaid matured Debentures, That portion of Long-term Borrowings repayable within 12 months, Interest accrued (whether due or not) on borrowings, Calls-in-Advance, Outstanding Expenses, Tax Payable, Incomes received-in-advance]*
4. Short-Term Provisions	*[e.g. Provision for Tax, Proposed Dividend, Provision for Employee Benefits to be settled within 12 months]*

CALCULATION OF CURRENT LIABILITIES

1. Current Liabilities = Short-Term Borrowings + Trade Payables + Other Current Liabilities + Short-Term Provisions
2. Current Liabilities = Current Assets – Working Capital
3. Current Liabilities = Total Debts [Whether Long-term *or* Short-term] – Debt

COMPUTATION OF CURRENT RATIO

Current Ratio is computed by dividing the Current Assets by the Current Liabilities. This ratio is usually expressed as a pure ratio e.g. 2 : 1. In the form of a formula, this ratio may be expressed as follows:

$$\textbf{Current Ratio} = \frac{\textbf{Current Assets}}{\textbf{Current Liabilities}}$$

TUTORIAL NOTES

1. *Current Ratio is calculated at a particular date and not for a particular period.*
2. *The excess of Current Assets over Current Liabilities is known as Working Capital.*

INTERPRETATION OF CURRENT RATIO

Current Ratio indicates rupees of current assets available for each rupee of current liability. Higher the ratio, greater the margin of safety for short-term creditors and vice versa.

Traditionally, a Current Ratio of 2 : 1 is considered to be a satisfactory ratio. On the basis of this traditional rule, if the Current Ratio is 2 *or* more, it means the firm is adequately liquid and has the ability to meet its current obligations but if the Current Ratio is *less* than 2, it means the firm has difficulty in meeting its current obligations. The logic behind this rule is that even if the value of current assets becomes half, the firm can still meet its short-term obligations.

A too high Current Ratio may be the result of excessive investment in current assets which may result in idle funds which further results in low profitability since idle funds earn nothing. On the other hand, a too low Current Ratio may be the result of inadequate investment in current assets which may result in low liquidity and may threaten the solvency of the enterprise. Higher liquidity means lower profitability and vice versa.

PRECAUTION WHILE USING CURRENT RATIO

While computing and using the Current Ratio, it must be ensured, (a) that the quality of both receivables (Trade Receivables and Bills Receivable) and inventory, has been carefully assessed and (b) that all Current Assets and Current Liabilities have been properly valued.

ILLUSTRATION 1

From the following information, calculate Current Ratio:

Particulars	₹	*Particulars*	₹
Trade Payables	70,000	Inventories	95,000
Advance Tax	4,000	Trade Receivables	3,40,000
Short-Term Borrowings	10,000	Current Investments	10,000
Accrued Incomes	2,000	Provision for Doubtful Debts	30,000
Other Current Liabilities	20,000	Cash & Cash Equivalents	10,000
Short-term Provisions	1,20,000	Short-term Loans & Advances	4,000
Prepaid Expenses	5,000		

SOLUTION

STEP 1: CALCULATION OF CURRENT ASSETS AND CURRENT LIABILITIES

Current Assets	₹	*Current Liabilities*	₹
Current Investments	10,000	Short-Term Borrowings	10,000
Inventories	95,000	Trade Payables	70,000
Trade Receivables	3,10,000	Other Current Liabilities	20,000
Cash and Cash Equivalents	10,000	Short-Term Provisions	1,20,000
Short-term Loans and Advances	4,000		
Other Current Assets	11,000		
[4,000 + 2,000 + 5,000]	4,40,000		2,20,000

Step 2: **Current Ratio** $= \frac{\textbf{Current Assets}}{\textbf{Current Liabilities}} = \frac{₹4,40,000}{₹2,20,000} = 2:1$

ILLUSTRATION 2

Current Assets ₹ 2,00,000, Inventories ₹ 1,00,000, Working Capital ₹ 1,20,000, Calculate Current Ratio.

SOLUTION

Step 1: Current Liabilities = Current Assets – Working Capital

= ₹ 2,00,000 – ₹ 1,20,000 = ₹ 80,000

Step 2: **Current Ratio** $= \frac{\textbf{Current Assets}}{\textbf{Current Liabilities}} = \frac{₹\ 2,00,000}{₹\ 80,000} = 2.5:1$

Note: *Inventories are already included in current assets.*

ILLUSTRATION 3

Trade Payables ₹ 20,000, Working Capital ₹ 3,60,000, Current Liabilities ₹ 1,20,000. Calculate Current Ratio.

SOLUTION

Step 1: Current Assets = Current Liabilities + Working Capital

= ₹ 1,20,000 + ₹ 3,60,000 = ₹ 4,80,000

Step 2: **Current Ratio** $= \frac{\textbf{Current Assets}}{\textbf{Current Liabilities}} = \frac{₹4,80,000}{₹\ 1,20,000} = 4:1$

Note: *Trade Payables are already included in Current Liabilities.*

ILLUSTRATIONS BASED ON SOME IMPORTANT RELATIONSHIPS

1.	Current Assets	= Total Assets – Non-Current Assets (e.g., Fixed Assets, Non-Current Investments, Long-term Loans & Advances)
2.	Current Assets	= Working Capital + Current Liabilities
3.	Current Liabilities	= Current Assets – Working Capital
4.	Current Liabilities	= Total Debt – Non-Current Liabilities (e.g., Long-term Borrowings, Long-term Provisions)

ILLUSTRATION 4

Working Capital ₹ 3,00,000, Total Assets ₹ 15,00,000, Non-Current Assets ₹ 11,00,000. Calculate Current Ratio.

SOLUTION

Step 1: Current Assets = Total Assets – Non-Current Assets

= ₹ 15,00,000 – ₹ 11,00,000 = ₹ 4,00,000

Step 2: Current Liabilities = Current Assets – Working Capital

= ₹ 4,00,000 – ₹ 3,00,000 = ₹ 1,00,000

Step 3: **Current Ratio** $= \frac{\textbf{Current Assets}}{\textbf{Current Liabilities}} = \frac{₹\ 4,00,000}{₹\ 1,00,000} = 4:1$

ILLUSTRATION 5

Working Capital ₹ 2,00,000, Total Debt ₹ 9,00,000, Non-Current Liabilities ₹ 8,00,000. Calculate Current Ratio.

SOLUTION

Step 1: Current Liabilities = **Total Debt – Non-Current Liabilities**

= ₹ 9,00,000 – ₹ 8,00,000 = ₹ 1,00,000

Step 2: Current Assets = **Working Capital + Current Liabilities**

= ₹ 2,00,000 + ₹ 1,00,000 = ₹ 3,00,000

Step 3: Current Ratio $= \dfrac{\textbf{Current Assets}}{\textbf{Current Liabilities}} = \dfrac{₹\ 3{,}00{,}000}{₹\ 1{,}00{,}000} = 3 : 1$

ILLUSTRATION 6

Total Debt ₹ 24,00,000, Total Assets ₹ 32,00,000, Fixed Assets ₹ 12,00,000, Non-Current Investments ₹ 2,00,000, Long-term Borrowings ₹ 8,00,000, Long-term Provisions ₹ 8,00,000, Long-term Loans & Advances ₹ 2,00,000. Calculate Current Ratio.

SOLUTION

Step 1: Current Assets = **Total Assets – Non-Current Assets**

= ₹ 32,00,000 – (₹ 12,00,000 + ₹ 2,00,000 + ₹ 2,00,000) = ₹ 16,00,000

Step 2: Current Liabilities = **Total Debt – Non-Current Liabilities**

= ₹ 24,00,000 – (₹ 8,00,000 + ₹ 8,00,000) = ₹ 8,00,000

Step 3: Current Ratio $= \dfrac{\textbf{Current Assets}}{\textbf{Current Liabilities}} = \dfrac{₹\ 16{,}00{,}000}{₹\ 8{,}00{,}000} = 2 : 1$

ILLUSTRATION 7

The ratio of Current Assets (₹ 3,00,000) to Current Liabilities (₹ 2,00,000) is 1.5 : 1. The accountant of this firm is interested in maintaining a Current Ratio of 2 : 1 by paying some part of current liabilities. You are required to suggest him the amount of current liabilities which must be paid for this purpose.

SOLUTION

Step 1: *Let the amount of Current Liabilities to be paid be X*

Step 2: Current Ratio $= \dfrac{\textbf{Current Assets}}{\textbf{Current Liabilities}} = \dfrac{3{,}00{,}000 - X}{2{,}00{,}000 - X} = 2$

or, ₹ 4,00,000 – 2X = ₹ 3,00,000 – X

X = ₹ 1,00,000

ILLUSTRATION 8

The ratio of Current Assets (₹ 5,00,000) to Current Liabilities (₹ 2,00,000) is 2.5 : 1. The accountant of this firm is interested in maintaining a Current Ratio of 2 : 1 by acquiring some current assets on credit. You are required to suggest him the amount of current assets which must be acquired for this purpose.

Solution

Step 1: *Let the amount of Current Assets to be acquired be X*

Step 2: Current Ratio $= \dfrac{\textbf{Current Assets}}{\textbf{Current Liabilities}} = \dfrac{₹\ 5{,}00{,}000 + X}{₹\ 2{,}00{,}000 + X} = 2$

$$₹\,4,00,000 + 2X = ₹\,5,00,000 + X$$
$$X = ₹\,1,00,000$$

ILLUSTRATION 9

A firm had Current Assets of ₹ 1,50,000. It then paid a Current Liability of ₹ 30,000. After this payment, the Current Ratio was 2 : 1. Determine the size of Current Liabilities and Working Capital after and before the payment was made.

SOLUTION

Step 1: *Let the Current Liabilities after payment be X*

$$\text{Current Ratio} = \frac{\textbf{Current Assets}}{\textbf{Current Liabilities}} = \frac{₹\,1,50,000 - ₹\,30,000}{X} = 2$$

$$2X = ₹\,1,20,000$$
$$X = ₹\,1,20,000/2 = ₹\,60,000$$

Step 2: Working Capital after payment = ₹ 1,20,000 – ₹ 60,000 = ₹ 60,000

Step 3: Current Liabilities before payment = Current liabilities after payment + Payment

= ₹ 60,000 + ₹ 30,000 = ₹ 90,000

Step 4: Working Capital before payment = ₹ 1,50,000 – ₹ 90,000 = ₹ 60,000

ILLUSTRATION 10

A firm had Current Liabilities of ₹ 90,000. It then acquired Stock-in-trade at a cost of ₹ 10,000 on credit. After this acquisition, the Current Ratio was 2 : 1. Determine the size of Current Assets and Working Capital after and before the Inventories was acquired.

SOLUTION

Step 1: *Let the Current assets after acquisition of Inventories be X*

$$\text{Current Ratio} = \frac{\textbf{Current Assets}}{\textbf{Current Liabilities}} = \frac{X}{₹\,90,000 + ₹\,10,000} = 2$$

$$X = ₹\,1,00,000 \times 2 = ₹\,2,00,000$$

Step 2: Working Capital after acquisition = ₹ 2,00,000 – ₹ 1,00,000 = ₹ 1,00,000

Step 3: Current Assets before acquisition

= Current Assets After acquisition – Purchase of Stock on credit

= ₹ 2,00,000 – ₹ 10,000 = ₹ 1,90,000

Step 4: Working Capital before acquisition = ₹ 1,90,000 – ₹ 90,000 = ₹ 1,00 000

IMPORTANT INSTRUCTION

To know the effect of a transaction on Current Ratio, Take the following Practical Steps:

Step 1: *Assume some figure of Current Assets and Current Liabilities.*

Step 2: *Put the effect of transaction in Assumed figures of Current Assets & Current Liabilities and Calculate the New figures.*

Step 3: *Calculate the New Current Ratio.*

Step 4: *Compare this New Current Ratio with Old Current Ratio to ascertain Improvement or Decline or no Change.*

ILLUSTRATION 11

State giving reason, whether the Current Ratio will improve *or* decline *or* will have no effect in each one of the following transactions if Current Ratio is (I) 2 : 1, (II) 1 : 1, (III) 0.8 : 1.

(a) Cash paid to Trade Payables
(b) Bills Receivable endorsed to creditors
(c) Bills Payable discharged
(d) Payment of Final Dividend already declared
(e) Purchase of Stock-in-trade on credit
(f) Bills Receivable endorsed to creditors dishonoured
(g) Purchase of Stock-in-trade for Cash
(h) Sale of Stock-in-trade (Costing ₹ 10,000) for ₹ 12,000
(i) Sale of Fixed Asset (Book Value ₹ 10,000) for ₹ 9,000

SOLUTION

I. If the Current Ratio is 2 : 1

Statement showing the Effect of Various Transactions on Current Ratio of 2 : 1

Transaction	*Effect on Current Ratio*	*Reason = Current Assets are more than Current Liabilities and ...*
(a)	Improve	Both the total Current Assets and total Current Liabilities are decreased by the same amount.
(b)	Improve	Both the total Current Assets and total Current Liabilities are decreased by the same amount.
(c)	Improve	Both the total Current Assets and total Current Liabilities are decreased by the same amount.
(d)	Improve	Both the total Current Assets and total Current Liabilities are decreased by the same amount.
(e)	Decline	Both the total Current Assets and total Current Liabilities are increased by the same amount.
(f)	Decline	Both the total Current Assets and total Current Liabilities are increased by the same amount.
(g)	No Effect	Neither the total Current Assets nor the total Current Liabilities are affected since there is only a conversion of one Current Asset into another Current Asset.
(h)	Improve	Total Current Assets are increased by ₹ 2,000 but total Current Liabilities remain unchanged.
(i)	Improve	Total Current Assets are increased by ₹ 9,000 but total Current Liabilities remain unchanged.

II. If the Current Ratio is 1 : 1

Statement showing the Effect of Various Transactions on Current Ratio of 1 : 1

Transaction	*Effect on Current Ratio*	*Reason = Current Assets are more than Current Liabilities and ...*
(a)	No effect	Both the total Current Assets and total Current Liabilities are decreased by the same amount.

(b)	No effect	Both the total Current Assets and total Current Liabilities are decreased by the same amount.
(c)	No effect	Both the total Current Assets and total Current Liabilities are decreased by the same amount.
(d)	No effect	Both the total Current Assets and total Current Liabilities are decreased by the same amount.
(e)	No effect	Both the total Current Assets and total Current Liabilities are increased by the same amount.
(f)	No effect	Both the total Current Assets and total Current Liabilities are increased by the same amount.
(g)	No Effect	Neither the total Current Assets nor the total Current Liabilities are affected since there is only a conversion of one Current Asset into another Current Asset.
(h)	Improve	Total Current Assets are increased by ₹ 2,000 (Profit) but total Current Liabilities remain unchanged.
(i)	Improve	Total Current Assets are increased by ₹ 9,000 but total Current Liabilities remain unchanged.

III. If the Current Ratio is 0.8 : 1

Statement showing the effect of Various Transactions on Current Ratio of 0.8 : 1

Transaction	*Effect on Current Ratio*	*Reason = Current Assets are more than Current Liabilities and ...*
(a)	Decline	Both the total Current Assets and total Current Liabilities are decreased by the same amount.
(b)	Decline	Both the total Current Assets and total Current Liabilities are decreased by the same amount.
(c)	Decline	Both the total Current Assets and total Current Liabilities are decreased by the same amount.
(d)	Decline	Both the total Current Assets and total Current Liabilities are decreased by the same amount.
(e)	Improve	Both the total Current Assets and total Current Liabilities are increased by the same amount.
(f)	Improve	Both the total Current Assets and total Current Liabilities are increased by the same amount.
(g)	No Effect	Neither the total Current Assets nor the total Current Liabilities are affected since there is only a conversion of one Current Asset into another Current Asset.
(h)	Improve	Total Current Assets are increased by ₹ 2,000 (Profit) but total Current Liabilities remain unchanged.
(i)	Improve	Total Current Assets are increased by ₹ 9,000 but total Current Liabilities remain unchanged.

12.0 QUICK RATIO [OR LIQUID RATIO *or* ACID TEST RATIO]

MEANING OF QUICK RATIO

Quick Ratio establishes a relationship between Quick Assets and Current Liabilities.

OBJECTIVE OF QUICK RATIO

The objective of this ratio is to measure the ability of the firm to meet its short-term obligations as and when due without relying upon the realization of Inventories.

COMPONENTS OF QUICK RATIO

There are two components of this ratio as follows:

1. **Quick Assets:** Quick Assets refer to those current assets which can be converted into cash immediately *or* at a short notice without a loss of value.

EXAMPLES OF QUICK ASSETS

1. Current Investments	*[e.g. Investments having maturity of more than 3 months but not more than 1 year from the date of acquisition]*
2. Trade Receivables	*[e.g. Trade Trade Receivables, Bills Receivables to be realized within 12 months]*
3. Cash and Cash Equivalents	*[e.g. Bank Balance, Cheques/Drafts on hand, Cash Balance, Investments having maturity of 3 months or less]*
4. Short-term Loans and Advances	*[e.g. Loans & Advances receivable within 12 months, Advance tax]*

TUTORIAL NOTES

1. *Inventories are not considered as quick assets because:*
   (a) *There is uncertainty as to whether or not and at what price the inventories can be sold;*
   (b) *Time is required to convert the raw-materials and work-in-progress into finished goods and to convert the finished goods into debtors.*
2. *Prepaid Expenses are not considered as quick assets because they usually cannot be converted into cash.*
3. *The 'Provision for doubtful Trade Receivables' is deducted from the total amount of Trade Receivables in order to ascertain the realisable value of Trade Receivables.*
4. *Non-realizable portion of Current Investments is also deducted from the total value of Current Investments in order to ascertain the realizable value of Current Investments.*
5. *Unless otherwise stated, it is assumed that Trade Receivables and Current Investments are realizable at their given book values.*

CALCULATION OF QUICK ASSETS

1. Quick Assets = Current Investments + Trade Receivables + Cash and Cash Equivalents + Short-term Loans and Advances
2. Quick Assets = Current Assets – Inventories – Other Current Assets

2. **Current Liabilities:** Current Liabilities refer to those liabilities which are expected to be settled within Operating Cycle *or* 12 months from the date of Balance Sheet.

EXAMPLES OF CURRENT LIABILITIES

1. Short-Term Borrowings	*[e.g. Loans repayable on demand or within 12 months, Deposits/Advances repayable within 12 months]*
2. Trade Payables	*[e.g. Trade Receivables, Bills Payables to be settled within 12 months]*

3. Other Current Liabilities	*[e.g. Bank Overdraft, Unpaid Dividend, Unpaid matured Deposits, Unpaid matured Debentures, That portion of Long-term Borrowings repayable within 12 months, Interest accrued (whether due or not) on borrowings, Calls-in-Advance, Outstanding Expenses, Tax Payable, Incomes received-in-advance]*
4. Short-Term Provisions	*[e.g. Provision for Tax, Proposed Dividend, Provision for Employee Benefits to be settled within 12 months]*

CALCULATION OF CURRENT LIABILITIES

1.	Current Liabilities	= Short-Term Borrowings + Trade Payables + Other Current Liabilities + Short-Term Provisions
2.	Current Liabilities	= Current Assets – Working Capital
	[**Note:** Working Capital = Current Assets – Current Liabilities]	
3.	Current Liabilities	= (Quick Assets + Inventories + Other Current Assets) – Working Capital
4.	Current Liabilities	= Total Debts – Non-Current Liabilities
5.	Current Liabilities	= Current Assets/Current Ratio

COMPUTATION OF QUICK RATIO

Quick ratio is computed by dividing the Quick Assets by the Current Liabilities. This ratio is usually expressed as a pure ratio e.g., 1 : 1. In the form of a formula, this ratio may be expressed as under:

$$\text{Quick Ratio} = \frac{\text{Quick Assets}}{\text{Current Liabilities}}$$

TUTORIAL NOTES

1. *Quick Ratio is calculated at particular date and not for a particular period.*
2. *The excess of Current Assets over Current Liabilities is known as Working Capital.*

INTERPRETATION OF QUICK RATIO

Quick Ratio indicates rupees of quick assets available for each rupee of current liability. Traditionally, a quick ratio of 1 : 1 is considered to be a satisfactory ratio. However, this traditional rule should not be used blindly since a firm having a quick ratio of more than 1, may not be meeting its short-term obligations in time if its current assets consist of doubtful and slow paying debtors while a firm having a quick ratio of *less* than 1, may be meeting its short-term obligations in time because of its very efficient inventory management.

PRECAUTION WHILE USING QUICK RATIO

While computing and using the quick ratio, it must be ensured, (a) that the quality of the receivables (debtors and bills receivable) has been carefully assessed and (b) that all Quick Assets and Current Liabilities have been properly valued.

13.0 DISTINCTION BETWEEN CURRENT RATIO AND QUICK RATIO

Basis of Distinction	*Current Ratio*	*Quick Ratio*
1. Relationship	Current Ratio shows relationship between Current Assets and Current Liabilities.	Quick Ratio shows relationship between Quick Assets and Current Liabilities.

2. Objective	Current Ratio measures ability to meet current obligations as and when they fall due for payment over a period normally not exceeding 12 months.	Quick Ratio measures enterprise's ability to meet current obligations without relying on the sale and collection of inventories.
3. Components of Ratio	The components of Current Ratio are Current Assets and Current Liabilities.	The components of Quick Ratio are Quick Assets and Current Liabilities.
4. Formula for Computation	Current Ratio = $\frac{\text{Current Assets}}{\text{Current Liabilities}}$	Quick Ratio = $\frac{\text{Quick Assets}}{\text{Current Liabilities}}$
5. Traditional Satisfactory Standard	It is 2 : 1.	It is 1 : 1.
6. Precaution	While computing and using Current Ratio, quality of both Inventories and Trade Receivables is required to be carefully assessed.	While computing and using Quick Ratio, quality of Trade Receivables is required to be carefully assessed (since the Inventories have already been excluded).

ILLUSTRATION 12

Current Assets ₹ 4,40,000, Inventories ₹ 95,000, Prepaid Expenses ₹ 5,000, Current Liabilities ₹ 3,40,000, Trade Payables ₹ 20,000. Calculate the Quick Ratio.

SOLUTION

Step 1: Quick Assets = **Current Assets – Inventories – Prepaid Expenses**

= ₹ 4,40,000 – ₹ 95,000 – ₹ 5,000 = ₹ 3,40,000

Step 2: Quick Ratio = $\frac{\textbf{Quick Assets}}{\textbf{Current Liabilities}} = \frac{₹\ 3,40,000}{₹\ 3,40,000} = 1:1$

Note: *Trade Payables are already included in Current Liabilities.*

ILLUSTRATION 13

Current Assets ₹ 2,00,000, Inventory ₹ 30,000, Prepaid Expenses ₹ 10,000, Working Capital ₹ 1,20,000. Calculate the Quick Ratio.

SOLUTION

Step 1: Current Liabilities = **Current Assets – Working Capital**

= ₹ 2,00,000 – ₹ 1,20,000 = ₹ 80,000

Step 2: Quick Assets = **Current Assets – Inventories – Prepaid Expenses**

= ₹ 2,00,000 – ₹ 30,000 – ₹ 10,000 = ₹ 1,60,000

Step 3: Quick Ratio = $\frac{\textbf{Quick Assets}}{\textbf{Current Liabilities}} = \frac{₹\ 1,60,000}{₹\ 80,000} = 2:1$

ILLUSTRATION 14

Current Liabilities ₹ 1,20,000, Working Capital ₹ 3,60,000, Trade Payables ₹ 20,000, Inventories ₹ 1,00,000, Prepaid Expenses ₹ 20,000. Calculate the Quick Ratio.

SOLUTION

Step 1: Current Assets = **Current Liabilities + Working Capital**

= ₹ 1,20,000 + ₹ 3,60,000 = ₹ 4,80,000

Step 2: Quick Assets = **Current Assets – Inventories – Prepaid Expenses**

= ₹ 4,80,000 – ₹ 1,00,000 – ₹ 20,000 = ₹ 3,60,000

Step 3: Quick Ratio = $\frac{\textbf{Quick Assets}}{\textbf{Current Liabilities}} = \frac{₹\ 3,60,000}{₹\ 1,20,000} = 3:1$

Note: *Trade Payables are already included in Current Liabilities.*

ILLUSTRATION 15

Liquid Assets ₹ 6,80,000, Inventories ₹ 1,90,000, Prepaid Expenses ₹ 10,000, Working Capital ₹ 2,00,000. Calculate the Current Ratio and Quick Ratio.

SOLUTION

Step 1: Current Assets = **Liquid Assets + Inventories + Prepaid Expenses**

= ₹6,80,000 + ₹1,90,000 + ₹ 10,000 = ₹ 8,80,000

Step 2: Current Liabilities = **Current Assets – Working Capital**

= ₹ 8,80,000 – ₹ 2,00,000 = ₹ 6,80,000

Step 3: Current Ratio = $\frac{\textbf{Current Assets}}{\textbf{Current Liabilities}} = \frac{₹\ 8,80,000}{₹\ 6,80,000} = 22:17$

Step 4: Quick Ratio = $\frac{\textbf{Quick Assets}}{\textbf{Current Liabilities}} = \frac{₹\ 6,80,000}{₹\ 6,80,000} = 1:1$

ILLUSTRATION 16

Working Capital ₹ 3,00,000, Total Assets ₹ 15,00,000, Non-Current Assets ₹ 11,00,000, Inventories ₹ 95,000, Prepaid Expenses ₹ 5,000. Calculate Current Ratio and Quick Ratio.

SOLUTION

Step 1: Current Assets = **Total Assets – Non-Current Assets**

= ₹ 15,00,000 – ₹ 11,00,000 = ₹ 4,00,000

Step 2: Quick Assets = **Current Assets – Inventories – Prepaid Expenses**

= ₹4,00,000 – ₹ 95,000 – ₹ 5,000 = ₹ 3,00,000

Step 3: Current Liabilities = **Current Assets – Working Capital**

= ₹ 4,00,000 – ₹ 3,00,000 = ₹ 1,00,000

Step 4: Current Ratio = $\frac{\textbf{Current Assets}}{\textbf{Current Liabilities}} = \frac{₹\ 4,00,000}{₹\ 1,00,000} = 4:1$

Step 5: Quick Ratio = $\frac{\textbf{Quick Assets}}{\textbf{Current Liabilities}} = \frac{₹\ 3,00,000}{₹\ 1,00,000} = 3:1$

ILLUSTRATION 17

Working Capital ₹ 2,00,000, Total Debt ₹ 9,00,000, Non-Current Liabilities ₹ 8,00,000, Inventories ₹ 95,000, Prepaid Expenses ₹ 5,000. Calculate Quick Ratio.

SOLUTION

Step 1: Current Liabilities = **Total Debt – Non-Current Liabilities**

= ₹ 9,00,000 – ₹ 8,00,000 = ₹ 1,00,000

Step 2: **Current Assets** = **Working Capital + Current Liabilities**

= ₹ 2,00,000 + ₹ 1,00,000 = ₹ 3,00,000

Step 3: **Quick Assets** = **Current Assets – Inventories – Prepaid Expenses**

= ₹ 3,00,000 – ₹ 95,000 – ₹ 5,000 = ₹ 2,00,000

Step 4: **Quick Ratio** $= \frac{\textbf{Quick Assets}}{\textbf{Current Liabilities}} = \frac{₹\ 2,00,000}{₹\ 1,00,000} = 2:1$

ILLUSTRATION 18

Total Debt ₹ 24,00,000, Total Assets ₹ 32,00,000, Fixed Assets ₹ 12,00,000, Non-Current Investments ₹ 2,00,000, Long-term Borrowings ₹ 8,00,000, Long-term Provisions ₹ 8,00,000, Long-term Loans & Advances ₹ 2,00,000, Inventories ₹ 3,80,000, Prepaid Expenses ₹ 20,000. Calculate Quick Ratio.

SOLUTION

Step 1: **Current Assets** = **Total Assets – Non-Current Assets**

= ₹ 32,00,000 – (₹ 12,00,000 + ₹ 2,00,000 + ₹ 2,00,000) = ₹ 16,00,000

Step 2: **Quick Assets** = **Current Assets – Inventories – Prepaid Expenses**

= ₹ 16,00,000 – ₹ 3,80,000 – ₹ 20,000 = ₹ 12,00,000

Step 3: Current Liabilities = **Total Debt – Non-Current Liabilities**

= ₹ 24,00,000 – (₹ 8,00,000 + ₹ 8,00,000) = ₹ 8,00,000

Step 4: **Quick Ratio** $= \frac{\textbf{Quick Assets}}{\textbf{Current Liabilities}} = \frac{₹\ 12,00,000}{₹\ 8,00,000} = 1.5:1$

ILLUSTRATION 19

Current Ratio 2.5 : 1, Inventories ₹ 60,000, Current Liabilities ₹ 80,000. Calculate the Liquid Ratio.

SOLUTION

Step 1: **Current Ratio** = **Current Assets/Current Liabilities = 2.5**

or, **Current Assets** = **Current Liabilities × Current Ratio**

or, **Current Assets** = ₹ 80,000 × 2.5 = ₹ 2,00,000

Step 2: **Liquid Assets** = **Current Assets – Inventories**

= ₹ 2,00,000 – ₹ 60,000 = ₹ 1,40,000

Step 3: **Liquid Ratio** $= \frac{\textbf{Liquid Assets}}{\textbf{Current Liabilities}} = \frac{₹\ 1,40,000}{₹\ 80,000} = 1.75:1$

ILLUSTRATION 20

X Ltd. has a Liquid Ratio of 1.5:1. Its Inventories is ₹ 60,000 and its Current Liabilities are ₹ 1,20,000. Calculate the Current Ratio.

SOLUTION

Step 1: **Liquid Ratio** = **Liquid Assets/Current Liabilities = 1.5**

or, **Liquid Assets** = **Current Liabilities × Liquid Ratio**

Liquid Assets = ₹ 1,20,000 × 1.5 = ₹ 1,80,000

Step 2: **Current Assets** = **Liquid Assets + Inventories**

= ₹ 1,80,000 + ₹ 60,000 = ₹ 2,40,000

Step 3: **Current Ratio** $= \frac{\textbf{Quick Assets}}{\textbf{Current Liabilities}} = \frac{₹\ 2,40,000}{₹\ 1,20,000} = 2:1$

ILLUSTRATION 21

X Ltd. has a Current Ratio of 2 : 1 and Quick Ratio of 1.5 : 1. Its Current Liabilities are ₹ 80,000. Calculate the value of Inventories.

SOLUTION

Step 1: Current Ratio = Current Assets/Current Liabilities = 2

Current Assets = Current Liabilities × Current Ratio

Current Assets = ₹ 80,000 × 2 = ₹ 1,60,000

Step 2: Quick Ratio = Quick Assets/Current Liabilities = 1.5

Quick Assets = Current Liabilities × Quick Ratio

Quick Assets = ₹ 80,000 × 1.5 = ₹ 1,20,000

Step 3: Inventories = Current Assets – Quick Assets

= ₹ 1,60,000 – ₹ 1,20,000 = ₹ 40,000

ILLUSTRATION 22

X Ltd. has a Current Ratio of 2.5 : 1 and Quick Ratio of 1.5 : 1. Its Current assets are ₹ 2,00,000. Calculate the Value of Inventories.

SOLUTION

Step 1: Current Ratio = Current Assets/Current Liabilities = 2.5

Current Liabilities = Current Assets/Current Ratio

Current Liabilities = ₹ 2,00,000/2.5 = ₹ 80,000

Step 2: Quick Ratio = Quick Assets/Current Liabilities = 1.5

Quick Assets = Current Liabilities × Quick Ratio

Quick Assets = ₹ 80,000 × 1.5 = ₹ 1,20,000

Step 3:Value of Inventories = Current Assets – Quick Assets

= ₹ 2,00,000 – ₹ 1,20,000 = ₹ 80,000

ILLUSTRATION 23

X Ltd. has a Current Ratio of 3 : 1. Its net Working Capital is ₹ 2,00,000 and its Inventory is ₹ 2,20,000. Calculate liquid assets.

SOLUTION

Step 1: Current Liabilities

Current Ratio = Current Assets/Current Liabilities = 3

Current Assets –3 Current Liabilities = 0 ......Eq. I

Current Assets – Current Liabilities = ₹ 2,00,000 ..... Eq. II

Subtracting Eq. II from Eq. I

2 Current Liabilities = ₹ 2,00,000

Current Liabilities = ₹ 2,00,000/2 = ₹ 1,00,000

Step 2: Current Assets = ₹ 1,00,000 × 3 = ₹ 3,00,000

Step 3: Liquid Assets = Current Assets – Inventory

= ₹ 3,00,000 – ₹ 2,20,000 = ₹ 80,000

ILLUSTRATION 24

X Ltd. has a Liquid Ratio of 1.5 : 1. Its Net Working Capital is ₹ 1,20,000 and its Inventory is ₹ 80,000. Calculate Current Assets.

SOLUTION

Step 1: Current Liabilities

$$\textbf{Liquid Ratio} = \frac{\textbf{Liquid Assets}}{\textbf{Current Liabilities}} = 1.5$$

or, $$= \frac{\textbf{Current Assets} - \textbf{Stock}}{\textbf{Current Liabilities}} = 1.5$$

or, Current Assets – ₹ 80,000 = 1.5 Current Liabilities

or, Current Assets –1.5 Current Liabilities = ₹ 80,000 ...... Eq. I

Working Capital = Current Assets – Current Liabilities

or, Current Assets – Current Liabilities = ₹ 1,20,000 ...... Eq. II

Subtracting Eq. II from Eq. I

0.5 Current Liabilities = ₹ 40,000

Current Liabilities = ₹ 40,000/0.5 = ₹ 80,000

Step 2: Current Assets = ₹ 80,000 + ₹ 1,20,000 = ₹ 2,00,000

ILLUSTRATION 25

X Ltd. has a Current Ratio of 3 : 1 and Liquid Ratio of 1 : 1. Its Working Capital is ₹ 2,00,000. Calculate the value of Inventories.

SOLUTION

Step 1: Current Assets & Current Liabilities

$$\textbf{Current Ratio} = \frac{\textbf{Current Assets (CA)}}{\textbf{Current Liabilities (CL)}} = 3$$

CA – 3CL = 0 ...... Eq. I

CA – CL = ₹ 2,00,000 ...... Eq. II

Subtracting Equation II from Equation I

2CL = ₹ 2,00,000

CL = ₹ 2,00,000/2 = ₹ 1,00,000

Current Assets = Current Liabilities × Current Ratio

= ₹ 1,00,000 × 3 = ₹ 3,00,000

Step 2: Quick Assets

$$\textbf{Quick Ratio} = \frac{\textbf{Quick Assets}}{\textbf{Current Liabilities}} = \frac{\text{Quick Assets}}{₹\ 1,00,000} = 1$$

Quick Assets = ₹ 1,00,000 × 1 = ₹ 1,00,000

Step 3: Inventories = Current Assets – Quick Assets

= ₹ 3,00,000 – ₹ 1,00,000 = ₹ 2,00,000

ILLUSTRATION 26

X Ltd. has a Current Ratio of 4.5 : 1 and Quick Ratio of 3 : 1. If its Inventories are ₹ 36,000, find out its Total Current Assets, and Total Current Liabilities and Quick Assets.

SOLUTION

Step 1: **Current Ratio** = $\frac{\textbf{Current Assets (CA)}}{\textbf{Current Liabilities (CL)}} = 4.5$

or, CA – 4.5 CL = 0 .... Eq. I

Step 2: **Quick Ratio** = **(CA – Stock)/CL = 3**

or, CA – ₹ 36,000 – 3CL = 0

or CA – 3CL = ₹ 36,000 .... Eq. II

Step 3: *Subtracting Equation II from Equation I*

1.5 CL = ₹ 36,000

CL = ₹ 36,000/1.5 = ₹ 24,000

Step 4: **CA** = ₹ 24,000 × 4.5 = ₹ 1,08,000

Step 5: **Quick Assets** = ₹ 1,08,000 – ₹ 36,000 = ₹ 72,000

ILLUSTRATION 27

The Quick Ratio of a company is 2 : 1. State, giving reason, which of the following would improve, reduce *or* not change the ratio:

(i) Purchase of Stock-in-trade for Cash; (ii) Cash collected from Trade Receivables; (iii) Sale of Stock-in-trade (costing ₹ 10,000) for ₹ 11,000 and (iv) Sale of an Office Furniture (Book value ₹ 10,000) for 9,000, (v) Payment of Dividend.

SOLUTION

EFFECT OF TRANSACTION ON QUICK RATIO

Transaction	*Effect*	*Reason*
(i)	**Reduce**	Quick Assets will decrease due ot reduction of Cash.
(ii)	**No Change**	Quick Assets will not change due ot conversion of Trade Receivables into cash.
(iii)	**Improve**	Quick Assets will increase due to increase in cash.
(iv)	**Improve**	Quick Assets will increase due to increase in cash.
(v)	**Improve**	Both the Quick Assets and Current Liabilities are decreased by the same amount.

14.0 SOLVENCY RATIOS

Meaning	Solvency Ratios measure the long-term financial solvency which means the enterprise's ability to pay the interest regularly and to repay the principal on maturity *or* in pre-determined instalments at due dates.
Solvency Ratios	Usually the following ratios are calculated to judge the long-term financial solvency of the enterprise: 1. Debt-Equity Ratio 2. Total Assets to Debt Ratio 3. Proprietary Ratio 4. Interest Coverage Ratio 5. Capital Gearing Ratio 6. Preference Dividend Coverage Ratio 7. Debt Service Coverage Ratio

15.0 DEBT-EQUITY RATIO

MEANING OF DEBT-EQUITY RATIO

Debt-Equity Ratio establishes a relationship between Debt (i.e., Non-Current Liabilities) and Equity (i.e., Shareholders' Funds).

OBJECTIVE OF DEBT-EQUITY RATIO

The basic objective of computing Debt-Equity ratio is to measure the long-term financial solvency. (i.e., the enterprise's ability to pay the interest regularly and to repay the principal on maturity *or* in pre-determined instalments at due dates).

COMPONENTS OF DEBT-EQUITY RATIO

There are two components of this ratio as follows:

1. **Debt** which mean Non-Current Liabilities (e.g. Long-term Borrowings like Debentures, Bonds, Term Loans From Banks, Financial Institutions, Long-term Loans & Advances, Long-term Provisions) which are expected to be settled after 12 months from the date of Balance Sheet.

CALCULATION OF DEBT

1. Debt = Long-term Borrowings + Long-term Provisions
2. Debt = Total Debt – Current Liabilities
3. Debt = Capital Employed – Equity
   [**Note:** Capital Employed = Equity + Debt]

2. Equity which mean Funds belonging to all the Shareholders (whether Equity *or* Preference).

CALCULATION OF EQUITY

Particulars	₹	Particulars	₹
Method I		**Method IV**	
A. Share Capital (Equity + Pref.)	....	A. Non-Current Assets	....
B. + Reserves & Surplus	....	B. + Current Assets	....
C. Equity [A + B]	....	C. – Current Liabilities	(..........)
		D. – Non-Current Liabilities	(..........)
		E. Equity	....
Method II		**Method V**	
A. Equity Share Capital	....	A. Non-Current Assets	....
B. + Pref. Share Capital	....	B. + Working Capital	....
C. + Reserves & Surplus	....	C. – Non-Current Liabilities	(..........)
D. Equity [A + B + C]	....	D. Equity	....
Method III		**Method VI**	
A. Capital Employed	....	A. Total Assets	....
B. – Non-Current Liabilities	(..........)	B. – Total Debts	(..........)
C. Equity	....	[Current + Non-Current]	
		C. Equity	....

COMPUTATION OF DEBT-EQUITY RATIO

Debt-Equity Ratio is computed by dividing the Debt by Equity. This ratio is usually expressed as a pure ratio e.g., 2 : 1. In the form of a formula, this ratio may be expressed as follows:

$$\text{Debt-Equity Ratio} = \frac{\textbf{Debt}}{\textbf{Equity}}$$

TUTORIAL NOTE

Debt-Equity Ratio is calculated at a particular date and not for a particular period.

INTERPRETATION OF DEBT-EQUITY RATIO

Debt-Equity Ratio indicates the margin of safety to long-term creditors. A low debt-equity ratio implies the use of more equity than debt which means a larger safety margin for creditors since owner's equity is treated as a margin of safety by creditors and vice versa. Traditionally, a Debt Equity Ratio of 2 : 1 is considered to be satisfactory which means debt could be twice the equity. The implications from the point of view of creditors and the firm may be seen as follows:

Case	*Implications from the point of view of*	
	Trade Payables	***Firm***
A. In case of Low Debt-Equity Ratio	Larger margin of safety since owner's equity is treated as margin of safety by creditors.	1. Debt servicing is *less* burdensome. 2. Less pressure and interference of creditors in management. 3. Capacity to raise additional debt. 4. Not much benefit of trading on equity when the firm earns a rate higher than the interest rate on borrowed funds.
B. In case of High Debt-Equity Ratio	Greater the risk to creditors	1. Debt servicing is burdensome under adverse business conditions. 2. Pressure & interference of creditors in management. 3. Difficulties in raising additional debt. 4. Benefits of trading on equity when the firm earns a rate higher than the interest rate on borrowed funds.

Thus, an enterprise should have neither a very high nor a very low ratio, it should have a satisfactory ratio. To judge whether the ratio is satisfactory *or* not, it should be compared with its own past ratios *or* with the ratio of similar enterprises in the same industry *or* with the industry average.

ILLUSTRATION 28

From the following information. Calculate Debt-Equity Ratio:

Particulars	₹
Equity Share Capital	1,50,000
Pref. Share capital	1,00,000
Reserves & Surplus	1,50,000
Long-term Borrowings	6,00,000
Long-term Provisions	2,00,000

SOLUTION

Step 1: **Debt** = **Long-term Borrowings + Long-term Provisions**

= ₹ 6,00,000 + ₹ 2,00,000 = ₹ 8,00,000

Step 2: **Equity** = **Equity Share Capital + Pref. Share Capital + Reserves & Surplus**

= ₹ 1,50,000 + ₹ 1,00,000 + ₹ 1,50,000 = ₹ 4,00,000

Step 3: Debt-Equity Ratio = $\frac{\textbf{Debt}}{\textbf{Equity}} = \frac{₹\,8,00,000}{₹\,4,00,000} = 2:1$

ILLUSTRATION 29

Fixed Assets (Gross) ₹ 12,00,000, Accumulated Depreciation ₹ 2,00,000, Non-Current Investments ₹ 20,000. Long-term Loans & Advances ₹ 80,000, Current Assets ₹ 5,00,000, Current Liabilities ₹ 4,00,000, 20% Long-term Borrowings ₹ 6,00,000, Long-term Provisions ₹ 2,00,000. Calculate Debt Equity Ratio.

SOLUTION

Step 1: **Debt** = **Long-term Borrowings + Long-term Provisions**

= ₹ 6,00,000 + ₹ 2,00,000 = ₹ 8,00,000

Step 2: **Equity** = **Non-Current Assets + Current Assets – Current Liabilities – Non-Current Liabilities**

= [(₹ 12,00,000 – ₹ 2,00,000) + ₹ 20,000 + ₹ 80,000] + ₹ 5,00,000 – ₹ 4,00,000 – (₹ 6,00,000 + ₹ 2,00,000) = ₹ 4,00,000

Step 3: Debt-Equity Ratio = $\frac{\textbf{Debt}}{\textbf{Equity}} = \frac{₹\,8,00,000}{₹\,4,00,000} = 2:1$

ILLUSTRATIONS BASED ON SOME IMPORTANT RELATIONSHIPS

1. Debt = Total Debt – Current Liabilities
2. Debt = Capital Employed – Equity
3. Capital Employed = Total Assets – Current Liabilities
4. Capital Employed = Non-Current Assets + Working Capital
5. Capital Employed = Equity + Debt
6. Equity = Equity Share Capital + Preference Share Capital + Reserves & Surplus
7. Equity = Non-Current Assets + Working Capital – Non-Current Liabilities
8. Equity = Capital Employed – Debt
9. Equity = Total Assets – Total Debt

ILLUSTRATION 30

Equity Shareholders' Funds ₹ 3,00,000, Reserves & Surplus ₹ 2,00,000, Preference Share Capital ₹ 1,00,000, Total Debt ₹ 11,40,000, Current Liabilities ₹ 3,40,000. Calculate Debt-Equity Ratio.

SOLUTION

Step 1: **Debt** = **Total Debt – Current Liabilities**

= ₹ 11,40,000 – ₹ 3,40,000 = ₹ 8,00,000

Step 2: **Equity** = **Equity Shareholders' Funds + Pref. Share Capital**

= ₹ 3,00,000 + ₹ 1,00,000 = ₹ 4,00,000

Step 3: Debt-Equity Ratio $= \frac{\textbf{Debt}}{\textbf{Equity}} = \frac{₹\,8,00,000}{₹\,4,00,000} = 2:1$

Note: *Reserves & Surplus are already adjusted in Equity Shareholders' Funds.*

ILLUSTRATION 31

Total Debt ₹ 24,00,000, Total Assets ₹ 28,00,000, Current Liabilities ₹ 8,00,000. Calculate Debt-Equity Ratio.

SOLUTION

Step 1: **Debt** = **Total Debt – Current Liabilities**

= ₹ 24,00,000 – ₹ 8,00,000 = ₹ 16,00,000

Step 2: **Equity** = **Total Assets – Total Debt**

= ₹ 28,00,000 – ₹ 24,00,000 = ₹ 4,00,000

Step 3: Debt-Equity Ratio $= \frac{\textbf{Debt}}{\textbf{Equity}} = \frac{₹\,16,00,000}{₹\,4,00,000} = 4:1$

ILLUSTRATION 32

Total Debt ₹ 6,00,000, Current Liabilities ₹ 2,00,000, Capital Employed ₹ 6,00,000. Calculate Debt-Equity Ratio.

SOLUTION

Step 1: **Debt** = **Total Debt – Current Liabilities**

= ₹ 6,00,000 – ₹ 2,00,000 = ₹ 4,00,000

Step 2: **Equity** = **Capital Employed – Debt**

= ₹ 6,00,000 – ₹ 4,00,000 = ₹ 2,00,000

Step 3: Debt-Equity Ratio $= \frac{\textbf{Debt}}{\textbf{Equity}} = \frac{₹\,4,00,000}{₹\,2,00,000} = 2:1$

ILLUSTRATION 33

Total Assets ₹ 14,00,000, Total Debt ₹ 12,00,000, Capital Employed ₹ 10,00,000. Calculate Debt-Equity Ratio.

SOLUTION

Step 1: **Equity** = **Total Assets – Total Debt**

= ₹ 14,00,000 – ₹ 12,00,000 = ₹ 2,00,000

Step 2: **Debt** = **Capital Employed – Equity**

= ₹ 10,00,000 – ₹ 2,00,000 = ₹ 8,00,000

Step 3: Debt-Equity Ratio $= \frac{\textbf{Debt}}{\textbf{Equity}} = \frac{₹\,8,00,000}{₹\,2,00,000} = 4:1$

ILLUSTRATION 34

X Ltd. has a Current Ratio of 3 : 1. Its net Working Capital is ₹ 2,00,000. Total Assets ₹ 3,50,000, Total Debt ₹ 3,00,000. Calculate Debt-Equity Ratio.

SOLUTION

Step 1: Current Assets and Current Liabilities

Current Ratio = **Current Assets/Current Liabilities** = 3

or, = Current Assets –3 Current Liabilities = 0 ......Eq. I

Working Capital = **Current Assets – Current Liabilities**

or, Current Assets – Current Liabilities = ₹ 2,00,000 ..... Eq. II

Subtracting Eq. II from Eq. I

2 Current Liabilities = ₹ 2,00,000

Current Liabilities = ₹ 2,00,000/2 = ₹ 1,00,000

Current Assets = ₹ 1,00,000 × 3 = ₹ 3,00,000

Step 2: Debt = Total Debt – Current Liabilities = ₹ 3,00,000 – ₹ 1,00,000 = ₹ 2,00,000

Step 3: Equity = Total Assets – Total Debt = ₹ 3,50,000 – ₹ 3,00,000 = ₹ 50,000

Step 4: Debt-Equity Ratio = Debt/Equity = ₹ 2,00,000/₹ 50,000 = 4 : 1

ILLUSTRATION 35

X Ltd. has a Liquid Ratio of 1.5 : 1. Its Net Working Capital is ₹ 1,20,000 and its Inventories are ₹ 80,000. Total Assets ₹ 3,80,000, Total Debt ₹ 2,80,000. Calculate Debt-Equity Ratio.

SOLUTION

Step 1: Current Assets and Current Liabilities

Liquid Ratio = **(CA – Stock)/CL** = 1.5

or, Current Assets – ₹ 80,000 = 1.5 Current Liabilities

or, Current Assets –1.5 Current Liabilities = ₹ 80,000 ...... Eq. I

Working Capital = **Current Assets – Current Liabilities**

or, Current Assets – Current Liabilities = ₹ 1,20,000 ...... Eq. II

Subtracting Eq. II from Eq. I

0.5 Current Liabilities = ₹ 40,000

Current Liabilities = ₹ 40,000/0.5 = ₹ 80,000

Current Assets = ₹ 80,000 + ₹ 1,20,000 = ₹ 2,00,000

Step 2: Debt = **Total Debt – Current Liabilities**

= ₹ 2,80,000 – ₹ 80,000 = ₹ 2,00,000

Step 3: Equity = **Total Assets – Total Debt**

= ₹ 3,80,000 – ₹ 2,80,000 = ₹ 1,00,000

Step 4: Debt-Equity Ratio = **Debt/Equity** = ₹ 2,00,000/₹ 1,00,000 = 2 : 1

ILLUSTRATION 36

Assuming that the Debt-Equity Ratio (defined as ratio of Debt to Equity) is 2, state, giving reason, whether this ratio will increase *or* decrease *or* will have no change in each one of the following cases:

(a) Purchase of a Fixed Asset on a credit of 2 months

(b) Purchase of a Fixed Asset on long-term deferred payment basis.

(c) Sale of a Fixed Asset (book value ₹ 4,000) at a loss of ₹ 3,000

(d) Sale of a Fixed Asset (book value ₹ 4,000) for ₹ 5,000
(e) Sale of a Fixed Asset (book value ₹ 4,000) for ₹ 4,000
(f) Issue of New Shares for cash
(g) Issue of New Shares against the purchase of a Fixed Asset
(h) Issue of Bonus Shares
(i) Redemption of Debentures for cash
(j) Conversion of Debentures into Equity Shares
(k) Declaration of a Final Dividend
(l) Payment of Final Dividend already declared
(m) Redemption of Redeemable Preference Shares
(n) Payment to Trade Creditors
(o) Discounting a Bill of Exchange of ₹ 50,000 at a discount of 10%.

SOLUTION

STATEMENT SHOWING THE EFFECT OF VARIOUS TRANSACTIONS ON DEBT-EQUITY RATIO OF 2 : 1

Transaction	*Effect on D/E Ratio*	*Reason*
(a)	No Effect	Neither the Debt nor the Equity are affected.
(b)	Increase	Debt is increased but Equity remains unchanged.
(c)	Increase	Equity is decreased by the amount of loss but Debt remains unchanged.
(d)	Decrease	Equity is increased by the amount of profit but Debt remains unchanged.
(e)	No Effect	Neither the Debt nor the Equity is affected.
(f)	Decrease	Equity is increased by the amount of issue of shares but Debt remains unchanged.
(g)	Decrease	Equity is increased by the amount of share capital issued but Debt remains unchanged.
(h)	No Effect	Neither the Debt nor the Equity is affected since there is only a conversion of accumulated profits into Share Capital.
(i)	Decrease	Debt is decreased but Equity remains unchanged.
(j)	Decrease	Debt is decreased and Equity is increased by the same amount.
(k)	No Effect	It represents merely the conversion of Provision into a Current Liability.
(l)	No Effect	Neither the Debt nor the Equity is affected.
(m)	Increase	Equity is decreased but Debt remains unchanged.
(n)	No Effect	Neither the Debt nor the Equity is affected.
(o)	Increase	Equity is decreased by ₹ 5,000 (discount) but Debt remains unchanged.

16.0 TOTAL ASSETS TO DEBT RATIO

MEANING OF TOTAL ASSETS TO DEBT RATIO

Total Assets to Debt Ratio establishes a relationship between Total Assets and Debt.

OBJECTIVE OF TOTAL ASSETS TO DEBT RATIO

The objective of computing Total Assets to Debt Ratio is to measure the safety margin available to the suppliers of long-term debts. It measures the extent to which debt is being covered by assets.

COMPONENTS OF TOTAL ASSETS TO DEBT RATIO

There are two components of this ratio as follows:

1. **Total Assets** mean all the Assets (i.e. Non-Current Assets & Current Assets).

CALCULATION OF TOTAL ASSETS

Particulars	₹
Method I	
A. Non-Current Assets (e.g. Net Fixed Assets, Non-Current Investments + Long-Term Loans & Advances)	....
B. + Current Assets	....
C. Total Assets [A + B]	....
Method II	
A. Shareholders' Funds	....
B. + Non-Current Liabilities (e.g. Long-term Borrowings, Long-term Provisions)	....
C. + Current Liabilities	....
D. Total Assets [A + B + C]	....
Method III	
A. Shareholders' Funds	....
B. + Total Debts [Whether Non-Current *or* Current]	....
C. Total Assets [A + B]	....
Method IV	
A. Capital Employed	....
B. + Current Liabilities	....
C. Total Assets [A + B]	....

2. **Debt** which means Non-Current Liabilities (e.g. Long-term Borrowings like Debentures, Bonds, Term Loans From Banks, Financial Institutions, Long-term Loans & Advances, Long-term Provisions) which are expected to be settled after 12 months from the date of Balance Sheet.

CALCULATION OF DEBT

1. Debt = Long-term Borrowings + Long-term Provisions
2. Debt = Total Debt – Current Liabilities
3. Debt = Capital Employed – Equity

   [**Note:** Capital Employed = Equity + Debt]

COMPUTATION OF TOTAL ASSETS TO DEBT RATIO

Total Assets to Debt Ratio is computed by dividing the Total Assets by the Debt. This ratio is usually expressed as a pure ratio e.g. 2 : 1. In the form of formula, this ratio may be expressed as follows:

$$\textbf{Total Assets to Debt Ratio} = \frac{\textbf{Total Assets}}{\textbf{Debt}}$$

TUTORIAL NOTE

Total Assets to Debt Ratio is calculated at a particular date and not for a particular period.

INTERPRETATION OF TOTAL ASSETS TO DEBT RATIO

Total Assets to Debt Ratio indicates the margin of safety to long-term creditors. A high Total Assets to Debt ratio implies the use of more Equity than Debt which means a larger safety margin for Long-term creditros since owner's equity is treated as a margin of safety by Long-term Creditors and vice versa.

ILLUSTRATION 37

Fixed Assets (Gross) ₹ 12,00,000, Accumulated Depreciation ₹ 2,00,000, Non-Current Investments ₹ 20,000, Long-term Loans & Advances ₹ 80,000, Current Assets ₹ 5,00,000, Current Liabilities ₹ 4,00,000, Long-term Borrowings ₹ 6,00,000, Long-term Provisions ₹ 2,00,000. Calculate Total Assets to Debt Ratio.

SOLUTION

Step 1: **Debt** = **Long-term Borrowings + Long-term Provisions**

= ₹ 6,00,000 + ₹ 2,00,000 = ₹ 8,00,000

Step 2: **Total Assets** = **Non-Current Assets + Current Assets**

= [(₹ 12,00,000 – ₹ 2,00,000) + ₹ 20,000 + ₹ 80,000] + ₹ 5,00,000

= ₹ 16,00,000

$$\textbf{Step 3: Total Assets to Debt Ratio} = \frac{\textbf{Total Assets}}{\textbf{Debt}} = \frac{₹\,16,00,000}{₹\,8,00,000} = 2:1$$

ILLUSTRATION 38

Equity Shareholders' Funds ₹ 3,00,000, Reserves & Surplus ₹ 1,00,000, Preference Share Capital ₹ 1,00,000, Total Debt ₹ 11,40,000, Current Assets ₹ 10,00,000, Working Capital ₹ 6,60,000. Calculate Total Assets to Debt Ratio.

SOLUTION

Step 1: Current Liabilities = **Current Assets – Working Capital**

= ₹ 10,00,000 – ₹ 6,60,000 = ₹ 3,40,000

Step 2: **Debt** = **Total Debt – Current Liabilities**

= ₹ 11,40,000 – ₹ 3,40,000 = ₹ 8,00,000

Step 3: Shareholders' Funds = **Equity Shareholders' Funds + Pref. Share Capital**

= ₹ 3,00,000 + ₹ 1,00,000 = ₹ 34,00,000

Step 4: **Total Assets** = **Shareholders' Funds + Total Debt**

= ₹ 4,00,000 + ₹ 11,40,000 = ₹ 15,40,000

$$\textbf{Step 5: Total Assets to Debt Ratio} = \frac{\textbf{Total Assets}}{\textbf{Debt}} = \frac{₹\,15,00,000}{₹\,8,00,000} = 77:40$$

Note: *Reserve & Surplus already included in Equity Shareholders' Funds.*

17.0 PROPRIETARY RATIO

MEANING OF PROPRIETARY RATIO

Proprietary Ratio measures a relationship between Proprietors' Funds and the Total Assets.

OBJECTIVE OF PROPRIETARY RATIO

The objective of computing this ratio is to measure the proportion of Total Assets financed by the Proprietors' Funds.

COMPONENTS OF PROPRIETARY RATIO

There are two components of this ratio as follows:

1. **Proprietors' Funds [or Shareholders' Funds]** which mean Funds belonging to all the Shareholders *(whether Equity or Preference)*.

CALCULATION OF PROPRIETORS' FUNDS [OR SHAREHOLDERS' FUNDS]

Particulars	₹	*Particulars*	₹
Method I		**Method IV**	
A. Share Capital (Equity + Pref.)	....	A. Non-Current Assets	....
B. + Reserves & Surplus	....	B. + Current Assets	....
C. Proprietors' Funds [A + B]	....	C. – Current Liabilities	(..........)
		D. – Non-Current Liabilities	(..........)
		E. Proprietors' Funds	....
Method II		**Method V**	
A. Equity Share Capital	....	A. Non-Current Assets	....
B. + Pref. Share Capital	....	B. + Working Capital	....
C. + Reserves & Surplus	....	C. – Non-Current Liabilities	(..........)
D. Proprietors' Funds [A + B + C]	....	D. Proprietors' Funds	....
Method III		**Method VI**	
A. Capital Employed	....	A. Total Assets	....
B. – Non-Current Liabilities	(..........)	B. – Total Debts [Current + Non-Current]	(..........)
C. Proprietors' Funds	....	C. Proprietors' Funds	....

2. **Total Assets** mean all the Assets (i.e. Non-Current Assets & Current Assets).

CALCULATION OF TOTAL ASSETS

Particulars	₹
Method I	
A. Non-Current Assets (e.g. Net Fixed Assets, Non-Current Investments + Long-Term Loans & Advances)	....
B. + Current Assets	....
C. Total Assets [A + B]	....
Method II	
A. Shareholders' Funds	....

B. + Non-Current Liabilities (e.g. Long-term Borrowings, Long-term Provisions)	....
C. + Current Liabilities	....
D. Total Assets [A + B + C]	....
Method III	
A. Shareholders' Funds	....
B. + Total Debts [Whether Non-Current *or* Current]	....
C. Total Assets [A + B]	....
Method IV	
A. Capital Employed	....
B. + Current Liabilities	....
C. Total Assets [A + B]	....

COMPUTATION OF PROPRIETARY RATIO

Proprietary Ratio is computed by dividing the Proprietors' Funds by Total Assets. It is expressed as a percentage. In the form of a formula, this ratio may be expressed as follows:

$$\textbf{Proprietary Ratio} = \frac{\textbf{Proprietors' Funds}}{\textbf{Total Assets}} \times 100$$

INTERPRETATION OF PROPRIETARY RATIO

Proprietary Ratio indicates the extent to which the assets of the enterprise have been financed out of Proprietors' Funds. A high proprietary ratio indicates the larger safety margin for creditors and the enterprise is not taking the benefit of trading on equity. A low proprietary ratio indicates the greater risk to creditors and the enterprise is taking the benefit of trading on equity.

ILLUSTRATION 39

From the following information, calculate Proprietary Ratio:

Share Capital	₹ 2,50,000	Reserves & Surplus	₹ 1,50,000
Non-Current Assets	₹ 11,00,000	Current Assets	₹ 5,00,000

SOLUTION

Step 1: Proprietors' Funds = **Share Capital + Reserves & Surplus**

= ₹ 2,50,000 + ₹ 1,50,000 = ₹ 4,00,000

Step 2: Total Assets = **Non-Current Assets + Current Assets**

= ₹ 11,00,000 + ₹ 5,00,000 = ₹ 16,00,000

$$\textbf{Step 3: Proprietary Ratio} = \frac{\textbf{Proprietors' Funds}}{\textbf{Total Assets}} \times 100 = \frac{₹\ 4,00,000}{₹\ 16,00,000} \times 100 = 25\%$$

ILLUSTRATION 40

From the following information, calculate Proprietary Ratio, Debt-Equity Ratio and Total Assets to Debt Ratio:

Net Fixed Assets ₹ 10,00,000, Non-Current Trade Investments ₹ 20,000. Long-term Loans & Advances ₹ 80,000. Current Assets ₹ 5,00,000, Equity Share Capital ₹ 1,50,000, 18% Pref. Share Capital ₹ 1,00,000, Reserves & Surplus ₹ 1,50,000, 12% Long-term Borrowings ₹ 6,00,000, Long-term Provisions ₹ 2,00,000, Current Liabilities ₹ 4,00,000.

SOLUTION

Step 1: **Debt** = **Long-term Borrowings + Long-term Provisions**

= ₹ 6,00,000 + ₹ 2,00,000 = ₹ 8,00,000

STEP 2: CALCULATION OF PROPRIETORS' FUNDS (OR EQUITY)

Liabilities Side Approach	₹	*Assets Side Approach*	₹
A. Equity Share Capital	1,50,000	A. Non-Current Assets [10,00,000 + 20,000 + 80,000]	11,00,000
B. + Pref. Share Capital	1,00,000		
C. + Reserves & Surplus	1,50,000	B. Current Assets	5,00,000
D. Proprietors' Funds	4,00,000	C. – Current Liabilities	4,00,000
		D. – Non-Current Liabilities [6,00,000 + 2,00,000]	8,00,000
		E. Proprietors' Funds	4,00,000

Step 3: **Total Assets** = **Non-Current Assets + Current Assets**

= ₹ 11,00,000 + ₹ 5,00,000 = ₹ 16,00,000

Step 4: Proprietary Ratio $= \frac{\textbf{Proprietors' Funds}}{\textbf{Total Assets}} \times \mathbf{100} = \frac{₹\ 4,00,000}{₹\ 16,00,000} \times 100 = 25\%$

Step 5: Debt-Equity Ratio $= \frac{\textbf{Debt}}{\textbf{Equity}} = \frac{₹\ 8,00,000}{₹\ 4,00,000} = 2:1$

Step 6: Total Assets to Debt Ratio $= \frac{\textbf{Total Assets}}{\textbf{Debt}} = \frac{₹\ 16,00,000}{₹\ 8,00,000} = 2:1$

ILLUSTRATION 41

Total Debt ₹ 24,00,000, Capital Employed ₹ 20,00,000, Current Assets ₹ 10,00,000, Working Capital ₹ 2,00,000. Calculate Debt-Equity Ratio, Total Assets to Debt Ratio and Proprietary Ratio.

SOLUTION

Step 1: Current Liabilities = **Current Assets – Working Capital**

= ₹ 10,00,000 – ₹ 2,00,000 = ₹ 8,00,000

Step 2: **Debt** = **Total Debt – Current Liabilities**

= ₹ 24,00,000 – ₹ 8,00,000 = ₹ 16,00,000

Step 3: **Total Assets** = **Capital Employed + Current Liabilities**

= ₹ 20,00,000 + ₹ 8,00,000 = ₹ 28,00,000

Step 4: Proprietors' Funds (or Equity) = Total Assets – Total Debt

= ₹ 28,00,000 – ₹ 24,00,000 = ₹ 4,00,000

or, = **Capital Employed – Debt**

= ₹ 20,00,000 – ₹ 16,00,000 = ₹ 4,00,000

Step 5: Debt-Equity Ratio = **Debt/Equity** = ₹ 16,00,000/₹ 4,00,000 = 4 : 1

Step 6: Total Assets to Debt Ratio = Total Assets/Debt = ₹ 28,00,000/₹ 16,00,000 = 7 : 4

Step 7: Proprietary Ratio $= \frac{\textbf{Proprietors' Funds}}{\textbf{Total Assets}} \times \mathbf{100} = \frac{₹\ 4,00,000}{₹\ 28,00,000} \times 100 = 14.29\%$

18.0 INTEREST COVERAGE RATIO (OR TIMES – INTEREST EARNED RATIO)

MEANING OF INTEREST COVERAGE RATIO

Interest Coverage Ratio estabilishes a relationship between Net Profit before Interest and Tax and Interest on Long-term Borrowings.

OBJECTIVE OF INTEREST COVERAGE RATIO

The objective of computing Interest Coverage Ratio is to measure the Debt Servicing Capacity of a firm so far as Fixed Interest on Long-term Borrowings is concerned.

COMPONENTS OF INTEREST COVERAGE RATIO

There are two components of Interest Coverage Ratio as follows:

1. **Net Profit before Interest and Tax**
2. **Interest on Long-term Borrowings**

COMPUTATION OF INTEREST COVERAGE RATIO

Interest Coverage Ratio is computed by dividing the Net Profit before Interest and Tax by Interest on Long-term Borrowings. This ratio is usually expressed as 'X' number of times. In the form of a formula, this ratio may be expressed as under:

$$\textbf{Interest Coverage Ratio} = \frac{\textbf{Net Profit before Interest and Tax}}{\textbf{Interest on Long-term Borrowings}} = \textbf{...Times}$$

INTERPRETATION OF INTEREST COVERAGE RATIO

Interest Coverage Ratio shows the number of times the amount of Interest on long-term Borrowings is covered by the profits out of which that will be paid. It indicates the limit beyond which the ability of the firm to service its debt would be adversely affected. ***For Example***, an Interest Coverage of 5 times would imply that even if the firm's Net Profit before Interest and Tax decreases by 80% of present level. The firm will still be able to pay interest out of profits. Higher the ratio, greater the firm's ability to pay interest but very high ratio may imply lesser use of debt and very effecient operations.

ILLUSTRATION 42

Net Profit before Interest and Tax ₹ 3,20,000. 10% Long term Borrowings ₹ 4,00,000. Calculate Interest Coverage Ratio.

SOLUTION

Step 1: Interest on Long-term Borrowing = ₹ 4,00,000 × 10/100 = ₹ 40,000

$$\textbf{Step 2: Interest Coverage Ratio} = \frac{\textbf{Net Profit before Interest and Tax}}{\textbf{Interest on Long-term Borrowings}}$$

$$= \frac{₹\ 3,20,000}{₹\ 40,000} = 8 \text{ times}$$

ILLUSTRATION 43

Net Profit after Interest and Tax ₹ 1,20,000, 10% Long-term Loan from Bank ₹ 1,20,000, 12% Debentures ₹ 4,00,000. Tax Rate 50%, Calculate the Interest Coverage Ratio.

SOLUTION

Step 1: Interest on Long-term Borrowings = [(₹ 1,20,000 × 10/100) + (₹ 4,00,000 × 12/100)]

= ₹ 60,000

Step 2: Net Profits before Interest and Tax

Particulars	₹
A. Net Profits after Interest and Tax	1,20,000
B. *Add:* Tax @ 50%	1,20,000
C. Net Profits after Interest but before Tax (A + B)	2,40,000
D. *Add:* Interest on Long-term Borrowings [(₹ 1,20,000 × 10/100) + (4,00,000 × 12/100)]	60,000
E. Net Profits before Interest and Tax (C + D)	3,00,000

Step 3: Interest Coverage Ratio $= \dfrac{\textbf{Net Profit before Interest and Taxes}}{\textbf{Interest on Long-term Borrowings}} = \dfrac{₹3{,}00{,}000}{₹60{,}000} = 5$ times

19.0 CAPITAL GEARING RATIO

MEANING OF CAPITAL GEARING RATIO

This ratio establishes a relationship between funds bearing Fixed Financial Payments and Equity Shareholder's Funds.

OBJECTIVE OF CAPITAL GEARING RATIO

The objective of computing this ratio is to measure the relative proportion of funds bearing Fixed Financial Payments to Equity Shareholder's Funds.

COMPONENTS OF CAPITAL GEARING RATIO

There are two components of this ratio as follows:—

1. **Funds bearing Fixed Financial Payments** e.g., Debentures,Bonds, Loans from financial institutions, Preference Share Capital.
2. **Equity Shareholder's Funds which means** equity share capital + Reserves & Surplus minus fictious assets.

COMPUTATION OF CAPITAL GEARING RATIO

This ratio is computed by dividing the funds bearing fixed financial payments by equity shareholder's funds. This ratio is usually expressed as a pure ratio e.g., 3 : 1. In the form of formula, this ratio may be expressed as follows

$$\text{Capital Gearing Ratio} = \frac{\text{Funds bearing Fixed Financial payments}}{\text{Equity Shareholders' Funds}}$$

TUTORIAL NOTE

Capital Gearing Ratio is calculated at a particular date and not for a particular period.

INTERPRETATION OF CAPITAL GEARING RATIO

It indicates the margin of safety available to suppliers of funds fixed financial payments. A high total Capital Gearing Ratio implies the use of *less* equity than funds bearing fixed financial payments which means a lower safty margin for funds bearing funds financial payments since owner's equity is treated as a margin of safty by the suppliers of funds bearing fixed financial payments and vice versa.

If the Capital Gearing Ratio is *less* than 1, the company is said to be lowly geared and if it is more than 1, it is said to be highly geared. Capital gearing shows the extent of the risk (in relation to payment of fixed financial payments) to which the company is subject and also the opportunity for trading on equity. Thus, the position highly geared and lowly geared company is as follows:

Basis of Comparison	Highly Geared Company	Lowly Geared Company
1. Risk	High	Low
2. Opportunity for Trading on Equity	High	Low
3. Equity Shareholders' Gain	Increases more if ROI > Rate of Interest & Pref. Dividend Decrease more if ROI < Rate Rate of Interest & Pre. Dividend	Increases *less* if ROI>Rate of Interest & Pref. Dividend Decreases *less* if ROI < Rate of Interest & Pref. Dividend

Thus, an enterprise should have neither a very high nor a very low ratio, it should have a satisfactory ratio. To judge whether the ratio is satisfactory *or* not, it should be compared with its own past ratios *or* with the ratio of similar enterprises in the same industry *or* with the industry average.

ILLUSTRATION 44

Calculate Capital Gearing Ratio from the following information:

15% Long-term Debts ₹ 8,00,000, 18% Preference Share Capital ₹ 1,00,000.

Equity Share Capital ₹ 2,00,000. Reserves & Surplus ₹ 1,50,000, Preliminary Expenses ₹ 50,000.

SOLUTION

$$\text{Capital Gearing Ratio} = \frac{\text{Funds bearing fixed Financial payments}}{\text{Equity Shareholders' Funds}}$$

$$= \frac{₹\,8{,}00{,}000 + ₹\,1{,}00{,}000}{₹\,2{,}00{,}000 + ₹\,1{,}50{,}000 - ₹\,50{,}000} = 3:1$$

20.0 PREFERENCE DIVIDEND COVERAGE RATIO

MEANING OF PREFERENCE DIVIDEND COVERAGE RATIO

This ratio establishes a relationship between net profits after interest and taxes and Preference Dividend on Preference Shares.

OBJECTIVE OF PREFERENCE DIVIDEND COVERAGE RATIO

The objective of computing this ratio is to measure the Preference Shares servicing capacity of a firm so far as Fixed Dividend on Preference Shares is concerned.

COMPONENTS OF PREFERENCE DIVIDEND COVERAGE RATIO

There are two components of this ratio as follows:

(i) Net profits after interest and taxes;

(ii) Preference Dividend on Preference Shares

COMPUTATION OF PREFERENCE DIVIDEND COVERAGE RATIO

This ratio is computed by dividing the net profits after interest and taxes by preference dividend on Preference Shares. This ratio is usually expressed as 'X' number of times. In the form of a formula, this ratio may be expressed as follows:

$$\text{Preference Dividend Coverage Ratio} = \frac{\text{Net Profit after interest and taxes}}{\text{Preference Dividend on Pref. Shares}}$$

INTERPRETATION OF PREFERENCE DIVIDEND COVERAGE RATIO

Preference Dividend Coverage Ratio shows the number of times the amount of Preference Dividend is covered by the profits out of which that will be paid. It indicates the limit beyond which the ability of the firm to service its preference share capital would be adversely affected. For instance, an preference dividend coverage of five times would imply that even if the firm's net profits after interest and tax decrease by 80% of the present level. The firm will still be able to pay preference dividend out of profits. Higher the ratio, greater the firm's ability to pay preference dividend but very high ratio may imply lesser use of preference share capital and very efficient operations.

ILLUSTRATION 45

Calculate Preference Dividend Coverage Ratio from the following information:

15% Debentures ₹ 8,00,000, Net Profit before Interest & Tax ₹ 6,00,000, Tax ₹ 50%. 16% ₹ 1,00,000 Pref. Shares of ₹ 100 each.

SOLUTION

Interest on Long-term Debt = ₹ 8,00,000 × 15/100 = ₹ 1,20,000

Net Profit after Interest & Tax = Net Profit before interest & tax – Interest – tax

= ₹ 6,00,000 – ₹ 1,20,000 – ₹ 2,40,000 = ₹ 2,40,000

Pref. Dividend = 16% of ₹ 1,00,000 = ₹ 16,000

$$\text{Pref. Dividend Coverage Ratio} = \frac{\text{Net Profit after Interest and Taxes}}{\text{Pref. Dividend on Pref. Share Capital}}$$

= ₹ 2,40,000/₹ 16,000 = 15 times

21.0 DEBT-SERVICE COVERAGE RATIO

MEANING OF DEBT-SERVICE COVERAGE RATIO

This ratio measures the relationship between Net Profits before Interest and Tax and Interest + Principal portion of instalment.

OBJECTIVE OF DEBT-SERVICE COVERAGE RATIO

The objective of computing this ratio is to determine the firm's capacity to pay off both the interest and principal portion of the instalment.

COMPONENTS OF DEBT-SERVICE COVERAGE RATIO

There are two components of this ratio as follows:

(i) Net Profit before Interest and Tax

(ii) Interest and Principal portion of Instalment

COMPUTATION OF DEBT-SERVICE COVERAGE RATIO

This ratio is calculated by dividing the Net Profit before Interest and Tax by the aggregate of Interest and Principal portion of Instalment. It is usually expressed in number of times. In the form of a formula, this ratio may be expressed as follows:

$$\text{Debt – Service Ratio} = \frac{\text{Net Profit before Interest and Tax}}{\text{Interest} + \dfrac{\text{Principal portion of instalment}}{1 - \text{Tax Rate}}} = \text{... times}$$

Note: *The principal portion of instalment is adjusted for tax effects since such payment is not deductible from net profit for tax purposes.*

INTERPRETATION OF DEBT-SERVICE COVERAGE RATIO

Debt-Service Coverage Ratio shows the number of times the amount of interest on long-term debts and the principal portion of instalment is covered by the profits out of which that will be paid. It indicates the limit beyond which the ability of the firm to service its debt would be adversely affected. For instance, an debt service of five times would imply that even if the firm's net profits before interest and tax decrease by 80% of the present level, the firm will still be able to pay interest and instalment out of profits. Higher the ratio, greater the firm's ability to pay current interest and instalment but very high ratio may imply lesser use of debt and very efficient operations.

Thus, an enterprise should have neither a very high nor a very low ratio, it should have a satisfactory ratio. To judge whether the ratio is satisfactory *or* not, it should be compared with its own past ratios *or* with the ratio of similar enterprises in the same industry *or* with the industry average.

ILLUSTRATION 46

Net profit before Interest and Tax ₹ 8,50,000, 10% Debentures (payable in 10 instalments) ₹ 7,00,000. Tax Rate 30%, Calculate Debt-Service Coverage Ratio.

SOLUTION

$$\text{Debt Service Coverage Ratio} = \frac{\text{Net Profit before Interest and Taxes}}{\text{Interest on Long-term Debt} + \dfrac{\text{Principal portion}}{1-\text{Tax Rate}}}$$

$$= \frac{₹\ 8,50,000}{₹\ 70,000 + \dfrac{₹\ 70,000}{(1-0.3)}} = 5 \text{ times}$$

ALTERNATIVE APPROACH I

Some Accountants who are interested in determining the firm's Operating capacity to pay off both interest and principal, prefer to calculate the Debt Service Coverage Ratio as follows:

$$\text{Debt-Service Coverage Ratio} = \frac{\text{Funds from operations before Interest and Taxes}}{\text{Interest} + \dfrac{\text{Principal portion}}{1-\text{Tax Rate}}}$$

Note: *Funds from operations before Interest and Taxes is computed as follows:*

A.	Net Profit before Interest and Taxes	XXX
B.	*Add:* Depreciation	XXX
C.	*Add:* Amortisation like goodwill, preliminary expenses	XXX
D.	*Add:* Non-Operating Adjustments like Loss on Sale of Fixed Assets	XXX
E.	Funds from operations	XXX

ILLUSTRATION 47

Net Profit before interest and tax ₹ 8,50,000, 10% Debentures (payable in 10 instalments) ₹ 7,00,000, Depreciation ₹ 1,00,000, Goodwill w/o ₹ 50,000, Loss on Sale of Fixed Assets ₹ 20,000, Tax Rate 30% Calculate Debt Service Coverage Ratio.

SOLUTION

STEP 1 — CASH FROM OPERATIONS BEFORE INTEREST AND TAX

A.	Net Profit before Interest and Tax	8,50,000
B.	*Add:* Depreciation	1,00,000

C. *Add:* Goodwill w/o	50,000
D. *Add:* Loss on Sale of Fixed Asset	20,000
E. Funds from Operations before Interest and Tax	10,20,000

Step 2 —

$$\text{Debt-Service coverage Ratio} = \frac{\text{Funds from operations before Interest and Taxes}}{\text{Interest} + \dfrac{\text{Principal portion}}{1-\text{Tax Rate}}}$$

$$= \frac{₹\ 10{,}20{,}000}{₹\ 70{,}000 + \dfrac{₹\ 70{,}000}{1-0.3}}$$

$$= ₹\ 10{,}20{,}000/₹\ 1{,}70{,}000 = 6 \text{ times}$$

ALTERNATIVE APPROACH II

Some Accountants who are interested in determining the firm's liquid capacity to pay off both interest and principal, prefer to calculate the Debt Service Coverage Ratio as follows:

Debt-Service Coverage Ratio = Cash from operations before Interest and TaxesInterest + Principal portion1 – Tax Rate

Note: Cash from operations before Interest and Taxes is computed as follows:

A. Net Profit before Interest and Taxes	xxx
B. *Add:* Depreciation	xxx
C. *Add:* Amortisation like goodwill, preliminary expenses	xxx
D. *Add:* Non-Operating Adjustments like Loss on Sale of Fixed Assets	xxx
E. *Add:* Decrease in Current Assets and Increase in Current Liabilities	xxx
F. *Less:* Increase in Current Assets and Decrease in Current Liabilities	(xxx)
G. Cash from operations	xxx

ILLUSTRATION 48

Net profit before interest and tax ₹ 8,50,000, 10% Debentures (payable in 10 instalments) ₹ 7,00,000, Depreciation ₹ 1,00,000, Goodwill w/o ₹ 50,000, Loss on Sale of Fixed Asset ₹ 20,000, Increase in Current Assets ₹ 3,10,000, Decrease in Current Liabilities ₹ 2,00,000, Tax Rate 30% Calculate Debt Service Coverage Ratio.

SOLUTION

STEP 1 — CASH FROM OPERATIONS BEFORE INTEREST AND TAX

A. Net Profit before Interest and Tax	8,50,000
B. *Add:* Depreciation	1,00,000
C. *Add:* Goodwill w/o	50,000
D. *Add:* Loss on Sale of Fixed Asset	20,000
E. *Less:* Increase in Current Assets	(3,10,000)
Decrease in Current Liabilities	(2,00,000)
F. Cash from Operations before Interest and Tax	5,10,000

Step 2 —

$$\text{Debt-Service coverage Ratio} = \frac{\text{Cash from operations before Interest and Taxes}}{\text{Interest} + \dfrac{\text{Principal portion}}{1 - \text{Tax Rate}}}$$

$$= \frac{₹\ 5,10,000}{₹\ 70,000 + \dfrac{₹\ 70,000}{1 - 0.3}}$$

$$= ₹\ 5,10,000/₹\ 1,70,000 = 3 \text{ times}$$

22.0 ACTIVITY RATIOS

Meaning	Activity Ratios measure the effectiveness with which a firm uses its available resources. These ratios help in commenting on the efficiency of the enterprise in managing its assets. These ratios are also called 'Turnover Ratios' since they indicate the speed with which the resources are being turned (or converted) into Revenue from Operations.
Activity Ratios	Usually the following Activity Turnover Ratios are calculated: 1. Capital Turnover Ratio 2. Fixed Assets Turnover Ratio 3. Current Assets Turnover Ratio 4. Net Working Capital Turnover Ratio 5. Inventory Turnover Ratio 6. Debtors Turnover Ratio 7. Creditors Turnover Ratio **TUTORIAL NOTE** *These ratios may be calculated with reference to **Revenue from Operations or Cost of Revenue from Operations** but the same basis (i.e., Revenue from Operations or Cost of Revenue from Operations) once selected, should be used on consistent basis so as to facilitate the comparison of figures of one year with that of another year.*

23.0 INVENTORY TURNOVER RATIO

MEANING OF INVENTORY TURNOVER

Inventory Turnover Ratio establishes a relationship between Cost of Revenue from Operations and Average Inventory.

OBJECTIVE OF INVENTORY TURNOVER

The objective of computing Inventory Turnover ratio is to determine the efficiency with which the Inventory of Finished Goods is converted into Revenue from Operations.

COMPONENTS OF INVENTORY TURNOVER

There are two components of Inventory Turnover Ratio as follows:

1. **Cost of Revenue from Operations**

   = Opening Inventory + Net Purchases + Direct Expenses – Closing Inventory

   or, = Cost of Materials Consumed + Purchases of Stock-in-Trade + Changes in Inventories of FInished Goods, Work-in-Progress and Stock-in-Trade + Direct Expenses

SOLUTION

Step 1: Cost of Revenue from Operations = (Cash Revenue from Operations + Credit Revenue from Operations) – Gross Profit

= (₹ 1,00,000 + ₹ 3,00,000) – (₹ 4,00,000 × 25/100)

= ₹ 3,00,000

Step 2: Inventory Turnover Ratio = $\dfrac{\textbf{Cost of Revenue from Operations}}{\textbf{Average Inventory}}$

3 = $\dfrac{₹\ 3,00,000}{\text{Average Inventory}}$

Average Inventory = ₹ 3,00,000/3 = ₹ 1,00,000

(OS + CS)/2 = ₹ 1,00,000

or, OS + CS = ₹ 1,00,000 × 2 = ₹ 2,00,000

OS + CS = ₹ 2,00,000 Eq. I

CS – 3 OS = 0 Eq. II

Subtracting Eq. II from Eq. I

4 OS = ₹ 2,00,000

OS = ₹ 2,00,000/4 = ₹ = 50,000

CS = ₹ 50,000 × 3 = ₹ 1,50,000

ILLUSTRATION 52

Cash Revenue from Operations 25% of total Revenue from Operations, Credit Revenue from Operations ₹ 3,00,000, Gross Profit 33-1/3% on Cost of Revenue from Operations, Inventory Turnover Ratio 3 Times, Inventory at the end was 3 times more than that in the beginning. Calculate Opening Inventory and Closing Inventory.

SOLUTION

Step 1: Cost of Revenue from Operations = Cash Revenue from Operations + Credit Revenue from Operations – Gross Profit

= ₹ 1,00,000 + ₹ 3,00,000 – (₹ 4,00,000 × 25/100)

= ₹ 3,00,000

Step 2: Inventory Turnover Ratio = $\dfrac{\textbf{Cost of Revenue from Operations}}{\textbf{Average Inventory}}$ = ₹ 3,00,000

3 = $\dfrac{₹\ 3,00,000}{\text{Average Inventory}}$

Average Inventory = ₹ 3,00,000/3 = ₹ 1,00,000

(OS + CS)/2 = ₹ 1,00,000

or, OS + CS = ₹ 1,00,000 × 2 = ₹ 2,00,000

OS + CS = ₹ 2,00,000 ...Eq. I

CS – 4OS = 0 ...Eq. II

Subtracting Eq. II from Eq. I

5 OS = ₹ 2,00,000

OS = ₹ 2,00,000/5 = ₹ 40,000

CS = ₹ 40,000 × 4 = ₹ 1,60,000

ILLUSTRATION 53

Cash Revenue from Operations 25% of total Revenue from Operations, Credit Revenue from Operations ₹ 3,00,000, Gross Profit 33-1/3% on Cost of Revenue from Operations, Inventory Turnover Ratio 3 Times. Inventory in the beginning was 1/3rd of Inventory at the end. Calculate Opening Inventory and Closing Inventory.

SOLUTION

Step 1: Cost of Revenue from Operations = (Cash Revenue from Operations + Credit Revenue from Operations) – Gross Profit

= (₹ 1,00,000 + ₹ 3,00,000) – (₹ 4,00,000 × 25/100)

= ₹ 3,00,000

Step 2: Inventory Turnover Ratio = $\dfrac{\textbf{Cost of Revenue from Operations}}{\textbf{Average Inventory}}$

$$3 = \frac{₹\ 3,00,000}{\text{Average Inventory}}$$

Average Inventory = ₹ 3,00,000/3 = ₹ 1,00,000

(OS + CS)/2 = ₹ 1,00,000

or, OS + CS = ₹ 1,00,000 × 2 = ₹ 2,00,000

OS + CS = ₹ 2,00,000 Eq. I

OS – 1/3CS = 0 Eq. II

Subtracting Eq. II from Eq. I

4/3 CS = ₹ 2,00,000

CS = ₹ 2,00,000 × 3/4 = ₹ 1,50,000

OS = ₹ 1,50,000 × 1/3 = ₹ 50,000

ILLUSTRATION 54

Inventory Turnover Ratio 5 times, Cash Revenue from Operations 33-1/3% of Total Revenue from Operations, Credit Revenue from Operations ₹ 16,80,000, Gross Profit @ 33-1/3% on Cost. Inventory in the beginning is 40% of the Inventory at the end.Calculate Opening Inventory and Closing Inventory.

SOLUTION

Step 1: Total Revenue from Operations

= Credit Revenue from Operations + Cash Revenue from Operations

= ₹ 16,80,000 + 50% of ₹ 16,80,000 = ₹ 16,80,000 + ₹ 8,40,000 = ₹ 25,20,000

Step 2: Cost of Revenue from Operations

= Total Revenue from Operations – Gross Profit

= ₹ 25,20,000 – 25% of ₹ 25,20,000 = ₹ 25,20,000 – ₹ 6,30,000 = ₹ 18,90,000

Step 3: Inventory Turnover Ratio = $\dfrac{\textbf{Cost of Re venue from Operations}}{\textbf{Average Inventory}}$

Average Inventory = ₹ 18,90,000/ 5 = ₹ 3,78,000

(OS + CS)/2 = ₹ 3,78,000

or, OS + CS = ₹ 3,78,000 × 2 = ₹ 7,56,000 ... Eq. I

Step 4: Formation of Second Equation

$$OS = 40\% \text{ of } CS$$

$$OS - 0.40\,CS = 0 \qquad \text{... Eq. II}$$

Subtracting Equation II from Equation I

$$1.4\,CS = ₹\,7{,}56{,}000$$

$$CS = ₹\,7{,}56{,}000/1.4 = ₹\,5{,}40{,}000$$

$$OS = 40\% \text{ of } ₹\,5{,}40{,}000 = ₹\,2{,}16{,}000$$

24.0 DEBTORS TURNOVER RATIO MEANING OF DEBTORS TURNOVER RATIO

Debtors Turnover Ratio establishes a relationship between Credit Revenue from Operations and Average Trade Receivables.

OBJECTIVE OF DEBTORS TURNOVER RATIO

The objective of computing Debtors Turnover Ratio is to determine the efficiency with which the Trade Receivables are managed and collected.

COMPONENTS OF DEBTORS TURNOVER RATIO

There are two components of Debtors Turnover Ratio as follows:

1. **Credit Revenue from Operations**
   = Revenue from Operations – Cash Revenue from Operations
2. **Average Trade Receivables**
   $$= \frac{\textbf{Opening Trade Receivables + Closing Trade Receivables}}{2}$$
   Note: Trade Receivables = Trade Debtors + Bills Receivable

TUTORIAL NOTES

1. *The term 'Trade Receivables' do not include Debtors which do not arise from the Sale of goods in which the enterprise deals in.*
2. ***The 'Provision for doubtful debts' is not deducted from the total amount of Trade Receivables since here, the purpose is to calculate the number of days for which Revenue from Operations are tied up in Trade Receivables and not to ascertain the Realizable Value of Trade Receivables. If the 'Provision for doubtful debts' were deducted, it would give an impression that a portion of Trade Receivables (to the extent of such provision) has already been collected.***
3. *If the figure of Average Trade Receivables cannot be ascertained due to the absence of the figure of Opening Trade Receivables, the figure of Closing Trade Receivables may be applied by giving a suitable note to that effect.*
4. *If the figure of Credit Revenue from Operations is not ascertainable, the figure of total Revenue from Operations given may be used assuming that all Revenue from Operations are credit Revenue from Operations.*

COMPUTATION OF DEBTORS TURNOVER RATIO

Debtors Turnover Ratio is computed by dividing the Credit Revenue from Operations by Average Trade Receivables. This ratio is usually expressed as 'x' number of times. In the form of a formula, this ratio may be expressed as follows:

$$\textbf{Debtors Turnover Ratio} = \frac{\textbf{Credit Revenue from Operations}}{\textbf{Average Trade Receivables}} = \textbf{. . . Times}$$

INTERPRETATION OF DEBTORS TURNOVER RATIO

Debtors Turnover Ratio indicates both the quality of Trade Receivables and the credit collection efforts of the enterprise. It indicates the speed with which the debtors are converted into cash each year. In general, a high ratio indicates the shorter collection period which implies prompt payments by Trade Receivables, and a low ratio indicates a longer collection period which implies delayed payments by Trade Receivables. However, too high ratio and too low ratio calls for further investigation. A too high ratio may be the result of a restrictive credit and collection policy which may curtail the Revenue from Operations and consequently profits. On the other hand, a too low ratio may be the result of liberal and inefficient credit and collection policy which may involve the risk of bad debts and burden of high interest cost involved in maintaining a higher level of Trade Receivables. Thus, a firm should neither have a very high nor a very low Debtors Turnover Ratio, but should have a satisfactory level.

DEBT COLLECTION PERIOD (OR TRADE RECEIVABLES VELOCITY)

Debt Collection Period shows an average period for which the Credit Revenue from Operations remains outstanding *or* the Average Credit Period actually enjoyed by the Trade Receivables. It measures the quality of Trade Receivables. It indicates the rapidity *or* slowness with which the money is collected from Trade Receivables. This period may be calculated as follows:

$$\textbf{Debt Collection Period} = \frac{\textbf{Average Trade Receivables}}{\textbf{Average Credit Revenue from Operations per day}}$$

= . . . Times

or,

$$= \frac{\textbf{12 months/52 weeks/365 days}}{\textbf{Debtors Turnover Ratio}} = \textbf{. . . Months/Weeks/Days}$$

Note: ***Average Credit Revenue from Operations per day***

$$= \frac{\textbf{Net Credit Revenue from Operations for the year}}{\textbf{No. of Working Days in the year}}$$

= ...per day

ILLUSTRATION 55

Calculate the Debtors Turnover Ratio and Average Debt Collection Period for the year from the following information:

Particulars	*Opening* ₹	*Closing* ₹
Trade Debtors	15,000	45,000
Bills Receivable	5,000	15,000
Provision for Doubtful Debts	1,500	4,500

Total Revenue from Operations ₹ 2,00,000, Cash Revenue from Operations ₹ 40,000.

SOLUTION

Step 1: Credit Revenue from Operations

= Total Revenue from Operations – Cash Revenue from Operations

= ₹ 2,00,000 – ₹ 40,000 = ₹ 1,60,000

Step 2: Average Trade Receivables

$$= \frac{\textbf{Opening Trade Receivables + Closing Trade Receivables}}{\textbf{2}}$$

$$= \frac{(₹\,15{,}000 + ₹\,5{,}000) + (₹\,45{,}000 + ₹\,15{,}000)}{2} = ₹\,40{,}000$$

Step 3: Debtors Turnover Ratio = $\frac{\textbf{Credit Revenue from Operations}}{\textbf{Average Trade Receivables}} = \frac{₹\,1,60,000}{₹\,40,000}$ = 4 times

Step 4: Average Debt Collection Period = $\frac{\textbf{12 months}}{\textbf{Debtors Turnover Ratio}} = \frac{\text{12 Months}}{\text{4 Times}}$ = 3 Months

ILLUSTRATION 56

Cash Revenue from Operations 33-1/3% of Credit Revenue from Operations, Cost of Revenue from Operations ₹ 3,00,000, Gross Profit 25% on Revenue from Operations,, Debtors Turnover Ratio 3 Times. Closing Trade Receivables were ₹ 1,00,000 in excess of Opening Trade Receivables. Calculate Opening Trade Receivables and Closing Trade Receivables.

SOLUTION:

Step 1: Total Revenue from Operations

= Cost of Revenue from Operations + Gross Profit

= ₹ 3,00,000 + (₹ 3,00,000 × 1/3) = ₹ 4,00,000

Step 2: Credit Revenue from Operations

= Total Revenue from Operations – Cash Revenue from Operations

= ₹ 4,00,000 – (₹ 4,00,000 × 25/100) = ₹ 3,00,000

Step 3: Debtors Turnover Ratio = $\frac{\textbf{Credit Revenue from Operations}}{\textbf{Average Trade Receivables}}$ = ₹ 3,00,000

Average Trade Receivables = ₹ 3,00,000/3 = ₹ 1,00,000

(OR + CR)/2 = ₹ 1,00,000

or, OR + CR = ₹ 1,00,000 × 2 = ₹ 2,00,000

OR + CR = ₹ 2,00,000 ...Eq. I

CR – OR = ₹ 1,00,000 ...Eq. II

Adding both the equations

2 CR = ₹ 3,00,000

CR = ₹ 3,00,000/2 = ₹ 1,50,000

OR = ₹ 1,50,000 – ₹ 1,00,000 = ₹ 50,000

ILLUSTRATION 57

Cash Revenue from Operations 33-1/3% of Credit Revenue from Operations, Cost of Revenue from Operations ₹ 3,00,000, Gross Profit 25% on Revenue from Operations,, Debtors Turnover Ratio 3 Times. Trade Receivables at the end were 3 times that in the beginning. Calculate Opening Trade Receivables and Closing Trade Receivables.

SOLUTION:

Step 1: Total Revenue from Operations

= Cost of Revenue from Operations + Gross Profit

= ₹ 3,00,000 + (₹ 3,00,000 × 1/3) = ₹ 4,00,000

Step 2: Credit Revenue from Operations

= Total Revenue from Operations – Cash Revenue from Operations

= ₹ 4,00,000 – (₹ 4,00,000 × 25/100) = ₹ 3,00,000

Step 3: Debtors Turnover Ratio = $\frac{\textbf{Credit Revenue from Operations}}{\textbf{Average Trade Receivables}} = \frac{₹3,00,000}{₹1,00,000} = 3$

Average Trade Receivables = ₹ 3,00,000/3 = ₹ 1,00,000

(OR +CR)/2 = ₹ 1,00,000

or, OR + CR = ₹ 1,00,000 × 2 = ₹ 2,00,000

OR + CR = ₹ 2,00,000 ...Eq. I

CR – 3 OR = 0 ...Eq. II

Subtracting Eq. II from Eq. I

4 OR = ₹ 2,00,000

OR = ₹ 2,00,000/4 = ₹ 50,000

CR = ₹ 50,000 × 3 = ₹ 1,50,000

ILLUSTRATION 58

Cash Revenue from Operations 33-1/3% of Credit Revenue from Operations, Cost of Revenue from Operations ₹ 3,00,000, Gross Profit 25% on Revenue from Operations, Debtors Turnover Ratio 3 Times. Trade Receivables at the end were 3 times more than that in the beginning. Calculate Opening Trade Receivables and Closing Trade Receivables.

SOLUTION

Step 1: Total Revenue from Operations

= Cost of Revenue from Operations + Gross Profit

= ₹ 3,00,000 + (₹ 3,00,000 × 1/3) = ₹ 4,00,000

Step 2: Credit Revenue from Operations

= Total Revenue from Operations – Cash Revenue from Operations

= ₹ 4,00,000 – (₹ 4,00,000 × 25/100) = ₹ 3,00,000

Step 3: Debtors Turnover Ratio = $\frac{\textbf{Credit Revenue from Operations}}{\textbf{Average Trade Receivables}} = \frac{₹3,00,000}{₹1,00,000} = 3 \text{ times}$

Average Trade Receivables = ₹ 3,00,000/3 = ₹ 1,00,000

(OR + CR)/2 = ₹ 1,00,000

or, OR + CR = ₹ 1,00,000 × 2 = ₹ 2,00,000

OR + CR = ₹ 2,00,000 ...Eq. I

CR – 4 OR = 0 ...Eq. II

Subtracting Eq. II from Eq. I

5 OR = ₹ 2,00,000

OR = ₹ 2,00,000/5 = ₹ 40,000

CR = ₹ 40,000 × 4 = ₹ 1,60,000

ILLUSTRATION 59

Cash Revenue from Operations 33-1/3% of Credit Revenue from Operations, Cost of Revenue from Operations ₹ 3,00,000, Gross Profit 25% on Revenue from Operations, Debtors Turnover Ratio 3 Times. Trade Receivables in the beginning were 1/3rd of Trade Receivables at the end. Calculate Opening Trade Receivables and Closing Trade Receivables.

SOLUTION

Step 1: Total Revenue from Operations

= Cost of Revenue from Operations + Gross Profit

= ₹ 3,00,000 + (₹ 3,00,000 × 1/3) = ₹ 4,00,000

Step 2: Credit Revenue from Operations

= Total Revenue from Operations – Cash Revenue from Operations

= ₹ 4,00,000 – (₹ 4,00,000 × 25/100) = ₹ 3,00,000

Step 3: Debtors Turnover Ratio = $\frac{\textbf{Credit Revenue from Operations}}{\textbf{Average Trade Receivables}} = \frac{₹\,3,00,000}{₹\,1,00,000} = 3$

Average Trade Receivables = ₹ 3,00,000/3 = ₹ 1,00,000

(OR + CR)/2 = ₹ 1,00,000

or, OR + CR = ₹ 1,00,000 × 2 = ₹ 2,00,000

OR + CR = ₹ 2,00,000 ...Eq. I

OR –1/3 CR = 0 ...Eq. II

Subtracting Eq. II from Eq. I

CR = ₹ 2,00,000

4/3 CR = ₹ 2,00,000

CR = ₹ 2,00,000 × 3/4 = ₹ 1,50,000

OR = ₹ 1,50,000/3 = ₹ 50,000

ILLUSTRATION 60

Average Debt Collection Period 2.4 months, Cash Revenue from Operations 33-1/3% of Credit Revenue from Operations, Inventory Turnover Ratio 5 times, Opening Inventory ₹ 5,40,000, Closing Inventory ₹ 2,16,000, Gross Profit @ 25% on Revenue from Operations. Trade Receivables in the beginning are 40% of the Trade Receivables at the end. Calculate Opening Trade Receivables and Closing Trade Receivables.

SOLUTION

Step 1: Inventory Turnover Ratio = $\frac{\textbf{Cost of Revenue from Operations}}{\textbf{Average Inventory}}$

Cost of Revenue from Operations = 5 × [(₹ 5,40,000 + ₹ 2,16,000)/2] = ₹ 18,90,000

Step 2: Revenue from Operations = Cost of Revenue from Operations + Gross Profit

= ₹ 18,90,000 + 33-1/3% of ₹ 18,90,000 = ₹ 25,20,000

Step 3: Credit Revenue from Operations

= Total Revenue from Operations – Cash Revenue from Operations

= ₹ 25,20,000 – 25% of ₹ 25,20,000 = ₹ 25,20,000 – ₹ 6,30,000 = ₹ 18,90,000

Step 4: Debtors Turnover Ratio = 12 Months/Average Debt Collection Period

= 12/2.4 = 5 Times

Step 5: Average Trade Receivables = $\frac{\textbf{Credit Revenue from Operations}}{\textbf{Debtors Turnover Ratio}}$

= ₹ 18,90,000 / 5 = ₹ 3,78,000

(OR + CR)/2 = ₹ 3,78,000

or, OR + CR = ₹ 3,78,000 × 2 = ₹ 7,56,000 ...Eq. I

Step 6: Formation of Second Equation

OR = 40% of CR

OR – 0.40 CR = 0 ...Eq. II

Subtracting Equation II from Equation I

1.4 CR = ₹ 7,56,000

CR = ₹ 7,56,000/1.4 = ₹ 5,40,000

OR = 40% of ₹ 5,40,000 = ₹ 2,16,000

25.0 CREDITORS TURNOVER RATIO

MEANING OF CREDITORS TURNOVER RATIO

Creditors Turnover Ratio establishes a relationship between Net Credit Purchases and Average Trade Payables.

OBJECTIVE OF CREDITORS TURNOVER RATIO

The objective of computing Creditors Turnover Ratio is to determine the efficiency with which the Trade Payables are managed and paid.

COMPONENTS OF CREDITORS TURNOVER RATIO

There are two components of Creditors Turnover ratio as follows:

1. **Net Credit Purchases = Net Purchases – Cash Purchases**
2. **Average Trade Payables** $= \dfrac{\textbf{Opening Trade Payables + Closing Trade Payables}}{\textbf{2}}$

Note: Trade Payables = Trade Creditors + Bills Payable

TUTORIAL NOTES

1. *The term 'Trade Payables' do not include Creditors which do not arise from the purchases of goods in which the enterprise deals in.*
2. *The 'Reserve for Discount on Trade Payables is not deducted from the total amount of Trade Payables since, here the purpose is to calculate the numbers of days for which the purchases remain outstanding and not to ascertain the net amount likely to be paid (after discount). If the 'Reserve for Discount on Trade Payables were deducted, it would give an impression that a portion of Trade Payables (to the extent of such reserve) has already been discharged.*
3. *If the figure of Average Trade Payables cannot be ascertained due to the absence of the figure of Opening Trade Payables, the figure of Closing Trade Payables may be applied by giving a suitable note to that effect.*
4. *If the figure of Net Credit Purchases is not ascertainable the figure of Total Purchases given may be applied assuming that all purchases are Credit Purchases.*

COMPUTATION OF CREDITORS TURNOVER RATIO

Creditors Turnover ratio is computed by dividing the Net Credit Purchases by Average Trade Receivables. This ratio is usually expressed as 'x' number of times. In the form of formula, this ratio may be expressed as follows:

$$\textbf{Creditors Turnover Ratio} = \frac{\textbf{Net Credit Purchases}}{\textbf{Average Trade Payables}} = \textbf{. . . Times}$$

INTERPRETATION OF CREDITORS TURNOVER RATIO

Creditors Turnover indicates the speed with which the Creditors turn over on an average each year. In general, a high ratio indicates the shorter payment period which implies either the availability of *less* credit *or* earlier payments and a low ratio indicates a larger payment period which implies either the availability of more credit *or* delayed payments.

AVERAGE DEBT PAYMENT

Average Debt payment period shows an average period for which the credit purchases remain outstanding *or* the average credit period actually availed of. This period may be calculated as follows:

$$\textbf{Average Debt Payment Period} = \frac{\textbf{Average Trade Payables}}{\textbf{Average Net Credit Purchases per day}} = \textbf{. . . Times}$$

$$\textbf{or,} \quad = \frac{\textbf{12 months/52 weeks/365 days}}{\textbf{Debtors Turnover Ratio}} = \textbf{. . . Months/Weeks/Days}$$

Note: ***Average Credit Revenue from Operations per day***

$$= \frac{\textbf{Net Credit Purchases for the year}}{\textbf{No. of Working Days in the year}} = \textbf{...per day}$$

ILLUSTRATION 61

Calculate the Creditors Turnover Ratio and Average Debt payment Period for the year from the following information:

Particulars	*Opening* ₹	*Closing* ₹
Trade Creditors	15,000	45,000
Bills Payable	5,000	15,000
Reserve for Discount on Trade Payables	1,500	4,500
Total Purchases ₹ 2,00,000, Cash Purchases ₹ 40,000.		

SOLUTION

Step 1: Net Credit Purchases = **Total Purchases – Cash Purchases**

$= ₹\ 2,00,000 - ₹\ 40,000 = ₹\ 1,60,000$

$$\textbf{Step 2: Average Trade Payables} = \frac{\textbf{Opening Trade Receivables + Closing Trade Receivables}}{\textbf{2}}$$

$$= \frac{(₹\ 15,000 + ₹\ 5,000) + (₹\ 45,000 + ₹\ 15,000)}{2} = ₹\ 40,000$$

$$\textbf{Step 3: Creditors Turnover Ratio} = \frac{\textbf{Net Credit Purchases}}{\textbf{Average Trade Payables}} = \frac{₹\ 1,60,000}{₹\ 40,000} = 4 \text{ times}$$

$$\textbf{Step 4: Average Debt Payment Period} = \frac{\textbf{12 months}}{\textbf{Debtors Turnover Ratio}} = \frac{12 \text{ Months}}{4 \text{ Times}} = 3 \text{ Months}$$

Note: *Reserve for Discount on Closing Trade Payables is not deducted from Trade Payables.*

ILLUSTRATION 62

Cash Purchases 25% of Total Purchases, Revenue from Operations ₹ 4,00,000, Gross Profit @ 25% on Revenue from Operations, Opening Inventory ₹ 1,00,000, Closing Inventory ₹ 2,00,000, Creditors Turnover Ratio 3 Times. Closing Trade Payables were ₹ 1,00,000 in excess of Opening Trade Payables. Calculate Opening Trade Payables and Closing Trade Payables.

SOLUTION

Step 1: Cost of Revenue from Operations

= Revenue from Operations – Gross Profit

= ₹ 4,00,000 – (25% of ₹ 4,00,000) = ₹ 3,00,000

Step 2: Total Purchases

= Cost of Revenue from Operations + Closing Inventory – Opening Inventory

= ₹ 3,00,000 + ₹ 2,00,000 – ₹ 1,00,000 = ₹ 4,00,000

Step 3: Net Credit Purchases = Total Purchases – Cash Purchases

= ₹ 4,00,000 – (25% of ₹ 4,00,000) = ₹ 3,00,000

Step 4: $\textbf{Creditors Turnover Ratio} = \dfrac{\textbf{Net Credit Purchases}}{\textbf{Average Trade Payables}}$

$$3 = \frac{₹\ 3{,}00{,}000}{\text{Average Trade Payables}}$$

Average Trade Payables = ₹ 3,00,000/3 = ₹ 1,00,000

(OP+CP)/2 = ₹ 1,00,000

or, OP + CP = ₹ 1,00,000 × 2 = ₹ 2,00,000 ...Eq.I

CP – OP = ₹ 1,00,000 ...Eq. II

Adding both the equations

2 CP = ₹ 3,00,000

CP = ₹ 3,00,000/2 = ₹ 1,50,000

OP = ₹ 1,50,000 – ₹ 1,00,000 = ₹ 50,000

ILLUSTRATION 63

Cash Purchases 25% of Total Purchases, Revenue from Operations ₹ 4,00,000, Gross Profit @ 25% on Revenue from Operations,Opening Inventory ₹ 1,00,000, Closing Inventory ₹ 2,00,000, Creditors Turnover Ratio 3 Times. Trade Payables at the end were 3 times that in the beginning. Calculate Opening Trade Payables and Closing Trade Payables.

SOLUTION

Step 1: Cost of Revenue from Operations= Revenue from Operations – Gross Profit

= ₹ 4,00,000 – (25% of ₹ 4,00,000) = ₹ 3,00,000

Step 2: Total Purchases

= Cost of Revenue from Operations + Closing Inventory – Opening Inventory

= ₹ 3,00,000 + ₹ 2,00,000 – ₹ 1,00,000 = ₹ 4,00,000

Step 3: Net Credit Purchases = Total Purchases – Cash Purchases

= ₹ 4,00,000 – (25% of ₹ 4,00,000) = ₹ 3,00,000

Step 4: $\textbf{Creditors Turnover Ratio} = \dfrac{\textbf{Net Credit Purchases}}{\textbf{Average Trade Payables}}$

$$3 = \frac{₹\ 3{,}00{,}000}{\text{Average Trade Payables}}$$

Average Trade Payables = ₹ 3,00,000/3 = ₹ 1,00,000

(OP+CP)/2 = ₹ 1,00,000

or, OP + CP = ₹ 1,00,000 × 2 = ₹ 2,00,000 ...Eq.I

CP – 3 OP = 0 ...Eq. II

Substracting Eq. II from I

4 OP = ₹ 2,00,000

OP = ₹ 2,00,000/4 = ₹ 50,000

CP = ₹ 50,000 × 3 = ₹ 1,50,000

ILLUSTRATION 64

Cash Purchases 25% of Total Purchases, Revenue from Operations ₹ 4,00,000, Gross Profit @ 25% on Revenue from Operations, Opening Inventory ₹ 1,00,000, Closing Inventory ₹ 2,00,000, Creditors Turnover Ratio 3 Times. Trade Payables at the end were 3 times more than that in the beginning. Calculate Opening Trade Payables and Closing Trade Payables.

SOLUTION

Step 1: Cost of Revenue from Operations = Revenue from Operations – Gross Profit

= ₹ 4,00,000 – (25% of ₹ 4,00,000) = ₹ 3,00,000

Step 2: Total Purchases

= Cost of Revenue from Operations + Closing Inventory – Opening Inventory

= ₹ 3,00,000 + ₹ 2,00,000 – ₹ 1,00,000 = ₹ 4,00,000

Step 3: Net Credit Purchases = Total Purchases – Cash Purchases

= ₹ 4,00,000 – (25% of ₹ 4,00,000) = ₹ 3,00,000

Step 4: Creditors Turnover Ratio = $\frac{\textbf{Net Credit Purchases}}{\textbf{Average Trade Payables}}$

$$3 = \frac{₹\ 3,00,000}{\text{Average Trade Payables}}$$

Average Trade Payables = ₹ 3,00,000/3 = ₹ 1,00,000

(OP+CP)/2 = ₹ 1,00,000

or, OP + CP = ₹ 1,00,000 × 2 = ₹ 2,00,000 ...Eq.I

CP – 4 OP = 0 ...Eq. II

Substracting Eq. II from I

5 OP = ₹ 2,00,000

OP = ₹ 2,00,000/5 = ₹ 40,000

CP = ₹ 40,000 × 4 = ₹ 1,60,000

ILLUSTRATION 65

Cash Purchases % of Net Credit Purchases, Revenue from Operations ₹ 4,00,000, Gross Profit @ 25% on Revenue from Operations, Opening Inventory ₹ 1,00,000, Closing Inventory ₹ 2,00,000, Creditors Turnover Ratio 3 Times. Trade Payables in the beginning were 1/3rd of Trade Payables at the end. Calculate Opening Trade Payables and Closing Trade Payables.

SOLUTION

Step 1: Cost of Revenue from Operations= Revenue from Operations – Gross Profit

= ₹ 4,00,000 – (25% of ₹ 4,00,000) = ₹ 3,00,000

Step 2: Total Purchases

= Cost of Revenue from Operations + Closing Inventory – Opening Inventory

= ₹ 3,00,000 + ₹ 2,00,000 – ₹ 1,00,000 = ₹ 4,00,000

Step 3: Net Credit Purchases = **Total Purchases – Cash Purchases**

= ₹ 4,00,000 – (25% of ₹ 4,00,000) = ₹ 3,00,000

Step 4: Creditors Turnover Ratio = $\frac{\textbf{Net Credit Purchases}}{\textbf{Average Trade Payables}}$

$$3 = \frac{₹\ 3,00,000}{\text{Average Trade Payables}}$$

Average Trade Payables = ₹ 3,00,000/3 = ₹ 1,00,000

(OP + CP)/2 = ₹ 1,00,000

or, OP + CP = ₹ 1,00,000 × 2 = ₹ 2,00,000 ...Eq.I

CP – 1/3 CP = 0 ...Eq. II

Substracting Eq. II from I

1 – 1/3 CP = ₹ 2,00,000

4/3 CP = ₹ 2,00,000

CP = ₹ 2,00,000 × 3/4 = ₹ 1,50,000

OP = ₹ 1,50,000/3 = ₹ 50,000

26.0 WORKING CAPITAL TURNOVER RATIO

MEANING OF WORKING CAPITAL TURNOVER RATIO

Working Capital Turnover ratio establishes a relationship between Revenue from Operations and Working Capital.

OBJECTIVE OF WORKING CAPITAL TURNOVER RATIO

The objective of computing Working Capital Turnover ratio is to determine the efficiency with which the Working Capital is utilised.

COMPONENTS OF WORKING CAPITAL TURNOVER RATIO

There are two components of Working Capital Turnover Ratio as follows:

1. **Revenue from Operations**

   = Credit Revenue from Operations + Cash Revenue from Operations

2. **Working Capital = Current Assets – Current Liabilities.**

COMPUTATION OF WORKING CAPITAL TURNOVER RATIO

Working Capital Turnover Ratio is computed by dividing the Revenue from Operations by the Working Capital. This ratio is usually expressed as 'x' number of times. In the form of a formula, this ratio may be expressed as follows:

$$\textbf{Working Capital Turnover Ratio} = \frac{\textbf{Revenue from Operations}}{\textbf{Working Capital}} = \textbf{... Times}$$

INTERPRETATION OF WORKING CAPITAL TURNOVER RATIO

Working Capital Turnover indicates the firm's ability to generate Revenue from Operations per rupee of Working Capital. In general, higher the ratio, the more efficient the management and utilisation of working capital and vice versa.

To judge whether the ratio is satisfactory *or* not, it should be compared with its own past ratios *or* with the ratio of similar enterprises in the same industry *or* with the industry average.

ILLUSTRATION 66

Current Assets ₹ 6,00,000, Current Liabilities ₹ 1,20,000, Credit Revenue from Operations ₹ 11,80,000, Cash Revenue from Operations ₹ 2,60,000. Calculate Working Capital Turnover Ratio.

SOLUTION:

Step 1: Revenue from Operations

= Cash Revenue from Operations + Credit Revenue from Operations – Revenue from Operations Returns

= ₹ 2,60,000 + ₹ 11,80,000 = ₹ 14,40,000

Step 2: Working Capital = Current Assets – Current Liabilities

= ₹ 6,00,000 – ₹ 1,20,000 = ₹ 4,80,000

Step 3: Working Capital Turnover Ratio $= \dfrac{\textbf{Revenue from Operations}}{\textbf{Working Capital}} = \dfrac{₹\,14,40,000}{₹\,4,80,000}$ = 3 times

ILLUSTRATION 67

Cost of Revenue from Operations ₹ 54,00,000. Gross Profit on Revenue from Operations 25%. Current Ratio 3, Current Liabilities ₹ 12,00,000, Calculate Working Capital Turnover Ratio.

SOLUTION

Step 1: Revenue from Operations

Let Revenue from Operations = ₹ 100, Gross Profit, = ₹ 25,

Cost of Revenue from Operations = ₹ 75

If Cost of Revenue from Operations is ₹ 75, then Revenue from Operations = ₹ 100

If Cost of Revenue from Operations is ₹ 54,00,000 then

Revenue from Operations = ₹100\₹75 × ₹ 54,00,000 = ₹ 72,00,000

Step 2: Working Capital

Current Ratio $= \dfrac{\textbf{Current Assets}}{\textbf{Current Liabilities}}$

$3 = \dfrac{\text{Current Assets}}{₹\,12,00,000}$

Current Assets = ₹ 12,00,000 × 3 = ₹ 36,00,000

Working Capital = ₹ 36,00,000 – ₹ 12,00,000 = ₹ 24,00,000

Step 3: Working Capital Tunrover Ratio = $\dfrac{\textbf{Revenue from Operations}}{\textbf{Working Capital}} = \dfrac{₹\,72,00,000}{₹\,24,00,000}$ = 3 times

ILLUSTRATION 68

Inventory Turnover Ratio 6 Times, Inventory ₹ 4,50,000. Gross Profit on Revenue from Operations 25%, Quick Ratio 2.25, Current Assets ₹ 18,00,000. Calculate Working Capital Turnover.

SOLUTION

Step 1: Cost of Revenue from Operations

Inventory Turnover $= \dfrac{\textbf{Cost of Revenue from Operations}}{\textbf{Average Inventory}}$

$6 = \dfrac{\text{Cost of Revenue from Operations}}{₹\,4,50,000}$

Cost of Revenue from Operations = ₹ 4,50,000 × 6 = ₹ 27,00,000

Step 2: Revenue from Operations

Let Revenue from Operations = ₹ 100, Goods Profit ₹ 25,

Cost of Revenue from Operations = ₹ 100 – ₹ 25 = ₹ 75

If Cost of Revenue from Operations is ₹ 75, then Revenue from Operations = ₹ 100

If Cost of Revenue from Operations is ₹ 27,00,000 then

Revenue from Operations $= \frac{₹100}{₹75} \times ₹27{,}00{,}000 = ₹36{,}00{,}000$

Step 3: Working Capital

$$\textbf{Quick Ratio} = \frac{\textbf{Current Assets – Inventory}}{\textbf{Current Liabilities}}$$

$$2.25 = \frac{₹18{,}00{,}000 - ₹4{,}50{,}000}{\text{Current Liabilities}}$$

Current Liabilities = (₹ 18,00,000 – ₹ 4,50,000)/2.25 = ₹ 6,00,000

Working Capital = ₹ 18,00,000 – ₹ 6,00,000 = ₹ 12,00,000

Step 4: Working Capital Tunrover Ratio $= \frac{\textbf{Revenue from Operations}}{\textbf{Working Capital}} = \frac{₹36{,}00{,}000}{₹12{,}00{,}000} = 3$ times

27.0 PROFITABILITY RATIOS

Meaning	Profitability Ratios measure management's overall effectiveness as shown by the returns generated on Revenue from Operations and Investment.
Profitability	The various types of profitability ratios are as follows: **I. Profitability Ratio In relation to Revenue from Operations:** 1. Gross Profit Ratio, 2. Operating Profit Ratio 3. Operating Ratio 4. Net Profit Ratio **II. Profitability Ratio In relation to Investment:** Raturn on Investment *or* Return on Capital Employed

28.0 GROSS PROFIT RATIO

MEANING OF GROSS PROFIT RATIO

Gross Profit Ratio measures the relationship between Gross Profit and Revenue from Operations.

OBJECTIVE OF GROSS PROFIT RATIO

The main objective of computing Gross Profit Ratio is to determine the efficiency with which production and/or purchase operations and selling operations are carried on.

COMPONENTS OF GROSS PROFIT RATIO

There are two components of Gross Profit Ratio as follows:

1. **Gross Profit**

   = Revenue from Operations (both Cash & Credit) – Cost of Revenue from Operations.

   Note: Cost of Revenue from Operations

   = Opening Inventory + Net Purchases + Direct Expenses – Closing Inventory

   or, = Average Inventory × Inventory Turnover Ratio

2. **Revenue from Operations**

   = Credit Revenue from Operations + Cash Revenue from Operations

COMPUTATION OF GROSS PROFIT RATIO

Gross Profit Ratio is computed by dividing the Gross Profit by the Revenue from Operations. It is expressed as percentage. In the form of a formula, this ratio may be expressed as follows:

$$\textbf{Gross Profit Ratio} = \frac{\textbf{Gross Profit}}{\textbf{Revenue from Operations}} \times 100 = \ldots\%$$

INTEPRETATION OF GROSS PROFIT

Gross Profit ratio indicates (a) an average Gross Margin earned on a Revenue from Operations of ₹ 100, (b) the limit beyond which the fall in Selling prices will definitely result in losses, and (c) what portion of Revenue from Operations is left to cover Operating Expenses (other than the Cost of Revenue from Operations) and Non-Operating Expenses. (e.g., Interest on Borrowings), to pay dividend and to create Reserves. In general Higher the ratio, the more efficient the production and/ or purchase management.

CAUSE OF INCREASE IN GROSS PROFIT RATIO

Gross Profit ratio may increase due to one of the following factors:

1. Higher Revenue from Operations Prices with constant Cost of Revenue from Operations;
2. Lower Cost of Revenue from Operations with constant Revenue from Operations Prices;
3. A combination of aforesaid two factors.

ILLUSTRATION 69

From the following information, Calculate Gross Profit Ratio:

Particulars	₹	*Particulars*	₹
Opening Inventory	50,000	Purchases	11,50,000
Cash Revenue from Operations	4,00,000	Wages	80,000
Credit Revenue from Operations	16,00,000	Carriage Inward	20,000
Closing Inventory	1,00,000	Depreciation	80,000
Interest & Dividend on		Finance Expenses:	
Long-term Investments	3,000	Cash Discount allowed to cus.	10,000
Profit on Sale of Long-term Invst.	2,000	Bad Debts	6,000
Compensation for acquisition of Land	1,000	Interest on Bills Payable	4,000
Value of Furniture lost by fire	6,000	Interest on Long-term Borrowings	1,20,000
Provision for Tax	2,40,000	Employees' Benefit Expense	1,00,000

SOLUTION

STEP 1: GROSS PROFIT

	Particulars	₹	₹
A	**Revenue from Operations (₹ 4,00,000 + ₹ 16,00,000)**		20,00,000
B	***Less:* Cost of Revenue from Operations:**		
	Opening Inventory	50,000	

	Purchases	11,50,000	
	Wages	80,000	
	Carriage inward	20,000	
	Less: Closing Inventory	(1,00,000)	(12,00,000)
C	**Gross Profit (A – B)**		8,00,000

Step 2: Gross Profit Ratio = $\frac{\textbf{Gross Profit}}{\textbf{Revenue from Operations}} \times \textbf{100} = \frac{₹\ 8,00,000}{₹\ 20,00,000} \times 100 = 40\%$

ILLUSTRATION 70

Average Inventory ₹ 80,000, Inventory Turnover Ratio 8 times, Average Trade Receivables ₹ 1,00,000, Average Debt Collection Period 2 months, Cash Revenue from Operations 25% of Revenue from Operations. Calculate Gross Profit Ratio.

SOLUTION

Step 1: Cost of Revenue from Operations

= Average Inventory × Inventory Turnover Ratio = ₹ 80,000 × 8 = ₹ 6,40,000

Step 2: Credit Revenue from Operations = Average Trade Receivables × Debtors Turnover Ratio

= ₹1,00,000 × (12/2) = ₹ 6,00,000

Step 3: Revenue from Operations

= Credit Revenue from Operations + Cash Revenue from Operations

= ₹ 6,00,000 +(₹ 6,00,000 × 1/3)= ₹ 8,00,000

Step 4: Gross Profit **= Revenue from Operations – Cost of Revenue from Operations**

= ₹ 8,00,000 – ₹ 6,40,000 = ₹ 1,60,000

Step 5: Gross Profit Ratio = $\frac{\textbf{Gross Profit}}{\textbf{Revenue from Operations}} \times \textbf{100} = \frac{₹1,60,000 \times 100}{₹8,00,000} = 20\%$

29.0 OPERATING RATIO

MEANING OF OPERATING RATIO

Operating Ratio measures the relationship between Operating Cost and Revenue from Operations.

OBJECTIVE OF OPERATING RATIO

The main objective of computing Operating Ratio is to determine the operational efficiency with which Production and/or Purchases and Selling Operations are carried on.

COMPONENTS OF OPERATING RATIO

There are two components of Operating Ratio as follows:

1. **Operating Cost** is the cost relating to the Operations of a business enterprise.

   Operating Cost = Cost of Revenue from Operations + Operating Expenses (e.g., Employees' Benefit Expense, Depreciation, Interest on Short-term Borrowings, Discount Allowed and Bad Debts).

2. **Revenue from Operations = Credit Revenue from Operations + Cash Revenue from Operations**

COMPUTATION OF OPERATING RATIO

Operating ratio is computed by dividing the Operating Cost by the Revenue from Operations. This ratio is expressed as a percentage. In the form of a formula, this ratio may be expressed as follows:

$$\textbf{Operating Ratio} = \frac{\textbf{Operating Cost}}{\textbf{Revenue from Operations}} \times 100 = \ldots\%$$

$$= \frac{\textbf{Cost of Revenue from Operations + Operating Expenses}}{\textbf{Revenue from Operations}} \times 100$$

where

1. **Cost of Revenue from Operations**

   = Opening Inventory + Purchases (both cash & Credit) + Direct Expenses + Manufacturing Expenses – Closing Inventory

   OR

   = Revenue from Operations – Gross Profit

   OR

   = Revenue from Operations + Gross Loss

   OR

   = Average Inventory × Inventory Turnover Ratio

2. **Operating Expenses = Employees' Benefit Expense + Depreciation + Interest on Short-term Borrowings + Discount Allowed + Bad Debts**

INTERPRETATION OF OPERATING RATIO

Operating Ratio indicates an Average Operating Cost incurred on a Revenue from Operations of ₹ 100. Lower the ratio, greater is the Operating Profit to cover the non-operating expenses, to pay dividend and to create reserves and vice versa.

TUTORIAL NOTE

Both Operating Profit Ratio and Operating Ratio are complementary to each other and thus, if one of such ratios is deducted from 100, another ratio may be obtained.

ILLUSTRATION 71

From the following information Calculate Operating Ratio.

Particulars	₹	*Particulars*	₹
Opening Inventory	50,000	Purchases	11,50,000
Cash Revenue from Operations	4,00,000	Wages	80,000
Credit Revenue from Operations	16,00,000	Carriage Inward	20,000
Closing Inventory	1,00,000	Depreciation	80,000
Interest & Dividend on		Finance Expenses:	
Long-term Investments	3,000	Cash Discount allowed to cus.	10,000
Profit on Sale of Long-term Invst.	2,000	Bad Debts	6,000
Compensation for acquisition of Land	1,000	Interest on Bills Payable	4,000
Value of Furniture lost by fire	6,000	Interest on Long-term Borrowings	1,20,000
Provision for Tax	2,40,000	Employees' Benefit Expense	1,00,000

SOLUTION

STEP 1: OPERATING COST

	Particulars	₹	₹
A	**Cost of Revenue from Operations:**		
	Opening Inventory	50,000	
	Purchases	11,50,000	
	Wages	80,000	
	Carriage inward	20,000	
	Less: Closing Inventory	(1,00,000)	12,00,000
B	***Add:* Operating Expenses:**		
	Employees' Benefit Expense	1,00,000	
	Depreciation	80,000	
	Cash Discount allowed	10,000	
	Bad Debts	6,000	
	Interest on Bills Payable	4,000	2,00,000
C	**Operating Cost (A + B)**		14,00,000

Step 2: Operating Ratio $= \dfrac{\textbf{Operating Cost}}{\textbf{Revenue from Operations}} \times 100 = \dfrac{₹\ 14,00,000}{₹\ 20,00,000} \times 100 = 70\%$

ILLUSTRATION 72

Operating Cost ₹ 27,20,000, Operating Expenses ₹ 3,20,000, Gross Profit Ratio 25%. Calculate Operating Ratio.

SOLUTION

Step 1: Cost of Revenue from Operations = Operating Cost – Operating Expenses
= ₹ 27,20,000 – ₹ 3,20,000 = ₹ 24,00,000

Step 2: Let Revenue from Operations = ₹ 100, Gross Profit = ₹ 25, Cost ₹ 75,
If Cost is ₹ 75, then **Revenue from Operations** = ₹ 100
If Cost is ₹ 24,00,000
then Revenue from Operations = ₹ 24,00,000 × 100/75 = ₹ 32,00,000

Step 3: Operating Ratio $= \dfrac{\textbf{Operating Cost}}{\textbf{Revenue from Operations}} \times 100 = \dfrac{₹\ 27,20,000}{₹\ 32,00,000} \times 100 = 85\%$

30.0 OPERATING PROFIT RATIO

MEANING OF OPERATING PROFIT RATIO

Operating Profit Ratio measures the relationship between Operating Profit and Revenue from Operations.

OBJECTIVE OF OPERATING PROFIT RATIO

The main objective of computing Operating Profit Ratio is to determine the operational efficiency of the management.

COMPONENTS OF OPERATING PROFIT RATIO

There are two components of Operating Profit Ratio as follows:

1. **Operating Profit = Gross Profit – Other Operating Expenses** (e.g., Employees' Benefit Expense, Depreciation, Interest on Short-term Borrowings, Discount Allowed and Bad Debts) and
   or, Operating Profit = Revenue from Operations – Operating Cost
2. **Revenue from Operations**
   = Credit Revenue from Operations + Cash Revenue from Operations
   or, = Cost of Revenue from Operations + Gross Profit

COMPUTATION OF OPERATING PROFIT RATIO

Operating Profit Ratio is computed by dividing the Operating Profit by the Revenue from Operations. It is expressed as a percentage. In the form of a formula, this ratio may be expressed as follows:

$$\textbf{Operating Profit Ratio} = \frac{\textbf{Operating Profit}}{\textbf{Revenue from Operations}} \times 100 = \ldots \%$$

INTERPRETATION OF OPERATING PROFIT RATIO

Operating Profit Ratio indicates (a) an average operating margin earned on Revenue from Operations of ₹ 100 and (b) what portion of Revenue from Operations is left to cover non-operating expenses, to pay dividend and to create reserves. In general, Higher the ratio, the more efficient is the operating management.

CAUSES FOR INCREASE IN OPERATING PROFIT RATIO

Operaing Profit Ratio may increase due to any one of the following factors:

1. Higher Gross Profit;
2. Lower Operating Expenses;
3. A combination of aforesaid two factors.

31.0 DISTINCTION BETWEEN OPERATING RATIO AND OPERATING PROFIT RATIO

Operating Ratio differs from Operating Profit Ratio in the following respects:

Basis of Distinction	*Operating Ratio*	*Operating Profit Ratio*
1. Relationship	It shows the relationship between Operating Cost and Revenue from Operations	It shows the relationship between Operating Profit and RFO.
2. Objective	The objective of computing this ratio is to determine the efficiency with which production/purchase & selling operations are carried on.	The objective of computing this ratio is to determine the operational efficiency of the management.
3. Interpretation	This ratio indicates an average operating cost incurred on a sales of ₹ 100.	This ratio indicates (a) an average operating margin as RFO of ₹ 100. (b) What portion of sales is left to over Non-Operating Expenses to pay Dividend and to create Reserves.
4. Formula	$\frac{\textbf{Operating Profit}}{\textbf{Revenue from Operations}} \times 100$	$\frac{\textbf{Operating Profit}}{\textbf{Revenue from Operations}} \times 100$

ILLUSTRATION 73

From the following information Calculate Operating Profit Ratio.

Particulars	₹	*Particulars*	₹
Opening Inventory	50,000	Purchases	11,50,000
Cash Revenue from Operations	4,00,000	Wages	80,000
Credit Revenue from Operations	17,00,000	Carriage Inward	20,000
Revenue from Operations Returns	1,00,000	Office & Adm. Expenses	1,00,000
Closing Inventory	1,00,000	Selling & Distribution Exp.	80,000
Interest & Dividend on		Finance Expenses:	
Long-term Investments	3,000	Cash Discount allowed to cus.	10,000
Profit on Sale of Long-term Invst.	2,000	Bad Debts	6,000
Compensation for acquisition of Land	1,000	Interest on Bills Payable	4,000
Value of Furniture lost by fire	6,000	Interest on Long-term Borrowings	1,20,000
Provision for Tax	2,40,000		

SOLUTION

STEP 1: OPERATING PROFIT

Particulars	₹	₹
A. Revenue from Operations		20,00,000
B. *Less:* Cost of Revenue from Operations:		
Opening Inventory	50,000	
Purchases	11,50,000	
Wages	80,000	
Carriage inward	20,000	
Less: Closing Inventory	(1,00,000)	(12,00,000)
C. Gross Profit (A – B)		8,00,000
D. *Less:* Operating Expenses:		
Employees' Benefit Expense	1,00,000	
Depreciation	80,000	
Cash Discount allowed	10,000	
Bad Debts	6,000	
Interest on Bills Payable	4,000	(2,00,000)
E. Operating Profit (C – D)		6,00,000

Step 2: Operating Profit Ratio $= \frac{\textbf{Operating Profit}}{\textbf{Revenue from Operations}} \times 100 = \frac{₹\,6,00,000}{₹\,20,00,000} \times 100 = 30\%$

ILLUSTRATION 74

Operating Cost ₹ 8,50,000, Gross Profit Ratio 20%, Operating Expenses ₹ 50,000. Calculate Operating Profit Ratio.

SOLUTION

Step 1: Cost of Revenue from Operations = Operating Cost – Operating Expenses

= ₹ 8,50,000 – ₹ 50,000 = ₹ 8,00,000

Step 2: Revenue from Operations = Cost of Revenue from Operations + Gross Profit

= ₹ 8,00,000 + (₹ 8,00,000 × 25/100) = ₹ 10,00,000

Step 3: Operating Profit = Revenue from Operations – Operating Cost

= ₹ 10,00,000 – ₹ 8,50,000 = ₹ 1,50,000

Step 4: $\textbf{Operating Profit Ratio} = \dfrac{\textbf{Operating Profit}}{\textbf{Revenue from Operations}} \times 100 = \dfrac{₹1,50,000}{₹10,00,000} \times 100 = 15\%$

ILLUSTRATION 75

Calculate Operating Profit Ratio if Operating Ratio is 20%.

SOLUTION

Operating Profit Ratio = 100% – Operating Ratio = 100% – 20% = 80%

32.0 NET PROFIT RATIO

MEANING OF NET PROFIT RATIO

Net Profit Ratio measures the relationship between Net Profit and Revenue from Operations.

OBJECTIVE OF NET PROFIT RATIO

The main objective of computing Net Profit ratio is to determine the overall profitability due to various factors such as operational efficiency, trading on equity etc.

COMPONENTS OF NET PROFIT RATIO

There are two components of Net Profit Ratio as follows:

1. **Net Profit = Revenue from Operations – Cost of Revenue from Operations – Operating Expenses – Non-Operating Expenses + Non-Operating Incomes**

   or, = Revenue from Operations – Operating Cost – Non-Operating Expenses + Non-Operating Incomes

   or, = Operating Profit – Non-Operating Expenses + Non-Operating Incomes
2. **Revenue from Operations = Credit Revenue from Operations + Cash Revenue from Operations**

COMPUTATION OF NET PROFIT RATIO

Net Profit Ratio is computed by dividing the Net Profit by the Revenue from Operations. The figure of Net Profit may be taken either before tax *or* after tax. It is expressed as a percentage. In the form of a formula, this ratio may be expressed as follows:

$$\textbf{Net Profit Ratio} = \frac{\textbf{Net Profit Before Tax}}{\textbf{Revenue from Operations}} \times 100 = \ldots\%$$

$$\textit{or, } \textbf{Net Profit Ratio} = \frac{\textbf{Net Profit After Tax}}{\textbf{Revenue from Operations}} \times 100 = \ldots\%$$

INTERPRETATION OF NET PROFIT RATIO

Net Profit Ratio indicates (a) an average Net Margin earned on a Revenue from Operations of ₹ 100 (b) what portion of Revenue from Operations is left to pay dividend and to create reserves, and (c) firm's capacity to withstand adverse economic conditions when selling price is declining, cost of production is rising and the demand for the product is falling. In general, Higher the ratio, greater is the capacity of the firm to withstand adverse economic conditions and vice versa.

ILLUSTRATION 76

From the following information Calculate Net Profit Ratio.

Particulars	₹	*Particulars*	₹
Opening Inventory	50,000	Purchases	11,50,000
Cash Revenue from Operations	4,00,000	Wages	80,000
Credit Revenue from Operations	17,00,000	Carriage Inward	20,000
Revenue from Operations Returns	1,00,000	Office & Adm. Expenses	1,00,000
Closing Inventory	1,00,000	Selling & Distribution Exp.	80,000
Interest & Dividend on		Finance Expenses:	
Long-term Investments	3,000	Cash Discount allowed to cus.	10,000
Profit on Sale of Long-term Invst.	2,000	Bad Debts	6,000
Compensation for acquisition of Land	1,000	Interest on Bills Payable	4,000
Value of Furniture lost by fire	6,000	Interest on Long-term Borrowings	1,20,000
Provision for Tax	2,40,000		

SOLUTION

STEP 1: NET PROFIT

	Particulars	₹	₹
A	**Revenue from Operations**		20,00,000
B	***Less:* Cost of Revenue from Operations:**		
	Opening Inventory	50,000	
	Purchases	11,50,000	
	Wages	80,000	
	Carriage inward	20,000	
	Less: Closing Inventory	(1,00,000)	(12,00,000)
C	**Gross Profit (A – B)**		8,00,000
D	***Less:* Operating Expenses:**		
	Employees' Benefit Expense	1,00,000	
	Depreciation	80,000	
	Cash Discount allowed	10,000	
	Bad Debts	6,000	
	Interest on Bills Payable	4,000	(2,00,000)
E	**Operating Profit (C – D)**		6,00,000
F	***Less:* Non-operating Expenses:**		
	Long-term Borrowings	1,20,000	
	Value of Furniture lost by fire	6,000	(1,26,000)

G	***Add:*** **Non-operating Incomes:**		
	Interest & Dividend as long-term investment	3,000	
	Profit an sale of long-term Investment	2,000	
	Compensation for acquisition of land	1,000	6,000
H	**Net Profit before tax (E – F + G)**		4,80,000
I	***Less:*** **Tax**		(2,40,000)
J	**Net Profit after tax (H – I)**		2,40,000

Step 2: Net Profit Ratio $= \dfrac{\textbf{Net Profit before tax}}{\textbf{Net Sales}} \times 100 = \dfrac{₹\,4,80,000}{₹\,20,00,000} \times 100 = 24\%$

or, **Net Profit Ratio** $= \dfrac{\textbf{Net Profit after tax}}{\textbf{Net Sales}} \times 100 = \dfrac{₹\,2,40,000}{₹\,20,00,000} \times 100 = 12\%$

ILLUSTRATION 77

Cash Revenue from Operations 25% of Revenue from Operations, Average Trade Receivables ₹ 1,50,000, Debtors Turnover Ratio 5, Gross Profit 2/3rd on Cost, Operating Expenses ₹ 1,00,000. Non-Operating Expenses ₹ 63,000, Non-Operating Incomes ₹ 3,000, Calculate Gross Profit Ratio, Operating Ratio, Operating Profit Ratio and Net Profit Ratio.

SOLUTION

Step 1: Credit Revenue from Operations

= Average Trade Receivables × Debtors Turnover Ratio

= ₹ 1,50,000 × 5 = ₹ 7,50,000

Step 2: Revenue from Operations = ₹ 7,50,000 + 33-1/3% ₹ 7,50,000 = ₹ 10,00,000

Step 3: Let Cost = ₹ 3, Gross Profit = 3 × 2/3 = ₹ 2, Revenue from Operations = ₹ 5

Step 4: Gross Profit = ₹ 10,00,000 × 2/5 = ₹ 4,00,000

Step 5: Cost of Revenue from Operations

= Revenue from Operations – Gross Profit

= ₹ 10,00,000 – ₹ 4,00,000 = ₹ 6,00,000

Step 6: Operating Cost = Cost of Revenue from Operations + Operating Expenses

= ₹ 6,00,000 + ₹ 1,00,000 = ₹ 7,00,000

Step 7: Operating Profit = Revenue from Operations – Operating Cost

= ₹ 10,00,000 – ₹ 7,00,000 = ₹ 3,00,000

Step 8: Net Profit = Operating Profit + Non-Operating Income – Non-Operating Expenses

= ₹ 3,00,000 + ₹ 3,000 – ₹ 63,000 = ₹ 2,40,000

Step 9: Gross Profit Ratio $= \dfrac{\textbf{Gross profit}}{\textbf{Revenue from Operations}} \times 100 = \dfrac{₹\,4,00,000}{₹\,10,00,000} \times 100 = 40\%$

Step 10: Operating Ratio $= \dfrac{\textbf{Operating Cost}}{\textbf{Revenue from Operations}} \times 100 = \dfrac{₹\,7,00,000}{₹\,10,00,000} \times 100 = 70\%$

Step 11: Operating Profit Ratio $= \dfrac{\textbf{Operating Profit}}{\textbf{Revenue from Operations}} \times 100 = \dfrac{₹\,3,00,000}{₹\,10,00,000} \times 100 = 30\%$

Step 12: Net Profit Ratio $= \dfrac{\textbf{Net Profit}}{\textbf{Revenue from Operations}} \times 100 = \dfrac{₹\,2,40,000}{₹\,10,00,000} \times 100 = 24\%$

ILLUSTRATION 78

Revenue from Operations ₹ 10,00,000, Gross Profit Ratio 25%, Operating Ratio 90%, Operating, ₹ 1,00,000. Non-Operating Expenses ₹ 5,000, Non-Operating Income ₹ 55,000. Calculate Net Profit Ratio.

SOLUTION

Step 1: Operating Profit Ratio = 100 – Operating Ratio = 100 – 90% = 10%

Step 2: Operating Profit = ₹ 10,00,000 × 10/100 = ₹ 1,00,000

Step 3: Net Profit **= Operating Profit + Non-Operating Incomes – Non-Operating Exp.**

= ₹ 1,00,000 + ₹ 55,000 – ₹ 5,000 = ₹ 1,50,000

Step 4: Net Profit Ratio $= \frac{\textbf{Net Profit}}{\textbf{Revenue from Operations}} \times \mathbf{100} = \frac{₹\ 1,50,000}{₹\ 10,00,000} \times 100 = 15\%$

33.0 RETURN ON TOTAL ASSETS [ROTA]

MEANING OF RETURN ON TOTAL ASSETS

Return of Total Assets Ratio measures a relationship between Net Profit before Interest and Tax, and Total Assets.

OBJECTIVE OF RETURN ON TOTAL ASSETS

The objective of computing Return on Total Assets Ratio is to find out how efficiently the Total Assets have been used by the management.

COMPONENTS OF RETURN ON TOTAL ASSETS

There are two components of Return on Total Assets Ratio as follows:

1. **Net Profit before Interest and Tax.**
2. **Total Assets** = All Assets *(excluding Fictitious Assets)*

   or, = Net Fixed Assets + Non-Current Investments + Current Assets

   or, = Shareholders'Funds + Total Debts

   or, = Capital Employed + Current Liabilities

COMPUTATION OF RETURN ON TOTAL ASSETS

Return on Total Assets Ratio is computed by dividing the Net Profit before Interest and Tax by Total Assets. This Ratio is expressed as a percentage. In the form of a formula, this ratio may be expressed as follows:

$$\textbf{Return on Total Assets} = \frac{\textbf{Net Profit before Interest and Tax}}{\textbf{Total Assets}} \times \mathbf{100} = \mathbf{...\%}$$

INTERPRETATION OF RETURN ON TOTAL ASSETS

Return on Total Assets Ratio indicates the firm's ability of generating profit per rupee of Total Assets. Higher the ratio, the more efficient the management and utilisation of total assets.

An enterprise should have a satisfactory ratio. To judge whether the ratio is satisfactory *or* not, it should be compared with its own past ratios *or* with the ratio of similar enterprises in the same industry *or* with the industry average.

ILLUSTRATION 79

From the following information, calculate Return on Total Assets.

Net Profit before Interest & Tax ₹ 6,00,000, Tax ₹ 1,50,000, Net Fixed Assets ₹ 10,00,000. Non-Current Investments ₹ 1,00,000, Current Assets ₹ 5,00,000, Equity Share Capital (₹ 10 each) ₹ 1,50,000, 20% Pref. Share Capital ₹ 1,00,000, Reserves & Surplus ₹ 1,50,000 (Opening Balance), 12.5% Debentures ₹ 8,00,000, Current Liabilities ₹ 4,00,000.

SOLUTION

Step 1: **Total Assets = Non-Current Assets + Current Assets**

= (₹ 10,00,000 + ₹ 1,00,000) + ₹ 5,00,000 = ₹ 16,00,000

Step 2: Return on Total Assets $= \dfrac{\textbf{Net Profit before Interest Tax}}{\textbf{Total Assets}} \times 100$

$= \dfrac{₹\ 6,00,000}{₹\ 16,00,000} \times 100 = 37.5\%$

34.0 RETURN ON INVESTMENT (ROI) [OR RETURN ON CAPITAL EMPLOYED]

MEANING OF RETURN ON INVESTMENT

Return on Investment Ratio measures a relationship between Net Profit before Interest and Tax and Capital Employed.

OBJECTIVE OF RETURN ON INVESTMENT

The objective of computing Return on Investment Ratio is to find out how efficiently the long-term funds supplied by the creditors and shareholders have been used.

COMPONENTS OF RETURN ON INVESTMENTS

There are two components of this ratio as follows:

1. **Net Profit before Interest, Tax & Pref. Dividend**
2. **Capital Employed** means long-term funds supplied by the long-term creditors and shareholders. It comprises the Nont-Current Liabilities and Shareholders' Funds. It can be calculated by any of the following methods:

CALCULATION OF CAPITAL EMPLOYED

Liabilities Side Approach	₹	*Assets Side Approach*	₹
A. Equity Share Capital	xxx	A. Non-Current Assets	xxx
B. + Pref. Share Capital	xxx	(Excluding Non-Trade Investments)	xxx
C. + Reserves & Surplus (Op. Bal.)	xxx	B. + Current Assets	xxx
D. + Non-Current Liabilities	xxx	C. – Current Liabilities	(xxx)
E. Capital Employed	xxx	D. Capital Employed	xxx

Thus,

1. **Capital Employed = Shareholders' Funds + Non-Current Liabilities**
2. **Capital Employed = (Share Capital + Reserves & Surplus) + Non-Current Liabilities**
3. **Capital Employed = [(Equity Share Capital + Pref. Share Capital + Reserves & Surplus)] + Non-Current Liabilities.**
4. **Capital Employed = Non-Current Assets (Excluding Non-Trade Investments) + Current Assets – Current Liabilities.**

5. **Capital Employed = Non-Current Assets (Excluding Non-Trade Investments) + Working Capital**
6. **Capital Employed = Total Assets (Excluding Non-Trade Investments) – Current Liabilities**

TUTORIAL NOTES

1. *Non-Operating Assets do not form part of Capital Employed (e.g., Non-Trade Investments, Advance for purchase of Fixed Assets, Capital Work-in-Progress.)*
2. *Income from Non-Operating Assets (if any) should also be excluded while calculating the Net Profit before Interest & Tax.*

COMPUTATION OF RETURN ON INVESTMENT

Reture on Investment ratio is computed by dividing the Net Profit before Interest and Tax by Capital Employed. It is expressed as a percentage. In the form of formula, this ratio may be expressed as follows:

$$\textbf{Return on Capital Employed} = \frac{\textbf{Net Profit before Interest, Tax \& Dividend}}{\textbf{Capital Employed}} \times 100 = \ldots\ \%$$

INTERPRETATION OF RETURN ON INVESTMENT

Return on Investment Ratio indicates the firm's ability of generating profit per rupee of Capital Employed. Higher the Ratio, the more efficient the management and utilisation of Capital Employed.

An enterprise should have a satisfactory ratio. To judge whether the ratio is satisfactory *or* not, it should be compared with its own past ratios *or* with the ratio of similar enterprises in the same industry *or* with the industry average.

USES OF RETURN ON INVESTMENT

The Return on Investment is a very important concept in the field of operational management and the financial management. Its managerial uses include the following:

1. It is a measure of overall profitability of an enterprise.
2. It can be used to measure and compare the performance of various divisions within an enterprise.
3. It can be used to compare the performance of various enterprises within an industry.
4. It can be used for evaluating Investment Decisions (or Capital Budgeting Decisions *or* Capital Expenditure Decisions) Investment Decision is a decision to invest in long-term assets. Other things remaining the same, the projects yielding higher Rate of Return on Investment may be selected.
5. It can be used for planning the Capital Structure. Capital Structure Decision is a decision to decide upon the proportion of various sources of long-term funds, viz., long-term debts, preference shares, equity funds (including retained earnings). A financial manager should not take the financial risk by employing the funds carrying fixed financial charges if he is not in position to generate a Rate of Return on Investment greater than the Rate of Fixed Financial Charges.
6. It can be used for determining the price of a product/contract. The price of a product/contract should be fixed in such a way that a reasonable rate of return on investment is obtained after recovering the operating cost of that product/contract.

ILLUSTRATION 80

From the following information, calculate Return on Capital Employed.

Net Profit after Interest & Tax ₹ 2,40,000, Tax ₹ 2,40,000, Net Fixed Assets ₹ 10,00,000, Non-Current Trade Investments ₹ 20,000. Long-term Loans & Advances ₹ 80,000. Current Assets ₹ 5,00,000, Equity Share Capital ₹ 1,50,000, 18% Pref. Share Capital ₹ 1,00,000, Reserves & Surplus ₹ 1,50,000, 20% Long-term Borrowings ₹ 6,00,000, Long-term Provisions ₹ 2,00,000, Current Liabilities ₹ 4,00,000.

SOLUTION

STEP 1: NET PROFIT BEFORE INTEREST & TAX

	Particulars	₹
A	Net Profit after interest & Tax	2,40,000
B	*Add:* Tax	2,40,000
C	Net Profit after Interest but before Tax (A + B)	4,80,000
D	*Add:* Interest on Long-term Borrowings	1,20,000
E	Net Profit before Interest & tax (C + D)	6,00,000

STEP 2: CAPITAL EMPLOYED

Liabilities Side Approach	₹	*Assets Side Approach*	₹
A. Equity Share Capital	1,50,000	A. Non-Current Assets	11,00,000
B. + Pref. Share Capital	1,00,000	[10,00,000 + 20,000 + 80,000]	
C. + Reserves & Surplus	1,50,000	B. Current Assets	5,00,000
D. + Non-Current Liabilities	8,00,000	C. – Current Liabilities	(4,00,000)
[6,00,000 + 2,00,000]		D. Capital Employed	12,00,000
E. Capital Employed	12,00,000		

Step 3: Return on Capital Employed $= \frac{\textbf{Net Profit before Interest, Tax \& Dividend}}{\textbf{Capital Employed}} \times 100$

$= \frac{₹ 6,00,000}{₹ 12,00,000} \times 100 = 50\%$

ILLUSTRATION 81

From the following information, calculate the Return on Investment:

Net Profit (after) Tax Ratio 12%. Tax Rate 50%, Revenue from Operations ₹ 20,00,000, 15% Long-term Borrowings ₹ 8,00,000, Equity Share Capital ₹ 1,50,000, Reserves & Surplurs ₹ 1,50,000, Securities Premium ₹ 50,000, 18% Pref. Share Capital ₹ 1,00,000,Current Liabilities ₹ 3,00,000

SOLUTION

Step 1: Net Profit after Tax = ₹ 20,00,000 × 12/100 = ₹ 2,40,000

Step 2: Net Profit before Tax **= Net Profit after Tax + Tax**

= ₹ 2,40,000 + (₹ 2,40,000 × 0.50/0.50) = ₹ 4,80,000

Step 3: Net Profit before Interest & Tax

= Net Profit before Tax + Interest on Long-term Borrowings

= ₹ 4,80,000 + (₹ 8,00,000 × 15/100) = ₹ 6,00,000

Step 4: Capital Employed = Shareholders' Funds + Non-Current Liabilities

= (₹ 1,50,000 + ₹ 1,50,000 + ₹ 1,00,000) + ₹ 8,00,000 = ₹ 12,00,000

Step 5: Return on Investment $= \dfrac{\textbf{Net Profit before Interest, Tax \& Dividend}}{\textbf{Capital Employed}} \times \mathbf{100}$

$= \dfrac{₹6,00,000}{₹12,00,000} \times 100 = 50\%$

Note: *Securities Premium is already included in Reserves & Surplus.*

ILLUSTRATION 82

From the following information, Calculate the Return on Investment:

Net Profit (after) Tax Ratio 24%. Tax Rate 50%, Revenue from Operations ₹ 15,00,000, Net Fixed Assets ₹ 7,50,000, Accumulated Depreciation ₹ 2,50,000, Non-Current Investment (Trade) ₹ 75,000, Current Assets ₹ 1,50,000, Trade Receivables ₹ 50,000, Total Debt ₹ 6,75,000, 15% Long-term Borrowings ₹ 6,00,000, Trade Payables ₹ 25,000.

SOLUTION

Step 1: Net Profit before Tax = ₹ 15,00,000 × 24/100 = ₹ 3,60,000

Step 2: Net Profit before Interest & Tax

= Net Profit before Tax + Interest on Long-term Borrowings

= ₹ 3,60,000 + (₹ 6,00,000 × 15/100) = ₹ 4,50,000

Step 3: Current Liabilities = Total Debt – Non-Current Liabilities

= ₹ 6,75,000 – ₹ 6,00,000 = ₹ 75,000

Step 4: Capital Employed = Net Fixed Assets + Non-Current Trade Investments + Current Assets – Current Liabilities

= ₹ 7,50,000 + ₹ 75,000 + ₹ 1,50,000 – ₹ 75,000 = ₹ 9,00,000

Step 5: Return on Investment $= \dfrac{\textbf{Net Profit before Interest, Tax \& Dividend}}{\textbf{Capital Employed}} \times \mathbf{100}$

$= \dfrac{₹4,50,000}{₹9,00,000} \times 100 = 50\%$

Notes:

1. *Accumulated Depreciation was already adjusted in Net Fixed Assets.*
2. *Trade Receivables are already included in Current Assets.*
3. *Trade Payables are already included in Current Liabilities.*

ILLUSTRATION 83

A Company's Return on Investment (ROI) is 25% before tax. Tax is paid by the Company at 30%. The company has a loan of ₹ 25 lakhs as part of the Capital employed on which interest is paid at 15% p.a. What is amount by which shareholders' gain from there being the Loan?

SOLUTION

Particulars	₹
A. Earning before Interest and tax (@ 25% on ₹ 25 lakhs)	6,25,000
B. *Less:* Interest @ 15% on ₹ 25 lakhs	3,75,000

C.	Earning after Interest (A – B)	2,50,000
D.	*Less:* Tax @ 30%	(75,000)
E.	Earnings after Tax	1,75,000
	Net Gain to Shareholders from there being Loan	1,75,000

35.0 RETURN ON SHAREHOLDERS' FUNDS (OR RETURN ON EQUITY) (ROE)

MEANING OF RETURN ON SHAREHOLDERS' FUNDS (OR RETURN ON EQUITY)

Return on Shareholders' Funds (or Return on Equity) Ratio measures a relationship between Net Profit after Interest and Tax, and Shareholders' Funds.

OBJECTIVE OF RETURN ON EQUITY

The objective of computing Return on Equity Ratio is to find out how efficiently the funds supplied by the Shareholders have been used.

COMPONENTS OF RETURN ON EQUITY

There are two components of Return on Equity ratio as follows:

1. **Net Profit after Interest and Tax**
2. **Shareholders' Funds** = All funds belonging to Shareholders.

TUTORIAL NOTE

Some accountants feel that the figure of 'Shareholders Funds' should be fairly representative of the shareholders' investment throughout the accounting period and therefore, they prefer to make use of the concept of 'Average Shareholders' Funds' which can be obtained by dividing the aggregate of the shareholders' funds at the beginning and at the end of the accounting period, by 2.

COMPUTATION OF RETURN ON EQUITY

Return on Equity Ratio is computed by dividing the Net Profit after Interest and Tax by Shareholders' Funds. It is expressed as a percentage. In the form of a formula, this ratio may be expressed as follows:

$$\textbf{Return on Shareholders' Funds} = \frac{\textbf{Net Profit after Interest and Tax}}{\textbf{Shareholder's Funds}} \times 100 = \ldots\%$$

INTERPRETATION OF RETURN ON EQUITY

Return on Equity Ratio indicates the firm's ability of generating profit per rupee of Shareholders' Funds. Higher the ratio, the more efficient the management and utilization of Shareholders' Funds.

An enterprise should have a satisfactory ratio. To judge whether the ratio is satisfactory *or* not, it should be compared with its own past ratios *or* with the ratio of similar enterprises in the same industry *or* with the industry average.

ILLUSTRATION 84

From the following information, calculate Return on Equity.

Net Profit before Interest & Tax ₹ 6,00,000, Tax ₹ 1,50,000, Net Fixed Assets ₹ 10,00,000. Non-Current Investments ₹ 1,00,000, Current Assets ₹ 5,00,000, Equity Share Capital (₹ 10 each) ₹ 1,50,000, 20% Pref. Share Capital ₹ 1,00,000, Reserves & Surplus ₹ 1,50,000 (Opening Balance), 12.5% Debentures ₹ 8,00,000, Current Liabilities ₹ 4,00,000.

SOLUTION

STEP 1: NET PROFIT AFTER INTEREST & TAX

Particulars	₹
A. Net Profit before Interest & Tax	6,00,000
B. *Less:* Interest on Debentures	(1,00,000)
C. Net Profit before tax	5,00,000
D. *Less:* Tax	(1,50,000)
E. Net Profit after Interest & Tax	3,50,000

STEP 2: CALCULATION OF SHAREHOLDERS'FUNDS (OR EQUITY)

Liabilities Side Approach	₹	*Assets Side Approach*	₹
A. Share Capital	2,50,000	A. Non-Current Assets	11,00,000
B. + Reserves & Surplus (Op)	1,50,000	B. Current Assets	5,00,000
C. Capital Employed	4,00,000	C. – Current Liabilities	(4,00,000)
		D. – Non-Current Liabilities	(8,00,000)
		E. Capital Employed	4,00,000

Step 3: Return on Shareholders' Funds

$$= \frac{\textbf{Net Profit after Interest and Tax}}{\textbf{Number of Equity Shares}} \times 100 = \frac{₹3,50,000}{₹4,00,000} \times 100 = 87.5\%$$

36.0 RETURN ON EQUITY SHAREHOLDERS' FUNDS

MEANING OF RETURN ON EQUITY SHAREHOLDERS' FUNDS

Return on Equity Shareholders' Funds Ratio measures a relationship between Net Profit after Interest, Tax, and Preference Dividend, and Equity Shareholders' Funds.

OBJECTIVE OF RETURN ON EQUITY SHAREHOLDERS' FUNDS

The objective of computing this ratio is to find out how efficiently the funds supplied by the equity shareholders have been used.

COMPONENTS OF RETURN ON EQUITY SHAREHOLDERS' FUNDS

There are two components of this ratio as follows:

1. **Net Profit after Interest, Tax and Preference Dividend** (including participating dividend if any, due to Participating Preference Shareholders).
2. **Equity Shareholders' Funds** = Equity Share Capital + Reserves and Surplus – Fictitious Assets (if any).

TUTORIAL NOTE

Some accountants feel that the figure of 'Total Assets' should be fairly representative of the investment in total assets throughout the accounting period and therefore, they prefer to make use of the concept of 'Average Assets' which can be obtained by dividing the aggregate of the total assets at the beginning and at the end of the accounting period, by 2.

COMPUTATION OF RETURN ON EQUITY SHAREHOLDERS' FUNDS

Return on Equity Shareholders' Funds Ratio is computed by dividing the Net Profit after Interest, Tax and Preference Dividend by Equity Shareholders' Funds. This ratio is expressed as a percentage. In the form of a formula, this ratio may be expressed as follows:

$$\textbf{Return on Equity Shareholders' Funds} = \frac{\textbf{Net Profit after Interest, Tax and Preference Dividend}}{\textbf{Equity Shareholders' Funds}} \times 100$$

INTERPRETATION OF RETURN ON EQUITY SHAREHOLDERS' FUNDS

Return on Equity Shareholders' Funds ratio indicates the firm's ability of generating profit per rupee of Equity Shareholders' Funds. Higher the ratio, the more efficient the management and utilisation of Equity Shareholders' Funds.

An enterprise should have a satisfactory ratio. To judge whether the ratio is satisfactory *or* not, it should be compared with its own past ratios *or* with the ratio of similar enterprises in the same industry *or* with the industry average.

ILLUSTRATION 85

From the following information, calculate Return on Equity Shareholders' Funds.

Net Profit before Interest & Tax ₹ 6,00,000, Tax ₹ 1,50,000, Net Fixed Assets ₹ 10,00,000. Non-Current Investments ₹ 1,00,000, Current Assets ₹ 5,00,000, Equity Share Capital (₹ 10 each) ₹ 1,50,000, 20% Pref. Share Capital ₹ 1,00,000, Reserves & Surplus ₹ 1,50,000 (Opening Balance), 12.5% Debentures ₹ 8,00,000, Current Liabilities ₹ 4,00,000.

SOLUTION

STEP 1: NET PROFIT AFTER INTEREST, TAX & PREF. DIVIDEND

Particulars	₹
A. Net Profit before Interest & Tax	6,00,000
B. *Less:* Interest on Debentures	(1,00,000)
C. Net Profit before tax	5,00,000
D. *Less:* Tax	(1,50,000)
E. Net Profit after Interest & Tax	3,50,000
F. *Less:* Pref. Dividend	(20,000)
G. Equity Shareholders' Funds	3,30,000

STEP 2: CALCULATION OF EQUITY SHAREHOLDERS'FUNDS

Liabilities Side Approach	₹	*Assets Side Approach*	₹
A. Equity Share Capital	1,50,000	A. Non-Current Assets	11,00,000
B. *Add:* Reserve & Surplus (op)	1,50,000	(10,00,000 + 1,00,000)	
C. Equity Shareholders' Funds	3,00,000	B. Current Assets	5,00,000
		C. *Less:* Current Liabilities	(4,00,000)
		D. Capital Employed (A + B – C)	12,00,000
		E. *Less:* Non-Current Liabilities	(8,00,000)
		F. Shareholders' Funds	4,00,000
		G. *Less:* Pref. Share Capital	(1,00,000)
		H. Equity Shareholders' Funds	3,00,000

Step 3: Return on Equity Shareholders' Funds

$$= \frac{\textbf{Net Profit after Interest, Tax and Pref. Dividend}}{\textbf{Equity Shareholders' Funds}} \times 100 = \frac{₹\ 3,30,000}{₹\ 3,00,000} \times 100 = 110\%$$

37.0 EARNING PER SHARE (EPS)

MEANING OF EARNING PER SHARE (EPS)

EPS measures the Earnings available to an Equity Shareholder on a per share basis.

OBJECTIVE OF EARNING PER SHARE (EPS)

The objective of computing EPS ratio is to measure the profitability of the firm on per equity share basis.

COMPONENTS OF EARNING PER SHARE (EPS)

1. **Net Profit after Interest, Tax and Preference Dividend;**
2. **Number of Equity Shares**

COMPUTATION OF EARNING PER SHARE (EPS)

EPS ratio is computed by dividing the Net Profit after Interest, Tax and Preference Dividend by the Number of Equity Shares. It is expressed as an absolute figure. In the form of a formula, this ratio may be expressed as follows:

$$\textbf{Earning Per Share (EPS)} = \frac{\textbf{Net Profit after Interest, Tax and Preference Dividend}}{\textbf{Number of Equity Shares}} \times 100 = ₹ \ldots \textbf{ per share}$$

INTERPRETATION OF EARNING PER SHARE (EPS)

In general, higher the EPS, better it is and vice versa. While interpreting this ratio, it must be seen whether there is any increase in Equity Shareholders' Funds as a result of retained earnings without any change in numbers of outstanding shares. For instance, in the case of a company which is following a practice of ploughing back of profits and which is not capitalising its profits by way of issue of bonus shares, the interpretation of EPS without considering the effect of profits ploughed back in the business on earnings, will not be appropriate. EPS helps in determining the market price of the equity shares of the company. It also helps in estimating the company's capacity to pay dividend.

An enterprise should have a satisfactory ratio. To judge whether the ratio is satisfactory *or* not, it should be compared with its own past ratios *or* with the ratio of similar enterprises in the same industry *or* with the industry average.

ILLUSTRATION 86

Net Profit before Interest & Tax ₹ 6,00,000, Equity Share Capital (₹ 10 each) ₹ 1,50,000. 12.5% Debentures ₹ 8,00,000, 20% Pref. Share Capital ₹ 1,00,000, Tax Rate 30%. Calculate the Earning Per Share.

SOLUTION

STEP 1: NET PROFIT AFTER INTEREST, TAX & PREF. DIVIDEND

Particulars	₹
A. Net Profit before Interest & Tax	6,00,000
B. *Less:* Interest on Debentures	(1,00,000)

C. Net Profit before tax	5,00,000
D. *Less:* Tax	(1,50,000)
E. Net Profit after Interest & Tax	3,50,000
F. *Less:* Pref. Dividend	(20,000)
G. Net Profit after Interest, Tax & Pref. Dividend	3,30,000

Step 2: Earning Per Share = $\frac{\textbf{Net Profit after Interest, Tax and Pref. Dividend}}{\textbf{Equity Shareholders' Funds}} \times \textbf{100}$

$= \frac{₹\ 3,30,000}{₹\ 15,000} = ₹\ 22$

38.0 DIVIDEND PER SHARE

MEANING OF DIVIDEND PER SHARE

This ratio measures the dividend distributed per equity share.

OBJECTIVE OF DIVIDEND PER SHARE

The objective of computing this ratio is to measure the dividend distributed per equity share.

COMPONENTS OF DIVIDEND PER SHARE

There are two components of this ratio as follows:

(i) Profits Distributed as dividend

(ii) Number of Equity Shares

Computation of Dividend Per Share

This ratio is computed by dividing the profit distributed as equity dividend by the number of equity shares. It is expressed as an absolute figure. In the form of a formula, this ratio may be expressed as follows:

$$\text{Dividend Per Share (EPS)} = \frac{\text{Profit distributed as Equity dividend}}{\text{Number of Equity Shares}} = ₹\text{... per share}$$

INTERPRETATION

In general, higher the DPS, better it is and vice versa. An enterprise should have a satisfactory ratio. To judge whether the ratio is satisfactory *or* not, it should be compared with its own past ratios *or* with the ratio of similar enterprises in the same industry *or* with the industry average.

ILLUSTRATION 87

Net Profit after Interest & Tax ₹ 3,30,000, Profit distributed as dividend ₹ 1,98,000., Equity Share Capital (₹ 10 each) ₹ 1,50,000. Calculate Dividend Per Share.

SOLUTION

$$\text{Dividend Per Share} = \frac{\text{Profit distributed as dividend}}{\text{Number of Equity Shares}} = ₹\ 1,98,000/15,000 = ₹\ 13.20$$

39.0 PRICE EARNING RATIO

MEANING OF PRICE EARNING RATIO

This ratio measures the relationship between the market price per share and earning per share.

OBJECTIVE

The objective of computing this ratio is to find out expectations of the shareholders about the earnings of the firm.

COMPONENTS

There are two components of this ratio as follows:

(i) Market Price Per Share, (ii) Earning Per Share (EPS).

COMPUTATION

This ratio is computed by dividing market price per share by the earning per share. It is usually expressed as a pure number. In the form of a formula, this ratio may be expressed as follows:

Note: *Market Price per share may be Average Share Price or Closing Share Price*

$$\text{Price-Earning Ratio} = \frac{\text{Market Price Per Share}}{\text{Earning Per Share EPS}}$$

INTERPRETATION

It indicates the number of times of EPS, the share is being quoted in the market. In other words, it indicates the payback period within which the prospective investor can recover his investment in a single share by way of Earning Per Share (EPS). Unless affected by speculation usually higher P/E Ratio indicates that the company is growing and has good earning prospects but a lower P/E ratio need not always necessarily mean that the company is not growing and has no good prospects as it happens in case of a closely held public company where only a few shares are available in the market for general investors who generally do not trade much in those limited shares.

ILLUSTRATION 88

Earning Per Share ₹ 13.20, Market Price Per Share ₹ 132. Calculate Price-Earning Ratio.

SOLUTION

$$\text{Price Earning Ratio} = \frac{\text{Market Price Per Share}}{\text{Earning Per Share}} = \frac{₹\,132}{₹\,13.20} = 10$$

40.0 DIVIDEND PAYOUT RATIO

MEANING DIVIDEND PAYOUT RATIO

This ratio measures the portion of earning per share distributed as dividend.

OBJECTIVE

The objective of computing this ratio is to measure the portion of EPS distributed as dividend.

COMPONENTS

There are two components of this ratio as follows:

(i) Earning Per Share (EPS)

(ii) Dividend Per Share (DPS)

COMPUTATION

This ratio is computed by dividing the DPS by EPS. It is usually expressed as a percentage. In the form of formula, this ratio may be expressed as follows:

$$\text{Dividend Payout Ratio} = \frac{\text{Dividend Per Share (DPS)}}{\text{Earning Per Share (ESP)}} \times 100$$

INTERPRETATION

In general higher the D/P Ratio, better it is. An enterprise should have a satisfactory ratio. To judge whether the ratio is satisfactory *or* not, it should be compared with its own past ratios *or* with the ratio of similar enterprises in the same industry *or* with the industry average.

ILLUSTRATION 89

Calculate Dividend Payout Ratio from the following:

Dividend Per Share ₹ 11.10, Earning Per Share ₹ 22.20.

SOLUTION

$$\text{Dividend Payout Ratio} = \frac{\text{Dividend Per Share (EPS)}}{\text{Earning Per Share (ESP)}} \times 100 = \frac{₹\ 13.20}{₹\ 22} \times 100 = 60\%$$

41.0 EARNING YIELD (EY)

MEANING OF EARNING YIELD

This ratio measures the relationship between Earning Per Share (EPS) and Maker price per share.

OBJECTIVE

The objective of computing this ratio is to measure the performance of earnings in relation to market price per share.

COMPONENTS

There are two components of this ratio as follows:

(i) Earning Per Share,

(ii) Market Price Per Share (preferably Average Market Price per share)

COMPUTATION

This ratio is computed by dividing the EPS by the market price per share. It is usually expressed as a percentage. In the form of a formula, this ratio may be expressed as follows:

$$\text{Earning yield} = \frac{\text{Earning Per Share (EPS)}}{\text{Market Price Per Share}} \times 100$$

INTERPRETATION

It indicates the return (in terms of EPS) on market price. It indicates earning as % of market price. In general higher the ratio, better it is.

An enterprise should have a satisfactory ratio. To judge whether the ratio is satisfactory *or* not, it should be compared with its own past ratios *or* with the ratio of similar enterprises in the same industry *or* with the industry average.

ILLUSTRATION 90

From the following. Calculate Earning Yield.

Earning Per Share ₹ 22, Market Price Per Share ₹ 132

SOLUTION

$$\text{Earning Yield} = \frac{\text{Earning Per Share (EPS)}}{\text{Market Price Per Share}} \times 100 = \frac{₹\ 22}{₹\ 132} \times 100 = 16.67\%$$

42.0 DIVIDEND YIELD (EY)

MEANING OF DIVIDEND YIELD

This ratio measure the relationship between Dividend Per Share (DPS) and Market Price per share.

OBJECTIVE

The objective of computing this ratio is to measure the performance of dividend in relation to market price per share.

COMPONENTS

There are two components of this ratio as follows:

(i) Dividend Per Share (DPS)

(ii) Market Price Per Share. (preferably Average Market Price Per Share)

COMPUTATION

This ratio is computed by dividing the DPS by the market price per share. It is usually expressed as a percentage. In the form of a formula, this ratio may be expressed as a percentage. In the form of a formula, this ratio may be expressed as follows:

$$\textbf{Dividend Yield} = \frac{\textbf{Dividend Per Share}}{\textbf{Market Price Per Share}} \times 100$$

INTERPRETATION

In indicates the return (in terms of DPS) on market price. It indicates dividend as % of market price. In general higher the ratio, better it is.

An enterprise should have a satisfactory ratio. To judge whether the ratio is satisfactory *or* not, it should be compared with its own past ratios *or* with the ratio of similar enterprises in the same industry *or* with the industry average.

ILLUSTRATION 91

From the following. Calculate Dividend Yield.

Dividend Per Share ₹ 13.20, Market Price Per Share ₹ 132

SOLUTION

$$\text{Earning Yield} = \frac{\text{Dividend Per Share (EPS)}}{\text{Earning Per Share (ESP)}} \times 100 = \frac{₹\ 13.20}{₹\ 132} \times 100\ = 10\%$$

43.0 MARKET RESPONSE RATIO

MEANING OF MARKET RESPONSE RATIO

This ratio measures a relationship between Market Value per share and Book Value per share.

OBJECTIVE

The objective of computing this ratio is to measure market response to the book value of a share.

COMPONENTS

There are two components of this ratio as follows:

(i) Market Value per share (preferably Average Market Price of a share)

(ii) Book Value per share which is computed by dividing Net Assets available for equity shareholders by Number of Equity Shares.

COMPUTATION

This ratio is computed by dividing the Market Price per share by Book Value per share. It is expressed as a percentage. In the form of a formula, this ratio may be expressed as follows:

$$\text{Market Value/Book Value} = \frac{\text{Market Value Per Share}}{\text{Book Value Per Share}} \times 100$$

$$\textit{or,} \quad = \frac{\text{Average/Closing Market Price Per Share}}{\text{Net Worth/No. of Equity Shares}} \times 100$$

INTERPRETATION

This ratio indicates market response to the book value of a share. Higher the ratio better is the shareholders' position in terms of capital gains. Price/Book Value is the price paid for the company's assets. Lower the price to book value, more attractive the Investment Opportunity.

However, price to book value should not be looked at in isolation. The quality of the Assets, Profitability, and Return on Equity should also be considered.

ILLUSTRATION 92

From the following, calculate the Market Response Ratio:

Market Value of an Equity Share ₹ 132

Book Value of an Equity Share ₹ 66

SOLUTION

$$\text{Market Value/Book Value} = \frac{\text{Market Value per share}}{\text{Book Value per share}} = \frac{₹\,132}{₹\,66} \times 100 = 200\%$$

ILLUSTRATION 93 [COMPREHENSIVE]

Following in the Balance Sheet of Tulsian Ltd as at 31.3.2015:

BALANCE SHEET OF TULSIAN LTD AS AT 31.03.2015

Particulars	*31.03.2015* ₹
I. EQUITY AND LIABILITIES	
(1) Shareholders' Funds	
(a) Share Capital (including 18% Pref. Share Capital ₹ 1,00,000)	2,00,000
(b) Reserves and Surplus	2,00,000
(2) Non-Current Liabilities	
Long-term Borrowings	8,00,000
(3) Current Liabilities	
Short-term Borrowings	40,000
Trade Payables	1,00,000
Other Current Liabilities	1,40,000
Short-term Provisions	1,20,000
Total	16,00,000

II.	**ASSETS**	
	(1) Non-Current Assets	
	Fixed Assets	10,00,000
	Non-Current Investments	1,00,000
	(2) Current Assets	
	Current Investments	20,000
	Inventories	1,90,000
	Trade Receivables	2,60,000
	Cash & Cash Equivalents	10,000
	Short-term Loans & Advances	10,000
	Other Current Assets(Prepaid Expenses)	10,000
	Total	16,00,000

Net Profit after Interest & Tax for the year 2014-2015 ₹ 2,40,000, Tax Rate 50%, Equity Dividend 60% of Earning Per Share, Operating Expenses ₹ 2,00,000, Market Price of an Equity Share ₹ 225, Net Sales ₹ 20,00,000, Sales Returns ₹ 1,00,000.

Required: (a) Gross Profit Ratio, (b) Operating Ratio, (c) Net Profit Ratio, (d) Return on Investment, (e) Earning Per Share, (f) Dividend per Share, (g) Price Earning Ratio. (h) Dividend Payout Ratio, (i) Earning Yield, (j) Dividend Yield, (k) Market Response Ratio.

SOLUTION

CALCULATION OF CAPITAL EMPLOYED

Liabilities Side Approach	₹	*Assets Side Approach*	₹
Equity Share Capital	1,00,000	Net Fixed Assets	10,00,000
Add: Reserves & Surplus	2,00,000	*Add:* Non-Current Investments	1,00,000
Equity Shareholders' Funds	3,00,000	*Add:* Current Assets	5,00,000
Add: Preference Share Capital	1,00,000	Total Assets	16,00,000
Shareholders' Funds	4,00,000	*Less:* Current Liabilities	(4,00,000)
Add: Long-term Debts	8,00,000		
Capital Employed	12,00,000	Capital Employed	12,00,000

CALCULATION OF NET PROFIT BEFORE INTEREST & TAX, GROSS PROFIT AND OPERATING COST

A.	Net Profit after Interest & Tax	2,40,000
B.	*Add:* Tax $\left[\frac{₹\ 2,43,000}{0.50} \times 0.50\right]$	2,40,000
C.	Net Profit Before Tax [A + B]	4,80,000
D.	*Add:* Interest on Long-term Debt [15% on ₹ 8,00,000]	1,20,000
E.	Net Profit Before Interest & Tax	6,00,000
F.	*Add:* Operating Expenses	2,00,000
G.	Gross Profit (F + G)	8,00,000
H.	Net Sales	20,00,000

I.	Cost of Goods Sold (I – H)	12,00,000
J.	Operating Cost (G + J)	14,00,000

(a) Gross Profit Ratio = $\frac{\text{Gross Profit}}{\text{Net Sales}}\times 100 = \frac{₹\ 8,00,000}{₹\ 20,00,000}\times 100 = 40\%$

(b) Operating Ratio = $\frac{\text{Operating Cost}}{\text{Net Sales}}\times 100 = \frac{₹\ 14,00,000}{₹\ 20,00,000}\times 100 = 70\%$

(c) Net Profit Ratio = $\frac{\text{Net Profit before tax}}{\text{Net Sales}}\times 100 = \frac{₹\ 4,86,000}{₹\ 20,00,000}\times 100 = 24.3\%$

or, Net Profit Ratio = $\frac{\text{Net Profit before tax}}{\text{Net Sales}}\times 100 = \frac{₹\ 2,43,000}{₹\ 20,00,000}\times 100 = 12.15\%$

(d) Return on Capital Employed *or* Investment $= \frac{\text{Net Profit Before Interest \& Tax}}{\text{Capital employed}}\times 100$

$= \frac{₹\ 6,00,000}{₹\ 12,00,000}\times 100 = 50\%$

(e) Earning Per Share = $\frac{\text{Net Profit after Interest, Tax and Preference Dividend}}{\text{Number of Equity Shares}} = \frac{₹\ 2,25,000}{10,000} = ₹\ 22.50$

(f) Dividend Per Share = $\frac{\text{Profit distributed as dividend}}{\text{Number of Equity Shares}} = \frac{₹\ 1,35,000}{10,000} = ₹\ 13.50$

(g) Price Earning Ratio = $\frac{\text{Market Price Per Share}}{\text{Earning Per Share}} = \frac{₹\ 225}{₹\ 22.50} = 10$

(h) Dividend Payout Ratio = $\frac{\text{Dividend Per Share}}{\text{Earning Per Share}} = \frac{₹\ 13.50}{₹\ 22.50}\times 100 = 60\%$

(i) Earning Yield = $\frac{\text{Earning Per Share}}{\text{Market Price Per Share}} = \frac{₹\ 22.50}{₹\ 225}\times 100 = 10\%$

(j) Dividend Yield = $\frac{\text{Dividend Per Share}}{\text{Market Price Per Share}} = \frac{₹\ 13.50}{₹\ 225}\times 100 = 6\%$

(k) Market Response Ratio = $\frac{\text{Market Price Per Share}}{\text{Book Value Per Share}} = \frac{₹\ 225}{₹\ 40}\times 100 = 562.50\%$

Note: Book Value Per Share = $\frac{\text{Equity Shareholders' Funds}}{\text{No. of Equity Shares}} = \frac{₹\ 4,00,000}{₹\ 10,000} = ₹\ 40$ per share.

44.0 INTER-FIRM COMPARISON

MEANING OF INTER-FIRM COMPARISON

Inter-firm comparison is a technique of comparing the information of similar other concerns for assessing its own performance and ascertaining the reasons for any difference in performance and efficiency. In this regard, financial statements as prepared by the concern are an important source of information. In order to evaluate and interpret the financial performance and efficiency of the concern, accounting ratios are extensively used. The same procedure may also be useful in comparing the inter-firm financial information.

ACCOUNTING RATIOS USED FOR INTER-FIRM COMPARISON

The important accounting ratios that may be used in inter-firm comparison are as follows:

1. **ROI:** The return on investment popularly known as ROI calculated as operating profit to operating assets provides an insight into the financial performance of the concern. This ratio can be broken into two components, viz., profit margin on sales and the turnover ratios to capital.

2. **Debt-Equity Ratio:** The debt-equity ratio, i.e., the ratio of long-term debt to the total of long-term funds i.e., capital and reserves, and long-term debt. A change in this ratio would indicate a change in the financial policy pursued by the company. Set against the ratio for the industry as a whole, it would indicate to what extent the particular company is deviating from the norms. Diversified business will be able to maintain a higher debt-equity ratio than a company which depends only on one product line. This is because profit volatility is relatively *less* in diversified business on the basis of which higher degree of leverage risk can be assumed.
3. **Current Ratio:** The current ratio which would indicate the efficiency with which the company would be able to meet its short-term commitments. Current Ratio higher than unity indicates that the business covers the Current Liabilities at least at the book value. Higher the current ratio, better is the Current Liabilities coverage. On the other hand, too high a current ratio may mean idle Working Capital.

Strictly speaking, these three ratios would be able to throw a good deal of light on the performance of the company. But these figures should be seen along with the progress in absolute terms. It is possible to maintain good ratios even in a declining business.

In this connection, it is necessary to point out that the criteria laid down for inter-firm comparison in respect of costs also hold good for comparison on the basis of accounting ratios. What may be suitable for a small firm may be unsuitable for a big one and vice-versa; the ratios worked out on the basis of financial statements in the case of old firms may not really be valid in terms whereas ratios in the case of new firm would be nearer the truth since the balance sheet figures would reflect more *or* less current values.

OBJECTIVES OF INTER-FIRM COMPARISON

Inter-firm comparison has been used on a large scale with the objectives of making choice of investment by potential investors. The investor conducts inter-firm comparison for determining the status of security of investment as also the returns in the form of dividends. Whereas the small investor who is interested in regular dividends conducts the analysis from the dividend and profitability angle, the large investors look to inter-firm comparison with a view to have not only returns but also to have the capital appreciation. This involves an inter-firm comparison of both profitability trends as also the trends pertaining to the quality, strength and fibre of share-holders' equity.

The technique of inter-firm comparison has also been increasingly applied by companies. The main objectives for which this technique is being used may be summarised as follows:

1. Diagnosing the real problems, over-all technical and accounting analysis, of each firm in relation to others, detecting weak spots and evaluating their real importance.
2. Helping the management to prepare specific plans of action under the existing circumstances after taking into account all relevant technical, financial and other factors.
3. Preparing the base for standardisation of products and practices, for uniform accounting systems and records, mutual exchange of information between firms and other factors.
4. Determining the conditions of a particular firm and special reasons of lower efficiency beyond the control due to geographical and other reasons, so that suggestions of allowing subsidies, loans and other amenities may be considered.
5. Facilitating introduction of collective incentive schemes and allowing the employees to understand the importance of such schemes.

In case of inter-firm comparison service, neither past performance as such nor arbitrary standard is followed but a direct and relevant yardstick having regard to the peculiarities of the industry and of the current business should be applied. The ultimate objective is to strive for better operational efficiency and better financial position of the industry as a whole due to the impact of individual striving in his field only. Every unit can focus its attention on its weakest spot. The most vulnerable points of the industry also come to broad day-light. By subscribing to the self-discipline,. the management has a constant review of the position. Otherwise, at times it may try an appraisal, and on other occasions appraisal may not be undertaken.

Thus, the objective of inter-firm comparison is to provide information regarding the competitive position of participating companies since it helps in improving the profitability and efficiency of these companies.

Some Performance indicators published in economic newspapers like Economic Times etc.

(a) Book Value per Share
(b) Earning Per Share (EPS)
(c) Dividend (%)
(d) Yield (%) = Equity Dividend × 100/Market Price
(e) Pay Out Ratio (%) = × 100
(f) Gross Margin/Sales (%)
(g) Gross Margin/Capital Employed (%)
(h) Price Earning Ratio (P/E)
(i) Current Ratio

45.0 INTERPRETATION OF RATIOS

Situation	Interpretation
1. High Current Ratio, High Quick Ratio	The proportion of either Cash *or* Debtors *or* both in the current assets in quite high.
2. High Current Ratio, Low Quick Ratio	The proportion of Stock in the current assets is quite high, i.e., Accumulation of Inventory
3. Low Current Ratio, High Quick Ratio	The proportion of bank overdraft in current liability is quite high & the firm is using quick liabilities as denominator while calculating quick liabilities.
4. Low Current Ratio, Low Quick Ratio	The proportion of either Cash *or* Debtors *or* both in the current assets is quite low & there is no accumulation of stock.
5. High Current Ratio, Low Capital Turnover Ratio	It indicates that the firm does not have profitable opportunities and is not in a position to employ the available funds hence it has idle funds. In other words, there is over capitalisation *or* under trading.
6. Low Current Ratio, High Capital Turnover Ratio	It indicates that the firm has profitable opportunities and is in a position to employ the available funds but it has shortage of funds. In other words, there is under capitalisation *or* over trading.
7. High Current Ratio, High Quick Ratio, Low Absolute Cash Ratio	The proportion of either Cash *or* Marketable Securities *or* both in the current assets is quite low but proportion of Debtors is quite high.
8. High Current Ratio, Low Quick Ratio, Low Absolute Cash Ratio	The proportion of Cash, Marketable Securities and Debtors in the current asses is quite low but proportion of Stock is quite high.
9. Low Current Ratio, Low Quick Ratio, Low Absolute Cash Ratio	The proportion of all the components of the current assets is quite low.
10. Increase in Stock Turnover and Debtors Turnover	Such increase causes decline in liquidity since the proportion of stock & debtors is quite low.

46.0 HOW TO CALCULATE VARIOUS ITEMS OF VARIOUS RATIOS

CALCULATION OF VARIOUS ITEMS BASED ON INCOME STATEMENT

	Particulars	₹	₹
A	**Revenue from Operations [Credit + Cash]**		....
B	***Less:* Cost of Revenue from Operations:**		
	Opening Inventory	....	
	Purchases [Net Credit Purchases + Cash Purchases]	....	
	Direct Expenses (e.g., Wages, Carriage/Feight Inward)	....	
	Less: Closing Inventory	(...........)	(...........)
C	**Gross Profit (A – B)**		....
D	***Less:* Operating Indirect Expenses: (e.g.)**		
	Employees' Benefit Expense	....	
	Depreciation	....	
	Cash Discount allowed	....	
	Bad Debts	....	
	Interest on Bills Payable	....	(..........)
E	**Operating Profit (C – D)**		....
F	***Less:* Non-Operating Expenses: (e.g.)**		
	Interest on Long-Term-Borrowings	....	
	Value of Fixed Assets lost by fire	....	(.........)
G	***Add:* Non-Operating Incomes: (e.g.)**		
	Interest & Dividend as Non-Current Investments	....	
	Profit an Sale of Non-Current Investments	....	
	Compensation for acquisition of land	....	....
H	**Net Profit before tax (E – F + G)**		....
I	***Less:* Tax**		(.........)
J	**Net Profit after tax (H – I)**		....

Note: Operating Cost = Cost of Revenue from Operations + Operating Expenses

CALCULATION OF VARIOUS ITEMS BASED ON BALANCE SHEET

	Particulars	₹
A.	Non-Current Assets (e.g. Net Fixed Assets, Non-Current Investments, Long-Term Loans Advances)	....
B.	Current Assets	....
C.	Total Assets [A + B]	....
D.	*Less:* Current Liabilities	(.........)
E.	Capital Employed [C – D]	....
F.	*Less:* Non-Current Liabilities (e.g. Long-term borrowings, Long-Term Provisions)	(.........)
G.	Shareholders' Funds/Proprietors' Funds/Equity [E – F]	....

Notes:

1. *Quick Assets = Current Assets – Inventory – Other Current Assets (e.g., Prepaid Expenses, Accrued Incomes, Advance Tax)*
2. *Working Capital = Current Assets – Current Liabilities*
3. *Total Debt = Current Liabilities + Non-Current Liabilities*
4. *Capital Employed = Non-Current Assets + Working Capital*
5. *Shareholders' Funds = Total Assets – Total Debt*
6. *Shareholders' Funds = Share Capital + Reserves & Surplus*
7. *Average Inventory = (Opening Inventory + Closing Inventory)/2*
8. *Average Trade Receivables = (Op. Trade Receivables + Cl. Trade Receivables)/2*
9. *Average Trade Payables = (Op. Trade Payables + Cl. Trade Payables)/2*

IMPORTANT POINTS TO REMEMBER

1. While calculating Current Ratio and Quick Ratio–

(i) The 'Provision for doubtful debts/bills' is deducted from the total amount of Trade Receivables.

(ii) Inventories and Prepaid Expenses are not considered as Quick Assets.

2. While calculating Inventory Turnover Ratio–

(i) If the figure of 'Average Inventory' cannot be ascertained due to the absence of the figure of 'Opening Inventory', the figure of 'Closing Inventory' may be applied by giving a suitable note to that effect.

(ii) If the figure of Cost of Revenue from Operations can not be ascertained, the figure of RFO may be used by giving a suitable note to that effect.

3. While calculating Debtors Turnover Ratio–

(i) The 'Provision for doubtful debts' is not deducted from the total amount of Trade Receivables.

(ii) If the figure of Average Trade Receivables cannot be ascertained due to the absence of the figure of Opening Trade Receivables, the figure of Closing Trade Receivables may be applied by giving a suitable note to that effect.

(iii) If the figure of Credit Revenue from Operations is not ascertainable, the figure of Total RFO given may be used assuming that all sales are credit sales.

4. While calculating Creditors Turnover Ratio–

(i) The 'Reserve for discount on creditors' is not deducted from the total amount of Trade Payables.

(ii) If the figure of Average Trade Payables cannot be ascertained due to the absence of the figure of Opening Trade Payables, the figure of Closing Trade Payables may be applied by giving a suitable note to that effect.

(iii) If the figure of Net Credit Purchases is not ascertainable the figure of Total Purchases given may be applied assuming that all purchases are credit purchases.

5. While calculating Net Profit Ratio, the figure of Net Profit may be taken either before tax *or* after tax.

6. Both Operating Profit Ratio and Operating Ratio are complementary to each other and thus, if one of such ratios is deducted from 100, another ratio may be obtained.

7. While calculating Return on Capital Employed/Return on Investment (ROI)–

(i) Non-Operating Assets do not form part of Capital Employed (e.g., Non-Trade Investments, Advance for purchase of Fixed Assets, Capital Work-in-Progress, Intangible Assets under development, Non-Trade Investments)

(ii) Income from Non -Operating Assets (if any) should also be excluded while calculating the Net Profit before Interest & Tax.

SOLVED PROBLEMS I

PROBLEM 1

From the following information, Calculate (a) Current Ratio (b) Quick Ratio, (c) Debt-Equity Ratio, (d) Total Assets to Debt Ratio, (e) Proprietary Ratio,:

BALANCE SHEET OF TULSIAN LTD AS AT 31.03.2015

Particulars	*31.03.2015* ₹
I. EQUITY AND LIABILITIES	
(1) Shareholders' Funds	
(a) Share Capital	4,00,000
(b) Reserves and Surplus	4,00,000
(2) Non-Current Liabilities	
Long-term Borrowings	10,00,000
Long-term Provisions	6,00,000
(3) Current Liabilities	
Short-term Borrowings	80,000
Trade Payables	2,00,000
Other Current Liabilities	2,80,000
Short-term Provisions	2,40,000
Total	32,00,000
II. ASSETS	
(1) Non-Current Assets	
Fixed Assets	10,00,000
Non-Current Investments	4,00,000
Long-term Loans & Advances	2,00,000
(2) Current Assets	
Current Investments	20,000
Inventories	7,90,000
Trade Receivables	7,60,000
Cash & Cash Equivalents	10,000
Short-term Loans & Advances	10,000
Other Current Assets(Prepaid Expenses)	10,000
Total	32,00,000

SOLUTION

(a) **Current Ratio** $= \frac{\textbf{Current Assets}}{\textbf{Current Liabilities}} = \frac{₹\,16,00,000}{₹\,8,00,000} = 2:1$

NOTE: CALCULATION OF CURRENT ASSETS AND CURRENT LIABILITIES

Current Assets	₹	*Current Liabilities*	₹
Current Investments	20,000	Short-Term Borrowings	80,000
Inventories	7,90,000	Trade Payables	2,00,000
Trade Receivables	7,60,000	Other Current Liabilities	2,80,000
Cash and Cash Equivalents	10,000	Short-Term Provisions	2,40,000
Short-term Loans and Advances	10,000		
Other Current Assets	10,000		
	16,00,000		8,00,000

(b) **Quick Ratio** $= \frac{\textbf{Quick Assets}}{\textbf{Current Liabilities}} = \frac{₹\,8,00,000}{₹\,8,00,000} = 1:1$

Note: **Quick Assets** = **Current Assets – Inventories – Prepaid Expenses**

= ₹ 16,00,000 – ₹ 7,90,000 – ₹ 10,000 = ₹ 8,00,000

(c) **Debt-Equity Ratio** $= \frac{\textbf{Debt}}{\textbf{Equity}} = \frac{₹\,16,00,000}{₹\,8,00,000} = 2:1$

Notes:

1. **Debt** = **Long-term Borrowings + Long-term Provisions**
   = ₹ 10,00,000 + ₹ 6,00,000 = ₹ 16,00,000
2. **Equity** = **Share Capital + Reserves & Surplus**
   = ₹ 4,00,000 + ₹ 4,00,000 = ₹ 8,00,000

(d)Total Assets to Debt Ratio $= \frac{\textbf{Total Assets}}{\textbf{Debt}} = \frac{₹\,32,00,000}{₹\,16,00,000} = 2:1$

Note: Total Assets = **Shareholders' Funds + Non-Current Liabilities + Current Liabilities**

= ₹ 8,00,000 + ₹ 16,00,000 + ₹ 8,00,000 = ₹ 32,00,000

(e) **Proprietary Ratio** $= \frac{\textbf{Proprietors' Funds}}{\textbf{Total Assets}} \times 100 = \frac{₹\,8,00,000}{₹\,32,00,000} \times 100 = 25\%$

PROBLEM 2

From the following calculate: (a) Gross Profit Ratio, (b) Operating Ratio, (c) Operating Profit Ratio, (d) Net Profit Ratio, (e) Inventory Turnover Ratio:

	₹		₹
Opening Inventory	1,00,000	Revenue from Operations	40,00,000
Purchases	23,00,000	Closing Inventory	2,00,000
Freight Inward	1,60,000	Interest & Dividend on	
Carriage Inward	40,000	Long-term Investments	6,000
Employees' Benefit Expense	2,00,000	Profit on Sale of	
Depreciation	1,60,000	Long term Investments	4,000
Finance Expenses:		Compensation for	

Cash discont allowed to Customers	20,000	acquisition of Land	2,000
Bad Debts	12,000	Value of Furniture lost by fire	12,000
Interest on Bills Payable	8,000	Provision for Tax	4,80,000
Interest on Debentures	2,40,000		

SOLUTION

(a) **Gross Profit Ratio** $= \dfrac{\textbf{Gross Profit}}{\textbf{Revenue from Operations}} \times \mathbf{100} = \dfrac{₹\,16,00000}{₹\,40,00,000} \times 100 = 40\%$

Notes:

1. **Cost of Revenue from Operations**

   = Opening Inventory + Purchases + Direct Expenses – Closing Inventory

   = ₹ 1,00,000 + ₹ 23,00,000 + (₹ 1,60,000 + ₹ 40,000) – ₹ 2,00,000 = ₹ 24,00,000

2. **Gross Profit** **= Revenue from Operations – Cost of RFO**

   = ₹ 40,00,000 – ₹ 24,00,000 = ₹ 16,00,000

(b) **Operating Ratio** $= \dfrac{\textbf{Operating Cost}}{\textbf{Revenue from Operations}} \times \mathbf{100} = \dfrac{₹\,28,00,000}{₹\,40,00,000} \times 100 = 70\%$

Notes:

Operating Cost = Cost of Revenue from Operations + Operating Expenses

= ₹ 24,00,000 + (₹ 2,00,000 + ₹ 1,60,000 + ₹ 12,000 + ₹ 20,000 + ₹ 8,000) = ₹ 28,00,000

(c) **Operating Profit Ratio** $= \dfrac{\textbf{Operating Profit}}{\textbf{Revenue from Operations}} \times \mathbf{100} = \dfrac{₹\,12,00,000}{₹\,40,00,000} \times 100 = 30\%$

Note: Operating Profit **= Revenue from Operations – Operating Cost**

= ₹ 40,00,000 – ₹ 28,00,000 = ₹ 12,00,000

or, **= 100% – Operating Ratio = 100% – 70% = 30%**

(d) **Net Profit Ratio** $= \dfrac{\textbf{Net Profit}}{\textbf{Revenue from Operations}} \times \mathbf{100} = \dfrac{₹\,4,80,000}{₹\,40,00,000} \times 100 = 12\%$

Note: Net Profit = Gross Profit – Operating Exp. – Non-Operating Exp. + Non-Operating Incomes – Tax

= ₹ 16,00,000 – ₹ 4,00,000 – ₹ 2,52,000 + ₹ 12,000 – ₹ 4,80,000 = ₹ 4,80,000

(e) **Inventory Turnover Ratio** $= \dfrac{\textbf{Cost of Revenue from Operations}}{\textbf{Average Inventory}}$

$= \dfrac{₹\,24,00,000}{₹\,1,50,000} = 16$ times

Note: Average Inventory **= (Opening Inventory + Closing Inventory)/2**

= (₹ 1,00,000 + ₹ 2,00,000)/2 = ₹ 1,50,000

PROBLEM 3

TULSIAN Ltd. provides you the following information:

Particulars	₹	*Particulars*	₹
Equity Share Capital (₹ 10 each)	3,00,000	Inventories	7,90,000
18% Pref. Share Capital	1,00,000	Trade Debtors	7,80,000
Debenture Redemption Reserve	1,60,000	Provision for Doubtful Debts	40,000
Profit & Loss A/c (Current year)	2,40,000	Current Investments	20,000
12% Debentures	10,00,000	Cash & Cash Equivalents	10,000
Long-term Provisions	6,00,000	Bills Receivables	20,000
Trade Creditors	1,40,000	Prepaid Expenses	10,000
Bills Payable	60,000	Short-term Loans & Advances	10,000
Outstanding Expenses	40,000	Provision for Tax	2,40,000
Short-term Bank Loan	80,000	Other Current Liabilities	2,40,000
Fixed Assets	10,00,000	Long-term Loans & Advances	2,00,000
Non-Current Investments	4,00,000		

Revenue from Operations for the year amounted to ₹ 20,00,000, Net Purchases ₹ 17,80,000, Opening Inventory ₹ 2,10,000. Operating Expenses ₹ 2,00,000.

Required: Calculate (a) Current Ratio (b) Quick Ratio, (c) Debt-Equity Ratio, (d) Total Assets to Debt Ratio, (e) Proprietary Ratio, (f) Interest Coverage Ratio, (g) Inventory Turnover Ratio. (h) Debtors Turnover Ratio, (i) Creditors Turnover Ratio, (j) Working Capital Turnover Ratio, (k) Gross Profit Ratio (l) Operating Ratio (m) Operating Profit Ratio (n) Net Profit Ratio.

SOLUTION

(a) **Current Ratio** $= \dfrac{\textbf{Current Assets}}{\textbf{Current Liabilities}} = \dfrac{₹\,16,00,000}{₹\,8,00,000} = 2:1$

CALCULATION OF CURRENT ASSETS AND CURRENT LIABILITIES

Current Assets	₹	*Current Liabilities*	₹
Current Investments	20,000	Short-Term Borrowings	80,000
Inventories	7,90,000	Trade Payables	2,00,000
Trade Receivables	7,60,000	Other Current Liabilities	2,80,000
Cash and Cash Equivalents	10,000	Short-Term Provisions	2,40,000
Short-term Loans and Advances	10,000		
Other Current Assets	10,000		
	16,00,000		8,00,000

(b) **Quick Ratio** $= \dfrac{\textbf{Quick Assets}}{\textbf{Current Liabilities}} = \dfrac{₹\,8,00,000}{₹\,8,00,000} = 1:1$

Note: **Quick Assets** = **Current Assets – Inventories – Prepaid Expenses**

= ₹ 16,00,000 – ₹ 7,90,000 – ₹ 10,000 = ₹ 8,00,000

(c) **Debt-Equity Ratio** $= \dfrac{\textbf{Debt}}{\textbf{Equity}} = \dfrac{₹\,16,00,000}{₹\,8,00,000} = 2:1$

Notes:

1. **Debt = Long-term Borrowings + Long-term Provisions**

   = ₹ 10,00,000 + ₹ 6,00,000 = ₹ 16,00,000

2. **Equity = Share Capital + Reserves & Surplus**

   = (₹ 3,00,000 + ₹ 1,00,000) + (₹ 1,60,000 + ₹ 2,40,000) = ₹ 8,00,000

(d) Total Assets to Debt Ratio $= \frac{\textbf{Total Assets}}{\textbf{Debt}} = \frac{₹\ 32,00,000}{₹\ 16,00,000} = 2:1$

Note: Total Assets = Shareholders' Funds + Non-Current Liabilities + Current Liabilities

= ₹ 8,00,000 + ₹ 16,00,000 + ₹ 8,00,000 = ₹ 32,00,000

(e) Proprietary Ratio $= \frac{\textbf{Proprietors' Funds}}{\textbf{Total Assets}} \times 100 = \frac{₹\ 8,00,000}{₹\ 32,00,000} \times 100 = 25\%$

(f) Interest Coverage Ratio $= \frac{\textbf{Net Profit before Interest and Tax}}{\textbf{Interest on Long-term Borrowings}} = \frac{₹\ 6,00,000}{₹\ 1,20,000} = 5 \text{ times}$

Note: Net Profit before Interest & Tax = Profit after Tax + Tax + Interest

= ₹ 2,40,000 + ₹ 2,40,000 + ₹ 1,20,000 = ₹ 6,00,000

(g) Inventory Turnover Ratio $= \frac{\textbf{Cost of Revenue from Operations}}{\textbf{Average Inventory}} = \frac{₹\ 12,00,000}{₹\ 5,00,000} = 2.4 \text{ times}$

Notes:

1. **Cost of Revenue from Operations**

   = Net Purchases + Opening Inventory – Closing Inventory

   = ₹ 17,80,000 + ₹ 2,10,000 – ₹ 7,90,000 = ₹ 12,00,000

2. **Average Inventory = (Opening Inventory + Closing Inventory)/2**

   = (₹ 2,10,000 + ₹ 7,90,000)/2 = ₹ 5,00,000

(h) Debtors Turnover Ratio $= \frac{\textbf{Credit Revenue from Operations}}{\textbf{Average Trade Receivables}}$

$= \frac{₹\ 20,00,000}{(₹\ 7,80,000 + ₹\ 20,000)} = 2.5 \text{ times}$

(i) Creditors Turnover Ratio $= \frac{\textbf{Net Credit Purchases}}{\textbf{Average Trade Payables}} = \frac{₹\ 17,80,000}{₹\ 2,00,000} = 8.9 \text{ times}$

(j) Working Capital Turnover Ratio $= \frac{\textbf{Revenue from Operations}}{\textbf{Working Capital}}$

$= \frac{₹\ 20,00,000}{₹\ 16,00,000 - ₹\ 8,00,000} = \frac{₹\ 20,00,000}{₹\ 8,00,000} = 2.5 \text{ times}$

(k) Gross Profit Ratio $= \frac{\textbf{Gross Profit}}{\textbf{Revenue from Operations}} \times 100 = \frac{₹\ 8,00,000}{₹\ 20,00,000} \times 100 = 40\%$

Note: Gross Profit = Revenue from Operations – Cost of Revenue from Operations

= ₹ 20,00,000 – ₹ 12,00,000 = ₹ 8,00,000

(l) Operating Ratio $= \frac{\textbf{Operating Cost}}{\textbf{Revenue from Operations}} \times 100 = \frac{₹\ 14,00,000}{₹\ 20,00,000} \times 100 = 70\%$

Note: Operating Cost = Cost of Revenue from Operations + Operating Exp.

= ₹ 12,00,000 + ₹ 2,00,000 = ₹ 14,00,000

(m) Operating Profit Ratio $= \frac{\textbf{Operating Profit}}{\textbf{Revenue from Operations}} \times 100 = \frac{₹\ 6,00,000}{₹\ 20,00,000} \times 100 = 30\%$

Note: Operating Profit = Revenue from Operations – Operating Cost
= ₹ 20,00,000 – ₹ 14,00,000 = ₹ 6,00,000

(n) **Net Profit Ratio** $= \dfrac{\textbf{Net Profit}}{\textbf{Revenue from Operations}} \times 100 = \dfrac{₹\ 2,40,000}{₹\ 20,00,000} \times 100$

Note: Net Profit = Gross Profit – Operating Exp. – Non-Operating Exp. – Tax
= ₹ 8,00,000 – ₹ 2,00,000 – ₹ 1,20,000 – ₹ 2,40,000 = ₹ 2,40,000

PROBLEM 4 [WHEN OPENING BALANCE SHEET IS GIVEN]

Following is the Balance Sheet as at 31st March, 2014;

Particulars	₹
I. EQUITY AND LIABILITIES	
(1) Shareholders' Funds	
Share Capital	2,50,000
Reserves & Surplus	2,10,000
(3) Non-Current Liabilities [15% Long-term Borrowings]	8,00,000
(4) Current Liabilities	4,00,000
Total	16,60,000
II. ASSETS	
(1) Non-Current Assets	
Fixed Assets	10,00,000
Non-Current Investments	
10% Trade Investments	1,00,000
10% Other Investments	60,000
(2) Current Assets	5,00,000
Total	16,60,000

Net Profit before Tax for the year 2014-2015, ₹ 4,86,000.

Required: Calculate Return on Investment for the year 2013-2014.

SOLUTION

STEP 1: NET PROFIT BEFORE INTEREST & TAX

	Particulars	₹
A	Net Profit before Tax	4,86,000
B	+ Interest on Long-term Borrowings [15% on ₹ 8,00,000]	1,20,000
C	– Interest on Non-Trade Investments [10% on ₹ 60,000]	(6,000)
D	Net Profit before Interest & Tax	6,00,000

STEP 2: CAPITAL EMPLOYED

Liabilities Side Approach	₹	*Assets Side Approach*	₹
A. Share Capital	2,50,000	A. Non-Current Assets	11,00,000
B. + Reserves & Surplus (Op)	2,10,000	[Ex. Non-Trade Investments]	

C. + Non-Current Liabilities	8,00,000	B. Current Assets	5,00,000
D. – Non-Trade Investments	(60,000)	C. – Current Liabilities	(4,00,000)
E. Capital Employed	12,00,000	D. Capital Employed	12,00,000

Step 3: Return on Capital Employed *or* Investment

$$= \frac{\textbf{Net Profit before Interest, Tax \& Dividend}}{\textbf{Capital Employed}} \times 100 = \frac{₹\ 6,00,000}{₹\ 12,00,000} \times 100 = 50\%$$

PROBLEM 5 [WHEN CLOSING BALANCE SHEET IS GIVEN]

Following is the Balance Sheet of the Tulsian Ltd. as at 31st March, 2015:

Particulars	₹
I. EQUITY AND LIABILITIES	
(1) Shareholders' Funds	
Share Capital	2,50,000
Reserves & Surplus (Profit for 2014-15 ₹ 4,86,000)	6,96,000
(3) Non-Current Liabilities [15% Long-term Borrowings]	8,00,000
(4) Current Liabilities	4,00,000
Total	21,46,000
II. ASSETS	
(1) Non-Current Assets	
Fixed Assets	9,00,000
Non-Current Investments	
10% Trade Investments	1,00,000
10% Other Investments	60,000
(2) Current Assets	10,86,000
Total	21,46,000

Required: Calculate Return on Investment for the year 2013-2014 with reference to Opening Capital Employed.

SOLUTION

STEP 1: NET PROFIT BEFORE INTEREST & TAX

Particulars	₹
A. Net Profit	4,86,000
B. + Interest on Long-term Borrowings [15% on ₹ 8,00,000]	1,20,000
C. – Interest on Non-Trade Investments [10% on ₹ 60,000]	(6,000)
D. Net Profit before Interest & Tax	6,00,000

STEP 2: CAPITAL EMPLOYED

Liabilities Side Approach	₹	*Assets Side Approach*	₹
A. Share Capital	2,50,000	A. Non-Current Assets [Ex. Non-Trade Investments]	10,00,000
B. + Reserves & Surplus (Op)	6,96,000		

C. + Non-Current Liabilities	8,00,000	B. Current Assets	10,86,000
D. – Non-Trade Investments	(60,000)	C. – Current Liabilities	(4,00,000)
E. – Current year's Profits	(4,86,000)	D. – Current year's Profits	(4,86,000)
F. Capital Employed	12,00,000	E. Capital Employed	12,00,000

Step 3: Return on Capital Employed *or* Investment

$$= \frac{\textbf{Net Profit before Interest, Tax \& Dividend}}{\textbf{Capital Employed}} \times 100 = \frac{₹\ 6,00,000}{₹\ 12,00,000} \times 100 = 50\%$$

PROBLEM 6

From the following information of BT Ltd, calculate (i) Debt-Equity Ratio and (ii) Net Profit Ratio: Cash Revenue from Operations, ₹ 10,00,000, Credit Revenue from Operations 120% of Cash Revenue from Operations, Cash Purchases ₹ 3,30,000, Credit Purchases 75% of Total Purchases, Opening Inventory ₹ 1,60,000, Closing Inventory 25% more than Opening Inventory, Direct Expenses ₹ 40,000, Operating Indirect Expenses 25% of Gross Profit, Non-Operating Expenses 20% of Operating Cost, Non-Operating Incomes 20% of Operating Profit, Trade Debtors ₹ 1,50,000, Other Quick Assets ₹ 45,000, Prepaid Expenses ₹ 5,000, Trade Creditors ₹ 1,50,000, Other Current Liabilities 12.5% of Current Assets, Net Fixed Assets ₹ 15,00,000, Non-Current Investments ₹ 80,000, Long-term Loans & Advances ₹ 20,000, Total Debt ₹ 14,00,000.

SOLUTION

(i) Debt-Equity Ratio $= \frac{\textbf{Debt}}{\textbf{Equity}} = \frac{₹\ 12,00,000}{₹\ 6,00,000} = 2:1$

Notes:

1. **Closing Inventory** = ₹ 1,60,000 + (₹ 1,60,000 × 25/100)= ₹ 2,00,000
2. **Current Assets = Trade Debtors +Other Quick Assets + Inventory + Prepaid Expenses**
   = ₹ 1,50,000 + ₹ 45,000 + ₹ 2,00,000 + ₹ 5,000 = ₹ 4,00,000
3. **Current Liabilities = Trade Creditors +Other Current Liabilities**
   = ₹ 1,50,000 + (₹ 4,00,000 × 12.5%)= ₹ 2,00,000
4. **Total Assets = Non-Current Assets + Current Assets**
   = (₹ 15,00,000 + ₹ 80,000 + ₹ 20,000) + ₹ 4,00,000 = ₹ 20,00,000
5. **Equity = Total Assets – Total Debt** = ₹ 20,00,000 – ₹ 14,00,000 = ₹ 6,00,000
6. **Long-term Debt = Total Debt – Current Liabilities**
   = ₹ 14,00,000 – ₹ 2,00,000 = ₹ 12,00,000

(ii) Net Profit Ratio $= \frac{\textbf{Net Profit}}{\textbf{Revenue from Operations}} \times 100 = \frac{₹\ 4,84,000}{₹\ 22,00,000} \times 100 = 22\%$

Notes:

1. **Revenue from Operations**
   = Cash Revenue from Operations + Credit Revenue from Operations
   = ₹ 10,00,000 +(₹ 10,00,000 × 120/100)= ₹ 22,00,000
2. **Net Purchases = Cash Purchases + Net Credit Purchases**
   = ₹ 3,30,000 +(₹ 3,30,000 × 75/25) = ₹ 13,20,000
3. **Closing Inventory** = ₹ 1,60,000 + (₹ 1,60,000 × 25/100) = ₹ 2,00,000
4. **Cost of Revenue from Operations**
   = Opening Inventory + Net Purchases + Direct Expenses – Closing Inventory
   = ₹ 1,60,000 + ₹ 13,20,000 + ₹ 40,000 – ₹ 2,00,000 = ₹ 13,20,000

5. **Gross Profit = Revenue from Operations – Cost of Revenue from Operations**
   = ₹ 22,00,000 – ₹ 13,20,000 = ₹ 8,80,000
6. **Operating Indirect Expenses** = ₹ 8,80,000 × 25/100 = ₹ 2,20,000
7. **Operating Cost = Cost of Revenue from Operations + Operating Expenses**
   = ₹ 13,20,000 + ₹ 2,20,000 = ₹ 15,40,000
8. **Non-Operating Expenses** = ₹ 15,40,000 × 20/100 = ₹ 3,08,000
9. **Operating Profit = Revenue from Operations – Operating Cost**
   = ₹ 22,00,000 – ₹ 15,40,000 = ₹ 6,60,000
10. **Non-Operating Incomes** = ₹ 6,60,000 × 20/100 = ₹ 1,32,000
11. **Net Profit = Operating Profit + Non-Operating Income – Non-Operating Expenses**
    = ₹ 6,60,000 + ₹ 1,32,000 – ₹ 3,08,000 = ₹ 4,84,000

Note: *Interest on Long-term Debt is already included in Non-Operating Expenses.*

PROBLEM 7

Liquid Ratio 1.5, Current Ratio 2, Inventory Turnover Ratio 6 times, Total Current Assets ₹ 8,00,000. Goods are sold at 20% profit on sales. Find out Annual Revenue from Operations.

SOLUTION

Step 1: Current Liabilities = **Current Assets/Current Ratio**
= ₹ 8,00,000/2 = ₹ 4,00,000

Step 2: Liquid Assets (LA) = **1.5 × Current Liabilities**
Liquid Assets = 1.5 × ₹ 4,00,000 = ₹ 6,00,000
Inventory = **Current Assets – Liquid Assets**
= ₹ 8,00,000 – ₹ 6,00,000 = ₹ 2,00,000

Step 3: Inventory Turnover Ratio = $\frac{\text{Cost of Goods Sold}}{\text{Average Inventory}}$

Cost of Goods sold = 6 × ₹ 2,00,000 = ₹ 12,00,000

Step 4: Let Total Revenue from Operations be X

Total Revenue from Operations = **Cost of Revenue from Operations + GP**
X = ₹ 12,00,000 + 20% of X
X = ₹ 12,00,000/0.80 = ₹ 15,00,000

PROBLEM 8

Current Ratio 2.5, Quick Ratio 1.5, Working Capital ₹ 1,20,000, Gross Profit @ 25% on Revenue from Operations was ₹ 1,00,000, Inventory Turnover Ratio 3 Times. Calculate Opening Inventory.

SOLUTION

Step 1: **Current Ratio** = $\frac{\textbf{Current Assets (CA)}}{\textbf{Current Liabilities (CL)}}$ = 2.5

CA – 2.5 CL = O Eq. I
CA – CL = ₹ 1,20,000 Eq. II

Subtracting Eq. II from Eq. I

$$1.5\ CL = ₹\ 1,20,000$$

$$CL = ₹\ 1,20,000/1.5 = ₹\ 80,000$$

CA = Current Liabilities × Current Ratio

$$= ₹\ 80,000 \times 2.5 = ₹\ 2,00,000$$

Step 2: **Quick Ratio** $= \dfrac{\text{Quick Assets}}{\text{Current Liabilities}} = \dfrac{\text{Quick Assets}}{₹\ 80,000} = 1.5$

Quick Assets = ₹ 80,000 × 1.5 = ₹ 1,20,000

Step 3: Closing Inventory = CA – QA = ₹ 2,00,000 – ₹ 1,20,000 = ₹ 80,000

Let the Revenue from Operations be = ₹ 4, Gross Profit = 25% of ₹ 4 = ₹ 1

Cost of Revenue from Operations = ₹ 4 – ₹ 1 = ₹ 3

If Gross Profit is ₹ 1, then Cost of Revenue from Operations = ₹ 3

If Gross Profit is ₹ 1,00,000, then Cost of Revenue from Operations = ₹ 3,00,000

Step 4: **Inventory Turnover Ratio** $= \dfrac{\textbf{Cost of Revenue from Operations}}{\textbf{Average Inventory}}$

$$= \frac{₹\ 3,00,000}{\text{Average Inventory}} = 3$$

Average Inventory = ₹ 3,00,000/3 = ₹ 1,00,000

$$\frac{OS + CS}{2} = ₹\ 1,00,000$$

$$OS + CS = ₹\ 1,00,000 \times 2 = ₹\ 2,00,000$$

$$OS = ₹\ 2,00,000 - ₹\ 80,000 = ₹\ 1,20,000$$

PROBLEM 9

Inventory Turnover Ratio 4 Times, Inventory at the end ₹ 20,000 more than that in the beginning, Revenue from Operations ₹ 3,00,000. Gross Profit Ratio 25%, Current Liabilities ₹ 40,000. Quick Ratio 0.75. Calculate Current Assets.

SOLUTION

Step 1: **Gross Profit = Revenue from Operations × GP Ratio**

= ₹ 3,00,000 × 25% = ₹ 75,000

Step 2: Cost of Revenue from Operations = Revenue from Operations – Gross Profit

= ₹ 3,00,000 – ₹ 75,000 = ₹ 2,25,000

Step 3: Average Inventory $= \dfrac{\textbf{Cost of Revenue from Operations}}{\textbf{Average Inventory}} = \dfrac{₹\ 2,25,000}{4} = ₹\ 56,250$

(Opening Inventory + Closing Inventory)/2 = ₹ 56,250

Closing Inventory + Opening Inventory = ₹ 56,250 × 2 = ₹ 1,12,500 ...Eq. I

Closing Inventory – Opening Inventory = ₹ 20,000 ...Eq. II

Adding Equation (i) & (ii)

2 Closing Inventory = ₹ 1,32,500

Closing Inventory = ₹ 1,32,500/2 = ₹ 66,250

Opening Inventory = ₹ 66,250 – ₹ 20,000 = ₹ 46,250

Step 4: **Quick Assets** = **Quick Ratio × Current Liabilities**

= ₹ 0.75 × ₹ 40,000 = ₹ 30,000

Step 5: **Current Assets** = **Quick Assets + Closing Inventory**

= ₹ 30,000 + ₹ 66,250 = ₹ 96,250

PROBLEM 10

Inventory Turnover Ratio 5 Times, Inventory at the end ₹ 15,000 more than Inventory in the beginning, Average Debt Collection period 3 Months, Gross Profit 33-1/3% cost, Current Liabilities ₹ 50,000, Average Trade Receivables ₹ 40,000, Cash Revenue from Operations 20% of Total Revenue from Operations, Trade Creditors ₹ 10,000, Current Ratio 2.25. Calculate Quick Assets.

SOLUTION

Step 1: Credit Revenue from Operations

= Debtors Turnovor Ratio × Average Trade Receivables

= ₹ 4 × ₹ 40,000 = 1,60,000

Total Revenue from Operations = $\frac{\text{Net Credit Sales}}{80\%} = \frac{1,60,000 \times 100}{80} = 2,00,000$

Step 2: Cost of Revenue from Operations

= Revenue from Operations – Gross Profit

= ₹ 2,00,000 – (25% of ₹ 2,00,000)

= ₹ 2,00,000 – ₹ 50,000 = ₹ 1,50,000

Step 3: Average Inventory = $\frac{\textbf{Cost of Revenue from Operations}}{\textbf{Stock Turnover Rario}} = \frac{₹\ 1,50,000}{5} = ₹\ 30,000$

(OS + CS)/2 = ₹ 30,000

CS + OS = ₹ 30,000 × 2 = ₹ 60,000 ...Eq. I

Closing Inventory – Opening Inventory = ₹ 15,000 ... Eq. II

Additing Equation (i) & (ii)

2 Closing Inventory = 75.000

Closing Inventory = ₹ 75,000/2 = ₹ 37.500

Opening Inventory = ₹ 37,500 – ₹ 15,000 = ₹ 22,500

Step 4: **Qulck Assets** = **Current Assets – Inventory**

= ₹ 1,12,500 – ₹ 37,500 = ₹ 75,000

PROBLEM 11

Average Debt Collection Period 4 Months, Inventory Turnover Ratio 3 Times, Average Trade Receivables ₹ 1,00,000. Cash Revenue from Operations being 25% of Total Revenue from Operations, Gross Profit Ratio 25%, Inventory at the end was 3 times that in the beginning. Calculate the amount of Opening Inventory and Closing Inventory.

SOLUTION

Step 1: Debtors Turnover Ratio = 12 Months/4 Months = 3 Times

$= \frac{\textbf{Credit Revenue from Operations}}{\textbf{Average Trade Receivables}} = 3 = \frac{\text{Credit Revenue from Operations}}{₹\ 1,00,000} = 3$

Credit Revenue from Operations = ₹ 1,00,000 × 3 = ₹ 3,00,000

Let Total Revenue from Operations be = ₹ 100

Cash Revenue from Operations = 25% of ₹ 100 = ₹ 25,

Credit Revenue from Operations = ₹ 100 – ₹ 25 = ₹ 75

If Credit Revenue from Operations are ₹ 75, then Total Revenue from Operations = ₹ 100

If Credit Revenue from Operations are ₹ 3,00,000, then

Total Revenue from Operations = ₹ 100 × ₹ 3,00,000/₹ 75 = ₹ 4,00,000

Gross Profit = 25% of ₹ 4,00,000 = ₹ 1,00,000

Step 2: Cost of Revenue from Operations

= Total Revenue from Operations – Gross Profit

= ₹ 4,00,000 – ₹ 1,00,000 = ₹ 3,00,000

Step 3: Inventory Turnover Ratio = $\frac{\textbf{Cost of Revenue from Operations}}{\textbf{Average Inventory}}$

$= \frac{₹\ 3,00,000}{\text{Average Stock}} = 3$

Average Inventory = ₹ 3,00,000/3 = ₹ 1,00,000

(OS + CS)/2 = ₹ 1,00,000

or OS + CS = ₹ 1,00,000 × 2 = ₹ 2,00,000 Eq. I

CS – 3OS = 0 Eq. II

Subtracting Eq. II from Eq. I

4 OS = ₹ 2,00,000

OS = ₹ 2,00,000/4 = ₹ 50,000

CS = ₹ 50,000 × 3 = ₹ 1,50,000.

PROBLEM 12

Debtors Turnover Ratio 4 times, Cost of Revenue from Operations ₹ 6,40,000, Gross Profit Ratio 20%, Closing Trade Receivables were ₹ 20,000 more than at the beginning, Cash Revenue from Operations being 33-1/3% of Credit Revenue from Operations. Opening Trade Receivables and Closing Trade Receivables

SOLUTION

Step 1: Credit Revenue from Operations

Let Total Revenue from Operations be X

Total Revenue from Operations = Cost of Revenue from Operations + Gross Profit

X = ₹ 6,40,000 + 20% of X

X = ₹ 6,40,000/0.80 = ₹ 8,00,000

Let Credit Revenue from Operations be X

Credit Revenue from Operations = Total Revenue from Operations – Cash Revenue from Operations

X = ₹ 8,00,000 – 1/3 X

X = ₹ 8,00,000 × 3/4 = ₹ 6,00,000

Step 2: Opening Trade Receivables and Closing Trade Receivables

Debtors Turnover Ratio = $\frac{\textbf{Credit Revenue from Operations}}{\textbf{Average Trade Receivables}}$

or **Average Trade Receivables** = ₹ 6,00,000/4 = ₹ 1,50,000

$$\frac{\textbf{Opening Trade Receivables + Closing Trade Receivables}}{\textbf{2}} = 1{,}50{,}000$$

Opening Trade Receivables + Closing Trade Receivables = ₹ 3,00,000 ...Eq. (i)

Closing Trade Receivables – Opening Trade Receivables = ₹ 20,000 ...Eq. (ii)

Adding equation (i) & (ii)

2 Closing Trade Receivables = ₹ 3,20,000

Closing Trade Receivables = ₹ 1,60,000

Opening Trade Receivables = ₹ 1,60,000 – ₹ 20,000 = ₹ 1,40,000

PROBLEM 13

Inventory Turnover Ratio 3 Times, Average Debt Collection Period 4 Months, Average Inventory ₹ 1,00,000, Cash Revenue from Operations being 33% of Credit Revenue from Operations, Gross Profit Ratio 25%, Debtors at the end were 3 times more than that in the beginning. Calculate the amount of Opening Trade Receivables and Closing Trade Receivables.

SOLUTION:

Step 1: Cost of Revenue from Operations

$$\textbf{Inventory Turnover Ratio} = \frac{\textbf{Cost of Revenue from Operations}}{\textbf{Average Inventory}} = 3 \text{ Times}$$

$$= \frac{\text{Cost of Goods Sold}}{₹\,1{,}00{,}000} = 3$$

Cost of Revenue from Operations = ₹ 1,00,000 × 3 = ₹ 3,00,000

Let the Revenue from Operations be = ₹ 100

Gross Profit = 25% of ₹ 100 = ₹ 25

Cost of Revenue from Operations = ₹ 100 – ₹ 25 = ₹ 75

Step 2: Credit Revenue from Operations

If the Cost of Revenue from Operations is ₹ 75, then Revenue from Operations = ₹ 100

If the Cost of Revenue from Operations is ₹ 3,00,000, then sales = $\frac{₹\,100 \times ₹\,3{,}00{,}000}{₹\,75}$

Total Revenue from Operations = ₹ 4,00,000

Let the Credit Revenue from Operations being ₹ 3

Cash Revenue from Operations = $33\frac{1}{3}$% of ₹ 3 = ₹ 1

Total Revenue from Operations = ₹ 3 + ₹ 1 = ₹ 4

If Total Revenue from Operations are ₹ 4, then Credit Revenue from Operations = ₹ 3

If Total Revenue from Operations are ₹ 4,00,000, then **Credit Revenue from Operations** = ₹ 3 × ₹ 4,00,000/₹ 4 = ₹ 3,00,000

Step 3: Opening and Closing Trade Receivables

$$\text{Debtors Turnover Ratio} = \frac{\textbf{12 Months}}{\textbf{Average Debt Collection Period}} = \frac{12}{4} = 3 \text{ Times}$$

$$\text{or,} \quad = \frac{\textbf{Credit Revenue from Operations}}{\textbf{Average Trade Receivables}} = 3$$

$$\text{or,} \quad = \frac{₹\,3{,}00{,}000}{\text{Average Debtors}} = 3$$

Average Trade Receivables = ₹ 3,00,000/3 = ₹ 1,00,000

or, (OR + CR)/2 = ₹ 1,00,000

or, OR + CR = ₹ 1,00,000 × 2 = ₹ 2,00,000 Eq. I

CR – 4 OR = 0 Eq. II

Substracting Eq. II for Eq. I

5 OR = ₹ 2,00,000

OR = ₹ 2,00,000/5 = ₹ 40,000

CR = ₹ 40,000 × 4 = ₹ 1,60,000

PROBLEM 14

Average Debt Collection Period 4 Months, Inventory Turnover Ratio 3 Times, Gross Profit Ratio 25%, Cash Revenue from Operations being 33-1/3% of Credit Revenue from Operations, Inventory at the end was 3 times that in the beginning. Trade Receivables at the end were 3 times more than that in the beginning. Bills Receivables in the beginning and at the end were ₹ 10,000 and ₹ 50,000 respectively. Gross Profit was ₹ 1,00,000. Calculate the amount of Opening Inventory, Closing Inventory, Opening Trade Debtors and Closing Trade Debtors.

SOLUTION

Step 1: Revenue from Operations = Gross Profit × $\frac{\textbf{100}}{\textbf{Gross Profit Rate}}$

= ₹ 1,00,000 × 100/25 = ₹ 4,00,000

Step 2: Gross Profit = ₹ 4,00,000 × 25/100 = ₹ 1,00,000

Step 3: Cost of Revenue from Operations = Revenue from Operations – Gross Profit

= ₹ 4,00,000 – ₹ 1,00,000 = ₹ 3,00,000

Step 4: Opening and Closing Inventory

$$\textbf{Inventory Turnover Ratio} = \frac{\textbf{Cost of Revenue from Operations}}{\textbf{Average Inventory}} = 3 \text{ Times}$$

$$= \frac{₹\ 3,00,000}{\text{Average Inventory}} = 3$$

Average Inventory = ₹ 3,00,000/3 = ₹ 1,00,000

(OS + CS)/2 = ₹ 1,00,000

OS + CS = ₹ 1,00,000 × 2 = ₹ 2,00,000 Eq. I

CS – 3OS = 0 Eq. II

Subtracting Eq. II from III Eq. I

4OS = ₹ 2,00,000

OS = ₹ 2,00,000/4 = ₹ 50,000

CS = ₹ 50,000 × 3 = ₹ 1,50,000

Step 5: Credit Revenue from Operations

Let the Credit Revenue from Operations be = ₹ 3

Cash Revenue from Operations = 33% of 3 = ₹ 1

Total Revenue from Operations = ₹ 3 + ₹ 1 = ₹ 4

If Total Revenue from Operations ₹ 4, then Credit Revenue from Operations = ₹ 3

If Total Revenue from Operations ₹ 4,00,000, then Credit Revenue from Operations

$$= \frac{₹\,3 \times ₹\,4{,}00{,}000}{₹\,4} = ₹\,3{,}00{,}000$$

Step 6: Opening and Closing Trade Receivables

$$\textbf{Debtors Turnover Ratio} = \frac{\textbf{12 Months}}{\textbf{Average Debt Collection Period}} = \frac{12}{4} = 3 \text{ Times}$$

$$= \frac{\textbf{Credit Revenue from Operations}}{\textbf{Average Trade Receivables}} = 3$$

$$= \frac{₹\,3{,}00{,}000}{\text{Average Trade Receivables}} = 3$$

Avg. Trade Receivables = ₹ 3,00,000 / 3 = ₹ 1,00,000

(OR + CR)/2 = ₹ 1,00,000

OR + CR = ₹ 1,00,000 × 2 = ₹ 2,00,000 Eq. I

CR – 4 OR = 0 Eq. II

Subtracting Eq. II from Eq. I

5 OR = ₹ 2,00,000

OR = ₹ 2,00,000/5 = ₹ 40,000

CR = ₹ 40,000 × 4 = ₹ 1,60,000

Opening Trade Debtors = ₹ 40,000 – ₹ 10,000 = ₹ 30,000

Closing Trade Debtors = ₹ 1,60,000 – ₹ 50,000 = ₹ 1,10,000

PROBLEM 15

From the following information, Calculate Closing Inventory, Share Capital and Fixed Assets:

Working Capital	₹ 1,20,000	Current Ratio	2.5
Reserves and Surplus	₹ 80,000	Quick Ratio	1.5
Non-Current Assets/Proprietary Funds	0.75	Bank Overdraft	₹ 20,000

There are neither Non-Current Liabilities nor Prepaid Expenses.

SOLUTION

Step 1: Current Assets and Current Liabilities

Current Assets – Current Liabilities = Working Capital = ₹ 1,20,000 Eq. I

Current Assets/Current Liabilities = 2.5

or, Current Assets – 2.5 Current Liabilities = 0 Eq. II

Subtracting Eq. II from Eq. I

1.5 Current Liabilities = ₹ 1,20,000

Current Liabilities = ₹ 1,20,000/1.5 = ₹ 80,000

Current Assets = ₹ 80,000 × 2.5 = 2,00,000

Step 2: Quick Assets = Current Liabilities × Quick Ratio = ₹ 80,000 × 1.5 = ₹ 1,20,000

Step 3: Closing Inventory = Current Assets – Quick Assets = ₹ 2,00,000 – ₹ 1,20,000 = ₹ 80,000

Step 4: Proprietary Funds + Current Liabilities = Non-Current Assets + Current Assets

Let us assume the Proprietary Funds be 'X'

X + ₹ 80.000 = .75X + ₹ 2,00,000

X – .75X = ₹ 2,00,000 – ₹ 80,000 = ₹ 1,20,000

X = ₹ 1,20,000/.25 = ₹ 4,80,000

Step 5: Share Capital = ₹ 4,80,000 – ₹ 80,000 = ₹ 4,00,000

Step 6: Non-Current Assets = 75% of ₹ 4,80,000 = ₹ 3,60,000

PROBLEM 16

Current Ratio 4.5, Quick Ratio 3 : 1, Inventory ₹ 72,000. Cash ₹ 4,000, Gross Profit @ 33-1/3% on Cost was ₹ 1,00,000, Cash Revenue from Operations being 33% of Credit sales; Debtors Turnover Ratio 3 Times. In current assets there was no asset other than Inventory, Trade Receivables and Cash. Calculate the Opening Trade Receivables.

SOLUTION

Step 1: Quick Assets

$$\textbf{Quick Ratio} = \frac{\textbf{Quick Assets (QA)}}{\textbf{Current Liabilities}} = \frac{\textbf{CA – Inventory}}{\textbf{CL}} = 3$$

$$= \frac{\text{CA} - ₹\ 72{,}000}{\text{CL}} = 3$$

CA – ₹ 72,000 = 3 CL

CA – 3 CL = ₹ 72,000

CA – 4.5 CL = 0

Subtracting Eq. II from Eq. I

1.5 CL = ₹ 72,000

CL = ₹ 72,000/1.5 = ₹ 48,000

CA = Current Liabilities × Current Ratio

= ₹ 48,000 × 4.5 = ₹ 2,16,000

QA = Current Liabilities × Quick Ratio

= ₹ 48,000 × 3 = ₹ 1,44,000

Step 2: Closing Trade Receivables = QA – Cash = ₹ 1,44,000 – ₹ 4,000 = ₹ 1,40,000

Step 3: Credit Revenue from Operations

Let the Cost of Revenue from Operations be ₹ 3

Gross Profit = 33 of ₹ 3 = ₹ 1

Revenue from Operations = ₹ 3 + ₹ 1 = ₹ 4

If Gross Profit is ₹ 1, then Revenue from Operations = ₹ 4

If Gross Profit is ₹ 1,00,000, then Revenue from Operations

= ₹ 4 × ₹ 1,00,000/₹ 1 = ₹ 4,00,000

Let the Credit Revenue from Operations be = 3

Cash Revenue from Operations = 33% of ₹ 3 = ₹ 1

Total Revenue from Operations = ₹ 3 + ₹ 1 = ₹ 4

If Total Revenue from Operations = ₹ 4, then Credit Revenue from Operations = ₹ 3

If Total Revenue from Operations ₹ 4,00,000, then Credit Revenue from Operations

$$= \frac{₹\ 3 \times ₹\ 4{,}00{,}000}{₹\ 4} = ₹\ 3{,}00{,}000$$

Step 4: Opening and Closing Trade Receivables

$$\textbf{Debtors Turnover Ratio} = \frac{\textbf{Credit Revenue from Operations}}{\textbf{Average Trade Receivables}} = 3$$

3 Average Trade Receivables= ₹ 3,00,000

Average Trade Receivables = ₹ 3,00,000/3 = ₹ 1,00,000

or, (OR + CR)/2 = ₹ 1,00,000

OR + CR = ₹ 1,00,000 × 2 = ₹ 2,00,000

OR = ₹ 2,00,000 – CR

OR = ₹ 2,00,000 – ₹ 1,40,000 = ₹ 60,000

PROBLEM 17

Following are the ratios relating to the trading activities of CAMHG Ltd.

Debtors Velocity 3 months; Inventory Velocity 6 months; Creditors' Velocity 2 months; Gross Profit Ratio 20%. Gross Profit for the year was ₹ 5,00,000, Inventory at the end was ₹ 20,000 more than what it was at the beginning of the year. Bills Payable and Bills Receivable were ₹ 36,667 and ₹ 60,000 respectively.

You are to ascertain the figures of:

(a) Revenue from Operations, (b) Trade Debtors, (c) Trade Creditors; and (d) Inventory.

SOLUTION:

(a) Revenue from Operations = Gross Profit/G.P. Ratio = ₹ 5,00,000/0.20 = ₹ 25,00,000

(b) Sundry Debtors

Debtors Turnover Ratio = 12/3 = 4 times

$$4 = \frac{\text{Credit Revenue from Operations}}{\text{Year end Debtors}}$$

Year end Debtors = ₹ 25,00,000/4 = ₹ 6,25,000

Trade Debtors = ₹ 6,25,000 – B/R of ₹ 60,000 = ₹ 5,65,000

(c) Sundry Creditors

Purchases = **Cost of Goods sold + Increase in Inventory**

= (₹ 25,00,000 – ₹ 5,00,000) + ₹ 20,000 = ₹ 20,20,000

Creditors Turnover Ratio = 12/2 = 6 times

$$6 = \frac{\text{Net Credit Purchases}}{\text{Year end Creditors}}$$

Year End Creditors = ₹ 20,20,000/6

Trade Creditors = ₹ 3,36,667 – B/P of ₹ 36,667 = ₹ 3,00,000

(d) Closing Inventory

$$\textbf{Inventory Turnover Ratio} = \frac{\textbf{Cost of Revenue from Operations}}{\textbf{Average Inventory}}$$

= 12 months/6 = 2 times

$$2 = \frac{₹\ 20,00,000}{\text{Average Stock}}$$

Average Inventory = ₹ 20,00,000/2 = ₹ 10,00,000

(OS + CS)/2 = ₹ 10,00,000

OS + CS = ₹ 10,00,000 × 2 = ₹ 20,00,000 Eq. I

CS – OS = ₹ 20,000. Eq. II

Adding both the Equations

2CS = ₹ 20,20,000

CS = ₹ 20,20,000/2 = ₹ 10,10,000

PROBLEM 18

Following are the ratios of the business of Tulsian Traders Ltd:

Average Collection period 3 months; Inventory Turnover Ratio 1.5 times; Average payment period 2 months; Gross Profit Ratio 25%; Opening Trade Receivables ₹ 6,00,000. Gross Profit ₹ 8,00,000

Closing Inventory of the year is ₹ 20,000 above the Opening Inventory. Closing Bills Receivable ₹ 50,000 and Closing Bills Payable ₹ 20,000.

Find out: (a) Revenue from Operations; (b) Closing Trade Debtors; (c) Closing Inventory; (d) Closing Trade Creditors.

SOLUTION

(a) Total Revenue from Operations:

Gross Profit Ratio = Gross Profit × 100/Revenue from Operations

25 = 8,00,000 × 100/Revenue from Operations

Revenue from Operations = 8,00,000 × 100/25 = ₹. 32,00,000

(b) Trade Debtors:

Average Collection Period = No. of months in year / Debtors Turnover Ratio

3 Months = 12 Months/Debtors Turnover ratio (DTR)

Debtors Turnover Ratio (DTR)= 12 Months/3 months = 4 Times

$$\textbf{Debtors Turnover Ratio (DTR)} = \frac{\textbf{Credit Revenue from Operations}}{\textbf{Average Trade Receivables}}$$

4 = 32,00,000/Average Trade Receivables

Average Trade Receivables = ₹. 32,00,000/4 = ₹. 8,00,000

Opening Receivables + Closing Receivables/2 = ₹ 8,00,000

Opening Receivables + Closing Receivables = ₹ 8,00,000 × 2 = ₹ 16,00,000

6,00,000 + Closing Receivables = ₹ 16,00,000

Closing Receivables = ₹ 16,00,000 – ₹ 6,00,000 = ₹ 10,00,000

Trade Debtors = Closing Trade Receivables – B/R

= ₹ 10,00,000 – ₹ 50,000 = ₹ 9,50,000

(c) Closing Inventory:

Cost of Revenue from Operations = Revenue from Operations – Gross profit

= ₹ 32,00,000 – 8,00,000 = ₹ 24,00,000

STR = Cost of Goods sold/Average Inventory

1.5 = 24,00,000/Average Inventory

Average Inventory = 24,00,000/1.5 = ₹ 16,00,000

Opening Inventory + Closing Inventory = ₹ 16,00,000 × 2 = ₹ 32,00,000 ...Eq I

Closing Inventory – Opening Inventory = ₹ 20,000 ...Eq II

Adding both the Equations

2 Closing Inventory = ₹ 32,00,000 + ₹ 20,000 = ₹ 32,20,000

Closing Inventory = ₹ 32,20,000/2 = ₹ 16,10,000

Opening Inventory = ₹ 16,10,000 – ₹ 20,000 = ₹ 15,90,000

(d) Trade Creditors:

Credit Purchases = Cost of Revenue from Operations + Closing Inventory – Opening Inventory.

= 24,00,000 + 16,10,000 – 15,90,000 = 24,20,000

Creditors Turnover Ratio = 12 Months/2 months = 6 times

Creditors Turnover Ratio = Net Credit Purchases/Average Payables

Average Trade Payables = ₹ 24,20,000/6 = 4,03,333

Trade Creditors = Average Trade Payables – B/P

= ₹ 4,03,333 – ₹ 20,000 = ₹ 3,83,333

Note: *In the absence of Opening Trade Payables, it seems that Closing Trade Payables have been used.*

PROBLEM 19

Calculate (a) Revenue from Operations (b) Cost of Revenue from Operations (c) Closing Inventory, (d) Working Capital, (e) Current Liabilities and (f) Current Assets from the following figures:

Debtors Turnover Ratio 4 Times, Inventory turnover Ratio 8 Times, Quick Ratio 1.5, Average Trade Receivables ₹ 1,80,000, Working Capital Turnover Ratio 8 Times, Prepaid, Expenses ₹ 5.000, Cash Revenue from Operations 25% of total Revenue from Operations. Gross Profit Ratio 33-1/3%. Closing Inventory was ₹ 10,000 in excess of Opening Inventory.

SOLUTION

(a) Revenue from Operations

$$\textbf{Debtors Turnover Ratio} = \frac{\textbf{Credit Revenue from Operations}}{\textbf{Average Trade Receivables}}$$

$$4 \text{ Times} = \frac{\text{Credit Revenue from Operations}}{₹\ 1,80,000}$$

Credit Revenue from Operations = ₹ 1,80,000 × 4 = ₹ 7,20,000

Let Total Revenue from Operations be X

Total Revenue from Operations = Cash Revenue from Operations + Credit Revenue from Operations

X = 25% of X + ₹ 7,20,000

X = ₹ 7,20,000/0.75 = ₹ 9,60,000

(b) Cost of Revenue from Operations = Revenue from Operations – Gross Profit

= ₹ 9,60,000 – 33-1/3% of ₹ 9,60,000 = ₹ 6,40,000

(c) Closing Inventory

$$\textbf{Inventory Turnover Ratio Sold} = \frac{\textbf{Cost of Revenue from Operations}}{\textbf{Average Inventory}}$$

8 Times = Average Inventory/6,40,000

8 × Average Inventory = ₹ 6,40,000

Average Inventory = ₹ 6,40,000/8 = ₹ 80,000

$(OS + CS)/2 = ₹ 80,000$

$OS + CS = ₹ 80,000 \times 2 = ₹ 1,60,000$ ... Eq. I

$CS - OS = ₹ 10,000$ ... Eq. II

Adding both the Equations

$2CS = ₹ 1,70,000$

$CS = ₹ 1,70,000/2 = ₹ 85,000$

(d) Working Capital

$$\textbf{Working Capital Turnover Ratio} = \frac{\textbf{Revenue from Operations}}{\textbf{Working Capital}}$$

$$8 \text{ Times} = \frac{₹ 9,60,000}{\text{Net Working Capital}}$$

Net Working Capital $= ₹ 9,60,000/8 = ₹ 1,20,000$

(e) Current Liabilities

$CA - CL = ₹ 1,20,000$ ...Eq.I

$$\textbf{Quick Ratio} = \frac{\textbf{QA}}{\textbf{CL}} = \frac{\textbf{CA – Inventory \& Prepaid Exp.}}{\textbf{CL}}$$

$$1.5 = \frac{CA - (₹85,000 + ₹5,000)}{CL}$$

$CA - 1.5\ CL = ₹ 90,000$ ...Eq. II

Subtracting Eq. II from Eq. I

$.5CL = ₹ 30,000$

$CL = ₹ 30,000/0.50 = ₹ 60,000$

(f) Current Assets (CA) $= ₹ 1,20,000 + ₹ 60,000 = ₹ 1,80,000$

PROBLEM 20

Calculate Opening and Closing Trade Receivables from the following information:

Current Ratio 5 : 3, Quick Ratio 3 : 5, Working Capital ₹ 1,00,000, Inventory Turnover Ratio 2 Times. Gross Profit Ratio 20%, Average Debt Collection Period 3 months, Cash Revenue from Operations being 33-1/3% of Credit Revenue from Operations. Closing Trade Receivables were ₹ 10,000 more than that at the beginning.

SOLUTION

Step 1: Current Assets & Current Liabilities

$$\text{Current Ratio} = \frac{\textbf{Current Assets (CA)}}{\textbf{Current Liabilities (CL)}} = \frac{5}{3}$$

$3CA = 5CL$

$CA = 5/3CL$ ...Eq. I

$CA - CL = ₹ 1,00,000$ ... Eq. II

Putting Eq. I in Eq. II

$CL - CL = ₹ 1,00,000$

$2CL = ₹ 3,00,000$

$CL = ₹ 3,00,000/2 = ₹ 1,50,000$

$CA = ₹ 1,50,000 + ₹ 1,00,000 = ₹ 2,50,000$

Step 2: Closing Inventory

$$\text{Quick Ratio} = \frac{QA}{CL} = \frac{CA - \text{Closing Inventory}}{CL} = \frac{3}{5}$$

$$5\,(CA - \text{Closing Inventory}) = 3CL$$

$$5CA - \text{Closing Inventory} = 3CL$$

$$-5\ \text{Closing Inventory} = 3CL - 5CA$$

$$-5\ \text{Closing Inventory} = (3 \times ₹\ 1,50,000) - (5 \times ₹\ 2,50,000)$$

$$\text{Closing Inventory} = \frac{₹4,50,000 - ₹12,50,000}{-5} = ₹\ 1,60,000$$

Step 3: Cost of Revenue from Operations

$$\textbf{Inventory Turnover Ratio} = \frac{\textbf{Cost of Revenue from Operations}}{\textbf{Average Inventory}}$$

$$2\ \text{Times} = \frac{\text{Cost of goods sold}}{₹\ 1,60,000}$$

Cost of Revenue from Operations = ₹ 1,60,000 × 2 = ₹ 3,20,000

Step 4: Credit Revenue from Operations

Revenue from Operations = Cost of Revenue from Operations + Gross Profit

Let Revenue from Operations be X

$$X = ₹\ 3,20,000 + 20\%\ \text{of}\ X$$

$$X = ₹\ 3,20,000/0.80 = ₹\ 4,00,000$$

Credit Revenue from Operations be X

Credit Revenue from Operations = Total Revenue from Operations – Cash Revenue from Operations

$$X = ₹\ 4,00,000 - 1/3\ \text{of}\ X$$

$$4/3X = ₹\ 4,00,000$$

$$X = ₹\ 4,00,000 \times 3/4 = ₹\ 3,00,000$$

Step 5: Opening and Closing Trade Receivables

$$\textbf{Debtors Turnover Ratio} = \frac{\textbf{12 Months}}{\textbf{Average Debt Collection Period}} = 12/3 = 4\ \text{times}$$

$$DTR = \frac{\textbf{Credit Revenue from Operations}}{\textbf{Average Trade Receivables}}$$

$$4 = \frac{₹\ 3,00,000}{\text{Average Trade Receivables}}$$

$$\text{Average Trade Receivables} = ₹\ 3,00,000/4 = ₹\ 75,000$$

$$(OR + CR)/2 = ₹\ 75,000$$

$$OR + CR = ₹\ 75,000 \times 2 = ₹\ 1,50,000 \quad \text{...Eq. I}$$

$$CR - OR = ₹\ 10,000 \quad \text{...Eq. II}$$

Adding both the equations

$$2\,CR = ₹\ 1,60,000$$

$$CR = ₹\ 1,60,000/2 = ₹\ 80,000$$

$$OR = ₹\ 80,000 - ₹\ 10,000 = ₹\ 70,000$$

PROBLEM 21

Calculate Working Capital Turnover Ratio from the following information:

Current Ratio 8 : 5, Quick Ratio 6 : 5, Inventory Turnover Ratio 5 Times, Closing Inventory was ₹ 96,000 *less* than that at the beginning. Gross Profit @ 25% on Cost, Average Debt Collection Period 3 months, Cash Revenue from Operations being 25% of Total Revenue from Operations, Opening Trade Debtors ₹ 1,40,000, Closing Bills Receivable ₹ 20,000, Opening Bills Receivable ₹ 10,000, Closing Trade Debtors ₹ 1,30,000.

SOLUTION

Step 1: Credit Revenue from Operations

$$\textbf{Debtors Turnover Ratio} = \frac{\textbf{12 Months}}{\textbf{Average Debt Collection Period}} = 12/3 = 4 \text{ times}$$

$$\textbf{DTR} = \frac{\textbf{Credit Revenue from Operations}}{\textbf{Average Trade Receivables}}$$

$$4 = \frac{\text{Credit Revenue from Operations}}{(₹\,1{,}40{,}000 + ₹\,10{,}000 + ₹\,1{,}30{,}000 + ₹\,20{,}000)/2}$$

Credit Revenue from Operations = ₹ 1,50,000 × 4 = ₹ 6,00,000

Step 2: Total Revenue from Operations

Let Total Revenue from Operations be X

Total Revenue from Operations = Credit Revenue from Operations + Cash Revenue from Operations

$$X = ₹\,6{,}00{,}000 + 25\% \text{ of } X$$

$$X = ₹\,6{,}00{,}000/0.75 = ₹\,8{,}00{,}000$$

$$\textbf{Gross Profit} = \textbf{Revenue from Operations – Cost of Revenue from Operations}$$

$$25\% \text{ of } X = ₹\,8{,}00{,}000 - X$$

$$X = ₹\,8{,}00{,}000/1.25 = ₹\,6{,}40{,}000$$

Step 3: Closing Inventory

$$\textbf{Inventory Turnover Ratio} = \frac{\textbf{Cost of Revenue from Operations}}{\textbf{Average Inventory}}$$

$$5 = \frac{₹\,6{,}40{,}000}{\text{Average Stock}}$$

$$\text{Average Inventory} = ₹\,6{,}40{,}000/5 = ₹\,1{,}28{,}000$$

$$(OS + CS)/2 = ₹\,1{,}28{,}000$$

$$OS + CS = ₹\,1{,}28{,}000 \times 2 = ₹\,2{,}56{,}000 \quad \text{... Eq. I}$$

$$OS - CS = ₹\,96{,}000 \quad \text{... Eq. II}$$

Adding the both equations

$$2OS = ₹\,3{,}52{,}000$$

$$OS = ₹\,3{,}52{,}000/2 = ₹\,1{,}76{,}000$$

$$CS = ₹\,1{,}76{,}000 - ₹\,96{,}000 = ₹\,80{,}000$$

Step 4: Current Assets & Current Liabilities

$$\textbf{Quick Ratio} = \frac{\textbf{Quick Assets}}{\textbf{Current Liabilities}} = \frac{\textbf{CA – Inventory}}{\textbf{Current Liabilities}}$$

$$6/5 = \frac{CA - ₹\,80{,}000}{\text{Current Liabilities}}$$

$$5CA - ₹\,4{,}00{,}000 = 6\,CL$$

$$5CA - 6CL = ₹\,4{,}00{,}000 \qquad \text{... Eq. I}$$

$$\text{Current Ratio} = \frac{CA}{CL} = \frac{8}{5}$$

$$5CA = 8CL$$

$$CA = \frac{8}{5}CL \qquad \text{...Eq. II}$$

Putting Eq. II In Eq. I

$$5 \times 8/5\,CL - 6\,CL = ₹\,4{,}00{,}000 \qquad \text{...Eq. III}$$

Multiplying Eq. III by 3

$$40\,CL - 30\,CL = ₹\,20{,}00{,}000$$

$$CL = ₹\,20{,}00{,}000/10 = ₹\,2{,}00{,}000$$

$$CA = \frac{8}{5} \times ₹\,2{,}00{,}000 = ₹\,3{,}20{,}000$$

Step 5: Working Capital Turnover Ratio

$$= \frac{\textbf{Revenue from Operations}}{\textbf{Working Capital}}$$

$$= \frac{₹\,8{,}00{,}000}{₹\,3{,}20{,}000 - ₹\,2{,}00{,}000} = 6.67 \text{ times}$$

SOLVED PROBLEMS II

PROBLEM 22

Bharat Ltd. provides you the following information:

Gross Profit Ratio 40%, Net Profit (after tax) 12%, Operating Ratio 70%, 15% Debt-Equity Ratio 2:1, Tax Rate 50%, Shareholders' Funds ₹ 4,00,000.

Required: Calculate (a) Gross Profit (b) Operating Expenses, (c) Interest Coverage Ratio, (d) Return on Capital Employed, (e) Return on Shareholders' Funds.

SOLUTION

Step 1: 15% Long-term Debt = ₹ 4,00,000 × 2 = ₹ 8,00,000 Interest on 15% Long-term Debt = 15% of ₹ 8,00,000 = ₹ 1,20,000

STEP 2: LET US ASSUME THE SALES BE X

A. Sales	x
B. *Less:* Cost of Goods Sold (b.f.)	0.6x
C. Gross Profit [A–B]	0.4x
D. *Less:* Operating Expenses (b.f.)	0.1x
E. Operating Profit @ 30%	0.3x
F. *Less:* Interest on Long-term Debt	1,20,000
G. Profit before Tax	0.3x – ₹ 1,20,000
H. *Less:* Tax @ 50%	50% (0.3x – ₹ 1,20,000)
I. Profit after tax	0.15x – ₹ 60,000

Step 3: Net Profit Ratio $= \dfrac{\text{Profit after tax}}{\text{Net Sales}} \times 100$

$$12\% = 0.15x - 60{,}000x$$

$$0.15x - 0.12x = ₹\,60{,}000$$

$$x = ₹\,60{,}000/0.03 = ₹\,20{,}00{,}000$$

Step 4:

(a) Gross Profit = 40% of ₹ 20,00,000 = ₹ 8,00,000

(b) Operating Expenses = 10% of ₹ 20,00,000 = ₹ 2,00,000

(c) Interest Coverage Ratio $= \dfrac{\text{Profit before interest \& tax}}{\text{Interest on Long-term Debt}}$

$$= \frac{30\% \text{ of } ₹\,20{,}00{,}000}{₹\,1{,}20{,}000} = 5 \text{ times}$$

(d) Return on Capital Employed $= \dfrac{\text{Profit before interest \& tax}}{\text{Capital Employed}} \times 100$

$$= \frac{30\% \text{ of } ₹\,20{,}00{,}000}{₹\,12{,}00{,}000} \times 100 = 50\%$$

(e) Return on Shareholders Funds $= \dfrac{\text{Profit after Interest \& Tax}}{\text{Shareholders' Funds}} \times 100$

$$= \frac{₹\,2{,}40{,}000}{₹\,4{,}00{,}000} \times 100 = 60\%$$

Note: Profit after Interest & Tax $= 50\%\,[0.30 \times (₹\,20{,}00{,}000) - ₹\,1{,}20{,}000]$

$$= 50\%\,[₹\,6{,}00{,}000 - ₹\,1{,}20{,}000] = ₹\,2{,}40{,}000$$

PROBLEM 23

From the following information, calculate Return on Total Assets and prepare the Balance Sheet:

Net Profit after Interest, Tax & Preference Dividend ₹ 2,22,000,Tax Rate 50%

18% Preference Share Capital?

15% Debentures?

Return on Capital Employed 50%

Return on Shareholders' Funds 60%

Return on Equity Shareholders' Funds 74%

Current Ratio 2:1

Net Fixed Assets ₹ 9,00,000

SOLUTION:

Equity Shareholders' Funds $= \dfrac{2{,}22{,}000}{74} \times 100 = ₹\,3{,}00{,}000$

Let Pref. Share Capital be x, Hence, Pref. Dividend = 18% x

Return on Shareholders' Funds $= \dfrac{\text{EAT}}{\text{Shareholders' Funds}} \times 100 = 60\%$

$$= 2{,}22{,}000 + 0.18x\ 3{,}00{,}000 + x = 0.6$$

$$2{,}22{,}000 + 0.18x = 1{,}80{,}000 + 0.6x$$

$$0.42x = 42{,}000$$

x = ₹ 1,00,000

Thus, Pref. Share Capital = ₹ 1,00,000

Earning after Tax = ₹ 2,22,000 + ₹ 18,000 = ₹ 2,40,000

Tax = 50% of EBT *or* 100% of EAT = ₹ 2,40,000

EBT = EAT + Tax = ₹ 2,40,000 + ₹ 2,40,000 = ₹ 4,80,000

Let 15% Debentures be y

Interest = 0.15 y

EBIT = EBT + Interest on Long-term Debt

EBIT = 4,80,000 + 0.15 y

$$\text{Return on Capital Employed} = \frac{\text{EBIT}}{\text{Capital Employed}} \times 100$$

= 4,80,000 + 0.15 y4,00,000 + y = 0.5

4,80,000 + 0.15y = 2,00,000 + 0.5y

0.35y = 2,80,000

y = ₹ 8,00,000

Thus, 15% Debentures = ₹ 8,00,000

Capital Employed = Shareholders' Funds + Long-term Debts

= (₹ 3,00,000 + ₹ 1,00,000) + ₹ 8,00,000

= ₹ 12,00,000

Working Capital = Capital Employed – Net Fixed Assets

= ₹ 12,00,000 – ₹ 9,00,000 = ₹ 3,00,000

or, CA – CL = ₹ 3,00,000 ... Eq. I

$$\text{Current Ratio} = \frac{CA}{CL} = 2:1$$

or, CA – 2CL = 0 ... Eq. II

Subtracting Eq. II from Eq. I

CL = ₹ 3,00,000

CA = ₹ 3,00,000 × 2 = ₹ 6,00,000

Total Assets = Fixed Assets + Current Assets

= ₹ 9,00,000 + ₹ 6,00,000 = ₹ 15,00,000

EBIT = ₹ 4,80,000 + 15% of ₹ 8,00,000

= ₹ 6,00,000

$$\text{Return on Total Assets} = \frac{\text{Earnings before Interest \& Tax}}{\text{Total Assets}} \times 100$$

$$= \frac{₹\,6,00,000}{₹\,15,00,000} \times 100 = 40\%$$

BALANCE SHEET AS AT ...... [*₹ in lakhs]*

Liabilities	₹	*Assets*	₹
Equity Share Holders' Funds	3	Fixed Assets	9
Preference Share Capital	1	Current Assets	6
15% Debentures	8		

Current Liabilities	3		
	15		15

PROBLEM 24

From the following information, prepare Trading, Profit and Loss Account, for the year ending 31st March, 2015 and the Balance Sheet of Tulsian Ltd. as at 31st March, 2015.

1. Current Ratio 2.5
2. Quick Ratio 1.5
3. Working Capital ₹ 1,20,000
4. Prepaid Expenses ₹ 35,000
5. Bank Overdraft ₹ 20,000
6. Working Capital Velocity 1.5 Months
7. Debtors' Velocity 3 months
8. Stock Velocity 3/4 Month
9. Cash Sales 33-1/3% of Credit Sales.
10. Closing Stock was ₹ 10,000 in excess of Opening Stock
11. Operating Ratio 75%
12. Provision for Tax @ 20%
13. Opening Balance of Profit and Loss A/c (cr) : ₹ 30,000
14. Opening Balance of General Reserve : ₹ 6,000
15. Transfer to General Reserve : 1/3 of Current year's Profits
16. Interim Dividend Paid : 37% of Paid up Capital
17. Debtors in the beginning were 3 times more than that at the end.
18. Current Assets consist of Cash, Marketing Securities, Stock, Debtors, Prepaid Expenses. Cash to Marketable Securities Ratio is 100%.
19. Fixed Assets to Proprietors' Funds 0.75
20. There are no long-term debts.

SOLUTION

TRADING AND PROFIT AND LOSS ACCOUNT OF TULSIAN LTD.

Dr. *For the year ending 31st March, 2015* *Cr.*

Particulars	₹	*Particulars*	₹
To Opening Stock	35,000	By Sales	9,60,000
To Purchases (Balancing Figure)	6,50,000	By Closing Stock	45,000
To Gross Profit c/d	3,20,000		
	10,05,000		10,05,000
To Expenses (Balancing Figure)	80,000	By Gross Profit b/d	3,20,000
To Provision for Tax (20% of ₹ 2,40,000)	48,000		
To Net Profit after tax c/d	1,92,000		
	3,20,000		3,20,000

To General Reserve	64,000	By Balance b/d	30,000
To Interim Dividend [37% of ₹ 4,00,000]	1,48,000	By Net Profit	1,92,000
To Balance c/d	10,000		
	2,22,000		2,22,000

BALANCE SHEET AS AT 31ST MARCH, 2015

Liabilities	₹	*Assets*	₹
Share Capital	4,00,000	Fixed Assets	3,60,000
Reserve and Surplus:		Current Assets:	
General Reserve [₹ 64,000 + ₹ 6,000]	70,000	Stock	45,000
Profit and Loss A/c	10,000	Debtors	72,000
Current Liabilities and Provisions:		Prepaid Expenses	35,000
Bank Overdraft	20,000	Marketable Securities	24,000
Provision for Tax	48,000	Cash	24,000
Other Current Liabilities	12,000		
	5,60,000		5,60,000

Working Notes:

(i) *Calculation of Current Assets and Current Liabilities*

Current Ratio = CA/CL = 2.5

CA = 2.5 CL

CA – 2.5CL = 0 ...(I)

Working Capital = CA – CL = ₹ 1,20,000 ...(ii)

Substituting Equation (i) in Equation (ii)

2.5 CL – CL = 1,20,000

CL = 1,20,000/1.5 = ₹ 80,000

CA = ₹ 80,000 × 2.5 = ₹ 2,00,000

(ii) *Calculation of Closing Stock*

$$\text{Quick Ratio} = \text{Quick Assets/CL} = \frac{\text{Current Assets} - \text{Stock} - \text{Prepaid Exp.}}{\text{CL}}$$

= ₹ 2,00,000 – Stock – ₹ 35,000₹ 80,000 = 1.5

Stock = ₹ 1,65,000 – (80,000 × 1.5) = ₹ 45,000

(iii) *Opening Stock* = ₹ 45,000 – ₹ 10,000 = ₹ 35,000

(iv) *Calculation of Total Sales*

$$\text{Working Capital Velocity} = \frac{12}{\text{Working Capital Turnover}} = 1.5$$

$$\text{Working Capital Turnover} = \frac{\text{Net Sales}}{\text{Working Capital}} = \frac{\text{Net Sales}}{₹\ 1,20,000} = 121.5 = 8$$

Net Sales = ₹ 1,20,000 × 8 = ₹ 9,60,000

(v) $$\text{Stock Turnover Ratio} = \frac{\text{Cost of Goods Sold}}{\text{Average Stock}} = 12/0.75 = 16$$

$$\text{Cost of Goods Sold} = 16\left(\frac{₹\ 4,00,000 + ₹\ 35,000}{2}\right)$$

= ₹ 6,40,000

(vi) Gross Profit = Net Sales – Cost of Goods Sold

= ₹ 9,60,000 – ₹ 6,40,000 = ₹ 3,20,000

(vii) Closing Debtors

Cash Sales + Cr. Sales = Net Sales

1/3x + x = ₹ 9,60,000

x = ₹ 9,60,000 × 3/4 = ₹ 7,20,000

Debtors Turnover Ratio = 12/3 = 4 times

Average Debtors = Net Cr. Sales / 4 = ₹ 7,20,000/4

(OD + CD)/2 = ₹ 1,80,000

OD + CD = ₹ 1,80,000 × 2 = ₹ 3,60,000 ...Eq. I

4CD – OD = 0 ... Eq. II

Adding both the equations

5CD = ₹ 3,60,000

CD = ₹ 3,60,000/5 = ₹ 72,000

(viii) Operating Profit before tax Ratio = 100 – Operating Ratio = 100% – 75% = 25%

= 25% of ₹ 9,60,000 = ₹ 2,40,000

(ix) *Calculation of Proprietors' Funds (Let us assume as X)*

Proprietors' Funds + CL = FA + CA

X + ₹ 80,000 = 0.75***x*** + ₹ 2,00,000

X = ₹ 1,20,000/0.25 = ₹ 4,80,000

(x) Fixed Assets = 75% of ₹ 4,80,000 = ₹ 3,60,000

(xi) New Reserve Created = ₹ 1,92,000 × 1/3 = ₹ 64,000

(xii) *Calculation of Share Capital (Let share capital be X).*

SC + Op. Reserve + New Reserve + Op. P&L + Balance of P&L = Proprietors' Funds

X + ₹ 6,000 + ₹ 64,000 + ₹ 30,000 + (₹ 1,92,000 – ₹ 64,000 – 0.37 X) = ₹ 4,80,000

X = ₹ 2,52,000/0.63 = ₹ 4,00,000

PROBLEM 25

From the following information, prepare Trading and Profit and Loss Account:

Debt-Equity Ratio (Long-term Debt/Shareholders' Funds)	2:1
Capital Gearing Ratio (Funds bearing fixed payments to Equity Shareholder's Funds)	3:1
15% Long-term Debts	₹ 8,00,000
Return on Equity Shareholder's Funds	25%
Tax Rate	50%
15% Preference Share Capital	?
Break-up of Cost-Profit:	
Materials	40%

Labour	25%
Manufacturing Expenses	10%
Depreciation on Plant	10%
Office & Selling Expenses	2.5%
Operating Profit	12.5%
	100%

SOLUTION

Dr. **TRADING & PROFIT & LOSS ACCOUNT FOR THE YEAR ENDING...** *Cr.*

Particulars	₹	*Particulars*	₹
To Material	9,60,000	By Sales	24,00,000
To Labour Expenses	6,00,000		
To Mfg. Expenses	2,40,000		
To Depreciation	2,40,000		
To Gross Profit @ 15%	3,60,000		
	24,00,000		24,00,000
To Office & Adm. Exp.	60,000	By Gross Profit	3,60,000
To Interest @ 15%	1,20,000		
To Tax 50%	90,000		
To Net Profit after Tax	90,000		
	3,60,000		3,60,000
To Preference Dividend	15,000	By Net Profit after Tax	90,000
To Balance for Equity Shareholders @ 25%	75,000		
	90,000		90,000

Working Notes:

(i) *Calculation of Equity Shareholders' Funds Long-term Debts*

$$\text{Debt Equity Ratio} = \frac{\text{Long-term Debts}}{\text{Shareholders' Funds}}$$

$$2 = ₹\ 8,00,000 / \text{Shareholders' Funds}$$

$$\text{Shareholders' Funds} = ₹\ 8,00,000/2 = ₹\ 4,00,000$$

Supposing Pref. Share Capital= x

$$\text{Equity Shareholders' Funds} = ₹\ 4,00,000 - x$$

(ii) *Calculation of Pref. Share Capital*

$$\text{Capital Gearing Ratio} = \frac{\text{Long-term Debts } \textit{plus} \text{ Pref. Share Capital}}{\text{Equity Shareholders' Funds}}$$

$$3 = \frac{₹\ 8,00,000 + x}{₹\ 4,00,000 - x}$$

$$₹\ 12,00,000 - 3x = ₹\ 8,00,000 + x$$

$$x = ₹\ 1,00,000$$

$$\text{Pref. Share Capital} = ₹\ 1,00,000$$

Equity Shareholders' Funds = ₹ 4,00,000 – ₹ 1,00,000 = ₹ 3,00,000

(iii) *Calculation of Operating Profit*

$$\text{Return on Equity} = \frac{\text{Net Profit after Int. Tax \& Pref. Div.}}{\text{Equity Shareholders' Funds}}$$

25% = x/₹ 3,00,000

x = ₹ 75,000

	Particulars	₹
A.	Net Profit after Int., Tax & Pref. Dividend	75,000
B.	*Add:* Pref. Dividend	15,000
C.	Net Profit after Int. & Tax (A+B)	90,000
D.	*Add:* Tax @ 50%	90,000
E.	Net Profit before Tax	1,80,000
F.	Interest on Long-term Debt @ 15% on ₹ 8,00,000	1,20,000
G.	Operating Profit (E + F)	3,00,000

(iv) *Calculation of Sales*

Operating Cost Ratio = 87.5%

(Material + Labour + Mfg. Exp. + Dep. + Office & Selling Exp.)

Operating Profit Ratio = 100 – 87.5% = 12.5%

= Operating Profit/Sales × 100

Sales = ₹ 3,00,000/12.5% = ₹ 24,00,000

Materials = 40% of ₹ 24,00,000 = ₹ 9,60,000

Labour = 25% of ₹ 24,00,000 = ₹ 6,00,000

Manufacturing Expenses = 10% of ₹ 24,00,000 = ₹ 2,40,000

Depreciation on Plant = 10% of ₹ 24,00,000 = ₹ 2,40,000

Office & Selling Expenses = 2.5% of ₹ 24,00,000 = ₹ 60,000

PROBLEM 26

Fill in the blanks in the following Trading and Profit & Loss Account for the year ended 31st March 2015 and the Balance Sheet as on 31st March 2015:

TRADING AND PROFIT & LOSS ACCOUNT OF X LTD.

Dr. *For the year ended 31st March 2015* Cr.

Particulars	₹	*Particulars*	₹
To Opening Stock	?	By Sales	?
To Purchases	?	By Closing Stock	?
	....		....
To Sundry Expenses	?	By Gross Profit b/d	?
To Provision for Tax	?		
To Net Profit after Tax	?		
	......		....

BALANCE SHEET OF X LTD. AS AT 31.3.2015

Liabilities	₹	*Assets*	₹
Share Capital:	...	Fixed Assets	?
Equity Share Capital		Investments	Nil
Current Assets:			
Preference Share Capital		Stock	?
Reserves & Surplus:	?	Trade Debtors	?
Profit & Loss A/c	?	Bills Receivables	40,000
Secured Loans:		Prepaid Expenses	?
Debentures	?	Cash & Bank Balances	?
Unsecured Loans:	Nil	Miscellaneous Expenditure:	Nil
Current Liabilities & Provisions:			
Trade Creditors	?		
Bills Payables	20,000		
Bank Overdraft	?		
Provision for Income Tax	?		
	?		?

Other Information:

1. Current Ratio	3
2. Quick Ratio	2
3. Working Capital	₹ 2,20,000
4. Cost of Goods Sold	₹ 6,40,000
5. Cash Purchases	₹ 1,40,000
6. Cash Sales	1/3rd of Credit Sales
7. Stock Velocity	1.5 months
8. Average Debt Collection Period	3 months
9. Creditors Velocity	3 months
10. Gross Profit Ratio	20%

11. Net Profit after tax to Equity Capital 10%
12. Stock as on 1.4.2014 was ₹ 10,000 in excess of the Stock as on 31.3.2015
13. Creditors on 31.3.2015 were *less* than that in the beginning of year by ₹ 45,000.
14. Debtors as on 1.4.2014 were ₹ 20,000 more than that at the end of the year.
15. Proprietary Ratio (Fixed Assets/Net Capital Employed) 0.75
16. Capital Gearing Ratio (Pref. Shares & Debentures to Equity Shareholders' Funds) 33 × 1/3%
17. Preference Share Capital to Debentures 3
18. General Reserve & Profit & Loss to Equity Capital 25%
19. Provision for Income Tax 10%

SOLUTION

TRADING AND PROFIT & LOSS ACCOUNT OF X LTD.

Dr. *For the year ended 31st March 2015* Cr.

Particulars	₹	*Particulars*	₹
To Opening Stock	85,000	By Sales	8,00,000
To Purchases	6,30,000	By Closing Stock	75,000
To Gross Profit c/d	1,60,000		
	8,75,000		8,75,000
To Sundry Expenses (b.f)	1,01,333	By Gross Profit b/d	1,60,000
To Provision for Tax	5,867		
To Net Profit after Tax	52,800		
	1,60,000		1,60,000

BALANCE SHEET OF X LTD. AS AT 31.3.2015

Liabilities	₹	*Assets*	₹
Share Capital:			
Equity Share Capital	5,28,000	Fixed Assets	6,60,000
Preference Share Capital	1,65,000	Investments	Nil
Reserves & Surplus:		Current Assets:	
General Reserve	79,200	Stock	75,000
Profit & Loss A/c	52,800	Trade Debtors	1,00,000
Secured Loans:		Bills Receivables	40,000
Debentures	55,000	Prepaid Expenses	35,000
Unsecured Loans:	Nil	Cash & Bank Balances	80,000
Current Liabilities & Provisions:			
Trade Creditors	80,000		
Bills Payables	20,000		
Bank Overdraft	4,133		
Provision for Income Tax	5,867		
	9,90,000		9,90,000

Working Notes:

(i) *Calculation of Total Current Assets, Total Current Liabilities & Stock & Prepaid expenses*

$$\text{Current Ratio} = \frac{\text{Current Assets (CA)}}{\text{Current Liabilities (CL)}} = 3$$

$$\text{Or CA} - 3\text{ CL} = 0 \qquad \text{.......... I}$$

$$\text{CA} - \text{CL} = ₹\ 2{,}20{,}000 \qquad \text{.......... II (given)}$$

Subtracting II from I equation

$$\text{CL} = ₹\ 1{,}10{,}000$$

$$\text{Therefore, CA} = ₹\ 1{,}10{,}000 \times 3 = ₹\ 3{,}30{,}000$$

$$\text{Quick Ratio} = \frac{\text{Quick Assets (QA)}}{\text{Current Liabilities (CL)}} = 2$$

= QA/₹ 1,10,000 = 2

QA = ₹ 2,20,000

Stock & Prepaid Expenses = CA – QA = ₹ 3,30,000 – ₹ 2,20,000 = ₹ 1,10,000

(ii) *Calculation of Closing Stock*

$$\text{Stock Velocity} = \frac{\text{12 Months}}{\text{Stock Turnover Ratio}}$$

1.5 = 12/Stock Turnover Ratio

or, Stock Turnover Ratio = 12/1.5 = 8 Times

or, 8 = Cost of Goods Sold/Average Stock

or, 8 = ₹ 6,40,000/Average Stock

or, Average Stock = ₹ 80,000

or, (Opening Stock + Closing Stock)/2 = ₹ 80,000

or, Opening Stock + Closing Stock = ₹ 1,60,000 I

Opening Stock – Closing Stock = ₹ 10,000 .... II (given)

Adding I & II Equations

2 Opening Stock = ₹ 1,70,000

or, Opening Stock = ₹ 85,000

Closing Stock = ₹ 85,000 – ₹ 10,000 = ₹ 75,000

(iii) *Calculation of Credit Sales*

If Gross Profit on Sales is 20%

Cost of Goods Sold to Sales Ratio is 80% (100% – 20%)

Thus, Sales = ₹ 6,40,000 × 100/80 = ₹ 8,00,000

Cash Sales = ₹ 8,00,000 × 25/100 = ₹ 2,00,000

Credit Sales = ₹ 6,00,000

(iv) *Calculation of Closing Total Debtors*

$$\text{Debtors' Velocity} = \frac{\text{12 Months}}{\text{Debtors' Turnover Ratio}}$$

3 = 12/Debtors, Turnover Ratio

or, Debtors' Turnover Ratio = 12/3 = 4 times

or, 4 = Net Credit Sales/Average Debtors

or, 4 = ₹ 6,00,000/Average Debtors

or, Average Debtors = ₹ 1,50,000

or, (Opening Drs. + Closing Drs.) / 2 = ₹ 1,50,000

or, Opening Drs. + Closing Drs. = ₹ 3,00,000 ... Eq. I

Opening Debtors – Closing Debtors = ₹ 20,000 ... Eq. II

Adding I & II Equations

2 Opening Debtors = ₹ 3,20,000

or, Opening Debtors = ₹ 1,60,000

Closing Debtors = ₹ 1,60,000 – ₹ 20,000 = ₹ 1,40,000

(v) Sundry Debtors = Total Debtors – B/R = ₹ 1,40,000 – ₹ 40,000 = ₹ 1,00,000

(vi) *Calculation of Credit Purchases*

TRADING ACCOUNT

Particulars	₹	*Particulars*	₹
To Opening Stock	85,000	By Sales	8,00,000
To Purchases	6,30,000	By Closing Stock	75,000
To Gross Profit c/d	1,60,000		
	8,75,000		8,75,000

Credit Purchases = ₹ 6,30,000 – ₹ 1,40,000 = ₹ 4,90,000

(vii) *Calculation of Closing Total Creditors*

Creditors' Velocity = 12 Months/Creditors Turnover Ratio

3 = 12/Creditors Turnover Ratio

or, Creditors Turnover Ratio = 12/3 = 4 times

or, 4 = Net Credit Purchases/Average Creditors

or, Average Creditors = ₹ 1,22,500

or, (Opening Crs. + Closing Crs.) /2 = ₹ 1,22,500

or, Opening Crs. + Closing Crs. = ₹ 2,45,000 ..... (I)

Opening Crs. – Closing Crs. = ₹ 45,000 ... (Given)

Adding I & II Equations

2 Opening Crs. = ₹ 2,90,000

or, Opening Creditors = ₹ 1,45,000

Closing Creditors = ₹ 1,45,000 – ₹ 45,000 = ₹ 1,00,000

(viii) Sundry Creditors = Total Creditors – B/P = ₹ 1,00,000 – ₹ 20,000 = ₹ 80,000

(ix) Prepaid Expenses = ₹ 1,10,000 – ₹ 75,000 = ₹ 35,000

(x) Cash & Bank Balances = Total Current Assets – Current Assets other than Cash

= ₹ 3,30,000 – ₹ 2,50,000 = ₹ 80,000

(xi) *Calculation of Net Capital Employed*

$$\text{Proprietory Ratio} = \frac{\text{Fixed Assets}}{\text{Net Capital Employed}} = 0.75$$

$$\text{or} = \frac{\text{Working Capital}}{\text{Net Capital Employed}} = 1 - 0.75 = 0.25$$

Net Capital Employed = ₹ 2,20,000/0.25 = ₹ 8,80,000

(xii) Fixed Assets = 75% of ₹ 8,80,000 = ₹ 6,60,000

(xiii) *Calculation of Pref. Shares & Debentures*

$$\text{Capital Gearing Ratio} = \frac{\text{Pref. Shares \& Deentures}}{\text{Equity Shareholders' Funds}}$$

$$1/3 = \frac{\text{Pref. Shares \& Debentures}}{\text{Capital Employed – Pref. Share \& Deb.}}$$

Taking Pref. Shares & Deb. As "x"

1/3 = x/₹ 8,80,000 – x)

x = 1/3₹ 880000 – x

x = (8,80,000/3) – (x/3)

3x + x = ₹ 8,80,000

x = ₹ 2,20,000

(xiv) Calculation of Debentures:

Pref. Shares + Debentures = ₹ 2,20,000

Taking Debentures as X

3 X + X = ₹ 2,20,000

X = ₹ 2,20,000/4 = ₹ 55,000

(xv) Pref. Shares Capital = ₹ 2,20,000 – ₹ 55,000 = ₹ 1,65,000

(xvi) Calculation of Equity Capital, Reserve & Profit & Loss

Taking Equity Capital as X

X + 0.15x + 0.10x = ₹ 6,60,000

1.25x = ₹ 6,60,000

x = ₹ 5,28,000

General Reserve = 15% of ₹ 5,28,000 = ₹ 79,200

Profit & Loss = 10% of ₹ 5,28,000 = ₹ 52,800

(xvii) Calculation of Provision for Tax

Let Net Profit before tax be x

Net Profit after tax = x – 10% of x

₹ 52,800 = 0.9x

X = 52,800/0.9 = ₹ 58,667

Provision for Tax = 10% of ₹ 58,667 = ₹ 5,867

(XVIII) CALCULATION OF BANK OVERDRAFT

A.	Total Current Liabilities		₹ 1,10,000
B.	Current Liabilities other than than Bank Overdraft		
	a) Trade Creditors	₹ 80,000	
	b) Bills Payables	₹ 20,000	
	c) Provision for Tax	₹ 5,867	₹ 1,05,867
C.	Bank Overdraft (A–B)		₹ 4,133

13 CASH FLOW STATEMENT

LEARNING OBJECTIVES

After studying this chapter, you should be able to understand:

- Meaning of Cash Flow Statement
- Objectives of Cash Flow Statement
- Uses/Advantages of Cash Flow Statement
- Limitations of Cash Flow Statement
- What is meant by the term 'Cash Flows'?
- Cash and Cash Equivalents
- Operating Activities
- Investing Activities
- Financial Activities
- Practical Steps involved in the Preparation of Cash Flow Statement

1.0 MEANING OF CASH FLOW STATEMENT

The Cash Flow Statement means the Statement of Changes in Cash and Cash equivalents during a particular accounting period. It shows—

1. Net Cash flows from Operating Activities;
2. Net Cash flows from Investing Activities;
3. Net Cash flows from Financing Activities;
4. Net Change in Cash and Cash Equivalents.

Notes:

1. *Cash Flow Statement is **not a substitute for Income Statement** because it does not disclose the calculation of Profit or Loss.*
2. *Cash Flow Statement is **not a substitute for Position Statement(Balance Sheet)** because it does not disclose the Total Financial Position [i.e. Total Equity,Non-Current Liabilities, Current Liabilities, Non-Current Assets and Current Assets].*
3. *Cash Flow Statement is historical in nature because it is prepared on the basis of Historical Financial Statements.*

2.0 OBJECTIVES OF CASH FLOW STATEMENT

The objectives of Cash Flow Statement are as follows:

1. **To ascertain Net Cash Flows from Operating, Investing and Financing Activities of an enterprise**

2. **To ascertain the Net Change in Cash & Cash Equivalents** indicating the aggregate of Net Cash Flows from Operating, Investing and Financing Activities of an enterprise between the dates of two consecutive Balance Sheets.

3.0 USES/ADVANTAGES OF CASH FLOW STATEMENT

The various uses of Cash Flow Statement are as follows:

1. **Facilitates to ascertain Net Cash flows:** Cash Flow Statement facilitates to ascertain Net Cash Flows from Operating, Investing and Financing Activities and Net Change in Cash and Cash Equivalents.
2. **Facilitates to evaluate Cash Financial Performance:** It facilitates to evaluate Cash Financial Performance by providing information on Net Cash flows from Operating Activities.
3. **Facilitates to evaluate Cash Financial Position:** It facilitates to evaluate Cash Financial Position by providing information on Net Cash flows from investing Activities and Financing Activities.
4. **Facilitates Efficient Cash Management:** The management can know the situation of shortage *or* surplus cash and can plan for the effective use of surplus cash *or* can make the necessary arrangement in case of an shortage of cash.
5. **Facilitates Comparison:** It facilitates the comparative study of the operating performance of different enterprises because it eliminates the effects of using different accounting treatments for the same transactions and events.
6. **Facilitates Capital Budgeting Decisions:** It facilitates Capital Budgeting Decisions by providing information on Net Cash flows from Investing Activities .
7. **Facilitates Capital Structure Decisions:** It facilitates Capital Structure Decisions by providing information on Net Cash flows from Financing Activities.
8. **Facilitates Planning:** The Projected Cash Flow Statement enables the management to plan its future investments, operating and financial activities such as the repayment of long-term loans and interest thereon, modernisation *or* expansion of plant, payment of cash dividend etc.
9. **Answers to some of the important financial questions:** As a tool of historical analysis, it provides an answer to some of the important financial questions such as:
   (i) How was it possible to distribute dividend in excess of current earnings *or* in the presence of a net loss for the period?
   (ii) Why has the cash decreased although the net income for the period has gone up?
   (iii) Why has the cash increased even though there has been a net loss for the period?
   (iv) What happened to the proceeds of the sale of land and equipments?
   (v) Why did the firm resort to long-term borrowings inspite of large profits?
   (vi) Why did the firm issue new equity *or* preference shares?
   (vii) How was the retirement of long-term debts *or* redemption of redeemable preference shares accomplished?

4.0 LIMITATIONS OF CASH FLOW STATEMENT

The major limitations of Cash Flow Statement are as follows:

1. Ignores Non-cash transactions	It ignores the non-cash transactions. In other words, it does not take into consideration those transactions which do not affect the cash ***For Example***, Issue of Shares against the purchase of Fixed Assets *or* Stock-in-trade, Conversion of Debentures into Shares.

2. Secondary Data Based Statement	It is a secondary data based statement. It merely rearranges the primary data already appearing in other statements viz., Income Statement and Balance Sheet.
3. Historical Statement	It is basically historical in nature because it is prepared on the basis of Historical Financial Statements.
4. Ignores Accural Concept	It ignores the Fundamental Assumption of Accural.

5.0 WHAT IS MEANT BY THE TERM 'CASH FLOWS'?

MEANING OF CASH FLOWS

Cash Flows are inflows and outflows of Cash and Cash equivalents.

MEANING OF CASH INFLOWS

Cash Inflow arises when the net effect of transaction is increase in the amount of **Cash *or* Cash Equivalents.**

MEANING OF CASH OUTFLOWS

Cash Outflow arises when the net effect of transaction is to decrease in the amount of **Cash *or* Cash Equivalents.**

EXAMPLES OF CASH FLOWS

Cash Inflows	***Cash Outflows***
1. Cash Sales of Goods	1. Cash Purchases of Goods
2. Cash received from Trade Debtors	2. Cash paid to Trade Creditors
3. Cash received from commission & Royalty	3. Operating Expenses paid (e.g. Salaries & Wages, Administration Exp. Selling Exp.)
4. Sale of Fixed Assets for Cash	4. Income Tax paid
5. Sale of Investments (whether Current *or* Non-Current) for Cash	5. Cash Purchase of Fixed Assets
6. Loans & Advances repayment received (whether Short term *or* Long term)	6. Cash Purchase of Investments (whether Short term *or* Long term)
7. Income received on Investments (whether Current *or* Non-Current)	7. Loans & Advances granted (whether Short term *or* Long term)
8. Issue of Equity Shares for Cash	8. Buy-back of Equity Shares for Cash
9. Issue of Preference Shares for Cash	9. Redemption of Preference Shares for Cash
10. Issue of Debentures for Cash	10. Redemption of Debentures for Cash
11. Loans taken (whether Short term *or* Long term)	11. Loans repaid (whether Short term *or* Long term)
	12. Interest on Debentures & Loans paid. (whether Short term ***or*** Long term)
	13. Final Dividend on Equity Shares paid.
	14. Dividend on Preference Shares paid.
	15. Interim Dividend on Equity Shares paid.

6.0 CASH AND CASH EQUIVALENTS

THE TERM 'CASH'

Meaning	Cash comprises Cash on hand and Demand Deposits with banks.
Examples	Cash in hand, Cash at Bank

THE TERM 'CASH EQUIVALENTS'

Meaning	Cash Equivalents are short term, highly liquid investments that are readily convertible into known amounts of cash and which are subject to an insignificant risk of changes in value.
Purpose	Cash Equivalents are held for the purpose of meeting short-term cash commitments rather than for Investment *or* other purposes.
Two Conditions for an Investment to qualify as a Cash Equivalent	1. It must be readily convertible to a known amount of cash. 2. It must be subject to an insignificant risk of changes in value. Therefore, an investment normally qualifies as a cash equivalent only when it has a **short maturity of, say, 3 months *or* less from the date of acquisition.**
Examples	Treasury Bills, Commercial Papers, Commercial Bills, Call Money, Certificate of Deposit

7.0 TRANSACTIONS NOT CONSIDERED AS CASH FLOWS

Meaning	Transactions which represent movements between items of Cash *or* Cash Equivalents are not considered as Cash Flows.
Reason	These components are part of the cash management of an enterprise rather than part of its Operating, Investing and Financing Activities.
Examples	1. Cash deposited into Bank; 2. Cash withdrawn from Bank; 3. Purchase/Sale of Short-term Marketable Securities (neither held as Current Investments nor held as Non-current Investments).

8.0 NON-CASH TRANSACTIONS

Meaning	Non-Cash transactions are those transactions which do not involve Cash.
Examples [Verification by Journal Entry]	1. **Issue of Equity Shares *or* Debentures against the purchase of an Asset** **JOURNAL ENTRY** Asset A/c Dr To Equity Share Capital A/c/Debentures A/c 2. **Issue of Equity Shares on conversion of Convertible** Debentures **JOURNAL ENTRY** Convertible Debentures A/c Dr To Equity Share Capital A/c

	3. Charging of Depreciation on a Fixed Tangible Asset **JOURNAL ENTRY** Depreciation A/c Dr To Fixed Tangible Asset A/c **4. Amortization of a Fixed Intangible Asset** **JOURNAL ENTRY** Profit & Loss A/c Dr To Intangible Asset A/c **5. Written off of an old Fixed Tangible Asset** **JOURNAL ENTRY** Profit & Loss A/c Dr To Fixed Tangible Asset A/c **6. Declaration of Final Dividend on Shares** **JOURNAL ENTRY:** Proposed Dividend A/c Dr To Dividend Payable A/c
Why ignored in CFS?	Non-Cash transactions are ignored while preparing Cash Flow Statement because these do not involve Cash.

9.0 OPERATING ACTIVITIES

MEANING OF OPERATING ACTIVITIES

Operating Activities are the principal revenue-producing activities of the enterprise and other activities that are not investing *or* financing activities.

EXAMPLES OF CASH FLOWS FROM OPERATING ACTIVITIES

Cash Inflows	***Cash Outflows***
1. Cash Sales of Goods 2. Cash received from Trade Debtors 3. Cash received from Trading Commission & Royalty	1. Cash Purchases of Goods 2. Cash paid to Trade Creditors 3. Operating Expenses paid (e.g. Salaries & Wages, Administration Exp. Selling Exp.) 4. Income Tax (related to Operating Activities only) paid.

TUTORIAL NOTE

In case of Financial Enterprises the following activities are classified as Operating Activities since they relate to the main revenue-producing activity of that enterprise:

1. *Purchases and Sales of Shares & Debentures of other companies for Cash*
2. *Dividend received on Shares of other companies*
3. *Interest received on Debentures of other companies*
4. *Loans & Advances granted*
5. *Interest received on Loans & Advances granted*

DISTINCTION BETWEEN NET PROFIT AND CASH FROM OPERATING ACTIVITIES

Basis of Distinction	*Net Profit*	*Cash from Operating Activities*
1. **Meaning**	It indicates the net result of Operating & non-operating activities carried out during an accounting year.	It indicates the Cash Flow as a result of operating activities.
2. **Non-Cash Operating Item (Depreciation)**	It is calculated **after taking into account the effect of non-cash operating items.**	It is calculated **excluding the effect of non-cash operating items** since these items merely represent the book entries.
3. **Non-Operating Items**	It is calculated **after taking into account the effect of non-operating items.**	It is calculated **excluding the effect of non-operating items** since these items do not relate to operating activities.

10.0 INVESTING ACTIVITIES

MEANING OF INVESTING ACTIVITIES

Investing Activities are the acquisition and disposal of Long-term Assets and other Investments not included in Cash Equivalents.

EXAMPLES OF INVESTING ACTIVITIES

Cash Inflows	*Cash Outflows*
1. Cash Sale of Fixed Assets	1. Cash Purchase of Fixed Assets
2. Cash Sale of Investments (whether Current *or* Non-Current)	2. Cash Purchase of Investments (whether Short term *or* Long term)
3. Loans & Advances repayment received (whether Short term *or* Long term)	3. Loans & Advances granted (whether Short term *or* Long term)
4. Income received on Investments (whether Current *or* Non-Current)	4. Brokerage paid on Purchase of Investments (whether Short term *or* Long term)

11.0 FINANCING ACTIVITIES

MEANING OF FINANCING ACTIVITIES

Financing Activities are activities that result in changes in the size and composition of the Owners' **Capital** (including Preference Share Capital in the case of a company) and Borrowings (whether Short term *or* Long term) of the enterprise.

EXAMPLES OF FINANCING ACTIVITIES

Cash Inflows	*Cash Outflows*
1. Issue of Equity Shares for Cash	1. Buy-back of Equity Shares for Cash.
2. Issue of Preference Shares for Cash	2. Redemption of Preference Shares for Cash.
3. Issue of Debentures for Cash	3. Redemption of Debentures for Cash
4. Loans taken (whether for short-term *or* long-term)	4. Loans repaid (whether Short term *or* Long term)

5. Interest received on Calls-in-arrears. (whether Short term *or* Long term).	5. Interest on Debentures & Loans paid 6. Final Dividend on Equity Shares paid 7. Dividend on Preference Shares paid 8. Interim Dividend on Equity Shares paid 9. Brokerage & Underwriting commission paid on Issue of Shares & Debentures.

ILLUSTRATION 1

Classify the following activities as (i) Operating Activities; (ii) Investing Activities; (iii) Financing Activities:

(i) Purchase of Machinery
(ii) Sale of Land
(iii) Payment of Income Tax
(iv) Refund of Income Tax
(v) Payment of Dividend
(vi) Receipt of Dividend
(vii) Payment of Interest on Debenture
(viii) Receipt of Interest on Debenture
(ix) Issue of Debentures
(x) Buy-back of Equity Shares

SOLUTION

(i) Investing Activity,
(ii) Investing Activity
(iii) Operating Activity,
(iv) Operating Activity
(v) Financing Activity,
(vi) Investing Activity
(vii) Financing Activity,
(viii) Investing Activity
(ix) Financial Activity,
(x) Financing Activity

ILLUSTRATION 2

Classify the following activities as (a) Operating Activities, (b) Investing Activities, (c) Financing Activities, (d) Cash *or* Cash Equivalents.

1. Purchase of Machinery	21. Dividend received on Shares
2. Issue of Equity Share Capital	22. Rent received on property
3. Cash Sales	23. Selling & Distribution Exp paid
4. Interest on Short-term Borrowings	24. Income Tax paid
5. Sale of Machinery	25. Dividend paid on Pref. Shares
6. Cash receipts from Debtors	26. Underwriting Commission paid
7. Commission and Royalty received	27. Rent paid
8. Purchase of Current Investments	28. Brokerage paid on issue of shares
9. Redemption of Preference shares	29. Brokerage paid on purchase of Investments
10. Cash Purchases of Goods	30. Bank Overdraft
11. Sale of Investments	31. Cash Credit
12. Purchase of Goodwill	32. Short-term Deposits having maturity of 3 months
13. Cash paid to suppliers of Goods.	33. Marketable Securities having maturity of 3 months
14. Interim Dividend paid on Equity Shares	
15. Wages & Salaries paid	

16. Sale of Patents	34. Refund of Income Tax received
17. Interest received on Debentures held as Investments	35. Discount allowed to customers
	36. Discount received from Suppliers
18. Interest paid on borrowings	37. Purchase of Marketable Securities having maturity of 6 months
19. Office & Adm. Expenses paid	
20. Manufacturing Overheads paid	

SOLUTION

CLASSIFICATION OF ACTIVITIES

(a) Operating Activities	3, 6, 7, 10, 13, 15, 19, 20, 23, 24, 27, 34, 35, 36
(b) Investing Activities	1, 5, 8, 11, 12, 16, 17, 21, 22, 29, 37
(c) Financing Activities	2, 4, 9, 14, 18, 25, 26, 28, 30, 31
(d) Cash *or* Cash Equivalents	32, 33

ILLUSTRATION 3

Classify the following activities as (i) Operating Activities; (ii) Investing Activities; (iii) Financing Activities in case of (a) a Manufacturing Enterprise; (b) a Financial Enterprise.

1. Purchase of Investments.
2. Proceeds from Sale of Investments.
3. Brokerage paid on purchase & sale of Investments.
4. Interest received on Debentures held as Investments.
5. Dividend received on shares held as Investments.
6. Loans & Advances made to third parties.
7. Receipts from the repayments of loans & advances made to third parties.
8. Receipt of Interest on loans & advances made to third parties.

SOLUTION

(a) In case of a **Manufacturing Enterprise**, all the given activities are **Investing Activities** since they relate to acquisition and disposal of long-term assets.

(b) In case of a **Financial Enterprise**, all the given activities are **Operating Activities** since they relate to the main revenue-producing activity of the enterprise.

ILLUSTRATION 4

Classify the following activities as (i) Operating Activities; (ii) Investing Activities; (iii) Financing Activities in case of (a) Manufacturing Enterprise; (b) a Real Estate Enterprise.

1. Purchase of Land.
2. Purchase of Building.
3. Sale of Land.
4. Sale of Building.
5. Brokerage paid on purchase and sale of Land & Building.
6. Rent received from a Building.
7. Payment of Construction Cost of a Building.

SOLUTION

(a) In case of a **Manufacturing Enterprise**, all the given activities are **Investing Activities** since they relate to acquisition and disposal of long-term assets.

(b) In case of a **Real Estate Enterprise**, all the given activities are **Operating Activities** since they relate to the main revenue-producing activity of the enterprise.

ILLUSTRATION 5

When is Dividend received considered as Operating Activity?

SOLUTION

Dividend received by a Financial Enterprise is considered as Operating Activity.

ILLUSTRATION 6

Classify the following into Operating, Investing and Financing Activities:

(a) Refund of Income Tax
(b) Sale of Shares & Debentures of other companies by a Finance Co
(c) Dividend on Shares and Interest on Debentures paid by a Mutual Fund Company
(d) Dividend on Shares and Interest on Debentures received by a Bank.
(e) Payment of Brokerage on Purchase of Shares of a Finance Company.

SOLUTION

(a) Operating Activity (b) Operating Activity (c) Financing Activity
(d) Investing Activity (e) Investing Activity

ILLUSTRATION 7

If you want neither Inflow nor Outflow of Cash, which of the following transactions will you select?

(a) A Long-term Loan from Bank
(b) Goodwill written off
(c) Issue of Equity Shares *or* Debentures against the purchase of a Fixed Asset
(d) Issue of Equity shares on conversion of Debentures
(e) Cash deposited into Bank
(f) Cash withdrawn from Bank
(g) Charging Depreciation on Furniture
(h) Declaration of Final Dividend
(i) Purchase of Stock-in-trade on credit

SOLUTION

(b) to (i)

ILLUSTRATION 8

Mention the net amount of 'Source' *or* 'Use' of Cash in the following cases:

1. When Fixed asset (having book value of ₹ 15,000) is sold at a loss of ₹ 5,000.

2. When Goods costing ₹ 10,000 are sold for ₹ 15,000.
3. When ₹ 19,000 received from a debtor and allowed ₹ 1,000 as discount.
4. When Discount of ₹ 1,000 is received on making payment to a creditor of ₹ 10,000.
5. When Issue of shares for ₹ 7,00,000 against purchase of business comprising of fixed assets ₹ 6,00,000; current assets ₹ 2,00,000 and took over current liabilities ₹ 1,00,000.
6. When Old Furniture (Book value ₹ 1,000) written off.
7. When Deferred Revenue Expenditure (₹ 1,000) charged to Profit.

SOLUTION

1. Source ₹10,000,
2. Source ₹ 15,000,
3. Source ₹19,000,
4. Use ₹ 9,000,
5. Nil because this transaction does not involve Cash.
6. Nil because this transaction does not involve Cash.
7. Nil because this transaction does not involve Cash.

12.0 HOW TO COMPUTE CASH FROM OPERATING ACTIVITIES

The amount of cash from operating activities may be computed by following either the Direct Method *or* the Indirect Method.

HOW TO COMPUTE NET CASH FLOW FROM OPERATING ACTIVITIES (UNDER DIRECT METHOD)

Particulars	₹	₹
A. Operating Receipts in Cash (e.g.)		
Cash Sales	xxx	
Cash receipts from Debtors	xxx	
Trading Commission received	xxx	xxx
B. Operating Payments in Cash (e.g.)		
Cash Purchases	xxx	
Cash paid to Suppliers	xxx	
Wages & Salaries paid	xxx	
Office and Administration Expenses paid	xxx	
Manufacturing Overheads paid	xxx	
Selling and Distribution Expenses paid	xxx	xxx
C. Cash generated from Operations before taxes (A – B)		xxx
D. Income Tax paid (Net of Refund of Tax)		xxx
E. Cash flow before extraordinary item (C – D)		xxx
F. Extraordinary item		xxx
G. Net Cash from (used in) Operating Activities		xxx

ILLUSTRATION 9

From the following particulars, Calculate Cash Flows from Operating Activities:

Particulars	₹	*Particulars*	₹
Cash Sales	2,00,000	Manufacturing Overheads paid	30,000
Cash Purchases	50,000	Office & Administration Exp. paid	20,000
Cash receipts from customers	4,00,000	Selling & Distribution Expenses paid	10,000
Cash paid to suppliers	1,00,000	Income Taxes paid	1,18,000
Trading Commission received	1,00,000	Insurance proceeds from earthquake	
Trading Commission Paid	25,000	disaster settlement	1,00,000
Wages & Salaries paid	40,000	Income Tax Refund received	3,000
Rent paid	10,000		

SOLUTION

CASH FLOW FROM OPERATING ACTIVITIES

Particulars	₹
A. Operating Receipts in Cash:	
Cash Sales	2,00,000
Cash receipts from customers	4,00,000
Trading Commission received	1,00,000
	7,00,000
B. Operating Payments in Cash:	
Cash Purchases	50,000
Cash paid to suppliers	1,00,000
Trading Commission paid	25,000
Wages & Salaries paid	40,000
Rent paid	10,000
Manufacturing Overheads paid	30,000
Office & Administrative Expenses paid	20,000
Selling & Distribution Expenses paid	10,000
	2,85,000
C. Cash generated from Operations before taxes [A – B]	4,15,000
D. Income Tax paid (Net of refund) [₹ 1,18,000 – ₹ 3,000]	1,15,000
E. Cash flow before extraordinary items	3,00,000
F. Insurance proceeds from earthquake disaster settlement	1,00,000
G. Net Cash from Operating Activities	4,00,000

HOW TO COMPUTE NET CASH FLOW FROM OPERATING ACTIVITIES (UNDER INDIRECT METHOD)

Particulars	₹	₹
Step 1: ***Calculate Net Profit before Taxation and Extraordinary Item as follows:***		
A. Closing Balance of P & L A/c		xxx

Less: Opening Balance of P&L A/c [or *Add:* Opening Bal. of P & L A/c (Dr.)]		xxx
Add: Proposed Dividend for the current year		xxx
Add: Interim Dividend paid during the current year		xxx
Add: Transfer to Reserve [or *Less:* Transfer from Reserve]		xxx
Add: Provision for Tax made during the Current Year		xxx
Less: Refund of Tax credited to P&L A/c		(xxx)
Less: Extraordinary item, if any, credited to P&L A/c (e.g., Insurance proceeds from earthquake disaster settlement)		(xxx)
Add: Extraordinary Debit Items (e.g., Loss due to earthquake)		xxx
B. Net Profit before Taxation and Extraordinary Item		xxx
Step 2: *Calculate Operating Profit before Working Capital Changes as follows:*		
A. Net Profit before Taxation and Extraordinary Item		xxx
B. Adjustments for Non-Cash and Non-Operating Items : (***For Example***)		
Depreciation	xxx	
Interest on Debentures & Loans (whether Short term *or* Long term)	xxx	
Preliminary Expenses/Underwriting Commission/Discount on	xxx	
Issue of Debentures/Shares written off	xxx	
Goodwill/Patents/Trade Marks/Copyright amortised	xxx	
Loss on Sale of Investments (whether Current *or* Non-Current).	xxx	
Premium payable on redemption of Preference shares/Debentures	xxx	
Interest Income from Investments (whether Current *or* Non-Current)	(xxx)	
Dividend Income	(xxx)	
Rental Income	(xxx)	
Profit on Sale of Investments (whether Current *or* Non-Current)	(xxx)	xxx
C. Operating Profit before Working Capital Changes		xxx
Step 3: *Calculate Cash from Operations before Tax & Extraordinary Item as follows:*		
A. Operating Profit before Working Capital Changes		xxx
B. Add : Changes in Current Assets (Excluding Cash and Cash Equivalents) &		
Current Liabilities (Excluding Bank Overdraft & Cash Credit):		
Decrease in Inventories, Trade Receivables etc.	xxx	
Increase in Trade Payables, O/s Exp. etc.	xxx	
Increase in Inventories, Trade Receivables etc.	(xxx)	
Decrease in Trade Payables, O/s Exp. etc.	(xxx)	xxx
C. Cash generated from Operations		xxx
Step 4: Calculate Cash generated from Operations after Tax but before Extraordinary Item as follows:		
A. Cash generated from Operations		xxx
B. *Less:* Income taxes paid (Including Advance Tax but Excluding Refund of Tax)		(xxx)
[**Note:** Income Tax should be related to Operating Activities only]		
C. Cash Flow before Extraordinary Item		xxx

Step 5: *Calculate Net Cash from (used in) Operating Activities as follows:*	
A. Cash Flow before Extraordinary Items	xxx
B. *Add:* Extraordinary Credit Items (e.g., Insurance proceeds from earthquake disaster settlement, Govt. Grant)	xxx
C. *Less:* Extraordinary Debit Items (e.g., Loss due to earthquake)	(xxx)
D. Net Cash Flow from (used in) Operating Activities	xxx

Note: *Negative items which are to be deducted have been shown in brackets.*

ILLUSTRATION 10

From the following information, calculate Net Profit before Taxation and Extraordinary Item:

Particulars	*Closing* ₹	*Opening* ₹
Profit & Loss Account	3,36,000	1,00,000
Reserve	1,50,000	50,000
Proposed Dividend	72,000	60,000

Interim Dividend paid during the year	90,000
Provision for Tax made during the current year	1,50,000
Refund of Tax	3,000
Loss due to Earthquake	2,00,000
Insurance Proceeds from earthquake disaster settlement	1,00,000

SOLUTION

CALCULATION OF NET PROFIT BEFORE TAXATION AND EXTRAORDINARY ITEM

Particulars	₹
A. Net Profit as per Profit & Loss A/c [₹ 3,36,000 – ₹ 1,00,000]	2,36,000
Add: Proposed Dividend for the current year	72,000
Add: Interim Dividend paid during the year	90,000
Add: Transfer to Reserve	1,00,000
Add: Provision for Tax made during the Current Year	1,50,000
Less: Refund of Tax	(3,000)
Add: Extraordinary Item (Loss due to Earthquake)	2,00,000
Less: Extraordinary items (i.e., Insurance proceeds from earthquake disaster settlement)	(1,00,000)
B. Net Profit before Taxation and Extraordinary Item	7,45,000

ILLUSTRATION 11

From the following information, calculate Net Cash Flow from Operating Activities:

Particulars	₹
Net Profit before Taxation and Extraordinary Item	7,45,000

Depreciation	1,40,000
Loss on Sale of Machinery	30,000
Interest on Debentures	24,850
Interest on Bank Loan	6,650
Goodwill amortised	9,000
Preliminary Expenses written off	2,000
Premium on Redemption of Preference Shares	10,000
Interest Income on Non-Current Investments	6,000
Interest Income on Current Investments	2,000
Profit on Sale of Current Investments	5,000
Loss on Sale of Non-Current Investments	10,000
Tax paid during the Current Year	1,18,000
Refund of Tax	3,000
Loss due to Earthquake	2,00,000
Insurance Proceeds from earthquake disaster settlement	1,00,000

POSITION OF CURRENT ASSETS & CURRENT LIABILITIES

Particulars	*Closing (₹)*	*Opening (₹)*
Inventories	1,06,000	1,00,000
Trade Receivables	10,000	6,70,000
Trade Payables	25,000	1,80,000
Outstanding Expenses	14,000	10,000
Cash & Cash Equivalents	30,000	49,000

SOLUTION

CALCULATION OF OPERATING PROFIT BEFORE WORKING CAPITAL CHANGES

Particulars		₹
A. Net Profit before Taxation and Extraordinary Item		7,45,000
B. *Adjustments for Non-Cash and Non-Operating Items:*		
Depreciation	1,40,000	
Loss on Sale of Machinery	30,000	
Interest on Debentures	24,850	
Interest on Bank Loan	6,650	
Goodwill amortised	9,000	
Preliminary Expenses written off	2,000	
Premium on Redemption of Preference Shares	10,000	
Interest Income on Non-Current Investments	(6,000)	
Interest Income on Current Investments	(2,000)	
Profit on Sale of Current Investments	(5,000)	
Loss on Sale of Non-Current Investments	10,000	2,19,500

C. Operating Profit before Working Capital Changes		9,64,500
D. Changes in Current Assets & Current Liabilities:		
Decrease in Inventories	6,000	
Increase in Trade Payables	1,55,000	
Increase in Trade Receivables	(6,60,000)	
Decrease in Outstanding Expenses	(4,000)	(5,03,000)
E. Cash generated from operations before Taxes		4,61,500
F. *Less:* Income taxes paid (Net of Refund) [₹ 1,18,000 – ₹ 3,000]		(1,15,000)
G. Cash Flow before Extraordinary Items		3,46,500
Add: Extraordinary items (i.e., Insurance proceeds from earthquake disaster settlement)		1,00,000
Less: Extraordinary items (i.e., Loss due to earthquake)		(2,00,000)
H. Net Cash Inflow from Operating Activities		2,46,500

ILLUSTRATION 12

From the following particulars, calculate the Net Cash Flow from Operating Activities:

(i) Profit made during the year was ₹ 1,00,000 after considering the following items:

Particulars	₹
(a) Depreciation on fixed assets	4,000
(b) Amortization of goodwill	2,000
(c) Transfer to Reserve	2,800
(d) Profit on Sale of Land	1,700
(e) Loss on Sale of Furniture	500
(f) Provision for Taxation	80,000

(ii) The following is the position of Current Assets and Current Liabilities

Particulars	*Closing (₹)*	*Opening (₹)*
Trade Receivables	6,000	4,800
Trade Payables	4,000	6,000
Inventories	3,200	4,000
Outstanding Expenses	2,400	1,600
Provision for Taxation	80,000	70,000

SOLUTION

CALCULATION OF NET CASH FLOW FROM OPERATING ACTIVITIES

Particulars		₹
Net Profit before Tax		1,82,800
Adjustments for Non-Cash and Non-Operating Items:		
Depreciation	4,000	
Goodwill amortized	2,000	
Loss on sale of Furniture	500	

Profit on sale of Land	(1,700)	4,800
Operating Profit before Working Capital Changes		1,87,600
Changes in Current Assets & Current Liabilities:		
Decrease in Inventories	800	
Increase in Outstanding Expenses	800	
Increase in Trade Receivables	(1,200)	
Decrease in Trade Payables	(2,000)	(1,600)
Cash generated from operations		1,86,000
Less: Income taxes paid (Net of Refund)		(70,000)
Net Cash Inflow from Operating Activities		1,16,000

Working Note:

CALCULATION OF NET PROFIT BEFORE TAX

Net Profit as per Profit & Loss A/c	1,00,000
Add: Transfer to Reserve	2,800
Add: Provision for Tax	80,000
Net Profit before Tax	1,82,800

TREATMENT OF SPECIAL ITEMS WHILE CALCULATING NET PROFIT BEFORE TAX

Item	*Treatment and Reason*	*Remarks*
Increase in General Reserve	**Add back** to Balance of P & L A/c to find out **Net Profit Before Tax** **Reason:** It represents an appropriation out of Current year's profits.	
Decrease in General Reserve	**Subtract** from Balance of P&L A/c to find out **Net Profit Before Tax** **Reason:** It represents utilization of past reserves and not of Current year's profits.	
Provision for Tax for Current Year	**Add back Tax provided** to Balance of P & L A/c to find out **Net Profit Before Tax** **Reason:** It is merely a book entry and does not involve any Cash outflow.	1. If only Opening & Closing amounts of Provision for Tax are given,Take Provision for Tax for Current Year as Tax provided during the current year. 2. **If Tax Paid is also given,** Prepare Provision for Tax Account to ascertain the amount of Tax provided during the current year.
Provision for Tax for Previous Year	**Subtract Tax paid** from Cash from Operating Activities before tax **Reason:** It involves Cash outflow.	1. If only Opening & Closing amounts of Provision for Tax are given, Take Provision for Tax for previous year as Tax paid during the current year. 2. **If Tax provided is also given,** Prepare Provision for Tax Account to ascertain the amount of Tax paid during the current year.

Proposed Dividend for Current Year [It represents the amount of dividend proposed by the Board of Directors for the current year.]	**Add back** to Balance of P & L A/c to find out **Net Profit Before Tax** **Reason:** It is merely a book entry and does not involve any Cash outflow.	
Interim Dividend Board of [An Interim Dividend is that dividend which is declared by the Directors for the current year during the current year.]	**Add back** to Balance of P & L A/c to find out **Net Profit Before Tax** **Reason:** It represents an appropriation out of Current Year's Profits.	
Dividend on Pref. Shares	**Add back** to Balance of P & L A/c to find out **Net Profit Before Tax** **Reason:** It represents an appropriation out of Current year's profits.	If the date of Fresh issue / Redemption of Pref. Shares is not given, Calculate Dividend on opening balance of Pref. Shares.

TREATMENT OF SPECIAL ITEMS WHILE CALCULATING CASH FROM OPERATING ACTIVITIES

Item	***Treatment and Reason***	***Remarks***
Depreciation for the Current year	**Add back** to Current year's profits in order to find out Cash from Operating Activities. **Reason:** It does not involve any Cash outflow.	In case of Missing Figure,Prepare Fixed Asset A/c (on WDV Basis) OR Provision for Depreciation A/c to ascertain the amount of Depreciation.
Loss on Sale of Fixed Asset / Investments	**Add back** to Current year's profits in order to find out Cash from Operating Activities. **Reason:** It does not represent an operating cost.	In case of Missing Figure, Prepare Fixed Asset A/c / Investments A/c to ascertain the amount of Loss on Sale.
1. Profit on Sale of Fixed Assets/ Investments **2. Income from Investments (whether Current *or* Non-Current)**	**Subtract** from Current year's profits in order to find out Cash from Operating Activities. **Reason:** It does not represent an operating income.	In case of Missing Figure, Prepare Fixed Asset A/c Investments A/c to ascertain the amount of Profit on Sale.
Goodwill/Patents Amortized	**Add back** to Current year's profits in order to find out Cash from Operating Activities. **Reason:** It merely represents a book entry and does not involve any Cash flow.	
Preliminary Expenses/ Discount on issue of Debentures written off	**Add back** to Current year's profits in order to find out Cash from Operating Activities. **Reason:** It merely represents a book entry and does not involve any Cash flow.	

Interest on Debentures/ Loans (whether disclosed as Current *or* Non-Current)	**Add back** to Current year's profits in order to find out Cash from Operating Activities. **Reason:** It does not represent an operating cost.	If the date of Fresh issue/ Redemption of Debentures is not given, Calculate Interest on opening balance of Debentures.
Premium on Redemption of Debentures/ Pref. Shares	**Add back** to Current year's profits in order to find out Cash from Operating Activities. **Reason:** It does not represent an operating cost.	
Increase in Provision for Doubtful Debts	**Add like** an Increase in Current Liability	
Decrease in Provision for Doubtful Debts	**Subtract like** a Decrease in Current Liability	
Increase in Inventories, Trade Receivables/ Payables against issue of Shares/Debentures	Exclude from Respective Closing Balances **Reason:** These do not involve any cash flow.	

ILLUSTRATION 13

From the following particulars, Calculate the Net Cash Flow from Operating Activities:

Particulars	*Closing* ₹	*Opening* ₹
Profit and Loss A/c	7,000	1,000
General Reserve	15,000	10,000
Proposed Dividend	25,000	21,000
Provision for Taxation	25,000	15,000
10% Debentures	25,000	21,000
Trade Payables	1,17,500	8,500
Machinery	44,000	50,000
Goodwill	8,000	10,000
Discount on issue of Debentures	—	200
Current Investments	8,000	3,000
Inventories	24,500	6,000
Trade Receivables	1,12,300	7,300
Cash & Cash Equivalents	17,700	0

Income tax paid during the year ₹ 20,000

SOLUTION

CALCULATION OF NET CASH FLOW FROM OPERATING ACTIVITIES

Particulars	₹	₹
Net Profit before Tax		66,000

Adjustments for Non-Cash and Non-Operating Items :		
Depreciation	6,000	
Discount on issue of Debentures	200	
Goodwill Amortised	2,000	
Interest on Debentures [₹ 21,000 × 10/110]	2,100	10,300
Operating Profit before Working Capital Changes		76,300
Changes in Current Assets & Current Liabilities:		
Increase in Trade Payables	1,09,000	
Increase in Inventories	(18,500)	
Increase in Trade Receivables	(1,05,000)	(14,500)
Cash generated from operations		61,800
Less: Income taxes paid		(20,000)
Net Cash Inflow from Operating Activities		41,800

Working Notes:

1. CALCULATION OF NET PROFIT BEFORE TAX

A.	**Closing balance as per Profit & Loss A/c:**	7,000
	Less: Opening Balance as per Profit & Loss A/c	1,000
	Add: Proposed Dividend for current year	25,000
	Add: Transfer to Reserve	5,000
	Add: Provision for Tax for current year	30,000
B.	**Net Profit before Tax**	66,000

2. *It has been assumed that new Debentures have been issued at the end of current accounting year*

Dr. **3. PROVISION FOR TAX ACCOUNT** *Cr.*

Particulars	₹	*Particulars*	₹
To Bank A/c	20,000	By Balance b/d	15,000
To Balance c/d	25,000	By P & L A/c (balancing figure)	30,000
	45,000		45,000

ILLUSTRATION 14

From the following particulars, Calculate the Net Cash Flow from Operating Activities:

Particulars	*Closing* ₹	*Opening* ₹
Profit & Loss A/c	7,000	1,000 (Dr)
General Reserve	10,000	15,000
Proposed Dividend	25,000	21,000
Provision for Taxation	25,000	15,000
15% Debentures	34,000	22,000

Trade Payables	22,000	24,000
Fixed Assets (Gross)	74,000	74,000
Accumulated Depreciation	30,000	24,000
10% Current Investments	20,000	10,000
Trade Receivables (Gross)	48,400	15,000
Provision for Doubtful Debts	10,000	5,000
Inventories	15,000	25,000
Cash & Cash Equivalents	5,600	1,000

Income tax provided during the year ₹ 30,000

SOLUTION

CALCULATION OF NET CASH FLOW FROM OPERATING ACTIVITIES

Particulars	₹	₹
Net Profit before Tax		58,000
Adjustments for Non-Cash and Non-Operating Items :		
Depreciation [₹ 30,000 – ₹ 24,000]		6,000
Interest on Debentures [₹ 22,000 × 15/100]		3,300
Interest Income on Current Investments		(1,000)
Operating Profit before Working Capital Changes		53,800
Changes in Current Assets & in Current Liabilities:		
Decrease in Inventories	10,000	
Increase in Trade Receivables (Gross)	(33,400)	
Increase in Provision for Doubtful Debts	5,000	
Decrease in Trade Payables	(2,000)	(20,400)
Cash generated from operations before tax		33,400
Less: Income taxes paid		(20,000)
Net Cash Inflow from Operating Activities		13,400

Working Notes:

1. CALCULATION OF NET PROFIT BEFORE TAX

	Particulars	₹
A.	Closing Balance as per Profit & Loss A/c	7,000
	Add: Opening Balance as per Profit & Loss A/c(Dr)	1,000
	Add: Proposed dividend	25,000
	Less: Transfer to Reserve	(5,000)
	Add: Provision for Tax	30,000
B.	Net Profit before Tax	58,000

Dr. **2. PROVISION FOR TAX ACCOUNT** Cr.

Particulars	₹	*Particulars*	₹
To Bank A/c (balancing figure)	20,000	By Balance b/d	15,000
To Balance c/d	25,000	By P & L A/c	30,000
	45,000		45,000

3. *It has been assumed that new Debentures have been issued at the end of current accounting year.*
4. *It has been assumed that new Current Investments have been acquired at the end of current accounting year.*

ILLUSTRATION 15

From the following information, calculate the Net Cash Flow from Operating Activities:

Particulars	*Closing* ₹	*Opening* ₹
Equity Share Capital	4,00,000	3,00,000
15% Preference Share Capital	1,00,000	1,50,000
General Reserve	70,000	40,000
Profit and Loss A/c	48,000	30,000
Proposed Dividend	50,000	42,000
Provision for Tax	50,000	40,000
Trade Payables	1,22,000	88,000
Tangible Fixed Assets	3,70,000	2,80,000
Intangible Assets [Goodwill]	90,000	1,15,000
Trade Receivables & Inventories	3,39,000	2,57,000

During the year a machine costing ₹ 50,000 (depreciation provided thereon ₹ 30,000) was sold for ₹ 10,000. A machine was purchased for ₹ 1,30,000. Interim Dividend paid, ₹ 20,000, Income-tax, ₹ 35,000 paid.

SOLUTION

CALCULATION OF NET CASH FLOW FROM OPERATING ACTIVITIES

Particulars	₹	₹
I. Cash Flow from Operating Activities		
A. Net Profit before tax		1,63,000
B. *Adjustments for Non-Cash and Non-Operating Items :*		
Depreciation	20,000	
Loss on Sale of Machinery	10,000	
Goodwill amortised	25,000	55,000
C. Operating Profit before Working Capital Changes		2,18,000
D. Changes in Current Assets & Current Liabilities:		
Increase in Trade Payables	34,000	

	Increase in Trade Receivables & Inventories	(82,000)	(48,000)
E.	Net Cash Flow from Operating Activities before Tax		1,70,000
F.	*Less:* Tax paid		(35,000)
G.	**Net Cash Inflow from Operating Activities after Tax**		1,35,000

Working Notes:

1. CALCULATION OF NET PROFIT BEFORE TAX

Particulars	₹
Closing Balance of P&L A/c	48,000
Less: Opening Balance of P&L A/c	(30,000)
Add: Transfer to Reserve	30,000
Add: Proposed Dividend	50,000
Add: Interim Dividend on Equity Shares	20,000
Add: Tax	45,000
Net Profit before Tax	1,63,000

Dr. **2. FIXED ASSETS ACCOUNT** *Cr.*

Particulars	₹	*Particulars*	₹
To Balance b/d	2,80,000	By Depreciation A/c (b.f.)	20,000
To Bank A/c (Purchases)	1,30,000	By Bank A/c (Sale)	10,000
		By P&L A/c (Loss) [₹20,000 - ₹10,000]	10,000
		By Balance c/d	3,70,000
	4,10,000		4,10,000

Dr. **3. PROVISION FOR TAX ACCOUNT** *Cr.*

Particulars	₹	*Particulars*	₹
To Bank A/c	35,000	By Balance c/d	40,000
To Balance c/d	50,000	By P & L A/c (balancing figure)	45,000
	85,000		85,000

ILLUSTRATION 16

From the following information, calculate the Net Cash Flow from Operating Activities:

Particulars	*Closing* ₹	*Opening* ₹
Equity Share Capital	5,50,000	4,50,000
5% Preference Share Capital	2,00,000	3,00,000
General Reserve	1,50,000	1,20,000
Profit and Loss A/c	1,50,000	(1,40,000)
Securities Premium	10,000	—

Provision for Tax	40,000	20,000
Non-Current Liabilities [8% Debentures]	2,60,000	1,50,000
Short-term Borrowings (8% Bank Loan)	40,000	50,000
Trade Payables	1,05,000	1,00,000
Tangible Fixed Assets	8,60,000	6,20,000
Intangible Assets [Goodwill]	15,000	20,000
Trade Receivables & Inventories	3,95,000	3,00,000
Other Non-Current Assets [Preliminary Exp.]	—	20,000

During the year a machinery costing ₹ 60,000 on which depreciation charged was ₹ 20,000 was sold for ₹ 20,000. Depreciation provided on Fixed Assets ₹ 60,000. Additional Debentures were issued at par on 1st October and Bank Loan was repaid on the same date. Dividend on equity shares @ 8% was paid on opening balance.Income Tax ₹ 45,000 has been provided during the year. Preference Shares were redeemed at a premium of 5% at the end of the year.

SOLUTION

CALCULATION OF NET CASH FLOW FROM OPERATING ACTIVITIES

Particulars	₹	₹
Net Profit before tax		4,16,000
Adjustment for Non-Cash and Non-Operating Items :		
Depreciation on Fixed Assets	60,000	
Loss on Sale of Machinery	20,000	
Interest on Debentures [(₹ 1,50,000 × 8/100) + (₹ 1,10,000 × 8/100 × 6/12)]	16,400	
Interest on Bank Loan [(₹ 50,000 × 8/100 × 6/12) + (₹ 40,000 × 8/100 × 6/12)	3,600	
Goodwill Amortised	5,000	
Preliminary Expenses Written off	20,000	
Premium on Redemption of Preference Shares	5,000	1,30,000
Operating Profit before Working Capital Changes		5,46,000
Changes in Current Assets & Current Liabilities:		
Increase in Trade Receivables & Inventories	(95,000)	
Increase in Trade Payables	5,000	(90,000)
Net Cash Flow from Operating Activities before Tax		4,56,000
Less: **Tax paid**		(35,000)
Net Cash Inflow from Operating Activities after Tax		4,21,000

Working Notes:

1. CALCULATION OF NET PROFIT BEFORE TAX

Particulars	₹
Closing Balance of P&L A/c	1,50,000
Add: Opening Balance of P&L A/c (Debit)	1,40,000
Add: Provision for tax	45,000

Add: Transfer to Reserve	30,000
Add: Dividend on Equity Shares	36,000
Add: Dividend on Preference Shares	15,000
Net Profit before Tax	4,16,000

Dr. **2. FIXED ASSETS ACCOUNT** *Cr.*

Particulars	₹	*Particulars*	₹
To Balance b/d	6,20,000	By Depreciation A/c	60,000
To Bank A/c (Purchases) (b.f.)	3,40,000	By Bank A/c (Sale)	20,000
		By P&L A/c (Loss)	20,000
		By Balance c/d	8,60,000
	9,60,000		9,60,000

Dr. **3. PROVISION FOR TAX ACCOUNT** *Cr.*

Particulars	₹	*Particulars*	₹
To Bank A/c (balancing figure)	35,000	By Balance c/d	40,000
To Balance c/d	50,000	By P & L A/c	45,000
	85,000		85,000

ILLUSTRATION 17

From the following information calculate Cash Flow from Operating Activities:

Particulars	*Closing* ₹	*Opening* ₹
Trade Payables	1,65,000	40,000
Intangible Assets [Goodwill]	21,000	10,000
Inventories	1,69,000	54,000
Trade Receivables	3,76,000	4,06,000

During the year, the business of Y Ltd. was purchased for ₹60,000 payable in fully paid equity shares of ₹10 each at 20% premium. The assets included Inventories ₹15,000. Trade Receivables ₹10,000 and machine ₹30,000. Trade Payables of ₹15,000 were also taken over. Net Profit before tax for the year was ₹ 7,98,000. Tax paid during the year ₹ 10,000.

SOLUTION

CALCULATION OF CASH FLOW FROM OPERATING ACTIVITIES

Particulars		₹
A. Net Profit before tax		7,98,000
B. *Add:* Goodwill amortised		9,000
C. Operating Profit before Working Capital Changes		8,07,000
D. Changes in Current Assets & Current Liabilities:		
Increase in Inventories [(1,69,000 – 15,000) – 54,000]	(1,00,000)	
Decrease in Trade Receivables [(3,76,000 – 10,000) – 4,06,000]	40,000	

	Increase in Trade Payables [(1,65,000 – 15,000) – 40,000]	1,10,000	50,000
E.	Net Cash Flow from Operating Activities before Tax		8,57,000
F.	*Less:* Tax paid		(10,000)
G.	Net Cash Inflow From Operating Activities After Tax		8,47,000

Note: Goodwill Amortised

= Goodwill Purchased + Opening Goodwill – Closing Goodwill

= [₹ 60,000 – (₹ 15,000 + ₹ 10,000 + ₹ 30,000 – ₹ 15,000] + ₹ 10,000 – ₹ 21,000 = ₹ 9,000

13.0 HOW TO COMPUTE CASH FLOW FROM INVESTING ACTIVITIES

TREATMENT OF SPECIAL ITEMS WHILE COMPUTING CASH FLOW FROM INVESTING ACTIVITIES

Item	Treatment	Reason
1. **Sale of Fixed Assets *or* Investments***	CashInflow from Investing Activities.	It involves Cash Inflow.
2. **Purchase of Fixed Assets *or* Investments***	Cash Outlow in Investing Activities.	It involves Cash Outflow.
3. **Interest *or* Dividend on Investments* *or* Rent from Property**	Cash Inflow from Investing Activities.	It represents the receipt of Non-Operating Income. **Note:** If the date of Fresh Purchase /Sale of Investments is not given, Calculate Interest on Opening Bal. of Investments.
4. **Increase in Accrued Interest on Investments***	**Subtract** from the Total Interest on Investments to ascertain the Net Amount of interest received.	It represents the amount of Interest not yet received.

**whether Current or Non-Current*

CALCULATION OF CASH FLOW FROM INVESTING ACTIVITIES

Particulars	₹
A. Cash Inflow from Investing Activities:	
Sale of Tangible Fixed Assets (e.g. Machinery) for cash	xxx
Sale of Intangible Assets (e.g. Goodwill/Patents/Trademark/Copyright) for cash	xxx
Sale of Investments(whether Current *or* Non-Current) for cash	xxx
Loans & Advances repayments received (whether Short term *or* Long term)	xxx
Incomes from Investments (whether Current *or* Non-Current)(***For Example***)	xxx
Dividend received on Shares held as Investments	xxx
Interest received on Debentures held as Investments	xxx
Rent received from Immovable Property held as Investments	xxx
	xxx
B. Cash used in Investing Activities:	
Purchase of Tangible Fixed Assets (e.g. Machinery) for cash	(xxx)

	Purchase of Intangible Assets (e.g. Goodwill/Patents/Trademark/Copyright) for cash	(xxx)
	Purchase of Investments(whether Current *or* Non-Current) for cash	(xxx)
	Loans & Advances granted (whether Short term *or* Long term)	(xxx)
		(xxx)
C.	**Net Cash Inflow from Investing Activities [if A > B]**	xxx
	or	***or***
	Net Cash used in Investing Activities [If A < B]	(xxx)

ILLUSTRATION 18

From the following particulars, Calculate Net Cash Flow from Investing Activities:

Particulars	*Closing* ₹	*Opening* ₹
Goodwill	90,000	1,10,000
Patents	1,15,000	90,000
Land	90,000	1,00,000
Plant & Machinery (Net)	1,60,000	1,80,000
Furniture (Gross)	4,25,000	2,00,000
Provision for Depreciation on Furniture	42,500	20,000
10% Non-Current Investments	1,10,000	1,50,000
10% Current Investments	60,000	50,000

SOLUTION

CALCULATION OF NET CASH FLOW FROM INVESTING ACTIVITIES

Particulars	₹
Purchase of Patents [₹ 1,15,000 – ₹ 90,000]	(25,000)
Sale of Land [₹ 1,00,000 – ₹ 90,000]	10,000
Purchase of Furniture [₹ 4,25,000 – ₹ 2,00,000]	(2,25,000)
Sale of Non-Current Investments [₹ 1,50,000 – ₹ 1,10,000]	40,000
Purchase of Current Investments [₹ 60,000 – ₹ 50,000]	(10,000)
Interest on 10% Non-Current Investments [₹ 1,50,000 × 10/100]	15,000
Interest on 10% Current Investments [₹ 50,000 × 10/100]	5,000
Net Cash used in Investing Activities	(1,90,000)

Notes:

1. *It has been assumed that Investments have been sold & purchased at the end of current accounting year.*
2. *Decrease in Goodwill represents Goodwill Amortised.*
3. *Decrease in Plant & Machinery (Net) represents Depreciation.*

HOW TO ASCERTAIN MISSING FIGURES (E.G. SALES, PURCHASES AND PROFIT/LOSS ON SALE) RELATED TO INVESTMENTS

To ascertain Missing Figures (e.g. Sales, Purchases and Profit/Loss on Sale) related to Investments, prepare Investments Account as follows:

Dr. **INVESTMENTS ACCOUNT** *Cr.*

Particulars	₹	*Particulars*	₹
To Balance b/d	....	By Bank A/c (Sale Proceeds)	....
To Bank A/c (Purchases)	....	By P&L A/c (Loss on Sale)	....
To P&L (Profit)	....	By Balance c/d	....
	....		....

ILLUSTRATION 19

Particulars	*Closing* ₹	*Opening* ₹
10% Non-Current Investments	1,60,000	60,000
10% Current Investments	60,000	20,000

At the end of the year Some Non-Current Investments costing ₹ 40,000 were sold at a loss of 1/3rd on sale and Some Current Investments costing ₹ 20,000 were sold at a profit of 25%. Net Profit before Tax ₹ 1,00,000. How will you disclose these items while preparing Cash Flow Statement as per AS–3 issued by ICAI?

SOLUTION

Dr. **1. NON-CURRENT INVESTMENTS ACCOUNT** *Cr.*

Particulars	₹	*Particulars*	₹
To Balance b/d	60,000	By Bank A/c [₹ 40,000 – ₹ 10,000]	30,000
To Bank A/c (Purchases) (b.f.)	1,40,000	By P&L A/c (Loss)	10,000
		By Balance c/d	1,60,000
	2,00,000		2,00,000

Dr. **2. CURRENT INVESTMENTS ACCOUNT** *Cr.*

Particulars	₹	*Particulars*	₹
To Balance b/d	20,000,	By Bank A/c	25,000
To Bank A/c (Purchase)	60,000	By Balance c/d	60,000
To P&L A/c (Profit) [25% of ₹ 20,000]	5,000		
	85,000		85,000

CASH FLOW STATEMENT FOR THE YEAR ENDED ...

A	**Cash Flow from Operating Activities**	₹
	Net Profit before Tax	1,00,000

	Add: Loss on Sale of Non-Current Investments	5,000
	Less: Profit on Sale of Current Investments	10,000
	Less: Interest Income on Non-Current Investments	6,000
	Less: Interest Income on Current Investments	2,000
	Operating Profit before Working Capital changes	87,000
B	**Cash Flow from Investing Activities**	
	Purchase of Non-Current Investments	(1,40,000)
	Purchase of Current Investments	(60,000)
	Interest Income on Non-Current Investments	6,000
	Interest Income on Current Investments	2,000
	Sale of Non-Current Investments	30,000
	Sale of Current Investments	25,000
	Cash used in Investing Activities	(1,37,000

ILLUSTRATION 20

Particulars	*Closing* ₹	*Opening* ₹
10% Non-Current Investments	1,60,000	60,000
10% Current Investments	60,000	20,000

At the end of the year Some Non-Current Investments costing ₹ 40,000 were sold at a loss of 1/3rd on sale and Some Current Investments costing ₹ 20,000 were sold at a profit of 25%. Profit / Loss on Investments was adjusted against the Capital Reserve. Net Profit before Tax ₹ 1,00,000. How will you disclose these items while preparing Cash Flow Statement as per AS–3 issued by ICAI?

SOLUTION

Dr. **1. NON-CURRENT INVESTMENTS ACCOUNT** *Cr.*

Particulars	₹	*Particulars*	₹
To Balance b/d	60,000	By Bank A/c [₹ 40,000 – ₹ 10,000]	30,000
To Bank A/c (Purchases) (b.f.)	1,40,000	By Capital Reserve A/c (Loss)	10,000
		By Balance c/d	1,60,000
	2,00,000		2,00,000

Dr. **2. CURRENT INVESTMENTS ACCOUNT** *Cr.*

Particulars	₹	*Particulars*	₹
To Balance b/d	20,000,	By Bank A/c	25,000
To Bank A/c (Purchase)	60,000	By Balance c/d	60,000
To Capital Reserve A/c (Profit) [25% of ₹ 20,000]	5,000		
	85,000		85,000

CASH FLOW STATEMENT OF TULSIAN LTD FOR THE YEAR ENDED 31ST DECEMBER, 2016

A	**Cash Flow from Operating Activities**	₹
	Net Profit before Tax	1,00,000
	Less: Interest Income on Non-Current Investments	6,000
	Less: Interest Income on Current Investments	2,000
	Operating Profit before Working Capital changes	92,000
B	**Cash Flow from Investing Activities**	
	Purchase of Non-Current Investments	(1,40,000)
	Purchase of Current Investments	(60,000)
	Interest Income on Non-Current Investments	6,000
	Interest Income on Current Investments	2,000
	Sale of Non-Current Investments	30,000
	Sale of Current Investments	25,000
	Cash used in Investing Activities	(1,37,000

HOW TO ASCERTAIN MISSING FIGURES (E.G. SALES, PURCHASES AND PROFIT/LOSS ON SALE) RELATED TO DEPRECIABLE FIXED ASSETS

To ascertain Missing Figures (e.g. Sales, Purchases and Profit/Loss on Sale) related to Depreciable Fixed Assets, prepare Fixed Assets Account as follows:

Dr. **FIXED ASSETS ACCOUNT** *Cr.*

Particulars	₹	*Particulars*	₹
To Balance b/d	....	By Depreciation A/c	....
To Bank A/c (Purchases)	....	By Bank A/c (Sale)	....
To Profit & Loss A/c (Profit)	....	By P&L A/c (loss)	....
To Equity Share Capital A/c (Purch.)	....	By Balance c/d	....
	....		....

ILLUSTRATION 21

Tangible Fixed Assets (Net): Closing ₹ 8,60,000, Opening ₹ 6,20,000. During the year a machine costing ₹ 60,000 (depreciation provided thereon ₹ 20,000) was sold at a loss of ₹ 10,000. Depreciation charged was ₹ 60,000. Net Profit before Tax ₹ 1,00,000. How will you disclose these items while preparing Cash Flow Statement as per AS–3 issued by ICAI?

SOLUTION

Dr. **FIXED ASSETS ACCOUNT** Cr.

Particulars	₹	*Particulars*	₹
To Balance b/d	6,20,000	By Depreciation A/c	60,000
To Bank A/c (Purchases) (b.f.)	3,40,000	By Bank A/c (Sale)	30,000
		By P&L A/c (Loss)	10,000
		By Balance c/d	8,60,000
	9,60,000		9,60,000

CASH FLOW STATEMENT FOR THE YEAR ENDED ...

A	**Cash Flow from Operating Activities**	₹
	Net Profit before Tax	1,00,000
	Add: Depreciation	60,000
	Add: Loss on Sale	10,000
	Operating Profit before Working Capital changes	1,70,000
B	**Cash Flow from Investing Activities**	
	Purchase of Machinery	(3,40,000)
	Sale of Machinery	30,000
	Cash used in Investing Activities	(3,10,000

ILLUSTRATION 22

Tangible Fixed Assets (Net): Closing ₹ 12,70,000, Opening ₹ 10,20,000. During the year a machine costing ₹ 1,40,000 (depreciation provided thereon ₹ 60,000) was sold for ₹ 50,000. Depreciation charged was ₹ 1,40,000. A machine costing ₹ 30,000 was purchased by issue of Equity Shares of ₹ 10 each at a premium of 20%.Net Profit before Tax ₹ 1,00,000. How will you disclose these items while preparing Cash Flow Statement as per AS–3 issued by ICAI?

SOLUTION

Dr. **FIXED ASSETS ACCOUNT** Cr.

Particulars	₹	*Particulars*	₹
To Balance b/d	10,20,000	By Bank A/c (Sale)	50,000
To Bank A/c (Purchases) (b.f.)	4,40,000	By P&L A/c (Loss on Sale)	30,000
To Equity Share Capital A/c	25,000	By Depreciation A/c	1,40,000
To Securities Premium	5,000	By Balance c/d	12,70,000
	14,90,000		14,90,000

CASH FLOW STATEMENT FOR THE YEAR ENDED ...

A	**Cash Flow from Operating Activities**	₹
	Net Profit before Tax	1,00,000
	Add: Depreciation	1,40,000
	Add: Loss on Sale	30,000
	Operating Profit before Working Capital changes	2,70,000
B	**Cash Flow from Investing Activities**	
	Purchase of Machinery	(4,40,000)
	Sale of Machinery	50,000
	Cash used in Investing Activities	(3,90,000

HOW TO ASCERTAIN MISSING FIGURES (E.G. SALES, PURCHASES AND PROFIT/LOSS ON SALE) RELATED TO DEPRECIABLE FIXED ASSETS WHEN PROVISION FOR DEPRECIATION ACCOUNT IS MAINTAINED

To ascertain Missing Figures (e.g. Sales, Purchases and Profit/Loss on Sale) related to Depreciable Fixed Assets when Provision for Depreciation Account is maintained, prepare the following three accounts as follows:

Dr. **1. FIXED ASSETS ACCOUNT (AT COST)** *Cr.*

Particulars	₹	*Particulars*	₹
To Balance b/d	....	By Machinery Disposal A/c	....
To Bank A/c (Purchases)	....	[T/f of Cost of Machine sold]	
To Equity Share Capital A/c (Purch.)	....	By Balance c/d	....
	....		....

Dr. **2. PROVISION FOR DEPRECIATION ACCOUNT** *Cr.*

Particulars	₹	*Particulars*	₹
To Machinery Disposal A/c	....	By Balance b/d	....
[T/f of Acc. Dep. on Machine sold]		By P&L A/c	
		(Dep. Provided during the	
To Balance c/d	....	current year)	....
	....		....

Dr. **3. MACHINERY DISPOSAL ACCOUNT** *Cr.*

Particulars	₹	*Particulars*	₹
To Plant & Machinery A/c (Cost)	....	By Provision for Depreciation A/c	....
To Profit & Loss A/c (Profit)	....	By Bank A/c (Sale proceeds)	....
		By Profit & Loss A/c (Loss on sale)	....
	....		....

ILLUSTRATION 23

Particulars	*Closing (₹)*	*Opening (₹)*
Tangible Fixed Assets	16,20,000	13,20,000
Accumulated Depreciation	3,80,000	3,00,000

During the year a machine having book value of ₹ 80,000 (depreciation provided thereon ₹ 60,000) was sold at a loss of ₹ 30,000. Net Profit before Tax ₹ 1,00,000. How will you disclose these items while preparing Cash Flow Statement as per AS–3 issued by ICAI?

SOLUTION

Dr. **1. FIXED ASSETS ACCOUNT (AT COST)** *Cr.*

Particulars	₹	*Particulars*	₹
To Balance b/d	13,20,000	By Machinery Disposal A/c	1,40,000
To Bank A/c (Purchases)	4,40,000	By Balance c/d	16,20,000
	17,60,000		17,60,000

Dr. **2. PROVISION FOR DEPRECIATION ACCOUNT** Cr.

Particulars	₹	Particulars	₹
To Machinery Disposal A/c	60,000	By Balance b/d	3,00,000
To Bank c/d	3,80,000	By P&L A/c (Depreciation for current year) (Balancing figure)	1,40,000
	4,40,000		4,40,000

Dr. **3. MACHINERY DISPOSAL ACCOUNT** Cr.

Particulars	₹	Particulars	₹
To Fixed Assets A/c	1,40,000	By Provision for Depreciation A/c	60,000
		By Bank A/c (b.f.)	50,000
		By Profit and Loss A/c (Loss)	30,000
	1,40,000		1,40,000

CASH FLOW STATEMENT FOR THE YEAR ENDED ...

A	**Cash Flow from Operating Activities**	₹
	Net Profit before Tax	1,00,000
	Add: Depreciation	1,40,000
	Add: Loss on Sale	30,000
	Operating Profit before Working Capital changes	2,70,000
B	**Cash Flow from Investing Activities**	
	Purchase of Machinery	(4,40,000)
	Sale of Machinery	50,000
	Cash used in Investing Activities	(3,90,000

ILLUSTRATION 24

Particulars	Closing ₹	Opening ₹
Tangible Fixed Assets	16,50,000	13,20,000
Accumulated Depreciation	3,80,000	3,00,000

During the year a machine having book value of ₹ 80,000 (depreciation provided thereon ₹ 60,000) was sold at a loss of 37.5%. A machine costing ₹ 30,000 was purchased by issue of Equity Shares of ₹ 10 each at a premium of 20%. Net Profit before Tax ₹ 1,00,000. How will you disclose these items while preparing Cash Flow Statement as per AS–3 issued by ICAI?

SOLUTION

Dr. **1. FIXED ASSETS ACCOUNT (AT COST)** Cr.

Particulars	₹	Particulars	₹
To Balance b/d	13,20,000	By Machinery Disposal A/c	1,40,000
To Bank A/c (Purchases)	4,40,000	By Balance c/d	16,50,000

To Equity Share Capital A/c	25,000		
To Securities Premium	5,000		
	17,90,000		17,90,000

Dr. **2. PROVISION FOR DEPRECIATION ACCOUNT** Cr.

Particulars	₹	*Particulars*	₹
To Machinery Disposal A/c	60,000	By Balance b/d	3,00,000
To Bank c/d	3,80,000	By P&L A/c (Depreciation for current year) (Balancing figure)	1,40,000
	4,40,000		4,40,000

Dr. **3. MACHINERY DISPOSAL ACCOUNT** Cr.

Particulars	₹	*Particulars*	₹
To Fixed Assets A/c	1,40,000	By Provision for Depreciation A/c	60,000
		By Bank A/c (b.f.)	50,000
		By Profit and Loss A/c (Loss)	30,000
	1,40,000		1,40,000

CASH FLOW STATEMENT FOR THE YEAR ENDED ...

A	**Cash Flow from Operating Activities**	₹
	Net Profit before Tax	1,00,000
	Add: Depreciation	1,40,000
	Add: Loss on Sale	30,000
	Operating Profit before Working Capital changes	2,70,000
B	**Cash Flow from Investing Activities**	
	Purchase of Machinery	(4,40,000)
	Sale of Machinery	50,000
	Cash used in Investing Activities	(3,90,000

ILLUSTRATION 25

Particulars	*Closing* ₹	*Opening* ₹
Tangible Fixed Assets	16,50,000	13,20,000
Accumulated Depreciation	3,80,000	3,00,000

During the year a machine costing ₹ 1,40,000 was sold at a loss of 37.5%. Depreciation of ₹ 1,40,000 was provided during the current year. A machine costing ₹ 30,000 was purchased by issue of Equity Shares of ₹ 10 each at a premium of 20%. Net Profit before Tax ₹ 1,00,000. How will you disclose these items while preparing Cash Flow Statement as per AS–3 issued by ICAI?

SOLUTION

Same as in case of Previous ILLUSTRATION.

ILLUSTRATION 26

From the following information, Calculate Net Cash Flow from Operating Activities and Investing Activities:

Particulars	*Closing* ₹	*Opening* ₹
Profit and Loss A/c	3,92,000	(1,08,000)
General Reserve	1,40,000	3,20,000
Proposed Dividend	1,50,000	1,20,000
Provision for Tax	40,000	20,000
Trade Payables	2,00,000	1,00,000
Tangible Fixed Assets (Net)	12,40,000	10,20,000
Intangible Assets [Goodwill]	1,000	10,000
10% Non-Current Investments	1,60,000	60,000
10% Current Investments	60,000	20,000
Trade Receivables & Inventories	5,20,000	4,60,000

During the year a machine costing ₹ 1,40,000 (depreciation provided thereon ₹ 60,000) was sold for ₹ 50,000. Depreciation charged was ₹ 1,40,000. Tax paid was ₹ 10,000.At the end of the year some Non-Current Investments costing ₹ 40,000 were sold at a profit of 25%,

SOLUTION

CALCULATION OF NET CASH FLOW FROM OPERATING ACTIVITIES AND INVESTING ACTIVITIES

Particulars	₹	₹
I. Cash Flow from Operating Activities:		
A. Net Profit before tax		5,00,000
B. Adjustments for Non-Cash and Non-Operating Items :		
Depreciation	1,40,000	
Loss on Sale of Machinery	30,000	
Goodwill amortised	9,000	
Profit on Sale of Non-Current Investments	(10,000)	
Interest Income on Non-Current Investments	(6,000)	
Interest Income on Current Investments	(2,000)	1,61,000
C. Operating Profit before Working Capital Changes		6,61,000
D. Changes in Current Assets & Current Liabilities:		
Increase in Trade Payables	1,00,000	
Increase in Trade Receivables & Inventories	(60,000)	40,000
E. Net Cash Flow from Operating Activities before Tax		7,01,000
F. *Less:* **Tax paid**		(10,000)
G. Net Cash Inflow from Operating Activities after Tax		6,91,000
II. Cash Flow from Investing Activities:		
Sale of Machinery		50,000

Purchases of Fixed Assets		(4,40,000)
Purchases of Non-Current Investments		(1,40,000)
Purchases of Current Investments		(40,000)
Sale of Non-Current Investments		50,000
Interest received on Non-Current Investments		6,000
Interest received on Current Investments		2,000
Net Cash used in Investing Activities		(5,12,000)

Working Notes:

1. CALCULATION OF NET PROFIT BEFORE TAX

Particulars	₹
Closing Balance of P&L A/c	3,92,000
Add: Opening Balance of P&L A/c (Debit)	1,08,000
*Less:*Transfer from Reserve	(1,80,000)
Add: Proposed Dividend	1,50,000
Add: Tax	30,000
Net Profit before Tax	5,00,000

Dr. **2. FIXED ASSETS ACCOUNT** *Cr.*

Particulars	₹	*Particulars*	₹
To Balance b/d	10,20,000	By Bank A/c (Sale)	50,000
To Bank A/c (Purchases) (b.f.)	4,40,000	By P&L A/c (Loss)	30,000
		By Depreciation A/c	1,40,000
		By Balance c/d	12,40,000
	14,60,000		14,60,000

Dr. **3. NON-CURRENT INVESTMENTS ACCOUNT** *Cr.*

Particulars	₹	*Particulars*	₹
To Balance b/d	60,000	By Bank A/c [₹ 40,000 + ₹ 10,000]	50,000
To Bank A/c (Purchases) (b.f.)	1,40,000	By Balance c/d	1,60,000
To Profit and Loss A/c (Profit) [₹ 40,000 × 25/100]	10,000		
	2,10,000		2,10,000

Dr. **4. PROVISION FOR TAX ACCOUNT** *Cr.*

Particulars	₹	*Particulars*	₹
To Bank A/c [Tax paid]	10,000	By Balance b/d	20,000
To Balance c/d	40,000	By Profit and Loss A/c (b.f.) [Provision made]	30,000
	50,000		50,000

14.0 HOW TO COMPUTE CASH FLOW FROM FINANCING ACTIVITIES

TREATMENT OF SPECIAL ITEMS WHILE CALCULATING CASH FROM FINANCING ACTIVITIES

Item	Treatment	Reason
1. Increase in Equity Share Capital/Pref. Share Capital/Debentures/ Loans*	Cash Inflow from Financing Activities.	It represents the issue of New Shares/Debentures.
2. Decrease in Equity Share Capital/ Pref. Share Capital/ Debentures/Loans*	Cash Outlow in Financing Activities.	It represents the buy-back of Equity Shares *or* Redemption of Pref. Share Capital/Debentures.
3. Increase in Securities Premium	Cash Inflow from Financing Activities.	It represents the issue of New Shares/Debentures at premium.
4. Increase in Discount on Issue of Debentures/ Shares	**Subtract** from the increase in amount of Share Capital/ Debentures to ascertain the Net amount of issue.	It represents the issue of New shares/Debentures at discount.
5. Increase in Underwriting Commission	Cash Outlow in Financing Activities.	It represents the payment of underwriting commission in raising Share Capital/ Debentures.
6. Interest on Debentures/ Loans*	Cash Outlow in Financing Activities.	It represents the payment of interest on Debentures. **Note:** *If the date of Fresh issue /Redemption of Debentures is not given, Calculate Interest on Opening Balance of Debentures.*
7. Increase in Unpaid Interest on Debentures/ Loans*	Subtract from the Total Interest on Debentures to ascertain the Net amount of Interest paid.	It represents the amount of Interest not yet paid.
8. Proposed Dividend for Previous Year [It represents the amount of dividend proposed by the Board of Directors for the Previous year.]	Cash Outlow in Financing Activities.	It represents the payment of Dividend.
9. Increase in Unclaimed Dividend	Subtract from the amount of Proposed Dividend for the previous year to ascertain the Net amount of dividend paid.	It represents the amount of Dividend not yet paid.
10. Interim Dividend [An Interim Dividend is that dividend which is declared by the Board of Directors for the current year during the current year.]	Cash Outlow in Financing Activities.	It represents the payment of Dividend.

11. Dividend on Pref. Shares	Cash Outlow in Financing Activities.	It represents the payment of Pref. Dividend. **Note:** *If the date of Fresh issue/ Redemption of Pref. Shares is not given, Calculate Dividend on Opening Balance of Pref. Share.*

*whether Short-term or Long-term

CALCULATION OF NET CASH FLOW FROM FINANCING ACTIVITIES

Particulars	₹
A. Cash Inflows from Financing Activities:	
Issue of Equity Share Capital for cash [including Premium but excl. Discount]	xxx
Issue of Pref. Share Capital for cash [including Premium but excl. Discount]	xxx
Issue of Debentures for cash [including Premium but excl. Discount]	xxx
Loans raised (whether Short term *or* Long term)	xxx
	xxx
B. Cash used in Financing Activities:	
Buy back of Equity Shares [including Premium]	(xxx)
Redemption of Preference Shares for cash [including Premium]	(xxx)
Redemption of Debentures for cash [including Premium]	(xxx)
Repayment of Loans (whether Short term *or* Long term)	(xxx)
Interim Dividend paid on Equity Shares	(xxx)
Final Dividend paid on Equity Shares	(xxx)
Final Dividend paid on Preference Shares	(xxx)
Interest paid on Debentures & Loans (whether Short term *or* Long term)	(xxx)
	(xxx)
C. Net Cash Inflow from Financing Activities [If A > B]	xxx
or	***or***
Net Cash Flow used in Financing Activities [If A < B]	(xxx)

ILLUSTRATION 27

From the following particulars, Calculate Net Cash Flow from Financing Activities:

Particulars	*Closing* ₹	*Opening* ₹
Equity Share Capital	4,00,000	3,00,000
Pref. Share Capital	1,00,000	1,50,000
Securities Premium	15,000	5,000
Proposed Dividend on Equity. Shares	35,000	30,000
Proposed Dividend on Pref. Shares	15,000	15,000
10% Debentures	4,00,000	3,00,000

SOLUTION

CALCULATION OF NET CASH FLOW FROM FINANCING ACTIVITIES

Particulars	₹
Proceeds from Issue of Equity Share Capital [(₹ 4,00,000 – ₹ 3,00,000) + ₹ 10,000 Premium]	1,10,000
Proceeds from Issue of Debentures [₹ 4,00,000 – ₹ 3,00,000]	1,00,000
Redemption of Preference Shares [₹ 1,50,000 – ₹ 1,00,000]	(50,000)
Interest on Debentures paid [₹ 3,00,000 × 10/100]	(30,000)
Dividend on Equity. Shares	(30,000)
Dividend on Pref. Shares	(15,000)
Net Cash Inflow from Financing Activities	85,000

Notes:

1. *It has been assumed that the new Debentures have been issued at par at the end of current accounting year.*
2. *It has been assumed that Preference Shares have been redeemed at the end of current accounting year.*

ILLUSTRATION 28

From the following particulars of BT Ltd., calculate Net Cash Flow from Financing Activities:

Particulars	*Closing* ₹	*Opening* ₹
Equity Share Capital	9,00,000	6,00,000
18% Pref. Share Capital	1,00,000	4,00,000
Securities Premium	1,30,000	1,00,000
14% Debentures	3,00,000	2,00,000

Additional Information: During the year Preference Dividend on preference shares and an Interim Dividend on equity shares @ 15% were paid on 30th Sept. New Shares and Debentures were issued on 1st Oct. Preference shares were redeemed at the end of the year at a premium of 5%. Such premium has been provided out of profits.

SOLUTION

CALCULATION OF NET CASH FLOW FROM FINANCING ACTIVITIES

Particulars	₹
Issue of Equity Share Capital [₹ 9,00,000 – ₹ 6,00,000 + ₹ 30,000 (Premium)]	3,30,000
Issue of Debentures [₹ 3,00,000 – ₹ 2,00,000]	1,00,000
Redemption of Preference Shares [₹ 3,00,000 + ₹ 15,000]	(3,15,000)
Interest paid on Debentures [(₹ 2,00,000 × 14/100) + ₹ 1,00,000 × 14/100 × 6/12)]	(35,000)
Interim Dividend paid on Equity Shares [₹ 6,00,000 × 15/100]	(90,000)
Dividend paid on Pref. Shares [₹ 4,00,000 × 18/100]	(72,000)
Net Cash used in Financing Activities	(82,000)

ILLUSTRATION 29

Particulars	*31.03.2016* ₹	*31.03.2015* ₹
14% Debentures	2,60,000	1,50,000
14% Short-term Bank Loan	40,000	50,000

New Debentures were issued on 01.01.2016 and Bank Loan was repaid on the same date. Unpaid Interest on Debentures on 31.03.2016 ₹ 10,000. Net Profit before Tax ₹ 1,00,000 How will you disclose these items while preparing Cash Flow Statement as per AS–3 issued by ICAI?

SOLUTION

CASH FLOW STATEMENT FOR THE YEAR ENDED 31ST MARCH, 2016

		₹
A	**Cash Flow from Operating Activities**	
	Net Profit before Tax	1,00,000
	Add: Interest on Debentures [(1,50,000 x 14%)+(1,10,000 x 14% x3/12]	24,850
	Add: Interest on Bank Loan [(50,000 x 14% x 9/12)+(40,000 x 14% x 3/12]	6,650
	Operating Profit before Working Capital changes	1,31,500
B	**Cash Flow from Financing activities**	
	Issue of Debentures	1,10,000
	Bank Loan repaid	(10,000)
	Interest on Debentures [24,850 – 10,000]	14,850
	Interest on Bank Loan	6,650
	Cash Flow from Financing activities	78,500

ILLUSTRATION 30

From the following information, Calculate Net Cash Flow from Operating Activities & Financing Activities:

Particulars	*31.03.2016* ₹	*31.03.2015* ₹
Equity Share Capital	5,50,000	4,50,000
5% Preference Share Capital	2,00,000	3,00,000
General Reserve	1,50,000	1,20,000
Profit and Loss A/c	1,50,000	(1,40,000)
Securities Premium	10,000	—
Provision for Tax	40,000	20,000
Non-Current Liabilities [8% Debentures]	2,60,000	1,50,000
Short-term Borrowings (8% Bank Loan)	40,000	50,000
Increase in Trade Payables	2,00,000	1,00,000
Increase in Trade Receivables & Inventories	5,20,000	4,60,000

Additional Information: During the year Additional Debentures were issued at par on 1st October, and Bank Loan was repaid on the same date. Dividend on equity shares @ 8% was paid on opening balance.Income Tax ₹ 45,000 has been provided during the year.Preference Shares were redeemed at a premium of 5% at the end of the year.

SOLUTION

CALCULATION OF CASH FLOW FROM OPERATING ACTIVITIES AND FINANCING ACTIVITIES

Particulars	₹	₹
I. Cash Flow from Operating Activities:		
Net Profit before tax		4,16,000
Adjustment for Non-Cash and Non-Operating Items :		
Interest on Debentures [(₹ 1,50,000 × 8/100) + (₹ 1,10,000 × 8/100 × 6/12)]		16,400
Interest on Bank Loan [(₹ 50,000 × 8/100 × 6/12) + (₹ 40,000 × 8/100 × 6/12)		3,600
Premium on Redemption of Preference Shares		5,000
Operating Profit before Working Capital Changes		4,41,000
Changes in Current Assets & Current Liabilities:		0
Increase in Trade Payables	1,00,000	
Increase in Trade Receivables & Inventories	(60,000)	40,000
Net Cash Flow from Operating Activities before Tax		4,81,000
Less: **Tax paid**		(35,000)
Net Cash Inflow from Operating Activities after Tax		4,46,000
II. Cash Flow from Financing Activities:		
Issue of Share Capital [₹ 1,00,000 + ₹ 10,000 (Premium)]		1,10,000
Issue of Debentures		1,10,000
Interest on Debentures		(16,400)
Interest on Bank Loan		(3,600)
Dividend on Equity Shares [₹4,50,000 × 8/100]		(36,000)
Dividend on Preference Shares [₹3,00,000 × 5/100]		(15,000)
Redemption of Preference Shares[₹ 1,00,000 + ₹ 5,000]		(1,05,000)
Bank Loan Repaid [₹ 50,000 + ₹ 40,000]		(10,000)
Net Cash from in Financing Activities		34,000

Working Notes:

1. CALCULATION OF NET PROFIT BEFORE TAX

Particulars	₹
Closing Balance of P&L A/c	1,50,000
Add: Opening Balance of P&L A/c (Debit)	1,40,000
Add: Provision for tax	45,000
Add: Transfer to Reserve	30,000
Add: Dividend on Equity Shares	36,000
Add: Dividend on Preference Shares	15,000
Net Profit before Tax	4,16,000

Dr. **2. PROVISION FOR TAX ACCOUNT** Cr.

Particulars	₹	*Particulars*	₹
To Bank A/c (balancing figure)	35,000	By Balance c/d	40,000
To Balance c/d	50,000	By P & L A/c	45,000
	85,000		85,000

15.0 PRACTICAL STEPS INVOLVED IN THE PREPARATION OF CASH FLOW STATEMENT

The various steps involved in the preparation of Cash Flow Statement are given below:

PRACTICAL STEPS INVOLVED IN THE PREPARATION OF CASH FLOW STATEMENT

Step 1: ***Calculate the Cash from Operating Activities.***

Step 2: ***Calculate the Cash Flow from Investing Activities.***

Step 3: ***Calculate the Cash Flow from Financing Activities.***

Step 4: ***Calculate the Net Increase (Decrease) in Cash and Cash Equivalents***

Step 4 = Step 1 + Step 2 + Step 3

Step 5: ***Calculate the Cash and Cash Equivalents at the Beginning of Period***

Step 6: ***Calculate the Cash and Cash Equivalents at the End of Period***

Step 6 = Step 4 + Step 5

IMPORTANT INSTRUCTIONS FOR WORKING NOTES

1. Net Profit before Tax	Calculate Net Profit before Tax *[Refer to Working Note No. 1 under Para 16.0].*
2. Fixed Assets Account	Prepare Fixed Assets Account to ascertain Missing Figures (e.g. Sales, Purchases and Profit/Loss on Sale) related to Depreciable Fixed Assets *[Refer to Working Note No. 2 under Para 16.0].*
3. Investments Account	Prepare Investments Account to ascertain Missing Figures (e.g. Sales, Purchases and Profit/Loss on Sale) related to Investments *[Refer to Working Note No. 3 under Para 16.0].*
4. Provision for Tax Account	Prepare Provision for Tax Account to ascertain Missing Figure (e.g. Tax provided *or* Tax paid) *[Refer to Working Note No. 4 under Para 16.0].*
5. Interest on Debentures/ Loans (whether Current *or* Non-Current)	Calculate Interest on Opening Balance of Debentures/Loan if the date of Fresh issue/Redemption of Debentures/Loan is not given.
6. Dividend on Pref.Shares	Calculate Dividend on Opening Balance of Pref. Shares if the date of Fresh issue /Redemption of Pref. Shares is not given.
7. Premium on Redemption of Pref. Share Capital/ Debentures	Calculate Premium on Redemption of Pref. Share Capital/ Debentures on Pref. Share Capital/Debentures redeemed during the year.
8. Interest on Investments (whether Current *or* Non-Current)	Calculate Interest at given % on Opening Balance of Investments if the date of Fresh Purchase/Sale of Investments is not given.

9. Proposed Dividend for Previous Year	Unless otherwise stated it is presumed that the 'Proposed Dividend for Previous Year' has been declared subsequently at the Annual General Meeting and has been paid during the current accounting period.
10. Provision for Tax for Previous Year	Unless otherwise stated, it presumed that the' Provision for Tax for Previous Year' has been paid subsequently during the current year.
11. Transactions which do not appear in CFS	1. Issue of Shares/Debentures on conversion of Debentures and 2. Purchase of an Asset against the issue of Shares/ Debentures **Reason:** These transactions do not involve any inflow/ outflow of cash.

PRECAUTIONS WHILE PREPARING CASH FLOW STATEMENT

1. *Check whether Current Year's Figures are given first or Previous Year's Figures are given first*
2. *Check whether Balance of Profit & Loss Account is Debit or Credit. If Balance of Profit & Loss Account is Debit, Add or Less very carefully.*
3. *Check whether Balance of General Reserve during current year has increased or decreased. If Balance of General Reserve during current year has decreased, Subtract Transfer from General Reserve from Closing Balance of Profit & Loss Account.*
4. *Check whether Interest % on Investments is given or not. If Interest % on Investments is given, Do not forget to make adjustment for Interest on Investments (whether Current or Non-Current) while computing Cash from Operating Activities and Investing Activities.*
5. *Do not forget to make adjustment for Interest on Borrowings (whether Short term or Long term) while computing Cash from Operating Activities and Financing Activities.*
6. *Exclude Increase in Inventories, Trade Receivables/ Payables against issue of Shares / Debentures from Respective Closing Balances. Reason: These do not involve any cash flow.*

16.0 FORMAT OF CASH FLOW STATEMENT

A Format of Cash Flow Statement is given below:

CASH FLOW STATEMENT OF M/S ....

for the year ended 31st March, ...

Particulars	₹	₹
I. Cash Flow from Operating Activities:		
A. *Net Profit before taxation, and extraordinary item*		xxx
B. *Adjustment for Non-Cash and Non-Operating Items:* ***(For Example)***		
Depreciation	xxx	
Interest on Debentures & Loans (whether Short term *or* Long term)	xxx	
Preliminary Expenses/Underwriting Commission/Discount on	xxx	
Issue of Debentures/Shares written of	xxx	
Goodwill/Patents/Trade Marks/Copyright amortised	xxx	
Loss on Sale of Investments (whether Current *or* Non-Current)	xxx	

	Premium payable on redemption of Preference shares/Debentures		
	Profit on Sale of Investments (whether Current *or* Non-Current)	(xxx)	
	Income from Investments (whether Current *or* Non-Current)	(xxx)	xxx
C.	*Operating Profit before Working Capital Changes*		xxx
D.	*Changes in Current Assets (Excluding Cash and Cash Equivalents) & Current Liabilities: (Excluding Bank over Draft & Cash Credit) other than due to issue of Shares /Debentures*		
	Decrease in Inventories	xxx	
	Decrease in Trade Receivables	xxx	
	Decrease in Prepaid expenses	xxx	
	Decrease in Accrued Commission	xxx	
	Increase in Trade Payables	xxx	
	Increase in Outstanding expenses	xxx	
	Increase in Commission received in advance	xxx	
	Increase in Provision for Doubtful Debts *or* Discount on Debtors	xxx	
	Increase in Inventories	(xxx)	
	Increase in Trade Receivables	(xxx)	
	Increase in Prepaid Expenses	(xxx)	
	Increase in Accrued Commission	(xxx)	
	Decrease in Trade Payables	(xxx)	
	Decrease in Outstanding expenses	(xxx)	
	Decrease in Commission received in advance	(xxx)	
	Decrease in Provision for Doubtful Debts/Discount on Debtors	(xxx)	xxx
E.	*Net Cash Flow from Operating Activities before Tax*	xxx	
F.	*Less: Income taxes paid (Net of Refund)*	(xxx)	
G.	*Net Cash Flow from Operating Activities before extraordinary item*	xxx	
H.	*Extraordinary items*		xxx
I.	*Net Cash Flow from (used in) Operating Activities*		xxx
II.	**Cash Flow from Investing Activities:**		
	Sale of Machinery/Land & Building for cash		xxx
	Sale of Investments (whether Current *or* Non-Current) for cash		xxx
	Sale of Patents/Trademarks/Copyrights for cash		xxx
	Income received from Investments (whether Current *or* Non-Current)	xxx	
	Purchase of Machinery/Land & Building for cash		(xxx)
	Purchase of Investments (whether Current *or* Non-Current) for cash		(xxx)
	Purchase of Patents/Trademarks/Copyrights/Goodwill for cash		(xxx)
	Net Cash Flow from (used in) Investing Activities		xxx
III.	**Cash Flow from Financing Activities:**		
	Issue of Share Capital for cash		xxx
	Issue of Debentures for cash		xxx

	Loans raised (whether Short term *or* Long term)		xxx
	Redemption of Preference Shares/Buy - back of Equity shares		(xxx)
	Redemption of Debentures for cash		(xxx)
	Loans repaid (whether Short term *or* Long term)		(xxx)
	Interest paid on Debentures/Loans(whether Short term *or* Long term)	(xxx)	
	Interim Dividend paid (Excluding Unpaid/Unclaimed)		(xxx)
	Final Dividend paid (Excluding Unpaid/Unclaimed)		(xxx)
	Net Cash Flow from (used in) Financing Activities		xxx
IV.	**Net Increase (Decrease) in Cash and Cash Equivalents [I + II + III]**	xxx	
V.	**Cash and Cash Equivalents at the Beginning of Period**		
	Cash in hand	xxx	
	Cash at bank	xxx	
	Cash Equivalents (Investments having maturity of 3 months *or* less)	xxx	
	Less: Bank Overdraft	(xxx)	xxx
VI.	**Cash and Cash Equivalents at End of Period [IV + V]**		
	Cash in hand	xxx	
	Cash at bank	xxx	
	Cash Equivalents (Investments having maturity of 3 months *or* less)	xxx	
	Less: Bank Overdraft	(xxx)	xxx

Working Notes:

1. CALCULATION OF NET PROFIT BEFORE TAX

Particulars	₹
Closing Balance of P&L A/c	xxx
Less: Opening Balance of P&L A/c(Cr.)[*Add:* Opening Balance of P&L A/c(Dr.)]	xxx
Add: Proposed Dividend for the current year.	xxx
Add: Interim Dividend paid during the Current year	xxx
Add: Transfer to Reserve [*Less:* Transfer from Reserve]	xxx
Add: Provision for Tax made during the Current Year	xxx
Less: Refund of Tax credited to P&L A/c	xxx
Net Profit before Tax	xxx

Dr. **2. FIXED ASSETS ACCOUNT** *Cr.*

Particulars	₹	*Particulars*	₹
To Balance b/d	…………	By Bank A/c (Sale)	…………
To Bank A/c (Purchases)	…………	By P&L A/c (Loss)	…………
To P & L A/c (Profit)		By Depreciation A/c	…………
To Equity Share Capital A/c (Purch.)	…………	By Balance c/d	…………
	…………		…………

Dr. **3. INVESTMENTS ACCOUNT** Cr.

Particulars	₹	*Particulars*	₹
To Balance b/d	....	By Bank A/c (Sale Proceeds)	....
To Bank A/c (Purchases)	....	By P&L A/c (Loss on Sale)	....
To P&L (Profit)	....	By Balance c/d	....
	....		....

Dr. **4. PROVISION FOR TAX ACCOUNT** Cr.

Particulars	₹	*Particulars*	₹
To Bank A/c	....	By Balance c/d	....
To Balance c/d	....	By P & L A/c	....
	....		....

ILLUSTRATION 31

From the following information, prepare a Cash Flow Statement:

BALANCE SHEETS AS AT ...

Particulars	*Note*	*31.03.2016* ₹	*31.03.2015* ₹
I. EQUITY AND LIABILITIES			
(1) Shareholders' Funds			
(a) Share Capital	1	5,00,000	4,50,000
(b) Reserves and Surplus	2	1,28,000	70,000
(2) Non-Current Liabilities		–	–
(3) Current Liabilities			
Trade Payables		99,000	75,000
Other Current Liabilities (Bank Overdraft)		23,000	13,000
Short-term Provisions	3	1,00,000	82,000
Total		8,50,000	6,90,000
II. ASSETS			
(1) Non-Current Assets			
Tangible Fixed Assets		3,70,000	2,80,000
Intangible Assets [Goodwill]		90,000	1,15,000
(2) Current Assets			
Current Investments		10,000	15,000
Cash & Cash Equivalents		41,000	23,000
Other Current Assets		3,39,000	2,57,000
Total		8,50,000	6,90,000

Notes to Accounts:

Particulars	*31.03.2016* ₹	*31.03.2015* ₹
1. Share Capital		
Equity Share Capital	4,00,000	3,00,000
15% Preference Share Capital	1,00,000	1,50,000
	5,00,000	4,50,000
2. Reserves and Surplus		
General Reserve	70,000	40,000
Profit and Loss A/c	48,000	30,000
Securities Premium	10,000	–
	1,28,000	70,000
3. Short-Term Provisions		
Proposed Dividend	50,000	42,000
Provision for Tax	50,000	40,000
	1,00,000	82,000

Additional Informtion: A machine costing ₹ 50,000 (depreciation provided thereon ₹ 30,000) was sold for ₹ 10,000. Depreciation charged during the year was ₹ 20,000. Interim Dividend paid, ₹ 20,000 paid, Income-tax, ₹ 35,000 paid.

SOLUTION

CASH FLOW STATEMENT
for the year ended 31st March, 2016

Particulars	₹	₹
I. Cash Flow from Operating Activities		
A. Net Profit before tax		1,63,000
B. Adjustments for Non-Cash and Non-Operating Items :		
Depreciation	20,000	
Loss on Sale of Machinery	10,000	
Goodwill amortised	25,000	55,000
C. Operating Profit before Working Capital Changes		2,18,000
D. Changes in Current Assets & Current Liabilities:		
Increase in Trade Payables	24,000	
Increase in Other Current Assets	(82,000)	(58,000)
E. Net Cash Flow from Operating Activities before Tax		1,60,000
F. *Less:* Tax paid		(35,000)
G. Net Cash Inflow from Operating Activities after Tax		1,25,000
II. Cash Flow from Investing Activities:		
Sale of Machinery		10,000

Purchases of Fixed Assets		(1,30,000)
Sale of Current Investments		5,000
Net Cash used in Investing Activities		(1,15,000)
III. Cash Flow from Financing Activities:		
Issue of Share Capital [₹ 1,00,000 + ₹ 10,000]		1,10,000
Interim Dividend paid on Equity Shares		(20,000)
Final Dividend paid		(42,000)
Redemption of Preference Shares		(50,000)
Net Cash used in Financing Activities		(2,000)
IV. Net Increase in Cash and Cash Equivalents [I + II + III]		8,000
V. Opening Cash and Cash Equivalents [₹ 23,000 – ₹ 13,000]		10,000
VI. Closing Cash and Cash Equivalents [₹ 41,000 – ₹ 23,000]		18,000

Working Notes:

1. CALCULATION OF NET PROFIT BEFORE TAX

Particulars	₹
Closing Balance of P&L A/c	48,000
Less: Opening Balance of P&L A/c	(30,000)
Add: Transfer to Reserve	30,000
Add: Proposed Dividend	50,000
Add: Interim Dividend on Equity Shares	20,000
Add: Tax	45,000
Net Profit before Tax	1,63,000

Dr. **2. FIXED ASSETS ACCOUNT** *Cr.*

Particulars	₹	*Particulars*	₹
To Balance b/d	2,80,000	By Depreciation A/c	20,000
To Bank A/c (Purchases) (b.f.)	**1,30,000**	By Bank A/c (Sale)	10,000
		By P&L A/c (Loss)	10,000
		By Balance c/d	3,70,000
	4,10,000		4,10,000

Dr. **3. PROVISION FOR TAX ACCOUNT** *Cr.*

Particulars	₹	*Particulars*	₹
To Bank A/c	35,000	By Balance c/d	40,000
To Balance c/d	50,000	By P & L A/c (balancing figure)	**45,000**
	85,000		85,000

ILLUSTRATION 32

From the following information, prepare a Cash Flow Statement:

BALANCE SHEETS AS AT ...

Particulars	*Note*	*31.03.2016* ₹	*31.03.2015* ₹
I. EQUITY AND LIABILITIES			
(1) Shareholders' Funds			
(a) Share Capital	1	7,50,000	7,50,000
(b) Reserves and Surplus	2	3,10,000	(20,000)
(2) Non-Current Liabilities [8% Debentures]		2,60,000	1,50,000
(3) Current Liabilities			
Short-term Borrowings (8% Bank Loan)		40,000	50,000
Trade Payables		1,05,000	1,00,000
Other Current Liabilities (Bank Overdraft)		15,000	10,000
Short term Provisions (Provision for tax)		50,000	40,000
Total		15,30,000	10,80,000
II. ASSETS			
(1) Non-Current Assets			
Tangible Fixed Assets		8,60,000	6,20,000
Intangible Assets [Goodwill]		15,000	20,000
Non-Current Investments		1,25,000	80,000
Other Non-Current Assets [Preliminary Exp.]		—	20,000
(2) Current Assets			
Current Investments		5,000	15,000
Cash & Cash Equivalents		1,30,000	25,000
Other Current Assets		3,95,000	3,00,000
Total		15,30,000	10,80,000

Notes to Accounts:

Particulars	*31.03.2016* ₹	*31.03.2015* ₹
1. Share Capital		
Equity Share Capital	5,50,000	4,50,000
5% Preference Share Capital	2,00,000	3,00,000
	7,50,000	7,50,000
2. Reserves and Surplus		
General Reserve	1,50,000	1,20,000
Profit and Loss A/c	1,50,000	(1,40,000)
Securities Premium	10,000	—
	3,10,000	(20,000)

Additional Information: A piece of machinery costing ₹ 60,000 on which depreciation charged was ₹ 20,000 was sold for ₹ 20,000. Depreciation provided on Fixed Assets ₹ 60,000. Preference Shares were redeemed at a premium of 5% at the end of the year. Additional Debentures were issued at par on 1st October, 2015 and Bank Loan was repaid on the same date. Dividend on equity shares @ 8% was paid on opening balance. Income Tax ₹ 45,000 has been provided during the year.

SOLUTION

CASH FLOW STATEMENT

for the year ended 31st March, 2016

Particulars	₹	₹
I. Cash Flow from Operating Activities:		
Net Profit before tax		4,16,000
Adjustment for Non-Cash and Non-Operating Items :		
Depreciation on Fixed Assets	60,000	
Loss on Sale of Machinery	20,000	
Interest on Debentures [(₹ 1,50,000 × 8/100) + (₹ 1,10,000 × 8/100 × 6/12)]	16,400	
Interest on Bank Loan [(₹ 50,000 × 8/100 × 6/12) + (₹ 40,000 × 8/100 × 6/12)	3,600	
Goodwill Amortised	5,000	
Preliminary Expenses Written off	20,000	
Premium on Redemption of Preference Shares	5,000	1,30,000
Operating Profit before Working Capital Changes		5,46,000
Changes in Current Assets & Current Liabilities:		
Increase in Other Current Assets	(95,000)	
Increase in Trade Payables	5,000	(90,000)
Net Cash Flow from Operating Activities before Tax		4,56,000
***Less:* Tax paid**		(35,000)
Net Cash Inflow from Operating Activities after Tax		4,21,000
II. Cash Flow from Investing Activities:		
Sale of Machinery		20,000
Purchase of Fixed Assets		(3,40,000)
Purchase of Non-Current Investments		(45,000)
Sale of Current Investments		10,000
Net Cash used in Investing Activities		(3,55,000)
III. Cash Flow from Financing Activities:		
Issue of Share Capital [₹ 1,00,000 + ₹ 10,000 (Premium)]		1,10,000
Issue of Debentures		1,10,000
Interest on Debentures		(16,400)
Interest on Bank Loan		(3,600)
Dividend on Equity Shares		(36,000)
Dividend on Preference Shares		(15,000)

	Redemption of Preference Shares[₹ 1,00,000 + ₹ 5,000]		(1,05,000)
	Bank Loan Repaid		(10,000)
	Net Cash from in Financing Activities		34,000
IV.	**Net Increase Cash and Cash Equivalents [I + II + III]**		1,00,000
V.	**Opening Cash and Cash Equivalents** [₹ 25,000 – ₹ 10,000]		15,000
VI.	**Closing Cash and Cash Equivalents** [₹ 1,30,000 – ₹ 15,000]		1,15,000

Working Notes:

1. CALCULATION OF NET PROFIT BEFORE TAX

Particulars	₹
Closing Balance of P&L A/c	1,50,000
Add: Opening Balance of P&L A/c (Debit)	1,40,000
Add: Provision for tax	45,000
Add: Transfer to Reserve	30,000
Add: Dividend on Equity Shares	36,000
Add: Dividend on Preference Shares	15,000
Net Profit before Tax	4,16,000

Dr. **2. FIXED ASSETS ACCOUNT** *Cr.*

Particulars	₹	*Particulars*	₹
To Balance b/d	6,20,000	By Depreciation A/c	60,000
To Bank A/c (Purchases) (b.f.)	3,40,000	By Bank A/c (Sale)	20,000
		By P&L A/c (Loss)	20,000
		By Balance c/d	8,60,000
	9,60,000		9,60,000

Dr. **3. PROVISION FOR TAX ACCOUNT** *Cr.*

Particulars	₹	*Particulars*	₹
To Bank A/c (balancing figure)	35,000	By Balance c/d	40,000
To Balance c/d	50,000	By P & L A/c	**45,000**
	85,000		85,000

ILLUSTRATION 33

From the following information, prepare a Cash Flow Statement:

BALANCE SHEETS AS AT ...

Particulars	*Note*	*31.03.2016* ₹	*31.03.2015* ₹
I. EQUITY AND LIABILITIES			
(1) Shareholders' Funds			
(a) Share Capital		12,50,000	10,00,000

(b) Reserves and Surplus	1	4,90,000	4,00,000
(2) Non-Current Liabilities [Loan]		4,00,000	5,00,000
(3) Current Liabilities			
Trade Payables		4,00,000	5,00,000
Short-term Provisions	2	1,85,000	1,50,000
Total		27,25,000	25,50,000
II. ASSETS			
(1) Non-Current Assets			
Tangible Fixed Assets	3	14,00,000	12,50,000
Non-Current Investments		50,000	1,00,000
(2) Current Assets			
Inventories		2,80,000	3,00,000
Trade Receivables		4,20,000	4,00,000
Cash & Cash Equivalents		5,75,000	5,00,000
Total		27,25,000	25,50,000

Notes to Accounts:

Particulars	*31.03.2016* ₹	*31.03.2015* ₹
1. Reserves and Surplus		
General Reserve	3,00,000	2,50,000
Profit and Loss A/c	1,80,000	1,50,000
Capital Reserve	10,000	—
	4,90,000	4,00,000
2. Short-Term Provisions		
Proposed Dividend	1,25,000	1,00,000
Provision for Tax	60,000	50,000
	1,85,000	1,50,000
3. Tangible Fixed Assets		
Land & Building	4,80,000	5,00,000
Machinery	9,20,000	7,50,000
	14,00,000	12,50,000

During the year the company purchased a machinery for ₹ 2,25,000. They paid ₹ 1,25,000 in cash and issued 10,000 equity shares of ₹ 10 each at par. The company sold some investments at a profit of ₹ 10,000, which was credited to Capital Reserve. Income-tax provided during the year ₹ 55,000.

SOLUTION

CASH FLOW STATEMENT FOR THE YEAR ENDING 31.03.2016

Particulars	₹
I. Cash Flows from Operating Activities	
Net Profit made during the year	2,60,000

	Adjustment for depreciation on Machinery	55,000
	Adjustment for depreciation Land and Building	20,000
	Operating profits before change in Working Capital	3,35,000
	Decrease in Inventories	20,000
	Increase in Trade Receivables	(20,000)
	Decrease in Trade Payables	(1,00,000)
	Income Tax paid	(45,000)
	Net Cash from operating activities	1,90,000
II.	**Cash flows from Investing Activities**	
	Purchase on Machinery	(1,25,000)
	Sale of Investments	60,000
	Cash flows from Investing Activities	(65,000)
III.	**Cash flows from Financing Activities**	
	Issue of Equity Shares (2,50,000 – 1,00,000)	1,50,000
	Repayment of Long term Loan	(1,00,000)
	Dividend Paid	(1,00,000)
	Cash flows from Financing Activities	(50,000)
	Net Increase in cash and cash equivalent	75,000
	Cash and cash equivalents at the beginning of the period	5,00,000
	Cash and cash equivalents at the end of the period	5,75,000

Working Notes:

1. NET PROFIT BEFORE TAX

Particulars	₹
Increase in P & L A/c (Cr.) Balance	30,000
Add: Transfer to general reserve	50,000
Add: Provision for taxation made during the year	55,000
Add: Proposed Dividend during the year	1,25,000
	2,60,000

Dr. **2. MACHINERY ACCOUNT** *Cr.*

Particulars	₹	*Particulars*	₹
To Balance b/d	7,50,000	By Depreciation A/c (Bal. Fig.)	55,000
To Bank A/c	1,25,000	By Balance c/d	9,20,000
To Equity Share Capital A/c	1,00,000		
	9,75,000		9,75,000

Dr. **3. PROVISION FOR TAXATION ACCOUNT** *Cr.*

Particulars	₹	*Particulars*	₹
To Cash A/c (Bal. Fig.)	45,000	By Balance b/d	50,000

To Bank A/c	60,000	By P & L A/c	55,000
	1,05,000		1,05,000

Dr. **4. PROPOSED DIVIDEND ACCOUNT** Cr.

Particulars	₹	*Particulars*	₹
To Dividend Payable A/c	1,00,000	By Balance b/d	1,00,000
To Balance c/d	1,25,000	By P & L A/c (bal. fig.)	1,25,000
	2,25,000		2,25,000

Dr. **5. INVESTMENTS ACCOUNT** Cr.

Particulars	₹	*Particulars*	₹
To Balance b/d	1,00,000	By Bank A/c	60,000
To Capital Reserve A/c	10,000	(Bal. figure for investment sold)	
(Profit on sale of investment)		By Balance c/d	50,000
	1,10,000		1,10,000

ILLUSTRATION 34

From the following information, prepare a Cash Flow Statement of SRCC Ltd.:

BALANCE SHEETS AS AT ...

Particulars	*Note*	*31.03.2016 (₹)*	*31.03.2015 (₹)*
I. EQUITY AND LIABILITIES			
(1) Shareholders' Funds			
(a) Share Capital	1	10,00,000	10,00,000
(b) Reserves and Surplus	2	5,62,000	2,32,000
(2) Non-Current Liabilities [14% Debentures]		2,60,000	1,50,000
(3) Current Liabilities			
Short-term Borrowings (14% Bank Loan)		40,000	50,000
Trade Payables		1,50,000	40,000
Other Current Liabilities	3	80,000	60,000
Short-term Provisions	4	1,90,000	1,40,000
Total		22,82,000	16,72,000
II. ASSETS			
(1) Non-Current Assets			
Tangible Fixed Assets (Net)		12,40,000	10,20,000
Intangible Assets [Goodwill]		1,000	10,000
10% Non-Current Investments		1,60,000	60,000
Other Non-Current Assets	5	1,000	2,000
(2) Current Assets			
10% Current Investments		60,000	20,000
Cash & Cash Equivalents		3,00,000	1,00,000

Other Current Assets		5,20,000	4,60,000
Total		22,82,000	16,72,000

Notes to Accounts:

Particulars	*31.03.2016 (₹)*	*31.03.2015 (₹)*
1. Share Capital		
Equity Share Capital	8,00,000	6,00,000
18% Preference Share Capital	2,00,000	4,00,000
	10,00,000	10,00,000
2. Reserves and Surplus		
General Reserve	1,40,000	3,20,000
Profit and Loss A/c	3,92,000	(1,08,000)
Securities Premium	30,000	20,000
	5,62,000	2,32,000
3. Other Current Liabilities		
Bank Overdraft	50,000	60,000
Unpaid Dividend	20,000	–
Unpaid Interest on Debentures	10,000	–
	80,000	60,000
4. Short-Term Provisions		
Proposed Dividend	1,50,000	1,20,000
Provision for Tax	40,000	20,000
	1,90,000	1,40,000
5. Other Non-Current Assets		
Underwriting Commission	1,000	—
Preliminary Expenses	—	2,000
	1,000	2,000

Additional Information:

(a) During the year a machine costing ₹ 1,40,000 (depreciation provided thereon ₹ 60,000) was sold for ₹ 50,000. Depreciation charged was ₹ 1,40,000. Tax paid was ₹ 10,000.

(b) At the end of the year some Non-Current Investments costing ₹ 40,000 were sold at a profit of 25%, New Shares and debentures were issued and Preference Shares were redeemed at a premium of 5%.

(c) An Interim Dividend @ 15% was paid on equity shares.

SOLUTION

CASH FLOW STATEMENT

for the year ended 31st March, 2016

Particulars	₹	₹
I. Cash Flow from Operating Activities:		
A. Net Profit before tax		5,90,000

B. Adjustments for Non-Cash and Non-Operating Items :		
Depreciation	1,40,000	
Loss on Sale of Machinery	30,000	
Interest on Debentures	21,000	
Interest on Bank Loan	7,000	
Goodwill amortised	9,000	
Preliminary Expenses written off	2,000	
Premium on Redemption of Preference Shares	10,000	
Profit on Sale of Non-Current Investments	(10,000)	
Interest Income on Non-Current Investments	(6,000)	
Interest Income on Current Investments	(2,000)	2,01,000
C. Operating Profit before Working Capital Changes		7,91,000
D. Changes in Current Assets & Current Liabilities:		
Increase in Other Current Assets	(60,000)	
Increase in Trade Payables	1,10,000	50,000
E. Net Cash Flow from Operating Activities before Tax		8,41,000
F. *Less:* Tax paid		(10,000)
G. Net Cash Inflow from Operating Activities after Tax		8,31,000
II. Cash Flow from Investing Activities:		
Sale of Machinery		50,000
Purchases of Fixed Assets		(4,40,000)
Purchases of Non-Current Investments		(1,40,000)
Purchases of Current Investments		(40,000)
Sale of Non-Current Investments		50,000
Interest received on Non-Current Investments		6,000
Interest received on Current Investments		2,000
Net Cash used in Investing Activities		(5,12,000)
III. Cash Flow from Financing Activities:		
Issue of Share Capital [₹ 2,00,000 + ₹ 10,000]		2,10,000
Issue of Debentures		1,10,000
Interest paid on Debentures [₹ 21,000 – ₹ 10,000]		(11,000)
Interest paid on Bank Loan		(7,000)
Interim Dividend paid on Equity Shares		(90,000)
Final Dividend paid [₹ 1,20,000 – ₹ 20,000]		(1,00,000)
Redemption of Preference Shares [₹ 2,00,000 + 5%]		(2,10,000)
Under writing commission paid		(1,000)
Bank Loan repaid		(10,000)
Net Cash used in Financing Activities		(1,09,000)
IV. Net Increase in Cash and Cash Equivalents [I + II + III]		2,10,000

V. Opening Cash and Cash Equivalents [₹ 1,00,000 – ₹ 60,000]		40,000
VI. Closing Cash and Cash Equivalents [₹ 3,00,000 – ₹ 50,000]		2,50,000

Working Notes:

1. CALCULATION OF NET PROFIT BEFORE TAX

Particulars	₹
Closing Balance of P&L A/c	3,92,000
Add: Opening Balance of P&L A/c (Debit)	1,08,000
Less: Transfer from Reserve	(1,80,000)
Add: Proposed Dividend	1,50,000
Add: Interim Dividend on Equity Shares	90,000
Add: Tax	30,000
Net Profit before Tax	5,90,000

Dr. **2. FIXED ASSETS ACCOUNT** *Cr.*

Particulars	₹	*Particulars*	₹
To Balance b/d	10,20,000	By Bank A/c (Sale)	50,000
To Bank A/c (Purchases) (b.f.)	4,40,000	By P&L A/c (Loss)	30,000
		By Depreciation A/c	1,40,000
		By Balance c/d	12,40,000
	14,60,000		14,60,000

Dr. **3. NON-CURRENT INVESTMENTS ACCOUNT** *Cr.*

Particulars	₹	*Particulars*	₹
To Balance b/d	60,000	By Bank A/c [₹ 40,000 + ₹ 10,000]	50,000
To Bank A/c (Purchases) (b.f.)	1,40,000	By Balance c/d	1,60,000
To Profit and Loss A/c (Profit) [₹ 40,000 × 25/100]	10,000		
	2,10,000		2,10,000

Dr. **4. PROVISION FOR TAX ACCOUNT** *Cr.*

Particulars	₹	*Particulars*	₹
To Bank A/c [Tax paid]	10,000	By Balance b/d	20,000
To Balance c/d	40,000	By Profit and Loss A/c (b.f.) [Provision made]	30,000
	50,000		50,000

ILLUSTRATION 35

From the following information, prepare a Cash Flow Statement:

BALANCE SHEETS AS AT ...

Particulars	*Note*	*31.03.2016* ₹	*31.03.2015* ₹
I. EQUITY AND LIABILITIES			
(1) Shareholders' Funds			
(a) Share Capital		7,87,500	6,75,000
(b) Reserves and Surplus	1	5,06,250	3,20,625
(2) Non-Current Liabilities [15% Debentures]		2,25,000	3,37,500
(3) Current Liabilities			
Trade Payables		2,81,250	1,80,000
Other Current Liabilities		13,500	11,250
Short-term Provisions	2	1,23,750	1,12,500
Total		19,37,250	16,36,875
II. ASSETS			
(1) Non-Current Assets			
Tangible Fixed Assets		13,50,000	11,25,000
Accumulated Depreciation		(2,81,250)	(2,25,000)
Non-Current Investments		2,02,500	2,02,500
(2) Current Assets			
Inventories		3,03,750	2,25,000
Trade Receivables		4,05,000	3,43,125
Provision for Doubtful debts		(56,250)	(45,000)
Other Current Assets (Prepaid Expenses)		13,500	11,250
Total		19,37,250	16,36,875

Notes to Accounts:

Particulars	*31.03.2016* ₹	*31.03.2015* ₹
1. Reserves and Surplus		
General Reserve	2,81,250	2,25,000
Profit and Loss A/c	2,13,750	95,625
Capital Reserve	11,250	—
	5,06,250	3,20,625
2. Short-Term Provisions		
Proposed Dividend	38,250	33,750
Provision for Tax	85,500	78,750
	1,23,750	1,12,500

Additional Information:

(i) During the year Fixed assets with a net book value of ₹ 11,250 (accumulated depreciation, ₹ 33,750) were sold for ₹ 9,000.

(ii) During the year Investments costing ₹ 90,000 were sold, and also Investments costing ₹ 90,000 were purchased. Profit on Sale was credited to Capital Reserve.

(iii) Debentures were retired at a Premium of 10%

(iv) Tax of ₹ 61,875 was paid during the year

(v) During the year, bad debts of ₹ 15,750 were written off against the provision for Doubtful Debt account

SOLUTION

CASH FLOW STATEMENT FOR THE YEAR ENDED 31ST MARCH, 2016

Particulars	₹	₹
I. Cash Flows from Operating Activities:		
A. Balance as per Profit and Loss Account		2,13,750
Less: Opening Balance as per Profit and Loss Account		(95,625)
Add: Proposed dividend for the current year		38,250
Add: Transfer to reserve		56,250
Add: Provision for Tax during the current year		68,625
B. Net Profit before Taxation, and Extraordinary item		2,81,250
C. *Add:* Items to be added		
Depreciation	90,000	
Intrest on Debentures	50,625	
Loss on sale of Fixed Assets	2,250	
Premium payable on redemption of Debentures	11,250	1,54,125
D. Operating Profit before Working Capital Changes		4,35,375
E. *Add:* Decrease in Current Assets and Increase in Current Liabilities		
Increase in Trade Payables	1,01,250	
Increase in other current liabities	2,250	
F. *Less:* Increase in Current Assets&Decrease in Current Libilities		
Increase in Inventories	78,750	
Increase in Trade Receivables	50,625	
Increase in Prepaid Expenses	2,250	(28125)
G. Cash generated from operations		4,07,250
H. *Less:* Income taxes paid		(61,875)
I. Net Cash from Operating Activties		3,45,375
II. Cash Flows from financing Activities:		
Proceeds from sale Assets		9,000
Proceeds from sale of Investments [₹ 90,000 + ₹ 11,250]		1,01,250
Purchase of Fixed Assets		(2,70,000)

	Purchase of Investments		(90,000)
	Net Cash used in Investing Activities		(2,49,750)
III.	**Cash Flow from Financing Activities:**		
	Proceeds from issuance of share capital		1,12,500
	Repayment of Debentures		(1,23,750)
	Interest paid on Debentures		(50,625)
	Final Dividend paid		(33,750)
	Net cash from Financing Activities		(95,625)
IV.	**Net Increase in cash and cash Equivalents [I + II + III]**		0
V.	**Cash and cash Equivalents at beginning of period**		0
VI.	**Cash and cash Equivalents at End of period [IV + V]**		0

Working Notes:

Dr. **1. FIXED ASSETS ACCOUNT** *Cr.*

Particulars	₹	*Particulars*	₹
To Balance b/d	11,25,000	By Fixed Assets Disposal A/c	45,000
To Bank (purchases) (Bal fig.)	2,70,000	By Balance c/d	13,50,000
	13,95,000		13,95,000

Dr. **2. ACCUMULATED DEPRECIATION ACCOUNT** *Cr.*

Particulars	₹	*Particulars*	₹
To Fixed Assets A/c	33,750	By Balance b/d	2,25,000
By Balance c/d	2,81,250	By Profit and Loss A/c	90,000
		(Provision for dep.) (Bal.fig.)	
	3,15,000		3,15,000

Dr. **3. FIXED ASSETS DISPOSAL ACCOUNT** *Cr.*

Particulars	₹	*Particulars*	₹
To Fixed Assets A/c	45,000	By Accumulated Dep,A/c	33,750
		By Bank A/c	9,000
		By Profit&Loss A/c (Loss)	2,250
	45,000		45,000

Dr. **4. PROVISION FOR TAX ACCOUNT** *Cr.*

Particulars	₹	*Particulars*	₹
To Bank A/c (Tax paid)	61,875	By Balance b/d	78,750
To Balance c/d	85,500	By P&L A/c (Prov.) (Bal.fig.)	68,625
	1,47,375		1,47,375

ILLUSTRATION 36

From the following information, prepare a Cash Flow Statement:

BALANCE SHEETS AS AT ...

Particulars	*Note*	*31.03.2016* ₹	*31.03.2015* ₹
I. EQUITY AND LIABILITIES			
(1) Shareholders' Funds			
(a) Share Capital		4,00,000	3,00,000
(b) Reserves and Surplus	1	1,45,000	1,02,000
(2) Non-Current Liabilities [10% Debentures]		1,00,000	1,50,000
(3) Current Liabilities			
Trade Payables		70,000	90,000
Other Current Liabilities (Dividend Payable)		4,000	—
Short-term Provisions	2	80,000	80,000
Total		7,99,000	7,22,000
II. ASSETS			
(1) Non-Current Assets			
Tangible Fixed Assets		4,29,250	2,98,000
Intangible Assets [Goodwill]		90,000	1,00,000
Non-Current Investments		60,000	1,00,000
(2) Current Assets			
Inventories		80,000	50,000
Trade Receivables		1,10,000	1,60,000
Cash & Cash Equivalents		24,000	10,000
Other Current Assets (Prepaid Expenses)		5,750	4,000
Total		7,99,000	7,22,000

Notes to Accounts:

Particulars	*31.03.2016* ₹	*31.03.2015* ₹
1. Reserves and Surplus		
General Reserve	1,00,000	80,000
Profit and Loss A/c	45,000	22,000
	1,45,000	1,02,000
2. Short-Term Provisions		
Proposed Dividend	40,000	30,000
Provision for Tax	40,000	50,000
	80,000	80,000

Additional Inofrmation:

1. 15% depreciation has been charged in the accounts on plant and machinery.

2. Old machines costing ₹.50,000 (WDV. ₹.20,000) have been sold for ₹.35,000.
3. A machine costing ₹.10,000 (WDV. ₹.3,000) has been discarded.
4. ₹.10,000 profit has been earned by sale of investments.
5. Debentures have been redeemed at 5% premium at the end.
6. ₹ 45,000 income tax has been paid and adjusted against Income Tax Provision Account.

SOLUTION

CASH FLOW STATEMENT FOR THE YEAR ENDING 31.03.2016

Particulars	₹	₹
I. **Cash Flows from Operating Activities**		
A. Closing balance as per Profit and Loss Account		45,000
Less: Opening Balance as per Profit and Loss Account		(22,000)
Add: Proposed dividend during the year		40,000
Add: Transfer to Reserve		20,000
Add: Provision for Tax		35,000
Add: Premium on Redemption of Debentures		2,500
B. Net Profit before taxation and extraordinary item		1,20,500
C. *Add:* Items to be added		
Depreciation	75,750	
Interest on Debentures	15,000	
Goodwill written off	10,000	
Loss on Machinery	3,000	1,03,750
D. *Less:* Items to be deducted		
Profit on sale of Machinery	(15,000)	
Profit on sale of Investments	(10,000)	(25,000)
E. Operating Profit before working capital changes [B + C – D]		1,99,250
F. Decrease in Trade Receivables		50,000
G. *Less:* Increase in Current Assets & Decrease in Current Liabilities		
Increase in Inventories	(30,000)	
Increase in Prepaid Expenses	(1,750)	
Decrease in Trade Payables	(20,000)	(51,750)
H. Cash generated from operations [E + F – G]		1,97,500
I. *Less:* Income taxes paid (Net of Refund)		(45,000)
J. Net Cash from Operating Activities		1,52,500
II. **Cash Flows from Investing Activities**		
Purchase of Machinery		(2,30,000)
Proceeds for sale of Machinery		35,000
Proceeds from sale of Investments		50,000
Net Cash used in investing activities		(1,45,000)

III.	**Cash Flows from Financing Activities**		
	Proceeds from issuance of share capital		1,00,000
	Redemption of Debentures		(52,500)
	Interest on Debentures		(15,000)
	Final dividend paid [₹.30,000 – ₹.4,000]		(26,000)
	Net Cash from financing activities		6,500
IV.	**Net Increase in Cash and Cash Equivalents [I + II + III]**		14,000
V.	**Cash and Cash Equivalents at beginning of Period**		10,000
VI.	**Cash and Cash Equivalents at end of Period [IV + V]**		24,000

Working Notes:

Dr. **1. PLANT AND MACHINERY ACCOUNT** *Cr.*

Particulars	₹	*Particulars*	₹
To Balance b/d	2,98,000	By Bank A/c (Sale)	35,000
To Bank A/c (Balancing figure)	2,30,000	By Profit and Loss A/c (written off)	3,000
To Profit and Loss A/c (Profit)	15,000	By Depreciation A/c	
		(4,29,250 × 15/85)	75,750
		By Balance c/d	4,29,250
	5,43,000		5,43,000

Dr. **2. PROVISION FOR TAX ACCOUNT** *Cr.*

Particulars	₹	*Particulars*	₹
To Bank A/c	45,000	By Balance b/d	50,000
To Balance c/d	40,000	By P&L A/c(b.f.)	35,000
	85,000		85,000

ILLUSTRATION 37

From the following information, prepare a Cash Flow Statement of IPCC (1) Ltd.:

BALANCE SHEETS AS AT ...

Particulars	*Note*	*31.03.2016* ₹	*31.03.2015* ₹
I. EQUITY AND LIABILITIES			
(1) Shareholders' Funds			
(a) Share Capital	1	10,25,000	10,00,000
(b) Reserves and Surplus	2	5,67,000	2,32,000
(2) Non-Current Liabilities [14% Debentures]		2,60,000	1,50,000
(3) Current Liabilities			
Short-term Borrowings (14% Bank Loan)		40,000	50,000
Trade Payables		1,50,000	40,000

Other Current Liabilities	3	80,000	60,000
Short-term Provisions	4	1,90,000	1,40,000
Total		23,12,000	16,72,000
II. ASSETS			
(1) Non-Current Assets			
Tangible Fixed Assets (Net)		12,70,000	10,20,000
Intangible Assets [Goodwill]		1,000	10,000
10% Non-Current Investments		1,60,000	60,000
Other Non-Current Assets	5	1,000	2,000
(2) Current Assets			
10% Current Investments		60,000	20,000
Cash & Cash Equivalents		3,00,000	1,00,000
Other Current Assets		5,20,000	4,60,000
Total		23,12,000	16,72,000

Notes to Accounts:

Particulars	*31.03.2016* ₹	*31.03.2015* ₹
1. Share Capital		
Equity Share Capital of ₹ 10 each	8,25,000	6,00,000
5% Preference Share Capital of ₹ 100 each	2,00,000	4,00,000
	10,25,000	10,00,000
2. Reserves and Surplus		
General Reserve	1,40,000	3,20,000
Profit and Loss A/c	3,92,000	(1,13,000)
Securities Premium	35,000	20,000
Capital Reserve	—	5,000
	5,67,000	2,32,000
3. Other Current Liabilities		
Bank Overdraft	50,000	60,000
Unpaid Dividend	20,000	–
Unpaid Interest on Debentures	10,000	–
	80,000	60,000
4. Short-Term Provisions		
Proposed Dividend	1,50,000	1,20,000
Provision for Tax	40,000	20,000
	1,90,000	1,40,000
5. Other Non-Current Assets		
Underwriting Commission	1,000	—
Preliminary Expenses	—	2,000
	1,000	2,000

Additional Information:

(a) During the year a machine costing ₹ 1,40,000 (depreciation provided thereon ₹ 60,000) was sold for ₹ 50,000. Depreciation charged was ₹ 1,40,000. A machine costing ₹ 30,000 was purchased by issue of Equity Shares of ₹ 10 each at a premium of 20%.

(b) At the end of the year Some Non-Current Investments costing ₹ 40,000 were sold at a loss of 25% and Some Current Investments costing ₹ 20,000 were sold at a profit of 25%. Profit / Loss on Investments was adjusted against the Capital Reserve.

(c) An Interim Dividend @ 15% was paid on equity shares on 31.12.2015. New Shares and Debentures were issued on 01.01.2016 and Bank Loan was repaid on the same date.

(d) Tax paid during the year was ₹ 10,000.

(e) Preference Shares were redeemed at the end of the year at a premium of 5%.

SOLUTION

CASH FLOW STATEMENT

for the year ended 31st March, 2016

Particulars	₹	₹
I. Cash Flow from Operating Activities:		
A. Net Profit before tax		5,95,000
B. Adjustments for Non-Cash and Non-Operating Items :		
Depreciation	1,40,000	
Loss on Sale of Machinery	30,000	
Interest on Debentures	24,850	
Interest on Bank Loan	6,650	
Goodwill amortised	9,000	
Preliminary Expenses written off	2,000	
Premium on Redemption of Preference Shares	10,000	
Interest Income on Non-Current Investments	(6,000)	
Interest Income on Current Investments	(2,000)	2,14,500
C. Operating Profit before Working Capital Changes		8,09,500
D. Changes in Current Assets & Current Liabilities:		
Increase in Other Current Assets	(60,000)	
Increase in Trade Payables	1,10,000	50,000
E. Net Cash Flow from Operating Activities before Tax		8,59,500
F. *Less:* Tax paid		(10,000)
G. Net Cash Inflow from Operating Activities after Tax		8,49,500
II. Cash Flow from Investing Activities:		
Sale of Machinery		50,000
Purchases of Fixed Assets		(4,40,000)
Purchases of Non-Current Investments		(1,40,000)
Purchases of Current Investments		(60,000)
Sale of Non-Current Investments		30,000
Sale of Current Investments		25,000

Interest received on Non-Current Investments		6,000
Interest received on Current Investments		2,000
Net Cash used in Investing Activities		(5,27,000)
III. Cash Flow from Financing Activities:		
Issue of Share Capital [₹ 2,00,000 + ₹ 10,000 (Premium in cash)]	2,10,000	
Issue of Debentures		1,10,000
Interest paid on Debentures [₹ 24,850 – ₹ 10,000]		(14,850)
Interest paid on Bank Loan		(6,650)
Interim Dividend paid on Equity Shares		(90,000)
Final Dividend paid [₹ 1,20,000 – ₹ 20,000]		(1,00,000)
Redemption of Preference Shares [₹ 2,00,000 + 5%]		(2,10,000)
Under writing commission paid		(1,000)
Bank Loan repaid		(10,000)
Net Cash used in Financing Activities		(1,12,500)
IV. Net Increase in Cash and Cash Equivalents [I + II + III]		2,10,000
V. Opening Cash and Cash Equivalents [₹ 1,00,000 – ₹ 60,000]		40,000
VI. Closing Cash and Cash Equivalents [₹ 3,00,000 – ₹ 50,000]		2,50,000

Working Notes:

1. CALCULATION OF NET PROFIT BEFORE TAX

Particulars	₹
Closing Balance of P&L A/c	3,92,000
Add: Opening Balance of P&L A/c (Debit)	1,13,000
Less: Transfer from Reserve	(1,80,000)
Add: Proposed Dividend	1,50,000
Add: Interim Dividend on Equity Shares	90,000
Add: Tax	30,000
Net Profit before Tax	5,95,000

Dr. **2. FIXED ASSETS ACCOUNT** *Cr.*

Particulars	₹	*Particulars*	₹
To Balance b/d	10,20,000	By Bank A/c (Sale)	50,000
To Bank A/c (Purchases) (b.f.)	4,40,000	By P&L A/c (Loss)	30,000
To Equity Share Capital A/c	25,000	By Depreciation A/c	1,40,000
To Securities Premium	5,000	By Balance c/d	12,70,000
	14,90,000		14,90,000

Dr. **3. NON-CURRENT INVESTMENTS ACCOUNT** *Cr.*

Particulars	₹	*Particulars*	₹
To Balance b/d	60,000	By Bank A/c [₹ 40,000 – ₹ 10,000]	30,000
To Bank A/c (Purchases) (b.f.)	1,40,000	By Capital Reserve A/c (Loss)	10,000

		By Balance c/d	1,60,000
	2,00,000		2,00,000

Dr. **4. CURRENT INVESTMENTS ACCOUNT** Cr.

Particulars	₹	*Particulars*	₹
To Balance b/d	20,000	By Bank A/c	25,000
To Bank A/c (Purchase)	60,000	By Balance c/d	60,000
To Capital Reserve A/c (Profit) [25% of ₹ 20,000]	5,000		
	85,000		85,000

Dr. **5. PROVISION FOR TAX ACCOUNT** Cr.

Particulars	₹	*Particulars*	₹
To Bank A/c [Tax paid]	10,000	By Balance b/d	20,000
To Balance c/d	40,000	By Profit and Loss A/c (b.f.) [Provision made]	30,000
	50,000		50,000

ILLUSTRATION 38

From the following information, prepare a Cash Flow Statement of IPCC (2) Ltd.:

BALANCE SHEETS AS AT ...

Particulars	*Note*	*31.03.2016* ₹	*31.03.2015* ₹
I. EQUITY AND LIABILITIES			
(1) Shareholders' Funds			
(a) Share Capital	1	10,50,000	10,00,000
(b) Reserves and Surplus	2	5,72,000	2,32,000
(2) Non-Current Liabilities [14% Debentures]		2,60,000	1,50,000
(3) Current Liabilities			
Short-term Borrowings (14% Bank Loan)		40,000	50,000
Trade Payables		1,65,000	40,000
Other Current Liabilities	3	80,000	60,000
Short-term Provisions	4	1,90,000	1,40,000
Total		23,57,000	16,72,000
II. ASSETS			
(1) Non-Current Assets			
Tangible Fixed Assets		16,50,000	13,20,000
Accumulated Depreciation		(3,80,000)	(3,00,000)
Intangible Assets [Goodwill]		21,000	10,000
10% Non-Current Investments		1,60,000	60,000

Other Non-Current Assets	5	1,000	2,000
(2) Current Assets			
10% Current Investments		60,000	20,000
Cash & Cash Equivalents		3,00,000	1,00,000
Inventories		1,69,000	54,000
Trade Receivables		3,76,000	4,06,000
Total		23,57,000	16,72,000

Notes to Accounts:

Particulars	*31.03.2016* ₹	*31.03.2015* ₹
1. Share Capital		
Equity Share Capital of ₹ 10 each	8,50,000	6,00,000
5% Preference Share Capital of ₹ 100 each	2,00,000	4,00,000
	10,50,000	10,00,000
2. Reserves and Surplus		
General Reserve	1,40,000	3,20,000
Profit and Loss A/c	3,92,000	(1,13,000)
Securities Premium	40,000	20,000
Capital Reserve	—	5,000
	5,72,000	2,32,000
3. Other Current Liabilities		
Bank Overdraft	50,000	60,000
Unpaid Dividend	20,000	–
Unpaid Interest on Debentures	10,000	–
	80,000	60,000
4. Short-Term Provisions		
Proposed Dividend	1,50,000	1,20,000
Provision for Tax	40,000	20,000
	1,90,000	1,40,000
5. Other Non-Current Assets		
Underwriting Commission	1,000	—
Preliminary Expenses		2,000
	1,000	2,000

Additional Information:

(a) During the year a machine having book value of ₹ 80,000 (depreciation provided thereon ₹ 60,000) was sold at a loss of 37.5%.

(b) On 01.01.2016, Some Non-Current Investments costing ₹ 1,40,000 were purchased and Some Non-Current Investments were sold at a loss of 1/3rd on sale. At the end of the year Some Current Investments costing ₹ 20,000 were sold at a profit of 25%. Profit / Loss on Investments was adjusted against the Capital Reserve.

(c) An Interim Dividend @ 15% was paid on equity shares on 31.12.2015. New Shares and Debentures were issued on 01.01.2016 and Bank Loan was repaid on the same date.

(d) Tax provided during the year was ₹ 30,000. Preference Shares were redeemed at the end of the year at a premium of 5%.

(e) On 01.01.2016, the Business of Y Ltd. was purchased for ₹ 60,000 payable in fully paid equity shares of ₹ 10 each at 20% premium. The assets included Stock ₹ 15,000. Debtors ₹ 10,000 and Machine ₹ 30,000. Creditors of ₹ 15,000 were also taken over.

SOLUTION

CASH FLOW STATEMENT

for the year ended 31st March, 2016

Particulars	₹	₹
I. Cash Flow from Operating Activities:		
A. Net Profit before tax		5,95,000
B. Adjustments for Non-Cash and Non-Operating Items :		
Depreciation	1,40,000	
Loss on Sale of Machinery	30,000	
Interest on Debentures	24,850	
Interest on Bank Loan	6,650	
Goodwill amortised	9,000	
Preliminary Expenses written off	2,000	
Premium on Redemption of Preference Shares	10,000	
Interest Income on Non-Current Investments	(8,500)	
Interest Income on Current Investments	(2,000)	2,12,000
C. Operating Profit before Working Capital Changes		8,07,000
D. Changes in Current Assets & Current Liabilities:		
Increase in Inventories [(1,69,000 – 15,000) – 54,000]	(1,00,000)	
Decrease in Trade Receivables [(3,76,000 – 10,000) – 4,06,000]	40,000	
Increase in Trade Payables [(1,65,000 – 15,000) – 40,000]	1,10,000	50,000
E. Net Cash Flow from Operating Activities before Tax		8,57,000
F. *Less:* Tax paid		(10,000)
G. Net Cash Inflow from Operating Activities after Tax		8,47,000
II. Cash Flow from Investing Activities:		
Sale of Machinery		50,000
Purchases of Fixed Assets		(4,40,000)
Purchases of Non-Current Investments		(1,40,000)
Purchases of Current Investments		(60,000)
Sale of Non-Current Investments		30,000
Sale of Current Investments		25,000
Interest received on Non-Current Investments		8,500
Interest received on Current Investments		2,000

Net Cash used in Investing Activities		(5,24,500)
III. Cash Flow from Financing Activities:		
Issue of Share Capital [₹ 2,00,000 + ₹ 10,000 (Premimum in cash)]		2,10,000
Issue of Debentures		1,10,000
Interest paid on Debentures [₹ 24,850 – ₹ 10,000]		(14,850)
Interest paid on Bank Loan		(6,650)
Interim Dividend paid on Equity Shares		(90,000)
Final Dividend paid [₹ 1,20,000 – ₹ 20,000]		(1,00,000)
Redemption of Preference Shares [₹ 2,00,000 + 5%]		(2,10,000)
Under writing commission paid		(1,000)
Bank Loan repaid		(10,000)
Net Cash used in Financing Activities		(1,12,500)
IV. Net Increase in Cash and Cash Equivalents [I + II + III]		2,10,000
V. Opening Cash and Cash Equivalents [₹ 1,00,000 – ₹ 60,000]		40,000
VI. Closing Cash and Cash Equivalents [₹ 3,00,000 – ₹ 50,000]		2,50,000

Working Notes:

1. CALCULATION OF NET PROFIT BEFORE TAX

Particulars	₹
Closing Balance of P&L A/c	3,92,000
Add: Opening Balance of P&L A/c (Debit)	1,13,000
Less: Transfer from Reserve	(1,80,000)
Add: Proposed Dividend	1,50,000
Add: Interim Dividend on Equity Shares	90,000
Add: Tax	30,000
Net Profit before Tax	5,95,000

Dr. **2. FIXED ASSETS ACCOUNT (AT COST)** *Cr.*

Particulars	₹	*Particulars*	₹
To Balance b/d	13,20,000	By Asset Sold A/c	1,40,000
To Bank A/c (Purchases)	4,40,000	By Balance c/d	16,50,000
To Business Purchase A/c	30,000		
	17,90,000		17,90,000

Dr. **3. PROVISION FOR DEPRECIATION ACCOUNT** *Cr.*

Particulars	₹	*Particulars*	₹
To Assets Sold A/c	60,000	By Balance b/d	3,00,000
To Bank c/d	3,80,000	By P&L A/c (Depreciation for current year) (Balancing figure)	1,40,000
	4,40,000		4,40,000

Dr. **4. ASSET SOLD ACCOUNT** *Cr.*

Particulars	₹	*Particulars*	₹
To Fixed Assets A/c	1,40,000	By Provision for Depreciation A/c	60,000
		By Bank A/c (b.f.)	50,000
		By Profit and Loss A/c (Loss)	30,000
	1,40,000		1,40,000

Dr. **5. NON-CURRENT INVESTMENTS ACCOUNT** *Cr.*

Particulars	₹	*Particulars*	₹
To Balance b/d	60,000	By Bank A/c [₹ 40,000 – ₹ 10,000]	30,000
To Bank A/c (Purchases) (b.f.)	1,40,000	By Capital Reserve A/c (Loss)	10,000
		By Balance c/d	1,60,000
	2,00,000		2,00,000

Dr. **6. CURRENT INVESTMENTS ACCOUNT** *Cr.*

Particulars	₹	*Particulars*	₹
To Balance b/d	20,000	By Bank A/c	25,000
To Bank A/c (Purchase)	60,000	By Balance c/d	60,000
To Capital Reserve A/c (Profit) [25% of ₹ 20,000]	5,000		
	85,000		85,000

Dr. **7. PROVISION FOR TAX ACCOUNT** *Cr.*

Particulars	₹	*Particulars*	₹
To Bank A/c [Tax paid] (b.f.)	10,000	By Balance b/d	20,000
To Balance c/d	40,000	By Profit and Loss A/c [Provision made]	30,000
	50,000		50,000

8. Goodwill Amortised = Goodwill Purchased + Opening Goodwill – Closing Goodwill
   = [₹ 60,000 – (₹ 15,000+ ₹ 10,000 + ₹ 30,000 – ₹ 15,000] + ₹ 10,000 – ₹ 21,000
   = ₹ 9,000
9. Following Items will not appear in the Cash Flow Statement since these are non- cash transactions:

   (i) Issue of Equity Shares for ₹ 50,000,(ii) Securities Premium of ₹ 10,000,(iii) Increase in Stock (₹ 15,000), Debtors (₹ 10,000), Creditors (₹ 15,000) and Machine(₹ 30,000) due to purchase of business.

ILLUSTRATION 39

10% Investments: Opening ₹ 1,00,000, Closing ₹ 80,000, Accrued Interest on Investments: Opening ₹ 2,000, Closing ₹ 3,000. How will you disclose these items while preparing Cash Flow Statement as per AS–3 issued by ICAI?

SOLUTION

A.	**Cash Flow from Operating Activities**	₹
	Net Profit as per Profit & Loss A/c	
	Less: Interest on 10% Investments	(10,000)
B.	**Cash Flow from Investing Activities**	
	Sale of 10% Investments [1,00,000 – 80,000]	20,000
	Interest on Investments [10,000 – (3,000 – 2,000)]	9,000

ILLUSTRATION 40

10% Debentures: Opening ₹ 2,00,000, Closing ₹ 1,40,000, Unpaid interest on Debentures: Opening ₹ 500, Closing ₹ 2,000. Debentures were redeemed at 5% premium at the end of the year. How will you disclose these items while preparing Cash Flow Statement as per AS–3 issued by ICAI?

SOLUTION

A.	**Cash Flow from Operating Activities**	
	Net Profit as per Profit & Loss A/c	
	Add: Premium on Redemption of Debentures	3,000
	Less: Interest on 10% Debentures	(20,000)
B.	**Cash Flow from Financing activities**	
	Interest on Debentures paid [20,000 – (2,000 – 500)]	(18,500)
	Redemption of Debentures [(2,00,000 – 1,40,000) + 5% premium]	(63,000)

ILLUSTRATION 41

Investment in Shares: Opening ₹ 10,000,Closing ₹ 35,000, Dividend received amounted to ₹ 2,100 which inciuded pre acquisition dividend of ₹ 600. How will you disclose these items while preparing Cash Flow Statement as per AS–3 issued by ICAI?

SOLUTION

A.	**Cash Flow from Operating Activities**	₹
	Net Profit as per Profit & Loss A/c	
	Less: Dividend (₹ 2,100 – ₹ 600)	(1,500)
B.	**Cash Flow from Investing Activities**	
	Purchase of investment in shares [(35,000 + 600) – 10,000]	(25,600)
	Dividend Income	2,100

ILLUSTRATION 42

Compensation received in a suit filed by the company ₹ 90,000 .How will you disclose this item while preparing Cash Flow Statement as per AS–3 issued by ICAI?

SOLUTION

A.	**Cash Flow from Operating Activities**	₹
	Net Profit as per Profit & Loss A/c	
	Less: Compensation received	(90,000)

B.	**Operating Profit before extraordinary items**	
	Add: Compensation received	90,000

ILLUSTRATION 43

Capital Grant: Opening ₹ Nil, Closing ₹ 8,00,000. Grant of ₹ 10,00,000 amortised in P&L A/c. How will you disclose these items while preparing Cash Flow Statement as per AS–3 issued by ICAI?

SOLUTION

A.	**Cash Flow from Operating Activities**	₹
	Net Profit as per Profit & Loss A/c	
	*Less:*Capital Grant amortised	(10,00,000)
B.	**Cash Flow from Financing activities**	
	Grant Received	18,00,000

ILLUSTRATION 44

Voluntary Separation Payments : Opening ₹ 65,000, Closing ₹ 1,25,000. Voluntary Separation Payments ₹ 50,000 adjusted against General Reserve. How will you disclose these items while preparing Cash Flow Statement as per AS–3 issued by ICAI?

SOLUTION

A.	**Cash Flow from Operating Activities**	₹
	Operating Profit before extraordinary items	
	Less: Voluntary Separation Payments [(125,000+50,000) – 65,000]	(1,10,000)

ILLUSTRATION 45

Debtors of ₹ 2,30,000 were written off against the Provision for Doubtful Debts A/c during the year. Short-term Investments (held for 2 months) costing ₹ 10,000 were sold for ₹ 12,000. How will you disclose these items while preparing Cash Flow Statement as per AS–3 issued by ICAI?

SOLUTION

Profit on sale of short term investments and debtors written off against provision for doubtful debts do not require any further adjustment in **Cash Flow Statement.**

ILLUSTRATION 46

Following are the Extracts of Balance Sheets of Tulsian Ltd.:

Paticulars	*31.3.2016 (₹)*	*31.3.2015 (₹)*
Equity Share Capital	9,10,000	5,00,000
General Reserve	2,10,000	2,50,000
Profit & Loss A/c	9,50,000	(40,000)
Securities Premium	50,000	—

Capital Redemption Reserve		1,00,000
Capital Grant	8,00,000	Nil
Convertible Debentures (into equity shares at 25% premium)	—	2,00,000
Trade Payables	1,00,000	1,05,000
Goodwill	15,000	—
Plant & Machinery	7,65,000	5,00,000
Inventories	95,640	54,000
Trade Receivables	7,50,000	6,25,000
Less: Provision for Doubtful Debts	(1,90,000)	(1,50,000)
Voluntary Separation Payments	1,25,000	65,000

Additional Information:

(a) Depreciation on Plant & Machinery written off @ 15%.

(b) It was decided to value Inventories at cost whereas previously the practice was to value Inventories at cost less 10%. However the closing stock on 31.03.2016 was correctly valued at cost.

(c) On 31st March 2016, the business of Y Ltd. was purchased for ₹ 60,000 payable in fully paid equity shares of ₹ 10 each at a premium of 20%. The assets included Inventories ₹ 26,640, Trade Receivables ₹ 10,000, and Machine ₹ 18,360. In addition Trade Payables of ₹ 15,000 were taken over.

(d) Debtors of ₹ 2,30,000 were written off against the Provision for Doubtful Debts A/c during the year. Grant of ₹ 10,00,000 amortised in P&L A/c. Compensation received in a suit filed by the company ₹ 90,000. Voluntary Separation Payments ₹ 50,000 adjusted against General Reserve.

Required: How will you disclose these items while preparing Cash Flow Statement as per AS–3 issued by ICAI.

SOLUTION

CASH FLOW STATEMENT OF TULSIAN LTD FOR THE YEAR ENDED 31ST MARCH, 2016

A	**Cash Flow from Operating Activities**		₹
	Net Profit [9,50,000 – (40,000) + 10,000 (t/f to Reserve)]		10,00,000
	Add: Depreciation [(7,65,000 x 15/85)]		1,35,000
	Add: Goodwill amortised		5,000
	[60,000 – (26,640 + 10,000 + 18,360 – 15,000)]–15,000		
	Less: Under valuation of Opening stock (54,000 × 10/90)		(6,000)
	Less: Compensation received		(90,000)
	Less: Capital Grant amortised		(10,00,000)
	Operating Profit before Working Capital changes		44,000
	Add: Increase in Provision for doubtful debts	40,000	
	Less: Increase in Inventories [(95,640 – 26,640) – (54,000 + 6,000)]	(9,000)	
	Increase in Trade Receivables [(7,50,000 – 10,000) – 6,25,000]	(1,15,000)	
	Decrease in Trade Payables [(1,05,000 – 15,000) – 1,00,000]	(10,000)	(94,000)

	Operating Profit before extraordinary items *Add:* Compensation received *Less:* Voluntary Separation Payments [(125,000+50,000) – 65,000] **Cash used in Operating Activities**		(50,000) 90,000 (1,10,000) (70,000)
B	**Cash Flow from Investing Activities**		
	Purchase of Machinery		(3,81,640)
	[(7,65,000+1,35,000) – 5,00,000 – 18,360]		
C	**Cash Flow from Financing Activities**		
	Issue of Equity Share Capital [(9,10,000 – 50,000 – 1,00,000 –1,60,000) – 5,00,000] Grant Received		1,00,000 18,00,000

Note: Debtors written off against provision for doubtful debts do not require any further adjustment in **Cash Flow Statement.**

SOLVED PROBLEMS

PROBLEM 1

CAMJI Limited provides you the following information for the preparation of Cash Flow Statement:

Particulars	(₹. *in lakhs*)
Net Profit	25,000
Dividend (including dividend tax) paid	8,535
Provision for Income Tax	5,000
Income tax paid during the year	4,248
Loss on sale of assets (net)	40
Book value of the assets sold	185
Depreciation charged to Profit and Loss Account	20,000
Amortisation of Capital grant	6
Profit on sale of Investments	100
Carrying amount of Investment sold	27,765
Interest income on investments	2,506
Interest expenses	10,000
Interest paid during the year	10,520
Increase in Working Capital (excluding Cash and Bank balance)	56,075
Purchase of fixed assets	14,560
Investment in joint venture	3,850
Expenditure on construction work in progress	34,740
Proceeds from calls in arrears	2
Receipt of grant for capital projects	12

Proceeds from long-term borrowings	25,980
Proceeds from short-term borrowings	20,575
Opening Cash and Bank balance	5,003
Closing Cash and Bank balance	6,988

SOLUTION

CASH FLOW STATEMENT

for the year ended 31st March.....

Particulars	*(₹. in lakhs)*
Cash flows from Operating Activities:	
Net Profit before taxation (₹. 25,000 + ₹. 5,000)	30,000
Adjustment for:	
Depreciation	20,000
Loss on sale of assets (Net)	40
Amortisation of capital grant	(6)
Profit on sale of investments	(100)
Interest income on investments	(2,506)
Interest expenses	10,000
Operating profit before working capital changes	57,428
Changes in working capital (excluding cash and bank balance)	(56,075)
Cash generated from operations	1,353
Income taxes paid	(4,248)
Net cash used in operating activities	(2,895)
Cash flows from Investing Activities:	
Sale of assets (185 – 40)	145
Sale of investments (27,765 + 100)	27,865
Interest income on investments	2,506
Purchase of fixed assets	(14,560)
Investment in joint venture	(3,850)
Expenditure on construction work-in-progress	(34,740)
Net cash used in investing activities	(22,634)
Cash flows from Financing Activities:	
Proceeds from calls in arrears	2
Receipts of grant for capital projects	12
Proceeds from long-term borrowings	25,980
Proceeds from short-term borrowings	20,575
Interest paid	(10,520)
Dividend (including dividend tax) paid	(8,535)
	27,514

Net increase in cash and cash equivalents	1,985
Cash and cash equivalents at the beginning of the period	5,003
Cash and cash equivalents at the end of the period	6,988

PROBLEM 2

J. Ltd. presents you the following information for the year ended 31st March, 2016:

Particulars	*(₹ in lacs)*
(i) Net profit before tax provision	36,000
(ii) Dividend paid	10,202
(iii) Income-tax paid	5,100
(iv) Book value of assets sold	222
Loss on sale of asset	48
(v) Depreciation debited in P&L Account	24,000
(vi) Capital grant received - amortized in P&L A/c	10
(vii) Book value of investment sold	33,318
Profit on sale of investment	120
(viii) Interest income from investment credited in P&L A/c	3,000
(ix) Interest expenditure debited in P&L A/c	12,000
(x) Interest actually paid (Financing activity)	13,042
(xi) Increase in working capital [Excluding cash and bank balance]	67,290
(xii) Purchase of fixed assets	22,092
(xiii) Expenditure on construction work	41,688
(xiv) Grant received for capital projects	18
(xv) Long term borrowings from banks	55,866
(xvi) Provision for Income-tax debited in P&L A/c	6,000
Cash and bank balance at the beginning	6,000
Cash and bank balance at the end	8,000

You are required to prepare a Cash Flow Statement as per AS 3 (Revised)

SOLUTION

CASH FLOW STATEMENT FOR THE YEAR ENDED 31ST MARCH, 2016

	Particulars	*(₹ in lacs)*
A	**Cash Flows from Operating Activities:**	
	Net profit before tax provision	36,000
	Add: Non-cash expenditures	
	Depreciation	24,000
	Loss on sale of assets	48
	Interest expenditure	12,000
		72,048

Less: Non-cash income	
Amortisation of capital grant received	(10)
Profit on sale of investments	(120)
Interest income from investment	(3,000)
Operating Profit before Working Capital Changed	68,918
Less: Increase in working capital	(67,290)
Cash from operations	1,628
Less: Income tax paid	(5,100)
Net cash used in operating activities	(3,472)
B. Cash flows from investing activities	
Sale of assets (222 – 48)	174
Sale of investments (33,318 + 120)	33,438
Interest income from investments	3,000
Purchase of fixed assets	(22,092)
Expenditure on construction work	(41,688)
Net cash used in investing activities	(27,168)
C. Cash flows from financing activities	
Grants for capital projects	18
Long term borrowings	55,866
Interest paid	(13,042)
Dividend paid	(10,202)
Net cash from financing activities	32,640
D. Net increase in Cash & Cash Equivalents	2,000
E. Cash & Cash Equivalents at the beginning of the year	6,000
F. Cash & Cash Equivalents at the end of the year	8,000

Note: No effect for 'provision for income tax debited in P&L A/c' has been given since the figure of 'net profit before tax provision' has been considered for calculation.

PROBLEM 3

Raj Ltd. gives you the following information for the year ended 31st March, 2016:

(i) Sales for the year ₹ 48,00,000. The Company sold goods for cash only.

(ii) Cost of goods sold was 75% of sales.

(iii) Closing inventory was higher than opening inventory by ₹ 50,000.

(iv) Closing Trade Payables exceed the Opening Trade Payables by ₹ 1,00,000

(v) Tax paid during the year amounts to ₹ 1,50,000.

(vi) Amounts paid to Trade Payables during the year ₹ 35,50,000.

(vii) Administrative and Selling expenses paid ₹ 3,60,000.

(viii) One new machinery was acquired during the year for ₹ 6,00,000.

(ix) Dividend paid during the year ₹ 1,20,000.

(x) Cash in hand and of Bank at the end ₹ 70,000.

(xi) Cash in hand and at Bank at the begining ₹ 50,000.

Required: Prepare Cash Flow Statement as per Accounting Standard 3.

SOLUTION

CASH FLOW STATEMENT FOR THE YEAR ENDED 31.3.2016

Particulars	₹
Cash flow from operating activities:	
Cash receipt from customers (sales)	48,00,000
Cash paid to suppliers and expenses (₹ 35,50,000 + ₹ 3,60,000)	(39,10,000)
Cash flow from operations	8,90,000
Less: Tax paid	(1,50,000)
Net cash from operating activities	7,40,000
Cash flow from investing activities:	
Purchase of fixed assets	(6,00,000)
Net cash used in investing activities	(6,00,000)
Cash flow from financing activities:	
Dividend Paid	(1,20,000)
Net cash from financing activities	(1,20,000)
Net Increase in Cash & Cash Equivalents	20,000
Cash & Cash Equivalents at the beginning of the year	50,000
Cash & Cash Equivalents at the end of the year	70,000

PROBLEM 4

The following figures have been extracted from the Books of X Ltd. for the year ended on 31.3.2016. You are required to prepare a cash flow statement.

(i) Net profit before taking into account Income Tax and Income from law suits but after taking into Account the following items was ₹ 20 lakhs:

- (a) Depreciation on Fixed Assets ₹ 5 lakhs.
- (b) Discount on issue of Debentures written off ₹ 30,000.
- (c) Interest on Debentures paid ₹ 3,50,000.
- (d) Books value of investments ₹ 3 lakhs (Sale of Investments for ₹ 3,20,000).
- (e) Interest received on investments ₹ 60,000.

(ii) Compensation received ₹ 90,000 by the company in a suit filed.

(iii) Income tax paid during the year ₹ 10,50,000.

(iv) 15,000, 10% preference shares of ₹ 100 each were redeemed at the end at a premium of 5%. Further the company issued 50,000 equity shares of ₹ 10 each at a premium of 20%. Dividend on preference shares were paid at the time of redemption.

(v) Final Dividends paid ₹ 5 lakhs and Interim dividend paid ₹ 3 lakhs.

(vi) Land was purchased for ₹ 2,40,000 for which the company issued 20,000 equity shares of ₹ 10 each at a premium of 20% to the land owner as consideration.

(vii) Current assets and Current liabilities in the beginning and at the end of the years were as detailed below:

Particulars	Opening ₹	Closing ₹
Inventories	12,00,000	13,18,000
Trade Receivables	2,58,000	2,53,100
Cash in hand	1,96,300	35,300
Trade Payables	2,11,000	2,11,300
Outstanding expenses	75,000	81,800

SOLUTION

CASH FLOW STATEMENT FOR THE YEAR ENDED 31ST MARCH, 2016

Particulars	₹
Net Profit before income tax and extraordinary items:	20,00,000
Adjustments for:	
Depreciation on Fixed Assets	5,00,000
Discount on issue of Debentures	30,000
Interest on Debentures paid	3,50,000
Interest on Investments received	(60,000)
Profit on Sale of Investments	(20,000)
Operating profit before working capital changes	28,00,000
Adjustments for:	
Increase in Inventories	(1,18,000
Decrease in Trade Receivables	4,900
Increase in Trade Payables	300
Increase in outstanding expenses	6,800
Cash flow from operation	26,94,000
Income Tax paid	(10,50,000)
	16,44,000
Cash flow from extraordinary items:	
Compensation received in a suit filed	90,000
Net Cash flow from operating activities	17,34,000
Cash flow from investing activities:	
Sale proceeds of investments	3,20,000
Interest received on investment	60,000
Net cash flow from investing activities	3,80,000
Cash flow from financing activities:	
Proceeds by issue of equity shares at a premium	6,00,000
Redemption of preference shares at a premium	(15,75,000)
Preference Dividend paid	(1,50,000)
Interest on debentures paid	(3,50,000)

Dividend paid (5,00,000 + 3,00,000)	(8,00,000)
	(22,75,000)
Net Decrease in Cash and Cash Equivalents	(1,61,000)
Cash & Cash Equivalents at the beginning of the year	1,96,300
Cash & Cash Equivalents at the end of the year	35,300

PROBLEM 5

From the following information, prepare a Cash Flow Statement:

BALANCE SHEETS AS AT ...

Particulars	*Note*	*31.03.2016* ₹	*31.03.2015* ₹
I. EQUITY AND LIABILITIES			
(1) Shareholders' Funds			
(a) Share Capital	1	18,80,000	16,00,000
(b) Reserves and Surplus	2	11,00,000	8,40,000
(2) Non-Current Liabilities [9% Debentures]		2,80,000	4,00,000
(3) Current Liabilities			
Trade Payables		5,20,000	4,80,000
Other Current Liabilities (Unpaid Dividend)		16,000	—
Short-term Provisions	3	4,84,000	4,80,000
Total		42,80,000	38,00,000
II. ASSETS			
(1) Non-Current Assets			
Tangible Fixed Assets		38,00,000	32,00,000
Accumulated Depreciation		(11,60,000)	(9,20,000)
Non-Current Investments		3,20,000	4,00,000
(2) Current Assets			
Cash & Cash Equivalents		10,000	10,000
Other Current Assets		13,10,000	11,10,000
Total		42,80,000	38,00,000

Notes to Accounts:

Particulars	*31.03.2016* ₹	*31.03.2015* ₹
1. Share Capital		
Equity Share Capital	16,00,000	12,00,000
10% Preference Share Capital	2,80,000	4,00,000
	18,80,000	16,00,000
2. Reserves and Surplus		
General Reserve	8,00,000	6,80,000

Profit and Loss A/c	2,60,000	1,60,000
Capital Reserve	40,000	—
	11,00,000	8,40,000
3. Short-Term Provisions		
Proposed Dividend	1,44,000	1,20,000
Provision for Tax	3,40,000	3,60,000
	4,84,000	4,80,000

Additional Information:

(i) The company sold one fixed asset for ₹ 1,00,000, the cost of which was ₹ 2,00,000 and the depreciation provided on it was ₹ 80,000. The company also decided to write off another fixed asset costing ₹ 56,000 on which depreciation amounting to ₹ 40,000 has been provided. Depreciation on fixed assets provided ₹ 3,60,000.

(ii) Sold some investment at a profit of ₹ 40,000, which was credited to capital reserve.

(iii) Debentures and preference share capital redeemed at 5% premium.

(iv) Company decided to value Inventories at cost, whereas previously the practice was to value Inventories at cost *less* 10%. The opening Inventories was ₹ 2,16,000. The Closing Inventories was correctly valued at ₹ 3,00,000.

SOLUTION

CASH FLOW STATEMENT FOR THE YEAR ENDED 31ST MARCH, 2016

Particulars	₹	₹
I. Cash Flow from operating activities		
Profit after appropriation		
Increase in Profit and Loss Account after inventory adjustment [₹ 2,60,000 – (₹ 1,60,000 + ₹ 24,000)]	76,000	
Transfer to general reserve	1,20,000	
Proposed dividend	1,44,000	
Provision for tax	3,40,000	
Net profit before taxation and extraordinary item	6,80,000	
Adjustments for:		
Depreciation	3,60,000	
Loss on sale of fixed assets	20,000	
Interest on Debentures	36,000	
Decrease in value of fixed assets	16,000	
Premium on redemption of preference share' capital	6,000	
Premium on redemption of debentures	6,000	
Operating profit before working capital changes	11,24,000	
Increase in Trade Payables (₹ 5,20,000 – ₹ 4,80,000)	40,000	
Increase in other current assets [₹ 13,10,000 – (₹ 11,10,000 + ₹ 24,000))	(1,76,000)	
Cash generated from operations	9,88,000	

	Income taxes paid	(3,60,000)	
	Net Cash from operating activities		6,28,000
II.	**Cash Flow from investing activities**		
	Purchase of fixed assets	(8,56,000)	
	Proceeds from sale of fixed assets	1,00,000	
	Proceeds from sale of investments	1,20,000	
	Net Cash from investing activities		(6,36,000)
III.	**Cash Flow from financing activities**		
	Proceeds from issuance of Share Capital		4,00,000
	Redemption of Preference Share Capital (₹ 1,20,000 + ₹ 6,000)		(1,26,000)
	Redemption of Debentures (₹ 1,20,000 + ₹ 6,000)		(1,26,000)
	Dividend paid (₹ 1,20,000 – ₹ 16,000)		(1,04,000)
	Interest on Debentures		(36,000)
	Net Cash from financing activities		8,000
	Net increase/decrease in cash and cash equivalent during the year		Nil
	Cash and Cash equivalent at the beginning of the year		10,000
	Cash and Cash equivalent at the end of the year		10,000

Working Notes:

(1) Revaluation of Inventories will increase opening Inventories by ₹ 24,000 (i.e. 2,16,000 × 10/90)

Opening of other current assets ₹ 11,10,000 + ₹ 24,000 = ₹ 11,34,000

Due to under valuation of Inventories, the opening balance of Profit and Loss Account be increase by ₹ 24,000.

The opening balance Profit and Loss Account after revaluation of Inventories will be

₹ 1,60,000 + ₹ 24,000 = ₹ 1,84,000

Dr. **2. INVESTMENTS ACCOUNT** *Cr.*

Particulars	₹	*Particulars*	₹
To Balance b/d	4,00,000	By Bank A/c (Balancing figure	1,20,000
To Capital Reserve Account	40,000	being investment sold)	
(Profit on sale of investment)		Balance c/d	3,20,000
	4,40,000		4,40,000

Dr. **3. FIXED ASSETS ACCOUNT** *Cr.*

Particulars	₹	*Particulars*	₹
To Balance b/d	32,00,000	By Bank A/c (sale of Assets)	1,00,000
To Bank A/c (Bal. figure	8,56,000	By Accumulated depreciation A/c	80,000
being assets purchased)		By Profit and Loss A/c	20,000
		(Loss on sale of assets)	
		By Accumulated Depreciation A/c	40,000

		By Profit and Loss A/c (Assets written off)	16,000
		By Balance c/d	38,00,000
	40,56,000		40,56,000

Dr. **4. ACCUMULATED DEPRECIATION ACCOUNT** *Cr.*

Particulars	₹	*Particulars*	₹
To Fixed Assets A/c	80,000	By Balance b/d	9,20,000
To Fixed Assets A/c	40,000	By Profit and Loss A/c	3,60,000
To Balance c/d	11,60,000	(Depreciation for the period)	
	12,80,000		12,80,000

PROBLEM 6

From the following information, prepare a Cash Flow Statement:

BALANCE SHEETS AS AT ...

Particulars	*Note*	*31.03.2016* ₹	*31.03.2015* ₹
I. EQUITY AND LIABILITIES			
(1) Shareholders' Funds			
(a) Share Capital	1	6,00,000	7,00,000
(b) Reserves and Surplus	2	3,60,000	2,75,000
(2) Non-Current Liabilities [9% Debentures]		2,00,000	—
(3) Current Liabilities			
Trade Payables		1,15,000	1,10,000
Other Current Liabilities		30,000	20,000
Short-term Provisions	3	1,85,000	1,20,000
Total		14,90,000	12,25,000
II. ASSETS			
(1) Non-Current Assets			
Tangible Fixed Assets	4	9,15,000	7,00,000
Non-Current Investments		50,000	80,000
Other Non-Current Assets	5	1,25,000	65,000
(2) Current Assets			
Inventories		95,000	90,000
Trade Receivables		2,40,000	2,00,000
Cash & Cash Equivalents		65,000	90,000
Total		14,90,000	12,25,000

Notes to Accounts:

Particulars	*31.03.2016* ₹	*31.03.2015* ₹
1. Share Capital		
Equity Share Capital	6,00,000	5,00,000
10% Preference Share Capital	—	2,00,000
	6,00,000	7,00,000
2. Reserves and Surplus		
General Reserve	1,00,000	2,50,000
Profit and Loss A/c	60,000	25,000
Capital Reserve	1,00,000	—
Capital Redemption Reserve	1,00,000	—
	3,60,000	2,75,000
3. Short-Term Provisions		
Proposed Dividend	90,000	60,000
Provision for Tax	95,000	60,000
	1,85,000	1,20,000
4. Tangible Fixed Assets		
Land & Building	1,50,000	2,00,000
Machinery	7,65,000	5,00,000
	9,15,000	7,00,000
5. Other Non-Current Assets		
Voluntary Separation Payments	1,25,000	65,000

Additional Information:

(i) A piece of land has been sold out for ₹ 1,50,000 (Cost: ₹ 1,20,000) and the balance land was revalued. Capital Reserve consisted of profit on sale and profit on revaluation.

(ii) During the year a plant was sold for ₹ 90,000 (Original Cost: ₹ 70,000 and W.D.V.: ₹ 50,000) and Debentures worth ₹ 1 lakhs was issued at par as part consideration for plant of ₹ 4.5 lakhs acquired. Depreciation @ 15% has been written off from Plant account but no depreciation has been charged on Land and Building.

(iii) Part of the investments (Cost ₹ 50,000) was sold for ₹ 70,000.

(iv) Income tax liability for the current year was estimated at ₹ 1,35,000.

(v) Pre-acquisition dividend received ₹ 5,000 was adjusted against cost of investment.

(vi) Voluntary separation cost of ₹ 50,000 was adjusted against General Reserve.

SOLUTION

CASH FLOW STATEMENT FOR THE YEAR ENDED 31ST MARCH, 2016

Particulars	₹
Net Profit before taxation	2,60,000
Adjustment for:	
Depreciation	1,35,000

Profit on sale of plant	(40,000)
Profit on sale of investments	(20,000)
Interest on debentures	18,000
Operating profit before working capital changes	3,53,000
Increase in Inventories	(5,000)
Increase in Trade Receivables	(40,000)
Increase in Trade Payables	5,000
Increase in other current liabilities	10,000
Cash generated from operations	3,23,000
Income taxes paid	(1,00,000)
	2,23,000
Voluntary separation payments	(1,10,000)
Net Cash from operating activities	1,13,000
Cash Flow from investing activities	
Proceeds from sale of land	1,50,000
Proceeds from sale of plant	90,000
Proceeds from sale of investments	70,000
Purchase of plant	(3,50,000)
Purchase of investments	(25,000)
Pre-acquisition dividend received	5,000
Net cash used in investing activities	(60,000)
Cash Flow from financing activities	
Proceeds from issue of equity shares	1,00,000
Proceeds from issue of debentures	1,00,000
Redemption of preference shares	(2,00,000)
Dividends paid	(60,000)
Interest paid on debentures	(18,000)
Net cash used in financing activities	(78,000)
Net decrease in cash and cash equivalents	(25,000)
Cash and cash equivalents at the beginning of the year	90,000
Cash and Cash equivalents at the end of the year	65,000

Working Notes:

1. NET PROFIT BEFORE TAXATION

Particulars	₹
Retained profit	60,000
Less: Opening Balance	(25,000)
Proposed dividend	90,000
Provision for taxation	1,35,000
	2,60,000

Dr. **2. LAND AND BUILDING ACCOUNT** Cr.

Particulars	₹	Particulars	₹
To Balance b/d	2,00,000	By Cash (Sale)	1,50,000
To Capital Reserve (Profit on sale)	30,000	By Balance c/d	1,50,000
To Capital Reserve (Revalua. Profit)	70,000		
	3,00,000		3,00,000

Dr. **3. PLANT AND MACHINERY ACCOUNT** Cr.

Particulars	₹	Particulars	₹
To Balance b/d	5,00,000	By Cash (Sale)	90,000
To Profit and Loss A/c	40,000	By Depreciation A/c (b.f.)	1,35,000
To Debentures	1,00,000	By Balance c/d	7,65,000
To Bank A/c	3,50,000		
	9,90,000		9,90,000

Dr. **4. INVESTMENTS ACCOUNT** Cr.

Particulars	₹	Particulars	₹
To Balance b/d	80,000	By Cash (Sale)	70,000
To Profit and Loss Account	20,000	By Dividend (Pre-acquisition)	5,000
To Bank A/c (Balancing figure)	25,000	By Balance c/d	50,000
	1,25,000		1,25,000

Dr. **5. PROVISION FOR TAXATION ACCOUNT** Cr.

Particulars	₹	Particulars	₹
To Bank (Balancing figure)	1,00,000	By Balance b/d	60,000
To Balance c/d	95,000	By Profit and Loss Account	1,35,000
	1,95,000		1,95,000

Dr. **6. CAPITAL RESERVE ACCOUNT** Cr.

Particulars	₹	Particulars	₹
To Balance c/d	1,00,000	By Profit on Sale of Land	30,000
		By Profit on Reval. of Land	70,000
	1,00,000		1,00,000

Dr. **7. GENERAL RESERVE ACCOUNT** Cr.

Particulars	₹	Particulars	₹
To Voluntary separation cost	50,000	By Balance b/d	2,50,000
To Capital redemption reserve	1,00,000		
To Balance c/d	1,00,000		
	2,50,000		2,50,000

Dr. **8. VOLUNTARY SEPARATION PAYMENTS ACCOUNT** Cr.

Particulars	₹	*Particulars*	₹
To balance b/d	65,000	By General Reserve	50,000
To Bank (Balancing figure)	1,10,000	By Balance c/d	1,25,000
	1,75,000		1,75,000

PROBLEM 7

From the following information, prepare a Cash Flow Statement:

BALANCE SHEETS AS AT ...

Particulars	*Note*	*31.03.2016* ₹	*31.03.2015* ₹
I. EQUITY AND LIABILITIES			
(1) Shareholders' Funds			
(a) Share Capital	1	3,50,000	3,00,000
(b) Reserves and Surplus	2	82,000	38,000
(2) Non-Current Liabilities			
(3) Current Liabilities			
Trade Payables		65,000	44,000
Other Current Liabilities (Dividend Payable)		4,000	—
Short-term Provisions	3	65,000	55,000
Total		5,66,000	4,37,000
II. ASSETS			
(1) Non-Current Assets			
Tangible Fixed Assets	4	2,66,000	1,90,000
Intangible Assets [Goodwill]		47,000	60,000
Non-Current Investments		35,000	10,000
(2) Current Assets			
Inventories		78,000	85,000
Trade Receivables		1,08,000	75,000
Cash & Cash Equivalents		32,000	17,000
Total		5,66,000	4,37,000

Particulars	*31.03.2016* ₹	*31.03.2015* ₹
1. Share Capital		
Equity Share Capital	2,50,000	1,50,000
8% Preference Share Capital	1,00,000	1,50,000
	3,50,000	3,00,000
2. Reserves and Surplus		
General Reserve	30,000	20,000

Profit and Loss A/c	27,000	18,000
Capital Reserve	25,000	—
	82,000	38,000
3. Short-Term Provisions		
Proposed Dividend	33,000	27,000
Provision for Tax	32,000	28,000
	65,000	55,000
4. Tangible Fixed Assets		
Land & Building	75,000	1,00,000
Machinery	1,91,000	90,000
	2,66,000	1,90,000

Addition Information:

(i) ₹ 18,000 depreciation has been written off Plant and Machinery and no depreciation has been charged on Land and Building.

(ii) A piece of land has been sold out and the balance has been revalued, profit on such sale and revaluation being transferred to Capital Reserve. There is no other entry in Capital Reserve Account.

(iii) A plant was sold for ₹ 12,000 (WDV being ₹ 15,000).

(iv) Dividend received amounted to ₹ 2,100 which included pre acquisition dividend of ₹ 600.

(v) An interim dividend of ₹ 10,000 has been paid.

SOLUTION

CASH FLOW STATEMENT FOR THE YEAR ENDING 31ST MARCH, 2016

Particulars	₹	₹
I. Cash Flows from Operating Activities		
A. Closing balance as per Profit and Loss Account		27,000
Less: Opening balance as per Profit and Loss Account		(18,000)
Add: Proposed dividend during the year		33,000
Add: Interim dividend paid during the year		10,000
Add: Transfer to reserve		10,000
Add: Provision for Tax		32,000
B. Net profit before taxation, and extra ordinary item		94,000
C. *Add:* Items to be added		
Depreciation	18,000	
Loss on sale of Plant	3,000	
Goodwill w/o	13,000	34,000
D. *Less:* Dividend Income		(1,500)
E. Operating profit before working capital changes [B + C – D]		1,26,500
F. *Add:* Decrease in Current Assets and Increase in current Liabilities		
Decrease in Inventories	7,000	

Increase in Trade Payables	21,000	28,000
G. *Less:* Increase in Trade Receivables (Gross)		(33,000)
H. Cash generated from operations [E + F – G]		1,21,500
I. *Less:* Income taxes paid		(28,000)
J. Net Cash from (used in) operating activities		93,500
II. Cash Flows from Investing Activities:		
Purchase of Plant		(1,34,000)
Sale of Land		50,000
Sale of Plant		12,000
Purchase of Investments		(25,600)
Dividend Received		2,100
Net Cash used in investing activities		(95,500)
III. Cash Flows from Financing Activities:		
Proceeds from issuance of share capital		1,00,000
Redemption of preference shares		(50,000)
Interim Dividend paid		(10,000)
Final Dividend paid [₹.27,000 – ₹.4,000]		(23,000)
Net Cash from Financing Activities		17,000
IV. Net Increase in Cash and Cash Equivalents [I + II + III]		15,000
V. Cash and Cash Equivalents at beginning of Period		17,000
VI. Cash and Cash Equivalents at end of Period [IV + V]		32,000

Working Notes:

Dr. **1. LAND AND BUILDING ACCOUNT** *Cr.*

Particulars	₹	*Particulars*	₹
To Balance b/d	1,00,000	By Bank A/c (sale)	50,000
To Capital Reserve A/c (Profit on sale and revaluation)	25,000	By Balance c/d	75,000
	1,25,000		1,25,000

Cr. **2. PLANT AND MACHINERY ACCOUNT** *Dr.*

Particulars	₹	*Particulars*	₹
To Balance b/d	90,000	By Depreciation A/c	18,000
To Bank A/c (Purchase)	1,34,000	By Bank A/c (Sale)	12,000
		By Profit and Loss A/c	
		By (Loss on sale)	3,000
		ByBalance c/d	1,91,000
	2,24,000		2,24,000

Dr. **3. INVESTMENTS ACCOUNT** *Cr.*

Particulars	₹	*Particulars*	₹
To Balance b/d	10,000	By Bank A/c (Div. received)	600
To Bank A/c (Purchases)	25,600	By Balance c/d	35,000
	35,600		35,600

4. It has been assumed that proposed dividend includes preference dividend also.

PROBLEM 8

From the following information, prepare a Cash Flow Statement:

BALANCE SHEETS AS AT ...

Particulars	*Note*	*31.03.2016* ₹ *'000*	*31.03.2015* ₹ *'000*
I. EQUITY AND LIABILITIES			
(1) Shareholders' Funds			
(a) Share Capital		1500	1250
(b) Reserves and Surplus		3410	1380
(2) Non-Current Liabilities [Long Term Debt]		1110	1040
(3) Current Liabilities			
Trade Payables		150	1890
Other Current Liabilities	1	630	1100
Total		6800	6660
II. ASSETS			
(1) Non-Current Assets			
Tangible Fixed Assets		2180	1910
Accumulated Depreciation		(1450)	(1060)
Non-Current Investments		2500	2500
(2) Current Assets			
Inventories		900	1950
Trade Receivables		1700	1200
Cash & Cash Equivalents		870	160
Other Current Assets (Interest Receivable)		100	—
Total		6800	6660

Notes to Accounts:

Particulars	*31.03.2016* ₹	*31.03.2015* ₹
1. Other Current Liabilities		
Interest Payable	230	100
Income Tax Payable	400	1000
	630	1100

STATEMENT OF PROFIT OR LOSS FOR THE YEAR ENDED 31.3.2016

Particulars	₹ *'000*
Sales	30,650
Cost of sales	(26,000)
Gross profit	4,650
Depreciation	(450)
Administrative and selling expenses	(910)
Interest expenses	(400)
Interest income	300
Dividend income	200
Net profit before taxation and extraordinary items	3,390
Extraordinary items:	
Insurance proceeds from earthquake disaster settlement	140
Net Profit after extraordinary items	3,530
Income tax	(300)
	3,230

Additional Information:

(i) An amount of ₹ 250 was raised from the issue of share capital and a further ₹250 was raised from long-term borrowings.

(ii) Interest expense was ₹ 400 of which ₹ 170 was paid during the period ₹ 100 relating to interest expense of the prior period was also paid during the period.

(iii) Dividends paid were ₹ 1,200.

(iv) Tax deducted at source on dividends received (including in the tax expense of ₹ 300 for the year) amounted to ₹ 40.

(v) During the period the enterprise acquired fixed assets for ₹ 350. The payment was made in cash.

(vi) Plant with original cost of ₹ 80 and accumulated depreciation of ₹ 60 was sold for ₹ 20.

(vii) Trade Receivables and Trade Payables include amounts relating to credit sales and credit purchase only.

SOLUTION

CASH FLOW STATEMENT (DIRECT METHOD)

Particulars	*(₹)*
Cash flows from Operating Activities	
Cash receipts from customers (30,650 + 1,200 – 1,700)	30,150
Cash paid to suppliers (24,950 + 1,890 – 150)	(26,690)
Cash paid to employees and for expenses	(910)
Cash generated from operations	2,550
Income tax paid (300 + 1000 – 400 – 40)	(860)
Cash flow before extraordinary item:	1,690
Proceeds from earthquake disaster settlement	140

Net cash from operating activities	1,830
Cash flows from Investing Activities	
Purchase of fixed assets	(350)
Proceeds from sale of equipment	20
Interest received (300 – 100)	200
Dividends received (200 – 40)	160
Net cash from investing activities	30
Cash flows from Financing Activities	
Proceeds from issuance of share capital	250
Proceeds from long term borrowings	250
Repayment of long term borrowings (1,040 + 250 – 1,110)	(180)
Interest paid (400 + 100 – 230)	(270)
Dividends paid	(1,200)
Net Cash used in financial activities	1,150
Net increase in cash and cash equivalents	710
Cash and Cash Equivalents at beginning of the period	160
Cash and Cash Equivalents at end of the period	870

Working Note:

CASH PAID TO SUPPLIERS, EMPLOYEES AND FOR EXPENSES

Particulars	₹
Cost of sales	26,000
Add: Closing Inventories	900
Less: Opening Inventories	(1,950)
Credit Purchases	24,950

PROBLEM 9

The following particulars relate to Bee Ltd., for the year ended 31st March, 2016:

(i) Furniture of Book Value of ₹ 15,500 was disposed off for ₹ 12,000.

(ii) Machinery costing ₹ 3,10,000 was purchased and ₹ 20,000 were spent on its erection.

(iii) Fully paid 8% preference shares of the face value of ₹ 10,00,000 were redeemed at a premium of 3%. In this connection 60,000 equity shares of ₹ 10 each were issued at a premium of ₹ 2 per share. The entire money being received with applications.

(iv) Dividend was paid as follows:

On 8% Preference Shares	₹ 40,000
On equity shares	₹ 1,10,000

(v) Total sales were ₹ 32,00,000 out of which cash sales were ₹ 11,50,000.

(vi) Total purchases were ₹ 8,00,000 including cash purchases of ₹ 60,000.

(vii) Total expenses were ₹ 12,40,000 charged to Profit and Loss A/c.

(viii) Taxes paid including dividend distribution tax of ₹ 22,500 were ₹ 3,30,000.

(ix) Closing Cash and cash equivalents were ₹ 1,25,000.

Prepare Cash Flow Statement as per AS 3 after taking into consideration the following also:

Particulars	*Opening (₹)*	*Closing (₹)*
Trade Receivables	1,50,000	1,47,000
Trade Payables	78,000	83,000
Unpaid Expenses	63,000	55,000

SOLUTION

CASH FLOW STATEMENT FOR THE YEAR ENDED 31ST MARCH, 2016

Particulars	₹
I. Cash Flow from Operating Activities	
Cash receipts from customers	32,03,000
Less: Cash paid to suppliers	(7,95,000)
Less: Cash paid for expenses	(12,48,000)
Casn generated from operations	11,60,000
Income tax paid (₹ 3,30,000 – ₹ 22,500)	(3,07,500)
Net Cash from Operating Activities	8,52,500
II. Cash Flows from Investing Activities	
Sale of Furniture	12,000
Purchase of Machinery	(3,30,000)
Net Cash used in Investing Activities	(3,18,000)
III. Cash Flow from Financing Activities	
Proceeds from issue of equity shares	7,20,000
Redemption of 8% preference shares	(10,30,000)
Dividend paid (₹ 40,000 + ₹ 1,10,000)	(1,50,000)
Dividend distribution tax paid	(22,500)
Net Cash used in Financing Activities	(4,82,500)
Net Increase in Cash and Cash equivalents	52,000
Add: Cash and Cash Equivalents at the beginning (Bal. fig)	73,000
Cash and Cash Equivalents at the end	1,25,000

Working Notes:

1. Credit sales = ₹32, 00,000 – ₹ 11,50,000 = ₹ 20,50,000

Dr. **2. TOTAL TRADE RECEIVABLES ACCOUNT** *Cr.*

Particulars	₹	*Particulars*	₹
To Balance b/d	1,50,000	By Cash/Bank A/c (Bal. fig.)	20,53,000
To Credit Sales	20,50,000	By Balance c/d	1,47,000
	22,00.000		22,00,000

3. Total Sale Receipts = ₹ 20,53,000 + ₹ 11,50,000 = ₹ 32,03,000
4. Credit Purchases = ₹ 8,00,000 – ₹ 60,0000 = ₹ 7,40,000

Dr. **5. TOTAL TRADE PAYABLES ACCOUNT** Cr.

Particulars	₹	*Particulars*	₹
To Cash/Bank A/c (Bal. fig.)	7,35,000	By Balance b/d	78,000
To Balance c/d	83,000	By Credit Purchases	7,40,000
	8,18,000		8,18,000

6. Total Payments to suppliers = ₹ 7,35,000 + ₹ 60,000 = ₹ 7,95,000
7. Payment for Expenses = ₹ 12,40,000 + ₹ 63,000 – ₹ 55,000 = ₹ 12,48,000

PROBLEM 10

From the following information, calculate Cash Flow from Operating Activities:

Cash Sales one forth of Net Credit Sales

Net Credit purchases are four times the Cash Purchases

Discount allowed to customers	₹ 6,000
Discount received from Suppliers	₹ 3,000
Returns Inward	₹ 10,000
Returns Outward	₹ 5,000
Office & Selling Expenses	₹ 51,000
Depreciation	₹ 19,000
Provision for Tax	₹ 40,000
Trading Commission earned	₹ 1,02,000
Total Sales (Net of Returns)	₹ 2,00,000
Total Purchases (Net of Returns)	₹ 1,00,000
Bad Debts	₹ 4,000

Particulars	*Opening*	*Closing*
Trade Receivables	₹ 1,00,000	₹ 2,00,000
Trade Payables	₹ 1,00,000	₹ 50,000
Outstanding Office & Selling Expenses	₹ 500	₹ 1,000
Prepaid Office & Selling Expenses	₹ 1,000	₹ 500
Accrued Trading Commission	₹ 1,000	₹ 2,000
Advance Trading Commission	₹ 2,000	₹ 1,000
Provision for Tax	₹ 50,000	₹ 60,000

SOLUTION

STATEMENT SHOWING THE COMPUTATION OF CASH FLOW FROM OPERATING ACTIVITIES

Particulars	₹
A. Operating Receipts in Cash:	
(a) Cash Sales	40,000
(b) Collection from Trade Receivables	50,000

(c) Trading Commission received	1,00,000
	1,90,000
B. Operating Payments in Cash:	
(a) Cash Purchases	20,000
(b) Payments made to Trade Payables	1,27,000
(c) Office & Selling Expenses paid	50,000
	1,97,000
C. Cash used in Operations before taxes	7,000
D. Income Tax paid	30,000
E. Net Cash used in Operating Activities	37,000

Working Notes:

1. *Calculation of Cash Sales, Net Credit Sales and Gross Credit Sales*

   Total Sales = Net Credit Sales + Cash Sales

   Let Net Credit Sales be X

   ₹ 2,00,000 = X + ¼X

   Multiplying the above equation by 4

   ₹ 8,00,000 = 4 X + X

   X = ₹ 8,00,000/5 = ₹ 1,60,000

   Cash Sales = ¼ × ₹ 1,60,000 = ₹ 40,000

   Gross Credit Sales = Net Credit Sales + Returns Inwara = ₹ 1,60,000 + ₹ 10,000 = ₹ 1,70,000

2. *Calculation of Cash Purchases, Net Credit Purchases and Gross Credit Purchases*

   Total Purchases = Net Credit Purchases + CasJrPurchases

   Let Cash Purchases be X

   ₹ 1,00,000 = 4X + X

   X = ₹ 1,00,000/5 = ₹ 20,000

   Net Credit Purchases = 4 × ₹ 20,000 = ₹ 80,000

   Gross Credit Purchases = Net Credit Purchases + Returns Outward

   = ₹ 80,000 + ₹ 5,000 = ₹ 85,000

Dr. **3. TOTAL TRADE RECEIVABLES ACCOUNT** Cr.

Particulars	₹	*Particulars*	₹
To Balance b/d	1,00,000	By Sales Returns	10,000
To Credit Sales	1,70,000	By Discount Allowed	6,000
		By Bad Debts	4,000
		By Cash Received (b.f.)	50,000
		By Balance c/d	2,00,000
	2,70,000		2,70,000

Dr. **4. TOTAL TRADE PAYABLES ACCOUNT** Cr.

Particulars	₹	Particulars	₹
To Purchases Returns	5,000	By Balance b/d	1,00,000
To Discount Received	3,000	By Credit Purchases	85,000
To Cash paid [Balancing Figure]	1,27,000		
To Balance c/d	50,000		
	1,85,000		1,85,000

Dr. **5. OFFICE & SELLING EXPENSES ACCOUNT** Cr.

Particulars	₹	Particulars	₹
To Prepaid Expenses A/c (in the beginning)	1,000	By Outstanding Expenses A/c (in the beginning)	500
To Bank A/c (Balancing figure)	50,000	By P & L A/c	51,000
To Outstanding Expenses A/c (af the end)	1,000	By Prepaid Expenses A/c (at the end)	500
	52,000		52,000

Dr. **6. TRADING COMMISSION ACCOUNT** Cr.

Particulars	₹	Particulars	₹
To Accrued Commission A/c (in the beginning)	1,000	By Advance Commission A/c	2,000
To P&L A/c	1,02,000	By Cash/Bank A/c (Balancing figure)	1,00,000
To Advance Commission A/c (at the end)	1,000	By Accrued Commission A/c (at the end)	2,000
	1,04,000		1,04,000

Dr. **7. PROVISION FOR TAX ACCOUNT** Cr.

Particulars	₹	Particulars	₹
To Bank A/c (Tax Paid) (Balancing figure)	30,000	By Balance b/d	50,000
		By P&L A/c (Provision made)	40,000
To Balance c/d	60,000		
	90,000		90,000

14 FUNDS FLOW STATEMENT

LEARNING OBJECTIVES

After studying this chapter, you should be able to understand:

- Meaning of Funds Flow Statement
- Objective of Funds Flow Statement
- Distinction between Funds Flow Statement and Position Statement
- Distinction between Funds Flow Statement and Income Statement
- Uses of Funds Flow Statement
- Limitations of Funds Flow Statement
- Preparation of Funds Flow Statement
- Preparation of Schedule of Changes in Working Capital
- Distinction between Funds Flow Statement and Schedule of Changes in Working Capital
- Analysis of the Changes in Non-current Items
- Funds from Operations
- Is Depreciation a Source of Funds?
- Format of Funds Flow Statement

1.0 MEANING OF FUNDS FLOW STATEMENT

The Funds Flow Statement consists of two terms 'Fund' and 'Flow'. Fund may be interpreted as cash *or* working capital *or* all financial resources. Flow means change *or* movement. Therefore, when the term 'Fund' is interpreted as 'working capital', the funds flow statement means statement of changes in working capital. It shows-

1. the specific sources from which working capital was generated by an enterprise.
2. the specific uses for which working capital was used by an enterprise.
3. Net change in working capital indicating the difference between the total sources and total uses.

Net working capital represents that portion of current assets which is financed through long-term sources.

Thus, Net Working Capital = Current Assets – Current Liabilities

This statement is also known as Statement of Sources and Applications of Funds, *or* Statement of Sources and Uses of Working Capital.

2.0 HOW TO DETERMINE WHETHER AN ASSET IS A CURRENT ASSET OR NON CURRENT ASSET

An asset is classified *either* as a current asset *or* as a non-current asset on the basis of the purpose for which an asset is held in the hands of user. If all the answers to the following questions are negative, the asset will be treated as a non-current asset.

Q 1. Whether it is Cash *or* Bank Balance.

Q 2. Whether it is expected to be converted into cash.

Q 3. Whether it is expected to be consumed in the production of goods *or* rendering services in the normal course of business.

For example:

Items / *Questions*	*Stock of Finished Goods*	*Stock of Raw Material & Work-in-Progress*	*Debtors & B/R*	*Land & Building*
Q 1	No	No	No	No
Q 2	Yes	No	Yes	No
Q 3	No	Yes	No	No
Result	Current Asset	Current Asset Asset	Current Asset	Non-current

Examples of Non-current Assets include Goodwill, Land & Building, Plant and Machinery, Furniture and Fixtures, Long-term Investments.

Examples of Non-current Liabilities include Share Capital, Long-term Loans, Debentures, Public Deposits Payable after 12 months from the date of Balance Sheet.

3.0 WHEN DOES THE FLOW OF WORKING CAPITAL ARISE?

The Working Capital flow arises when the net effect of a transaction is *either* to increase *or* decrease the amount of working capital. The transaction which affects both a Current Account (e.g., account of current asset *or* current liability) and a Non-Current Account (e.g., account of non-current asset *or* non-current liability), causes a change in working capital.

4.0 SOURCES OF FUND

Any transaction which increases the amount of working capital is a source of working capital. The working capital increases if a transaction increases current assets *or* decreases current liabilities. The major sources of working capital are summarised as follows:-

1. Issue of shares (whether Equity *or* Preference) for Cash
2. Raising of Long-term Debt (e.g., issue of debentures for Cash)
3. Sale of Non-current Assets for Cash
4. Non-operating Incomes (e.g., Dividend and Interest on Investment)
5. Funds from Operations

5.0 APPLICATIONS OF FUND

Any transaction which decreases the amount of working capital is an application of working capital. The working capital decreases if a transaction decreases current assets *or* increases current liabilities. The major uses of working capital are summarised as follows:-

1. Redemption of Redeemable Preference Shares for Cash and Buyback of shares
2. Repayment of Long-term Debt

3. Purchase of Non-current Assets for Cash
4. Payment of cash dividend (whether Final *or* Interim)
5. Funds used in Operations
6. Non-operating Expenses (e.g., Payment of Preliminary Expenses, Payment of Underwriting Commission)

ILLUSTRATION 1

State, which of the following would result in inflow/outflow of funds if the funds were defined as Working Capital?

(a) Purchase of stock-in-trade on credit;
(b) Purchases of a fixed asset on a credit of two months;
(c) Purchase of a fixed asset on long-term deferred payment basis;
(d) Sale of Stock-in-trade at profit for cash;
(e) Sale of a fixed asset (book value ₹ 7,000) at a loss of ₹ 6,000.
(f) Cash collected from debtors.
(g) Cash paid to creditors
(h) Bills receivables endorsed to creditors;
(i) B/R endorsed to creditors, dishonored;
(j) Issue of shares against a purchase of fixed asset;
(k) Issue of fully paid Bonus Shares;
(l) Payment of Final dividend already declared;
(m) Redemption of Debentures by converting them into equity shares;
(n) Writing off Bad Debts against a Provision for Doubtful Debts.

SOLUTION

STATEMENT SHOWING THE EFFECT OF VARIOUS TRANSACTIONS ON WORKING CAPITAL

Case	*Effect on Working Capital*	*Reason*
(a)	No Effect	Both the total current assets and all current liabilities are increased by the same amount.
(b)	Outflow	Total current liabilities are increased but total current assets remain unchanged.
(c)	No Effect	Neither the total current assets *nor* the total current liabilities are affected since both the total non-current assets and total non-current liabilities are increased by the same amount.
(d)	Inflow	Total current assets are increased by the amount of profit but total current liabilities remain unchanged.
(e)	Inflow	Total current assets are increased by ₹ 1,000 but total current liabilities remain unchanged.
(f)	No Effect	Neither the total current assets *nor* the total current liabilities are affected since there is only a conversion of one current asset into another current asset.

(g)	No Effect	Both the total current assets and total current liabilities are decreased by the same amount.
(h)	No Effect	Both the total assets and total current liabilities are decreased by the same amount.
(i)	No Effect	Both the total current assets and total current liabilities are increased by the same amount.
(j)	No Effect	Neither the total current assets *nor* the total current liabilities are affected since both the total non-current assets and total non-current liabilities are increased by the same amount.
(k)	No Effect	Neither the total current assets *nor* the total current liabilities are affected since there is only a conversion of accumulated profits into share capital.
(l)	No Effect	Both the total current assets and total current liabilities are decreased by the same amount.
(m)	No Effect	Neither the total current assets *nor* the total current liabilities are affected since there is only a conversion of one non-current account into another non-current account.
(n)	No Effect	Neither the total current assets *nor* the total current liabilities are affected.

6.0 PERIOD OF FUNDS FLOW STATEMENT

To provide a comparative view of the movements of funds, this statement should be prepared and published for the period covered by the Profit and Loss Account and for the corresponding previous period.

7.0 OBJECTIVE OF FUNDS FLOW STATEMENT

The basic objective of funds flow statement is to indicate the sources from which the funds (i.e., working capital) were obtained and the specific uses to which such funds (i.e., working capital) were applied between the dates of two Balance Sheets.

8.0 DISTINCTION BETWEEN FUNDS FLOW STATEMENT AND POSITION STATEMENT

Funds Flow Statement and Position Statement can be distinguished as under:-

Basis of Distinction	Position Statement	Funds Flow Statement
1. Meaning	It is a **statement of assets and liabilities** of an enterprise.	It is a **statement of changes in assets and liabilities** of an enterprise.
2. Objective	It is prepared to **ascertain the financial position** at a particular date.	It is prepared to **indicate how the financial position has changed** during a specific period.
3. Legal obligation to prepare	Schedule VI to the Companies Act **requires** every company to prepare a Balance Sheet.	There exists **no legal obligation** to prepare Fund Flow Statement.
4. Prescribed Form	Company's Balance Sheet is required to be prepared in a **prescribed form.**	Fund Flow Statement is not required to be prepared in a **prescribed form.**
5. Headings	The headings used in horizontal Balance Sheet are 'Assets' and'Liabilities'.	The headings used in Funds Flow Statement are **'Sources of Funds' and 'Application of Funds'.**

6. **Treatment of retained earnings**	Retained earnings are treated as **sources** of funds.	**All earnings** (whether retained *or* distributed) are treated as **source of funds.**
7. **Basic data required for preparation**	It is prepared with the help of **ledger balances and additional information.**	It is prepared with the help of **two consecutive Balance Sheets** and additional information.

9.0 DISTINCTION BETWEEN FUNDS FLOW STATEMENT AND INCOME STATEMENT

Funds Flow Statement and an Income Statement can be distinguished as follows:-

Basis of Distinction	Income Statement	Funds Flow Statement
1. **Meaning**	It summarises the results of operating activities during a particular period.	It is a statement of changes in assets and liabilities of an enterprise.
2. **Objective**	It is prepared to ascertain how the profit was earned.	It is prepared to ascertain how the profit has been utilized.
3. **Legal obligation to prepare**	Schedule VI to the Companies Act requires every company to prepare an Income Statement.	There exists no legal obligation to prepare Fund Flow Statement.
4. **Basic data required for preparation**	It is prepared with the help of nominal accounts and additional information.	It is prepared with the help of two consecutive Balance Sheets and additional information.
5. **Treatment of difference**	An excess of incomes over expenses is known as net profit and vice versa is known as net loss.	An excess of sources over applications is known as increase in working capital and vice versa is known as decrease in working capital.
6. **Basis for one source *or* all sources of funds**	It provides a basis for the calculation of funds from operations which is one of the sources of funds.	It shows the funds from various sources (including funds from operations).

10.0 USES OF FUNDS FLOW STATEMENT

The various uses of funds flow statement are summarised as under:-

(a) As a tool of historical analysis, it provides an answer to some of the important financial questions such as:

(i) How was it possible to distribute dividend in excess of current earnings *or* in the presence of a net loss for the period? (i.e., the firm might have raised funds from other sources also in addition to funds from operations).

(ii) Why dividends are not paid though company earned higher profits than previous year.

(iii) Why has the net working capital decreased although the net income for the period has gone up? (i.e., the firm might have applied the funds more than the sources of funds).

(iv) Why has the net working capital increased even though there has been a net loss for the period? (i.e., the firm might have raised the funds more than the application of funds).

(v) What happened to the proceeds of the sale of plant and equipment? (e.g., the firm might have purchased some fixed assets *or* it might have redeemed the redeemable debentures *or* preference shares).

(vi) Why did the firm resort to long-term borrowings inspite of large profits?

(vii) Why did the firm issue new equity *or* preference shares?

(viii) How was the retirement of long-term debts *or* redemption of redeemable preference shares accomplished? (e.g., the firm might have issued new shares).

(b) As a tool of planning, the Projected Fund Flow Statement enables the management to plan its future investments, operating and financial activities such as the repayment of long-term loans and interest thereon, modernisation *or* expansion of plant, payment of cash dividend etc.

(c) Along with a Schedule of Changes in Components of Working Capital, the Funds Flow Statement helps in managing and utilizing the working capital. The management can know the adequacy *or* otherwise of the working capital and can plan for the effective use of surplus working capital *or* can make arrangement in case of inadequacy of working capital. Besides this, the management can identify the magnitude and directions of changes in various components of working capital and if there is any undesired situation such as heavy inventory accumulations, heavy funds locked up in receivables than normally required, the necessary corrective action may be taken so as to achieve the desired level thereof.

11.0 LIMITATIONS OF FUNDS FLOW STATEMENT

The major limitations of Funds Flow Statement are summarised below:

1. **Ignores the Non-fund Transactions** - It ignores the non-fund transactions. In other words, it does not take into consideration those transactions which do not affect the working capital e.g., issue of shares against the purchase of fixed assets, conversion of debentures into equity shares.
2. **Secondary Data Based Statement** - It is a secondary data based statement. It merely rearranges the primary data already appearing in other statements, viz., Income Statement and Balance Sheet.
3. **Historical Statement** - It is basically historical in nature unless Projected Fund Flow Statements are prepared to plan for the future.

12.0 PREPARATION OF FUNDS FLOW STATEMENT

The various practical steps involved in the preparation of Funds Flow Statement are given below:

PRACTICAL STEPS INVOLVED IN THE PREPARATION OF FUNDS FLOW STATEMENT

Step 1: Prepare Schedule of Changes in Components of Working Capital.

Step 2: Analyse the Changes in non-current assets and non-current liabilities to find out whether there is inflow *or* outflow of funds on account of these non-current items.

Step 3: Compute the Funds from Operations.

Step 4: Prepare Funds Flow Statement.

13.0 PREPARATION OF SCHEDULE OF CHANGES IN WORKING CAPITAL

PRACTICAL STEPS INVOLVED IN THE PREPARATION OF SCHEDULE OF CHANGES IN WORKING CAPITAL

The various practical steps involved in the preparation of Schedule of Changes in Working Capital are given below:

Practical Steps involved in the preparation of Schedule of Changes in Working Capital

Step 1: Enter the names of Current Assets in 'Particular Column.'

Step 2: Enter the amounts of Current Assets for previous year in 'Previous Year Column'

Step 3: Enter the amounts of Current Assets for Current Year in 'Current Year Column'.

Step 4: Enter the increase in a Current Asset in 'Increase in Working Capital Column and decrease in a Current Asset in 'Decrease in Working Capital Column.

Step 5: Total 'Previous year Column' and 'Current Year Column' for Current Assets separately.

Step 6: Enter the names of Current Liabilities in 'Particulars Column'

Step 7: Enter the amounts of Current Liabilities for previous year in 'Previous Year Column'.

Step 8: Enter the amounts of Current Liabilities for current year in 'Current Year Column.'

Step 9: Enter the increase in a Current Liability in 'Decrease in Working Capital column' and decrease in a Current Liability in 'Increase in Working Capital Column'.

Step 10: Total 'Previous Year Column' and 'Current Year Column' for Current Liabilities separately.

Step 11: Calculate the Working Capital for previous year and current year by taking out the difference between Current Assets and Current Liabilities and enter in 'Previous Year Column' and 'Current Year Column' respectively.

Step 12: Calculate the difference between the Working Capital for current year and Working Capital for previous year and enter Increase in Working Capital in 'Previous Year Column' and 'Decrease in Working Capital Column' and decrease in working capital in 'Current Year Column' and 'Increase in Working Capital Column'.

Step 13: Total 'Previous year Column', 'Current year Column', 'Increase in working Capital Column' and 'Decrease in Working Capital Column.'

PURPOSE OF SCHEDULE OF CHANGES IN WORKING CAPITAL

The purpose of preparing this statement is to arrive at a single figure of net increase *or* decrease in working capital at the end of the period as compared with that of the beginning.

INTERPRETATION OF CHANGE IN WORKING CAPITAL

An increase in working capital means applying long-term funds towards short-term needs and a decrease in working capital means applying short-term funds towards long-term needs.

FORMAT OF SCHEDULE OF CHANGES IN WORKING CAPITAL

A format of Schedule of Changes in Components of Working Capital is shown below:

SCHEDULE OF CHANGES IN WORKING CAPITAL

(1) *Particulars*	*Absolute Amounts*		*Changes in Working Capital*	
	(2) *Previous Year* ₹	*(3)* *Current Year* ₹	*(4)* *Increase* ₹	*(5)* *Decrease* ₹
A. Current Assets:				
(a) Stock-in-trade	...	...	...	...
(b) Debtors (Gross)	...	...	...	...
(c) Cash Balance	...	...	...	...
(d) Bank Balance	...	...	...	...
(e) Bills Receivable	...	...	...	...
(f) Prepaid Expenses	...	...	...	...

(g) Accrued Incomes	...	...	...	...
(h) Short-term Loans and Advances	...	...	...	...
(i) Marketable Investments (Short-term)	...	...	...	...
	...	...	...	...
B. Current Liabilities:				
(a) Creditors for goods	...	...	...	...
(b) Bills Payable	...	...	...	...
(c) Outstanding Expenses	...	...	...	...
(d) Bank Overdraft	...	...	...	...
(e) Unclaimed/Unpaid dividend	...	...	...	...
(f) Unaccrued Incomes	...	...	...	...
(g) Short-term Loans and Advances	...	...	...	...
(h) Provision for Doubtful Debt	...	...	...	...
(I) Provision for Discount on Debtors	...	...	...	...
(j) Dividend Payable	...	...	...	...
(k) Income Tax Payable	...	...	...	...
(l) Provision for Legal Damages	...	...	...	...
	...	...	...	...
C. Working Capital (A – B)	...	...	...	...
D. Increase In Working Capital	...	...	...	...
Or				
Decrease in Working Capital	...	...	...	...
	...	...	...	...

Tutorial Notes

(i) If all the debtors are considered as good, the debtors will be shown in the schedule at gross figure and the Provision for doubtful debts will not appear in the schedule. However, Provision for Discount on debtors (if any) will appear in the schedule.

(ii) If 'Provision for Tax' is treated as a current item, then this item will appear as a Current liability in the 'Schedule'.

(iii) The figures of Marketable Investments given in the Balance Sheets should not again be adjusted for purchase, sale *or* profit/loss on sale of such investments made during the accounting period.

14.0 DISTINCTION BETWEEN FUNDS FLOW STATEMENT AND SCHEDULE OF CHANGES IN WORKING CAPITAL

Funds Flow Statement and Schedule of Changes in Components of Working Capital can be distinguished as follows:-

Basis of Distinction	Funds Flow Statement	Schedule of Changes in Working Capital
1. Meaning	It contains the sources of funds, uses of funds and the change in net working capital.	It contains the various items of current assets, current liabilities and changes therein, working

		capital for the previous year and for current year and the net increase/ decrease in working capital as compared to previous year.
2. Objective	It is prepared to ascertain how the financial position has changed during a particular period.	It is prepared to ascertain how the various components of working capital have changed during a particular period.
3. Disclosure of Changes in Non-Current items	Changes in non-current items are shown in Funds Flow Statement.	Changes in non-current items are not shown in this schedule.
4. Disclosure of Funds from operations	Funds from operations are shown in Funds Flow Statement.	Funds from operations are not shown in this schedule.

ILLUSTRATION 2

How will you deal with the following while preparing the Schedule of Changes in Working Capital'? (a) Increase in Patents (b) Decrease in Stock (c) Decrease in Goodwill (d) Increase in Debtors (e) Decrease in Land & Building (f) Decrease in Marketable Securities (g) Increase in Long-term Investments (h) Decrease in Creditors (i) Increase in Share Capital (j) Increase in Bank overdraft (k) Decrease in Debentures (l) Decrease in Dividend Payable (m) Increase in Securities Premium (n) Increase in Bills Payable (o) Decrease in Public Deposits (due after 2 years) (p) Decrease in Unclaimed Dividend (q) Decrease in Preliminary Expenses (r) Increase in Discount on Issue of Debentures (s) Decrease in Interest accrued and due on Secured Loans (t) Decrease in Interest accrued but not due on Unsecured Loans.

SOLUTION

Items to be shown as increase in working capital-(d), (h), (l), (p), (t)

Items to be shown as decrease in working capital-(b), (f), (j), (n)

Items not to be shown in Schedule-(a), (c), (e), (g), (i), (k), (m), (o), (q), (r), (s)

ILLUSTRATION 3

From the following Balance Sheets of TULSIAN Ltd., prepare Schedule of Changes in Working Capital:

Particulars	*31.3.2015* ₹	*31.3.2016* ₹
Equity Share Capital	3,00,000	4,00,000
Pref. Share Capital	1,50,000	1,00,000
General Reserve	40,000	70,000
Securities Premium	5,000	15,000
Profit & Loss A/c	23,000	54,000
Debentures	3,20,000	4,20,000
Creditors for Goods	30,000	50,000
Bills Payables	20,000	30,000
Commission received-in-advance	3,000	2,000

Outstanding Expenses	2,000	1,000
Bank Overdraft (Canara Bank)	19,000	14,000
Provision for Taxation	38,000	50,000
Proposed Dividend	42,000	50,000
Provision for Doubtful Debt	4,000	5,000
Provision for Legal Damages	2,000	–
Provision for Discount on Debtors	1,000	2,000
Goodwill	1,15,000	90,000
Patents	90,000	1,15,000
Land	1,00,000	90,000
Plant & Machinery (Net)	1,80,000	1,70,000
Furniture	10,000	2,25,000
Investments	2,00,000	1,80,000
Stock	77,000	1,09,000
Debtors	1,60,000	2,00,000
Bills Receivable	20,000	30,000
Marketable Securities	3,000	2,000
Accrued Interest	1,000	3,000
Cash in hand	5,000	4,000
Cash at Dena Bank	10,000	6,000
Prepaid Expenses	10,000	8,000
Preliminary Expenses	5,000	3,000
Underwriting Comm.	3,000	8,000
Discount on Issue of Debentures	10,000	20,000

SOLUTION

SCHEDULE OF CHANGES IN WORKING CAPITAL

Particulars	*31st March*		*Changes in Working Capital*	
	2015 ₹	*2016* ₹	*Increase* ₹	*Decrease* ₹
A. Current Assets:				
Stock	77,000	1,09,000	32,000	
Debtors	1,60,000	2,00,000	40,000	
Bills Receivables	20,000	30,000	10,000	
Marketable Securities	3,000	2,000		1,000
Accrued Interest	1,000	3,000	2,000	
Cash-in-hand	5,000	4,000		1,000
Cash at Dena Bank	10,000	6,000		4,000
Prepaid Expenses	10,000	8,000		2,000
	2,86,000	3,62,000		

B. Current Liabilities:				
Creditors for Goods	30,000	50,000		20,000
Bills Payables	20,000	30,000		10,000
Outstanding Expenses	2,000	1,000	1,000	
Commission received-in-advance	3,000	2,000	1,000	
Bank O/D (Canara Bank)	19,000	14,000	5,000	
Provision for Doubtful Debts	4,000	5,000		1,000
Provision for Legal Damages	2,000	–	2,000	
Provision for Discount on Debtors	1,000	2,000		1,000
	81,000	1,04,000		
C. Working Capital [A – B]	2,05,000	2,58,000		
D. Increase in Working Capital	53,000			53,000
	2,58,000	2,58,000	93,000	93,000

ILLUSTRATION 4

Assuming that all debtors are good in Illustration 3. Prepare Schedule of Changes in Working Capital.

SOLUTION

SCHEDULE OF CHANGES IN WORKING CAPITAL

Particulars	*31st March*		*Changes in Working Capital*	
	2015 ₹	*2016* ₹	*Increase* ₹	*Decrease* ₹
A. Current Assets:				
Stock	77,000	1,09,000	32,000	
Debtors	1,60,000	2,00,000	40,000	
Bills Receivables	20,000	30,000	10,000	
Marketable Securities	3,000	2,000		1,000
Accrued Interest	1,000	3,000	2,000	
Cash-in-hand	5,000	4,000		1,000
Cash at Dena Bank	10,000	6,000		4,000
Prepaid Expenses	10,000	8,000		2,000
	2,86,000	3,62,000		
B. Current Liabilities:				
Creditors for goods	30,000	50,000		20,000
Bills Payables	20,000	30,000		10,000
Outstanding Expenses	2,000	1,000	1,000	
Commission received-in-advance	3,000	2,000	1,000	
Bank O/D (Canara Bank)	19,000	14,000	5,000	
Provision for Discount on Debtors	1,000	2,000		1,000

Provision for Legal Damages	2,000	–	2,000	
	77,000	99,000		
C. Working Capital [A – B]	2,09,000	2,63,000		
D. Increase in Working Capital	54,000			54,000
	2,63,000	2,63,000	93,000	93,000

Note: Provision for Doubtful Debts has not been shown in the Schedule because it is basically 'Reserve for Doubtful Debts.' Since all debtors have been considered as good, there is no need for creating any 'Provision for Doubtful Debts.' Such excess provision is treated as Reserve.

15.0 ANALYSIS OF THE CHANGES IN NON-CURRENT ITEMS

To identify whether there is an inflow *or* outflow of funds on account of non-current items, the accounts of all non-current items (like Fixed Assets, Investments (Long-term), Goodwill, Patents, Trademarks, Preliminary Expenses, Underwriting Commission, Discount on issue of Shares/Debentures, Equity Share Capital, Preference Share Capital, Debentures, Long-term Loans) should be prepared after taking into consideration the following:

(a) Opening Balance (given in Opening Balance Sheet)

(b) Closing Balance (given in Closing Balance Sheet)

(c) Relevant Additional Information (if any given)

The following table summarises the meaning, accounting treatment and reasoning for treatment of changes in various non-current items in the absence of any additional information:

Non-current Items	Meaning	Treatment	Reasoning for Treatment
I. Intangible Non-Current Assets (e.g. Goodwill, Patents, Trademarks, Copy-rights)			
(a) *Increase*	It represents the amount of purchase.	Show as an application of Fund in Funds Flow Statement.	It involves an outflow of fund.
(b) *Decrease*	It represents the amount amortised/written off.	Add back to the current years' profits to find out funds from operations.	It merely represents a book entry and does not involve any outflow of fund.
II. Tangible Non-depreciable Non-current Assets (e.g. Investments)			
(a) *Increase*	It represents the amount of purchase.	Show as an application of Funds in Funds Flow Statement.	It involves an outflow of fund.
(b) *Decrease*	It represents the amount of sale proceeds.	Show as a Source of Funds in Fund Flow Statement.	It involves an inflow of fund.

III. Tangible Depreciable Non-current Assets (e.g. Land and Building, Plant & Machinery)			
(a) *Increase*	It represents the amount of purchase.	Show as an Application of Fund in Funds Flow Statement.	It involves an outflow of fund.
(b) *Decrease*	It represents the amount of depreciation provided during the year.	Add back to the current years' profits to find out funds from operations.	It merely represents a book entry and does not involve any outflow of fund.
IV. Fictitious Assets other than Discount (e.g. Preliminary Expenses, Underwriting Commission)			
(a) *Increase*	It represents the pay-ment.	Show as an Application of Funds in Funds Flow Statement.	It involves an outflow of fund.
(b) *Decrease*	It represents the amount written off.	Add back to the current years' profits to find out funds from operations.	It merely represents a book entry and does not involve any outflow of fund.
V. Discount allowed on Issue of Shares/ Debentures			
(a) *Increase*	It represents the amount of discount allowed on issue of shares/ debentures.	Deduct from the in-crease in Share Capital/ Debenture to ascertain the net amount of issue (which is shown as a Funds Flow Statement)	It represents *less* in-flow of funds on issue of shares/ debentures to the extent of dis-count allowed, source of funds in
(b) *Decrease*	It represents the amount written off.	Add back to the current years' profits to find out funds from operations.	It merely represents a book entry and does not involve any outflow of funds.
VI. Share Capital, Debentures, Long-term Loans			

(a) *Increase*	It represents an issue of new shares/ debentures *or* raising a fresh loan.	Show as a source of funds in Funds Flow Statement. **Note:** While calculating the amount of source, premium (if any received) should be added to *or* discount (if any allowed) should be deducted from the amount of increase.	It involves an inflow of funds.
(b) *Decrease*	It represents the re-payment of Redeemable Pref. Shares/ Debentures/Long-term Loan *or* buy-back of shares.	Show as an application of funds in Funds Flow Statement. **Note:** While calculating the amount of application, premium on redemption (if any paid) should be added to the amount of decrease.	It involves an outflow of fund.
VII. General Reserve account			
(a) *Increase*	It represents transfer of profits from P & L A/c.	Add back to the current years' profits to find out funds from operations.	It merely represents a book entry and does not involve any flow of funds.
(b) *Decrease*	It represents transfer of profit from General Reserve to P & L A/c.	Deduct from the current years' profits to find out funds from operations.	It merely represents a book entry and does not involve any flow of funds.
VIII. Securities Premium A/c			
(a) *Increase*	It represents the amount of premium received on issue of securities.	Add to the increase in securities to ascertain the total amount of issue (which is shown as a received. source of funds in Funds Flow Statement).	It represents more in-flow of funds on issue of securities to the extent of premium
(b) *Decrease*	It represents the amount of premium utilized for: (i) Writing off prelimi-nary expenses, un-derwriting commission, Discount on issue of shares/ debentures or	No treatment is required but it may be noted that an amount of decrease in preliminary exp./ underwriting comm./Discount allowed, to the extent of decrease in securities premium, shall not be added back to current years' profits.	

	(ii) Providing for pre-mium on redemption of redee- mable pref-erence shares/ debentures	No treatment is re-quired but it may be noted that premium paid on redemption to the extent of decrease in securities premium, shall not be added back to current years' profits.	
IX. Proposed Dividend			
(a) *Previous year's*	It represents the amount of final divi-dend declared for the previous year but paid during the current year.	Show as an Application of Funds in Funds Flow Statement.	It involves an outflow of funds.
(b) *Current year's*	It represents the amount of dividend proposed by the Board of Directors for the current year.	Add back to the current year's profits to find out funds from operations.	It is merely a book en-try and does not in-volve outflow of funds.
X. Increase in	It represents transfer of Profits from P&L A/c.	Treatment is similar to that of General Reserve (as discussed earlier in item VII).	Increase in Provision when all debtors are good, is treated as Reserve.

ILLUSTRATION 5

How will you deal with the following items while preparing Funds Flow Statement if no other information is given:

1. Increase/Decrease in Balance of Patents.
2. Increase/Decrease in Balance of Land.
3. Increase/Decrease in Balance of Investments.
4. Increase/Decrease in Balance of Plant & Machinery.
5. Increase/Decrease in Balance of Underwriting Commission.
6. Increase/Decrease in Balance of Discount on Issue of Debentures.
7. Increase/Decrease in Balance of Share Capital.
8. Increase/Decrease in Balance of Securities Premium.
9. Increase/Decrease in Balance of General Reserve.
10. Increase/Decrease in Balance of Provision for Doubtful Debts (if all debtors have been considered good)
11. Increase/Decrease in Balance of Debentures.
12. Proposed Dividend for previous year & current year.
13. Provision for Tax for previous year & current year.

SOLUTION

Item	Accounting Treatment	
	In case of Increase	**In case of Decrease**
1. Patents	Treat as Application of Funds	Add back to the current years' profits to find out Funds from Operations (FFO).
2. Land	Treat as Application of Funds	Treat as Source of Funds
3. Investments	Treat as Application of Funds	Treat as Source of Funds.
4. Plant & Machinery	Treat as Application of Funds	**Add back** to the current years' profits to find out Funds from Operations (FFO).
5. Underwriting Commission	Treat as Application of Funds	**Add back** to the current years' profits to find out Funds from Operations (FFO).
6. Discount on Issue of Debentures	It is **deducted from the increase** in Debentures to ascertain the net amount of issue as source of funds.	**Add back** to the current years' profits to find out Funds from Operations (FFO).
7. Share Capital	Treat as Source of Funds	Treat as Application of Funds.
8. Securities Premium	It is **added to the increase** in securities to ascertain the total amount of issue as source of funds.	(i) **No treatment** is required but it may be noted that an amount of decrease in preliminary exp./ underwriting comm./ Discount allowed, to the extent of decrease in securities premium, shall not be added back to current years' profits. (ii) **No treatment** is required but it may be noted that premium paid on redemption to the extent of decrease in securities premium, shall not be added back to current years' profits.
9. General Reserve	**Add back** to the current years' profits to find out Funds from Operation.	It is **deducted** from the current years' profits to find out Funds from Operation (FFO).
10. Provision for Doubtful	**Add back** to the current years' profits to find out funds from Operation.	It is **deducted** from the current year' profits to find out Funds from Operation (FFO).
11. Debentures	Treat as Source of Funds	Treat as Application of Funds.
12. Proposed Dividend		
(a) For the Current Year	**Add back** to current years' profits to find out Funds from Operations.	
(b) For the Previous Year	Treat as Application of Funds	

13. Provision for Tax (If treated as non-current)	
(a) For the Current Year	**Add back** to current years' profits to find out Funds from Operations.
(b) For the Previous Year	Treat as Application of Funds

ILLUSTRATION 6

How will you deal with the following items while preparing Funds Flow Statements if no other information is given:

1. Decrease in Balance of Goodwill
2. Increase in Balance of Patent
3. Decrease in Balance of Land
4. Decrease in Balance of Plant & Machinery
5. Increase in Balance of Furniture
6. Decrease in Balance of Investments
7. Decrease in Balance of Preliminary Expenses
8. Increase in Balance of Discount on Issue of Debentures
9. Increase in Equity Share Capital
10. Decrease in Pref. Share Capital
11. Increase in General Reserve
12. Increase in Securities Premium
13. Increase in Debentures
14. Proposed Dividend for Previous year
15. Proposed Dividend for Current Year
16. Provision for Tax for Previous Year
17. Provision for Tax for Current Year

SOLUTION

Item	Accounting Treatment
1. Decrease in Balance of Goodwill	Add back to current year's profits to find out Funds from Operations (FFO)
2. Increase in Balance of Patent	Application of Fund
3. Decrease in Balance of Land	Sources of Fund
4. Decrease in Balance of Plant & Machinery	Add back to current year's profits to find out Funds from Operations (FFO)
5. Increase in Balance of Furniture	Application of Fund
6. Decrease in Balance of Investments	Sources of Fund
7. Decrease in Balance of Preliminary Expenses	Add back to current year's profits to find out Funds from Operations (FFO)
8. Increase in Balance of Discount on Issue of Debentures	It is deducted from the increase in Debenture to ascertain the net amount of issue as Source of Funds

9. Increase in Equity Share Capital	Sources of Fund
10. Decrease in Pref. Share Capital	Application of Fund
11. Increase in General Reserve	Add back to current year's profits to find out Funds from Operations (FFO)
12. Increase in Securities Premium	It is added to the increase in securities to ascertain the total amount of issue as source of fund.
13. Increase in Debentures	Sources of Fund
14. Proposed Dividend for Previous year	Application of Fund
15. Proposed Dividend for Current Year	Add back to current year's profits to find out Funds from Operations (FFO)
16. Provision for Tax for Previous Year	Application of Fund
17. Provision for Tax for Current Year	Add back to current year's profits to find out Funds from Operations (FFO)

16.0 FUNDS FROM OPERATIONS

MEANING OF FUNDS FROM OPERATIONS

Funds from operations refer to those funds which are generated in the business as a result of carrying out the operations during the normal course of the business and are computed by taking out the difference between the operating revenues that provided funds during the accounting period and operating expenses that involved an outflow of funds during the accounting period.

DISTINCTION BETWEEN NET PROFIT AND FUNDS FROM OPERATIONS

Net Profit can be distinguished from Funds from Operations as follows:

Basis of Distinction	Net Profit	Funds from Operations
1. Meaning	It indicates the net results of operating & non-operating activities carried on during an accounting year.	It indicates the working capital flow as a result of operating activities.
2. Non-cash operating items (Depreciation)	It is calculated after taking into account the effect of non-cash operating items.	It is calculated excluding the effect of non-cash operating items since these items represent merely the book entries.
3. Non-operating Items	It is calculated after taking into account the effect of non-operating items.	It is calculated excluding the effect of non-operating items since these items do not relate to operating activities.

METHODS OF COMPUTATION OF FUNDS FROM OPERATIONS

The amount of funds from operations may be computed *either* following Direct Method *or* Indirect Method as follows:-

DIRECT METHOD

Under direct method the fund from Operations is computed as follows:

Statement showing the computation of Funds from Operations (Under Direct Method)

Particulars	₹	₹	₹
A. Operating Revenues			
Cash Sales		xxx	
Credit Sales		xxx	
Other operating revenues (e.g., Trading Commission earned)		xxx	xxx
B. *Less:* Total Operating Cost (other than Depreciation)			
(a) Cost of Goods Sold:			
(i) Opening Stock	xxx		
(ii) Purchases	xxx		
(iii) Direct Expenses	xxx		
(iv) *Less:* Closing Stock	xxx	xxx	
(b) Office and Administration Expenses (including outstanding but excluding prepaid)		xxx	
(c) Selling and Distribution Expenses (including outstanding but excluding prepaid)		xxx	xxx
C. Funds from Operations (A- B)			xxx

Note: Provision for Tax is not deducted when the Tax is treated as a non-current item.

ILLUSTRATION 7

Calculate the Funds from Operations in each of the following alternative cases:

Case I Operating Revenue ₹ 1,00,000, Operating Cost (includes Depreciation ₹ 10,000) ₹ 70,000.

Case II Opening Stock ₹ 10,000, Purchases ₹ 3,20,000, Closing Stock ₹ 30,000, Sales ₹ 8,10,000, Wages ₹ 10,000, Rent paid ₹ 25,000, Salaries paid ₹ 1,00,000, Commission allowed ₹ 3,000, Provision for Doubtful Debts ₹ 3,000, Provision for Legal Damages ₹ 5,000, Discount allowed ₹ 2,000, Refund of Tax ₹ 2,000, Provision for Taxation ₹ 1,50,000, Provision for Depreciation ₹ 50,000.

Case III Gross Profit ₹ 2,50,000, Wages ₹ 5,000, Cost of Goods sold ₹ 1,50,000, Rent paid ₹ 12,500, Salaries paid ₹ 50,000, Commission be allowed ₹ 1,500. Discount allowed ₹ 1,000, Provision for Doubtful Debts ₹ 2,500, Provision for Legal Damages ₹ 1,500, Provision for Taxation ₹ 75,000, Refund of Tax ₹ 1,000, Provision for Depreciation ₹ 25,000.

SOLUTION

Case I Funds from Operations = Operating Revenue – Operating Cost (other than Depreciation)

= ₹ 1,00,000 – 60,000 = ₹ 40,000

Case II Funds from Operations = Sales – Cost of goods sold – Operating Expenses (other than depreciation)

= ₹ 8,10,000 – (₹ 10,000 + ₹ 3,20,000 + ₹ 10,000 – ₹ 30,000) – (₹ 25,000 + ₹ 1,00,000 + ₹ 3,000 + ₹ 3,000 + ₹ 5,000 + ₹ 2,000)

= ₹ 3,62,000.

Case III Funds from Operations = Gross Profit – Operating Expenses (other than depreciation)

= ₹ 2,50,000 – (₹ 12,500 + ₹ 50,000 + ₹ 1,500 + ₹ 1,000 + ₹ 2,500 + ₹ 1,500) = ₹ 1,81,000

INDIRECT METHOD

Under indirect method fund from Operations is computed as follows:

DR. ADJUSTED PROFIT AND LOSS ACCOUNT CR.

Particulars	₹	*Particulars*	₹
To Depreciation	xxx	By Opening Balance (Cr.)	xxx
To Loss on Sale of non-current Assets	xxx	By Gain from sale of non-current Assets	xxx
To Goodwill/Patent/Trade mark/other intangible assets amortized	xxx	By Transfer fees	xxx
		By Dividend and Interest on Investments	xxx
To Discount on Issue of Shares/Debentures etc., written off	xxx	By Rent Received	xxx
		By Compensation on acquisition of Non-Current Assets	xxx
To Transfer to Reserves	xxx	By Refund of Taxes	xxx
To Reserve for Doubtful Debts (if all debtors are good)	xxx	By Profit on Revaluation of Assets	xxx
To Interim Dividend (for Current year)	xxx	By Funds from Operations *(Balancing figure)*	xxx
To Proposed Dividend (for Current year)	xxx		xxx
To Provision for Tax (for Current year)	xxx		
To Closing Balance (Cr.)	xxx		
	xxx		xxx

TUTORIAL NOTES

(i) In case, the opening balance of P & L A/c is a debit balance (which represents loss), it should be shown on the debit side of Adjusted P & L A/c and similarly if the closing balance of P & L A/c is a debit balance (which represents loss), it should be shown on the credit side of Adjusted P & L A/c.

(ii) Provision for Tax is not shown on the debit side of Adjusted P & L A/c if this item is treated as a current item.

Note: Provision for Tax has been treated as 'Non-Current Item' in this Chapter.

ILLUSTRATION 8

For calculating funds from operations from a given figure of Net Profits earned during the year, how will you deal with the following if the Net Profit has been computed after considering them?

(a) Depreciation on plant (b) Outstanding Office Expenses (c) Prepaid Selling expenses (d) Discount allowed (e) Commission allowed (f) Bad Debts (g) Provision for Doubtful Debt (h) Provision for Doubtful Debt (if all debtors are considered as good) (i) Provision for Discount on debtors (j) Provision for Legal Damages (k) Loss on sale of Plant (l) Expenses on issue of shares (m) Brokerage on issue of debentures (n) Underwritten Commission w/o (o) Goodwill w/o (p) Advertisement Suspense w/o (q) Transfer to General Reserve (r) Transfer to Sinking Fund for Debentures (s) Transfer to Sinking Fund for machine replacement (t) Premium on redemption of debentures (u) Interim Dividend (v) Proposed Dividend for Current year (w) Accrued Commission (x) Profit on sale of marketable securities (y) Interest and Dividend on Marketable securities (z) Profit on sale of Long-term investments (aa) Interest and Dividend on Long-term investments (ab) Compensation for acquisition of land (ac) Discount received.

SOLUTION

Items to be added to Net Profit-(a), (h), (k), (l) to (s), (t), (u), (v)

Items to be subtracted from Net Profit-(z), (aa), (ab)

Items ***neither*** **to be added** ***nor*** **to be subtracted**-(b), (c), (d), (e), (f), (g), (i), (j), (w), (x), (y), (ac).

ILLUSTRATION 9

For calculating 'Funds from Operations' from a given figure of 'Net Profits' earned during a year, how will you deal with the following?

Decrease in Goodwill, Decrease in Plant & Machinery Account, Decrease in Land Account, Decrease in Investments, Decrease in Discount on Issue of Debentures A/c, Increase in Preliminary Expenses, Decrease in Share Capital, Decrease in Debentures, Increase in General Reserve, Increase in Securities Premium Account, Previous year's Proposed Dividend, Loss on sale of a machine, Profit on sale of investments, Loss on sale of marketable securities, Interest & Dividend on Long--term Investments.

SOLUTION

Item	Whether to be added to *or* subtracted from the figure of Net Profit earned
Decrease in Goodwill	To be added
Decrease in Plant & Machinery Account	To be added on account of depreciation
Decrease in Land Account	Neither to be added *nor* to be subtracted
Decrease in Investment Account	Neither to be added *nor* to be subtracted
Decrease in Discount on issue of Debentures A/c	To be added
Increase in Preliminary Expenses	Neither to be added *nor* to be subtracted
Decrease in Share Capital	Neither to be added *nor* to be subtracted
Decrease in Debentures	Neither to be added *nor* to be subtracted
Increase in General Reserve	To be added
Increase in Securities Premium Account	Neither to be added *nor* to be subtracted
Previous year's Proposed Dividend	Neither to be added *nor* to be subtracted
Loss on sale of a machine	To be added
Profit on sale of investments A/c	To be subtracted if not credited to Capital Reserve A/c
Loss on sale of Marketable Securities	Neither to be added *nor* to be subtracted
Interest & Dividend on Long-term Investment	To be subtracted

ILLUSTRATION 10

Calculate the Funds from Operations in each of the following alternative cases:

Case I Operating Profit ₹ 62,400, Provision for Depreciation ₹ 10,000, Provision for Taxation ₹ 30,000, Refund of Tax ₹ 400, Provision for doubtful debts ₹ 1,000, Office & Admn. Exp. ₹ 50,000.

Case II Net Profit after tax ₹ 1,65,000, Provision for Depreciation ₹ 50,000, Provision for Taxation ₹ 1,50,000, Refund of Tax ₹ 2,000, Profit on Sale of a fixed asset ₹ 3,000, Loss on sale of Investments ₹ 10,000, Interest received ₹ 1,000. Rent received ₹ 2,000, Dividend received ₹ 7,000, Discount allowed on issue of debentures written off ₹ 500, Cost of issue of shares written off ₹ 600, Preliminary Expenses written off ₹ 200, Goodwill written off ₹ 500, Underwriting Commission written off ₹ 200.

Case III Closing Balance of P & L A/c ₹ 1,00,000, Depreciation ₹ 10,000, Non-operating Expenses & losses w/o ₹ 30,000, Non-operating Incomes ₹ 20,000, Opening Balance of P&L A/c ₹ 30,000.

SOLUTION

Case I Funds from Operations = Operating Profit + Provision for Depreciation

= ₹ 62,400 + ₹ 10,000 = ₹ 72,400

Case II Funds from Operations = Net Profit after tax + Provision for Depreciation + Loss on sale of Investment + Discount on issue of Debentures w/o + Cost of Issue of Shares w/o + Preliminary Expenses w/o + Goodwill w/o + Under Comm. w/o – Profit on sale of a Fixed Asset – Interest received – Rent received – Dividend Received + Provision for Tax – Refund of Tax

= ₹ 1,65,000 + ₹ 50,000 + ₹ 10,000 + ₹ 500 + ₹ 600 + ₹ 200 + ₹ 500 + ₹ 200 – ₹ 3,000 – ₹ 1,000 – ₹ 2,000 – ₹ 7,000 + ₹ 1,50,000 – ₹ 2,000 = ₹ 3,62,000.

Case III Funds from Operations = Closing Balance of P&L A/c + Depreciation + Non Operating Expenses & losses w/o – Non-operating Incomes – Opening Balance of P&L A/c

= ₹ 1,00,000 + ₹ 10,000 + ₹ 30,000 – ₹ 20,000 – ₹ 30,000

= ₹ 90,000

ILLUSTRATION 11

Calculate Funds from Operations from the following information:

Dr. **PROFIT & LOSS ACCOUNT** *Cr.*

Particulars	₹	*Particulars*	₹
To Office & Adm. Expenses	10,000	By Gross Profit b/d	1,17,000
To Selling Expenses	10,000	By Profit on sale of	
To Provision for Doubtful Debts	1,000	Land & Building	10,000
To Provision for Legal Damages	1,000	By Profit on sale of	
To Depreciation	5,000	Marketable Securities	1,500
To Loss on Sale of Machine	6,000	By Interest & Dividend on	
To Goodwill Amortised	10,000	Investment	1,000
To Preliminary Expenses w/o	3,000	By Interest on Marketable	
To Provision for Discount on Debtors	5,000	Securities	400
To Provision for Tax	40,000	By Refund of Taxes	15,000
To Transfer to Reserve	5,000	By Compensation received	4,000
To Proposed Dividend	25,000	By Discount received from suppliers	40
To Interim Dividend	10,000	By Rent received	1,000
To Net Profit	19,000	By Commission Accrued	60
	1,50,000		1,50,000

SOLUTION

Dr. **ADJUSTED PROFIT & LOSS ACCOUNT** *Cr.*

Particulars	₹	*Particulars*	₹
To Depreciation	5,000	By Profit on sale of Land & Building	10,000

To Loss on Sale of Machine	6,000	By Interest & Dividend on Investment	1,000
To Goodwill Amortised	10,000	By Compensation Received	4,000
To Preliminary Exp. w/o	3,000	By Refund of Taxes	15,000
To Transfer to Reserve	5,000	By Rent Received	1,000
To Proposed Dividend	25,000	By Funds from operations	92,000
To Interim Dividend	10,000	*(Balancing figure)*	
To Provision for tax	40,000		
To Net Profit	19,000		
	1,23,000		1,23,000

ILLUSTRATION 12

Following are the extracts from the Balance Sheets of X Ltd.

Particulars	*As at 31.03.2015* ₹	*As at 31.03.2016* ₹
Securities Premium Account	3,000	9,000
General Reserve	24,000	42,000
Profit and Loss account	21,000	28,800
Provision for Taxation	24,000	30,000
Proposed Dividend	25,200	30,000
Goodwill	69,000	54,000
Patents and Trade Marks	54,000	69,000
Fixed Assets (Net)	60,000	42,000
Preliminary Expenses	3,000	1,800
Underwriting Commission	1,800	3,000

Note: There was no sale/purchase of fixed assets during 2015-2016.

Required: Compute the funds from operations.

SOLUTION

Dr. **ADJUSTED PROFIT & LOSS ACCOUNT** *Cr.*

Particulars	₹	*Particulars*	₹
To Depreciation	18,000	By Balance b/d	21,000
To Goodwill w/o	15,000	By Funds from Operations	1,20,000
To Preliminary Expenses w/o	1,200	*(Balancing figure)*	
To Transfer to Reserve	18,000		
To Proposed Dividend	30,000		
To Provision for Tax	30,000		
To Balance c/d	28,800		
	1,41,000		1,41,000

ILLUSTRATION 13

Calculate Funds from Operations from the following information:

Particulars	*As at 31.3.2015*	*As at 31.3.2016*
Profit and Loss Appropriation (Cr.)	12,00,000	15,00,000
General Reserve (Cr.)	22,00,000	25,00,000
Goodwill (Dr.)	5,70,000	4,70,000
Preliminary Expenses (Dr.)	1,20,000	90,000
Accumulated Depreciation on Fixed Assets (Cr.)	7,70,000	9,40,000

During the year the dividend paid was ₹ 3,00,000. and there were no purchase *or* sale of fixed assets.

SOLUTION

Particulars	₹
A. Increase in Profit and Loss Appropriation balance (₹ 15,00,000 – ₹ 12,00,000)	3,00,000
B. *Add:* Transfer to General Reserve	3,00,000
Dividend paid	3,00,000
C. Net Income for the year [A + B]	9,00,000
D. *Add:* Goodwill written-off	1,00,000
Preliminary expenses written-off	30,000
Depreciation written-off	1,70,000
E. Funds from Operations [C + D]	12,00,000

ILLUSTRATION 14

Calculate Funds from Operations from the following information:

Particulars	*31.3.2015* ₹	*31.3.2016* ₹
Profit & Loss Account	30,000	35,000
General Reserve	10,000	15,000
Provision for Depreciation on Plant	30,000	35,000
Goodwill	15,000	7,500
Preliminary Expenses	5,000	2,500

During the year an item of plant costing ₹ 20,000 having book value of ₹ 14,000 was sold for ₹ 18,000.

SOLUTION

Dr. **ADJUSTED PROFIT & LOSS ACCOUNT** *Cr.*

Particulars	₹	*Particulars*	₹
To Depreciation	11,000	By Balance b/d	30,000
To Goodwill w/o	7,500	By Profit on Sale of Plant	4,000
To Preliminary Exp. w/o	2,500	By Funds from Operations (b.f.)	27,000

To Transfer to Reserve	5,000		
To Balance c/d	35,000		
	61,000		61,000

Working Note:

Dr. **PROVISION FOR DEPRECIATION ON PLANT ACCOUNT** *Cr.*

Particulars	₹	*Particulars*	₹
To Accumulated Depreciation on Plant Sold	6,000	By Balance b/d	30,000
		By P & L A/c (b.f.)	11,000
To Balance c/d	35,000		
	41,000		41,000

ILLUSTRATION 15

Calculate the Funds from Operations from the information given below as on 31st March, 2016.

(a) Increase in Balance of P & L A/c during the year ended 31st March, 2016 ₹ 6,50,000

(b) Gain on sale of building ₹ 35,500

(c) Goodwill appears in the books as on 1.4.2015 at ₹ 1,80,000 out of which 10 per cent has been written off during the year.

(d) Old machinery worth ₹ 8,000 has been sold during the year for ₹ 6,500.

(e) ₹ 1,25,000 have been transferred to the General Reserve.

(f) Depreciation has been provided during the year on machinery and furniture at 20%, on written down value.

The written down value of machinery and furniture as on 31.03.2016 was ₹ 5,20,000.

SOLUTION

Particulars	₹	₹
A. Net Profit for the year		6,50,000
B. *Add:*		
(i) Depreciation	1,30,000	
(ii) Goodwill w/o	18,000	
(iii) Loss on Sale of Machinery	1,500	
(iv) Transfer to Reserve	1,25,000	2,74,500
C. *Less:* Gain on Sale of Building		(35,500)
D. Funds from Operations (A + B – C)		8,89,000

Working Notes:

(i) W.D.V. of machinery and furniture as on 1.4.2015

= ₹ 5,20,000 + 25% of ₹ 5,20,000 = ₹ 6,50,000

(ii) Depreciation = 20% of ₹ 6,50,000 = ₹ 1,30,000

ILLUSTRATION 16

Calculate funds from operations from the following Balance Sheets of Tulsian Ltd. :

Particulars	*31.3.2015* ₹	*31.3.2016* ₹
Equity Share Capital	3,00,000	4,00,000
Pref. Share Capital	1,50,000	1,00,000
General Reserve	40,000	70,000
Securities Premium	5,000	15,000
P & L A/c	23,000	54,000
Debentures	3,20,000	4,20,000
Provision for Taxation	40,000	50,000
Proposed Dividend	42,000	50,000
Provision for Doubtful Debt	4,000	5,000
Other Current Liabilities	75,000	99,000
Goodwill	1,15,000	90,000
Patents	90,000	1,15,000
Land	1,00,000	90,000
Plant & Machinery (Net)	1,80,000	1,70,000
Furniture	10,000	2,25,000
Investments	2,00,000	1,80,000
Debtors	1,60,000	2,00,000
Other Current Assets	1,26,000	1,62,000
Preliminary Expenses	5,000	3,000
Underwriting Commission	3,000	8,000
Discount on Issue of Debentures	10,000	20,000

SOLUTION

Dr. **ADJUSTED PROFIT & LOSS ACCOUNT** *Cr.*

Particulars	₹	*Particulars*	₹
To Depreciation	10,000	By Opening Balance	23,000
To Goodwill Amortised	25,000	By Funds from Operations	1,98,000
To Preliminary Exp. w/o	2,000	*(Balancing figure)*	
To Transfer to Reserve	30,000		
To Proposed Dividend	50,000		
To Provision for Tax	50,000		
To Closing Balance	54,000		
	2,21,000		2,21,000

ILLUSTRATION 17

Assuming that all debtors in Illustration 16 are good, Calculate Funds from Operations.

SOLUTION

Dr. **ADJUSTED PROFIT & LOSS ACCOUNT** *Cr.*

Particulars	₹	*Particulars*	₹
To Depreciation	10,000	By Opening Balance	23,000
To Goodwill Amortised	25,000	By Funds from Operations	
To Preliminary Exp. w/o	2,000	*(Balancing figure)*	1,99,000
To Transfer to Reserve	30,000		
To Proposed Dividend	50,000		
To Provision for Doubtful Debt	1,000		
To Provision for Tax	50,000		
To Closing Balance	54,000		
	2,22,000		2,22,000

Note: An increase in 'Provision for Doubtful Debts' has been added back to current year's profits in order to find out funds from operations since it is an appropriation out of profit (since all debtors have been considered as good).

17.0 IS DEPRECIATION A SOURCE OF FUNDS?

In general depreciation is not a source of funds since *neither* the current assets *nor* the current liabilities are affected. On providing depreciation, only the fixed assets and the current year's profits are deceased by the amount of depreciation.

The depreciation is added back to the profits merely to determine the actual working capital flow from operations since the profits are ascertained after debiting the item 'depreciation' which does not affect the working capital. If the depreciation were a source of funds, all enterprises having shortage of funds could have improved their financial position by providing more and more depreciation.

However, the following points should be noted regarding the depreciation:

1. Depreciation can indirectly influence the flow of funds by affecting the tax liability. For instance, more depreciation means *less* tax liability *or less* outflow of funds to income-tax authorities.
2. In case the fixed assets are hired by an enterprise and hire charges (which undoubtedly include a depreciation charge) are paid for their use, funds from operations are reduced to that extent.
3. In case of manufacturing concern, when current assets include closing inventories and the value of closing inventories includes the depreciation on fixed assets as an element of cost, depreciation acts as a source of funds in such a case.

18.0 FORMAT OF FUNDS FLOW STATEMENT

The fund flow statement can be presented *either* in 'T' form *or* in Single Columnar Form. In Single Columnar Form, first the Sources of funds and then the Application of Funds are shown. In 'T' Form, sources of funds are shown on the left-hand side and the application of funds are shown on the right-hand side. A format of Fund Flow Statement in 'T' form is shown below:

FUNDS FLOW STATEMENT OF M/S ....

for the period ended....

Sources of Funds	₹	*Applications of Funds*	₹
Issue of Shares (including Premium but net of Discount)	xxx	Redemption of Redeemable Preference Shares (including premium on redemption)	xxx
Issue of Debentures (including Premium but net of Discount)	xxx	Redemption of Debentures (including premium on redemption)	xxx
		Buy-back of Shares	xxx
Raising of Non-current Loans/deposits	xxx	Repayment of Non-current Loans/ Deposits	xxx
Sale of Non-current Assets	xxx	Purchase of Non-current Assets	xxx
Non-operating Incomes (e.g. Dividend, Interest, Rent Received)	xxx	Payment of Final Dividends (for previous year)	xxx
		Payment of Interim Dividend	xxx
Funds from Operations	xxx	Payment of Tax	xxx
Decrease in Working Capital	xxx	Payment of Non-operating Expenses	xxx
		Funds used in Operations	xxx
		Increase in Working Capital	xxx
	xxx		xxx

TUTORIAL NOTES

(i) Issue of Shares/Debentures on purchase of a non-current asset, *or* on conversion of Debentures and the purchase of a Non-current Asset against the issue of Shares/Debentures do not appear in the Funds Flow Statement (prepared on Working Capital Basis) because these transactions do not involve any inflow/outflow of working Capital.

(ii) Payment of tax is not shown as an application of funds if this item is treated as a current item.

ILLUSTRATION 18

From the following Balance Sheets of TULSIAN Ltd., prepare Schedule of Changes in Working Capital and Funds Flow Statement:

Particulars	*31.3.2015* ₹	*31.3.2016* ₹
Equity Share Capital	3,00,000	4,00,000
Pref. Share Capital	1,50,000	1,00,000
General Reserve	40,000	70,000
Securities Premium	5,000	15,000
Profit & Loss A/c	23,000	54,000
Debentures	3,20,000	4,20,000
Creditors for Goods	30,000	50,000
Bills Payables	20,000	30,000
Outstanding Expenses	2,000	1,000

Commission received-in-advance	3,000	2,000
Bank Overdraft (Canara Bank)	19,000	14,000
Provision for Taxation	38,000	50,000
Proposed Dividend	42,000	50,000
Provision for Doubtful Debt	4,000	5,000
Provision for Legal Damages	2,000	–
Provision for Discount on Debtors	1,000	2,000
Goodwill	1,15,000	90,000
Patents	90,000	1,15,000
Land	1,00,000	90,000
Plant & Machinery (Net)	1,80,000	1,70,000
Furniture	10,000	2,25,000
Investments	2,00,000	1,80,000
Stock	77,000	1,09,000
Debtors	1,60,000	2,00,000
Bills Receivable	20,000	30,000
Marketable Securities	3,000	2,000
Accrued Interest	1,000	3,000
Cash in hand	5,000	4,000
Cash at Dena Bank	10,000	6,000
Prepaid Expenses	10,000	8,000
Preliminary Expenses	5,000	3,000
Underwriting Comm.	3,000	8,000
Discount on Issue of Debentures	10,000	20,000

SOLUTION

SCHEDULE OF CHANGES IN WORKING CAPITAL

Particulars	*31st March*		*Changes in Working Capital*	
	2015 ₹	*2016* ₹	*Increase* ₹	*Decrease* ₹
A. Current Assets:				
Stock	77,000	1,09,000	32,000	
Debtors	1,60,000	2,00,000	40,000	
Bills Receivables	20,000	30,000	10,000	
Marketable Securities	3,000	2,000		1,000
Accrued Interest	1,000	3,000	2,000	
Cash-in-hand	5,000	4,000		1,000
Cash at Dena Bank	10,000	6,000		4,000
Prepaid Expenses	10,000	8,000		2,000
	2,86,000	3,62,000		

B. Current Liabilities:				
Creditors for Goods	30,000	50,000		20,000
Bills Payables	20,000	30,000		10,000
Outstanding Expenses	2,000	1,000	1,000	
Commission received-in-advance	3,000	2,000	1,000	
Bank O/D (Can Bank)	19,000	14,000	5,000	
Provision for Doubtful Debts	4,000	5,000		1,000
Provision for Legal Damages	2,000	-	2,000	
Provision for Discount on Debtors	1,000	2,000		1,000
	81,000	1,04,000		
C. Working Capital [A – B]	2,05,000	2,58,000		
D. Increase in Working Capital	53,000			53,000
	2,58,000	2,58,000	93,000	93,000

FUNDS FLOW STATEMENT
FOR THE YEAR ENDING ON 31.3.2016

Sources	₹	*Applications*	₹
Issue of Equity Shares		Redemption of Red. Pref. Shares	50,000
(including premium)	1,10,000	Purchase of Patents	25,000
[₹ 1,00,000 + ₹ 10,000]		Purchase of Furniture	2,15,000
Issue of Debentures		Payment of Underwriting Commission	5,000
(Net of Discount)		Payment of Tax	38,000
(₹ 1,00,000 – ₹ 10,000)	90,000	Payment of Final Dividend	42,000
Sale of Land	10,000	Increase in Working Capital	53,000
Sale of Investments	20,000		
Funds from operations	1,98,000		
	4,28,000		4,28,000

Working Notes:

(I) CALCULATION OF FUNDS FROM OPERATIONS
ADJUSTED PROFIT & LOSS ACCOUNT

Dr. *Cr.*

Particulars	₹	*Particulars*	₹
To Depreciation	10,000	By Opening Balance	23,000
To Goodwill Amortised	25,000	By Funds from Operations	1,98,000
To Preliminary Exp. w/o	2,000	*(Balancing figure)*	
To Transfer to Reserve	30,000		
To Proposed Dividend	50,000		
To Provision for Tax	50,000		
To Closing Balance	54,000		
	2,21,000		2,21,000

(ii) Provision for Tax has been treated as non-current item.

(iii) It has been assumed that the sales of land and investments are at book values and as a result there is *neither* profit *nor* loss on sale.

ILLUSTRATION 19

Prepare the Funds Flow Statement and Schedule of Changes in Working Capital if all debtors are good in Illustration 18.

SOLUTION

SCHEDULE OF CHANGES IN WORKING CAPITAL

Particulars	*31st March*		*Changes in Working Capital*	
	2015 ₹	*2016* ₹	*Increase* ₹	*Decrease* ₹
A. Current Assets:				
Stock	77,000	1,09,000	32,000	
Debtors	1,60,000	2,00,000	40,000	
Bills Receivables	20,000	30,000	10,000	
Marketable Securities	3,000	2,000		1,000
Accrued Interest	1,000	3,000	2,000	
Cash-in-hand	5,000	4,000		1,000
Cash at Dena Bank	10,000	6,000		4,000
Prepaid Expenses	10,000	8,000		2,000
	2,86,000	3,62,000		
B. Current Liabilities:				
Creditors for Goods	30,000	50,000		20,000
Bills Payables	20,000	30,000		10,000
Outstanding Expenses	2,000	1,000	1,000	
Commission received-in-advance	3,000	2,000	1,000	
Bank O/D (Can Bank)	19,000	14,000	5,000	
Provision for Legal Damages	2,000	-	2,000	
Provision for Discount on Debtors	1,000	2,000		1,000
	77,000	99,000		
C. Working Capital [A – B]	2,09,000	2,63,000		
D. Increase in Working Capital	54,000			54,000
	2,63,000	2,63,000	93,000	93,000

FUNDS FLOW STATEMENT
for the year ending on 31.3.2016

Sources	₹	*Applications*	₹
Issue of Equity Shares		Redemption of Red. Pref. Shares	50,000

(including premium)	1,10,000	Purchase of Patents	25,000
[₹ 1,00,000 + ₹ 10,000]		Purchase of Furniture	2,15,000
Issue of Debentures		Payment of Underwriting Commission	5,000
(Net of Discount)		Payment of Tax	38,000
(₹ 1,00,000 – ₹ 10,000)	90,000	Payment of Final Dividend	42,000
Sale of Land	10,000	Increase in Working Capital	54,000
Sale of Investments	20,000		
Funds from operations	1,99,000		
	4,29,000		4,29,000

Working Notes:

(I) CALCULATION OF FUNDS FROM OPERATIONS
ADJUSTED PROFIT & LOSS ACCOUNT

Dr. *Cr.*

Particulars	₹	*Particulars*	₹
To Depreciation	10,000	By Opening Balance	23,000
To Goodwill Amortised	25,000	By Funds from Operations	1,99,000
To Preliminary Exp. w/o	2,000	*(Balancing figure)*	
To Transfer to Reserve	30,000		
To Proposed Dividend	50,000		
To Provision for Tax	50,000		
To Increase in Provision for Doubtful Debts [₹ 5,000 – ₹ 4,000]	1,000		
To Closing Balance	54,000		
	2,22,000		2,22,000

(ii) Provision for Tax has been treated as non-current item.

(iii) It has been assumed that the sales of land and investments are at book values and as a result there is *neither* profit *nor* loss on sale.

ILLUSTRATION 20

From the following Balance Sheets of X Ltd., prepare Funds Flow Statement:

Particulars	*31.3.2015* ₹	*31.3.2016* ₹
Equity Share Capital	3,00,000	4,00,000
Redeemable Preference Share Capital	1,50,000	1,00,000
General Reserve	40,000	70,000
Profit & Loss A/c	30,000	48,000
Creditors	55,000	83,000
Bills Payable	20,000	16,000
Provision for Taxation	40,000	50,000
Proposed Dividend	42,000	50,000

Goodwill	1,15,000	90,000
Land & Building	2,00,000	1,70,000
Plant	80,000	2,00,000
Debtors	1,60,000	2,00,000
Stock	77,000	1,09,000
Bills Receivable	20,000	30,000
Cash in hand	15,000	10,000
Cash at Bank	10,000	8,000

Additional Information:

(a) Depreciation of ₹ 10,000 and ₹ 20,000 has been charged on plant and land and buildings respectively,

(b) An interim dividend of ₹ 20,000 has been paid, and

(c) Income-tax ₹ 35,000 has been paid.

SOLUTION

FUNDS FLOW STATEMENT
FOR THE PERIOD ENDING ON 31ST MARCH 2016

Sources	₹	*Applications*	₹
Issue of Equity Shares	1,00,000	Redemption of Red. Pref. Shares	50,000
Sale of Land & Building	10,000	Purchase of Plant	1,30,000
Funds from Operations	2,18,000	Payment of Final Dividend	42,000
		Payment of Interim Dividend	20,000
		Payment of Tax	35,000
		Increase in Working Capital	51,000
	3,28,000		3,28,000

SCHEDULE OF CHANGES IN COMPONENTS OF WORKING CAPITAL

Particulars	*31st March*		*Changes in Working Capital*	
	2015 ₹	*2016* ₹	*Increase* ₹	*Decrease* ₹
A. Current Assets:				
(a) Stock	77,000	1,09,000	32,000	
(b) Debtors	1,60,000	2,00,000	40,000	
(c) Cash	15,000	10,000		5,000
(d) B/R	20,000	30,000	10,000	
(e) Cash at Bank	10,000	8,000		2,000
	2,82,000	3,57,000		
B. Current Liabilities:				
(a) Creditors	55,000	83,000		28,000
(b) Bills Payables	20,000	16,000	4,000	

	75,000	99,000		
C. Working Capital (A – B)	2,07,000	2,58,000		
D. Increase in Working Capital	51,000			51,000
	2,58,000	2,58,000	86,000	86,000

Working Notes:

Dr. **(I) PLANT ACCOUNT** *Cr.*

Particulars	₹	*Particulars*	₹
To Balance b/d	80,000	By Depreciation A/c	10,000
To Bank A/c (Purchases) (b.f.)	1,30,000	By Balance c/d	2,00,000
	2,10,000		2,10,000

Dr. **(II) LAND & BUILDING ACCOUNT** *Cr.*

Particulars	₹	*Particulars*	₹
To Balance b/d	2,00,000	By Depreciation A/c	20,000
		By Bank A/c (b.f.)	10,000
		By Balance c/d	1,70,000
	2,00,000		2,00,000

Dr. **(III) PROVISION FOR TAXATION ACCOUNT** *Cr.*

Particulars	₹	*Particulars*	₹
To Bank A/c	35,000	By Balance b/d	40,000
To Balance c/d	50,000	By P & L A/c (b.f.)	45,000
	85,000		85,000

Dr. **(IV) ADJUSTED PROFIT AND LOSS ACCOUNT** *Cr.*

Particulars	₹	*Particulars*	₹
To Depreciation	30,000	By Balance b/d	30,000
To Goodwill written off	25,000	By Funds from Operations	
To Proposed Dividend	50,000	*(Balancing figure)*	2,18,000
To Interim Dividend	20,000		
To Transfer to General Reserve	30,000		
To Provision for Tax	45,000		
To Balance c/d	48,000		
	2,48,000		2,48,000

ILLUSTRATION 21

From the following particulars, prepare Funds Flow Statement.

Particulars	*31.3.2016* ₹	*31.3.2015* ₹
Equity Share Capital	80,000	55,000
12% Pre. Share Capital	20,000	25,000

General Reserve	4,000	4,000
Profit & Loss Ac	2,400	2,000
13% Debentures	14,000	12,000
Creditors & B/R	19,000	23,000
Outstanding Exp.	3,000	1,000
Provision for Taxation	8,400	6,000
Proposed Dividend	11,600	10,000
Bank Overdraft	13,600	25,000
Fixed Assets	80,000	82,000
Less: Accumulated Depreciation	(30,000)	(22,000)
	50,000	60,000
Debtors & B/R	49,000	20,600
Stock	70,000	80,000
Marketable Securities	5,000	2,000
Cash & Bank	2,000	400

Additional Information:

(a) Provision for tax made ₹ 9,400

(b) Fixed assets, sold for ₹ 10,000 their cost ₹ 20,000 and accumulated depreciation till date of sale on them ₹ 6,000;

(c) An Interim Dividend paid during the year ₹ 9,000.

SOLUTION

FUNDS FLOW STATEMENT

for the Year ending on 31st March, 2016

Sources	₹	*Applications*	₹
Issue of Equity Shares	25,000	Redemption of Pref. Shares	5,000
Issue of Debentures	2,000	Purchase of Fixed Assets	18,000
Sale of Fixed Assets	10,000	Payment of Interim Dividend	9,000
Funds from Operations	48,400	Payment of Final Dividend	10,000
		Payment of Tax	7,000
		Increase in Working Capital	36,400
	85,400		85,400

SCHEDULE OF CHANGES IN COMPONENTS OF WORKING CAPITAL

Particulars	*31st March*		*Changes in Working Capital*	
	2015 ₹	*2016* ₹	*Increase* ₹	*Decrease* ₹
A. Current Assets:				
Debtors & B/R	20,600	49,000	28,400	
Stock	80,000	70,000		10,000
Marketable Securities	2,000	5,000	3,000	

Cash at Bank	400	2,000	1,600	
	1,03,000	1,26,000		
B. Current Liabilities:				
Creditors & B/P	23,000	19,000	4,000	
Outstanding Expenses	1,000	3,000	2,000	
Bank Overdraft	25,000	13,600	11,400	
	49,000	35,600		
C. Working Capital (A – B)	54,000	90,400		
D. Increase in Working Capital	36,400	–		36,400
	90,400	90,400	48,400	48,400

Working Notes:

Dr. **(I) FIXED ASSETS ACCOUNT** *Cr.*

Particulars	₹	*Particulars*	₹
To Balance b/d	82,000	By Asset Sold A/c	20,000
To Bank A/c (Purchases) (b.f.)	18,000	By Balance c/d	80,000
	1,00,000		1,00,000

Dr. **(II) ACCUMULATED DEPRECIATION ACCOUNT** *Cr.*

Particulars	₹	*Particulars*	₹
To Asset Sold A/c	6,000	By Balance b/d	22,000
To Balance c/d	30,000	By P & L A/c	
		(Depreciation for current year)	14,000
	36,000		36,000

Dr. **(II) ASSET SOLD ACCOUNT** *Cr.*

Particulars	₹	*Particulars*	₹
To Fixed Assets A/c	20,000	By Accumulated Depreciation A/c	6,000
		By Bank A/c	10,000
		By P & L A/c (Loss)	4,000
	20,000		20,000

Dr. **(IV) PROVISION FOR TAXATION ACCOUNT** *Cr.*

Particulars	₹	*Particulars*	₹
To Bank A/c (b.f.)	7,000	By Balance b/d	6,000
To Balance c/d	8,400	By P & L A/c	9,400
	15,400		15,400

Dr. **(V) ADJUSTED PROFIT & LOSS ACCOUNT** Cr.

Particulars	₹	*Particulars*	₹
To Depreciation	14,000	By Balance b/d	2,000
To Loss on Sale of machine	4,000	By Funds from Operations	48,400
To Interim Dividend	9,000	*(Balancing figure)*	
To Proposed Dividend	11,600		
To Provision for Tax	9,400		
To Balance c/d	2,400		
	50,400		50,400

ILLUSTRATION 22

From the following particulars, prepare a statement showing application and source of funds.

Particulars	*31.3.2015* ₹	*31.3.2016* ₹
Equity Share Capital	3,00,000	3,50,000
18% Pref. Share Capital	2,00,000	1,00,000
14% Debentures	1,00,000	2,00,000
Reserves	1,10,000	2,70,000
Current Liabilities	80,000	1,60,000
Fixed Assets (Net)	5,10,000	6,20,000
Investments	30,000	80,000
Current Assets	2,40,000	3,75,000
Discount on Debentures	10,000	5,000

You are informed that during the year:

(a) A machine with a book value of ₹ 40,000 was sold for ₹ 25,000.

(b) Preference Share redemption was done at a premium of 15% on 31.3.2016.

(c) An Interim Dividend @ 15% was paid on equity shares. New shares were issued on 31.3.2016.

(d) Depreciation charged during the year was ₹ 60,000.

SOLUTION

FUNDS FLOW STATEMENT

for the year ending on 31st March, 2016

Sources	₹	*Applications*	₹
Issue of Shares	50,000	Purchase of Investments	50,000
Issue of Debentures	1,00,000	Redemption of Red. Pref. Shares	1,15,000
Sale of Fixed Assets	25,000	Payment of Pref. Dividend	36,000
Funds from Operations	3,36,000	Payment of Interim Dividend	45,000
		Purchase of Fixed Asset	2,10,000
		Increase in Working Capital	55,000
	5,11,000		5,11,000

SCHEDULE OF CHANGES IN COMPONENTS OF WORKING CAPITAL

Particulars	*31st March*		*Changes in Working Capital*	
	2015 ₹	*2016* ₹	*Increase* ₹	*Decrease* ₹
A. Current Assets	2,40,000	3,75,000	1,35,000	
B. Current Liabilities	80,000	1,60,000		80,000
C. Working Capital (A – B)	1,60,000	2,15,000		
D. Increase in Working Capital	55,000			55,000
	2,15,000	2,15,000	1,35,000	1,35,000

Working Notes:

Dr. **(I) FIXED ASSETS ACCOUNT (AT W.D.V.)** *Cr.*

Particulars	₹	*Particulars*	₹
To Balance b/d	5,10,000	By Bank A/c	25,000
To Bank A/c (Purchases) *(Balancing figure)*	2,10,000	By P & L A/c (Loss on Sale)	15,000
		By Depreciation A/c	60,000
		By Balance c/d	6,20,000
	7,20,000		7,20,000

Dr. **(II) RESERVES ACCOUNT** *Cr.*

Particulars	₹	*Particulars*	₹
To Balance c/d	2,70,000	By Balance b/d	1,10,000
		By P & L A/c (b.f.)	1,60,000
	2,70,000		2,70,000

Dr. **(III) ADJUSTED PROFIT & LOSS ACCOUNT** *Cr.*

Particulars	₹	*Particulars*	₹
To Depreciation	60,000	By Funds for operations *(Balancing figure)*	3,36,000
To Discount on Issue of Debentures	5,000		
To Loss on Sale of Machine	15,000		
To Pref. Dividend	36,000		
To Interim Dividend (Equity) [15% on ₹ 3,00,000]	45,000		
To Premium on Red. of Pref. Shares	15,000		
To Transfer to Reserve	1,60,000		
	3,36,000		3,36,000

ILLUSTRATION 23

From the following particulars, prepare Funds Flow statement:

Particulars	*31.3.2016* ₹	*31.3.2015* ₹
Equity Share Capital	3,50,000	3,00,000
18% Pref. Share Capital	1,00,000	2,00,000
14% Debentures	2,00,000	1,00,000
Reserves	2,70,000	1,10,000
Current Liabilities	1,45,000	70,000
Provision for Doubtful Debts	15,000	10,000
Fixed Assets	6,20,000	5,10,000
Investments	80,000	30,000
Current Assets	3,75,000	2,40,000
Discount on Issue of Debentures	5,000	10,000

The Provision for depreciation stood at ₹ 1,50,000 on 31st March, 2015 and at ₹ 1,90,000 on 31st March, 2016. During the year:-

(a) A machine costing ₹ 70,000 (book value ₹ 40,000) was disposed off for ₹ 25,000.

(b) Preference share redemption was carried out at a premium of 5% on 31.3.2016.

(c) Dividend @ 15% was paid on equity shares. New shares were issued on 31.3.2016.

SOLUTION

FUNDS FLOW STATEMENT

For the year ending on 31st March. 2016

Sources	₹	*Applications*	₹
Issue of Shares	50,000	Purchase of Investments	50,000
Issue of Debentures	1,00,000	Redemption of Red. Pref. Shares	1,05,000
Sale of Fixed Assets	25,000	Payment of Equity Dividend	45,000
Funds from operations	3,36,000	Purchase of Fixed Assets	2,20,000
		Increase in Working Capital	55,000
		Payment of Preference Dividend	36,000
	5,11,000		5,11,000

SCHEDULE OF CHANGES IN COMPONENTS OF WORKING CAPITAL

Particulars	*31st March*		*Changes in Working Capital*	
	2015 ₹	*2016* ₹	*Increase* ₹	*Decrease* ₹
A. Current Assets	2,30,000	3,60,000	1,30,000	–
(Net of provision for Doubtful debts)				
B. Current Liabilities	(70,000)	(1,45,000)	–	75,000
C. Working Capital (A – B)	1,60,000	2,15,000		
D. Increase in Working Capital	55,000	–	–	55,000
	2,15,000	2,15,000	1,30,000	1,30,000

Working Notes:

Dr. **(I) FIXED ASSETS (AT COST)** *Cr.*

Particulars	₹	*Particulars*	₹
To Balance b/d	6,60,000	By Asset Sold A/c	70,000
To Bank A/c (purchases) (b.f.)	2,20,000	By Balance c/d	8,10,000
	8,80,000		8,80,000

Dr. **(II) PROVISION FOR DEPRECIATION ACCOUNT** *Cr.*

Particulars	₹	*Particulars*	₹
To Asset Sold A/c	30,000	By Balance b/d	1,50,000
To Balance c/d	1,90,000	By P & L A/c	
		(Depreciation for current year)	70,000
		(Balancing figure)	
	2,20,000		2,20,000

Dr. **(III) ASSET SOLD ACCOUNT** *Cr.*

Particulars	₹	*Particulars*	₹
To Fixed Assets A/c	70,000	By Provision for Depreciation A/c	30,000
		By Bank A/c	25,000
		By P & L A/c	15,000
	70,000		70,000

Dr. **(IV) RESERVES ACCOUNT** *Cr.*

Particulars	₹	*Particulars*	₹
To Balance c/d	2,70,000	By Balance b/d	1,10,000
		By P & L A/c	1,60,000
	2,70,000		2,70,000

Dr. **(IV) ADJUSTED PROFIT & LOSS ACCOUNT** *Cr.*

Particulars	₹	*Particulars*	₹
To Depreciation	70,000	By Funds from Operations	3,36,000
To Discount on Issue of		*(Balancing figure)*	
Debentures w/o	5,000		
To Loss on Sale of Machine	15,000		
To Interim Dividend			
[15% on ₹ 3,00,000]	45,000		
To Premium on Red. of Pref. Shares	5,000		
To Preference Dividend	36,000		
To Transfer to Reserve	1,60,000		
	3,36,000		3,36,000